THIRD EDITION

Contemporary Mathematics

for Business and Consumers

ROBERT A. BRECHNER
MIAMI-DADE COMMUNITY COLLEGE

THOMSON
SOUTH-WESTERN

Australia · Canada · Mexico · Singapore · Spain · United Kingdom · United States

THOMSON
SOUTH-WESTERN

Student Edition

Contemporary Mathematics for Business and Consumers
Robert A. Brechner

Editor-in-Chief:
Jack Calhoun

Team Leader:
Melissa S. Acuña

Acquisitions Editor:
Charles E. McCormick

Developmental Editor:
Mardell Toomey

Marketing Manager:
Mignon Tucker

Senior Production Editor:
Marci Combs

Manufacturing Coordinator:
Diane Lohman

Project Management:
Elm Street Publishing Services, Inc.

Compositor:
Pre-Press Company, Inc.

Printer:
Courier Companies,
Kendallville, IN

Design Project Manager:
Michelle Kunkler

Internal Designer:
Van Mua

Cover Designer:
Van Mua

Cover Image:
© Digital Vision

Photo Researcher:
Linda Blundell

Printed in the United States of America
3 4 5 05 04

For more information contact South-Western,
5191 Natorp Boulevard,
Mason, Ohio 45040.
Or you can visit our Internet site at:
http://www.swcollege.com

ISBN: 0-324-30104-9 (text + cd)
0-324-18589-8 (text only)
0-03-035433-1 (cd only)

Dedication

To Shari Joy, my wife and partner.
You are a world of happiness and
celebration for me.
I can imagine no other place
for my heart!
I love you.

ABOUT THE AUTHOR

Robert A. Brechner is Professor, School of Business, at Miami-Dade Community College, the largest multi-campus community college in the country. For the past 36 years he has taught Business Math, Principles of Business, Marketing, Advertising, Public Relations, Management, and Personal Finance. He has been Adjunct Professor at Florida Atlantic University, Boca Raton, International Fine Arts College, Miami, and Florida International University School of Journalism and Mass Communications.

Bob holds a Bachelor of Science degree in Industrial Management from the Georgia Institute of Technology in Atlanta, Georgia. He also has a Masters of Business Administration from Emory University, also in Atlanta.

He consults widely with industrial companies and has published the following books: *Annuities and Sinking Funds* (Prentice Hall); *Guidelines for the New Manager* (The Dryden Press); and *A Little Math With Your Business* (The Dryden Press). Bob is a member of the American Mathematical Association of Two-Year Colleges, the National Council of Teachers of Mathematics, and the Florida Association of Community Colleges.

Bob lives in Coconut Grove, Florida, with his wife, Shari Joy. He enjoys spending his free time playing tennis, running, boating, and cooking.

Bob encourages feedback and suggestions for future editions from all those who use the text. Students and instructors can contact him toll-free at 1.888.284.MATH or by e-mail at bizmath@aol.com or via the textbook's Web site www.contemporarymath.com.

BUSINESS FIRST

Not a math book using business examples, *Contemporary Mathematics for Business and Consumers* is a business book using math to solve real-world business problems. This unique text divides each chapter into sections that contain specific Performance Objectives. These objectives reflect actual business situations, and students learn to use math to make decisions within those situations. A captivating and student-friendly style ensures student comprehension, while the abundant exercises reinforce vital material.

Razor sharp and newly updated in its third edition, *Contemporary Mathematics* is the book today's students need for success in their future business and personal financial endeavors.

If knowledge is the currency of the New Economy, this is where Wealth is Created.
—Goizueta Business School
Emory University

FEATURES OF BRECHNER, *CONTEMPORARY MATHEMATICS FOR BUSINESS AND CONSUMERS,* THIRD EDITION

Contemporary Mathematics for Business and Consumers is a 21-chapter adventure into today's business world and its associated mathematical procedures. The book is designed to provide solid math preparation and foundation for students going on to courses and careers in accounting, marketing, retailing, banking, office administration, finance, insurance, real estate, and business administration.

In addition, it is ideal for use in small businesses or for personal finance applications. This is not just a textbook but a "reference manual" for consumers and businesspersons alike. When used in conjunction with the MathCue.Business tutorial software, *Contemporary Math* becomes an even more powerful and dynamic teaching and learning tool.

The book begins with a business-oriented review of the basic mathematical operations, whole numbers, fractions, and decimals. Once students have mastered these basics, they are introduced to the concept of equations and how they are used to solve business problems. Next students learn the all-important concept of percents and how they are used in today's business jargon to express numbers and numerical changes. After percents, each subsequent chapter presents a business math topic that utilizes the students' knowledge of the basic operations, equations, and percents.

In keeping with the philosophy of "practice makes perfect," the text contains well over 2,000 realistic business math exercises—many with multiple steps and answers—designed to prepare students to use math to make business decisions and develop critical-thinking and problem-solving skills. Consistent with AMATYC standards, many exercises ask students to make choices and then substantiate their answers in their own written words. This technique helps students visualize how what they are learning connects to real-world applications rather than simply memorizing a series of mathematical steps.

Many of the exercises in each chapter are written in a "you are the manager of" format, to enhance student involvement. The exercises cover a full range of difficulty levels, from those designed for beginners to those requiring moderate to challenge-level skills. The exercises also reflect today's diverse and ever-changing American workplace and marketplace, with increasing importance given to the service sector.

Text Organization

Chapter material is divided into Sections. Each section is then subdivided into numbered Performance Objectives. Each chapter begins with a page-referenced "contents" list of the sections and objectives to be covered. This feature gives students an overview of what lies ahead and how best to schedule their study time. This modular approach allows instructors the flexibility to customize their courses' chapter content and order of presentation to best meet the needs of their particular students.

Textual Material

Chapter material and explanations are "business-realistic" and up-to-date. They reflect current dates, products, services, names, trends, and prices. Important terminology appears in bold-faced type with complete definitions in the Marginal Glossary opposite each term. Realistic business and government forms, including tables, checks, bank statements, credit card statements, and invoices, are prevalent throughout the text.

Step-by-Step Approach

After the text explanation, the math sequence of each Performance Objective is illustrated using a step-by-step approach that is easy for students to follow and remember. These "step" elements are easily distinguishable by their highlighted design for ease in looking them up while working problems or reviewing material.

Examples with Solution Strategies

Following each step-by-step sequence is an Example problem with corresponding Solution Strategy. The Example and Solution Strategy provides a worked-out solution and example with explanation, notes to the students, and calculator sequences for difficult computations.

EXAMPLE

Jim Patterson has a revolving department store credit account, with an annual percentage rate of 18%. Jim's previous balance from last month is $322.40. During the month, he purchased shirts for $65.60 and a baseball bat for $43.25. He returned a tie for a credit of $22.95 and made a $50 payment. If the department store uses the unpaid balance method, what is the amount of the finance charge on the account and what is Jim's new balance?

SOLUTION STRATEGY

Step 1. $\text{Periodic rate} = \frac{\text{Annual percentage rate}}{12}$

Try-It Exercises

Following each Example and Solution Strategy is a Try-It Exercise, which provides a chance for students to try the math procedure they have just learned. The worked-out solutions to the Try-It Exercises follow each chapter's summary chart. The solutions provide students with immediate feedback as to their understanding of the material and their ability to solve related math problems.

TRY-IT | EXERCISE

1. Heather Hogan has a BankCard account with an annual percentage rate of 15%. Her previous month's balance is $214.90. During the month of July, Heather's account showed the following activity:

Everybody's Business

Everybody's Business

Shortcut

"New Balance" can be calculated by adding the finance charge to the last "Unpaid Balance" of the month.

$427.28 + $3.89 = $431.37

Everybody's Business provides students with helpful Learning Tips and interesting Real-World Connections. Found in the margins, these provide students with useful hints and shortcuts relating to the math procedures, as well as conceptual understanding of how the material is applied in the business world.

Calculator Sequences

Easy to read calculator sequences with icons provide students with a "walk-through" illustration of how to solve various business problems using a calculator.

Calculator Sequence: 1 [+] .05 [y^x] 6 [×] 5000 [=] 6,700.4782

Section Review Exercises

One of the most important features of this textbook is the Section Review Exercises, a comprehensive set of 25 to 50 numeric and word problems at the end of each Section. These exercises allow the student to review manageable amounts of material from only two or three Performance Objectives as they work through the chapter, rather than having to wait until the entire chapter has been covered. Section Review Exercises allow the instructor the flexibility to assign homework or class practice problems without having to complete the whole chapter.

REVIEW EXERCISES | CHAPTER 13—SECTION I

Calculate the missing information on the following revolving charge accounts. Interest is calculated on the unpaid or previous month's balance:

	Previous Balance	Annual Percentage Rate (APR)	Monthly Periodic Rate	Finance Charge	Purchases and Cash Advances	Payments and Credits	New Balance
1.	$167.88	18%	1.5%	$2.52	$215.50	$50.00	$335.90
2.	$35.00	12%	1%	.35	$186.40	$75.00	$146.75
3.	$455.12	21%	1.75%	7.96	$206.24	$125.00	$544.32

Business Decision Exercises

BUSINESS DECISION

Pick the Right Plastic

16. On October 22, you plan to purchase a $3,000 computer by using one of your two credit cards. The Silver Card charges 18% interest and calculates interest on the previous month's balance. The Gold Card charges 18% interest and calculates interest based on the average daily balance. Both cards have a $0 balance as of October 1.

Your plan is to make a $1,000 payment in November, a $1,000 payment in December, and pay off the remaining balance in January. All your payments will be received and posted on the 10th of each month. No other charges will be made on the account.

The final problem in each set of Section Review Exercises and the Assessment Test is a multi-step student involvement exercise describing an in-depth business scenario. These challenge-level problems are designed to test students' ability to apply critical thinking in a decision-making situation. Frequently, they contain material that students will encounter in later chapters.

Many of these exercises ask students to make choices and then substantiate their answers in their own written words. The Business Decision exercises can be used as Collaborative Learning Activities in class or for homework.

Formula Recap Chart

Located before the chapter summary charts, this list contains all of the important formulas used in the chapter. This recap is useful to the students as a quick reference for doing homework or reviewing for a test.

CHAPTER FORMULAS

$$\text{Periodic rate} = \frac{\text{Annual percentage rate}}{12}$$

$$\text{Finance charge} = \text{Previous month's balance} \times \text{Periodic rate}$$

$$\text{Average daily balance} = \frac{\text{Sum of daily balances}}{\text{Days in billing cycle}}$$

$$\text{Finance charge} = \text{Average daily balance} \times \text{Periodic rate}$$

$$\text{New balance} = \text{Previous balance} + \text{Finance charge} + \text{Purchases and cash advances} - \text{Payments and credits}$$

✦ SUMMARY CHART ✦
SECTION I: Open-End Credit—Charge Accounts, Credit Cards, and Lines of Credit

Topic	P/O, Page	Important Concepts	Illustrative Examples
Calculating Finance Charge and New Balance by Using Previous Month's Balance Method	13–1 405	1. Divide the annual percentage rate by 12 to find the monthly or periodic interest rate. 2. Calculate the finance charge by multiplying the previous month's balance by the periodic interest rate from Step 1. 3. Total all the purchases and cash advances for the month. 4. Total all the payments and credits for the month. 5. Use the following formula to determine the new balance: $\text{New bal} = \text{Prev bal} + \text{Fin chg} + \text{Purch \& csh} - \text{Pmts \& crd}$	Calculate the finance charge and the new balance of an account with an annual percentage rate of 15%. Previous month's bal = \$186.11 Purchases = \$365.77 Payments = \$200.00 Periodic rate $= \frac{15}{12} = 1.25\%$ Finance charge = 186.11 × .0125 = <u>\$2.33</u> New balance = 186.11 + 2.33 + 365.77 − 200.00 = <u>\$354.21</u>

Chapter Summary Chart

This extensive chart provides a comprehensive page-referenced review of each Performance Objective in the chapter. It contains a review of the important concepts, steps, and formulas for every topic, with a new illustrative example and worked-out solution for each topic. It is an invaluable tool for the student to use in learning and reviewing the chapter material or studying for an exam.

Assessment Tests

This section provides a comprehensive set of exercises. As with the Section Review Exercises, these are business-realistic in nature and are designed to promote critical-thinking and problem-solving ability. Many of these problems have multiple parts that build on previous answers and previously learned material.

CHAPTER 13 I ASSESSMENT TEST

1. Valerie Mebust's revolving charge account has an annual percentage rate of 16%. The previous month's balance was \$345.40. During the current month, Valerie's purchases and cash advances amounted to \$215.39, and her payments and credits totaled \$125.00.

a. What is the monthly periodic rate of the account?

$$\text{Periodic rate} = \frac{16\%}{12} = \underline{1.33\%}$$

b. What is the amount of the finance charge?

$$345.40 \times 1.33\% = \underline{\$4.59}$$

c. What is Valerie's new balance?

Name ________________

Class ________________

Answers

3. \$4.46
\$724.12

4. \$724.12
\$12.09
\$839.64

Grading Panels

The grading panels are found in the margins of the Assessments Tests. These answer blanks are for students to use in answering each question and instructors to use in grading student work. The grading panel is set up in a vertical list format, allowing the instructor to place an answer template next to it for easy evaluation.

The Business Math Times

All the Math That's Fit to Learn

The Business Math Times

Volume XIII | **Consumer and Business Credit** | One Dollar

1,562 Hippos!

A billion credit cards combined would

"Quote . . . Unquote"

Education is when you read the fine print.
Experience is what you get if you don't.
—*Pete Seeger*

Debt is saving in reverse.
—*Peter Lynch*

services. Today, credit cards are accepted at more than 23 million locations in more than 300 countries.

parking meters, pay for a Big Mac, or use them to make pay phone calls.

In Germany, most citizens have a

Designed to stimulate students' curiosity, each chapter ends with a newspaper-style feature called *The Business Math Times.* Newly revised for the Third Edition, these pages present interesting business news, insights, and statistics; career information; Internet references; amusing quotes and cartoons; and challenging brainteasers.

Collaborative Learning Activities

In keeping with AMATYC standards, the Collaborative Learning Activities provide valuable opportunities to reinforce the concept of teamwork and polish presentation skills. Activities range from interviews to research, with emphasis on the application of mathematical concepts to real-world situations. These activities are located in Appendix A of the text.

Answers to Odd-Numbered Problems

Appendix B contains answers to the odd-numbered questions in the text. This feature allows students to easily check their progress on class assignments or homework.

ABOUT THE AUTHOR OF MATHCUE.BUSINESS

The author of numerous software packages, George Bergeman has taught mathematics for more than 25 years. His teaching career began at a small college in West Africa as a Peace Corps volunteer and continues at Northern Virginia Community College, one of the largest multi-campus community colleges in the country. Teaching awards have included Faculty Member of the Year honors at his campus.

In 1983, George developed a small program for use in statistics classes. Students and instructors responded positively, and in 1985 an expanded version was published along with an accompanying workbook.

Since then, George has developed a variety of software packages to accompany texts in statistics, calculus, developmental mathematics, finite mathematics, and a special favorite—Bob Brechner's *Contemporary Mathematics for Business and Consumers*. By drawing upon his teaching experiences and day-to-day contact with students and faculty, he has endeavored to develop software that provides targeted, effective, and easy-to-use support for instruction.

George lives with his wife, Clarissa, near Washington, DC, and they have one daughter, Jessica, now living in San Francisco. In his free time, he enjoys accompanying his wife and their dog to dog shows, and he flies an ultralight airplane.

MathCue.Business WITH INTERNET-BASED COURSE MANAGEMENT—FREE—WITH EACH NEW COPY OF BRECHNER, *CONTEMPORARY MATHEMATICS FOR BUSINESS AND CONSUMERS*, THIRD EDITION

MathCue.Business

MathCue.Business is a comprehensive software package specifically designed to accompany **Contemporary Mathematics for Business and Consumers,** Third Edition.

Developed by George W. Bergeman, who has taught math for more than 25 years and created instructional software for the last 17 years, **MathCue.Business** is both a learning and assessment tool. Instructional content is provided both on CD and on the Internet. **MathCue.Business** benefits students and instructors alike and includes these key features:

MathCue.Business Primary Modes

- **Tutorial-Practice:** Presents and scores problems and provides step-by-step solutions for each problem. Gives immediate feedback.
- **Test:** Sessions are scored only after they are finished. *Not only does the software create, display, and grade problems, it also shows students how to solve any questions that they missed.* Use for practice tests, tests, retests, and testing to mastery.

Both **Tutorial-Practice** and **Test** modes randomly generate large numbers of problems keyed to performance objectives in the text. Sessions are easily customized to include problems from one or more performance objectives in order to provide highly targeted tutorial sessions and various types of tests.

Customized session setups may be saved and later used repeatedly to generate multiple problem sets. Because the problems are randomly generated, each session is unique.

Extremely detailed score summaries are provided for each session.

Exclusive MathCue.Business Tool

- **Solution Finder:** Students *enter their own* basic math problems and receive step-by-step help. Solution Finder simulates the experience of asking a tutor how to solve a problem and receiving a complete explanation.

Optional Internet-Based Course Management

- **MathCue.Business Syllabus:** Allows instructors to schedule a sequence of customized, highly targeted sessions.
- **MathCue.Business Grade Book:** Automatically tracks student progress. The grade book includes a listing of session grades for all students in a section and session-by-session details of each student's work. An item analysis feature facilitates assessment of class-wide strengths and weaknesses. Instructors may specify various grading options.
- **MathCue.Business Communications:** Facilitates instructor-student communication. Instructors may send messages to an entire class or to selected groups or individuals.

The **Student Version** and the new **Internet-Based Course Management System** offer a wide variety of instructional options. Some instructors prefer to use the software for informal tutoring while others create a complete, customized tutoring and testing environment that takes full advantage of the electronic **Syllabus** and **Grade Book** features in **MathCue.Business.**

MathCue.Business *Tutorial-Practice* and *Test* Modes

MathCue.Business is a targeted, customizable tool for both learning and assessment.

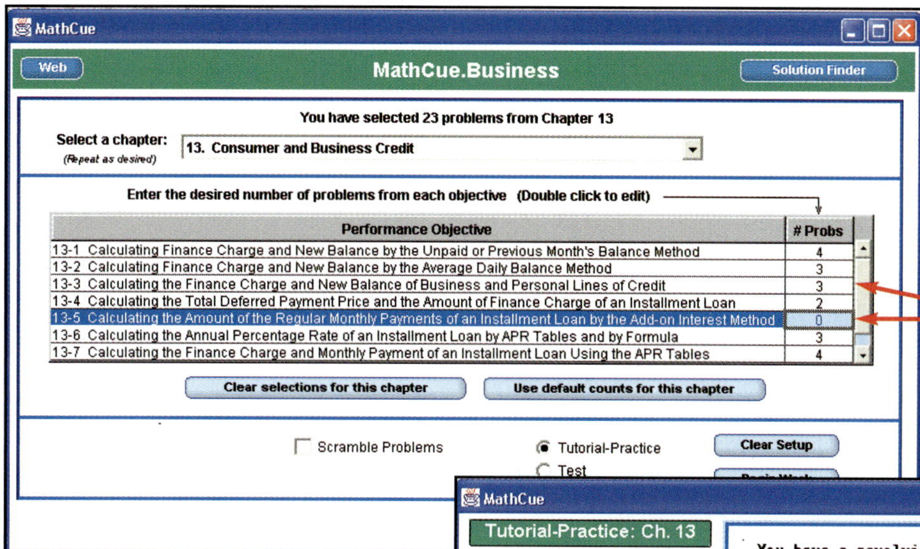

Create customized *Practice Test* or *Test* sessions by specifying the exact number of problems desired from each Performance Objective.

Objectives can be included or excluded as appropriate.

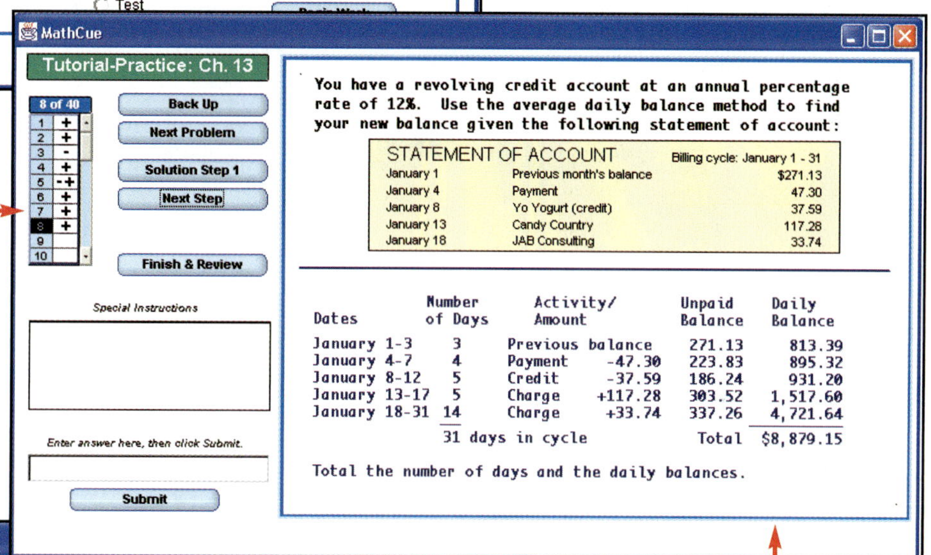

Grading panel tracks session progress.

A complete step-by-step solution is provided for every problem. (In test mode, the solutions are given after the test is completed.)

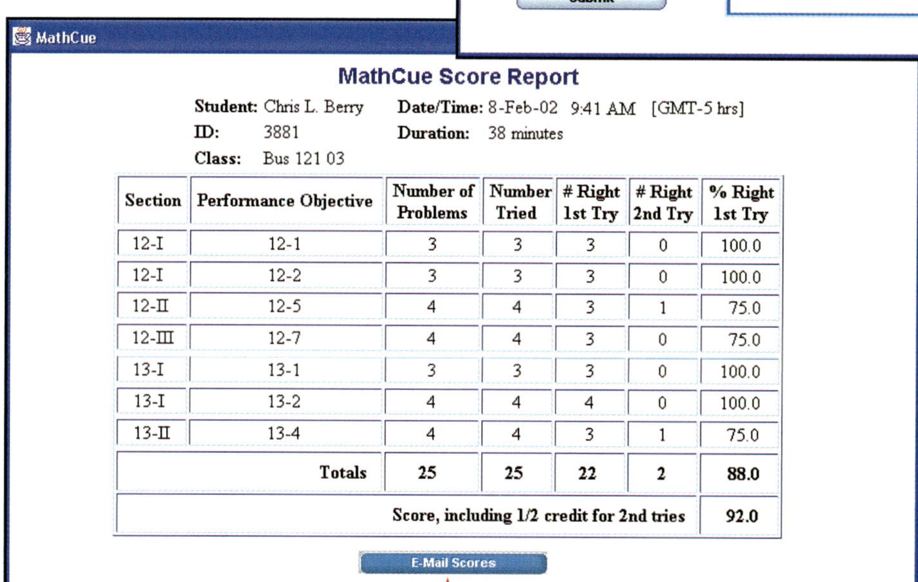

Extremely detailed results summaries help both students and instructors evaluate proficiency.

E-mail scores to the instructor.

MathCue.Business Solution Finder

MathCue.Business Solution Finder lets *students ask the questions.* This unique, built-in tool allows students to enter their own basic math problems and receive step-by-step help as if they were working with a tutor. **Solution Finder** is especially helpful to students who can't find a tutor or are reluctant to reveal their confusion to another person.

Students use **Solution Finder** for help solving a variety of basic math problems. Furthermore, as they proceed through their course, **Solution Finder** serves as a personal coach when students need help reviewing fundamental skills that are incorporated in more advanced topics.

Solution Finder is automatically disabled during testing.

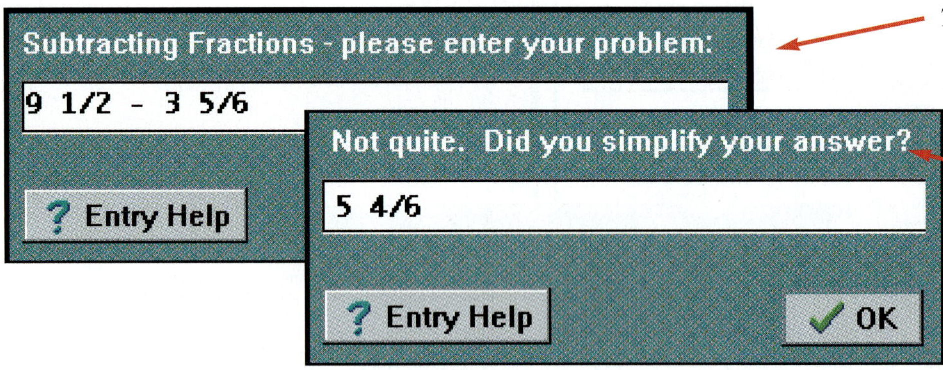

The STUDENT enters a problem.

Like a tutor, the software asks students to try to answer the problem. It then evaluates and responds to this answer.

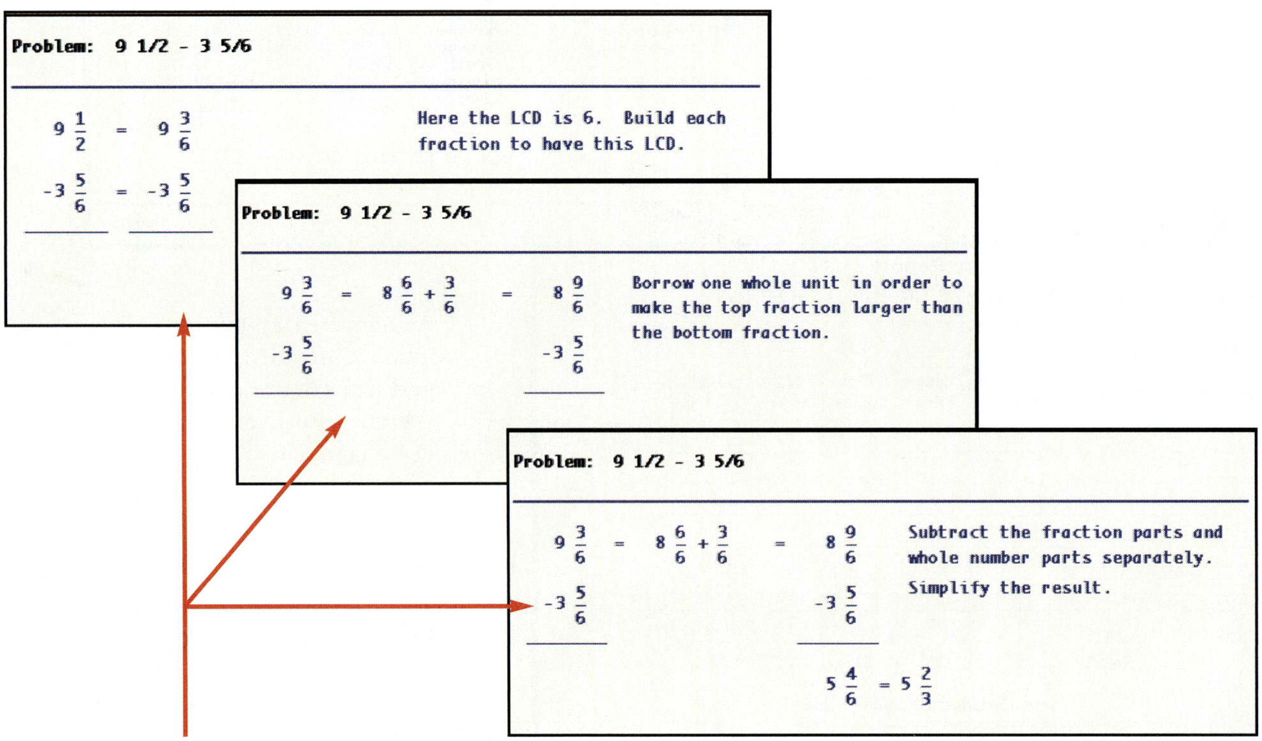

Solution Finder displays a full solution with a complete step-by-step explanation to the problem entered by the student.

MathCue.Business Internet Course Management

Instructors use the optional **MathCue.Business Course Management Version** to manage their classes and to schedule and track customized *Tutorial-Practice* and *Test* sessions. Features include:

MathCue.Business Syllabus allows instructors to create and schedule customized sessions:

- Each session may include problems from any combination of performance objectives.
- Instructors specify mode (*Tutorial-Practice* or *Test*), grading weight, date available, due date, and late penalties.

MathCue.Business Grade Book automatically tracks students' results.

- Drill-down grade reports include *Class Overviews, Student Grade Summaries* showing a record of each student's session-by-session work, and *Session Results* showing the details of each individual session.
- Instructors specify grading preferences and may override grades.
- Statistical summaries, sorting, and item analysis options help instructors evaluate results.

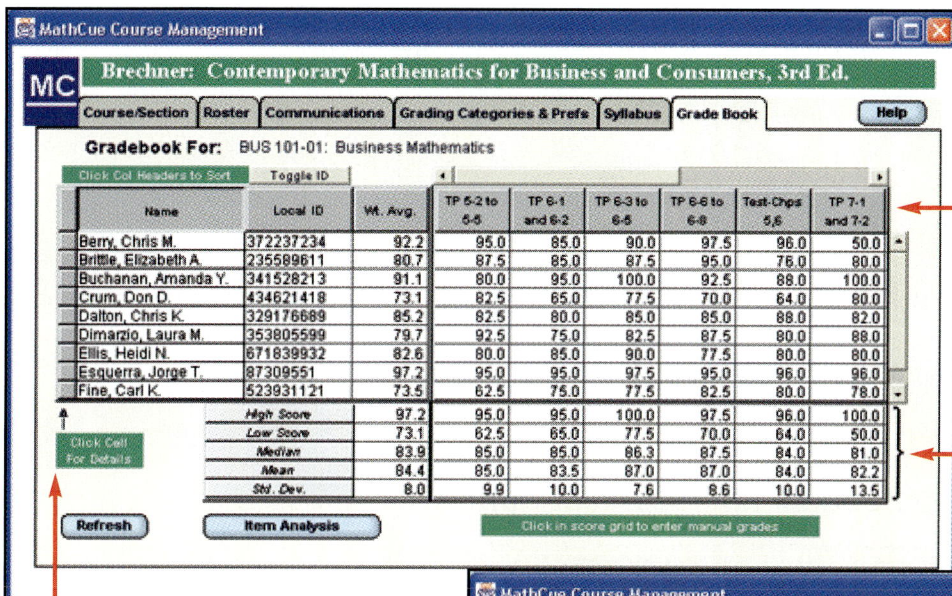

Click on any heading to sort scores based on that heading.

Summary statistics aid in analyzing results.

Drill down to see the grade summary for any individual student.

An *Item Analysis* shows how the class as a whole performs on each performance objective in a session.

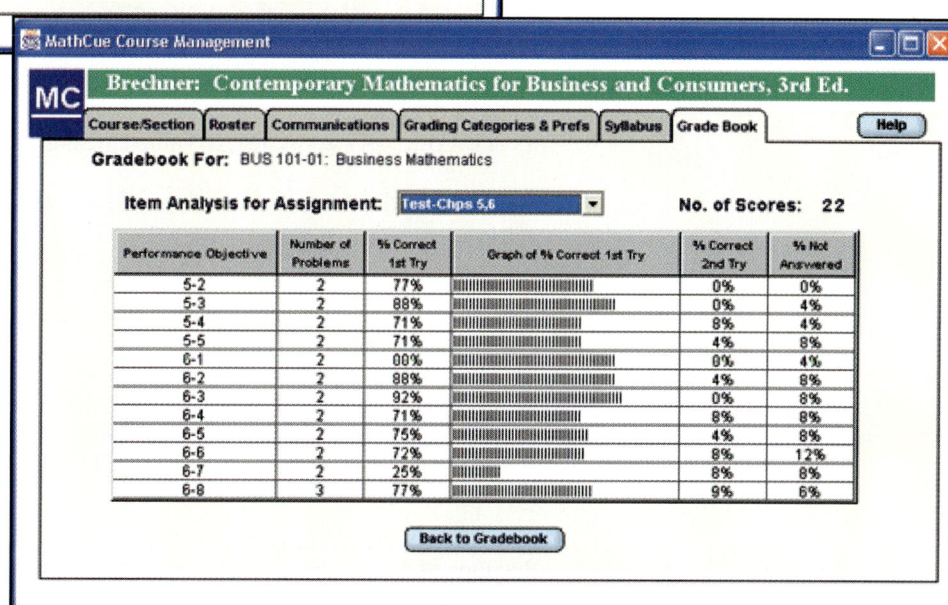

Supplements to Accompany *Contemporary Mathematics*

The learning package provided with *Contemporary Mathematics* was specifically designed to meet the needs of instructors facing a variety of teaching conditions and to enhance students' experience of the subject. We have attempted to address both the traditional and the innovative classroom environment by providing an array of quality, fundamental, and technologically advanced items to bring a contemporary, real-world feel to the study of business mathematics.

At http://brechner.swcollege.com Students and Instructors Will Find:

- An additional set of comprehensive homework or extra credit assignments for each chapter. These problems are designed to supplement and enhance the student's business math learning experience.
- Additional information and links related to the textbook topics including math basics, banking and financial services, marketing, accounting, insurance, taxes, and investments.
- The latest payroll and tax tables and charts from the Internal Revenue Service can be downloaded from this site.
- An extensive Research Library is included with links to major business and financial news organizations, business and computer publications, government departments, and research sites that give students and professors access to the latest business news.
- Business Careers contains links to sites providing career advice and employment information, sample employment tests, as well as homework help and study tips.
- Links to mathematical games and other fun and challenging math activities.

For Instructors Only:

- In addition to being available on a CD-ROM, the Instructor's Resource Database is available for download from the instructor's site.
- PowerPoint Solutions to all Section Review Exercises in the text will be included.
- Excel Templates with Answers.

Online Course Management Software

Go beyond the classroom with WebTutor. It offers in-depth content with concept presentations, flashcards, audio clips, Internet links, discussion questions, and tutorials. An internal e-mail system, chat and discussion areas, search capabilities, calendars, custom printing features, and instructor customization options provide an unparalleled level of functionality. Visit http://www.swcollege.com/elearning.html for more information.

Annotated Instructor's Edition of *Contemporary Mathematics* (ISBN 0-324-18588-X)

This valuable teaching aid includes annotated worked-out solutions for all problems and exercises as well as helpful marginal teaching notes and collaborative learning activities. These annotations appear in blue for clarity and ease of duplication. An icon in the margin highlights references to teaching and solution transparencies.

Student Resource Manual (ISBN 0-03-035478-1)

This supplement is available as a recommended support item for students. It contains reproductions of tables, charts, and formulas from the text for easy reference during tests or comprehensive reviews. It also contains additional material on business measurements, the metric system, and international applications, including currency conversion and import/export issues. More than 400 additional review exercises cover each chapter in the main text, providing another source of practice problems. This manual can be ordered at a minimal cost through the bookstore as a stand-alone supplement or shrinkwrapped with the text. The third edition SRM also includes a calculator workbook of a 10-key or financial calculator. Practice problems are included.

PowerPoint Solutions (ISBN 0-03-035463-3)

The worked-out solutions to all of the Section Review Exercises are available on PowerPoint slides, as well as on transparencies. This gives the instructor the option of going over the solutions to these exercises electronically in class or making the slides available to the students in a lab for them to check their work on their own time. The Third Edition PowerPoint slides also include chapter outlines and key concepts for classroom lectures.

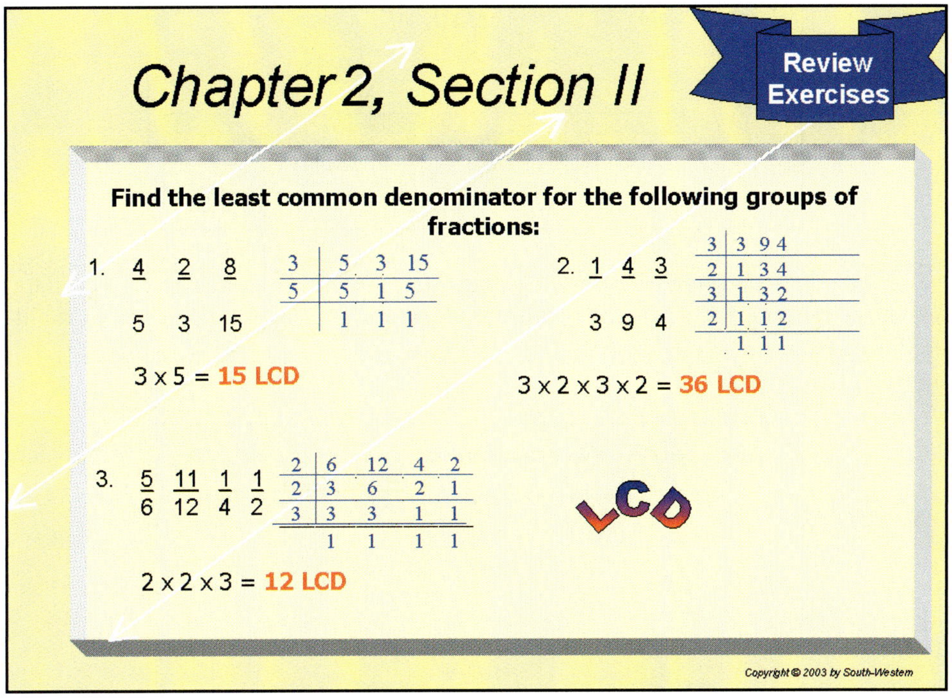

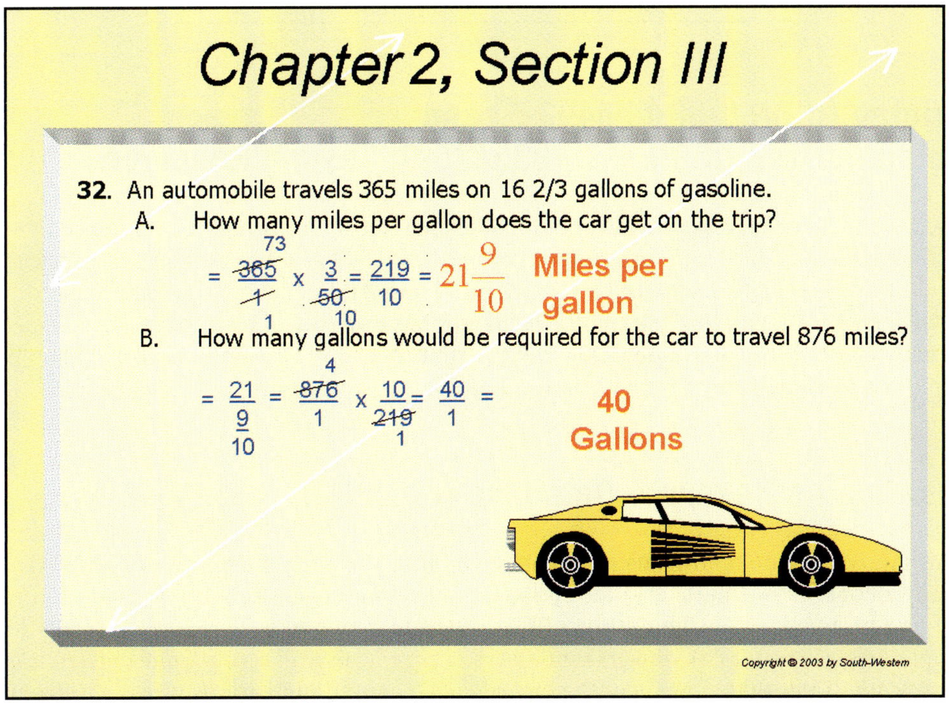

Teaching (ISBN 0-03-035486-2) and Solutions (ISBN 0-03-035471-4) Transparency Acetate Package

Available in acetate form are more than 200 two- and four-color **teaching transparencies** derived from figures, exhibits, and Try-It Exercises in the text. These provide an easy display format to reinforce important concepts.

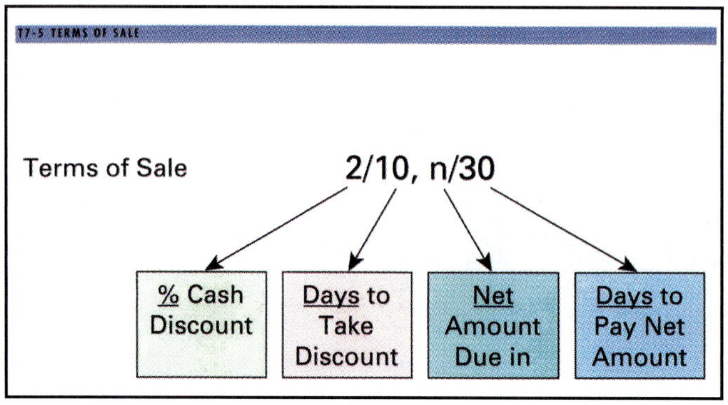

Also provided are **solution transparencies** keyed to the review exercises in each chapter. Icons in the Annotated Instructor's Edition indicate where the transparencies should be used during lecture.

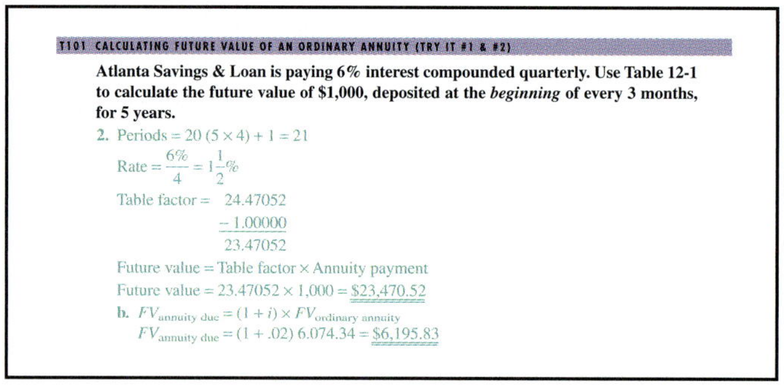

Printed (ISBN 0-03-035493-5) and Computerized (ISBN 0-03-035426-9) Testing Resources

These valuable resources provide additional testing items for instructor's reference in four distinct formats. The Test Bank contains more than 2,500 problems ranging from vocabulary reviews and matching to drill and word problems. Additional multiple choice questions have been added with this edition. Each chapter has a variety of tests and practice quizzes already created for easy duplication and distribution. This Test Bank is also available in Windows software format from Thomson Learning Testing Tools™.

Instructor's Resource Database (ISBN 0-03-035441-2)

This innovative tool allows instructors to customize their teaching notes for class. Every chapter contains a general chapter outline and teaching suggestions, ideas, and problem-solving hints based on the author's 36 years of teaching experience, and suggestions from our class testers, reviewers, and users. There is also a section on using *The Business Math Times* that appears at the end of each chapter and various ways to utilize the

"Collaborative Learning Activities." Finally, there are numerous suggestions and instructions for using the MathCue.Business Tutorial Software and the PowerPoint electronic transparencies, and incorporating video into the classroom. A new section has been added to the Third Edition "Questions Students Always Ask." This will be especially helpful for adjunct instructors.

Spreadsheet Exercises

New for the Third Edition, these Excel exercises help students to understand the concepts presented in the text and to apply the topics in a realistic and meaningful manner. These exercises are designed to help students learn how Excel (and spreadsheets in general) can be used to perform calculations and display results in mathematical and financial contexts. In addition, they will enhance students' problem analysis skills by requiring careful consideration of the inputs and outputs involved in a variety of business situations.

Unique to *Contemporary Mathematics for Business and Consumers,* each chapter includes Excel exercises presented at three levels of difficulty:

- **Beginner**—In Level 1 exercises, students are asked to enter the appropriate data. All formulas and labels are provided.
- **Intermediate**—In Level 2 exercises, students must determine which formulas are needed, then enter them as well as the data.
- **Advanced**—In Level 3 exercises, students demonstrate a mastery of Excel by creating all aspects of the spreadsheet from a given set of data.

Videos

There is video support to accompany this text that will bring topics to life for students, increasing their enjoyment of business math as well as their understanding. A description of our video offerings is available on our Web site.

Web Site

- Web site: http://brechner.swcollege.com. Our Web site provides support for both instructors and students. Features include downloadable supplements, research library, career advice, and interactive learning tools.
- Web Tutor on Blackboard (ISBN 0-324-18649-5); Web Tutor on WebCT (ISBN 0-324-18650-9): These online learning aids include discussion questions, flashcards, multiple-choice quizzes, and links to MathCue and the product support site.

Contributors to *Contemporary Mathematics*

Contemporary Mathematics for Business and Consumers benefited from the valuable input of instructors throughout the country. I would like to especially thank those who responded to our questions about how they teach business math and those who reviewed various parts of the manuscript and/or allowed this book to be tested by their classes.

Reviewers:

Alton Amidon, Pamlico Community College
Carol Baker, Napa Valley Community College
Christine F. Belles, Macomb Community College
Don Boyer, Jefferson College
Natalie Card, Utah Valley State College
Milton Cohen, Fairfax Community Adult Education
Frank DiFerdinando, Hudson County Community College
Elizabeth Domenico, Gaston College
J.D. Dulgeroff, San Bernardino Valley Community College
Acie B. Earl, Black Hawk Community College
Rene Garcia, Miami-Dade Community College, Wolfson Campus
Patricia Gardner, San Bernardino Valley College
Glen Gelderloos, Grand Rapids Community College
Cecil Green, Riverside Community College

Stephen W. Griffin, Tarrant County Junior College, South Campus
James Grigsby, Lake Sumter Community College
Paul Grutsis, San Bernardino Valley College
Giselle Halpern, El Camino Community College
John Heinsius, Modesto Junior College
Phil C. Kopriva, San Francisco Community College District
Rosemarie LeFebvre, Mohave Community College
Gwendolyn Loftis, Rose State College
Paul H. Martin, Aims Community College
Sharon Meyer, Pikes Peak Community College
Zo Miller, Rose State College
Jack L. Nelson, Ferris State University
Wayne A. Paper, Hawkeye Institute of Technology
Wayne Price, Napa Valley Community College
Barbara Rosenthal, Miami-Dade Community College, Wolfson Campus
Ben Sadler, Miami-Dade Community College, Wolfson Campus
Amy Shinoki, Kapiolani Community College
David D. Stringer, DeAnza College
Lynette Teal, Western WI Technical College
Steven Teeter, Utah Valley State College
Charles Webb, Miami-Dade Community College, Wolfson Campus
Gregory J. Worosz, Schoolcraft College

Phone Survey Respondents:

Jeffrey Abrams, Newport Business Institute
Terry Alexander, Denver Technical College
Charles Anderson, TN Technology Center at Livingston
David Blum, Moraine Park Technical College
Rita Boetell, Bakersfield College
Barry Brandbold, Aaker's Business College
Norma Broadway, Hinds Community College
Howard Bryan, Santa Rosa Junior College
Dr. Bob Bulls, J.S. Reynolds County College
Roy Bunek, Fugazzi College
Patricia Calloway, East Mississippi County College
Lisa Campenella, ICSI (Allentown, PA)
John H. Carpenter, Polk Community College
Roger D. Chagnon, Jamestown Business College
Victor Clearsuas, Holyoke Community College
Carol Coeyman, Yorktown Business Institute
George Converse, Stone Academy
Ron Cooley, South Suburban College
William S. Dahlman, Premier Career College
Nancy Degnan, Sawyer School
Karen Desele, Gillette
Joe D. DiCostanzo, Johnson County Community College
Stephen Ernest, Baton Rouge School of Computers
Carol Ferguson, Rock Valley College
Mark Finger, Madison Area Technical College
Dennis Franklin, Culinary Arts Institute
Rachael Freuche, Indiana Business College
Rick Gallardo, International Business College
Miriam Gateley, Valencia Community College
Cynthia Gerber, Indiana Business College
Jeff Gordon, San Joaquin Valley College
Carolyn Green, Universal Business & Media School
Bob Grenier, Vatterott College
Ray Hale, Rets Medical & Business Institute
Michael Hlebik, Erie Business School
Bill Holbrook, Owensboro Junior College of Business
Brenda Holmes, Northwest Mississippi Community College
John Hudson, National Business College
Jared Jay, American Commercial College
Joanne Kaufman, Metro Business College
Patti Koluda, Yakima Valley County College
Janice Lawrence, Northwestern Business College
Suzann Lewison, Southwestern WI Technical College
Marvin Mai, Empire College
Jackie Marshall, Ohio Business College
Faye Massey, Northwest Mississippi Community College
Cheryl McGahee, Guilford Community College
Mary Jo McKinney, American School of Business
Hugh McNiece, Lincolnland County College
Rose Miller, Milwaukee Area Technical College
Charlene Mulleollan, Dubois Business College
Jim Murray, Western WI Technical College
Steve O'Rourke, Newcastle Business School
Peggy Peterson, Rasmusson College
Barbara Portzen, Mid State Technical College
Edward Pratowski, Dorsey Business School
Rose Ramirez, MTL Business College of Stockton
Bill Rleodarmer, Haywood County College
Linda Rockwall, Ridley Lowell Business & Technical Institute
Steve Shaw, Tidewater Tech
Susan Shaw, Southwestern Business College
Chuck Sherryll, Community College of Aurora
Forrest Simmons, Portland Community College
Eileen Snyder, Harrisburg Area Community College
Adina Solomon, Vatterott College
Walter Soroka, Newcastle School of Trade
Teresa Stephenson, Indianapolis Business School
Mary Susa, Mid-State Technical College
Kermit Swanson, Rasmussen College
Paula Terrones, College of Office Technology
Arthur Walter, Suffolk Community College
Winston Wrenn, Draughton Junior College
Gaylon Wright, Angelina College
Sandra Young, Business Institute of Pennsylvania

I would like to extend personal thanks to the many academic and business information contributors who helped me develop this book:

Santiago Alan
Bob Albrecht
John Aldrich
John Anderson
Vince Arenas
Marcie Bader

Christine Balmori
Robert Barton
Charlie Beavin
Jessica Bergeman
Ed Blakemore
Joan Braverman
Martha Cavalaris
Patricia Conroy
Ralph Covert
Nancy De La Vega
Elliott Denner
John Dunham
Ivan Figueroa
Mario Font
Butch Gemin
Blanca Gonzalez
Abdul Hamza
Lionel Howard
Scott Isenberg
Al Kahn
Joseph Kreutle
Kimberly Lipscomb
Jaime Lopez
Jane Mangrum
Jim McHugh
Marvin Mai
Noemi McPherson
Sharon Meyer
Rolando Montoya
Joseph Moutran
Sylvia Ratner
Cheryl Robinson
Brian Rochlin
Michael Roher
Howard Schoninger
Richard Waldman
Joseph Walzer
Kathryn Warren
Larry Zigler

Also, I would like to thank the corporate and government organizations that I used as examples and sources of information in preparing and developing this book:

Aetna
Ann Taylor
AMR Corporation
Arthur Andersen & Company
Bank of America
Barnett Banks, Inc.
Board of Governors, Federal Reserve System
Bureau of Labor Statistics
Citicorp Financial Services
Dell
Dow Jones, Inc., *The Wall Street Journal*
Federal Express
Goodrich
Harcourt General, Inc.
Harley-Davidson
Home Depot
Internal Revenue Service
Kellogg
Knight-Ridder, Inc., *The Miami Herald*
Macy's
MasterCard International
Microsoft
Office Depot
Popular Bank of Florida
Radio Shack
Reebok, Inc.
Ryder
Smith Barney Shearson
State of Florida, Department of Revenue
Target
Time, Inc., *Fortune Magazine*
Town & Country
Toyota Motors
Toys 'R' Us, Inc.
Transamerica Life Companies
Transocean
Tribune
Tupperware
U.S. Department of Commerce
U.S. Department of Housing and Urban Development
U.S. Government Printing Office, *Statistical Abstract of the United States*
U.S. Timber
Wal-Mart, Inc.
Walt Disney Company
Winn-Dixie Stores, Inc.

I would like to gratefully acknowledge and thank all of the team members at both Harcourt and our new home, South-Western Thomson, for making the transition to a new company and the third edition so smooth and complete. Like Olympians handing off the baton in a relay race, you didn't miss a beat!

Special thanks to publisher Mike Roche, market strategist Julie Conover, acquisitions editor Tracy Morse, and developmental editor Heather Hogan for the handoff; and to vice president and team leader Melissa Acuña, senior acquisitions editor Charles McCormick, developmental editor Mardell Toomey, marketing manager Mignon Tucker, and production editor Marcella Combs for the running catch. I am thrilled to be associated with such talented and dedicated professionals, and look forward to a long and wonderful relationship.

Thanks also to director of technology Tim Butz, media/technology editor Diane Van Bakel, and media developmental editor Christine Wittmer for your technical expertise and valuable input; to picture and rights editor Linda Blundell, for being there—long after, and to career school channel manager Brian Joyner, for your terrific support and energy.

My heartfelt thanks are also extended to the staff at Elm Street Publishing Services, especially production manager Isabel Fiore and project editor Steven Knoerr, copyeditor Paula Stephenson, and proofreader Charlotte Hyland. You have all been a pleasure to work with, and I hope we can do an encore performance in the future.

To my supplement preparers, many thanks for the following great works:

- Test Bank—Chuck Trester, Northeast Wisconsin Technical College; Milt Cohen, Fairfax Community Adult Education; Ann Germain, Cosumnes River College; and Virginia Choate, test bank verifier.
- Spreadsheet Exercises—George Bergeman, Northern Virginia Community College; Maria Castro.
- Instructor's Resource Database—Heidi Gahler Bolong, Yakima Valley Community College.
- PowerPoint Solutions—Tina Pitt, Heald College.
- Student Resource Manual—Claudia Babich; and Terri D. Bellman, Coastal Bend College.

Finally, I would like to acknowledge my good friend, colleague, and software maven, George Bergeman. A world of thanks for your endless support and a fabulous new edition of Mathcue.Business, student tutorial software. Truly, developed by a beautiful mind!

Robert A. Brechner
February 2002

CONTENTS IN BRIEF

CONTENTS

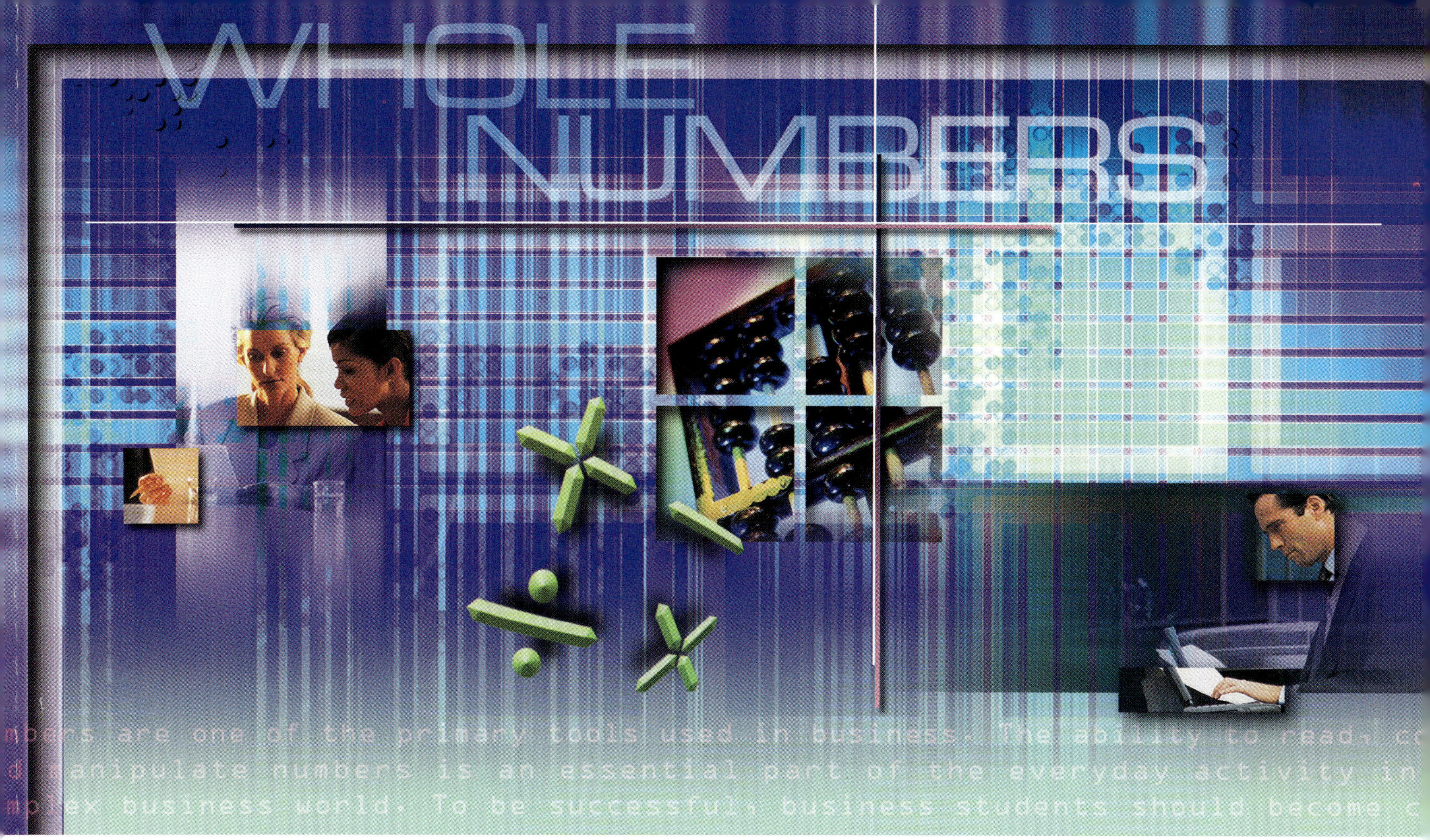

CHAPTER 1

Whole Numbers

PERFORMANCE OBJECTIVES

Section I The Decimal Number System: Whole Numbers

1-1 Reading and writing whole numbers in numerical and word form. (p. 2)
1-2 Rounding whole numbers to a specified place value. (p. 4)

Section II Addition and Subtraction of Whole Numbers

1-3 Adding whole numbers and verifying your answers. (p. 8)
1-4 Subtracting whole numbers and verifying your answers. (p. 10)

Section III Multiplication and Division of Whole Numbers

1-5 Multiplying whole numbers and verifying your answers. (p. 16)
1-6 Dividing whole numbers and verifying your answers. (p. 19)

SECTION I

THE DECIMAL NUMBER SYSTEM: WHOLE NUMBERS

Numbers are one of the primary tools used in business. The ability to read, comprehend, and manipulate numbers is an essential part of the everyday activity in today's complex business world. To be successful, business students should become competent and confident in dealing with numbers.

We shall begin our study of business mathematics with whole numbers and their basic operations—addition, subtraction, multiplication, and division. The material in this chapter is based on the assumption that you have a basic working knowledge of these operations. Our goal is to review these fundamentals and build accuracy and speed. This arithmetic review will set the groundwork for our study of fractions, decimals, and percents. Most business math applications involve calculations using these components.

decimal number system
A system using the 10 Hindu-Arabic symbols, 0 through 9. In this place-value system, the position of a digit to the left or right of the decimal point affects its value.

decimal point
A dot written in a decimal number to indicate where the place values change from whole numbers to decimals.

The number system most widely used in the world today is known as the Hindu-Arabic, or **decimal number system.** This system is far superior to any other for today's complex business calculations. It derives its name from the Latin words *decimus,* meaning 10th, and *decem,* meaning 10. The decimal system is based on 10s, with the starting point marked by a dot known as the **decimal point.** The decimal system uses the 10 familiar Hindu-Arabic symbols or digits:

0, 1, 2, 3, 4, 5, 6, 7, 8, 9

1-1 Reading and Writing Whole Numbers in Numerical and Word Form

whole number
Any number, 0 or greater, that does not contain a decimal or fraction. Whole numbers are found to the left of the decimal point. Also known as an integer. For example, 6, 25, and 300 are whole numbers.

The major advantage of our decimal system over previous systems is that the position of a digit to the left or right of the decimal point affects its value. This enables us to write any number with only the 10 single-digit numbers, 0 through 9. For this reason, we have given names to the places or positions. In this chapter we work with places to the left of the decimal point, **whole numbers.** The next two chapters are concerned with the places to the right of the decimal point, fractions and decimals.

The Hindu-Arabic, or decimal number system, is based on an ancient system of counting, yet it remains the system best suited for today's complex scientific and business calculations.

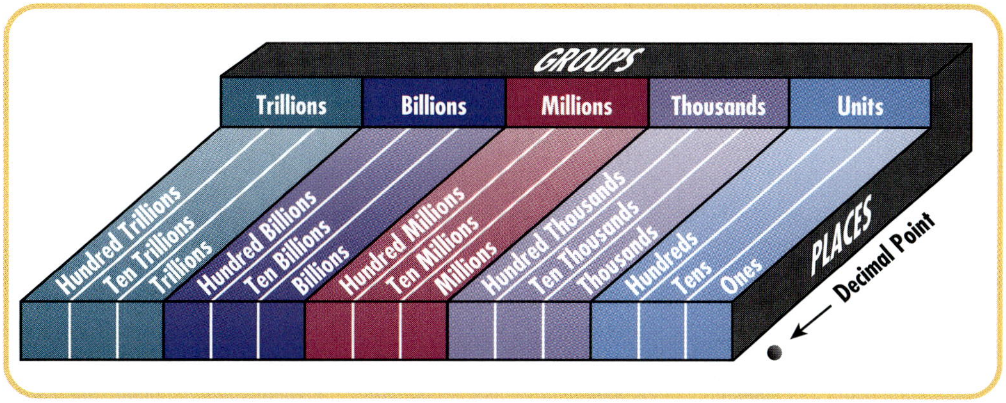

EXHIBIT 1-1

Whole Number Place Value Chart

When whole numbers are written, a decimal point is understood to be located on the right of the number. For example, the number **27** is actually

27.

The decimal point is not displayed until we write a decimal number or dollars and cents, such as 27.25 inches or $27.25.

Exhibit 1-1 illustrates the first 15 places, and five groups, of the decimal number system. Note that our system is made up of groups of three places, separated by commas, each with their own name. Whole numbers start at the understood decimal point and increase in value from right to left. Each group contains the same three places: one, 10, and 100. Note that each place increases by a factor of "times 10." The group names are units, thousands, millions, billions, and trillions.

STEPS FOR READING AND WRITING WHOLE NUMBERS:

Step 1. Beginning at the right side of the number, insert a comma every three digits to mark the groups.

Step 2. Beginning from left to right, name the digits and the groups. The units group and groups that have all zeros are not named.

Step 3. When writing whole numbers in word form, the numbers from 21 to 99 are hyphenated (except for the decades, e.g., thirty). For example, 83 would be written eighty-three.

Note: The word *and* should *not* be used in reading or writing whole numbers. It represents the decimal point and will be covered in Chapter 3.

Everybody's Business

Real-World Connection

In text, large numbers, in the millions and greater, may be easier to read by writing the "zero's portion" in words. For example, 44,000,000,000,000 may be written as 44 trillion.

EXAMPLES

Read and write the following whole numbers in numerical and word form:

a. 14296 **b.** 560

c. 2294857 **d.** 184910

e. 3004959001 **f.** 24000064

For additional help with whole numbers, visit our Web site at www.contemporarymath.com.

SOLUTION STRATEGY

Following the steps above, we insert the commas to mark the groups, then read and write the numbers from left to right.

	Number	Numerical Form	Word Form
a.	14296	14,296	fourteen thousand, two hundred ninety-six
b.	560	560	five hundred sixty
c.	2294857	2,294,857	two million, two hundred ninety-four thousand, eight hundred fifty-seven
d.	184910	184,910	one hundred eighty-four thousand, nine hundred ten
e.	3004959001	3,004,959,001	three billion, four million, nine hundred fifty-nine thousand, one
f.	24000064	24,000,064	twenty-four million, sixty-four

TRY-IT | EXERCISES

Read and write the following whole numbers in numerical and word form:

1. 49588 **2.** 804 **3.** 1928837 **4.** 900015

5. 6847365911 **6.** 2000300007

Check your answers with the solutions on page 27.

1-2 Rounding Whole Numbers to a Specified Place Value

rounded numbers
Numbers that are approximations or estimates of exact numbers. For example, 50 is the rounded number of the exact number 49.

In many business applications, an approximation of an exact number may be more desirable to use than the number itself. Approximations, or **rounded numbers,** are easier to refer to and remember. For example, if a grocery store carries 9,858 items on its shelves, you would probably say that it carries 10,000 items. If you drive 1,593 miles, you would say that the trip is 1,600 miles. Another rounding application in business involves money. If your company has profits of $1,302,201, you might refer to this exact amount by the rounded number $1,300,000. Money amounts are usually rounded to the nearest cent, although they could also be rounded to the nearest dollar or to any other place.

estimate
To calculate approximately the amount or value of something. The number 50 would be an estimate of 49.

rounding all the way
A process of rounding numbers to the first digit. Used to prework a problem to an estimated answer. For example, 2,865 rounded all the way is 3,000.

Rounded numbers are frequently used to **estimate** an answer to a problem, before working that problem. Estimation approximates the exact answer. By knowing an estimate of an answer in advance, you will be able to catch many math errors. When using estimation to prework a problem, you can generally round off to the first digit, which is called **rounding all the way.**

Once you have rounded to the first digit, perform the indicated math procedure. This can often be done quickly and will give you a ballpark or general idea of the actual answer. In the example below, the estimated answer of 26,000 is a good indicator of the "reasonableness" of the actual answer.

Original Calculation	Estimated Solution (rounding all the way)	Actual Solution
19,549	20,000	19,549
+ 6,489	+ 6,000	+ 6,489
	26,000	26,038

If, for example, you had mistakenly added for a total of 23,038 instead of 26,038, your estimate would have immediately indicated that something was wrong.

Form **1040** Department of the Treasury—Internal Revenue Service
U.S. Individual Income Tax Return **200X** (99) IRS Use Only—Do not write or staple in this space.

For the year Jan. 1–Dec. 31, 2001, or other tax year beginning , 2001, ending , 20 OMB No. 1545-0074

Label (See instructions on page 19.) **Use the IRS label.** Otherwise, please print or type. LABEL HERE

Your first name and initial: *John Q* | Last name: *Public* | Your social security number: *123 45 6789*
If a joint return, spouse's first name and initial | Last name | Spouse's social security number
Home address (number and street). If you have a P.O. box, see page 19.: *301 Main Street* | Apt. no.
City, town or post office, state, and ZIP code. If you have a foreign address, see page 19.: *Anytown FL 30301*

Important! You **must** enter your SSN(s) above.

Presidential Election Campaign (See page 19.)
Note. Checking "Yes" will not change your tax or reduce your refund.
Do you, or your spouse if filing a joint return, want $3 to go to this fund? ▶ You ☐ Yes ☐ No Spouse ☐ Yes ☐ No

Filing Status Check only one box.
1 ☑ Single
2 ☐ Married filing joint return (even if only one had income)
3 ☐ Married filing separate return. Enter spouse's social security no. above and full name here. ▶
4 ☐ Head of household (with qualifying person). (See page 19.) If the qualifying person is a child but not your dependent, enter this child's name here. ▶
5 ☐ Qualifying widow(er) with dependent child (year spouse died ▶). (See page 19.)

Exemptions
6a ☑ **Yourself.** If your parent (or someone else) can claim you as a dependent on his or her tax return, **do not** check box 6a
b ☐ **Spouse**
c **Dependents:** (1) First name, Last name | (2) Dependent's social security number | (3) Dependent's relationship to you | (4) ✓ if qualifying child for child tax credit (see page 20)
If more than six dependents, see page 20.
d Total number of exemptions claimed

No. of boxes checked on 6a and 6b: *1*
No. of your children on 6c who: • lived with you • did not live with you due to divorce or separation (see page 20)
Dependents on 6c not entered above
Add numbers entered on lines above ▶ *1*

		Line	Amount
Income	7 Wages, salaries, tips, etc. Attach Form(s) W-2	7	25,275
Attach Forms W-2 and W-2G here. Also attach Form(s) 1099-R if tax was withheld.	8a **Taxable** interest. Attach Schedule B if required	8a	200
	b **Tax-exempt** interest. **Do not** include on line 8a 8b		
	9 Ordinary dividends. Attach Schedule B if required	9	
	10 Taxable refunds, credits, or offsets of state and local income taxes (see page 22)	10	575
	11 Alimony received	11	
	12 Business income or (loss). Attach Schedule C or C-EZ	12	2,300
	13 Capital gain or (loss). Attach Schedule D if required. If not required, check here ▶ ☐	13	
	14 Other gains or (losses). Attach Form 4797	14	
If you did not get a W-2, see page 21.	15a Total IRA distributions 15a; b Taxable amount (see page 23)	15b	
	16a Total pensions and annuities 16a; b Taxable amount (see page 23)	16b	
	17 Rental real estate, royalties, partnerships, S corporations, trusts, etc. Attach Schedule E	17	4,600
Enclose, but do not attach, any payment. Also, please use Form 1040-V.	18 Farm income or (loss). Attach Schedule F	18	
	19 Unemployment compensation	19	
	20a Social security benefits 20a; b Taxable amount (see page 25)	20b	
	21 Other income. List type and amount (see page 27)	21	
	22 Add the amounts in the far right column for lines 7 through 21. This is your **total income** ▶	22	32,950
Adjusted Gross Income	23 IRA deduction (see page 27) 23: 500		
	24 Student loan interest deduction (see page 28) 24		
	25 Archer MSA deduction. Attach Form 8853 25		
	26 Moving expenses. Attach Form 3903 26		
	27 One-half of self-employment tax. Attach Schedule SE 27		
	28 Self-employed health insurance deduction (see page 30) 28		
	29 Self-employed SEP, SIMPLE, and qualified plans 29		
	30 Penalty on early withdrawal of savings 30		
	31a Alimony paid b Recipient's SSN ▶ 31a		
	32 Add lines 23 through 31a	32	500
	33 Subtract line 32 from line 22. This is your **adjusted gross income** ▶	33	32,450

For Disclosure, Privacy Act, and Paperwork Reduction Act Notice, see page 72. Cat. No. 11320B Form **1040** (2001)

Everybody's Business

Real-World Connection

The Internal Revenue Service requires that monetary amounts reported on income tax forms be rounded to the nearest dollar.

Skills you acquire in this course will be applied frequently in your roles as a consumer and a businessperson.

STEPS FOR ROUNDING WHOLE NUMBERS TO A SPECIFIED PLACE VALUE:

Step 1. Determine the place to which the number is to be rounded.

Step 2a. If the digit to the right of the place being rounded is 5 or more, increase the digit in that place by 1.

Step 2b. If the digit to the right of the place being rounded is 4 or less, do not change the digit in the place being rounded.

Step 3. Change all digits to the right of the place being rounded to zeros.

EXAMPLES

Round the following numbers to the indicated place:

a. 1,867 to tens
b. 760 to hundreds
c. 129,338 to thousands
d. 293,847 to hundred thousands
e. 97,078,838,576 to billions
f. 85,600,061 all the way

SOLUTION STRATEGY

Following the steps above, locate the place to be rounded, use the digit to the right of that place to determine whether to round up or leave it as is, then change all digits to the right of the place being rounded to zeros.

	Place Indicated	Rounded Number
a. 1,867 to tens	1,867	1,870
b. 760 to hundreds	760	800
c. 129,338 to thousands	129,338	129,000
d. 293,847 to hundred thousands	293,847	300,000
e. 97,078,838,576 to billions	97,078,838,576	97,000,000,000
f. 85,600,061 all the way	85,600,061	90,000,000

TRY-IT | EXERCISES

Round the following numbers to the indicated place:

7. 51,667 to hundreds
8. 23,441 to tens
9. 175,445,980 to ten thousands

10. 59,561 all the way
11. 14,657,000,138 to billions

12. 8,009,070,436 to ten millions

Check your answers with the solutions on page 27.

REVIEW EXERCISES | CHAPTER 1—SECTION I

Read and write the following whole numbers in numerical and word form:

Number	Numerical Form	Word Form
1. 22938	________	______________________
2. 1573	________	______________________
3. 184	________	______________________
4. 984773	________	______________________
5. 2433590	________	______________________
6. 49081472	________	______________________

Write the following whole numbers in numerical form:

7. One hundred eighty-three thousand, six hundred twenty-two ________

8. Two million, forty-three thousand, twelve ________

9. One thousand, nine hundred thirty-six ________

Match the following numbers in word form with the numbers in numerical form:

10. One hundred two thousand, four hundred seventy ___	**a.** 11,270
11. One hundred twelve thousand, seven hundred forty-three ___	**b.** 102,470
12. Twelve thousand, seven hundred forty-three ___	**c.** 102,740
13. Eleven thousand, two hundred seventy ___	**d.** 112,743
14. One hundred two thousand, seven hundred forty ___	**e.** 12,743

Round the following numbers to the indicated place:

15. 1,757 to tens ________

16. 32,475 to thousands ________

17. 235,376 to hundreds ________

18. 559,443 to ten thousands ________

19. 8,488,710 to millions ________

20. 45,699 all the way ________

21. 1,325,669,226 to hundred millions ________

22. 23,755 all the way ________

23. 18,750,000,000 to billions ________

24. 860,002 to hundred thousands ________

BUSINESS DECISION

Up or Down?

25. You are responsible for writing a monthly stockholder's recap report about your company. Your boss has given you the flexibility to round the numbers to tens, hundreds, thousands, or not at all depending on which is the most beneficial for the company's image. For each of the following numbers for the past month, make a rounding choice and explain your reasoning:

a. 75,469—number of items manufactured ________________

b. $245,833—your department's net sales for the month ________________

c. 5,648—defective items manufactured ________________

d. $649,341—total company profit ________________

e. 149 new customers ________________

SECTION II

ADDITION AND SUBTRACTION OF WHOLE NUMBERS

Addition and subtraction are the most basic mathematical operations. They are used in almost all business calculations. In business, amounts of things or dollars are often combined or added to determine the total. Likewise, subtraction is frequently used to determine an amount of something after it has been reduced in quantity. Typical examples might be a decrease in inventory or a reduction of a bank account balance when writing checks. This section reviews the basics of addition and subtraction. With practice, it will help increase your accuracy and speed.

It is important for businesspeople to be able to do the basic mathematical calculations by hand. In business, you may not always have a calculator when you need to do math. For now, put aside your calculator. Use only pencil and paper to compute the exercises in the next few sections. After this review chapter, you will be asked to use your calculators once again.

Everybody's Business

Real-World Connection

Basic math proficiency without calculators is important. Calculators are not permitted on most employment tests and Civil Service exams.

1-3 Adding Whole Numbers and Verifying Your Answers

Addition is the mathematical process of computing sets of numbers to find their sum, or total. The numbers being added are known as **addends,** and the result or answer of the addition is known as the **sum, total,** or **amount.** The "+" symbol represents addition and is called the **plus sign.**

1,932	addend
2,928	addend
+ 6,857	addend
11,717	total

addition
The mathematical process of computing sets of numbers to find their sum or total.

addends
Any of a set of numbers being added in an addition problem. For example, 4 and 1 are the addends of the addition problem 4 + 1 = 5.

sum, total, or amount
The result or answer of an addition problem. The number 5 is the sum or total of 4 + 1 = 5.

plus sign
The symbol "+" representing addition.

STEPS FOR ADDING WHOLE NUMBERS:

Step 1. Write the whole numbers in columns so that you line up the place values—units, tens, hundreds, thousands, and so on.

Step 2. Add the digits in each column, starting on the right with the units column.

Step 3. When the total in a column is greater than nine, write the units digit and carry the tens digit to the top of the next column to the left.

VERIFYING ADDITION

Generally, when adding the digits in each column, we add from top to bottom. An easy and commonly used method of verifying your addition is to add the numbers again, but this time from bottom to top. By adding the digits in the *reverse* order, you will check your answer without making the same error twice.

For illustrative purposes, addition verification will be rewritten in reverse. In actuality, you do not have to rewrite the numbers, just add them from bottom to top. As mentioned earlier, speed and accuracy will be achieved with practice.

ADDITION SHORTCUT

Once you become proficient at verifying addition, you can speed up your addition by recognizing and combining two numbers that add up to 10, such as 1 + 9, 2 + 8, 6 + 4, 5 + 5, and so on. After you have mastered combining two numbers, try combining three numbers that add up to 10, such as 3 + 3 + 4, 2 + 5 + 3, 4 + 4 + 2, and so on.

A WORD ABOUT WORD PROBLEMS

In business math, calculations are only a part of the story! Business math, most importantly, requires the ability to (a) understand and analyze the facts of business situations; (b) determine what information is given and what is missing; and (c) decide what strategy and procedure is required to solve for an answer. Business application word problems are an important part of each chapter's subject matter. As you progress through the course, your ability to analyze and solve these business situations will improve. Now, start slowly, and relax!

EXAMPLES

Add the following sets of whole numbers. Verify your answers by adding in reverse:

a.
```
   40,562
   29,381
 + 60,095
```

b. 2,293 + 121 + 7,706 + 20 + 57,293 + 4

c. A furniture manufacturing company has 229 employees in the cutting department, 439 employees in the assembly department, and 360 in the finishing department. There are 57 warehouse workers, 23 salespeople, 4 bookkeepers, 12 secretaries, and 5 executives. How many people work for this company?

SOLUTION STRATEGY

a. Step 1. Write the numbers in columns so that the place values line up. In this example they are already lined up.

Step 2. Add the digits in each column, starting with the units column.

```
   11 2
   40,562
   29,381
 + 60,095
  130,038
```

Units column: 2 + 1 + 5 = 8 Enter the 8 under the units column.

Tens column: 6 + 8 + 9 = 23 Enter the 3 under the tens column and carry the 2 to the hundreds column.

Hundreds column: 2 + 5 + 3 + 0 = 10 Enter the 0 under the hundreds column and carry the 1 to the thousands column.

Thousands column: 1 + 0 + 9 + 0 = 10 Enter the 0 under the thousands column and carry the 1 to the ten thousands column.

Ten thousands column: 1 + 4 + 2 + 6 = 13 Enter the 3 under the ten thousands column and the 1 under the hundred thousands column.

Verification:

```
   11 2
   60,095
   29,381
 + 40,562
  130,038
```

Everybody's Business

Overcoming Math Anxiety

Math! It often transforms otherwise excellent students into a state of absolute anxiety.

The following are a few pointers to help you reduce the anxiety and learn a new and essential life-skill, mathematics:

- Not everybody learns at the same speed. It may take you a little longer; that's OK!
- Everybody makes mistakes. View them as learning opportunities, not as failures.
- Attendance is very important. A missed class is hard to make up.
- Read the textbook—don't just skip to the exercises.
- Don't memorize. Try to understand the concepts.
- Do your homework and be ready to ask questions about things you don't understand.
- Woodrow Wilson said, "I not only use all the brains that I have, but all that I can borrow." Study with a friend; test each other.
- Relax!

b. Addition	Verification
1121	1121
2,293	4
121	57,293
7,706	20
20	7,706
57,293	121
+ 4	+ 2,293
67,437 ←	67,437

c. Addition	Verification
23	23
229	5
439	12
360	4
57	23
23	57
4	360
12	439
+ 5	+ 229
1,129 ←	1,129

TRY-IT | EXERCISES

Add the following sets of whole numbers and verify your answers:

13.

$$\begin{array}{r} 39{,}481 \\ 5{,}594 \\ +\ 11{,}029 \\ \hline \end{array}$$

14. 6,948 + 330 + 7,946 + 89 + 5,583,991 + 7 + 18,606

15. Paulo's Italian Restaurant served 183 meals on Monday, 228 meals on Tuesday, 281 meals on Wednesday, 545 meals on Thursday, and 438 meals on Friday. On the weekend they served 1,157 meals. How many total meals were served that week?

Check your answers with the solutions on page 27.

1-4 Subtracting Whole Numbers and Verifying Your Answers

subtraction
The mathematical process of taking away, or deducting, an amount from a given number.

minuend
In subtraction, the original number. The amount from which another number, the subtrahend, is subtracted. For example, 5 is the minuend of the subtraction problem 5 − 1 = 4.

subtrahend
The amount being taken or subtracted from the minuend. For example, 1 is the subtrahend of 5 − 1 = 4.

difference or remainder
The number obtained when one number is subtracted from another. The answer or result of subtraction. For example, 4 is the difference or remainder of 5 − 1 = 4.

minus sign
The symbol "−" representing subtraction.

Subtraction is the mathematical computation of taking away, or deducting, an amount from a given number. Subtraction is the opposite of addition. The original or top number is the **minuend,** the amount we are subtracting from the original number is the **subtrahend,** and the answer is the **remainder,** or **difference.** The "−" symbol represents subtraction and is called the **minus sign.** In subtraction, the answer or difference is usually a positive number. Sometimes, however, the subtrahend will be larger than the minuend, resulting in a negative number.

$$\begin{array}{rl} 938{,}477 & \text{minuend} \\ -\ \ 4{,}482 & \text{subtrahend} \\ \hline 933{,}995 & \text{difference} \end{array}$$

STEPS FOR SUBTRACTING WHOLE NUMBERS:

Step 1. Write the whole numbers in columns so that the place values line up.

Step 2. Starting with the units column, subtract the digits.

Step 3. When a column cannot be subtracted, you must "borrow" a digit from the column to the left of the one you are working in.

VERIFYING SUBTRACTION

An easy and well-known method of verifying subtraction is to add the difference and the subtrahend. If you subtracted correctly, this total will equal the minuend.

Subtraction	Verification
200 minuend	150 difference
− 50 subtrahend	+ 50 subtrahend
150 difference	200 minuend

EXAMPLES

Subtract the following whole numbers and verify your answers:

a. 4,968 − 192

b. 189,440 − 1,347

c. On Monday morning, Appliance Depot had 165 microwave ovens in inventory. During the week the store had a clearance sale and sold 71 of the ovens. How many ovens remain in stock for next week?

SOLUTION STRATEGY

a.

Step 1. Write the numbers in columns so that the place values are lined up. In this problem they are already lined up.

```
    8
 4,968
 − 192
 4,776
```

Step 2. Starting with the units column, subtract the digits.

Units column: 8 − 2 = 6 Enter the 6 under the units column.

Tens column: 6 − 9 can't be subtracted so we must borrow a digit, 10, from the hundreds column of the minuend. This reduces the 9 to an 8 and gives us a 10 to add to the 6, making it 16.

Now we can subtract 9 from 16 to get 7. Enter the 7 under the tens column.

Hundreds column: 8 − 1 = 7. Enter the 7 under the hundreds column.

Thousands column: This column has no subtrahend, so just bring down the 4 from the minuend to the answer line.

Verification:

```
    1
 4,776
 + 192
 4,968
```

b. **Subtraction** / **Verification**

```
      33            11
 189,440       188,093
 −  1,347      +  1,347
 188,093       189,440
```

c. **Subtraction** / **Verification**

```
  0       1
 165      94
 − 71    + 71
  94     165
```

Everybody's Business

Learning Tip

Because each place value increases by a factor of 10 as we move from right to left (units, tens, hundreds, etc.), when we borrow a digit, we are actually borrowing a 10.

TRY-IT | EXERCISES

Subtract the following whole numbers and verify your answers:

16. 98,117
− 7,682

17. 12,395 − 5,589

18. Don Robinson has $4,589 in his checking account. If he writes a check for $344, how much will be left in the account?

Check your answers with the solutions on page 27.

REVIEW EXERCISES | CHAPTER 1—SECTION II

Add the following numbers:

1. 45
27
+ 19

2. 548
229
4,600
+ 62,660

3. 339
1,236
5,981
3,597
+ 8,790

4. 2,359
8,511
+ 14,006

5. 733
401
1,808
24,111
+ 10,595

6. 2,339 + 118 + 3,650 + 8,770 + 81 + 6 = _______

7. 12,554 + 22,606 + 11,460 + 20,005 + 4,303 = _______

Estimate the following by rounding each number all the way, then add to find the exact answer:

	Rounded Estimate	Exact Answer
8. 288 512 3,950 + 1,944	________	________

	Rounded Estimate	Exact Answer
9. 38,599 3,116 + 129	________	________
10. 318,459 +283,405	________	________

11. A toy manufacturer makes 2,594 stuffed animals in January; 2,478 in February; and 1,863 in March.

a. Round each number to the nearest hundred, and add to get an *estimate* of the production.

b. What was the *exact* amount of production for the three-month period?

12. While shopping, Alex Johnson purchases items for $3, $24, $13, $2, and $175. How much did he spend?

13. The following chart shows the output of Dandy Dry Cleaners and Laundry for last week. Total each column to get the *daily totals.* Total each row to get the *total items* per clothing category. What is the week's *grand total?*

Dandy Dry Cleaners and Laundry

	Monday	Tuesday	Wednesday	Thursday	Friday	Total Items
Shirts	342	125	332	227	172	______
Slacks	298	267	111	198	97	______
Suits	66	85	121	207	142	______
Dresses	98	48	79	118	103	______
Daily Totals	____	____	____	____	____ **Grand Total**	______

14. A farmer plants 350 acres of soybeans, 288 acres of corn, 590 acres of wheat, and 43 acres of assorted vegetables. In addition, the farm has 9 acres for grazing and 4 acres for the barnyard and farmhouse. What is the total acreage of the farm?

15. ABC Office Machines pays its sales staff a salary of $575 per month, plus commissions. Last month Anita Covington earned commissions of $129, $216, $126, $353, and $228. What was Anita's total income for the month?

Subtract the following numbers:

16. 354 − 48

17. 5,596 − 967

18. 95,490 − 73,500

19. 339,002 − 60,911

20. 2,000,077 − 87,801

21. $185 minus $47

22. 67,800 – 9,835

23. $308 less $169

24. Subtract 264 from 1,893

25. 8,906,000 from 12,396,700

26. Tom Watson had $153 in his wallet this morning. During the day he spent $5 for breakfast, $43 on a pair of pants, and $29 on a shirt.

a. How much did he spend?

b. How much did Tom have left?

27. Last year Jan Hopkins earned $27,000. She paid $5,490 in income taxes and $1,290 for social security. How much did Jan have left after these deductions?

28. The beginning inventory of the European Shoe Salon for August was 850 pairs of shoes. On the 9th, they received a shipment from the factory of 297 pairs. On the 23rd, another shipment of 188 pairs arrived. When inventory was taken at the end of the month, there were 754 pairs left. How many pairs of shoes were sold that month?

29. An electrician starts the day with 650 feet of wire on his truck. In the morning he cuts off pieces 26, 78, 45, and 89 feet long. During lunch he goes to an electrical supply warehouse and buys another 250 feet of wire. In the afternoon he uses lengths of 75, 89, and 120 feet. How many feet of wire are still on the truck at the end of the day?

30. A moving company's truck picks up loads of furniture weighing 5,500 pounds, 12,495 pounds, and 14,562 pounds. The truck weighs 11,480 pounds and the driver weighs 188 pounds. If a bridge has a weight limit of 42,500 pounds, is the truck within the weight limit to cross the bridge?

BUSINESS DECISION

Personal Balance Sheet

31. Personal financial statements are important indicators of your financial position. When compared over a period of time, they tell a story of where you have been, and where you are going, financially. The balance sheet, the income statement, and the cash flow statement are the most commonly used financial statements.

A personal *balance sheet* is the financial picture of how much "wealth" you have accumulated, as of a certain date. It specifically lists your *assets*, what you own; and your *liabilities*, what you owe. Your current *net worth* is the difference between the assets and the liabilities.

Net worth = Assets − Liabilities

John and Lori Turner have asked for your help in preparing a personal balance sheet. They have listed the following assets and liabilities: current value of home, \$144,000; audio/video equipment, \$1,340; automobiles, \$17,500; personal property, \$4,350; computer, \$3,700; mutual funds, \$26,700; 401k retirement plan, \$53,680; jewelry, \$4,800; certificates of deposit, \$19,300; stock investments, \$24,280; furniture and other household goods, \$8,600; Wal-Mart and Sears charge accounts balance, \$4,868; automobile loan balance, \$8,840; home mortgage balance, \$106,770; Visa and MasterCard balances, \$4,211; savings account balance, \$3,700; Lori's night school tuition loan balance, \$2,750; checking account balance, \$1,385; signature loan balance, \$6,350.

Use the data provided and the personal balance sheet that follows to calculate the following for the Turners:

a. Total assets

b. Total liabilities

c. Net worth

d. Explain the importance of the personal balance sheet. How often should this information be updated?

e. (optional) Prepare a personal balance sheet for yourself or your family.

Personal Balance Sheet

Assets		
CURRENT ASSETS		
Checking account	______	
Savings account	______	
Certificates of deposit	______	
Other	______	
Total Current Assets		______
LONG-TERM ASSETS		
Investments		
Retirement plans	______	
Stocks	______	
Bonds	______	
Mutual funds	______	
Other	______	
Personal		
Home	______	
Automobiles	______	
Furniture	______	
Personal property	______	
Jewelry	______	
Other	______	
Other	______	
Total Long-Term Assets		______
TOTAL ASSETS		$______

Liabilities		
CURRENT LIABILITIES		
Store charge accounts	______	
Credit card accounts	______	
Other current debt	______	
Total Current Liabilities		______
LONG-TERM LIABILITIES		
Home mortgage	______	
Automobile loan	______	
Education loan	______	
Other loan	______	
Other loan	______	
Total Long-Term Liabilities		______
TOTAL LIABILITIES		$______

NET WORTH		
Total Assets	______	
Total Liabilities	− ______	
NET WORTH		$______

SECTION III

MULTIPLICATION AND DIVISION OF WHOLE NUMBERS

Multiplication and division are the next two mathematical procedures used with whole numbers. Both are found in business as often as addition and subtraction. In reality, most business problems involve a combination of procedures. For example, invoices, which are a detailed list of goods and services sold by a company, require multiplication of items by the price per item, and then addition to reach a total. From the total, discounts are frequently subtracted, or transportation charges added.

A working knowledge of all math fundamentals is essential for success in today's business world. A little extra time spent on these basics now will go a long way toward making the remainder of this course a much easier and richer learning experience.

1-5 Multiplying Whole Numbers and Verifying Your Answers

Multiplication of whole numbers is actually a shortcut method for addition. Let's see how this works. If a clothing store buys 12 pairs of jeans at \$29 per pair, what is the total cost of the jeans? One way to solve this problem is to add \$29 + \$29 + . . . , 12 times. It's not hard to see how tedious this repeated addition becomes, especially with large numbers. Imagine a chain of stores such as The Limited ordering 2,500 pairs of jeans. Calculating the amount of this order by addition would be out of the question! By using multiplication, the total cost can be found in one step: 2,500 × \$29 = \$72,500.

multiplication
The combination of two integers in which the number of times one is represented is determined by the value of the other.

Multiplication is the combination of two whole numbers in which the number of times one is represented is determined by the value of the other. These two whole numbers are known as factors. The number being multiplied is the **multiplicand,** and the number by which the multiplicand is multiplied is the **multiplier.** The answer to a multiplication problem is the **product.** Intermediate answers are called partial products.

$$\begin{array}{rl} 258 & \text{multiplicand or factor} \\ \times\quad 43 & \text{multiplier or factor} \\ \hline 774 & \text{partial product 1} \\ 10\,32\ & \text{partial product 2} \\ \hline 11{,}094 & \text{product} \end{array}$$

In mathematics, the **times sign**—represented by the symbols "×" and "•" and "()"—is used to indicate multiplication. For example, 12 times 18 can be expressed as

$$12 \times 18 \qquad 12 \cdot 18 \qquad (12)(18) \qquad 12(18)$$

Note: The symbol • is *not* a decimal point.

multiplicand
In multiplication, the number being multiplied. For example, 5 is the multiplicand of 5 × 4 = 20.

multiplier
The number by which the multiplicand is multiplied. For example, 4 is the multiplier of 5 × 4 = 20.

product
The answer or result of multiplication. The number 20 is the product of 5 × 4 = 20.

times sign
The symbol "×" representing multiplication. Also represented by a dot "•" or parentheses "( )".

STEPS FOR MULTIPLYING WHOLE NUMBERS:

Step 1. Write the multiplication factors in columns so that the place values line up.

Step 2. Multiply each digit of the multiplier, starting with units, times the multiplicand. Each will yield a partial product whose units digit appears under the corresponding digit of the multiplier.

Step 3. Add the digits in each column of the partial products, starting on the right with the units column.

Everybody's Business

Learning Tip

In multiplication the factors are interchangeable. For example, 15 times 5 gives the same product as 5 times 15.

Multiplication is usually expressed with the larger factor on top as the multiplicand, and the smaller factor placed under it as the multiplier.

MULTIPLICATION SHORTCUTS

The following shortcuts can be used to make multiplication easier and faster:

1. **When the multiplier has a 0 in one or more of its middle digits,** there is no need to write a whole line of zeros as a partial product. Simply place a 0 in the next partial product row, directly below the 0 in the multiplier, and go on to the next digit in the multiplier. The next partial product will start on the same row, one place to the left of the 0, and directly below its corresponding digit in the multiplier. For example, consider 554 times 103.

Long way:
$$\begin{array}{r} 554 \\ \times\ 103 \\ \hline 1\,662 \\ 0\,00\ \\ 55\,4\quad \\ \hline 57{,}062 \end{array}$$

Shortcut:
$$\begin{array}{r} 554 \\ \times\ 103 \\ \hline 1\,662 \\ 55\,40\ \\ \hline 57{,}062 \end{array}$$

2. **When multiplying any number times zero,** the resulting product is *always* zero. For example,

$$573 \times 0 = 0 \qquad 0 \times 34 = 0 \qquad 1{,}254{,}779 \times 0 = 0$$

3. **When multiplying a number times one, the product is that number itself.** For example,

$$1{,}844 \times 1 = 1{,}844 \qquad 500 \times 1 = 500 \qquad 1 \times 894 = 894$$

4. **When a number is multiplied by 10, 100, 1,000, 10,000, 100,000, and so on,** simply add the zeros of the multiplier to the end of that number. For example,

$$792 \times 100 = 792 + 00 = 79{,}200 \qquad 9{,}345 \times 1{,}000 = 9{,}345 + 000 = 9{,}345{,}000$$

5. **When the multiplicand and/or the multiplier have zeros at the end,** multiply the two numbers without the zeros, and then add that number of zeros to the product. For example,

$$130 \times 90 = \begin{array}{r} 13 \\ \times\ 9 \\ \hline 117 \end{array} + 00 = 11{,}700$$

$$5{,}800 \times 3{,}400 = \begin{array}{r} 58 \\ \times\ 34 \\ \hline 232 \\ 1\,74\ \\ \hline 1{,}972 \end{array} + 0000 = 19{,}720{,}000$$

VERIFYING MULTIPLICATION

To check your multiplication for accuracy, divide the product by the multiplier. If the multiplication was correct, this will yield the multiplicand. For example,

Multiplication	Verification	Multiplication	Verification
48		527	
× 7		× 18	
336	336 ÷ 7 = 48	4 216	
		5 27	
		9,486	9,486 ÷ 18 = 527

EXAMPLES

Multiply the following numbers and verify your answers by division:

a. 2,293 × 45 **b.** 59,300 × 180 **c.** 436 × 2,027 **d.** 877 × 1 **e.** 6,922 × 0

f. A new plastic parts molding machine produces 85 parts per minute. How many parts can this machine produce in an hour? If a company has 15 of these machines and they run for 8 hours per day, what is the total output of parts per day?

SOLUTION STRATEGY

a.
2,293
× 45
11 465
91 72
103,185

This is a standard multiplication problem with two partial products. Always be sure to keep your columns lined up. The answer, 103,185, can be verified by division: 103,185 ÷ 45 = 2,293

b.
593
× 18
4 744
5 93
10,674 + 000 = 10,674,000

In this problem we remove the three zeros, multiply, and then add back the zeros.
Verification: 10,674 ÷ 18 = 593

c.
2027
× 436
12 162
60 81
810 8
883,772

This is another standard multiplication problem. Note that the larger number was made the multiplicand (top), and the smaller number became the multiplier. This makes the problem easier to work.
Verification: 883,772 ÷ 436 = 2,027

d. 877 × 1 = 877 — Remember, any number multiplied by 1 is that number.

e. 6,922 × 0 = 0 — Remember, any number multiplied by 0 is 0.

f. 85 parts per minute × 60 minutes per hour = 5,100 parts per hour
5,100 parts per hour × 15 machines = 76,500 parts per hour, all machines
76,500 parts per hour × 8 hours per day = 612,000 parts per day, total production

TRY-IT | EXERCISES

Multiply the following numbers and verify your answers:

19. $\begin{array}{r} 8{,}203 \\ \times\ 508 \\ \hline \end{array}$ **20.** $\begin{array}{r} 5{,}400 \\ \times\ 250 \\ \hline \end{array}$ **21.** $\begin{array}{r} 3{,}370 \\ \times\ 4{,}002 \\ \hline \end{array}$ **22.** 189×169

23. A typical plasterer can finish 150 square feet of interior wall per hour. If he works 6 hours per day

(a.) How many square feet can he finish?

(b.) If a contractor hires four plasterers, how many feet can they finish in a 5-day week?

Check your answers with the solutions on page 27.

1-6 Dividing Whole Numbers and Verifying Your Answers

Just as multiplication is a shortcut for repeated addition, division is a shortcut for repeated subtraction. Let's say while shopping you want to know how many \$5 items you can purchase with \$45. You could get the answer by finding out how many times 5 can be subtracted from 45. You would begin by subtracting 5 from 45 to get 40; then subtracting 5 from 40 to get 35; 5 from 35 to get 30; and so on, until you got to 0. Quite tedious, but it does give you the answer, 9. By using division, we simply ask, how many \$5 are contained in \$45? By dividing 45 by 5 we get the answer in one step ($45 \div 5 = 9$). Because division is the opposite of multiplication, we can verify our answer by multiplying 5 times 9 to get 45.

Division of whole numbers is the process of determining how many times one number is contained within another number. The number being divided is called the **dividend,** the number doing the dividing is called the **divisor,** and the answer is known as the **quotient.** When the divisor has only one digit, as in 100 divided by 5, it is called short division. When the divisor has more than one digit, as in 100 divided by 10, it is known as long division.

The "÷" symbol represents division, and is known as the **division sign.** For example, $12 \div 4$ is read "12 divided by 4." Another way to show division is

$$\frac{12}{4}$$

This also reads "12 divided by 4." To actually solve the division, we use the sign $\overline{)\quad}$. The problem is then written as $4\overline{)12}$. As in addition, subtraction, and multiplication, proper alignment of the digits is very important.

$$\frac{\text{Dividend}}{\text{Divisor}} = \text{Quotient} \qquad \text{Divisor}\overline{)\text{Dividend}}^{\ \text{Quotient}}$$

When the divisor divides evenly into the dividend, it is known as even division. When the divisor does not divide evenly into the dividend, the answer then becomes a quotient plus a **remainder.** The remainder is the amount left over after the division is completed.

division
The mathematical process of determining how many times one number is contained within another number.

dividend
In division, the quantity being divided. For example, 20 is the dividend of $20 \div 5 = 4$.

divisor
The quantity by which another quantity, the dividend, is being divided. The number doing the dividing. For example, 5 is the divisor of $20 \div 5 = 4$.

quotient
The answer or result of division. The number 4 is the quotient of $20 \div 5 = 4$.

division sign
The symbol "÷" representing division.

remainder
In uneven division, the amount left over after the division is completed. For example, 2 is the remainder of $22 \div 5 = 4$, R2.

This is known as uneven division. In this chapter, a remainder of 3, for example, will be expressed as R 3. In Chapter 2, remainders will be expressed as fractions, and in Chapter 3, remainders will be expressed as decimals.

VERIFYING DIVISION

To verify even division, multiply the quotient by the divisor. If the problem was worked correctly, this will yield the dividend. To verify uneven division, multiply the quotient by the divisor, and add the remainder to the product. If the problem was worked correctly, this will yield the dividend.

EVEN DIVISION ILLUSTRATED

$$\frac{850 \text{ (dividend)}}{25 \text{ (divisor)}} = 34 \text{ (quotient)}$$

```
     34
25)850
   75↓
   100
   100
     0
```

Verification: $34 \times 25 = 850$

UNEVEN DIVISION ILLUSTRATED

$$\frac{850 \text{ (dividend)}}{20 \text{ (divisor)}} = 42 \text{ R}10 \text{ (quotient)}$$

```
     42 R10
20)850
   80↓
    50
    40
    10
```

Verification: $42 \times 20 = 840$
$+10$
850

DIVISION SHORTCUT

When both the dividend and the divisor end in one or more zeros, you can remove an *equal* number of zeros from each and then divide. This gives the same answer with much less work. For example, 7,000 divided by 200 is the same as 70 divided by 2. *Note:* Although 7,000 has three zeros, you can't remove three zeros, because 200 has only two zeros.

$$\frac{7000}{200} = 35 \qquad \frac{70}{2} = 35$$

STEPS FOR DIVIDING WHOLE NUMBERS:

Step 1. Determine the first group of digits in the dividend that the divisor will divide into at least once. This group will contain an equal or larger number of places than the divisor. Divide, and place the partial quotient over the last digit in that group.

Step 2. Multiply the partial quotient by the divisor. Place it under the first group of digits and subtract.

Step 3. From the dividend, bring down the next digit after the first group of digits.

Step 4. Repeat Steps 1, 2, and 3, until all of the digits in the dividend have been brought down.

EXAMPLES

Divide the following numbers and verify your answers:

a. $210 \div 7$ **b.** $185 \div 9$ **c.** $\frac{1{,}508}{6}$ **d.** $\frac{14{,}000}{3{,}500}$

e. A rancher has a roll of rope containing 650 feet. How many 8-foot pieces can be cut from this roll?

SOLUTION STRATEGY

a.

```
    30
 7)210
   21
    00
```

This is an example of even division. Note that there is no remainder.

Verification: $30 \times 7 = \underline{\underline{210}}$

b.

```
    20 R 5
 9)185
   18
     5
```

This example illustrates uneven division. Note that there is a remainder.

Verification: $20 \times 9 = 180$
$+ 5$
$\underline{\underline{185}}$

c.

```
    251 R 2
 6)1508
   12
    30
    30
     08
      6
      2
```

This is another example of uneven division. Be sure to keep the digits properly lined up.

Verification: $251 \times 6 = 1{,}506$
$+ \quad 2$
$\underline{\underline{1{,}508}}$

d.

```
      4
 35)140
    140
      0
```

In this example, we simplify the division by deleting two zeros from the dividend and the divisor.

Verification: $4 \times 35 = \underline{\underline{140}}$

e.

```
    81 R 2
 8)650
   64
    10
     8
     2
```

In this word problem, we want to know how many 8-foot pieces of rope are contained in a 650-foot roll. The dividend is 650 and the divisor is 8. The quotient, 81 R 2, means that 81 whole pieces of rope can be cut from the roll, with some left over, but not enough for another whole piece.

Verification: $81 \times 8 = 648$
$+ 2$
$\underline{\underline{650}}$

TRY-IT | EXERCISES

Divide the following numbers and verify your answers:

24. $910 \div 35$ **25.** $1{,}503 \div 160$ **26.** $\frac{3{,}358}{196}$ **27.** $\frac{175{,}000}{12{,}000}$

28. Nutone Industries has 39 production line workers, each making the same amount of money. If last week's total payroll amounted to $18,330, how much did each employee earn?

Check your answers with the solutions on page 27.

REVIEW EXERCISES | CHAPTER 1—SECTION III

Multiply the following numbers and verify your answers:

1. 589×19

2. $1{,}292 \times 158$

3. 327×900

4. $76{,}000 \times 45$

5. $56{,}969 \times 1{,}000$

6. Multiply \$4 times 501

7. 23×570

8. What is 475 times 12?

Estimate the following by rounding each number all the way, then multiply to get the exact answer:

	Rounded Estimate	Exact Answer
9. 202×490	________	________
10. 515×180	________	________
11. 17×11	________	________

12. Sara Gomez earns \$6 per hour. How much does Sara make in a 35-hour week?

13. Tom DeWitt has a car that averages 19 miles per gallon. If the gas tank holds 21 gallons, how many miles can he travel on a tank of gas?

14. To earn extra money while attending college, you work as a cashier in a restaurant.

a. Find the total bill for the following food order: three sirloin steak dinners at \$12 each; two baked chicken specials at \$7 each; four steak burger platters at \$5 each; two extra salads at \$2 each; six drinks at \$1 each; and tax of \$7.

b. How much change will you give back if the check is paid with a \$100 bill?

15. A Norton press can print 620 posters per hour. A Cramden press can print 1,035 posters per hour. If Printmasters has three Norton presses and five Cramden presses, how many posters can be printed in a 10-hour day?

Divide the following numbers:

16. 4,500 ÷ 35 **17.** 74,770 ÷ 5,700 **18.** $\frac{60{,}000}{250}$ **19.** $\frac{236{,}500{,}000}{4{,}300{,}000}$

Estimate the following by rounding each number to hundreds, then divide to get the exact answer:

	Rounded Estimate	Exact Answer
20. 890 ÷ 295	________	________
21. 1,499 ÷ 580	________	________
22. 57,800 ÷ 102	________	________

23. A roofer has 50,640 square feet of roofing material. If the average roof requires 8,440 square feet of material, how many roofs can he cover?

24. A calculator uses eight circuit boards, each containing 450 parts. A company has 421,215 parts in stock.

a. How many calculators can it manufacture?

b. How many parts will be left?

25. John Fernandez borrows $24,600 from the Friendly Bank and Trust Co. The interest charge amounts to $8,664. What equal monthly payments must John make in order to pay back the loan, with interest, in 36 months?

26. You have just purchased a 65-acre ranch for a price of $780 per acre. In addition, the house was valued at $125,000 and the equipment amounted to $22,300.

a. What was the total price of your purchase?

b. Since the owner was anxious to sell, he offered to finance the ranch for you with a no-interest mortgage loan. What would your monthly payments be to pay off the loan in 10 years?

c. Besides the mortgage payment, you are required to make monthly property tax and insurance payments. If property tax is $3,000 per year and insurance is $2,400 per year, how much would these items add to your monthly expenses for the ranch?

BUSINESS DECISION

Estimating a Tile Job

27. You are the owner of The Tile Galleria. Chuck and Jill have asked you to give them an estimate for tiling four rooms of their house. The living room is 15 feet × 23 feet; the dining room is 12 feet × 18 feet; the kitchen is 9 feet × 11 feet; and the study is 10 feet × 12 feet.

a. How many square feet of tile are required for each room? (Multiply the length times the width.)

b. What is the total number of square feet to be tiled?

c. If the tile for the kitchen and study costs $4 per square foot, and the tile for the living and dining rooms costs $3 per square foot, what is the total cost of the tile?

d. If your company charges $2 per square foot for installation, what is the total cost of the tile job?

e. If Chuck and Jill have saved $4,500 for the tile job, have they saved enough money? If not, how much more do they need?

✦ SUMMARY CHART ✦

SECTION I: The Decimal Number System: Whole Numbers

Topic	P/O[1], Page	Important Concepts	Illustrative Examples
Reading and Writing Whole Numbers in Numerical and Word Form	1-1 2	1. Insert the commas every three digits to mark the groups, beginning at the right side of the number. 2. From left to right, name the places and the groups. Groups that have all zeros are not named. 3. When writing whole numbers in word form, the numbers from 21 to 99 are hyphenated. *Note:* The word *and* should *not* be used in reading or writing whole numbers.	The number 15538 takes on the numerical form 15,538 and is read, "fifteen thousand, five hundred thirty-eight." The number 22939643 takes on the numerical form 22,939,643 and is read, "twenty-two million, nine hundred thirty-nine thousand, six hundred forty-three." The number 1000022 takes on the numerical value 1,000,022 and is read, "one million, twenty-two."
Rounding Whole Numbers to a Specified Place Value	1-2 4	1. Determine the place to which the number is to be rounded. 2a. If the digit to the right of the one being rounded is 5 or more, increase the digit in the place being rounded by 1. 2b. If the digit to the right of the one being rounded is 4 or less, do not change the digit in the place being rounded. 3. Change all digits to the right of the place being rounded to zeros.	1,449 rounded to tens = 1,450 255 rounded to hundreds = 300 345,391 rounded to thousands = 345,000 68,658,200 rounded to millions = 69,000,000 768,892 rounded all the way = 800,000

SECTION II: Addition and Subtraction of Whole Numbers

Adding Whole Numbers	1-3 8	1. Write the whole numbers in columns so that the place values line up. 2. Add the digits in each column, starting on the right with the units column. 3. When the total in a column is greater than 9, write the units digit and carry the tens digit to the top of the next column to the left. To verify addition, add the numbers in reverse, from bottom to top.	2 1 1 1,931 addend 2,928 addend + 5,857 addend 10,716 sum Verification: 2 1 1 5,857 2,928 + 1,931 10,716

[1]Performance Objective.

SECTION II: (continued)

Topic	P/O, Page	Important Concepts	Illustrative Examples
Subtracting Whole Numbers	1-4 10	1. Write the whole numbers in columns so that the place values line up. 2. Starting with the units column, subtract the digits. 3. When a column cannot be subtracted, borrow a digit from the column to the left of the one you are working in. To verify subtraction, add the difference and the subtrahend; this should equal the minuend.	34,557 minuend − 6,224 subtrahend 28,333 difference Verification: 28,333 + 6,224 34,557

SECTION III: Multiplication and Division of Whole Numbers

Multiplying Whole Numbers	1-5 16	1. Write the multiplication factors in columns so that the place values are lined up. 2. Multiply each digit of the multiplier, starting with units, times the multiplicand. Each will yield a partial product whose units digit appears under the corresponding digit of the multiplier. 3. Add the digits in each column of the partial products, starting on the right, with the units column. To verify multiplication, divide the product by the multiplier. If the multiplication is correct, this should yield the multiplicand.	258 multiplicand or factor × 43 multiplier or factor 774 partial product 1 10 32 partial product 2 11,094 product Verification: $\frac{11,094}{43} = 258$
Dividing Whole Numbers	1-6 19	1. The number being divided is the dividend. The number by which we are dividing is the divisor. The answer is known as the quotient. $\text{Divisor}\overline{)\text{Dividend}}$ with Quotient above 2. If the divisor does not divide evenly into the dividend, the quotient will have a remainder. To verify division, multiply the divisor by the quotient and add the remainder. If the division is correct, this will yield the dividend.	Divide six hundred fifty by twenty-seven. $650 \div 27 = \frac{650}{27} =$ 24 R 2 27)650 54 110 108 2 Verification: 27 × 24 = 648 + 2 = 650

TRY-IT EXERCISE | SOLUTIONS

	Numerical Form	Word Form
1.	49,588	Forty-nine thousand, five hundred eighty-eight
2.	804	Eight hundred four
3.	1,928,837	One million, nine hundred twenty-eight thousand, eight hundred thirty-seven
4.	900,015	Nine hundred thousand, fifteen
5.	6,847,365,911	Six billion, eight hundred forty-seven million, three hundred sixty-five thousand, nine hundred eleven
6.	2,000,300,007	Two billion, three hundred thousand, seven

7. 51,700 **8.** 23,440 **9.** 175,450,000 **10.** 60,000 **11.** 15,000,000,000 **12.** 8,010,000,000

13. $39{,}481 + 5{,}594 + 11{,}029 = 56{,}104$ *Verify:* $11{,}029 + 5{,}594 + 39{,}481 = 56{,}104$

14. $6{,}948 + 330 + 7{,}946 + 89 + 5{,}583{,}991 + 7 + 18{,}606 = 5{,}617{,}917$ *Verify:* $18{,}606 + 7 + 5{,}583{,}991 + 89 + 7{,}946 + 330 + 6{,}948 = 5{,}617{,}917$

15. $183 + 228 + 281 + 545 + 438 + 1{,}157 = 2{,}832$ meals *Verify:* $1{,}157 + 438 + 545 + 281 + 228 + 183 = 2{,}832$ meals

16. $98{,}117 - 7{,}682 = 90{,}435$ *Verify:* $90{,}435 + 7{,}682 = 98{,}117$

17. $12{,}395 - 5{,}589 = 6{,}806$ *Verify:* $6{,}806 + 5{,}589 = 12{,}395$

18. $\$4{,}589 - 344 = \$4{,}245$ left in account *Verify:* $\$4{,}245 + 344 = \$4{,}589$

19.
```
    8,203
  ×   508
   65 624
 4 101 50
4,167,124
```
Verify: $\frac{4{,}167{,}124}{508} = 8{,}203$

20.
```
    5,400
  ×   250
  270 000
 1 080 50
1,350,000
```
Verify: $\frac{1{,}350{,}000}{250} = 5{,}400$

21.
```
     3,370
  ×  4,002
     6 740
  13 480 00
13,486,740
```
Verify: $\frac{13{,}486{,}740}{4{,}002} = 3{,}370$

22. 189×169
```
   189
 × 169
  1 701
 11 34
 18 9
 31,941
```
Verify: $\frac{31{,}941}{169} = 189$

23. 150×6 = **a.** 900 sq ft per day

900×4 plasterers = 3,600 sq ft per day

$3{,}600 \times 5$ days = **b.** 18,000 sq ft in 5 days

24. $910 \div 35 = 26$
```
     26
35)910
   70
   210
   210
     0
```
Verify: $26 \times 35 = 910$

25. $1{,}503 \div 160 = 9$ R63
```
        9 R63
160)1,503
    1 440
       63
```
Verify: $160 \times 9 = 1{,}140$; $1{,}140 + 63 = 1{,}503$

26. $3{,}358 \div 196 = 17$ R26
```
        17 R26
196)3,358
    196
    1 398
    1 372
       26
```
Verify: $196 \times 17 = 3{,}332$; $3{,}332 + 26 = 3{,}358$

27. $175 \div 12 = 14$ R7
```
     14 R7
12)175
   12
    55
    48
     7
```
Verify: $12 \times 14 = 168$; $168 + 7 = 175$

28. $\frac{18{,}330}{39}$ = $470 per employee
```
      470
39)18,330
   15 6
    2 73
    2 73
       0
```
Verify: $39 \times 470 = 18{,}330$

Name ____________________

Class ____________________

Answers

1. ____________________
2. ____________________
3. ____________________
4. ____________________
5. ____________________
6. ____________________
7. ____________________
8. ____________________
9. ____________________
10. ____________________
11. ____________________
12. ____________________
13. ____________________
14. ____________________
15. ____________________
16. ____________________
17. ____________________

For additional practice exercises, visit our Web site at www.contemporarymath.com.

CHAPTER 1 | ASSESSMENT TEST

Read and write the following whole numbers in numerical and word form:

Number	Numerical Form	Word Form
1. 200049	______	____________________
2. 52308411	______	____________________

Write the following whole numbers in numerical form:

3. Three hundred sixteen thousand, two hundred twenty-nine

4. Four million, five hundred sixty thousand

Round the following numbers to the indicated place:

5. 18,334 to hundreds

6. 3,545,687 all the way

7. 256,733 to ten thousands

Perform the indicated operation for the following:

8.
$$\begin{array}{r} 1{,}860 \\ 429 \\ 133 \\ +\ 1{,}009 \\ \hline \end{array}$$

9.
$$\begin{array}{r} 927 \\ -\ 828 \\ \hline \end{array}$$

10.
$$\begin{array}{r} 207 \\ \times\ 106 \\ \hline \end{array}$$

11. $42\overline{)1876}$

12.
$$\begin{array}{r} 3{,}505 \\ \times\ 290 \\ \hline \end{array}$$

13.
$$\begin{array}{r} 6{,}800 \\ 919 \\ 201 \\ +\ 14{,}338 \\ \hline \end{array}$$

14. $150{,}000 \div 188$

15. $1{,}205 - 491$

16. The following chart shows Melody Music Shop's product sales for last week. Use addition and subtraction to fill in the blank spaces. What is the week's grand total?

Melody Music Shop

	Monday	Tuesday	Wednesday	Thursday	Friday	Saturday	Total Units
Records	82	____	68	57	72	92	427
Tapes	29	69	61	____	82	75	____
CDs	96	103	71	108	112	159	____
Daily Totals	____	____	____	223	____	____	Grand Total ____

17. You are the bookkeeper for Melody Music, in problem 16. If records sell for \$9 each, tapes sell for \$6 each, and CDs sell for \$13 each, what was the total dollar sales for last week?

Name ____________

Class ____________

Answers

18. ____________

19. a. ____________

b. ____________

20. ____________

21. a. ____________

b. ____________

22. ____________

18. A 1,600-acre farm was sold for a total of $235,000. If the house and equipment are worth $68,600 and the land represents the balance, what was the price paid per acre for the land?

19. A summer camp has budgeted $85,500 for a new fleet of sailboats. The boat selected is a deluxe model costing $4,500.

 a. How many boats can be purchased by the camp?

 b. If instead a standard model were chosen costing $3,420, how many boats could be purchased?

20. Jeffrey Miller makes a salary of $23,440 per year plus a commission of $300 per month. What is his weekly income? (There are 52 weeks in a year.)

21. You are in charge of putting together the annual stockholder's luncheon for your company. The meal will cost $13 per person; entertainment will cost $2,100; facility rental is $880; invitations and annual report printing costs are $2,636; and other expenses come to $1,629. If 315 stockholders plan to attend:

 a. What is the total cost of the luncheon?

 b. What is the cost per stockholder?

22. Century Bank requires mortgage loan applicants to have a gross monthly income of five times the amount of their monthly payment. How much monthly income must Jennifer Adams have to qualify for a payment of $865?

Name ____________________

Class ____________________

Answers

23. ____________________

24. ____________________

25. ____________________

26. a. ____________________

b. ____________________

27. ____________________

28. a. ____________________

b. ____________________

23. Magi Khoo had $868 in her checking account on April 1. During the month she wrote checks for $15, $123, $88, $276, and $34. She also deposited $45, $190, and $436. What is the balance in her checking account at the end of April?

24. Last week, the *More Joy,* a commercial fishing boat, brought in 360 pounds of tuna, 225 pounds of halibut, and 570 pounds of snapper. At the dock, the catch was sold to Atlantic Seafood Wholesalers. The tuna brought $3 per pound; the halibut, $4 per pound; and the snapper, $5 per pound. If fuel and crew expenses amounted to $1,644, how much profit did Captain Bob make on this trip?

25. Samuel Charles bought 2,000 shares of stock at $62 per share. Six months later he sold the 2,000 shares at $87 per share. If the total stockbroker's commission was $740, how much profit did he make on this transaction?

26. A movie was estimated to cost $24,890,000 to produce.

a. If the actual cost was $32,009,770, by how much was the movie over budget?

b. If ticket sales grossed $50,000,000 how much was the profit?

27. The Virginia City Mining Company produces 40 tons of ore in an 8-hour shift. The mine operates continuously—three shifts per day, 7 days per week. How many tons of ore can be extracted in 6 weeks?

28. The Krypton Corporation purchased a new building for $165,000. After a down payment of $45,600, the balance was paid in equal monthly payments, with no interest.

a. If the loan was paid off in 2 years, how much were the monthly payments?

b. If the loan was paid off in 5 years, how much *less* were the monthly payments?

Name ______________________

Class ______________________

Answers

29. ______________________

30. ______________________

31. a. ______________________

b. ______________________

c. ______________________

d. ______________________

29. A flatbed railroad car weighs 150 tons empty and 420 tons loaded with 18 equal-weight trailers. How many tons does each trailer weigh?

30. Star-Bright Security charges $14 per hour for security guards. The guards are paid $8 per hour. If Star-Bright has 30 guards, each working a 25-hour week, how much profit did the company make last week?

BUSINESS DECISION

Buy Right—Sleep Tight

31. You are interested in purchasing either a king-size bed set or two twin-size sets. In today's newspaper you notice that Mattress Magic is having a sale on Serta Perfect Sleeper bedding. Answer the following questions, based on the advertisement below:

a. In the *Katrina* line, which size, king or two twins, would be the better deal, and by how much?

b. In the *Lennox* line, which size, king or two twins, would be the better deal, and by how much?

c. In the *Tresco* line, which size, king or two twins, would be the better deal, and by how much?

d. Also in today's newspaper, you find another advertisement for the *Tresco* line of Serta bedding at Bradley's Department Store. It reads as follows:

> Sale
> **Serta Tresco Twin Bed Sets**
> **Buy Any 3 Pieces At Regular Price**
> **And Get The 4th One**
> **FREE!**

If Bradley's regular price on *Tresco* twin pieces is $425 each, how does this sale compare with the *Tresco* offer at Mattress Magic?

All the Math That's Fit to Learn

The Business Math Times

Volume I | Whole Numbers | One Dollar

Gazillions!

Most people can comprehend numbers up to a few hundred-thousand, or perhaps a million, but after that, numbers become pretty hard to imagine. The same applies to small numbers.

In business, numbers can range up to hundreds of millions, and even billions. When it comes to trillions, we are beyond any single company's numbers. Trillions define numbers for industries, governments, and worldwide references.

Beyond that, you are in the realm of subjects such as medicine; computer science; astrophysics, chemistry, astronomy; and, of course, bragging. The chart (at right) shows the prefix, name, and number in digital and scientific notation form of some very large numbers. Note that each number gets larger by three places each time.

There are names for each of the next 13 three-digit number groups—that brings us to 63 zeros. The next group has 100 zeros, and is known as **googol**. After that, if you need more, there's the exponential number, **googolplex**, which is 10 raised to the googol power.

Then what? Are numbers infinite? No matter what size number your mind can imagine, it's not the biggest; you can always add at least a 1 to it.

Yottabytes

Now that kilo-, mega-, and even gigabytes of computer memory have become commonplace, it's time to learn the next set of exponential prefixes destined to become part of our modern vocabulary.

If you use the Internet, you know approximately how long it takes to download a few hundred kilobyte or one megabyte file. According to the National Institute of Standards and Technology, it would take more than 5 trillion years to download a one yottabyte file.

"Quote . . . Unquote"

The Greatest Risk Is Not Taking One.
—*AIG, advertisement*

Success In Business is 1% Inspiration and 99% Perspiration.
—*Thomas Edison*

Really Big Numbers

Prefix	Word Name	Number	Scientific Notation
Kilo-	One thousand	1,000	1×10^{3}
Mega-	One million	1,000,000	1×10^{6}
Giga-	One billion	1,000,000,000	1×10^{9}
Tere-	One trillion	1,000,000,000,000	1×10^{12}
Peta-	One quadrillion	1,000,000,000,000,000	1×10^{15}
Exa-	One quintillion	1,000,000,000,000,000,000	1×10^{18}
Zetta-	One sextillion	1,000,000,000,000,000,000,000	1×10^{21}
Yotta-	One septillion	1,000,000,000,000,000,000,000,000	1×10^{24}

Let's Get Scientific

Scientific notation is used to express very large or very small numbers. For example, if you wanted to express the number seventy-five trillion, the distance in miles between two galaxies, you would write 75,000,000,000,000.

In scientific notation for large numbers, the numbers are written with exponents. Here are the rules for large numbers:

1. The first factor is greater than or equal to 1, and is less than 10.
2. The second factor is a power of 10, in exponential form.
3. The number of places to the right of the first nonzero number becomes the exponent.

In our example of 75 trillion miles, the first nonzero number is 7. There are 13 digits to the right of the 7, so 13 is the exponent. The number would be written as:

$$\mathbf{7.5 \times 10^{13}}$$

Although numbers involving money are not commonly written in scientific notation, try it on Bill Gates's 2001 net worth of $58,700,000,000

$$\mathbf{5.87 \times 10^{10}}$$

Speaking of Numbers

Did you know that when we count, or specify a total number of items, we are using **cardinal numbers**. *Ten,* for example, is a cardinal number. **Ordinal numbers** are used to show order. *Tenth* is an ordinal number, and can be written in shortened form as "10th."

Brainteaser

"A" NUMBER

If you were to spell out numbers, beginning with the number 1, how far would you have to go until you found the letter "A"?

Answers to all "Brainteasers" can be found in the next chapter's issue of *The Business Math Times.*

CHAPTER 2

Fractions

PERFORMANCE OBJECTIVES

SECTION I

UNDERSTANDING AND WORKING WITH FRACTIONS

fractions
A mathematical way of expressing a part of a whole thing. For example, $\frac{1}{4}$ is a fraction expressing one part out of a total of four parts.

Fractions are a mathematical way of expressing a part of a whole thing. The word fraction comes from a Latin word meaning "break." Fractions result from breaking a unit into a number of equal parts. This concept is used quite commonly in business. We may look at sales for $\frac{1}{2}$ the year, or reduce prices by $\frac{1}{4}$ for a sale. A new production machine in your company may be $1\frac{3}{4}$ times faster than the old one, or you might want to cut $5\frac{3}{4}$ yards of fabric from a roll of material. Just like whole numbers, fractions can be added, subtracted, multiplied, divided, and even combined with whole numbers. This chapter introduces you to the various types of fractions and shows you how they are used in the business world.

2-1 Distinguishing among the Various Types of Fractions

numerator
The number on top of the division line of a fraction. It represents the dividend in the division. In the fraction $\frac{1}{4}$, 1 is the numerator.

denominator
The number on the bottom of the division line of a fraction. It represents the divisor in the division. In the fraction $\frac{1}{4}$, 4 is the denominator.

division line
The horizontal or slanted line separating the numerator from the denominator. The symbol representing "divided by" in a fraction. In the fraction $\frac{1}{4}$, the line between the 1 and the 4 is the division line.

Technically, fractions express the relationship between two numbers, set up as a division. The **numerator** is the number on the top of the fraction. It represents the dividend in the division. The **denominator** is the bottom number of the fraction. It represents the divisor. The numerator and the denominator are separated by a horizontal or slanted line, known as the **division line.** This line means "divided by." For example, the fraction 2/3, or $\frac{2}{3}$, read as "two-thirds," means 2 divided by 3, or $2 \div 3$.

Remember, fractions express parts of a whole unit. The unit may be dollars, feet, ounces, or anything. The denominator describes how many total parts are in the unit. The numerator represents how many of the total parts we are describing or referring to. For example, a pizza (the whole unit) is divided into eight slices (total equal parts, denominator). As a fraction, the whole pizza would be represented as $\frac{8}{8}$. If five of the slices were eaten (parts referred to, numerator), what fraction represents the part that was eaten? The answer would be the fraction $\frac{5}{8}$, read "five-eighths." However, because five slices were eaten out of a total of eight, three slices, or $\frac{3}{8}$, of the pizza is left.

common or proper fraction
A fraction in which the numerator is smaller than the denominator. Represents less than a whole unit. The fraction $\frac{1}{4}$ is a common or proper fraction.

Fractions such as $\frac{3}{8}$ and $\frac{5}{8}$, in which the numerator is smaller than the denominator, represent less than a whole unit and are known as **common,** or **proper fractions.** Some examples of proper fractions would be

$\frac{3}{16}$ three-sixteenths $\quad \frac{1}{4}$ one-fourth $\quad \frac{9}{32}$ nine-thirty-seconds

improper fraction
A fraction in which the denominator is equal to or less than the numerator. Represents one whole unit or more. The fraction $\frac{4}{1}$ is an improper fraction.

When a fraction's denominator is equal to or less than the numerator, it represents one whole unit or more, and is known as an **improper fraction.** Some examples of improper fractions are

$\frac{9}{9}$ nine-ninths $\quad \frac{15}{11}$ fifteen-elevenths $\quad \frac{19}{7}$ nineteen-sevenths

mixed number
A number that combines a whole number with a proper fraction. The fraction $10\frac{1}{4}$ is a mixed number.

A number that combines a whole number with a proper fraction is known as a **mixed number.** Some examples of mixed numbers are

$3\frac{1}{8}$ three and one-eighth $\quad 7\frac{11}{16}$ seven and eleven-sixteenths

$46\frac{51}{60}$ forty-six and fifty-one-sixtieths

EXAMPLES

For each of the following, identify the type of fraction, and write it in word form:

a. $\frac{45}{16}$ $\quad$ **b.** $14\frac{2}{5}$ $\quad$ **c.** $\frac{11}{12}$

SOLUTION STRATEGY

a. $\frac{45}{16}$ This is an improper fraction because the denominator, 16, is less than the numerator, 45. In word form we say, "forty-five-sixteenths." It could also be read as "45 divided by 16," or "45 over 16."

b. $14\frac{2}{5}$ This is a mixed number because it combines the whole number 14 with the fraction $\frac{2}{5}$. In word form this is read, "fourteen and two-fifths."

c. $\frac{11}{12}$ This is a common or proper fraction because the numerator, 11, is less than the denominator, 12. This fraction is read, "eleven-twelfths." It could also be read, "11 over 12" or "11 divided by 12."

Everybody's Business

Learning Tip

A **complex fraction** is one in which the numerator or the denominator, or both, are fractions.

Examples: $\frac{\frac{2}{3}}{6}, \frac{9}{\frac{3}{4}}, \frac{\frac{7}{8}}{\frac{1}{4}}$

Can you solve them?

(*Answers:* $\frac{1}{9}$, 12, $3\frac{1}{2}$)

TRY-IT | EXERCISES

For each of the following, identify the type of fraction, and write it in word form:

1. $76\frac{3}{4}$ **2.** $\frac{3}{5}$ **3.** $\frac{18}{18}$ **4.** $\frac{33}{8}$

Check your answers with the solutions on page 63.

2-2 Converting Improper Fractions to Whole or Mixed Numbers

It often becomes necessary to change or convert an improper fraction into a whole or mixed number. For example, final answers cannot be left as improper fractions; they must be converted.

STEPS FOR CONVERTING IMPROPER FRACTIONS TO WHOLE OR MIXED NUMBERS:

Step 1. Divide the numerator of the improper fraction by the denominator.

Step 2a. If there is no remainder, the improper fraction becomes a whole number.

Step 2b. If there is a remainder, write the whole number and then write the fraction as

$$\textbf{Whole number} = \frac{\textbf{Remainder}}{\textbf{Divisor}}$$

EXAMPLES

Convert the following improper fractions to whole or mixed numbers:

a. $\frac{30}{5}$ **b.** $\frac{9}{2}$

SOLUTION STRATEGY

a. $\frac{30}{5} = \underline{\underline{6}}$

When we divide the numerator, 30, by the denominator, 5, we get the whole number 6. There is no remainder.

b. $\frac{9}{2} = 2\overline{)9} = \underline{\underline{4\frac{1}{2}}}$

This improper fraction divides 4 times with a remainder of 1, therefore it will become a mixed number. In this case, the 4 is the whole number. The remainder, 1, becomes the numerator of the new fraction; the divisor, 2, becomes the denominator.

TRY-IT | EXERCISES

Convert the following improper fractions to whole or mixed numbers:

5. $\frac{8}{3}$ **6.** $\frac{25}{4}$ **7.** $\frac{39}{3}$

Check your answers with the solutions on page 63.

Construction workers must accurately measure and calculate various lengths of building materials by using fractions.

Everybody's Business

Real-World Connection

Certain calculators have a fraction key, $a\frac{b}{c}$, that allows you to enter fractions. For example, $\frac{2}{3}$ would be entered as [2] [$a\frac{b}{c}$] [3] and would appear as 2⌟3. The mixed fraction $25\frac{2}{3}$ would be entered as [25] [$a\frac{b}{c}$] [2] [$a\frac{b}{c}$] [3] and would appear as 25⌟2⌟3.

Fraction calculators express answers in fractional notation, and are a handy tool for measuring materials without having to convert fractions to decimals. They are particularly useful in the construction, medical, and food trades.

2-3 Converting Mixed Numbers to Improper Fractions

STEPS FOR CONVERTING A MIXED NUMBER TO AN IMPROPER FRACTION:

Step 1. Multiply the denominator by the whole number.

Step 2. Add the numerator to the product from Step 1.

Step 3. Place the total from Step 2 as the "new" numerator.

Step 4. Place the original denominator as the "new" denominator.

EXAMPLES

Convert the following mixed numbers to improper fractions:

a. $5\frac{2}{3}$ **b.** $9\frac{5}{6}$

SOLUTION STRATEGY

a. $5\frac{2}{3} = \underline{\underline{\frac{17}{3}}}$

In this example, we multiply the denominator, 3, by the whole number, 5, and add the numerator, 2, to get 17 ($3 \times 5 + 2 = 17$). We then place the 17 over the original denominator, 3.

b. $9\frac{5}{6} = \underline{\underline{\frac{59}{6}}}$

In this example, we multiply the denominator, 6, by the whole number, 9, and add the numerator, 5, to get 59 ($6 \times 9 + 5 = 59$). We then place the 59 over the original denominator, 6.

TRY-IT | EXERCISES

Convert the following mixed numbers to improper fractions:

8. $2\frac{3}{4}$ **9.** $9\frac{1}{5}$ **10.** $22\frac{5}{8}$

Check your answers with the solutions on page 63.

2-4 Reducing Fractions to Lowest Terms

When working with fractions, it is often necessary to reduce them to lowest terms. For example, when the final answer to a math problem contains a fraction, it is common practice to reduce that fraction to its lowest terms. Thus, you would express an answer of $\frac{4}{8}$ as $\frac{1}{2}$, or $\frac{6}{9}$ as $\frac{2}{3}$. Fractions may be reduced to lower terms or raised to higher terms without changing the value of the fraction.

Reducing a fraction means finding whole numbers, called common divisors or common factors, that divide evenly into both the numerator and denominator of the fraction. For example, the fraction $\frac{24}{48}$ can be reduced to $\frac{12}{24}$, by the common divisor 2. The new fraction, $\frac{12}{24}$, can be further reduced to $\frac{4}{8}$ by the common divisor 3, and to $\frac{1}{2}$, by the common divisor 4. When a fraction has been reduced to the point where there are no common divisors left, other than 1, it is said to be **reduced to lowest terms.**

The largest number that is a common divisor of a fraction is known as the **greatest common divisor.** It reduces the fraction to lowest terms in one step. In the example of $\frac{24}{48}$ above, we could have used 24, the greatest common divisor, to reduce the fraction to $\frac{1}{2}$.

reduce to lowest terms
The process of dividing whole numbers, known as common divisors or common factors, into both the numerator and denominator of a fraction. Used for expressing fractions as final answers. For example, $\frac{5}{20}$ reduces to $\frac{1}{4}$ by the common divisor, 5.

greatest common divisor
The largest number that is a common divisor of a fraction. Used to reduce a fraction to lowest terms in one step. For example, 5 is the greatest common divisor of $\frac{5}{20}$.

a. Reducing Fractions by Inspection

Reducing fractions by inspection or observation is often a trial-and-error procedure. Sometimes a fraction's common divisors are obvious; other times they are more difficult to determine. The following rules of divisibility may be helpful:

RULES OF DIVISIBILITY

A Number Is Divisible by	Conditions
2	If the last digit is 0, 2, 4, 6, or 8.
3	If the sum of the digits is divisible by 3.
4	If the last two digits are divisible by 4.
5	If the last digit is 0 or 5.
6	If the number is divisible by 2 and 3, or if it is even and the sum of the digits is divisible by 3.
8	If the last three digits are divisible by 8.
9	If the sum of the digits is divisible by 9.
10	If the last digit is 0.

When buying gas, the price per gallon is frequently quoted as a fraction. The price of 1.83^9 is read as "one dollar, eighty-three and 9/10ths cents."

EXAMPLE

Use observation and the rules of divisibility to reduce $\frac{48}{54}$ to lowest terms.

SOLUTION STRATEGY

$\frac{48}{54} = \frac{48 \div 2}{54 \div 2} = \frac{24}{27}$ Because the last digit of the numerator is 8 and the last digit of the denominator is 4, they are both divisible by 2.

$\frac{24}{27} = \frac{24 \div 3}{27 \div 3} = \frac{8}{9}$ Because the sum of the digits of the numerator, 2 + 4, and the denominator, 2 + 7, are both divisible by 3, the fraction is divisible by 3.

$\frac{48}{54} = \frac{8}{9}$ Because no numbers other than 1 divide evenly into the new fraction $\frac{8}{9}$, it is now reduced to lowest terms.

b. Reducing Fractions by the Greatest Common Divisor Method

The best method for reducing a fraction to lowest terms is to divide the numerator and the denominator by the greatest common divisor, because this accomplishes the task in one step. When the greatest common divisor is not obvious to you, use the following steps to determine it:

STEPS FOR DETERMINING THE GREATEST COMMON DIVISOR OF A FRACTION:

Step 1. Divide the numerator of the fraction into the denominator.

Step 2. Take the remainder from Step 1 and divide it into the divisor from Step 1.

Step 3. Repeat this division process until the remainder is either 0 or 1.

- If the remainder is 0, the last divisor is the greatest common divisor.
- If the remainder is 1, the fraction cannot be reduced and is therefore in lowest terms.

EXAMPLE

Reduce the fraction $\frac{63}{231}$ by finding the greatest common divisor.

SOLUTION STRATEGY

$63\overline{)231}$ = 3; 231 − 189 = 42

Divide the numerator, 63, into the denominator, 231. This leaves a remainder of 42.

$42\overline{)63}$ = 1; 63 − 42 = 21

Next, divide the remainder, 42, into the previous divisor, 63. This leaves a remainder of 21.

$21\overline{)42}$ = 2; 42 − 42 = 0

Then, divide the remainder, 21, into the previous divisor, 42. Because this leaves a remainder of 0, the last divisor, 21, is the greatest common divisor of the original fraction.

$\frac{63 \div 21}{231 \div 21} = \frac{3}{11}$

By dividing both the numerator and the denominator by the greatest common divisor, 21, we get the fraction, $\frac{3}{11}$, which is the original fraction reduced to lowest terms.

TRY-IT | EXERCISES

Reduce the following fractions to lowest terms:

11. $\frac{30}{55}$ **12.** $\frac{72}{148}$ **13.** $\frac{270}{810}$ **14.** $\frac{175}{232}$

Check your answers with the solutions on page 63.

2-5 Raising Fractions to Higher Terms

Raising a fraction to higher terms is a procedure sometimes needed in addition and subtraction. It is the opposite of reducing fractions to lower terms. In reducing, we used common divisors; in raising fractions we use common multiples. To **raise to higher terms,** simply multiply the numerator and denominator of a fraction by a **common multiple.**

For example, if we want to raise the fraction $\frac{3}{4}$ by a factor of 7, multiply the numerator and the denominator by 7. This procedure raises the fraction to $\frac{21}{28}$.

$$\frac{3 \times 7}{4 \times 7} = \frac{21}{28}$$

It is important to remember that the value of the fraction has not changed by raising it; we have simply divided the "whole" into more parts. Therefore $\frac{3}{4}$ has the same value as $\frac{21}{28}$. The fraction $\frac{7}{7}$, which we used as the common multiple, reduces to 1 ($7 \div 7 = 1$). Because the common multiple equals 1, multiplying it by a fraction does not change the value of that fraction.

In fractions, remember the denominator indicates how many total parts make up the whole, whereas the numerator indicates how many of those parts we are describing.

raise to higher terms
The process of multiplying whole numbers, known as common multiples, by the numerator and denominator of a fraction. Sometimes needed in addition and subtraction of fractions. For example, $\frac{5}{20}$ is the fraction $\frac{1}{4}$ raised to higher terms, 20ths, by the common multiple, 5.

common multiples
Whole numbers used to raise fractions to higher terms. The common multiple 5 raises the fraction $\frac{1}{4}$ to $\frac{5}{20}$.

STEPS FOR RAISING A FRACTION TO A NEW DENOMINATOR:

Step 1. Divide the original denominator into the new denominator. The resulting quotient is the common multiple that raises the fraction.

Step 2. Multiply the numerator and the denominator of the original fraction by the common multiple.

Everybody's Business

Learning Tip

Sometimes it is difficult to determine which of two fractions is the larger or smaller number. By converting them to **like fractions** (same denominator), the answer will become evident.

For example:

Which fraction is larger, $\frac{4}{5}$ or $\frac{5}{6}$?

$\frac{4}{5} = \frac{24}{30}$, whereas $\frac{5}{6} = \frac{25}{30}$

EXAMPLES

Convert the following fractions to higher terms, as indicated:

a. $\frac{2}{3}$ to fifteenths **b.** $\frac{3}{5}$ to fortieths

SOLUTION STRATEGY

a. $\frac{2}{3} = \frac{?}{15}$ — In this example, we are raising the fraction $\frac{2}{3}$ to the denominator 15.

$15 \div 3 = 5$ — Divide the original denominator, 3, into 15. This yields the common multiple, 5.

$\frac{2 \times 5}{3 \times 5} = \underline{\underline{\frac{10}{15}}}$ — Now, multiply both the numerator and denominator by the common multiple, 5.

b. $\frac{3}{5} = \frac{?}{40}$ Here, the indicated denominator is 40.

$40 \div 5 = 8$ Dividing 5 into 40, we get the common multiple, 8.

$\frac{3 \times 8}{5 \times 8} = \underline{\underline{\frac{24}{40}}}$ Now raise the fraction by multiplying the numerator, 3, and the denominator, 5, by 8.

TRY-IT | EXERCISES

Convert the following fractions to higher terms, as indicated:

15. $\frac{7}{8}$ to sixty-fourths

16. $\frac{3}{7}$ to thirty-fifths

Check your answers with the solutions on page 64.

REVIEW EXERCISES | CHAPTER 2—SECTION I

For each of the following, identify the type of fraction, and write it in word form:

1. $23\frac{4}{5}$ **2.** $\frac{12}{12}$ **3.** $\frac{15}{9}$ **4.** $\frac{7}{16}$ **5.** $2\frac{1}{8}$

Convert the following improper fractions to whole or mixed numbers:

6. $\frac{26}{8}$ **7.** $\frac{20}{6}$ **8.** $\frac{92}{16}$

9. $\frac{64}{15}$ **10.** $\frac{88}{11}$ **11.** $\frac{33}{31}$

Convert the following mixed numbers to improper fractions:

12. $6\frac{1}{2}$ **13.** $11\frac{4}{5}$ **14.** $25\frac{2}{3}$

15. $18\frac{5}{8}$ **16.** $1\frac{5}{9}$ **17.** $250\frac{1}{4}$

Use inspection or the greatest common divisor to reduce the following fractions to their lowest terms:

18. $\frac{21}{35}$ **19.** $\frac{9}{12}$ **20.** $\frac{18}{48}$ **21.** $\frac{216}{920}$

22. $\frac{27}{36}$ **23.** $\frac{14}{112}$ **24.** $\frac{9}{42}$ **25.** $\frac{95}{325}$

26. $\frac{8}{23}$ **27.** $\frac{78}{96}$ **28.** $\frac{30}{150}$ **29.** $\frac{85}{306}$

Convert the following fractions to higher terms, as indicated:

30. $\frac{2}{3}$ to twenty-sevenths **31.** $\frac{3}{4}$ to forty-eighths **32.** $\frac{7}{8}$ to eightieths

33. $\frac{11}{16}$ to sixty-fourths **34.** $\frac{1}{5}$ to hundredths **35.** $\frac{3}{7}$ to ninety-eighths

36. $\frac{3}{5} = \frac{\quad}{25}$ **37.** $\frac{5}{8} = \frac{\quad}{64}$ **38.** $\frac{5}{6} = \frac{\quad}{360}$ **39.** $\frac{9}{13} = \frac{\quad}{182}$

40. $\frac{23}{24} = \frac{\quad}{96}$ **41.** $\frac{2}{9} = \frac{\quad}{72}$ **42.** $\frac{3}{8} = \frac{\quad}{4{,}000}$

43. A wedding cake was cut into 40 slices. If 24 of the slices were eaten, what fraction represents the eaten portion of the cake? Reduce your answer to lowest terms.

44. In last year's Indianapolis 500 car race, 11 of the 33 starters were still running at the end. What fraction represents the portion of the total cars that dropped out of the race?

BUSINESS DECISION

The Wrench Sale

45. You work in the tool department of a Home Depot store. Your manager asks you to set up a point-of-purchase display for a set of 10 wrenches that are on sale this week. He asks you to arrange them in order from smallest to largest on the display board. When you open the box, you find the following sizes in inches: $\frac{9}{32}, \frac{5}{8}, \frac{5}{16}, \frac{1}{2}, \frac{3}{16}, \frac{3}{4}, \frac{7}{8}, \frac{5}{32}, \frac{1}{4}, \frac{3}{8}$.

a. Rearrange the wrenches by size, from smallest to largest.

b. Next, your manager tells you that the sale will be for "1/3 off" the regular price of $57, and has asked you to calculate the "sale price" to be printed on the sign.

c. After the sale is over, your manager asks you for the sales figures on the wrench promotion. If 150 sets were sold that week, what amount of revenue will you report?

d. If $6,000 in sales was expected, what reduced fraction represents the sales actually attained?

SECTION II

ADDITION AND SUBTRACTION OF FRACTIONS

Adding and subtracting fractions occurs frequently in business. Quite often, we must combine or subtract quantities expressed as fractions. To add or subtract fractions, the denominators must be the same. If they are not, we must find a common multiple, or **common denominator,** of all the denominators in the problem. The most efficient common denominator to use is the **least common denominator, or LCD.** By using the LCD you avoid raising fractions to terms higher than necessary.

common denominator
A common multiple of all the denominators in an addition or subtraction of fractions problem. A common denominator of the fractions $\frac{1}{4} + \frac{3}{5}$ is 40.

least common denominator (LCD)
The smallest and, therefore, most efficient common denominator in addition or subtraction of fractions. Avoids raising the fraction to terms higher than necessary. The least common denominator of the fractions $\frac{1}{4} + \frac{3}{5}$ is 20.

prime number
A whole number divisible only by itself and 1. For example, 2, 3, 5, 7, and 11 are prime numbers.

2-6 Determining the Least Common Denominator (LCD) of Two or More Fractions

Finding least common denominators, or LCDs, involves a series of divisions using prime numbers. A **prime number** is a whole number divisible only by itself and 1. Some examples of prime numbers are

2, 3, 5, 7, 11, 13, 17, 19, 23, 29, 31, and so on

STEPS FOR FINDING THE LEAST COMMON DENOMINATOR OF TWO OR MORE FRACTIONS:

Step 1. Write all the denominators in a row.

Step 2. Find a prime number that divides evenly into any of the denominators. Write that prime number to the left of the row, and divide. Place all quotients and undivided numbers in the next row down.

Step 3. Repeat this process until the new row contains all ones.

Step 4. Multiply all the prime numbers on the left together to get the LCD of the fractions.

EXAMPLE

Find the least common denominator of the fractions $\frac{3}{4}, \frac{1}{5}, \frac{4}{9},$ and $\frac{5}{6}$.

SOLUTION STRATEGY

The following chart shows our solution. Note that the first row contains the original denominators. The first prime number, 2, divides evenly into the 4 and the 6. The quotients, 2 and 3, and the nondivisible numbers, 5 and 9, are brought down to the next row.

The same procedure is repeated with the prime numbers 2, 3, 3, and 5. When the bottom row becomes all ones, we multiply all the prime numbers to get the LCD, 180.

Prime Number	Denominators			
2	4	5	9	6
2	2	5	9	3
3	1	5	9	3
3	1	5	3	1
5	1	5	1	1
	1	1	1	1

$2 \times 2 \times 3 \times 3 \times 5 = \underline{\underline{180}} = \text{LCD}$

Everybody's Business

Learning Tip

Answers to fraction problems should always be reduced to lowest terms.

TRY-IT EXERCISE

17. Find the least common denominator of $\frac{3}{8}, \frac{4}{5}, \frac{4}{15},$ and $\frac{11}{12}$.

Check your answer with the solution on page 64.

2-7 Adding Fractions and Mixed Numbers

Now that you have learned to convert fractions to higher and lower terms and find least common denominators, you are ready to add and subtract fractions. We shall learn to add and subtract fractions with the same denominator, fractions with different denominators, and mixed numbers.

Adding Fractions with the Same Denominator

Proper fractions that have the same denominator are known as **like fractions.**

like fractions
Proper fractions that have the same denominator. For example, $\frac{1}{4}$ and $\frac{3}{4}$ are like fractions.

STEPS FOR ADDING LIKE FRACTIONS:

Step 1. Add all the numerators and place the total over the original denominator.

Step 2. If the result is a proper fraction, reduce it to lowest terms.

Step 3. If the result is an improper fraction, convert it to a whole or a mixed number.

EXAMPLE

Add $\frac{4}{15} + \frac{2}{15}$

SOLUTION STRATEGY

$$\frac{4}{15} + \frac{2}{15} = \frac{4+2}{15} = \frac{6}{15} = \frac{2}{5}$$

Because these are like fractions, we simply add the numerators, 4 + 2, and place the total, 6, over the original denominator, 15. This gives us the fraction $\frac{6}{15}$, which reduces by 3 to $\frac{2}{5}$.

TRY-IT | EXERCISE

Add and reduce to lowest terms:

18. $\frac{3}{25} + \frac{9}{25} + \frac{8}{25}$

Check your answer with the solution on page 64.

Adding Fractions with Different Denominators

unlike fractions
Proper fractions that have different denominators. Must be converted to like fractions before adding or subtracting. For example, $\frac{1}{4}$ and $\frac{1}{3}$ are unlike fractions.

Proper fractions that have different denominators are known as **unlike fractions.** Unlike fractions must first be converted to like fractions before they can be added.

STEPS FOR ADDING UNLIKE FRACTIONS:

Step 1. Find the least common denominator of the unlike fractions.

Step 2. Raise all fractions to the terms of the LCD, making them like fractions.

Step 3. Follow the same procedure used for adding like fractions.

EXAMPLE

Add $\frac{3}{8} + \frac{5}{7} + \frac{1}{2}$

SOLUTION STRATEGY

Prime Number	Denominator		
2	8	7	2
2	4	7	1
2	2	7	1
7	1	7	1
	1	1	1

$2 \times 2 \times 2 \times 7 = 56$

These are unlike fractions and must be converted to obtain the same denominator.

First, find the LCD, 56.

$$\frac{3}{8} = \frac{21}{56}$$
$$\frac{5}{7} = \frac{40}{56}$$
$$+\frac{1}{2} = \frac{28}{56}$$
$$\frac{89}{56} = 1\frac{33}{56}$$

Next raise each fraction to fifty-sixths.

Then add the fractions and convert the answer, an improper fraction, to a mixed number.

TRY-IT EXERCISE

Add and reduce to lowest terms:

19. $\frac{1}{6} + \frac{3}{5} + \frac{2}{3}$

Check your answer with the solution on page 64.

Adding Mixed Numbers

STEPS FOR ADDING MIXED NUMBERS:

Step 1. Add the fractional parts. If the sum is an improper fraction, convert it to a mixed number.

Step 2. Add the whole numbers.

Step 3. Add the fraction from Step 1 to the whole number from Step 2.

Step 4. Reduce the sum to lowest terms.

EXAMPLE

Add $15\frac{3}{4} + 18\frac{5}{8}$

SOLUTION STRATEGY

$$15\frac{3}{4} = 15\frac{6}{8}$$
$$+\ 18\frac{5}{8} = 18\frac{5}{8}$$
$$33\frac{11}{8} = 33 + 1\frac{3}{8} = 34\frac{3}{8}$$

First add the fractional parts, using 8 as the LCD. Because $\frac{11}{8}$ is an improper fraction, convert it to the mixed number, $1\frac{3}{8}$.

Next add the whole numbers, $15 + 18 = 33$. Then add the fraction and the whole number to get the answer, $34\frac{3}{8}$.

TRY-IT EXERCISE

Add and reduce to lowest terms:

20. $45\frac{1}{4} + 16\frac{5}{9} + \frac{1}{3}$

Check your answer with the solution on page 64.

2-8 Subtracting Fractions and Mixed Numbers

In addition, we add the numerators of like fractions. In subtraction, we subtract the numerators of like fractions. If the fractions have different denominators, first raise the fractions to the terms of the least common denominator, then subtract.

STEPS FOR SUBTRACTING LIKE FRACTIONS:

Step 1. Subtract the numerators and place the difference over the original denominator.

Step 2. Reduce the fraction to lowest terms.

EXAMPLE

Subtract $\frac{9}{16} - \frac{5}{16}$

SOLUTION STRATEGY

$$\begin{array}{r} \frac{9}{16} \\ -\ \frac{5}{16} \\ \hline \frac{4}{16} = \underline{\underline{\frac{1}{4}}} \end{array}$$

In this example, the denominators are the same so we simply subtract the numerators, $9 - 5$, and place the difference, 4, over the original denominator, 16. Then reduce the fraction $\frac{4}{16}$ to lowest terms, $\frac{1}{4}$.

TRY-IT | EXERCISE

Subtract and reduce to lowest terms:

21. $\frac{11}{25} - \frac{6}{25}$

Check your answer with the solution on page 64.

Subtracting Fractions with Different Denominators

Unlike fractions must first be converted to like fractions before they can be subtracted.

STEPS FOR SUBTRACTING UNLIKE FRACTIONS:

Step 1. Find the least common denominator.

Step 2. Raise each fraction to the denominator of the LCD.

Step 3. Follow the same procedure used to subtract like fractions.

EXAMPLE

Subtract $\frac{7}{9} - \frac{1}{2}$

SOLUTION STRATEGY

$$\begin{array}{rcr} \frac{7}{9} & = & \frac{14}{18} \\ -\frac{1}{2} & = & \frac{9}{18} \\ \hline & & \frac{5}{18} \end{array}$$

In this example, we must first find the least common denominator. By inspection we can see that the LCD is 18.

Next raise both fractions to eighteenths. Now subtract the numerators, 14 − 9, and place the difference, 5, over the common denominator, 18. Because it cannot be reduced, $\frac{5}{18}$ is the final answer.

TRY-IT | EXERCISE

Subtract and reduce to lowest terms:

22. $\frac{5}{12} - \frac{2}{9}$

Check your answer with the solution on page 64.

Subtracting Mixed Numbers

STEPS FOR SUBTRACTING MIXED NUMBERS:

Step 1. If the fractions of the mixed numbers have the same denominator, subtract them and reduce to lowest terms.

Step 2. If the fractions do not have the same denominator, raise them to the denominator of the LCD, and subtract.

Step 3. Subtract the whole numbers.

Step 4. Add the difference of the whole numbers and the difference of the fractions.

Note: When the numerator of the fraction in the minuend is less than the numerator of the fraction in the subtrahend, we must *borrow* one whole unit from the whole number of the minuend. This will be in the form of the LCD/LCD and is added to the fraction of the minuend.

EXAMPLES

Subtract: **a.** $15\frac{2}{3} - 9\frac{1}{5}$ **b.** $7\frac{1}{8} - 2\frac{3}{4}$

SOLUTION STRATEGY

a.

$$\begin{array}{rcr} 15\frac{2}{3} & = & 15\frac{10}{15} \\ -\ 9\frac{1}{5} & = & -9\frac{3}{15} \\ \hline & & 6\frac{7}{15} \end{array}$$

In this example raise the fractions to fifteenths; LCD = 5 × 3 = 15.

Then subtract the fractions to get $\frac{7}{15}$.

Now subtract the whole numbers, 15 − 9, to get the whole number 6.

By combining the 6 and the $\frac{7}{15}$, we get the final answer, $6\frac{7}{15}$.

> **Everybody's Business**
>
> **Learning Tip**
>
> Remember, when you borrow "one" in subtraction, you are borrowing a whole unit expressed in terms of the common denominator.
>
> Such as,
>
> $$\frac{4}{4}, \frac{5}{5}, \frac{8}{8}, \frac{24}{24}$$
>
> Don't forget to add this to the existing fraction.

b.

$$\begin{array}{rcrcr} 7\frac{1}{8} = & 7\frac{1}{8} & = 6\frac{8}{8} + \frac{1}{8} & = & 6\frac{9}{8} \\ -2\frac{3}{4} = & -2\frac{6}{8} & = & & -2\frac{6}{8} \\ \hline & & & & 4\frac{3}{8} \end{array}$$

In this example, after raising $\frac{3}{4}$ to $\frac{6}{8}$, we find that we cannot subtract $\frac{6}{8}$ from $\frac{1}{8}$. We must *borrow* one whole unit, $\frac{8}{8}$, from the whole number, 7, making it a 6 ($8 \div 8 = 1$).

By adding $\frac{8}{8}$ to $\frac{1}{8}$, we get $\frac{9}{8}$.

Now we can subtract $\frac{9}{8} - \frac{6}{8}$, to get $\frac{3}{8}$.

We now subtract the whole numbers, $6 - 2 = 4$. By combining the whole number, 4, and the fraction, $\frac{3}{8}$, we get the final answer, $4\frac{3}{8}$.

TRY-IT | EXERCISES

Subtract the following mixed numbers and reduce to lowest terms:

23. $6\frac{3}{4} - 4\frac{2}{3}$

24. $25\frac{2}{9} - 11\frac{5}{6}$

Check your answers with the solutions on page 64.

REVIEW EXERCISES | CHAPTER 2—SECTION II

Find the least common denominator for the following groups of fractions:

1. $\frac{4}{5}, \frac{2}{3}, \frac{8}{15}$

2. $\frac{1}{3}, \frac{4}{9}, \frac{3}{4}$

3. $\frac{5}{6}, \frac{11}{12}, \frac{1}{4}, \frac{1}{2}$

4. $\frac{1}{6}, \frac{19}{24}, \frac{2}{3}, \frac{3}{5}$

5. $\frac{21}{25}, \frac{9}{60}, \frac{7}{20}, \frac{1}{3}$

6. $\frac{5}{12}, \frac{9}{14}, \frac{2}{3}, \frac{7}{10}$

Add the following fractions, and reduce to lowest terms:

7. $\frac{5}{6} + \frac{1}{2}$

8. $\frac{2}{3} + \frac{3}{4}$

9. $\frac{5}{8} + \frac{13}{16}$

10. $\frac{9}{32} + \frac{29}{32}$

11. $\frac{1}{2} + \frac{4}{5} + \frac{7}{20}$

12. $\frac{3}{4} + \frac{7}{8} + \frac{5}{16}$

13. $\frac{11}{12} + \frac{3}{5} + \frac{19}{30}$

14. $5\frac{4}{7} + \frac{2}{3}$

15. $7\frac{1}{2} + 2\frac{7}{8} + 1\frac{1}{6}$

16. $13\frac{5}{9} + 45\frac{1}{3} + 9\frac{7}{27}$

17. Michael Stone ran $3\frac{1}{2}$ miles on Monday, $2\frac{4}{5}$ miles on Tuesday, and $4\frac{1}{8}$ miles on Wednesday. What is Michael's total mileage for the 3 days?

18. Sanford Distributors shipped three packages to San Francisco weighing $45\frac{1}{5}$, $126\frac{3}{4}$, and $88\frac{3}{8}$ pounds. What was the total weight of the shipment?

19. At a farmer's market you buy $6\frac{3}{10}$ pounds of red onions and $4\frac{1}{3}$ pounds of yellow onions. What is the total weight of the purchase?

20. BrewMasters Coffee Co. purchased $12\frac{1}{2}$ tons of coffee beans in January, $15\frac{4}{5}$ tons in February, and $34\frac{7}{10}$ tons in March. What was the total weight of the purchases?

Subtract the following fractions, and reduce to lowest terms:

21. $\frac{5}{6} - \frac{1}{6}$

22. $\frac{4}{7} - \frac{1}{8}$

23. $\frac{2}{3} - \frac{1}{18}$

24. $\frac{3}{4} - \frac{9}{16}$

25. $12\frac{3}{5} - 4\frac{1}{3}$

26. $8\frac{1}{4} - 5\frac{2}{3}$

27. $28\frac{4}{9} - 1\frac{4}{5}$

28. $8\frac{11}{12} - 8\frac{3}{8}$

29. Bill North sold $18\frac{4}{5}$ of his $54\frac{2}{3}$ acres of land. How many acres does Bill have left?

30. A water tank weighs $1{,}877\frac{5}{8}$ pounds full and $343\frac{1}{4}$ pounds empty. How many pounds of water does the tank hold?

31. A roll of flexible tubing is 136 feet long. John Hiffman cut lengths of $7\frac{2}{3}$, $16\frac{1}{5}$, and $21\frac{1}{2}$ from the roll.

a. How many feet did he cut?

b. How much tubing is left on the roll?

32. Charlie Winters weighed $196\frac{1}{2}$ pounds when he decided to lose some weight. At the end of the first month he weighed $191\frac{3}{8}$ pounds

a. How much did he lose that month?

b. If his goal is $186\frac{3}{4}$ pounds, how much more does he have to lose?

33. An electric sanding machine reduced a table top from $\frac{5}{8}$ inch to $\frac{5}{16}$ inch thick. How much of the wood was sanded off?

34. Michael Angelo, a painter, used $6\frac{4}{5}$ gallons of paint on the exterior of a house and $9\frac{3}{4}$ gallons on the interior.

a. What is the total amount of paint used on the house?

b. If an additional $8\frac{3}{5}$ gallons was used on the garage, what is the total amount of paint used on the house and garage?

c. Rounding your answer from part b "up" to the next whole gallon, calculate the total cost of the paint, if you paid $23 for each gallon.

BUSINESS DECISION

The Red-Eye Express

35. You are an executive with All-Star Corporation in Atlanta, Georgia. The company president was scheduled to make an important sales presentation tomorrow afternoon in Seattle, Washington, but has now asked you to take his place.

The trip consists of a $2\frac{1}{2}$ hour flight from Atlanta to Dallas, a $1\frac{1}{4}$ hour layover in Dallas, and then a $3\frac{3}{4}$ hour flight to Portland. There is a $1\frac{1}{2}$ hour layover in Portland and then a $\frac{3}{4}$ hour flight to Seattle. Seattle is on Pacific Time, which is 3 hours earlier than Eastern Time in Atlanta.

a. If you depart Atlanta tonight at 11:30 P.M., and all flights are on schedule, what time will you arrive in Seattle?

b. If your return flight is scheduled to leave Seattle at 10:10 P.M. tomorrow night, with the same flight times and layovers in reverse, what time are you scheduled to arrive in Atlanta?

c. If the leg from Dallas back to Atlanta is $\frac{2}{3}$ of an hour longer than scheduled due to headwinds, what time will you actually arrive?

SECTION III

MULTIPLICATION AND DIVISION OF FRACTIONS

In addition and subtraction we were concerned with common denominators; however, in multiplication and division common denominators are not required. This simplifies the process considerably.

2-9 Multiplying Fractions and Mixed Numbers

STEPS FOR MULTIPLYING FRACTIONS:

Step 1. Multiply all the numerators to form the new numerator.

Step 2. Multiply all the denominators to form the new denominator.

Step 3. If necessary, reduce the answer to lowest terms.

cancellation
When multiplying fractions, cancellation is the process of finding a common factor that divides evenly into at least one numerator and one denominator. A useful shortcut that simplifies multiplication and often leaves the answer in lowest terms. The common factor 2 can be used to cancel $\frac{1}{\overset{}{\underset{2}{\cancel{4}}}} \times \frac{\overset{3}{\cancel{6}}}{7}$ to $\frac{1}{2} \times \frac{3}{7}$.

A procedure known as **cancellation** can serve as a useful shortcut when multiplying fractions. Cancellation simplifies the numbers with which we are dealing and often leaves the answer in lowest terms.

STEPS FOR APPLYING CANCELLATION:

Step 1. Find a common factor that divides evenly into at least one of the denominators and one of the numerators.

Step 2. Divide that common factor into the denominator and numerator, thereby reducing it.

Step 3. Repeat this process until there are no more common factors.

Step 4. Multiply the fractions as before.

EXAMPLES

Multiply the following fractions:

a. $\frac{5}{7} \times \frac{3}{4}$ **b.** $\frac{2}{3} \times \frac{7}{8}$

SOLUTION STRATEGY

a. $\frac{5}{7} \times \frac{3}{4}$

In this example, there are no common factors between the numerators and the denominators; therefore we cannot use cancellation.

$$\frac{5 \times 3}{7 \times 4} = \underline{\underline{\frac{15}{28}}}$$

Multiply the numerators, 5×3, to form the new numerator, 15; and multiply the denominators, 7×4, to form the new denominator, 28. This fraction does not reduce.

b. $$\frac{2}{3} \times \frac{7}{8}$$

In this example, the 2 in the numerator and the 8 in the denominator have the common factor of 2.

$$\frac{\overset{1}{\cancel{2}}}{3} \times \frac{7}{\underset{4}{\cancel{8}}} =$$

Dividing each by the common factor reduces the 2 to a 1 and the 8 to a 4.

$$\frac{1 \times 7}{3 \times 4} = \underline{\underline{\frac{7}{12}}}$$

Now multiply the simplified numbers; 1×7 forms the numerator, 7, and 3×4 forms the denominator, 12. The resulting product is $\frac{7}{12}$.

TRY-IT | EXERCISE

Multiply and reduce to lowest terms:

25. $\frac{12}{21} \times \frac{7}{8}$

Check your answer with the solution on page 64.

Multiplying Mixed Numbers

STEPS FOR MULTIPLYING MIXED NUMBERS:

Step 1. Convert all mixed numbers to improper fractions.

Step 2. Multiply as before, using cancellation wherever possible.

Step 3. If the answer is an improper fraction, convert it to a whole or mixed number.

Step 4. Reduce to lowest terms.

Note: When multiplying fractions by whole numbers, change the whole numbers to fractions by placing them over 1. For example, the whole number 9 becomes the fraction $\frac{9}{1}$.

EXAMPLES

Multiply:

a. $3\frac{3}{4} \times 5\frac{1}{2}$ **b.** $12\frac{5}{6} \times 4$

SOLUTION STRATEGY

a. $$3\frac{3}{4} \times 5\frac{1}{2}$$

In this example, convert the mixed numbers to improper fractions; $3\frac{3}{4}$ becomes $\frac{15}{4}$, and $5\frac{1}{2}$ becomes $\frac{11}{2}$.

$$\frac{15}{4} \times \frac{11}{2}$$

$$\frac{15 \times 11}{4 \times 2} = \frac{165}{8} = \underline{\underline{20\frac{5}{8}}}$$

After multiplying the numerators together and the denominators together, we get the improper fraction $\frac{165}{8}$, which converts to the mixed number $20\frac{5}{8}$.

b.

$$12\frac{5}{6} \times 4$$

This example demonstrates a mixed number multiplied by a whole number.

$$\frac{77}{6} \times \frac{4}{1}$$

The mixed number $12\frac{5}{6}$ converts to the improper fraction $\frac{77}{6}$. The whole number, 4, expressed as a fraction, becomes $\frac{4}{1}$.

$$\frac{77}{\overset{}{\underset{3}{\cancel{6}}}} \times \frac{\overset{2}{\cancel{4}}}{1}$$

Before multiplying, cancel the 4 in the numerator and the 6 in the denominator by the common factor, 2.

$$\frac{77 \times 2}{3 \times 1} = \frac{154}{3} = \underline{\underline{51\frac{1}{3}}}$$

After multiplying, convert the improper fraction $\frac{154}{3}$ to the mixed number $51\frac{1}{3}$.

TRY-IT | EXERCISES

Multiply and reduce to lowest terms:

26. $8\frac{2}{5} \times 6\frac{1}{4}$

27. $45 \times \frac{4}{9} \times 2\frac{1}{4}$

Check your answers with the solutions on page 64.

Everybody's Business

Learning Tip

The number *after* the "÷" sign is the divisor.

This is the number that gets inverted when dividing.

2-10 Dividing Fractions and Mixed Numbers

In division of fractions, it is important to identify which fraction is the dividend and which is the divisor. In whole numbers, we found that a problem such as 12 ÷ 5 is read, "12 divided by 5." The 12 therefore is the dividend and the 5 is the divisor. Fractions work in the same way. The number *after* the "÷" sign is the divisor. In the problem $\frac{3}{4} \div \frac{2}{3}$, for example, $\frac{3}{4}$ is the dividend and $\frac{2}{3}$ is the divisor.

$$\text{Dividend} \div \text{Divisor} = \frac{\text{Dividend}}{\text{Divisor}} = \text{Divisor}\overline{)\text{Dividend}}$$

invert
To turn upside down. For example, $\frac{1}{4}$ inverted becomes $\frac{4}{1}$. In division of fractions, the divisor is inverted.

reciprocals
Numbers whose product is 1. Inverted numbers are also known as reciprocals of each other. The fractions $\frac{1}{4}$ and $\frac{4}{1}$ are reciprocals since $\frac{1}{4} \times \frac{4}{1} = 1$.

Division of fractions requires that we **invert** the divisor. To invert means to turn upside down. By inverting a fraction, the numerator becomes the denominator, and the denominator becomes the numerator. For example, the fraction $\frac{5}{12}$ becomes $\frac{12}{5}$ when inverted. The inverted fraction is also known as a **reciprocal.** Therefore $\frac{5}{12}$ and $\frac{12}{5}$ are reciprocals of each other.

As in multiplication, division requires that mixed numbers be converted to improper fractions.

STEPS FOR DIVIDING FRACTIONS:

Step 1. Identify the fraction that is the divisor, and invert.

Step 2. Change the "divided by" sign, ÷, to a "multiplied by" sign, ×.

Step 3. Multiply the fractions.

Step 4. Reduce the answer to lowest terms.

EXAMPLES

Divide the following fractions:

a. $\frac{4}{5} \div \frac{2}{3}$ **b.** $6\frac{3}{8} \div 2\frac{1}{2}$ **c.** $12\frac{1}{6} \div 3$

SOLUTION STRATEGY

a. $\frac{4}{5} \div \frac{2}{3} = \frac{4}{5} \times \frac{3}{2}$

In this example, invert the divisor, $\frac{2}{3}$, to form its reciprocal, $\frac{3}{2}$, and change the sign from "÷" to "×."

$\frac{\overset{2}{\cancel{4}}}{5} \times \frac{3}{\underset{1}{\cancel{2}}} = \frac{6}{5} = \underline{\underline{1\frac{1}{5}}}$

Now multiply in the usual manner. Note that the 4 in the numerator and the 2 in the denominator can be reduced by the common factor, 2. The answer, $\frac{6}{5}$, is an improper fraction and must be converted to the mixed number $1\frac{1}{5}$.

b. $6\frac{3}{8} \div 2\frac{1}{2} = \frac{51}{8} \div \frac{5}{2}$

First, convert the mixed numbers to the improper fractions $\frac{51}{8}$ and $\frac{5}{2}$, and state them again as a division.

$\frac{51}{8} \times \frac{2}{5}$

Next invert the divisor, $\frac{5}{2}$, to its reciprocal, $\frac{2}{5}$, and change the sign from "÷" to "×."

$\frac{51}{\underset{4}{\cancel{8}}} \times \frac{\overset{1}{\cancel{2}}}{5} = \frac{51}{20} = \underline{\underline{2\frac{11}{20}}}$

Now multiply in the usual way. Note that the 2 in the numerator and the 8 in the denominator can be reduced by the common factor, 2. The answer, $\frac{51}{20}$, is an improper fraction and must be converted to the mixed number $2\frac{11}{20}$.

c. $12\frac{1}{6} \div 3 = \frac{73}{6} \div \frac{3}{1}$

In this example, we have a mixed number that must be converted to the improper fraction, $\frac{73}{6}$, and a whole number, 3, that converts to $\frac{3}{1}$.

$\frac{73}{6} \times \frac{1}{3}$

The fraction $\frac{3}{1}$ is the divisor and must be inverted to its reciprocal, $\frac{1}{3}$. The sign is changed from "÷" to "×."

$\frac{73}{6} \times \frac{1}{3} = \frac{73}{18} = \underline{\underline{4\frac{1}{18}}}$

The answer is the improper fraction $\frac{73}{18}$, which converts to the mixed number $4\frac{1}{18}$.

Everybody's Business

Real-World Connection

According to *The Wall Street Journal*, the problem below was a question on the Jersey City High School admissions exam in June 1885! Try this for practice:

Divide the difference between 37 hundredths and 95 thousandths by 25 hundred-thousandths and express the result in words.

Answer: one thousand, one hundred

TRY-IT EXERCISES

Divide the following fractions and mixed numbers:

28. $\frac{14}{25} \div \frac{4}{5}$ **29.** $11\frac{3}{16} \div 8\frac{2}{3}$ **30.** $18 \div 5\frac{3}{5}$

Check your answers with the solutions on page 64.

REVIEW EXERCISES | CHAPTER 2—SECTION III

Multiply the following fractions and reduce to lowest terms. Use cancellation whenever possible:

1. $\frac{2}{3} \times \frac{4}{5}$

2. $\frac{5}{6} \times \frac{1}{4}$

3. $\frac{1}{2} \times \frac{4}{9}$

4. $\frac{7}{8} \times \frac{1}{3} \times \frac{4}{7}$

5. $\frac{16}{19} \times \frac{5}{8}$

6. $\frac{25}{51} \times \frac{2}{5}$

7. $\frac{8}{11} \times \frac{33}{40} \times 4$

8. $\frac{2}{3} \times \frac{2}{3} \times 6$

9. $8\frac{1}{5} \times 2\frac{2}{3}$

10. $\frac{1}{2} \times \frac{2}{3} \times \frac{4}{5} \times \frac{3}{4} \times 5$

11. $\frac{1}{5} \times \frac{1}{5} \times \frac{1}{5}$

12. $\frac{2}{3} \times 5\frac{4}{5} \times 9$

13. A recent market research survey showed that $\frac{3}{8}$ of the people interviewed preferred decaffeinated coffee over regular.

a. What fraction of the people preferred regular coffee?

b. If 4,400 persons were interviewed, how many preferred regular coffee?

14. Geoff Seeger earns $1\frac{3}{5}$ times as much as Stan Freeman. If Stan earns $375 per week, how much does Geoff earn per week?

15. A driveway requires $9\frac{1}{2}$ truckloads of gravel. If the truck holds $4\frac{5}{8}$ cubic yards of gravel, how many total cubic yards of gravel are used for the driveway?

16. Molly borrowed $4,200 from the bank. If she has already repaid $\frac{3}{7}$ of the loan, what is the remaining balance owed to the bank?

17. Mat Mesaros works $36\frac{4}{5}$ hours per week for 3 weeks on Project 1, and $27\frac{2}{3}$ hours per week for $7\frac{1}{2}$ weeks on Project 2. What is the total number of hours spent on both projects?

18. Three partners share a business. Sam owns $\frac{3}{8}$, Anita owns $\frac{2}{5}$, and David owns the rest. If the profits this year are $150,000, how much does each partner receive?

Divide the following fractions and reduce to lowest terms:

19. $\frac{5}{6} \div \frac{3}{8}$

20. $\frac{7}{10} \div \frac{1}{5}$

21. $\frac{2}{3} \div \frac{5}{8}$

22. $7 \div \frac{4}{5}$

23. $\frac{1}{3} \div \frac{5}{6}$

24. $\frac{9}{16} \div \frac{9}{16}$

25. $4\frac{4}{5} \div \frac{7}{8}$

26. $21\frac{1}{2} \div 5\frac{2}{3}$

27. $18 \div \frac{18}{19}$

28. $12 \div 1\frac{3}{5}$

29. $\frac{15}{60} \div \frac{7}{10}$

30. $1\frac{1}{5} \div 10$

31. Dream Homes, Inc., a builder of custom homes, owns $126\frac{1}{2}$ acres of undeveloped land. If the property is divided into $2\frac{3}{4}$-acre pieces, how many homesites can be developed?

32. An automobile travels 365 miles on $16\frac{2}{3}$ gallons of gasoline.

a. How many miles per gallon does the car get on the trip?

b. How many gallons would be required for the car to travel 876 miles?

33. Spencer's Department Store purchases 600 straw baskets from a wholesaler.

a. In the first week, $\frac{2}{5}$ of the baskets are sold. How many are sold?

b. By the third week, only $\frac{3}{20}$ remain. How many baskets are left?

34. A hardware supply company buys nails in bulk from the manufacturer and packs them into $2\frac{4}{5}$-pound boxes. How many boxes can be filled from 518 pounds of nails?

35. The chef at the Sizzling Steakhouse has 140 pounds of sirloin steak on hand for Saturday night. If each portion is $10\frac{1}{2}$ ounces, how many sirloin steak dinners can be served? Round to the nearest whole dinner. (There are 16 ounces in a pound.)

36. Engineers at United Electronics use special silver wire to manufacture fuzzy logic circuit boards. The wire comes in 840-foot rolls that cost $1,200 each. Each board requires $4\frac{1}{5}$ feet of wire.

a. How many circuit boards can be made from each roll?

b. What is the cost of wire per circuit board?

37. Southern Reflective Signs makes speed limit signs for the state department of transportation. By law, these signs must be displayed every $\frac{5}{8}$ of a mile. How many signs will be required on a new highway that is $34\frac{3}{8}$ miles long?

38. You are making a batch of corn flake-crusted chicken for a party. The recipe calls for one pound of crushed corn flakes. How many $\frac{11}{16}$ ounce individual-sized boxes will it take to make the chicken? (There are 16 ounces in a pound.)

BUSINESS DECISION

Dinner Special

39. You are the owner of The Gourmet Diner. On Wednesday nights you offer a special of "Buy one dinner, get one free dinner—of equal or lesser value." Michael and Ernie come in for the special. Michael chooses chicken Parmesan for $15, and Ernie chooses a $10 barbecue-combo platter.

a. Excluding tax and tip, how much should each pay, to share the check fairly?

b. If sales tax and tip amount to $\frac{1}{5}$ of the total of the two dinners, how much is that?

c. If they decide to split the tax and tip in the same ratio as the dinners, how much more does each owe?

✦ SUMMARY CHART ✦

SECTION I: Understanding and Working with Fractions

Topic	P/O, Page	Important Concepts	Illustrative Examples
Distinguishing among the Various Types of Fractions	2-1 34	Common or proper fraction: A fraction representing less than a whole unit, where the numerator is less than the denominator. Improper fraction: A fraction representing one whole unit or more, where the denominator is equal to or less than the numerator. Mixed number: A number that combines a whole number with a proper fraction.	Proper $\frac{4}{7}, \frac{2}{3}, \frac{93}{124}$ Improper $\frac{5}{4}, \frac{7}{7}, \frac{88}{51}, \frac{796}{212}, \frac{1{,}200}{1{,}200}$ Mixed $12\frac{2}{5}, 4\frac{5}{9}, 78\frac{52}{63}$
Converting Improper Fractions to Whole or Mixed Numbers	2-2 35	1. Divide the numerator of the improper fraction by the denominator. 2a. If there is no remainder, the improper fraction becomes a whole number. 2b. If there is a remainder, write the whole number and then write the fraction as $\text{Whole Number}\frac{\text{Remainder}}{\text{Divisor}}$	$\frac{68}{4} = 17$ $\frac{127}{20} = 6\frac{7}{20}$
Converting Mixed Numbers to Improper Fractions	2-3 36	1. Multiply the denominator by the whole number. 2. Add the numerator to the product from Step 1. 3. Place the total from Step 2 as the new numerator. 4. Place the original denominator as the new denominator.	$15\frac{3}{4} = \frac{(15 \times 4) + 3}{4} = \frac{63}{4}$

SECTION I: (continued)

Topic	P/O, Page	Important Concepts	Illustrative Examples
Reducing Fractions to Lowest Terms by Inspection	2-4a 37	Reducing a fraction means finding whole numbers, called common divisors or common factors, that divide evenly into both the numerator and denominator of the fraction. When a fraction has been reduced to the point where there are no common divisors left other than 1, it is said to be reduced to lowest terms.	$\frac{24}{120} = \frac{24 \div 3}{120 \div 3} = \frac{8}{40} =$ $\frac{8}{40} = \frac{8 \div 2}{40 \div 2} = \frac{4}{20} =$ $\frac{4}{20} = \frac{4 \div 4}{20 \div 4} = \frac{1}{5}$
Finding the Greatest Common Divisor (Reducing Shortcut)	2-4b 38	The largest number that is a common divisor of a fraction is known as the greatest common divisor (GCD). It reduces the fraction to lowest terms in one step. To find the GCD: 1. Divide the numerator of the fraction into the denominator. 2. Take the remainder from Step 1 and divide it into the divisor from Step 1. 3. Repeat this division process until the remainder is either 0 or 1. If the remainder is 0, the last divisor is the greatest common divisor. If the remainder is 1, the fraction cannot be reduced and is therefore in lowest terms.	What greatest common divisor will reduce the fraction $\frac{48}{72}$? $72 \div 48 = 1$, $72 - 48 = 24$ → $48 \div 24 = 2$, $48 - 48 = 0$ The greatest common divisor is 24.
Raising Fractions to Higher Terms	2-5 39	To raise a fraction to a new denominator: 1. Divide the original denominator into the new denominator. The resulting quotient is the common multiple that raises the fraction. 2. Multiply the numerator and the denominator of the original fraction by the common multiple.	Raise $\frac{5}{8}$ to forty-eighths: $\frac{5}{8} = \frac{?}{48}$ $48 \div 8 = 6$ $\frac{5 \times 6}{8 \times 6} = \frac{30}{48}$

SECTION II: Addition and Subtraction of Fractions

Topic	P/O, Page	Important Concepts	Illustrative Examples
Understanding Prime Numbers	2-6 42	A prime number is a whole number greater than 1 that is divisible only by 1 and itself. Prime numbers are used to find the least common denominator.	Examples of prime numbers: 2, 3, 5, 7, 11, 13, 17, 19, 23, 29

SECTION II: (continued)

Topic	P/O, Page	Important Concepts	Illustrative Examples
Determining the Least Common Denominator (LCD) of Two or More Fractions	2-6 42	1. Write all the denominators in a row. 2. Find a prime number that divides evenly into any of the denominators. Write that prime number to the left of the row, and divide. Place all quotients and undivided numbers in the next row down. 3. Repeat this process until the new row contains all ones. 4. Multiply all the prime numbers on the left together, to get the LCD of the fractions.	Find the LCD of $\frac{2}{9}, \frac{5}{6}, \frac{1}{4}$, and $\frac{4}{5}$. **Prime Number — Denominators** 3 — 9 6 4 5 2 — 3 2 4 5 2 — 3 1 2 5 3 — 3 1 1 5 5 — 1 1 1 5 1 1 1 1 LCD $= 3 \times 2 \times 2 \times 3 \times 5 = 180$
Adding Like Fractions	2-7 43	1. Add all the numerators and place the total over the original denominator. 2. If the result is a proper fraction, reduce it to lowest terms. 3. If the result is an improper fraction, convert it to a whole or a mixed number.	Add $\frac{8}{9}, \frac{4}{9}$, and $\frac{1}{9}$ $\frac{8+4+1}{9} = \frac{13}{9} = 1\frac{4}{9}$
Adding Unlike Fractions	2-7 44	1. Find the least common denominator of the unlike fractions. 2. Raise each fraction to the terms of the LCD, thereby making them like fractions. 3. Add the like fractions.	Add $\frac{2}{3} + \frac{5}{7}$ LCD $= 3 \times 7 = 21$ $\frac{2 \times 7}{21} + \frac{5 \times 3}{21} = \frac{14 + 15}{21} =$ $\frac{29}{21} = 1\frac{8}{21}$
Adding Mixed Numbers	2-7 45	1. Add the whole numbers. 2. Add the fractions and reduce to lowest terms. If they are improper, convert to whole or mixed numbers. 3. Add the whole numbers from Step 1 and the fractions from Step 2 to get the total.	Add $3\frac{3}{4} + 4\frac{1}{8}$ $3 + 4 = 7$ $\frac{3}{4} + \frac{1}{8} = \frac{(3 \times 2) + 1}{8} = \frac{7}{8}$ $7 + \frac{7}{8} = 7\frac{7}{8}$
Subtracting Like Fractions	2-8 46	1. Subtract the numerators and place the difference over the original denominator. 2. Reduce the fraction to lowest terms.	Subtract $\frac{11}{12} - \frac{5}{12}$ $\frac{11-5}{12} = \frac{6}{12} = \frac{1}{2}$
Subtracting Unlike Fractions	2-8 46	1. Find the least common denominator. 2. Raise each fraction to the denominator of the LCD. 3. Subtract the like fractions.	Subtract $\frac{7}{8} - \frac{2}{3}$ LCD $= 8 \times 3 = 24$ $\frac{21}{24} - \frac{16}{24} = \frac{5}{24}$

SECTION II: (continued)

Topic	P/O, Page	Important Concepts	Illustrative Examples
Subtracting Mixed Numbers	2-8 47	1. If the fractions of the mixed numbers have the same denominator, subtract them and reduce to lowest terms. 2. If the fractions do not have the same denominator, raise them to the denominator of the LCD, and subtract. 3. Subtract the whole numbers. 4. Add the difference of the whole numbers and the difference of the fractions.	Subtract $15\frac{5}{8} - 12\frac{1}{2}$ $15\frac{5}{8} = 15\frac{5}{8}$ $-12\frac{1}{2} = -12\frac{4}{8}$ $= 3\frac{1}{8}$
Subtracting Mixed Numbers, Using Borrowing	2-8 47	When the numerator of the fraction in the minuend is less than the numerator of the fraction in the subtrahend, we must borrow one whole unit from the whole number of the minuend. This will be in the form of the LCD/LCD and is added to the fraction of the minuend. Now, subtract as before.	Subtract $6\frac{1}{7} - 2\frac{5}{7}$ $6\frac{1}{7} = 5\frac{7}{7} + \frac{1}{7} = 5\frac{8}{7}$ $-2\frac{5}{7}$ $\quad$ $-2\frac{5}{7}$ $=3\frac{3}{7}$

SECTION III: Multiplication and Division of Fractions

Multiplying Fractions	2-9 52	1. Multipy all the numerators to form the new numerator. 2. Multiply all the denominators to form the new denominator. 3. If necessary, reduce the answer to lowest terms.	Multiply $\frac{5}{8} \times \frac{2}{3}$ $\frac{5}{8} \times \frac{2}{3} = \frac{10}{24} = \frac{5}{12}$
Multiplying Fractions, Using Cancellation	2-9 52	Cancellation simplifies the numbers and leaves the answer in lowest terms. 1. Find a common factor that divides evenly into at least one of the denominators and one of the numerators. 2. Divide that common factor into the denominator and the numerator, thereby reducing it. 3. Repeat this process until there are no more common factors. 4. Multiply the fractions. The resulting product will be in lowest terms.	Use cancellation to solve the multiplication problem above: Cancellation Method: $\frac{5}{8} \times \frac{2}{3} = \frac{5}{\cancel{8}_{4}} \times \frac{\cancel{2}^{1}}{3} = \frac{5}{12}$

SECTION III: (continued)

Topic	P/O, Page	Important Concepts	Illustrative Examples
Multiplying Mixed Numbers	2-9 53	1. Convert all mixed numbers to improper fractions. 2. Multiply, using cancellation wherever possible. 3. If the answer is an improper fraction, convert it to a whole or mixed number. 4. Reduce to lowest terms. *Note:* When multiplying fractions by whole numbers, change the whole numbers to fractions by placing them over 1.	Multiply $3\frac{1}{2} \times 2\frac{3}{8}$ $3\frac{1}{2} = \frac{7}{2} \quad 2\frac{3}{8} = \frac{19}{8}$ $\frac{7}{2} \times \frac{19}{8} = \frac{133}{16} = 8\frac{5}{16}$
Dividing Fractions and Mixed Numbers	2-10 54	Division of fractions requires that we invert the divisor, or turn it upside down. The inverted fraction is also known as a reciprocal. Dividing fractions: 1. Convert all mixed numbers to improper fractions. 2. Identify the fraction that is the divisor, and invert it. 3. Change ÷ to ×. 4. Multiply the fractions. 5. Reduce the answer to lowest terms.	Divide $\frac{11}{12} \div \frac{2}{3}$ $\frac{11}{12}$ is the dividend $\frac{2}{3}$ is the divisor $\frac{11}{12} \div \frac{2}{3} = \frac{11}{12} \times \frac{3}{2}$ $\frac{11}{\cancel{12}_4} \times \frac{\cancel{3}^1}{2} = \frac{11}{8} = 1\frac{3}{8}$

TRY-IT EXERCISE | SOLUTIONS

1. Mixed fraction Seventy-six and three-fourths

2. Common or proper fraction Three-fifths

3. Improper fraction Eighteen-eighteenths

4. Improper fraction Thirty-three-eighths

5. $8 \div 3 = 2\frac{2}{3}$

6. $25 \div 4 = 6\frac{1}{4}$

7. $39 \div 3 = 13$

8. $\frac{11}{4}$ $(2 \times 4 + 3 = 11)$

9. $\frac{46}{5}$ $(9 \times 5 + 1 = 46)$

10. $\frac{181}{8}$ $(22 \times 8 + 5 = 181)$

11. $\frac{30 \div 5}{55 \div 5} = \frac{6}{11}$

$30\overline{)55}$ = 1; 30; 25

$25\overline{)30}$ = 1; 25; 5

$5\overline{)25}$ = 5; 25; 0

12. $\frac{72 \div 4}{148 \div 4} = \frac{18}{37}$

$72\overline{)148}$ = 2; 144; 4

$4\overline{)72}$ = 18; 72; 0

13. $\frac{270 \div 270}{810 \div 270} = \frac{1}{3}$

$270\overline{)810}$ = 3; 810; 0

14. At lowest terms

$175\overline{)232}$ = 1; 175; 57

$57\overline{)175}$ = 3; 171; 4

$4\overline{)57}$ = 14; 4; 17; 16; 1

15. $\dfrac{7 \times 8}{8 \times 8} = \dfrac{56}{64} \quad (64 \div 8 = 8)$

16. $\dfrac{3 \times 5}{7 \times 5} = \dfrac{15}{35} \quad (35 \div 7 = 5)$

17.
$$\begin{array}{c|cccc} 2 & 8 & 5 & 15 & 12 \\ \hline 2 & 4 & 5 & 15 & 6 \\ \hline 2 & 2 & 5 & 15 & 3 \\ \hline 3 & 1 & 5 & 15 & 3 \\ \hline 5 & 1 & 5 & 5 & 1 \\ \hline & 1 & 1 & 1 & 1 \end{array}$$

$2 \times 2 \times 2 \times 3 \times 5 = 120 = \text{LCD}$

18. $\dfrac{3}{25} + \dfrac{9}{25} + \dfrac{8}{25} = \dfrac{3 + 9 + 8}{25} = \dfrac{20}{25} = \dfrac{4}{5}$

19.
$$\begin{array}{rcr} \dfrac{1}{6} & = & \dfrac{5}{30} \\ \dfrac{3}{5} & = & \dfrac{18}{30} \\ +\dfrac{2}{3} & = & +\dfrac{20}{30} \\ \hline & & \dfrac{43}{30} = 1\dfrac{13}{30} \end{array}$$

20.
$$\begin{array}{rcr} 45\dfrac{1}{4} & = & 45\dfrac{9}{36} \\ 16\dfrac{5}{9} & = & 16\dfrac{20}{36} \\ +\ \dfrac{1}{3} & = & +\ \dfrac{12}{36} \\ \hline & & 61\dfrac{41}{36} = 61 + 1\dfrac{5}{36} = 62\dfrac{5}{36} \end{array}$$

21.
$$\begin{array}{r} \dfrac{11}{25} \\ -\dfrac{6}{25} \\ \hline \dfrac{5}{25} = \dfrac{1}{5} \end{array}$$

22.
$$\begin{array}{rcr} \dfrac{5}{12} & = & \dfrac{15}{36} \\ -\dfrac{2}{9} & = & -\dfrac{8}{36} \\ \hline & & \dfrac{7}{36} \end{array}$$

23.
$$\begin{array}{rcr} 6\dfrac{3}{4} & = & 6\dfrac{9}{12} \\ -4\dfrac{2}{3} & = & -4\dfrac{8}{12} \\ \hline & & 2\dfrac{1}{12} \end{array}$$

24.
$$\begin{array}{rcrcr} 25\dfrac{2}{9} & = & 25\dfrac{4}{18} = 24\dfrac{18}{18} + \dfrac{4}{18} & = & 24\dfrac{22}{18} \\ -11\dfrac{5}{6} & = & -11\dfrac{15}{18} = & & -11\dfrac{15}{18} \\ \hline & & & & 13\dfrac{7}{18} \end{array}$$

25. $\dfrac{\overset{1}{\overset{3}{\cancel{12}}}}{\underset{1}{\underset{3}{\cancel{21}}}} \times \dfrac{\overset{1}{\cancel{7}}}{\underset{2}{\cancel{8}}} = \dfrac{1}{2}$

26. $8\dfrac{2}{5} \times 6\dfrac{1}{4} = \dfrac{\overset{21}{\cancel{42}}}{\underset{1}{\cancel{5}}} \times \dfrac{\overset{5}{\cancel{25}}}{\underset{2}{\cancel{4}}} = \dfrac{105}{2} = 52\dfrac{1}{2}$

27. $45 \times \dfrac{4}{9} \times 2\dfrac{1}{4} = \dfrac{45}{1} \times \dfrac{\overset{1}{\cancel{4}}}{\underset{1}{\cancel{9}}} \times \dfrac{\overset{1}{\cancel{9}}}{\underset{1}{\cancel{4}}} = \dfrac{45}{1} = 45$

28. $\dfrac{14}{25} \div \dfrac{4}{5} = \dfrac{\overset{7}{\cancel{14}}}{\underset{5}{\cancel{25}}} \times \dfrac{\overset{1}{\cancel{5}}}{\underset{2}{\cancel{4}}} = \dfrac{7}{10}$

29. $11\dfrac{3}{16} \div 8\dfrac{2}{3} = \dfrac{179}{16} \div \dfrac{26}{3} = \dfrac{179}{16} \times \dfrac{3}{26} = \dfrac{537}{416} = 1\dfrac{121}{416}$

30. $18 \div 5\dfrac{3}{5} = \dfrac{18}{1} \div \dfrac{28}{5} = \dfrac{\overset{9}{\cancel{18}}}{1} \times \dfrac{5}{\underset{14}{\cancel{28}}} = \dfrac{45}{14} = 3\dfrac{3}{14}$

CHAPTER 2 | ASSESSMENT TEST

Name ____________

Class ____________

Identify the type of fraction and write it in word form:

1. $\frac{18}{11}$ **2.** $4\frac{1}{6}$ **3.** $\frac{13}{16}$

Convert to whole or mixed numbers:

4. $\frac{57}{9}$ **5.** $\frac{125}{5}$

Convert to improper fractions:

6. $12\frac{3}{4}$ **7.** $9\frac{5}{9}$

Reduce to lowest terms:

8. $\frac{96}{108}$ **9.** $\frac{26}{65}$

Convert to higher terms, as indicated:

10. $\frac{4}{5}$ to twenty-fifths **11.** $\frac{3}{13} = \frac{}{78}$

Find the least common denominator for the following fractions:

12. $\frac{3}{4}, \frac{19}{20}, \frac{1}{6}, \frac{3}{5}, \frac{8}{15}$

Solve the following problems and reduce to lowest terms:

13. $\frac{3}{4} - \frac{1}{18}$ **14.** $\frac{2}{3} + \frac{1}{6} + \frac{11}{12}$ **15.** $\frac{2}{3} \div \frac{1}{8}$ **16.** $\frac{5}{6} \times \frac{1}{4}$

17. $\frac{2}{5} \times 5\frac{3}{8} \times 2$ **18.** $6\frac{5}{6} - \frac{17}{18}$ **19.** $4\frac{1}{2} + 5\frac{5}{6} + 3$ **20.** $25\frac{1}{2} \div 1\frac{2}{3}$

Answers

1. ____________
2. ____________
3. ____________
4. ____________
5. ____________
6. ____________
7. ____________
8. ____________
9. ____________
10. ____________
11. ____________
12. ____________
13. ____________
14. ____________
15. ____________
16. ____________
17. ____________
18. ____________
19. ____________
20. ____________

Name ______________________

Class ______________________

Answers

21. ______________________

22. ______________________

23. ______________________

24. a. ______________________

b. ______________________

25. a. ______________________

b. ______________________

26. ______________________

21. The Number Crunchers, an accounting firm, has 161 employees. If $\frac{3}{7}$ of them are certified public accountants, how many CPAs are there?

22. Northeastern Coal mined $6\frac{2}{3}$ tons on Monday, $7\frac{3}{4}$ tons on Tuesday, and $4\frac{1}{2}$ tons on Wednesday. If the goal is to mine 25 tons this week, how many more tons must be mined?

23. A blueprint of a house has a scale of 1 inch equals $4\frac{1}{2}$ feet. If the living room wall measures $5\frac{1}{4}$ inches on the drawing, what is the actual length of the wall?

24. On a canned fruit assembly line, a large container holds 255 gallons of fruit salad.

a. If each can holds $\frac{5}{12}$ of a gallon, how many cans does the container fill?

b. If the process uses $2\frac{3}{4}$ containers per hour, how many cans are packed in an 8-hour day?

25. A developer owns three lots measuring $1\frac{2}{3}$ acres each, four lots measuring $2\frac{1}{2}$ acres each, and one lot measuring $3\frac{3}{8}$ acres.

a. What is the total acreage owned by the developer?

b. If each acre is worth $10,000, what is the total value of the properties?

26. A manufacturer has been using glass jars weighing $11\frac{2}{3}$ ounces each. If the company switches to plastic jars, each weighing $7\frac{3}{4}$ ounces, how many ounces would be saved per 48-jar carton?

Name ____________________

Class ____________________

Answers

27. a. ____________________

b. ____________________

28. a. ____________________

b. ____________________

29. ____________________

____

____

____

27. You are a sales representative for Century Marine Equipment. Last year you sold \$490,000 in marine products.

a. If this year you expect to sell $\frac{1}{5}$ more, how much will your sales be?

b. If you are paid a commission of $\frac{1}{12}$ of sales, how much will you earn this year?

28. During a spring clearance sale, JCPenney advertises $\frac{1}{4}$ off the list price of Model II microwave ovens, and an additional $\frac{1}{5}$ off the sale price for ovens that are scratched or dented.

a. If the list price of a Model II is \$240, what is the sale price?

b. What is the price of a scratched one?

29. Among other ingredients, a recipe for linguini with red sauce calls for the following: 24 ounces linguini pasta, $6\frac{2}{5}$ tablespoons minced garlic, 5 cups fresh tomatoes, and 10 tablespoons Parmesan cheese. If the recipe serves eight people, recalculate the quantities to serve five people.

Pasta:

Garlic:

Tomatoes:

Cheese:

Name ______________________

Class ______________________

Answers

30. a. ______________________

b. ______________________

31. a. ______________________

b. ______________________

30. A house has 4,400 square feet. The bedrooms occupy $\frac{2}{5}$ of the space, the living and dining rooms occupy $\frac{1}{4}$ of the space, the garage represents $\frac{1}{10}$ of the space, and the balance is split evenly among three bathrooms and the kitchen.

a. How many square feet are in each bath and kitchen?

b. If the owner wants to increase the size of the garage by $\frac{1}{8}$, how many square feet will the new garage have?

31. Compact disks are $\frac{3}{32}$ inch thick.

a. How tall is a spindle of 50 CDs, plus a base of $\frac{1}{4}$ inch?

b. How tall is a spindle of 100 CDs, with the same $\frac{1}{4}$ inch base?

BUSINESS DECISION

Hong Kong Custom Tailors

Name ______________________

Class ______________________

32. Hong Kong Custom Tailors buys fabric in rolls containing 171 yards each. Pants require $2\frac{3}{4}$ yards of material, vests require $\frac{7}{8}$ of a yard, and jackets take $3\frac{1}{2}$ yards.

a. How many yards of material are required for each complete suit?

b. How many suits can be made from each roll?

c. If each roll of 100 percent wool material costs $1,800, what is the cost of material per suit?

d. If the company adds labor and overhead charges of $290 per suit, and profit of $100 per suit, how much should they charge for a custom-made suit?

Answers

32. a. ______________________

b. ______________________

c. ______________________

d. ______________________

All the Math That's Fit to Learn

The Business Math Times

Volume II | **Fractions** | One Dollar

The History of Fractions, 101

The history of fractions began with human observation of the divisions found in nature. These include such things as the divisions of the day, the month, the seasons, and the patterns of nature. The use of fractions increased over time as growing societies needed ways to meausre goods and currency in commerce.

More than 4,000 years ago, ancient Babylonian astronomers used fractions made by dividing a "whole" into 60 parts, then dividing each of those parts into 60 parts, and so on. This system is still used for telling time and for measuring angles in minutes and seconds. The ancient Chinese developed *decimal* fractions made by dividing units over and over again by 10.

Egyptian mathematicians who helped build the pyramids used only fractions with 1 in the numerator. These are known as *unit* fractions. The use of only unit fractions made it necessary to express other fractional parts as sums. For example, $\frac{3}{4}$ is expressed in unit fractions as $\frac{1}{2} + \frac{1}{4}$.

About 2,000 years ago, the ancient Greeks wrote fractions with the numerator on the bottom and the denominator on the top. Later they changed to the current notation, with the denominator on the bottom. Hindu mathematicians in India adopted this method of writing fractions.

DENNIS THE MENACE

"CUT IT UP INTO A **LOT** OF SLICES, MOM. I'M REALLY HUNGRY!"

"Quote . . . Unquote"

Practice is nine-tenths.
—*Emerson*

Whether you think you can or you think you can't, you are right.
—*Henry Ford*

During the A.D. 700s, Arabs conquered parts of India. There, they learned today's method of writing fractions and the decimal number system. During the next 300 years, the Arabs spread that knowledge through western Asia, across northern Africa, and into Spain.

During the late 1400s, several arithmetic books that explained the use of fractions and the decimal system were published in Europe. Following the publication of the books, large numbers of Europeans began to use fractions to perform everyday calculations.

Today, fractions are an important means of expressing rates, ratios, and division, as well as measuring inches, cups, pounds, and other units in the inch-pound system of measurement.

For more information, visit our web site at www.contemporarymath.com.

All About Money—Wealth and Riches

- Although money cannot buy happiness, our word *wealth* is from *wela*, Anglo-Saxon for happiness and well-being.
- If you were a king in the old days, you would expect to be rich. In fact, our word *rich* comes from *rex*, Latin for king.

Decimals Replace Fractions in Stock Market Trading

In 2000, by congressional mandate and a direct order from the Securities and Exchange Commission, stocks began trading and being quoted in dollars and cents (decimals) rather than in fractions.

American investors for centuries had quoted stock prices in fractions based on eighths of a dollar, such as $\$15\frac{3}{8}$. Some trading systems used smaller fractions such as sixteenths, thirty-seconds, and even sixty-fourths.

Stocks now not only are quoted but also are traded in dollars and cents. In the past, when stocks were traded in increments of eighths, for example, stocks went up and down in eighths of a dollar, or about $.13. Using decimals, stocks now can change by as little as $.01, thereby lowering brokerage commissions.

Brainteaser

YOUR LAST ODD DAY ON EARTH

The numerical format for November 17, 1999, is 11-17-1999. All of the digits are odd numbers. The next "odd" day was 11-19-1999—just two days later.

a. What is the date of the next odd day?

b. What was the date of the even day before 2-2-2000?

Answer to Last Issue's Brainteaser

The first number that contains the letter "a" is: thousand.

CHAPTER 3

Decimals

PERFORMANCE OBJECTIVES

Section I Understanding Decimal Numbers

3-1 Reading and writing decimal numbers in numerical and word form. (p. 72)
3-2 Rounding decimal numbers to a specified place value. (p. 75)

Section II Decimal Numbers and the Fundamental Processes

3-3 Adding and subtracting decimals. (p. 77)
3-4 Multiplying decimals. (p. 78)
3-5 Dividing decimals. (p. 80)

Section III Conversion of Decimals to Fractions and Fractions to Decimals

3-6 Converting decimals to fractions. (p. 87)
3-7 Converting fractions to decimals. (p. 88)

SECTION I

UNDERSTANDING DECIMAL NUMBERS

In Chapter 1, we learned that the position of the digits in our number system affects their value. In whole numbers, we dealt with the positions or places to the left of the decimal point. In decimal numbers, we deal with the places to the right of the decimal point. These places express values that are less than whole numbers.

Just as with fractions, decimals are a way of expressing *parts* of a whole thing. Decimals are used extensively in business applications. Transactions involving dollars and cents are decimals. Percents, an integral part of business, use decimals in their calculation, and frequently fractions are written in decimal form to accommodate digital displays, such as in calculators and other digital readouts. In this chapter you learn to read, write, and work problems involving all types of decimal numbers.

3-1 Reading and Writing Decimal Numbers in Numerical and Word Form

decimal numbers, or decimals
Amounts less than whole, or less than one. For example, .44 is a decimal number.

decimal point
A dot written in a decimal number to indicate where the place values change from whole numbers to decimal numbers.

mixed decimals
Decimals written in conjunction with whole numbers. For example, 2.44 is a mixed decimal.

By definition, **decimal numbers,** or **decimals,** are amounts less than whole, or less than one. They are preceded by a dot known as the **decimal point** and are written .31 or 0.31, for example. The zero is used to ensure that the decimal point is not missed. Often, decimals are written in conjunction with whole numbers. These are known as **mixed decimals.** In mixed decimals, the decimal point separates the whole numbers from the decimal, such as 4.31.

The place value chart, shown in Exhibit 3-1, expands the whole number chart from Chapter 1 to include the places representing decimals. In decimals, the value of each place, starting at the decimal point and moving from left to right, decreases by a factor of 10. The names of the places on the decimal side end in *ths;* they are tenths, hundredths, thousandths, ten-thousandths, hundred-thousandths, and millionths.

To read or write decimal numbers in words, you must read or write the decimal part as if it were a whole number, then name the place value of the last digit on the right. For example, .0594 would be read as "five hundred ninety-four ten-thousandths."

In reading and writing mixed decimals, the decimal point should be read as "and." For example, 81.205 would be read as "eighty-one and two hundred five thousandths." If the

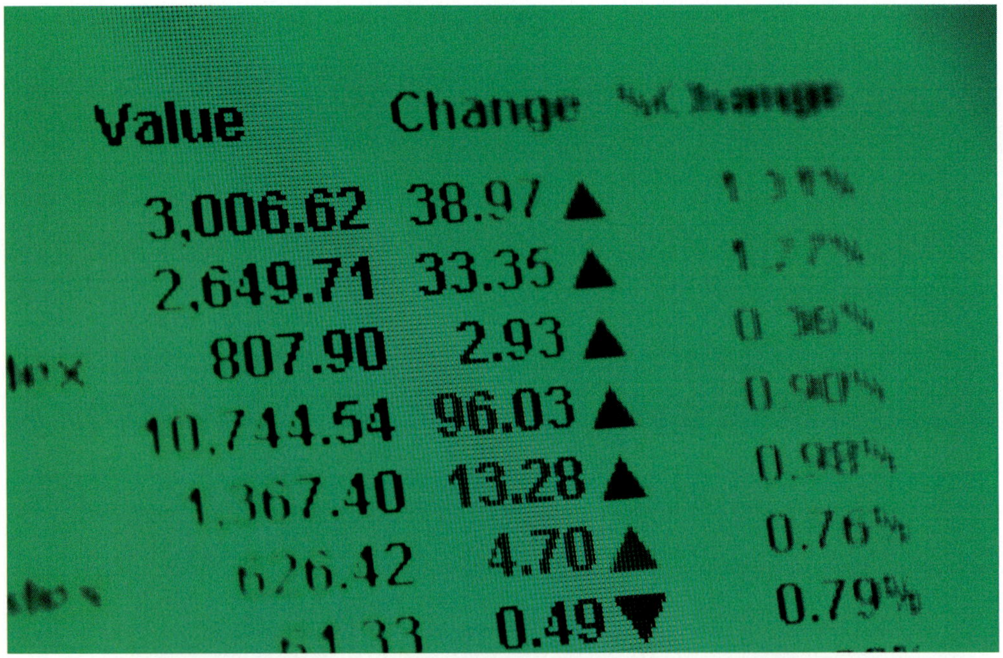

Dollars and cents are expressed as decimals. The numbers to the left of the decimal point represent whole dollars; the numbers to the right represent parts of a dollar, or cents.

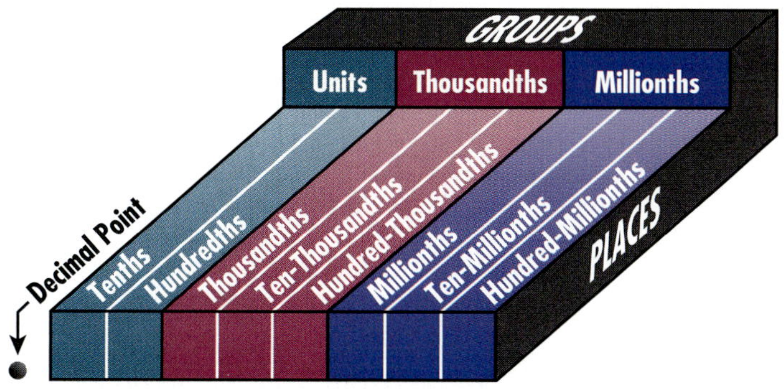

EXHIBIT 3-1
Decimal Numbers Place Value Chart

decimal has a fraction at the end, simply read them together, using the place value of the last digit of the decimal. For example, $.12\frac{1}{2}$ would be read as "twelve and one-half hundredths."

When a dollar sign ($) precedes a number, the whole number value represents dollars and the decimal value represents cents. The decimal point is read as "and." For example, $146.79 would be read as "one hundred forty-six dollars and seventy-nine cents."

Everybody's Business
Learning Tip
When reading numbers, remember that decimals start with the "tenths" place, whereas whole numbers start with the "ones" place.
Don't forget that the word "and" is used to represent the decimal point.

EXAMPLES

Read and write the following numbers in word form:

a. .18 **b.** .0391 **c.** .00127 **d.** 34.892 **e.** 1,299.008 **f.** $.328\frac{2}{3}$

Write the following decimal numbers in numerical form:

g. Three hundred seventy-two ten-thousandths
h. Sixteen thousand and forty-one hundredths
i. Twenty-five and sixty-three and one-half thousandths

SOLUTION STRATEGY

a. .18

Strategy: In this example, write the number eighteen. Because the last digit, 8, is in the hundredths place, the decimal would be written:

Eighteen hundredths

b. .0391

Strategy: Write the number three hundred ninety-one. The last digit, 1, is in the ten-thousandths place; therefore the decimal would be written:

Three hundred ninety-one ten-thousandths

c. .00127

Strategy: Write the number one hundred twenty-seven. The last digit, 7, is in the hundred-thousandths place; therefore the decimal would be written:

One hundred twenty-seven hundred-thousandths

> **Everybody's Business**
>
> **Learning Tip**
>
> Try this for practice:
>
> You are driving to a new restaurant in an unfamiliar area. A highway billboard directs you to make a right turn at an intersection $4\frac{3}{5}$ miles ahead. If your odometer reads 16,237.8, at what mileage should you make the turn?
>
> Solution:
>
> $4\frac{3}{5} = 4.6$ 16,237.8 + 4.6 = 16,242.4 miles

d. 34.892

Strategy: This example is a mixed decimal. First, write the whole number, thirty-four. The decimal point is represented by the word *and.* Now write the decimal part as the number, eight hundred ninety-two. The last digit, 2, is in the thousandths place; therefore the mixed decimal is written:

Thirty-four and eight hundred ninety-two thousandths

e. 1,299.008

Strategy: This example is also a mixed decimal. Start by writing the whole number, one thousand, two hundred ninety-nine. Write "and" for the decimal point, and write the number eight. Because the last digit, 8, is in the thousandths place, the mixed decimal is written:

One thousand, two hundred ninety-nine and eight thousandths

f. $.328\frac{2}{3}$

Strategy: This decimal has a fraction at the end. Start by writing the number, three hundred twenty-eight. Write "and," then write the fraction, two-thirds. Because the last digit of the decimal, 8, is in the thousandths place, it is written:

Three hundred twenty-eight and two-thirds thousandths

g. Three hundred seventy-two ten-thousandths

Strategy: Write three hundred seventy-two in numerical form. Place the last digit, 2, in the ten-thousandths place. Because ten thousand has four zeros, this is four places to the right of the decimal point. Note that we have to add a zero in the tenths place for the last digit, 2, to be in the ten-thousandths place.

.0372

h. Sixteen thousand and forty-one hundredths

Strategy: Write the whole number sixteen thousand. Place the decimal point for the word *and.* Write the number forty-one, and place the last digit, 1, in the hundredths place. Note that hundred has two zeros; therefore the hundredths place is two places to the right of the decimal point.

16,000.41

i. Twenty-five and sixty-three and one-half thousandths

Strategy: Write the whole number twenty-five. Place the decimal point for the word *and.* Write the number sixty-three, and place the fraction one-half after it. Write the last digit, 3, in the thousandths place, three places to the right of the decimal point.

$25.063\frac{1}{2}$

TRY-IT EXERCISES

Read and write the following decimal numbers in word form:

1. .64 **2.** .492 **3.** .10019 **4.** 579.0004 **5.** 26.708 **6.** $.33\frac{1}{3}$

Write the following words in numerical form:

7. Two hundred seventy-two and ninety-four hundred-thousandths

8. Eleven and three and one-quarter thousandths

Check your answers with the solutions on page 93.

3-2 Rounding Decimal Numbers to a Specified Place Value

Rounding decimals is important in business because frequently numbers contain many more decimal places than necessary. For money amounts, we round to the nearest cent, or hundredth place. For other business applications, we usually do not go beyond thousandths as a final answer.

Rounding decimal numbers is much like rounding whole numbers. In whole numbers, after rounding, we substitute zeros for the remaining spaces to the right of the rounded digit to preserve the place value of the number. In rounding decimals, we do not add zeros, just drop the rest of the digits.

Everybody's Business
Real-World Connection

The Margin of Victory
Fractions and decimals are used in all forms of racing to express the time differences among the competitors. Sometimes these can be extremely close.

- In 1997, in the closest race in Indy car history, first and second place were separated by only twenty-seven thousandths (.027) of a second—and that's after 500 miles!
- In 2001, a 500-mile NASCAR race in Atlanta ended even closer when Kevin Harvic edged out Jeff Gordon by six one-thousandths (.006) of a second. (See photo below.)

STEPS TO ROUND DECIMALS TO A SPECIFIED PLACE VALUE:

Step 1. Determine the place to which the decimal is to be rounded.

Step 2a. If the digit to the right of the one being rounded is 5 or more, increase the digit in the place being rounded by 1.

Step 2b. If the digit to the right of the one being rounded is 4 or less, do not change the digit in the place being rounded.

Step 3. Delete all digits to the right of the one being rounded.

EXAMPLES

Round the following numbers to the indicated place:

a. .0292 to hundredths **b.** .33945 to thousandths **c.** 36.798 to tenths

d. 177.0212782 to hundred-thousandths **e.** $46.976 to cents **f.** $66.622 to dollars

SOLUTION STRATEGY

	Decimal Number	Indicated Place	Rounded Number
a.	.0292	.0292	.03
b.	.33945	.33945	.339
c.	36.798	36.798	36.8
d.	177.0212782	177.0212782	177.02128
e.	$46.976	$46.976	$46.98
f.	$66.622	$66.622	$67

TRY-IT | EXERCISES

Round the following numbers to the indicated place:

9. 5.78892 to thousandths **10.** .004522 to ten-thousandths **11.** $345.8791 to cents

12. 76.03324 to hundredths **13.** $766.43 to dollars **14.** 34,956.1229 to tenths

Check your answers with the solutions on page 93.

REVIEW EXERCISES | CHAPTER 3—SECTION I

Write the following decimal numbers in word form:

1. .21 **2.** 3.76 **3.** .092 **4.** 14.659 **5.** 98,045.045

6. .000033 **7.** .00938 **8.** $36.99\frac{2}{3}$ **9.** $.00057\frac{1}{2}$ **10.** $2,885.59

Write the following decimal numbers in numerical form:

11. Eight tenths

12. Twenty-nine thousandths

13. Sixty-seven thousand, three hundred nine and four hundredths

14. Eleven hundred fifty-four dollars and thirty-four cents

15. One hundred eighty-three thousand and one hundred eighty-three ten-thousandths

Round the following numbers to the indicated place:

16. .448557 to hundredths **17.** 123.0069 to thousandths

18. .9229388 to ten-thousandths **19.** .0100393 to hundred-thousandths

20. $688.75 to dollars **21.** $14.59582 to cents **22.** 88.964 to tenths

23. 43.0056 to hundredths **24.** 1.344 to hundredths **25.** 45.80901 to whole numbers

BUSINESS DECISION

Tech Talk

26. You are the assistant to the production manager for Dynamo Industries. When you arrived at work, there was a message on your answering machine from an important client with a rush order. It stated the following:

Hi! This is Warren Jasper from Precision Fabricators. We need sixteen, three and three-quarter-inch widgets with a gap of fifty-seven thousandths; twenty, four and three-eighth-inch widgets with a gap of two hundred forty-nine ten-thousandths; and twenty-five widget connectors with clamps that adjust from one and twenty-three hundredths inches to five and three hundred seventy-six thousandths. Please bill and ship the order to the usual address. Thanks.

a. Write this order in numerals for the production department to process.

Dynamo Industries—Production Order

Quantity	Description

b. If widgets cost $4.80 per inch, regardless of gap size, and connectors cost $17.95 each, calculate the total cost of the order.

SECTION II

DECIMAL NUMBERS AND THE FUNDAMENTAL PROCESSES

In business, working with decimals is an everyday occurrence. As you shall see, performing the fundamental processes of addition, subtraction, multiplication, and division on decimal numbers is very much like performing them on whole numbers. As before, the alignment of the numbers is very important. The difference is in the handling and placement of the decimal point.

3-3 Adding and Subtracting Decimals

In adding and subtracting decimals we follow the same procedure as we did with whole numbers. As before, be sure that you line up all the place values, including the decimal points.

STEPS FOR ADDING AND SUBTRACTING DECIMALS:

Step 1. Line up all the place values and decimal points vertically.

Step 2. (Optional) Add zeros to the right of the decimal numbers that do not have enough places.

Step 3. Perform the addition or subtraction, working from right to left.

Step 4. Place the decimal point in the answer in the same position (column) as in the problem.

Everybody's Business

Real-World Connection

Did you know the Romans called the total of addition problems *res summa*, the highest thing. Later this was shortened to *summa*, which is why we call addition answers *sums*.

In addition, the Romans always added a column of numbers from the bottom, putting the total at the top! This explains why we still say, "to add up."

EXAMPLES

a. Add 45.3922 + .0019 + 2.9 + 1,877.332

b. Add \$37.89 + \$2.76

c. Subtract 87.06 − 35.2

d. Subtract \$67.54 from \$5,400

SOLUTION STRATEGY

These examples are solved by lining up the decimal points, then performing the indicated operation as if they were whole numbers.

a.	b.	c.	d.
45.3922	\$37.89	87.06	\$5,400.00
.0019	+ 2.76	− 35.20	− 67.54
2.9000	\$40.65	51.86	\$5,332.46
+ 1,877.3320			
1,925.6261			

TRY-IT | EXERCISES

Perform the indicated operation:

15. 35.7008 + 311.2 + 84,557.54

16. \$65.79 + \$154.33

17. Subtract 57.009 from 186.7

18. \$79.80 minus \$34.61

Check your answers with the solutions on page 93.

3-4 Multiplying Decimals

> **Everybody's Business**
> **Learning Tip**
> When adding, subtracting, multiplying, or dividing decimals, numbers should not be rounded until the final answer—unless you are estimating.
> If the situation involves money, final answers should be rounded to the nearest cent.

Decimals are multiplied in the same way as whole numbers, except we must now deal with placing the decimal point in the answer. The rule is that there must be as many decimal places in the product as there are total decimal places in the multiplier and the multiplicand. This may require adding zeros to the product.

STEPS FOR MULTIPLYING DECIMALS:

Step 1. Multiply the numbers as if they are whole numbers. Disregard the decimal points.

Step 2. Total the number of decimal places in the multiplier and the multiplicand.

Step 3. Insert the decimal point in the product, giving it the same number of decimal places as the total from Step 2.

Step 4. If necessary, place zeros to the left of the product to provide the correct number of digits.

EXAMPLE

Multiply 125.4 by 3.12.

SOLUTION STRATEGY

125.4	1 decimal place
× 3.12	2 decimal places
2508	
1254	
3762	
391.248	3 decimal places

EXAMPLE

To illustrate a situation where we must add zeros to the product, multiply .0004 × 6.3.

SOLUTION STRATEGY

6.3	1 decimal place
× .0004	4 decimal places
.00252	5 decimal places

Here, we had to add 2 zeros to the left of the product to make five decimal places.

MULTIPLICATION SHORTCUT

Whenever you are multiplying a decimal by a power of 10, such as 10, 100, 1,000, 10,000, etc., count the number of zeros in the multiplier and move the decimal point in the multiplicand the same number of places to the right. If necessary, add zeros to the product to provide the required places.

EXAMPLES

To illustrate the multiplication shortcut, multiply 138.57 by 10, 100, 1,000, and 10,000.

SOLUTION STRATEGY

138.57 × 10 = 1,385.7	Decimal moved 1 place to the right
138.57 × 100 = 13,857.	Decimal moved 2 places to the right
138.57 × 1,000 = 138,570.	Decimal moved 3 places to the right—1 zero added
138.57 × 10,000 = 1,385,700.	Decimal moved 4 places to the right—2 zeros added

TRY-IT | EXERCISES

Multiply the following decimals:

19. 876.66 × .045

20. 4,955.8 × 2.9

21. $65.79 × 558

22. .00232 by 1,000

Check your answers with the solutions on page 93.

3-5 Dividing Decimals

In division of decimals, be aware of the decimal points. The basic rule is that you cannot divide with a decimal in the divisor. If there is a decimal, you must convert it to a whole number before dividing.

STEPS FOR DIVIDING DECIMALS IF THE DIVISOR IS A WHOLE NUMBER:

Step 1. Place the decimal point in the quotient directly above the decimal point in the dividend.

Step 2. Divide the numbers.

EXAMPLE

Divide: 8.50 ÷ 25

SOLUTION STRATEGY

```
                   .34
8.50 ÷ 25 = 25)8.50
                 7 5
                 1 00
                 1 00
                    0
```

In this example, the divisor, 25, is a whole number, so we place the decimal point in the quotient directly above the decimal point in the dividend, and then divide. The answer is .34.

STEPS FOR DIVIDING DECIMALS IF THE DIVISOR IS A DECIMAL NUMBER:

Step 1. Move the decimal point in the divisor to the right until it becomes a whole number.

Step 2. Move the decimal point in the dividend the same number of places as you moved it in the divisor. It may be necessary to add zeros to the right of the dividend if there are not enough places.

Step 3. Place the decimal point in the quotient directly above the decimal point in the dividend.

Step 4. Divide the numbers.

Note: All answers involving money should be rounded to the nearest cent. This means dividing until the quotient has a thousandths place, and then rounding back to hundredths. For example, $45.671 = $45.67 or $102.879 = $102.88.

EXAMPLE

Divide: 358.75 ÷ 17.5

SOLUTION STRATEGY

358.75 ÷ 17.5 =

17.5)358.75

175)3587.5

In this example, the divisor, 17.5, is a decimal with one place. To make it a whole number, move the decimal point one place to the right. Now move the decimal point in the dividend one place to the right.

```
       20.5
175)3587.5
    350
      87 5
      87 5
         0
```

Then place the decimal point in the quotient above the decimal point in the dividend.

Now divide the numbers. The answer is 20.5.

DIVISION SHORTCUT

Whenever you divide a decimal by a power of 10, such as 10, 100, 1,000, 10,000, etc., count the number of zeros in the divisor and move the decimal point in the dividend the same number of places to the left. It may be necessary to add zeros to provide the required places.

EXAMPLES

To illustrate the division shortcut, divide 43.78 by 10, 100, 1,000, and 10,000.

SOLUTION STRATEGY

$43.78 \div 10 = 4.378$ Decimal moved 1 place to the left

$43.78 \div 100 = .4378$ Decimal moved 2 places to the left

$43.78 \div 1{,}000 = .04378$ Decimal moved 3 places to the left—1 zero added

$43.78 \div 10{,}000 = .004378$ Decimal moved 4 places to the left—2 zeros added

TRY-IT | EXERCISES

Divide the following decimals:

23. $716.8 \div 16$ **24.** $21.336 \div .007$ **25.** $\$3,191.18 \div 42.1$ **26.** $2.03992 \div 1,000$

Check your answers with the solutions on page 93.

REVIEW EXERCISES | CHAPTER 3—SECTION II

Perform the indicated operation for the following:

1. $2.03 + 56.003$

2. $.006 + 12.33$

3. $\$24.66 + \$19.72 + \$.89$

4. $54.669 + 121.3393 + 7.4$

5. $.000494 + 45.776 + 16.008 + 91$

6. $495.09 - 51.05$

7. $58.043 - 41.694$

8. $\$70.55 - \$12.79$

9. $1.71 − $.84

10. 28.90922 − 16.41

11. The Fancy Fruit Company shipped 218 pounds of strawberries, 186.9 pounds of cherries, and 374.85 pounds of apples to the Ritz Hotel. What was the total weight of the order?

12. Ed Diamond wants to build a fence around his property. If the dimensions of the land are 145.66 feet, 97.1 feet, 164.09 feet, and 103.6 feet, what is the total length of the fence?

13. While at the mall, Maria Gomez spends $46.50 for a blouse, $39.88 for a skirt, and $51.99 for a pair of shoes. What is the total amount of Maria's purchases?

14. On a recent trip, Edward Burton filled up his gas tank four times with the following quantities of gasoline: 23.4 gallons, 19.67 gallons, 21.008 gallons, and 16.404 gallons. How many gallons did Edward use?

15. Last week, Carley Hopkins ran a 5-kilometer race in 26.696 minutes. This week she ran a race in 24.003 minutes. What is the difference in Carley's times?

16. Before dieting, John Richards weighed 188.75 pounds. After three weeks, he weighed 179.46. How much weight did John lose?

17. In a manufacturing process, three pieces of wood are glued together. In thickness, they measure .65 inch, .0591 inch, and 1.6 inches.

 a. What is the total thickness of the pieces?

 b. If these pieces are fit into a space measuring 3.94 inches, how much room is left for other parts?

18. On Monday an electrician used 184.66 feet of wire; on Tuesday he used 121.03 feet.

 a. How many total feet did he use?

 b. If he started with a roll 445 feet in length, how much wire remains on the roll?

19. Sandy's checking account had a starting balance of $1,850.37. During the week, Sandy wrote checks for $131.57, $533.19, $51.50, and $8.70. He also made deposits of $422.17 and $88.66. What is the new balance of the checking account?

20. A milk tanker truck weighs 57,699 pounds empty. After filling up at the dairy, the truck weighed 64,707.2 pounds.

 a. How many pounds of milk did the truck pick up?

 b. At the end of the day the truck weighed 59,202.9 pounds. How much milk did the truck deliver?

Multiply the following decimals:

21. $\begin{array}{r} 45.77 \\ \times \quad 12 \\ \hline \end{array}$ **22.** $\begin{array}{r} 494.09 \\ \times \quad .81 \\ \hline \end{array}$ **23.** $\begin{array}{r} 2.311 \\ \times \quad 3.2 \\ \hline \end{array}$ **24.** $\begin{array}{r} 112.005 \\ \times \; 10{,}000 \\ \hline \end{array}$ **25.** $\begin{array}{r} .00202 \\ \times \quad 24 \\ \hline \end{array}$

26. 15.032 × 1.008 **27.** 45.0079 × 1,000 **28.** .3309 × 100,000

Divide the following decimals, rounding to hundredths where necessary:

29. 24.6 ÷ 19 **30.** .593 ÷ 8.6 **31.** 18.69 ÷ 1,000 **32.** $24.50 ÷ 9

33. $72\overline{)266.4}$ **34.** $23.18\overline{)139.08}$ **35.** $.04\overline{)62.2}$ **36.** $4.6\overline{)1000}$

37. The Cardwell Corporation purchases 23 fax machines for its office staff. Each of the machines costs $345.50. What is the total cost of the machines?

38. A developer is building 13 homes at one time. Each roof measures 45.7 feet by 68.55 feet.

a. What is the total square feet per roof? (Multiply length by width.)

b. What is the total square feet of roof for the entire project?

c. If the roofing company charges $4.15 per square foot, what is the total cost of the roofs?

39. a. What is the cost of a dress requiring 3.63 yards of material, if the material is $12.59 per yard?

b. How much is saved on the dress if material costing $9.45 per yard is used instead?

40. A vegetable wholesaler sold 1,168.07 pounds of potatoes, 1,246.11 pounds of lettuce, and 1,217.82 pounds of onions on Monday.

a. What is the total pounds the wholesaler sold?

b. If the wholesaler had eight customers on Monday, what was the average pounds per sale?

41. Jerry Kreshover has a car with a gas tank that holds 19.48 gallons. If the car averages 16.22 miles per gallon, how many miles can he drive on a tank? (Round to the nearest whole mile.)

42. Danny Alioto purchases 153.6 square yards of carpeting on sale for $13.70 per yard.

a. What is the cost of the carpet?

b. Normally, this carpeting sells for $19.69 per yard. How much does Danny save by purchasing during the sale?

43. Debbie Ogilvy started the day with $65.78 in her purse. During the day she spent $13.58 at the bookstore, $34.62 at the supermarket, and $11.86 at the dry cleaner. On the way home, she cashed a check for $40.00.

a. How much cash did Debbie have that evening?

b. If her spending budget was $50.00 per day, was she over or under budget for the day? By how much?

44. Jim Fowler bought a car at Municipal Auto Sales for $14,566.90. The sticker price was $17,047.88.

a. How much did Jim save from the sticker price?

b. The tax was $957.70, and the registration and license plate cost $65.40. What is the total cost of the car?

c. If Jim makes a down payment of $4,550 and gets an interest-free car loan from Municipal, what will the equal monthly payments be for 48 months?

45. Boxes of candy are 5.77 inches high.

a. How many boxes can be stacked in a container 86.55 inches high?

b. If each box weighs 1.4 pounds, and the container weighs 6 pounds, what is the total weight of a filled container?

c. If freight charges to Toledo, Ohio, are $1.48 per pound, what is the total cost to ship the container?

BUSINESS DECISION

Pepsi, Please!

46. Jim Patterson owns a PepsiCo vending truck that holds 360 quarts of soda. Last Saturday at a carnival, Jim sold out completely. He sells a 10-ounce Pepsi for $1.25. There are 16 ounces in a pint and 2 pints in a quart.

a. How many drinks did he serve?

b. How much money did he take in for the day?

c. For the next carnival, Jim is considering switching to either a 12-ounce drink for $1.65 or a 16-ounce drink for $1.95. As his business advisor, what size do you recommend, assuming each would be a sellout?

SECTION III

CONVERSION OF DECIMALS TO FRACTIONS AND FRACTIONS TO DECIMALS

Changing a number from decimal form to its fractional equivalent, or changing a number in fractional form to its decimal equivalent, is common in the business world. For example, a builder or an architect may use fractions when dealing with the measurements of a project but convert to decimals when calculating the cost of materials.

3-6 Converting Decimals to Fractions

Keep in mind that decimals are another way of writing fractions whose denominators are powers of 10 (10, 100, 1,000). When you are converting a mixed decimal, the whole number is added to the new fraction, resulting in a mixed fraction.

STEPS FOR CONVERTING DECIMALS TO THEIR FRACTIONAL EQUIVALENT:

Step 1. Write the decimal as a fraction by making the decimal number, without the decimal point, the numerator.

Step 2. The denominator is 1 followed by as many zeros as there are decimal places in the original decimal number.

Step 3. Reduce the fraction to lowest terms.

Everybody's Business

Learning Tip

When converting decimals to fractions, verbally "say" the decimal and then write down what you said as a fraction. For example:

- .85 would be verbally stated as "eighty-five hundredths" and written as $\frac{85}{100}$.
- .655 would be verbally stated as "six hundred fifty-five thousandths" and written as $\frac{655}{1000}$.

EXAMPLES

Convert the following decimals to their fractional equivalent, reducing where possible:

a. .64 **b.** .125 **c.** .0457 **d.** 17.31

SOLUTION STRATEGY

a. $.64 = \frac{64}{100} = \frac{16}{25}$

In this example, 64 becomes the numerator. Because there are two decimal places, the denominator is 1 with two zeros. Then reduce the fraction.

b. $.125 = \frac{125}{1000} = \frac{1}{8}$

Once again, the decimal becomes the numerator, 125. This decimal has three places; therefore, the denominator will be 1 followed by three zeros. The resulting fraction is then reduced to lowest terms.

c. $.0457 = \frac{457}{10{,}000}$

This fraction does not reduce.

d. $17.31 = 17 + \frac{31}{100} = 17\frac{31}{100}$

This mixed decimal results in a mixed fraction. It cannot be reduced.

TRY-IT | EXERCISES

Convert the following decimals to their fractional equivalent, reducing where possible:

27. .875 **28.** 23.076 **29.** .0004 **30.** 84.75

Check your answers with the solutions on page 93.

3-7 Converting Fractions to Decimals

In Chapter 2, we learned that fractions are actually a way of expressing a division, with the line separating the numerator and the denominator representing "divided by."

$$\frac{\text{Numerator (dividend)}}{\text{Denominator (divisor)}} \longrightarrow \text{Denominator}\overline{)\text{Numerator}}$$

In business, decimal numbers are usually rounded to three places (thousandths) or less. When expressing money, round to the nearest hundredth, or cent.

> **Everybody's Business**
> **Learning Tip**
> When fractions such as $\frac{2}{3}$ are converted to decimals, the result is a *repeating decimal.* These may be written as .666, or for business applications, rounded to tenths or hundredths.
>
> Others include: $\frac{1}{3}, \frac{1}{6}, \frac{5}{6}, \frac{1}{9}, \frac{4}{9}, \frac{23}{9}$.

STEPS FOR CONVERTING FRACTIONS TO DECIMALS:

Step 1. Divide the numerator by the denominator.

Step 2. Add a decimal point and zeros, as necessary, to the numerator (dividend).

EXAMPLES

Convert the following fractions to their decimal equivalents, rounding to hundredths:

a. $\frac{3}{5}$ **b.** $\frac{1}{3}$ **c.** $\frac{23}{9}$ **d.** $15\frac{3}{8}$

SOLUTION STRATEGY

a. $\frac{3}{5} = 5\overline{)3.0}$ = .6 = $\underline{\underline{.6}}$

In this example, the numerator, 3, becomes the dividend, with a decimal point and zero added. The denominator, 5, becomes the divisor.

b. $\frac{1}{3} = 3\overline{)1.0000}$ = .3333 = $\underline{\underline{.33}}$

In this example, the division is uneven and goes on and on, so we round the quotient to hundredths.

c. $\frac{23}{9} = 9\overline{)23.00000}$ = 2.55555 = $\underline{\underline{2.56}}$

Improper fractions result in mixed decimals. Note that the quotient was rounded because of an endlessly repeating decimal.

d. $15\frac{3}{8} = 15 + 8\overline{)3.000}$ = .375 = $\underline{\underline{15.38}}$

This example contains a whole number. Remember to add it to the resulting decimal.

TRY-IT | EXERCISES

Convert the following fractions to their decimal equivalents, rounding to hundredths where necessary:

31. $\frac{4}{5}$ **32.** $84\frac{2}{3}$ **33.** $\$6\frac{3}{4}$ **34.** $\frac{5}{2}$ **35.** $\frac{5}{8}$

Check your answers with the solutions on page 93.

REVIEW EXERCISES | CHAPTER 3—SECTION III

Convert the following decimals to fractions and reduce to lowest terms:

1. .125 **2.** 4.75 **3.** .008 **4.** 93.0625 **5.** 14.82

Convert the following fractions to decimals, rounding the quotients to hundredths:

6. $\frac{9}{16}$ **7.** $5\frac{2}{3}$ **8.** $24\frac{1}{8}$ **9.** $\frac{55}{45}$ **10.** $\frac{3}{5}$

For the following numbers, perform the indicated operation:

11. $34.55 + 14.08 + 9\frac{4}{5}$

12. $565.809 - 224\frac{3}{4}$

13. $12\frac{1}{2} \div 2.5$

14. $\$35.88 \times 21\frac{1}{4}$

15. a. How many eight-slice pizzas must you purchase to feed 24 women, who eat $2\frac{1}{8}$ slices each, and 20 men, who eat $3\frac{3}{4}$ slices each? (Round to the nearest whole pizza.)

b. If each pizza costs $11.89, what is the total cost?

16. Janice buys $4\frac{3}{5}$ pounds of potatoes at $.75 per pound. What is the cost of the potatoes?

17. a. What is the total cost of fuel for a 3,003 mile trip, if your vehicle gets 15.4 miles per gallon and the average cost of gasoline is $\$1.42\frac{9}{10}$? Round to the nearest cent.

b. While on the trip, you paid $368.50 for engine repairs and $37.80 for a new battery. In addition, tolls amounted to $45.75 and parking averaged $4.50 per day for nine days. What was the cost per mile for the trip? Round to the nearest tenth of a cent.

18. You are the purchasing manager for Visual Graphics, a company that uses specially treated photo paper. The yellow paper costs $.07\frac{1}{5}$ per sheet and the blue paper costs $.05\frac{3}{8}$ per sheet. If you order 15,000 yellow sheets and 26,800 blue sheets, what is the total cost of the order?

19. Magic City taxicabs charge $1.20 for the first $\frac{1}{4}$ of a mile, and $.35 for each additional $\frac{1}{4}$ of a mile. What is the cost of a trip from the airport to downtown, a distance of $8\frac{3}{4}$ miles?

BUSINESS DECISION

The $\frac{7}{8}$ths Sale

20. You are the manager of The Aces, an upscale men's clothing store in a large shopping mall. The store has an interesting and successful promotion called "The $\frac{7}{8}$ths Sale." On the seventh and eighth day of each month, the store offers all merchandise at a sale price of $\frac{7}{8}$ths of the regular price. When the seventh or eighth falls on a Saturday, an "extra" $\frac{1}{5}$ off is given that day.

a. If on Friday, the 7th, Steve chooses two shirts and one sport coat totaling $260 at regular price, how much is the sale price of the merchandise?

b. What happens if Steve waits until the next day?

c. The owner asks for your opinion about changing the sale to "$\frac{9}{10}$ths" on the ninth and tenth days of each month. If you tried it a few times and found that the sales were the same as when you used the $\frac{7}{8}$ths promotion, what would you recommend to the boss?

d. How much will the store "save" in discounts using your choice from part **c**, on a day with $25,000 in sales based on the regular price?

✦ SUMMARY CHART ✦

SECTION I: Understanding Decimal Numbers

Topic	P/O, Page	Important Concepts	Illustrative Examples
Reading and Writing Decimals in Numerical and Word Form	3-1 72	In decimals, the value of each place, starting at the decimal point and moving from left to right, decreases by a factor of 10. The names of the places end in *ths;* they are tenths, hundredths, thousandths, ten-thousandths, hundred-thousandths, and millionths. 1. To write decimal numbers in words, write the decimal part as a whole number, then add the place value of the last digit on the right. 2. When writing mixed decimals, the decimal point should be read as "and." 3. If the decimal ends in a fraction, read them together, using the place value of the last digit of the decimal. 4. When a dollar sign ($) precedes a number, the whole number value represents dollars, the decimal value represents cents, and the decimal point is read as "and."	*Decimal Numbers* .0691 is six hundred ninety-one ten-thousandths Twenty-one ten-thousandths is .0021 *Mixed Decimals* 51.305 is fifty-one and three hundred five thousandths Eighteen and thirty-six thousandths is 18.036 *Decimals with Fractions* $.22\frac{1}{2}$ is twenty-two and one-half hundredths Seventeen and one-half hundredths is $.17\frac{1}{2}$ *Dollars and Cents* $946.73 is nine hundred forty-six dollars and seventy-three cents Six dollars and twelve cents is $6.12
Rounding Decimal Numbers to a Specified Place Value	3-2 75	1. Determine the place to which the decimal is to be rounded. 2a. If the digit to the right of the one being rounded is 5 or more, increase the digit in the place being rounded by 1. 2b. If the digit to the right of the one being rounded is 4 or less, do not change the digit in the place being rounded. 3. Delete all digits to the right of the one being rounded.	.645 rounded to hundredths is .65 42.5596 rounded to tenths is 42.6 .00291 rounded to thousandths is .003 $75.888 rounded to cents is $75.89

SECTION II: Decimal Numbers and the Fundamental Processes

Topic	P/O, Page	Important Concepts	Illustrative Examples
Adding and Subtracting Decimals	3-3 77	1. Line up all the place values, including the decimal points. 2. The decimal point in the answer will appear in the same position (column) as in the problem. 3. You may add zeros to the right of the decimal numbers that do not have enough places.	Addition: 2,821.049 12.500 + 143.008 2,976.557 Subtraction: 194.1207 − 45.3400 148.7807

SECTION II: (continued)

Topic	P/O, Page	Important Concepts	Illustrative Examples
Multiplying Decimals	3-4 78	1. Multiply the numbers as if they are whole numbers, disregarding the decimal points. 2. Total the number of decimal places in the multiplier and the multiplicand. 3. Insert the decimal point in the product, giving it the same number of decimal places as the total from Step 2. 4. If necessary, place zeros to the left of the product to provide the correct number of digits. *Note:* If the situation involves money, answers should be rounded to the nearest cent.	Multiply 224.5 by 4.53 224.5 1 decimal place × 4.53 2 decimal places 6 735 112 25 898 0 1,016.985 3 decimal places
Multiplication Shortcut: Powers of 10	3-4 79	When multiplying a decimal times a power of 10 (such as 10, 100, 1,000, 10,000, etc.): 1. Count the number of zeros in the multiplier and move the decimal point in the multiplicand the same number of places to the right. 2. If necessary, add zeros to the product to provide the required places.	.064 × 10 = .64 1 place .064 × 100 = 6.4 2 places .064 × 1,000 = 64 3 places .064 × 10,000 = 640 4 places .064 × 100,000 = 6,400 5 places
Dividing Decimals	3-5 80	*If the divisor is a whole number:* 1. Place the decimal point in the quotient directly above the decimal point in the dividend. 2. Divide the numbers. *If the divisor is a decimal number:* 1. Move the decimal point in the divisor to the right until it becomes a whole number. 2. Move the decimal point in the dividend the same number of places you moved it in the divisor. It may be necessary to add zeros to the right of the dividend if there are not enough places. 3. Place the decimal point in the quotient directly above the decimal point in the dividend. 4. Divide the numbers. *Note:* All answers involving money should be rounded to the nearest cent.	Divide: 9.5 ÷ 25 .38 25)9.50 7 5 2 00 2 00 0 Divide: 14.3 ÷ 2.2 2.2)14.3 6.5 22)143.0 132 11 0 11 0 0
Division Shortcut: Powers of 10	3-5 81	When dividing a decimal by a power of 10 (10, 100, 1,000, 10,000, etc.): 1. Count the number of zeros in the divisor, and move the decimal point in the dividend the same number of places to the left. 2. It may be necessary to add zeros to provide the required number of decimal places.	21.69 ÷ 10 = 2.169 1 place 21.69 ÷ 100 = .2169 2 places 21.69 ÷ 1,000 = .02169 3 places 21.69 ÷ 10,000 = .002169 4 places

SECTION III: Conversion of Decimals to Fractions and Fractions to Decimals

Topic	P/O, Page	Important Concepts	Illustrative Examples
Converting Decimals to Fractions	3-6 87	1. Write the decimal as a fraction by making the decimal number, without the decimal point, the numerator. 2. The denominator is "1" followed by as many zeros as there are decimal places in the original decimal number. 3. Reduce the fraction to lowest terms.	$.88 = \frac{88}{100} = \frac{22}{25}$ $5.57 = 5 + \frac{57}{100} = 5\frac{57}{100}$
Converting Fractions to Decimals	3-7 88	1. Divide the numerator by the denominator. 2. Add a decimal point and zeros, as necessary, to the numerator.	$\frac{4}{5} = 5\overline{)4.0}$ → .8 $\frac{22}{4} = 4\overline{)22.0}$ → 5.5

TRY-IT EXERCISE | SOLUTIONS

1. Sixty-four hundredths
2. Four hundred ninety-two thousandths
3. Ten thousand nineteen hundred-thousandths
4. Five hundred seventy-nine and four ten-thousandths
5. Twenty-six and seven hundred eight thousandths
6. Thirty-three and one-third hundredths
7. 272.00094
8. $11.003\frac{1}{4}$
9. 5.78892 = 5.789
10. .004522 = .0045
11. \$345.8791 = \$345.88
12. 76.03324 = 76.03
13. \$766.43 = \$766
14. 34,956.1229 = 34,956.1

15.
```
      35.7008
     311.2000
 + 84,557.5400
   84,904.4408
```

16.
```
 $ 65.79
 +154.33
 $220.12
```

17.
```
  186.700
 − 57.009
  129.691
```

18.
```
  $79.80
 − 34.61
  $45.19
```

19.
```
  876.66
 ×  .045
 4 38330
35 0664
39.44970
```

20.
```
   4,955.8
  ×    2.9
   4 460 22
   9 911 6
  14,371.82
```

21.
```
    $65.79
  ×    558
    526 32
   3 289 5
  32 895
$36,710.82
```

22. .00232 × 1,000 = 2.32

Move decimal three places to the right

23.
```
    44.8
16)716.8
   64
    76
    64
    12 8
    12 8
       0
```

24.
```
  3048
7)21336
  21
   33
   28
    56
    56
     0
```

25.
```
      $75.8
421)31911.8
    2947
     2441
     2105
      336 8
      336 8
          0
```

26. 2.03992 ÷ 1,000 = .00203992

Move decimal three places to the left

27. $\frac{875}{1000} = \frac{7}{8}$

28. $23\frac{76}{1000} = 23\frac{19}{250}$

29. $\frac{4}{10000} = \frac{1}{2500}$

30. $84\frac{75}{1000} = 84\frac{3}{4}$

31. $\frac{4}{5} = .8$
```
   .8
5)4.0
  4 0
    0
```

32. $84\frac{2}{3} = 84.67$
```
           .666
84 + 3)2.000
        1 8
          20
          18
           20
           18
            2
```

33. $\$6\frac{3}{4} = \$6.75$
```
         .75
6 + 4)3.00
       2 8
         20
         20
          0
```

34. $\frac{5}{2} = 2.5$
```
  2.5
2)5.0
  4
  1 0
  1 0
    0
```

35. $\frac{5}{8} = .63$
```
  .625
8)5.000
  4 8
    20
    16
     40
     40
      0
```

Name ____________________

Class ____________________

Answers

1. ____________________
2. ____________________
3. ____________________
4. ____________________
5. ____________________
6. ____________________
7. ____________________
8. ____________________
9. ____________________
10. ____________________
11. ____________________
12. ____________________
13. ____________________
14. ____________________
15. ____________________
16. ____________________
17. ____________________
18. ____________________
19. ____________________
20. ____________________
21. ____________________
22. ____________________
23. ____________________
24. ____________________
25. ____________________

CHAPTER 3 | ASSESSMENT TEST

Write the following decimal numbers in word form:

1. .61 **2.** 34.581 **3.** $119.85 **4.** $.09\frac{3}{7}$ **5.** .0495

Write the following decimal numbers in numerical form:

6. Nine hundred sixty-seven ten-thousandths

7. Five and fourteen thousandths

8. Eight hundred forty-three and two tenths

9. Sixteen dollars and fifty-seven cents

Round the following numbers to the indicated place:

10. .44857 to hundredths

11. 995.06966 to thousandths

12. $127.94 to dollars

13. 4.6935 to tenths

Perform the indicated operation for the following:

14. 6.03 + 45.168

15. $1.58 + $15.63 + $19.81 + $.17

16. .0031 + 69.271 + 193.55 + 211

17. 23.0556 − 15.35

18. $95.67 − $2.84

19. .802 − .066

20. $\begin{array}{r} 14.74 \\ \times\ 15 \\ \hline \end{array}$

21. $\begin{array}{r} .008 \\ \times\ .024 \\ \hline \end{array}$

22. .9912 × 100,000

23. .503 ÷ 1.2575

24. 79.3 ÷ 10,000

25. $150.48 ÷ 7.5

Name ______________________

Class ______________________

Convert the following decimals to fractions and reduce to lowest terms:

26. 12.035

27. .0441

Convert the following fractions to decimals. Round the quotients to hundredths.

28. $\frac{8}{29}$

29. $3\frac{1}{9}$

30. $\frac{95}{42}$

31. John Leahy went shopping for a stereo. He purchased an AM-FM tuner for $335.79, a control amplifier for $435.67, and a CD player for $287.99. He also bought 2 CDs for $11.88 each and 3 CDs for $14.88 each. What was the total of his purchase?

32. Mike's Bikes has a 22-inch off-road racer on sale this month for $239.95. If the original price of the bike was $315.10, how much would a customer save buying it on sale?

33. Stan and Myra Jordan both work for the Caliper Company. Stan earns $17.75 per hour as a technician and Myra earns $19.50 per hour as a research analyst. Last week Stan worked 43.22 hours and Myra worked 37.6 hours. What was their combined total earnings for the week?

34. A ream of paper contains 500 sheets and costs $7.50. What is the cost per sheet?

35. Use the accompanying Sports Authority advertisement for Wilson tennis balls to answer the following:

a. How much is saved if a customer buys the tennis balls on sale?

b. What is the sale price per can of balls?

c. To the nearest cent, how much is the savings per ball?

d. Which offer brings The Sports Authority more revenue, selling 400 packages of tennis balls in a week at the sale price, or selling 350 packages per week at the regular price?

Answers

26. ______________________

27. ______________________

28. ______________________

29. ______________________

30. ______________________

31. ______________________

32. ______________________

33. ______________________

34. ______________________

35. a. ______________________

b. ______________________

c. ______________________

d. ______________________

Name ______________

Class ______________

Answers

36. a. ______________

b. ______________

37. ______________

38. a. ______________

b. ______________

c. ______________

39. a. ______________

b. ______________

36. Great Impressions, a printing company, charges $.066 per page for color brochures.

a. What is the cost of 10,000 copies of a four-page brochure?

b. If Payless Printers will do the job for $.061, how much can be saved by using them to print the brochure?

37. Lynn Henn owes the Mountain City Bank $34,880.41 for her home mortgage. If she makes monthly payments of $546.11 for two years, what is the balance remaining on the loan?

38. The Enchanted Island Theme Park took in $663,750 in June on ticket sales.

a. If 35,400 people attended the park, what was the average price per ticket?

b. If, on the average, each person spent $4.70 on food, how much did the park make on food?

c. What was the total revenue for the tickets and the food?

39. As the food manager for a local charity, you are planning a fund-raising pasta party. Spaghetti sells for $1.79 per 16-ounce box.

a. If the average adult serving is $5\frac{3}{4}$ ounces, and the average child eats $3\frac{1}{2}$ ounces, how many boxes will you have to purchase to serve 36 adults and 46 children?

b. What is the total cost of the spaghetti?

Name ______________

Class ______________

40. John Young wanted to make some money at a flea market. He purchased 55 small orchids from a nursery for a total of $233.75, three bags of potting soil for $2.75 each, and 55 ceramic pots at $4.60 each. After planting the orchids in the pots, John sold each plant for $15.50 at the next flea market.

a. What was his total cost per potted plant?

b. How much profit did John make on this venture?

BUSINESS DECISION

Qualifying for a Mortgage

41. You are a loan officer at the Front Range Savings and Loan. Mr. and Mrs. Winston are in your office to apply for a mortgage loan on a house they want to buy. The house has a market value of $180,000. Your bank requires $\frac{1}{5}$ of the market value as a down payment.

a. What is the amount of the down payment?

b. What is the amount of the mortgage for which the Winstons are applying?

c. The current annual interest rate for a 30-year mortgage is 9 percent. At that rate, the monthly payments for principal and interest on the loan will be $8.05 for every $1,000 financed. What is the amount of the principal and interest portion of the Winston's monthly payment?

d. What is the total amount of interest that will be paid over the life of the loan?

e. Your bank also requires that the monthly mortgage payments include property tax and homeowner's insurance payments. If the property tax is $1,710.00 per year and the property insurance is $1,458.00 per year, what is the total monthly payment for PITI (principal, interest, taxes, and insurance)?

f. To qualify for the loan, bank rules state that mortgage payments cannot exceed $\frac{1}{4}$ of the combined monthly income of the family. If the Winstons earn $5,350 per month, will they qualify for this loan?

g. What monthly income would be required to qualify for this size mortgage payment?

Answers

40. a. ______________

b. ______________

41. a. ______________

b. ______________

c. ______________

d. ______________

e. ______________

f. ______________

g. ______________

All the Math That's Fit to Learn

The Business Math Times

Volume III | **Decimals** | One Dollar

Inside Intel

Intel is a $33.7-billion technical giant of the computer and Internet age. Since 1971, the company has developed and manufactured microprocessors primarily for desktop and laptop computers.

A *microprocessor* is an integrated circuit built on a tiny piece of silicon. It contains thousands, or even millions, of transistors, which are interconnected via superfine traces of aluminum. The transistors work together to store and manipulate data so that the microprocessor can perform a wide variety of useful functions dictated by software.

One of the most common tasks microprocessors perform is to serve as the basis for personal computers, but they deliver "intelligence" to countless other devices. For example, they may give your telephone speed-dial and redial options, automatically turn down your house's thermostat at night, and make your car safer and more energy efficient.

Intel spends more than $4 billion per year on research and development of faster, smaller, and better products related to computing. Their products range from PC and server processors to optical and wireless networks for the automotive and biomedical industries.

Where it's @ www.intel.com

"Quote . . . Unquote"

The only place where success comes before work is in the dictionary.
—*Vidal Sassoon,* entrepreneur

There is only one boss. The customer. And he can fire everybody in the company from the chairman on down, simply by spending his money somewhere else.
—*Sam Walton,* founder, Wal-Mart

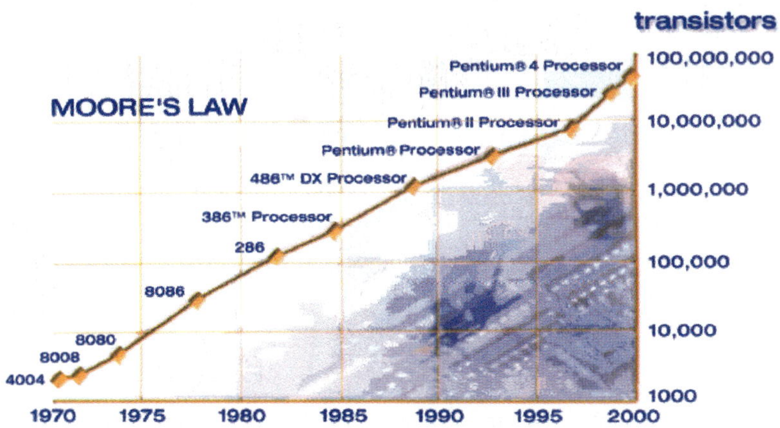

Moore's Law

Gordon E. Moore, co-founder and chairman emeritus of Intel Corporation, in 1965 predicted that the number of transistors per integrated computer circuit—and thus performance—would double every eighteen months through 1975. He made his observation just four years after the first integrated circuit was discovered. The media called his observation "Moore's Law," and the name has stuck ever since.

Through technology, Moore's Law has maintained far past 1975, and still holds true today. More transistors mean more calculations, or "speed," per second. Intel's mission is to continue to break down barriers to Moore's Law: Consider that Intel's first microprocessor, the 4004, ran at 108 kilohertz (108,000 hertz) compared to the Pentium 4 with speeds of more than 1.5 gigahertz (1.5 billion hertz).

If automobile speed had increased similarly over the same period, you could now drive from San Francisco to New York in about one second!

Nano is Next

In 1999, scientists devised a new way to make computer chips the size of molecules. The technology, known as molecular electronics or nanotechnology, is important because today's silicon chips are expected to hit their capacity within 15 years.

Nano, from the Greek word for *dwarf,* means a billionth. A nanometer is one billionth of a meter, or about three times the size of a single atom. A million nano-sized objects could be packed in the period at the end of this sentence.

Brainteaser

GET THE POINT!

What mathematical symbol can you place between the number 1 and the number 2, to yield a new number, larger than 1, but less than 2?

ANSWER TO LAST ISSUE'S BRAINTEASER

The next odd day will be 1-1-3111
The last even day before 2-2-2000 was 8-28-888!

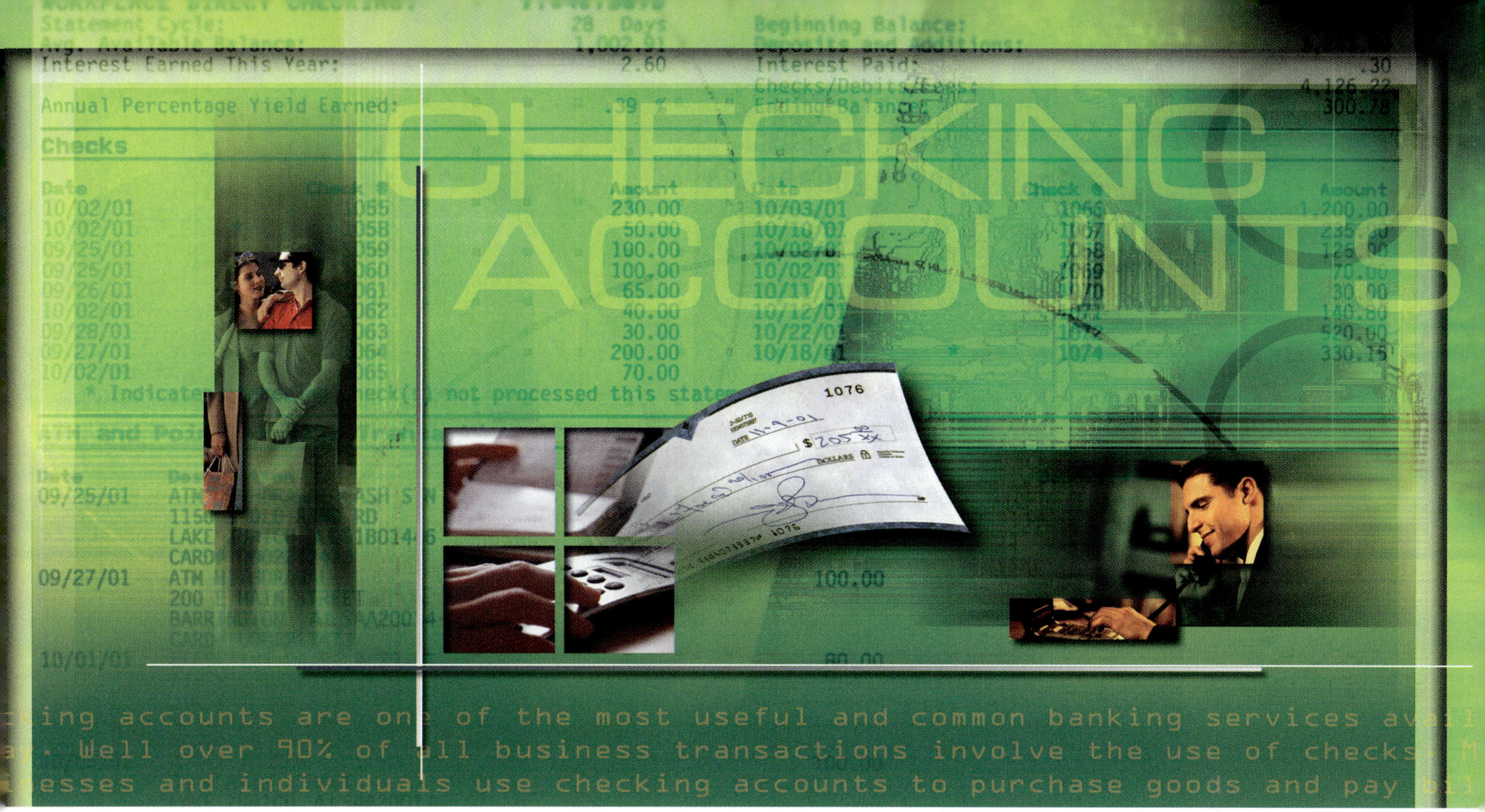

CHAPTER 4

Checking Accounts

PERFORMANCE OBJECTIVES

Section I Understanding and Using Checking Accounts

4-1 Opening a checking account and understanding how the various forms are used. (p. 100)
4-2 Writing checks in proper form. (p. 103)
4-3 Endorsing checks by using blank, restrictive, and full endorsements. (p. 104)
4-4 Preparing deposit slips in proper form. (p. 106)
4-5 Using check stubs or checkbook registers to record account transactions. (p. 107)

Section II Bank Statement Reconciliation

4-6 Understanding the bank statement. (p. 115)
4-7 Preparing a bank statement reconciliation. (p. 116)

SECTION I UNDERSTANDING AND USING CHECKING ACCOUNTS

Checking accounts are one of the most useful and common banking services available today. Well over 90 percent of all business transactions involve the use of checks. Most businesses and individuals use checking accounts to purchase goods and pay bills, because checks are convenient to use, are safer than cash, and provide an accurate record of the transactions.

Checking accounts are offered by banks, savings and loan institutions, and credit unions. For the purpose of this chapter, the word *bank* will be used to represent any of these institutions. Recently, decreased government regulation has increased the competition among banking institutions, and as a consequence, a variety of new services and options have been offered to the banking customer. Some checking accounts even pay interest on the balances maintained in the account.

Although checking account options, charges, and restrictions are too numerous and varied to list here, before opening a checking account, a business or individual should shop for those that best fit their financial needs. Some important things to consider are monthly service charges, check printing charges, minimum balance requirements, interest paid on the account, availability of automated teller machines (ATMs) and electronic funds transfer (EFT), overdraft privileges, and for businesses, services such as note collection and payroll assistance. Bank customers may also be offered free traveler's checks, free safe-deposit boxes, and even credit cards and loans at preferred rates.

4-1 Opening a Checking Account and Understanding How the Various Forms Are Used

After you have chosen a bank, the account is usually opened by a new accounts officer or clerk. The customer is assigned an account number and is given a **signature card** that is filled out and signed by all persons authorized to sign checks on the account. The bank uses the signature card to verify the authenticity of the signature on your checks.

After the initial paperwork has been completed, the customer will place an amount of money into the account as an opening balance. Funds added to a checking account are known as **deposits.** The bank will then give the **depositor** a checkbook containing checks and deposit slips.

signature card
A card signed by all persons authorized to sign checks on the account. Used by the bank to verify the authenticity of the signatures on checks.

deposits
Funds added to a checking account.

depositor
A person who deposits money in a checking account.

Everybody's Business
Real-World Connection
According to the American Bankers Association, there are more than 273,000 ATMs in the United States, performing more than 13.2 billion transactions annually. That's more than 1.5 million every hour. The average withdrawal amount is $60.

Automatic teller machines are one of the many services that banks provide.

Checks, or **drafts,** are negotiable instruments ordering the bank to pay money from the checking account to the name written on the check. The person or business named on the check to receive the money is known as the **payee.** The person or business issuing the check is known as the **payor.**

Checks are available in many sizes, colors, and designs; however, they all contain the same fundamental elements. Exhibit 4-1 shows a check with the major parts labeled. Look at the illustration carefully, and familiarize yourself with the various parts of the check.

Deposit slips, or deposit tickets, are printed forms with the depositor's name, address, account number, and space for the details of the deposit. Deposit slips are used to record money, both cash and checks, being *added* to the checking account. They are presented to the bank teller along with the items to be deposited. When a deposit is completed, the depositor receives a copy of the deposit slip as a receipt, or proof of the transaction. The deposit should also be recorded by the depositor on the current check stub, or in the check register. Exhibit 4-2 is an example of a deposit slip.

Either **check stubs** or a **check register** can be used to keep track of the checks written, the deposits added, and the current account balance. It is very important to keep these records accurate and up to date. This will prevent the embarrassing error of writing checks with insufficient funds in the account.

Check stubs, with checks attached by perforation, are usually a bound part of the checkbook. A sample check stub with a check is shown in Exhibit 4-3. Note that the check number is preprinted on both the check and the attached stub. Each stub is used to record the issuing of its corresponding check and any deposits made on that date.

Check registers are the alternative method for keeping track of checking account activity. They are a separate booklet of forms, rather than stubs attached to each check. A sample check register is shown in Exhibit 4-4. Note that space is provided for all the pertinent information required to keep an accurate and up-to-date running balance of the account.

check or draft
A written order to a bank by a depositor to pay the amount specified on the check from funds on deposit in a checking account.

payee
The person or business named on the check to receive the money.

payor
The person or business issuing the check.

deposit slip
Printed forms with the depositor's name, address, account number, and space for the details of the deposit. Used to record money, both cash and checks, being added to the checking account.

check stub
A bound part of the checkbook, attached by perforation to checks. Used to keep track of the checks written, deposits, and current account balance of a checking account.

check register
A separate booklet of blank forms used to keep track of all checking account activity. An alternative to the check stub.

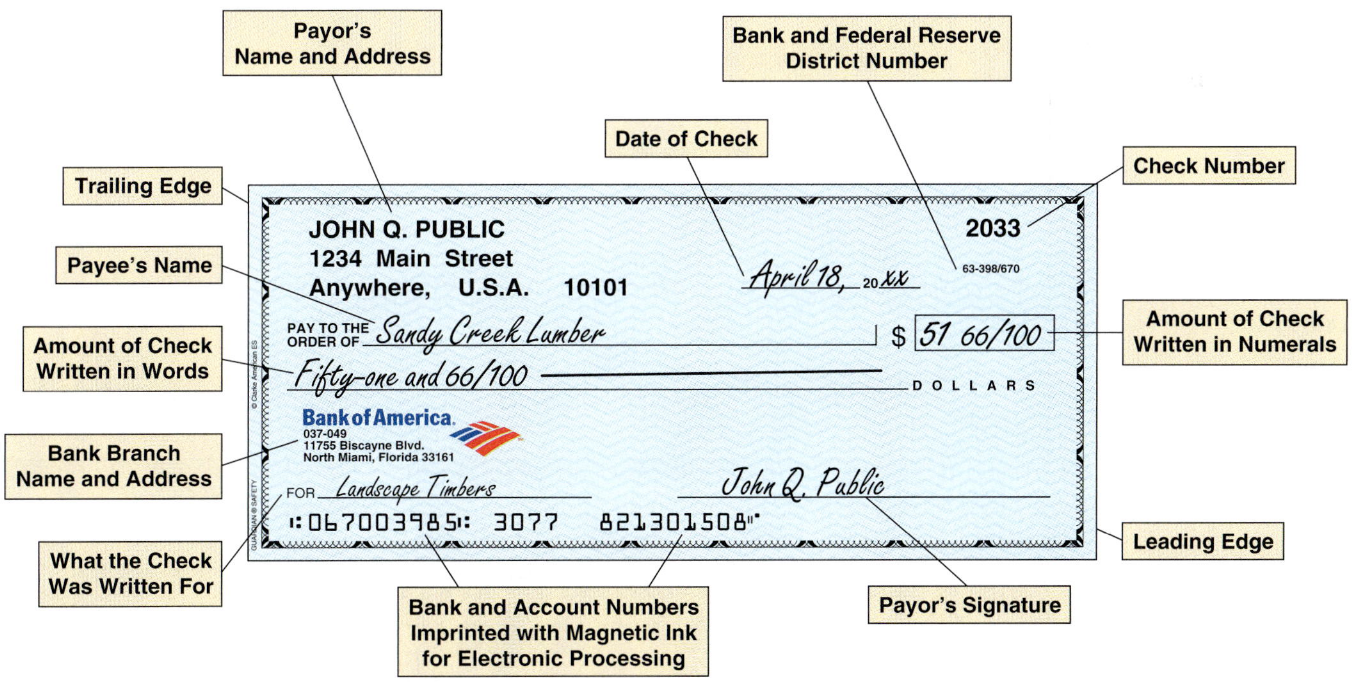

EXHIBIT 4-1
Check

EXHIBIT 4-2
Deposit Slip

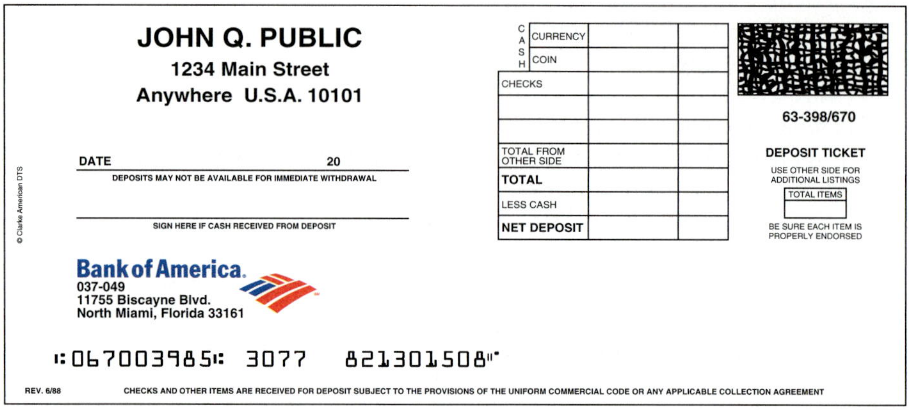
JOHN Q. PUBLIC
1234 Main Street
Anywhere U.S.A. 10101
DATE 20
DEPOSITS MAY NOT BE AVAILABLE FOR IMMEDIATE WITHDRAWAL
SIGN HERE IF CASH RECEIVED FROM DEPOSIT
Bank of America
037-049
11755 Biscayne Blvd.
North Miami, Florida 33161
CASH CURRENCY
COIN
CHECKS
TOTAL FROM OTHER SIDE
TOTAL
LESS CASH
NET DEPOSIT
63-398/670
DEPOSIT TICKET
USE OTHER SIDE FOR ADDITIONAL LISTINGS
TOTAL ITEMS
BE SURE EACH ITEM IS PROPERLY ENDORSED
⑆067003985⑆ 3077 821301508⑈
REV. 6/88
CHECKS AND OTHER ITEMS ARE RECEIVED FOR DEPOSIT SUBJECT TO THE PROVISIONS OF THE UNIFORM COMMERCIAL CODE OR ANY APPLICABLE COLLECTION AGREEMENT

EXHIBIT 4-3
Check Stub with Check

IF TAX DEDUCTIBLE CHECK HERE $
3078
20
TO
FOR
	DOLLARS	CENTS
BAL. FWD.		
DEPOSIT		
DEPOSIT		
TOTAL		
THIS ITEM		
SUB-TOTAL		
OTHER DEDUCT. (IF ANY)		
BAL. FWD.		

JOHN Q. PUBLIC
1234 Main Street
Anywhere, U.S.A. 10101
3078
63-398/670
20
PAY TO THE ORDER OF $
DOLLARS
Bank of America
037-049
11755 Biscayne Blvd.
North Miami, Florida 33161
FOR
⑆067003985⑆ 3077 821301508⑈

EXHIBIT 4-4
Check Register

PLEASE BE SURE TO **DEDUCT** ANY BANK CHARGES THAT APPLY TO YOUR ACCOUNT.

CHECK NUMBER	DATE	DESCRIPTION OF TRANSACTION	AMOUNT OF PAYMENT OR WITHDRAWAL (–)		✓	AMOUNT OF DEPOSIT OR INTEREST (+)		BALANCE FORWARD		
		To								
		For						Bal.		
		To								
		For						Bal.		
		To								
		For						Bal.		
		To								
		For						Bal.		
		To								
		For						Bal.		
		To								
		For						Bal.		

4-2 Writing Checks in Proper Form

When a checking account is opened, you will choose the color and style of your checks. The bank will then order custom-printed checks with your name, address, and account number identifications. The bank will provide you with some blank checks and deposit slips to use until your printed ones arrive.

Checks should be typed or neatly written in ink. There are six parts to be filled in when writing a check.

> **Everybody's Business**
>
> **Real-World Connection**
>
> When there is a discrepancy between the numerical and written word amount of a check, banks consider the *written word amount* as official.
>
> **Learning Tip**
>
> Don't forget, when writing the amount of a check in word form, that the word *and* represents the decimal point.

STEPS FOR WRITING CHECKS IN PROPER FORM:

Step 1. Enter the *date* of the check in the space provided.

Step 2. Enter the name of the person or business to whom the check is written, the payee, in the space labeled "*pay to the order of.*"

Step 3. Enter the amount of the check, in numerical form, in the space with the dollar sign, $. The dollar amount should be written close to the $ sign so additional digits cannot be added. The cents may be written as xx/100 or .xx.

Step 4. Enter the amount of the check, this time written in word form, on the next line down, labeled *dollars.* As before, the cents should be written as xx/100 or .xx. A horizontal, wavy line is then written to the end of the line.

Step 5. The space labeled *memo* is used to write the purpose of the check. Although it is optional, it's a good idea to use this space so you will not forget why the check was written.

Step 6. The space in the lower right-hand corner of the check is for the signature. It should be written exactly as it is on the signature card.

EXAMPLE

Write a check for Bill Pearson to the Fifth Avenue Flower Shop, for a ceramic planter, in the amount of $83.73, on June 7, 20xx.

SOLUTION STRATEGY

Here is the check for Bill Pearson, written in proper form. Note that the amount, $83.73, is written $83 73/100, and the name is signed as it is printed on the check.

TRY-IT | EXERCISE

1. Use the following blank to write a check for Carolyn Richards to Snappy Photo Service for developing four rolls of film in the amount of $41.88 on April 27.

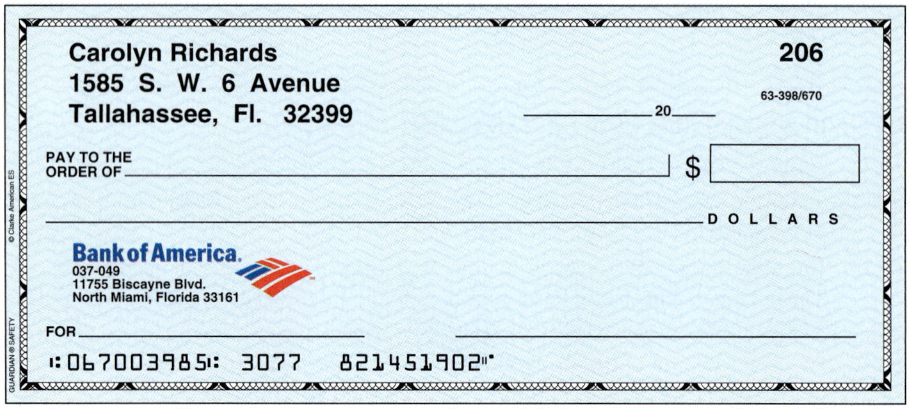
Carolyn Richards
1585 S. W. 6 Avenue
Tallahassee, Fl. 32399

206
63-398/670
20____

PAY TO THE ORDER OF ____________ $

____________ DOLLARS

Bank of America.
037-049
11755 Biscayne Blvd.
North Miami, Florida 33161

FOR ____________

⑆067003985⑆ 3077 8214519O2⑈

Check your answer with the solution on page 126.

4-3 Endorsing Checks by Using Blank, Restrictive, and Full Endorsements

endorsement
The signature and instructions on the back of a check instructing the bank on what to do with that check.

blank endorsement
An endorsement used when the payee wants to cash a check.

restrictive endorsement
An endorsement used when the payee wants to deposit a check into his or her account.

full endorsement
An endorsement used when the payee wants to transfer a check to another party.

When you receive a check, you may either cash it, deposit it into your account, or transfer it to another party. The **endorsement** on the back of the check instructs the bank what to do. Federal regulations require that specific areas of the reverse side of checks be designated for the payee and bank endorsements. Your endorsement should be written within the $1\frac{1}{2}$-inch space at the trailing edge of the check, as shown in Exhibit 4-5. The space is usually labeled "ENDORSE HERE."

There are three types of endorsements with which you should become familiar: blank endorsements, restrictive endorsements, and full endorsements, which are shown in Exhibits 4-6, 4-7, and 4-8.

A **blank endorsement** is used when you want to cash the check. You, as the payee, simply sign your name exactly as it appears on the front of the check. Once you have endorsed a check in this manner, anyone who has possession of the check can cash it. For this reason, you should use blank endorsements cautiously.

A **restrictive endorsement** is used when you want to deposit the check into your account. In this case, you endorse the check "for deposit only," sign your name as it appears on the front, and write your account number.

A **full endorsement** is used when you want to transfer the check to another party. In this case, you endorse the check "pay to the order of," write the name of the person or business to whom the check is being transferred, and sign your name and account number.

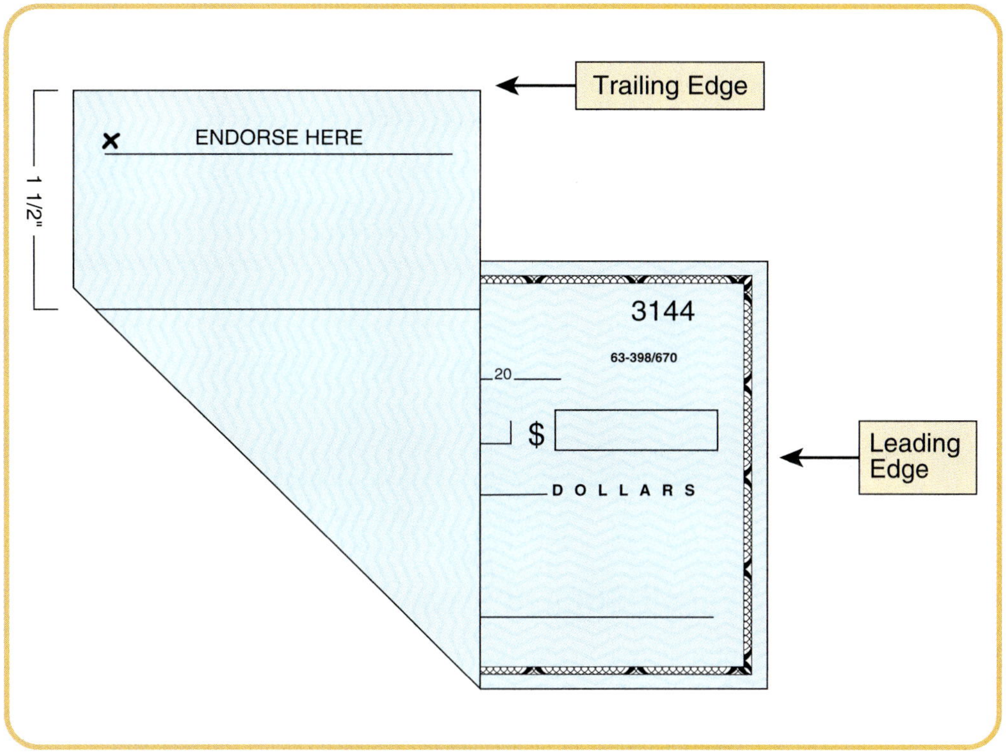

EXHIBIT 4-5
Endorsement Space

EXHIBIT 4-6
Blank Endorsement

EXHIBIT 4-7
Restrictive Endorsement

EXHIBIT 4-8
Full Endorsement

EXAMPLES

You have just received a check. Your account number is #2922-22-33-4. Write the following endorsements and identify what type they are:

a. Allowing you to cash the check.
b. Allowing you to deposit the check into your checking account.
c. Allowing the check to be transferred to your partner Sam Johnson.

SOLUTION STRATEGY

a. Blank Endorsement
Your Signature
2922-22-33-4

b. Restrictive Endorsement
for deposit only
Your Signature
2922-22-33-4

c. Full Endorsement
pay to the order of
Sam Johnson
Your Signature
2922-22-33-4

TRY-IT | EXERCISES

You have just received a check. Your account number is #696-339-1028. Write the following endorsements in the space provided and identify what type they are:

2. Allowing the check to be transferred to your friend Roz Reitman.
3. Allowing you to cash the check.
4. Allowing you to deposit the check in your checking account.

2. ______________ **3.** ______________ **4.** ______________

Check your answers with the solutions on page 126.

4-4 Preparing Deposit Slips in Proper Form

Deposit slips are filled out and presented to the bank along with the funds being deposited. They are dated and list the currency, coins, individual checks, and the total amount of the deposit. Note on the sample deposit slip, Exhibit 4-9, that John Q. Public took $100.00 in cash out of the deposit, which required him to sign the deposit slip.

EXHIBIT 4-9
Completed Deposit Slip

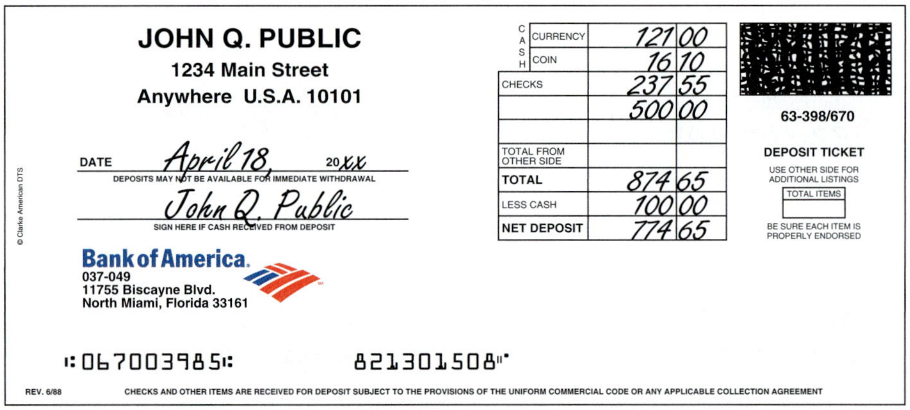
JOHN Q. PUBLIC
1234 Main Street
Anywhere U.S.A. 10101

DATE April 18, 20xx
DEPOSITS MAY NOT BE AVAILABLE FOR IMMEDIATE WITHDRAWAL
John Q. Public
SIGN HERE IF CASH RECEIVED FROM DEPOSIT

CASH: CURRENCY	121	00
CASH: COIN	16	10
CHECKS	237	55
	500	00
TOTAL FROM OTHER SIDE		
TOTAL	874	65
LESS CASH	100	00
NET DEPOSIT	774	65

63-398/670
DEPOSIT TICKET
USE OTHER SIDE FOR ADDITIONAL LISTINGS
TOTAL ITEMS
BE SURE EACH ITEM IS PROPERLY ENDORSED

© Clarke American DTS

Bank of America.
037-049
11755 Biscayne Blvd.
North Miami, Florida 33161

⑆067003985⑆ 821301508⑈

REV. 6/88
CHECKS AND OTHER ITEMS ARE RECEIVED FOR DEPOSIT SUBJECT TO THE PROVISIONS OF THE UNIFORM COMMERCIAL CODE OR ANY APPLICABLE COLLECTION AGREEMENT

EXAMPLE

Prepare a deposit slip for Rob Donaldson, based on the following information:

a. Date: June 4, 20xx
b. $127 in currency
c. $3.47 in coins
d. A check for $358.89 and a check for $121.68

SOLUTION STRATEGY

ROB DONALDSON
4500 Main Highway
Sacramento, Ca. 95818

DATE *June 4* 20*xx*
DEPOSITS MAY NOT BE AVAILABLE FOR IMMEDIATE WITHDRAWAL

SIGN HERE IF CASH RECEIVED FROM DEPOSIT

Bank of America
037-049
11755 Biscayne Blvd.
North Miami, Florida 33161

⑆067003985⑆ 602183386⑈

CASH CURRENCY	127	00
CASH COIN	3	47
CHECKS	358	89
	121	68
TOTAL FROM OTHER SIDE		
TOTAL	611	04
LESS CASH		
NET DEPOSIT	611	04

63-398/670
DEPOSIT TICKET
USE OTHER SIDE FOR ADDITIONAL LISTINGS
TOTAL ITEMS
BE SURE EACH ITEM IS PROPERLY ENDORSED

REV. 6/88 CHECKS AND OTHER ITEMS ARE RECEIVED FOR DEPOSIT SUBJECT TO THE PROVISIONS OF THE UNIFORM COMMERCIAL CODE OR ANY APPLICABLE COLLECTION AGREEMENT

TRY-IT EXERCISE

5. Fill out the deposit slip for Dawson Electronics, based on the following information:

a. Date: November 11, 20xx
b. $3,549 in currency
c. 67 quarters, 22 dimes, and 14 nickels
d. A check for $411.92, and a check for $2,119.56

DAWSON ELECTRONICS
12155 Miller Road
New Orleans, La. 70144

DATE 20
DEPOSITS MAY NOT BE AVAILABLE FOR IMMEDIATE WITHDRAWAL

SIGN HERE IF CASH RECEIVED FROM DEPOSIT

Bank of America
037-049
11755 Biscayne Blvd.
North Miami, Florida 33161

⑆067003985⑆ 536101902⑈

CASH CURRENCY		
CASH COIN		
CHECKS		
TOTAL FROM OTHER SIDE		
TOTAL		
LESS CASH		
NET DEPOSIT		

63-398/670
DEPOSIT TICKET
USE OTHER SIDE FOR ADDITIONAL LISTINGS
TOTAL ITEMS
BE SURE EACH ITEM IS PROPERLY ENDORSED

REV. 6/88 CHECKS AND OTHER ITEMS ARE RECEIVED FOR DEPOSIT SUBJECT TO THE PROVISIONS OF THE UNIFORM COMMERCIAL CODE OR ANY APPLICABLE COLLECTION AGREEMENT

Check your answer with the solution on page 126.

Everybody's Business
Real-World Connection

It is important to keep accurate checkbook records and reconcile the account balance each month. "It's your money." Banks can and do make mistakes!

Inaccurate record keeping on the part of the account holder can cause embarrassment due to incorrect balances, as well as service charges for "bounced" checks.

4-5 Using Check Stubs or Checkbook Registers to Record Account Transactions

In part 4-1 we learned that some people use check stubs to keep records and some use check registers. Exhibit 4-10 shows a check and its corresponding stub properly filled out. Note that the check number is printed on the stub. The stub is used to record the amount of the check, the date, the payee, and the purpose of the check. In addition, the stub also records

✦ EXHIBIT 4-10 ✦
Check with Filled-Out Stub

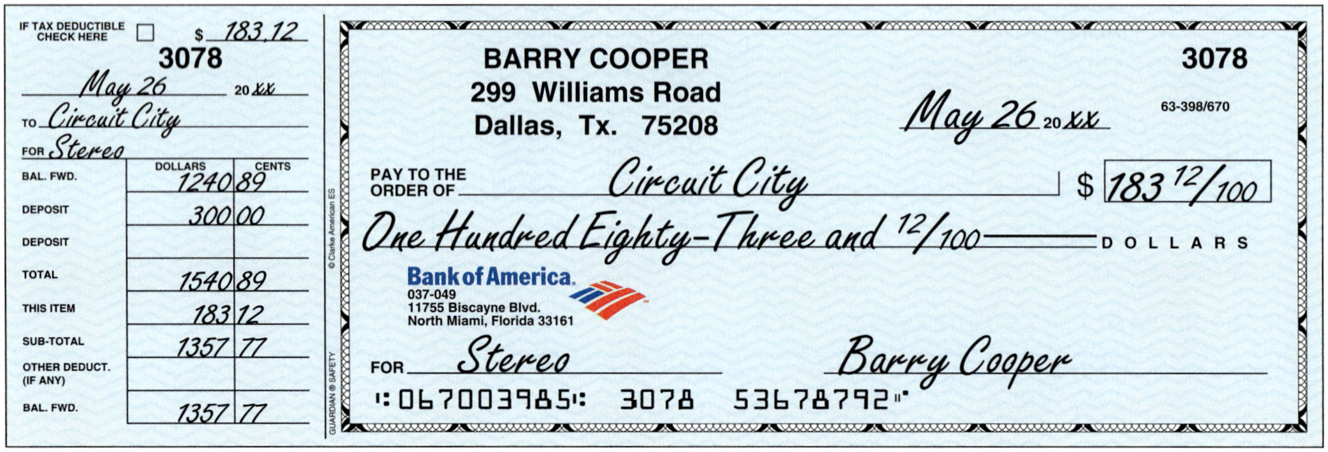

IF TAX DEDUCTIBLE CHECK HERE ☐ $ 183.12
3078
May 26 20 xx
TO Circuit City
FOR Stereo

	DOLLARS	CENTS
BAL. FWD.	1240	89
DEPOSIT	300	00
DEPOSIT		
TOTAL	1540	89
THIS ITEM	183	12
SUB-TOTAL	1357	77
OTHER DEDUCT. (IF ANY)		
BAL. FWD.	1357	77

BARRY COOPER
299 Williams Road
Dallas, Tx. 75208
3078
63-398/670
May 26 20 xx
PAY TO THE ORDER OF Circuit City $ 183 12/100
One Hundred Eighty-Three and 12/100 DOLLARS
Bank of America
037-049
11755 Biscayne Blvd.
North Miami, Florida 33161
FOR Stereo Barry Cooper
⑆067003985⑆ 3078 53678792⑈

✦ EXHIBIT 4-11 ✦
Filled-Out Check Register

PLEASE BE SURE TO **DEDUCT** ANY BANK CHARGES THAT APPLY TO YOUR ACCOUNT.

CHECK NUMBER	DATE	DESCRIPTION OF TRANSACTION	AMOUNT OF PAYMENT OR WITHDRAWAL (−)	✓	AMOUNT OF DEPOSIT OR INTEREST (+)	BALANCE FORWARD 560 00
450	1/6	To Mastercard For	34 60			Bal. 525 40
451	1/8	To State Farm Insurance For	166 25			Bal. 359 15
	1/12	To Deposit For			340 00	Bal. 699 15
452	1/13	To Walgreens For	15 50			Bal. 683 65
	1/15	To Deposit For			88 62	Bal. 772 27
	1/17	To ATM-Withdrawal For	100 00			Bal. 672 27
453	1/21	To Time-Life Books For	24 15			Bal. 648 12

the balance forwarded from the last stub, deposits made since the previous check, and the new balance of the account, after deducting the current check and any other charges.

Check registers record the same information as the stub but in a different format. Exhibit 4-11 shows a check register properly filled out. The starting balance is located in the upper right-hand corner. In keeping a check register, it is your option to write it single spaced or double spaced. Remember, in reality you would use *either* the check stub or the checkbook register.

EXAMPLE

From the following information, complete the two check stubs and the check register in proper form:

a. Starting balance $1,454.21.

b. January 14, 20xx, check #056 issued to Paints & Pails Hardware for a ladder in the amount of $69.97.

c. January 19, 20xx, deposit of $345.00.

d. February 1, 20xx, check #057 issued to Northern Power & Light for electricity bill, in the amount of $171.55.

SOLUTION STRATEGY

Below are the properly completed stubs and register. Note that the checks were subtracted from the balance and the deposits were added to the balance.

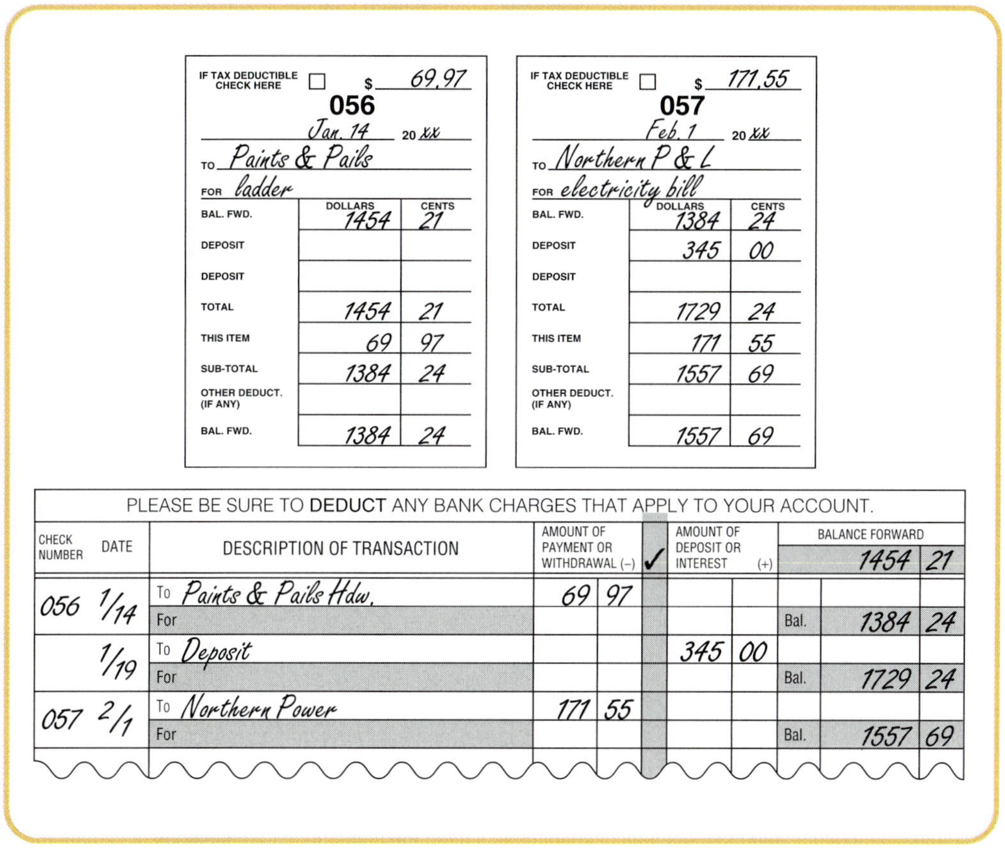

IF TAX DEDUCTIBLE CHECK HERE ☐ $ 69.97
056
Jan. 14 20 xx
TO Paints & Pails
FOR ladder

	DOLLARS	CENTS
BAL. FWD.	1454	21
DEPOSIT		
DEPOSIT		
TOTAL	1454	21
THIS ITEM	69	97
SUB-TOTAL	1384	24
OTHER DEDUCT. (IF ANY)		
BAL. FWD.	1384	24

IF TAX DEDUCTIBLE CHECK HERE ☐ $ 171.55
057
Feb. 1 20 xx
TO Northern P & L
FOR electricity bill

	DOLLARS	CENTS
BAL. FWD.	1384	24
DEPOSIT	345	00
DEPOSIT		
TOTAL	1729	24
THIS ITEM	171	55
SUB-TOTAL	1557	69
OTHER DEDUCT. (IF ANY)		
BAL. FWD.	1557	69

PLEASE BE SURE TO **DEDUCT** ANY BANK CHARGES THAT APPLY TO YOUR ACCOUNT.

CHECK NUMBER	DATE	DESCRIPTION OF TRANSACTION	AMOUNT OF PAYMENT OR WITHDRAWAL (−)	✓	AMOUNT OF DEPOSIT OR INTEREST (+)	BALANCE FORWARD	1454.21
056	1/14	To Paints & Pails Hdw.	69.97				
		For				Bal.	1384.24
	1/19	To Deposit			345.00		
		For				Bal.	1729.24
057	2/1	To Northern Power	171.55				
		For				Bal.	1557.69

TRY-IT EXERCISE

6. From the following information, complete the two check stubs and the check register on page 110, in proper form:

a. Starting balance $887.45.

b. March 12, 20xx, check #137 issued to Nathan & David Hair Stylists for a permanent and manicure in the amount of $55.75.

c. March 16, 20xx, deposits of $125.40 and $221.35.

d. March 19, 20xx, check #138 issued to Complete Auto Service for car repairs in the amount of $459.88.

IF TAX DEDUCTIBLE CHECK HERE ☐ $______
137
______ 20___
TO ______
FOR ______

	DOLLARS	CENTS
BAL. FWD.		
DEPOSIT		
DEPOSIT		
TOTAL		
THIS ITEM		
SUB-TOTAL		
OTHER DEDUCT. (IF ANY)		
BAL. FWD.		

IF TAX DEDUCTIBLE CHECK HERE ☐ $______
138
______ 20___
TO ______
FOR ______

	DOLLARS	CENTS
BAL. FWD.		
DEPOSIT		
DEPOSIT		
TOTAL		
THIS ITEM		
SUB-TOTAL		
OTHER DEDUCT. (IF ANY)		
BAL. FWD.		

PLEASE BE SURE TO **DEDUCT** ANY BANK CHARGES THAT APPLY TO YOUR ACCOUNT.

CHECK NUMBER	DATE	DESCRIPTION OF TRANSACTION	AMOUNT OF PAYMENT OR WITHDRAWAL (−)	✓	AMOUNT OF DEPOSIT OR INTEREST (+)	BALANCE FORWARD
		To				
		For				Bal.
		To				
		For				Bal.
		To				
		For				Bal.
		To				
		For				Bal.
		To				
		For				Bal.
		To				
		For				Bal.

Check your answer with the solution on page 127.

REVIEW EXERCISES I CHAPTER 4—SECTION I

You are the owner of the Ultimate Care Car Wash. Using the blanks provided, write out the following checks, in proper form:

1. Check #2550, September 14, 20xx, in the amount of $345.54, to the Silky Soap Company, for 300 gallons of liquid soap.

ULTIMATE CARE CAR WASH
214 Collings Blvd.
Durham, N.C. 27704

2550
63-398/670

______ 20___

PAY TO THE ORDER OF ______ $ ______

______ DOLLARS

Bank of America
037-049
11755 Biscayne Blvd.
North Miami, Florida 33161

FOR ______ ______

⑆067003985⑆ 3077 821301508⑈

©Clarke American ES
GUARDIAN ® SAFETY

2. Check #2551, September 20, 20xx, in the amount of $68.95, to the Tidy Towel Service, for six dozen wash rags.

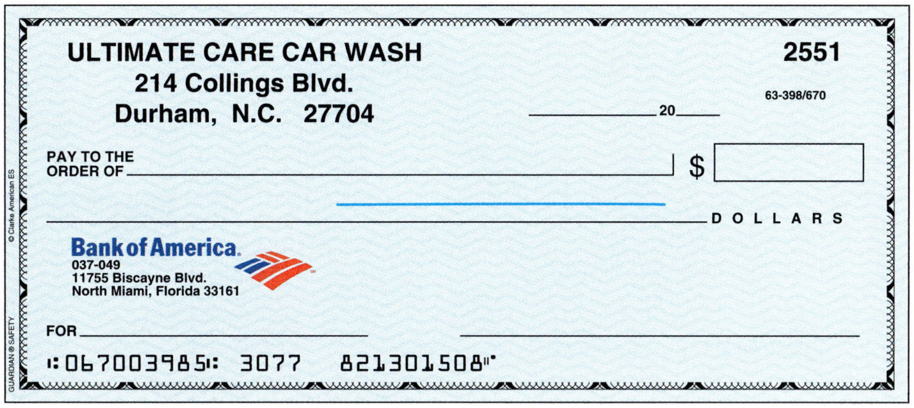
ULTIMATE CARE CAR WASH
214 Collings Blvd.
Durham, N.C. 27704
2551
63-398/670
20
PAY TO THE ORDER OF $
DOLLARS
Bank of America
037-049
11755 Biscayne Blvd.
North Miami, Florida 33161
FOR
⑆067003985⑆ 3077 821301508⑈

3. Check #2552, September 23, 20xx, in the amount of $644.30, to the Arch Creek Valley Water Dept., for August service.

ULTIMATE CARE CAR WASH
214 Collings Blvd.
Durham, N.C. 27704
2552
63-398/670
20
PAY TO THE ORDER OF $
DOLLARS
Bank of America
037-049
11755 Biscayne Blvd.
North Miami, Florida 33161
FOR
⑆067003985⑆ 3077 821301508⑈

You have just received a check. Your account number is #099-506-8. Write the following endorsements in the space provided below, and identify what type they are:

4. Allowing you to deposit the check into your account.
5. Allowing you to cash the check.
6. Allowing you to transfer the check to your friend David Sporn.

4. ______________ **5.** ______________ **6.** ______________

7. Properly fill out the deposit slip for The Williamson Corp., based on the following information:
   a. Date: July 9, 20xx.
   b. $1,680 in currency.
   c. $62.25 in coins.
   d. Checks in the amount of $2,455.94; $4,338.79; and $1,461.69.

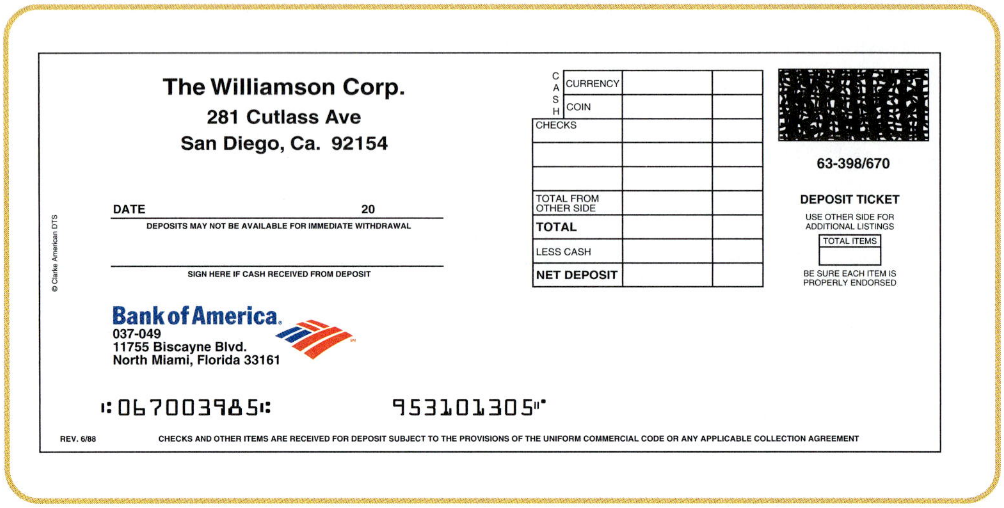
The Williamson Corp.
281 Cutlass Ave
San Diego, Ca. 92154

DATE 20
DEPOSITS MAY NOT BE AVAILABLE FOR IMMEDIATE WITHDRAWAL
SIGN HERE IF CASH RECEIVED FROM DEPOSIT

CASH	CURRENCY		
	COIN		
CHECKS			
TOTAL FROM OTHER SIDE			
TOTAL			
LESS CASH			
NET DEPOSIT			

63-398/670
DEPOSIT TICKET
USE OTHER SIDE FOR ADDITIONAL LISTINGS
TOTAL ITEMS
BE SURE EACH ITEM IS PROPERLY ENDORSED

© Clarke American DTS

Bank of America.
037-049
11755 Biscayne Blvd.
North Miami, Florida 33161

⑆067003985⑆ 953101305⑈

REV. 6/88 CHECKS AND OTHER ITEMS ARE RECEIVED FOR DEPOSIT SUBJECT TO THE PROVISIONS OF THE UNIFORM COMMERCIAL CODE OR ANY APPLICABLE COLLECTION AGREEMENT

8. Properly fill out the deposit slip for Sally Randall, based on the following information:
   a. Date: December 18, 20xx.
   b. A check for $651.03.
   c. $150 cash withdrawal.

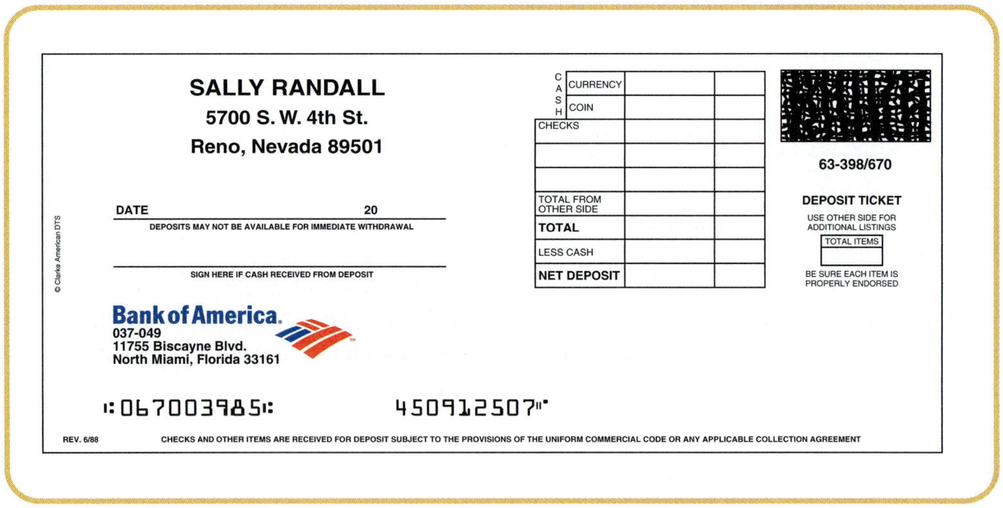
SALLY RANDALL
5700 S. W. 4th St.
Reno, Nevada 89501

DATE 20
DEPOSITS MAY NOT BE AVAILABLE FOR IMMEDIATE WITHDRAWAL
SIGN HERE IF CASH RECEIVED FROM DEPOSIT

CASH	CURRENCY		
	COIN		
CHECKS			
TOTAL FROM OTHER SIDE			
TOTAL			
LESS CASH			
NET DEPOSIT			

63-398/670
DEPOSIT TICKET
USE OTHER SIDE FOR ADDITIONAL LISTINGS
TOTAL ITEMS
BE SURE EACH ITEM IS PROPERLY ENDORSED

© Clarke American DTS

Bank of America.
037-049
11755 Biscayne Blvd.
North Miami, Florida 33161

⑆067003985⑆ 450912507⑈

REV. 6/88 CHECKS AND OTHER ITEMS ARE RECEIVED FOR DEPOSIT SUBJECT TO THE PROVISIONS OF THE UNIFORM COMMERCIAL CODE OR ANY APPLICABLE COLLECTION AGREEMENT

9. From the following information, complete the three check stubs, in proper form:
   a. Starting balance $265.73.
   b. February 12, 20xx, check #439, in the amount of $175.05, to The Biloxie Bank, for a car payment.
   c. February 15, deposit of $377.10.

d. February 18, check #440, in the amount of $149.88, to Fitness Equipment Co., for a set of dumbbells.

e. February 22, deposit of $570.00.

f. February 27, check #441, in the amount of $23.40, to Royalty Cleaners, for dry cleaning.

IF TAX DEDUCTIBLE CHECK HERE ☐ $______

______ 20____

TO ______

FOR

	DOLLARS	CENTS
BAL. FWD.		
DEPOSIT		
DEPOSIT		
TOTAL		
THIS ITEM		
SUB-TOTAL		
OTHER DEDUCT. (IF ANY)		
BAL. FWD.		

IF TAX DEDUCTIBLE CHECK HERE ☐ $______

440

______ 20____

TO ______

FOR

	DOLLARS	CENTS
BAL. FWD.		
DEPOSIT		
DEPOSIT		
TOTAL		
THIS ITEM		
SUB-TOTAL		
OTHER DEDUCT. (IF ANY)		
BAL. FWD.		

IF TAX DEDUCTIBLE CHECK HERE ☐ $______

441

______ 20____

TO ______

FOR

	DOLLARS	CENTS
BAL. FWD.		
DEPOSIT		
DEPOSIT		
TOTAL		
THIS ITEM		
SUB-TOTAL		
OTHER DEDUCT. (IF ANY)		
BAL. FWD.		

10. From the following information, complete the checkbook register below:

a. Starting balance $479.20.

b. April 7, 20xx, deposit of $766.90.

c. April 14, 20xx, check #1207, in the amount of $45.65, to Mario's Supermarket, for groceries.

d. April 16, ATM withdrawal, $125.00.

e. April 17, check #1208, in the amount of $870.00, to Howard Properties, Inc., for rent.

f. April 21, 20xx, deposit of $1,350.00.

g. April 27, check #1209, in the amount of $864.40, to Elegant Decor, for a dining room set.

PLEASE BE SURE TO **DEDUCT** ANY BANK CHARGES THAT APPLY TO YOUR ACCOUNT.

CHECK NUMBER	DATE	DESCRIPTION OF TRANSACTION	AMOUNT OF PAYMENT OR WITHDRAWAL (–)	AMOUNT OF DEPOSIT OR INTEREST (+)	BALANCE FORWARD
		To			
		For			Bal.
		To			
		For			Bal.
		To			
		For			Bal.
		To			
		For			Bal.
		To			
		For			Bal.
		To			
		For			Bal.

BUSINESS DECISION

Teller Training

11. You are the training director for tellers at a large local bank. As part of a new training program that you are developing, you have decided to give teller trainees a "sample" deposit slip, check, and check register, with common errors on them. The trainees must find and correct the errors. Your task is to create the three documents.

a. On a separate sheet of paper, list some "typical errors" that bank customers might make on a deposit slip, a check, and a check register.

b. Use the blank deposit slip, check, and check register below to create "filled-out" versions, each with one error you named for that document in part **a.** You make up all the details; names, dates, numbers, etc.

c. After completing part **b.**, exchange documents with another student in the class, and try to find and correct the errors. (If this is a homework assignment, bring a copy of each document you created to class for the exchange. If this is an in-class assignment, temporarily trade texts with the other student, after completing part **b.**)

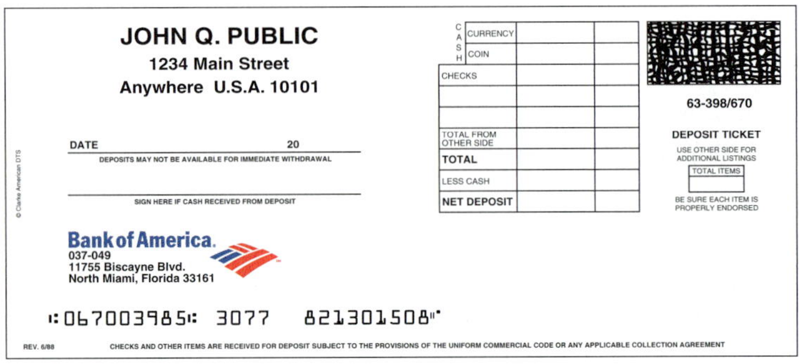

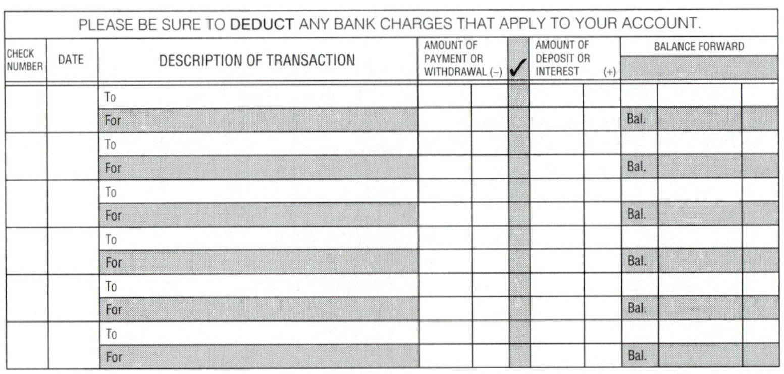

SECTION II

BANK STATEMENT RECONCILIATION

Each month the bank sends to the account holder a record of all checking account activity known as the bank statement, or statement of account. In addition, most banks send back the checks that have been paid out of the account. These are known as **canceled checks.** Banks that do not send the canceled checks with the statements retain them at the bank for a period of time and then copy them on microfilm for future reference. When a depositor needs a canceled check as proof of payment, for example, the bank will send a copy of it for a small service charge.

canceled checks
Checks that have been paid out of the account; usually sent back to the account holder each month along with the bank statement.

4-6 Understanding the Bank Statement

Bank statements vary widely in style from bank to bank; however, most contain essentially the same information. Exhibit 4-12 is an example of a typical bank statement. Note that it shows the balance brought forward from the last statement; the deposits and credits that have been added to the account during the month; the checks and debits that have been subtracted from the account during the month; any service charges assessed to the account; and the current or ending balance.

bank statement
A monthly summary of the activities in a checking account, including debits, credits, and beginning and ending balance. Sent by the bank to the account holder.

Bank of America
037-049
11755 Biscayne Blvd.
North Miami, Florida 33161

STATEMENT DATE
11-2-20xx

John Q. Public
1234 Main St.
Anywhere, U.S.A. 10101

CHECKING ACCOUNT SUMMARY
10-1-20xx THRU 10-31-20xx

ACCOUNT NUMBER
82-1301-508

Previous Balance	Deposits & Credits Number	Total	Checks & Debits Number	Total	Current Balance
775.20	3	3,228.11	7	2,857.80	1,145.51

CHECKING ACCOUNT TRANSACTIONS

DATE	AMOUNT	DESCRIPTION	BALANCE
10-2	125.00	Check #445	650.20
10-4	357.18	Deposit	1,007.38
10-7	884.22	Check #446	123.16
10-13	1,409.30	EFT Payroll Deposit	1,532.46
10-15	12.95	Check #447	1,519.51
10-16	326.11	Check #448	1,193.40
10-22	200.00	ATM Withdrawal	993.40
10-25	1,461.63	Deposit	2,455.03
10-27	1,294.52	Check #449	1,160.51
10-31	15.00	Service Charge	1,145.51

EXHIBIT 4-12
Bank Statement

Credits are additions to the account, such as interest earned, notes collected, and electronic fund transfers of direct deposit payroll checks. **Debits** are subtractions from the account, such as automatic teller machine (ATM) withdrawals, monthly service charges, check printing charges, nonsufficient fund (NSF) fees, and returned items. A **nonsufficient fund (NSF) fee** is a fee charged by the bank when a check is written without sufficient funds in the account to cover the amount of that check. **Returned items** are checks from others that you deposited into your account but were returned to your bank unpaid because the person or business issuing the check had insufficient funds in its account to cover the check. Banks usually charge a **returned item fee** when this occurs.

credits
Additions to a checking account, such as deposits and interest earned.

debits
Subtractions from a checking account, such as service charges.

nonsufficient fund (NSF) fees
A fee charged by the bank when a check is written without sufficient funds in the account to cover the amount of that check.

returned item
A check that you deposited into your account but was returned to your bank unpaid because the person or business issuing the check had insufficient funds in its account to cover the check.

returned item fee
A fee charged to your checking account when a check you deposit becomes a returned item.

bank statement reconciliation
The process of adjusting the bank and checkbook balances to reflect the actual current balance of the checking account.

outstanding checks
Checks that have been written but have not yet reached the bank and therefore do not appear on the current bank statement.

deposits in transit
Deposits made close to the statement date, or by mail, which do not clear in time to appear on the current bank statement.

adjusted checkbook balance
The checkbook balance minus service charges and other debits plus interest earned and other credits.

adjusted bank balance
The bank balance minus outstanding checks plus deposits in transit.

4-7 Preparing a Bank Statement Reconciliation

When the statement arrives from the bank each month, the depositor must compare the bank balance with the balance shown in the checkbook. Usually, the balances are not the same because during the month some account activity has taken place without being recorded by the bank, and other activities have occurred without being recorded in the checkbook. The process of adjusting the bank and checkbook balances to reflect the actual current balance is known as **bank statement reconciliation.** When we use the word *checkbook* in this chapter, we are actually referring to the records kept by the depositor on the check stubs or in the checkbook register.

Before a statement can be reconciled, you must identify and total all the checks that have been written but have not yet reached the bank. These are known as **outstanding checks.** Outstanding checks are found by comparing and checking off each check in the checkbook with those shown on the statement. Any checks not appearing on the statement are outstanding checks.

Sometimes deposits are made close to the statement date, or by mail, and do not clear the bank in time to appear on the current statement. These are known as **deposits in transit.** Just like outstanding checks, deposits in transit must be identified and totaled. Once again, this is done by comparing and checking off the checkbook records with the deposits shown on the bank statement.

A bank statement is reconciled when the **adjusted checkbook balance** is equal to the **adjusted bank balance.** Most bank statements have a form on the back to use in reconciling the account. Exhibit 4-13 is an example of such a form and is used in this chapter.

CHECKBOOK BALANCE	$	STATEMENT BALANCE	$
Add: Interest Earned & Other Credits		Add: Deposits in Transit	
SUB TOTAL		SUB TOTAL	
Deduct: Service Charges & Other Debits		Deduct: Outstanding Checks	
ADJUSTED CHECKBOOK BALANCE		ADJUSTED STATEMENT BALANCE	

Checks Outstanding		
No.	Amount	
Total		

✦ **EXHIBIT 4-13** ✦
Bank Statement Reconciliation Form

STEPS FOR PREPARING A BANK STATEMENT RECONCILIATION:

Step 1. Calculate the adjusted checkbook balance:

a. Look over the bank statement and find any credits not recorded in the checkbook, such as interest earned or notes collected, and *add* them to the checkbook balance to get a subtotal.

b. Locate any charges or debits, such as service charges, NSF fees, or returned items, that have been recorded in the checkbook, and *subtract* them from the subtotal from Step 1a.

Step 2. Calculate the adjusted bank balance:

a. Locate all of the deposits in transit and *add* them to the statement balance to get a subtotal.

b. Locate and total all outstanding checks and *subtract* them from the subtotal from Step 2a.

Step 3. Compare the adjusted balances:

a. If they are equal, the statement has been reconciled.

b. If they are not equal, an error exists that must be found and corrected. The error is either in the checkbook or on the bank statement.

EXAMPLE

Prepare a bank reconciliation for Winston Hill from the following bank statement and checkbook records:

Grove Isle Bank

STATEMENT DATE
8-2-20xx

WINSTON HILL
1190 Cherry Lane
Baltimore, Md. 21222

CHECKING ACCOUNT SUMMARY
7-1-20xx THRU 7-31-20xx

ACCOUNT NUMBER
82-1301-508

Previous Balance	Deposits & Credits Number	Deposits & Credits Total	Checks & Debits Number	Checks & Debits Total	Current Balance
1,233.40	3	2,445.80	7	2,158.92	1,520.28

CHECKING ACCOUNT TRANSACTIONS

DATE	AMOUNT	DESCRIPTION	BALANCE
7-3	450.30	Check #1209	783.10
7-6	500.00	Deposit	1,283.10
7-10	47.75	Check #1210	1,235.35
7-13	1,300.00	EFT Payroll Deposit	2,535.35
7-15	312.79	Check #1212	2,222.56
7-17	547.22	Check #1214	1,675.34
7-22	350.00	ATM Withdrawal	1,325.34
7-24	645.80	Deposit	1,971.14
7-28	430.86	Check #1215	1,540.28
7-30	20.00	Service Charge	1,520.28

Everybody's Business

Learning Tip

When a bank statement arrives, the balance on that statement will not agree with the checkbook balance until the account has been *reconciled.* Remember that ***both*** balances need to be adjusted.

To determine which balance, the checkbook or the bank, gets adjusted for various situations, ask, "who didn't know?" For example,

- The bank *"didn't know"* about outstanding checks and deposits in transit; therefore these adjustments are made to the bank balance.
- The checkbook *"didn't know"* the amount of the service charges and other debits or credits. These adjustments are made to the checkbook.

PLEASE BE SURE TO **DEDUCT** ANY BANK CHARGES THAT APPLY TO YOUR ACCOUNT.

CHECK NUMBER	DATE	DESCRIPTION OF TRANSACTION	AMOUNT OF PAYMENT OR WITHDRAWAL (−)		✓	AMOUNT OF DEPOSIT OR INTEREST (+)			BALANCE FORWARD	
									1233	40
1209	7/1	To *Stillwell Supply Co.*	450	30						
		For						Bal.	783	10
	7/6	To *Deposit*				500	00			
		For						Bal.	1283	10
1210	7/8	To *Food Spot*	47	75						
		For						Bal.	1235	35
1211	7/10	To *Delta Airlines*	342	10						
		For						Bal.	893	25
	7/13	To *Payroll Deposit*				1300	00			
		For						Bal.	2193	25
1212	7/13	To *Hyatt Hotel*	312	79						
		For						Bal.	1880	46
1213	7/15	To *Wall Street Journal*	75	00						
		For						Bal.	1805	46
1214	7/15	To *Builder's Depot*	547	22						
		For						Bal.	1258	24
	7/21	To *ATM Withdrawal*	350	00						
		For						Bal.	908	24
	7/24	To *Deposit*				645	80			
		For						Bal.	1554	04
1215	7/25	To *Williams Roofing*	430	86						
		For						Bal.	1123	18
	7/31	To *Deposit*				550	00			
		For						Bal.	1673	18
		To								
		For						Bal.		

SOLUTION STRATEGY

Below is the properly completed reconciliation form. Note that the adjusted checkbook balance equals the adjusted bank statement balance. The balances are now reconciled. After some practice, the format will become familiar to you, and you should no longer need the form.

CHECKBOOK BALANCE	$ 1,673.18	**STATEMENT BALANCE**	$ 1,520.28
Add: Interest Earned & Other Credits		**Add:** Deposits in Transit	550.00
SUB TOTAL	1,673.18	**SUB TOTAL**	2,070.28
Deduct: Service Charges & Other Debits	20.00	**Deduct:** Outstanding Checks	417.10
ADJUSTED CHECKBOOK BALANCE	1,653.18	**ADJUSTED STATEMENT BALANCE**	1,653.18

Reconciled Balances

Checks Outstanding

No.	Amount	
1211	342	10
1213	75	00
Total	417	10

TRY-IT | EXERCISE

7. Using the form provided, reconcile the following bank statement and checkbook records for Penny Hart:

Grove Isle Bank

STATEMENT DATE
4-3-20xx

PENNY HART
4121 Pinetree Rd.
Bangor, Maine 04401

CHECKING ACCOUNT SUMMARY
3-1-20xx THRU 3-31-20xx

ACCOUNT NUMBER
097440

Previous Balance	Deposits & Credits Number	Deposits & Credits Total	Checks & Debits Number	Checks & Debits Total	Current Balance
625.40	3	1,790.00	8	690.00	1,725.40

CHECKING ACCOUNT TRANSACTIONS

DATE	AMOUNT	DESCRIPTION	BALANCE
3-3	34.77	Check #338	590.63
3-6	750.00	Payroll- EFT Deposit	1,340.63
3-10	247.05	Check #340	1,093.58
3-13	390.00	Deposit	1,483.58
3-15	66.30	Check #342	1,417.28
3-17	112.18	Check #343	1,305.10
3-22	150.00	ATM Withdrawal	1,155.10
3-24	650.00	Deposit	1,805.10
3-28	50.00	Check #345	1,755.10
3-30	17.70	Check printing charge	1,737.40
3-31	12.00	Service charge	1,725.40

PLEASE BE SURE TO **DEDUCT** ANY BANK CHARGES THAT APPLY TO YOUR ACCOUNT.

CHECK NUMBER	DATE	DESCRIPTION OF TRANSACTION	AMOUNT OF PAYMENT OR WITHDRAWAL (−)	✓	AMOUNT OF DEPOSIT OR INTEREST (+)	BALANCE FORWARD
						625 40
338	3/2	To Naples Pet Shop	34 77			
		For				Bal. 590 63
	3/5	To Deposit			750 00	
		For				Bal. 1340 63
339	3/5	To Alison Company	19 83			
		For				Bal. 1320 80
340	3/9	To Silver Software	247 05			
		For				Bal. 1073 75
	3/12	To Deposit			390 00	
		For				Bal. 1463 75
341	3/12	To The Book Shelf	57 50			
		For				Bal. 1406 25
342	3/13	To Wal-Mart	66 30			
		For				Bal. 1339 95
343	3/15	To S.E. Office Supply	112 18			
		For				Bal. 1227 77
	3/22	To ATM Withdrawal	150 00			
		For				Bal. 1077 77
	3/24	To Deposit			650 00	
		For				Bal. 1727 77
344	3/24	To Flower Decor, Inc.	119 32			
		For				Bal. 1608 45
345	3/28	To Cablevision, Inc.	50 00			
		For				Bal. 1558 45
	3/30	To Deposit			240 23	
		For				Bal. 1798 68

CHECKBOOK BALANCE	$	STATEMENT BALANCE	$
Add: Interest Earned & Other Credits		**Add:** Deposits in Transit	
SUB TOTAL		SUB TOTAL	
Deduct: Service Charges & Other Debits		**Deduct:** Outstanding Checks	
ADJUSTED CHECKBOOK BALANCE		ADJUSTED STATEMENT BALANCE	

Reconciled Balances

Checks Outstanding

No.	Amount	
Total		

Check your answers with the solutions on page 127.

REVIEW EXERCISES | CHAPTER 4—SECTION II

1. On April 3, Skeeter King received her bank statement, showing a balance of $1,637.93. Her checkbook showed a balance of $1,493.90. Outstanding checks were $224.15, $327.80, $88.10, $122.42, and $202.67. There was an $8.00 service charge, and the deposits in transit amounted to $813.11. Use the form below to reconcile Skeeter's account.

CHECKBOOK BALANCE	$	STATEMENT BALANCE	$
Add: Interest Earned & Other Credits		Add: Deposits in Transit	
SUB TOTAL		SUB TOTAL	
Deduct: Service Charges & Other Debits		Deduct: Outstanding Checks	
ADJUSTED CHECKBOOK BALANCE		ADJUSTED STATEMENT BALANCE	

Reconciled Balances

Checks Outstanding		
No.	Amount	
Total		

2. Bob Albrecht received his bank statement on July 5, showing a balance of $2,663.31. His checkbook had a balance of $1,931.83. The statement showed a service charge of $15.80 and a note collected by the bank for Bob, in the amount of $200.00. (A note collected is a payment owed to Bob by someone who makes that payment directly to Bob's bank account.) The deposits in transit totaled $314.12, and the outstanding checks were for $182.00, $261.40, and $418.00. Use the form below to reconcile Bob's account.

CHECKBOOK BALANCE	$	STATEMENT BALANCE	$
Add: Interest Earned & Other Credits		Add: Deposits in Transit	
SUB TOTAL		SUB TOTAL	
Deduct: Service Charges & Other Debits		Deduct: Outstanding Checks	
ADJUSTED CHECKBOOK BALANCE		ADJUSTED STATEMENT BALANCE	

Reconciled Balances

Checks Outstanding		
No.	Amount	
Total		

3. On December 2, Marcy Diaz received her bank statement showing a balance of $358.97. Her checkbook showed a balance of $479.39. There was a check printing charge of $13.95, and interest earned was $6.40. The outstanding checks were for $22.97, $80.36, $19.80, and $4.50. The deposits in transit totaled $240.50. Use the form below to reconcile Marcy's account.

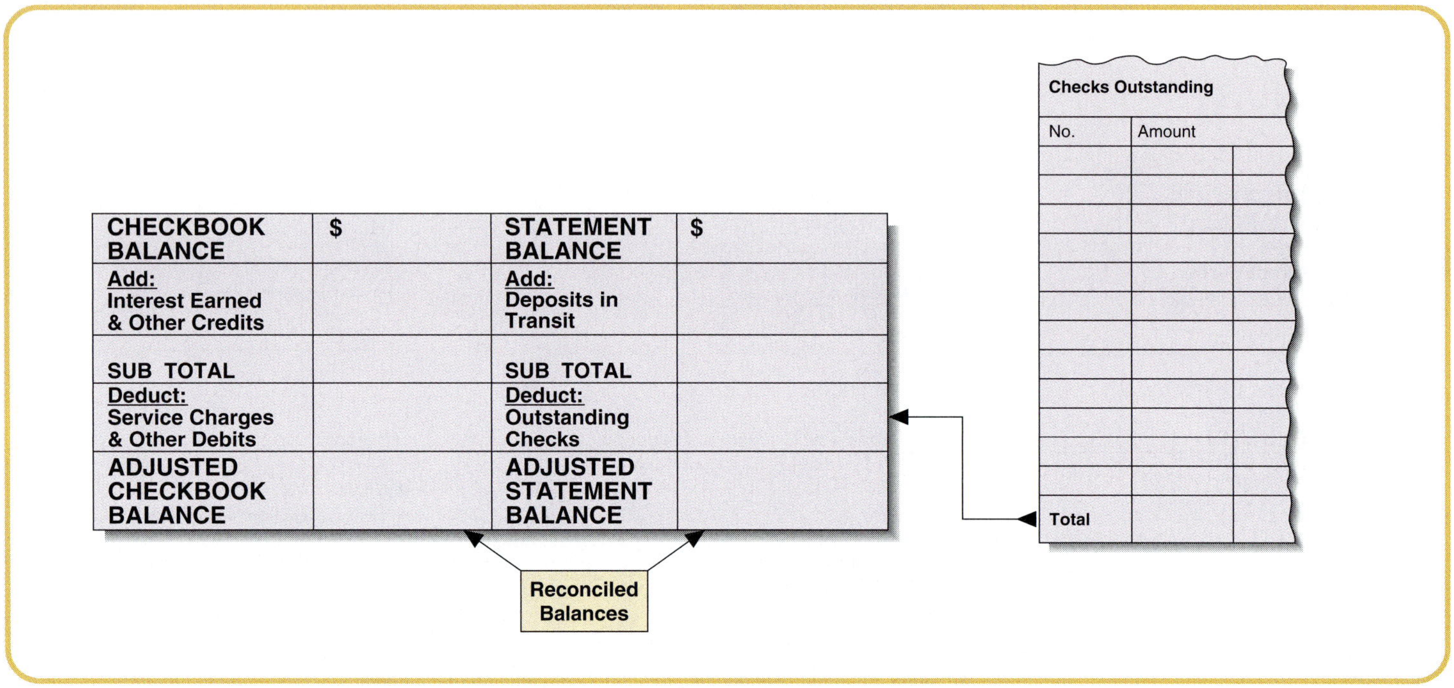

BUSINESS DECISION

Choosing a Bank

4. You are looking for a bank in which to open a checking account for your new part-time business. You estimate that in the first year you will be writing 30 checks per month and will make three balance inquiries per month. Your average daily balance is estimated to be $900 for the first six months and $2,400 for the next six months.

Use the following information to solve the problem.

Bank	Monthly Fees and Conditions
Intercontinental Bank	$15.00 with $1,000 min. daily balance -or- $25.00 under $1,000 min. daily balance
City National Bank	$4.50 plus $.50 per check over 10 checks monthly $1.00 per balance inquiry
Bank of America	$6 plus $.25 per check $2.00 per balance inquiry
First Union Bank	$9 plus $.15 per check $1.50 per balance inquiry

a. Calculate the cost of doing business with each bank for a year.

Intercontinental Bank: City National Bank:

Bank of America: First Union Bank:

b. Which bank should you choose for your checking account?

✦ SUMMARY CHART ✦
SECTION I: Understanding and Using Checking Accounts

Topic	P/O, Page	Important Concepts	Illustrative Examples
Checks	4-1 100 4-2 103	Checks, or drafts, are negotiable instruments ordering the bank to pay money from the checking account to the name written on the check. The person or business named on the check to receive the money is known as the payee. The person or business issuing the check is known as the payor.	See Check, with Parts Labeled Exhibit 4-1, p. 101 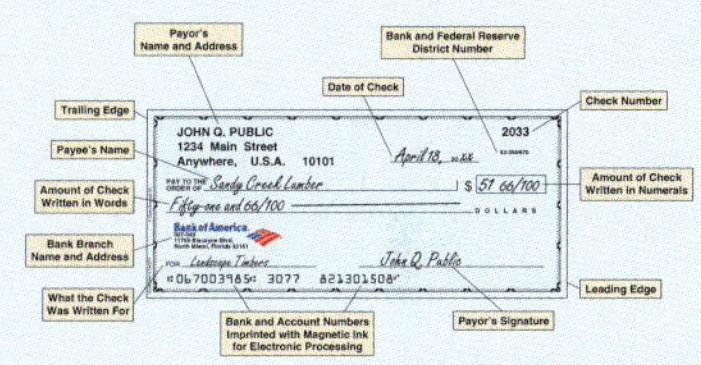
Deposit Slips	4-1 101	Deposit slips or deposit tickets are printed forms with the depositor's name, address, account number, and space for the details of the deposit. Deposit slips are used to record money, both cash and checks, being added to the checking account. They are presented to the bank teller along with the items to be deposited. When a deposit is completed, the depositor receives a copy of the deposit slip as a receipt, or proof of the transaction.	See Deposit Slip Exhibit 4-2, p. 102 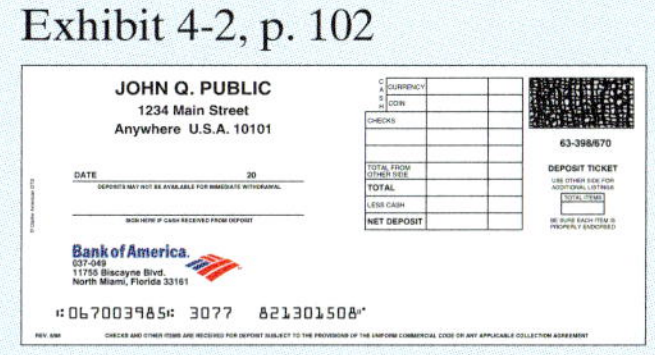 See Completed Deposit Slip Exhibit 4-9, p. 106 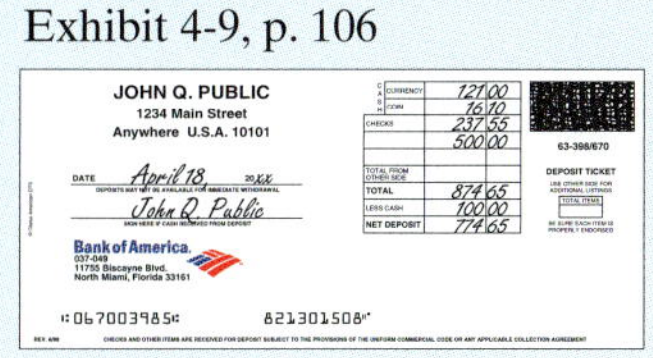

SECTION I: (continued)

Topic	P/O, Page	Important Concepts	Illustrative Examples
Check Stubs	4-1 101 4-5 108	Check stubs, with checks attached by perforation, are a bound part of the checkbook. The check number is preprinted on both the check and the attached stub. Each stub is used to record the issuing of its corresponding check, and any deposits made on that date.	See Check Stub with Check Exhibit 4-3, p. 102 
Check Registers	4-1 101 4-5 108	Check registers are the alternative method for keeping track of checking account activities. They are a separate booklet of forms, rather than stubs attached to each check. Space is provided for all the pertinent information required to keep an accurate and up-to-date running balance of the account.	See Check Register Exhibit 4-4, p. 102 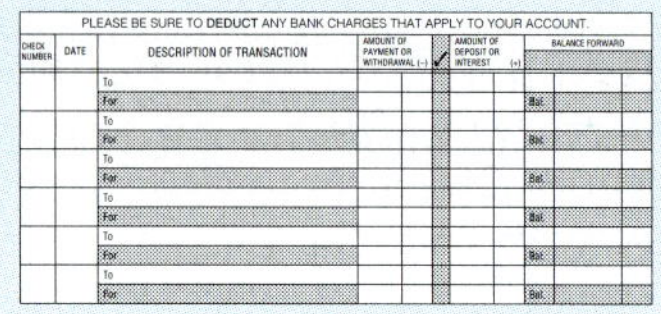
Endorsements	4-3 104	When you receive a check, you may either cash it, deposit it in your account, or transfer it to another party. The endorsement on the back of the check instructs the bank on what to do. Your endorsement should be written within the $1\frac{1}{2}$-inch space at the trailing edge of the check.	See Endorsement Space Exhibit 4-5, p. 105 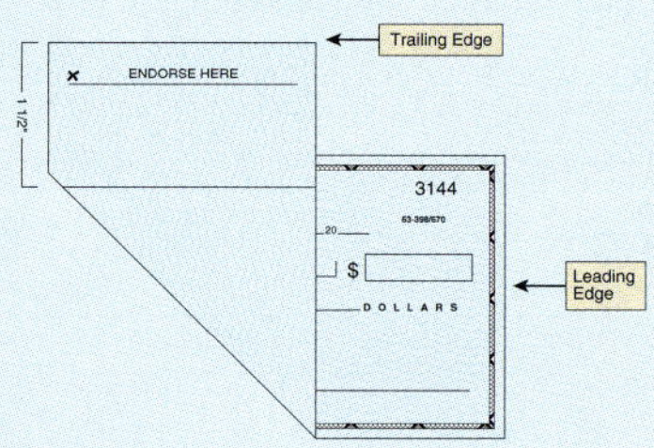
Blank Endorsement	4-3 104	A blank endorsement is used when you want to cash the check. You, as the payee, simply sign your name exactly as it appears on the front of the check. Once you have endorsed a check in this manner, anyone who has possession of the check can cash it.	See Blank Endorsement Exhibit 4-6, p. 105 
Restrictive Endorsement	4-3 104	A restrictive endorsement is used when you want to deposit the check into your account. In this case, you endorse the check "for deposit only," sign your name as it appears on the front, and write your account number.	See Restrictive Endorsement Exhibit 4-7, p. 105 

SECTION I: (continued)

<table>
<tr><th>Topic</th><th>P/O, Page</th><th>Important Concepts</th><th>Illustrative Examples</th></tr>
<tr><td>Full Endorsement</td><td>4-3
104</td><td>A full endorsement is used when you want to transfer the check to another party. In this case, you endorse the check "pay to the order of," write the name of the person or business to whom the check is being transferred, and sign your name and account number.</td><td>See Full Endorsement
Exhibit 4-8, p. 105
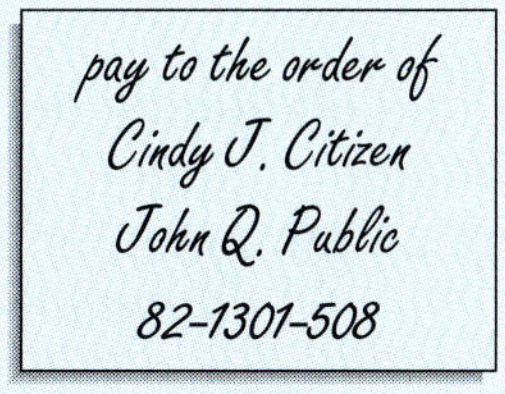
</td></tr>
</table>

SECTION II: Bank Statement Reconciliation

<table>
<tr><td>Bank Statements</td><td>4-6
115</td><td>Bank statements are a recap of the checking account activity for the month. They show the balance brought forward from the last statement, the deposits and credits that have been added to the account during the month, the checks and debits that have been subtracted from the account during the month, service charges assessed to the account, and the current or ending balance.</td><td>See Bank Statement
Exhibit 4-12, p. 115
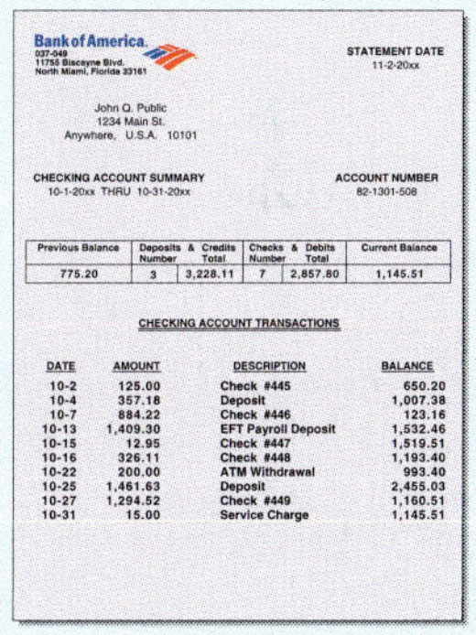
Bank of America
037-049
11755 Biscayne Blvd.
North Miami, Florida 33161
STATEMENT DATE
11-2-20xx
John Q. Public
1234 Main St.
Anywhere, U.S.A. 10101
CHECKING ACCOUNT SUMMARY
10-1-20xx THRU 10-31-20xx
ACCOUNT NUMBER
82-1301-508
<table>
<tr><th>Previous Balance</th><th>Deposits & Credits Number</th><th>Deposits & Credits Total</th><th>Checks & Debits Number</th><th>Checks & Debits Total</th><th>Current Balance</th></tr>
<tr><td>775.20</td><td>3</td><td>3,228.11</td><td>7</td><td>2,857.80</td><td>1,145.51</td></tr>
</table>
CHECKING ACCOUNT TRANSACTIONS
<table>
<tr><th>DATE</th><th>AMOUNT</th><th>DESCRIPTION</th><th>BALANCE</th></tr>
<tr><td>10-2</td><td>125.00</td><td>Check #445</td><td>650.20</td></tr>
<tr><td>10-4</td><td>357.18</td><td>Deposit</td><td>1,007.38</td></tr>
<tr><td>10-7</td><td>884.22</td><td>Check #446</td><td>123.16</td></tr>
<tr><td>10-13</td><td>1,409.30</td><td>EFT Payroll Deposit</td><td>1,532.46</td></tr>
<tr><td>10-15</td><td>12.95</td><td>Check #447</td><td>1,519.51</td></tr>
<tr><td>10-16</td><td>326.11</td><td>Check #448</td><td>1,193.40</td></tr>
<tr><td>10-22</td><td>200.00</td><td>ATM Withdrawal</td><td>993.40</td></tr>
<tr><td>10-25</td><td>1,461.63</td><td>Deposit</td><td>2,455.03</td></tr>
<tr><td>10-27</td><td>1,294.52</td><td>Check #449</td><td>1,160.51</td></tr>
<tr><td>10-31</td><td>15.00</td><td>Service Charge</td><td>1,145.51</td></tr>
</table></td></tr>
<tr><td>Bank Statement Reconciliation</td><td>4-7
116</td><td>1. Calculate the adjusted checkbook balance:
a. Locate any credits on the statement not recorded in the checkbook, such as interest earned or notes collected, and add them to the checkbook balance to get a subtotal.
b. Subtract any debits or charges such as service charges, NSF fees, or returned items from the subtotal above.
2. Calculate the adjusted bank balance:
a. Locate all the deposits in transit and add them to the checkbook balance to get a subtotal.
b. Locate all outstanding checks and subtract them from the subtotal above.
3. Compare the adjusted balances:
a. If they are equal, the statement has been reconciled.
b. If they are not equal, an error exists that must be found and corrected. The error is either in the checkbook or on the bank statement.</td><td>See Blank Reconciliation Form
Exhibit 4-13, p. 116
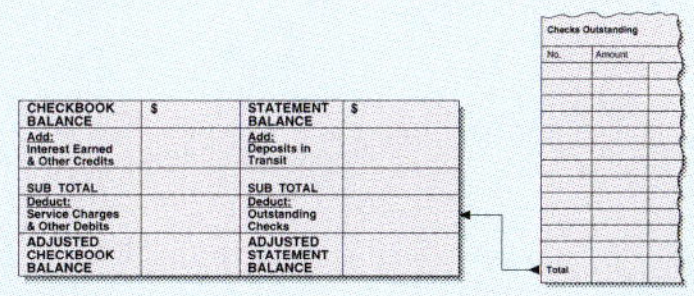
<table>
<tr><td>CHECKBOOK BALANCE</td><td>$</td><td>STATEMENT BALANCE</td><td>$</td></tr>
<tr><td>Add: Interest Earned & Other Credits</td><td></td><td>Add: Deposits in Transit</td><td></td></tr>
<tr><td>SUB TOTAL</td><td></td><td>SUB TOTAL</td><td></td></tr>
<tr><td>Deduct: Service Charges & Other Debits</td><td></td><td>Deduct: Outstanding Checks</td><td></td></tr>
<tr><td>ADJUSTED CHECKBOOK BALANCE</td><td></td><td>ADJUSTED STATEMENT BALANCE</td><td></td></tr>
</table>
Checks Outstanding
<table>
<tr><th>No.</th><th>Amount</th></tr>
<tr><td>Total</td><td></td></tr>
</table></td></tr>
</table>

TRY-IT EXERCISE | SOLUTIONS

1.

Carolyn Richards
1585 S. W. 6 Avenue
Tallahassee, Fl. 32399

206

April 27 20 xx

63-398/670

PAY TO THE ORDER OF Snappy Photo Service $ 41 88/100

Forty-one and 88/100 DOLLARS

Bank of America
037-049
11755 Biscayne Blvd.
North Miami, Florida 33161

FOR Film Developing Carolyn Richards

⑆067003985⑆ 3077 821451902⑈

2. Pay to the order of
Roz Reitman
Your Signature
696-339-1028
Full Endorsement

3. Your Signature
696-339-1028
Blank Endorsement

4. for deposit only
Your Signature
696-339-1028
Restrictive Endorsement

5.

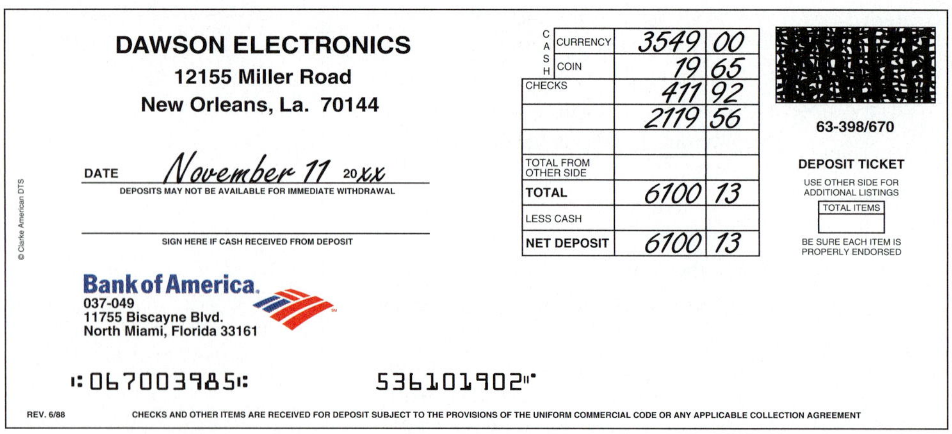

DAWSON ELECTRONICS
12155 Miller Road
New Orleans, La. 70144

DATE November 11 20xx
DEPOSITS MAY NOT BE AVAILABLE FOR IMMEDIATE WITHDRAWAL

SIGN HERE IF CASH RECEIVED FROM DEPOSIT

CASH CURRENCY	3549	00
CASH COIN	19	65
CHECKS	411	92
	2119	56
TOTAL FROM OTHER SIDE		
TOTAL	6100	13
LESS CASH		
NET DEPOSIT	6100	13

63-398/670

DEPOSIT TICKET
USE OTHER SIDE FOR ADDITIONAL LISTINGS
TOTAL ITEMS
BE SURE EACH ITEM IS PROPERLY ENDORSED

Bank of America
037-049
11755 Biscayne Blvd.
North Miami, Florida 33161

⑆067003985⑆ 536101902⑈

REV. 6/88 CHECKS AND OTHER ITEMS ARE RECEIVED FOR DEPOSIT SUBJECT TO THE PROVISIONS OF THE UNIFORM COMMERCIAL CODE OR ANY APPLICABLE COLLECTION AGREEMENT

6.

IF TAX DEDUCTIBLE CHECK HERE ☐	$ 55.75	
137		
March 12 20 xx		
TO Nathan & David		
FOR perm & manicure		
	DOLLARS	CENTS
BAL. FWD.	887	45
DEPOSIT		
DEPOSIT		
TOTAL	887	45
THIS ITEM	55	75
SUB-TOTAL	831	70
OTHER DEDUCT. (IF ANY)		
BAL. FWD.	831	70

IF TAX DEDUCTIBLE CHECK HERE ☐	$ 459.88	
138		
March 19 20 xx		
TO Complete Auto Service		
FOR Car repair		
	DOLLARS	CENTS
BAL. FWD.	831	70
DEPOSIT 3/16	125	40
DEPOSIT 3/16	221	35
TOTAL	1178	45
THIS ITEM	459	88
SUB-TOTAL	718	57
OTHER DEDUCT. (IF ANY)		
BAL. FWD.	718	57

PLEASE BE SURE TO **DEDUCT** ANY BANK CHARGES THAT APPLY TO YOUR ACCOUNT.

CHECK NUMBER	DATE	DESCRIPTION OF TRANSACTION	AMOUNT OF PAYMENT OR WITHDRAWAL (−)	✓	AMOUNT OF DEPOSIT OR INTEREST (+)	BALANCE FORWARD	
						887	45
137	3/12	To Nathan & David Hair Stylists	55.75				
		For				Bal. 831	70
	3/16	To Deposit			125.40		
		For				Bal. 957	10
	3/16	To Deposit			221.35		
		For				Bal. 1178	45
138	3/19	To Complete Auto Service	459.88				
		For				Bal. 718	57

7.

CHECKBOOK BALANCE	$ 1,798.68	STATEMENT BALANCE	$ 1,725.40
Add: Interest Earned & Other Credits		**Add:** Deposits in Transit	240.23
SUB TOTAL	1,798.68	SUB TOTAL	1,965.63
Deduct: Service Charges & Other Debits	29.70	**Deduct:** Outstanding Checks	196.65
ADJUSTED CHECKBOOK BALANCE	1,768.98	ADJUSTED STATEMENT BALANCE	1,768.98

Reconciled Balances

Checks Outstanding

No.	Amount	
339	19	83
341	57	50
344	119	32
Total	196	65

CHAPTER 4 | ASSESSMENT TEST

1. As the purchasing manager for Fuzzy Logic Industries, write a check dated April 29, 20xx, in the amount of $24,556.00, to Outback Electronics, Inc., for circuit boards.

FUZZY LOGIC INDUSTRIES
12221 Keystone Blvd
Greenville, S.C. 29610

206

63-398/670

_______ 20____

PAY TO THE ORDER OF ______________________ $ [ ]

______________________ DOLLARS

Bank of America.
037-049
11755 Biscayne Blvd.
North Miami, Florida 33161

FOR ____________ ____________

⑆067003985⑆ 3077 731021807⑈

2. You have just received a check. Your account number is #9299-144-006. Write the following endorsements in the space provided below, and identify what type they are:

a. Allowing the check to be transferred to Expo, Inc.

b. Allowing you to cash the check.

c. Allowing you to deposit the check into your account.

a. ____________ **b.** ____________ **c.** ____________

3. As cashier for the Country Kitchen Cafe, it is your responsibility to make the daily deposits. Complete the deposit slip below, based on the following information:

a. Date: January 20, 20xx.

b. Checks totaling $344.20.

c. Currency of $547.00.

d. Coins: 125 quarters, 67 dimes, 88 nickels, and 224 pennies.

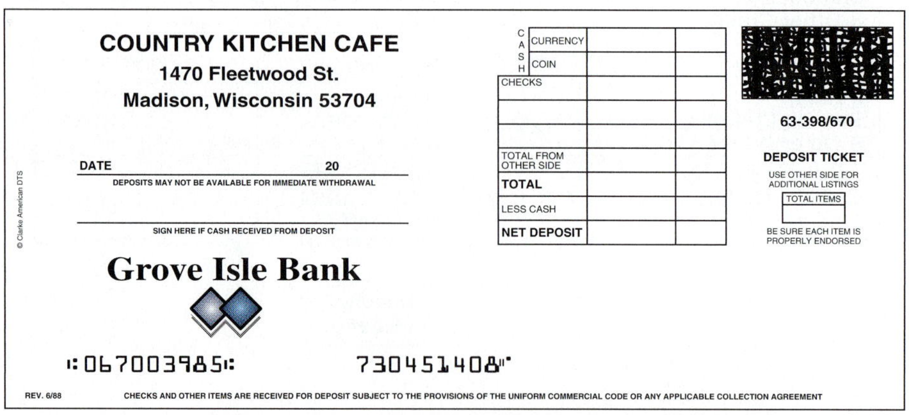

COUNTRY KITCHEN CAFE
1470 Fleetwood St.
Madison, Wisconsin 53704

DATE ____________ 20____
DEPOSITS MAY NOT BE AVAILABLE FOR IMMEDIATE WITHDRAWAL

____
SIGN HERE IF CASH RECEIVED FROM DEPOSIT

Grove Isle Bank

CASH CURRENCY		
CASH COIN		
CHECKS		
TOTAL FROM OTHER SIDE		
TOTAL		
LESS CASH		
NET DEPOSIT		

63-398/670

DEPOSIT TICKET
USE OTHER SIDE FOR ADDITIONAL LISTINGS
TOTAL ITEMS
BE SURE EACH ITEM IS PROPERLY ENDORSED

⑆067003985⑆ 730451408⑈

REV. 6/88 CHECKS AND OTHER ITEMS ARE RECEIVED FOR DEPOSIT SUBJECT TO THE PROVISIONS OF THE UNIFORM COMMERCIAL CODE OR ANY APPLICABLE COLLECTION AGREEMENT

4. From the following information, complete the two check stubs and the check register below:

a. Starting balance: $463.30.

b. April 15, 20xx, check #450, issued to the Keystone Market, for groceries, in the amount of $67.78.

c. April 17, ATM withdrawal of $250.

d. April 19, deposit of $125.45.

e. April 20, deposit of $320.00.

f. April 27, check #451, in the amount of $123.10, to Ace Appliance, Inc., for refrigerator repair.

IF TAX DEDUCTIBLE CHECK HERE ☐ $______

__________ 20____

TO __________

FOR __________

	DOLLARS	CENTS
BAL. FWD.		
DEPOSIT		
DEPOSIT		
TOTAL		
THIS ITEM		
SUB-TOTAL		
OTHER DEDUCT. (IF ANY)		
BAL. FWD.		

IF TAX DEDUCTIBLE CHECK HERE ☐ $______

__________ 20____

TO __________

FOR __________

	DOLLARS	CENTS
BAL. FWD.		
DEPOSIT		
DEPOSIT		
TOTAL		
THIS ITEM		
SUB-TOTAL		
OTHER DEDUCT. (IF ANY)		
BAL. FWD.		

PLEASE BE SURE TO **DEDUCT** ANY BANK CHARGES THAT APPLY TO YOUR ACCOUNT.

CHECK NUMBER	DATE	DESCRIPTION OF TRANSACTION	AMOUNT OF PAYMENT OR WITHDRAWAL (−)	AMOUNT OF DEPOSIT OR INTEREST (+)	BALANCE FORWARD
		To			
		For			Bal.
		To			
		For			Bal.
		To			
		For			Bal.
		To			
		For			Bal.
		To			
		For			Bal.
		To			
		For			Bal.

5. On October 1, Jennifer Bernhard received her bank statement showing a balance of $440.22. Her checkbook records indicate a balance of $338.97. There was a service charge for the month of $14.40 on the statement. The outstanding checks were for $47.10, $110.15, $19.80, and $64.10. The deposits in transit totaled $125.50. Use the following form to reconcile Jennifer's checking account.

CHECKBOOK BALANCE	$	STATEMENT BALANCE	$
Add: Interest Earned & Other Credits		**Add:** Deposits in Transit	
SUB TOTAL		SUB TOTAL	
Deduct: Service Charges & Other Debits		**Deduct:** Outstanding Checks	
ADJUSTED CHECKBOOK BALANCE		ADJUSTED STATEMENT BALANCE	

Reconciled Balances

Checks Outstanding		
No.	Amount	
Total		

6. Prepare a bank reconciliation for Avis Sohn from the following checkbook records and bank statement.

PLEASE BE SURE TO **DEDUCT** ANY BANK CHARGES THAT APPLY TO YOUR ACCOUNT.

CHECK NUMBER	DATE	DESCRIPTION OF TRANSACTION	AMOUNT OF PAYMENT OR WITHDRAWAL (−)		✓	AMOUNT OF DEPOSIT OR INTEREST (+)		BALANCE FORWARD		
									879	36
801	10/1	To Technique Photo Lab	236	77						
		For						Bal.	642	59
	10/6	To Deposit				450	75			
		For						Bal.	1,093	34
802	10/8	To L.L. Bean	47	20						
		For						Bal.	1,046	14
803	10/10	To Sam Newman	75	89						
		For						Bal.	970	25
	10/13	To Deposit				880	34			
		For						Bal.	1,850	59
804	10/13	To Sheraton Hotel	109	00						
		For						Bal.	1,741	59
805	10/15	To American Express	507	82						
		For						Bal.	1,233	77
	10/20	To ATM Withdrawal	120	00						
		For						Bal.	1,113	77
	10/24	To Deposit				623	50			
		For						Bal.	1,737	27
	10/27	To Deposit				208	40			
		For						Bal.	1,945	67
806	10/28	To K-Mart	48	25						
		For						Bal.	1,897	42
		To								
		For						Bal.		
		To								
		For						Bal.		

Aloha Bank

STATEMENT DATE
11-2-20xx

Avis Sohn
1127 Pineapple Place
Honolulu, Hawaii 96825

CHECKING ACCOUNT SUMMARY
10-1-20xx THRU 10-31-20xx

ACCOUNT NUMBER
449-56-7792

Previous Balance	Deposits & Credits Number	Deposits & Credits Total	Checks & Debits Number	Checks & Debits Total	Current Balance
879.36	3	1,954.59	7	1,347.83	1,486.12

CHECKING ACCOUNT TRANSACTIONS

DATE	AMOUNT	DESCRIPTION	BALANCE
10-3	236.77	Check #801	642.59
10-6	450.75	Deposit	1,093.34
10-10	324.70	Returned Item	768.64
10-13	880.34	EFT Payroll Deposit	1,648.98
10-15	75.89	Check #803	1,573.09
10-17	507.82	Check #805	1,065.27
10-22	120.00	ATM Withdrawal	945.27
10-24	623.50	Deposit	1,568.77
10-28	48.25	Check #806	1,520.52
10-30	34.40	Check printing charge	1,486.12

CHECKBOOK BALANCE	$	STATEMENT BALANCE	$
Add: Interest Earned & Other Credits		**Add:** Deposits in Transit	
SUB TOTAL		SUB TOTAL	
Deduct: Service Charges & Other Debits		**Deduct:** Outstanding Checks	
ADJUSTED CHECKBOOK BALANCE		ADJUSTED STATEMENT BALANCE	

Reconciled Balances

Checks Outstanding

No.	Amount	
Total		

BUSINESS DECISION

Choosing a Bank with Interest

7. Sometimes banks offer checking accounts that earn interest on the average daily balance of the account each month. This interest is calculated using a formula known as the simple interest formula. The formula is written as:

Interest = Principal × Rate × Time   I = PRT

The formula states that the amount of **Interest** earned on the account is equal to the **Principal** (average daily balance) times the **Rate** (interest rate per year—expressed as a decimal) times the **Time** (expressed in years—use $\frac{1}{12}$ to represent one month of a year).

a. If you have not already done so, complete the Business Decision, Choosing a Bank, in Section II, page 122.

b. Use the simple interest formula to calculate the amount of interest you would earn per month, if the Intercontinental Bank were offering 2 percent interest per year on checking accounts. (Note that your average daily balance changes from $900 to $2,400 in the last six months of the year.)

c. How much interest would you earn per month at Bank of America if they were offering 1.5 percent interest per year on checking accounts? Round to the nearest cent, when necessary.

d. Recalculate the cost of doing business with Intercontinental Bank and Bank of America for a year.

e. Based on this new information, which of the four banks should you choose for your checking account?

All the Math That's Fit to Learn

The Business Math Times

Volume IV | **Checking Accounts** | One Dollar

Check On It!

Did you know that checks became popular around the early 1500s, in Holland? At that time, Amsterdam was a major international shipping and trading center. People who had accumulated cash began depositing it with Dutch "cashiers," for a fee, as a safer alternative to keeping the money at home.

The business concept of writing and depositing checks as a method of arranging payments soon spread to England and thereafter around the world.

The word "check" originated in England in the mid-1700s when serial numbers were placed on the documents as a way to keep track of, or "check" on a financial transaction. The first printed checks are traced to 1762 and British banker Lawrence Childs.

Those little paper notes called checks began circulating in the United States one year after the National Banking Act of 1864 established the dollar as the national currency. Now, more than 65 billion checks are written in the United States each year, and the number grows annually.

Choosing the right checking account, and maintaining it properly, should be a priority item in your personal finance planning. The wrong choice can cost you a considerable amount of money over the years.

Please visit our Web site at www.bankrate.com

THE LOCKHORNS

"Something's wrong, Leroy ... it balances."

"Quote . . . Unquote"

Banks will lend you money if you can prove you don't need it.
—*Mark Twain*

We don't look for people who *never fail.*
We look for people who *never give up.*
—*Tenneco, Inc.*

Branching Out

Actual and projected number of U.S. households that bank online, in millions

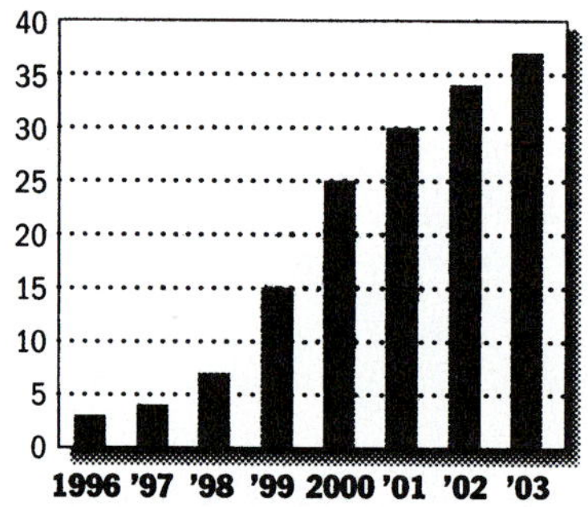

Source: Gartner Group

Stashing Cash

Estimated U.S. deposits of online banking customers, in billions of dollars

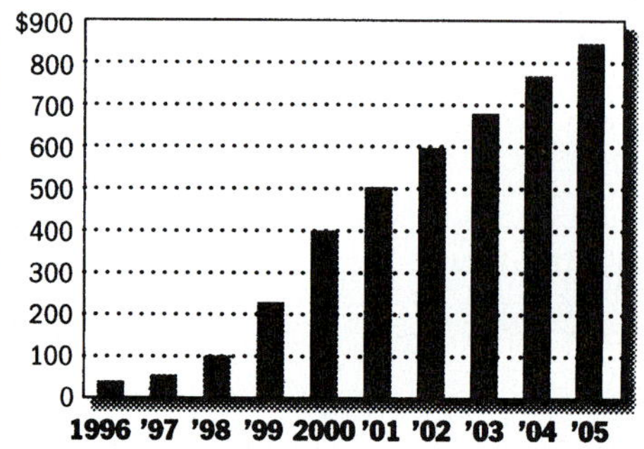

Clicks or Bricks?

When independent online banks started appearing in 1997, many people believed they would revolutionize retail banking. Although they have had some very good times and some not-so-good times in their short history, they still beat their offline counterparts by a wide margin when it comes to fees.

According to Bankrate.com, Internet banks remain in a class by themselves relative to the offerings of traditional "brick-and-mortar" banks.

From *The Wall Street Journal* charts above, you can see how quickly online banking is catching on. From the chart below, you may get an idea of why!

	Online Bank	Offline Bank
Yields:	3.78%	1.17%
Av. Fees:	$5.25	$10.77
No Fees:	46%	7.1%
Min. Bal. for interest:	$831.25	$2,337.70
NSF fee:	$23.54	$24.45

It's a Holdup!

It's not the kind of holdup involving guns and masks, but the kind where a bank takes your money and refuses to let you have it for several days.

These are legal "holdups," sanctioned by the federal government. According to law, there are three standard hold periods: one, two, and five business days.

Knowing when you can get your money from the check you just deposited is more important than ever. Debit cards and speedy electronic check clearing have increased the chances of spending deposits too soon!

Consumers should know their bank's policy on the length of fund "holds," and should also look into overdraft protection.

Brainteaser

YOU CAN COUNT ON IT!

How long would it take a bank teller to count one billion $1 bills, if they were counted continuously at the rate of one bill per second?

ANSWER TO LAST ISSUE'S BRAINTEASER

A decimal point 1.2

CHAPTER

5

Using Equations to Solve Business Problems

PERFORMANCE OBJECTIVES

Section I Solving Basic Equations

5-1 Understanding the concept, terminology, and rules of equations. (p. 136)
5-2 Solving equations for the unknown and proving the solution. (p. 137)
5-3 Writing expressions and equations from written statements. (p. 144)

Section II Using Equations to Solve Business-Related Word Problems

5-4 Setting up and solving business-related word problems by using equations. (p. 148)
5-5 Understanding and solving ratio and proportion problems. (p. 154)

SECTION I

SOLVING BASIC EQUATIONS

formula
A mathematical representation of a fact, rule, principle, or other logical relation in which letters represent number quantities. An example is the simple interest formula, $I = PRT$, where interest equals principal times rate times time.

One of the primary objectives of business mathematics is to describe business situations and solve business problems. Many business problems requiring a mathematical solution have been converted to formulas used to solve those problems. A **formula** is a mathematical statement describing a real-world situation in which letters represent number quantities. A typical example of a formula follows:

Business Situation: Revenue less expenses is profit

Mathematical Formula: Revenue − Expenses = Profit

or

$$R - E = P$$

By knowing the numerical value of any two of the three parts, we can use the formula to determine the unknown part. Formulas are a way of standardizing repetitive business situations. They are used in almost every aspect of business activity and are an essential tool for the businessperson. Later in the book, we see formulas applied to topics such as markup and markdown, percents, interest rates, financial ratios, inventory, and depreciation.

As valuable and widespread as formulas are, they cannot anticipate all business situations. Today, businesspeople must have the ability to analyze the facts of a situation and devise custom-made formulas to solve business problems. These formulas are actually mathematical equations.

In this important chapter, you learn to write and solve equations. At first, some of the concepts may seem a bit strange. Equations use letters of the alphabet as well as numbers. Do not be intimidated! After some practice, you will be able to write and solve equations comfortably.

equation
A mathematical statement expressing a relationship of equality; usually written as a series of symbols that are separated into left and right sides and joined by an equal sign. $X + 7 = 10$ is an equation.

expression
A mathematical operation or a quantity stated in symbolic form, not containing an equal sign. $X + 7$ is an expression.

variables (unknowns)
The part of an equation that is not given. In equations, the unknowns are variables (letters of the alphabet), which are quantities having no fixed value. In the equation $X + 7 = 10$, X is the unknown or variable.

constants (knowns)
The portion or parts of an equation that are given. In equations, the knowns are constants (numbers), which are quantities having a fixed value. In the equation $X + 7 = 10$, 7 and 10 are the knowns or constants.

terms
The knowns (constants) and unknowns (variables) of an equation. In the equation $X + 7 = 10$, X, 7, and 10 are the terms.

solve an equation
The process of finding the numerical value of the unknown in an equation.

5-1 Understanding the Concept, Terminology, and Rules of Equations

In English, we write by using words to form complete thoughts known as sentences. Equations convert written sentences describing business situations into mathematical sentences. When the statement contains an equal sign, =, it is an **equation.** If it does not contain an equal sign, it is simply an **expression.** Equations express business problems in their simplest form. There are no adjectives or words of embellishment, just the facts.

$S + 12$ is an *expression* $S + 12 = 20$ is an *equation*

An equation is a mathematical statement using numbers, letters, and symbols to express a relationship of equality. Equations have an expression on the left side and an expression on the right side, connected by an equal sign.

Letters of the alphabet are used to represent unknown quantities in equations and are called **variables.** In the equation above, S is the variable, or the **unknown.** The 12 and the 20 are the **constants,** or **knowns.** Variables and constants are also known as the **terms** of the equation. The plus sign and the equal sign separate the terms and describe the relationship between them.

To **solve an equation** means to find the numerical value of the unknown. From our equation $S + 12 = 20$, what value of S would make the equation true? Is it 6? No, 6 plus 12 is 18, and 18 does not equal 20. Is it 10? No, 10 plus 12 is 22, and 22 does not equal 20. How about 8? Yes, 8 plus 12 does equal 20.

$$S + 12 = 20$$
$$8 + 12 = 20$$
$$20 = 20$$

By substituting 8 for the variable, *S,* we have found the value of the unknown that satisfies the equation and makes it true: 20 equals 20. The numerical value of the variable that makes the equation true, in this case, 8, is known as the **solution,** or **root,** of the equation.

Today, managers must have the ability to analyze the facts of a business problem and devise custom-made formulas to solve them.

5-2 Solving Equations for the Unknown and Proving the Solution

In solving equations, we use the same basic operations we used in arithmetic: addition, subtraction, multiplication, and division. The meanings of the signs $+$, $-$, $\times$, and $\div$ are still the same. Equations have a few new designations, however, that we must learn.

Multiplication of 5 times *Y,* for example, may be written as

$$5 \times Y$$

$$5 \cdot Y$$

$$5(Y)$$

$$5Y$$

The number 5 in the term $5Y$ is known as the **coefficient** of the term. In cases in which there is no numerical coefficient written, such as *W,* the coefficient is understood to be a 1. Therefore, $1W = W$.

Division in equations is indicated by the fraction bar, just as in Chapter 2. For example, the term 5 divided by *Y* would be written as

$$\frac{5}{Y}$$

It is important to remember that an equation is a statement of *equality.* The left side must always *equal* the right side. To solve equations, we must move or **transpose** all the unknowns to one side and all the knowns to the other side. It is customary for the unknowns to be on the left side and the knowns to be on the right side, such as $X = 7$.

Transposing involves the use of inverse or opposite operations. To transpose a term in an equation, (a) note the operation indicated and (b) apply the *opposite* operation to both sides of the equation, as follows:

Operation Indicated		Opposite Operation
Addition	→	Subtraction
Subtraction	→	Addition
Multiplication	→	Division
Division	→	Multiplication

solution, or root
The numerical value of the unknown that makes the equation true. In the equation $X + 7 = 10$, for example, 3 is the solution, because $3 + 7 = 10$.

coefficient
A number or quantity placed before another quantity, indicating multiplication. For example, 4 is the coefficient in the expression 4*C.* This indicates 4 multiplied by *C.*

transpose
To bring a term from one side of an equation to the other, with corresponding change of sign.

STEPS FOR SOLVING EQUATIONS AND PROVING THE SOLUTION:

Step 1. Transpose all the unknowns to the left side of the equation and all the knowns to the right side of the equation.

Rule 1–To solve equations with more than one operation, perform the addition and subtraction first, then the multiplication and division.

Rule 2–Parentheses, if any, must be cleared before any other operations are performed. To clear parentheses, multiply the coefficient by each term inside the parentheses.

$$2(4X + 7) = 2(4X) + 2(7) = 8X + 14$$

Step 2. Prove the solution by substituting your answer for the letter or letters in the original equation. If the left and right sides are *equal,* the equation is true, and your answer is correct.

EXAMPLE

Solve the equation $X + 4 = 15$ and prove the solution.

SOLUTION STRATEGY

The equation $X + 4 = 15$ indicates addition (+4). To solve for *X*, apply the opposite operation, subtraction. Subtract 4 from each side.

$$\begin{array}{rcr} X + 4 & = & 15 \\ -\ 4 & & -\ 4 \\ \hline X \quad & = & 11 \end{array}$$

$$\underline{\underline{X = 11}}$$

Proof: The solution can easily be proven by substituting our answer (11) for the letter or letters in the original equation. If the left and right sides are equal, the equation is true and the solution is correct.

$$X + 4 = 15$$

$$\boxed{11} + 4 = 15$$

$$\underline{\underline{15 = 15}}$$

Everybody's Business

Learning Tip

Remember, an equation is a statement of "equality." The left side must always equal the right side. The word *equation,* in fact, is derived from the word *equal.*

Real-World Connection

The equal sign, two parallel lines (=), was invented in the sixteenth century by Robert Recorde. He stated, "Nothing can be more equal than parallel lines!"

Other related mathematical symbols are:

- $\approx$ is approximately equal to
- $\neq$ is not equal to
- $\geq$ is greater than or equal to
- $\leq$ is less than or equal to

EXAMPLE

Solve the equation $H - 20 = 44$ and prove the solution.

SOLUTION STRATEGY

The equation $H - 20 = 44$ indicates subtraction (−20). To solve for *H*, apply the opposite operation, addition. Add 20 to each side of the equation.

$$\begin{array}{rcr} H - 20 & = & 44 \\ +\ 20 & & +\ 20 \\ \hline H \quad & = & 64 \end{array}$$

$$\underline{\underline{H = 64}}$$

Proof: Substitute 64 for *H*:

$$H - 20 = 44$$

$$\boxed{64} - 20 = 44$$

$$\underline{\underline{44 = 44}}$$

TRY-IT | EXERCISES

Solve the following equations for the unknown and prove your solutions:

1. $W + 10 = 25$ **2.** $A - 8 = 40$ **3.** $Q + 30 = 100$ **4.** $L - 3 = 7$

Check your answers with the solutions on pages 163–164.

EXAMPLE

Solve the equation $9T = 36$ and prove the solution.

SOLUTION STRATEGY

The equation $9T = 36$ indicates multiplication. $9T$ means 9 times T. To solve for T, apply the opposite operation. Divide both sides of the equation by 9.

$$9T = 36$$

$$\frac{\cancel{9}T}{\cancel{9}} = \frac{36}{9}$$

$$\underline{\underline{T = 4}}$$

Proof:

$$9T = 36$$

$$9(4) = 36$$

$$\underline{\underline{36 = 36}}$$

EXAMPLE

Solve the equation $\frac{M}{5} = 4$ and prove the solution.

SOLUTION STRATEGY

The equation $\frac{M}{5} = 4$ indicates division. To solve for M, do the opposite operation. Multiply both sides of the equation by 5.

$$(\cancel{5})\frac{M}{\cancel{5}} = 4(5)$$

$$\underline{\underline{M = 20}}$$

Proof:

$$\frac{M}{5} = 4$$

$$\frac{20}{5} = 4$$

$$\underline{\underline{4 = 4}}$$

TRY-IT EXERCISES

Solve the following equations for the unknown and prove your solutions:

5. $15L = 75$ 5

6. $\frac{Z}{8} = 2$ 16

7. $16F = 80$ 5

8. $\frac{C}{9} = 9$ 81

Check your answers with the solutions on page 164.

MULTIPLE OPERATIONS

Frequently, more than one operation is required to solve an equation. When this occurs, the "order" in which the calculations are performed becomes important.

EXAMPLE

Solve the equation $7R - 5 = 51$ and prove the solution.

SOLUTION STRATEGY

The equation $7R - 5 = 51$ indicates subtraction and multiplication. Following the rule for multiple operations, begin by adding 5 to each side of the equation.

$$\begin{array}{rcr} 7R - 5 & = & 51 \\ +5 & & +5 \\ \hline 7R & = & 56 \end{array}$$

$$7R = 56$$

Next, divide both sides of the equation by 7.

$$\frac{\not{7}R}{\not{7}} = \frac{56}{7}$$

$$\underline{\underline{R = 8}}$$

Proof:

$$7R - 5 = 51$$

$$7(8) - 5 = 51$$

$$56 - 5 = 51$$

$$\underline{\underline{51 = 51}}$$

EXAMPLE

Solve the equation $\frac{x}{2} + 20 = 34$ and prove the solution.

SOLUTION STRATEGY

The equation $\frac{x}{2} + 20 = 34$ indicates addition and division. Following the rule for multiple operations, begin by subtracting 20 from each side.

$$\begin{array}{rcr} \frac{X}{2} + 20 & = & 34 \\ -20 & & -20 \\ \hline \frac{X}{2} & = & 14 \end{array}$$

$$\frac{X}{2} = 14$$

Next, multiply each side by 2.

$$(\not{2})\frac{X}{\not{2}} = 14(2)$$

$$\underline{\underline{X = 28}}$$

Proof:

$$\frac{X}{2} + 20 = 34$$

$$\frac{28}{2} + 20 = 34$$

$$14 + 20 = 34$$

$$\underline{\underline{34 = 34}}$$

TRY-IT | EXERCISES

Solve the following equations for the unknown and prove the solutions:

9. $12N + 14 = 50$

10. $3W - 4 = 26$

11. $\frac{F}{3} - 6 = 2$

12. $\frac{Z}{5} + 15 = 24$

Check your answers with the solutions on page 164.

Parentheses

Sometimes, parentheses are used in equations. They contain a number just outside the left-hand parentheses known as the coefficient and two or more terms inside the parentheses. An example is $5(3X + 6)$.

> **PARENTHESES RULE**
>
> In solving equations, parentheses must be removed before any other operations are performed. To remove parentheses, multiply the coefficient by each term inside the parentheses.

To apply this rule to the example above,

$$5(3X + 6)$$

$$5(3X) + 5(6)$$

$$15X + 30$$

In equations, when terms with *like* signs are multiplied, the result is a positive and contains a plus sign. For example, $+5(+4) = +20$; and $-5(-4) = +20$. When terms with *unlike* signs are multiplied, the result is a negative and contains a minus sign. For example, $+5(-4) = -20$.

EXAMPLE

Solve the equation $8(2K - 4) = 48$ and prove the solution.

SOLUTION STRATEGY

Because this equation contains parentheses, we must begin there. Following the rule for removing parentheses, multiply the coefficient, 8, by each term inside the parentheses.

$$8(2K - 4) = 48$$

$$8(2K) - 8(4) = 48$$

$$16K - 32 = 48$$

Now solve the equation as before, by isolating the unknown, *K,* on the left side of the equal sign. Remember, add and subtract first, then multiply and divide.

$$\begin{array}{rcr} 16K - 32 & = & 48 \\ +\ 32 & & +32 \\ \hline 16K \qquad & = & 80 \end{array}$$

$$16K = 80$$

$$\frac{\cancel{16}K}{\cancel{16}} = \frac{80}{16}$$

$$\underline{\underline{K = 5}}$$

Proof:

$$8(2K - 4) = 48$$

$$8(2\{5\} - 4) = 48$$

$$8(10 - 4) = 48$$

$$8(6) = 48$$

$$\underline{\underline{48 = 48}}$$

TRY-IT | EXERCISES

Solve the following equations for the unknown and prove the solutions:

13. $4(5G + 6) = 64$

14. $6(3H - 5) = 42$

Check your answers with the solutions on page 164.

When equations contain unknowns that appear two or more times, they must be combined.

STEPS FOR COMBINING MULTIPLE UNKNOWNS:

Step 1. To combine unknowns, they must be on the same side of the equation. If they are not, move them all to the same side.

$$5X = 12 + 2X$$
$$5X - 2X = 12$$

Step 2. Once the unknowns are on the same side of the equation, add or subtract their coefficients as indicated:

$$5X - 2X = 12$$
$$3X = 12$$

EXAMPLE

Solve the equation $4C + 7 - C = 25 - 6C$ and prove the solution.

SOLUTION STRATEGY

To solve this equation, we begin by combining the two terms on the left side that contain C: $4C - C = 3C$. This leaves

$$3C + 7 = 25 - 6C$$

Next move the $-6C$ to the left side by adding $+6C$ to both sides of the equation.

$$\begin{array}{rcl} 3C + 7 &=& 25 - 6C \\ +6C & & +6C \\ \hline 9C + 7 &=& 25 \end{array}$$

Now that all the terms containing the unknown, C, have been combined, we can solve the equation.

$$\begin{array}{rcl} 9C + 7 &=& 25 \\ -7 & & -7 \\ \hline 9C &=& 18 \end{array}$$

$$\frac{\not{9}C}{\not{9}} = \frac{18}{9}$$

$$\underline{\underline{C = 2}}$$

Proof:

$$4C + 7 - C = 25 - 6C$$
$$4(2) + 7 - 2 = 25 - 6(2)$$
$$8 + 7 - 2 = 25 - 12$$
$$\underline{\underline{13 = 13}}$$

TRY-IT | EXERCISES

Solve the following equations for the unknown and prove the solutions:

15. $X + 3 = 18 - 4X$

16. $9S + 8 - S = 2(2S + 8)$

Check your answers with the solutions on page 164.

> **Everybody's Business**
>
> **Learning Tip**
>
> When a written statement has no action word (verb), it is an expression. When there is a verb, such as "is," it represents an equal sign, and the statement is an equation.

5-3 Writing Expressions and Equations from Written Statements

Expressions and equations are created from written statements by identifying the unknowns and the knowns and determining the mathematical relationship between them. The variables are assigned letters of the alphabet. The letter X is commonly used to represent the unknown. The relationship between the knowns and the unknowns involves either addition, subtraction, multiplication, or division, or a combination of two or more of these.

STEPS FOR WRITING EXPRESSIONS AND EQUATIONS:

Step 1. Read the written statement carefully.

Step 2. Using the following chart, identify and underline the key words and phrases.

Step 3. Convert the words to numbers and mathematical symbols.

KEY WORDS AND PHRASES FOR CREATING EQUATIONS

Equal Sign: is, are, was, equals, gives, giving, leaves, leaving, makes, denotes

Addition: and, added to, totals, the sum of, plus, more than, larger than, increased by, greater than, exceeds

Subtraction: less, less than, smaller than, minus, difference between, decreased by, reduced by

Multiplication: of, times, product of, multiplied by, twice, double, triple, at, @

Division: divide, divided by, the average of, divided into, the quotient of, the ratio of

Parentheses: times the quantity of

EXAMPLES

For the following statements, underline the key words and translate into *expressions:*

a. A number increased by 18

b. 19 times W

c. 12 less than S

d. $\frac{2}{3}$ of Y

e. 9 more than 2 times R

f. 4 times the quantity of X and 8

SOLUTION STRATEGY

Key Words	Expression
a. A number increased by 18	$N + 18$
b. 19 times W	$19W$
c. 12 less than S	$S - 12$
d. $\frac{2}{3}$ of Y	$\frac{2}{3}Y$
e. 9 more than 2 times R	$2R + 9$
f. 4 times the quantity of X and 8	$4(X + 8)$

TRY-IT | EXERCISES

For the following statements, underline the key words and translate into *expressions:*

17. The sum of twice E and 9

18. 6 times N divided by Z

6n ÷ Z

19. 8 less than half of F

8 − F/2

20. $45.75 more than the product of X and Y

$45.75 + XY

21. The difference of Q and 44

Q − 44

22. R times A times B

RAB

Check your answers with the solutions on page 164.

EXAMPLES

For the following statements, underline the key words and translate into *equations:*

a. A number decreased by 14 is 23

b. 8 less than $3D$ leaves 19

c. A number totals 4 times the quantity of V and N

d. The cost of X lbs at $3 per lb is $12

e. Cost is the product of price and quantity

f. The sum of liabilities and capital is assets

SOLUTION STRATEGY

Key Words	Equations
a. A number decreased by 14 is 23	$X - 14 = 23$
b. 8 less than $3D$ leaves 19	$3D - 8 = 19$
c. A number totals 4 times the quantity of V and N	$X = 4(V + N)$
d. The cost of X lbs at $3 per lb is $12	$3X = 12$
e. Cost is the product of price and quantity	$C = PQ$
f. The sum of liabilities and capital is assets	$L + C = A$

TRY-IT | EXERCISES

For the following statements, underline the key words and translate into *equations:*

23. What number increased by 32 yields 125?

24. 21 less than twice C gives 9.

21 − 2C = 9

25. 5 more than 6 times a number, plus 3 times that number, is 25.

5 + 6n

26. The cost of G gallons at \$1.33 per gallon equals \$34.40.

1.33g = 34.40

27. The area of a rectangle is the length times the width.

A = l x w

28. (Challenge) What number less 12 is the average of A, B, and C?

Check your answers with the solutions on page 165.

REVIEW EXERCISES | CHAPTER 5—SECTION I

Solve the following equations for the unknown and prove your solutions:

1. $B + 11 = 24$

2. $C - 16 = 5$

3. $S + 35 = 125$

4. $M - 58 = 12$

5. $21K = 63$

6. $\frac{Z}{3} = 45$

7. $50Y = 375$

8. $\frac{L}{5} = 8$

9. $6G + 5 = 29$

10. $\frac{D}{3} - 5 = 15$

11. $25A - 11 = 64$

12. $\frac{R}{5} + 33 = 84$

13. $3(4X + 5) = 63$

14. $C + 5 = 26 - 2C$

15. $12(2D - 4) = 72$

16. $14V + 5 - 5V = 4(V + 5)$

17. $Q + 20 = 3(9 - 2Q)$

For the following statements, underline the key words and translate into *expressions:*

18. 5 times G divided by R

19. The sum of 5 times F and 33

20. 6 less than one-fourth of C

21. 550 more than the product of H and P

22. T times B times 9

23. The difference of $8Y$ and 128

24. 7 times the quantity of X and 7

25. 40 more than $\frac{3}{4}$ of B

For the following statements, underline the key words and translate into *equations:*

26. A number increased by 24 is 35.

27. A number totals 5 times B and C.

28. 12 less than $4G$ leaves 33.

29. The cost of R at \$5.75 each is \$28.75.

30. Cost per person is the total cost divided by the number of persons.

31. 4 more than 5 times a number, plus 2 times that number, is that number increased by 40.

BUSINESS DECISION

Grouping Symbols

32. In algebra, grouping symbols are used to arrange numbers, variables, and operations. In this chapter you learned to use the grouping symbols known as parentheses ( ). In addition to parentheses, other symbols used in algebra for grouping are brackets [ ] and braces { }. When solving equations with multiple grouping symbols, always start with the innermost symbols, and work to the outside.

In business, you may encounter situations that require you to set up equations with more than just parentheses. For practice, solve the following equation.

$$X = 6(2 + [3\{9 - 3\} + \{8 + 1\} - 4])$$

SECTION II

USING EQUATIONS TO SOLVE BUSINESS-RELATED WORD PROBLEMS

Everybody's Business

Learning Tip

This is the real "bottom line" of equations: the ability to analyze a business situation, convert it to an equation, and solve it. Proficiency will come with practice.

In business, most of the math encountered is in the form of business-situation word problems. Variables such as profits, production units, inventory, employees, money, customers, and interest rates are constantly interacting mathematically. Your boss will not ask you simply to add, subtract, multiply, or divide but will ask for information requiring you to perform these functions in a business context. Business students must be able to analyze a business situation requiring math, set up the situation in a mathematical expression or equation, and work it out to a correct solution.

5-4 Setting Up and Solving Business-Related Word Problems by Using Equations

In Section I of this chapter we learned to create and solve equations from written statements. Let's see how to apply these skills in business situations. You will learn a logical procedure for setting up and solving business-related word problems. Some problems have more than one way to arrive at an answer. The key, once again, is not to be intimidated. Learning to solve word problems requires practice, and the more you do it, the easier it will become and the more comfortable you will feel with it.

SHOE

STEPS FOR SETTING UP AND SOLVING WORD PROBLEMS:

Step 1. **Understand the situation.** If the problem is written, read it carefully, perhaps a few times. If the problem is verbal, write down the facts of the situation.

Step 2. **Take inventory.** Identify all the parts of the situation. These parts can be any variables, such as dollars, people, boxes, tons, trucks, anything! Separate them into knowns and unknowns.

Step 3. **Make a plan—create an equation.** The object is to solve for the unknown. Ask yourself what math relationship exists between the knowns and the unknowns. Use the chart of key words and phrases on page 144 to help you write the equation.

Step 4. **Work out the plan—solve the equation.** Remember, to solve an equation you must move the unknowns to one side of the equal sign and the knowns to the other.

Step 5. **Check your solution.** Does your answer make sense? Is it exactly correct? It is a good idea to estimate an approximate answer by using rounded numbers. This will let you know if your answer is in the correct range. If it is not, either the equation is set up incorrectly or the solution is wrong. If this occurs, you must go back and start again.

Now let's see how this works. The following examples illustrate several common business situations and their solutions.

EXAMPLE

On Tuesday, the Jiffy Car Wash took in \$360 less in wash business than in wax business. If the total sales for the day were \$920, what were the sales for each service?

SOLUTION STRATEGY

Reasoning: Wax sales plus wash sales equal the total sales, \$920.

$$\text{Let } X = \$ \text{ amount of wax sales}$$

$$\text{Let } X - 360 = \$ \text{ amount of wash sales}$$

$$\begin{aligned} X + X - 360 &= 920 \\ +360 &\quad +360 \\ X + X &= 1{,}280 \end{aligned}$$

$$2X = 1{,}280$$

$$\frac{2X}{2} = \frac{1{,}280}{2}$$

$$X = 640 \qquad \text{wax sales} = \$640$$

$$X - 360 = 640 - 360 = 280 \qquad \text{wash sales} = \$280$$

Proof:

$$X + X - 360 = 920$$

$$640 + 640 - 360 = 920$$

$$920 = 920$$

Everybody's Business

Learning Tip

Frequently, the left side of an equation represents the "interaction" of the variables, and the right side shows the "result" of that interaction.

In this example, the left side is the interaction (in this case, addition) of the wax and wash sales. The right side is the result, or total.

Interaction		Result
$X + X - 360$	=	920

TRY-IT | EXERCISE

29. José and Bob are salesmen for Superior Electronics. Last week José sold 12 fewer DVD players than Bob. Together they sold 44. How many did each sell?

Check your answer with the solution on page 165.

EXAMPLE

Consolidated Equipment, Inc., spends $\frac{1}{4}$ of total revenue on employee payroll expenses. If last week's payroll amounted to \$5,000, what was the revenue for the week?

SOLUTION STRATEGY

Reasoning: $\frac{1}{4}$ of revenue is the week's payroll, \$5,000.

Let R = revenue for the week

$$\frac{1}{4}R = 5{,}000$$

$$(\cancel{4})\frac{1}{\cancel{4}}R = 5{,}000(4)$$

$$R = 20{,}000 \qquad \underline{\underline{\text{Revenue for the week} = \$20{,}000}}$$

Proof:

$$\frac{1}{4}R = 5{,}000$$

$$\frac{1}{4}(20{,}000) = 5{,}000$$

$$\underline{\underline{5{,}000 = 5{,}000}}$$

TRY-IT | EXERCISE

30. One-third of the checking accounts at the Hemisphere National Bank earn interest. If 2,500 accounts are this type, how many total checking accounts does the bank have?

Check your answer with the solution on page 165.

EXAMPLE

Micron Systems, Inc., has 25 shareholders. If management decides to split the \$80,000 net profit equally among the shareholders, how much will each receive?

SOLUTION STRATEGY

Reasoning: Profit per shareholder is the net profit, \$80,000, divided by the number of shareholders.

Let P = Profit per shareholder

$$P = \frac{80{,}000}{25}$$

$$P = 3{,}200 \qquad \text{Profit per shareholder} = \$3{,}200$$

Proof:

$$P = \frac{80{,}000}{25}$$

$$3{,}200 = \frac{80{,}000}{25}$$

$$3{,}200 = 3{,}200$$

TRY-IT | EXERCISE

31. American Trade and Export, Inc., fills an order for 58 cartons of merchandise weighing a total of 7,482 pounds. What is the weight per carton?

Check your answer with the solution on page 165.

EXAMPLE

HiFi Associates sold 144 CD players last week. If five times as many single CD models sold as carousel models, how many of each were sold?

SOLUTION STRATEGY

Reasoning: Carousel models plus single CD models equals total CD players sold, 144.

Let X = carousel models

Let $5X$ = single CD models

$$X + 5X = 144$$

$$6X = 144$$

$$\frac{\cancel{6}X}{\cancel{6}} = \frac{144}{6}$$

$$X = 24 \qquad \text{carousel models sold} = 24$$

$$5X = 5(24) = 120 \qquad \text{single CD models sold} = 120$$

Proof:

$$X + 5X = 144$$

$$24 + 5(24) = 144$$

$$24 + 120 = 144$$

$$144 = 144$$

TRY-IT | EXERCISE

32. Super Discount Department Store sells three times as much in soft goods, such as clothing and linens, as it sells in hard goods, such as furniture and appliances. If total store sales on Saturday were \$180,000, how much of each category was sold?

Check your answer with the solution on page 166.

EXAMPLE

Yesterday, the Bay City recycling van picked up a total of 4,500 pounds of material. If newspaper weighed three times as much as aluminum cans and aluminum weighed twice as much as glass, what was the weight of each material?

SOLUTION STRATEGY

Reasoning: Glass plus aluminum plus newspaper amounts to the total material, 4,500 pounds.

Hint: Let the least (smallest) element equal X. That way the larger ones will be multiples of X. By doing this, you avoid having fractions in your equation.

Let X = pounds of glass

Let $2X$ = pounds of aluminum

Let $3(2X)$ = pounds of newspaper

$$X + 2X + 3(2X) = 4{,}500$$

$$X + 2X + 6X = 4{,}500$$

$$9X = 4{,}500$$

$$\frac{\cancel{9}X}{\cancel{9}} = \frac{4{,}500}{9}$$

$X = 500$ glass collected = 500 pounds

$2X = 2(500) = 1{,}000$ aluminum collected = 1,000 pounds

$3(2X) = 3(1{,}000) = 3{,}000$ newspaper collected = 3,000 pounds

Proof:

$$X + 2X + 3(2X) = 4{,}500$$

$$500 + 2(500) + 3(2\{500\}) = 4{,}500$$

$$500 + 1{,}000 + 3{,}000 = 4{,}500$$

$$4{,}500 = 4{,}500$$

TRY-IT | EXERCISE

33. Last week El Dorado Furniture sold 520 items. They sold twice as many sofas as chairs and four times as many chairs as tables. How many were sold of each product?

Check your answer with the solution on page 166.

EXAMPLE

Chicken Delight sells whole chicken dinners for \$12.00 and half chicken dinners for \$8.00. Yesterday they sold a total of 400 dinners and took in \$4,200. How many of each size dinner were sold? What were the dollar sales of each size dinner?

SOLUTION STRATEGY

Reasoning: The sum of the price multiplied by the quantity of each item is total sales, \$4,200.

Hint: This type of problem requires that we multiply the price of each item by the quantity. We know that a total of 400 dinners were sold, therefore,

$$\text{Let } X = \text{quantity of whole chicken dinners}$$

$$\text{Let } 400 - X = \text{quantity of half chicken dinners}$$

Note: By letting X equal the more expensive item, we avoid dealing with negative numbers.

$$\text{Price times quantity of whole chicken dinners} = \$12X$$

$$\text{Price times quantity of half chicken dinners} = \$8(400 - X)$$

$$\begin{aligned} 12X + 8(400 - X) &= 4{,}200 \\ 12X + 3{,}200 - 8X &= 4{,}200 \\ 4X + 3{,}200 &= 4{,}200 \\ -3{,}200 &\quad -3{,}200 \\ 4X \qquad &= 1{,}000 \end{aligned}$$

$$\frac{\not{4}X}{\not{4}} = \frac{1{,}000}{4}$$

$X = 250$ — Quantity of whole chicken dinners = 250

$400 - X = 400 - 250 = 150$ — Quantity of half chicken dinners = 150

Proof:

$$\begin{aligned} 12X + 8(400 - X) &= 4{,}200 \\ 12(250) + 8(400 - 250) &= 4{,}200 \\ 3{,}000 + 8(150) &= 4{,}200 \\ 3{,}000 + 1{,}200 &= 4{,}200 \\ 4{,}200 &= 4{,}200 \end{aligned}$$

Now that we have calculated the quantity sold of each size dinner, we can find the dollar sales:

Reasoning: Dollar sales are the price per dinner multiplied by the quantity sold.

Let S = dollar sales

Whole chicken dinners: $S = \$12(250) = \underline{\$3{,}000 \text{ in sales}}$

Half chicken dinners: $S = \$8(150) = \underline{\$1{,}200 \text{ in sales}}$

TRY-IT | EXERCISE

34. Auto Zone sells a regular car battery for $70 and a heavy-duty model for $110. If they sold 40 batteries yesterday for a total of $3,400, how many of each type battery were sold? What were the dollar sales of each type?

Check your answer with the solution on page 166.

5-5 Understanding and Solving Ratio and Proportion Problems

ratio
A fraction that describes a comparison of two numbers or quantities. For example, five cats for every three dogs would be a ratio of 5 to 3, written as 5 : 3.

Many business problems and situations are expressed as ratios. A **ratio** is a fraction that describes a comparison of two numbers or quantities. In business, numbers often take on much more meaning when compared with other numbers in the form of a ratio.

For example, a factory has an output of 40 units per hour. Is this good or bad? If we also know that the industry average is 20 units per hour, we can set up a ratio of our factory, 40, compared with the industry average, 20.

$$\frac{\text{Factory}}{\text{Industry}} = \frac{40}{20} = 40 : 20 \quad \text{Expressed verbally, we say, "40 to 20"}$$

Because ratios are fractions, we can reduce our fraction and state that our factory output is 2 to 1 over the industry average. If the industry average changed to 40, the ratio would be $\frac{40}{40}$, or 1 to 1. Had the industry average been 80, the ratio would be $\frac{40}{80}$, or 1 to 2.

Ratios can compare anything: money, weights, measures, output, or individuals. The units do not have to be the same. If we can buy 9 ounces of shampoo for $2.00, this is actually a ratio of ounces to dollars, or 9 : 2.

proportion
A statement showing that two ratios are equal. For example, 9 is to 3 as 3 is to 1, written 9 : 3 = 3 : 1.

A **proportion** is a statement showing that two ratios are equal. Proportions are equations, with "as" being the equal sign. For example, we could say, "9 is to 2 as 18 is to 4."

$$\frac{9}{2} = \frac{18}{4} \quad \text{or} \quad 9 : 2 = 18 : 4$$

This means that if we can buy 9 ounces for $2.00, we can buy 18 ounces for $4.00. Proportions with three knowns and one unknown become a very useful business tool. For example, if we can buy 9 ounces for $2.00, how many ounces can we buy for $7.00? This proportion, 9 is to 2 as X is to 7, would be written as

$$\frac{9 \text{ ounces}}{\$2.00} = \frac{X \text{ ounces}}{\$7.00} \quad \text{or} \quad 9 : 2 = X : 7$$

STEPS FOR SOLVING PROPORTION PROBLEMS USING CROSS-MULTIPLICATION:

Step 1. Let X represent the unknown quantity.

Step 2. Set up the equation with one ratio (expressed as a fraction) on each side of the equal sign.

Step 3. Multiply the numerator of the first ratio by the denominator of the second and place the product to the left of the equal sign.

Step 4. Multiply the denominator of the first ratio by the numerator of the second and place the product to the right of the equal sign.

Step 5. Solve the equation for X.

Everybody's Business

Learning Tip

Remember, when setting up a proportion, the variables of both ratios must be in the same "order"—numerator to denominator. For example:

$$\frac{\text{dollars}}{\text{donuts}} = \frac{\text{dollars}}{\text{donuts}}$$

EXAMPLE

If a car can travel 350 miles on 16 gallons of fuel, how many gallons would be required to complete a trip of 875 miles?

SOLUTION STRATEGY

This business situation can be solved by using a proportion. The equation reads "350 miles is to 16 gallons as 875 miles is to X gallons."

$$\frac{350}{16} = \frac{875}{X}$$

Using cross-multiplication to solve the equation:

$$350X = 16(875)$$

$$350X = 14{,}000$$

$X = 40$ 40 gallons of fuel are required for the car to travel 875 miles.

TRY-IT EXERCISE

35. If Wilbur earns \$87.50 for 7 hours of work, how much can he expect to earn in a 35-hour week?

Check your answer with the solution on page 167.

REVIEW EXERCISES | CHAPTER 5—SECTION II

Set up and solve equations for the following business situations:

1. Kathy and Karen work in a boutique. During a sale, Kathy sold eight less dresses than Karen. If together they sold 86 dresses, how many did each sell?

2. One-fifth of the employees of Consolidated Widget Corporation work in the Midwest region. If the company employs 252 workers in that region, what is the total number of employees working for Consolidated?

3. Blue Ridge Mountain Water, Inc., received an order for 456 gallon jugs of water. If Blue Ridge packs the gallons in cartons containing four jugs each, how many cartons will be required to fill the order?

4. Sylvia's Bookstore makes four times as much money in paperback books as in hardcover books. If last month's sales totaled $124,300, how much was sold of each type book?

5. At Bertram Industries, a new production machine can make five more than twice the production per hour of the old machine. If the new machine can produce 41 units per hour, how many does the old machine produce?

6. Toy World, a retail toy chain, placed a seasonal order for stuffed animals from a distributor. Large animals cost $20.00 and small ones cost $14.00.

   a. If the total cost of the order was $7,320 for 450 pieces, how many of each size were ordered?

   b. What was the dollar amount of each size ordered?

7. Robbins and Bryant invested $89,600 in a business. If Bryant invested three times as much as Robbins, how much did each invest?

8. An estate is to be distributed among a wife, three children, and two grandchildren. The children will each receive three times as much as each grandchild, and the wife will receive four times as much as each child. If the estate amounted to $115,000, how much will each person receive?

9. Yesterday, Town and Country Fashions had seven less than three-fourths of its sales transactions paid for by charge cards. If 209 transactions were charged, how many total transactions took place?

10. The deluxe model of a KitchenAid oven costs $46 more than twice the cost of the standard model. If together they cost $1,234, what is the cost of each model?

11. PC Solutions sells standard keyboards for $84.00 and extended keyboards for $105.00. Last week the store sold three times as many standard keyboards as extended. If total keyboard sales were $4,998, how many of each type were sold?

12. The Michigan plant of DynoTech Industries is four times as old as the Ohio plant. If the difference in the ages of the two plants is 9 years, what is the age of each?

13. The Cookie Jar sells oatmeal cookies for $1.30 per pound and peanut butter cookies for $1.60 per pound.

a. If total cookie sales last week amounted to 530 pounds, valued at $755, how many pounds of each type of cookie were sold?

b. What dollar amount of each type was sold?

14. One-ninth of Superior Plastics' sales are made in New England. If New England sales amount to $600,000, what are the total sales of the company?

2 15. If a 48-piece set of stainless steel flatware costs $124.80 at Crate and Barrel, what is the cost per piece?

16. What is the total cost to ship an order weighing 1,860 pounds, if the breakdown is $.04 per pound for packing, $.02 per pound for insurance, $.13 per pound for transportation, and $132.40 for the crate?

Use ratio and proportion to solve the following business situations:

1 17. If the interest on a $4,600 loan is $370, what would be the interest on a loan of $9,660?

3 18. At Tropical Fruit Distributors, Inc., the ratio of fruits to vegetables sold is 5 to 3. If 1,848 pounds of vegetables are sold, how many pounds of fruit are sold?

19. If auto insurance costs $6.52 per $1,000 of coverage, what is the cost to insure a car valued at $17,500?

20. A recipe for turkey stuffing calls for three eggs for every $12\frac{1}{2}$ ounces of corn bread. If a dinner party requires $87\frac{1}{2}$ ounces of corn bread for stuffing, how many eggs should be used?

21. An architect uses a scale of $\frac{3}{4}$ inch to represent 1 foot on a blueprint for a building. If the east wall of the building is 36 feet long, how long will the line be on the blueprint?

22. If a car goes 48 miles per hour at 3,300 rpm (revolutions per minute) of the engine, how fast will it go at 4,000 rpm in the same gear?

23. KwikPrint has a press that can print 5,800 brochures per hour. How many can be printed during a $3\frac{1}{4}$-hour run?

24. A local airport handles passenger to cargo traffic in a ratio of 8 to 5. If 45 cargo planes landed yesterday, how many passenger flights came in?

25. Eighty ounces of Happy Lawn fertilizer covers 1,250 square feet of lawn.

a. How many ounces would be required to cover a 4,000-square-foot lawn?

b. If Happy Lawn costs $1.19 for a 32-ounce bag, what is the total cost to fertilize the lawn?

BUSINESS DECISION

The Aspect Ratio

26. Wide-screen televisions have screens that are shaped like those in a movie theater. They are known as a 16 : 9 aspect ratio screen. This means that the ratio of the width to the height is in the ratio of 16 to 9. In most cases, the cabinet dimensions are the same ratio. More conventional TVs have screens with an aspect ratio of 4 : 3, width to height.

You are a salesperson for Galaxy Electronics, an upscale audio/video equipment store. Customers switching from conventional to wide-screen models often have questions about the size of set that will fit in their wall units or shelves that previously held the conventional 4 : 3 sets.

a. James Yamamoto, one of your customers, has a conventional TV that is 36 inches wide. What is the height of that TV?

b. If James purchases a wide-screen TV with a cabinet 36 inches wide, what would be the height of that set? Round to a tenth.

c. As an astute salesperson, you know that wide-screen TV cabinets require less height than conventional models, so you often suggest that there may be room for a larger set in the current space. If the next larger size wide-screen is 26 inches high, how much shelf space, in width, would be required? Round to a tenth.

d. As it turns out, there was room for the larger set, and you made the sale! Your commission amounts to $\frac{1}{25}$ of your sales revenue. If the small set is priced at \$3,500 and the larger one is \$4,800, how much extra commission did you earn by suggesting the larger size?

✦ SUMMARY CHART ✦
SECTION I: Solving Basic Equations

Topic	P/O, Page	Important Concepts	Illustrative Examples
Solving Equations by Using Inverse or Opposite Operations	5-2 137	To solve equations we must move or transpose all the unknowns to one side and isolate all the knowns on the other side. It is customary for the unknowns to be on the left side and the knowns to be on the right side, such as $X = 33$. To solve for the unknown value, apply an inverse or opposite operation to both sides of the equation. **Operation—Opposite** Addition ⟶ Subtraction Subtraction ⟶ Addition Multiplication ⟶ Division Division ⟶ Multiplication	Solve the equation $R + 7 = 12$ The equation indicates addition; therefore, use the opposite operation: subtract 7 from both sides: $R + 7 = 12$ $\quad - 7 = -7$ $R \quad = 5$ $\quad$ $\underline{\underline{R = 5}}$ Solve the equation $W - 4 = 30$ The equation indicates subtraction; therefore, use the opposite operation: add 4 to both sides: $W - 4 = 30$ $\quad + 4 = +4$ $W \quad = 34$ $\quad$ $\underline{\underline{W = 34}}$ Solve the equation $3G = 18$ The equation indicates multiplication; therefore, use the opposite operation: divide both sides by 3: $\frac{3G}{3} = \frac{18}{3}$ $\quad$ $\underline{\underline{G = 6}}$ Solve the equation $\frac{T}{5} = 9$ The equation indicates division; therefore, use the opposite operation: multiply both sides by 5: $(5)\frac{T}{5} = 9(5)$ $\quad$ $\underline{\underline{T = 45}}$

SECTION I: (continued)

Topic	P/O, Page	Important Concepts	Illustrative Examples
Solving Equations Containing Multiple Operations	5-2 140	Multiple Operation Rule: To solve equations with more than one operation, perform the addition and subtraction first, then do the multiplication and division.	Solve the equation $5X - 4 = 51$ $5X - 4 = 51$ $\underline{+4 \quad +4}$ $5X = 55$ $\frac{5X}{5} = \frac{55}{5}$ $X = 11$
Solving Equations Containing Parentheses	5-2 141	To remove parentheses, multiply the coefficient by each term inside the parentheses. Sign Rules: When like signs are multiplied, the result is positive. For example, $5(5) = 25$, and $-5(-5) = 25$. When unlike signs are multiplied, the result is negative. For example, $5(-5) = -25$.	Solve the equation $3(4S - 5) = 9$ To remove the parentheses, multiply the coefficient, 3, by both terms inside the parentheses: $3(4S - 5) = 9$ $3(4S) - 3(5) = 9$ $12S - 15 = 9$ $12S = 24$ $S = 2$
Solving Equations by Combining Unknowns	5-2 143	To combine unknowns in an equation, add or subtract their coefficients. If the unknowns are on opposite sides of the equal sign, first move them all to one side.	Solve the equation $3B + 5 - B = 7$ $3B + 5 - B = 7$ $2B + 5 = 7$ $2B = 2$ $B = 1$
Writing Expressions and Equations from Written Statements	5-3 144	Expressions and equations are created from written statements by identifying the unknowns and the knowns and determining the mathematical relationship between them. The variables are assigned letters of the alphabet. The relationship between the knowns and the unknowns involve addition, subtraction, multiplication, and division, or a combination of two or more. Key words indicate what relationship exists between the terms (see chart, page 144). If the written statement has a verb, such as "is," the statement is an equation.	A number increased by 44 $X + 44$ 6 more than 3 times U $3U + 6$ 3 times the sum of C and 9 $3(C + 9)$ 7 less than 4 times M leaves 55 $4M - 7 = 55$ 2 less than 5 times a number, plus 9 times that number, is 88 $5X - 2 + 9X = 88$

SECTION II: Using Equations to Solve Business-Related Word Problems

Topic	P/O, Page	Important Concepts	Illustrative Examples
Solving Business-Related Equations	5-4 149	Example 1: Mary and Beth sell furniture at Futura Designs. Last week Mary sold eight less recliner chairs than Beth. Together they sold 30. How many chairs did each sell?	Solution: *Reasoning:* Beth's sales plus Mary's sales equal total sales, 30 Let X = Beth's sales Let $X - 8$ = Mary's sales $X + X - 8 = 30$ $2X - 8 = 30$ $2X = 38$ $X = 19$ chairs = Beth's sales $X - 8 = 11$ chairs = Mary's sales
Solving Business-Related Equations	5-4 150	Example 2: One-fourth of the employees at Atlantic Distributors work in the accounting division. If there are 45 workers in this division, how many people work for Atlantic?	Solution: *Reasoning:* $\frac{1}{4}$ of the total employees are in accounting, 45. Let X = total employees Let $\frac{1}{4}X$ = accounting employees $\frac{1}{4}X = 45$ $(4)\frac{1}{4}X = 45(4)$ $X = 180$ = Total employees
Solving Business-Related Equations	5-4 151	Example 3: Longhorn Industries, a small manufacturing company, made a profit of $315,000 last year. If the nine investors decide to evenly split this profit, how much will each receive?	Solution: *Reasoning:* Each investor's share is the total profit divided by the number of investors. Let X = each investor's share $X = \frac{315,000}{9}$ $X = \$35,000$ = Investor's share
Solving Business-Related Equations	5-4 151	Example 4: The Pet Carnival sells four times as much in cat supplies as in fish supplies. If total sales last week were $6,800, how much of each category was sold?	Solution: *Reasoning:* Fish supplies plus cat supplies equals total, $6,800. Let X = fish supplies Let $4X$ = cat supplies $X + 4X = 6,800$ $5X = 6,800$ $X = \$1,360$ = Fish supplies $4X = \$5,440$ = Cat supplies

SECTION II: (continued)

Topic	P/O, Page	Important Concepts	Illustrative Examples
Solving Business-Related Equations	5-4 153	Example 5: The Image, a men's clothing store, sells suits for \$275 and sport coats for \$180. Yesterday they made 20 sales, for a total of \$4,360. a. How many suits and how many sport coats were sold? b. What were the dollar sales of each?	Solution a: *Reasoning:* The sum of the price multiplied by the quantity of each item is the total sales, \$4,360. Let X = suit sales Let $20 - X$ = sport coat sales $275X + 180(20 - X) = 4{,}360$ $275X + 3{,}600 - 180X = 4{,}360$ $95X + 3{,}600 = 4{,}360$ $95X = 760$ $X = 8$ = Number of suits sold $(20 - X) - 12$ = Sport coats sold Solution b: 8 suits × \$275 each = \$2,200 12 coats × \$180 each = \$2,160
Solving Business Problems by Using Ratio and Proportion	5-5 154	A ratio is a fraction that describes a comparison of two numbers or quantities. A proportion is a statement showing that two ratios are equal. Proportions are equations with "as" being the equal sign and "is to" being the division bar. Proportion problems are solved by cross-multiplication: 1. Let X represent the unknown quantity. 2. Set up the equation with one ratio on each side of the equal sign. 3. Multiply the numerator of the first ratio by the denominator of the second and place the product to the left of the equal sign. 4. Multiply the denominator of the first ratio by the numerator of the second and place the product to the right of the equal sign. 5. Solve the equation for X.	Example 1: 12 is to 42 as 6 is to X $\frac{12}{42} = \frac{6}{X}$ $12X = 42(6)$ $12X = 252$ $X = 21$ Example 2: If Larry works 6 hours for \$150.00, how much can he expect to earn in a 42-hour week? $\frac{6}{150} = \frac{42}{X}$ $6X = 150(42)$ $6X = 6{,}300$ $X = \$1{,}050$ = Larry's salary for 42 hours work

TRY-IT EXERCISE | SOLUTIONS

1. $W + 10 = 25$

$$\begin{aligned} W + 10 &= 25 \\ -10 &\quad -10 \\ W &= 15 \\ W &= 15 \end{aligned}$$

Proof:

$$\begin{aligned} W + 10 &= 25 \\ 15 + 10 &= 25 \\ 25 &= 25 \end{aligned}$$

2. $A - 8 = 40$

$$\begin{aligned} A - 8 &= 40 \\ +8 &\quad +8 \\ A &= 48 \\ A &= 48 \end{aligned}$$

Proof:

$$\begin{aligned} A - 8 &= 40 \\ 48 - 8 &= 40 \\ 40 &= 40 \end{aligned}$$

3. $Q + 30 = 100$

$$\begin{aligned} Q + 30 &= 100 \\ -30 &\quad -30 \\ Q &= 70 \\ Q &= 70 \end{aligned}$$

Proof:

$$\begin{aligned} Q + 30 &= 100 \\ 70 + 30 &= 100 \\ 100 &= 100 \end{aligned}$$

4.
$$\begin{aligned} L - 3 &= 7 \\ L - 3 &= 7 \\ +3 \quad &\ \ +3 \\ L \quad &= 10 \\ L &= 10 \end{aligned}$$

Proof:
$$\begin{aligned} L - 3 &= 7 \\ 10 - 3 &= 7 \\ 7 &= 7 \end{aligned}$$

5.
$$\begin{aligned} 15L &= 75 \\ \frac{15L}{15} &= \frac{75}{15} \\ L &= 5 \end{aligned}$$

Proof:
$$\begin{aligned} 15L &= 75 \\ 15(5) &= 75 \\ 75 &= 75 \end{aligned}$$

6.
$$\begin{aligned} \frac{Z}{8} &= 2 \\ (8)\frac{Z}{8} &= 2(8) \\ Z &= 16 \end{aligned}$$

Proof:
$$\begin{aligned} \frac{Z}{8} &= 2 \\ \frac{16}{8} &= 2 \\ 2 &= 2 \end{aligned}$$

7.
$$\begin{aligned} 16F &= 80 \\ \frac{16F}{16} &= \frac{80}{16} \\ F &= 5 \end{aligned}$$

Proof:
$$\begin{aligned} 16F &= 80 \\ 16(5) &= 80 \\ 80 &= 80 \end{aligned}$$

8.
$$\begin{aligned} \frac{C}{9} &= 9 \\ (9)\frac{C}{9} &= 9(9) \\ C &= 81 \end{aligned}$$

Proof:
$$\begin{aligned} \frac{C}{9} &= 9 \\ \frac{81}{9} &= 9 \\ 9 &= 9 \end{aligned}$$

9.
$$\begin{aligned} 12N + 14 &= 50 \\ 12N + 14 &= 50 \\ -14 \quad &\ \ -14 \\ 12N \quad &= 36 \\ \frac{12N}{12} &= \frac{36}{12} \\ N &= 3 \end{aligned}$$

Proof:
$$\begin{aligned} 12N + 14 &= 50 \\ 12(3) + 14 &= 50 \\ 36 + 14 &= 50 \\ 50 &= 50 \end{aligned}$$

10.
$$\begin{aligned} 3W - 4 &= 26 \\ 3W - 4 &= 26 \\ +4 \quad &\ \ +4 \\ 3W \quad &= 30 \\ \frac{3W}{3} &= \frac{30}{3} \\ W &= 10 \end{aligned}$$

Proof:
$$\begin{aligned} 3W - 4 &= 26 \\ 3(10) - 4 &= 26 \\ 30 - 4 &= 26 \\ 26 &= 26 \end{aligned}$$

11.
$$\begin{aligned} \frac{F}{3} - 6 &= 2 \\ \frac{F}{3} - 6 &= 2 \\ +6 \quad &\ \ +6 \\ \frac{F}{3} \quad &= 8 \\ (3)\frac{F}{3} &= 8(3) \\ F &= 24 \end{aligned}$$

Proof:
$$\begin{aligned} \frac{F}{3} - 6 &= 2 \\ \frac{24}{3} - 6 &= 2 \\ 8 - 6 &= 2 \\ 2 &= 2 \end{aligned}$$

12.
$$\begin{aligned} \frac{Z}{5} + 15 &= 24 \\ \frac{Z}{5} + 15 &= 24 \\ -15 \quad &\ \ -15 \\ \frac{Z}{5} \quad &= 9 \\ (5)\frac{Z}{5} &= 9(5) \\ Z &= 45 \end{aligned}$$

Proof:
$$\begin{aligned} \frac{Z}{5} + 15 &= 24 \\ \frac{45}{5} + 15 &= 24 \\ 9 + 15 &= 24 \\ 24 &= 24 \end{aligned}$$

13.
$$\begin{aligned} 4(5G + 6) &= 64 \\ 20G + 24 &= 64 \\ 20G + 24 &= 64 \\ -24 \quad &\ \ -24 \\ 20G \quad &= 40 \\ \frac{20G}{20} &= \frac{40}{20} \\ G &= 2 \end{aligned}$$

Proof:
$$\begin{aligned} 4(5G + 6) &= 64 \\ 4(5\{2\} + 6) &= 64 \\ 4(10 + 6) &= 64 \\ 4(16) &= 64 \\ 64 &= 64 \end{aligned}$$

14.
$$\begin{aligned} 6(3H - 5) &= 42 \\ 18H - 30 &= 42 \\ 18H - 30 &= 42 \\ +30 \quad &\ \ +30 \\ 18H \quad &= 72 \\ \frac{18H}{18} &= \frac{72}{18} \\ H &= 4 \end{aligned}$$

Proof:
$$\begin{aligned} 6(3H - 5) &= 42 \\ 6(3\{4\} - 5) &= 42 \\ 6(12 - 5) &= 42 \\ 6(7) &= 42 \\ 42 &= 42 \end{aligned}$$

15.
$$\begin{aligned} X + 3 &= 18 - 4X \\ X + 3 &= 18 - 4X \\ +4X \quad &\quad\ \ +4X \\ 5X + 3 &= 18 \\ 5X + 3 &= 18 \\ -3 \quad &\ \ -3 \\ 5X \quad &= 15 \\ \frac{5X}{5} &= \frac{15}{5} \\ X &= 3 \end{aligned}$$

Proof:
$$\begin{aligned} X + 3 &= 18 - 4X \\ 3 + 3 &= 18 - 4(3) \\ 6 &= 18 - 12 \\ 6 &= 6 \end{aligned}$$

16.
$$\begin{aligned} 9S + 8 - S &= 2(2S + 8) \\ 9S + 8 - S &= 4S + 16 \\ 8S + 8 &= 4S + 16 \\ 8S + 8 &= 4S + 16 \\ -4S \quad &\quad -4S \\ 4S + 8 &= \quad +16 \\ 4S + 8 &= 16 \\ -8 \quad &\ \ -8 \\ 4S \quad &= 8 \\ \frac{4S}{4} &= \frac{8}{4} \\ S &= 2 \end{aligned}$$

Proof:
$$\begin{aligned} 9S + 8 - S &= 2(2S + 8) \\ 9(2) + 8 - 2 &= (2\{2\} + 8) \\ 18 + 8 - 2 &= 2(4 + 8) \\ 24 &= 2(12) \\ 24 &= 24 \end{aligned}$$

17. The sum of twice E and 9

$2E + 9$

18. 6 times N divided by Z

$\frac{6N}{Z}$

19. 8 less than half of F

$\frac{1}{2}F - 8$

20. \$45.75 more than the product of X and Y

$XY + \$45.75$

21. The difference of Q and 44

$Q - 44$

22. R times A times B

RAB

23. What number increased by 32 yields 125?

$$X + 32 = 125$$

24. 21 less than twice C gives 9.

$$2C - 21 = 9$$

25. 5 more than 6 times a number, plus 3 times that number, is 25.

$$6X + 5 + 3X = 25$$

26. The cost of G gallons at \$1.33 per gallon equals \$34.40.

$$\$1.33G = \$34.40$$

27. The area of a rectangle is the length times the width.

$$A = LW$$

28. What number less 12 is the average of A, B, and C?

$$X - 12 = \frac{A + B + C}{3}$$

29. *Reasoning:* José's sales and Bob's sales equal total sales, 44.

Let X = Bob's sales

Let $X - 12$ = José's sales

$$X + X - 12 = 44$$
$$2X - 12 = 44$$
$$2X = 56$$
$$\frac{2X}{2} = \frac{56}{2}$$
$$X = 28$$
$$X - 12 = 28 - 12 = 16$$

Bob's sales = 28 DVD players

José's sales = 16 DVD players

Proof:

$$X + X - 12 = 44$$
$$28 + 28 - 12 = 44$$
$$44 = 44$$

30. *Reasoning:* $\frac{1}{3}$ of the total checking accounts are interest-earning, 2,500.

Let C = total checking accounts

$$\frac{1}{3}C = 2{,}500$$
$$(3)\frac{1}{3}C = 2{,}500(3)$$
$$C = 7{,}500$$

Total checking accounts = 7,500

Proof:

$$\frac{1}{3}C = 2{,}500$$
$$\frac{1}{3}(7{,}500) = 2{,}500$$
$$2{,}500 = 2{,}500$$

31. *Reasoning:* Weight per carton equals the total weight divided by the number of cartons.

Let W = weight per carton

$$W = \frac{7{,}482}{58}$$
$$W = 129$$

Weight per carton = 129 pounds

Proof:

$$W = \frac{7{,}482}{58}$$
$$129 = \frac{7{,}482}{58}$$
$$129 = 129$$

32. *Reasoning:* Soft goods plus hard goods equals total store sales, \$180,000.

$$\text{Let } X = \text{hard goods}$$
$$\text{Let } 3X = \text{soft goods}$$
$$X + 3X = \$180{,}000$$
$$4X = 180{,}000$$
$$\frac{4X}{4} = \frac{180{,}000}{4}$$
$$X = 45{,}000 \qquad \text{hard goods} = \$45{,}000$$
$$3X = 3(45{,}000) = 135{,}000 \qquad \text{soft goods} = \$135{,}000$$

Proof:

$$X + 3X = 180{,}000$$
$$(45{,}000) + 3(45{,}000) = 180{,}000$$
$$45{,}000 + 135{,}000 = 180{,}000$$
$$180{,}000 = 180{,}000$$

33. *Reasoning:* Tables plus chairs plus sofas equals total items sold, 520.

$$\text{Let } X = \text{tables}$$
$$\text{Let } 4X = \text{chairs}$$
$$\text{Let } 2(4X) = \text{sofas}$$
$$X + 4X + 2(4X) = 520$$
$$X + 4X + 8X = 520$$
$$13X = 520$$
$$\frac{13X}{13} = \frac{520}{13}$$
$$X = 40 \qquad \text{tables sold} = 40$$
$$4X = 4(40) = 160 \qquad \text{chairs sold} = 160$$
$$2(4X) = 2(4\{40\}) = 2(160) = 320 \qquad \text{sofas sold} = 320$$

Proof:

$$X + 4X + 2(4X) = 520$$
$$(40) + 4(40) + 2(4\{40\}) = 520$$
$$40 + 160 + 2(160) = 520$$
$$40 + 160 + 320 = 520$$
$$520 = 520$$

34. *Reasoning:* The sum of the price of each item multiplied by the quantity of each item is the total sales, \$3,400.
Remember: Let X equal the more expensive item, thereby avoiding negative numbers.

Let X = Quantity of heavy-duty batteries
Let $40 - X$ = Quantity of regular batteries
Price times quantity of heavy-duty batteries = $\$110X$
Price times quantity of regular batteries = $\$70(40 - X)$

$$110X + 70(40 - X) = 3{,}400$$
$$110X + 2{,}800 - 70X = 3{,}400$$
$$40X + 2{,}800 = 3{,}400$$
$$40X = 600$$
$$\frac{40X}{40} = \frac{600}{40}$$
$$X = 15 \qquad \text{Quantity of heavy-duty batteries} = 15$$
$$40 - X = 40 - 15 = 25 \qquad \text{Quantity of regular batteries} = 25$$

Proof:

$$110X + 70(40 - X) = 3{,}400$$
$$110(15) + 70(40 - 15) = 3{,}400$$
$$1{,}650 + 70(25) = 3{,}400$$
$$1{,}650 + 1{,}750 = 3{,}400$$
$$3{,}400 = 3{,}400$$

Now that we have calculated the quantity of each size battery, we can find the dollar sales:
Reasoning: Dollar sales are the price per battery multiplied by the quantity sold.

Let S = dollar sales
Heavy-duty battery: $S = \$110(15) =$ \$1,650 in sales
Regular battery: $S = \$70(25) =$ \$1,750 in sales

35.

$$\frac{87.50}{7} = \frac{X}{35}$$

$$7X = 87.50(35)$$

$$7X = 3{,}062.50$$

$$\frac{\cancel{7}X}{\cancel{7}} = \frac{3{,}062.50}{7}$$

$$X = 437.50$$

Wilbur would earn $437.50 for 35 hours of work.

Proof:

$$\frac{87.50}{7} = \frac{X}{35}$$

$$\frac{87.50}{7} = \frac{437.50}{35}$$

$$12.50 = 12.50$$

Name ______________________

Class ______________________

Answers

1. ______________________
2. ______________________
3. ______________________
4. ______________________
5. ______________________
6. ______________________
7. ______________________
8. ______________________
9. ______________________
10. ______________________
11. ______________________
12. ______________________
13. ______________________
14. ______________________
15. ______________________
16. ______________________
17. ______________________
18. ______________________
19. ______________________

____

20. ______________________

CHAPTER 5 | ASSESSMENT TEST

Solve the following equations for the unknown, and prove your solutions:

1. $T + 45 = 110$

65

2. $G - 24 = 75$

99

3. $11K = 165$

15

4. $3(2C - 5) = 45$

5. $8X - 15 = 49$

6. $\frac{S}{7} = 12$

7. $B + 5 = 61 - 6B$

8. $\frac{N}{4} - 7 = 8$

9. $4(3X + 8) = 212$

For the following statements, underline the key words and translate into *expressions:*

10. 15 less than one-ninth of P

11. The difference of $4R$ and 108

12. 3 times the quantity of H less 233

13. 24 more than the product of Z and W

For the following statements, underline the key words and translate into *equations:*

14. A number decreased by 4 is 25

15. A number totals 4 times C and L

16. The cost of Q at \$4.55 each is \$76.21

17. 14 less than $3F$ leaves 38

18. 2 more than 6 times a number, and 7 times that number, is that number decreased by 39

Set up and solve equations for each of the following business situations:

19. At a recent boat show, Nautica Marine sold five more boats than Blue Water Marine. If together they sold 33 boats, how many were sold by each company?

20. One-seventh of the customers responding to a survey at Westland Department Store were not satisfied with the merchandise selection. If 145 customers were not satisfied, how many customers responded to the survey?

21. Creative Communications ordered three dozen cordless phones from the manufacturer. If the total order amounted to \$1,980.00, what was the cost of each phone?

22. The Bon Appetit Bakery makes $4\frac{1}{2}$ times as much money on donuts as muffins. If total sales were \$44,000 for May, what dollar amount of each was sold?

23. A regular light bulb uses 20 watts less than twice the power of an energy-saver light bulb. If the regular bulb uses 170 watts, how much does the energy-saver bulb use?

24. The Royal Peacock, a men's clothing store, ordered short-sleeve shirts for \$23 each and long-sleeve shirts for \$28.50 each from Tommy Hilfiger.

a. If the total order amounted to \$9,862.50 for 375 shirts, how many of each were ordered?

b. What was the dollar amount of each type of shirt ordered?

25. Ace Hardware is offering a 140-piece mechanics tool set plus a \$65 tool chest for \$226. What is the cost per tool?

26. Denski and Schwartz invested \$195,000 in a business venture. If Schwartz invested $2\frac{1}{4}$ times as much as Denski, how much did each invest?

Name ____________________

Class ____________________

Answers

21. ____________________

22. ____________________

____

23. ____________________

24. a. ____________________

____

b. ____________________

____

25. ____________________

26. ____________________

____

Name ______________________

Class ______________________

Answers

27. a. ______________________

____

b. ______________________

____

28. ______________________

29. ______________________

30. ______________________

31. ______________________

32. ______________________

33. ______________________

27. A Dairy Queen ice cream shop sells sundaes for \$3.60 and banana splits for \$4.25. The shop sells four times as many sundaes as banana splits.

a. If total sales amount to \$3,730.00, how many of each dish are sold?

b. What are the dollar sales of each?

28. What is the total cost to ship an order weighing 420 pounds if the breakdown is \$.18 per pound for packing, \$.12 per pound for insurance, \$.37 per pound for transportation, and \$148.60 for the shipping crate?

Use ratio and proportion to solve the following business situations:

29. At The Sports Authority, the inventory ratio of equipment to clothing is 8 to 5. If the clothing inventory amounts to \$65,000, what is the amount of the equipment inventory?

30. If the interest on a \$6,000 loan is \$400, what would be the interest on a loan of \$2,250?

31. If property insurance costs \$.75 per \$100 of coverage, how much will it cost Albright Enterprises to insure a building and equipment worth \$182,000?

32. A recipe calls for $1\frac{1}{2}$ tablespoons of minced garlic for every $\frac{1}{4}$ pound of pasta. How much garlic would be required for $2\frac{1}{2}$ pounds of pasta?

33. A contractor is using a blueprint for a shopping center with a scale of 1.25 inches equals 4 feet. If a concrete slab is 18.75 inches on the blueprint, how many feet long is the slab?

Name ____________

Class ____________

BUSINESS DECISION

Managing *The Chronicle*

34. You have just been hired as advertising manager of *The Daily Chronicle,* a not-very-successful newspaper. In the past, *The Chronicle* contained one-half advertising and one-half news stories. Current industry research indicates a newspaper must have three times as much advertising as news stories to make money. In addition, the advertising must be divided in the following ratio: 5 to 3 to 1, retail advertising to national advertising to classified advertising. *The Chronicle* is typically 48 pages in length.

a. How many pages should be advertising and how many should be news stories?

b. Based on the industry ratios, how should the pages be divided among the three types of advertising?

c. After you made the changes in the advertising distribution ratios, your newspaper began making a profit—for the first time in years. If last year's total advertising revenue was $810,000, how much was earned by each type of advertising?

d. When you accepted the job of advertising manager, in addition to your salary, you were promised a $\frac{1}{50}$ share of each year's revenue from retail and classified advertising, and $\frac{1}{75}$ share for national. How much bonus will you receive for last year's sales?

Answers

34. a. ____________

____

b. ____________

____

____

c. ____________

____

____

d. ____________

All the Math That's Fit to Learn

The Business Math Times

Volume V | Using Equations to Solve Business Problems | One Dollar

The History of Algebra, 101

Algebra is one of the chief branches of mathematics. Mastery of mathematics depends on a sound understanding of algebra.

Engineers and scientists use algebra every day. Business and industry rely on algebra to help solve many problems that are beyond the range of arithmetic alone.

Algebra was invented in Arabia. The term derives from the Arabic *al-jabr* or literally "the reunion of broken parts." As well as its mathematical meaning, the word also means the surgical treatment of fractures. It gained widespread use through the title of a book *ilm al-jabr wa'l-mukabala*—the science of restoring what is missing and equating like with like—written by the mathematician Abu Ja'far Muhammad.

The Arabic word *shei* means "something," or "the unknown." When it was translated into English, *shei* became "xei," and "X" became the letter of choice to represent the unknown in equations.

As long ago as 2000 B.C., the Babylonians and the Egyptians posed problems that used algebra for their solution. For example, on the Rhind Papyrus, dating from about 1650 B.C., problem 24 asks for the value of "heap" if heap and a seventh of heap is 19. In modern terminology and notation, this problem could be formulated as, "What number plus a seventh of that number is 19?"

$$X + \tfrac{1}{7}X = 19$$

"Quote . . . Unquote"

I hear and I forget. I see and I remember. I do and I understand.
—*Confucius*

The magic formula that successful businesses have discovered is to treat customers like guests and employees like people
—*Tom Peters*

Evolution of Math Teaching

- **1960s:** A peasant sells a bag of potatoes for $10. His costs amount to $\frac{4}{5}$ of his selling price. What is his profit?
- **1970s:** A farmer sells a bag of potatoes for $10. His costs amount to $\frac{4}{5}$ of his selling price, that is, $8. What is his profit?
- **1970s** (new math): A farmer exchanges a set *P* of potatoes with set *M* of money. The cardinality of the set *M* is equal to 10, and each element of *M* is worth $1. What is the cardinality of the set of profits?
- **1980s:** A farmer sells a bag of potatoes for $10. His production costs are $8, and his profit is $2. Underline the word "potatoes" and discuss with your classmates.
- **1990s:** A farmer sells a bag of potatoes for $10. His or her production costs are 0.80 of his or her revenue. On your calculator, graph revenue versus cost. Run the POTATO program to determine the profit. Write a brief essay that analyzes this example in the real world.
- **2000s:** E-mail your assignment to your instructor's virtual grade book and discuss the results with the class in the chat room. See you at graduation!

Your Next PC

During the next decade the personal computer will change dramatically both in the workplace and at home. Experts predict that we will soon enter the post-PC era, in which smaller, less powerful devices such as set-top boxes and PDAs will replace the PCs.

In business, desktop computers are being replaced with wireless mobile computers. This enables employees to roam freely around the office—no longer "tied" to their desks.

At home, the PC trend is just the opposite. Instead of becoming more mobile, most analysts believe the home PC will become a behind-the-scenes centerpiece of a network, linking everything from the television to the toaster to the thermostat.

"Just a darn minute! Yesterday you said X equals two!"

Brainteaser

HOLD THE ANCHOVIES

Pizza Palace sold 100 pizzas in five days, each day selling six more than the day before. How many pizzas were sold on the first day?

ANSWER TO LAST ISSUE'S BRAINTEASER

31.7 years

1 minute = $1 × 60 = $60
1 hour = $60 × 60 = $3,600
1 day = $3,600 × 24 = $86,400
1 year = $86,000 × 365 = $31,536,000

$$\frac{1{,}000{,}000{,}000}{31{,}536{,}000} = 31.7 \text{ years}$$

CHAPTER 6

Percents and Their Applications in Business

PERFORMANCE OBJECTIVES

Section I Understanding and Converting Percents

6-1 Converting percents to decimals and decimals to percents. (p. 174)
6-2 Converting percents to fractions and fractions to percents. (p. 176)

Section II Using the Percentage Formula to Solve Business Problems

6-3 Solving for the portion. (p. 181)
6-4 Solving for the rate. (p. 182)
6-5 Solving for the base. (p. 184)

Section III Solving Other Business Problems Involving Percents

6-6 Determining rate of increase or decrease. (p. 189)
6-7 Determining amounts in increase or decrease situations. (p. 192)
6-8 Understanding and solving problems involving percentage points. (p. 194)

SECTION I

UNDERSTANDING AND CONVERTING PERCENTS

Percents are a way of expressing a quantity with relation to a whole.

It takes only a glance at the business section of a newspaper or an annual report of a company to see how extensively percents are applied in business. Percents are the primary way of measuring change among business variables. For example, a business might report "revenue is up 6% this year" or "expenses have been cut by 2.3% this month." Interest rates, commissions, and many taxes are expressed in percent form. You may have heard phrases like these: "Sunnyside Bank charged 12% on the loan," "A real estate broker made 5% commission on the sale of the property," or "The state charges a $6\frac{1}{2}$% sales tax." Even price changes are frequently advertised as percents, "Sears Dishwasher Sale—All Models, 25% off!"

To this point, we have learned that fractions and decimals are ways of representing parts of a whole. Percents are another way of expressing quantity with relation to a whole. **Percent** means *per hundred* or *parts per hundred* and is represented by the **percent sign, %.** Percents are numbers equal to a fraction with a denominator of 100. Five percent, for example, means five parts out of 100 and may be written in the following ways:

$$5 \text{ percent} \qquad 5\% \qquad 5 \text{ hundredths} \qquad \frac{5}{100} \qquad .05$$

Before performing any mathematical calculations with percents, they must be converted to either decimals or fractions. Although this function is performed automatically by the percent key on a calculator, Section I of this chapter covers the procedures for making these conversions manually. Sections II and III introduce you to some important applications of percents in business.

percent
A way of representing the parts of a whole. Percent means *per hundred* or *parts per hundred.*

percent sign
The symbol, %, used to represent percents. For example, 1 percent would be written 1%.

6-1 Converting Percents to Decimals and Decimals to Percents

Because percents are numbers expressed as parts per 100, the percent sign, %, means multiplication by $\frac{1}{100}$. Therefore, 25% means

$$25\% = 25 \times \frac{1}{100} = \frac{25}{100} = .25$$

Everybody's Business
Learning Tip
To divide a number by 100, move the decimal point two places to the left. Add zeros as needed.

Remember, if there is no decimal point, it is understood to be to the right of the digit in the ones place. (24 = 24.)

STEPS FOR CONVERTING A PERCENT TO A DECIMAL:

Step 1. Remove the percent sign.

Step 2. Divide by 100.

Step 3. If the percent is a fraction, such as $\frac{3}{8}$%, or a mixed number, such as $4\frac{3}{4}$%, first change the fraction to a decimal, then follow Steps 1 and 2 above.

$$\frac{3}{8}\% = .375\% = .00375 \qquad 4\frac{3}{4}\% = 4.75\% = .0475$$

Step 4. If the percent is a fraction such as $\frac{2}{3}$%, which converts to a repeating decimal, .66666, round the decimal to hundredths, .67, then follow Steps 1 and 2 above.

$$\frac{2}{3}\% = .67\% = .0067$$

EXAMPLES

Convert the following percents to decimals:

a. 44% **b.** 233% **c.** 56.4% **d.** .68% **e.** $18\frac{1}{4}\%$ **f.** $\frac{1}{8}\%$ **g.** $9\frac{1}{3}\%$

SOLUTION STRATEGY

Remove the percent sign and move the decimal point two places to the left:

a. 44% = .44 **b.** 233% = 2.33 **c.** 56.4% = .564 **d.** .68% = .0068

e. $18\frac{1}{4}\% = 18.25\% = .1825$ **f.** $\frac{1}{8}\% = .125\% = .00125$ **g.** $9\frac{1}{3}\% = 9.33\% = .0933$

TRY-IT | EXERCISES

Convert the following percents to decimals:

1. 27% **2.** 472% **3.** 93.7% **4.** .81% **5.** $12\frac{3}{4}\%$ **6.** $\frac{7}{8}\%$

Check your answers with the solutions on page 201.

STEPS FOR CONVERTING A DECIMAL OR WHOLE NUMBER TO A PERCENT:

Step 1. Multiply by 100.

Step 2. Add a percent sign to the number.

Step 3. If there are fractions involved, such as $\frac{3}{4}$, convert them to decimals first, then proceed with Steps 1 and 2 above.

$$\frac{3}{4} = .75 = 75\%$$

Everybody's Business

Learning Tip

To multiply a number by 100, move the decimal point two places to the right. Add zeros as needed. As a "navigational aid" to the direction of the decimal point, consider the words *decimal* and *percent* as written alphabetically, with "decimal" preceding "percent."

- When converting from decimal to percent, the decimal moves **right**

  decimal ⟶ percent

- When converting from percent to decimal, the decimal moves **left**

  decimal ⟵ percent

EXAMPLES

Convert the following decimals or whole numbers to percents:

a. .5 **b.** 3.7 **c.** .044 **d.** $.09\frac{3}{5}$ **e.** 7 **f.** $6\frac{1}{2}$

SOLUTION STRATEGY

Move the decimal point two places to the right and add a percent sign.

a. .5 = 50% **b.** 3.7 = 370% **c.** .044 = 4.4%

d. $.09\frac{3}{5} = .096 = 9.6\%$ **e.** 7 = 700% **f.** $6\frac{1}{2} = 6.5 = 650\%$

TRY-IT | EXERCISES

Convert the following decimals or whole numbers to percents:

7. .8 **8.** 1.4 **9.** .0023 **10.** $.016\frac{2}{5}$ **11.** 19 **12.** $.57\frac{2}{3}$

Check your answers with the solutions on page 201.

6-2 Converting Percents to Fractions and Fractions to Percents

STEPS FOR CONVERTING A PERCENT TO A FRACTION:

Step 1. Remove the percent sign.

Step 2. (*If the percent is a whole number*) Write a fraction with the percent as the numerator and 100 as the denominator. If that fraction is improper, change it to a mixed number. Reduce the fraction to lowest terms.

or

Step 2. (*If the percent is a fraction*) Multiply the number by $\frac{1}{100}$ and reduce to lowest terms.

or

Step 2. (*If the percent is a decimal*) Convert it to a fraction and multiply by $\frac{1}{100}$. Reduce to lowest terms.

EXAMPLES

Convert the following percents to reduced fractions, mixed numbers, or whole numbers:

a. 3% **b.** 57% **c.** $2\frac{1}{2}\%$ **d.** 150% **e.** 4.5% **f.** 600%

SOLUTION STRATEGY

a. $3\% = \frac{3}{100}$

b. $57\% = \frac{57}{100}$

c. $2\frac{1}{2}\% = \frac{5}{2} \times \frac{1}{100} = \frac{5}{200} = \frac{1}{40}$

d. $150\% = \frac{150}{100} = 1\frac{50}{100} = 1\frac{1}{2}$

e. $4.5\% = 4\frac{1}{2}\% = \frac{9}{2} \times \frac{1}{100} = \frac{9}{200}$

f. $600\% = \frac{600}{100} = 6$

TRY-IT | EXERCISES

Convert the following percents to reduced fractions, mixed numbers, or whole numbers:

13. 9% **14.** 23% **15.** 75% **16.** 225% **17.** 8.7% **18.** 1,000%

Check your answers with the solutions on page 201.

STEPS FOR CONVERTING FRACTIONS OR MIXED NUMBERS TO PERCENTS:

Step 1. Change the fraction to a decimal by dividing the numerator by the denominator.

Step 2. Multiply by 100. (Move the decimal point two places to the right. Add zeros as needed.)

Step 3. Write a percent sign after the number.

Everybody's Business

Learning Tip

Use the % key on your calculator to save the step of multiplying by 100.

For example: $\frac{44}{50} = .88 = 88\%$.

Calculator sequence:

44 [÷] 50 [%] = 88

Note: Scientific and business calculators require pushing the [=] button after the % key; common arithmetic calculators do not.

EXAMPLES

Convert the following fractions or mixed numbers to percents:

a. $\frac{1}{10}$ **b.** $\frac{69}{100}$ **c.** $\frac{15}{4}$ **d.** $4\frac{3}{8}$ **e.** $\frac{18}{25}$ **f.** $13\frac{1}{2}$

SOLUTION STRATEGY

Change the fractions to decimals by dividing the denominator into the numerator, then move the decimal point two places to the right and add a percent sign.

a. $\frac{1}{10} = .10 = \underline{\underline{10\%}}$

b. $\frac{69}{100} = .69 = \underline{\underline{69\%}}$

c. $\frac{15}{4} = 3\frac{3}{4} = 3.75 = \underline{\underline{375\%}}$

d. $4\frac{3}{8} = 4.375 = \underline{\underline{437.5\%}}$

e. $\frac{18}{25} = .72 = \underline{\underline{72\%}}$

f. $13\frac{1}{2} = 13.5 = \underline{\underline{1350\%}}$

TRY-IT | EXERCISES

Convert the following fractions or mixed numbers to percents:

19. $\frac{1}{5}$ **20.** $\frac{70}{200}$ **21.** $\frac{23}{5}$ **22.** $6\frac{9}{10}$ **23.** $\frac{45}{54}$ **24.** $140\frac{1}{8}$

Check your answers with the solutions on pages 201–202.

REVIEW EXERCISES | CHAPTER 6—SECTION I

Convert the following percents to decimals:

1. 28% **2.** 76% **3.** 13.4% **4.** 121% **5.** 42.68%

6. $6\frac{1}{2}\%$ **7.** .02% **8.** $\frac{3}{5}\%$ **9.** $125\frac{1}{6}\%$ **10.** 2,000%

Convert the following decimals or whole numbers to percents:

11. 3.5 **12.** .11 **13.** 46 **14.** $.34\frac{1}{2}$ **15.** .00935

16. $.9\frac{3}{4}$ **17.** 164 **18.** .04 **19.** 5.33 **20.** $1.15\frac{5}{8}$

Convert the following percents to reduced fractions, mixed numbers, or whole numbers:

21. 5% **22.** 75% **23.** 89% **24.** 230% **25.** 38%

26. 37.5% **27.** $62\frac{1}{2}\%$ **28.** 450% **29.** 125% **30.** .8%

Convert the following fractions or mixed numbers to percents:

31. $\frac{3}{4}$ **32.** $\frac{1}{8}$ **33.** $\frac{12}{5}$ **34.** $6\frac{3}{10}$ **35.** $\frac{125}{100}$

36. $\frac{78}{24}$ **37.** $\frac{3}{16}$ **38.** $4\frac{1}{5}$ **39.** $\frac{35}{100}$ **40.** $\frac{375}{1,000}$

BUSINESS DECISION

Enhancing the Pie

41. You have been asked to make a presentation about the Walt Disney Company. In your research, you locate the accompanying pie chart, which shows company revenue, by category, expressed in billions of dollars.

To enhance your presentation, you have decided to convert the dollar amounts to percents, and display both numbers.

a. What is the total revenue?

b. Express the revenue from each category (numerator) as a fraction of the total revenue (denominator).

Broadcast Cable

Parks Studio

Internet Products

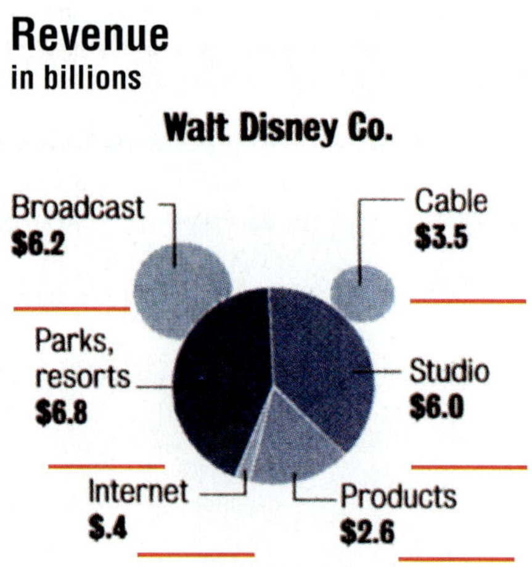

c. Convert each fraction from part **b** to a percent, rounded to a tenth, and enter your answers on the red lines.

Broadcast	Cable
Parks	Studio
Internet	Products

d. What is the percent breakdown between the Broadcast and Cable categories? Round to a tenth

Broadcast

Cable

e. (Optional) Using your percentages from part **d** and the template below, construct a pie chart of the revenue breakdown between Broadcast and Cable. Use different colors or shading to enhance your presentation.

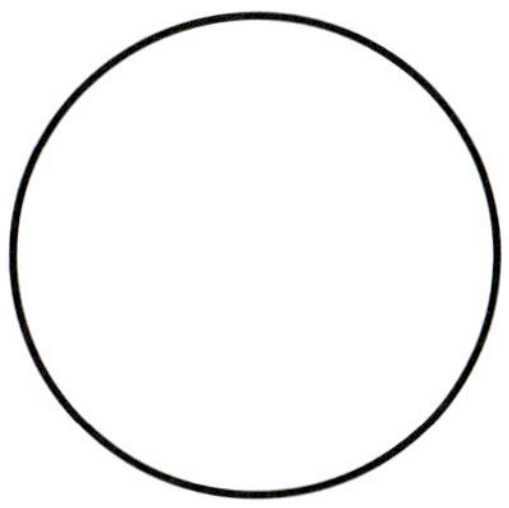

SECTION II

USING THE PERCENTAGE FORMULA TO SOLVE BUSINESS PROBLEMS

Now that we have learned to manipulate percents, let's look at some of their practical applications in business. Percent problems involve the use of equations known as the percentage formulas. These formulas have three variables: the **base,** the **portion,** and the **rate.** In business situations, two of the variables will be given and are the *knowns*; one of the variables will be the *unknown.*

base
The variable of the percentage formula that represents 100%, or the whole thing.

portion
The variable of the percentage formula that represents a part of the base.

rate
The variable of the percentage formula that defines how much or what part the portion is of the base. The rate is the variable with the percent sign.

Once the variables have been properly identified, the equations are simple to solve. The variables have the following characteristics, which should be used to help identify them:

BASE: The base is the number that represents 100%, or the whole thing. It is the starting point, the beginning, or total value of something. The base is often preceded by the word *of* in the written statement of the situation because it is multiplied by the rate.

PORTION: The portion is the number that represents a part of the base. The portion is always in the same terms as the base. For example, if the base is dollars, the portion is dollars; if the base is people, the portion is people; if the base is production units, the portion will be production units. The portion often has a unique characteristic that is being measured or compared with the base. For example, if the base is the total number of cars in a parking lot, the portion could be the part of the total cars that are convertibles (the unique characteristic).

RATE: The rate is easily identified. It is the variable with the % sign or the word *percent.* It defines what part the portion is of the base. If the rate is less than 100%, the portion is less than the base. If the rate is 100%, the portion is equal to the base. If the rate is more than 100%, the portion is greater than the base.

The following percentage formulas are used to solve percent problems:

$$\textbf{Portion} = \textbf{Rate} \times \textbf{Base} \qquad P = R \times B$$

$$\textbf{Rate} = \frac{\textbf{Portion}}{\textbf{Base}} \qquad R = \frac{P}{B}$$

$$\textbf{Base} = \frac{\textbf{Portion}}{\textbf{Rate}} \qquad B = \frac{P}{R}$$

> **Everybody's Business**
> **Learning Tip**
> Don't confuse the word *percentage* with the percent, or rate. The *percentage* means the portion, not the rate.

STEPS FOR SOLVING PERCENTAGE PROBLEMS:

Step 1. Identify the two knowns and the unknown.

Step 2. Choose the formula that solves for that unknown.

Step 3. Solve the equation by substituting the known values for the letters in the formula.

Hint: By remembering the one basic formula, $P = R \times B$, you can derive the other two by using your knowledge of solving equations from Chapter 5. Because multiplication is indicated, we isolate the unknown by performing the inverse or opposite operation, division.

To solve for rate, R, divide both sides of the equation by B:

$$P = R \times B \longrightarrow \frac{P}{B} = \frac{R \times \cancel{B}}{\cancel{B}} \longrightarrow \frac{P}{B} = R$$

To solve for base, B, divide both sides of the equation by R:

$$P = R \times B \longrightarrow \frac{P}{R} = \frac{\cancel{R} \times B}{\cancel{R}} \longrightarrow \frac{P}{R} = B$$

Another method for remembering the percentage formulas is by using the Magic Triangle.

The Magic Triangle

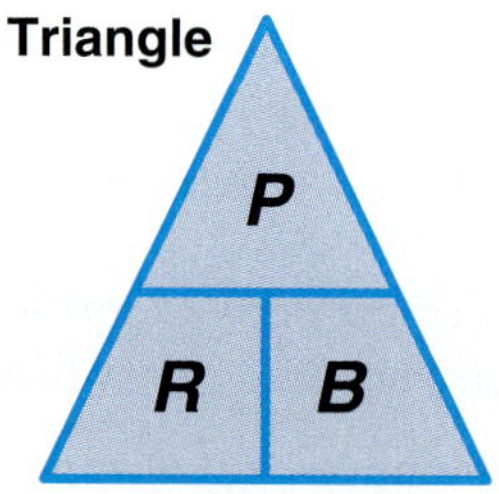

The triangle is divided into three sections, representing the portion, rate, and base. By circling or covering the letter in the triangle that corresponds to the *unknown* of the problem, the triangle will "magically" reveal the correct formula to use.

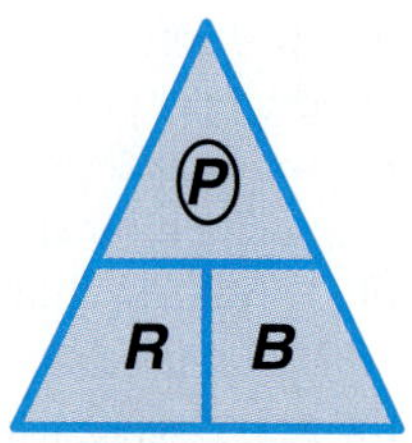

$P = R \times B$

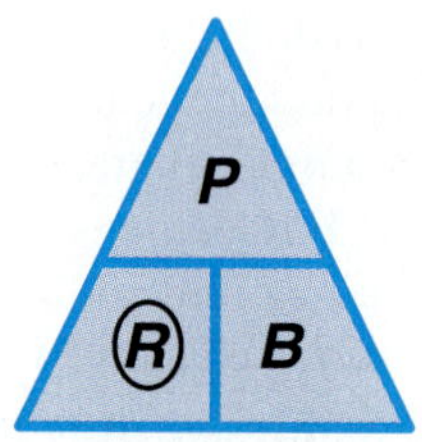

$R = \frac{P}{B}$

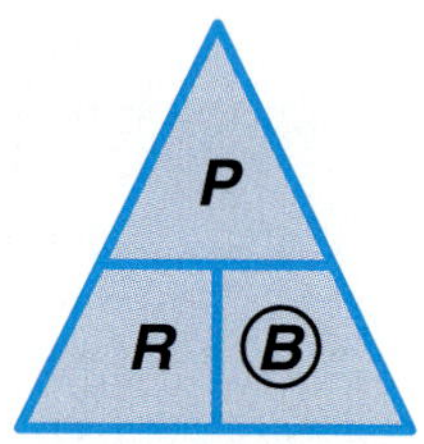

$B = \frac{P}{R}$

6-3 Solving for the Portion

Remember, the portion is a part of the whole and will always be in the same terms as the base. It is found by multiplying the rate times the base: $P = R \times B$. The following examples will demonstrate solving for the portion.

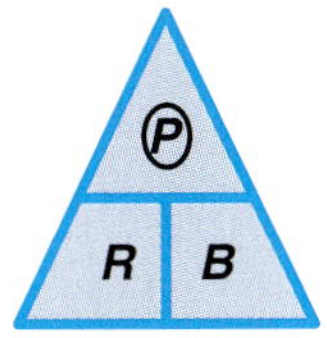

$P = R \times B$

EXAMPLE

What is the portion if the base is \$400 and the rate is 12%?

SOLUTION STRATEGY

In this basic problem, simply substitute the known numbers for the letters in the formula, portion = rate × base. In this problem, 12% is the rate, and \$400 is the base. Do not forget to convert the percent (rate) to a decimal by deleting the % sign and moving the decimal point two places to the left (12% = .12).

$$P = R \times B$$

$$P = 12\% \times 400 = .12 \times 400 = 48$$

$$\underline{\underline{\text{Portion} = \$48}}$$

Everybody's Business

Shortcut

Remember to use the % key on your calculator.

12 [%] [×] 400 [=] 48

EXAMPLE

What number is 43.5% of 250?

SOLUTION STRATEGY

In this problem, the rate is easily identified as the term with the % sign. The base, or whole amount, is preceded by the word *of*. We use the formula portion = rate × base, substituting the knowns for the letters that represent them.

$$P = R \times B$$

$$P = 43.5\% \times 250 = .435 \times 250 = 108.75$$

$$\underline{\underline{\text{Portion} = 108.75}}$$

EXAMPLE

Motorola made 6,000 radios last week. If 2% of them were defective, how many defective radios were produced?

SOLUTION STRATEGY

To solve this problem, we must first identify the variables. Because 2% has the percent sign, it is the rate. The terms are radios; the total number of radios (6,000) is the base. The unique characteristic of the portion, the unknown, is that they were defective.

$$P = R \times B$$

$$P = 2\% \times 6{,}000 = .02 \times 6{,}000 = 120$$

$$\underline{\underline{\text{Portion} = 120 = \text{Number of defective radios last week}}}$$

TRY-IT | EXERCISES

Solve the following for the portion:

25. What is the portion if the base is 980 and the rate is 55%?

26. What number is 72% of 3,200?

27. Gulf Stream Industries has 1,250 employees. 16% constitute the sales staff. How many employees are in sales?

28. If Sunshine Savings & Loan requires a 15% down payment on a mortgage loan, what is the down payment needed to finance a $148,500 home?

Check your answers with the solutions on page 202.

6-4 Solving for the Rate

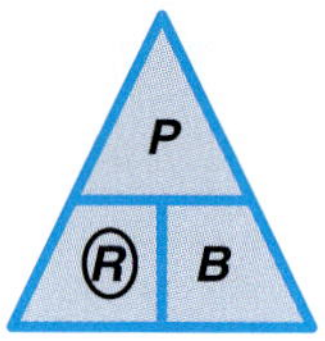

$$R = \frac{P}{B}$$

The rate is the variable that describes what part of the base is represented by the portion. It is *always* the term with the percent sign. When solving for the rate, your answer will be a decimal. Be sure to convert the decimal to a percent by moving the decimal point two places to the right and adding a percent sign. We use the formula

$$\text{Rate} = \frac{\text{Portion}}{\text{Base}} \quad \text{or} \quad R = \frac{P}{B}$$

The following examples demonstrate solving for the rate.

Everybody's Business

Learning Tip

Remember, the rate expresses "what part" the portion is of the base.

- When the rate is less than 100%, the portion is *less* than the base.
- When the rate is more than 100%, the portion is *more* than the base.
- When the rate is 100%, the portion *equals* the base.

EXAMPLE

What is the rate if the base is 160 and the portion is 40?

SOLUTION STRATEGY

In this basic problem, we simply substitute the known numbers for the letters in the formula.

$$\text{Rate} = \frac{\text{Portion}}{\text{Base}}$$

$$R = \frac{P}{B}$$

$$R = \frac{40}{160} = .25 = 25\%$$

$$\underline{\underline{\text{Rate} = 25\%}}$$

EXAMPLE

What percent of 700 is 56?

SOLUTION STRATEGY

This problem asks what percent, indicating that the rate is the unknown. The 700 is preceded by the word *of* and is therefore the base. The 56 is part of the base and is therefore the portion. Once again we use the formula $R = P \div B$, substituting the knowns for the letters that represent them.

$$R = \frac{P}{B}$$

$$R = \frac{56}{700} = .08 = 8\%$$

Rate = 8%

EXAMPLE

Pet Supermarket placed an order for 560 fish tanks. If only 490 tanks were delivered, what percent of the order was received?

SOLUTION STRATEGY

The first step in solving this problem is to identify the variables. The statement asks "what percent," therefore, the rate is the unknown. Because 560 is the total order, it is the base; 490 is a part of the total and is therefore the portion. Note that the base and the portion are in the same terms, fish tanks; the unique characteristic of the portion is that 490 tanks *were delivered*.

$$R = \frac{P}{B}$$

$$R = \frac{490}{560} = .875 = 87.5\%$$

Rate = 87.5% = Percent of the order received

TRY-IT | EXERCISES

Solve the following for the rate, rounding to tenths when necessary:

29. What is the rate if the base is 21 and the portion is 9?

30. 67 is what percent of 142?

31. A contract called for 18,000 square feet of tile to be installed in a shopping mall. In the first week 5,400 feet of tile was completed. What percent of the job has been completed?

32. During a recent sale, Image Makers, a boutique, sold $5,518 in men's business suits. If total sales amounted to $8,900, what percent of the sales were suits?

Check your answers with the solutions on page 202.

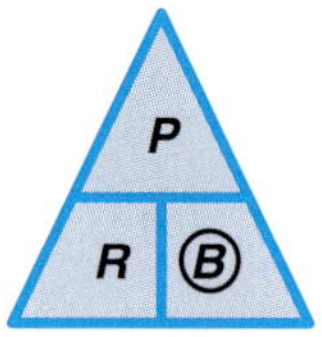

$B = \frac{P}{R}$

6-5 Solving for the Base

To solve business situations in which the whole or total amount is the unknown, we use the formula

$$\text{Base} = \frac{\text{Portion}}{\text{Rate}} \quad \text{or} \quad B = \frac{P}{R}$$

The following examples illustrate solving for the base.

EXAMPLE

What is the base if the rate is 21% and the portion is 58.8?

SOLUTION STRATEGY

In this basic problem, we simply substitute the known values for the letters in the formula. Remember, the rate must be converted from a percent to a decimal.

$$B = \frac{P}{R}$$

$$B = \frac{58.8}{21\%} = \frac{58.8}{.21} = 280$$

$$\underline{\underline{\text{Base} = 280}}$$

EXAMPLE

75 is 15% of what number?

SOLUTION STRATEGY

Remember, the base is usually identified as the value preceded by "of" in the statement. In this case, that value is the unknown. Because 15 has the percent sign, it is the rate and 75 is the part of the whole, or the portion.

$$B = \frac{P}{R}$$

$$B = \frac{75}{15\%} = \frac{75}{.15} = 500$$

$$\underline{\underline{\text{Base} = 500}}$$

EXAMPLE

Gold's Sporting Goods reports that 28% of total shoe sales are from Nike products. If last week's Nike sales were $15,400, what is the total amount of sales for the week?

SOLUTION STRATEGY

In this problem, the total amount of sales, the base, is unknown. Because 28% has the percent sign, it is the rate, and $15,400 is the portion. Note again, the portion is in the same terms as the base, dollar sales; however, the unique characteristic is that the portion represents Nike sales.

$$B = \frac{P}{R}$$

$$B = \frac{15{,}400}{28\%} = \frac{15{,}400}{.28} = 55{,}000$$

$$\underline{\underline{\text{Base} = \$55{,}000 = \text{Total sales for the week}}}$$

TRY-IT | EXERCISES

Solve the following for the base, rounding answers to hundredths or the nearest cent when necessary:

33. What is the base if the rate is 40% and the portion is 690?

34. $550 is 88% of what amount?

35. In a machine shop, 35% of the motor repairs are for broken shafts. If 126 motors had broken shafts last month, how many total motors were repaired?

36. At Office Depot, 75% of the copy paper sold is letter size. If 3,420 reams of letter size were sold, how many total reams of copy paper were sold?

Check your answers with the solutions on page 202.

REVIEW EXERCISES | CHAPTER 6—SECTION II

Solve the following for the portion, rounding to hundredths when necessary:

1. 15% of 380 is ______

2. 3.6% of 1,800 is ______

3. 200% of 45 is ______

4. $5\frac{1}{2}\%$ of $600 is ______

5. What is the portion if the base is 450 and the rate is 19%?

6. What is the portion if the base is 1,650 and the rate is 150%?

7. What number is 35.2% of 184?

8. What number is .8% of 500?

9. What number is $15\frac{4}{5}$% of 360?

10. What number is 258% of 2,500?

Solve the following for the rate, rounding to a tenth percent when necessary:

11. 40 is _______ % of 125

12. _______ % of 50 is 23

13. 600 is _______ % of 240

14. What is the rate if the base is 288 and the portion is 50?

15. What is the rate if the portion is 21.6 and the base is 160?

16. What is the rate if the base is $3,450 and the portion is $290?

17. What percent of 77 is 23?

18. What percent of 1,600 is 1,900?

19. 68 is what percent of 262?

20. $7.80 is what percent of $58.60?

Solve the following for the base, rounding to hundredths when necessary:

21. 69 is 15% of _______

22. 360 is 150% of _______

23. 6.45 is $18\frac{1}{2}$% of _______

24. What is the base if the rate is 16.8% and the portion is 451?

25. What is the base if the portion is 10 and the rate is $2\frac{3}{4}$%?

26. What is the base if the portion is $4,530 and the rate is 35%?

27. 60 is 15% of what number?

28. 160 is 130% of what number?

29. \$46.50 is $86\frac{2}{3}\%$ of what number?

30. .55 is 21.4% of what number?

Solve the following word problems for the portion, rate, or base:

31. Sharon Gibson owns 37% of a travel agency. If the total worth of the business is \$160,000, how much is Sharon's share?

32. What is the sales tax rate in a state where the tax on a purchase of \$464.00 is \$25.52?

33. *The Daily Times* reports that 28% of its advertising is for department stores. If department store advertising amounts to \$46,200, what is the total advertising revenue of the newspaper?

34. A Nissan assembly line produced 1,650 cars on Tuesday. If 759 of the cars were convertibles, what percent of the production was convertibles?

35. If Alton Amidon, a real estate agent, earned $6\frac{1}{2}\%$ commission on the sale of property valued at \$210,000, how much was Alton's commission?

36. Thirty percent of the inventory of a Nine West shoe store is in high heels. If the store has 846 pairs of high heels in stock, how many total pairs of shoes are in the inventory?

37. In a state with sales tax of $3\frac{1}{4}\%$, what is the tax on a purchase of \$4,380?

38. Friendly Ford advertised a down payment of \$1,200 on a Mustang valued at \$14,700. What is the percent of the down payment? Round to a tenth percent.

39. Judith Matsumoto, a sales associate for a large company, successfully makes the sale on 40% of her presentations. If she made 25 presentations last week, how many sales did she make?

40. A quality control process finds 17.2 defects for every 8,600 units of production. What percent of the production is defective?

41. The Parker Company employs 68 part-time workers. If this represents 4% of the total work force, how many individuals work for the company?

42. Twenty-six percent of the clerical workers responding to a survey used WordPerfect as their primary word processing software. If 1,900 persons were interviewed, how many used WordPerfect?

43. A corporation earned $457,800 last year. If its tax rate is $13\frac{3}{8}\%$, how much tax was paid?

44. In June, the New York Yankees won 15 games and lost 9. What percent of the games did they win? (*Hint:* Use total games played as the base.)

45. In its first "On The Street" survey, the National Highway Traffic Safety Administration reported that at any given daytime moment, about 3% of Americans behind the wheel are also talking on hand-held cell phones. The survey estimates this to be about 500,000 drivers.

a. Based on this information, how many total drivers are on the road at any given daytime moment? Round to the nearest hundred.

b. If data collectors observed a total of 12,000 cars in their survey, how many of those had drivers using cell phones?

c. According to the survey, women use cell phones more than men, 3.4% to 2.7%. If total drivers are 52% women and 48% men, use your answer from part **a** to find the number of women and men using phones, at any given time. Round to the nearest whole person.

BUSINESS DECISION

The Banquet

46. You are the catering manager for the Post Hotel. Last Saturday, your staff catered a wedding reception in the main ballroom, during which 152 chicken dinners, 133 steak dinners, and 95 fish dinners were served. All dinners are the same price. The hotel charges "per person" for catered events.

a. What percent of the total meals served was each type of dinner?

b. If $13,300 was charged for all the meals, how much revenue did each type produce?

c. If a 20% price increase goes into effect next month, what will be the new price per meal?

d. When photographers, florists, DJs, bands, and other outside vendors are booked through your office for events at the hotel, a $5\frac{1}{2}$% "finder's fee" is charged. Last year, $175,000 of such services were booked. How much did the hotel make on this service?

e. If your boss is expecting $11,000 in "finder's fee" revenue next year, what amount of these services must be booked?

SECTION III

SOLVING OTHER BUSINESS PROBLEMS INVOLVING PERCENTS

In addition to the basic percentage formulas, percents are used in many other ways in business. Measuring increases and decreases, comparing results from one year with another, and reporting economic activity and trends are just a few of these applications.

The ability of managers to make correct decisions is fundamental to success in business. These decisions require accurate and up-to-date information. Measuring percent changes in business activity is an important source of this information. Percents often describe a situation in a more informative way than simply the raw data alone.

For example, a company reports a profit of $50,000 for the year. Although the number $50,000 is correct, it does not give a perspective of whether that amount of profit is good or bad. A comparison to last year's figures, using percents, might reveal that profits are up 45% over last year, or profits are down 66.8%. Significant news!

> **Everybody's Business**
> **Learning Tip**
> It is important to remember, when solving percentage problems that involve "change" from an original number to a new number, the original number is always the *base* and represents 100%.

6-6 Determining Rate of Increase or Decrease

In calculating the rate of increase or decrease of something, we use the same percentage formula concepts as before. Rate of change means percent change, therefore the *rate* is the unknown. Once again we use the formula $R = P \div B$. Rate of change situations contain an original amount of something, which either increases or decreases to a new amount.

Predicting the probability of an event occurring is often expressed as a percent. For example, a weather forecast might include "a 50% chance of snow tonight."

In solving these problems, the original amount is always the base. The difference between the original and the new is the portion. The unknown is the rate, which describes the percent change between the two amounts.

STEPS FOR DETERMINING THE RATE OF INCREASE OR DECREASE:

Step 1. Identify the original and the new amounts, and find the *difference* between them.

Step 2. Using the rate formula, $R = P \div B$, substitute the difference from Step 1 for the portion, and the original amount for the base.

Step 3. Solve the equation for R. Remember, your answer will be in decimal form, which must be converted to a percent.

The following examples illustrate how this procedure is applied.

EXAMPLE

If a number increases from 60 to 75, what is the rate of increase?

SOLUTION STRATEGY

In this basic situation, a number changes from 60 to 75, and we are looking for the percent change; in this case it is an increase. The original amount is 60; the new amount is 75.

The portion is the difference between the amounts, 75 − 60 = 15, and the base is the original amount, 60. We now substitute these values into the formula,

$$R = \frac{P}{B} = \frac{15}{60} = .25 = 25\%$$

$$\underline{\underline{\text{Rate of increase} = 25\%}}$$

EXAMPLE

A number decreased from 120 to 80. What is the percent decrease?

SOLUTION STRATEGY

This problem illustrates a number decreasing in value. The unknown is the rate of decrease. We identify the original amount as 120, and the new amount as 80.

The difference between them is the portion: 120 − 80 = 40. The original amount, 120, is the base. Now apply the formula:

$$R = \frac{P}{B} = \frac{40}{120} = .333 = 33.3\%$$

Rate of decrease = 33.3%

EXAMPLE

Last year Continental Furniture had a work force of 360 employees. This year there are 504 employees. What is the rate of change in the number of employees?

SOLUTION STRATEGY

The key to solving this problem is to properly identify the variables. The problem asks "what is the rate"; therefore, the rate is the unknown. The original amount, 360 employees, is the base. The difference between the two amounts, 504 − 360 = 144, is the portion. We now apply the rate formula:

$$R = \frac{P}{B} = \frac{144}{360} = .4 = 40\%$$

Rate of increase in employees = 40%

EXAMPLE

Action Sporting Goods had revenue of $122,300 in May and $103,955 in June. What is the percent change in revenue from May to June?

SOLUTION STRATEGY

In this problem, the rate of change, the unknown, is a decrease. The original amount, $122,300, is the base. The difference between the two amounts, $122,300 − $103,955 = $18,345, is the portion. We apply the rate formula:

$$R = \frac{P}{B} = \frac{18,345}{122,300} = .15 = 15\%$$

Rate of decrease in revenue = 15%

TRY-IT | EXERCISES

Solve the following problems for the rate of increase or decrease, rounding to a tenth percent when necessary:

37. If a number increases from 650 to 948, what is the rate of increase?

38. If a number decreases from 21 to 15, what is the rate of decrease?

39. When Leonardo Mendez was promoted from supervisor to manager he received a salary increase from $450 to $540 per week. What was the percent change in his salary?

40. You are the production manager for the Keystone Corporation. After starting a quality control program on the production line, defects per day dropped from 60 to 12. Top management was very pleased with your results but wanted to know what percent decrease this change represented. Calculate the percent change in defects.

Check your answers with the solutions on page 202.

6-7 Determining Amounts in Increase or Decrease Situations

Finding the New Amount after a Percent Change

Sometimes the original amount of something and the rate of change will be known and the new amount, after the change, will be the unknown. For example, if a store sold $5,000 in merchandise on Tuesday and 8% more on Wednesday, what are Wednesday's sales?

Keep in mind that the original amount, or beginning point, is always the base and represents 100%. Because the new amount is the total of the original amount, 100%, and the amount of increase, 8%, the rate of the new amount is 108% (100% + 8%). If the rate of change had been a decrease instead of an increase, the rate would have been 8% less than the base, or 92% (100% − 8%).

The unknown in this situation, the new amount, is the portion; therefore, we use the formula Portion = Rate × Base.

Everybody's Business

Learning Tip

Remember, if the rate of change is an increase, *add* that rate to 100%.

If the rate of change is a decrease, *subtract* that rate from 100%.

STEPS FOR DETERMINING THE NEW AMOUNT AFTER A PERCENT CHANGE:

Step 1. In the formula Portion = Rate × Base, substitute the original amount, or starting point, for the base.

Step 2a. If the rate of change is an increase, add that rate to 100% to determine the rate.

Step 2b. If the rate of change is a decrease, subtract that rate from 100% to determine the rate.

Step 3. Solve the equation for the portion.

The following examples illustrate how these problems are solved.

EXAMPLE

Progressive Insurance estimated that the number of claims on homeowner's insurance would increase by 15%. If the company received 1,240 claims last year, how many can it expect this year?

SOLUTION STRATEGY

Last year's claims, the original amount, is the base. Because the rate of change is an increase, we find the rate by adding that change to 100% (100% + 15% = 115%). Now substitute these values in the portion formula.

$$P = R \times B$$

$$P = 115\% \times 1{,}240 = 1.15 \times 1{,}240 = 1{,}426$$

Portion = 1,426 = Number of homeowner's claims expected this year

EXAMPLE

Scotty's Drive-in Restaurant sold 25% fewer milk shakes this week than last week. If they sold 380 shakes last week, how many did they sell this week?

SOLUTION STRATEGY

Because this situation represents a percent decrease, the rate is determined by subtracting the rate of decrease from 100% (100% − 25% = 75%). As usual, the base is the original amount.

$$P = R \times B$$

$$P = 75\% \times 380 = .75 \times 380 = 285$$

$$\underline{\underline{\text{Portion} = 285 = \text{Number of milk shakes sold this week}}}$$

TRY-IT | EXERCISES

Solve the following business situations for the new amount, after a percent change:

41. Maxwell Imports had a computer with a 28 gigabyte hard drive. If it was replaced with a new model containing 60% more capacity, how many gigabytes would the new hard drive have?

42. Rapid Transfer has delivery trucks that cover 20% fewer miles per week during the winter snow season. If the truck averages 650 miles per week during the summer, how many miles can be expected per week during the winter?

Check your answers with the solutions on page 202.

Finding the Original Amount before a Percent Change

In another business situation involving percent change, the new amount is known and the original amount, the base, is unknown. For example, a car dealer sold 42 cars today. If this represents a 20% increase from yesterday, how many cars were sold yesterday? Solving for the original amount is a base problem, therefore we use the formula:

$$\text{Base} = \frac{\text{Portion}}{\text{Rate}}$$

STEPS FOR DETERMINING THE ORIGINAL AMOUNT BEFORE A PERCENT CHANGE:

Step 1. In the formula Base = Portion ÷ Rate, substitute the new amount for the portion.

Step 2a. If the rate of change is an increase, add that rate to 100% to determine the rate.

Step 2b. If the rate of change is a decrease, subtract that rate from 100% to determine the rate.

Step 3. Solve the equation for the base.

The following examples illustrate how these problems are solved.

EXAMPLE

Sunbelt Technologies found that after an advertising campaign, business in April increased 12% over March. If April sales were $53,760, how much were the sales in March?

SOLUTION STRATEGY

April's sales, the new amount, is the portion. Because the rate of change is an increase, we find the rate by adding that change to 100%. 100% + 12% = 112%.

$$B = \frac{P}{R}$$

$$B = \frac{53{,}760}{112\%} = \frac{53{,}760}{1.12} = 48{,}000$$

$$\underline{\underline{\text{Base} = \$48{,}000 = \text{March sales}}}$$

EXAMPLE

At Circuit City the price of a Sony VCR dropped by 15% to \$425. What was the original price?

SOLUTION STRATEGY

Because this situation represents a percent decrease, the rate is determined by subtracting the rate of decrease from 100%. 100% − 15% = 85%. The portion is the new amount, \$425. The original price, the base, is the unknown. Using the formula for the base,

$$B = \frac{P}{R}$$

$$B = \frac{425}{85\%} = \frac{425}{.85} = 500$$

$$\underline{\underline{\text{Base} = \$500 = \text{Original price of VCR}}}$$

TRY-IT | EXERCISES

Solve the following business situations for the original amount, before a percent change:

43. A harvester can cover 90 acres per day with a new direct-drive system. If this represents an increase of 20% over the conventional chain-drive system, how many acres per day were covered with the old chain-drive?

44. The water level in a large holding tank decreased to 12 feet. If it is down 40% from last week, what was last week's level?

Check your answers with the solutions on page 202.

6-8 Understanding and Solving Problems Involving Percentage Points

percentage points
A way of expressing a change from an original amount to a new amount, without using a percent sign.

Percentage points are another way of expressing a change from an original amount to a new amount, without using a percent sign. When percentage points are used, it is assumed that the base amount, 100%, stays constant. For example, if a company's market share increased from 40 to 44 percent of a total market, this is expressed as an increase of 4 percentage points.

The actual percent change in business, however, is calculated by using the formula:

$$\text{Rate of change} = \frac{\text{Change in percentage points}}{\text{Original amount of percentage points}}$$

In this illustration, the change in percentage points is 4, and the original amount of percentage points is 40; therefore,

$$\text{Rate of change} = \frac{4}{40} = .10 = \underline{\underline{10\% \text{ increase in business}}}$$

Everybody's Business

Learning Tip

Calculating percentage points is an application of the rate formula, Rate = Portion ÷ Base, with the change in percentage points as the *portion* and the original percentage points as the *base*.

EXAMPLE

When a competitor built a better mouse trap, a company's market share dropped from 55 to 44 percent of the total market, a drop of 11 percentage points. What percent decrease in business did this represent?

SOLUTION STRATEGY

In this problem, the change in percentage points is 11, and the original market share is 55. Using the formula to find rate of change:

$$\text{Rate of change} = \frac{\text{Change in percentage points}}{\text{Original amount of percentage points}}$$

$$\text{Rate of change} = \frac{11}{55} = .2 = 20\%$$

$$\underline{\underline{\text{Rate of change} = 20\% = \text{Decrease in market share}}}$$

TRY-IT EXERCISE

45. **Prior to an election, a political research firm announced that a candidate for mayor had gained 8 percentage points in the polls that month, from 20 to 28 percent of the total registered voters. What is the candidate's actual percent increase in voters?**

Check your answer with the solution on page 202.

REVIEW EXERCISES | CHAPTER 6—SECTION III

Solve the following increase or decrease problems for the unknown, rounding decimals to hundredths and percents to the nearest tenth:

1. If a number increases from 320 to 440, what is the rate of increase?

2. If a number decreases from 56 to 49, what is the rate of decrease?

3. What is the rate of change if the price of an item rises from \$123.00 to \$154.00?

4. What is the rate of change if the number of employees in a company decreases from 133 to 89?

5. 50 increased by 20% = _______

6. 750 increased by 60% = _______

7. 25 decreased by 40% = _______

8. 3,400 decreased by 18.2% = _______

9. 2,500 increased by 300% = _______

10. \$46 decreased by $10\frac{1}{2}$% = _______

11. Allied Plumbing sold 2,390 feet of $\frac{5}{8}$-inch galvanized pipe in July. If 2,558 feet were sold in August, what is the percent increase in pipe footage sales?

12. At a Safeway Supermarket the price of yellow onions dropped from \$.59 per pound to \$.45 per pound.

a. What is the percent decrease in the price of onions?

b. Tomatoes are expected to undergo the same percent decrease in price. If they currently sell for \$1.09 per pound, what will be the new price of tomatoes?

13. At a Sports Authority store 850 tennis rackets were sold last season.

a. If business is predicted to be 30% higher this season, how many rackets should be ordered from the distributor?

b. If racket sales break down into 40% graphite and 60% wood, how many of each type should be ordered?

14. Metro Toyota sold 112 cars this month. If that is 40% better than last month, how many cars were sold last month?

15. The Andretti Racing Team increased the horsepower of an engine from 340 to 440 by converting to fuel injection. What was the percent increase in horsepower?

16. The second shift of a factory produced 17,010 units. If this was $5\frac{1}{2}$% less than shift 1, how many units were produced on the first shift?

17. Housing prices in San Francisco have increased 37.5% over the price of homes 5 years ago.

a. If $80,000 was the average price of a house 5 years ago, what is the average price of a house today?

b. Economists predict that next year housing prices will drop by 4%. Based on your answer from part **a**, what will the average price of a house be next year?

18. After a vigorous promotion campaign, Kellogg's Frosted Flakes increased its market share from 5.4% to 8.1%, a rise of 2.7 percentage points. What percent increase in sales does this represent?

19. Recent economic reports indicate that unemployment in Winter Haven dropped from 8.8% to 6.8% in the past quarter, a decrease of 2 percentage points. What percent decrease does this represent?

BUSINESS DECISION

More Volume Isn't Just Noise

20. Using stock market data accumulated since 1954, statisticians at the popular Wall Street newspaper *Investor's Business Daily* (*IBD*) have observed that the greatest stock market winners (stocks that have doubled or tripled or more in price within any one-year period) have factors with certain "critical characteristics."

One of the factors identified by *IBD* is known as **Volume Percent Change**, and is listed in their stock market tables in a column labeled: **Vol % Chg**. Volume Percent Change identifies stocks with unusual changes in daily trading volume that wouldn't be detected in standard stock tables.

Volume Percent Change shows each stock's prior day's volume in terms of the percentage the stock traded above or below its average daily volume for the past fifty trading days.

Stocks with a Volume Percent Change of +50% or more are boldfaced in the *IBD* stock listings, allowing easy identification of stocks with significant increases in volume. For example, a +200 means that stock traded 200% more volume yesterday than the average daily volume over the past fifty trading days.

a. Using the partial stock listing below, calculate and fill in the missing information for *IBD*.

Company	50-day Av	Volume	Vol % Chg
Clarabell Group, Inc.	436,900	544,200	______
Morgan Motors, Inc.	88,300	172,400	______
StarTrek International	36,600	______	−32.2
Titan Manufacturing, Inc.	______	1,347,300	+162.8
Winkie-Dink Industries	500,400	426,700	______

b. Which of the stocks should be listed in boldface type?

c. (Optional) Obtain a current copy of *Investor's Business Daily,* or go to *www.investors.com*. Bring to class business stories, tables, and charts in which percents are used. Share your findings with the class.

CHAPTER FORMULAS

Portion = Rate × Base

Rate = Portion ÷ Base

Base = Portion ÷ Rate

SUMMARY CHART

SECTION I: Understanding and Converting Percents

Topic	P/O, Page	Important Concepts	Illustrative Examples
Converting a Percent to a Decimal	6-1 174	1. Remove the percent sign. 2. Move the decimal point two places to the left. 3. If the percent is a fraction, such as $\frac{4}{5}\%$, or a mixed number, such as $9\frac{1}{2}\%$, first change the fraction part to a decimal, then follow Steps 1 and 2.	$28\% = .28$ $159\% = 1.59$ $.37\% = .0037$ $\frac{4}{5}\% = .8\% = .008$ $9\frac{1}{2}\% = 9.5\% = .095$
Converting a Decimal or Whole Number to a Percent	6-1 175	1. Move the decimal point two places to the right. 2. Add a percent sign to the number. 3. If there are fractions involved, convert them to decimals first, then proceed with Steps 1 and 2.	$.8 = 80\%$ $2.9 = 290\%$ $.075 = 7.5\%$ $3 = 300\%$ $\frac{1}{2} = .5 = 50\%$
Converting a Percent to a Fraction	6-2 176	1. Remove the percent sign. 2. *(If the percent is a whole number)* Write a fraction with the percent as the numerator and 100 as the denominator. Reduce to lowest terms. or 2. *(If the percent is a fraction)* Multiply the number by $\frac{1}{100}$ and reduce to lowest terms. or 2. *(If the percent is a decimal)* Convert it to a fraction and multiply by $\frac{1}{100}$. Reduce to lowest terms.	$7\% = \frac{7}{100}$ $60\% = \frac{60}{100} = \frac{3}{5}$ $400\% = \frac{400}{100} = 4$ $2.1\% = 2\frac{1}{10}\% = \frac{21}{10} \times \frac{1}{100} = \frac{21}{1{,}000}$ $5\frac{3}{4}\% = \frac{23}{4} \times \frac{1}{100} = \frac{23}{400}$
Converting Fractions or Mixed Numbers to Percents	6-2 177	1. Change the fraction to a decimal by dividing the numerator by the denominator. 2. Move the decimal point two places to the right. 3. Write a percent sign after the number.	$\frac{1}{8} = .125 = 12.5\%$ $\frac{16}{3} = 5.333 = 533.3\%$ $12\frac{3}{4} = 12.75 = 1{,}275\%$

SECTION II: Using the Percentage Formula to Solve Business Problems

Topic	P/O, Page	Important Concepts	Illustrative Examples
Solving for the Portion	6-3 181	The portion is the number that represents a part of the base. To solve for portion, use the formula Portion = Rate × Base 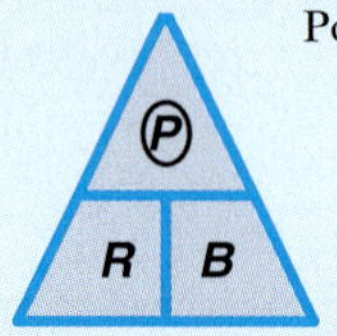 	15% of Meridian Enterprise's employees got raises this year. If 1,800 individuals work for the company, how many got raises? $P = .15 \times 1{,}800 = 270$ <u>270 employees got raises this year</u>
Solving for the Rate	6-4 182	The rate is the variable that describes what part of the base is represented by the portion. It is always the term with the percent sign. To solve for rate, use the formula $\text{Rate} = \dfrac{\text{Portion}}{\text{Base}}$ 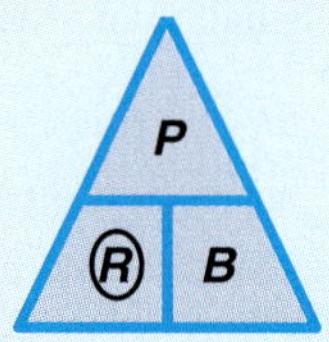 	28 out of 32 warehouses owned by Rio Distributors passed safety inspection. What percent of the warehouses passed? $\text{Rate} = \dfrac{28}{32} = .875 = 87.5\%$ <u>87.5% passed inspection</u>
Solving for the Base	6-5 184	Base is the variable that represents 100%, the starting point, or the whole thing. To solve for base, use the formula $\text{Base} = \dfrac{\text{Portion}}{\text{Rate}}$ 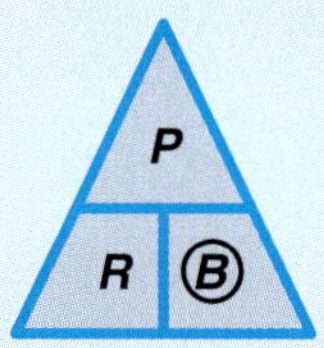 	34.3% of Delta Tile's sales are from customers west of the Mississippi River. If those sales last year were \$154,350, what are the company's total sales? $\text{Base} = \dfrac{154{,}350}{.343} = \$450{,}000$ <u>Total sales = \$450,000</u>

SECTION III: Solving Other Business Problems Involving Percents

Determining Rate of Increase or Decrease	6-6 190	1. Identify the original and the new amounts, and find the difference between them. 2. Using the rate formula $R = P \div B$, substitute the difference from Step 1 for the portion and the original amount for the base. 3. Solve the equation for R.	A price rises from \$45 to \$71. What is the rate of increase? $\text{Portion} = 71 - 45 = 26$ $\text{Rate} = \dfrac{P}{B} = \dfrac{26}{45} = .5778 = \underline{\underline{57.8\%}}$ What is the rate of decrease from 152 to 34? $\text{Portion} = 152 - 34 = 118$ $\text{Rate} = \dfrac{P}{B} = \dfrac{118}{152} = .776 = \underline{\underline{77.6\%}}$

SECTION III: (continued)

Topic	P/O, Page	Important Concepts	Illustrative Examples
Determining New Amount after a Percent Change	6-7 192	Solving for the new amount is a portion problem, therefore we use the formula Portion = Rate × Base 1. Substitute the original amount for the base. 2a. If the rate of change is an increase, add that rate to 100%. 2b. If the rate of change is a decrease, subtract that rate from 100%.	Dixie Plastics projects a 24% increase in sales for next year. If sales this year were $172,500, what sales can be expected next year? Rate = 100% + 24% = 124% $P = R \times B = 1.24 \times 172{,}500$ $P = 213{,}900$ Projected sales = $213,900
Determining Original Amount before a Percent Change	6-7 193	Solving for the original amount is a base problem, therefore we use the formula $\text{Base} = \dfrac{\text{Portion}}{\text{Rate}}$ 1. Substitute the new amount for the portion. 2a. If the rate of change is an increase, add that rate to 100%. 2b. If the rate of change is a decrease, subtract that rate from 100%.	If a DVD was marked down by 30% to $16.80, what was the original price? Portion = 100% − 30% = 70% $\text{Base} = \dfrac{P}{R} = \dfrac{16.80}{.7} = 24$ Original price = $24.00
Solving Problems Involving Percentage Points	6-8 194	Percentage points are another way of expressing a change from an original amount to a new amount, without using the percent sign. When percentage points are used, it is assumed that the base amount, 100%, stays constant. The actual percent change in business, however, is calculated by using the formula $\%\text{ Change} = \dfrac{\text{Change in percentage points}}{\text{Original percentage points}}$	After an intensive advertising campaign, Alpha Industries' market share increased from 21 to 27%, an increase of 6 percentage points. What percent increase in business does this represent? $\%\text{ change} = \dfrac{6}{21} = .2857 = 28.6\%$ % increase in business = 28.6%

TRY-IT EXERCISE | SOLUTIONS

1. $27\% = \underline{.27}$

2. $472\% = \underline{4.72}$

3. $93.7\% = \underline{.937}$

4. $.81\% = \underline{.0081}$

5. $12\frac{3}{4}\% = 12.75\% = \underline{.1275}$

6. $\frac{7}{8}\% = .875\% = \underline{.00875}$

7. $.8 = \underline{80\%}$

8. $1.4 = \underline{140\%}$

9. $.0023 = \underline{.23\%}$

10. $.016\frac{2}{5} = 1.6\frac{2}{5}\% = \underline{1.64\%}$

11. $19 = \underline{1{,}900\%}$

12. $.57\frac{2}{3} = 57\frac{2}{3}\% = \underline{57.67\%}$

13. $9\% = \underline{\frac{9}{100}}$

14. $23\% = \underline{\frac{23}{100}}$

15. $75\% = \frac{75}{100} = \underline{\frac{3}{4}}$

16. $225\% = \frac{225}{100} = 2\frac{25}{100} = \underline{2\frac{1}{4}}$

17. $8.7\% = 8\frac{7}{10}\% = \frac{87}{10} \times \frac{1}{100} = \underline{\frac{87}{1{,}000}}$

18. $1{,}000\% = \frac{1{,}000}{100} = \underline{10}$

19. $\frac{1}{5} = .2 = \underline{20\%}$

20. $\frac{70}{200} = .35 = \underline{\underline{35\%}}$ **21.** $\frac{23}{5} = 4\frac{3}{5} = 4.6 = \underline{\underline{460\%}}$ **22.** $6\frac{9}{10} = 6.9 = \underline{\underline{690\%}}$ **23.** $\frac{45}{54} = .8333 = \underline{\underline{83.33\%}}$

24. $140\frac{1}{8} = 140.125 = \underline{\underline{14{,}012.5\%}}$ **25.** $P = R \times B = .55 \times 980 = \underline{\underline{539}}$ **26.** $P = R \times B = .72 \times 3{,}200 = \underline{\underline{2{,}304}}$

27. $P = R \times B = .16 \times 1{,}250 = \underline{\underline{200}}$ salespeople **28.** $P = R \times B = .15 \times 148{,}500 = \underline{\underline{\$22{,}275}}$ down payment

29. $R = \frac{P}{B} = \frac{9}{21} = .4285 = \underline{\underline{42.9\%}}$ **30.** $R = \frac{P}{B} = \frac{67}{142} = .4718 = \underline{\underline{47.2\%}}$ **31.** $R = \frac{P}{B} = \frac{5{,}400}{18{,}000} = .3 = \underline{\underline{30\%}}$ of job completed

32. $R = \frac{P}{B} = \frac{5{,}518}{8{,}900} = .62 = \underline{\underline{62\%}}$ suits **33.** $B = \frac{P}{R} = \frac{690}{.4} = \underline{\underline{1{,}725}}$ **34.** $B = \frac{P}{R} = \frac{550}{.88} = \underline{\underline{\$625}}$

35. $B = \frac{P}{R} = \frac{126}{.35} = \underline{\underline{360}}$ motors **36.** $B = \frac{P}{R} = \frac{3{,}420}{.75} = \underline{\underline{4{,}560}}$ reams of paper

37. Portion = Increase = 948 − 650 = 298

Base = Original number = 650

$R = \frac{P}{B} = \frac{298}{650} = .45846 = \underline{\underline{45.8\%}}$ increase

38. Portion = Decrease = 21 − 15 = 6

Base = Original number = 21

$R = \frac{P}{B} = \frac{6}{21} = .2857 = \underline{\underline{28.6\%}}$ decrease

39. Portion = Increase = \$540 − \$450 = \$90

Base = Original number = \$450

$R = \frac{P}{B} = \frac{90}{450} = .2 = \underline{\underline{20\%}}$ increase

40. Portion = Decrease = 60 − 12 = 48

Base = Original number = 60

$R = \frac{P}{B} = \frac{48}{60} = .8 = \underline{\underline{80\%}}$ decrease

41. Rate = 100% + 60% = 160%

$P = R \times B = 1.6 \times 28 = \underline{\underline{44.8}}$ gigabytes

42. Rate = 100% − 20% = 80%

$P = R \times B = .8 \times 650 = \underline{\underline{520}}$ miles per week

43. Rate = 100% + 20% = 120%

$B = \frac{P}{R} = \frac{90}{1.2} = \underline{\underline{75}}$ acres per day

44. Rate = 100% − 40% = 60%

$B = \frac{P}{R} = \frac{12}{.6} = \underline{\underline{20}}$ feet

45. $R = \frac{P}{B} = \frac{8}{20} = .4 = \underline{\underline{40\%}}$ increase in voters

CHAPTER 6 | ASSESSMENT TEST

Name ______________________

Class ______________________

Convert the following percents to decimals:

1. 88% **2.** $3\frac{3}{4}\%$ **3.** 59.68% **4.** 422% **5.** $\frac{9}{16}\%$

Convert the following decimals or whole numbers to percents:

6. 12.6 **7.** .681 **8.** 53 **9.** $24\frac{4}{5}$ **10.** .0929

Convert the following percents to reduced fractions, mixed numbers, or whole numbers:

11. 19% **12.** 217% **13.** 7.44% **14.** 126% **15.** $25\frac{2}{5}\%$

Convert each of the following fractions or mixed numbers to percents:

16. $\frac{4}{5}$ **17.** $\frac{5}{9}$ **18.** $\frac{33}{4}$ **19.** $56\frac{3}{10}$ **20.** $\frac{745}{100}$

Solve the following for the portion, rate, or base, rounding decimals to hundredths and percents to the nearest tenth when necessary:

21. 24% of 1,700 = **22.** 56 is _____ % of 125 **23.** 91 is 88% of ____

24. What number is 45% of 680? **25.** $233.91 is what percent of $129.95?

26. 315 is 126% of _____ **27.** 60 increased by 15% = _____

28. If a number increases from 47 to 70.5, what is the rate of increase?

29. What is the base if the portion is 444 and the rate is 15%?

Answers

1. ______________________
2. ______________________
3. ______________________
4. ______________________
5. ______________________
6. ______________________
7. ______________________
8. ______________________
9. ______________________
10. ______________________
11. ______________________
12. ______________________
13. ______________________
14. ______________________
15. ______________________
16 ______________________
17. ______________________
18. ______________________
19. ______________________
20. ______________________
21. ______________________
22. ______________________
23. ______________________
24. ______________________
25. ______________________
26. ______________________
27. ______________________
28. ______________________
29. ______________________

Name ____________________

Class ____________________

Answers

30. ____________________

31. ____________________

32. ____________________

33. ____________________

34. ____________________

35. ____________________

36. a. ____________________

b. ____________________

c. ____________________

30. What is the portion if the base is 900 and the rate is $12\frac{3}{4}\%$?

31. What is 100% of 1,492?

32. 7,000 decreased by 62% = _____

Solve the following word problems for the unknown, rounding decimals to hundredths and percents to the nearest tenth when necessary:

33. An ad for JCPenney read, "This week only, all merchandise 35% off!" If a television set normally sells for $349.95, what is the amount of the savings?

34. If 453 runners out of 620 completed a marathon, what percent of the runners finished the race?

35. A letter carrier can deliver mail to 112 homes per hour by walking and 168 homes per hour by driving. By what percent is productivity increased by driving?

36. Last year Microtech's corporate jet required $23,040 in maintenance and repairs.

a. If this represents 32% of the total operating costs of the airplane, what was the total cost to fly the plane for the year?

b. If the plane flew 300,000 miles last year, what is the cost per mile to operate the plane?

c. Liberty Leasing offered a deal whereby it would operate the plane for Microtech for only $.18 per mile. What is the percent decrease in operating expense per mile being offered by Liberty?

Name ______________________

Class ______________________

37. Last year the Vista Corporation had sales of $343,500. If this year's sales are forecast to be $415,700, what is the percent increase in sales?

Answers

37. ______________________

38. ______________________

39. a. ______________________

b. ______________________

40. ______________________

41. ______________________

42. ______________________

43. a. ______________________

b. ______________________

38. After a 15% pay raise, Tricia Rivers now earns $27,600. What was her salary before the raise?

39. A freight container weighed 360 percent of its empty weight when it was full.

a. If the full weight was 1,800 pounds, what was the weight of the empty container?

b. What percent of the total loaded weight of the container was the merchandise?

40. Three of every seven sales transactions at Dollar Discount are on credit cards. What percent of the transactions are *not* credit card sales?

41. A pre-election survey shows that an independent presidential candidate has increased his popularity from 26.5 percent to 31.3 percent of the electorate, an increase of 4.8 percentage points. What percent does this increase represent?

42. By what percent is a 100-watt light bulb brighter than a 60-watt bulb?

43. Use the accompanying article from *The New York Times* to answer the following:

a. What is Hitachi's total work force?

b. What percent of the job cuts were in Japan?

Hitachi to Cut 4% of Its Work Force

Hitachi, Japan's largest private employer, said it would cut 4 percent of its work force, or 14,700 jobs, by March — 10,200 in Japan and the remaining 4,500 overseas. Hitachi, which expects a $1.2 billion loss for the year, joined Fujitsu, Toshiba and Kyocera in announcing major staff reductions recently.

Name ____________________

Class ____________________

Answers

44. a. ____________________

b. ____________________

45. ____________________

46. a. ____________________

b. ____________________

c. ____________________

____

47. a. ____________________

____

____

____

____

b. ____________________

44. Eddie Dawson, an ice cream vendor, pays $17.50 for a five-gallon container of premium ice cream. From this quantity, he sells 80 scoops at $.90 per scoop. If he sold smaller scoops, he could sell 98 scoops from the same container; however, he could only charge $.80 per scoop. As his accountant, you are asked the following questions:

a. If he switches to the smaller scoops, by how much will his profit per container go up or down? (Profit = Sales − Expenses.)

b. By what percent will the profit change?

45. An insurance adjuster for Kemper found that 12% of a shipment was damaged in transit. If the damaged goods amounted to $4,870, what was the total value of the shipment?

46. A state had 1,350,000 registered vehicles last year.

a. If 405,000 are leased, what percent of the total vehicles are *owned?*

b. If the state charges each owned vehicle a $5 highway tax per year and each leased vehicle an $8 highway tax per year, how much highway tax was collected last year?

c. What is the percent breakdown of owned and leased vehicles' dollar contribution as a percent of the total highway tax fund?

47. Wayne Leonida, a contractor, built a warehouse complex for the following costs: land, $12,000; concrete and steel work, $34,500; plumbing and electrical, $48,990; general carpentry and roof, $42,340; and all other expenses, $34,220.

a. What percent of the total cost is represented by each category of expenses?

b. When the project was completed, Wayne sold the entire complex for 185% of its cost. What was the selling price of the complex?

48. From the accompanying *USA Today* Snapshot, calculate the percent change in salary for each sport and enter your answers on the appropriate red lines. Round to a whole percent.

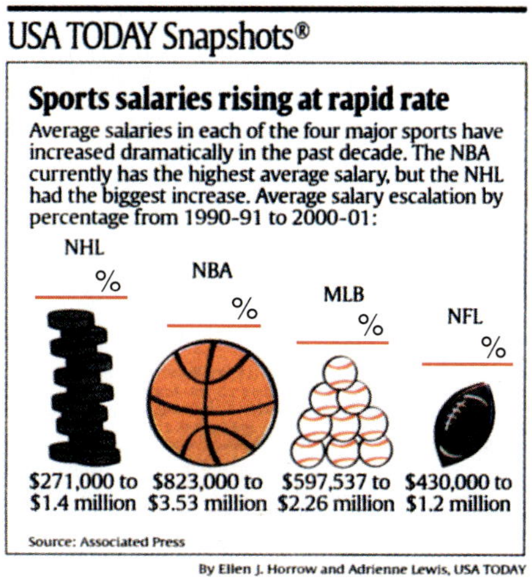

BUSINESS DECISION

Allocating Overhead Expenses

49. You are the owner of a chain of three successful restaurants, with the following number of seats in each location: airport, 340 seats; downtown, 218 seats; and suburban, 164 seats.

a. If the liability insurance premium is $16,000 per year, how much of that premium should be allocated to each of the restaurants, based on percent of total seating capacity? (Round each percent to tenths.)

b. If you open a fourth location at the beach, with 150 seats, and the liability insurance premium increases by 18%, what is the new allocation of insurance premium among the four locations?

c. (Optional) What other expenses could be allocated to the 4 restaurants?

d. (Optional) What other ways, besides seating capacity, could you use to allocate expenses?

Name ______________________

Class ______________________

Answers

48. ______________________

____

____

____

49. a. ______________________

____

____

b. ______________________

____

____

____

____

c. ______________________

d. ______________________

All the Math That's Fit to Learn

The Business Math Times

Volume VI | **Percents and Their Applications in Business** | One Dollar

When "Close Enough" Isn't

People often say, "It's close enough, it's only a small percentage!" But is it? What would constitute an ambitious but realistic error—or conversely, success—rate?

How about 99%? A 99% success rate would be a great batting average but a pretty crummy surgical success rate. Each day in the United States, 67,000 Americans undergo surgery. A 99% success rate would mean that 670 of those surgeries would not be successful. Assuming a six-day surgical workweek, that comes to 4,020 failures a week and 210,000 a year. Not very good!

What if the performance standard were set at 99.9% by some everyday organizations? This one-tenth of 1% failure rate would result in some startling numbers:

- 2 million documents would be lost by the IRS each year.
- 22,000 checks would be deducted from the wrong bank account in the next hour.
- 2,488,000 books would be shipped in the next year with the wrong cover.
- 45,000 American Express credit card statements would be sent to the wrong person.
- 18,322 pieces of mail would be mishandled in the next hour.
- 315 entries in Webster's *New International Dictionary* would be misspelled.
- $833,000,000 in individual income tax would not be collected.

"Our forecast was only 5,000% off, which is a 10,000% improvement in our forecasting."

"Quote . . . Unquote"

You miss 100% of the shots you never take
—*Wayne Gretzky*

Your imagination is your preview of life's coming attractions
—*Albert Einstein*

Office Furniture Goes 24/7

There is a famous photograph from the 1950s that shows offices, with row after row of secretaries and desks. The apparently endless grid of identical cubicles symbolizes the corporate mind-set of an earlier generation.

In many young corporations today, that conventional office layout has been totally redesigned. Gone are the old icons—the steel filing cabinet, the cubicle, the conference table. The concept of the workplace is adapting to the changes in the economy, technology, and the way people live.

With laptops, the Internet, cell phones, and faxes, the workplace can be anywhere and everywhere. The boundaries between work and personal space have blurred.

Many furniture companies have responded to the new work attitudes with softer, curving forms that embrace rather than alienate the worker.

In Europe, designers created the "communicating scarf," a cuddly thing containing a communication system with phone, computer screen, and keyboard. Wrap it around your face and you can telecommunicate as you stroll down the boulevard.

A Dutch designer, Hella Jongerius, developed a line called "My Soft Office" that includes a bed with a computer screen in its mattress and keyboard and mouse embedded in a "smart pillow."

"It's like velvet handcuffs," says consultant Eric Kuhn. "The digital era has taken 9 to 5 and turned it into a constant flow of connectedness. The tyranny of the 24-hour work day is undeniable. It's a state that some workers now call e-mail jail."

According to market researcher Madelyn Hochstein, businesses that want to attract bright young people in their mid-twenties need to recognize that the traditional boundaries between work and social life have disappeared. Ms Hochstein calls them the "whatever generation." They want social integration. They have parties in the office at 2 p.m. They sleep in the office. "It's become as much a home as a workplace and vice versa—their homes have become workplaces!"

Brainteaser

FOR ALL THE MARBLES

A bag contains three blue, four red, and three yellow marbles. How many blue marbles must be added to the bag for it to contain 75% blue marbles?

ANSWER TO LAST ISSUE'S BRAINTEASER

8 Pizzas

Let X = Pizzas sold on the first day

$$X + (X + 6) + (X + 12) + (X + 18) + (X + 24) = 100$$
$$5X + 60 = 100$$
$$5X = 40$$
$$\underline{\underline{X = 8}}$$

CHAPTER 7

Invoices, Trade Discounts, and Cash Discounts

PERFORMANCE OBJECTIVES

Section I The Invoice

7-1 Reading and understanding the parts of an invoice. (p. 210)
7-2 Extending and totaling an invoice. (p. 214)

Section II Trade Discounts—Single

7-3 Calculating the amount of a single trade discount. (p. 218)
7-4 Calculating net price by using the net price factor, complement method. (p. 218)
7-5 Calculating trade discount rate when list price and net price are known. (p. 219)

Section III Trade Discounts—Series

7-6 Calculating net price and trade discount amount by using a series of trade discounts. (p. 224)
7-7 Calculating the net price of a series of trade discounts by using the net price factor, complement method. (p. 224)
7-8 Calculating the amount of a trade discount by using a single equivalent discount. (p. 226)

Section IV Cash Discounts and Terms of Sale

7-9 Calculating cash discounts and net amount due. (p. 232)
7-10 Calculating net amount due, with credit given for partial payment. (p. 234)
7-11 Determining discount date and net date by using various dating methods. (p. 235)

SECTION I

THE INVOICE

invoice
A document detailing a sales transaction, containing a list of goods shipped or services rendered, with an account of all costs.

In business, merchandise is bought and sold many times as it passes from the manufacturer through wholesalers and retailers to the final consumer. Bills of sale or **invoices** are business documents used to keep track of these sales and purchases. From the seller's point of view, they are sales invoices; from the buyer's point of view, they are purchase invoices, or purchase orders.

Invoices are a comprehensive record of a sales transaction. They show what merchandise or services have been sold, to whom, in what quantities, at what price, and under what conditions and terms. They vary in style and format from company to company, but most contain essentially the same information. Invoices are used extensively in business, and it is important to be able to read and understand them. In this chapter, you become familiar with how businesses use invoices and the math applications that relate to them.

7-1 Reading and Understanding the Parts of an Invoice

Exhibit 7-1 shows a typical format used in business for an invoice. The important parts have been labeled and are explained in Exhibit 7-2. Some of the terms have page references, which direct you to the sections in this chapter that further explain those terms and their business math applications. Exhibit 7-2 also presents some of the most commonly used invoice abbreviations. These pertain to merchandise quantities and measurements.

EXHIBIT 7-1
Typical Invoice Format

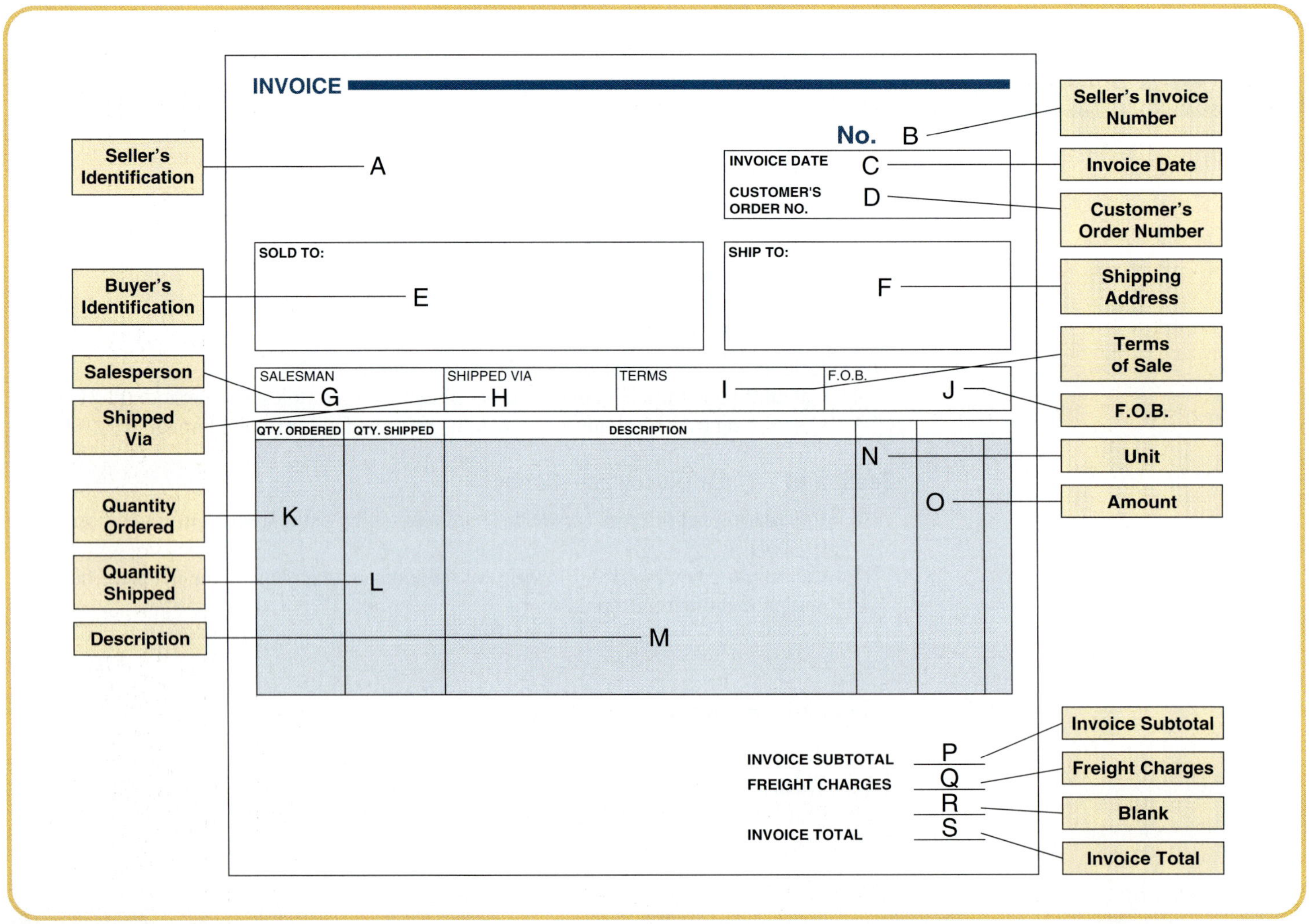

When companies ship and receive quantities of merchandise, invoices and purchase orders are used to record the details of the transaction.

With some practice, these terms and abbreviations will become familiar to you. Take some time to look them over before you continue reading.

Freight Terminology

Two frequently used freight terms that you should become familiar with are **F.O.B. shipping point** and **F.O.B. destination. F.O.B.** means "free on board" or "freight on board." These terms define who pays the freight charges and when the title (ownership) of the

F.O.B.
Term used in quoting shipping charges meaning "free on board" or "freight on board."

F.O.B. shipping point
The buyer pays all transportation charges from the vendor's location.

F.O.B. destination
The seller pays all transportation charges to the buyer's store or warehouse.

EXHIBIT 7-2

Invoice Terminology and Abbreviations

Invoice Terminology

- **A Seller's Identification**—Name, address, and logo or corporate symbol of the seller
- **B Seller's Invoice Number**—Seller's identification number of the transaction
- **C Invoice Date**—Date the invoice was written
- **D Customer's Order Number**—Buyer's identification number of the transaction
- **E Buyer's Identification**—Name and mailing address of the buyer
- **F Shipping Address**—Address where merchandise will be shipped
- **G Salesperson**—Name of salesperson credited with the sale
- **H Shipped Via**—Name of freight company handling the shipment
- **I Terms**—Terms of sale—Section detailing date of payment and cash discount (p. 232)
- **J F.O.B.**—"Free on board"—Section detailing who pays the freight charges (pp. 211–212)
- **K Quantity Ordered**—Number of units ordered
- **L Quantity Shipped**—Number of units shipped
- **M Description**—Detailed description of the merchandise, including model numbers
- **N Unit**—Price per unit of merchandise
- **O Amount**—Extended total—Quantity in units times the unit price for each line (p. 214)
- **P Invoice Subtotal**—Total of the "amount" column—Merchandise total (p. 214)
- **Q Freight Charges**—Shipping charges—Cost to physically transport the merchandise from the seller to the buyer (p. 212)
- **R Blank Line**—Line used for other charges, such as insurance or handling
- **S Invoice Total**—Total amount of the invoice—Includes merchandise plus all other charges (p. 214)

Invoice Abbreviations

ea.	each	pr.	pair	in.	inch	oz	ounce
dz. or doz.	dozen	dm. or drm.	drum	ft	foot	g or gr	gram
gr. or gro.	gross	bbl.	barrel	yd	yard	kg	kilogram
bx.	box	sk.	sack	mm	millimeter	pt	pint
cs.	case	@	at	cm	centimeter	qt	quart
ct. or crt.	crate	C.	100 items	m	meter	gal	gallon
ctn. or cart.	carton	M.	1,000 items	lb	pound	cwt	hundred weight

EXHIBIT 7-3

Freight Terminology

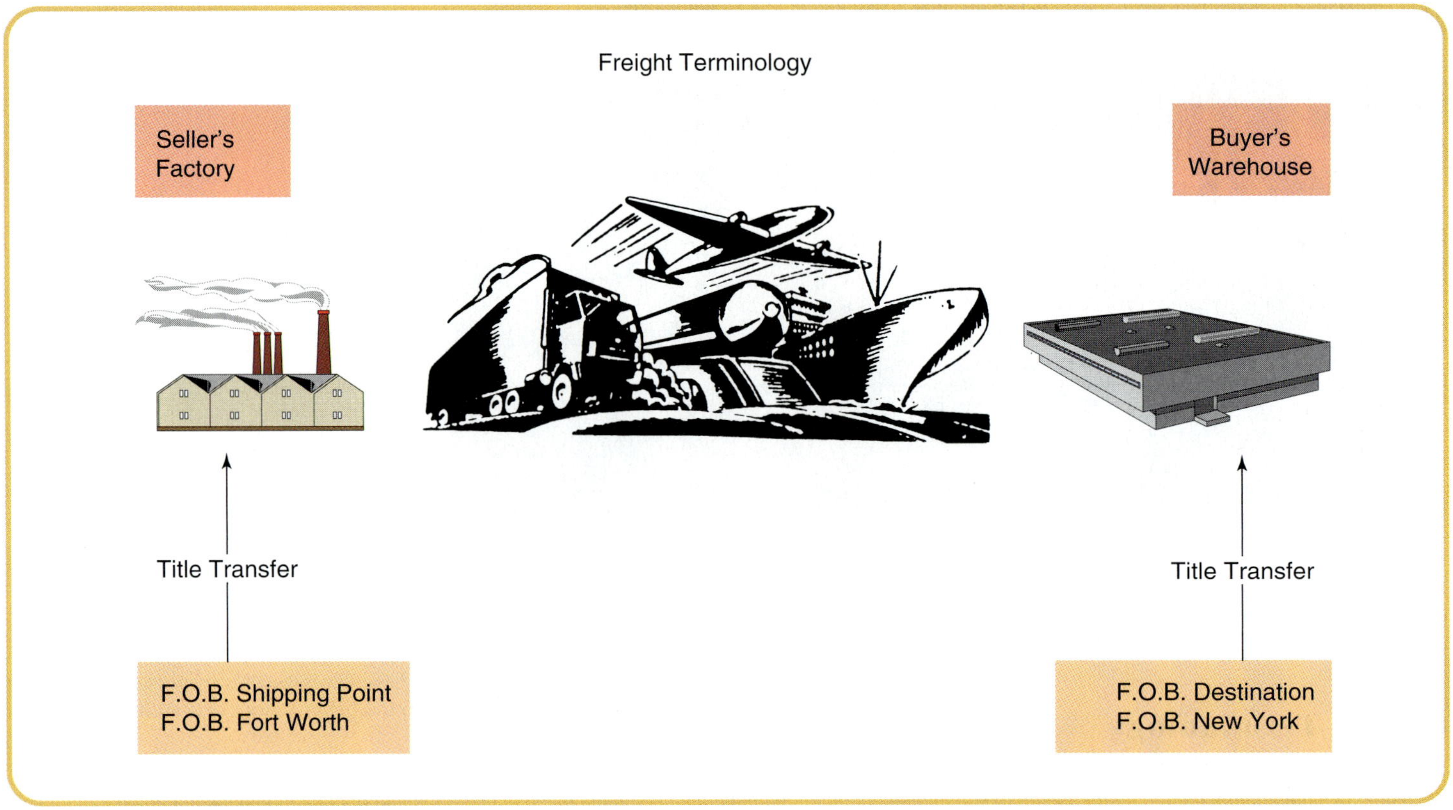

goods is transferred from the seller to the buyer. Ownership becomes important when insurance claims must be filed due to problems in shipment. Freight terms, such as terms of sale, are a negotiable issue between the seller and the buyer.

> **Everybody's Business**
>
> **Real-World Connection**
>
> Trade and Cash Discounts, as well as Markup and Markdown (Chapter 8), are particularly important concepts for those seeking careers related to the marketing channels, such as manufacturer's sales or wholesale or retail buying and merchandising.

F.O.B. Shipping Point When the terms are F.O.B. shipping point, the freight charges are paid by the buyer. The merchandise title is transferred to the buyer at the manufacturer's factory, or at a shipping point such as a railroad freight yard or air freight terminal. From this point, the buyer is responsible for the merchandise.

F.O.B. Destination When the shipping terms are F.O.B. destination, the seller is responsible for the shipping charges to the destination. The destination is usually the buyer's store or warehouse.

Sometimes the freight terms are stated as F.O.B. with the name of a city. For example, if the seller is in Ft. Worth and the buyer is in New York, F.O.B. Ft. Worth means the title is transferred in Ft. Worth, and the buyer pays the shipping charges from Ft. Worth to New York. If the terms are F.O.B. New York, the seller pays the shipping charges to New York and then the title is transferred to the buyer. Exhibit 7-3 illustrates these transactions.

EXAMPLE

From the following Whole Grain invoice, identify the indicated parts.

a. Seller	______	**b.** Invoice number	______
c. Invoice date	______	**d.** Cust. order #	______
e. Buyer	______	**f.** Terms of sale	______

INVOICE

Whole Grain Co.
697 Canyon Road
Boulder, CO 80304

No. 2112

INVOICE DATE	August 19, 200X
CUSTOMER'S ORDER NO.	B-1623

SOLD TO:	SHIP TO:
A & P SUPERMARKETS 565 North Avenue Atlanta, Georgia 30348	DISTRIBUTION CENTER 1424 Peachtree Road Atlanta, Georgia 30341

SALESPERSON	SHIPPED VIA	TERMS	F.O.B.
H. L. Mager	Terminal Transport	Net - 45 Days	Boulder, CO

QTY. ORDERED	QTY. SHIPPED	DESCRIPTION		UNIT	AMOUNT	
55 cs.	55 cs.	Corn Crunchies	24 ounce	22.19	$1220	45
28 cs.	28 cs.	Fruit and Nut Flakes	24 ounce	19.34	541	52
41 cs.	22 cs.	Rice and Wheat Flakes	16 ounce	21.14	465	08

INVOICE SUBTOTAL	2,227.05
FREIGHT CHARGES	67.45
INSURANCE	33.00
INVOICE TOTAL	$2,327.50

g. Shipping address ______ **h.** Salesperson ______
i. Shipped via ______ **j.** Insurance ______
k. Freight charges ______ **l.** Invoice subtotal ______
m. Unit price—Fruit and Nut Flakes ______ **n.** Invoice total ______

SOLUTION STRATEGY

a. Seller	Whole Grain	**b.** Invoice number	2112
c. Invoice date	August 19, 200X	**d.** Cust. order #	B-1623
e. Buyer	A & P Supermarkets	**f.** Terms of sale	Net 45 days
g. Shipping address	1424 Peachtree Rd	**h.** Salesperson	H. L. Mager
i. Shipped via	Terminal transport	**j.** Insurance	$33.00
k. Freight charges	$67.45	**l.** Invoice subtotal	$2,227.05
m. Unit price—Fruit and Nut Flakes	$19.34	**n.** Invoice total	$2,327.50

TRY-IT EXERCISE

1. From the following FotoFair invoice, identify the indicated parts:

a. Buyer ______ **b.** Invoice number ______
c. Invoice date ______ **d.** Amount—Model 55 ______
e. Seller ______ **f.** Terms of sale ______

INVOICE

No. 44929

FotoFair Corporation
3900 Crescent Way
Knoxville, TN 37996

INVOICE DATE	November 27, 200X
CUSTOMER'S ORDER NO.	09022

SOLD TO:	SHIP TO:
SHUTTERBUG CAMERA SHOPS 1518 N. W. 123rd. Street Chicago, Illinois 60613	Warehouse 1864 N. W. 123rd. Street Chicago, Illinois 60613

SALESPERSON	SHIPPED VIA	TERMS	F.O.B.
J. Herman	Federal Express	Net - 30 Days	Knoxville, TN

QTY. ORDERED	QTY. SHIPPED	DESCRIPTION	UNIT	AMOUNT	
160	160	Model 55 Instant Cameras	23.40	$3,744	00
120	120	Model 75 Instant Cameras	41.88	5,025	60
12cs.	12cs.	Developer Fluid	9.20	110	40
19bx.	19bx.	Photo developing paper - 8 x 10	12.50	237	50

INVOICE SUBTOTAL	9,117.50
FREIGHT CHARGES	183.70
INVOICE TOTAL	$9,301.20

g. Shipping address ________ **h.** Salesperson ________

i. Shipped via ________ **j.** F.O.B. ________

k. Freight charges ________ **l.** Invoice subtotal ________

m. Unit price—Model 75 ________ **n.** Invoice total ________

Check your answers with the solutions on page 247.

7-2 Extending and Totaling an Invoice

invoice subtotal
The amount of all merchandise or services on the invoice before adjustments.

invoice total
The final amount due from the buyer to the seller.

Extending an invoice is the process of computing the value in the Total or Amount column for each line of the invoice. This number represents the total dollar amount of each type of merchandise or service being purchased. The **invoice subtotal** is the amount of all items on the invoice before shipping and handling charges, insurance, and other adjustments, such as discounts, returns, and credits. The **invoice total** is the final amount due from the buyer to the seller.

STEPS TO EXTEND AND TOTAL AN INVOICE:

Step 1. For each line of the invoice, multiply the number of items by the cost per item.

$$\text{Extended total} = \text{Number of items} \times \text{Cost per item}$$

Step 2. Add all extended totals to get the invoice subtotal.

Step 3. Calculate the invoice total by adding the shipping charges and insurance to the subtotal and taking into account any other adjustments that may be involved in the transaction.

EXAMPLE

From the following invoice, extend each line to the total column and calculate the invoice subtotal and total.

Stock #	Quantity	Unit	Merchandise Description	Unit Price	Total
4334	17	ea.	15" B & W Monitors	$244.00	______
1217	8	ea.	13" Color Monitors	525.80	______
2192	2	doz.	Connecting Cables	24.50	______
5606	1	bx.	15" Anti-Glare Filters	365.90	______
				Invoice Subtotal	______
				Shipping Charges	$244.75
				Invoice Total	______

SOLUTION STRATEGY

					Total
B & W Monitors	17	×	$244.00	=	$4,148.00
Color Monitors	8	×	525.80	=	4,206.40
Connecting Cables	2	×	24.50	=	49.00
Anti-Glare Filters	1	×	365.90	=	365.90
			Invoice Subtotal		$8,769.30
			Shipping Charges		+ 244.75
			Invoice Total		$9,014.05

TRY-IT EXERCISE

2. From the following invoice, extend each line to the total column and calculate the invoice subtotal and total.

Stock #	Quantity	Unit	Merchandise Description	Unit Price	Total
R443	125	ea.	Food Processors	$ 89.00	______
B776	24	ea.	Microwave Ovens	225.40	______
Z133	6	doz.	12" Mixers	54.12	______
Z163	1	bx.	Mixer Covers	166.30	______
				Invoice Subtotal	______
				Shipping Charges	$194.20
				Invoice Total	______

Check your answers with the solutions on page 247.

REVIEW EXERCISES | CHAPTER 7—SECTION I

What word is represented by each of the following abbreviations?

1. bx. ________ **2.** pt ________ **3.** drm. ________ **4.** kg ________

5. gro. ________ **6.** oz ________ **7.** M. ________ **8.** cwt ________

Using the Frasier invoice below, extend each line to the amount column and calculate the subtotal and total. Then answer questions 9–22. (*Note:* Although 26 boxes of 2-inch reflective tape were ordered, only 11 boxes were shipped. Charge only for the boxes shipped.)

> **Everybody's Business**
>
> **Real-World Connection**
>
> Frequently, merchandise that is ordered from vendors is "out of stock" and goes into back-order status.
>
> As a general rule, companies charge only for the merchandise that is shipped.

INVOICE

Frasier Manufacturing
486 5th Avenue
Eureka, CA 95501

No. R-7431

INVOICE DATE June 16, 200X
CUSTOMER'S ORDER NO. 12144

SOLD TO:
J. M. Hardware Supply
2051 West Adams Blvd.
Lansing, MI 48901

SHIP TO:
SAME

SALESPERSON	SHIPPED VIA	TERMS	F.O.B.
H. Marshall	Gilbert Trucking	Net 30 Days	Effingham, IL

QTY. ORDERED	QTY. SHIPPED	DESCRIPTION	UNIT	AMOUNT
16 cases	16 cases	Masking Tape ½" Standard	21.90	
12 cases	12 cases	Masking Tape 1½" Standard	26.79	
26 Boxes	11 Boxes	2" Reflective Tape	88.56	
37 cases	37 cases	Sand Paper Assorted	74.84	

INVOICE SUBTOTAL ______
FREIGHT CHARGES 61.45
INVOICE TOTAL ______

9. Seller ______

10. Invoice number ______

11. Invoice date ______

12. Cust. order # ______

13. Buyer ______

14. Terms of sale ______

15. Shipping address ______

16. Salesperson ______

17. Shipped via ______

18. Insurance ______

19. Freight charges ______

20. Unit price—2" Tape ______

21. Invoice subtotal ______

22. Invoice total ______

BUSINESS DECISION

Accounts Payable

23. You are the accounts payable manager for The Linen Closet. The following invoice is due for payment to one of your vendors, Hamilton Mills.

a. Check the invoice for errors, and correct any you find.

INVOICE

Hamilton Mills
115 Rock Creek Road
Charlotte, North Carolina 28235

No. 49485

INVOICE DATE July 9, 200x
CUSTOMER'S ORDER NO. 49485

SOLD TO:	SHIP TO:
The Linen Closet 406 Maple Road Franklin, VA 23851	SAME

SALESPERSON	SHIPPED VIA	TERMS	F.O.B.
	Federal Express	Net 30 Days	Franklin, VA

QTY. ORDERED	QTY. SHIPPED	DESCRIPTION	UNIT	AMOUNT	
42	ea.	Sheets, king	$45.10	1,894	20
65	ea.	Sheets, queen	$37.60	2,444	00
26	pkg.	Pillow Cases, queen	$17.85	464	10
55	pkg.	Pillow Cases, std.	$14.35	789	25
8	ea.	Shams	$33.25	366	00

INVOICE SUBTOTAL	5,957.55
FREIGHT CHARGES	132.50
INSURANCE	21.15
INVOICE TOTAL	$6,111.20

b. Your inventory manager reports that there were three king-size sheets and five queen-size sheets returned, along with four packages of queen pillow cases. Calculate the revised total due.

c. The vendor has offered a 4% early payment discount that applies only to the merchandise, not the shipping or insurance. What is the amount of the discount?

d. What is the new balance due after the discount?

TRADE DISCOUNTS—SINGLE

SECTION II

The path merchandise travels as it moves from the manufacturer through wholesalers and retailers to the ultimate consumer is known as a channel of distribution or trade channel. The businesses that form these channels are said to be "in the trade." In today's complex economy, a number of different trade channels are used to move goods and services efficiently.

trade discount
Reductions from the manufacturer's list price given to businesses that are "in the trade," for performance of marketing functions.

list price
Suggested retail selling price of an item, set by the manufacturer or supplier. The original price from which discounts are taken.

Trade discounts are reductions from the manufacturer's suggested **list price.** They are given to businesses at various levels of the trade channel for the performance of marketing functions. These functions may include activities such as selling, advertising, storage, service, and display.

Manufacturers print catalogs showcasing their merchandise. Often, these catalogs contain the manufacturer's suggested list or retail prices. Businesses in the trade receive price sheets from the manufacturer listing the trade discounts, in percent form, associated with each item in the catalog. By issuing updated price sheets of trade discounts, manufacturers have the flexibility of changing the prices of their merchandise without the expense of reprinting the entire catalog.

Trade discounts are sometimes quoted as a single discount and sometimes as a series or chain of discounts. The number of discounts is dependent on the extent of the marketing services performed by the channel member.

7-3 Calculating the Amount of a Single Trade Discount

The amount of a single trade discount is calculated by multiplying the list price by the trade discount percent.

Trade discount amount = List price × Trade discount percent

EXAMPLE

What is the amount of the trade discount on merchandise with a list price of $2,800 and a trade discount of 45%?

SOLUTION STRATEGY

Trade discount amount = List price × Trade discount percent

Trade discount amount = 2,800 × .45 = $1,260

TRY-IT | EXERCISE

3. A retail gift shop buys merchandise with a list price of $7,600 from a wholesaler of novelty items and toys. The wholesaler extends a 30% trade discount to the retailer. What is the amount of the trade discount?

Check your answer with the solution on page 247.

7-4 Calculating Net Price by Using the Net Price Factor, Complement Method

net price
The amount a business actually pays for the merchandise after the discount has been deducted.

The **net price** is the amount a business actually pays for the merchandise after the discount has been deducted. It may be calculated by subtracting the amount of the trade discount from the list price.

Net price = List price − Trade discount amount

Frequently, merchants are more interested in knowing the net price of an item than the amount of the trade discount. In that case, the net price can be calculated directly from the list price without first finding the amount of the discount.

The list price of an item is considered to be 100%. If, for example, the trade discount on an item is 40% of the list price, the net price will be 60%, because the two must equal 100%. This 60%, the complement of the trade discount percent (100% − 40%), is the portion of the list price that *is* paid. Known as the **net price factor,** it is usually written in decimal form.

net price factor
The percent of the list price a business pays for merchandise. It is the multiplier used to calculate the net price.

STEPS TO CALCULATE NET PRICE BY USING THE NET PRICE FACTOR:

Step 1. Calculate the net price factor, complement of the trade discount percent:

Net price factor = 100% − Trade discount percent

Step 2. Calculate the net price:

Net price = List price × Net price factor

Note: This procedure can be combined into one step by the formula:

Net price = List price (100% − Trade discount percent)

Everybody's Business

Learning Tip

Complements are two numbers that add up to 100%. The trade discount percent and the net price factor are complements of each other. This means that if we know one of them, the other can be found by subtracting from 100%.

EXAMPLE

Calculate the net price of merchandise listing for $900 less a trade discount of 45%.

SOLUTION STRATEGY

Net price = List price (100% − Trade discount percent)

Net price = 900 (100% − 45%)

Net price = 900 (.55) = $495

TRY-IT EXERCISE

4. A hardware store bought paint supplies listing for $2,100 with a single trade discount of 35%. What is the net price of the order?

Check your answer with the solution on page 247.

7-5 Calculating Trade Discount Rate When List Price and Net Price Are Known

The trade discount rate can be calculated by using the now-familiar percentage formula, Rate = Portion ÷ Base. For this application, the amount of the trade discount is the portion, or numerator, and the list price is the base, or denominator.

$$\text{Trade discount rate} = \frac{\text{Amount of trade discount}}{\text{List price}}$$

STEPS FOR CALCULATING TRADE DISCOUNT RATE:

Step 1. Calculate the amount of the trade discount:

$$\text{Trade discount amount} = \text{List price} - \text{Net price}$$

Step 2. Calculate the trade discount rate:

$$\text{Trade discount rate} = \frac{\text{Amount of trade discount}}{\text{List price}}$$

EXAMPLE

Oxford Manufacturing sells tools to American Garden Supply. In a recent transaction, the list price of an order was $47,750, and the net price of the order was $32,100. Calculate the amount of the trade discount? What was the trade discount rate? Round your answer to the nearest tenth percent.

SOLUTION STRATEGY

$$\text{Trade discount amount} = \text{List price} - \text{Net price}$$

$$\text{Trade discount amount} = 47{,}750 - 32{,}100 = \underline{\underline{\$15{,}650}}$$

$$\text{Trade discount rate} = \frac{\text{Amount of trade discount}}{\text{List price}}$$

$$\text{Trade discount rate} = \frac{15{,}650}{47{,}750} = .3277 = \underline{\underline{32.8\%}}$$

TRY-IT | EXERCISE

5. Proline Sporting Goods recently sold tennis rackets listing for $109,500 to The Sports Authority. The net price of the order was $63,300. What was the amount of the trade discount? What was the trade discount rate? Round your answer to the nearest tenth percent.

Check your answer with the solution on page 248.

REVIEW EXERCISES | CHAPTER 7—SECTION II

Calculate the following trade discounts. Round all answers to the nearest cent.

	List Price	Trade Discount Rate	Trade Discount
1.	$860.00	30%	______
2.	125.50	12%	______
3.	41.75	19%	______
4.	499.00	8%	______
5.	88.25	50%	______

Calculate the following trade discounts and net prices to the nearest cent.

	List Price	Trade Discount Rate	Trade Discount	Net Price
6.	$286.00	25%	______	______
7.	134.79	40%	______	______
8.	21.29	18%	______	______
9.	959.00	55%	______	______

Calculate the following net price factors and net prices by using the complement method. Round all answers to the nearest cent.

	List Price	Trade Discount Rate	Net Price Factor	Net Price
10.	$3,499.00	37%	______	______
11.	565.33	24%	______	______
12.	1,244.25	45.8%	______	______
13.	4.60	$12\frac{3}{4}$%	______	______

Calculate the following trade discounts and trade discount rates. Round answers to the nearest tenth percent.

	List Price	Trade Discount	Trade Discount Rate	Net Price
14.	$4,500.00	______	______	$3,565.00
15.	345.50	______	______	225.00
16.	2.89	______	______	2.15

17. Find the amount of the trade discount on a television set that has a list price of $799.95 less a trade discount of 30%.

18. Find the amount of the trade discount on a set of fine china that lists for $345.70 less 55%.

19. What is the amount of the trade discount offered to a shoe store for merchandise purchased at a total list price of $7,800 less a trade discount of 25%?

20. Kalaidoscope for Kids, a chain of clothing stores, purchased merchandise with a total list price of $25,450 from Sandy Sport, a manufacturer. The order has a trade discount of 34%.

a. What is the amount of the trade discount?

b. What is the net amount Kalaidoscope owes Sandy Sport for the merchandise?

21. Bay Street Market ordered twelve cases of soup with a list price of $18.90 per case, and eight cases of baked beans with a list price of $33.50 per case. The wholesaler offered a 39% trade discount to Bay Street Market.

a. What is the total extended list price of the order?

b. What is the total amount of the trade discount on this order?

c. What is the total net amount Bay Street Market owes the wholesaler for the order?

22. An item with a trade discount of 41% has a list price of $289.50. What is the net price?

23. Gilbert Miranda, owner of Innovations Hair Boutique, places an order for beauty supplies from a wholesaler. The list price of the order is $2,800. If the vendor offers Gilbert a trade discount of 46%, what is the net price of the order?

24. A watch has a list price of $889.00 and can be bought by Sterling Jewelers for a net price of $545.75.

a. What is the amount of the trade discount?

b. What is the trade discount rate?

25. You are the buyer for the housewares department of a large department store. A number of vendors in your area carry similar lines of merchandise. On sets of microwavable serving bowls, Kitchen Magic offers a list price of $400 per dozen, less a 38% trade discount. Pro-Chef offers a similar set for a list price of $425, less a 45% trade discount.

a. Which vendor is offering the lower net price?

b. If you order 500 dozen sets of the bowls, how much money will be saved by using the lower-priced vendor?

BUSINESS DECISION

Quantity Discount

26. You are the purchasing manager for VisionMaster, a company that manufactures scanners and other computer peripherals. Your vendor for scanner motors, Enfield Industries, is now offering "quantity discounts" in the form of instant rebates and lower shipping charges, as follows:

Quantity	Net Price	Rebate	Shipping
1–500 motors	$16	none	$1.30
501–1,000 motors	16	$1.20	.90
1,001–2,000 motors	16	1.80	.60

a. Calculate the cost of the motors, including shipping charges, for each category.

b. If you usually purchase 400 motors per month, what percent would be saved per motor by ordering 800 every two months? Round to a tenth percent.

c. What percent would be saved per motor by ordering 1,200 every three months? Round to a tenth percent.

d. How much money can be saved in a year by purchasing the motors every three months instead of every month?

e. (Optional) What other factors, besides price, should be considered before changing your purchasing procedures?

SECTION III

TRADE DISCOUNTS—SERIES

Trade discounts are frequently offered by manufacturers to wholesalers and retailers in a series of two or more, known as **chain** or **series trade discounts.** For example, a series of 25% and 10% is verbally stated as "25 and 10." It is written 25/10. A three-discount series is written 25/10/5. Multiple discounts are given for many reasons. Some of the more common ones follow:

chain, or series, trade discount
Term used when a vendor offers a buyer more than one trade discount.

Position or Level in the Channel of Distribution A manufacturer might sell to a retailer at 30% trade discount, whereas a wholesaler in the same channel might be quoted a 30% and a 15% trade discount.

Volume Buying Many manufacturers and wholesalers grant an extra discount for buying a large volume of merchandise. For example, any purchase more than 5,000 units at one time may earn an extra 7% trade discount. Retailers with many stores or those with large storage capacity can enjoy a considerable savings (additional trade discounts) by purchasing in large quantities.

Advertising and Display Additional discounts are often given to retailers and wholesalers who heavily advertise and aggressively promote a manufacturer's line of merchandise.

Competition Competitive pressures often cause extra trade discounts to be offered. In certain industries, such as household products and consumer electronics, price wars are not an uncommon occurrence.

> **Everybody's Business**
> **Learning Tip**
> Remember, when calculating the net price by using a series of trade discounts, you *cannot* simply add the trade discounts together. Each discount must be applied to a successively lower base.

7-6 Calculating Net Price and Trade Discount Amount by Using a Series of Trade Discounts

Finding net price with a series of trade discounts is accomplished by taking each trade discount, one at a time, from the succeeding net price until all discounts have been deducted. Note that you *cannot* simply add the trade discounts together. They must be calculated individually, unless we use the net price factor method—a handy shortcut. Trade discounts can be taken in any order, although they are usually listed and calculated in descending order.

For illustrative purposes, let's begin with an example of how to calculate a series of trade discounts one at a time; then we shall try the shortcut method.

EXAMPLE

Calculate the net price and trade discount amount for merchandise with a list price of $2,000 less trade discounts of 30/20/15.

SOLUTION STRATEGY

$2,000	$2,000	$1,400	$1,400	$1,120	$1,120	
× .30	− 600	× .20	− 280	× .15	− 168	
$600	$1,400	$280	$1,120	$168	$952	= Net price

Trade discount amount = List price − Net price

Trade discount amount = 2,000 − 952 = $1,048

TRY-IT | EXERCISE

6. **Northwest Publishers sold an order of books to The Bookworm, Inc., a chain of bookstores. The list price of the order was $25,000. The Bookworm buys in volume from Northwest. They also prominently display and heavily advertise Northwest's books. Northwest, in turn, gives The Bookworm a series of trade discounts, amounting to 35/20/10. Calculate the net price of the order and the amount of the trade discount.**

Check your answers with the solutions on page 248.

7-7 Calculating the Net Price of a Series of Trade Discounts by Using the Net Price Factor, Complement Method

As a shortcut, the net price can be calculated directly from the list price, bypassing the trade discount, by using the net price factor as before. Remember, the net price factor is the complement of the trade discount percent. With a series of discounts, we must find the complement of each trade discount to calculate the net price factor of the series.

The net price factor indicates to buyers what percent of the list price they actually *do* pay. For example, if the net price factor of a series of discounts is calculated to be .665, this means that the buyer is paying 66.5% of the list price.

STEPS TO CALCULATE NET PRICE OF A SERIES OF DISCOUNTS BY USING THE NET PRICE FACTOR:

Step 1. Find the complement of the trade discounts in the series by subtracting each from 100% and converting them to decimal form.

Step 2. Calculate the net price factor of the series by multiplying all the decimals together.

Step 3. Calculate the net price by multiplying the list price by the net price factor:

$$\text{Net price} = \text{List price} \times \text{Net price factor}$$

EXAMPLE

The Crystal Gallery purchased merchandise from a manufacturer in Italy with a list price of $37,000 less trade discounts of 40/25/10. Calculate the net price factor and the net price of the order.

SOLUTION STRATEGY

Step 1. Subtract each trade discount from 100% and convert to decimals.

$$\begin{array}{r} 100\% \\ -\ 40\% \\ \hline 60\% \end{array} = .6 \qquad \begin{array}{r} 100\% \\ -\ 25\% \\ \hline 75\% \end{array} = .75 \qquad \begin{array}{r} 100\% \\ -\ 10\% \\ \hline 90\% \end{array} = .9$$

Step 2. Multiply all the complements together to get the net price factor.

$$\text{Net price factor} = .6 \times .75 \times .9$$

$$\text{Net price factor} = \underline{\underline{.405}}$$

Step 3.

$$\text{Net price} = \text{List price} \times \text{Net price factor}$$

$$\text{Net price} = 37{,}000 \times .405$$

$$\text{Net price} = \underline{\underline{\$14{,}985}}$$

TRY-IT | EXERCISE

7. Something's Fishy, a pet shop, always gets a 30/20/12 series of trade discounts from the Clearview Fish Tank Company. In June, the shop ordered merchandise with a list price of $3,500. In September, the shop placed an additional order listing for $5,800.

a. What is the net price factor for the series of trade discounts?

b. What is the net price of the merchandise purchased in June?

c. What is the net price of the merchandise purchased in September?

Check your answers with the solutions on page 248.

7-8 Calculating the Amount of a Trade Discount by Using a Single Equivalent Discount

single equivalent discount
A single trade discount that equates to all the discounts in a series or chain.

Sometimes retailers and wholesalers want to know the one single discount rate that equates to a series of trade discounts. This is known as the **single equivalent discount.** We have already learned that the trade discounts *cannot* simply be added together.

Here is the logic: The list price of the merchandise is 100%. If the net price factor is the part of the list price that is paid, then 100% minus the net price factor is the part of the list price that *is* the trade discount. The single equivalent discount, therefore, is the complement of the net price factor (100% − Net price factor percent).

STEPS TO CALCULATE THE SINGLE EQUIVALENT DISCOUNT AND THE AMOUNT OF A TRADE DISCOUNT:

Step 1. Calculate the net price factor as before, by subtracting each trade discount from 100% and multiplying them all together in decimal form.

Step 2. Calculate the single equivalent discount by subtracting the net price factor in decimal form from 1.

Single equivalent discount = 1 − Net price factor

Step 3. Find the amount of the trade discount by multiplying the list price by the single equivalent discount.

Trade discount amount = List price × Single equivalent discount

EXAMPLE

Calculate the single equivalent discount and amount of the trade discount on merchandise listing for $10,000, less trade discounts of 30/10/5.

SOLUTION STRATEGY

Step 1. Calculate the net price factor:

$$\begin{array}{ccccccc} 100\% & & 100\% & & 100\% & & \\ -\ 30\% & & -\ 10\% & & -\ 5\% & & \\ \hline .70 & \times & .90 & \times & .95 & = & .5985 = \text{Net price factor} \end{array}$$

Step 2. Calculate the single equivalent discount:

Single equivalent discount = 1 − Net price factor

Single equivalent discount = 1 − .5985 = .4015

Note: 40.15% is the single equivalent discount of the series 30%, 10%, and 5%.

Step 3. Calculate the trade discount amount:

Trade discount amount = List price × Single equivalent discount

Trade discount amount = $10,000 × .4015 = $4,015

TRY-IT | EXERCISE

8. The Rainbow Appliance Center purchased an order of dishwashers and ovens listing for \$36,800. The manufacturer allows Rainbow a series of trade discounts of 25/15/10. What are the single equivalent discount and the amount of trade discount?

Check your answers with the solutions on page 248.

REVIEW EXERCISES | CHAPTER 7—SECTION III

Calculate the following net price factors and net prices. For convenience, round net price factors to five decimal places when necessary:

	List Price	Trade Discount Rates	Net Price Factor	Net Price
1.	\$360.00	12/10		
2.	425.80	18/15/5		
3.	81.75	20/10/10		
4.	979.20	15/10/5		
5.	7.25	25/15/10$\frac{1}{2}$		
6.	.39	20/9/8		

Calculate the following net price factors and single equivalent discounts. Round to five places when necessary.

	Trade Discount Rates	Net Price Factor	Single Equivalent Discount
7.	15/10		
8.	20/15/12		
9.	25/15/7		
10.	30/5/5		
11.	35/15/7.5		

Complete the following table. Round net price factors to five decimal places when necessary.

	List Price	Trade Discount Rates	Net Price Factor	Single Equivalent Discount	Trade Discount	Net Price
12.	\$7,800.00	15/5/5				
13.	1,200.00	20/15/7				
14.	560.70	25/15/5				
15.	883.50	18/12/9				
16.	4.89	12/10/10				
17.	2,874.95	30/20/5.5				

18. What is the net price factor of a 25/10 series of trade discounts?

19. What is the net price factor of a 35/15/10 series of discounts?

20. Toy Town orders toys, games, and videos with a list price of $10,300 less trade discounts of 25/15/12.

a. What is the net price factor?

b. What is the net price of the order?

21. Contempo Designs places an order for furniture listing for $90,500 less trade discounts of 25/20.

a. What is the net price factor?

b. What is the net price of the order?

22. If a supplier offers you trade discounts with a net price factor of .5788, what is the single equivalent discount?

23. A vendor offers trade discounts of 25/15/10.

a. What is the net price factor?

b. What is the single equivalent discount?

24. An order of lightbulbs listing for $9,500 has trade discounts of 25/13/8.

a. What is the net price factor?

b. What is the single equivalent discount?

c. What is the amount of the trade discount?

d. What is the net price of the order?

25. Shari's Boutique is offered a line of blouses that list for $700 per dozen from a clothing manufacturer. They are offering trade discounts of 35/25/5.

a. What is the net price per dozen Shari will pay for the blouses?

b. What is the single equivalent discount of this deal?

26. The Speedy Auto Service Center can buy auto parts from Southeast Auto Supply at a series discount of 20/15/5 and from Northwest Auto Supply for 25/10/8.

a. Which auto parts supplier offers a better deal to Speedy?

b. If Speedy orders $15,000 in parts at list price per month, how much will they save in a year by choosing the lower-priced supplier?

27. Toshiba offers wholesalers a series discount of 35/20/20 and retailers a series discount of 35/20. A television set has a list price of $560.

a. What is the price the wholesaler pays?

b. What is the price to the retailer?

28. Taylor Pharmacy buys merchandise from B. G. Distributors with a series discount of 35/15/7.

a. What is the single equivalent discount?

b. What is the amount of the trade discount on an order with a list price of $5,700?

29. Certified Food Distributors received the following items at a discount of 25/20/10: 18 cases of marinara sauce listing at $26.80 per case and 45 cases of tomato sauce listing at $22.50 per case.

a. What is the total list price of this order?

b. What is the amount of the trade discount?

c. What is the net price of the order?

30. Shopper's Mart purchased the following items. Calculate the extended total after the trade discounts for each line, the invoice subtotal, and the invoice total:

Quantity	Unit	Merchandise	Unit List	Trade Discounts	Extended Total
150	ea.	Blenders	$ 59.95	20/15/15	________
400	ea.	Toasters	39.88	20/10/10	________
18	doz.	Coffee Mills	244.30	30/9/7	________
12	doz.	Juicers	460.00	25/10/5	________
				Invoice subtotal	________
		Extra $5\frac{1}{2}$% volume discount on total order			________
				Invoice total	________

BUSINESS DECISION

Negotiate and Save

31. Referring back to Exercise 30, you have just been hired as the new buyer for the kitchen division of Shopper's Mart, a general merchandise retailer. After looking over the discounts offered to the previous buyer by the vendor, you decide to ask for better discounts.

After negotiating with the vendor's salesperson, you now can buy blenders at trade discounts of 20/20/15, and juicers at 25/15/10. In addition, the vendor has increased the volume discount to $6\frac{1}{2}$%.

a. How much would have been saved with your new discounts, based on the quantites of the previous order (Exercise 30)?

b. As a result of your negotiations, the vendor has offered an additional discount of 2% of the total amount due if the invoice is paid within 15 days instead of the usual 30 days. What would be the amount of this discount?

c. (Optional) Contact some companies in your area, such as manufacturers, wholesalers, or retailers, that ship and receive quantities of merchandise. Speak with an employee in the shipping, purchasing, or sales department. Identify yourself as a student of business math from your school who is doing a class research assignment. Obtain information about any or all of the following, and report your findings to the class:

- What products they sell
- Who their customers are
- Invoices and purchase orders they use (obtain samples, if possible)
- Trade discounts they offer their customers and receive from their vendors
- Terms of sale, and cash discounts they offer and receive
- Career advice

SECTION IV

CASH DISCOUNTS AND TERMS OF SALE

As merchandise physically arrives at the buyer's back door, the invoice ordinarily arrives by mail through the front door. What happens next? The invoice has a section entitled **terms of sale.** The terms of sale are the details of when the invoice must be paid and whether any additional discounts will be offered.

Commonly, manufacturers allow wholesalers and retailers 30 days or even longer to pay the bill. In certain industries, the time period is as much as 60 or 90 days. This is known as the **credit period.** This gives the buyer time to unpack and check the order, and more important, begin selling the merchandise. This credit period clearly gives the wholesaler and retailer an advantage. They can generate revenue by selling merchandise that they have not paid for yet.

To encourage them to pay the bill earlier than the **net date,** or **due date,** sellers frequently offer buyers an optional extra discount, over and above the trade discounts. This is known as a **cash discount.** Cash discounts are an extra few percent offered as an incentive for early payment of the invoice, usually within 10 to 15 days after the **invoice date.** This is known as the **cash discount period.** The last date for a buyer to take advantage of a cash discount is known as the **discount date.**

terms of sale
The details of when an invoice must be paid, and if a cash discount is being offered.

credit period
The time period that the seller allows the buyer to pay an invoice.

net date, due date
The last day of the credit period.

cash discount
An extra discount offered by the seller as an incentive for early payment of an invoice.

invoice date
The date an invoice is written. The beginning of the discount and credit periods when ordinary dating is used.

cash discount period
The time period in which a buyer can take advantage of the cash discount.

discount date
The last day of the discount period.

The Importance of Cash Discounts

Both buyers and sellers benefit from cash discounts. Sellers get their money much sooner, which improves their cash flow, whereas buyers get an additional discount, which lowers their merchandise cost, thereby raising their margin or gross profit.

Cash discounts generally range from an extra 1% to 5% off the net price of the merchandise. A 1% to 5% discount may not seem significant, but it is. Let's say that an invoice is due in 30 days; however, a distributor would like payment sooner. They might offer the retailer a cash discount of 2% if the bill is paid within 10 days rather than 30 days. If the retailer chooses to take the cash discount, he or she must pay the bill by the 10th day after the date of the invoice. Note that this is *20 days* earlier than the due date. The retailer is therefore receiving a 2% discount for paying the bill 20 days early.

The logic: There are 18.25 twenty-day periods in a year (365 days divided by 20 days). By multiplying the 2% discount by the 18.25 periods, we see that on a yearly basis, 2% cash discounts can *theoretically* amount to 36.5%. Very significant!

Everybody's Business
Real-World Connection
Cash discounts are so important to wholesaler's and retailer's "profit picture" that frequently they borrow the money on a short-term basis to take advantage of the cash discount savings. This procedure is covered in Chapter 10, "Simple Interest."

7-9 Calculating Cash Discounts and Net Amount Due

Cash discounts are offered in the terms of sale. A transaction with no cash discount would have terms of sale of net 30, for example. This means the **net amount** of the invoice is due in 30 days. If a cash discount is offered, the terms of sale would be written as 2/10, n/30. This means a 2% cash discount may be taken if the invoice is paid within 10 days; if not, the net amount is due in 30 days. See Exhibit 7-4.

net amount
The amount of money due from the buyer to the seller.

EXHIBIT 7-4
Terms of Sale

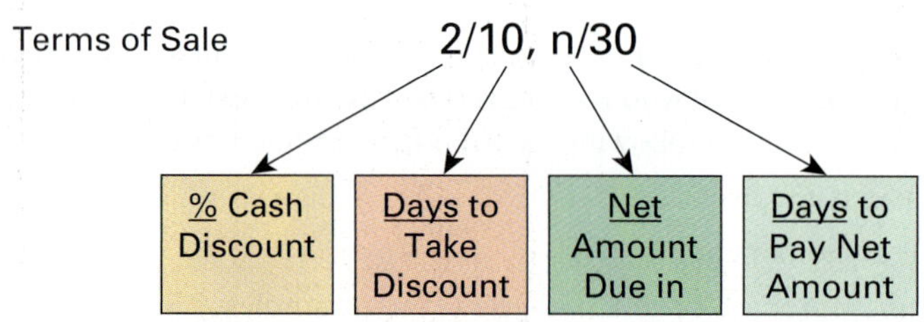

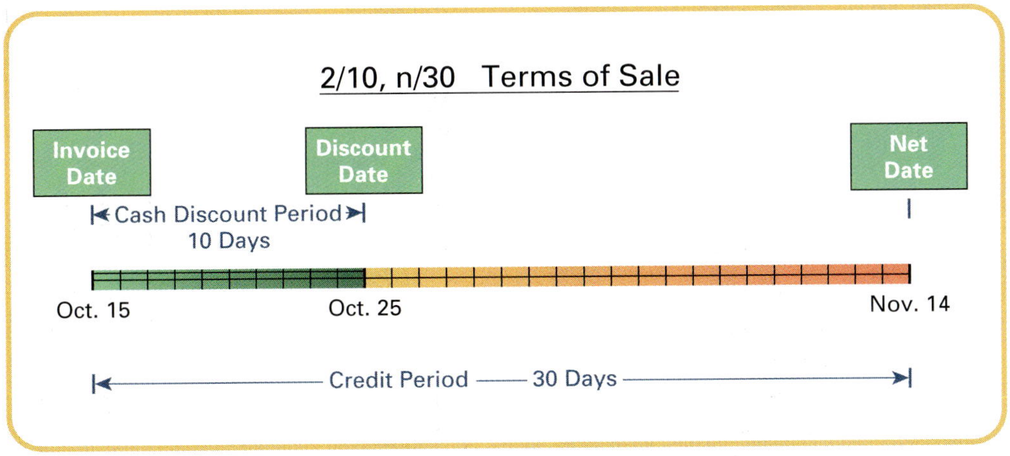

EXHIBIT 7-5
Terms of Sale Time Line

Exhibit 7-5 shows a time line of the discount period and credit period on an invoice, dated October 15. The 2/10, n/30 terms of sale stipulate a cash discount if the bill is paid within 10 days. If not, the balance is due in 30 days. As you can see, the cash discount period runs for 10 days from the invoice date, October 15 to October 25. The credit period, 30 days, extends from the invoice date through November 14.

Sometimes, two cash discounts are offered, such as 3/15, 1/25, n/60. This means a 3% cash discount is offered if the invoice is paid within 15 days, a 1% cash discount if the invoice is paid within 25 days, with the net amount due in 60 days.

Cash discounts cannot be taken on freight charges or returned goods, only on the net price of the merchandise. If freight charges are included in the amount of an invoice, they must be subtracted before taking the cash discount. After the cash discount has been deducted, the freight charges are added back to get the invoice total.

If arriving merchandise is damaged or is not what was ordered, those goods will be returned to the vendor. The amount of the returned goods must also be subtracted from the amount of the invoice. They are no longer a part of the transaction.

STEPS TO CALCULATE CASH DISCOUNT AND NET AMOUNT DUE:

Step 1. Calculate the amount of the cash discount by multiplying the cash discount percent by the net price of the merchandise:

Cash discount = Net price × Cash discount percent

Step 2. Calculate the net amount due by subtracting the amount of the cash discount from the net price:

Net amount due = Net price − Cash discount

Note: As with trade discounts, buyers are frequently more interested in the net amount due than the amount of the discount. When that is the case, we can simplify the calculation by using the complement method to determine the net amount due.

Net amount due = Net price (100% − Cash discount percent)

Everybody's Business

Learning Tip

Remember, freight charges or returned items are not subject to cash discounts. These must be deducted from the invoice before the cash discount is applied. After the discount is taken, freight charges, if any, are added back to get the invoice total.

EXAMPLE

A retailer buys merchandise from a supplier with an invoice amount of $16,000. The terms of sale are 2/10, n/30. What is the amount of the cash discount? What is the net amount due on this order if the bill is paid by the 10th day?

SOLUTION STRATEGY

Cash discount = Net price × Cash discount percent

Cash discount = 16,000 × .02 = $320

Net amount due = Net price − Cash discount

Net amount due = 16,000 − 320 = $15,680

TRY-IT | EXERCISE

9. Melody Music ordered cassette tapes and compact discs from a supplier with a net price of $8,300 and terms of sale of 3/15, n/45. What is the amount of the cash discount? What is the net amount due if the bill is paid by the 15th day?

Check your answers with the solutions on page 248.

7-10 Calculating Net Amount Due, with Credit Given for Partial Payment

Sometimes buyers do not have all the money needed to take advantage of the cash discount. Manufacturers and suppliers usually allow them to pay part of the invoice by the discount date and the balance by the end of the credit period. These **partial payments** earn partial cash discount credit. In this situation, we must calculate how much **partial payment credit** is given.

partial payment
When a portion of the invoice is paid within the discount period.

partial payment credit
The amount of the invoice paid off by the partial payment.

Here is how it works: Assume a cash discount of 4/15, n/45 is offered to a retailer. A 4% cash discount means that the retailer will pay 96% of the bill (100% − 4%) and receive 100% credit. Another way to look at it is that every $.96 paid toward the invoice earns $1.00 credit. We must determine how many $.96s are in the partial payment. This will tell us how many $1.00s of credit we receive.

Everybody's Business
Real-World Connection
The extension of partial payment credit by vendors is important to small retailers who don't always have the cash flow to take advantage of the full cash discount.

STEPS TO CALCULATE PARTIAL PAYMENT CREDIT AND NET AMOUNT DUE:

Step 1. Calculate the amount of credit given for a partial payment by dividing the partial payment by the complement of the cash discount percent:

$$\text{Partial payment credit} = \frac{\text{Partial payment}}{100\% - \text{Cash discount percent}}$$

Step 2. Calculate the net amount due by subtracting the partial payment credit from the net price:

$$\text{Net amount due} = \text{Net price} - \text{Partial payment credit}$$

EXAMPLE

Happy Feet, a chain of children's shoe stores, receives an invoice from a tennis shoe manufacturer on September 3, with terms of 3/20, n/60. The net price of the order is $36,700. Happy Feet wants to send a partial payment of $10,000 by the discount date and the balance on the net date. How much credit does Happy Feet get for the partial payment? What is the remaining net amount due to the manufacturer?

EXAMPLE

If an invoice dated April 14 is due in 75 days, what is the net date?

SOLUTION STRATEGY

Step 1. From the calendar, April 14 is day number 104.
Step 2. $104 + 75 = 179$
Step 3. From the calendar, day number 179 is June 28.

Terms of Sale—Dating Methods

Ordinary Dating

Ordinary dating is when the discount period and the credit period start on the date of the invoice. It is the most common method of dating the terms of sale. The last day to take advantage of the cash discount, the discount date, is found by adding the number of days in the discount period to the date of the invoice. For example, to receive a cash discount, an invoice dated November 8 with terms of 2/10, n/30 should be paid no later than November 18 (November 8 + 10 days). The last day to pay the invoice, the net date, is found by adding the number of days in the credit period to the invoice date. With terms of 2/10, n/30, the net date would be December 8 (November 8 + 30 days). If the buyer does not pay the bill by the net date, the seller may impose a penalty charge for late payment.

ordinary dating
When the discount period and credit period start on the invoice date.

EXAMPLE

AccuCare Pharmacy receives an invoice from Sterling Drug Wholesalers for merchandise on August 19. The terms of sale are 3/10, n/45. If AccuCare elects to take the cash discount, what is the discount date? If AccuCare does not take the cash discount, what is the last day to pay the bill?

SOLUTION STRATEGY

Find the discount date by adding the number of days in the discount period to the date of the invoice.

Discount date = August 19 + 10 days = August 29

If the discount is not taken, find the net date by adding the number of days in the credit period to the invoice date.

August 19 + 45 days = 12 days left in August (31 − 19)
+ 30 days in September
+ 3 days in October
45 days

The net date, the 45th day, is October 3

TRY-IT EXERCISE

11. Premier Printing buys ink and paper from a supplier with an invoice date of June 11. If the terms of sale are 4/10, n/60, what is the discount date and what is the net date of the invoice?

Check your answers with the solutions on page 248.

EOM or Proximo Dating

EOM dating
End-of-month dating. Depending on invoice date, terms of sale start at the end of the month of the invoice or the end of the following month.

proximo, or prox
Another name for EOM dating. Means "in the following month."

EOM dating, or end-of-month dating, means that the terms of sale start *after* the end of the month of the invoice. Another name for this dating method is **proximo,** or **prox.** Proximo means "in the following month." For example, 2/10 EOM, or 2/10 proximo, means that a 2% cash discount will be allowed if the bill is paid 10 days after the *end of the month* of the invoice. This is the case for any invoice dated from the 1st to the 25th of a month. If an invoice is dated the 26th of the month or later, the terms of sale begin *after* the end of the *following* month. Unless otherwise specified, the net amount is due *20 days* after the discount date.

EXAMPLES

a. What are the discount date and the net date of an invoice dated March 3, with terms of 3/15 EOM?

b. What are the discount date and the net date of an invoice dated March 27, with terms of 3/15 EOM?

SOLUTION STRATEGY

a. Because the invoice date is between the 1st and the 25th of the month, March 3, the discount date on terms of 3/15 EOM would be 15 days *after* the end of the month of the invoice. The net date will be 20 days later.

Discount date = 15 days after the end of March = April 15

Net date = April 15 + 20 days = May 5

b. Because the invoice date is after the 26th of the month, March 27, the discount date on terms of 3/15 EOM would be 15 days *after* the end of the month *following* the invoice month. The net date will be 20 days later.

Discount date = 15 days after the end of April = May 15

Net date = May 15 + 20 days = June 4

TRY-IT | EXERCISE

12. a. What are the discount date and the net date of an invoice dated November 18, with terms of 3/15 EOM?

b. What are the discount date and the net date of an invoice dated November 27, with terms of 3/15 EOM?

Everybody's Business
Learning Tip
Remember, when using extra dating, unless otherwise specified, the net date is 20 days after the discount date.

Check your answers with the solutions on page 248.

ROG Dating

ROG dating
Receipt of goods dating. Terms of sale begin on the date the goods are received by the buyer.

Receipt of goods or **ROG dating** is a common method used when shipping times are long, such as with special or custom orders. When ROG dating is used, the terms of sale begin the day the goods are received at the buyer's location. With this method, the buyer does not have to pay for the merchandise before it arrives. An example would be 2/10 ROG. As usual, the net date is 20 days after the discount date.

EXAMPLE

What are the discount date and the net date for an invoice dated June 23 if the shipment arrives on August 16 and the terms are 3/15 ROG?

SOLUTION STRATEGY

In this case, the discount period starts on August 16, the date the shipment arrives. The net date will be 20 days after the discount date.

Discount date = August 16 + 15 days = August 31

Net date = August 31 + 20 days = September 20

TRY-IT | EXERCISE

13. What are the discount date and the net date of an invoice dated October 11 if the shipment arrives on December 29 and the terms are 2/20 ROG?

Check your answers with the solutions on page 248.

Extra Dating

The last dating method commonly used in business today is called **Extra, Ex,** or **X dating.** With this dating method, the seller offers an extra discount period to the buyer as an incentive for purchasing slow-moving or out-of-season merchandise, such as Christmas goods in July or bathing suits in January. An example would be 3/10, 60 extra. This means the buyer gets a 3% cash discount in 10 days plus 60 *extra* days, or a total of 70 days. Once again, unless otherwise specified, the net date is 20 days after the discount date.

extra, ex, or x dating
The buyer receives an extra discount period as an incentive to purchase slow-moving or out-of-season merchandise.

EXAMPLE

What are the discount date and the net date of an invoice dated February 9, with terms of 3/15, 40 Extra?

SOLUTION STRATEGY

These terms, 3/15, 40 Extra, give the retailer 55 days (15 + 40) from February 9 to take the cash discount. The net date will be 20 days after the discount date.

Discount date = February 9 + 55 days = April 5

Net date = April 5 + 20 days = April 25

TRY-IT | EXERCISE

14. What are the discount date and the net date of an invoice dated February 22, with terms of 4/20, 60 Extra?

Check your answers with the solutions on page 248.

REVIEW EXERCISES | CHAPTER 7—SECTION IV

Calculate the cash discount and the net amount due for each of the following transactions:

	Amount of Invoice	Terms of Sale	Cash Discount	Net Amount Due
1.	$15,800.00	3/15, n/30	______	______
2.	12,660.00	2/10, n/45	______	______
3.	2,421.00	4/10, n/30	______	______
4.	6,940.20	2/10, n/30	______	______
5.	9,121.44	$3\frac{1}{2}$/15, n/60	______	______

For the following transactions, calculate the credit given for the partial payment and the net amount due on the invoice:

	Amount of Invoice	Terms of Sale	Partial Payment	Credit for Partial Payment	Net Amount Due
6.	$8,303.00	2/10, n/30	$2,500	______	______
7.	1,344.60	3/10, n/45	460	______	______
8.	5,998.20	4/15, n/60	3,200	______	______
9.	7,232.08	$4\frac{1}{2}$/20, n/45	5,500	______	______

Using the ordinary dating method, calculate the discount date and the net date for the following transactions:

	Date of Invoice	Terms of Sale	Discount Date(s)	Net Date
10.	November 4	2/10, n/45	______	______
11.	April 23	3/15, n/60	______	______
12.	August 11	3/20, n/45	______	______
13.	January 29	2/10, 1/20, n/60	______	______
14.	July 8	4/25, n/90	______	______

Using the EOM, ROG, and Extra dating methods, calculate the discount date and the net date for the following transactions. Unless otherwise specified, the net date is 20 days after the discount date:

	Date of Invoice	Terms of Sale	Discount Date	Net Date
15.	December 5	2/10, EOM	______	______
16.	June 27	3/15, EOM	______	______
17.	September 1	3/20, ROG Rec'd Oct. 3	______	______
18.	February 11	2/10, 60 Extra	______	______
19.	May 18	4/25, EOM	______	______
20.	October 26	2/10, ROG Rec'd Nov. 27	______	______

21. The Apollo Company received an invoice from a vendor on April 12 in the amount of $1,420.00. The terms of sale were 2/15, n/45. The invoice included freight charges of $108. The vendor sent $250 in merchandise that was not ordered. These goods will be returned by Apollo. (Remember, no discounts on freight or returned goods.)

a. What are the discount date and the net date?

b. What is the amount of the cash discount?

c. What is the net amount due?

22. An invoice is dated August 29 with terms of 4/15 EOM.

a. What is the discount date?

b. What is the net date?

23. An invoice dated January 15 has terms of 3/20 ROG. The goods are delayed in shipment and arrive on March 2.

a. What is the discount date?

b. What is the net date?

24. What payment should be made on an invoice in the amount of $3,400 dated August 7 if the terms of sale are 3/15, 2/30, n/45 and the bill is paid on

a. August 19?

b. September 3?

25. City Cellular purchased $28,900 in portable phones and beepers on April 25. The terms of sale were 4/20, 3/30, n/60. Freight terms were F.O.B. destination. Returned goods amounted to $650.

a. What is the net amount due if City Cellular sends the manufacturer a partial payment of $5,000 on May 20?

b. What is the net date?

c. If the manufacturer charges a $4\frac{1}{2}$% late fee, how much would City Cellular owe if they did not pay the balance by the net date?

BUSINESS DECISION

The Employment Test

2

26. As part of the employment interview for an accounting job at StereoMaster Stores, you have been asked to answer the following questions, based on an invoice from one of StereoMaster's vendors, Target Electronic Wholesalers.

TARGET
ELECTRONIC WHOLESALERS
1979 N.E. 123 Street
Jacksonville, Florida 32204

Sold to: StereoMaster Stores
480 McDowell Rd.
Phoenix, AZ 85008

Invoice Date: June 28, 200X

Terms of Sale: 3/15,n/30 ROG

Quantity	Stock #	Description	Unit Price	Amount
50	4811V	AM-FM Stereo Receivers	$297.50	______
25	511CX	CD Players-8 bit	132.28	______
40	6146M	VCR-Super VHS	658.12	______
20	1031A	D.A.T. Recorders	591.00	______
			Merchandise Total	______
			Insurance & Freight charges	$1,150.00
			Invoice Total	______

a. Extend each line and calculate the merchandise total and the total amount of the invoice, using the space provided on the invoice.

b. What is the discount date and the net date if the shipment arrived on July 16?

c. While in transit, five CD players and four D.A.T. recorders were damaged and will be returned. What is the amount of the returned merchandise? What is the revised merchandise total?

d. What are the amount of the cash discount and the net amount due if the discount is taken?

e. If StereoMaster sends in a partial payment of $20,000 within the discount period, what is the net balance still due?

CHAPTER FORMULAS

The Invoice

Extended total = Number of items × Cost per item

Trade Discounts—Single

Trade discount amount = List price × Trade discount percent

Net price = List price − Trade discount amount

Net price = List price (100% − Trade discount percent)

$$\text{Trade discount rate} \quad \frac{\text{Amount of trade discount}}{\text{List price}}$$

Trade Discounts—Series

Net price = List price × Net price factor

Single equivalent discount = 1 − Net price factor

Trade discount amount = List price × Single equivalent discount

Cash Discounts and Terms of Sale

Net amount due = Net price (100% − Cash discount percent)

$$\text{Partial payment credit} = \frac{\text{Partial payment}}{100\% - \text{Cash discount percent}}$$

Net amount due = Net price − Partial payment credit

✦ SUMMARY CHART ✦

SECTION I: The Invoice

Topic	P/O, Page	Important Concepts	Illustrative Examples
Reading and Understanding the Parts of an Invoice	7-1 210	Refer to Exhibits 7-1, 7-2, and 7-3.	
Extending and Totaling an Invoice	7-2 214	**Extended amount =** **Number of items × Cost per item** **Invoice subtotal =** **Total of extended amount column** **Invoice total =** **Invoice subtotal − Other charges**	The Great Subversion, a sandwich shop, ordered 25 lbs. of ham at \$3.69 per pound, and 22 lbs. of cheese at \$4.25 per pound. There is a \$7.50 delivery charge. Extend each item and find the invoice subtotal and invoice total. 25 × 3.69 = 92.25 Ham 22 × 4.25 = 93.50 Cheese 185.75 Subtotal + 7.50 Delivery \$193.25 Invoice total

SECTION II: Trade Discounts—Single

Topic	P/O, Page	Important Concepts	Illustrative Examples
Calculating the Amount of a Single Trade Discount	7-3 218	Trade discounts are reductions from the manufacturer's list price given to businesses in the trade for the performance of various marketing functions. **Trade discount amount =** **List price × Trade discount percent**	The Sunglass King ordered merchandise from a manufacturer with a list price of \$12,700. Because they are in the trade, Sunglass King gets a 35% trade discount. What is the amount of the trade discount? Trade disc = 12,700 × .35 = \$4,445
Calculating Net Price by Using the Net Price Factor, Complement Method	7-4 219	**Net price factor =** **100% − Trade discount percent** **Net price =** **List price (100% − Trade discount%)**	From the previous problem, use the net price factor to find the net price of the order for Sunglass King. Net price = 12,700(100% − 35%) Net price = 12,700 × .65 = \$8,255
Calculating Trade Discount Rate When List Price and Net Price Are Known	7-5 219	$\text{Trade discount rate} = \dfrac{\text{Amount of trade discount}}{\text{List price}}$	Cycle World Bike Shop orders merchandise listing for \$5,300 from Schwinn. The shop receives a \$2,110 trade discount. What is the trade discount rate? $\text{Trade disc rate} = \dfrac{2{,}100}{5{,}300} = 39.8\%$

SECTION III: Trade Discounts—Series

Topic	P/O, Page	Important Concepts	Illustrative Examples
Calculating Net Price and Trade Discount Amount by Using a Series of Trade Discounts	7-6 224	Net price is found by taking each trade discount in the series from the succeeding net price until all discounts have been deducted. **Trade discount = List price − Net price**	An invoice with merchandise listing for $4,700 was entitled to trade discounts of 20% and 15%. What is the net price and the amount of the trade discount? 4,700 × .20 = 940 4,700 − 940 = 3,760 3,760 × .15 = 564 3,760 − 564 = $3,196 Net price Trade discount = 4,700 − 3,196 = $1,504
Calculating Net Price of a Series of Trade Discounts by Using the Net Price Factor, Complement Method	7-7 225	Net price factor is found by subtracting each trade discount from 100% (complement) and multiplying these complements together. **Net price = List price × Net price factor**	Use the net price factor method to verify your answer to the previous problem. 100% 100% −20% −15% .80 × .85 = .68 Net price factor Net price = 4,700 × .68 = $3,196
Calculating the Amount of a Trade Discount by Using a Single Equivalent Discount	7-8 226	**Single equivalent discount =** **1 − Net price factor** **Trade discount =** **List price × Single equivalent discount**	What is the single equivalent discount in the previous problem? Use this to verify your trade discount answer. Single equivalent discount = 1 − .68 = .32 Trade discount = 4,700 × .32 = $1,504

Section IV: Cash Discounts and Terms of Sale

Topic	P/O, Page	Important Concepts	Illustrative Examples
Calculating Cash Discounts and Net Amount Due	7-9 233	Terms of sale are the details of when an invoice must be paid and if a cash discount is offered. Cash discount is an extra discount offered by the seller as an incentive for early payment of an invoice. **Cash discount =** **Net price × Cash discount percent** **Net amount due =** **Net price − Cash discount**	Wilbur's Auto Parts orders merchandise for $1,800 including $100 in freight charges. Wilbur's gets a 3% cash discount. What is the amount of the cash discount and the net amount due? 1,800 − 100 = 1,700 Net price Cash discount = 1,700 × .03 = $51 1,700 − 51 = 1,649 + 100 Freight $1,749 Net amount due

SECTION IV: (continued)

Topic	P/O, Page	Important Concepts	Illustrative Examples
Calculating Net Amount Due, with Credit Given for Partial Payment	7-10 234	$\text{Partial payment credit} = \dfrac{\text{Partial payment}}{100\% - \text{Cash discount percent}}$ Net amount due = Net price − Partial payment credit	Elite Fashions makes a partial payment of $3,000 on an invoice of $7,900. The terms of sale are 3/15, n/30. What is the amount of the partial payment credit, and how much does Elite Fashions still owe on the invoice? $\text{Part pmt credit} = \dfrac{3{,}000}{100\% - 3\%} = \underline{\underline{\$3{,}092.78}}$ Net amount due = 7,900.00 − 3,092.78 = $\underline{\underline{\$4{,}807.22}}$
Determining Discount Date and Net Date by Using Various Dating Methods	7-11 235	Discount date: last date to take advantage of a cash discount. Net date: last date to pay an invoice without incurring a penalty charge.	
Ordinary Dating	7-11 237	Ordinary dating: discount period and the credit period start on the date of the invoice.	Mayor's Jewelers receives an invoice for merchandise on March 12 with terms of 3/15, n/30. What are the discount date and the net date? Disc date = March 12 + 15 days = March 27 Net date = March 12 + 30 days = April 11
EOM or Proximo Dating Method	7-11 238	EOM means end of month. It is a dating method in which the terms of sale start *after* the end of the month of the invoice. If the invoice is dated after the 25th of the month, the terms of sale start *after* the end of the *following* month. Unless otherwise specified, the net date is *20 days* after the discount date. *Proximo* or prox. is another name for EOM dating. It means "in the following month."	Superior Cleaning Service buys supplies with terms of sale of 2/10, EOM. What are the discount date and the net date if the invoice date is a. May 5? b. May 27? a. May 5 invoice terms start *after* the end of May: Discount date = June 10 Net date = June 10 + 20 days = June 30 b. May 27 invoice terms start *after* the end of the *following* month, June: Discount date = July 10 Net date = July 10 + 20 days = July 30

SECTION IV: (continued)

Topic	P/O, Page	Important Concepts	Illustrative Examples
ROG Dating Method	7-11 238	ROG means receipt of goods. It is a dating method in which the terms of sale begin on the date the goods are received rather than the invoice date. This is used to accommodate long shipping times. Unless otherwise specified, the net date is *20 days* after the discount date.	An invoice dated August 24 has terms of 3/10 ROG. If the merchandise arrives on October 1, what are the discount date and the net date? Disc date = October 1 + 10 days = October 11 Net date = October 11 + 20 days = October 31
Extra Dating Method	7-11 239	Extra, Ex, or X is a dating method in which the buyer receives an extra period of time before the terms of sale begin. Vendors use extra dating as an incentive to entice buyers to purchase out-of-season or slow-moving merchandise. Unless otherwise specified, the net date is *20 days* after the discount date.	Lacy's Linen Shop buys merchandise from a vendor with terms of 3/15, 60 Extra. The invoice is dated December 11. What are the discount date and the net date? Disc date = December 11 + 75 days = February 24 Net date = February 24 + 20 = March 16

TRY-IT EXERCISE | SOLUTIONS

1. a. Shutterbug Camera Shops
b. 44,929
c. November 27, 200X
d. $3,744.00
e. FotoFair Corporation
f. Net—30 days
g. 1864 N.W. 123rd St. Chicago, IL 60613
h. J. Herman
i. Federal Express
j. Knoxville, TN
k. $183.70
l. $9,117.50
m. $41.88
n. $9,301.20

2.

Stock #	Quantity	Unit	Merchandise Description	Unit Price	Total
R443	125	ea.	Food Processors	$ 89.00	$11,125.00
B776	24	ea.	Microwave Ovens	225.40	5,409.60
Z133	6	doz.	12" Mixers	54.12	324.72
Z163	1	bx.	Mixer Covers	166.30	166.30
				Invoice Subtotal	17,025.62
				Shipping Charges	194.20
				Invoice Total	$17,219.82

3. Trade discount amount = List price × Trade discount percent
Trade discount amount = 7,600 × .30 = $2,280.00

4. Net price = List price (100% − Trade discount percent)
Net price = 2,100 (100% − 35%)
Net price = 2,100 × .65 = $1,365.00

5. Trade discount amount = List price − Net price

Trade discount amount = 109,500 − 63,300 = $46,200

$$\text{Trade discount rate} = \frac{\text{Amount of trade discount}}{\text{List price}} = \frac{46{,}200}{109{,}500} = 42.2\%$$

6.

25,000	25,000	16,250	16,250	13,000	13,000	
× .35	− 8,750	× .20	− 3,250	× .10	− 1,300	
8,750	16,250	3,250	13,000	1,300	$11,700	= Net price

Trade discount amount = 25,000 − 11,700 = $13,300

7. a.

100%		100%		100%	
− 30%		− 20%		−12%	
.7	×	.8	×	.88	= .4928 = Net price factor

b. Net price = List price × Net price factor

Net price = 3,500 × .4928 = $1,724.80

c. Net price = List price × Net price factor

Net price = 5,800 × .4928 = $2,858.24

8.

100%		100%		100%	
− 25%		− 15%		− 10%	
.75	×	.85	×	.9	= .57375 = Net price factor

Single equivalent discount = 1 − Net price factor

Single equivalent discount = 1 − .57375 = .42625

Trade discount amount = List price × Single equivalent discount

Trade discount amount = 36,800.00 × .42625 = $15,686.00

9. Cash discount = Net price × Cash discount percent

Cash discount = 8,300.00 × .03 = $249.00

Net amount due = Net price − Cash discount

Net amount due = 8,300.00 − 249.00 = $8,051.00

10. $$\text{Partial payment credit} = \frac{\text{Partial payment}}{100\% - \text{Cash discount percent}}$$

$$\text{Partial payment credit} = \frac{20{,}000.00}{100\% - 4\%} = \frac{20{,}000.00}{.96} = \$20{,}833.33$$

Net amount due = Net price − Partial payment credit

Net amount due = 45,300.00 − 20,833.33 = $24,466.67

11. Discount date = June 11 + 10 days = June 21

Net date = June 11 + 60 days

30 Days in June
− 11 Discount date
19 June
31 July
− 10 Aug → August 10
60 days

12. a. Discount date = 15 days after end of November = December 15

Net date = December 15 + 20 days = January 4

b. Discount date = 15 days after end of December = January 15

Net date = January 15 + 20 days = February 4

13. Discount date = December 29 + 20 days = January 18

Net date = January 18 + 20 days = February 7

14. Discount date = February 22 + 80 days = May 13

Net date = May 13 + 20 days = June 2

CHAPTER 7 | ASSESSMENT TEST

Name ______________________

Class ______________________

Answer the following questions based on the Sunshine Industries invoice below:

1. Who is the vendor?

2. What is the date of the invoice?

3. What is the stock # of rockers?

4. What does dz. mean?

5. What is the unit price of lounge covers?

6. What is the destination?

7. What is the extended total for chaise lounges with no armrest?

8. Who pays the freight if the terms are F.O.B. shipping point?

9. What is the invoice subtotal?

10. What is the invoice total?

Answers

1. ______________________

2. ______________________

3. ______________________

4. ______________________

5. ______________________

6. ______________________

7. ______________________

8. ______________________

9. ______________________

10. ______________________

Sunshine Industries
Patio Furniture Manufacturers
1930 Main Street
Ft. Worth, Texas 76102

SOLD TO: Patio Magic Stores
3386 Fifth Avenue
Raleigh, NC 27613

DATE: November 2

INVOICE # B-112743

TERMS OF SALE: Net 30 days **SHIPPING INFO: Fed-Ex Freight**

STOCK #	QUANTITY	UNIT	MERCHANDISE DESCRIPTION	UNIT PRICE	TOTAL
1455	40	ea.	Chaise Lounges with armrest	$169.00	______
1475	20	ea.	Chaise Lounges—no armrest	127.90	______
4387	24	ea.	Rocker Chairs	87.70	______
8100	3	dz.	Plastic Lounge Covers	46.55	______
			INVOICE SUBTOTAL:		______
			Packing and Handling:		$125.00
			Shipping charges:		477.50
			INVOICE TOTAL:		______

Name ____________________

Class ____________________

Answers

11. ____________________

12. a. ____________________

b. ____________________

13. ____________________

14. a. ____________________

b. ____________________

15. ____________________

11. E-Z Shop Grocery Store receives an invoice for the purchase of merchandise with a list price of $5,500. Because they are in the trade, E-Z Shop gets a 27% trade discount. What is the amount of the trade discount?

12. Natureland Garden Supply buys lawnmowers that list for $679.95 less a 30% trade discount.

a. What is the amount of the trade discount?

b. What is the net price of each lawnmower?

13. Billy's BBQ Restaurant places an order with a meat and poultry supplier listing for $1,250. They receive a trade discount of $422 on the order. What is the trade discount rate on this transaction?

14. Exotic Gardens Florist Shop purchases an order of imported roses with a list price of $2,375 less trade discounts of 15/20/20.

a. What is the amount of the trade discount?

b. What is the net amount of the order?

15. All-American Sports can purchase sneakers for $450 per dozen less trade discounts of 14/12 from Ideal Shoes. Fancy Footwear is offering the same sneakers for $435 less trade discounts of 18/6. Which supplier offers a lower net price?

Name ______________________

Class ______________________

Answers

16. a. ______________________

b. ______________________

17. a. ______________________

b. ______________________

18. a. ______________________

b. ______________________

19. a. ______________________

b. ______________________

16. a. What is the net price factor for trade discounts of 25/15/10?

b. Use that net price factor to find the net price of a couch listing for $800.

17. a. What is the net price factor of the trade discount series 20/15/11?

b. What is the single equivalent discount?

18. The Empress Carpet Company orders merchandise for $17,700, including $550 in freight charges, from Mohawk Carpet Mill on May 4. Carpets valued at $1,390 will be returned because they are damaged. The terms of sale are 2/10, n/30 ROG. The shipment arrives on May 26, and Empress wants to take advantage of the cash discount.

a. By what date must Empress pay the invoice?

b. As the bookkeeper for Empress, how much will you send to Mohawk?

19. Super Suds Laundry receives an invoice for detergent dated April 9 with terms of 3/15, n/30.

a. What is the discount date?

b. What is the net date?

Name ____________________

Class ____________________

Answers

19. c. ____________________

d. ____________________

20. a. ____________________

b. ____________________

c. ____________________

c. If the invoice terms are changed to 3/15 EOM, what is the new discount date?

d. What is the new net date?

20. Ned's Sheds purchases building materials from Grove Lumber for $3,700 with terms of 4/15, n/30. The invoice is dated October 17. Ned's decides to send in a $2,000 partial payment.

a. By what date must the partial payment be sent to take advantage of the cash discount?

b. What is the net date?

c. If partial payment was sent by the discount date, what is the balance still due on the order?

BUSINESS DECISION

The Busy Executive

21. You are a salesperson for Victory Lane Wholesale Auto Parts. You have just taken a phone order from one of your best customers, Champion Motors. Because you were busy when the call came in, you recorded the details of the order on a notepad.

Phone Order Notes

- The invoice date is April 4, 200X.
- The customer order no. is 443B.
- Champion Motors's warehouse is located at 7011 N.W. 4th Avenue, Columbus, Ohio 43205.
- Terms of sale—3/15, n/45.
- The order will be filled by D. Watson.
- The goods will be shipped by truck.
- Champion Motors's home office is located next to the warehouse at 7013 N.W. 4th Avenue.
- Champion ordered 44 car batteries, stock #394, listing for $69.95 each, and 24 truck batteries, stock #395, listing for $89.95 each. These items get trade discounts of 20/15.
- Champion also ordered 36 cases of 10W/30 motor oil, stock #838-W, listing for $11.97 per case, and 48 cases of 10W/40 super-oil, stock #1621S, listing for $14.97 per case. These items get trade discounts of 20/20/12.
- The freight charges for the order amount to $67.50.
- Insurance charges amount to $27.68.

Name ______________________

Class ______________________

Answers

21. a. ______________________

b. ______________________

c. ______________________

d ______________________

e. ______________________

a. Transfer your notes to the invoice below, extend each line, and calculate the total.

b. What is the discount date of the invoice? April 19th

c. If Champion sends a partial payment of $1,200 by the discount date, what is the balance due on the invoice? ~~2971.15~~ 3066.33

d. What is the net date of the invoice? May 19th

e. Your company has a policy of charging a 5% late fee if invoice payments are more than five days late. What is the amount of the late fee that Champion will be charged if it fails to pay the balance due on time? ~~21~~ ~~153.52~~ 153.52

INVOICE

Victory Lane
Wholesale Auto Parts
422 Riverfront Road
Cincinnati, Ohio 45244

Invoice # ~~April 4th 2004~~

Invoice Date: April 4th ~~April 4th 2004~~

Sold To: 7013 N.W. 4th Avenue Columbus, Ohio 43205

Ship To: ~~Champion Motors Wire~~ 7011 N.W. 4th Ave. Columbus, Ohio 43205

Customer Order No.	Salesperson	Ship Via	Terms of Sale	Filled By
443B	B. Schlegel	truck	3/15, n/45	D. Watson

Quantity Ordered	Stock Number	Description	Unit List Price	Trade Discounts	Extended Amount
44	394	car batteries	69.95	20/15	~~3077.80~~ 2092.90
24	395	truck batteries	89.95	20/15	1467.98
36	838-W	10W/30 motor oil	11.97	20/20/12	242.69
48	162158	10W/40 motor oil	14.97	20/20/12	404.69

Invoice Subtotal	4208.26
Shipping Charges	67.50
Insurance	27.68
Invoice Total	4303.44

1237.11 .5432 2154.8

All the Math That's Fit to Learn

The Business Math Times

Volume VII | Invoices, Cash Discounts, and Trade Discounts | One Dollar

Entrepreneurs Lite

Thinking about leaving your job and starting your own business? Is franchising right for you?

There are many advantages to starting a business by joining an established franchise system. Franchises provide a strong brand name, training programs that teach you how to run the business, and support programs that provide assistance and advice once you have the business up and running.

Becoming a franchisee in a well-established franchise system has many advantages over starting a new business independently, but it is not for everyone.

Franchisees are not entrepreneurs in the classic sense. Entrepreneurs want to make their own decisions. They like to experiment with the menu, services, décor, advertising, staff uniforms, and suppliers. They have the need to develop and operate the business based on their own vision of how things should operate.

If a true entrepreneur were allowed to operate a franchise, there would be little consistency between one location and the next. Consumers stopping off to get their favorite hamburger might find that their local McDonald's, Burger King, or Wendy's was now serving Chinese food!

Good franchisees aren't so much entrepreneurs as they are "entrepreneurs lite." They are provided with a system of doing business and standards for using that system. The secret of success for most franchise chains is the promise of consistency. Successful franchisees improve the performance of their system through better execution, not change.

"Congratulations on reaching ten million dollars in sales! What will be your goal for this afternoon?"

"Quote . . . Unquote"

Don't squander time, for that is the stuff life is made of.
—*Benjamin Franklin*

There is only one valid definition of business purpose: to create a customer.
—*Peter Drucker*

Top 10 Franchise Opportunities (2001)

Franchise	Number of Units	Start-up Costs ($000)	Royalty Fee %
1. Subway	15,249	73–185	8.0
2. Mail Boxes, Etc.	4,430	156–226	5.0
3. McDonald's	27,903	523–1.5 mil.	12.5+
4. Jiffy Lube	2,185	199–229	5.0
5. Taco Bell	5,670	281–560	5.5
6. Quizno's	1,182	190–245	7.0
7. Sonic Drive-In Rest.	2,268	621–1.2 mil.	1.0–5.0
8. Radio Shack	7,356	85	0
9. GNC	4,509	163–207	6.0
10. Jani-King	8,188	14–66	10.0

Franchise Frenzy!

A franchise is a form of business in which you (the franchisee) purchase the rights to sell the products or services of another company (the franchisor) under their usually well-known brand name and reputation. By contractual agreement you have to run the franchise within certain "rules of operation" and pay the parent company a percent of sales known as a "royalty fee."

In recent years, franchising has grown to become a sizeable portion of the American economy. This year, franchises are expected to ring up sales of more than $1 trillion in the United States and billions more worldwide.

Everything from soft drinks to soft pretzels, transmissions to tacos, pest control to pizza, and burgers to bagels has franchises. The latest trend is to combine two or more franchises in one location, such as a Baskin-Robbins ice cream store inside a Dunkin' Donuts shop.

Each year, *Entrepreneur Magazine* publishes a list entitled "Franchise 500," which ranks America's best franchise opportunities based on franchisee value. The rankings consider numerous factors, some of which are weighed more heavily than others. The most important factors include financial strength and stability, growth rate, and size of the system.

Brainteaser

THE INVOICE

One third of an invoice is for computers, one fourth is for printers, and the remaining $10,000 is for monitors. What is the total amount of the invoice?

ANSWER TO LAST ISSUE'S BRAINTEASER

18 marbles

If X is the number of blue marbles to be added to the bag, then

$$\frac{3 + X}{10 + X} = \frac{3}{4}$$

$$12 + 4X = 30 + 3X$$

$$\underline{\underline{X = 18}}$$

CHAPTER

8

Markup and Markdown

PERFORMANCE OBJECTIVES

Section I Markup Based on Cost

8-1 Understanding and using the retailing equation to find cost, amount of markup, and selling price of an item. (p. 256)

8-2 Calculating percent markup based on cost. (p. 258)

8-3 Calculating selling price when cost and percent markup based on cost are known. (p. 259)

8-4 Calculating cost when selling price and percent markup based on cost are known. (p. 259)

Section II Markup Based on Selling Price

8-5 Calculating percent markup based on selling price. (p. 263)

8-6 Calculating selling price when cost and percent markup based on selling price are known. (p. 264)

8-7 Calculating cost when selling price and percent markup based on selling price are known. (p. 265)

8-8 Converting percent markup based on cost to percent markup based on selling price, and vice versa. (p. 266)

Section III Markdowns, Multiple Operations, and Perishable Goods

8-9 Determining the amount of markdown and the markdown percent. (p. 270)

8-10 Determining the sale price after a markdown and the original price before a markdown. (p. 272)

8-11 Computing the final selling price after a series of markups and markdowns. (p. 273)

8-12 Calculating the selling price of perishable goods. (p. 274)

SECTION I

MARKUP BASED ON COST

Determining an appropriate selling price for a company's goods or services is an extremely important function in business. The price must be attractive to potential customers, yet sufficient to cover expenses and provide the company with a reasonable profit.

cost of goods sold
The cost of the merchandise sold during an operating period. One of two major expense categories of a business.

operating expenses, or overhead
All business expenses, other than cost of merchandise, required to operate a business, such as payroll, rent, utilities, and insurance.

markup, markon, margin
The amount added to the cost of an item to cover the operating expenses and profit. It is the difference between the cost and the selling price.

retailing equation
The selling price of an item is equal to the cost plus the markup.

In business, expenses are separated into two major categories. The first is the **cost of goods sold.** To a manufacturer, this expense would be the cost of production; to a wholesaler or retailer, the expense is the price paid to a manufacturer or distributor for the merchandise. The second category includes all the other expenses required to operate the business, such as salaries, rent, utilities, taxes, insurance, advertising, and maintenance. These expenses are known as **operating expenses,** overhead expenses, or simply **overhead.**

The amount added to the cost of an item to cover the operating expenses and profit is known as the **markup, markon,** or **margin.** It is the difference between the cost and the selling price of an item. Markup is applied at all levels of the marketing channels of distribution. This chapter deals with the business math applications involved in the pricing of goods and services.

8-1 Understanding and Using the Retailing Equation to Find Cost, Amount of Markup, and Selling Price of an Item

The fundamental principle on which business operates is to sell goods and services for a price high enough to cover all expenses and provide the owners with a reasonable profit. The formula that describes this principle is known as the **retailing equation.** The equation states that the selling price of an item is equal to the cost plus the markup.

Selling price = Cost + Markup

Using the abbreviations *C* for cost, *M* for markup, and *SP* for selling price, the formula is written as

$$SP = C + M$$

According to the retailing equation, the selling price of merchandise is equal to the cost plus the markup.

To illustrate, if a camera costs a retailer \$60 and a \$50 markup is added to cover operating expenses and profit, the selling price of the camera would be \$110.

\$60 (cost) + \$50 (markup) = \$110 (selling price)

In Chapter 5, we learned that equations are solved by isolating the unknown on one side and the knowns on the other. Using this theory, when the amount of markup is the unknown, the equation can be rewritten as

Markup = Selling price − Cost $\qquad M = SP - C$

When the cost is the unknown, the equation becomes

Cost = Selling price − Markup $\qquad C = SP - M$

The following examples illustrate how these formulas are used to determine the dollar amount of cost, markup, and selling price.

EXAMPLE

Gary's Gifts pays $8.00 for a picture frame. If a markup of $6.50 is added, what is the selling price of the frame?

SOLUTION STRATEGY

Because selling price is the unknown variable, we use the formula $SP = C + M$ as follows:

$$SP = C + M$$

$$SP = 8.00 + 6.50 = 14.50$$

$$\text{Selling price} = \underline{\underline{\$14.50}}$$

EXAMPLE

Office Mart buys printing calculators from Taiwan for $22.50 each. If they are sold for $39.95, what is the amount of the markup?

SOLUTION STRATEGY

Because the markup is the unknown variable, we use the formula $M = SP - C$ as follows:

$$M = SP - C$$

$$M = 39.95 - 22.50 = 17.45$$

$$\text{Markup} = \underline{\underline{\$17.45}}$$

EXAMPLE

Food Fair Supermarkets sell Corn Crunchies for $3.29 per box. If the markup on this item is $2.12, how much did the store pay for the cereal?

SOLUTION STRATEGY

Because the cost is the unknown variable in this problem, we use the formula $C = SP - M$.

$$C = SP - M$$

$$C = 3.29 - 2.12 = 1.17$$

$$\text{Cost} = \underline{\underline{\$1.17}}$$

TRY-IT | EXERCISES

For each of the following, use the basic retailing equation to solve for the unknown:

1. Ceramic planters cost the manufacturer $6.80 per unit to produce. If a markup of $9.40 each is added to the cost, what is the selling price per planter?

2. The SuperSport sells a dozen golf balls for $28.50. If the distributor was paid $16.75, what is the amount of the markup?

3. After a wholesaler adds a markup of $75.00 to a television set, it is sold to a retail store for $290.00. What is the wholesaler's cost?

Check your answers with the solutions on page 284.

Everybody's Business

Real-World Connection

Many retailers use a psychological pricing strategy known as **odd pricing,** whereby prices are set to end in odd numbers such as $.79, $2.47, or $9.95.

Theoretically, customers perceive odd prices as being substantially below even prices, and therefore a bargain. For example, $299.95 is "perceived" as being much lower than $300.00.

Retailers, to psychologically project a prestigious image for their products, use **even pricing** such as $10.00 or $500.00.

8-2 Calculating Percent Markup Based on Cost

In addition to being expressed in dollar amounts, markup is frequently expressed as a percent. There are two ways of representing markup as a percent: based on cost and based on selling price. Manufacturers and most wholesalers use cost as the base in calculating the percent markup because cost figures are readily available to them. When markup is based on cost, the cost is 100%, and the markup is expressed as a percent of that cost. Retailers, however, use selling price figures as the base of most calculations, including percent markup. In retailing, the selling price represents 100%, and the markup is expressed as a percent of that selling price.

Everybody's Business

Learning Tip

Note that *percent markup based on cost* calculations are an application of *rate of increase,* covered in Chapter 6. In the percentage formula, the markup (portion) represents the amount of the increase, and the cost (base) represents the original amount.

In Chapter 6, we used the percentage formula, Portion = Rate × Base. To review these variables, portion is a *part* of a whole amount, base is the *whole amount,* and the rate, as a percent, describes what part the portion is of the base. When we calculate markup as a percent, we are actually solving a rate problem, using the formula: Rate = Portion ÷ Base.

When the markup is based on cost, the percent markup is the rate, the dollar amount of markup is the portion, and the cost, representing 100%, is the base. The answer will describe what percent the markup is of the cost, therefore it is called percent **markup based on cost.** We use the formula

markup based on cost
When cost is 100%, and the markup is expressed as a percent of that cost.

$$\text{Percent markup based on cost (rate)} = \frac{\text{Markup (portion)}}{\text{Cost (base)}} \quad \text{or} \quad \%M_{\text{COST}} = \frac{M}{C}$$

Everybody's Business

Learning Tip

A shortcut for calculating the factors of the retailing equation is to use the **markup table.** The cells represent cost, markup, and selling price, in both dollars and percents.

Markup Table

	$	%
C		
+MU		
SP		

Step 1. Fill in the given information using 100% for the base, and *X* for the unknown. (blue)

Step 2. Calculate the figure for the remaining cell (red) in the column without the *X*.

89.60 − 56.00 = 33.60

	$	%
C	56.00	100
+MU	33.60	*X*
SP	89.60	

Then form a box. (green)

The figures in the box form a proportion.

$$\frac{56}{33.60} = \frac{100}{X}$$

Step 3. Solve for *X* by cross-multiplying the corner figures in the box.

$$56X = 33.60(100)$$

$$X = \frac{3{,}360}{56} = \underline{\underline{60\%}}$$

EXAMPLE

A manufacturer produces stainless steel sinks at a cost of $56.00 each. If the sinks are sold to distributors for $89.60 each, what are the amount of the markup and the percent markup based on cost?

SOLUTION STRATEGY

$$M = SP - C$$

$$M = 89.60 - 56.00 = 33.60$$

$$\text{Markup} = \underline{\underline{\$33.60}}$$

$$\%M_{\text{COST}} = \frac{M}{C}$$

$$\%M_{\text{COST}} = \frac{33.60}{56.00} = .6$$

$$\text{Percent markup based on cost} = \underline{\underline{60\%}}$$

TRY-IT | EXERCISE

4. A wholesaler buys lamps for $45 and sells them for $63. What is the amount of the markup and the percent markup based on cost?

Check your answers with the solutions on page 284.

8-3 Calculating Selling Price When Cost and Percent Markup Based on Cost Are Known

From the basic retailing equation, we know that the selling price is equal to the cost plus the markup. When the markup is based on cost, the cost equals 100%, and the selling price equals 100% plus the percent markup. If, for example, the percent markup is 30%, then

Selling price = Cost + Markup

Selling price = 100% + 30%

Selling price = 130% *of* the cost

Because "of" means multiply, we multiply the cost by (100% plus the percent markup)

Selling price = Cost(100% + Percent markup based on cost)

$$SP = C(100\% + \%M_{COST})$$

EXAMPLE

A watch costs $50.00 to produce. If the manufacturer wants a 70% markup based on cost, what should be the selling price of the watch?

SOLUTION STRATEGY

$$SP = C(100\% + \%M_{COST})$$

$$SP = 50.00(100\% + 70\%)$$

$$SP = 50.00(170\%) = 50.00(1.7) = 85$$

Selling price = $85.00

100 + 70 = 170

	$	%
C	50.00	100
+MU		70
SP	*X*	170

Note: When the green box has six cells, use the four corner figures.

$$100X = 50(170)$$

$$X = \$85.00$$

TRY-IT EXERCISE

5. Capital Appliances buys toasters for $38.00. If a 65% markup based on cost is desired, what should be the selling price of the toaster?

Check your answer with the solution on page 284.

8-4 Calculating Cost When Selling Price and Percent Markup Based on Cost Are Known

To calculate cost when selling price and percent markup on cost are known, let's use our knowledge of solving equations from Chapter 5. Because we are dealing with the same three variables from the last section, simply solve the equation $SP = C(100\% + \%M_{COST})$ for the cost. Cost, the unknown, is isolated to one side of the equation by dividing both sides by (100% + Percent markup).

$$\text{Cost} = \frac{\text{Selling price}}{100\% + \text{Percent markup on cost}} \qquad C = \frac{SP}{100\% + \%M_{COST}}$$

$100 + 50 = 150$

	$	%
C	*X*	100
+MU		50
SP	66.00	150

$150X = 66(100)$

$X = \$44.00$

EXAMPLE

A Nose for Clothes sells a blouse for $66.00. If a 50% markup based on cost is used, what is the cost of the blouse?

SOLUTION STRATEGY

$$\text{Cost} = \frac{\text{Selling price}}{100\% + \text{Percent markup on cost}}$$

$$\text{Cost} = \frac{66.00}{100\% + 50\%} = \frac{66.00}{150\%} = \frac{66.00}{1.5} = 44.00$$

$$\text{Cost} = \underline{\underline{\$44.00}}$$

TRY-IT | EXERCISE

6. General Electric sells automatic coffee makers to distributors for $39.00. If a 30% markup based on cost is used, how much did it cost to manufacture the coffee maker?

Check your answer with the solution on page 284.

REVIEW EXERCISES | CHAPTER 8—SECTION I

For the following items, calculate the missing information, rounding dollars to the nearest cent and percents to the nearest tenth percent:

	Item	Cost	Amount of Markup	Selling Price	Percent Markup Based on Cost
1.	television set	$161.50	______	$299.95	______
2.	bookcase	$32.40	$21.50	______	______
3.	automobile	______	$5,400.00	$12,344.80	______
4.	dress	$75.00	______	______	80%
5.	vacuum cleaner	______	______	$249.95	60%
6.	hat	$46.25	$50.00	______	______
7.	computer	$1,350.00	______	$3,499.00	______
8.	treadmill	______	$880.00	$2,335.00	______
9.	1 lb potatoes	$.58	______	______	130%
10.	wallet	______	______	$44.95	75%

Solve the following word problems, rounding dollars to the nearest cent and percents to the nearest tenth:

11. Alarm clocks cost the manufacturer $56.10 per unit to produce. If a markup of $29.80 is added to the cost, what is the selling price per clock?

12. The Image Boutique sells dress shirts for \$22.88. If the cost per shirt is \$15.50, what is the amount of the markup?

13. After a wholesaler adds a markup of \$125.00 to a stereo, it is sold for \$320.00. What is the cost of the stereo?

14. Circuit City purchases flat-screen computer monitors from ViewSonic for \$275.59.

a. What is the amount of the markup?

b. What is the present markup based on cost?

15. The Holiday Card Shop purchased stationery for \$2.44 per box. A \$1.75 markup is added to the stationery. 2

a. What is the selling price?

b. What is the percent markup based on cost?

16. The Electronic Warehouse adds a \$4.60 markup to calculators and sells them for \$9.95.

a. What is the cost of the calculators?

b. What is the percent markup based on cost?

17. The Green Thumb Garden Shop purchases automatic lawn sprinklers for \$12.50 from the manufacturer. If a 75% markup based on cost is added, at what retail price should the sprinklers be marked? 1

18. Golden Auto Supply purchases water pumps from the distributor for $35.40 each. If Golden adds a 120% markup based on cost, at what retail price should the pumps be sold?

19. A department store sells refrigerators at retail for $875.88. If a 50% markup based on cost is added, what is the cost of the refrigerator?

20. What is the cost of a printer that sells at retail for $1,750, with a 70% markup based on cost?

21. **a.** What is the amount of markup on the leather computer case shown here if the cost is $58.25?

b. What is the percent markup based on cost?

22. If the real wood filing cabinet shown here is marked up by $97.30,

a. What is the cost?

b. What is the percent markup based on cost?

23. **a.** What is the cost of the backpack shown here if the markup is 70% based on the cost?

b. What is the amount of the markup?

BUSINESS DECISION

Keystone Markup

24. In department and specialty store retailing, a common markup strategy is to double the cost of an item to arrive at a selling price. This strategy is known as **keystoning** the markup, and is widely used in apparel, cosmetics, fashion accessories, shoes, and other categories of merchandise.

The reasoning for the high amount of markup is that these stores have particularly high operating expenses. In addition, they have a continuing need to update fixtures and remodel stores to attract customers.

You are the buyer in the women's shoe department of the Roma Grande department store. You normally keystone your markups on certain shoes and handbags. This amount of markup allows you enough gross margin so that you can lower prices when "sales" occur, and still have a profitable department.

a. If you are looking for a line of handbags that will retail for \$120, what is the most you can pay for the bags?

b. At a women's wear trade show, you find a line of handbags that you like with a suggested retail price of \$130.00. The vender has offered you trade discounts of 30/20/5. Will this series of trade discounts allow you to keystone the handbags?

c. The vender tells you that the first two discounts, 30% and 20%, are fixed, but the 5% is negotiable. What trade discount, rounded to a whole percent, should you ask for, in order to keystone the markup?

SECTION II

MARKUP BASED ON SELLING PRICE

In Section I, we calculated markup as a percentage of the cost of an item. The cost was the base and represented 100%. As noted, this method is primarily used by manufacturers and wholesalers. In this section, the markup is calculated as a percentage of the selling price; therefore, the selling price will be the base and represent 100%. This practice is used by most retailers, because most retail records and statistics are kept in sales dollars.

8-5 Calculating Percent Markup Based on Selling Price

The calculation of percent **markup based on selling price** is the same as that for percent markup based on cost, except the base (the denominator) changes from cost to selling price. Remember, finding percent markup is a rate problem, using the now familiar percentage formula, Rate = Portion ÷ Base.

markup based on selling price When selling price is 100%, and the markup is expressed as a percent of that selling price.

For this application of the formula, the percent markup based on selling price is the rate, the amount of the markup is the portion, and the selling price is the base. The formula is

$$\text{Percent markup based on selling price (rate)} = \frac{\text{Markup (portion)}}{\text{Selling price (base)}} \quad \text{or} \quad \%M_{SP} = \frac{M}{SP}$$

$125 - 60 = 65$

	\$	%
C	60.00	
+MU	65.00	*X*
SP	125.00	100

$125X = 65(100)$

$X = \underline{\underline{\$52.00}}$

EXAMPLE

American Hardware & Garden Supply purchases electric drills for \$60.00 each. If it sells the drills for \$125, what is the amount of the markup, and what is the percent markup based on selling price?

SOLUTION STRATEGY

$$M = SP - C$$

$$M = 125 - 60 = 65$$

$$\text{Markup} = \underline{\underline{\$65.00}}$$

$$\%M_{SP} = \frac{M}{SP}$$

$$\%M_{SP} = \frac{65}{125} = .52$$

$$\text{Percent markup based on selling price} = \underline{\underline{52\%}}$$

TRY-IT | EXERCISE

7. Playtime Toys buys bicycles from the distributor for \$94.50 each. If the bikes sell for \$157.50, what is the amount of the markup and what is the percent markup based on selling price?

Check your answers with the solutions on page 284.

8-6 Calculating Selling Price When Cost and Percent Markup Based on Selling Price Are Known

When the percent markup is based on selling price, remember that the selling price is the base and represents 100%. This means the percent cost plus the percent markup must equal 100%. If, for example, the markup is 25% of the selling price, the cost must be 75% of the selling price,

$$\text{Cost} + \text{Markup} = \text{Selling price}$$

$$75\% + 25\% = 100\%$$

Because the percent markup is known, the percent cost will always be the complement, or

$$\% \text{ Cost} = (100\% - \text{Percent markup based on selling price})$$

Because the selling price is the base, we can solve for the selling price by using the percentage formula Base = Portion ÷ Rate, where the cost is the portion and the percent cost or (100% − Percent markup on selling price) is the rate.

$$\text{Selling price} = \frac{\text{Cost}}{100\% - \text{Percent markup on selling price}} \quad \text{or} \quad SP = \frac{C}{100\% - \%M_{SP}}$$

EXAMPLE

Stylistic Furniture purchases wall units from the manufacturer for $550. If the store policy is to mark up all merchandise 60% based on the selling price, what is the retail selling price of the wall units?

SOLUTION STRATEGY

$$SP = \frac{C}{100\% - \%M_{SP}}$$

$$SP = \frac{550}{100\% - 60\%} = \frac{550}{40\%} = 1{,}375$$

Selling price = $\underline{\underline{\$1{,}375}}$

100 − 60 = 40

	$	%
C	550.00	40
+*MU*		60
SP	*X*	100

$40X = 550(100)$

$X = \underline{\underline{\$1{,}375.00}}$

TRY-IT EXERCISE

8. Grand Prix Menswear buys suits for $169.00 from the manufacturer. If a 35% markup based on selling price is the objective, what should be the selling price of the suit?

Check your answer with the solution on page 284.

8-7 Calculating Cost When Selling Price and Percent Markup Based on Selling Price Are Known

Often, retailers know how much their customers are willing to pay for an item. The following procedure is used to determine the most a store can pay for an item and still get the intended markup.

To calculate the cost of an item when the selling price and percent markup based on selling price are known, we use a variation of the formula used in the last section. To solve for cost, we must isolate cost on one side of the equation by multiplying both sides of the equation by (100% − Percent markup). This yields the equation for cost:

$$\text{Cost} = \text{Selling price}(100\% - \text{Percent markup on selling price})$$

$$C = SP(100\% - \%M_{SP})$$

EXAMPLE

A buyer for a chain of boutiques is looking for a line of dresses to retail for $120. If a 40% markup based on selling price is the objective, what is the most the buyer can pay for these dresses and still get the intended markup?

100 − 40 = 60

	$	%
C	*X*	60
+*MU*		40
SP	120.00	100

$100X = 120(60)$

$X = \underline{\underline{\$72.00}}$

SOLUTION STRATEGY

$$C = SP(100\% - \%M_{SP})$$

$$C = 120(100\% - 40\%) = 120(.6) = 72$$

$$\text{Cost} = \underline{\underline{\$72.00}}$$

TRY-IT | EXERCISE

9. What is the most a gift shop buyer can pay for a clock if he wants a 55% markup based on selling price and expects to sell the clock for $79 at retail?

Check your answer with the solution on page 284.

8-8 Converting Percent Markup Based on Cost to Percent Markup Based on Selling Price, and Vice Versa

> **Everybody's Business**
> **Learning Tip**
> The percent markup on cost is always *greater* than the corresponding percent markup on selling price because markup on cost uses cost as the base, which is *less* than the selling price. In the percentage formula, the lower the base, the greater the rate.
> The exception is when merchandise is sold at a loss, where the selling price is "below cost."

Converting Percent Markup Based on Cost to Percent Markup Based on Selling Price

When percent markup is based on cost, it can be converted to percent markup based on selling price by using the following formula:

$$\textbf{Percent markup based on selling price} = \frac{\textbf{Percent markup based on cost}}{\textbf{100\% + Percent markup based on cost}}$$

EXAMPLE

If a bookcase is marked up 60% based on cost, what is the corresponding percent markup based on selling price?

SOLUTION STRATEGY

$$\text{Percent markup based on selling price} = \frac{\text{Percent markup based on cost}}{100\% + \text{Percent markup based on cost}}$$

$$\text{Percent markup based on selling price} = \frac{60\%}{100\% + 60\%} = \frac{.6}{1.6} = .375$$

$$\text{Percent markup based on selling price} = \underline{\underline{37.5\%}}$$

TRY-IT | EXERCISE

10. A photocopier is marked up 50% based on cost. What is the corresponding percent markup based on selling price?

Check your answer with the solution on page 284.

Converting Percent Markup Based on Selling Price to Percent Markup Based on Cost

When percent markup is based on selling price, it can be converted to percent markup based on cost by the formula:

$$\text{Percent markup based on cost} = \frac{\text{Percent markup based on selling price}}{100\% - \text{Percent markup based on selling price}}$$

EXAMPLE

A Sony stereo is marked up 25% based on selling price at Circuit City. What is the corresponding percent markup based on cost? Round your answer to the nearest tenth percent.

SOLUTION STRATEGY

$$\text{Percent markup based on cost} = \frac{\text{Percent markup based on selling price}}{100\% - \text{Percent mkarup based on selling price}}$$

$$\text{Percent markup based on cost} = \frac{25\%}{100\% - 25\%} = \frac{.25}{.75} = .3333$$

$$\text{Percent markup based on cost} = \underline{\underline{33.3\%}}$$

TRY-IT EXERCISE

11. A video game is marked up 75% based on selling price at Playtime Toys. What is the corresponding percent markup based on cost? Round your answer to the nearest tenth percent.

Check your answer with the solution on page 284.

REVIEW EXERCISES | CHAPTER 8—SECTION II

For the following items, calculate the missing information, rounding dollars to the nearest cent and percents to the nearest tenth:

	Item	Cost	Amount of Markup	Selling Price	Percent Markup Based on Cost	Percent Markup Based on Selling Price
1.	sink	$65.00	$50.00	________		________
2.	textbook	$34.44	________	$51.50		________
3.	telephone	$75.00	________	________		45%
4.	bicycle	________	________	$133.50		60%
5.	magazine				60%	________
6.	flashlight				________	35%
7.	doll house	$71.25	________	$165.99	________	________
8.	1 qt. milk	$1.18	$.79	________	________	________
9.	truck	$15,449.00	________	________	________	38%
10.	sofa	________	________	$1,299.00	________	55%
11.	fan				150%	________
12.	drill				________	47%

Solve the following word problems, rounding dollars to the nearest cent and percents to the nearest tenth:

13. If the Sony computer shown here has a cost of $544.00,
    a. What is the amount of the markup?
    b. What is the percent markup based on selling price?

14. A distributor purchases tractors at a cost of $6,500 and sells them for $8,995.
    a. What is the amount of the markup?
    b. What is the percent markup based on selling price?

15. Waterbed City purchases beds from the manufacturer for $212.35. If the store policy is to mark up all merchandise 42% based on selling price, what is the retail selling price of the beds?

16. Cindy's Sundries purchases color film for $2.67 per roll. If Cindy's policy is to mark up all film 30% based on selling price, what is the retail selling price per roll?

17. If this lantern flashlight has a markup of 28% based on selling price,
    a. What is the cost?
    b. What is the amount of the markup?
    c. What is the percent markup based on cost?

18. A buyer for a shoe store chain is looking for a line of men's shoes to retail for $79.95. If the objective is a 55% markup based on selling price, what is the most that the buyer can pay for the shoes to still get the desired markup?

19. If the markup on a washing machine is 43% based on selling price, what is the corresponding percent markup based on cost?

20. If the markup on an oven is 200% based on cost, what is the corresponding percent markup based on selling price?

21. A pillow has a cost of $21.50 and a selling price of $51.99.

a. What is the amount of markup on the pillow?

b. What is the percent markup based on cost?

c. What is the corresponding percent markup based on selling price?

22. If a pair of running shoes has a 45% markup based on selling price,

a. What is the cost?

b. What is the amount of markup?

c. If the store changed to a 90% markup based on cost, what would be the new selling price?

BUSINESS DECISION

Increasing the Margin

23. If Target paid \$37.50 for the vacuum cleaner shown here,

a. What is the percent markup based on selling price?

b. If Target pays \$1.50 to the insurance company for each replacement policy sold, what is the percent markup based on selling price when a customer buys the vacuum cleaner and a policy?

c. If 6,000 vacuum cleaners are sold in a season, and 40% are sold with the insurance policy, how much additional "markup dollars," or **gross margin,** was made by offering the policy?

d. (Optional) As a housewares buyer for Target, what is your opinion of such policies regarding their effect on the "profit picture" of the department? How can you sell more policies?

SECTION III

MARKDOWNS, MULTIPLE OPERATIONS, AND PERISHABLE GOODS

markdown
A price reduction from the original selling price of merchandise.

markdown cancellation
Raising prices back to the original selling price after a sale is over.

The original selling price of merchandise usually represents only a temporary situation, based on customer and competitor reaction to that price. A price reduction from the original selling price of merchandise is known as a **markdown.** Markdowns are frequently used in retailing because of errors in initial pricing or merchandise selection. For example, the original price may have been set too high, or the buyer ordered the wrong styles, sizes, or quantities of merchandise.

Most markdowns should not be regarded as losses but as sales promotion opportunities used to increase sales and profits. When a sale has been concluded, raising prices back to the original selling price is known as a **markdown cancellation.** This section deals with the mathematics of markdowns, a series of markups and markdowns, and the pricing of perishable merchandise.

8-9 Determining the Amount of Markdown and the Markdown Percent

sale price
The promotional price of merchandise, after a markdown.

A markdown is a reduction from the original selling price of an item to a new **sale price.** To determine the amount of a markdown, we use the formula

Amount of markdown = Original selling price − Sale price

Prudent shoppers often spend time comparing products in order to make "informed" buying decisions.

For example, if a sweater was originally marked at $89.95 and then was sale priced at $59.95, the amount of the markdown would be $30.00 ($89.95 − $59.95 = $30.00).

To find the markdown percent, we use the percentage formula once again, Rate = Portion ÷ Base, where the markdown percent is the rate, the amount of the markdown is the portion, and the original selling price is the base:

$$\text{Markdown percent} = \frac{\text{Amount of markdown}}{\text{Original selling price}}$$

EXAMPLE

A lamp that originally sold for $60 was marked down and sold for $48. What are the amount of the markdown and the markdown percent?

SOLUTION STRATEGY

Amount of markdown = Original selling price − Sale price

Amount of markdown = 60 − 48 = 12

Amount of markdown = $12.00

$$\text{Markdown percent} = \frac{\text{Amount of markdown}}{\text{Original selling price}} = \frac{12}{60} = .2$$

Markdown percent = 20%

Everybody's Business

Learning Tip

Note that *markdown percent* calculations are an application of *rate of decrease,* covered in Chapter 6.

In the percentage formula, the markdown (portion) represents the amount of the decrease, and the original selling price (base) represents the original amount.

TRY-IT EXERCISE

12. An FM radio that originally sold for $75 was marked down and sold for $56. What are the amount of the markdown and the markdown percent? Round your answer to the nearest tenth percent.

Check your answers with the solutions on page 284.

8-10 Determining the Sale Price after a Markdown and the Original Price before a Markdown

Determining Sale Price after a Markdown

In markdown calculations, the original selling price is the base, or 100%. After a markdown is subtracted from that price, the new price represents (100% − Markdown percent) *of* the original price. For example, if a chair is marked down 30%, the sale price would be 70% (100% − 30%) of the original price.

To find the new sale price after a markdown, we use the familiar percentage formula, Portion = Rate × Base, where the sale price is the portion, the original price is the base, and (100% − Markdown percent) is the rate.

$$\textbf{Sale price} = \textbf{Original selling price}(100\% - \textbf{Markdown percent})$$

EXAMPLE

A men's shop originally sold a line of ties for $55 each. If the manager decides to mark them down 40% for a clearance sale, what is the sale price of a tie?

SOLUTION STRATEGY

Remember, if the markdown is 40%, the sale price must be 60% (100% − 40%) *of* the original price.

$$\text{Sale price} = \text{Original selling price }(100\% - \text{Markdown percent})$$

$$\text{Sale price} = \$55(100\% - 40\%) = 55(.6) = 33$$

$$\text{Sale price} = \underline{\underline{\$33}}$$

TRY-IT | EXERCISE

13. A lumber yard originally sold paneling for $27.50 per sheet. When the stock was almost depleted, the price was marked down 60% to make room for incoming merchandise. What was the sale price per sheet of paneling?

Check your answer with the solution on page 284.

Finding the Original Price before a Markdown

To find the original selling price before a markdown, we use the sale price formula solved for the original selling price. The original selling price is isolated to one side by dividing both sides of the equation by (100% − Markdown percent). *Note:* This is actually the percentage formula Base = Portion ÷ Rate, with the original selling price as the base.

$$\textbf{Original selling price} = \frac{\textbf{Sale price}}{100\% - \textbf{Markdown percent}}$$

EXAMPLE

What was the original selling price of Rollerblades, currently on sale for $99 after a 25% markdown?

SOLUTION STRATEGY

Reasoning: $99 = 75%(100% − 25%) *of* the original price. Solve for the original price.

$$\text{Original selling price} = \frac{\text{Sale price}}{100\% - \text{Markdown percent}} = \frac{99}{100\% - 25\%} = \frac{99}{.75} = 132$$

Original selling price = $132

TRY-IT EXERCISE

14. What was the original selling price of a briefcase, currently on sale for $79 after a 35% markdown? Round your answer to the nearest cent.

Check your answer with the solution on page 284.

8-11 Computing the Final Selling Price after a Series of Markups and Markdowns

Products that do not undergo seasonal fluctuations in sales, such as food, tools, tires, and furniture, are known as **staple goods.** These products are usually marked up once and perhaps marked down occasionally, on sale. **Seasonal goods,** such as men's and women's fashion items, snow shovels, bathing suits, and holiday merchandise, may undergo many markups and markdowns during their selling season. Merchants must continually adjust prices as the season progresses. Getting caught with an excessive amount of out-of-season inventory can ruin an otherwise bright profit picture. Christmas decorations in January or snow tires in June are virtually useless profit-wise!

staple goods
Products, considered basic and routinely purchased, that do not undergo seasonal fluctuations in sales, such as food, tools, and furniture.

seasonal goods
Products that undergo seasonal fluctuations in sales, such as fashion apparel and holiday merchandise.

EXAMPLE

In March, a boutique purchased designer bathing suits for $50 each. The original markup was 60% based on the selling price. In May, the shop took a 25% markdown by having a sale. After three weeks, the sale was over and all merchandise was marked up 15%. By July, many of the bathing suits were still in stock, so the shop took a 30% markdown to stimulate sales. At the end of August, the balance of the bathing suits were put on clearance sale, with a final markdown of another 25%. What was the final selling price of the bathing suits? Round your answer to the nearest cent.

Everybody's Business

Learning Tip

In a series of markups and markdowns, each calculation is based on the *previous* selling price.

SOLUTION STRATEGY

When solving a series of markups and markdowns, remember that each should be based on the previous selling price. Use the formulas presented in this chapter, and take each step one at a time.

Step 1. Find the original selling price, with markup based on the selling price:

$$\text{Selling price} = \frac{\text{Cost}}{100\% - \text{Percent markup}} = \frac{50}{100\% - 60\%} = \frac{50}{.4} = 125$$

Original selling price = $125

Step 2. Calculate the 25% markdown in May:

Sale price = Original selling price (100% − Markdown percent)

Sale price = 125(100% − 25%) = 125(.75) = 93.75

Sale price = $93.75

Step 3. Calculate the after-sale 15% markup:
Remember, the base is the previous selling price, $93.75.

Selling price = Sale price (100% + Percent markup)

Selling price = 93.75(100% + 15%) = 93.75(1.15) = 107.81

Selling price = $107.81

Step 4. Calculate the July 30% markdown:

Sale price = Previous selling price (100% − Markdown percent)

Sale price = 107.81 (100% − 30%) = 107.81(.7) = 75.47

Sale price = $75.47

Step 5. Calculate the final 25% markdown:

Sale price = Previous selling price (100% − Markdown percent)

Sale price = 75.47(100% − 25%) = 75.47(.75) = 56.60

Final sale price = $56.60

TRY-IT | EXERCISE

15. In September, a tire shop in Chicago purchased snow tires from a distributor for $48.50 each. The original markup was 55% based on the selling price. In November, the tires were marked down 30% and put on sale. In December, they were marked up 20%. In February, the tires were again on sale at 30% off, and in March were cleared out with a final 25% markdown. What was the final selling price of the tires? Round your answer to the nearest cent.

Check your answer with the solution on page 284.

8-12 Calculating the Selling Price of Perishable Goods

perishable goods
Products that have a certain shelf life and then no value at all, such as fruits, vegetables, flowers, and dairy products.

Out-of-season merchandise still has some value, whereas **perishable goods** (such as fruits, vegetables, flowers, and dairy products) have a certain shelf life and then no value at all. For sellers of this type of merchandise to achieve their intended markups, the selling price must be based on the quantity of products sold at the original price. The quantity sold is calculated as total items less spoilage. For example, if a tomato vendor anticipates a 20% spoilage rate, the selling price of the tomatoes should be calculated based on 80% of the original stock. To calculate the selling price of perishables, use the formula

$$\textbf{Selling price of perishables} = \frac{\textbf{Total expected selling price}}{\textbf{Total quantity} - \textbf{Anticipated spoilage}}$$

EXAMPLE

The Farmer's Market buys 1,500 pounds of fresh peaches at a cost of $.60 a pound. If a 15% spoilage rate is anticipated, at what price per pound should the peaches be sold to achieve a 50% markup based on selling price? Round your answer to the nearest cent.

SOLUTION STRATEGY

Step 1. Find the total expected selling price: The total expected selling price is found by applying the selling price formula, $SP = C \div (100\% - \%M_{SP})$. The cost will be the total pounds times the price per pound, $1{,}500 \times \$.60 = \$900$.

$$SP = \frac{\text{Cost}}{100\% - \%M_{SP}} = \frac{900}{100\% - 50\%} = \frac{900}{.5} = 1{,}800$$

Total expected selling price = $\underline{\underline{\$1{,}800}}$

Step 2. Find the anticipated spoilage: To find the amount of anticipated spoilage, use the formula,

$$\text{Anticipated spoilage} = \text{Total quantity} \times \text{Spoilage rate}$$

$$\text{Anticipated spoilage} = 1{,}500 \times 15\% = 1{,}500(.15) = 225$$

$$\text{Anticipated spoilage} = \underline{\underline{225 \text{ pounds}}}$$

Step 3. Calculate the selling price of the perishables:

$$\text{Selling price of perishables} = \frac{\text{Total expected selling price}}{\text{Total quantity} - \text{Anticipated spoilage}}$$

$$\text{Selling price} = \frac{\$1{,}800}{1{,}500 - 225} = \frac{\$1{,}800}{1{,}275} = 1.4117$$

$$\text{Selling price of peaches} = \underline{\underline{\$1.41 \text{ per pound}}}$$

TRY-IT | EXERCISE

16. Exotic Gardens, a chain of flower shops, purchases 800 dozen roses for Valentine's Day at a cost of $6.50 per dozen. If a 10% spoilage rate is anticipated, at what price per dozen should the roses be sold to achieve a 60% markup based on selling price? Round your answer to the nearest cent.

Check your answer with the solution on page 284.

REVIEW EXERCISES | CHAPTER 8—SECTION III

For the following items, calculate the missing information, rounding dollars to the nearest cent and percents to the nearest tenth:

Item	Original Selling Price	Amount of Markdown	Sale Price	Markdown Percent
1. fish tank	$189.95	$28.50	________	________
2. sneakers	$53.88	________	$37.50	________
3. cantaloupe	________	$.39	$1.29	________

	Item	Original Selling Price	Amount of Markdown	Sale Price	Markdown Percent
4.	CD player	$264.95	________	________	30%
5.	1 yd carpet	________	________	$24.66	40%
6.	suitcase	$68.00	________	$51.99	________
7.	chess set	$115.77	$35.50	________	________
8.	necklace	________	$155.00	$235.00	________
9.	copier	$1,599.88	________	________	35%
10.	pen	________	________	$15.90	25%

Solve the following word problems, rounding dollars to the nearest cent and percents to the nearest tenth:

11. A cellular phone that originally sold for $235.75 was marked down and sold for $189.95.

a. What is the amount of the markdown?

b. What is the markdown percent?

12. A set of glasses that originally sold for $34.88 was marked down by $12.11.

a. What is the sale price?

b. What is the markdown percent?

13. a. What is the amount of the markdown on these notebooks?

b. What is the markdown percent?

c. If the sale price is then marked up by 40%, what is the new selling price?

14. Office Headquarters, a retail store, originally sold file cabinets for $68.50. If they were put on sale at a markdown of 35%, what is the sale price?

15. Home Library, a book store, sold dictionaries for $75.00. If they were put on clearance sale at 60% off, what is the sale price?

16. What was the original selling price of a fax machine, currently on sale for $154.99 after a 38% markdown?

17. A lamp is on sale for $63.25, after a markdown of 45%. What was the original selling price of the lamp?

18. From the Office Depot coupon shown here,

a. Calculate the markdown percent.

b. If the offer was changed to "Buy 3, Get 2 Free," what is the new markdown percent?

c. Which offer is more profitable for the store? Explain.

19. In February, Golf World, a retail shop, purchased golf clubs for $453.50 per set. The original markup was 35% based on selling price. In April, the shop took a 20% markdown by having a special sale. After two weeks, the sale was over and the clubs were marked up 10%. In June, it offered a storewide sale of 15% off all merchandise, and in September, a final 10% markdown was taken on the clubs. What was the final selling price of the golf clubs?

20. The Farmer's Market purchases 460 pounds of sweet potatoes at $.76 per pound. If a 10% spoilage rate is anticipated, at what price per pound should the sweet potatoes be sold to achieve a 35% markup based on selling price?

21. A microwave oven cost The Electronic Warehouse $141.30 and was initially marked up by 55% based on selling price. In the next few months the item was marked down 20%, marked up 15%, marked down 10%, and marked down a final 10%. What was the final selling price of the microwave oven?

22. The Goldenflake Bakery makes 200 cherry cheesecakes at a cost of $2.45 each. If a spoilage rate of 5% is anticipated, at what price should the cakes be sold to achieve a 40% markup based on cost?

23. a. What is the markdown percent of the rebate offered by the manufacturer of this fax machine?

b. If during a sale, Best Buy offered an additional 20% off the "after rebate" price, what would be the new sale price of the fax machine?

BUSINESS DECISION

The Permanent Markdown

24. You are the manager of WorldWide Athlete, a chain of six sporting goods shops in your area. The shops sell 12 racing bikes per week at a retail price of $679.99. Recently, you put the bikes on sale at $599.99. At the sale price, 15 bikes were sold during the one-week sale.

a. What was your markdown percent on the bikes?

b. What is the percent increase in number of bikes sold each week during the sale?

c. How much more revenue would be earned in six months by permanently selling the bikes at the lower price, rather than having a one-week sale, each month? (6 sale weeks in 26 weeks)

d. (Optional) As manager of WorldWide, would you recommend this permanent price reduction? Explain.

CHAPTER FORMULAS

$$\text{Selling price} = \text{Cost} + \text{Markup}$$

$$\text{Cost} = \text{Selling price} - \text{Markup}$$

$$\text{Markup} = \text{Selling price} - \text{Cost}$$

$$\text{Percent markup}_{\text{COST}} = \frac{\text{Markup}}{\text{Cost}}$$

$$\text{Percent markup}_{SP} = \frac{\text{Markup}}{\text{Selling price}}$$

$$\text{Selling price} = \text{Cost}(100\% + \%\text{Markup}_{\text{COST}})$$

$$\text{Cost} = \frac{\text{Selling price}}{100\% + \%\text{Markup}_{\text{COST}}}$$

$$\text{Selling price} = \frac{\text{Cost}}{100\% - \%\text{Markup}_{SP}}$$

$$\text{Cost} = \text{Selling price}(100\% - \%\text{Markup}_{SP})$$

$$\%\text{Markup}_{SP} = \frac{\%\text{Markup}_{\text{COST}}}{100\% + \%\text{Markup}_{\text{COST}}}$$

$$\%\text{Markup}_{\text{COST}} = \frac{\%\text{Markup}_{SP}}{100\% - \%\text{Markup}_{SP}}$$

$$\text{Markdown} = \text{Original price} - \text{Sale price}$$

$$\text{Sale price} = \text{Original price} - \text{Markdown}$$

$$\text{Original price} = \text{Sale price} + \text{Markdown}$$

$$\text{Markdown\%} = \frac{\text{Markdown}}{\text{Original price}}$$

$$\text{Sale price} = \text{Original price}(100\% - \text{Markdown\%})$$

$$\text{Original price} = \frac{\text{Sale price}}{100\% - \text{Markdown\%}}$$

$$\text{Selling price}_{\text{Perishables}} = \frac{\text{Expected selling price}}{\text{Total quantity} - \text{Spoilage}}$$

✦ SUMMARY CHART ✦

SECTION I: Markup Based on Cost

Topic	P/O, Page	Important Concepts	Illustrative Examples
Using the Basic Retailing Equation	8-1 256	The basic retailing equation can be applied to solve for selling price *(SP)*, cost *(C)*, and amount of markup *(M)*. **Selling price = Cost + Markup** $SP = C + M$ **Cost = Selling price − Markup** $C = SP - M$ **Markup = Selling price − Cost** $M = SP - C$	1. What is the selling price of a lamp that costs $86.00 and has a $55.99 markup? $SP = 86.00 + 55.99$ Selling price = $\underline{\underline{\$141.99}}$ 2. What is the cost of a radio that sells for $125.50 and has a $37.29 markup? $C = 125.50 - 37.29$ Cost = $\underline{\underline{\$88.21}}$ 3. What is the markup on a set of dishes costing $53.54 and selling for $89.95? $M = 89.95 - 53.54$ Markup = $\underline{\underline{\$36.41}}$
Calculating Percent Markup Based on Cost	8-2 258	$\%\text{Markup}_{\text{COST}} = \dfrac{\text{Markup}}{\text{Cost}}$ $\%M_{\text{COST}} = \dfrac{M}{C}$	A calculator costs $25.00. If the markup is $10.00, what is the percent markup based on cost? $\%M_{\text{COST}} = \dfrac{10.00}{25.00} = .4$ $\%M_{\text{COST}} = \underline{\underline{40\%}}$
Calculating Selling Price	8-3 259	**Selling price = Cost (100% + %Markup$_{\text{COST}}$)** $SP = C(100\% + \%M_{\text{COST}})$	A fax machine costs $260 to manufacture. What should be the selling price if a 60% markup based on cost is desired? $SP = 260(100\% + 60\%)$ $SP = 260(1.6) = 416$ Selling price = $\underline{\underline{\$416.00}}$
Calculating Cost	8-4 259	$\text{Cost} = \dfrac{\text{Selling price}}{100\% + \text{Markup}_{\text{COST}}}$ $C = \dfrac{SP}{100\% + \%M_{\text{COST}}}$	What is the cost of a chair with a selling price of $250 and a 45% markup based on cost? $C = \dfrac{250}{100\% + 45\%} = \dfrac{250}{1.45}$ Cost = $\underline{\underline{\$172.41}}$

SECTION II: Markup Based on Selling Price

Topic	P/O, Page	Important Concepts	Illustrative Examples
Calculating Percent Markup Based on Selling Price	8-5 264	$\%\text{Markup}_{SP} = \dfrac{\text{Markup}}{\text{Selling price}}$ $\%M_{SP} = \dfrac{M}{SP}$	What is the percent markup on the selling price of a Xerox copier with a selling price of $400.00 and a markup of $188.00? $\%M_{SP} = \dfrac{188.00}{400.00} = .47$ $\%M_{SP} = \underline{\underline{47\%}}$
Calculating Selling Price	8-6 265	$\text{Selling price} = \dfrac{\text{Cost}}{100\% - \%\text{Markup}_{SP}}$ $SP = \dfrac{C}{100\% - \%M_{SP}}$	What is the selling price of a quart of milk with a cost of $1.19 and a 43% markup based on selling price? $SP = \dfrac{1.19}{100\% - 43\%} = \dfrac{1.19}{.57}$ $SP = \underline{\underline{\$2.09}}$
Calculating Cost	8-7 265	$\text{Cost} = \text{Selling price}\,(100\% - \%\text{Markup}_{SP})$ $C = SP(100\% - \%M_{SP})$	What is the most a hardware store can pay for a drill if it will have a selling price of $65.50 and a 45% markup based on selling price? $C = 65.50(100\% - 45\%)$ $C = 65.50(.55)$ $\text{Cost} = \underline{\underline{\$36.03}}$
Converting Percent Markup Based on Cost to Percent Markup Based on Selling Price	8-8 266	$\%\text{Markup}_{SP} = \dfrac{\%\text{Markup}_{COST}}{100\% + \%\text{Markup}_{COST}}$ $\%M_{SP} = \dfrac{\%M_{COST}}{100\% + \%M_{COST}}$	If a hair dryer is marked up 70% based on cost, what is the corresponding percent markup based on selling price? $\%M_{SP} = \dfrac{70\%}{100\% + 70\%} = \dfrac{.7}{1.7}$ $\%M_{SP} = \underline{\underline{.4118 = 41.2\%}}$
Converting Percent Markup Based on Selling Price to Percent Markup Based on Cost	8-8 267	$\%\text{Markup}_{COST} = \dfrac{\%\text{Markup}_{SP}}{100\% - \%\text{Markup}_{SP}}$ $\%M_{COST} = \dfrac{\%M_{SP}}{100\% - \%M_{SP}}$	If a toaster is marked up 35% based on selling price, what is the corresponding percent markup based on cost? $\%M_{COST} = \dfrac{35\%}{100\% - 35\%} = \dfrac{.35}{.65}$ $\%M_{COST} = \underline{\underline{.5384 = 53.8\%}}$

SECTION III: Markdowns, Multiple Operations, and Perishable Goods

Topic	P/O, Page	Important Concepts	Illustrative Examples
Calculating Markdown and Markdown Percent	8-9 270	Markdown = Original price − Sale price $MD = \text{Orig} - \text{Sale}$ $\text{Markdown } \% = \frac{\text{Markdown}}{\text{Original price}}$ $MD\% = \frac{MD}{\text{Orig}}$	Calculate the amount of markdown and the markdown percent of a television set that originally sold for $425.00 and was then put on sale for $299.95. $MD = 425.00 - 299.95$ Markdown = $125.05 $MD\% = \frac{125.05}{425.00} = .2942$ Markdown % = 29.4%
Determining the Sale Price after a Markdown	8-10 272	Sale price = Original selling price (100% − Markdown %) Sale = Orig (100% − MD%)	What is the sale price of a computer that originally sold for $2,500.00 and was then marked down by 35%? Sale = 2,500(100% − 35%) Sale = 2,500(.65) = 1,625 Sale price = $1,625.00
Determining the Original Selling Price before a Markdown	8-10 272	$\text{Original price} = \frac{\text{Sale price}}{100\% - \text{Markdown}\%}$ $\text{Orig} = \frac{\text{Sale}}{100\% - MD\%}$	What is the original selling price of an exercise bicycle, currently on sale at Sears for $235.88 after a 30% markdown? $\text{Orig} = \frac{235.88}{100\% - 30\%} = \frac{235.88}{.7}$ Original price = $336.97
Computing the Final Selling Price after a Series of Markups and Markdowns	8-11 273	To solve for the final selling price after a series of markups and markdowns, calculate each step based on the previous selling price.	Compute the final selling price of an umbrella costing $27.50, with the following seasonal activity: a. Initial markup, 40% on cost b. 20% markdown c. 15% markdown d. 10% markup e. Final clearance, 25% markdown a. Initial 40% markup: $SP = C(100\% + \%M_{\text{COST}})$ $SP = 27.50(100\% + 40\%)$ $SP = 27.50(1.4) = 38.50$ Original price = $38.50 b. 20% markdown: Sale = Orig (100% − MD%) Sale = 38.50(100% − 20%) Sale = 38.50(.8) Sale price = $30.80

SECTION III: (continued)

Topic	P/O, Page	Important Concepts	Illustrative Examples
			c. 15% markdown: Sale = Orig (100% − MD%) Sale = 30.80(100% − 15%) Sale = 30.80(.85) Sale price = $26.18 d. 10% markup: SP = sale price (100% + M%) SP = 26.18(100% + 10%) SP = 26.18(1.10) Selling price = $28.80 e. Final 25% markdown: Sale = Orig (100% − MD%) Sale = 28.80(100% − 25%) Sale = 28.80(.75) Final selling price = $21.60
Calculating the Selling Price of Perishable Goods	8-12 274	$\text{Selling price}_{\text{Perishables}} = \dfrac{\text{Total expected selling price}}{\text{Total quantity} - \text{Anticipated spoilage}}$ $SP_{\text{perish}} = \dfrac{\text{Exp } SP}{\text{Quan} - \text{Spoil}}$	A grocery store purchases 250 pounds of apples from a wholesaler for $.67 per pound. If a 10% spoilage rate is anticipated, what selling price per pound will yield a 45% markup based on cost? Total Cost = 250 lb @ .67 = $167.50 Exp SP = C(100% + M_{COST}) Exp SP = 167.50(100% + 45%) Exp SP = 167.50(1.45) = $242.88 $SP_{\text{perish}} = \dfrac{242.88}{250 - 25} = \dfrac{242.88}{225}$ SP_{perish} = $1.08 per lb

TRY-IT EXERCISE | SOLUTIONS

1. $SP = C + M = 6.80 + 9.40 = \underline{\underline{\$16.20}}$

2. $M = SP - C = 28.50 - 16.75 = \underline{\underline{\$11.75}}$

3. $C = SP - M = 290.00 - 75.00 = \underline{\underline{\$215.00}}$

4. $M = SP - C = 63.00 - 45.00 = \underline{\underline{\$18.00}}$

$$\%M_{COST} = \frac{M}{C} = \frac{18.00}{45.00} = .4 = \underline{\underline{40\%}}$$

5. $SP = C(100\% + \%M_{\text{COST}}) = 38.00\,(100\% + 65\%) = 38.00(1.65) = \underline{\underline{\$62.70}}$

6. $$C = \frac{SP}{100\% + \%M_{\text{COST}}} = \frac{39.00}{100\% + 30\%} = \frac{39.00}{1.3} = \underline{\underline{\$30.00}}$$

7. $M = SP - C = 157.50 - 94.50 = \underline{\underline{\$63.00}}$

$$\%M_{SP} = \frac{M}{SP} = \frac{63.00}{157.50} = .40 = \underline{\underline{40\%}}$$

8. $$SP = \frac{C}{100\% - \%M_{SP}} = \frac{169.00}{100\% - 35\%} = \frac{169.00}{.65} = \underline{\underline{\$260.00}}$$

9. $C = SP(100\% - \%M_{SP}) = 79.00(100\% - 55\%) = 79.00(.45) = \underline{\underline{\$35.55}}$

10. $$\%M_{SP} = \frac{\%M_{\text{COST}}}{100\% + \%M_{\text{COST}}} = \frac{50\%}{100\% + 50\%} = \frac{.5}{1.5} = .333 = \underline{\underline{33.3\%}}$$

11. $$\%M_{\text{COST}} = \frac{\%M_{SP}}{100\% - \%M_{SP}} = \frac{75\%}{100\% - 75\%} = \frac{.75}{.25} = 3 = \underline{\underline{300\%}}$$

12. MD = Original price − Sale price = 75.00 − 56.00 = $\underline{\underline{\$19.00}}$

$$MD\% = \frac{MD}{\text{Original price}} = \frac{19.00}{75.00} = .2533 = \underline{\underline{25.3\%}}$$

13. Sale price = Original price $(100\% - MD\%) = 27.50(100\% - 60\%) = 27.50(.4) = \underline{\underline{\$11.00}}$

14. $$\text{Original price} = \frac{\text{Sale price}}{100\% - MD\%} = \frac{79.00}{100\% - 35\%} = \frac{79.00}{.65} = \underline{\underline{\$121.54}}$$

15. $$SP = \frac{C}{100\% - \%M_{SP}} = \frac{48.50}{100\% - 55\%} = \frac{48.50}{.45} = \$107.78$$

Markdown #1: Original price$(100\% + MD\%) = 107.78(.7) = \$75.45$

20% markup: $75.45(100\% + 20\%) = 75.45(1.2) = \$90.54$

Markdown #2: Original price$(100\% - MD\%) = 90.54(.7) = \$63.38$

Final markdown: Original price$(100\% - MD\%) = 63.38(.75) = \underline{\underline{\$47.54}}$

16. Total cost = 800 dozen @ \$6.50 = \$5,200.00

$$\text{Expected selling price} = \frac{C}{100\% - \%M_{SP}} = \frac{5{,}200.00}{100\% - 60\%} = \frac{5{,}200}{.4} = \$13{,}000$$

$$SP_{\text{perish}} = \frac{\text{Expected } SP}{\text{Total quantity} - \text{Spoilage}} = \frac{13{,}000.00}{800 - 80} = \frac{13{,}000.00}{720} = \underline{\underline{\$18.06 \text{ per doz.}}}$$

CHAPTER 8 | ASSESSMENT TEST

Name ____________

Class ____________

Solve the following word problems, rounding dollars to the nearest cent and percents to the nearest tenth:

1. Vacuum cleaners cost the manufacturer $83.22 to produce. If a markup of $69.38 is added to the cost, what is the selling price per unit?

2. Modernage Furniture sells desks for $346.00. If the desks cost $212.66, what is the amount of the markup?

3. After Southwest Food Wholesalers adds a markup of $15.40 to a case of tomato sauce, it sells for $33.98. What is the wholesaler's cost per case?

4. If The Phone Store adds a $53.00 markup to each Panasonic phone shown here,

a. What is the cost?

b. What is the percent markup based on selling price?

c. What is the percent markup based on cost?

5. Cody's Western Wear purchases shirts for $47.50 each. A $34.00 markup is added to the shirts.

a. What is the selling price?

b. What is the percent markup based on cost?

c. What is the percent markup based on selling price?

Answers

1. ____________
2. ____________
3. ____________
4. a. ____________
   b. ____________
   c. ____________
5. a. ____________
   b. ____________
   c. ____________

Name ______________________

Class ______________________

Answers

6. ______________________
7. ______________________
8. a. ______________________
   b. ______________________
9. a. ______________________
   b. ______________________
10. a. ______________________
    b. ______________________

6. Macy's purchases imported perfume for $24.30 per ounce. If the store policy is to mark up all merchandise in that department 39% based on selling price, what is the retail selling price of the perfume?

7. The Carpet Gallery is looking for a new line of nylon carpeting to retail at $39.88 per square yard. If management wants a 60% markup based on selling price, what is the most that can be paid for the carpeting to still get the desired markup?

8. a. If the markup on a lamp is 50% based on selling price, what is the corresponding percent markup based on cost?

b. If the markup on a VCR is 120% based on cost, what is the corresponding percent markup based on selling price?

9. a. What is the markdown percent of the tennis racquet?

b. If the store offered an additional 15% off on all merchandise in the store on "Sale Sunday," what is the new sale price of the racquet?

10. A three-day cruise on the Bahamas Fiesta originally selling for $988 was marked down by $210 at the end of the season.

a. What is the sale price of the cruise?

b. What is the markdown percent?

11. TV City originally sold 12-inch portables for $277. If they are put on sale at a markdown of 22%, what is the sale price of the TV sets?

12. What was the original selling price of a computer, currently on sale for $2,484.00 after a 20% markdown?

13. Outdoor World brought in a line of basketball hoops shown here for the summer season. The store uses a 55% markup based on selling price.

a. If they were originally priced at $124.99, what was the cost?

b. As the summer progressed, they were marked down 25%, marked up 15%, marked down 20%, and cleared out in October at a final 25%-off sale. What was the final selling price of the hoops?

14. The Epicure Market prepares fresh gourmet entrees each day. On Wednesday, 80 baked chicken dinners were made at a cost of $3.50 each. A 10% rate of spoilage is anticipated.

a. At what price should the dinners be sold to achieve a 60% markup based on selling price?

b. If Epicure offers a $1.00-off coupon in a newspaper advertisement, what markdown percent does the coupon represent?

Name ______________________

Class ______________________

Answers

11. ______________________

12. ______________________

13. a. ______________________

b. ______________________

14. a. ______________________

b. ______________________

Name ____________________

Class ____________________

Answers

15. a. ____________________

b. ____________________

c. ____________________

d. ____________________

16. a. ____________________

15. a. What is the original selling price of the guitar shown here, if the $1,999.99 sale price represents 20% off?

b. How much did the store pay for the guitar if the initial markup was 150% based on cost?

c. What is the markup based on selling price?

d. If next month the guitar is scheduled to be on sale for $1,599.99, what is the markdown percent?

BUSINESS DECISION

Maintained Markup

16. The markup that a retail store actually realizes on the sale of their goods is called **maintained markup.** It is what is achieved after "retail reductions" (markdowns) have been subtracted from the initial markup. Maintained markup is one of the "keys to profitability" in retailing. It is the difference between the actual selling price and the cost, and therefore has a direct effect on net profits.

$$\text{Maintained markup} = \frac{\text{Actual selling price} - \text{Cost}}{\text{Actual selling price}}$$

You are the buyer for The Emporium, a chain of four men's clothing stores. For the fall season you purchased a line of men's dress shirts with a manufacturer's suggested retail price of $29.50. Your cost was $16.00 per shirt.

a. What is the initial markup based on selling price?

Name ______________________

Class ______________________

b. The shirts did not sell as expected at the regular price, so you marked them down to $21.99, and sold them out. What is the maintained markup on the shirts?

c. When you complained to the manufacturer's sales representative about having to take excessive markdowns in order to sell their merchandise, they offered a $2.00 rebate per shirt. What is your new maintained markup?

Answers

16. b. ______________________

c. ______________________

All the Math That's Fit to Learn

The Business Math Times

Volume VIII | **Markup and Markdown** | One Dollar

Consumer Trends

According to futurist and marketing consultant Faith Popcorn, the following are some consumer trends to look out for:

Time is the new money. People would rather spend money than time. By 2010, 90% of all consumer goods will be home-delivered.

Women are the "king" of retailing. They control 80% of household spending and influence 90% of all car purchases. They also own 53% of all stocks.

Polluted air, contaminated water, and tainted food have people concerned. Bottled water sales are booming. Even McDonald's has its own brand. Also, 73% of Americans use antibacterial soap, and hand sanitizers are a $100-million business.

Health consciousness is in. Organics are a $7.6 billion business, up 200% in the last five years. GNC is opening more than a store a day; it does $4.2 billion in annual sales. Fitness club membership is up 64% over the last seven years for those aged 39 to 54.

People are cocooning. Staying, playing, and working safely at home is more prevalent. Home improvement is a $143-billion business. Home Depot has 700 stores, with 1,300 more on the way. QVC has 5 million couch shoppers. HSN sends out 62,000 packages per day.

THE WALL STREET JOURNAL

"We make money the old-fashioned way... first we undercut the competition into bankruptcy, and then we jack up the prices!"

"Quote . . . Unquote"

Rule 1: The customer is always right.
Rule 2: If the customer is ever wrong, refer to rule 1.
—*Stew Leonard*

Competition is a lot like cod liver oil.
First it makes you sick. Then it makes you better.
—*Advance Micro Devices, Inc.*

Top 10 Retailers

Rank	Company	Volume ($000)	Earnings (loss) ($000)	Stores
1	Wal-Mart	$193,295,000	$6,295,000	4,190
2	Kroger	49,000,400	1,126,800	3,660
3	Home Depot	45,738,000	2,581,000	1,134
4	Sears	40,937,000	1,343,000	2,960
5	Kmart	37,028,000	(244,000)	2,150
6	Albertson's	36,762,000	765,000	2,533
7	Target	36,362,000	1,264,000	1,307
8	JCPenney	32,649,000	(409,000)	3,725
9	Costco	32,164,296	631,437	335
10	Safeway	31,976,900	1,091,900	1,688

Top 10 Specialty Stores

Rank	Company	Volume ($000)	Earnings (loss) ($000)	Stores
1	Best Buy	$15,326,552	$395,839	1,741
2	Gap	13,673,460	877,497	3,676
3	Circuit City	12,959,028	160,802	636
4	Office Depot	11,569,696	49,332	1,020
5	Toys'R' Us	11,332,000	404,000	1,586
6	Staples	10,673,671	59,712	1,305
7	Limited	10,104,606	427,905	2,739
8	TJX	9,579,006	538,066	1,483
9	CompUSA	6,150,000	n.a.	226
10	Office Max	5,156,392	(133,166)	995

Brainteaser

THE BIKE SALE

A bicycle, originally priced at less than $100, was on sale at a 25% discount. When the original price, a whole number of dollars, was marked down, the new price was also a whole number of dollars.

What is the largest possible number of dollars in the original price of the bicycle?

ANSWER TO LAST ISSUE'S BRAINTEASER

Total invoice = $24,000

$$X = 1/3X + 1/4X + 10{,}000$$
$$X = 7/12X + 10{,}000$$
$$X - 7/12X = 10{,}000$$
$$5/12X = 10{,}000$$
$$X = \underline{\underline{\$24{,}000}}$$

CHAPTER 9

Payroll

PERFORMANCE OBJECTIVES

Section I Employee's Gross Earnings and Incentive Pay Plans

9-1 Prorating annual salary on the basis of weekly, biweekly, semimonthly, and monthly pay periods. (p. 292)
9-2 Calculating gross pay by hourly wages, including regular and overtime rates. (p. 293)
9-3 Calculating gross pay by straight and differential piecework schedules. (p. 294)
9-4 Calculating gross pay by straight and incremental commission, salary plus commission, and drawing accounts. (p. 296)

Section II Employee's Payroll Deductions

9-5 Computing FICA taxes, both social security and Medicare, withheld from an employee's paycheck. (p. 302)
9-6 Calculating an employee's federal income tax withholding (FIT) by the percentage method. (p. 304)
9-7 Determining an employee's total withholding for federal income tax, social security, and Medicare using the combined wage bracket tables. (p. 307)

Section III Employer's Payroll Expenses and Record Keeping Responsibilities

9-8 Computing FICA tax for employers and self-employment tax for self-employed persons. (p. 313)
9-9 Computing the amount of state unemployment taxes (SUTA) and federal unemployment taxes (FUTA). (p. 314)
9-10 Calculating employer's fringe benefit expenses. (p. 315)
9-11 Understanding Internal Revenue Service payroll forms. (p. 317)

SECTION I

EMPLOYEE'S GROSS EARNINGS AND INCENTIVE PAY PLANS

Because payroll is frequently a company's largest operating expense, efficient payroll preparation and record keeping are extremely important functions in any business operation. Although today most businesses computerize their payroll functions, it is important for businesspeople to understand the processes and procedures involved.

Employers are responsible for paying employees for services rendered to the company over a period of time. In addition, the company is responsible for withholding certain taxes and other deductions from an employee's paycheck and depositing those taxes with the Internal Revenue Service (IRS) through authorized financial institutions. Other deductions, such as insurance premiums and charitable contributions, are also disbursed by the employer to the appropriate place.

gross pay, or gross earnings
Total amount of earnings due an employee for work performed before payroll deductions are withheld.

net pay, or net earnings, or take-home pay
The actual amount of the employee's paycheck after all payroll deductions have been withheld.

In business, the term **gross pay** or **gross earnings** means the *total* amount of earnings due an employee for work performed before payroll deductions are withheld. The **net pay, net earnings,** or **take-home pay** is the actual amount of the employee's paycheck after all payroll deductions have been withheld. This concept is easily visualized by the formula

$$\text{Net pay} = \text{Gross pay} - \text{Total deductions}$$

This chapter deals with the business math involved in payroll management: the computation of employee gross earnings, calculating withholding taxes and other deductions, and the associated governmental deposits, regulations, and record keeping requirements.

9-1 Prorating Annual Salary on the Basis of Weekly, Biweekly, Semimonthly, and Monthly Pay Periods

salary
A fixed gross amount of pay, equally distributed over periodic payments, without regard to the number of hours worked.

Employee compensation takes on many forms in the business world. Employees who hold managerial, administrative, or professional positions are paid a salary. A **salary** is a fixed gross amount of pay, equally distributed over periodic payments, without regard to the number of hours worked. Salaries are usually expressed as an annual, or yearly, amount. For example, a corporate accountant might receive an annual salary of $50,000.

Although salaries may be stated as annual amounts, they are usually distributed to employees on a more timely basis. A once-a-year paycheck would be a real trick to manage! Employees are most commonly paid in one of the following ways:

Weekly	52 paychecks per year	Annual salary ÷ 52
Biweekly	26 paychecks per year	Annual salary ÷ 26
Semimonthly	24 paychecks per year	Annual salary ÷ 24
Monthly	12 paychecks per year	Annual salary ÷ 12

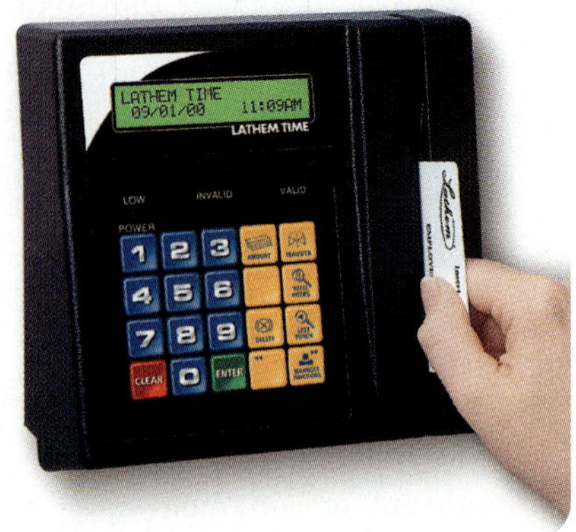

Time clocks are used by many companies to keep track of employees' work hours.

EXAMPLE

What is the weekly, biweekly, semimonthly, and monthly amount of gross pay for a corporate accountant with an annual salary of $50,000?

SOLUTION STRATEGY

The amount of gross pay per period is determined by dividing the annual salary by the number of pay periods per year.

$$\text{Weekly pay} = \frac{50{,}000}{52} = \underline{\underline{\$961.54}}$$

$$\text{Biweekly pay} = \frac{50{,}000}{26} = \underline{\underline{\$1{,}923.08}}$$

$$\text{Semimonthly pay} = \frac{50{,}000}{24} = \underline{\underline{\$2{,}083.33}}$$

$$\text{Monthly pay} = \frac{50{,}000}{12} = \underline{\underline{\$4{,}166.67}}$$

TRY-IT | EXERCISE

1. An executive of a large manufacturing company earns a gross annual salary of $43,500. What is the weekly, biweekly, semimonthly, and monthly pay for this employee?

Check your answers with the solutions on page 329.

9-2 Calculating Gross Pay by Hourly Wages, Including Regular and Overtime Rates

Wages are earnings for routine or manual work, usually based on the number of hours worked. An **hourly wage** or **hourly rate** is the amount an employee is paid for each hour worked. The hourly wage is the most frequently used pay method and is designed to compensate employees for the amount of time spent on the job. The Fair Labor Standards Act of 1938, a federal law, specifies that a standard work week is 40 hours, and **overtime,** amounting to at least $1\frac{1}{2}$ times the hourly rate, must be paid for all hours worked over 40 hours per week. Paying an employee $1\frac{1}{2}$ times the hourly rate is known as **time-and-a-half.**

Many companies have taken overtime a step farther than required by compensating employees at time-and-a-half for all hours over 8 hours per day instead of 40 hours per week. Another common payroll benefit is when companies pay **double time,** twice the hourly rate, for holidays, midnight shifts, and weekend hours.

wages
Earnings for routine or manual work, usually based on the number of hours worked.

hourly wage, or hourly rate
The amount an employee is paid for each hour worked.

overtime
According to federal law, the amount an employee is paid for each hour worked over 40 hours per week.

time-and-a-half
Overtime rate amounting to one and a half times the hourly rate.

double time
Overtime rate usually paid for holidays, midnight shifts, and weekend hours, amounting to twice the hourly rate.

STEPS TO CALCULATE AN EMPLOYEE'S GROSS PAY BY HOURLY WAGES:

Step 1. Calculate an employee's regular gross pay for working 40 hours or less:

Regular pay = Hourly rate × Regular hours worked

Step 2. Calculate an employee's overtime pay by chain multiplying the hourly rate by the overtime factor by the number of overtime hours.

Overtime pay = Hourly rate × Overtime factor × Overtime hours worked

Step 3. Calculate total gross pay:

Total gross pay = Regular pay + Overtime pay

Everybody's Business

Real-World Connection

Payroll is a very important business responsibility. Employees must be paid on a regular basis, and accurate records must be kept for government reporting.

- Payroll is usually one of the largest "expense" categories of a company.
- The department responsible for the payroll function may be called Payroll, Personnel, or Human Resources.
- In recent years, companies have evolved that specialize in doing payroll. When a business hires an outside firm to perform a function such as payroll, this is known as *outsourcing*.

EXAMPLE

Kathryn Warren earns \$8.00 per hour as a checker on an assembly line. If her overtime rate is time-and-a-half, what is Kathryn's total gross pay for working 46 hours last week?

SOLUTION STRATEGY

To find Kathryn's total gross pay, compute her regular pay plus overtime pay.

Regular pay = Hourly rate × Regular hours worked

Regular pay = 8.00 × 40 = \$320.00

Overtime pay = Hourly rate × Overtime factor × Overtime hours worked

Overtime pay = 8.00 × 1.5 × 6 = \$72.00

Total gross pay = Regular pay + Overtime pay

Total gross pay = 320.00 + 72.00 = \$392.00

TRY-IT | EXERCISE

2. John Murdock works as a delivery truck driver for \$6.50 per hour, with time-and-a-half for overtime and double time on Sundays. What is John's total gross pay for last week if he worked 45 hours on Monday through Saturday, plus a 4-hour shift on Sunday?

Check your answer with the solution on page 329.

9-3 Calculating Gross Pay by Straight and Differential Piecework Schedules

piecework
Pay rate schedule based on an employee's production output, not hours worked.

straight piecework plan
Pay per unit of output, regardless of output quantity.

differential piecework plan
Greater incentive method of compensation than straight piecework, where pay per unit increases as output goes up.

A **piecework** pay rate schedule is not based on time but on production output. The incentive is that the more units the worker produces, the more money he or she makes. A **straight piecework plan** is when the worker receives a certain amount of pay per unit of output, regardless of output quantity. A **differential piecework plan** gives workers a greater incentive to increase output, because the rate per unit increases as output goes up. For example, a straight piecework plan might pay \$3.15 per unit, whereas a differential plan might pay \$3.05 for the first 50 units produced, \$3.45 for units 51–100, and \$3.90 for any units over 100.

STEPS TO CALCULATE GROSS PAY BY PIECEWORK:

Straight Piecework:

Step 1. Total gross pay under a straight piecework schedule is calculated by multiplying the number of pieces or output units by the rate per unit.

Total gross pay = Output quantity × Rate per unit

Differential Piecework:

Step 1. Multiply the number of output units at each level by the rate per unit at that level.

Step 2. Find the total gross pay by adding the total from each level.

EXAMPLE

Kim Evans works on a hat assembly line. Kim gets paid at a straight piecework rate of $.35 per hat. What is Kim's total gross pay for last week if she produced 1,655 hats?

SOLUTION STRATEGY

Total gross pay = Output quantity × Rate per unit

Total gross pay = 1,655 × .35 = $579.25

TRY-IT | EXERCISE

3. Nestor Blanco works at a tire manufacturing plant. He is on a straight piecework rate of $.41 per tire. What is Nestor's total gross pay for last week if he produced 950 tires?

Check your answer with the solution on page 329.

EXAMPLE

Susan Woods assembled 190 watches last week. Calculate her total gross pay based on the following differential piecework schedule:

Pay Level	Watches Assembled	Rate per Watch
1	1–100	$2.45
2	101–150	$2.75
3	Over 150	$3.10

SOLUTION STRATEGY

To find Susan's total gross earnings, we calculate her earnings at each level of the pay schedule and add the totals. In this case, she will be paid for all of level 1, all of level 2, and for 40 watches at level 3 (190 − 150).

Level pay = Output × Rate per piece

Level 1 = 100 × 2.45 = $245.00

Level 2 = 50 × 2.75 = $137.50

Level 3 = 40 × 3.10 = $124.00

Total gross pay = Level 1 + Level 2 + Level 3

Total gross pay = 245.00 + 137.50 + 124.00 = $506.50

TRY-IT | EXERCISE

4. You are the payroll manager for Royal Toys, Inc., a manufacturer of small plastic toys. Your production workers are on a differential piecework schedule as follows:

Pay Level	Toys Produced	Rate per Toy
1	1–300	$.68
2	301–500	$.79
3	501–750	$.86
4	Over 750	$.94

Calculate last week's total gross pay for the following employees:

Name	Toys Produced	Total Gross Pay
C. Gomez	515	______
L. Clifford	199	______
M. Maken	448	______
B. Nathan	804	______

Check your answers with the solutions on page 329.

9-4 Calculating Gross Pay by Straight and Incremental Commission, Salary Plus Commission, and Drawing Accounts

Straight and Incremental Commission

commission
Percentage method of compensation primarily used to pay employees who sell a company's goods and services.

straight commission
Commission based on a specified percentage of the sales volume attained by an employee.

incremental commission
Greater incentive method of compensation than straight commission, whereby higher levels of sales earn increasing rates of commission.

Commission is a method of compensation primarily used to pay employees who sell a company's goods or services. **Straight commission** is based on a single specified percentage of the sales volume attained. For example, Delta Distributors pays its sales staff a commission of 8% on all sales. **Incremental commission** is much like the differential piecework rate, whereby higher levels of sales earn increasing rates of commission. An example would be 5% commission on all sales up to $70,000; 6% on sales greater than $70,000 and up to $120,000; and 7% commission on any sales greater than $120,000.

STEPS TO CALCULATE GROSS PAY BY COMMISSION:

Straight Commission:

Step 1. Total gross pay under a straight commission schedule is calculated by multiplying the total sales by the commission rate.

Total gross pay = Total sales × Commission rate

Incremental Commission:

Step 1. Multiply the total sales at each level by the commission rate for that level.

Step 2. Find the total gross pay by adding the total from each level.

EXAMPLE

Tropicana Wholesalers pays its sales force a commission rate of 6% of all sales. What is the total gross pay for an employee who sold $113,500 last month?

SOLUTION STRATEGY

Total gross pay = Total sales × Commission rate

Total gross pay = 113,500 × .06 = $6,810

TRY-IT | EXERCISE

5. Alisa Madden sells for South Hills Designs, a manufacturer of women's clothing. Alisa is paid a straight commission of 2.4%. If her sales volume last month was $233,760, what is her total gross pay?

Check your answer with the solution on page 329.

EXAMPLE

Stockton Industries pays its sales representatives on the following incremental commission schedule:

Level	Sales Volume	Commission Rate (%)
1	$1–$50,000	4
2	$50,001–$150,000	5
3	Over $150,000	6.5

What is the total gross pay for a sales rep who sold $162,400 last month?

SOLUTION STRATEGY

Using an incremental commission schedule, we find the pay for each level and then add the totals from each level. In this problem, the sales rep will be paid for all of level 1, all of level 2, and for $12,400 of level 3 ($162,400 − $150,000).

Level pay = Sales per level × Commission rate

Level 1 pay = 50,000 × .04 = $2,000.00

Level 2 pay = 100,000 × .05 = $5,000.00

Level 3 pay = 12,400 × .065 = $806.00

Total gross pay = Level 1 + Level 2 + Level 3

Total gross pay = 2,000.00 + 5,000.00 + 806.00 = $7,806.00

TRY-IT | EXERCISE

6. Roger Fine sells copiers for Sharp Business Products. He is on an incremental commission schedule of 1.7% of sales up to $100,000 and 2.5% on sales greater than $100,000. What is Roger's total gross pay for last month if his sales volume was $184,600?

Check your answer with the solution on page 329.

Salary Plus Commission

A variation of straight and incremental commission pay schedules is the **salary plus commission,** whereby the employee is paid a guaranteed salary plus a commission on sales over a certain specified amount. To calculate the total gross pay, find the amount of commission and add it to the salary.

salary plus commission
A guaranteed salary plus a commission on sales over a certain specified amount.

EXAMPLE

Angus McDonald works on a pay schedule of $1,500 per month salary plus a 3% commission on all sales greater than $40,000. If he sold $60,000 last month, what is Angus's total gross pay?

SOLUTION STRATEGY

To solve for Angus's total gross pay, add his monthly salary to his commission for the month.

Commission = Commission rate × Sales subject to commission

Commission = 3%(60,000 − 40,000)

Commission = .03 × 20,000 = $600

Total gross pay = Salary + Commission

Total gross pay = $1,500 + $600 = $2,100

TRY-IT | EXERCISE

7. Ronnie Jerome is a salesperson for Continental Supply, Inc. He is paid a salary of $1,400 per month plus a commission of 4% on all sales greater than $20,000. If Ronnie sold $45,000 last month, what was his total gross earnings?

Check your answer with the solution on page 329.

Draw against Commission

In certain industries and at certain times of the year, sales fluctuate significantly. To provide salespeople on commission with at least some income during slack periods of sales, a drawing account is used. A **drawing account,** or **draw against commission,** is a commission paid in advance of sales and later deducted from the commissions earned. If a period goes by when the salesperson does not earn enough commission to cover the draw, the unpaid balance carries over to the next period.

drawing account, or draw against commission
Commission paid in advance of sales and later deducted from the commission earned.

EXAMPLE

Charlie Sparkle is a salesperson for Dynamo Corp. The company pays 8% commission on all sales, and gives Charlie a $1,500 per month draw against commission. If he receives his draw at the beginning of the month and then sells $58,000 during the month, how much commission is owed to Charlie?

SOLUTION STRATEGY

To find the amount of commission owed to Charlie, find the total amount of commission he earned and subtract $1,500, the amount of his draw against commission.

Commission = Total sales × Commission rate

Commission = $58,000 × 8% = $4,640

Commission owed = Commission − Amount of draw

Commission owed = 4,640 − 1,500 = $3,140

TRY-IT | EXERCISE

8. Holly Smith sells for Panorama Products, Inc. She is on a 3.5% straight commission with a $2,000 drawing account. If she is paid the draw at the beginning of the month and then sells $120,000 during the month, how much commission is owed to Holly?

Check your answer with the solution on page 329.

REVIEW EXERCISES | CHAPTER 9—SECTION I

Calculate the gross earnings per pay period for the following pay schedules:

	Annual Salary	Monthly	Semimonthly	Biweekly	Weekly
1.	$15,000.00				
2.	$44,200.00				
3.	$100,000.00				
4.		$1,800.00			
5.			$1,450.00		
6.				$875.00	
7.					$335.00

8. Tristine James has gross earnings of $1,600 semimonthly. If her company switches pay schedules from semimonthly to biweekly, what are Tristine's new gross earnings?

9. The president and founder of a large corporation earns a salary of $2,000,000 per year. What are the gross earnings of this executive on a monthly pay schedule?

10. Brooke Wright works 40 hours per week. At the rate of $7.60 per hour, what are her gross weekly earnings?

11. Shelly Torres works for a company that pays time-and-a-half for all hours worked over 40. If she earns $8.70 per hour, what are her gross weekly earnings for a 51-hour week?

12. Joe Martin earns $6.25 per hour for regular time up to 40 hours, time-and-a-half for overtime, and double time for the midnight shift. Last week, Joe worked 58 hours, including 6 on the midnight shift. What are his gross earnings?

As the payroll manager for Oxford Systems, Inc., it is your task to complete the following weekly payroll record. The company pays overtime for all hours worked over 40 at the rate of time-and-a-half (round answers to the nearest cent, when necessary).

	Employee	M	T	W	T	F	S	S	Hourly Rate	Total Hours	Overtime Hours	Regular Pay	Overtime Pay	Total Pay
1	**13.** Williams	7	8	5	8	8	0	0	$5.70					
	14. Tanner	6	5	9	8	10	7	0	$9.50					
2	**15.** Gomez	8	6	11	7	12	0	4	$7.25					
	16. Wells	9	7	7	7	9	0	8	$14.75					

17. Tracy Stuart assembles circuit boards for United Electronics. She is paid a straight piecework rate of $6.50 per board. If she assembled 88 units last week, what were her gross earnings?

18. Bill Kingman works for a company that manufactures small appliances. Bill is paid $2.00 for each toaster, $4.60 for each microwave oven, and $1.55 for each food blender he assembles. If he produced 56 toasters, 31 microwave ovens, and 79 blenders, what were his total weekly gross earnings?

You are the payroll manager for Glitzy Garments, a manufacturer of women's apparel. Your workers are paid per garment sewn on a differential piecework schedule as follows:

Pay Level	Garments Produced	Rate per Garment
1	1–50	$3.60
2	51–100	$4.25
3	101–150	$4.50
4	Over 150	$5.10

Calculate last week's total gross pay for each of the following employees:

Employee	Garments Produced	Total Gross Pay
19. Johnston, C.	109	
20. Barber, W.	83	
21. Lynn, K.	174	

22. What is the total gross pay for a salesperson on a straight commission of 4.7% if his or her sales volume is $123,200?

23. What is the total gross pay for a salesperson on an incremental commission schedule of 1.2% of sales up to $200,000 and 1.5% on sales greater than $200,000 if last month's sales volume was $284,300?

24. Bertrand Dorcy is a salesperson for a company that pays a salary of $770 per month plus a commission of $8\frac{1}{2}$% of all sales greater than $10,000. If he sold $25,880 last month, what was his total gross pay?

25. Tom Wilson is a sales representative for General Industries. He is paid a 2.8% straight commission with a $1,200 drawing account. If he receives the draw at the beginning of the month and then sells $162,000 during the month, how much commission is owed to Tom?

26. Jenifer Brunner works for Escapade selling clothing. She is on a salary of $140 per week plus a commission of 7% of her sales. Last week, she sold 19 dresses at $79.95 each, 26 skirts at $24.75 each, and 17 jackets at $51.50 each. What were her total gross earnings for the week?

27. Jason Ford is a waiter in a restaurant that pays a salary of $22 per day. He also averages tips of 18% of his total gross food orders. Last week, he worked 6 days and had total food orders of $2,766.50. What was his total gross pay for the week?

BUSINESS DECISION

Play Ball

28. You are the official scorekeeper for a professional baseball team. You earn $140 per home game and $195 for each away game. The regular season is 162 games, evenly split between home and away. Last season, the team also made the playoffs and got into the World Series. The playoffs were an extra 12 games (five at home and seven away), paying an additional $75 each over and above your regular game pay. The six World Series games (three home and three away) paid an additional $120 each over and above your playoff game pay.

a. Calculate your total earnings for last season.

b. The Bonus! Your annual bonus is 5% of your total earnings for the season. Because your team won the World Series, all of the employees in the organization are also entitled to a share of the "Champions" bonus of $1,000,000, offered by the television network that carried the games. You have been with the team for a number of years and your portion of the "Champions" bonus this year is $\frac{1}{370}$. Calculate the amount of your bonuses, and your total compensation for the year:

SECTION II

EMPLOYEE'S PAYROLL DEDUCTIONS

"Hey! What happened to my paycheck?" This is the typical reaction of employees on seeing their paychecks for the first time after a raise or a promotion. As we shall see, gross pay is by no means the amount of money that the employee takes home.

deductions, or withholdings
Funds withheld from an employee's paycheck.

mandatory deductions
Deductions withheld from an employee's paycheck by law: social security, Medicare, and federal income tax.

voluntary deductions
Deductions withheld from an employee's paycheck by request of the employee, such as insurance premiums, dues, loan payments, and charitable contributions.

Employers, by federal law, are required to deduct or withhold certain funds, known as **deductions** or **withholdings**, from an employee's paychecks. Employee payroll deductions fall into two categories: mandatory and voluntary. The three major **mandatory deductions** most workers in the United States are subject to are social security, Medicare, and federal income tax. Other mandatory deductions, found only in some states, are state income tax and state disability insurance.

In addition to the mandatory deductions, employees may also choose to have **voluntary deductions** taken out of their paychecks. Some examples include payments for life or health insurance premiums, union or professional organization dues, credit union savings deposits or loan payments, stock or bond purchases, and charitable contributions.

After all the deductions have been subtracted from the employee's gross earnings, the remaining amount is known as net or take-home pay.

Net pay = Gross pay − Total deductions

9-5 Computing FICA Taxes, Both Social Security and Medicare, Withheld from an Employee's Paycheck

Federal Insurance Contribution Act (FICA)
Federal legislation, enacted in 1937 during the Great Depression, to provide retirement funds and hospital insurance for retired and disabled workers. Today, FICA is divided into two categories, social security and Medicare.

wage base
The amount of earnings up to which an employee must pay social security tax.

In 1937 during the Great Depression, Congress enacted legislation known as the **Federal Insurance Contribution Act (FICA)** with the purpose of providing monthly benefits to retired and disabled workers and to the families of deceased workers. This social security tax, which is assessed to virtually every worker in the United States, is based on a certain percent of the worker's income up to a specified limit or **wage base** per year. When the tax began in 1937, the tax rate was 1% up to a wage base of $3,000. At that time, the maximum a worker could be taxed per year for social security was $30.00 (3,000 × .01).

Today, the FICA tax is divided into two categories. **Social security tax** (OASDI, which stands for Old Age, Survivors, and Disability Insurance) is a retirement plan, and **Medicare** tax is for health care and hospital insurance. The social security wage base changes every year. For the most current information, consult the Internal Revenue Service, *Circular E: Employer's Tax Guide*. In 2002, the following rates and wage base were in effect for the FICA tax and should be used for all exercises in this chapter:

	Tax Rate	Wage Base
Social Security (OASDI)	6.2%	\$84,900
Medicare	1.45%	no limit

social security tax (OASDI)
Old Age, Survivors, and Disability Insurance—a federal tax, based on a percentage of a worker's income up to a specified limit or wage base, for the purpose of providing monthly benefits to retired and disabled workers and to the families of deceased workers.

When an employee reaches the wage base for the year, he or she is no longer subject to the tax. In 2002, the maximum social security tax per year was \$5,263.80 (84,900 × .062). There is no limit on the amount of Medicare tax. The 1.45% is in effect regardless of how much an employee earns.

Medicare tax
A federal tax used to provide health care benefits and hospital insurance to retired and disabled workers.

EXAMPLE

What are the withholdings for social security and Medicare for an employee with gross earnings of \$650 per week?

SOLUTION STRATEGY

To find the withholdings, we apply the tax rates for social security (6.2%) and Medicare (1.45%) to the gross earnings for the week:

$$\text{Social security tax} = \text{Gross earnings} \times 6.2\%$$

$$\text{Social security tax} = 650 \times .062 = \underline{\underline{\$40.30}}$$

$$\text{Medicare tax} = \text{Gross earnings} \times 1.45\%$$

$$\text{Medicare tax} = 650 \times .0145 = 9.425 = \underline{\underline{\$9.43}}$$

TRY-IT | EXERCISE

9. What are the withholdings for social security and Medicare for an employee with gross earnings of \$5,000 per month?

Check your answers with the solutions on page 329.

Mandatory payroll deductions enacted into law by Congress include social security, Medicare, and federal income tax.

Reaching the Wage Base Limit

In the pay period when an employee's year-to-date (YTD) earnings reach and surpass the wage base for social security, the tax is applied only to the portion of the earnings below the limit.

Everybody's Business
Real-World Connection
The current FICA deductions and wage base are listed in the IRS publication *Circular E, Employer's Tax Guide*.
This and other tax forms and publications can be obtained by calling the IRS at 1-800-TAX FORM or from their Web site, www.irs.gov.

EXAMPLE

Claudia Babich has earned \$82,300 so far this year. Her next paycheck, \$5,000, will put her earnings over the wage base limit for social security. What is the amount of Claudia's social security deduction for that paycheck?

SOLUTION STRATEGY

To calculate Claudia's social security deduction, first determine how much more she must earn to reach the wage base of \$84,900.

Earnings subject to tax = Wage base − Year-to-date earnings

Earnings subject to tax = 84,900 − 82,300 = \$2,600

Social security tax = Earnings subject to tax × 6.2%

Social security tax = \$2,600 × .062 = \$161.20

TRY-IT | EXERCISE

10. Jaime Lopez has year-to-date earnings of \$79,700. If his next paycheck is for \$6,000, what is the amount of his social security deduction?

Check your answer with the solution on page 329.

9-6 Calculating an Employee's Federal Income Tax Withholding (FIT) by the Percentage Method

federal income tax (FIT)
A graduated tax, based on gross earnings, marital status, and number of exemptions, that is paid by all workers earning over a certain amount of money in the United States.

withholding allowance, or exemption
An amount that reduces an employee's taxable income. Employees are allowed one exemption for themselves, one for their spouse if the spouse does not work, and one for each dependent child or elderly parent living with the taxpayer but not working.

percentage method
An alternate method to the wage bracket tables, used to calculate the amount of an employee's federal income tax withholding.

In addition to social security and Medicare tax withholdings, an employer is also responsible, by federal law, for withholding an appropriate amount of **federal income tax (FIT)** from each employee's paycheck. This graduated tax allows the government a steady flow of tax revenues throughout the year. Self-employed persons must send quarterly tax payments based on estimated earnings to the Internal Revenue Service.

The amount of income tax withheld from an employee's paycheck is determined by his or her amount of gross earnings, marital status, and the number of **withholding allowances** or **exemptions** claimed. Employees are allowed one exemption for themselves, one for their spouse if the spouse does not work, and one for each dependent child or elderly parent living with the taxpayer but not working.

Each employee is required to complete a form called W-4, Employee's Withholding Allowance Certificate, shown in Exhibit 9-1. The information provided on this form is used by the employer in calculating the amount of income tax withheld from the paycheck.

The **percentage method** for determining the amount of federal income tax withheld from an employee's paycheck is used by companies whose payroll processing is on a computerized system. The amount of tax withheld is based on the amount of gross earning, the marital status of the employee, and the number of withholding allowances claimed.

The percentage method of calculating federal income tax requires the use of two tables. The first is the Percentage Method—Amount for One Withholding Allowance Table, Exhibit 9-2. This table shows the dollar amount of one withholding allowance, for the various payroll periods. The second, Exhibit 9-3, is the Rate Tables for Percentage Method of Withholding. These tables reflect the latest tax rates resulting from the Economic Growth and Tax Relief Reconciliation Act of 2001.

EXHIBIT 9-1
Employee W-4 Form

Cut here and give Form W-4 to your employer. Keep the top part for your records.

Form **W-4** | **Employee's Withholding Allowance Certificate** | OMB No. 1545-0010
Department of the Treasury
Internal Revenue Service
▶ **For Privacy Act and Paperwork Reduction Act Notice, see page 2.**
20XX

1 Type or print your first name and middle initial | Last name | 2 Your social security number

Home address (number and street or rural route) | 3 ☐ Single ☐ Married ☐ Married, but withhold at higher Single rate.
Note: *If married, but legally separated, or spouse is a nonresident alien, check the Single box.*

City or town, state, and ZIP code | 4 **If your last name differs from that on your social security card, check here. You must call 1-800-772-1213 for a new card.** ▶ ☐

5 Total number of allowances you are claiming (from line **H** above **or** from the applicable worksheet on page 2) | 5 |
6 Additional amount, if any, you want withheld from each paycheck . . . . | 6 | $
7 I claim exemption from withholding for 2001, and I certify that I meet **both** of the following conditions for exemption:
- Last year I had a right to a refund of **all** Federal income tax withheld because I had **no** tax liability **and**
- This year I expect a refund of **all** Federal income tax withheld because I expect to have **no** tax liability.

If you meet both conditions, write "Exempt" here . . . . ▶ | 7 |

Under penalties of perjury, I certify that I am entitled to the number of withholding allowances claimed on this certificate, or I am entitled to claim exempt status.
Employee's signature
(Form is not valid
unless you sign it.) ▶ **Date** ▶

8 Employer's name and address (Employer: Complete lines 8 and 10 only if sending to the IRS.) | 9 Office code (optional) | 10 Employer identification number

Cat. No. 10220Q

STEPS TO CALCULATE THE INCOME TAX WITHHELD USING THE PERCENTAGE METHOD:

Step 1. Using the proper payroll period, multiply one withholding allowance, Exhibit 9-2, by the number of allowances claimed by the employee.

Step 2. Subtract that amount from the employee's gross earnings to find the wages subject to federal income tax.

Step 3. From Exhibit 9-3, locate the proper segment (Table 1, 2, 3, or 4) corresponding to the employee's payroll period. Within that segment, use the *left* side (a) for single employees and the *right* side (b) for married employees.

Step 4. Locate the "Over—" and "But not over—" brackets containing the employee's taxable wages from Step 2. The tax is listed to the right as a percent or a dollar amount and a percent.

Payroll Period	One Withholding Allowance
Weekly	$55.77
Biweekly	111.54
Semimonthly	120.83
Monthly	241.67
Quarterly	725.00
Semiannually	1,450.00
Annually	2,900.00
Daily or miscellaneous (each day of the payroll period	11.15

EXHIBIT 9-2
Percentage Method Withholding Allowances

EXHIBIT 9-3

Tables for Percentage Method of Withholding

Tables for Percentage Method of Withholding

TABLE 1—WEEKLY Payroll Period

(a) SINGLE person (including head of household)—

If the amount of wages (after subtracting withholding allowances) is: Not over $51 . . . . . The amount of income tax to withhold is: $0

Over—	But not over—		of excess over—
$51	—$552 . .	15%	—51
$552	—$1,196 . .	$75.15 plus 27%	—552
$1,196	—$2,662 . .	$249.03 plus 30%	—1,196
$2,662	—$5,750 . .	$688.83 plus 35%	—2,662
$5,750	. . . . . .	$1,769.63 plus 38.6%	—5,750

(b) MARRIED person—

If the amount of wages (after subtracting withholding allowances) is: Not over $124 . . . . The amount of income tax to withhold is: $0

Over—	But not over—		of excess over—
$124	—$960 . .	15%	—$124
$960	—$2,023 . .	$125.40 plus 27%	—$960
$2,023	—$3,292 . .	$412.41 plus 30%	—$2,023
$3,292	—$5,809 . .	$793.11 plus 35%	—$3,292
$5,809	. . . . . .	$1,674.06 plus 38.6%	—$5,809

TABLE 2—BIWEEKLY Payroll Period

(a) SINGLE person (including head of household)—

If the amount of wages (after subtracting withholding allowances) is: Not over $102 . . . . The amount of income tax to withhold is: $0

Over—	But not over—		of excess over—
$102	—$1,104 . .	15%	—$102
$1,104	—$2,392 . .	$150.30 plus 27%	—$1,104
$2,392	—$5,323 . .	$498.06 plus 30%	—$2,392
$5,323	—$11,500 . .	$1,377.36 plus 35%	—$5,323
$11,500	. . . . . .	$3,539.31 plus 38.6%	—$11,500

(b) MARRIED person—

If the amount of wages (after subtracting withholding allowances) is: Not over $248 . . . . The amount of income tax to withhold is: $0

Over—	But not over—		of excess over—
$248	—$1,919 . .	15%	—$248
$1,919	—$4,046 . .	$250.65 plus 27%	—$1,919
$4,046	—$6,585 . .	$824.94 plus 30%	—$4,046
$6,585	—$11,617 . .	$1,586.64 plus 35%	—$6,585
$11,617	. . . . . .	$3,347.84 plus 38.6%	—$11,617

TABLE 3—SEMIMONTHLY Payroll Period

(a) SINGLE person (including head of household)—

If the amount of wages (after subtracting withholding allowances) is: Not over $110 . . . . The amount of income tax to withhold is: $0

Over—	But not over—		of excess over—
$110	—$1,196 . .	15%	—$110
$1,196	—$2,592 . .	$162.90 plus 27%	—$1,196
$2,592	—$5,767 . .	$539.82 plus 30%	—$2,592
$5,767	—$12,458 . .	$1,492.32 plus 35%	—$5,767
$12,458	. . . . . .	$3,834.17 plus 38.6%	—$12,458

(b) MARRIED person—

If the amount of wages (after subtracting withholding allowances) is: Not over $269 . . . . The amount of income tax to withhold is: $0

Over—	But not over—		of excess over—
$269	—$2,079 . .	15%	—$269
$2,079	—$4,383 . .	$271.50 plus 27%	—$2,079
$4,383	—$7,133 . .	$893.58 plus 30%	—$4,383
$7,133	—$12,585 . .	$1,718.58 plus 35%	—$7,133
$12,585	. . . . . .	$3,626.78 plus 38.6%	—$12,585

TABLE 4—MONTHLY Payroll Period

(a) SINGLE person (including head of household)—

If the amount of wages (after subtracting withholding allowances) is: Not over $221 . . . . The amount of income tax to withhold is: $0

Over—	But not over—		of excess over—
$221	—$2,392 . .	15%	—$221
$2,392	—$5,183 . .	$325.65 plus 27%	—$2,392
$5,183	—$11,533 . .	$1,079.22 plus 30%	—$5,183
$11,533	—$24,917 . .	$2,984.22 plus 35%	—$11,533
$24,917	. . . . . .	$7,668.62 plus 38.6%	—$24,917

(b) MARRIED person—

If the amount of wages (after subtracting withholding allowances) is: Not over $538 . . . . The amount of income tax to withhold is: $0

Over—	But not over—		of excess over—
$538	—$4,158 . .	15%	—$538
$4,158	—$8,767 . .	$543.00 plus 27%	—$4,158
$8,767	—$14,267 . .	$1,787.43 plus 30%	—$8,767
$14,267	—$25,171 . .	$3,437.43 plus 35%	—$14,267
$25,171	. . . . . .	$7,253.83 plus 38.6%	—$25,171

EXAMPLE

Maritza Marrero is a manager for Global Travel. She is single and is paid $750 weekly. She claims two withholding allowances. Using the percentage method, calculate the amount of income tax that should be withheld from her paycheck each week.

SOLUTION STRATEGY

From Exhibit 9-2, the amount of one withholding allowance for an employee paid weekly is $55.77. Next, multiply this amount by the number of allowances claimed, two.

$$\$55.77 \times 2 = \$111.54$$

Subtract that amount from the gross earnings to get taxable income.

$$\$750.00 - \$111.54 = \$638.46$$

From Exhibit 9-3, find the tax withheld from Maritza's paycheck in Table 1(a), Weekly payroll period, Single person. Maritza's taxable wages of $638.46 fall in the category over $552, but not over $1,196. The tax, therefore, is $75.15 plus 27% of the excess over $552.

$$\text{Tax} = 75.15 + 27\%(638.46 - 552.00)$$

$$\text{Tax} = 75.15 + .27(86.46)$$

$$\text{Tax} = 75.15 + 23.34 = \underline{\underline{\$98.49}}$$

TRY-IT | EXERCISE

11. Tara Raussen is married, claims five exemptions, and earns $2,350 per month. As the payroll manager of Tara's company, use the percentage method to calculate the amount of income tax that must be withheld from her paycheck.

Check your answer with the solution on page 330.

9-7 Determining an Employee's Total Withholding for Federal Income Tax, Social Security, and Medicare Using the Combined Wage Bracket Tables

In 2001, the IRS introduced **combined wage bracket tables** that can be used to determine the combined amount of income tax, social security, and Medicare that must be withheld from an employee's gross earnings each pay period. These tables are found in *Publication 15-A: Employer's Supplemental Tax Guide*. This publication contains a complete set of tables for both single and married people, covering weekly, biweekly, semimonthly, monthly, and even daily pay periods. The wage bracket method is used primarily by companies whose payroll is done manually, without the aid of a computer.

Exhibit 9-4 shows a portion of the wage bracket tables for Married Persons—Weekly Payroll Period and Exhibit 9-5 shows a portion of the wage bracket table for Single Persons—Monthly Payroll Period. Use these tables to solve wage bracket problems in this chapter.

combined wage bracket tables
IRS tables used to determine the combined amount of income tax, social security, and Medicare that must be withheld from an employee's gross earnings each pay period.

STEPS TO FIND THE TOTAL INCOME TAX, SOCIAL SECURITY, AND MEDICARE WITHHELD BY USING THE COMBINED WAGE BRACKET TABLE:

Step 1. Based on the employee's marital status and period of payment, find the corresponding table (Exhibit 9-4 or 9-5).

Step 2. Note that the two left-hand columns, labeled "At least" and "But less than," are the wage brackets. Scan down these columns until you find the bracket containing the gross pay of the employee.

Step 3. Scan across the row of that wage bracket to the intersection of the column containing the number of withholding allowances claimed by the employee.

Step 4. The number in that column, on the wage bracket row, is the amount of combined tax withheld.

Everybody's Business

Real-World Connection

All employees must have a Social Security number. Applications are available at all U.S. post offices.

Social Security numbers are used by the IRS as a taxpayer identification number as well as by banks, credit unions, and other financial institutions for reporting income from savings and other investments.

Information about an individual's Social Security account can be obtained by filing a Form 7004-SM—*Request for Earnings and Benefit Estimate Statement*. These can be obtained by calling the Social Security Administration at 1-800-772-1213.

EXHIBIT 9-4

Payroll Deductions—Married, Paid Weekly

MARRIED Persons—WEEKLY Payroll Period

And the wages are–		And the number of withholding allowances claimed is—										
At least	But less than	0	1	2	3	4	5	6	7	8	9	10
		The amount of income, social security, and Medicare taxes to be withheld is—										
$740	**$750**	$149.99	$141.99	$132.99	$124.99	$116.99	$107.99	$99.99	$91.99	$82.99	$74.99	$65.99
750	**760**	152.76	143.76	135.76	127.76	118.76	110.76	101.76	93.76	85.76	76.76	68.76
760	**770**	154.52	146.52	137.52	129.52	121.52	112.52	104.52	96.52	87.52	79.52	70.52
770	**780**	157.29	148.29	140.29	132.29	123.29	115.29	106.29	98.29	90.29	81.29	73.29
780	**790**	159.05	151.05	142.05	134.05	126.05	117.05	109.05	101.05	92.05	84.05	75.05
790	**800**	161.82	152.82	144.82	136.82	127.82	119.82	110.82	102.82	94.82	85.82	77.82
800	**810**	163.58	155.58	146.58	138.58	130.58	121.58	113.58	105.58	96.58	88.58	79.58
810	**820**	166.35	157.35	149.35	141.35	132.35	124.35	115.35	107.35	99.35	90.35	82.35
820	**830**	168.11	160.11	151.11	143.11	135.11	126.11	118.11	110.11	101.11	93.11	84.11
830	**840**	170.88	161.88	153.88	145.88	136.88	128.88	119.88	111.88	103.88	94.88	86.88
840	**850**	172.64	164.64	155.64	147.64	139.64	130.64	122.64	114.64	105.64	97.64	88.64
850	**860**	175.41	166.41	158.41	150.41	141.41	133.41	124.41	116.41	108.41	99.41	91.41
860	**870**	177.17	169.17	160.17	152.17	144.17	135.17	127.17	119.17	110.17	102.17	93.17
870	**880**	179.94	170.94	162.94	154.94	145.94	137.94	128.94	120.94	112.94	103.94	95.94
880	**890**	181.70	173.70	164.70	156.70	148.70	139.70	131.70	123.70	114.70	106.70	97.70
890	**900**	184.47	175.47	167.47	159.47	150.47	142.47	133.47	125.47	117.47	108.47	100.47
900	**910**	186.23	178.23	169.23	161.23	153.23	144.23	136.23	128.23	119.23	111.23	102.23
910	**920**	189.00	180.00	172.00	164.00	155.00	147.00	138.00	130.00	122.00	113.00	105.00
920	**930**	190.76	182.76	173.76	165.76	157.76	148.76	140.76	132.76	123.76	115.76	106.76
930	**940**	193.53	184.53	176.53	168.53	159.53	151.53	142.53	134.53	126.53	117.53	109.53
940	**950**	195.29	187.29	178.29	170.29	162.29	153.29	145.29	137.29	128.29	120.29	111.29
950	**960**	198.06	189.06	181.06	173.06	164.06	156.06	147.06	139.06	131.06	122.06	114.06
960	**970**	200.82	191.82	182.82	174.82	166.82	157.82	149.82	141.82	132.82	124.82	115.82
970	**980**	203.59	193.59	185.59	177.59	168.59	160.59	151.59	143.59	135.59	126.59	118.59
980	**990**	207.35	196.35	187.35	179.35	171.35	162.35	154.35	146.35	137.35	129.35	120.35
990	**1,000**	211.12	198.12	190.12	182.12	173.12	165.12	156.12	148.12	140.12	131.12	123.12
1,000	**1,010**	214.88	200.88	191.88	183.88	175.88	166.88	158.88	150.88	141.88	133.88	124.88
1,010	**1,020**	217.65	202.65	194.65	186.65	177.65	169.65	160.65	152.65	144.65	135.65	127.65
1,020	**1,030**	221.41	206.41	196.41	188.41	180.41	171.41	163.41	155.41	146.41	138.41	129.41
1,030	**1,040**	225.18	210.18	199.18	191.18	182.18	174.18	165.18	157.18	149.18	140.18	132.18
1,040	**1,050**	227.94	212.94	200.94	192.94	184.94	175.94	167.94	159.94	150.94	142.94	133.94
1,050	**1,060**	231.71	216.71	203.71	195.71	186.71	178.71	169.71	161.71	153.71	144.71	136.71
1,060	**1,070**	235.47	220.47	205.47	197.47	189.47	180.47	172.47	164.47	155.47	147.47	138.47
1,070	**1,080**	238.24	223.24	208.24	200.24	191.24	183.24	174.24	166.24	158.24	149.24	141.24
1,080	**1,090**	242.00	227.00	212.00	202.00	194.00	185.00	177.00	169.00	160.00	152.00	143.00
1,090	**1,100**	245.77	230.77	215.77	204.77	195.77	187.77	178.77	170.77	162.77	153.77	145.77
1,100	**1,110**	249.53	234.53	218.53	206.53	198.53	189.53	181.53	173.53	164.53	156.53	147.53
1,110	**1,120**	252.30	237.30	222.30	209.30	200.30	192.30	183.30	175.30	167.30	158.30	150.30
1,120	**1,130**	256.06	241.06	226.06	211.06	203.06	194.06	186.06	178.06	169.06	161.06	152.06
1,130	**1,140**	259.83	244.83	229.83	214.83	204.83	196.83	187.83	179.83	171.83	162.83	154.83
1,140	**1,150**	262.59	247.59	232.59	217.59	207.59	198.59	190.59	182.59	173.59	165.59	156.59
1,150	**1,160**	266.36	251.36	236.36	221.36	209.36	201.36	192.36	184.36	176.36	167.36	159.36
1,160	**1,170**	270.12	255.12	240.12	225.12	212.12	203.12	195.12	187.12	178.12	170.12	161.12
1,170	**1,180**	272.89	257.89	242.89	227.89	213.89	205.89	196.89	188.89	180.89	171.89	163.89
1,180	**1,190**	276.65	261.65	246.65	231.65	216.65	207.65	199.65	191.65	182.65	174.65	165.65
1,190	**1,200**	280.42	265.42	250.42	235.42	220.42	210.42	201.42	193.42	185.42	176.42	168.42
1,200	**1,210**	284.18	269.18	253.18	238.18	223.18	212.18	204.18	196.18	187.18	179.18	170.18
1,210	**1,220**	286.95	271.95	256.95	241.95	226.95	214.95	205.95	197.95	189.95	180.95	172.95
1,220	**1,230**	290.71	275.71	260.71	245.71	230.71	216.71	208.71	200.71	191.71	183.71	174.71
1,230	**1,240**	294.48	279.48	264.48	249.48	233.48	219.48	210.48	202.48	194.48	185.48	177.48
1,240	**1,250**	297.24	282.24	267.24	252.24	237.24	222.24	213.24	205.24	196.24	188.24	179.24
1,250	**1,260**	301.01	286.01	271.01	256.01	241.01	226.01	215.01	207.01	199.01	190.01	182.01
1,260	**1,270**	304.77	289.77	274.77	259.77	244.77	229.77	217.77	209.77	200.77	192.77	183.77
1,270	**1,280**	307.54	292.54	277.54	262.54	247.54	232.54	219.54	211.54	203.54	194.54	186.54
1,280	**1,290**	311.30	296.30	281.30	266.30	251.30	236.30	222.30	214.30	205.30	197.30	188.30
1,290	**1,300**	315.07	300.07	285.07	270.07	255.07	240.07	225.07	216.07	208.07	199.07	191.07
1,300	**1,310**	318.83	303.83	287.83	272.83	257.83	242.83	227.83	218.83	209.83	201.83	192.83
1,310	**1,320**	321.60	306.60	291.60	276.60	261.60	246.60	231.60	220.60	212.60	203.60	195.60
1,320	**1,330**	325.36	310.36	295.36	280.36	265.36	250.36	235.36	223.36	214.36	206.36	197.36
1,330	**1,340**	329.13	314.13	299.13	284.13	268.13	253.13	238.13	225.13	217.13	208.13	200.13
1,340	**1,350**	331.89	316.89	301.89	286.89	271.89	256.89	241.89	227.89	218.89	210.89	201.89
1,350	**1,360**	335.66	320.66	305.66	290.66	275.66	260.66	245.66	230.66	221.66	212.66	204.66
1,360	**1,370**	339.42	324.42	309.42	294.42	279.42	264.42	248.42	233.42	223.42	215.42	206.42
1,370	**1,380**	342.19	327.19	312.19	297.19	282.19	267.19	252.19	237.19	226.19	217.19	209.19
1,380	**1,390**	345.95	330.95	315.95	300.95	285.95	270.95	255.95	240.95	227.95	219.95	210.95
$1,390 and over		Do not use this table. See page 37 for instructions.										

✦ **EXHIBIT 9-5** ✦

Payroll Deductions—Single, Paid Monthly

SINGLE Persons—**MONTHLY** Payroll Period

And the wages are–		And the number of withholding allowances claimed is—										
At least	But less than	0	1	2	3	4	5	6	7	8	9	10
		The amount of income, social security, and Medicare taxes to be withheld is—										
$2,440	**$2,480**	$532.19	$488.19	$451.19	$415.19	$379.19	$343.19	$306.19	$270.19	$234.19	$198.19	$188.19
2,480	**2,520**	546.25	497.25	460.25	424.25	388.25	352.25	315.25	279.25	243.25	207.25	191.25
2,520	**2,560**	560.31	506.31	469.31	433.31	397.31	361.31	324.31	288.31	252.31	216.31	194.31
2,560	**2,600**	573.37	515.37	478.37	442.37	406.37	370.37	333.37	297.37	261.37	225.37	197.37
2,600	**2,640**	587.43	524.43	487.43	451.43	415.43	379.43	342.43	306.43	270.43	234.43	200.43
2,640	**2,680**	601.49	536.49	496.49	460.49	424.49	388.49	351.49	315.49	279.49	243.49	206.49
2,680	**2,720**	615.55	550.55	505.55	469.55	433.55	397.55	360.55	324.55	288.55	252.55	215.55
2,720	**2,760**	629.61	563.61	514.61	478.61	442.61	406.61	369.61	333.61	297.61	261.61	224.61
2,760	**2,800**	642.67	577.67	523.67	487.67	451.67	415.67	378.67	342.67	306.67	270.67	233.67
2,800	**2,840**	656.73	591.73	532.73	496.73	460.73	424.73	387.73	351.73	315.73	279.73	242.73
2,840	**2,880**	670.79	605.79	541.79	505.79	469.79	433.79	396.79	360.79	324.79	288.79	251.79
2,880	**2,920**	684.85	619.85	553.85	514.85	478.85	442.85	405.85	369.85	333.85	297.85	260.85
2,920	**2,960**	698.91	632.91	567.91	523.91	487.91	451.91	414.91	378.91	342.91	306.91	269.91
2,960	**3,000**	711.97	646.97	581.97	532.97	496.97	460.97	423.97	387.97	351.97	315.97	278.97
3,000	**3,040**	726.03	661.03	596.03	542.03	506.03	470.03	433.03	397.03	361.03	325.03	288.03
3,040	**3,080**	740.09	675.09	610.09	551.09	515.09	479.09	442.09	406.09	370.09	334.09	297.09
3,080	**3,120**	754.15	689.15	623.15	560.15	524.15	488.15	451.15	415.15	379.15	343.15	306.15
3,120	**3,160**	768.21	702.21	637.21	572.21	533.21	497.21	460.21	424.21	388.21	352.21	315.21
3,160	**3,200**	781.27	716.27	651.27	586.27	542.27	506.27	469.27	433.27	397.27	361.27	324.27
3,200	**3,240**	795.33	730.33	665.33	600.33	551.33	515.33	478.33	442.33	406.33	370.33	333.33
3,240	**3,280**	809.39	744.39	679.39	613.39	560.39	524.39	487.39	451.39	415.39	379.39	342.39
3,280	**3,320**	823.45	758.45	692.45	627.45	569.45	533.45	496.45	460.45	424.45	388.45	351.45
3,320	**3,360**	837.51	771.51	706.51	641.51	578.51	542.51	505.51	469.51	433.51	397.51	360.51
3,360	**3,400**	850.57	785.57	720.57	655.57	589.57	551.57	514.57	478.57	442.57	406.57	369.57
3,400	**3,440**	864.63	799.63	734.63	669.63	603.63	560.63	523.63	487.63	451.63	415.63	378.63
3,440	**3,480**	878.69	813.69	748.69	682.69	617.69	569.69	532.69	496.69	460.69	424.69	387.69
3,480	**3,520**	892.75	827.75	761.75	696.75	631.75	578.75	541.75	505.75	469.75	433.75	396.75
3,520	**3,560**	906.81	840.81	775.81	710.81	645.81	587.81	550.81	514.81	478.81	442.81	405.81
3,560	**3,600**	919.87	854.87	789.87	724.87	658.87	596.87	559.87	523.87	487.87	451.87	414.87
3,600	**3,640**	933.93	868.93	803.93	738.93	672.93	607.93	568.93	532.93	496.93	460.93	423.93
3,640	**3,680**	947.99	882.99	817.99	751.99	686.99	621.99	577.99	541.99	505.99	469.99	432.99
3,680	**3,720**	962.05	897.05	831.05	766.05	701.05	636.05	587.05	551.05	515.05	479.05	442.05
3,720	**3,760**	976.11	910.11	845.11	780.11	715.11	649.11	596.11	560.11	524.11	488.11	451.11
3,760	**3,800**	989.17	924.17	859.17	794.17	728.17	663.17	605.17	569.17	533.17	497.17	460.17
3,800	**3,840**	1,003.23	938.23	873.23	808.23	742.23	677.23	614.23	578.23	542.23	506.23	469.23
3,840	**3,880**	1,017.29	952.29	887.29	821.29	756.29	691.29	626.29	587.29	551.29	515.29	478.29
3,880	**3,920**	1,031.35	966.35	900.35	835.35	770.35	705.35	639.35	596.35	560.35	524.35	487.35
3,920	**3,960**	1,045.41	979.41	914.41	849.41	784.41	718.41	653.41	605.41	569.41	533.41	496.41
3,960	**4,000**	1,058.47	993.47	928.47	863.47	797.47	732.47	667.47	614.47	578.47	542.47	505.47
4,000	**4,040**	1,072.53	1,007.53	942.53	877.53	811.53	746.53	681.53	623.53	587.53	551.53	514.53
4,040	**4,080**	1,086.59	1,021.59	956.59	890.59	825.59	760.59	695.59	632.59	596.59	560.59	523.59
4,080	**4,120**	1,100.65	1,035.65	969.65	904.65	839.65	774.65	708.65	643.65	605.65	569.65	532.65
4,120	**4,160**	1,114.71	1,048.71	983.71	918.71	853.71	787.71	722.71	657.71	614.71	578.71	541.71
4,160	**4,200**	1,127.77	1,062.77	997.77	932.77	866.77	801.77	736.77	671.77	623.77	587.77	550.77
4,200	**4,240**	1,141.83	1,076.83	1,011.83	946.83	880.83	815.83	750.83	685.83	632.83	596.83	559.83
4,240	**4,280**	1,155.89	1,090.89	1,025.89	959.89	894.89	829.89	764.89	698.89	641.89	605.89	568.89
4,280	**4,320**	1,169.95	1,104.95	1,038.95	973.95	908.95	843.95	777.95	712.95	650.95	614.95	577.95
4,320	**4,360**	1,184.01	1,118.01	1,053.01	988.01	923.01	857.01	792.01	727.01	662.01	624.01	587.01
4,360	**4,400**	1,197.07	1,132.07	1,067.07	1,002.07	936.07	871.07	806.07	741.07	675.07	633.07	596.07
4,400	**4,440**	1,211.13	1,146.13	1,081.13	1,016.13	950.13	885.13	820.13	755.13	689.13	642.13	605.13
4,440	**4,480**	1,225.19	1,160.19	1,095.19	1,029.19	964.19	899.19	834.19	768.19	703.19	651.19	614.19
4,480	**4,520**	1,239.25	1,174.25	1,108.25	1,043.25	978.25	913.25	847.25	782.25	717.25	660.25	623.25
4,520	**4,560**	1,253.31	1,187.31	1,122.31	1,057.31	992.31	926.31	861.31	796.31	731.31	669.31	632.31
4,560	**4,600**	1,266.37	1,201.37	1,136.37	1,071.37	1,005.37	940.37	875.37	810.37	744.37	679.37	641.37
4,600	**4,640**	1,280.43	1,215.43	1,150.43	1,085.43	1,019.43	954.43	889.43	824.43	758.43	693.43	650.43
4,640	**4,680**	1,294.49	1,229.49	1,164.49	1,098.49	1,033.49	968.49	903.49	837.49	772.49	707.49	659.49
4,680	**4,720**	1,308.55	1,243.55	1,177.55	1,112.55	1,047.55	982.55	916.55	851.55	786.55	721.55	668.55
4,720	**4,760**	1,322.61	1,256.61	1,191.61	1,126.61	1,061.61	995.61	930.61	865.61	800.61	734.61	677.61
4,760	**4,800**	1,335.67	1,270.67	1,205.67	1,140.67	1,074.67	1,009.67	944.67	879.67	813.67	748.67	686.67
4,800	**4,840**	1,349.73	1,284.73	1,219.73	1,154.73	1,088.73	1,023.73	958.73	893.73	827.73	762.73	697.73
4,840	**4,880**	1,363.79	1,298.79	1,233.79	1,167.79	1,102.79	1,037.79	972.79	906.79	841.79	776.79	711.79
4,880	**4,920**	1,377.85	1,312.85	1,246.85	1,181.85	1,116.85	1,051.85	985.85	920.85	855.85	790.85	724.85
4,920	**4,960**	1,391.91	1,325.91	1,260.91	1,195.91	1,130.91	1,064.91	999.91	934.91	869.91	803.91	738.91
4,960	**5,000**	1,404.97	1,339.97	1,274.97	1,209.97	1,143.97	1,078.97	1,013.97	948.97	882.97	817.97	752.97
5,000	**5,040**	1,419.03	1,354.03	1,289.03	1,224.03	1,158.03	1,093.03	1,028.03	963.03	897.03	832.03	767.03

$5,040 and over — Do not use this table. See page 37 for instructions.

EXAMPLE

Use the combined wage bracket tables to determine the amount of income tax, social security, and Medicare withheld from the monthly paycheck of Cherie Norvell, a single employee, claiming three withholding allowances and earning $2,675 per month.

SOLUTION STRATEGY

To find Cherie Norvell's monthly income tax withholding, choose the table for Single Persons—Monthly Payroll Period, Exhibit 9-5. Scanning down the "At least" and "But less than" columns, we find the wage bracket containing Cherie's earnings: "At least 2,640—But less than 2,680."

Next, scan across that row from left to right to the "3" withholding allowances column. The number at that intersection, $460.49, is the total combined tax to be withheld from Cherie's paycheck.

TRY-IT | EXERCISE

12. Using the combined wage bracket tables, what is the total amount of income tax, social security, and Medicare that should be withheld from Shane Davis's weekly paycheck of $835 if he is married and claims two withholding allowances?

Check your answer with the solution on page 330.

REVIEW EXERCISES | CHAPTER 9—SECTION II

Solve the following problems using 6.2%, up to $84,900, for social security tax, and 1.45%, no wage limit, for Medicare tax:

1. What are the withholdings for social security and Medicare for an employee with gross earnings of $825 per week?

2. What are the withholdings for social security and Medicare for an employee with gross earnings of $1,400.00 paid semimonthly?

3. Don Tweedt is an executive with Federal Distributors. His gross earnings are $8,800 per month.

a. What are the withholdings for social security and Medicare for Don in his January paycheck?

b. In what month will Don's salary reach the social security wage base limit?

c. What are the social security and Medicare tax withholdings for Don in the month named in part **b**?

4. Gloria Lewin has biweekly gross earnings of $1,750. What are her total social security and Medicare tax withholdings for a whole year?

As payroll manager for Andretti Enterprises, it is your task to calculate the monthly social security and Medicare withholdings for the following employees:

	Employee	Year-to-Date Earnings	Current Month	Social Security	Medicare
5.	Chad, J.	$23,446	$3,422	_______	_______
6.	Graham, C.	$14,800	$1,540	_______	_______
7.	Potter, R.	$83,215	$4,700	_______	_______
8.	Andretti, K.	$145,000	$12,450	_______	_______

Use the percentage method of income tax calculation to complete the following payroll roster:

	Employee	Marital Status	Withholding Allowances	Pay Period	Gross Earnings	Income Tax Withholding
9.	Needle, B.	M	2	Weekly	$594	_______
10.	White, W.	S	0	Semimonthly	$1,227	_______
11.	Benator, B.	S	1	Monthly	$4,150	_______
12.	Ismart, D.	M	4	Biweekly	$1,849	_______

Use the combined wage bracket tables, Exhibits 9-4 and 9-5, to solve Exercises 13–19.

13. How much combined tax should be withheld from the paycheck of a married employee earning $1,075 per week and claiming four withholding allowances?

14. How much combined tax should be withheld from the paycheck of a single employee earning $3,185 per month and claiming zero withholding allowances?

15. Earl Campbell is single, claims one withholding allowance, and earns $2,670 per month. Calculate the amount of Earl's paycheck after his employer withholds social security, Medicare, and federal income tax.

	Employee	Marital Status	Withholding Allowances	Pay Period	Gross Earnings	Combined Withholding
16.	Milton, A.	S	3	Monthly	$4,633	______
17.	Wallace, P.	M	5	Weekly	$937	______
18.	Blount, S.	M	4	Weekly	$1,172	______
19.	Cairns, K.	S	1	Monthly	$3,128	______

BUSINESS DECISION

Take Home Pay

20. You are the payroll manager for the Golden Tropic Resort. Stuart Spector, the marketing director, earns a salary of $43,200 per year, payable monthly. He is married and claims four withholding allowances. His social security number is 444-44-4444.

In addition to federal income tax, social security, and Medicare, Stuart pays 2.3% state income tax, $\frac{1}{2}$% for state disability insurance (both based on gross earnings), $23.74 for term life insurance, $122.14 to the credit union, and $40 to the United Way.

Fill out the following payroll voucher for Stuart for the month of April:

Golden Tropic Resort

Payroll Voucher

Employee: ____________ Tax Filing Status: ________

SSN: ____________ Withholding Allowances: ____

Full-time Pay Period From ________ To ________

Primary Withholdings:

Federal income tax ________

Social security ________

Medicare ________

State income tax ________

State disability ________

Additional Withholdings:

____

____

____

____

Gross Earnings: ________

− Total withholdings: ________

NET PAY ________

SECTION III

EMPLOYER'S PAYROLL EXPENSES AND RECORD KEEPING RESPONSIBILITIES

To this point we have discussed payroll deductions from the employee's point of view. Now let's take a look at the payroll expenses and record keeping responsibilities of the employer. According to the Fair Labor Standards Act, employers are required to maintain complete and up-to-date earnings records for each employee. These records are a quarterly (every 13 weeks) summary of an employee's gross earnings and payroll deductions.

Employers are responsible for the payment of four payroll taxes: social security, Medicare, state unemployment tax (SUTA), and federal unemployment tax (FUTA). In addition, most employers are responsible for a variety of **fringe benefits** that are offered to their employees. These are benefits over and above an employee's normal earnings and can be a significant expense to the employer. Some typical examples are retirement plans, stock option plans, holiday leave, sick days, health and dental insurance, and tuition reimbursement. This section deals with the calculation of these employer taxes and other payroll expenses.

fringe benefits
Employer provided benefits and service packages, over and above an employee's paycheck, such as pension funds, paid vacations, sick leave, and health insurance.

"I can offer you a company car, your own parking space, three week's vacation each year, full health and dental benefits, a private office with a window, and a salary of $43 a week."

9-8 Computing FICA Tax for Employers and Self-Employment Tax for Self-Employed Persons

Employer's FICA Tax

Employers are required to *match* all FICA tax payments, both social security and Medicare, made by each employee. For example, if a company withheld a total of $23,000 in FICA taxes from its employee paychecks this month, the company would be responsible for a matching share of $23,000.

EXAMPLE

A company has 25 employees, each with gross earnings of $250 per week. What are the total social security and Medicare taxes that should be withheld from the employee paychecks, and what is the employer's share of FICA for the first quarter of the year?

SOLUTION STRATEGY

To solve for the total FICA tax due quarterly from the employees and the employer, first calculate the tax due per employee per week, multiply by 25 to find the total weekly FICA for all employees, then multiply by 13 weeks to find the total quarterly amount withheld from all employees. The employer's share will be an equal amount.

Social security tax = Gross earnings × 6.2% = 250 × .062 = $15.50
Medicare tax = Gross earnings × 1.45% = 250 × .0145 = $3.63
Total FICA tax per employee per week = $15.50 + $3.63 = $19.13

Total FICA tax per week = FICA tax per employee × 25 employees
Total FICA tax per week = 19.13 × 25 = $478.25

Total FICA tax per quarter = Total FICA tax per week × 13 weeks
Total FICA tax per quarter = 478.25 × 13 = 6,217.25

Total FICA tax per quarter—Employee's share = $\underline{\underline{\$6,217.25}}$
Total FICA tax per quarter—Employer's share = $\underline{\underline{\$6,217.25}}$

TRY-IT | EXERCISE

13. The Evergreen Tree Service has 18 employees, 12 with gross earnings of $350 per week and six with gross earnings of $425 per week. What are the employee's share and the employer's share of the social security and Medicare tax for the first quarter of the year?

Check your answers with the solutions on page 330.

Self-Employment Tax

Self-employed persons are responsible for social security and Medicare taxes at twice the rate deducted for employees. Technically, they are the employee and the employer and therefore must pay both shares. For a self-employed person, the social security and Medicare tax rates are twice the normal rates, as follows:

	Tax Rate	Wage Base
Social Security	12.4% (6.2% × 2)	\$84,900
Medicare	2.9% (1.45% × 2)	No limit

EXAMPLE

What are the social security and Medicare taxes due on gross earnings of \$3,560 per month for a self-employed person?

SOLUTION STRATEGY

To find the amount of tax due, apply the self-employed tax rates to the gross earnings.

Social security tax = Gross earnings × Tax rate = \$3,560 × 12.4%

Social security tax = 3,560 × .124 = \$441.44

Medicare tax = Gross earnings × Tax rate = \$3,560 × 2.9%

Medicare tax = 3,560 × .029 = \$103.24

TRY-IT | EXERCISE

14. Linda Miller, a self-employed commercial artist, had total gross earnings of \$60,000 last year. What is the amount of the social security and Medicare taxes that Linda was required to send the IRS each quarter?

Check your answers with the solutions on page 330.

9-9 Computing the Amount of State Unemployment Taxes (SUTA) and Federal Unemployment Taxes (FUTA)

Federal Unemployment Tax Act (FUTA)
A federal tax that is paid by employers for each employee, to provide unemployment compensation to workers who have lost their jobs.

State Unemployment Tax Act (SUTA)
A state tax that is paid by employers for each employee, to provide unemployment compensation to workers who have lost their jobs.

The **Federal Unemployment Tax Act (FUTA),** together with state unemployment systems, provides for payments of unemployment compensation to workers who have lost their jobs. Most employers are responsible for both a federal and a state unemployment tax.

In 2002, the FUTA tax was 6.2% of the first \$7,000 of wages paid to each employee during the year. Generally, an employer can take a credit against the FUTA tax for amounts paid into state unemployment funds. These state taxes are commonly known as the **State Unemployment Tax Act (SUTA)**. This credit cannot be more than 5.4% of the first \$7,000 of employees' taxable wages.

SUTA tax rates vary from state to state according to the employment record of the company. These merit-rating systems, found in many states, provide significant SUTA tax savings to companies with good employment records.

For companies with full and timely payments to the state unemployment system, the FUTA tax rate is .8% (6.2% FUTA rate − 5.4% SUTA credit).

EXAMPLE

Continental Industries, Inc., had a total payroll of $50,000 last month. Continental pays a SUTA tax rate of 5.4%, and a FUTA rate of 6.2% less the SUTA credit. If none of the employees had reached the $7,000 wage base, what is the amount of SUTA and FUTA tax the company must pay?

SOLUTION STRATEGY

To calculate the SUTA and FUTA taxes, apply the appropriate tax rates to the gross earnings subject to the tax, in this case, all the gross earnings.

$$\text{SUTA tax} = \text{Gross earnings} \times 5.4\%$$

$$\text{SUTA tax} = 50{,}000 \times .054 = \underline{\underline{\$2{,}700}}$$

The FUTA tax rate will be .8%. Remember, it is actually 6.2% less the 5.4% credit.

$$\text{FUTA tax} = \text{Gross earnings} \times .8\%$$

$$\text{FUTA tax} = 50{,}000 \times .008 = \underline{\underline{\$400}}$$

TRY-IT | EXERCISE

15. Gourmet Catering had a total payroll of $10,000 last month. Gourmet pays a SUTA tax rate of 5.4% and a FUTA rate of 6.2% less the SUTA credit. If none of the employees had reached the $7,000 wage base, what is the amount of SUTA and FUTA tax the company must pay?

Check your answers with the solutions on page 330.

9-10 Calculating Employer's Fringe Benefit Expenses

In addition to compensating employees with a paycheck, most companies today offer employee fringe benefit and services packages. These packages include a wide variety of benefits such as pension plans, paid vacations and sick leave, day-care centers, tuition assistance, and health insurance. Corporate executives may receive benefits such as company cars, first-class airline travel, and country club memberships. At the executive level of business, these benefits are known as **perquisites** or **perks**.

perquisites, or **perks**
Executive-level fringe benefits such as first-class airline travel, company cars, and country club membership.

Over the past decade, employee benefits have become increasingly important to workers. They have grown in size to the point where today total benefits may cost a company as much as 40 to 50% of payroll. Frequently, employees are given a *menu* of fringe benefits to choose from, up to a specified dollar amount. These plans are known as **cafeteria-style**, or **flexible benefit programs.**

cafeteria-style, or **flexible benefit program**
A plan whereby employees are given a menu of fringe benefits to choose from, up to a specified dollar amount.

STEPS TO CALCULATE EMPLOYER'S FRINGE BENEFITS EXPENSE:

Step 1. If the fringe benefit is a percent of gross payroll, multiply that percent by the amount of the gross payroll. If the fringe benefit is a dollar amount per employee, multiply that amount by the number of employees.

Step 2. Find the total fringe benefits by adding all the individual fringe benefit amounts.

(continued)

(continued)

Step 3. Calculate the fringe benefit percent by using the percentage formula, Rate = Portion ÷ Base, with total fringe benefits as the portion and gross payroll as the base (remember to convert your answer to a percent).

$$\text{Fringe benefit percent} = \frac{\text{Total fringe benefits}}{\text{Gross payroll}}$$

Everybody's Business
Real-World Connection

Although paid vacations and health insurance are still the most popular among company-sponsored benefits, there is a trend today toward more "work-life initiatives." These are benefits that help employees balance their professional and personal lives such as child-care assistance and flexible work hours.

In a full-employment economy, employers often use fringe benefits to attract good workers away from the competition. These may include such perks as golf, tennis, scuba, or even flying lessons, automobiles, and mortgage assistance programs.

EXAMPLE

In addition to its gross payroll of \$150,000 per month, General Distributors, Inc., with 75 employees, pays 7% of payroll to a retirement fund, 9% for health insurance, and \$25 per employee for a stock purchase plan.

a. What are the company's monthly fringe benefit expenses?

b. What percent of payroll does this represent?

SOLUTION STRATEGY

a. To solve for monthly fringe benefits, compute the amount of each benefit, then add them to find the total.

Retirement fund expense = Gross payroll × 7%

Retirement fund expense = 150,000 × .07 = \$10,500

Health insurance expense = Gross payroll × 9%

Health insurance expense = 150,000 × .09 = \$13,500

Stock plan expense = Number of employees × \$25

Stock plan expense = 75 × 25 = \$1,875

Total fringe benefits = Retirement + Health + Stock

Total fringe benefits = 10,500 + 13,500 + 1,875 = \$25,875

b.

$$\text{Fringe benefit percent} = \frac{\text{Total fringe benefits}}{\text{Gross payroll}} = \frac{25{,}875}{150{,}000} = .1725 = \underline{\underline{17.25\%}}$$

Paid vacation time is one of the many fringe benefits offered by employers today.

TRY-IT | EXERCISE

16. Consolidated Enterprises employs 250 workers with a gross payroll of \$123,400 per week. Fringe benefits are 5% of gross payroll for sick days and holiday leave, 8% for health insurance, and \$12.40 per employee for dental insurance.

a. What is the total weekly cost of fringe benefits for Consolidated?

b. What percent of payroll does this represent?

c. What is the cost of these fringe benefits to the company for a year?

Check your answers with the solutions on page 330.

9-11 Understanding Internal Revenue Service Payroll Forms

Form 1040-ES Estimated Quarterly Tax Voucher for Self-Employed Persons

Earlier, we learned that self-employed persons must pay the self-employment tax, the equivalent of the employer's and employee's share of social security and Medicare tax. In addition, those who are self-employed are required to pay quarterly federal income tax on their gross earnings. When earnings are listed on an annual basis, divide the annual earnings by 4 to get quarterly earnings.

$$\text{Quarterly earnings} = \frac{\text{Estimated annual earnings}}{4\ (\text{quarters})}$$

Exhibit 9-6 illustrates the Internal Revenue Service Form 1040-ES. Note that it requires the taxpayer's name, address, social security number, amount of payment, and the current date.

Everybody's Business

Real-World Connection

The IRS requires that quarterly estimated tax payments be made on the following dates:

First payment	April 15, current year
Second payment	June 15, current year
Third payment	Sept. 15, current year
Fourth payment	Jan. 15, next year

Note: If any payment date falls on a Saturday, Sunday, or legal holiday, use the next business day.

You may use your American Express Card, Discover Card, or MasterCard to make estimated tax payments. Call toll free or access by Internet one of the service providers listed below and follow the instructions of the provider. Each provider will charge a convenience fee based on the amount you are paying.

- Official Payments Corporation
  1-800-2PAY-TAX (1-800-272-9829)
  www.officialpayments.com
- PhoneCharge, Inc.
  1-888-ALLTAXX (1-888-255-8229)
  www.about1888alltaxx.com

EXAMPLE

Diana Farrell is a self-employed marketing consultant. Her estimated annual earnings this year are $90,000. Her social security tax rate is 12.4% up to the wage base, Medicare is 2.9%, and her estimated federal income tax rate is 24%. How much quarterly estimate tax must Diana send to the IRS each quarter?

SOLUTION STRATEGY

$$\text{Quarterly earnings} = \frac{\text{Estimated annual earnings}}{4\ (\text{quarters})} = \frac{90{,}000}{4} = \$22{,}500$$

Note: In the first three quarters of the year, Diana's quarterly tax will be equal. In the fourth quarter, her wages will reach the social security wage base. In that quarter, she will pay less taxes.

FIRST, SECOND, AND THIRD QUARTERS:

Social security = 22,500.00 × 12.4% = $2,790.00

Medicare = 22,500.00 × 2.9% = $652.50

Income tax = 22,500.00 × 24% = $5,400.00

Quarterly tax = 2,790.00 + 652.50 + 5,400.00 = $8,842.50

FOURTH QUARTER:

Wages subject to social security = 84,900.00 − 67,500.00 = $17,400.00

Social security = 17,400.00 × 12.4% = $2,157.60

Medicare = 22,500.00 × 2.9% = $652.50

Income tax = 22,500.00 × 24% = $5,400.00

Quarterly tax = 2,157.60 + 652.50 + 5,400.00 = $8,210.10

EXHIBIT 9-6

Estimated Tax Payment Voucher

Form **1040-ES** Department of the Treasury Internal Revenue Service | **20XX** **Payment Voucher 4** | OMB No. 1545-0087

File only if you are making a payment of estimated tax by check or money order. Mail this voucher with your check or money order payable to the **"United States Treasury."** Write your social security number and "2001 Form 1040-ES" on your check or money order. Do not send cash. Enclose, but do not staple or attach, your payment with this voucher.

Calendar year—Due Jan. 15,

Amount of estimated tax you are paying by check or money order. $

Type or print

Your first name and initial	Your last name	Your social security number
If joint payment, complete for spouse		
Spouse's first name and initial	Spouse's last name	Spouse's social security number
Address (number, street, and apt. no.)		
City, state, and ZIP code (If a foreign address, enter city, province or state, postal code, and country.)		

For Privacy Act and Paperwork Reduction Act Notice, see instructions on page 5.

Page 6

TRY-IT | EXERCISE

17. Steven Knoerr is a self-employed freelance editor and project director for a large publishing company. His annual salary this year is estimated to be $100,000, with a federal income tax rate of 20%. What is the amount of estimated tax that Steven must send to the IRS each quarter?

Check your answer with the solution on page 330.

Everybody's Business

Real-World Connection

Penalties apply if you do not make required deposits on time, make deposits for less than the required amount, or if you do not use EFTPS when required. For amounts not deposited properly or in a timely manner, the penalty rates are:

Penalty	Reason for Penalty
2%	Deposits made 1 to 5 days late
5%	Deposits made 6 to 15 days late
10%	Deposits made 16 or more days late
10%	Not using EFTPS when required
15%	Amounts still unpaid more than 10 days after IRS notice

Form 8109 Federal Tax Deposit Coupon

After employers withhold social security, Medicare, and income taxes from employee paychecks, these funds must be combined with the employer's share of FICA and deposited in an authorized financial institution or a Federal Reserve Bank or branch in the employer's area. These deposits must be made monthly if the total taxes withheld for the previous year were less than $50,000, and semiweekly, by electronic deposit, if the taxes withheld last year amounted to more than $50,000. Electronic deposits are made by using the new Electronic Federal Tax Payment System (EFTPS). For new employers with no taxes withheld last year, the deposits are made monthly.

Form 8109, Exhibit 9-7, is used as a *deposit slip* to accompany these deposits. The form requires the name and address of the employer; the amount of the deposit; the type of tax, which in this case is known as 941; the tax period; and the telephone number.

Form 941 Employer's Quarterly Federal Tax Return

According to the IRS, more than 30 million 940 and 941 tax forms are filed each year by employers. Employers are required to file Form 941, Employer's Quarterly Federal Tax Return, by the end of the month following each quarter to inform the IRS of the total amount of social security, Medicare, and income tax withheld from employee paychecks during the quarter and the amount of the employer's share of social security and Medicare taxes. Form 941 appears in Exhibit 9-8.

Note that Line 1 shows number of employees; Line 3 shows the total income tax withheld from employee's wages; Line 8 shows total social security and Medicare taxes; and Line 11 shows total taxes. If the total deposits for the quarter, Line 14, are more than $500 and deposited on time, then Line 15, balance due, will be zero.

Federal Tax Deposit (FTD) Coupon

(Use a soft lead pencil when completing Form 8109 or 8109-B)

Mark the "X" in this box only if there is a change to Employer Identification Number (EIN) or Name.

See instructions on page 1.

BANK NAME/ DATE STAMP

2 AMOUNT OF DEPOSIT (Do NOT type, please print.)

DOLLARS | CENTS

EIN 12-3456789 111111

1

LILIAN SMITH & PAUL JONES
L & P GRAPHICS
2025 MAIN STREET
ANYTOWN, MD 99999

IRS USE ONLY

3 Darken only one TYPE OF TAX

941	945
990-C	1120
943	990-T
720	990-PF
CT-1	1042
940	

and

4 Darken only one TAX PERIOD

- 1st Quarter
- 2nd Quarter
- 3rd Quarter
- 4th Quarter

62

Telephone number ( ) ________ 5

FOR BANK USE IN MICR ENCODING

Federal Tax Deposit Coupon
Form 8109 (Rev. 10-96)

✦ **EXHIBIT 9-7** ✦

Federal Tax Deposit Coupon

Form **941** (Rev. October 2001) Department of the Treasury Internal Revenue Service (99)

Employer's Quarterly Federal Tax Return

▶ See separate instructions revised January 2001 for information on completing this return.

Please type or print.

Enter state code for state in which deposits were made **only** if different from state in address to the right ▶ (see page 2 of instructions).

Name (as distinguished from trade name) — Date quarter ended

Trade name, if any — Employer identification number

Address (number and street) — City, state, and ZIP code

OMB No. 1545-0029

T
FF
FD
FP
I
T

If address is different from prior return, check here ▶ — IRS Use

If you do not have to file returns in the future, check here ▶ ☐ and enter date final wages paid ▶

If you are a seasonal employer, see **Seasonal employers** on page 1 of the instructions and check here ▶ ☐

1	Number of employees in the pay period that includes March 12th . ▶ 1	
2	Total wages and tips, plus other compensation	2
3	Total income tax withheld from wages, tips, and sick pay	3
4	Adjustment of withheld income tax for preceding quarters of calendar year	4
5	Adjusted total of income tax withheld (line 3 as adjusted by line 4—see instructions)	5
6	Taxable social security wages . . . 6a × 12.4% (.124) =	6b
	Taxable social security tips . . . 6c × 12.4% (.124) =	6d
7	Taxable Medicare wages and tips . . . 7a × 2.9% (.029) =	7b
8	Total social security and Medicare taxes (add lines 6b, 6d, and 7b). Check here if wages are not subject to social security and/or Medicare tax ▶ ☐	8
9	Adjustment of social security and Medicare taxes (see instructions for required explanation) Sick Pay $ ____ ± Fractions of Cents $ ____ ± Other $ ____ =	9
10	Adjusted total of social security and Medicare taxes (line 8 as adjusted by line 9—see instructions)	10
11	**Total taxes** (add lines 5 and 10)	11
12	Advance earned income credit (EIC) payments made to employees	12
13	Net taxes (subtract line 12 from line 11). **If $2,500 or more, this must equal line 17, column (d) below (or line D of Schedule B (Form 941))**	13
14	Total deposits for quarter, including overpayment applied from a prior quarter	14
15	**Balance due** (subtract line 14 from line 13). See instructions	15

16 **Overpayment.** If line 14 is more than line 13, enter excess here ▶ $ ________ and check if to be: ☐ Applied to next return **or** ☐ Refunded.

- **All filers:** If line 13 is less than $2,500, you need not complete line 17 or Schedule B (Form 941).
- **Semiweekly schedule depositors:** Complete Schedule B (Form 941) and check here ▶ ☐
- **Monthly schedule depositors:** Complete line 17, columns (a) through (d), and check here ▶ ☐

17 Monthly Summary of Federal Tax Liability. Do not complete if you were a semiweekly schedule depositor.

(a) First month liability	(b) Second month liability	(c) Third month liability	(d) Total liability for quarter

Sign Here Under penalties of perjury, I declare that I have examined this return, including accompanying schedules and statements, and to the best of my knowledge and belief, it is true, correct, and complete.

Signature ▶ Print Your Name and Title ▶ Date ▶

For Privacy Act and Paperwork Reduction Act Notice, see back of Payment Voucher. Cat. No. 17001Z Form **941** (Rev. 10-2001)

✦ **EXHIBIT 9-8** ✦

Employer's Quarterly Federal Tax Return

EXHIBIT 9-9

Employer's Annual FUTA Return

Form **940-EZ**

Department of the Treasury
Internal Revenue Service (99)

Employer's Annual Federal Unemployment (FUTA) Tax Return

► **See separate Instructions for Form 940-EZ for information on completing this form.**

OMB No. 1545-1110

T	
FF	
FD	
FP	
I	
T	

You must complete this section. ▶

Name (as distinguished from trade name) Calendar year

Trade name, if any

Address and ZIP code Employer identification number

*Answer the questions under **Who May Use Form 940-EZ** on page 2. If you cannot use Form 940-EZ, you must use Form 940.*

A Enter the amount of contributions paid to your state unemployment fund. (see separate instructions) . . . ► $ ....

B (1) Enter the name of the state where you have to pay contributions . . . . ► ....

(2) Enter your state reporting number as shown on your state unemployment tax return ►

If you will not have to file returns in the future, check here (see **Who Must File** in separate instructions), **and complete and sign the return.** ► ☐

If this is an Amended Return, check here . . . . ► ☐

Part I Taxable Wages and FUTA Tax

1	Total payments (including payments shown on lines 2 and 3) during the calendar year for services of employees			1	
2	Exempt payments. (Explain all exempt payments, attaching additional sheets if necessary.) ►	2			
3	Payments of more than $7,000 for services. Enter only amounts over the first $7,000 paid to each employee. **(see separate instructions)**	3			
4	Add lines 2 and 3			4	
5	**Total taxable wages** (subtract line 4 from line 1) . . . . ►			5	
6	**FUTA tax.** Multiply the wages on line 5 by .008 and enter here. **(If the result is over $100, also complete Part II.)**			6	
7	Total FUTA tax deposited for the year, including any overpayment applied from a prior year			7	
8	**Balance due** (subtract line 7 from line 6). Pay to the **"United States Treasury."** . . . . ► If you owe more than $100, see **Depositing FUTA tax** in separate instructions.			8	
9	**Overpayment** (subtract line 6 from line 7). Check if it is to be: ☐ **Applied to next return** or ☐ **Refunded** ►			9	

Part II Record of Quarterly Federal Unemployment Tax Liability (Do not include state liability.) **Complete only if line 6 is over $100.**

Quarter	First (Jan. 1 – Mar. 31)	Second (Apr. 1 – June 30)	Third (July 1 – Sept. 30)	Fourth (Oct. 1 – Dec. 31)	Total for year
Liability for quarter					

Third Party Designee Do you want to allow another person to discuss this return with the IRS (see instructions page 4)? ☐ **Yes.** Complete the following. ☐ **No**

Designee's name ► Phone no. ► ( ) Personal identification number (PIN) ►

Under penalties of perjury, I declare that I have examined this return, including accompanying schedules and statements, and, to the best of my knowledge and belief, it is true, correct, and complete, and that no part of any payment made to a state unemployment fund claimed as a credit was, or is to be, deducted from the payments to employees.

Signature ► **Title (Owner, etc.)** ► **Date** ►

For Privacy Act and Paperwork Reduction Act Notice, see separate instructions. ▼ **DETACH HERE** ▼ Cat. No. 10983G Form **940-EZ** (2001)

Form 940-EZ Employer's Annual Federal Unemployment (FUTA) Tax Return

Employers are required to file a FUTA tax return each year. Exhibit 9-9 is an example of such a return. Note that the wages over $7,000, the wage base, Line 3, are subtracted from the total wages, Line 1, to get total taxable wages, Line 5. Also note, as we learned in this chapter, the FUTA tax rate is .8%, or .008 (Line 6).

REVIEW EXERCISES | CHAPTER 9—SECTION III

1. Universal Systems, Inc., has 40 employees on the assembly line, each with gross earnings of $325 per week.

a. What is the total social security and Medicare taxes that should be withheld from the employee paychecks each week?

b. What is the employer's share of these taxes for the first quarter of the year?

2. VIP Industries has 24 employees, 15 with gross earnings of $345 per week and nine with gross earnings of $385 per week. What is the total social security and Medicare tax that the company must send to the Internal Revenue Service for the first quarter of the year?

3. What are the social security and Medicare taxes due on gross earnings of $2,800 per month for a self-employed person?

4. John Carey is a self-employed painter. Last year, he had total gross earnings of $38,700. How much must he send to the IRS for his quarterly social security and Medicare payments?

5. Bill Ronald earns $21,450 annually as a line supervisor for Blossom Manufacturers.

a. If the SUTA tax rate is 5.4% of the first $7,000 earned in a year, how much SUTA tax must Blossom pay each year for Bill?

b. If the FUTA tax rate is 6.2% of the first $7,000 earned in a year minus the SUTA tax paid, how much FUTA tax must the company pay each year for Bill?

6. Annie Engstrom worked part time last year as a cashier in a supermarket. Her total gross earnings were $6,443.00.

a. How much SUTA tax must the supermarket pay to the state for Annie?

b. How much FUTA tax must be paid for her?

7. Riteway Roofing Company has three installers. Larry earns \$355 per week, Curly earns \$460 per week, and Moe earns \$585 per week. The company's SUTA rate is 5.4%, and the FUTA rate is 6.2% minus the SUTA. As usual, these taxes are paid on the first \$7,000 of each employee's earnings.

   a. How much SUTA and FUTA tax does Riteway owe for the first quarter of the year?

   b. How much SUTA and FUTA tax does Riteway owe for the second quarter of the year?

3

8. Metro Limousine Service employs 166 workers and has a gross payroll of \$154,330 per week. Fringe benefits are $4\frac{1}{2}\%$ of gross payroll for sick days and maternity leave, 7.4% for health insurance, 3.1% for the retirement fund, and \$26.70 per employee for a stock purchase plan.

   a. What is the total weekly cost of fringe benefits for the company?

   b. What percent of payroll does this represent?

   c. What is the company's annual cost of fringe benefits?

9. Bill Hendee, a self-employed sales consultant, has an estimated gross salary of \$300,000 this year. His social security tax rate is 12.4% up to the wage base, Medicare is 2.9%, and his estimated federal income tax rate is 31%.

   a. How much quarterly estimate tax must Bill send to the IRS for each quarter?

b. What form should he use?

10. You are the payroll manager for Biltmore International, Inc.

a. According to IRS deposit rules, if your company's tax liability last year was $70,000, when are the deposits due and how do you make these payments?

b. What form should accompany these deposits?

c. How often must you file a tax return for Biltmore?

d. What IRS form should you use for this purpose?

BUSINESS DECISION

New Fringe Benefits

11. You are the Human Resource Director for Monterey International, a cellular phone company with 800 employees. Top management has asked you to implement three additional fringe benefits that were negotiated with employee representatives and agreed upon by a majority of the employees. These include group term life insurance, a group legal services plan, and a "wellness center."

The life insurance is estimated to cost $260 per employee per quarter. The legal plan will cost $156 semiannually per employee. The company will contribute 40% to the life insurance premium and 75% to the cost of the legal services plan. The employees will pay the balance through payroll deductions from their biweekly paychecks. In addition, they will be charged $\frac{1}{4}$% of their gross earnings per paycheck for maintaining the wellness center. The company will pay the initial cost of $500,000 to build the center. This expense will be spread over 5 years.

a. What total amount should be deducted *per paycheck* for these new fringe benefits, for an employee earning $41,600 per year?

b. What is the total *annual* cost of the new fringe benefits to the company?

CHAPTER FORMULAS

Hourly Wages

Regular pay = Hourly rate × Regular hours worked

Overtime pay = Hourly rate × Overtime factor × Overtime hours worked

Total gross pay = Regular pay + Overtime pay

Piecework

Total gross pay = Output quantity × Rate per unit

Commission

Total gross pay = Total sales × Commission rate

Payroll Deductions

Total deductions = Social security + Medicare + Income tax + Voluntary deductions

Net pay = Gross pay − Total deductions

Fringe Benefits

$$\text{Fringe benefit percent} = \frac{\text{Total fringe benefits}}{\text{Gross payroll}}$$

Estimated Quarterly Tax

$$\text{Quarterly earnings} = \frac{\text{Estimated annual earnings}}{4\ (\text{quarters})}$$

✦ SUMMARY CHART ✦

SECTION I: Employee's Gross Earnings and Incentive Pay Plans

Topic	P/O, Page	Important Concepts	Illustrative Examples
Prorating Annual Salary to Various Pay Periods	9-1 292	Salaried employees are most commonly paid based on one of the following pay schedules: *Weekly:* 52 paychecks per year Annual salary ÷ 52 *Biweekly:* 26 paychecks per year Annual salary ÷ 26 *Semimonthly:* 24 paychecks per year Annual salary ÷ 24 *Monthly:* 12 paychecks per year Annual salary ÷ 12	What are the gross earnings of an employee with an annual salary of $40,000 based on weekly, biweekly, semimonthly, and monthly pay schedules? $\text{Weekly} = \frac{40{,}000}{52} = \underline{\underline{\$769.23}}$ $\text{Biweekly} = \frac{40{,}000}{26} = \underline{\underline{\$1{,}538.46}}$ $\text{Semimonthly} = \frac{40{,}000}{24} = \underline{\underline{\$1{,}666.67}}$ $\text{Monthly} = \frac{40{,}000}{12} = \underline{\underline{\$3{,}333.33}}$

SECTION I: (continued)

<table>
<tr><th>Topic</th><th>P/O, Page</th><th>Important Concepts</th><th>Illustrative Examples</th></tr>
<tr><td>Calculating Gross Pay by Regular Hourly Wages and Overtime</td><td>9-2
293</td><td>An hourly wage is the amount an employee is paid for each hour worked.
Regular time specifies that a standard work week is 40 hours.
Overtime amounting to at least time-and-a-half must be paid for all hours over 40. Some employers pay double time for weekend, holiday, and midnight shifts.
Regular pay =
Hourly rate × Hours worked
Overtime pay =
Hourly rate × Overtime factor × Hours worked
Total gross pay =
Regular pay + Overtime pay</td><td>Sandi Yee earns $9.50 per hour as a supervisor in a plant. If her overtime rate is time-and-a-half and holidays are double time, what is Sandi's total gross pay for working 49 hours last week, including 4 holiday hours?
Regular pay =
9.50 × 40 = $380.00
Time-and-a-half pay =
9.50 × 1.5 × 5 = $71.25
Double-time pay =
9.50 × 2 × 4 = $76.00
Total gross pay =
380.00 + 71.25 + 76.00 = $527.25</td></tr>
<tr><td>Calculating Straight and Differential Piecework Wages</td><td>9-3
294</td><td>A piecework pay rate schedule is based on production output, not time. Straight piecework pays the worker a certain amount of pay per unit, regardless of quantity. In differential piecework, the rate per unit increases as output quantity goes up.
Total gross pay =
Output quantity × Rate per unit</td><td>A factory pays its workers $2.50 per unit of production. What is the gross pay of a worker producing 233 units?
Gross pay =
233 × 2.50 = $582.50
A factory pays its production workers $.54 per unit up to 5,000 units and $.67 per unit above 5,000 units. What is the gross pay of an employee who produces 6,500 units?
5,000 × .54 = 2,700
+ 1,500 × .67 = 1,005
Total gross pay = $3,705</td></tr>
<tr><td>Calculating Straight and Incremental Commission</td><td>9-4
296</td><td>Commission is a method of compensation primarily used to pay employees selling goods and services. Straight commission is based on a single specified percentage of the sales volume attained. Incremental commission, like differential piecework, is when various levels of sales earn increasing rates of commission.
Total gross pay =
Total sales × Commission rate</td><td>A company pays 4% straight commission on all sales. What is the gross pay of an employee who sells $135,000?
Gross pay =
135,000 × .04 = $5,400.00
A company pays incremental commissions of 3.5% on sales up to $100,000 and 4.5% on all sales greater than $100,000. What is the gross pay of an employee selling $164,000?
100,000 × .035 = 3,500.00
+ 64,000 × .045 = 2,880.00
Gross pay = $6,380.00</td></tr>
</table>

SECTION I: (continued)

<table>
<tr><th>Topic</th><th>P/O, Page</th><th>Important Concepts</th><th>Illustrative Examples</th></tr>
<tr><td>Calculating Salary Plus Commissions</td><td>9-4
297</td><td>Salary plus commission is a pay schedule whereby the employee receives a guaranteed salary in addition to a commission on sales over a certain specified amount.</td><td>An employee is paid a salary of $350 per week plus a 2% commission on sales greater than $8,000. If Jeff sold $13,400 last week, how much did he earn?
350 + 2% (13,400 − 8,000)
350 + .02 × 5,400
350 + 108 = $458.00</td></tr>
<tr><td>Computing Gross Earnings with Drawing Accounts</td><td>9-4
298</td><td>A drawing account, or draw against commission, is a commission paid in advance of sales and later deducted from the commission earned.</td><td>Jim Hall sells for a company that pays $6\frac{1}{2}\%$ commission with a $600 per month drawing account. If Jim takes the draw and then sells $16,400 in goods, how much commission is he owed?
(16,400 × .065) − 600
1,066 − 600 = $466.00</td></tr>
</table>

SECTION II: Employee's Payroll Deductions

<table>
<tr><td>Computing FICA Taxes, Both Social Security and Medicare</td><td>9-5
302</td><td>FICA taxes are divided into two categories: social security and Medicare. When employees reach the wage base for the year, they are no longer subject to the tax.

| | Tax Rate | Wage Base |
| Social Security | 6.2% | $84,900 |
| Medicare | 1.45% | no limit |</td><td>What are the FICA tax withholdings for social security and Medicare for an employee with gross earnings of $760 per week?
Social security =
$760 × 6.2% = $47.12
Medicare =
$760 × 1.45% = $11.02</td></tr>
<tr><td>Calculating Federal Income Tax by Using Percentage Method</td><td>9-6
304</td><td>1. Multiply one withholding allowance, in Exhibit 9-2, by the number of allowances the employee claims.
2. Subtract that amount from the employee's gross earnings to find the income subject to income tax.
3. Determine the amount of tax withheld from the appropriate section of Exhibit 9-3.</td><td>Gisele Valdivia is single, earns $1,800 per week as a loan officer for Bank of America, and claims three withholding allowances. Calculate the amount of federal income tax withheld from Gisele's weekly paycheck.
From Exhibit 9-2:
$55.77 × 3 = $167.31
Taxable income =
$1,800 − $167.31 = $1,632.69
From Exhibit 9-3:
Withholding tax =
$249.03 + 30%(1,632.69 − 1,196.00)
249.03 + .3(436.69)
249.03 + 131.01 = $380.04</td></tr>
</table>

SECTION II: (continued)

Topic	P/O, Page	Important Concepts	Illustrative Examples
Determining an Employee's Total Withholding for Federal Income Tax, Social Security, and Medicare Using the Combined Wage Bracket Tables	9-7 307	1. Based on marital status and payroll period, choose either Exhibit 9-4 or 9-5. 2. Scan down the left-hand columns until you find the bracket containing the gross pay of the employee. 3. Scan across the row of that wage bracket to the intersection of that employee's "withholding allowances claimed" column. 4. The number in that column, on the wage bracket row, is the amount of combined withholding tax.	What amount of combined tax should be withheld from the monthly paycheck of a single employee claiming two withholding allowances and earning $3,495 per month? Use Exhibit 9-5. Scan down the wage brackets to $3,480—$3,520. Scan across to "2" withholding allowances to find the tax, $761.75

SECTION III: Employer's Payroll Expenses and Record Keeping Responsibilities

Topic	P/O, Page	Important Concepts	Illustrative Examples
Computing FICA Tax for Employers	9-8 313	Employers are required to match all FICA tax payments made by each employee.	Last month, a company withheld a total of $3,400 in FICA taxes from employee paychecks. What is the company's FICA liability? The company is responsible for a matching amount withheld from the employees, $3,400
Calculating Self-Employment Tax	9-8 314	Self-employed persons are responsible for social security and Medicare taxes at twice the rate deducted for employees. Technically, they are the employee and the employer, therefore they must pay both shares, as follows: ***Social Security*** **12.4% (6.2% × 2), wage base $84,900** ***Medicare*** **2.9% (1.45% × 2), no limit**	What are the social security and Medicare taxes due on gross earnings of $4,260 per month for a self-employed person? *Social security* Gross earnings × 12.4% = 4,260 × .124 = $528.24 *Medicare* Gross earnings × 2.9% = 4,260 × .029 = 123.54
Calculating State Unemployment Tax (SUTA) and Federal Unemployment Tax (FUTA)	9-9 314	SUTA and FUTA taxes provide for unemployment compensation to workers who have lost their jobs. These taxes are paid by the employer. The SUTA tax rate is 5.4% of the first $7,000 of earnings per year by each employee. The FUTA tax rate is 6.2% of the first $7,000 minus the SUTA tax paid (6.2% − 5.4% = .8%).	Chang Enterprises had a total payroll of $40,000 last month. If none of the employees have reached the $7,000 wage base, what is the amount of SUTA and FUTA tax due? SUTA = 40,000 × 5.4% = $2,160 FUTA = 40,000 × .8% = $320

SECTION III: (continued)

Topic	P/O, Page	Important Concepts	Illustrative Examples
Calculating Employer's Fringe Benefit Expenses	9-10 315	In addition to compensating employees with a paycheck, most companies offer benefit packages that may include pensions, paid sick days, tuition assistance, and health insurance. Fringe benefits represent a significant expense to employers. $\text{Fringe benefit percent} = \frac{\text{Total fringe benefits}}{\text{Gross payroll}}$	Northern Industries employs 48 workers and has a monthly gross payroll of $120,000. In addition, the company pays 6.8% to a pension fund, 8.7% for health insurance, and $30 per employee for a stock purchase plan. What are Northern's monthly fringe benefit expenses? What percent of payroll does this represent? 120,000 × 6.8% = 8,160 120,000 × 8.7% = 10,440 48 × $30 = + 1,440 Total fringe benefits $20,040 $\text{Fringe ben.\%} = \frac{20{,}040}{120{,}000} = 16.7\%$
Filing Form 1040-ES—Quarterly Estimate Tax for Self-Employed	9-11 317	Each quarter, self-employed persons must send to the IRS Form 1040-ES along with a tax payment for social security, Medicare, and income tax. $\text{Quarterly earnings} = \frac{\text{Annual earnings}}{4(\text{quarters})}$	Jane Perez is self-employed as a decorator. She estimates her annual earnings this year to be $44,000. On what quarterly earnings should her taxes be based? $\text{Qtly earnings} = \frac{44{,}000}{4} = \$11{,}000$
Filing Form 8109—Federal Tax Deposit Coupon	9-11 318	Form 8109 is used as a deposit slip when employers send social security, Medicare, and income tax payments to the IRS. Deposits must be made monthly if last year's deposits were less than $50,000 and semiweekly by electronic payment, if last year's deposits were more than $50,000.	Last year, a restaurant deposited $72,000 with the IRS for employee withholdings. How often and how must deposits be made this year? Because last year's amount was greater than $50,000, deposits must be made semiweekly, by using EFTPS, this year.
Filing Form 941—Employer's Quarterly Federal Tax Return	9-11 318	IRS Form 941 is filed quarterly by employers to report: 1. Amount of employee FICA tax withheld from gross earnings. 2. Employer's share of FICA. 3. Amount of federal income tax withheld from employees' gross earnings.	The Appleton Corp. withheld $5,360 in FICA taxes and $12,920 in federal income tax from its employees' gross earnings in the first quarter. How much should be reported on Form 941? Employees' FICA $5,360 Employer's share 5,360 Income tax + 12,920 Total deposits for qtr. $23,640

TRY-IT EXERCISE | SOLUTIONS

1. Weekly pay $= \dfrac{\text{Annual salary}}{52} = \dfrac{43{,}500}{52} = \underline{\underline{\$836.54}}$

Biweekly pay $= \dfrac{\text{Annual salary}}{26} = \dfrac{43{,}500}{26} = \underline{\underline{\$1{,}673.08}}$

Semimonthly pay $= \dfrac{\text{Annual salary}}{24} = \underline{\underline{\$1{,}812.50}}$

Monthly pay $= \dfrac{\text{Annual salary}}{12} = \underline{\underline{\$3{,}625.00}}$

2. Regular pay = Hourly rate × Number of hours worked
Regular pay = 6.50 × 40 = $\underline{\underline{\$260}}$

Time-and-a-half pay = Hourly rate × Overtime factor × Hours worked
Time-and-a-half pay = 6.50 × 1.5 × 5 = $\underline{\underline{\$48.75}}$

Double time pay = Hourly rate × Overtime factor × Hours worked
Double time pay = 6.50 × 2 × 4 = $\underline{\underline{\$52.00}}$

Total gross pay = Regular pay + Overtime pay
Total gross pay = 260.00 + 48.75 + 52.00 = $\underline{\underline{\$360.75}}$

3. Total gross pay = Output quantity × Rate per unit
Total gross pay = 950 × .41 = $\underline{\underline{\$389.50}}$

4. Level pay = Output × Rate per piece

Gomez:	300 × .68 =	$204.00
	200 × .79 =	158.00
	15 × .86 =	+ 12.90
		$\underline{\underline{\$374.90}}$ Total gross pay
Clifford:	199 × .68 =	$\underline{\underline{\$135.32}}$ Total gross pay
Maken:	300 × .68 =	$204.00
	148 × .79 =	+ 116.92
		$\underline{\underline{\$320.92}}$ Total gross pay
Nathan:	300 × .68 =	$204.00
	200 × .79 =	158.00
	250 × .86 =	215.00
	54 × .94 =	+ 50.76
		$\underline{\underline{\$627.76}}$ Total gross pay

5. Total gross pay = Total sales × Commission rate
Total gross pay = 233,760 × .024 = $\underline{\underline{\$5{,}610.24}}$

6. Level pay = Sales per level × Commission rate
Level pay = 100,000 × .017 = $1,700.00
84,600 × .025 = + 2,115.00
$\underline{\underline{\$3{,}815.00}}$

7. Commission = Commission rate × Sales subject to commission
Commission = 4%(45,000 − 20,000)
Commission = .04 × 25,000 = $1,000

Total gross pay = Salary + Commission
Total gross pay = 1,400 + 1,000 = $\underline{\underline{\$2{,}400}}$

8. Commission = Total sales × Commission rate
Commission = 120,000 × 3.5% = $4,200
Commission owed = Commission − Amount of draw
Commission owed = 4,200 − 2,000 = $\underline{\underline{\$2{,}200}}$

9. Social security tax = Gross earnings × 6.2%
Social security tax = 5,000 × .062 = $\underline{\underline{\$310}}$

Medicare tax = Gross earnings × 1.45%
Medicare tax = 5,000 × .0145 = $\underline{\underline{\$72.50}}$

10. Earnings subject to tax = Wage base − Year-to-date earnings
Earnings subject to tax = 84,900 − 79,700 = $5,200
Social security tax = Earnings subject to tax × 6.2%
Social security tax = 5,200 × .062 = $\underline{\underline{\$322.40}}$

11. From Exhibit 9-2:
Withholding allowance = 1 allowance × exemptions
Withholding allowance = $241.67 × 5 = $1,208.35

Taxable income = Gross pay − Withholding allowance
Taxable income = 2,350 − 1,208.35 = $1,141.65

From Exhibit 9-3, Table 4(b):
Category $538 to $4,158
Withholding tax = 15% of amount greater than $538
Withholding tax = 15% (1,141.65 − 538.00)
Withholding tax = .15 ($603.65) = $90.55

12. From Exhibit 9-4
$835 Weekly, married, 2 Allowances = $153.88

13. *12 employees @ $350*
Social security = 350 × .062 = 21.70
Medicare = 350 × .0145 = 5.08

Total FICA per employee = 21.70 + 5.08 = $26.78
Total FICA per week = 26.78 × 12 employees = $321.36
Total FICA per quarter = 321.36 × 13 weeks = $4,177.68

6 employees @ $425
Social security = 425 × .062 = 26.35
Medicare = 425 × .0145 = 6.16
Total FICA per employee = 26.35 + 6.16 = $32.51

Total FICA per week = 32.51 × 6 employees = $195.06
Total FICA per quarter = 195.06 × 13 weeks = $2,535.78
Total FICA per quarter:
Employees' share = 4,177.68 + 2,535.78 = $6,713.46
Employer's share = 4,177.68 + 2,535.78 = $6,713.46

14. $\text{Quarterly earnings} = \frac{\text{Annual earnings}}{4} = \frac{60{,}000}{4} = \$15{,}000$
Social security = Gross earnings × Tax rate
Social security = 15,000 × .124 = $1,860
Medicare tax = Gross earnings × Tax rate
Medicare tax = 15,000 × .029 = $435

15. SUTA tax = Gross earnings × 5.4%
SUTA tax = 10,000 × .054 = $540
FUTA tax = Gross earnings × .8%
FUTA tax = 10,000 × .008 = $80

16. a. Fringe benefits
Sick days = Gross payroll × 5%
Sick days = 123,400 × .05 = $6,170
Health ins = Gross payroll × 8%
Health ins = 123,400 × .08 = $9,872
Dental ins = Number of employees × 12.40
Dental ins = 250 × 12.40 = $3,100
Total fringe benefits = 6,170 + 9,872 + 3,100 = $19,142

b. $\text{Fringe benefit percent} = \frac{\text{Total fringe benefits}}{\text{Gross payroll}}$

$\text{Fringe benefit percent} = \frac{19{,}142}{123{,}400} = .155 = 15.5\%$

c. Yearly fringe benefits = Weekly total × 52
Yearly fringe benefits = 19,142 × 52 = $995,384

17. $\text{Quarterly earnings} = \frac{\text{Annual earnings}}{4}$

$\text{Quarterly earnings} = \frac{100{,}000.00}{4} = \$25{,}000.00$

First, second, and third quarters
Social security = 25,000.00 × .124 = 3,100.00
Medicare = 25,000.00 × .029 = 725.00
Income tax = 25,000.00 × .20 = 5,000.00
Quarterly tax = 3,100.00 + 725.00 + 5,000.00 = $8,825.00

Fourth quarter Social security limit reached

Wage base − Year-to-date earnings =
Wages subject to social security
84,900.00 − 75,000.00 = 9,900.00 subject to social security
Social security = 9,900.00 × .124 = 1,227.60
Medicare = 25,000.00 × .029 = 725.00
Income tax = 25,000.00 × .20 = 5,000.00
Quarterly tax = 1,227.60 + 725.00 + 5,000.00 = $6,952.60

CHAPTER 9 | ASSESSMENT TEST

Name ______________________

Class ______________________

1. Jorge Kevin earns $2,800 semimonthly as a congressional aide for a senator in the state legislature.

a. How much are his annual gross earnings?

b. If the senator switches pay schedules from semimonthly to biweekly, what will Jorge's new gross earnings be per payroll period?

2. Hazel Kates works 40 hours per week. At the rate of $8.05 per hour, what are her gross weekly earnings?

3. Reagann Keller earns $7.45 per hour for regular time up to 40 hours, time-and-a-half for overtime, and double time for the midnight shift. If Reagann worked 56 hours last week, including 4 on the midnight shift, how much are her gross earnings?

4. Tiffany Francis assembles electric fans for the Hunter Corporation. She is paid on a differential piecework rate of $2.70 per fan for the first 160 fans and $3.25 for each fan over 160. If she assembled 229 units last week, how much were her gross earnings?

5. You work in the payroll department of Sanders Manufacturing. The following piece rate schedule is used for computing earnings for assembly line workers. As an overtime bonus, on Saturdays, each unit produced counts as $1\frac{1}{2}$ units.

1–100	$2.30
101–150	2.60
151–200	2.80
over 200	3.20

Calculate the gross earnings for the following employees:

	Employee	Mon.	Tues.	Wed.	Thurs.	Fri.	Sat.	Total Units	Gross Earnings
a.	Anderson	0	32	16	36	27	12		
b.	Cavalcante	18	26	24	10	13	0		
c.	West	26	42	49	51	34	20		

Answers

1. a. ______________________

b. ______________________

2. ______________________

3. ______________________

4. ______________________

5. a. ______________________

b. ______________________

c. ______________________

Name ______________________

Class ______________________

Answers

6. ______________________
7. ______________________
8. ______________________
9. ______________________
10. ______________________
11. ______________________
____

12. a. ______________________
____

b. ______________________

c. ______________________
____

6. What is the total gross pay for a salesperson on a straight commission of 7.8% if his or her sales volume is $123,800?

7. What is the total gross pay for a salesperson on an incremental commission schedule of 4.3% of sales up to $50,000 and 5.3% on sales greater than $50,000 if last month's sales volume was $71,700?

8. Erin Williams works in the telemarketing division for a company that pays a salary of $735 per month plus a commission of $3\frac{1}{2}$% of all sales greater than $15,500. If she sold $45,900 last month, what was her total gross pay?

9. Julie Oliver is on a 2.1% straight commission with a $700 drawing account. If she is paid the draw at the beginning of the month and then sells $142,100 during the month, how much commission is owed to Julie?

10. Dennis Morgan is the first mate on a charter fishing boat. He is paid a salary of $40.00 per day. He also averages tips amounting to 12% of the $475 daily charter rate. Last month during a fishing tournament, Dennis worked 22 days. What were his total gross earnings for the month?

Solve the following problems, using 6.2% up to $84,900 for social security withholding and 1.45% for Medicare:

11. What are the withholdings for social security and Medicare for an employee with gross earnings of $725 per week?

12. Mark Goodwin is an executive with Metro Distributors. His gross earnings are $7,750 per month.

a. What are the withholdings for social security and Medicare for Mark's January paycheck?

b. In what month will his salary reach the social security wage base limit?

c. What are the social security and Medicare tax withholdings for Mark in the month named in part **b**?

Name ____________

Class ____________

Answers

13. a. ____________

b. ____________

c. ____________

14. ____________

15. ____________

16. ____________

Use the *percentage method* to solve the following:

13. Larry Alison is single, claims one withholding allowance, and earns $2,120 per month.

a. What is the amount of Larry's paycheck after his employer withholds social security, Medicare, and income tax?

b. If Larry gets married and changes to two withholding allowances, what will be the new amount of his paycheck?

c. If he then gets a 15% raise, what is the new amount of his paycheck?

Use the *combined wage bracket tables* for Exercises 14 and 15 (Exhibits 9-4 and 9-5).

14. How much combined tax should be withheld from the paycheck of a married employee earning $910 per week and claiming three withholding allowances?

15. How much combined tax should be withheld from the paycheck of a single employee earning $4,458 per month and claiming zero withholding allowances?

16. Kay Allen is married, claims five withholding allowances, and earns $3,200 per month. In addition to social security, Medicare, and FIT, Kay pays 2.1% state income tax, $\frac{1}{2}$% for state disability insurance (both based on gross income), $43.11 for life insurance, and $72.30 to the credit union. As payroll manager for Kay's company, calculate her net take-home pay per month.

Name ______________________

Class ______________________

Answers

17. a. ______________________

____

b. ______________________

____

18. ______________________

____

19. a. ______________________

b. ______________________

17. The Hastings Corporation has 83 employees on the assembly line, each with gross earnings of $329 per week.

a. What are the total social security and Medicare taxes that should be withheld from the employee paychecks each week?

b. What is the total social security and Medicare that Hastings should send to the IRS for the first quarter of the year?

18. Mark Levin is a self-employed mechanic. Last year, he had total gross earnings of $44,260. What are Mark's quarterly social security and Medicare payments due the IRS?

19. Lizzy Losi earns $28,330 annually as a supervisor for the International Bank.

a. If the SUTA tax rate is 5.4% of the first $7,000 earned in a year, how much SUTA tax must the bank pay each year for Lizzy?

b. If the FUTA tax rate is 6.2% of the first $7,000 earned in a year minus the SUTA tax paid, how much FUTA tax must the bank pay each year for Lizzy?

20. Striker Exporting has three warehouse employees: John Abner earns $422 per week, Anne Clark earns $510 per week, and Todd Corbin earns $695 per week. The company's SUTA tax rate is 5.4%, and the FUTA rate is 6.2% minus the SUTA. As usual, these taxes are paid on the first $7,000 of each employee's earnings.

a. How much SUTA and FUTA tax does the company owe on these employees for the first quarter of the year?

b. How much SUTA and FUTA tax does Striker owe for the second quarter of the year?

12

Name ____________

Class ____________

Answers

20. a. ____________

____

b. ____________

____

21. a. ____________

b. ____________

c. ____________

21. Flamingo Developers employs 150 workers and has a gross payroll of $282,100 per week. Fringe benefits are $6\frac{1}{2}$% of gross payroll for sick days and holiday leave, 9.1% for health and hospital insurance, 4.6% for the retirement fund, and $10.70 per employee for a stock purchase plan.

a. What is the total weekly cost of fringe benefits for the company?

b. What percent of payroll does this represent?

c. What is the company's annual cost of fringe benefits?

Name ____________

Class ____________

Answers

22. a. ____________

____

b. ____________

23. a. ____________

22. Pat Ayres is self-employed with an annual salary of $86,000. Her social security tax rate is 12.4%, Medicare is 2.9%, and her estimated federal income tax rate is 14%.

    a. How much quarterly estimate tax must Pat send to the IRS each quarter?

    b. What form should she use?

BUSINESS DECISION

The Bride, the Groom, and the Taxman

23. Two of your friends, John and Carmen, have been living together for a year. John earns $3,000 per month as the manager of a Radio Shack Store. Carmen is a sophomore at college and is not currently working. They plan to marry but cannot decide whether to get married now or wait a year or two.

    After studying the payroll chapter in your business math class, you inform John that married couples generally pay less income taxes and that if they got married now instead of waiting he would have less income tax withheld from his paychecks. John's current tax filing status is single, one exemption. If he and Carmen got married he could file as married, two exemptions. Use the percentage method and Exhibits 9-2 and 9-3 to calculate the following:

    a. How much income tax is withheld from John's paycheck each month now?

b. How much income tax would be withheld from John's check if he and Carmen got married?

Name ______________________

Class ______________________

Answers

23. b. ______________________

c. ______________________

c. Assuming Carmen has 3 more years of full-time college before going to work and John expects a 10% raise in 1 year and a 15% raise the year after, what is the total 3-year tax advantage of their getting married now?

All the Math That's Fit to Learn

The Business Math Times

Volume IX | **Payroll** | One Dollar

The Payroll Function

More than 70% of the gross federal revenues of the United States, nearly $1.2 trillion, are collected through the payroll withholdings from more than 135 million workers.

Those federal revenues fund the activities relating to the safety and well-being of the American public. These include public education, national defense, interstate highways, national parks, health and human service initiatives, and social security.

In addition to paying workers accurately and on time, the payroll function plays a key roll in government programs including the enforcement of fair labor standards, child support regulations, social security taxes and benefits, unemployment insurance, and Medicare.

Tax Facts

- In 2000, the IRS received more than 125 million individual income tax returns and predicts an increase of 20 million by 2008.
- The top 1% ($270,000 income) pay about 35% of all federal personal income taxes. The top 5% ($115,000 income) pay 54%.

Social Security

The United States did not have social security on a national level until 1935, when the Social Security Act was passed as part of President Franklin Delano Roosevelt's "New Deal" program.

"Quote . . . Unquote"

Don't just make a living, design a life
—*Jim Rohn*

If you aren't fired with enthusiasm, you'll be fired with enthusiasm
—*Vince Lombardi*

The act established two social insurance programs: a federal-state program of unemployment compensation and a federal program of old-age retirement insurance. The compulsory old-age insurance pays benefits proportionate to prior earnings for persons over 65.

The rate of the tax was originally set at 1% with a $3,000 wage base limit. Increases in social security retirement benefits and wage bases are tied to increases in the Consumer Price Index.

If you are age 25 or older and have ever worked in a job covered by social security, you should be receiving your social security statement every year; about three months before your birthday.

The burden is on you to check that the Social Security Administration has your correct records and that you will receive the proper amount of benefits. The agency can tell you right now what your projected benefit will be.

To check out your records, visit www.ssa.gov or call the toll free SSA line at 1-800-772-1213.

Medicare

In 1965, Congress enacted the Medicare program providing medical benefits for persons over the age of 65, and an accompanying Medicaid program for the indigent, regardless of age. The initial tax rate was .35%.

Medicare is funded by a 1.45% tax on the earnings of employees; that amount is matched by the employer. Over 40 million Americans are enrolled in Medicare. Expenditures today exceed $200 billion per year.

Top 10 Employers in the U.S.

	Employer	Employees
1.	Wal-Mart	1,244,000
2.	General Motors	386,000
3.	United Parcel Service	359,000
4.	Ford Motor	345,991
5.	General Electric	341,000
6.	Sears, Roebuck and Co.	323,000
7.	IBM	316,303
8.	JCPenney	267,000
9.	Kmart	252,000
10.	Citigroup	237,500

For additional information, visit our web site at: www.contemporarymath.com

Brainteaser

THE JOB OFFER

A painter agrees to work under the condition that he is paid $55.00 for every day he works, and he must pay $66.00 for every day he does not work. At the end of 30 days, he has earned $924.00. How many days did he work?

ANSWER TO LAST ISSUE'S BRAINTEASER

$96.00

Because 25% is equivalent to $\frac{1}{4}$, you are looking for the largest multiple of 4 that is less than 100.

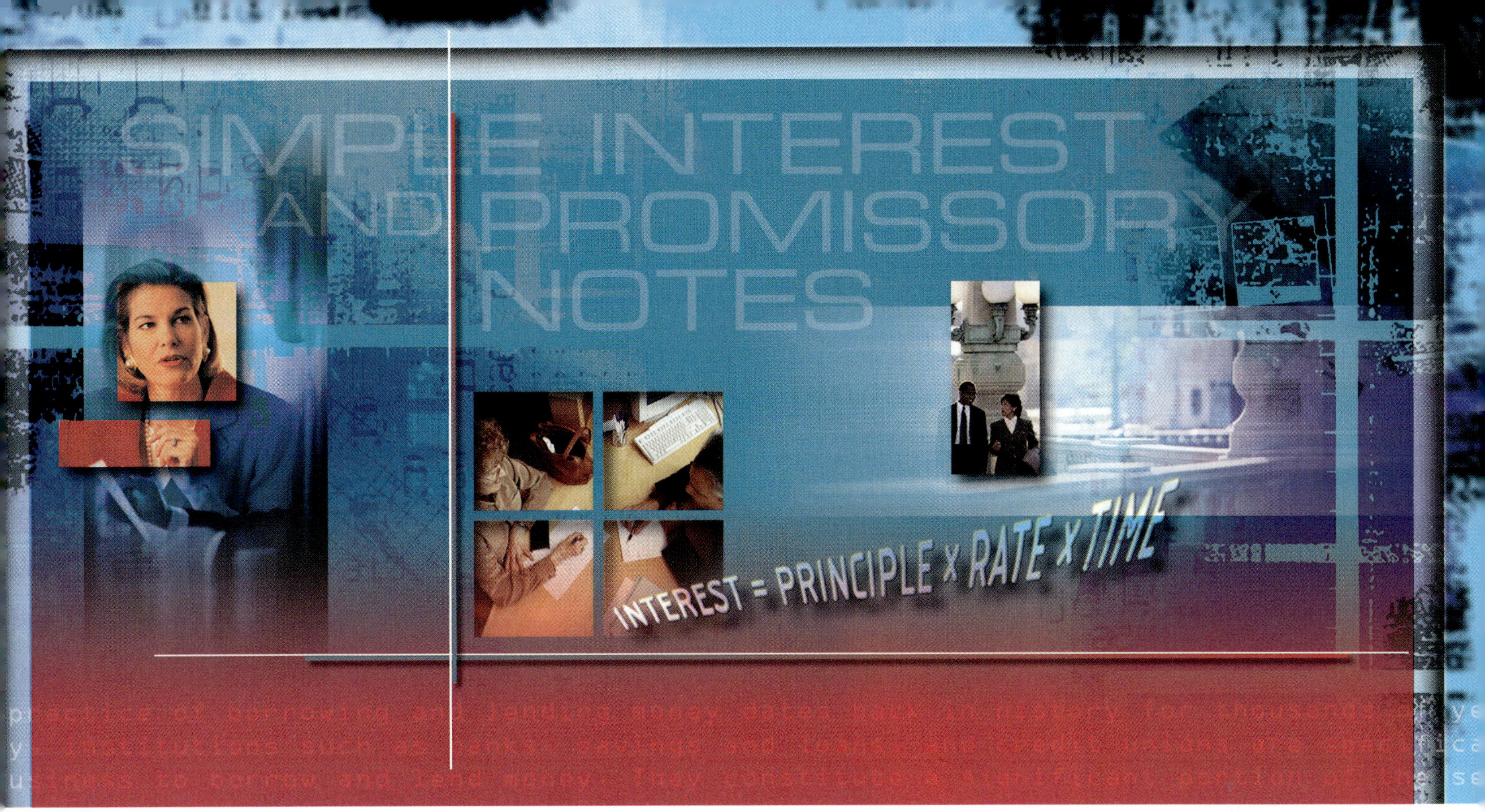

CHAPTER

10

Simple Interest and Promissory Notes

PERFORMANCE OBJECTIVES

Section I Understanding and Computing Simple Interest

10-1 Computing simple interest for loans with terms of years or months. (p. 340)
10-2 Calculating simple interest for loans with terms of days by using the exact interest and ordinary interest methods. (p. 342)
10-3 Calculating the maturity value of a loan. (p. 343)
10-4 Calculating the number of days of a loan. (p. 344)
10-5 Determining the maturity date of a loan. (p. 345)

Section II Using the Simple Interest Formula

10-6 Solving for the principal. (p. 349)
10-7 Solving for the rate. (p. 350)
10-8 Solving for the time. (p. 351)
10-9 Calculating loans involving partial payments before maturity. (p. 352)

Section III Understanding Promissory Notes and Discounting

10-10 Calculating bank discount and proceeds for simple discount notes. (p. 359)
10-11 Calculating true or effective rate of interest for a simple discount note. (p. 360)
10-12 Discounting notes before maturity. (p. 361)

SECTION I

UNDERSTANDING AND COMPUTING SIMPLE INTEREST

The practice of borrowing and lending money dates back in history for thousands of years. Today, institutions such as banks, savings and loans, and credit unions are specifically in business to borrow and lend money. They constitute a significant portion of the service sector of the American economy.

interest
The price or rental fee charged by a lender to a borrower for the use of money.

principal
A sum of money, either invested or borrowed, on which interest is calculated.

rate
The percent that is charged or earned for the use of money per year.

time
Length of time, expressed in days, months, or years, of an investment or loan.

simple interest
Interest calculated solely on the principal amount borrowed or invested. It is calculated only *once* for the entire time period of the loan.

compound interest
Interest, calculated at regular intervals, on the principal and previously earned interest. Covered in Chapter 11.

Interest is the rental fee charged by a lender to a business or individual for the use of money. The amount of interest charged is determined by three factors: the amount of money being borrowed or invested, known as the **principal;** the percent of interest charged on the money per year, known as the **rate;** and the length of time of the loan, known as **time.** The manner in which the interest is computed is an additional factor that influences the amount of interest. The two most commonly used methods in business today for computing interest are simple and compound.

Simple interest means that the interest is calculated *only once* for the entire time period of the loan. At the end of the time period, the borrower repays the principal plus the interest. Simple interest loans are usually made for short periods of time, such as a few days, weeks, or months. **Compound interest** means that the interest is calculated *more than once* during the time period of the loan. When compound interest is applied to a loan, each succeeding time period accumulates interest on the previous interest, in addition to interest on the principal. Compound interest loans are generally for time periods of a year or longer.

This chapter discusses the concepts of simple interest; simple discount, which is a variation of a simple interest loan; and promissory notes. Chapter 11 covers the concepts and calculations related to compound interest and present value.

10-1 Computing Simple Interest for Loans with Terms of Years or Months

Simple interest is calculated by using a formula known as the simple interest formula. It is stated as

$$\text{Interest} = \text{Principal} \times \text{Rate} \times \text{Time}$$

$$I = PRT$$

When using the simple interest formula, the time factor, T, must be expressed in years or a fraction of a year.

Banking institutions all over the world are in business specifically to borrow and lend money, at a profitable rate of interest.

SIMPLE INTEREST FORMULA—YEARS OR MONTHS

YEARS

When the time period of a loan is a year or longer, use the number of years as the time factor, converting fractional parts to decimals. For example, the time factor for a 2-year loan is 2, 3 years is 3, $1\frac{1}{2}$ years is 1.5, and $4\frac{3}{4}$ years is 4.75.

MONTHS

When the time period of a loan is for a specified number of months, express the time factor as a fraction of a year. The number of months is the numerator, and 12 months (1 year) is the denominator. A loan for 1 month would have a time factor of $\frac{1}{12}$, a loan for 2 months would have factor of $\frac{2}{12}$ or $\frac{1}{6}$, a 5-month loan would use $\frac{5}{12}$ as the factor, a loan for 18 months would use $\frac{18}{12}$ or $1\frac{1}{2}$, written as 1.5.

Everybody's Business

Real-World Connection

Business and personal financial decisions involve a concept known as *opportunity cost.* Like time, money used in one way cannot be used in other ways. Financial choices are always a series of "trade-offs."

If you buy a car with your savings, you give up the interest that money could earn. If you invest the money, you don't get the car. If you borrow money to buy the car, you have to pay interest for its use.

When making financial choices such as saving, spending, investing, or borrowing, you should consider the interest-earning ability of that money as an opportunity cost.

EXAMPLE

What is the amount of interest for a loan of $8,000, at 9% interest, for 1 year?

SOLUTION STRATEGY

To solve this problem, we apply the simple interest formula,

$$\text{Interest} = \text{Principal} \times \text{Rate} \times \text{Time}$$

$$\text{Interest} = 8{,}000 \times 9\% \times 1$$

$$\text{Interest} = 8{,}000 \times .09 \times 1$$

$$\text{Interest} = \underline{\underline{\$720}}$$

EXAMPLE

What is the amount of interest for a loan of $16,500, at $12\frac{1}{2}$% interest, for 7 months?

SOLUTION STRATEGY

In this example, the rate is converted to .125, and the time factor is expressed as a fraction of a year, $\frac{7}{12}$.

$$\text{Interest} = \text{Principal} \times \text{Rate} \times \text{Time}$$

$$\text{Interest} = 16{,}500 \times .125 \times \frac{7}{12}$$

$$\text{Interest} = \underline{\underline{\$1{,}203.13}}$$

Calculator Sequence: 16500 [×] .125 [×] 7 [÷] 12 [=] $\underline{\underline{\$1{,}203.13}}$

TRY-IT EXERCISES

Find the amount of interest on each of the following loans:

	Principal	Rate (%)	Time
1.	$4,000	7	$2\frac{1}{4}$ years
2.	$45,000	$9\frac{3}{4}$	3 months
3.	$130,000	10.4	42 months

Check your answers with the solutions on page 370.

10-2 Calculating Simple Interest for Loans with Terms of Days by Using the Exact Interest and Ordinary Interest Methods

There are two methods for calculating the time factor, *T,* when applying the simple interest formula using days. Because time must be expressed in years, loans whose terms are given in days must be made into a fractional part of a year. This is done by dividing the days of a loan by the number of days in a year.

exact interest
Interest calculation method using 365 days (366 in leap year) as the time factor denominator.

ordinary interest, or banker's rule
Interest calculation method using 360 days as the time factor denominator.

SIMPLE INTEREST FORMULA—DAYS

EXACT INTEREST

The first method for calculating the time factor is known as **exact interest.** Exact interest uses *365 days* as the time factor denominator. This method is used by government agencies, the Federal Reserve Bank, and most credit unions.

$$\text{Time} = \frac{\text{Number of days of a loan}}{365}$$

ORDINARY INTEREST

The second method for calculating the time factor is known as **ordinary interest.** Ordinary interest uses *360 days* as the denominator of the time factor. This method dates back to the time before electronic calculators and computers. In the past, when calculating the time factor manually, a denominator of 360 was easier to use than 365.

Regardless of today's electronic sophistication, banks and most other lending institutions still use ordinary interest because it yields a somewhat higher amount of interest than the exact interest method. Over the years, ordinary interest has become known as the **banker's rule.**

$$\text{Time} = \frac{\text{Number of days of a loan}}{360}$$

EXAMPLE

Using the exact interest method, what is the amount of interest on a loan of $4,000, at 7% interest, for 88 days?

SOLUTION STRATEGY

Because we are looking for exact interest, we will use 365 days as the denominator of the time factor in the simple interest formula:

$$\text{Interest} = \text{Principal} \times \text{Rate} \times \text{Time}$$

$$\text{Interest} = 4{,}000 \times .07 \times \frac{88}{365}$$

$$\text{Interest} = 67.506849$$

$$\text{Interest} = \underline{\underline{\$67.51}}$$

Calculator Sequence: 4000 [×] .07 [×] 88 [÷] 365 [=] $\underline{\underline{\$67.51}}$

EXAMPLE

Using the ordinary interest method, what is the amount of interest on a loan of $19,500, at 12% interest, for 160 days?

SOLUTION STRATEGY

Because we are looking for ordinary interest, we will use 360 days as the denominator of the time factor in the simple interest formula:

$$\text{Interest} = \text{Principal} \times \text{Rate} \times \text{Time}$$

$$\text{Interest} = 19{,}500 \times .12 \times \frac{160}{360}$$

$$\text{Interest} = \underline{\underline{\$1{,}040.00}}$$

Calculator Sequence: 19500 [×] .12 [×] 160 [÷] 360 [=] $\underline{\underline{\$1{,}040.00}}$

TRY-IT | EXERCISES

4. Sandra Miller goes to the bank and borrows \$15,000, at $9\frac{1}{2}$%, for 250 days. If the bank uses the ordinary interest method, how much interest will Sandra have to pay?

5. David Hall goes to a credit union and borrows \$23,000, at 8%, for 119 days. If the credit union calculates interest by the exact interest method, what is the amount of interest on the loan?

Check your answers with the solutions on page 370.

10-3 Calculating the Maturity Value of a Loan

When the time period of a loan is over, the loan is said to mature. At that time, the borrower repays the original principal plus the interest. The total payback of principal and interest is known as the **maturity value** of a loan. Once the interest has been calculated, the maturity value can be found by using the formula:

maturity value
The total payback of principal and interest of an investment or loan.

Maturity value = Principal + Interest

$$MV = P + I$$

For example, if a loan for \$50,000 had interest of \$8,600, the maturity value would be found by adding the principal and the interest: 50,000 + 8,600 = \$58,600.

Maturity value can also be calculated directly, without first calculating the interest, by using the following formula:

Maturity value = Principal (1 + Rate × Time)

$$MV = P(1 + RT)$$

> **Everybody's Business**
> **Learning Tip**
> When using the maturity value formula, $MV = P(1 + RT)$, the order of operation is
> - Multiply rate times time
> - Add the 1
> - Multiply by the principal

EXAMPLE

What is the maturity value of a loan for \$25,000, at 11%, for $2\frac{1}{2}$ years?

SOLUTION STRATEGY

Because this example asks for the maturity value, not the amount of interest, we shall use the formula for finding maturity value directly, $MV = P(1 + RT)$. Remember to multiply the rate and time first, then add the 1. Note that the time, $2\frac{1}{2}$ years, should be converted to the decimal equivalent 2.5 for ease in calculation.

$$\text{Maturity value} = \text{Principal } (1 + \text{Rate} \times \text{Time})$$

$$\text{Maturity value} = 25{,}000(1 + .11 \times 2.5)$$

$$\text{Maturity value} = 25{,}000(1 + .275)$$

$$\text{Maturity value} = 25{,}000(1.275)$$

$$\text{Maturity value} = \underline{\underline{\$31{,}875}}$$

TRY-IT | EXERCISES

6. What is the amount of interest and the maturity value of a loan for \$15,400, at $6\frac{1}{2}$% simple interest, for 24 months? (Use the formula $MV = P + I$.)

7. Precision Air Taxi Service borrowed \$450,000, at 8% simple interest, for 9 months, to purchase a new airplane. Use the formula $MV = P(1 + RT)$ to find the maturity value of the loan.

Check your answers with the solutions on page 370.

10-4 Calculating the Number of Days of a Loan

loan date
The first day of a loan.

due date, or maturity date
The last day of a loan.

The first day of a loan is known as the **loan date** and the last day is known as the **due date** or **maturity date.** When these dates are known, the number of days of the loan can be calculated by using the days in each month chart and the steps that follow:

Days in Each Month

28 Days	30 Days	31 Days
February	April	January
(29 leap year)	June	March
	September	May
	November	July
		August
		October
		December

STEPS FOR DETERMINING THE NUMBER OF DAYS OF A LOAN:

Step 1. Determine the number of days remaining in the first month by subtracting the loan date from the number of days in that month.

Step 2. List the number of days for each succeeding whole month.

Step 3. List the number of loan days in the last month.

Step 4. Add the days from Steps 1, 2, and 3.

Everybody's Business

Learning Tip

An alternate method for calculating the number of days of a loan is to use the Days-in-a-Year Calendar, Exhibit 7-6, page 236.

Subtract the "day number" of the loan date from the "day number" of the maturity date. If the maturity date is in the next year, add 365 to that day number, then subtract. *Note:* In leap years, add 1 to the day numbers, beginning with March 1.

EXAMPLE

Claudia Ruiz borrowed money from the Capital Bank on August 18 and repaid the loan on November 27. For how many days was this loan?

SOLUTION STRATEGY

The number of days from August 18 to November 27 would be calculated as follows:

Step 1.	Days remaining in first month	Aug. 31		
		Aug. − 18		
		13 →	August	13 days
Step 2.	Days in succeeding whole months →		September	30 days
			October	31 days
Step 3.	Days of loan in last month →		November	+ 27 days
Step 4.	Add the days		Total	101 days

TRY-IT | EXERCISES

8. A loan was made on April 4 and had a due date of July 18. What is the number of days of the loan?

9. Ben Rakusin borrowed $3,500 on June 15, at 11% interest. If the loan was due on October 9, what was the amount of interest on Ben's loan using the exact interest method?

Check your answers with the solutions on page 370.

10-5 Determining the Maturity Date of a Loan

When the loan date and number of days of the loan are known, the maturity date can be found as follows:

Everybody's Business

Learning Tip

An alternate method for calculating the maturity date of a loan is to use the Days-in-a-Year Calendar, Exhibit 7-6, page 236. Follow the steps for finding a future date, page 236.

STEPS FOR DETERMINING THE MATURITY DATE OF A LOAN:

Step 1. Find the number of days remaining in the first month by subtracting the loan date from the number of days in that month.

Step 2. Subtract the days remaining in the first month (Step 1) from the number of days of the loan.

Step 3. Continue subtracting the number of days in each succeeding whole month, until you reach a month in which the difference is less than the total days in that month. At that point, the maturity date will be the day of that month that corresponds to the difference.

EXAMPLE

What is the maturity date of a loan that was taken out on April 14 for 85 days?

SOLUTION STRATEGY

Step 1.	Days remaining in first month	30	Days in April
		− 14	Loan date April 14
	Days remaining in April	16	

Step 2. Subtract remaining days in first month from days of the loan		85	Days of the loan
		− 16	Days remaining in April
	Difference	69	
Step 3. Subtract succeeding whole months		69	Difference
		− 31	Days in May
	Difference	38	
		38	Difference
		− 30	Days in June
	Difference	8	

At this point, the difference, 8, is less than the number of days in the next month, July, therefore the maturity date is July 8.

TRY-IT | EXERCISES

10. What is the maturity date of a loan taken out on September 9 for 125 days?

Everybody's Business
Real-World Connection
In business, due dates that fall on weekends or holidays are commonly advanced to the next business day.

11. On October 21, Anita Louise went to the Castle Rock Bank and took out a loan for $9,000, at 10% ordinary interest, for 80 days. What is the maturity value and maturity date of this loan?

Check your answers with the solutions on page 370.

REVIEW EXERCISES | CHAPTER 10—SECTION I

Find the amount of interest on each of the following loans:

	Principal	Rate (%)	Time	Interest
1.	$5,000	8	2 years	______
2.	$75,000	$10\frac{3}{4}$	6 months	______
3.	$100,000	12.7	18 months	______
4.	$80,000	15	$3\frac{1}{2}$ years	______
5.	$6,440	$5\frac{1}{2}$	7 months	______
6.	$13,200	9.2	$4\frac{3}{4}$ years	______

Use the exact interest method (365 days) and the ordinary interest method (360 days) to compare the amount of interest for the following loans:

	Principal	Rate (%)	Time (days)	Exact Interest	Ordinary Interest
7.	$45,000	13	100	______	______
8.	$184,500	$15\frac{1}{2}$	58	______	______
9.	$32,400	8.6	241	______	______
10.	$7,230	9	18	______	______
11.	$900	$10\frac{1}{4}$	60	______	______
12.	$100,000	10	1	______	______

13. $2,500	12	74	________	________
14. $350	14.1	230	________	________
15. $50,490	$9\frac{1}{4}$	69	________	________
16. $486,000	$13\frac{1}{2}$	127	________	________

Find the amount of interest and the maturity value of the following loans (use the formula $MV = P + I$ to find the maturity values):

Principal	Rate (%)	Time	Interest	Maturity Value
17. $54,000	11.9	2 years	________	________
18. $125,000	$12\frac{1}{2}$	5 months	________	________
19. $33,750	8.4	10 months	________	________
20. $91,000	$9\frac{1}{4}$	$2\frac{1}{2}$ years	________	________

Find the maturity value of the following loans (use $MV = P(1 + RT)$ to find the maturity values):

Principal	Rate (%)	Time	Maturity Value
21. $1,500	9	2 years	________
22. $18,620	$10\frac{1}{2}$	30 months	________
23. $1,000,000	11	3 years	________
24. $750,000	13.35	11 months	________

From the following information, determine the number of days of each loan:

Loan Date	Due Date	Number of Days
25. September 5	December 12	________
26. June 27	October 15	________
27. January 23	November 8	________
28. March 9	July 30	________

From the following information, determine the maturity date of each loan:

Loan Date	Time of Loan (days)	Maturity Date
29. October 19	45	________
30. February 5	110	________
31. May 26	29	________
32. July 21	200	________
33. December 6	79	________

Solve the following word problems:

34. On April 12, Sharon Meyer borrowed $5,000 from her credit union at 9% for 80 days. The credit union uses the ordinary interest method.

a. What is the amount of interest on the loan?

b. What is the maturity value of the loan?

c. What is the maturity date of the loan?

35. What is the maturity value of a $60,000 loan, for 100 days, at 12.2% interest, using the exact interest method?

36. Playtime Toys borrowed $350,000 at 9% interest on July 19 for 120 days.

    a. If the bank uses the ordinary interest method, what is the amount of interest on the loan?

    b. What is the maturity date?

37. Brady Black missed an income tax payment of $9,000. The Internal Revenue Service charges a 13% simple interest penalty calculated by the exact interest method. If the tax was due on April 15 but was paid on August 19, what is the amount of the penalty charge?

BUSINESS DECISION

Competing Banks

38. You are the accounting manager for Eurostyle, Inc., a manufacturer of men's and women's clothing. The company needs to borrow $1,800,000 for 90 days in order to purchase a large quantity of material at "closeout" prices. The interest rate for such loans at your bank, Century Bank, is 11%, using ordinary interest.

    a. What is the amount of interest on this loan?

    b. After making a few "shopping" calls, you find that Metro Bank will lend at 11%, using exact interest. What is the amount of interest on this offer?

c. In order to keep your business, Century Bank has counteroffered with a loan at 10.5%, using ordinary interest. What is the amount of interest on this offer?

d. (Challenge) If Metro wants to beat Century's last offer (part **c**) by charging $1,250 less interest, what rate, rounded to hundredths, must they quote, using exact interest?

SECTION II

USING THE SIMPLE INTEREST FORMULA

In Section I, we used the simple interest formula, $I = PRT$, to solve for the interest. Frequently in business, however, the principal, rate, or time might be the unknown factor. Remember from Chapter 5 that an equation can be solved for any of the variables by isolating that variable to one side of the equation. In this section, we convert the simple interest formula to equations that solve for each of the other variable factors.

If you find this procedure difficult or hard to remember, use the Magic Triangle, as we did in Chapter 6, to calculate the portion, rate, and base. Remember, to use the Magic Triangle, cover the variable you are solving for and the new formula will "magically" appear!

Magic Triangle
Simple Interest Formula

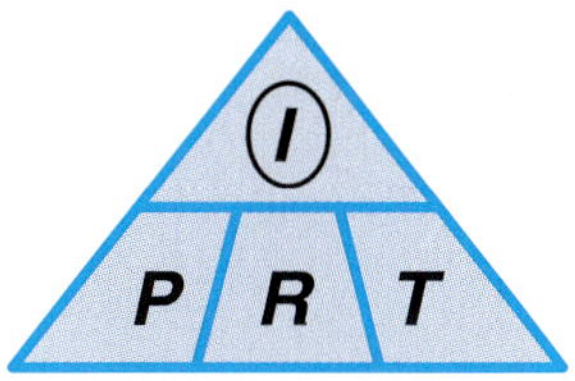

$$I = PRT$$

10-6 Solving for the Principal

When using the simple interest formula to solve for principal, P, we isolate the P on one side of the equation by dividing both sides of the equation by RT. This yields the new equation:

$$\text{Principal} = \frac{\text{Interest}}{\text{Rate} \times \text{Time}} \qquad P = \frac{I}{RT}$$

We can also find the formula in the Magic Triangle by covering the unknown variable, P, as follows:

Magic Triangle
Solving for Principal

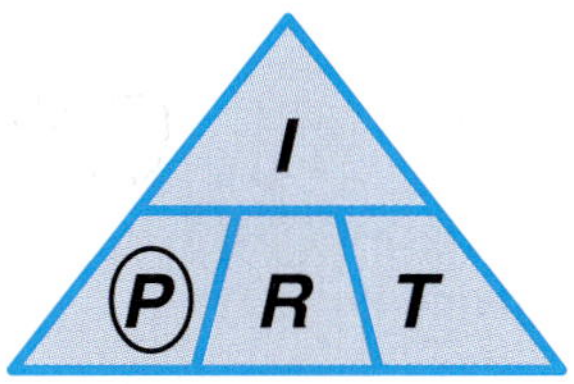

$$P = \frac{I}{RT}$$

Everybody's Business

Learning Tip

This formula provides a good opportunity to use your calculator's memory keys. Use M+ to store a number in memory, and MR to retrieve it.

Some financial and scientific calculators use STO (store) and RCL (recall) keys for the memory function.

EXAMPLE

A bank loaned a business money at 8% interest for 90 days. If the amount of interest was \$4,000, use the ordinary interest method to find the amount of principal borrowed.

SOLUTION STRATEGY

To solve for the principal, we use the formula $P = \dfrac{I}{RT}$.

$P = \dfrac{I}{RT}$	Substitute the known variables into the equation.
$P = \dfrac{4{,}000}{.08 \times \dfrac{90}{360}}$	Calculate the denominator first. Calculator sequence: .08 × 90 ÷ 360 M+
$P = \dfrac{4{,}000}{.02}$	Next, divide the numerator by the denominator. Calculator sequence: 4000 ÷ MR = 200,000
Principal = \$200,000	The company borrowed \$200,000 from the bank.

TRY-IT | EXERCISE

12. Walzer Industries borrowed money at 9% interest for 125 days. If the interest charge was \$560, use the ordinary interest method to calculate the amount of principal of the loan.

Check your answer with the solution on page 370.

10-7 Solving for the Rate

When solving the simple formula for rate, the answer will be a decimal that must be converted to a percent. In business, interest rates are always expressed as a percent.

When the rate is the unknown variable, we isolate the R on one side of the equation by dividing both sides of the equation by PT. This yields the new equation:

$$\text{Rate} = \frac{\text{Interest}}{\text{Principal} \times \text{Time}} \qquad R = \frac{I}{PT}$$

We can also find the formula in the Magic Triangle by covering the unknown variable, R, as follows:

Magic Triangle
Solving for Rate

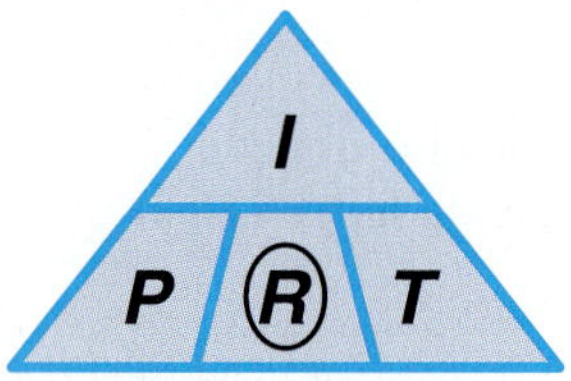

$$R = \frac{I}{PT}$$

EXAMPLE

What is the rate of interest on a loan of $5,000, for 125 days, if the amount of interest is $166, using the ordinary interest method? Round your answer to the nearest hundredth percent.

SOLUTION STRATEGY

To solve for the rate, we use the formula $R = \frac{I}{PT}$.

$R = \frac{I}{PT}$ — Substitute the known variables into the equation.

$R = \frac{166}{5{,}000 \times \frac{125}{360}}$ — Calculate the denominator first.

Calculator sequence: 5000 × 125 ÷ 360 M+

$R = \frac{166}{1{,}736.1111}$ — Next, divide the numerator by the denominator. *Note:* Don't round the denominator. Calculator sequence: 166 ÷ MR = .095616

$R = .095616$ — Round the answer to the nearest hundredth percent.

Rate = 9.56% — The bank charged 9.56% interest.

TRY-IT | EXERCISE

13. What is the rate of interest on a loan of $25,000, for 245 days, if the amount of interest is $1,960, using the ordinary interest method? Round your answer to the nearest hundredth percent.

Check your answer with the solution on page 370.

10-8 Solving for the Time

When solving the simple interest formula for time, a whole number in the answer represents years and a decimal represents a portion of a year. The decimal should be converted to days by multiplying it by 360 for ordinary interest or by 365 for exact interest.

For example, an answer of 3 means 3 years. An answer of 3.23 means 3 years and .23 of the next year. Assuming ordinary interest, multiply the decimal portion of the answer, .23, by 360. This gives 82.8, which represents the number of days. The total time of the loan would be 3 years and 83 days.

When using the simple interest formula to solve for time, *T*, we isolate the *T* on one side of the equation by dividing both sides of the equation by *PR*. This yields the new equation:

$$\text{Time} = \frac{\text{Interest}}{\text{Principal} \times \text{Rate}} \qquad T = \frac{I}{PR}$$

We can also find the formula in the Magic Triangle by covering the unknown variable, *T*, as follows:

Magic Triangle
Solving for Time

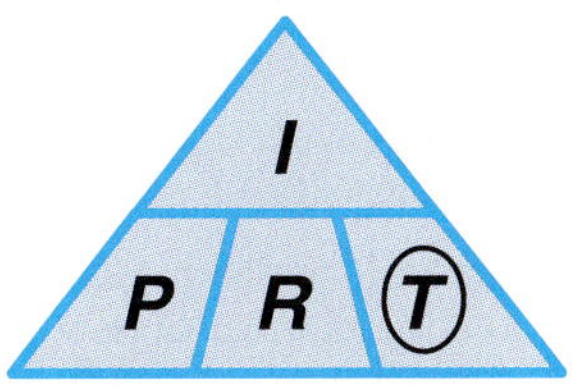

$$T = \frac{I}{PR}$$

> **Everybody's Business**
> **Learning Tip**
> Lending institutions consider any part of a day to be a full day. When calculating time, *T*, any fraction of a day is rounded up to the next higher day, even if it is less than .5.
> For example, 25.1 days would round up to 26 days.

EXAMPLE

What would be the time period of a loan for $7,600, at 11% ordinary interest, if the amount of interest is $290?

SOLUTION STRATEGY

To solve for the time, we use the formula $T = \frac{I}{PR}$.

$T = \frac{I}{PR}$	Substitute the known variables into the equation.
$T = \frac{290}{7{,}600 \times .11}$	Calculate the denominator first. Calculator sequence: 7600 [×] .11 [M+]
$T = \frac{290}{836}$	Next, divide the numerator by the denominator. Calculator sequence: 290 [÷] [MR] [=] .3468899
$T = .3468899$ years	Because the answer is a decimal, the time is less than 1 year. Using ordinary interest, we multiply the entire decimal by 360 to find the number of days of the loan.
$T = .3468899 \times 360$	Remember, do not round off; use the entire decimal.
Time = 124.8 or <u>125 days</u>	

TRY-IT | EXERCISE

14. What is the time period of a loan for $15,000, at 9.5% ordinary interest, if the amount of interest is $650?

Check your answer with the solution on page 370.

10-9 Calculating Loans Involving Partial Payments before Maturity

U.S. rule
Method for distributing early partial payments of a loan, whereby the payment is first used to pay off the accumulated interest to date, with the balance used to reduce the principal.

Frequently, businesses and individuals who have borrowed money for a specified length of time find that they want to save some interest by making one or more partial payments on the loan before the maturity date. The most commonly used method for this calculation is known as the **U.S. rule.** The rule states that when a partial payment is made on a loan, the payment is first used to pay off the accumulated interest to date, and the balance is used to reduce the principal. In this application, the ordinary interest method (360 days) will be used for all calculations.

STEPS FOR CALCULATING MATURITY VALUE OF A LOAN AFTER ONE OR MORE PARTIAL PAYMENTS:

Step 1. Using the simple interest formula, with *ordinary* interest, compute the amount of interest due from the date of the loan to the date of the partial payment.

Step 2. Subtract the interest from Step 1 from the partial payment. This pays the interest to date.

Step 3. Subtract the balance of the partial payment, after Step 2, from the original principal of the loan. This gives the new adjusted principal.

Step 4. If another partial payment is made, repeat Steps 1, 2, and 3, using the adjusted principal and the number of days since the last partial payment.

Step 5. After all partial payments have been credited to the loan, the maturity value is computed by adding the interest since the last partial payment to the adjusted principal.

Everybody's Business
Learning Tip
Remember to use *ordinary interest,* 360 days, for all calculations involving partial payments.

EXAMPLE

Ivan Figueroa borrowed $10,000 at 9% interest for 120 days. On day 30, Ivan made a partial payment of $2,000. On day 70, he made a second partial payment of $3,000. What is the final amount due on the loan?

SOLUTION STRATEGY

To help you visualize the details of a loan with partial payments, construct a time-line such as the one illustrated in Exhibit 10-1.

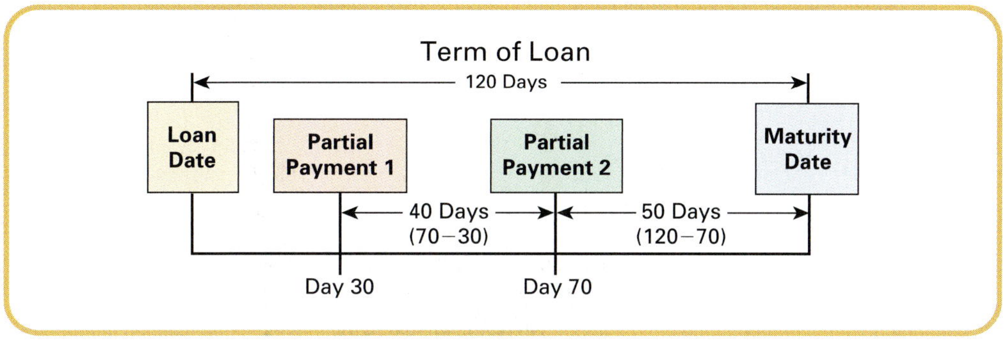

✦ EXHIBIT 10-1 ✦
Partial Payment Time Line

Step 1. Compute the interest from the date of the loan to the partial payment. In this problem, the first partial payment was made on day 30.

$$I = PRT$$

$$I = 10{,}000 \times .09 \times \frac{30}{360} = 75$$

$$I = \$75.00$$

Step 2. Subtract the interest from the partial payment.

$2,000 partial payment
− 75 accumulated interest
$1,925 amount of partial payment left to reduce the principal

Step 3. Reduce the principal.

$10,000 original principal
− 1,925 amount of partial payment used to reduce principal
$8,075 new adjusted principal

Step 4. A second partial payment of $3,000 was made on day 70. We now repeat Steps 1, 2, and 3 to properly credit the second partial payment. Remember, use the new adjusted principal and 40 days (70 − 30 = 40) for this calculation.

Step 1.

$$I = PRT$$

$$I = \$8{,}075 \times .09 \times \frac{40}{360}$$

$I = \$80.75$ accumulated interest since last partial payment

Step 2.

$3,000.00 partial payment
− 80.75 accumulated interest
$2,919.25 amount of partial payment left to reduce the principal

Step 3.

$8,075.00	principal
− 2,919.25	amount of partial payment used to reduce principal
$5,155.75	new adjusted principal

Step 5. Once all partial payments have been credited, we find the maturity value of the loan by calculating the interest due from the last partial payment to the maturity date and adding it to the last adjusted principal. *Note:* The last partial payment was made on day 70 of the loan, therefore, 50 days remain on the loan (120 − 70 = 50 days).

$$I = PRT$$

$$I = \$5{,}155.75 \times .09 \times \frac{50}{360}$$

$I = \$64.45$ interest from last partial payment to maturity date

Maturity Value = Principal + Interest

Maturity Value = $5,155.75 + $64.45

Maturity Value = $5,220.20

TRY-IT | EXERCISE

15. Staci Shanahan borrowed $15,000 at 12% ordinary interest for 100 days. On day 20 of the loan, she made a partial payment of $4,000. On day 60, she made another partial payment of $5,000. What is the final amount due on the loan?

Check your answer with the solution on page 370.

REVIEW EXERCISES | CHAPTER 10—SECTION II

Compute the principal for the following loans (use ordinary interest when time is stated in days):

	Principal	Rate (%)	Time	Interest
1.	________	12	2 years	$300
2.	________	9	$1\frac{1}{2}$ years	$675
3.	________	8	9 months	$3,000
4.	________	10.7	90 days	$5,350
5.	________	13.1	210 days	$917

Compute the rate for the following loans (round answers to the nearest tenth percent; use ordinary interest when time is stated in days):

	Principal	Rate (%)	Time	Interest
6.	$5,000	________	3 years	$1,200
7.	$1,800	________	5 months	$105
8.	$48,000	________	60 days	$728
9.	$4,600	________	168 days	$275
10.	$125,000	________	2 years	$18,750

Use the ordinary interest method to compute the time for the following loans (round answers to the next higher day, when necessary):

	Principal	Rate (%)	Time	Interest
11.	$18,000	12	________	$948
12.	$7,900	10.4	________	$228
13.	$4,500	$9\frac{3}{4}$	________	$375
14.	$25,000	8.9	________	$4,450
15.	$680	15	________	$51

Calculate the missing information for the following loans (round percents to the nearest tenth and days to the next higher day, when necessary):

	Principal	Rate (%)	Time (days)	Interest Method	Interest	Maturity Value
16.	$16,000	13	________	Ordinary	$760	________
17.	________	9.5	100	Exact	$340	________
18.	$3,600	_____	160	Exact	$225	________
19.	$25,500	$11\frac{1}{4}$	300	Ordinary	________	________
20.	________	10.4	________	Exact	$4,000	$59,000

Solve the following word problems:

21. Williamson Motors, a Chevrolet dealership, borrowed $225,000 on April 16 to purchase a shipment of new cars. The interest rate was 9.3% using the ordinary interest method. The amount of interest was $9,600. 3

a. For how many days was the loan?

b. What was the maturity date of the loan?

22. Steven Teeter took out a loan for $3,500 at the Fortune Bank for 270 days. If the bank uses the ordinary interest method, what rate of interest was charged if the amount of interest was $269? Round your answer to the nearest tenth percent. 1

23. Kathleen Murphrey borrowed money to buy a car at 13.5% simple interest from her credit union. If the loan was repaid in 2 years and the amount of interest was $2,700, how much did Kathleen borrow? 2

24. What is the maturity date of a loan for $5,000, at 15% exact interest, taken out on June 3? The amount of interest on the loan was $150.

25. What rate of interest was charged on an ordinary interest loan for $135,000, if the interest was $4,400 and the time period was from January 16 to April 27? Round your answer to the nearest tenth percent.

26. Rossen Garcia deposited $8,000 in a savings account paying 6.25% simple interest. How long will it take for her investment to amount to $10,000?

27. Don Boyer borrowed $10,000 at 12% ordinary interest for 60 days. On day 20 of the loan, Don made a partial payment of $4,000. What is the new maturity value of the loan?

28. Standard Plumbing Supplies borrowed $60,000 on March 15 for 90 days. The rate was 13% using the ordinary interest method. On day 25 of the loan, Standard made a partial payment of $16,000, and on day 55 of the loan Standard made a second partial payment of $12,000.

a. What is the new maturity value of the loan?

b. What is the maturity date of the loan?

29. a. How many years will it take $5,000 invested at 8% simple interest to double to $10,000?

b. How long will it take if the interest rate is increased to 10%?

BUSINESS DECISION

The Opportunity Cost

30. You are the owner of four Speedy Auto Lube locations. You have a business loan with Continental Bank taken out 60 days ago, and due in 90 days. The amount of the loan is $40,000, and the rate is 9.5%, using ordinary interest.

You currently have some excess cash. You have the choice of sending Continental $25,000 now as a partial payment on your loan, or purchasing $25,000 of motor oil and filters for your inventory at a special discount price that is "10% off" your normal cost of these items.

a. How much interest will you save on this loan if you make the partial payment and don't buy the merchandise?

b. How much will you save by purchasing the discounted merchandise and not making the partial payment?

c. (Optional) What other factors should you consider before making this decision?

SECTION III

UNDERSTANDING PROMISSORY NOTES AND DISCOUNTING

promissory note
A debt instrument in which one party agrees to repay money to another, within a specified period of time. Promissory notes may be noninterest-bearing, at no interest, or interest-bearing, at a specified rate of interest.

Technically, the document that states the details of a loan, and is signed by the borrower, is known as a **promissory note.** *Promissory* means it is a promise to pay the principal back to the lender on a certain date. *Note* means that the document is a negotiable instrument and can be transferred or sold to others not involved in the original loan. Much like a check, with proper endorsement by the payee, the note can be transferred to another person, company, or lending institution.

Promissory notes are either noninterest-bearing or interest-bearing. When a note is noninterest-bearing, the maturity value equals the principal, because there is no interest being charged. With interest-bearing notes, the maturity value equals the principal plus the interest.

Exhibit 10-2 is an example of a typical promissory note with its parts labeled. Notice the similarity between a note and a check. A list explaining the labels follows.

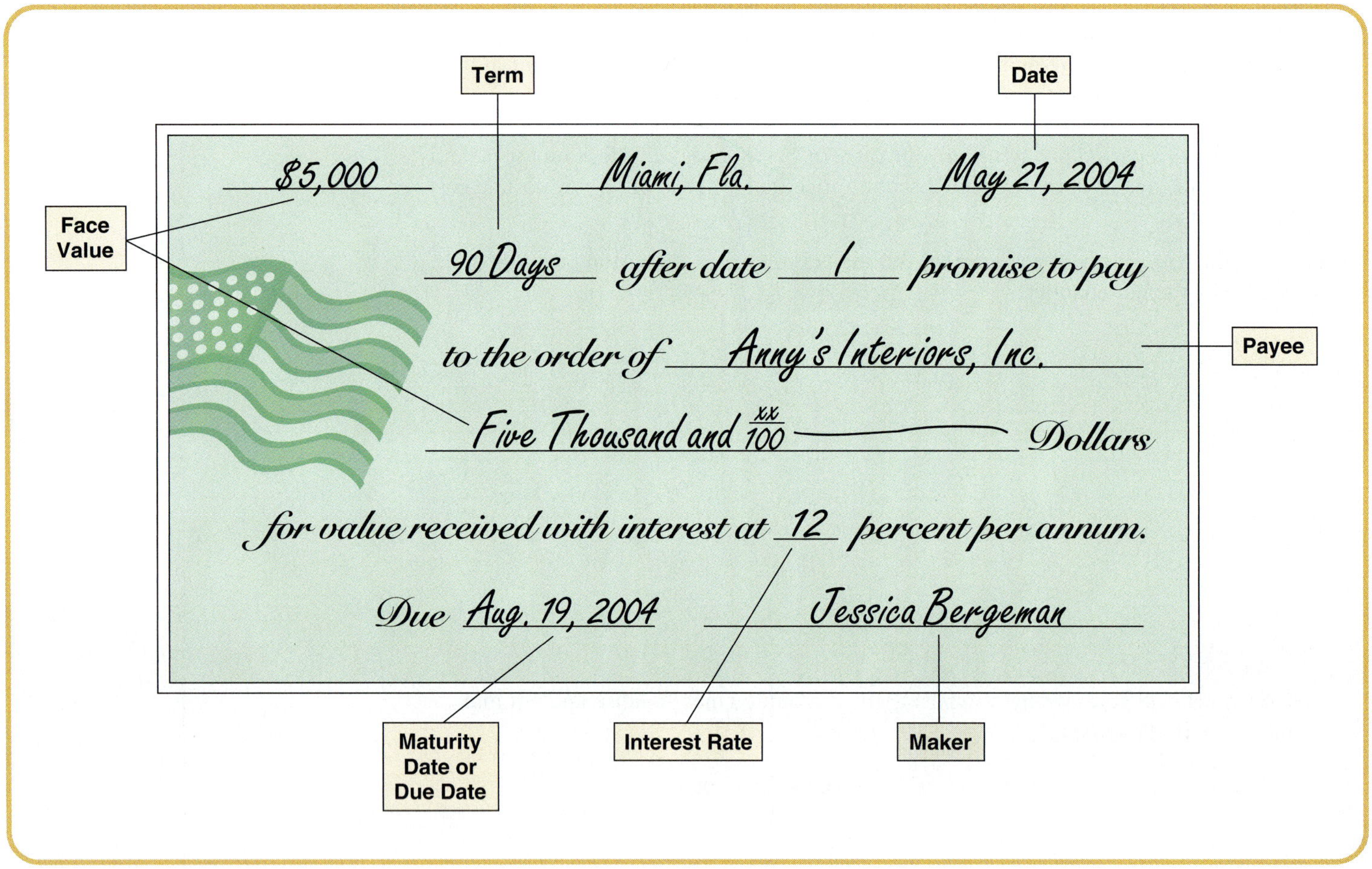

✦ **EXHIBIT 10-2** ✦
Interest-Bearing Promissory Note

Everybody's Business
Real-World Connection
Discounting is used in the purchase of government Treasury bonds, notes, and bills. These are actually loans to the U. S. government.

Maker: The person or company borrowing the money and issuing the note.

Payee: The person or institution lending the money and receiving the payment.

Term: The time period of the note, usually stated in days. (Use ordinary interest.)

Date: The date that the note is issued.

Face Value or Principal: The amount of money borrowed.

Interest Rate: The annual rate of interest being charged.

Maturity Date or Due Date: The date when maturity value is due the payee.

10-10 Calculating Bank Discount and Proceeds for Simple Discount Notes

To this point, we have been dealing with simple interest notes in which the interest was added to the principal to determine the maturity value. Another way of lending money is to deduct the interest from the principal at the beginning of the loan and give the borrower the difference. These are known as **simple discount notes.** When this method is used, the amount of interest charged is known as the **bank discount,** and the amount that the borrower receives is known as the **proceeds.** When the term of the note is over, the borrower will repay the entire principal or face value of the note as the maturity value.

For example, Julie goes to a bank and signs a simple interest note for $5,000. If the interest charge amounts to $500, she will receive $5,000 at the beginning of the note and repay $5,500 on maturity of the note. If the bank used a simple discount note for Julie's loan, the bank discount (interest) would be deducted from the face value (principal). Julie's proceeds on the loan would be $4,500, and on maturity she would pay $5,000.

simple discount note
Promissory note in which the interest is deducted from the principal at the beginning of the loan.

bank discount
The amount of interest charged (deducted from principal) on a discounted promissory note.

proceeds
The amount of money that the borrower receives at the time a discounted note is made.

Bank Discount

Because bank discount is the same as interest, we use the formula $I = PRT$ as before, substituting bank discount for interest, face value for principal, and discount rate for interest rate. *Note:* Use ordinary interest, 360 days, for simple discount notes whose terms are stated in days.

Bank discount = Face value × Discount rate × Time

Proceeds

The proceeds of a note are calculated using the following formula:

Proceeds = Face value − Bank discount

EXAMPLE

What are the bank discount and proceeds of a $7,000 note at a 14% discount rate for 270 days?

SOLUTION STRATEGY

Bank discount = Face value × Discount rate × Time

$$\text{Bank discount} = \$7{,}000 \times .14 \times \frac{270}{360}$$

Bank discount = $\underline{\underline{\$735}}$

Proceeds = Face value − Bank discount

Proceeds = $7,000 − $735

Proceeds = $\underline{\underline{\$6{,}265}}$

TRY-IT | EXERCISE

16. Daryl Fox signed a $20,000 simple discount promissory note at the Manhattan International Bank. The discount rate is 13%, and the term of the note is 330 days. What is the amount of the bank discount, and what are Daryl's proceeds on the loan?

Check your answers with the solutions on page 370.

10-11 Calculating True or Effective Rate of Interest for a Simple Discount Note

In a simple interest note, the borrower receives the full face value, whereas with a simple discount note, the borrower receives only the proceeds. Because the proceeds are less than the face value, the stated discount rate is not the true or actual interest rate of the note.

true, or effective interest rate
The actual interest rate charged on a discounted note. Takes into account the fact that the borrower does not receive the full amount of the principal.

To protect the consumer, the U. S. Congress has passed legislation requiring all lending institutions to quote the **true** or **effective interest rate** for all loans. Effective interest rate is calculated by substituting the bank discount for interest, and the proceeds for principal, in the rate formula,

$$\text{Effective interest rate} = \frac{\text{Bank discount}}{\text{Proceeds} \times \text{Time}}$$

EXAMPLE

What is the effective interest rate of a simple discount note for $10,000, at a bank discount rate of 14%, for a period of 90 days? (Round to the nearest tenth percent.)

SOLUTION STRATEGY

To find the effective interest rate, we must first calculate the amount of the bank discount and the proceeds of the note, then substitute these numbers in the effective interest rate formula.

Step 1. Bank Discount

$$\text{Bank discount} = \text{Face value} \times \text{Discount rate} \times \text{Time}$$

$$\text{Bank discount} = 10{,}000 \times .14 \times \frac{90}{360}$$

$$\text{Bank discount} = \underline{\underline{\$350}}$$

Step 2. Proceeds

$$\text{Proceeds} = \text{Face value} - \text{Bank discount}$$

$$\text{Proceeds} = 10{,}000 - 350$$

$$\text{Proceeds} = \underline{\underline{\$9{,}650}}$$

Step 3. Effective Interest Rate

$$\text{Effective interest rate} = \frac{\text{Bank discount}}{\text{Proceeds} \times \text{Time}}$$

$$\text{Effective interest rate} = \frac{350}{9{,}650 \times \frac{90}{360}}$$

$$\text{Effective interest rate} = \frac{350}{2{,}412.50}$$

$$\text{Effective interest rate} = .14507 \text{ or } \underline{\underline{14.5\%}}$$

TRY-IT | EXERCISE

17. What is the effective interest rate of a simple discount note for $40,000, at a bank discount rate of 11%, for a period of 270 days? Round your answer to hundredths.

Check your answer with the solution on page 371.

10-12 Discounting Notes before Maturity

Frequently in business, companies extend credit to their customers by accepting short-term promissory notes as payment for goods or services. These notes are simple interest and are usually for less than 1 year. Prior to the maturity date of these notes, the payee (lender) may take the note to a bank and sell it. This is a convenient way for a company or individual to *cash in* a note at any time before maturity. This process is known as **discounting a note.**

discounting a note
A process whereby a company or individual can *cash in* or sell a promissory note, at a discount, at any time before maturity.

When a note is discounted at a bank, the original payee receives the proceeds of the discounted note, and the bank (the new payee) receives the maturity value of the note when it matures. The time period used to calculate the proceeds is from the date the note is discounted to the maturity date. This is known as the **discount period.**

discount period
The time period between the date a note is discounted and the maturity date. Used to calculate the proceeds of a discounted note.

Exhibit 10-3 illustrates the time-line for a 90-day simple interest note discounted on the 60th day.

STEPS FOR DISCOUNTING A NOTE BEFORE MATURITY:

Step 1. Calculate the maturity value of the note. If the original note was noninterest-bearing, the maturity value will be the same as the face value. If the original note was interest-bearing, the maturity value should be calculated as usual:

Maturity value = Principal (1 + Rate × Time)

Step 2. Determine the number of days or months of the discount period. The discount period is used as the numerator of the time in Step 3.

Step 3. Calculate the amount of the bank discount by using the following formula. *Note:* Use ordinary interest, 360 days, for discounting a note before maturity, when the terms are stated in days.

Bank discount = Maturity value × Discount rate × Time

Step 4. Calculate the proceeds of the note by using the formula:

Proceeds = Maturity value − Bank discount

Everybody's Business

Real-World Connection

Many companies are forced to extend credit to their business customers due to "competitive pressures," not because they want to be in the loan business. Discounting the note at their bank is a way of getting their money sooner.

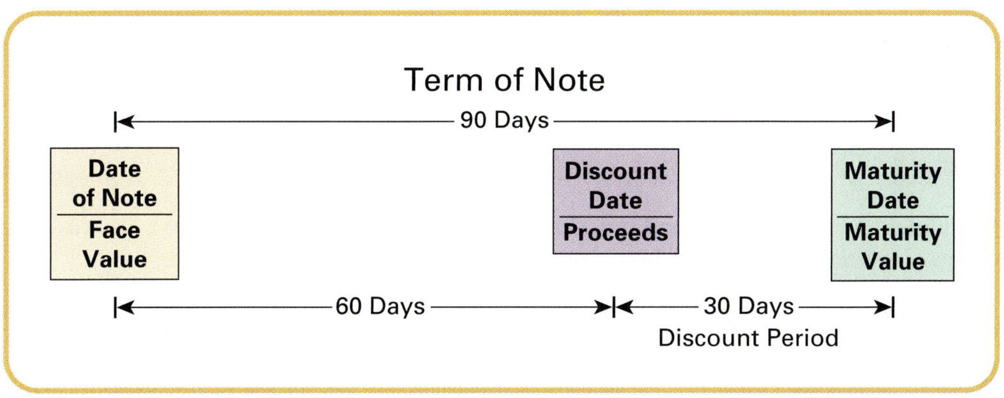

EXHIBIT 10-3
Time-Line for Discounted Note

EXAMPLE

Bradley Distributors received a $15,000 promissory note for 150 days at 12% simple interest from one of its customers. After 90 days, Bradley needed cash so it discounted the note at the InterAmerican Bank at a discount rate of 14%. What are the proceeds Bradley will receive from the discounted note?

SOLUTION STRATEGY

Step 1. Calculate the maturity value of the original note:

$$\text{Maturity value} = \text{Principal}\,(1 + \text{Rate} \times \text{Time})$$

$$\text{Maturity value} = 15{,}000\left(1 + .12 \times \frac{150}{360}\right)$$

$$\text{Maturity value} = 15{,}000\,(1 + .05) = 15{,}000(1.05)$$

$$\text{Maturity value} = \underline{\underline{\$15{,}750}}$$

Step 2. Find the days of the discount period: In this example, the note was discounted after 90 days of a 150-day note, therefore the discount period is 60 days (150 − 90 = 60).

Step 3. Calculate the amount of the bank discount:

$$\text{Bank discount} = \text{Maturity value} \times \text{Discount rate} \times \text{Time}$$

$$\text{Bank discount} = \$15{,}750 \times .14 \times \frac{60}{360}$$

$$\text{Bank discount} = \underline{\underline{\$367.50}}$$

Step 4. Calculate the proceeds of the discounted note:

$$\text{Proceeds} = \text{Maturity value} - \text{Bank discount}$$

$$\text{Proceeds} = \$15{,}750.00 - \$367.50$$

$$\text{Proceeds} = \underline{\underline{\$15{,}382.50}}$$

TRY-IT | EXERCISE

18. Lakeside Lumber received a $35,000 promissory note at 10% simple interest for 6 months from one of its customers. After 4 months, the note was discounted at the Goldenview Bank at a discount rate of 14%. What are the proceeds Lakeside will receive from the discounted note?

Check your answer with the solution on page 371.

REVIEW EXERCISES | CHAPTER 10—SECTION III

Calculate the bank discount and proceeds for the following simple discount notes (use the ordinary interest method, 360 days, when applicable):

	Face Value	Discount Rate (%)	Term	Bank Discount	Proceeds
1.	$4,500	13	6 months	________	________
2.	$235	11.3	50 days	________	________

3.	$1,850	$12\frac{1}{2}$	1 year		
4.	$35,000	9.65	11 months		
5.	$7,800	$8\frac{1}{4}$	130 days		

Using ordinary interest, 360 days, calculate the missing information for the following simple discount notes:

	Face Value	Discount Rate (%)	Date of Note	Term (days)	Maturity Date	Bank Discount	Proceeds
6.	$16,800	10	June 3	80			
7.	$5,000	14.7	April 16		July 9		
8.	$800	12.1	Sept. 3	109			
9.	$1,300	$9\frac{1}{2}$	Aug. 19		Nov. 27		
10.	$75,000	15	May 7	53			

Using ordinary interest, 360 days, calculate the bank discount, proceeds, and effective rate for the following simple discount notes (round effective rate to the nearest hundredth percent):

	Face Value	Discount Rate (%)	Term (days)	Bank Discount	Proceeds	Effective Rate (%)
11.	$2,700	14	126			
12.	$6,505	10.39	73			
13.	$3,800	$14\frac{1}{2}$	140			
14.	$95,000	9.7	45			
15.	$57,500	$12\frac{3}{4}$	230			

The following interest-bearing promissory notes were discounted at a bank by the payee before maturity. Use the ordinary interest method, 360 days, to calculate the missing information:

	Face Value	Interest Rate (%)	Date of Note	Term of Note (days)	Maturity Date	Maturity Value	Date of Discount	Discount Period (days)	Discount Rate (%)	Proceeds
16.	$2,500	12	Mar. 4	70			Apr. 15		13	
17.	$4,000	10.4	Dec. 12	50			Jan. 19		15	
18.	$850	$13\frac{1}{2}$	June 7	125			Sept. 3		16.5	

Use the ordinary interest method, 360 days, to solve the following word problems:

19. Lisa Figueroa signed a $24,000 simple discount promissory note at the Central Bank. The discount rate is 14%, and the note was made on February 19 for 50 days.

a. What proceeds will Lisa receive on the note?

b. What is the maturity date of the note?

20. Jeff Foran signed a $10,000 simple discount promissory note at a bank discount rate of 13%. If the term of the note was 125 days, what was the effective rate of interest of the note? Round your answer to the nearest hundredth percent.

21. Berkshire Manufacturing received a $40,000 promissory note at 12% simple interest for 95 days from one of its customers. On day 70, Berkshire discounted the note at the Weston Hills Bank at a discount rate of 15%. The note was made on September 12.

a. What is the maturity date of the note?

b. What is the maturity value of the note?

c. What is the discount date of the note?

d. What proceeds will Berkshire receive after discounting the note?

BUSINESS DECISION

Timing the Discount?

22. Jim Collins is the accounting manager for Mountaineer, Inc., a manufacturer of custom motor homes. In order to get an order from Motor Homes of America, Jim has just accepted a 90-day, 9.5% promissory note for $600,000.

You are a manager for Atlantic Bank, and Jim is one of your clients. Atlantic's discount rate currently is 16%. Jim's goal is to discount the note as soon as possible, but not until the proceeds are at least equal to the face value of the note, $600,000.

a. As his banker, Jim has asked you to "run the numbers" at 10-day intervals, starting with day 20, and advise him when he can discount the note and still receive his $600,000.

b. (Challenge) Calculate the exact day the note should be discounted to meet Jim's goal.

CHAPTER FORMULAS

$$\text{Interest} = \text{Principal} \times \text{Rate} \times \text{Time}$$

$$\text{Time (exact interest)} = \frac{\text{Number of days of a loan}}{365}$$

$$\text{Time (ordinary interest)} = \frac{\text{Number of days of a loan}}{360}$$

$$\text{Maturity value} = \text{Principal} + \text{Interest}$$

$$\text{Maturity value} = \text{Principal}\ (1 + \text{Rate} \times \text{Time})$$

$$\text{Principal} = \frac{\text{Interest}}{\text{Rate} \times \text{Time}}$$

$$\text{Rate} = \frac{\text{Interest}}{\text{Principal} \times \text{Time}}$$

$$\text{Time} = \frac{\text{Interest}}{\text{Principal} \times \text{Rate}}$$

$$\text{Bank discount} = \text{Face value} \times \text{Discount rate} \times \text{Time}$$

$$\text{Proceeds} = \text{Face value} - \text{Bank discount}$$

$$\text{Effective interest rate} = \frac{\text{Bank discount}}{\text{Proceeds} \times \text{Time}}$$

✦ SUMMARY CHART ✦

SECTION I: Understanding and Computing Simple Interest

Topic	P/O, Page	Important Concepts	Illustrative Examples
Computing Simple Interest for Loans With Terms of Years or Months	10-1 340	Simple interest is calculated by using the formula $I = PRT$. **Interest = Principal × Rate × Time** *Note:* Time is always expressed in years or fractions of a year.	What is the amount of interest for a loan of \$20,000, at 12% simple interest, for 9 months? $I = 20{,}000 \times .12 \times \frac{9}{12}$ Interest = $\underline{\underline{\$1{,}800.00}}$

SECTION I: (continued)

Topic	P/O, Page	Important Concepts	Illustrative Examples
Calculating Interest for Loans with Terms of Days by the Exact Interest Method	10-2 342	Exact interest uses *365 days* as the time factor denominator. $\text{Time} = \dfrac{\text{Number of days of a loan}}{365}$	Using the exact interest method, what is the amount of interest on a loan of \$5,000, at 8%, for 95 days? $I = PRT$ $I = 5{,}000 \times .08 \times \dfrac{95}{36}$ Interest = $\underline{\underline{\$104.11}}$
Calculating Interest for Loans with Terms of Days by the Ordinary Interest Method	10-2 342	Ordinary interest uses *360 days* as the time factor denominator. $\text{Time} = \dfrac{\text{Number of days of a loan}}{360}$	Using the ordinary interest method, what is the amount of interest on a loan of \$8,000, at 9%, for 120 days? $I = PRT$ $I = 8{,}000 \times .09 \times \dfrac{120}{360}$ Interest = $\underline{\underline{\$240.00}}$
Calculating the Maturity Value of a Loan	10-3 343	When the time period of a loan is over, the loan is said to mature. The total payback of principal and interest is known as the maturity value of a loan. **Maturity value = Principal + Interest** **Maturity value = Principal(1 + Rate × Time)**	What is the maturity value of a loan for \$50,000, at 12% interest, for 3 years? $MV = 50{,}000(1 + .12 \times 3)$ $MV = 50{,}000(1.36)$ Maturity Value = $\underline{\underline{\$68{,}000.00}}$
Calculating the Number of Days of a Loan	10-4 344	1. Determine the number of days remaining in the first month by subtracting the loan date from the number of days in that month. 2. List the number of days for each succeeding whole month. 3. List the number of loan days in the last month. 4. Add the days from Steps 1, 2, and 3.	Santos Blan borrowed money from the Republic Bank on May 5 and repaid the loan on August 19. For how many days was this loan? May 31 − May 5 26 days in May 61 June–July + 19 August 106 Days

SECTION I: (continued)

Topic	P/O, Page	Important Concepts	Illustrative Examples
Determining the Maturity Date of a Loan	10-5 345	1. Determine the number of days remaining in the first month. 2. Subtract days from Step 1 from number of days in the loan. 3. Subtract days in each succeeding whole month until you reach a month in which the difference is less than the days in that month. The maturity date will be the day of that month that corresponds to the difference.	What is the maturity date of a loan taken out on June 9 for 100 days? June 30 June − 9 21 days in June 100 days of the loan − 21 days in June 79 − 31 days in July 48 − 31 days in August 17 At this point, the difference, 17, is less than the days in September; therefore the maturity date is September 17.

SECTION II: Using the Simple Interest Formula

Topic	P/O, Page	Important Concepts	Illustrative Examples
Solving for the Principal	10-6 349	$\text{Principal} = \dfrac{\text{Interest}}{\text{Rate} \times \text{Time}}$ 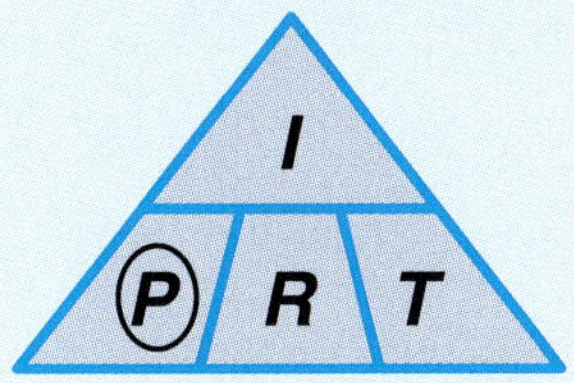	Shana Lum borrowed money at 10% interest for 2 years. If the interest charge was $800, how much principal did Shana borrow? $\text{Principal} = \dfrac{800}{.10 \times 2} = \dfrac{800}{.2}$ $\text{Principal} = \underline{\underline{\$4{,}000.00}}$
Solving for the Rate	10-7 350	$\text{Rate} = \dfrac{\text{Interest}}{\text{Principal} \times \text{Time}}$ 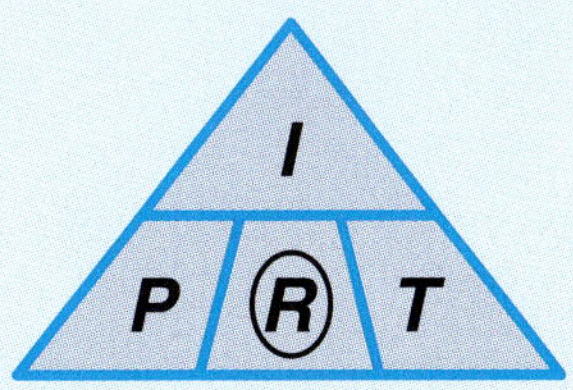	Glenn Hartmann borrowed $3,000 for 75 days. If the interest was $90 using ordinary interest, what was the rate on Glenn's loan? $\text{Rate} = \dfrac{90}{3{,}000 \times \dfrac{70}{360}} = \dfrac{90}{625}$ $\text{Rate} = .144 = \underline{\underline{14.4\%}}$

SECTION II: (continued)

Topic	P/O, Page	Important Concepts	Illustrative Examples
Solving for the Time	10-8 351	When solving for time, whole numbers are years, and decimals are multiplied by 360 or 365 to get days. Any fraction of a day should be rounded up to the next higher day, because lending institutions consider any portion of a day to be another day. $\text{Time} = \dfrac{\text{Interest}}{\text{Principal} \times \text{Rate}}$ 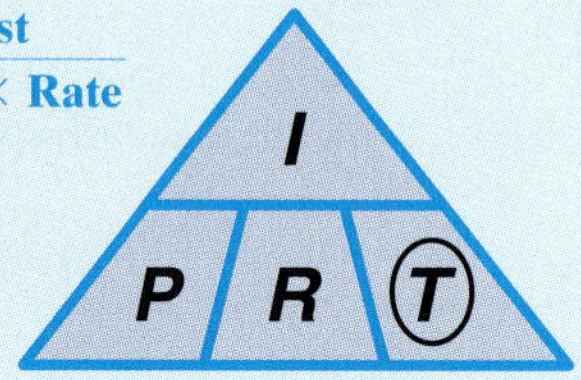	What is the time period of a loan for \$20,000 at 9% ordinary interest if the amount of interest is \$1,000? $\text{Time} = \dfrac{1{,}000}{20{,}000 \times .09} = \dfrac{1{,}000}{1{,}800}$ Time = .5555555 × 360 199.99 = 200 days
Calculating Loans Involving Partial Payments before Maturity	10-9 352	1. Compute the interest due from the date of loan to the date of partial payment. 2. Subtract the interest (Step 1) from the partial payment. 3. The balance of the partial payment is used to reduce the principal. 4. Maturity value is computed by adding the interest since the last partial payment to the adjusted principal.	Larry Mager borrowed \$7,000 at 10% ordinary interest for 120 days. On day 90, Larry made a partial payment of \$3,000. What is the new maturity value of the loan? $I = PRT$ $I = 7{,}000 \times .10 \times \dfrac{90}{360} = \$175$ \$3,000 partial payment − 175 accumulated interest \$2,825 reduces principal \$7,000 original principal − 2,825 \$4,175 adjusted principal Days remaining = 120 − 90 = 30 $I = PRT$ $I = 4{,}175 \times .10 \times \dfrac{30}{360} = \$34.79$ Maturity value = $P + I$ $MV = 4{,}175.00 + 34.79$ Maturity value = \$4,209.79

Section III: Understanding Promissory Notes and Discounting

Topic	P/O, Page	Important Concepts	Illustrative Examples
Calculating Bank Discount and Proceeds for a Simple Discount Note	10-10 359	With discounting, the interest, known as the bank discount, is deducted from the face value of the loan. The borrower gets the difference, known as the proceeds. **Bank discount = Face value × Discount rate × Time** **Proceeds = Face value − Bank discount**	What are the bank discount and proceeds of a $10,000 note discounted at 12% for 6 months? Bank disc $= 10{,}000 \times .12 \times \frac{6}{12}$ Bank disc = $600 Proceeds = 10,000 − 600 = $9,400
Calculating True or Effective Rate of Interest for a Simple Discount Note	10-11 360	Because the proceeds are less than the face value of a loan, the true or effective interest rate is higher than the stated bank discount rate. $\text{Effective rate} = \frac{\text{Bank discount}}{\text{Proceeds} \times \text{Time}}$	What is the effective rate of a simple discount note for $20,000, at a bank discount of 15%, for a period of 9 months? Bank disc $= FV \times R \times T$ Bank disc $= 20{,}000 \times .15 \times \frac{9}{12}$ Bank disc = $2,250 Proceeds = Face Value − Discount Proceeds = 20,000 − 2,250 Proceeds = $17,750 Effective rate $= \frac{2{,}250}{17{,}750 \times \frac{9}{12}}$ Effective rate = 16.9%
Discounting Notes before Maturity	10-12 361	Frequently companies extend credit to their customers by accepting short-term promissory notes as payment for goods or services. These notes can be cashed in early by discounting them at a bank and receiving the proceeds. 1. Calculate the maturity value. $MV = P(1 + RT)$ 2. Determine the discount period. 3. Calculate the bank discount. **Bank discount** $= MV \times R \times T$ 4. Calculate the proceeds. **Proceeds** $= MV -$ **Discount**	Dixie Food Wholesalers received a $100,000 promissory note for 6 months, at 11% interest, from SuperSaver Supermarkets. If Dixie discounts the note after 4 months at a discount rate of 15%, what proceeds will they receive? $MV = 100{,}000\left(1 + .11 \times \frac{6}{12}\right)$ $MV = \$105{,}500$ Discount period = 2 months (6 − 4) Bank disc $= 105{,}500 \times .15 \times \frac{2}{12}$ Bank disc = $2,637.50 Proceeds = 105,500.00 − 2,637.50 Proceeds = $102,862.50

TRY-IT EXERCISE | SOLUTIONS

1. $I = PRT = 4{,}000 \times .07 \times 2.25 = \underline{\underline{\$630.00}}$

2. $I = PRT = 45{,}000 \times .0975 \times \frac{3}{12} = \underline{\underline{\$1{,}096.88}}$

3. $I = PRT = 130{,}000 \times .104 \times \frac{42}{12} = \underline{\underline{\$47{,}320.00}}$

4. $I = PRT = 15{,}000 \times .095 \times \frac{250}{360} = \underline{\underline{\$989.58}}$

5. $I = PRT = 23{,}000 \times .08 \times \frac{119}{365} = \underline{\underline{\$599.89}}$

6. $I = PRT = 15{,}400 \times .065 \times \frac{24}{12} = \underline{\underline{\$2{,}002.00}}$

$MV = P + I = 15{,}400 + 2{,}002 = \underline{\underline{\$17{,}402.00}}$

7. $MV = P(1 + RT) = 450{,}000\left(1 + .08 \times \frac{9}{12}\right) = \underline{\underline{\$477{,}000.00}}$

8. Days of loan $=$

$$\begin{array}{rr} 30 & \\ -\ 4 & \\ \hline 26 \text{ days} & \to 26 \text{ April} \\ & 61 \text{ May–June} \\ & +\ 18 \text{ July} \\ \hline & \underline{105 \text{ days}} \end{array}$$

9. Days of loan $=$

$$\begin{array}{rr} 30 & \\ -\ 15 & \\ \hline 15 \text{ days} & \to 15 \text{ June} \\ & 92 \text{ July–Sept.} \\ & +\ 9 \text{ Oct.} \\ \hline & \underline{116 \text{ days}} \end{array}$$

$I = PRT = 3{,}500 \times .11 \times \frac{116}{365} = \underline{\underline{\$122.36}}$

10.

$$\begin{array}{lr} \text{Days in Sept.} & 30 \\ \text{Loan date} & -\ 9 \\ \hline \text{Days of Sept.} & 21 \end{array}$$

$$\begin{array}{rl} 125 & \text{Days of loan} \\ -\ 21 & \text{Days of Sept.} \\ \hline 104 & \\ -\ 31 & \text{October} \\ \hline 73 & \\ -\ 30 & \text{November} \\ \hline 43 & \\ -\ 31 & \text{December} \\ \hline 12 & \to \underline{\underline{\text{January 12}}} \end{array}$$

11. $MV = P(1 + RT) = 9{,}000\left(1 + .10 \times \frac{80}{360}\right) = \underline{\underline{\$9{,}200.00}}$

Maturity date $=$

$$\begin{array}{rr} 31 & \\ -\ 21 & \\ \hline 10 \text{ days} & \to 10 \text{ Oct.} \\ & 61 \text{ Nov.–Dec.} \\ & +\ 9 \text{ Jan.} \to \underline{\underline{\text{January 9}}} \\ \hline & 80 \text{ days} \end{array}$$

12. $P = \dfrac{I}{RT} = \dfrac{560}{.09 \times \frac{125}{360}} = \underline{\underline{\$17{,}920.00}}$

13. $R = \dfrac{I}{PT} = \dfrac{1{,}960}{25{,}000 \times \frac{245}{360}} = \underline{\underline{11.52\%}}$

14. $T = \dfrac{I}{PR} = \dfrac{650}{15{,}000 \times .095} = .4561404$

$$\begin{array}{r} .4561404 \\ \times \quad 360 \\ \hline 164.2 = \underline{\underline{165 \text{ days}}} \end{array}$$

15. $I = PRT = 15{,}000 \times .12 \times \frac{20}{360} = \$100$ 1st Part pay = 20 days

$$\begin{array}{rl} 4{,}000 & \text{pmt} \\ -\ 100 & \text{int} \\ \hline 3{,}900 & \end{array} \qquad \begin{array}{rl} 15{,}000 & \\ -\ 3{,}900 & \\ \hline 11{,}100 & \text{Adj. Prin.} \end{array}$$

$I = PRT = 11{,}100 \times .12 \times \frac{40}{360} = \$148$ 2nd Part pay = 40 days (60 − 20)

$$\begin{array}{rl} 5{,}000 & \text{pmt} \\ -\ 148 & \text{int} \\ \hline 4{,}852 & \end{array} \qquad \begin{array}{rl} 11{,}100 & \\ -\ 4{,}852 & \\ \hline 6{,}248 & \text{Adj. Prin.} \end{array}$$

Days remaining = 40 (100 − 60)

$I = PRT = 6{,}248 \times .12 \times \frac{40}{360} = \$83.31$

Final due $= P + I = 6{,}248.00 + 83.31 = \underline{\underline{\$6{,}331.31}}$

16. Bank discount $= FV \times R \times T = 20{,}000 \times .13 \times \frac{330}{360} = \underline{\underline{\$2{,}383.33}}$

Proceeds $= FV - \text{Disc} = 20{,}000 - 2{,}383.33 = \underline{\underline{\$17{,}616.67}}$

17. Bank discount $= FV \times R \times T = 40{,}000 \times .11 \times \frac{270}{360} = \$3{,}300.00$

Proceeds $= FV - \text{Disc} = 40{,}000 - 3{,}300 = \$36{,}700.00$

Effective rate $= \frac{\text{Bank discount}}{\text{Proceeds} \times \text{Time}} = \frac{3{,}300}{36{,}700 \times \frac{270}{360}} = \underline{\underline{11.99\%}}$

18. $MV = P(1 + RT) = 35{,}000\left(1 + .10 \times \frac{6}{12}\right) = \$36{,}750$

Discount period $= \begin{array}{r} 6 \text{ months} \\ -\ 4 \text{ months} \\ \hline 2 \text{ months} \end{array}$

Bank discount $= MV \times R \times T = 36{,}750 \times .14 \times \frac{2}{12} = \$857.50$

Proceeds $= MV - \text{Disc} = \$36{,}750.00 - 857.50 = \underline{\underline{\$35{,}892.50}}$

Name ______________________

Class ______________________

Answers

1. ______________________
2. ______________________
3. ______________________
4. ______________________
5. ______________________
6. ______________________
7. ______________________
8. ______________________
9. ______________________
10. ______________________
11. ______________________
12. ______________________
13. ______________________
14. ______________________

CHAPTER 10 | ASSESSMENT TEST

Using the exact interest method (365 days), find the amount of interest on the following loans:

	Principal	Rate (%)	Time (days)	Exact Interest
1.	$15,000	13	120	________
2.	$1,700	$12\frac{1}{2}$	33	________

Using the ordinary interest method (360 days) find the amount of interest on the following loans:

	Principal	Rate (%)	Time (days)	Ordinary Interest
3.	$20,600	12	98	________
4.	$286,000	$13\frac{1}{2}$	224	________

What is the maturity value of the following loans (use $MV = P(1 + RT)$ to find the maturity values):

	Principal	Rate (%)	Time	Maturity Value
5.	$15,800	14	4 years	________
6.	$120,740	$11\frac{3}{4}$	7 months	________

From the following information, determine the number of days of each loan:

	Loan Date	Due Date	Number of Days
7.	April 16	August 1	________
8.	October 20	December 18	________

From the following information, determine the maturity date of each loan:

	Loan Date	Time Loan (days)	Maturity Date
9.	November 30	55	________
10.	May 15	111	________

Compute the principal for the following loans (round answers to the nearest cent):

	Principal	Rate (%)	Time	Interest
11.	________	12	2 years	$2,800
12.	________	$10\frac{1}{2}$	10 months	$5,900

Compute the rate for the following loans (round answers to the nearest tenth percent):

	Principal	Rate (%)	Time	Interest
13.	$2,200	________	4 years	$800
14.	$50,000	________	9 months	$4,500

Name ______________

Class ______________

Use the ordinary interest method to compute the time for the following loans (round answers to the next higher day, when necessary):

	Principal	Rate (%)	Time (days)	Interest
15.	$13,500	13	________	$350
16.	$7,900	10.4	________	$625

Calculate the missing information for the following loans (round percents to the nearest tenth, and days to the next higher day, when necessary):

	Principal	Rate (%)	Time (days)	Interest Method	Interest	Maturity Value
17.	$13,000	14	________	Ordinary	$960	________
18.	________	12.2	133	Exact	$1,790	________
19.	$2,500	________	280	Ordinary	$295	________

Using ordinary interest, calculate the missing information for the following simple discount notes:

	Face Value	Discount Rate (%)	Date of Note	Term (days)	Maturity Date	Bank Discount	Proceeds
20.	$50,000	13	Apr. 5	________	Aug. 14	________	________
21.	$875,000	$9\frac{1}{2}$	Oct. 25	87	________	________	________

Using ordinary interest (360 days), calculate the bank discount, proceeds, and effective rate for the following simple discount notes (round effective rate to the nearest hundredth percent):

	Face Value	Discount Rate (%)	Term (days)	Bank Discount	Proceeds	Effective Rate (%)
22.	$22,500	$10\frac{1}{2}$	60	________	________	________
23.	$290,000	11.9	110	________	________	________

The following interest-bearing promissory notes were discounted at a bank by the payee before maturity. Use the ordinary interest method (360 days) to solve for the missing information:

	Face Value	Interest Rate (%)	Date of Note	Term of Note (days)	Maturity Date	Maturity Value	Date Note Discounted	Discount Period (days)	Discount Rate (%)	Proceeds
24.	$8,000	11	Jan. 12	83	________	________	Mar. 1	________	15	________
25.	$5,500	$13\frac{1}{2}$	June 17	69	________	________	July 22	________	13.7	________

Answers

15. ______________

16. ______________

17. ______________

18. ______________

19. ______________

20. ______________

21. ______________

22. ______________

23. ______________

24. ______________

25. ______________

Name ______________________

Class ______________________

Answers

26. a. ______________________

b. ______________________

c. ______________________

27. ______________________

28. ______________________

Solve the following word problems:

26. On May 23, Carol Baker borrowed $4,000 from the Summerville Credit Union at 13% for 160 days. The credit union uses the exact interest method.

a. What was the amount of interest on the loan?

b. What was the maturity value of the loan?

c. What is the maturity date of the loan?

27. Robert Romero missed an income tax payment of $2,600. The Internal Revenue Service charges a 15% simple interest penalty calculated by the exact interest method. If the tax was due on April 15 but was paid on July 17, what is the amount of the penalty charge?

2600 x 15% x 93/365 $99.37

28. Sam Green borrowed money to buy furniture from his credit union at 13.2% simple interest. If the loan was repaid in $2\frac{1}{2}$ years and the amount of interest was $1,320, how much did Sam borrow?

Name ____________________

Class ____________________

Answers

29. ____________________

30. ____________________

31. ____________________

32. a. ____________________

b. ____________________

29. Jeff Lukenbill took out a loan for $5,880 at the Northern Trust Bank for 110 days. The bank uses the ordinary method for calculating interest. What rate of interest was charged if the amount of interest was $275? Round to the nearest tenth percent.

30. Jody St. John deposited $2,000 in a savings account paying 6% ordinary interest. How long will it take for her investment to amount to $2,600?

31. Ann Veith borrowed $16,000 at 14% ordinary interest, for 88 days. On day 30 of the loan, she made a partial payment of $7,000. What is the new maturity value of the loan?

32. Samson Industries borrowed $40,000 on April 6 for 66 days. The rate was 14% using the ordinary interest method. On day 25 of the loan Samson made a partial payment of $15,000, and on day 45 of the loan Samson made a second partial payment of $10,000.

a. What is the new maturity value of the loan?

b. What is the maturity date of the loan?

Name ____________________

Class ____________________

Answers

33. a. ____________________

b. ____________________

c. ____________________

34. a. ____________________

b. ____________________

c. ____________________

d. ____________________

33. Ransford Morgan signed a $30,000 simple discount promissory note at the Plantation Bank. The discount rate was 13%, ordinary interest, and the note was made on August 9 for 95 days.

a. What proceeds will Ransford receive on the note?

30,000 x 13% x 95/360 = 1029.17
30,000 − 1029.17 = 28970.83

b. What is the maturity date of the note?

Nov 12th

c. What is the effective rate of interest of the note? Round the answer to the nearest hundredth percent.

1029.17 / (28970.83 x 95/360)   13.46%

34. Schoninger Publishing, Inc., received a $70,000 promissory note at 12% ordinary interest for 60 days from one of its customers. After 20 days, Schoninger discounted the note at the Bank of Keystone Point at a discount rate of 14.5%. The note was made on March 21.

a. What is the maturity date of the note?

b. What is the maturity value of the note?

c. What is the discount date of the note?

d. What proceeds will Schoninger receive after discounting the note?

Name ____________________

Class ____________________

3

BUSINESS DECISION

Borrowing to Take Advantage of a Cash Discount

35. You are the accountant for Leather City, a retail furniture store. Recently, an order of sofas and chairs was received from a manufacturer with terms of 3/15, n/45. The order amounted to $230,000, and Leather City can borrow money at 13% ordinary interest.

 a. How much can be saved by borrowing the funds for 30 days to take advantage of the cash discount? (Remember, Leather City only has to borrow the net amount due, after the cash discount is taken.)

 b. What would you recommend?

Answers

35. a. ____________________

 b. ____________________

Everybody's Business

Real-World Connection

This Business Decision illustrates an important business concept, borrowing money to take advantage of a cash discount.

Note how much can be saved by taking the cash discount, even if the money is borrowed.

For a review of cash discounts, see Section IV, Chapter 7.

All the Math That's Fit to Learn

The Business Math Times

Volume X | Simple Interest and Promissory Notes | One Dollar

U.S. Treasury Securities

The U.S. Treasury issues securities to raise the money needed to operate the Federal government and to pay off maturing debt. These securities are a safe and secure investment option because the full faith and credit of the government guarantees that interest and principal payments will be paid on time.

The government sells Treasury bills, notes, and bonds to individual investors in $1,000 increments. Treasury *bills* are short-term securities that mature in one year or less from their issue date. *Notes* mature in more than a year, but not more than 10 years. *Bonds* have the longest term, maturing more than 10 years from their issue date.

These securities are actually **discounted loans** to our government that range in time from a few weeks to many years. When investors buy "loans," they are essentially lending the government the proceeds. At maturity, the investor is paid the face value.

For example, if you bought a $10,000, 5%, 26-week Treasury bill for $9,750 and held it until maturity, it would be worth $10,000 and your interest would be $250.

The Federal Reserve System

The Federal Reserve System, the "Fed," is the central banking system of the United States.

The Fed serves as the banker to both the banking community and the government. It also issues the national currency, conducts monetary policy, and plays a major role in the supervision and regulation of banks and bank holding companies.

The Fed's actions generally have a significant effect on U.S. interest rates and, subsequently, on stock, bond, and other financial markets. The Fed is best known for the influence it has on interest rates by "loosening" or "tightening" the money supply. This is basically the amount of money available at any one time in the U.S. financial system.

The Federal Reserve's open market operations are the most flexible and most frequently used instrument of controlling the money supply. When the FOMC (Federal Open Market Committee) decides that the money supply is growing too slowly, the Fed may purchase U.S. government securities, thus injecting cash into the financial system and expanding the monetary base. This enables banks to create additional deposits, which constitute a major portion of the money supply.

Conversely, should the money supply grow more rapidly than is desired, the Fed will sell securities on the open market. Such sales reduce bank reserves and thus the ability of the banking system to create deposits. Generally, the less money there is, the higher is its cost—the rate of interest.

Also among its controls, the Fed can make changes in the discount rate. When banks seek additional reserves by borrowing from the Fed, a change in the discount rate makes such borrowing either more or less expensive and consequently changes the rate that banks charge their customers (see chart).

Pepper . . . and Salt

THE WALL STREET JOURNAL

"The businessman's lunch comes with a complimentary glass of wine with which to toast the drop in interest rates."

"Quote . . . Unquote"

Banks do not raise or lower interest rates depending upon how they feel about it. A bank buys money like a grocer buys bananas—and then adds on salaries and rent and sells the product.

—*Llewellyn Jenkins, American banker*

The best ideas come after you think you've run out of them.

—*Dove Chocolate*

Fed & Bank Rate Comparison

Year	Discount Rate	Prime Rate
1990	7.00%	10.00%
1991	5.00%	7.50%
1992	3.00%	6.00%
1993	3.00%	6.00%
1994	4.75%	7.75%
1995	4.50%	8.50%
1996	5.00%	8.25%
1997	5.00%	8.50%
1998	4.75%	8.00%
1999	5.00%	8.25%
2000	6.00%	9.50%
2001	2.00%	5.50%
2002	1.25%	4.75%

Brainteaser

THE SALES REPORT

When the sales manager of a dealership that sells cars and motorcycles was asked how many vehicles he sold last week, he replied, "We sold 30 motors and 100 tires."

From this information, calculate the number of cars sold and the number of motorcycles sold.

ANSWER TO LAST ISSUE'S BRAINTEASER

24 days

Let X = days worked

Let $(30 - X)$ = days not worked

Solve the equation:

$$55X - 66(30 - X) = 924$$

CHAPTER

11

Compound Interest and Present Value

PERFORMANCE OBJECTIVES

Section I Compound Interest—The Time Value of Money

11-1 Manually calculating compound amount (future value) and compound interest. (p. 381)

11-2 Computing compound amount (future value) and compound interest by using compound interest tables. (p. 383)

11-3 Creating compound interest table factors for periods beyond the table. (p. 386)

11-4 Calculating annual percentage yield (APY) or effective interest rate (p. 387)

11-5 (Optional) Calculating compound amount (future value) by using the compound interest formula. (p. 388)

Section II Present Value

11-6 Calculating the present value of a future amount by using present value tables. (p. 392)

11-7 Creating present value table factors for periods beyond the table. (p. 394)

11-8 (Optional) Calculating present value of a future amount by using the present value formula. (p. 395)

SECTION I

COMPOUND INTEREST—THE TIME VALUE OF MONEY

compound interest
Interest that is applied a number of times during the term of a loan or investment. Interest paid on principal and previously earned interest.

In Chapter 10 we studied simple interest, in which the formula $I = PRT$ was applied once during the term of a loan or investment to find the amount of interest. In business, another common way of calculating interest is by a method known as *compounding,* or **compound interest,** in which the interest calculation is applied a number of times during the term of the loan or investment.

Compound interest yields considerably higher interest than simple interest because the investor is earning interest on the interest. With compound interest, the interest earned for each period is reinvested or added to the previous principal before the next calculation or compounding. The previous principal plus interest then becomes the new principal for the next period. For example, $100 invested at 8% interest is worth $108 after the first year ($100 principal + $8 interest). If the interest is not withdrawn, the interest for the next period will be calculated based on $108 principal.

As this compounding process repeats itself each period, the principal keeps growing by the amount of the previous interest. As the number of compounding periods increases, the amount of interest earned grows dramatically, especially when compared with simple interest, as illustrated in Exhibit 11-1.

the time value of money
The idea that money "now," or in the present, is more desirable than the same amount of money in the future, because it can be invested and earn interest as time goes by.

This chapter introduces you to an all-important business concept, the **time value of money.** Consider this: If you were owed $1,000, would you rather have it now or 1 year from now? If you answered "now," you already have a feeling for the concept. Money "now," or in the *present,* is more desirable than the same amount of money in the *future,* because it can be invested and earn interest as time goes by.

Everybody's Business

Real World Connection

Today, most banks, savings and loan institutions, and credit unions pay compound interest on depositor's money. The U.S. government also uses compounding for savings bonds.

✦ See "Putting Your Money to Work!" in this chapter's issue of *The Business Math Times,* page 408.

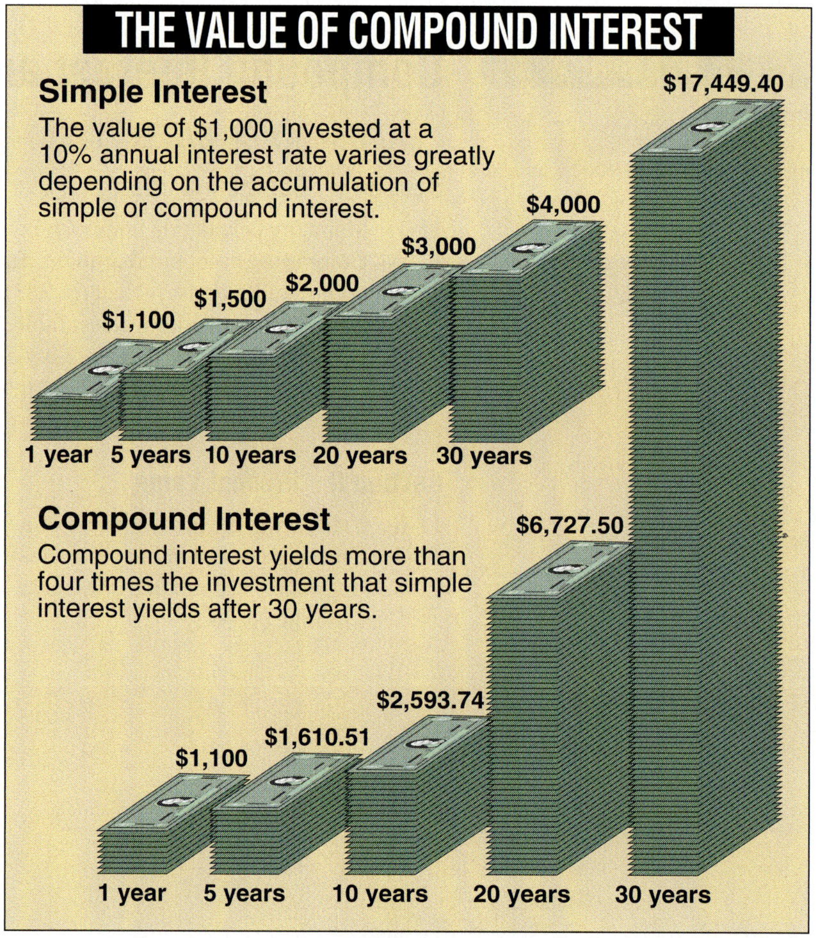

✦ **EXHIBIT 11-1** ✦
The Time Value of Money

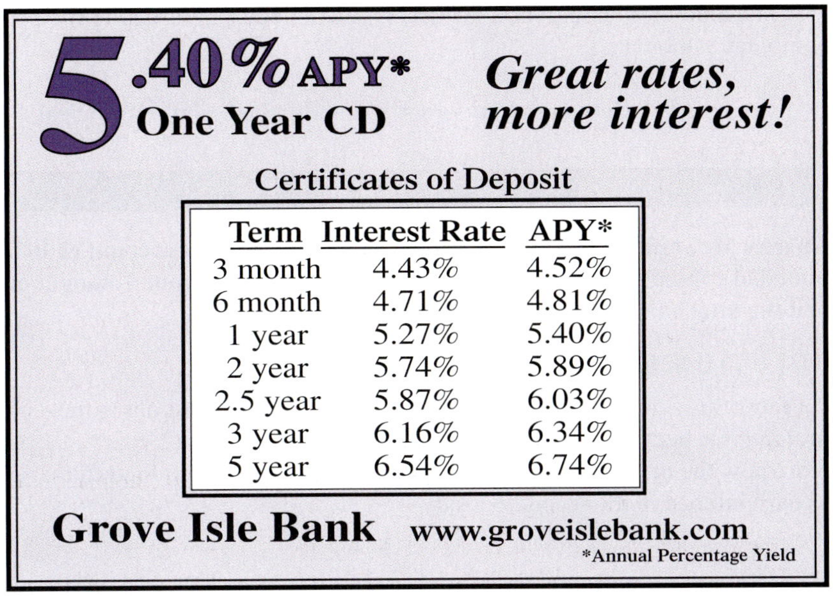

Certificates of deposit, CDs, as well as passbook and money market accounts are based on compound interest.

In this chapter you learn to calculate the **compound amount (future value)** of an investment at compound interest, when the **present amount (present value)** is known. You also learn to calculate the present value that must be deposited now, at compound interest, to yield a known future amount. See Exhibit 11-2.

compound amount, or future value (FV) The total amount of principal and accumulated interest at the end of a loan or investment.

present amount, or present value (PV) An amount of money that must be deposited today, at compound interest, to provide a specified lump sum of money in the future.

11-1 Manually Calculating Compound Amount (Future Value) and Compound Interest

Compounding divides the time of a loan or investment into compounding periods or simply periods. To manually calculate the compound amount or future value of an investment, we must compound or calculate the interest as many times as there are compounding periods, at the interest rate per period.

For example, an investment made for 5 years at 12% compounded annually (once per year) would have five compounding periods (5 years × 1 period per year), each at 12%. If the same investment was compounded semiannually (two times per year), there would be 10 compounding periods (5 years × 2 periods per year), each at 6% (12% annual rate ÷ 2 periods per year).

EXHIBIT 11-2
Present Value and Future Value at Compound Interest

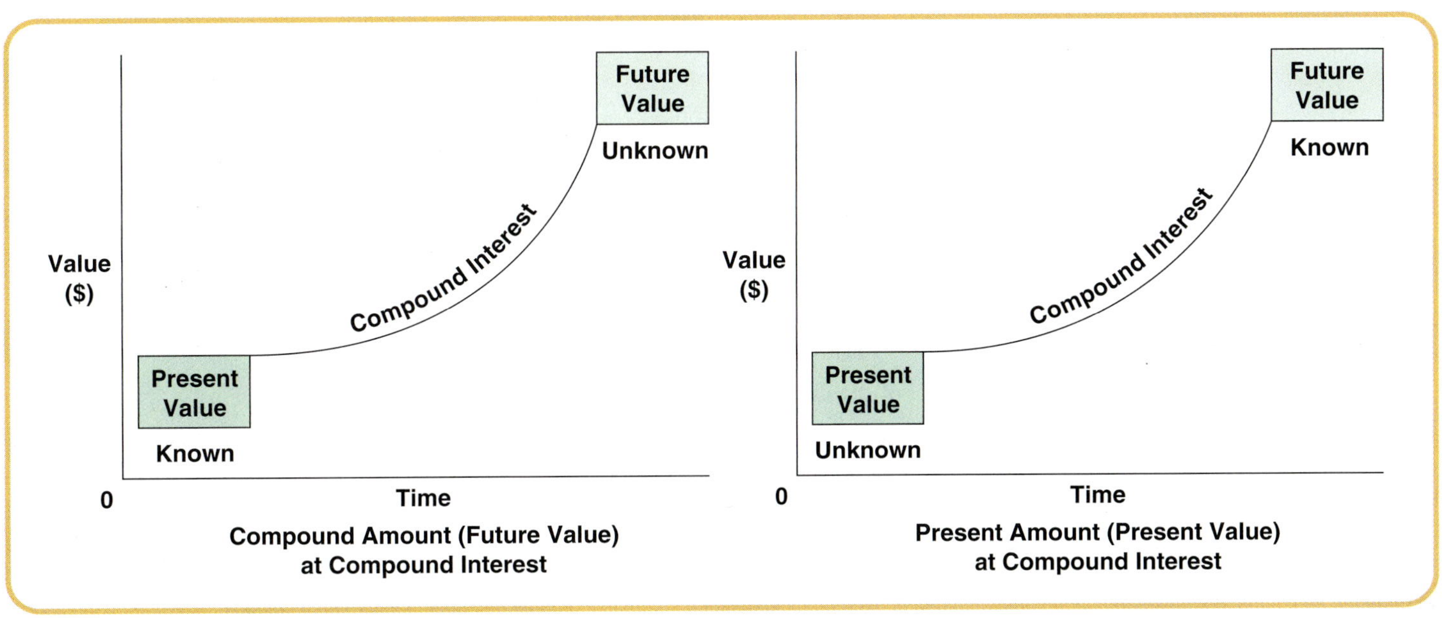

The amount of compound interest is calculated by subtracting the principal from the compound amount.

Compound interest = Compound amount − Principal

"I feel like a million bucks, compounded annually, of course."

EXAMPLE

Charles McCormick invested \$5,000 in a passbook savings account at 10% interest, compounded annually, for 2 years. Manually calculate the compound amount of the investment and the total amount of compound interest Charles earned.

SOLUTION STRATEGY

To solve this compound interest problem manually, we must apply the simple interest formula twice, because there are two compounding periods (2 years × 1 period per year). Note how the interest from the first period is reinvested or added to the original principal to earn interest in the second period.

Original principal	\$5,000.00	
Interest — period 1	+ 500.00	($I = PRT = 5{,}000.00 \times .10 \times 1$)
Principal — period 2	5,500.00	
Interest — period 2	+ 550.00	($I = PRT = 5{,}500.00 \times .10 \times 1$)
Compound Amount	\$6,050.00	

Compound Amount	\$6,050.00
Principal	− 5,000.00
Compound Interest Earned	\$1,050.00

EXAMPLE

Manually recalculate the compound amount and compound interest from the previous example by using semiannual compounding (two times per year). How much more interest would Charles earn if the bank offered semiannual compounding?

SOLUTION STRATEGY

To solve this compound interest problem, we must apply the simple interest formula four times, because there are four compounding periods (2 years × 2 periods per year). Note that the time factor is now $\frac{6}{12}$ or $\frac{1}{2}$, because semiannual compounding means every 6 months.

Original principal	\$5,000.00	
Interest — period 1	+ 250.00	($I = PRT = 5{,}000.00 \times .10 \times \frac{1}{2}$)
Principal — period 2	5,250.00	
Interest — period 2	+ 262.50	($I = PRT = 5{,}250.00 \times .10 \times \frac{1}{2}$)
Principal — period 3	5,512.50	
Interest — period 3	+ 275.63	($I = PRT = 5{,}512.50 \times .10 \times \frac{1}{2}$)
Principal — period 4	5,788.13	
Interest — period 4	+ 289.41	($I = PRT = 5{,}788.13 \times .10 \times \frac{1}{2}$)
Compound Amount	\$6,077.54	

Compound Amount	\$6,077.54
Principal	− 5,000.00
Compound Interest	\$1,077.54

For the same investment variables, semiannual compounding yields \$27.54 more than annual compounding:

Interest with semiannual compounding	\$1,077.54
Interest with annual compounding	−\$1,050.00
	\$27.54

TRY-IT | EXERCISE

1. Debbie Anderson invested \$10,000 at 12% interest, compounded semiannually, for 3 years. Manually calculate the compound amount and the compound interest of Debbie's investment.

Check your answer with the solution on page 402.

11-2 Computing Compound Amount (Future Value) and Compound Interest by Using Compound Interest Tables

You do not have to work many compound interest problems manually, particularly those with numerous compounding periods, before you start wishing for an easier way! In actuality, there are two other methods for solving compound interest problems. The first uses a compound interest formula, and the second uses compound interest tables.

The compound interest formula, $A = P(1 + i)^n$, contains an exponent and therefore requires the use of a calculator with an exponential function key. The use of the compound interest formula is covered in Performance Objective 11-5.

A compound interest table, such as Table 11-1 on page 384, is a useful set of factors that represents the future value of \$1.00 at various interest rates for a number of compounding periods. Because these factors are based on \$1.00, the future values of other principal amounts are found by multiplying the appropriate table factor by the number of dollars of principal.

Compound amount (future value) = Table factor × Principal

To use the compound interest tables, we must know the number of compounding periods and the interest rate per period. The following chart shows the various compounding options and the corresponding number of periods per year. *Note:* The greater the number of compounding periods per year, the higher the interest earned on the investment. Today, interest can actually be calculated on a continuous basis—that is, up to the minute. In competitive markets, many banks offer continuous compounding as an incentive to attract new deposits.

To find the number of compounding periods of an investment, multiply the number of years by the number of periods per year.

Compounding periods = Years × Periods per year

To find the interest rate per period, divide the annual or nominal rate by the number of periods per year.

$$\textbf{Interest rate per period} = \frac{\textbf{Nominal rate}}{\textbf{Periods per year}}$$

Everybody's Business

The Rule of 72

There is an easy method for calculating how long it takes an amount of money to double in value at compound interest. Simply divide the number 72 by the interest rate. The result is the number of years it takes to double in value.

$$\text{Years to double} = \frac{72}{\text{Compound interest rate}}$$

- For example, if you invested money at 6% compound interest, it would take 12 years ($\frac{72}{6} = 12$) to double your money.
- If you were able to find an investment that paid 9% interest, you could double your money in 8 years ($\frac{72}{9} = 8$).

EXHIBIT 11-3
Compounding Periods per Year

Interest Compounded		Compounding Periods per Year
Annually	Every year	1
Semiannually	Every 6 months	2
Quarterly	Every 3 months	4
Monthly	Every month	12
Daily	Every day	365
Continuously		Infinite

✦ **TABLE 11-1** ✦

Compound Interest Table (Future Value of $1 at Compound Interest)

Periods	$\frac{1}{2}\%$	1%	$1\frac{1}{2}\%$	2%	3%	4%	5%	6%	7%	8%	Periods
1	1.00500	1.01000	1.01500	1.02000	1.03000	1.04000	1.05000	1.06000	1.07000	1.08000	1
2	1.01003	1.02010	1.03023	1.04040	1.06090	1.08160	1.10250	1.12360	1.14490	1.16640	2
3	1.01508	1.03030	1.04568	1.06121	1.09273	1.12486	1.15763	1.19102	1.22504	1.25971	3
4	1.02015	1.04060	1.06136	1.08243	1.12551	1.16986	1.21551	1.26248	1.31080	1.36049	4
5	1.02525	1.05101	1.07728	1.10408	1.15927	1.21665	1.27628	1.33823	1.40255	1.46933	5
6	1.03038	1.06152	1.09344	1.12616	1.19405	1.26532	1.34010	1.41852	1.50073	1.58687	6
7	1.03553	1.07214	1.10984	1.14869	1.22987	1.31593	1.40710	1.50363	1.60578	1.71382	7
8	1.04071	1.08286	1.12649	1.17166	1.26677	1.36857	1.47746	1.59385	1.71819	1.85093	8
9	1.04591	1.09369	1.14339	1.19509	1.30477	1.42331	1.55133	1.68948	1.83846	1.99900	9
10	1.05114	1.10462	1.16054	1.21899	1.34392	1.48024	1.62889	1.79085	1.96715	2.15892	10
11	1.05640	1.11567	1.17795	1.24337	1.38423	1.53945	1.71034	1.89830	2.10485	2.33164	11
12	1.06168	1.12683	1.19562	1.26824	1.42576	1.60103	1.79586	2.01220	2.25219	2.51817	12
13	1.06699	1.13809	1.21355	1.29361	1.46853	1.66507	1.88565	2.13293	2.40985	2.71962	13
14	1.07232	1.14947	1.23176	1.31948	1.51259	1.73168	1.97993	2.26090	2.57853	2.93719	14
15	1.07768	1.16097	1.25023	1.34587	1.55797	1.80094	2.07893	2.39656	2.75903	3.17217	15
16	1.08307	1.17258	1.26899	1.37279	1.60471	1.87298	2.18287	2.54035	2.95216	3.42594	16
17	1.08849	1.18430	1.28802	1.40024	1.65285	1.94790	2.29202	2.69277	3.15882	3.70002	17
18	1.09393	1.19615	1.30734	1.42825	1.70243	2.02582	2.40662	2.85434	3.37993	3.99602	18
19	1.09940	1.20811	1.32695	1.45681	1.75351	2.10685	2.52695	3.02560	3.61653	4.31570	19
20	1.10490	1.22019	1.34686	1.48595	1.80611	2.19112	2.65330	3.20714	3.86968	4.66096	20
21	1.11042	1.23239	1.36706	1.51567	1.86029	2.27877	2.78596	3.39956	4.14056	5.03383	21
22	1.11597	1.24472	1.38756	1.54598	1.91610	2.36992	2.92526	3.60354	4.43040	5.43654	22
23	1.12155	1.25716	1.40838	1.57690	1.97359	2.46472	3.07152	3.81975	4.74053	5.87146	23
24	1.12716	1.26973	1.42950	1.60844	2.03279	2.56330	3.22510	4.04893	5.07237	6.34118	24
25	1.13280	1.28243	1.45095	1.64061	2.09378	2.66584	3.38635	4.29187	5.42743	6.84848	25

Periods	9%	10%	11%	12%	13%	14%	15%	16%	17%	18%	Periods
1	1.09000	1.10000	1.11000	1.12000	1.13000	1.14000	1.15000	1.16000	1.17000	1.18000	1
2	1.18810	1.21000	1.23210	1.25440	1.27690	1.29960	1.32250	1.34560	1.36890	1.39240	2
3	1.29503	1.33100	1.36763	1.40493	1.44290	1.48154	1.52088	1.56090	1.60161	1.64303	3
4	1.41158	1.46410	1.51807	1.57352	1.63047	1.68896	1.74901	1.81064	1.87389	1.93878	4
5	1.53862	1.61051	1.68506	1.76234	1.84244	1.92541	2.01136	2.10034	2.19245	2.28776	5
6	1.67710	1.77156	1.87041	1.97382	2.08195	2.19497	2.31306	2.43640	2.56516	2.69955	6
7	1.82804	1.94872	2.07616	2.21068	2.35261	2.50227	2.66002	2.82622	3.00124	3.18547	7
8	1.99256	2.14359	2.30454	2.47596	2.65844	2.85259	3.05902	3.27841	3.51145	3.75886	8
9	2.17189	2.35795	2.55804	2.77308	3.00404	3.25195	3.51788	3.80296	4.10840	4.43545	9
10	2.36736	2.59374	2.83942	3.10585	3.39457	3.70722	4.04556	4.41144	4.80683	5.23384	10
11	2.58043	2.85312	3.15176	3.47855	3.83586	4.22623	4.65239	5.11726	5.62399	6.17593	11
12	2.81266	3.13843	3.49845	3.89598	4.33452	4.81790	5.35025	5.93603	6.58007	7.28759	12
13	3.06580	3.45227	3.88328	4.36349	4.89801	5.49241	6.15279	6.88579	7.69868	8.59936	13
14	3.34173	3.79750	4.31044	4.88711	5.53475	6.26135	7.07571	7.98752	9.00745	10.14724	14
15	3.64248	4.17725	4.78459	5.47357	6.25427	7.13794	8.13706	9.26552	10.53872	11.97375	15
16	3.97031	4.59497	5.31089	6.13039	7.06733	8.13725	9.35762	10.74800	12.33030	14.12902	16
17	4.32763	5.05447	5.89509	6.86604	7.98608	9.27646	10.76126	12.46768	14.42646	16.67225	17
18	4.71712	5.55992	6.54355	7.68997	9.02427	10.57517	12.37545	14.46251	16.87895	19.67325	18
19	5.14166	6.11591	7.26334	8.61276	10.19742	12.05569	14.23177	16.77652	19.74838	23.21444	19
20	5.60441	6.72750	8.06231	9.64629	11.52309	13.74349	16.36654	19.46076	23.10560	27.39303	20
21	6.10881	7.40025	8.94917	10.80385	13.02109	15.66758	18.82152	22.57448	27.03355	32.32378	21
22	6.65860	8.14027	9.93357	12.10031	14.71383	17.86104	21.64475	26.18640	31.62925	38.14206	22
23	7.25787	8.95430	11.02627	13.55235	16.62663	20.36158	24.89146	30.37622	37.00623	45.00763	23
24	7.91108	9.84973	12.23916	15.17863	18.78809	23.21221	28.62518	35.23642	43.29729	53.10901	24
25	8.62308	10.83471	13.58546	17.00006	21.23054	26.46192	32.91895	40.87424	50.65783	62.66863	25

STEPS FOR USING COMPOUND INTEREST TABLES:

Step 1. Scan across the top row to find the interest rate per period.

Step 2. Look down that column to the row corresponding to the number of periods.

Step 3. The table factor at the intersection of the rate per period column and the number of periods row is the future value of $1.00 at compound interest. Multiply the table factor by the principal to determine the compound amount.

Compound amount = Table factor × Principal

EXAMPLE

Steven Knoerr invested $1,200, at 8% interest compounded quarterly, for 5 years. Use Table 11-1 to find the compound amount of Steven's investment. What is the amount of the compound interest?

SOLUTION STRATEGY

To solve this compound interest problem, we must first find the interest rate per period and the number of compounding periods.

$$\text{Interest rate per period} = \frac{\text{Nominal rate}}{\text{Periods per year}}$$

$$\text{Interest rate per period} = \frac{8\%}{4} = 2\%$$

$$\text{Compounding periods} = \text{Years} \times \text{Periods per year}$$

$$\text{Compounding periods} = 5 \times 4 = 20$$

Now find the table factor by scanning across the top row of the compound interest table to 2% and down the 2% column to 20 periods. The table factor at that intersection is 1.48595. The compound amount is found by multiplying the table factor by the principal:

$$\text{Compound amount} = \text{Table factor} \times \text{Principal}$$

$$\text{Compound amount} = 1.48595 \times 1{,}200 = \underline{\underline{\$1{,}783.14}}$$

The amount of interest is found by subtracting the principal from the compound amount.

$$\text{Compound interest} = \text{Compound amount} - \text{Principal}$$

$$\text{Compound interest} = 1{,}783.14 - 1{,}200.00 = \underline{\underline{\$583.14}}$$

TRY-IT | EXERCISE

2. Patricia Martinez invested $20,000, at 14% interest compounded semiannually, for 8 years. Use Table 11-1 to find the compound amount of Patricia's investment. What is the amount of compound interest Patricia earned?

Check your answers with the solutions on page 402.

11-3 Creating Compound Interest Table Factors for Periods beyond the Table

When the number of periods of an investment is greater than the number of periods provided by the compound interest table, you can compute a new table factor by multiplying the factors for any two periods that add up to the number of periods required. For answer consistency in this chapter, use the two table factors that represent *half* of the periods required. For example,

20 periods + 20 periods → 40 periods   20 periods + 21 periods → 41 periods

STEPS FOR CREATING NEW COMPOUND INTEREST TABLE FACTORS:

Step 1. For the stated interest rate per period, find the two table factors that represent *half* of the periods required.

Step 2. Multiply the two table factors from Step 1 to form the new factor.

Step 3. Round the new factor to five decimal places.

EXAMPLE

Calculate a new table factor and find the compound amount of $10,000, invested at 12% compounded monthly, for 3 years.

SOLUTION STRATEGY

This investment requires a table factor for 36 periods (12 periods per year for 3 years). Because Table 11-1 only provides factors up to 25 periods, we must create one using the steps above.

Step 1. At 12% interest compounded monthly, the rate per period is 1%. Because we are looking for 36 periods, we shall use the factors for 18 and 18 periods, at 1%.

Table factor for 18 periods, 1% = 1.19615

Table factor for 18 periods, 1% = 1.19615

Step 2. Multiply the factors for 18 and 18 periods:

$$1.19615 \times 1.19615 = 1.4307748$$

Step 3. Round to five decimal places:

The new table factor for 36 periods is 1.43077.

The compound amount of the $10,000 investment is

Compound amount = Table factor × Principal

Compound amount = 1.43077 × 10,000 = $14,307.70

TRY-IT | EXERCISE

3. Blake Moore invests $3,500, at 16% interest compounded quarterly, for 7 years. Calculate a new table factor and find the compound amount of Blake's investment.

Check your answer with the solution on page 402.

Compounding	Interest Earned
Annually	$12.00
Semiannually	$12.36
Quarterly	$12.55
Monthly	$12.68

EXHIBIT 11-4
Compound Interest Earned on $100 at 12%

11-4 Calculating Annual Percentage Yield (APY) or Effective Interest Rate

In describing investments and loans, the advertised or stated interest rate is known as the **annual** or **nominal rate.** It is also the rate used to calculate the compound interest. Consider, however, what happens to an investment of $100 at 12% nominal interest.

As we learned in Performance Objective 11-2, the greater the number of compounding periods per year, the higher the amount of interest earned. Although the nominal interest rate is 12%, with monthly compounding the $100 earns more than 12%. This is why many investment offers today advertise daily or continuous compounding. How much are these investments really earning?

The **annual percentage yield (APY)** or **effective rate** reflects the real rate of return on an investment. APY is calculated by finding the total compound interest earned in 1 year and dividing by the principal. *Note:* This is actually the simple interest formula solved for rate from Chapter 10, $R = I \div PT$, where T is equal to 1.

annual or nominal rate
The advertised or stated interest rate of an investment or loan. The rate used to calculate the compound interest.

annual percentage yield (APY) or effective rate
The real or true rate of return on an investment. It is the total compound interest earned in 1 year divided by the principal. The more compounding periods per year, the higher the APY.

$$\text{Annual percentage yield (APY)} = \frac{\text{Total compound interest earned in 1 year}}{\text{Principal}}$$

From the $100 investment example above, the annual percentage yield is the same as the nominal rate when interest is compounded annually; however, it jumps to 12.36% when the compounding is changed to semiannually and to 12.68% when compounded monthly.

Everybody's Business

Real-World Connection

Regulation DD of the Truth in Savings Law, enacted by Congress in 1993, requires banks and other depository institutions to fully disclose the terms of deposit accounts to consumers. The major provisions of the regulation require institutions to:

- Provide consumer account holders with written information about important terms of an account, including the **annual percentage yield.**
- Provide fee and other information on any periodic statement sent to consumers.
- Use certain methods to determine the balance on which interest is calculated.
- Comply with special requirements when advertising deposit accounts.

EXAMPLE

What is the compound amount, compound interest, and annual percentage yield of $4,000, invested for 1 year at 8%, compounded semiannually?

SOLUTION STRATEGY

First we must find the total compound interest earned in 1 year. We can find the compound amount using the factor for 4%, two periods, from Table 11-1.

$$\text{Compound amount} = \text{Table factor} \times \text{Principal}$$

$$\text{Compound amount} = 1.08160 \times 4{,}000 = \underline{\underline{\$4{,}326.40}}$$

$$\text{Compound interest} = \text{Compound amount} - \text{Principal}$$

$$\text{Compound interest} = 4{,}326.40 - 4{,}000 = \underline{\underline{\$326.40}}$$

$$\text{Annual percentage yield} = \frac{\text{Total compound interest earned in 1 year}}{\text{Principal}}$$

$$\text{Annual percentage yield} = \frac{326.40}{4{,}000.00} = \underline{\underline{8.16\%}}$$

TRY-IT | EXERCISE

4. Mignon Tucker invested $7,000 in a certificate of deposit for 1 year, at 6% interest, compounded quarterly. What is the compound amount, compound interest, and annual percentage yield of Mignon's investment? (Round the APY to the nearest hundredth percent.)

Check your answers with the solutions on page 402.

11-5 (Optional) Calculating Compound Amount (Future Value) by Using the Compound Interest Formula

If your calculator has an exponential function key, y^x, you can calculate the compound amount of an investment by using the compound interest formula.

The compound interest formula states:

$$A = P(1 + i)^n$$

where

A = Compound amount

P = Principal

i = Interest rate per period (expressed as a decimal)

n = Total compounding periods (years × periods per year)

STEPS FOR SOLVING THE COMPOUND INTEREST FORMULA:

Step 1. Add the 1 and the interest rate per period, i.

Step 2. Raise the sum from Step 1 to the nth power, using the y^x key on your calculator.

Step 3. Multiply the principal, P, by the answer from Step 2.

Calculator Sequence: 1 [+] i [y^x] n [×] P [=] A

EXAMPLE

Use the compound interest formula to calculate the compound amount of $5,000 invested, at 10% interest compounded semiannually, for 3 years.

SOLUTION STRATEGY

This problem is solved by substituting the investment information into the compound interest formula. It is important to solve the formula in the sequence of steps as outlined above. Note that the rate per period, i, is 5% (10% ÷ 2 periods per year). The total number of periods, the exponent n, is 6 (3 years × 2 periods per year).

$$A = P(1 + i)^n$$

$$A = 5{,}000(1 + .05)^6$$

$$A = 5{,}000(1.05)^6$$

$$A = 5{,}000(1.3400956) = 6{,}700.4782 = \underline{\underline{\$6{,}700.48}}$$

Calculator Sequence: 1 [+] .05 [y^x] 6 [×] 5000 [=] $\underline{\underline{6{,}700.4782}}$

TRY-IT | EXERCISE

5. Use the compound interest formula to calculate the compound amount of $3,000, invested at 8% interest compounded quarterly, for 5 years.

Check your answer with the solution on page 402.

REVIEW EXERCISES | CHAPTER 11—SECTION I

For the following investments, find the total number of compounding periods and the interest rate per period:

	Term of Investment	Nominal (Annual) Rate (%)	Interest Compounded	Compounding Periods	Rate per Period (%)
1.	3 years	13	annually	______	______
2.	5 years	16	quarterly	______	______
3.	12 years	8	semiannually	______	______
4.	6 years	18	monthly	______	______
5.	4 years	14	quarterly	______	______
6.	9 years	10.5	semiannually	______	______
7.	9 months	12	quarterly	______	______

Manually calculate the compound amount and compound interest for the following investments:

	Principal	Term of Investment (years)	Nominal Rate (%)	Interest Compounded	Compound Amount	Compound Interest
8.	$4,000	2	10	annually	______	______
9.	$10,000	1	12	quarterly	______	______
10.	$8,000	3	8	semiannually	______	______

Using Table 11-1, calculate the compound amount and compound interest for the following investments:

	Principal	Term of Investment (years)	Nominal Rate (%)	Interest Compounded	Compound Amount	Compound Interest
11.	$7,000	4	13	annually	______	______
12.	$11,000	6	14	semiannually	______	______
13.	$5,300	3	8	quarterly	______	______
14.	$67,000	2	18	monthly	______	______
15.	$25,000	15	11	annually	______	______
16.	$400	2	6	monthly	______	______
17.	$8,800	$12\frac{1}{2}$	10	semiannually	______	______

The following investments require table factors for periods beyond the table. Create the new table factor, rounded to five places, and calculate the compound amount for each:

	Principal	Term of Investment (years)	Nominal Rate (%)	Interest Compounded	New Table Factor	Compound Amount
18.	$13,000	3	12	monthly	______	______
19.	$19,000	29	9	annually	______	______
20.	$34,700	11	16	quarterly	______	______
21.	$10,000	40	13	annually	______	______
22.	$1,000	16	14	semiannually	______	______

For the following investments, compute the amount of compound interest earned in 1 year and the annual percentage yield (APY):

	Principal	Nominal Rate (%)	Interest Compounded	Compound Interest Earned in 1 Year	Annual Percentage Yield (APY)
23.	$5,000	10	semiannually	______	______
24.	$2,000	13	annually	______	______
25.	$36,000	12	monthly	______	______
26.	$1,000	8	quarterly	______	______

Solve the following word problems by using either Table 11-1 or the optional compound interest formula, $A = P(1 + i)^n$:

27. Marie Stewart invested $3,000 at the Independent Bank, at 6% interest compounded quarterly.

a. What is the annual percentage yield of this investment?

b. What will Marie's investment be worth after 6 years?

28. As a savings plan for college, the Chongs deposited $10,000 in an account paying 8% compounded annually when their son Masahiro was born. How much will the account be worth when Masahiro is 18 years old?

29. Southeastern Supply, Inc., deposited \$500,000 in an account earning 12% compounded monthly. This account is intended to pay for the construction of a new warehouse. How much will be available for the project in $2\frac{1}{2}$ years?

30. The First National Bank is offering a 6-year certificate of deposit (CD) at 4% interest, compounded quarterly; Second National Bank is offering a 6-year CD at 5% interest, compounded annually. 2

a. If you were interested in investing \$8,000 in one of these CDs, calculate the compound amount of each offer.

b. What is the annual percentage yield of each CD?

c. (Optional) If Third National Bank has a 6-year CD at 4.5% interest compounded monthly, use the compound interest formula to the compound amount of this offer.

BUSINESS DECISION

Daily Compounding

31. As an incentive to attract savings deposits, most financial institutions today offer **daily** or even **continuous compounding.** This means that savings or passbook accounts, as well as CDs, earn interest compounded each day, or even more frequently—continuously, such as every hour or even every minute. Let's take a look at daily compounding.

To calculate the compound amount, A, of an investment with daily compounding, use the compound interest formula, modified as follows:

- Rate per period (daily) $= \frac{i}{365}$ (nominal interest rate, i, divided by 365)
- Number of periods (days), n, = number of days of the investment.

$$A = P\left(1 + \frac{i}{365}\right)^n$$

Calculator Sequence: (1 + (i ÷ 365)) y^x n × P = A

a. On April 19, John Smith deposited $2,700 in a passbook savings account at 3.5% interest compounded daily. What is the compound amount of his account on August 5?

b. Using daily compounding, recalculate the compound amount for each of the certificates of deposit in Exercise 30.

SECTION II

PRESENT VALUE

In Section I we learned how to find a future value when the present value was known. Let's take a look at the reverse situation, also commonly found in business. When a future value (an amount needed in the future) is known, the present value is the amount that must be invested today to accumulate with compound interest to that future value. For example, if a corporation wants $100,000 in 5 years (future value—known) to replace its fleet of trucks, what amount must be invested today (present value—unknown) at 8% compounded quarterly to achieve this goal? See Exhibit 11-5.

Everybody's Business

Learning Tip

Which table to use—Compound Interest (Table 11-1) or Present Value (Table 11-2)?

Note that the Compound Interest Table factors are all *greater* than 1, whereas the Present Value Table factors are all *less* than 1.

- When solving for compound amount, a future amount *greater* than the present, use the table with factors *greater* than 1—Compound Interest Table.
- When solving for present value, a present amount *less* than the future, use the table with factors *less* than 1—Present Value Table.

11-6 Calculating the Present Value of a Future Amount by Using Present Value Tables

Just as there are compound interest tables to aid in the calculation of compound amounts, present value tables help calculate the present value of a known future amount. Table 11-4, page 393, is such a table. Note that it is similar to the compound interest table in that the table factors are based on various interest rates per period, for many periods.

EXHIBIT 11-5
Present Value to Future Value

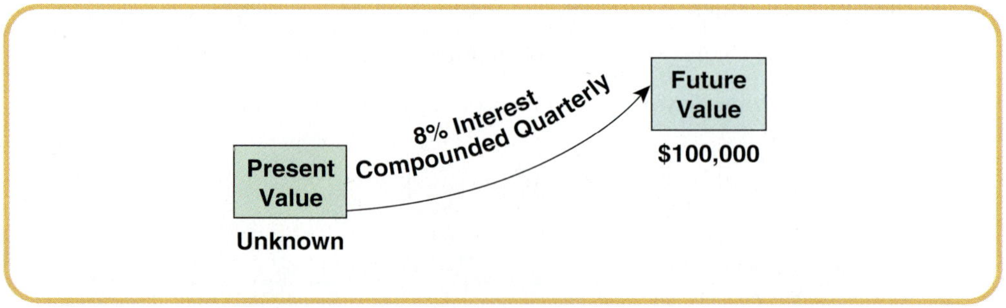

✦ TABLE 11-2 ✦

Present Value Table (Present Value of $1 at Compound Interest)

Periods	$\frac{1}{2}$%	1%	$1\frac{1}{2}$%	2%	3%	4%	5%	6%	7%	8%	Periods
1	0.99502	0.99010	0.98522	0.98039	0.97087	0.96154	0.95238	0.94340	0.93458	0.92593	1
2	0.99007	0.98030	0.97066	0.96117	0.94260	0.92456	0.90703	0.89000	0.87344	0.85734	2
3	0.98515	0.97059	0.95632	0.94232	0.91514	0.88900	0.86384	0.83962	0.81630	0.79383	3
4	0.98025	0.96098	0.94218	0.92385	0.88849	0.85480	0.82270	0.79209	0.76290	0.73503	4
5	0.97537	0.95147	0.92826	0.90573	0.86261	0.82193	0.78353	0.74726	0.71299	0.68058	5
6	0.97052	0.94205	0.91454	0.88797	0.83748	0.79031	0.74622	0.70496	0.66634	0.63017	6
7	0.96569	0.93272	0.90103	0.87056	0.81309	0.75992	0.71068	0.66506	0.62275	0.58349	7
8	0.96089	0.92348	0.88771	0.85349	0.78941	0.73069	0.67684	0.62741	0.58201	0.54027	8
9	0.95610	0.91434	0.87459	0.83676	0.76642	0.70259	0.64461	0.59190	0.54393	0.50025	9
10	0.95135	0.90529	0.86167	0.82035	0.74409	0.67556	0.61391	0.55839	0.50835	0.46319	10
11	0.94661	0.89632	0.84893	0.80426	0.72242	0.64958	0.58468	0.52679	0.47509	0.42888	11
12	0.94191	0.88745	0.83639	0.78849	0.70138	0.62460	0.55684	0.49697	0.44401	0.39711	12
13	0.93722	0.87866	0.82403	0.77303	0.68095	0.60057	0.53032	0.46884	0.41496	0.36770	13
14	0.93256	0.86996	0.81185	0.75788	0.66112	0.57748	0.50507	0.44230	0.38782	0.34046	14
15	0.92792	0.86135	0.79985	0.74301	0.64186	0.55526	0.48102	0.41727	0.36245	0.31524	15
16	0.92330	0.85282	0.78803	0.72845	0.62317	0.53391	0.45811	0.39365	0.33873	0.29189	16
17	0.91871	0.84438	0.77639	0.71416	0.60502	0.51337	0.43630	0.37136	0.31657	0.27027	17
18	0.91414	0.83602	0.76491	0.70016	0.58739	0.49363	0.41552	0.35034	0.29586	0.25025	18
19	0.90959	0.82774	0.75361	0.68643	0.57029	0.47464	0.39573	0.33051	0.27651	0.23171	19
20	0.90506	0.81954	0.74247	0.67297	0.55368	0.45639	0.37689	0.31180	0.25842	0.21455	20
21	0.90056	0.81143	0.73150	0.65978	0.53755	0.43883	0.35894	0.29416	0.24151	0.19866	21
22	0.89608	0.80340	0.72069	0.64684	0.52189	0.42196	0.34185	0.27751	0.22571	0.18394	22
23	0.89162	0.79544	0.71004	0.63416	0.50669	0.40573	0.32557	0.26180	0.21095	0.17032	23
24	0.88719	0.78757	0.69954	0.62172	0.49193	0.39012	0.31007	0.24698	0.19715	0.15770	24
25	0.88277	0.77977	0.68921	0.60953	0.47761	0.37512	0.29530	0.23300	0.18425	0.14602	25

Periods	9%	10%	11%	12%	13%	14%	15%	16%	17%	18%	Periods
1	0.91743	0.90909	0.90090	0.89286	0.88496	0.87719	0.86957	0.86207	0.85470	0.84746	1
2	0.84168	0.82645	0.81162	0.79719	0.78315	0.76947	0.75614	0.74316	0.73051	0.71818	2
3	0.77218	0.75131	0.73119	0.71178	0.69305	0.67497	0.65752	0.64066	0.62437	0.60863	3
4	0.70843	0.68301	0.65873	0.63552	0.61332	0.59208	0.57175	0.55229	0.53365	0.51579	4
5	0.64993	0.62092	0.59345	0.56743	0.54276	0.51937	0.49718	0.47611	0.45611	0.43711	5
6	0.59627	0.56447	0.53464	0.50663	0.48032	0.45559	0.43233	0.41044	0.38984	0.37043	6
7	0.54703	0.51316	0.48166	0.45235	0.42506	0.39964	0.37594	0.35383	0.33320	0.31393	7
8	0.50187	0.46651	0.43393	0.40388	0.37616	0.35056	0.32690	0.30503	0.28478	0.26604	8
9	0.46043	0.42410	0.39092	0.36061	0.33288	0.30751	0.28426	0.26295	0.24340	0.22546	9
10	0.42241	0.38554	0.35218	0.32197	0.29459	0.26974	0.24718	0.22668	0.20804	0.19106	10
11	0.38753	0.35049	0.31728	0.28748	0.26070	0.23662	0.21494	0.19542	0.17781	0.16192	11
12	0.35553	0.31863	0.28584	0.25668	0.23071	0.20756	0.18691	0.16846	0.15197	0.13722	12
13	0.32618	0.28966	0.25751	0.22917	0.20416	0.18207	0.16253	0.14523	0.12989	0.11629	13
14	0.29925	0.26333	0.23199	0.20462	0.18068	0.15971	0.14133	0.12520	0.11102	0.09855	14
15	0.27454	0.23939	0.20900	0.18270	0.15989	0.14010	0.12289	0.10793	0.09489	0.08352	15
16	0.25187	0.21763	0.18829	0.16312	0.14150	0.12289	0.10686	0.09304	0.08110	0.07078	16
17	0.23107	0.19784	0.16963	0.14564	0.12522	0.10780	0.09293	0.08021	0.06932	0.05998	17
18	0.21199	0.17986	0.15282	0.13004	0.11081	0.09456	0.08081	0.06914	0.05925	0.05083	18
19	0.19449	0.16351	0.13768	0.11611	0.09806	0.08295	0.07027	0.05961	0.05064	0.04308	19
20	0.17843	0.14864	0.12403	0.10367	0.08678	0.07276	0.06110	0.05139	0.04328	0.03651	20
21	0.16370	0.13513	0.11174	0.09256	0.07680	0.06383	0.05313	0.04430	0.03699	0.03094	21
22	0.15018	0.12285	0.10067	0.08264	0.06796	0.05599	0.04620	0.03819	0.03162	0.02622	22
23	0.13778	0.11168	0.09069	0.07379	0.06014	0.04911	0.04017	0.03292	0.02702	0.02222	23
24	0.12640	0.10153	0.08170	0.06588	0.05323	0.04308	0.03493	0.02838	0.02310	0.01883	24
25	0.11597	0.09230	0.07361	0.05882	0.04710	0.03779	0.03038	0.02447	0.01974	0.01596	25

STEPS FOR USING PRESENT VALUE TABLES:

Step 1. Scan across the top row to find the interest rate per period.

Step 2. Look down that column to the row corresponding to the number of periods.

Step 3. The table factor found at the intersection of the rate per period column and the number of periods row is the present value of $1.00 at compound interest. Multiply the table factor by the compound amount to determine the present value:

Present value = Table factor × Compound amount (future value)

EXAMPLE

Mardell Toomey wants $5,000 in 8 years. Use Table 11-2 to find how much Mardell must invest now at 6% interest compounded semiannually to have $5,000, 8 years from now.

SOLUTION STRATEGY

To solve this present value problem, we shall use 3% per period (6% nominal rate ÷ 2 periods per year) and 16 periods (8 years × 2 periods per year).

Step 1. Scan across the top row of the present value table to 3%.

Step 2. Look down that column to the row corresponding to 16 periods.

Step 3. Find the table factor at the intersection of Steps 1 and 2, and multiply it by the compound amount to find the present value. Table factor = .62317.

Present value = Table factor × Compound amount

Present value = .62317 × 5,000 = $3,115.85

TRY-IT | EXERCISE

6. Baron von Keller III wants to renovate his castle in Germany in 3 years. He estimates the cost to be $300,000. Use Table 11-2 to find how much the Baron must invest now at 8% interest compounded quarterly to have $300,000, 3 years from now.

Check your answer with the solution on page 402.

11-7 Creating Present Value Table Factors for Periods beyond the Table

Just as with the compound interest tables, there may be times when the number of periods of an investment or loan is greater than the number of periods provided by the present value tables. When this occurs, you can create a new table factor by multiplying the table factors for any two periods that add up to the number of periods required.

For answer consistency in this chapter, use the two table factors that represent *half* of the periods required. For example,

20 periods + 20 periods → 40 periods

20 periods + 21 periods → 41 periods

STEPS FOR CREATING NEW TABLE FACTORS:

Step 1. For the stated interest rate per period, find the two table factors that represent *half* of the periods required.

Step 2. Multiply the two table factors from Step 1 to form the new factor.

Step 3. Round the new factor to five decimal places.

EXAMPLE

Calculate a new table factor and find the present value of $2,000, if the interest rate is 12% compounded quarterly, for 8 years.

SOLUTION STRATEGY

This investment requires a table factor for 32 periods, four periods per year for 8 years. Because Table 11-4 only provides factors up to 25 periods, we must create one by using the steps above.

Step 1. At 12% interest compounded quarterly, the rate per period is 3%. Because we are looking for 32 periods, we shall use the factors for 16 and 16 periods, at 3%.

Table factor for 16 periods, 3% = .62317

Table factor for 16 periods, 3% = .62317

Step 2. Multiply the factors for 16 and 16 periods:

$$.62317 \times .62317 = .3883408$$

Step 3. Rounding to five decimal places, the new table factor for 32 periods is $\underline{\underline{.38834}}$. The present value of the $2,000 investment is

Present value = Table factor × Compound amount

Present value = .38834 × 2,000 = $\underline{\underline{\$776.68}}$

TRY-IT | EXERCISE

7. Calculate a new table factor and find the present value of $8,500, if the interest rate is 6% compounded quarterly, for 10 years.

Check your answer with the solution on page 402.

11-8 (Optional) Calculating Present Value of a Future Amount by Using the Present Value Formula

If your calculator has an exponential function key, y^x, you can calculate the present value of an investment by using the present value formula.

The present value formula states:

$$PV = \frac{A}{(1 + i)^n}$$

where

PV = Present value

A = Compound amount

i = Interest rate per period (expressed as a decimal)

n = Total compounding periods (years × periods per year)

STEPS FOR SOLVING THE PRESENT VALUE FORMULA:

Step 1. Add the 1 and the interest rate per period, i.

Step 2. Raise the sum from Step 1 to the nth power, using the y^x key on your calculator.

Step 3. Divide the compound amount, A, by the answer from Step 2.

Calculator Sequence: 1 [+] i [y^x] n [=] [M+] A [÷] [MR] [=] PV

EXAMPLE

Use the present value formula to calculate the present value of $3,000, if the interest rate is 16% compounded quarterly, for 6 years.

SOLUTION STRATEGY

This problem is solved by substituting the investment information into the present value formula. It is important to solve the formula in the sequence of steps as outlined. Note the rate per period, i, is 4% (16% ÷ 4 periods per year). The total number of periods, the exponent n, is 24 (6 years × 4 periods per year).

$$\text{Present value} = \frac{A}{(1 + i)^n}$$

$$\text{Present value} = \frac{3{,}000}{(1 + .04)^{24}}$$

$$\text{Present value} = \frac{3{,}000}{(1.04)^{24}}$$

$$\text{Present value} = \frac{3{,}000}{2.5633041} = \underline{\underline{\$1{,}170.36}}$$

Calculator Sequence: 1 [+] .04 [y^x] 24 [=] [M+] 3000 [÷] [MR] [=] $1,170.36

TRY-IT | EXERCISE

8. Ernie and Roni Sanchez want to accumulate $30,000, 17 years from now, as a college fund for their baby son, Michael. Use the present value formula to calculate how much they must invest now, at an interest rate of 8% compounded semiannually, to have $30,000 in 17 years.

Check your answer with the solution on page 402.

REVIEW EXERCISES | CHAPTER 11—SECTION II

For the following investments, calculate the present value (principal) and the compound interest. Use Table 11-2 (round your answers to the nearest cent):

	Compound Amount	Term of Investment	Nominal Rate (%)	Interest Compounded	Present Value	Compound Interest
1.	$6,000	3 years	9	annually		
2.	$24,000	6 years	14	semiannually		
3.	$650	5 years	8	quarterly		
4.	$2,000	12 years	6	semiannually		
5.	$50,000	25 years	11	annually		
6.	$14,500	18 months	10	semiannually		
7.	$9,800	4 years	12	quarterly		
8.	$100,000	10 years	9	annually		
9.	$250	1 year	18	monthly		
10.	$4,000	27 months	8	quarterly		

The following investments require table factors for periods beyond the table. Create the new table factor, rounded to five places, and calculate the present value for each:

	Compound Amount	Term of Investment (years)	Nominal Rate (%)	Interest Compounded	New Table Factor	Present Value
11.	$12,000	10	16	quarterly		
12.	$33,000	38	7	annually		
13.	$1,400	12	12	quarterly		
14.	$1,000	45	13	annually		
15.	$110,000	17	8	semiannually		

Solve the following word problems by using either Table 11-2 or the optional present value formula:

$$PV = \frac{A}{(1 + i)^n}$$

16. How much must be invested today at 6% compounded quarterly to have $8,000 in 3 years?

17. Irene McGuinness is planning a vacation in Europe in 4 years, after graduation. She estimates that she will need $3,500 for the trip.

a. If her bank is offering 4-year certificates of deposit with 8% interest compounded quarterly, how much must Irene invest now to have the money for the trip?

b. How much compound interest will be earned on the investment?

18. Sunshine Homes, a real estate development company, is planning to build five custom homes, each costing \$125,000, in $2\frac{1}{2}$ years. The Bank of Aventura pays 6% interest compounded semiannually. How much should the company invest now to have sufficient funds to build the homes in the future?

19. Ben Whitney estimates that he will need \$25,000 to set up a law office in 7 years, when he graduates from law school.

a. How much must Ben invest now at 12% interest compounded quarterly to achieve his goal?

b. How much compound interest will he earn on the investment?

20. American Airlines intends to pay off a \$20,000,000 bond issue that comes due in 4 years. How much must the company set aside now, at 6% interest compounded monthly, to accumulate the required amount of money?

BUSINESS DECISION

The Inflation Factor

21. You are the finance manager for All-Ways Manufacturing. The company plans to purchase \$1,000,000 in new assembly line machinery in 5 years.

a. How much must be set aside now, at 6% interest compounded semiannually, to accumulate the \$1,000,000 in 5 years?

b. If the inflation rate on this type of equipment is 4% per year, what will be the cost of the equipment in 5 years, adjusted for inflation?

c. Use the inflation-adjusted cost of the equipment to calculate how much must be set aside now.

d. (Optional) Use the present value formula to calculate how much would be required now if you found a bank that offered 6% interest compounded daily.

CHAPTER FORMULAS

Compound interest = Compound amount − Principal

Compounding periods = Years × Periods per year

$$\text{Interest rate per period} = \frac{\text{Nominal rate}}{\text{Periods per year}}$$

Compound amount = Table factor × Principal

$$\text{Annual percentage yield (APY)} = \frac{\text{Total interest earned in 1 year}}{\text{Principal}}$$

$$\text{Compound amount} = \text{Principal}(1 + \text{interest})^{\text{periods}}$$

Present value = Table factor × Compound amount

$$\text{Present value} = \frac{\text{Compound amount}}{(1 + \text{interest})^{\text{periods}}}$$

✦ SUMMARY CHART ✦

SECTION I: Compound Interest—The Time Value of Money

Topic	P/O, Page	Important Concepts	Illustrative Examples
Manually Calculating Compound Amount (Future Value)	11-1 381	In compound interest, the interest is applied a number of times during the term of an investment. Compound interest yields considerably higher interest than simple interest because the investor is earning interest on the interest. Interest can be compounded annually, semiannually, quarterly, monthly, daily, and continuously. 1. Determine number of compounding periods (years × periods per year). 2. Apply the simple interest formula, $I = PRT$, as many times as there are compounding periods, adding interest to principal before each succeeding calculation.	Manually calculate the compound amount of a $1,000 investment at 8% interest compounded annually for 2 years. Original principal 1,000.00 Interest—period 1 + 80.00 Principal—period 2 1,080.00 Interest—period 2 + 86.40 Compound Amount $1,166.40

SECTION I: (continued)

Topic	P/O, Page	Important Concepts	Illustrative Examples
Calculating Amount of Compound Interest	11-1 382	Amount of compound interest is calculated by subtracting the original principal from the compound amount. **Compound interest = Compound amount − Principal**	What is the amount of compound interest earned in the problem above? $1,166.40 − $1,000 = $166.40
Computing Compound Amount (Future Value) by Using the Compound Interest Tables	11-2 383	1. Scan across the top row of Table 11-1 to find the interest rate per period. 2. Look down that column to the row corresponding to the number of compounding periods. 3. The table factor found at the intersection of the rate per period column and the periods row is the future value of $1.00 at compound interest. **Compound amount = Table factor × Principal**	Use Table 11-1 to find the compound amount of an investment of $2,000, at 12% interest compounded quarterly, for 6 years. Rate = 3% per period (12% ÷ 4) Periods = 24 (6 years × 4) Table factor = 2.03279 Compound amount = 2.03279 × 2,000 = $4,065.58
Creating Compound Interest Table Factors for Periods beyond the Table	11-3 386	1. For the stated interest rate per period, find the two table factors that represent *half* of the periods required. 2. Multiply the two table factors from Step 1 to form the new factor. 3. Round the new factor to five decimal places.	Create a new table factor for 5% interest for 30 periods. Multiply the 5% factors for 15 and 15 periods from Table 11-1. 5%, 15 periods = 2.07893 5%, 15 periods = × 2.07893 30 4.3219499 New factor, rounded = 4.32195
Calculating Annual Percentage Yield (APY) or Effective Interest Rate	11-4 387	To calculate annual percentage yield, divide total compound interest earned in 1 year by the principal. $\text{Annual percentage yield (APY)} = \dfrac{\text{1 year compound interest}}{\text{Principal}}$	What is the annual percentage yield of $5,000 invested for 1 year at 12% compounded monthly? From Table 11-2, we use the table factor for 12 periods, 1%, to find the compound amount: 1.12683 × 5,000 = 5,634.15 Interest = Cmp amt − Principal Int = 5,634.15 − 5,000 = 634.15 $\text{APY} = \dfrac{634.15}{5{,}000} = 12.68\%$
(Optional) Calculating Compound Amount (Future Value) by Using the Compound Interest Formula	11-5 388	In addition to the compound interest tables, another method for calculating compound amount is by the compound interest formula. $A = P(1 + i)^n$ **where** A = **Compound amount** P = **Principal** I = **Interest rate per period (decimal form)** n = **Number of compounding periods**	What is the compound amount of $3,000 invested at 8% interest compounded quarterly for 10 years? $A = P(1 + i)^n$ $A = 3{,}000(1 + .02)^{40}$ $A = 3{,}000(1.02)^{40}$ $A = 3{,}000(2.2080396)$ $A = \$6{,}624.12$

SECTION II: Present Value

Topic	P/O, Page	Important Concepts	Illustrative Examples
Calculating the Present Value of a Future Amount by Using the Present Value Tables	11-6 394	When the future value, an amount needed in the future, is known, the present value is the amount that must be invested today to accumulate, with compound interest, to that future value. 1. Scan across the top row of Table 11-2 to find the rate per period. 2. Look down that column to the row corresponding to the number of periods. 3. The table factor found at the intersection of the rate per period column and the periods row is the present value of $1.00 at compound interest. **Present value = Table factor × Compound amount**	How much must be invested now at 10% interest compounded semiannually to have $8,000, 9 years from now? Rate = 5% (10% ÷ 2) Periods = 18 (9 years × 2) Table factor = .41552 Present value = .41552 × 8,000 Present value = $3,324.16
Creating Present Value Table Factors for Periods beyond the Table	11-7 395	1. For the stated interest rate per period, find the two table factors that represent *half* of the periods required. 2. Multiply the two table factors from Step 1 for the new factor. 3. Round the new factor to five decimal places.	Create a new table factor for 6% interest for 41 periods. Multiply the 6% factors for 21 and 20 periods from Table 11-2. 6%, 21 periods = .29416 6%, 20 periods = × .31180 41 .0917191 New factor, rounded = .09172
(Optional) Calculating Present Value of a Future Amount by Using the Present Value Formula	11-8 395–396	If your calculator has an exponential function key, y^x, you can calculate the present value of an investment by using the present value formula. $PV = \frac{A}{(1+i)^n}$ **where** PV **= Present value** A **= Compound amount** i **= Interest rate per period (decimal form)** n **= Total compounding periods**	How much must be invested now in order to have $12,000 in 10 years, if the interest rate is 12% compounded quarterly? Present value $= \frac{12{,}000}{(1+.03)^{40}}$ $PV = \frac{12{,}000}{(1.03)^{40}} = \frac{12{,}000}{3.2620378}$ Present value = $3,678.68

TRY-IT EXERCISE | SOLUTIONS

1.

10,000.00	Original principal
+ 600.00	($I = PRT = 10{,}000 \times .12 \times \frac{1}{2} = 600$)
10,600.00	Principal period 2
+ 636.00	($I = PRT = 10{,}600 \times .12 \times \frac{1}{2} = 636$)
11,236.00	Principal period 3
+ 674.16	($I = PRT = 11{,}236 \times .12 \times \frac{1}{2} = 674.16$)
11,910.16	Principal period 4
+ 714.61	($I = PRT = 11{,}910.16 \times .12 \times \frac{1}{2} = 714.61$)
12,624.77	Principal period 5
+ 757.49	($I = PRT = 12{,}624.77 \times .12 \times \frac{1}{2} = 757.49$)
13,382.26	Principal period 6
+ 802.94	($I = PRT = 13{,}382.26 \times .12 \times \frac{1}{2} = 802.94$)
$14,185.20	Compound amount

Compound interest = 14,185.20 − 10,000.00 = $4,185.20

2. 7%, 16 periods

Compound amount = Table factor × Principal

Compound amount = 2.95216 × 20,000 = $59,043.20

Compound interest = Compound amount − Principal

Compound interest = 59,043.20 − 20,000.00 = $39,043.20

3. Table factor required = 4%, 28 periods

4%, 14 periods: 1.73168

4%, 14 periods: × 1.73168

28 periods 2.9987156 = 2.99872 new factor 4%, 28 periods

Compound amount = 2.99872 × 3,500 = $10,495.52

4. $1\frac{1}{2}$%, 4 periods

Compound amount = 1.06136 × 7,000 = $7,429.52

Compound interest = 7,429.52 − 7,000.00 = $429.52

$$\text{Annual percentage yield} = \frac{\text{1 year interest}}{\text{Principal}} = \frac{429.52}{7{,}000.00} = 6.14\%$$

5. $A = P(1 + i)^n$ $P = \$3{,}000$

$$i = \frac{8\%}{4} = .02$$

$$n = 5 \times 4 = 20$$

$$A = 3{,}000(1 + .02)^{20}$$

$$A = 3{,}000(1.02)^{20}$$

$$A = 3{,}000(1.4859474)$$

$$A = \$4{,}457.84$$

6. 2%, 12 periods

Present value = Table factor × Compound amount

Present value = .78849 × 300,000 = $236,547.00

7. Table factor required = $1\frac{1}{2}$%, 40 periods

$1\frac{1}{2}$%, 20 periods: .74247

$1\frac{1}{2}$%, 20 periods: × .74247

40 periods = .5512617 = .55126 new factor $1\frac{1}{2}$%, 40 periods

Present value = .55126 × 8,500 = $4,685.71

8. $PV = \frac{A}{(1 + i)^n}$ $A = 30{,}000$

$$i = \frac{8\%}{2} = .04$$

$$n = 17 \times 2 = 34$$

$$PV = \frac{30{,}000}{(1 + .04)^{34}}$$

$$PV = \frac{30{,}000}{(1.04)^{34}}$$

$$PV = \frac{30{,}000}{3.7943163} = \$7{,}906.56$$

CHAPTER 11 | ASSESSMENT TEST

Name ______________

Class ______________

Using Table 11-1, calculate the compound amount and compound interest for the following investments:

	Principal	Term of Investment (years)	Nominal Rate (%)	Interest Compounded	Compound Amount	Compound Interest
1.	$14,000	6	14	semiannually	________	________
2.	$7,700	5	6	quarterly	________	________
3.	$3,000	1	18	monthly	________	________
4.	$42,000	19	11	annually	________	________

The following investments require table factors for periods beyond the table. Create the new table factor and calculate the compound amount for each:

	Principal	Term of Investment (years)	Nominal Rate (%)	Interest Compounded	New Table Factor	Compound Amount
5.	$20,000	11	16	quarterly	________	________
6.	$10,000	4	6	monthly	________	________

For the following investments, compute the amount of compound interest earned in 1 year and the annual percentage yield (round APY to the nearest hundredth percent):

	Principal	Nominal Rate (%)	Interest Compounded	Compound Interest Earned in 1 Year	Annual Percentage Yield (APY)
7.	$8,500	12	monthly	________	________
8.	$1,000,000	8	quarterly	________	________

Calculate the present value (principal) and the compound interest for the following investments. Use Table 11-2 (round answers to the nearest cent):

	Compound Amount	Term of Investment	Nominal Rate (%)	Interest Compounded	Present Value	Compound Interest
9.	$150,000	22 years	15	annually	________	________
10.	$20,000	30 months	14	semiannually	________	________
11.	$900	$1\frac{3}{4}$ years	18	monthly	________	________
12.	$5,500	15 months	8	quarterly	________	________

The following investments require table factors for periods beyond the table. Create the new table factor and the present value for each:

	Compound Amount	Term of Investment (years)	Nominal Rate (%)	Interest Compounded	New Table Factor	Present Value
13.	$1,300	4	12	monthly	________	________
14.	$100,000	50	5	annually	________	________

Solve the following word problems by using either Tables 11-1 and 11-2 or the optional compound interest and present value formulas. When necessary, create new table factors (round dollars to the nearest cent and percents to the nearest hundredth):

15. What is the compound amount and compound interest of $36,000 invested at 12% compounded semiannually for 7 years?

Answers

1. ______________
2. ______________
3. ______________
4. ______________
5. ______________
6. ______________
7. ______________
8. ______________
9. ______________
10. ______________
11. ______________
12. ______________
13. ______________
14. ______________
15. ______________

Name ______________________

Class ______________________

Answers

16. ______________________

17. ______________________

____

18. ______________________

19. ______________________

20. ______________________

16. What is the present value of $73,000 in 11 years if the interest rate is 8% compounded semiannually?

17. What is the compound amount and compound interest of $15,000 invested at 6% compounded quarterly for 27 months?

18. What is the annual percentage yield of a $10,000 investment, for 1 year, at 12% interest compounded monthly?

19. Geoff and Audrey Coll want to save $50,000 in $5\frac{1}{2}$ years to redecorate their house. If the Bank of Kendall is paying 8% interest compounded quarterly, how much must they deposit now to have the money for the project?

20. What is the present value of $100,000 in 3 years if the interest rate is 6% compounded monthly?

Name ____________________

Class ____________________

Answers

21. a. ____________________

b. ____________________

22. ____________________

23. ____________________

24. a. ____________________

b. ____________________

____

21. Jennifer Langer invested \$8,800 at the Worthington Credit Union at 12% interest compounded quarterly.

a. What is the annual percentage yield of this investment?

b. What will Jennifer's investment be worth after 6 years?

22. Swifty Delivery Service uses vans costing \$13,800 each. How much will the company have to invest today to accumulate enough money to buy six new vans at the end of 4 years? Swifty's bank is currently paying 12% interest compounded quarterly.

23. While rummaging through the attic, you discover a savings account left to you by your rich Uncle David. When you were 5 years old, he invested \$20,000 in your name, at 6% interest compounded semiannually. If you are now 20 years old, how much is the account worth?

24. Wentworth Industries is planning to expand its production facility in a few years. New plant construction costs are estimated to be \$4.50 per square foot. The company invests \$850,000 today at 8% interest compounded quarterly.

a. How many square feet of new facility could be built after $3\frac{1}{2}$ years?

b. If the company waits 5 years, but construction costs increase to \$5.25 per square foot, how many square feet could be built? What do you recommend?

Name ____________________

Class ____________________

Answers

25. a. ____________________

b. ____________________

26. a. ____________________

b. ____________________

25. Over the past 10 years you made the following investments:

1. Deposited $10,000 at 8% compounded semiannually, in a 3-year certificate of deposit.
2. After the 3 years, you took the maturity value (principal and interest) of that CD and added another $5,000 to buy a 4-year, 6% certificate compounded quarterly.
3. When that certificate matured, you added another $8,000 and bought a 3-year, 7% certificate compounded annually.

a. What was the total worth of your investment when the last certificate matured?

b. What is the total amount of compound interest earned over the 10-year period?

Everybody's Business

Real World Connection

Pay Me Now, Pay Me Later is a good example of how the "time value of money" concept can be applied in business. Remember:

When interest can be earned, money today is more desirable than the same amount of money in the future

BUSINESS DECISION

Pay Me Now, Pay Me Later

26. You are the owner of an apartment building that is being offered for sale for $1,500,000. You receive an offer from a prospective buyer who wants to pay you $500,000 now, $500,000 in 6 months, and $500,000 in 1 year.

a. What is the actual present value of this offer, considering you can earn 12% interest compounded monthly on your money?

b. If another buyer offers to pay you $1,425,000 cash now, which is a better deal?

c. Because you understand the "time value of money" concept, you have negotiated a deal with the original buyer from part **a**, whereby you will accept the three-payment offer but will charge 12% interest, compounded monthly, on the two delayed payments.

Calculate the total purchase price under this new arrangement.

Name ______________________

Class ______________________

Answers

26. c. ______________________

d. ______________________

d. Now, calculate the present value of the new deal, to verify that you will receive the original asking price of $1,500,000 for your apartment building.

All the Math That's Fit to Learn

The Business Math Times

Volume XI | **Compound Interest and Present Value** | One Dollar

Putting Your Money to Work!

CHECKING ACCOUNTS

In Chapter 4, we learned about checking accounts. The money left in checking accounts is known as **demand deposits,** since it can be withdrawn "on demand," without advance notice. Over the years, these basic, no-frills accounts have lost popularity because they do not pay interest on the depositor's money.

Today, banks offer checking accounts that do pay interest. These accounts, commonly called **NOW accounts** (negotiable order of withdrawal), allow unlimited check writing but require minimum balances ranging from a few hundred dollars to a few thousand dollars.

Another popular form of deposit account is known as a **money market account.** These pay even higher interest rates than NOW accounts but have check writing limitations.

SAVINGS ACCOUNTS

One common form of savings account is called a **passbook savings account.** These are a safe place to keep money; however, the interest rates paid are not very competitive and there are no check writing privileges.

Another form of time deposit, **certificates of deposit (CDs)** pay higher interest than passbook savings accounts. These are notes issued by commercial banks or other financial institutions. They guarantee a depositor a predetermined rate of interest for specified periods of time, ranging from 30 days to 10, or even 15 years.

CREDIT UNION ACCOUNTS

Credit unions offer accounts that are similar to accounts at other depository institutions, but have different names. Credit union members have "share draft" accounts, rather than checking; "share" accounts, rather than savings; and "share certificate" accounts, rather than certificates of deposit.

For more information, visit our Web site at www.contemporarymath.com

Pepper . . . and Salt

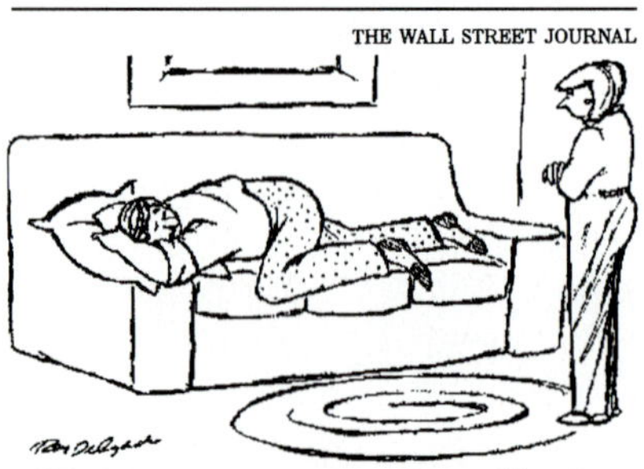

"Don't worry, my money is working for me."

"Quote . . . Unquote"

Compounding is mankind's greatest invention because it allows for the reliable, systematic accumulation of wealth.
—*Albert Einstein*

Remember that time is money.
—*Benjamin Franklin*

The Magic of Compounding!

NEW YORK, NEW YORK

In 1626, Peter Minuit, a Dutch colonial governor in America, purchased New Amsterdam, the settlement that later became New York City, from one of the Algonquin-speaking tribes. The purchase price was trinkets and trade goods valued at 60 Dutch guilders; a sum later calculated as $24.

At first, this might seem like an incredibly low price. But wait! Let's put the time value of money to work.

A. If the $24 had been invested at 6% interest compounded annually, by 2003, 377 years later, how much would the $24 be worth?

B. If they could have invested the money at 8% compounded annually instead of 6%, how much would the $24 be worth?

The solutions appear in the next issue of *The Business Math Times* on page 442.

Brainteaser

I SEE THE LIGHT!

If a digital clock is the only light in an otherwise totally dark room, at what time will the room be the darkest? Brightest?

ANSWER TO LAST ISSUE'S BRAINTEASER

20 cars and 10 motorcycles

Let C = number of cars and
M = number of motorcycles

$$C + M = 30$$
$$M = 30 - C$$
$$4C + 2M = 100$$
$$4C + 2(30 - C) = 100$$
$$4C + 60 - 2C = 100$$
$$2C = 40$$
$$C = 20, M = 10$$

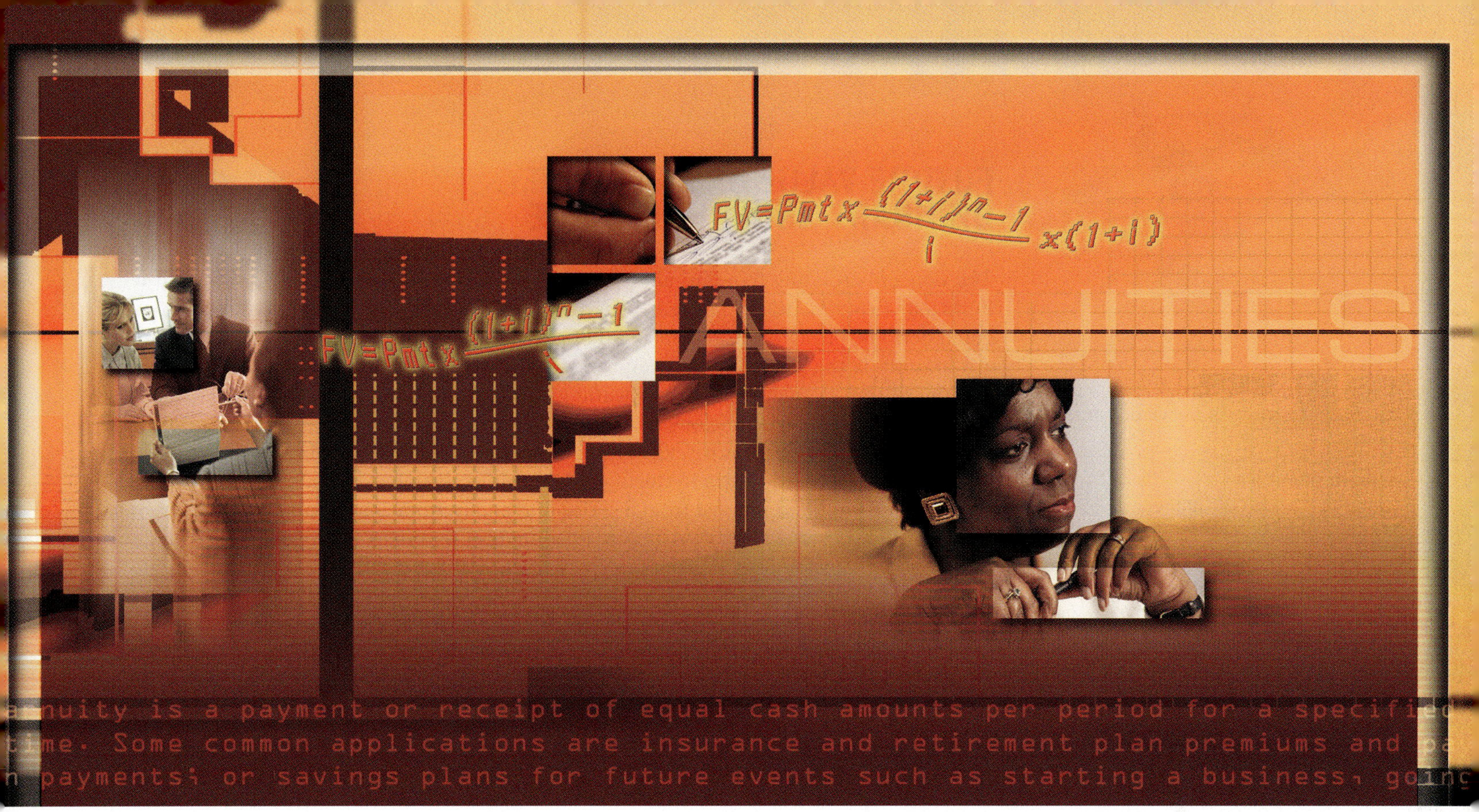

CHAPTER

12

Annuities

PERFORMANCE OBJECTIVES

Section I Future Value of an Annuity: Ordinary and Annuity Due

12-1 Calculating the future value of an ordinary annuity by using tables. (p. 410)
12-2 Calculating the future value of an annuity due by using tables. (p. 413)
12-3 (Optional) Calculating the future value of an ordinary annuity and an annuity due by formula. (p. 415)

Section II Present Value of an Annuity

12-4 Calculating the present value of an ordinary annuity by using tables. (p. 419)
12-5 Calculating the present value of an annuity due by using tables. (p. 421)
12-6 (Optional) Calculating the present value of an ordinary annuity and an annuity due by formula. (p. 422)

Section III Sinking Funds and Amortization

12-7 Calculating the amount of a sinking fund payment by table. (p. 426)
12-8 Calculating the amount of an amortization payment by table. (p. 427)
12-9 (Optional) Calculating sinking fund payments by formula. (p. 428)
12-10 (Optional) Calculating amortization payments by formula. (p. 429)

SECTION I

FUTURE VALUE OF AN ANNUITY: ORDINARY AND ANNUITY DUE

annuity
Payment or receipt of equal amounts of money per period for a specified amount of time.

simple annuity
Annuity in which the number of compounding periods per year coincides with the number of annuity payments per year.

complex annuity
Annuity in which the annuity payments and compounding periods do not coincide.

annuities certain
Annuities that have a specified number of time periods.

contingent annuities
Annuities based on an uncertain time period, such as the life of a person.

The concepts relating to compound interest in Chapter 11 were mainly concerned with lump sum investments or payments. Frequently in business, situations involve a series of equal periodic payments or receipts, rather than lump sums. These are known as annuities. An **annuity** is the payment or receipt of *equal* cash amounts per period for a specified amount of time. Some common applications are insurance and retirement plan premiums and payouts; loan payments; or savings plans for future events such as starting a business, going to college, or purchasing expensive items such as real estate or business equipment.

In this chapter, you learn to calculate the future value of an annuity, the amount accumulated at compound interest from a series of equal periodic payments. You also learn to calculate the present value of an annuity, the amount that must be deposited now at compound interest to yield a series of equal periodic payments. Exhibit 12-1 graphically shows the difference between a future value annuity and a present value annuity.

All the exercises in this chapter are of the type known as **simple annuities.** This means that the number of compounding periods per year coincides with the number of annuity payments per year. For example, if the annuity payments are monthly, the interest is compounded monthly; if the annuity payments are made every 6 months, the interest is compounded semiannually. **Complex annuities** are those in which the annuity payments and compounding periods do not coincide.

As with compound interest, annuities can be calculated manually, by tables, and by formulas. Manual computation is useful for illustrative purposes; however, it is too tedious because it requires a calculation for each period. The table method is the easiest and most widely used and is the basis for this chapter's exercises. As in Chapter 11, there are formulas to calculate annuities; however, they require calculators with the exponential function key, y^x, and the change-of-sign key, $+/-$. These optional Performance Objectives are for students with business, financial, or scientific calculators.

12–1 Calculating the Future Value of an Ordinary Annuity by Using Tables

Annuities are categorized into annuities certain and contingent annuities. **Annuities certain** are those that have a specified number of periods, such as $200 per month for 5 years, or $500 semiannually for 10 years. **Contingent annuities** are based on an uncertain time period, such as a retirement plan that is payable only for the lifetime of the retiree. This chapter is concerned only with annuities certain.

EXHIBIT 12-1
Time Line Illustrating Present and Future Value of Annuities

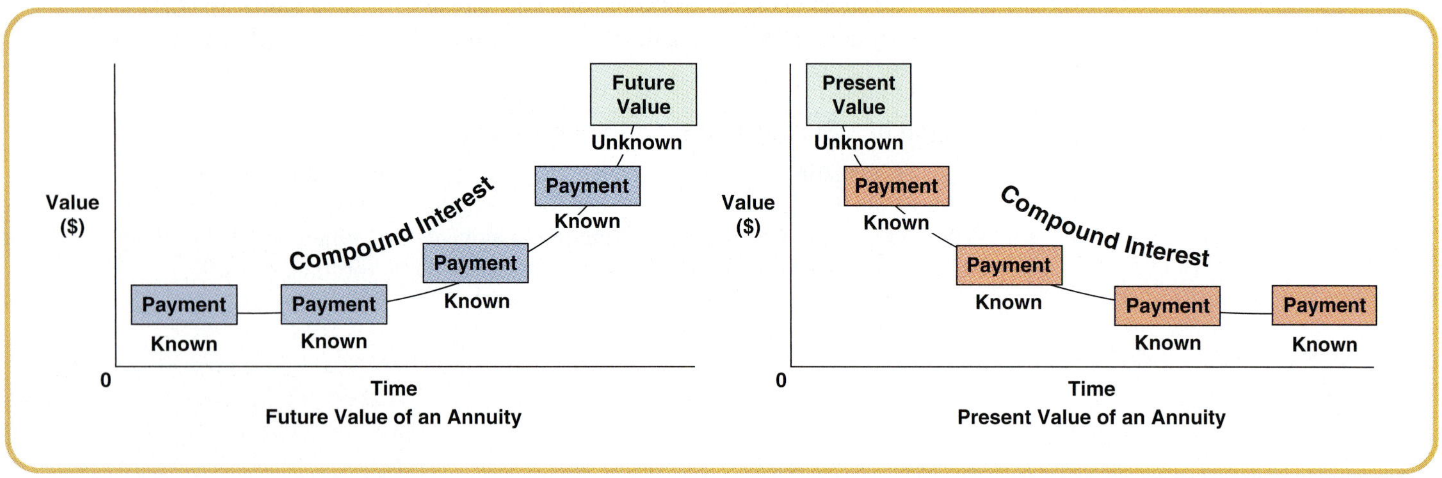

When the annuity payment is made at the end of each period, it is known as an **ordinary annuity.** When the payment is made at the beginning of each period, it is called an **annuity due.** A salary paid at the end of each month is an example of an ordinary annuity. A mortgage payment or rent paid at the beginning of each month is an example of an annuity due.

The **future value of an annuity** is also known as the amount of an annuity. It is the total of the annuity payments plus the accumulated compound interest on those payments.

For illustrative purposes, consider the following example, calculated manually.

ordinary annuity
Annuity that is paid or received at the end of each time period.

annuity due
Annuity that is paid or received at the beginning of each time period.

future value of an annuity
The total amount of the annuity payments and the accumulated interest on those payments. Also known as the amount of an annuity.

EXAMPLE

What is the future value of an ordinary annuity of $10,000 per year, for 4 years, at 6% interest compounded annually?

SOLUTION STRATEGY

Because this is an ordinary annuity, the payment is made at the *end* of each period, in this case years. Each interest calculation uses $I = PRT$, with $R = .06$ and $T = 1$ year.

Time	Balance	
Beginning of period 1	0	
	+ 10,000.00	First annuity payment (end of period 1)
End of period 1	10,000.00	
Beginning of period 2	10,000.00	
	600.00	Interest earned, period 2 (10,000.00 × .06 × 1)
	+ 10,000.00	Second annuity payment (end of period 2)
End of period 2	20,600.00	
Beginning of period 3	20,600.00	
	1,236.00	Interest earned, period 3 (20,600.00 × .06 × 1)
	+ 10,000.00	Third annuity payment (end of period 3)
End of period 3	31,836.00	
Beginning of period 4	31,836.00	
	1,910.16	Interest earned, period 4 (31,836.00 × .06 × 1)
	+ 10,000.00	Fourth annuity payment (end of period 4)
End of period 4	$43,746.16	Future value of the ordinary annuity

As you can see, calculating annuities this way is tedious. An annuity of 10 years, with payments made monthly, would require 120 calculations. As with compound interest, we shall use tables to calculate the future value (amount) of an annuity.

STEPS FOR CALCULATING FUTURE VALUE (AMOUNT) OF AN ORDINARY ANNUITY:

Step 1. Calculate the interest rate per period for the annuity (nominal rate ÷ periods per year).

Step 2. Determine the number of periods of the annuity (years × periods per year).

Step 3. From Table 12-1, locate the ordinary annuity table factor at the intersection of the rate column and the periods row.

Step 4. Calculate the future value of the ordinary annuity by using the formula:

$$\text{Future value (ordinary annuity)} = \text{Ordinary annuity table factor} \times \text{Annuity payment}$$

Everybody's Business

Learning Tip

The procedure for using the annuity tables, Tables 12-1 and 12-2, is the same as we used with the compound interest and present value tables in Chapter 11.

Table factors are found at the intersection of the "rate per period" column and the "number of periods" row.

✦ TABLE 12-1 ✦

Future Value (Amount) of an Ordinary Annuity of $1.00

Periods	$\frac{1}{2}$%	1%	$1\frac{1}{2}$%	2%	3%	4%	5%	6%	7%	8%	Periods
1	1.00000	1.00000	1.00000	1.00000	1.00000	1.00000	1.00000	1.00000	1.00000	1.00000	1
2	2.00500	2.01000	2.01500	2.02000	2.03000	2.04000	2.05000	2.06000	2.07000	2.08000	2
3	3.01502	3.03010	3.04522	3.06040	3.09090	3.12160	3.15250	3.18360	3.21490	3.24640	3
4	4.03010	4.06040	4.09090	4.12161	4.18363	4.24646	4.31013	4.37462	4.43994	4.50611	4
5	5.05025	5.10101	5.15227	5.20404	5.30914	5.41632	5.52563	5.63709	5.75074	5.86660	5
6	6.07550	6.15202	6.22955	6.30812	6.46841	6.63298	6.80191	6.97532	7.15329	7.33593	6
7	7.10588	7.21354	7.32299	7.43428	7.66246	7.89829	8.14201	8.39384	8.65402	8.92280	7
8	8.14141	8.28567	8.43284	8.58297	8.89234	9.21423	9.54911	9.89747	10.25980	10.63663	8
9	9.18212	9.36853	9.55933	9.75463	10.15911	10.58280	11.02656	11.49132	11.97799	12.48756	9
10	10.22803	10.46221	10.70272	10.94972	11.46388	12.00611	12.57789	13.18079	13.81645	14.48656	10
11	11.27917	11.56683	11.86326	12.16872	12.80780	13.48635	14.20679	14.97164	15.78360	16.64549	11
12	12.33556	12.68250	13.04121	13.41209	14.19203	15.02581	15.91713	16.86994	17.88845	18.97713	12
13	13.39724	13.80933	14.23683	14.68033	15.61779	16.62684	17.71298	18.88214	20.14064	21.49530	13
14	14.46423	14.94742	15.45038	15.97394	17.08632	18.29191	19.59863	21.01507	22.55049	24.21492	14
15	15.53655	16.09690	16.68214	17.29342	18.59891	20.02359	21.57856	23.27597	25.12902	27.15211	15
16	16.61423	17.25786	17.93237	18.63929	20.15688	21.82453	23.65749	25.67253	27.88805	30.32428	16
17	17.69730	18.43044	19.20136	20.01207	21.76159	23.69751	25.84037	28.21288	30.84022	33.75023	17
18	18.78579	19.61475	20.48938	21.41231	23.41444	25.64541	28.13238	30.90565	33.99903	37.45024	18
19	19.87972	20.81090	21.79672	22.84056	25.11687	27.67123	30.53900	33.75999	37.37896	41.44626	19
20	20.97912	22.01900	23.12367	24.29737	26.87037	29.77808	33.06595	36.78559	40.99549	45.76196	20
21	22.08401	23.23919	24.47052	25.78332	28.67649	31.96920	35.71925	39.99273	44.86518	50.42292	21
22	23.19443	24.47159	25.83758	27.29898	30.53678	34.24797	38.50521	43.39229	49.00574	55.45676	22
23	24.31040	25.71630	27.22514	28.84496	32.45288	36.61789	41.43048	46.99583	53.43614	60.89330	23
24	25.43196	26.97346	28.63352	30.42186	34.42647	39.08260	44.50200	50.81558	58.17667	66.76476	24
25	26.55912	28.24320	30.06302	32.03030	36.45926	41.64591	47.72710	54.86451	63.24904	73.10594	25
26	27.69191	29.52563	31.51397	33.67091	38.55304	44.31174	51.11345	59.15638	68.67647	79.95442	26
27	28.83037	30.82089	32.98668	35.34432	40.70963	47.08421	54.66913	63.70577	74.48382	87.35077	27
28	29.97452	32.12910	34.48148	37.05121	42.93092	49.96758	58.40258	68.52811	80.69769	95.33883	28
29	31.12439	33.45039	35.99870	38.79223	45.21885	52.96629	62.32271	73.63980	87.34653	103.96594	29
30	32.28002	34.78489	37.53868	40.56808	47.57542	56.08494	66.43885	79.05819	94.46079	113.28321	30
31	33.44142	36.13274	39.10176	42.37944	50.00268	59.32834	70.76079	84.80168	102.07304	123.34587	31
32	34.60862	37.49407	40.68829	44.22703	52.50276	62.70147	75.29883	90.88978	110.21815	134.21354	32
33	35.78167	38.86901	42.29861	46.11157	55.07784	66.20953	80.06377	97.34316	118.93343	145.95062	33
34	36.96058	40.25770	43.93309	48.03380	57.73018	69.85791	85.06696	104.18375	128.25876	158.62667	34
35	38.14538	41.66028	45.59209	49.99448	60.46208	73.65222	90.32031	111.43478	138.23688	172.31680	35
36	39.33610	43.07688	47.27597	51.99437	63.27594	77.59831	95.83632	119.12087	148.91346	187.10215	36

EXAMPLE

Kelly Waterman deposited $3,000 at the *end* of each year for 8 years in her savings account. If her bank paid 5% interest compounded annually, use Table 12-1 to find the future value of Kelly's account.

SOLUTION STRATEGY

Step 1. The rate period is 5% (5% ÷ 1 period per year).

Step 2. The number of periods is eight (8 years × 1 period per year).

Step 3. From Table 12-1, the table factor for 5%, eight periods is 9.54911.

Step 4. Future value = Table factor × Annuity payment

Future value = 9.54911 × 3,000 = $28,647.33

✦ **TABLE 12-1** ✦ (continued)

Periods	9%	10%	11%	12%	13%	14%	15%	16%	17%	18%	Periods
1	1.00000	1.00000	1.00000	1.00000	1.00000	1.00000	1.00000	1.00000	1.00000	1.00000	1
2	2.09000	2.10000	2.11000	2.12000	2.13000	2.14000	2.15000	2.16000	2.17000	2.18000	2
3	3.27810	3.31000	3.34210	3.37440	3.40690	3.43960	3.47250	3.50560	3.53890	3.57240	3
4	4.57313	4.64100	4.70973	4.77933	4.84980	4.92114	4.99338	5.06650	5.14051	5.21543	4
5	5.98471	6.10510	6.22780	6.35285	6.48027	6.61010	6.74238	6.87714	7.01440	7.15421	5
6	7.52333	7.71561	7.91286	8.11519	8.32271	8.53552	8.75374	8.97748	9.20685	9.44197	6
7	9.20043	9.48717	9.78327	10.08901	10.40466	10.73049	11.06680	11.41387	11.77201	12.14152	7
8	11.02847	11.43589	11.85943	12.29969	12.75726	13.23276	13.72682	14.24009	14.77325	15.32700	8
9	13.02104	13.57948	14.16397	14.77566	15.41571	16.08535	16.78584	17.51851	18.28471	19.08585	9
10	15.19293	15.93742	16.72201	17.54874	18.41975	19.33730	20.30372	21.32147	22.39311	23.52131	10
11	17.56079	18.53117	19.56143	20.65458	21.81432	23.04452	24.34928	25.73290	27.19994	28.75514	11
12	20.14072	21.38428	22.71319	24.13313	25.65018	27.27075	29.00167	30.85017	32.82393	34.93107	12
13	22.95338	24.52271	26.21164	28.02911	29.98470	32.08865	34.35192	36.78620	39.40399	42.21866	13
14	26.01919	27.97498	30.09492	32.39260	34.88271	37.58107	40.50471	43.67199	47.10267	50.81802	14
15	29.36092	31.77248	34.40536	37.27971	40.41746	43.84241	47.58041	51.65951	56.11013	60.96527	15
16	33.00340	35.94973	39.18995	42.75328	46.67173	50.98035	55.71747	60.92503	66.64885	72.93901	16
17	36.97370	40.54470	44.50084	48.88367	53.73906	59.11760	65.07509	71.67303	78.97915	87.06804	17
18	41.30134	45.59917	50.39594	55.74971	61.72514	68.39407	75.83636	84.14072	93.40561	103.74028	18
19	46.01846	51.15909	56.93949	63.43968	70.74941	78.96923	88.21181	98.60323	110.28456	123.41353	19
20	51.16012	57.27500	64.20283	72.05244	80.94683	91.02493	102.44358	115.37975	130.03294	146.62797	20
21	56.76453	64.00250	72.26514	81.69874	92.46992	104.76842	118.81012	134.84051	153.13854	174.02100	21
22	62.87334	71.40275	81.21431	92.50258	105.49101	120.43600	137.63164	157.41499	180.17209	206.34479	22
23	69.53194	79.54302	91.14788	104.60289	120.20484	138.29704	159.27638	183.60138	211.80134	244.48685	23
24	76.78981	88.49733	102.17415	118.15524	136.83147	158.65862	184.16784	213.97761	248.80757	289.49448	24
25	84.70090	98.34706	114.41331	133.33387	155.61956	181.87083	212.79302	249.21402	292.10486	342.60349	25
26	93.32398	109.18177	127.99877	150.33393	176.85010	208.33274	245.71197	290.08827	342.76268	405.27211	26
27	102.72313	121.09994	143.07864	169.37401	200.84061	238.49933	283.56877	337.50239	402.03234	479.22109	27
28	112.96822	134.20994	159.81729	190.69889	227.94989	272.88923	327.10408	392.50277	471.37783	566.48089	28
29	124.13536	148.63093	178.39719	214.58275	258.58338	312.09373	377.16969	456.30322	552.51207	669.44745	29
30	136.30754	164.49402	199.02088	241.33268	293.19922	356.78685	434.74515	530.31173	647.43912	790.94799	30
31	149.57522	181.94342	221.91317	271.29261	332.31511	407.73701	500.95692	616.16161	758.50377	934.31863	31
32	164.03699	201.13777	247.32362	304.84772	376.51608	465.82019	577.10046	715.74746	888.44941	1103.49598	32
33	179.80032	222.25154	275.52922	342.42945	426.46317	532.03501	664.66552	831.26706	1040.48581	1303.12526	33
34	196.98234	245.47670	306.83744	384.52098	482.90338	607.51991	765.36535	965.26979	1218.36839	1538.68781	34
35	215.71075	271.02437	341.58955	431.66350	546.68082	693.57270	881.17016	1120.71295	1426.49102	1816.65161	35
36	236.12472	299.12681	380.16441	484.46312	618.74933	791.67288	1014.34568	1301.02703	1669.99450	2144.64890	36

TRY-IT | EXERCISE

1. City National Bank is paying 8% interest compounded quarterly. Use Table 12-1 to find the future value of $1,000 deposited at the *end* of every 3 months for 6 years.

Check your answer with the solution on page 437.

12-2 Calculating the Future Value of an Annuity Due by Using Tables

Once again, for illustrative purposes, let's manually calculate the future value of the annuity from Performance Objective 12-1, page 411. This time, however, it is an annuity due.

EXAMPLE

What is the amount of an annuity due of $10,000 per year, for 4 years, at 6% interest compounded annually?

SOLUTION STRATEGY

Because this is an annuity due, the payment is made at the *beginning* of each period. Each interest calculation uses $I = PRT$, with $R = .06$ and $T = 1$ year.

Time	Balance	
Beginning of period 1	10,000.00	First annuity payment (beginning of period 1)
	+ 600.00	Interest earned, period 1 (10,000.00 × .06 × 1)
End of period 1	10,600.00	
Beginning of period 2	10,600.00	
	10,000.00	Second annuity payment (beginning of period 2)
	+ 1,236.00	Interest earned, period 2 (20,600.00 × .06 × 1)
End of period 2	21,836.00	
Beginning of period 3	21,836.00	
	10,000.00	Third annuity payment (beginning of period 3)
	+ 1,910.16	Interest earned, period 3 (31,836.00 × .06 × 1)
End of period 3	33,746.16	
Beginning of period 4	33,746.16	
	10,000.00	Fourth annuity payment (beginning of period 4)
	+ 2,624.76	Interest earned, period 4 (43,746.16 × .06 × 1)
End of period 4	$46,370.92	

When calculating the future value of an annuity due, the table factor is found by using the same table as ordinary annuities (Table 12-1), with some modifications in the steps. With annuities due, you must *add* one period to the number of periods and *subtract* 1.00000 from the table factor.

STEPS FOR CALCULATING FUTURE VALUE (AMOUNT) OF AN ANNUITY DUE:

Step 1. Calculate the number of periods of the annuity (years × periods per year), and add one period to the total.

Step 2. Calculate the interest rate per period (nominal rate ÷ periods per year).

Step 3. From Table 12-1, locate the table factor at the intersection of the rate column and the periods row.

Step 4. Subtract 1.00000 from the ordinary annuity table factor to get the annuity due table factor.

Step 5. Calculate the future value of the annuity due by the formula:

Future value (annuity due) = Annuity due table factor × Annuity payment

EXAMPLE

Eric Ziegler deposited $60 at the *beginning* of each month, for 2 years, at his credit union. If the interest rate was 12% compounded monthly, use Table 12-1 to calculate the future value of Eric's account.

SOLUTION STRATEGY

Step 1. Number of periods of the annuity due is 24 (2 × 12) + 1 for a total of 25.

Step 2. Interest rate per period is 1% (12% ÷ 12).

Step 3. The ordinary annuity table factor at the intersection of the rate column and the periods row is 28.24320.

Step 4. Subtract 1.00000 from table factor:

$$\begin{array}{rl} 28.24320 & \text{ordinary annuity table factor} \\ -\ 1.00000 & \\ \hline 27.24320 & \text{annuity due table factor} \end{array}$$

Step 5. Future value = Annuity due table factor × Annuity payment

Future value = 27.24320 × 60 = $1,634.59

TRY-IT EXERCISE

2. Atlanta Savings & Loan is paying 6% interest compounded quarterly. Use Table 12-1 to calculate the future value of $1,000, deposited at the *beginning* of every 3 months for 5 years.

Check your answer with the solution on page 437.

12-3 (Optional) Calculating the Future Value of an Ordinary Annuity and an Annuity Due by Formula

Students with financial, business, or scientific calculators may use the following formulas to solve for the future value of an ordinary annuity and the future value of an annuity due.

Everybody's Business

Learning Tip

Note that the annuity due formula is the same as the ordinary annuity formula except it is multiplied by $(1 + i)$. This is to account for the additional period of the annuity due.

Future value of an ordinary annuity

$$FV = Pmt \times \frac{(1+i)^n - 1}{i}$$

Future value of an annuity due

$$FV = Pmt \times \frac{(1+i)^n - 1}{i} \times (1+i)$$

where

FV = future value

Pmt = annuity payment

i = interest rate per period (nominal rate ÷ periods per year)

n = number of periods (years × periods per year)

Ordinary Annuity
Calculator Sequence: 1 [+] i [=] [y^x] n [−] 1 [÷] i [×] Pmt [=] $FV_{\text{ordinary annuity}}$

Annuity Due
Calculator Sequence: 1 [+] i [=] [×] $FV_{\text{ordinary annuity}}$ [=] $FV_{\text{annuity due}}$

EXAMPLES

a. What is the future value of an ordinary annuity of $100 per month, for 3 years, at 12% interest compounded monthly?

b. What is the future value of this investment if it is an annuity due?

SOLUTION STRATEGY

a. For this future value of an ordinary annuity problem, we use $i = 1\%$ (12% ÷ 12) and $n = 36$ periods (3 years × 12 periods per year).

$$FV = Pmt \times \frac{(1 \times i)^n - 1}{i}$$

$$FV = 100 \times \frac{(1 + .01)^{36} - 1}{.01}$$

$$FV = 100 \times \frac{(1.01)^{36} - 1}{.01}$$

$$FV = 100 \times \frac{1.4307688 - 1}{.01}$$

$$FV = 100 \times \frac{.4307688}{.01}$$

$$FV = 100 \times 43.07688 = \underline{\underline{\$4,307.69}}$$

Calculator Sequence: 1 [+] .01 [=] [y^x] 36 [−] 1 [÷] .01 [×] 100 [=] $\underline{\underline{\$4,307.69}}$

b. To solve the problem as an annuity due, rather than an ordinary annuity, multiply $(1 + i)$, for one extra compounding period, by the future value of the ordinary annuity.

$$FV_{\text{annuity due}} = (1 + i) \times FV_{\text{ordinary annuity}}$$

$$FV_{\text{annuity due}} = (1 + .01) \times 4,307.69$$

$$FV_{\text{annuity due}} = (1.01) \times 4,307.69 = \underline{\underline{\$4,350.77}}$$

Calculator Sequence: 1 [+] .01 [=] [×] 4,307.69 [=] $\underline{\underline{\$4,350.77}}$

TRY-IT | EXERCISE

3. Melissa Acuna invested $250 at the *end* of every 3-month period, for 5 years, at 8% interest compounded quarterly.

a. How much is Melissa's investment worth after 5 years?

b. If Melissa would have invested the money at the *beginning* of each 3-month period, rather than at the end, how much would be in the account?

Check your answers with the solutions on page 437.

REVIEW EXERCISES | CHAPTER 12—SECTION I

Use Table 12-1 to calculate the future value of the following ordinary annuities:

	Annuity Payment	Payment Frequency	Time Period (years)	Nominal Rate (%)	Interest Compounded	Future Value of the Annuity
1.	$1,000	every 3 months	4	8	quarterly	________
2.	$2,500	every 6 months	5	10	semiannually	________
3.	$10,000	every year	10	9	annually	________

4.	$200	every month	2	12	monthly	__________
5.	$1,500	every 3 months	7	16	quarterly	__________

Use Table 12-1 to calculate the future value of the following annuities due:

	Annuity Payment	Payment Frequency	Time Period (years)	Nominal Rate (%)	Interest Compounded	Future Value of the Annuity
6.	$400	every 6 months	12	10	semiannually	__________
7.	$1,000	every 3 months	3	8	quarterly	__________
8.	$50	every month	$2\frac{1}{2}$	18	monthly	__________
9.	$2,000	every year	25	5	annually	__________
10.	$4,400	every 6 months	8	6	semiannually	__________

Solve the following exercises by using Table 12-1:

11. Grove Isle Savings & Loan is paying 6% interest compounded monthly. How much will $100 deposited at the *end* of each month be worth after 2 years?

12. Emory Distributors, Inc., deposits $5,000 at the *beginning* of each 3-month period for 6 years in an account paying 8% interest compounded quarterly.

a. How much will be in the account at the end of the 6-year period?

b. What is the total amount of interest earned in this account?

13. When Brian Gonzalez was born, his parents began depositing $500 at the *beginning* of every year into an annuity to save for his college education. If the account paid 7% interest compounded annually for the first 10 years and then dropped to 5% for the next 8 years, how much is the account worth now that Brian is 18 years old and is ready for college?

Everybody's Business

Exercise #13, Solution Hint

Once you have determined the account value after the first 10 years, don't forget to apply 5% compound interest to that value for the remaining 8 years.

14. Surfside Hardware has been in business for a few years and is doing well. The owner has decided to save for a future expansion to a second location. He invests $1,000 at the *end* of every month at 12% interest compounded monthly.

a. How much will be available for the second store after $2\frac{1}{2}$ years?

b. (Optional) Use the formula for an ordinary annuity to calculate how much would be in the account if the owner saved for 5 years.

c. (Optional) Use the formula for an annuity due to calculate how much would be in the account after 5 years if it had been an annuity due.

BUSINESS DECISION

Planning Your Nest Egg

15. As part of your retirement plan, you have decided to deposit $3,000 at the *beginning* of each year into an account paying 5% interest compounded annually.

a. How much would the account be worth after 10 years?

b. How much would the account be worth after 20 years?

c. When you retire in 30 years, what will be the total worth of the account?

d. If you found a bank that paid 6% interest compounded annually, rather than 5%, how much more would you have in the account after 30 years?

PRESENT VALUE OF AN ANNUITY

SECTION II

In Section I of this chapter, we learned to calculate the future value of annuities. These business situations require that a series of equal payments be made into an account, such as a savings account; it starts with nothing and accumulates at compound interest to a future amount. Now, consider the opposite situation. What if we wanted an account from which we could withdraw a series of equal payments over a period of time? This business situation requires that a lump sum amount be deposited at compound interest now to yield the specified annuity payments. This lump sum required at the beginning is known as the **present value of an annuity.**

present value of an annuity Lump sum amount of money that must be deposited today to provide a specified series of equal payments (annuity) in the future.

Let's look at a business situation using this type of annuity. A company owes $10,000 interest to bondholders at the end of each month for the next 3 years. The company decides to set up an account with a lump sum deposit now, which at compound interest will yield the $10,000 monthly payments for 3 years. After 3 years, the debt will have been paid, and the account will be zero.

Just as in Section I, present value annuities can be ordinary, whereby withdrawals from the account are made at the *end* of each period, or annuity due, in which the withdrawals are made at the *beginning.* As with future value annuities, we shall use tables to calculate the present value of an annuity. Once again, in addition to tables, present value annuities can be solved by using formulas requiring a calculator with a y^x key.

12-4 Calculating the Present Value of an Ordinary Annuity by Using Tables

Table 12-2, Present Value of an Ordinary Annuity, is used to calculate the lump sum required to be deposited now to yield the annuity payment.

STEPS FOR CALCULATING PRESENT VALUE OF AN ORDINARY ANNUITY:

Step 1. Calculate the interest rate per period for the annuity (nominal rate ÷ periods per year).

Step 2. Determine the number of periods of the annuity (years × periods per year).

Step 3. From Table 12-2, locate the present value table factor at the intersection of the rate column and the periods row.

Step 4. Calculate the present value of an ordinary annuity by using the formula:

$$\text{Present value (ordinary annuity)} = \text{Ordinary annuity table factor} \times \text{Annuity payment}$$

EXAMPLE

How much must be deposited now, at 9% compounded annually, to yield an annuity payment of $5,000 at the end of each year, for 10 years?

SOLUTION STRATEGY

Step 1. The rate per period is 9% (9% ÷ 1 period per year).

Step 2. The number of periods is 10 (10 years × 1 period per year).

Step 3. From Table 12-2, the table factor for 9%, 10 periods is 6.41766.

Step 4. Present value = Table factor × Annuity payment

Present value = 6.41766 × 5,000 = $32,088.30

✦ TABLE 12-2 ✦

Present Value (Amount) of an Ordinary Annuity of $1.00

Periods	$\frac{1}{2}$%	1%	$1\frac{1}{2}$%	2%	3%	4%	5%	6%	7%	8%	Periods
1	0.99502	0.99010	0.98522	0.98039	0.97087	0.96154	0.95238	0.94340	0.93458	0.92593	1
2	1.98510	1.97040	1.95588	1.94156	1.91347	1.88609	1.85941	1.83339	1.80802	1.78326	2
3	2.97025	2.94099	2.91220	2.88388	2.82861	2.77509	2.72325	2.67301	2.62432	2.57710	3
4	3.95050	3.90197	3.85438	3.80773	3.71710	3.62990	3.54595	3.46511	3.38721	3.31213	4
5	4.92587	4.85343	4.78264	4.71346	4.57971	4.45182	4.32948	4.21236	4.10020	3.99271	5
6	5.89638	5.79548	5.69719	5.60143	5.41719	5.24214	5.07569	4.91732	4.76654	4.62288	6
7	6.86207	6.72819	6.59821	6.47199	6.23028	6.00205	5.78637	5.58238	5.38929	5.20637	7
8	7.82296	7.65168	7.48593	7.32548	7.01969	6.73274	6.46321	6.20979	5.97130	5.74664	8
9	8.77906	8.56602	8.36052	8.16224	7.78611	7.43533	7.10782	6.80169	6.51523	6.24689	9
10	9.73041	9.47130	9.22218	8.98259	8.53020	8.11090	7.72173	7.36009	7.02358	6.71008	10
11	10.67703	10.36763	10.07112	9.78685	9.25262	8.76048	8.30641	7.88687	7.49867	7.13896	11
12	11.61893	11.25508	10.90751	10.57534	9.95400	9.38507	8.86325	8.38384	7.94269	7.53608	12
13	12.55615	12.13374	11.73153	11.34837	10.63496	9.98565	9.39357	8.85268	8.35765	7.90378	13
14	13.48871	13.00370	12.54338	12.10625	11.29607	10.56312	9.89864	9.29498	8.74547	8.24424	14
15	14.41662	13.86505	13.34323	12.84926	11.93794	11.11839	10.37966	9.71225	9.10791	8.55948	15
16	15.33993	14.71787	14.13126	13.57771	12.56110	11.65230	10.83777	10.10590	9.44665	8.85137	16
17	16.25863	15.56225	14.90765	14.29187	13.16612	12.16567	11.27407	10.47726	9.76322	9.12164	17
18	17.17277	16.39827	15.67256	14.99203	13.75351	12.65930	11.68959	10.82760	10.05909	9.37189	18
19	18.08236	17.22601	16.42617	15.67846	14.32380	13.13394	12.08532	11.15812	10.33560	9.60360	19
20	18.98742	18.04555	17.16864	16.35143	14.87747	13.59033	12.46221	11.46992	10.59401	9.81815	20
21	19.88798	18.85698	17.90014	17.01121	15.41502	14.02916	12.82115	11.76408	10.83553	10.01680	21
22	20.78406	19.66038	18.62082	17.65805	15.93692	14.45112	13.16300	12.04158	11.06124	10.20074	22
23	21.67568	20.45582	19.33086	18.29220	16.44361	14.85684	13.48857	12.30338	11.27219	10.37106	23
24	22.56287	21.24339	20.03041	18.91393	16.93554	15.24696	13.79864	12.55036	11.46933	10.52876	24
25	23.44564	22.02316	20.71961	19.52346	17.41315	15.62208	14.09394	12.78336	11.65358	10.67478	25
26	24.32402	22.79520	21.39863	20.12104	17.87684	15.98277	14.37519	13.00317	11.82578	10.80998	26
27	25.19803	23.55961	22.06762	20.70690	18.32703	16.32959	14.64303	13.21053	11.98671	10.93516	27
28	26.06769	24.31644	22.72672	21.28127	18.76411	16.66306	14.89813	13.40616	12.13711	11.05108	28
29	26.93302	25.06579	23.37608	21.84438	19.18845	16.98371	15.14107	13.59072	12.27767	11.15841	29
30	27.79405	25.80771	24.01584	22.39646	19.60044	17.29203	15.37245	13.76483	12.40904	11.25778	30
31	28.65080	26.54229	24.64615	22.93770	20.00043	17.58849	15.59281	13.92909	12.53181	11.34980	31
32	29.50328	27.26959	25.26714	23.46833	20.38877	17.87355	15.80268	14.08404	12.64656	11.43500	32
33	30.35153	27.98969	25.87895	23.98856	20.76579	18.14765	16.00255	14.23023	12.75379	11.51389	33
34	31.19555	28.70267	26.48173	24.49859	21.13184	18.41120	16.19290	14.36814	12.85401	11.58693	34
35	32.03537	29.40858	27.07559	24.99862	21.48722	18.66461	16.37419	14.49825	12.94767	11.65457	35
36	32.87102	30.10751	27.66068	25.48884	21.83225	18.90828	16.54685	14.62099	13.03521	11.71719	36

TRY-IT | EXERCISE

4. **The Coconut Grove Playhouse wants $20,000 at the end of each 6-month theater season for renovations and new stage and lighting equipment. How much must be deposited now, at 8% compounded semiannually, to yield this annuity payment for the next 6 years?**

Check your answer with the solution on page 437.

12-5 Calculating the Present Value of an Annuity Due by Using Tables

Present values of annuities due are calculated by using the same table as ordinary annuities, with some modifications in the steps.

TABLE 12-2 (continued)

Periods	9%	10%	11%	12%	13%	14%	15%	16%	17%	18%	Periods
1	0.91743	0.90909	0.90090	0.89286	0.88496	0.87719	0.86957	0.86207	0.85470	0.84746	1
2	1.75911	1.73554	1.71252	1.69005	1.66810	1.64666	1.62571	1.60523	1.58521	1.56564	2
3	2.53129	2.48685	2.44371	2.40183	2.36115	2.32163	2.28323	2.24589	2.20958	2.17427	3
4	3.23972	3.16987	3.10245	3.03735	2.97447	2.91371	2.85498	2.79818	2.74324	2.69006	4
5	3.88965	3.79079	3.69590	3.60478	3.51723	3.43308	3.35216	3.27429	3.19935	3.12717	5
6	4.48592	4.35526	4.23054	4.11141	3.99755	3.88867	3.78448	3.68474	3.58918	3.49760	6
7	5.03295	4.86842	4.71220	4.56376	4.42261	4.28830	4.16042	4.03857	3.92238	3.81153	7
8	5.53482	5.33493	5.14612	4.96764	4.79877	4.63886	4.48732	4.34359	4.20716	4.07757	8
9	5.99525	5.75902	5.53705	5.32825	5.13166	4.94637	4.77158	4.60654	4.45057	4.30302	9
10	6.41766	6.14457	5.88923	5.65022	5.42624	5.21612	5.01877	4.83323	4.65860	4.49409	10
11	6.80519	6.49506	6.20652	5.93770	5.68694	5.45273	5.23371	5.02864	4.83641	4.65601	11
12	7.16073	6.81369	6.49236	6.19437	5.91765	5.66029	5.42062	5.19711	4.98839	4.79322	12
13	7.48690	7.10336	6.74987	6.42355	6.12181	5.84236	5.58315	5.34233	5.11828	4.90951	13
14	7.78615	7.36669	6.98187	6.62817	6.30249	6.00207	5.72448	5.46753	5.22930	5.00806	14
15	8.06069	7.60608	7.19087	6.81086	6.46238	6.14217	5.84737	5.57546	5.32419	5.09158	15
16	8.31256	7.82371	7.37916	6.97399	6.60388	6.26506	5.95423	5.66850	5.40529	5.16235	16
17	8.54363	8.02155	7.54879	7.11963	6.72909	6.37286	6.04716	5.74870	5.47461	5.22233	17
18	8.75563	8.20141	7.70162	7.24967	6.83991	6.46742	6.12797	5.81785	5.53385	5.27316	18
19	8.95011	8.36492	7.83929	7.36578	6.93797	6.55037	6.19823	5.87746	5.58449	5.31624	19
20	9.12855	8.51356	7.96333	7.46944	7.02475	6.62313	6.25933	5.92884	5.62777	5.35275	20
21	9.29224	8.64869	8.07507	7.56200	7.10155	6.68696	6.31246	5.97314	5.66476	5.38368	21
22	9.44243	8.77154	8.17574	7.64465	7.16951	6.74294	6.35866	6.01133	5.69637	5.40990	22
23	9.58021	8.88322	8.26643	7.71843	7.22966	6.79206	6.39884	6.04425	5.72340	5.43212	23
24	9.70661	8.98474	8.34814	7.78432	7.28288	6.83514	6.43377	6.07263	5.74649	5.45095	24
25	9.82258	9.07704	8.42174	7.84314	7.32998	6.87293	6.46415	6.09709	5.76623	5.46691	25
26	9.92897	9.16095	8.48806	7.89566	7.37167	6.90608	6.49056	6.11818	5.78311	5.48043	26
27	10.02658	9.23722	8.54780	7.94255	7.40856	6.93515	6.51353	6.13636	5.79753	5.49189	27
28	10.11613	9.30657	8.60162	7.98442	7.44120	6.96066	6.53351	6.15204	5.80985	5.50160	28
29	10.19828	9.36961	8.65011	8.02181	7.47009	6.98304	6.55088	6.16555	5.82039	5.50983	29
30	10.27365	9.42691	8.69379	8.05518	7.49565	7.00266	6.56598	6.17720	5.82939	5.51681	30
31	10.34280	9.47901	8.73315	8.08499	7.51828	7.01988	6.57911	6.18724	5.83709	5.52272	31
32	10.40624	9.52638	8.76860	8.11159	7.53830	7.03498	6.59053	6.19590	5.84366	5.52773	32
33	10.46444	9.56943	8.80054	8.13535	7.55602	7.04823	6.60046	6.20336	5.84928	5.53197	33
34	10.51784	9.60857	8.82932	8.15656	7.57170	7.05985	6.60910	6.20979	5.85409	5.53557	34
35	10.56682	9.64416	8.85524	8.17550	7.58557	7.07005	6.61661	6.21534	5.85820	5.53862	35
36	10.61176	9.67651	8.87859	8.19241	7.59785	7.07899	6.62314	6.22012	5.86171	5.54120	36

STEPS FOR CALCULATING PRESENT VALUE OF AN ANNUITY DUE:

Step 1. Calculate the number of periods of the annuity (years × periods per year), and *subtract* one period from the total.

Step 2. Calculate the interest rate per period (nominal rate ÷ periods per year).

Step 3. From Table 12-2, locate the table factor at the intersection of the rate column and the periods row.

Step 4. Add 1.00000 to the ordinary annuity table factor to get the annuity due table factor.

Step 5. Calculate the present value of an annuity due by the formula

$$\text{Present value (annuity due)} = \text{Ordinary annuity table factor} \times \text{Annuity payment}$$

Everybody's Business

Learning Tip

The procedure for finding the present value table factor for an annuity due is the *opposite* of that for future value factors. This time you must subtract a period and add a 1.00000.

EXAMPLE

How much must be deposited now, at 10% compounded semiannually, to yield an annuity payment of $2,000 at the beginning of each 6-month period for 7 years?

SOLUTION STRATEGY

Step 1. The number of periods for the annuity due is 14 (7 years × 2 periods per year) less 1 period = 13.

Step 2. The rate per period is 5% (10% ÷ 2 periods per year).

Step 3. From Table 12-2, the ordinary annuity table factor for 5%, 13 periods is 9.39357.

Step 4. Add 1 to the table factor from Step 3 to get 10.39357, the annuity due table factor.

Step 5. Present value (annuity due) = Table factor × Annuity payment

Present value = 10.39357 × 2,000 = $20,787.14

TRY-IT | EXERCISE

5. You are the accountant at Central Lumber, Inc. Based on sales and expense forecasts, you have estimated that $10,000 must be sent to the Internal Revenue Service for income tax payments at the *beginning* of each 3-month period for the next 3 years. How much must be deposited now, at 6% compounded quarterly, to yield the annuity payment needed?

Check your answer with the solution on page 437.

12-6 (Optional) Calculating the Present Value of an Ordinary Annuity and an Annuity Due by Formula

Students with financial, business, or scientific calculators may use the following formulas to solve for the present value of an ordinary annuity and the present value of an annuity due. Note that the annuity due formula is the same as the ordinary annuity formula, except it is multiplied by $(1 + i)$. This is to account for the fact that with an annuity due each payment earns interest for one additional period, because payments are made at the beginning of each period, not the end.

Present value of an ordinary annuity

$$PV = Pmt \times \frac{1 - (1 + i)^{-n}}{i}$$

Present value of an annuity due

$$PV = Pmt \times \frac{1 - (1 + i)^{-n}}{i} \times (1 + i)$$

where

PV = present value (lump sum)

Pmt = annuity payment

i = interest rate per period (nominal rate ÷ periods per year)

n = number of periods (years × periods per year)

Ordinary Annuity
Calculator Sequence: 1 [+] i [=] [y^x] n [+/−] [=] [M+] 1 [−] [MR] [÷] i [×] Pmt [=] PV

Annuity Due
Calculator Sequence: 1 [+] i [=] [×] $PV_{\text{ordinary annuity}}$ [=] $PV_{\text{annuity due}}$

EXAMPLES

a. What is the present value of an ordinary annuity of \$100 per month, for 4 years, at 12% interest compounded monthly?

b. What is the present value of this investment if it is an annuity due?

SOLUTION STRATEGY

a. For this present value of an ordinary annuity problem, we use $i = 1\%$ (12% ÷ 12) and $n = 48$ periods (4 years × 12 periods per year).

$$PV = Pmt \times \frac{1 - (1 + i)^{-n}}{i}$$

$$PV = 100 \times \frac{1 - (1 + .01)^{-48}}{.01}$$

$$PV = 100 \times \frac{1 - (1.01)^{-48}}{.01}$$

$$PV = 100 \times \frac{1 - .6202604}{.01}$$

$$PV = 100 \times \frac{.3797396}{.01}$$

$$PV = 100 \times 37.97396 = \underline{\underline{\$3,797.40}}$$

Calculator Sequence:
1 [+] .01 [=] [y^x] 48 [+/−] [=] [M+] 1 [−] [MR] [÷] .01 [×] 100 [=] $\underline{\underline{\$3,797.40}}$

b. To solve as an annuity due, rather than an ordinary annuity, multiply the present value of the ordinary annuity by $(1 + i)$, for one extra compounding period.

$$PV_{\text{annuity due}} = (1 + i) \times PV_{\text{ordinary annuity}}$$

$$PV_{\text{annuity due}} = (1 + .01) \times 3,797.40$$

$$PV_{\text{annuity due}} = (1.01) \times 3,797.40 = \underline{\underline{\$3,835.37}}$$

Calculator Sequence: 1 [+] .01 [=] [×] 3,797.40 [=] $\underline{\underline{\$3,835.37}}$

TRY-IT | EXERCISE

6. Use the present value of an annuity formula to solve the following:

a. Ben Sadler wants \$500 at the *end* of each 3-month period for the next 6 years. If Ben's bank is paying 8% interest compounded quarterly, how much must he deposit now in order to receive the desired ordinary annuity?

b. If Ben wants the payments at the *beginning* of each 3-month period, rather than at the end, how much would he have to deposit?

Check your answers with the solutions on page 437.

REVIEW EXERCISES | CHAPTER 12—SECTION II

Use Table 12-2 to calculate the present value of the following ordinary annuities:

	Annuity Payment	Payment Frequency	Time Period (years)	Nominal Rate (%)	Interest Compounded	Present Value of the Annuity
1.	$300	every 6 months	7	10	semiannually	________
2.	$2,000	every year	20	7	annually	________
3.	$1,600	every 3 months	6	12	quarterly	________
4.	$1,000	every month	$1\frac{3}{4}$	6	monthly	________
5.	$8,500	every 3 months	3	16	quarterly	________

Use Table 12-2 to calculate the present value of the following annuities due:

	Annuity Payment	Payment Frequency	Time Period (years)	Nominal Rate (%)	Interest Compounded	Present Value of the Annuity
6.	$1,400	every year	10	11	annually	________
7.	$1,300	every 3 months	4	12	quarterly	________
8.	$500	every month	$2\frac{1}{4}$	18	monthly	________
9.	$7,000	every 6 months	12	8	semiannually	________
10.	$4,000	every year	18	7	annually	________

Solve the following exercises by using Table 12-2:

11. Transamerica Savings & Loan is paying 6% interest compounded monthly. How much must be deposited now to withdraw $400 at the end of each month for 2 years?

12. Maureen Staudt wants to receive $2,000 at the beginning of each year for the next 10 years. How much should be deposited now at 6% compounded annually to accomplish this goal?

2 **13.** As the chief accountant for the Worthington Corporation, you have estimated that the company must pay $100,000 income tax to the IRS at the end of each quarter this year. How much should be deposited now at 8% interest compounded quarterly to meet this tax obligation?

3 **14.** Georgiann Adams is the grand prize winner in a college tuition essay contest sponsored by a local scholarship fund. The winner receives $2,000 at the beginning of each year for the next 4 years. How much should be invested at 7% interest compounded annually to pay the prize?

BUSINESS DECISION

The Settlement

15. Churchill Enterprises has been awarded an insurance settlement of $5,000 at the end of each 6-month period for the next 10 years.

a. As their accountant, calculate how much the insurance company must set aside now, at 6% interest compounded semiannually, to pay this obligation to Churchill.

b. (Optional) Use the present value of an ordinary annuity formula to calculate how much the insurance company would have to invest now if the Churchill settlement was changed to $2,500 at the end of each 3-month period for 10 years, and the insurance company could earn 8% interest compounded quarterly.

c. (Optional) Use the present value of an annuity due formula to calculate how much the insurance company would have to invest now if the Churchill settlement was paid at the beginning of each 3-month period rather than at the end.

SECTION III

SINKING FUNDS AND AMORTIZATION

Sinking funds and amortization are two common applications of annuities. In the previous sections of this chapter, the amount of the annuity payment was known and you were asked to calculate the future or present value (lump sum) of the annuity. In this section, the future or present value of the annuity is known, and the amount of the payments is calculated.

A sinking fund situation occurs when the future value of an annuity is known, and the payment required each period to amount to that future value is the unknown. **Sinking funds** are accounts used to set aside equal amounts of money at the end of each period, at compound interest, for the purpose of saving for a future obligation. Businesses use sinking funds to accumulate money for such things as new equipment, facility expansion, and other expensive items needed in the future. Another common use is to retire financial obligations such as bond issues that come due at a future date. Individuals can use sinking funds to save for a college education, a car, the down payment on a house, or a vacation.

sinking fund
Account used to set aside equal amounts of money at the end of each period, at compound interest, for the purpose of saving for a future obligation.

Amortization is the opposite of a sinking fund. **Amortization** is a financial arrangement whereby a lump-sum obligation is incurred at compound interest now (present value) and is paid off or liquidated by a series of equal periodic payments for a specified amount of time. With amortization the amount of the loan or obligation is given, and the equal payments that will amortize or pay off the obligation must be calculated. Some business uses of amortization would be paying off loans or liquidating insurance or retirement funds.

amortization
A financial arrangement whereby a lump-sum obligation is incurred at compound interest now, such as a loan, and is paid off or liquidated by a series of equal periodic payments for a specified amount of time.

In this section, you learn to calculate the sinking fund payment required to save for a future amount and the amortization payment required to liquidate a present amount. We assume that all annuities are ordinary, with payments made at the *end* of each period. As in previous sections, these exercises can be calculated by tables and by formulas.

> **Everybody's Business**
> **Real-World Connection**
> Mortgages, which are real estate loans, are a common example of amortization. More detailed coverage, including the preparation of amortization schedules, is found in Chapter 14.

12-7 Calculating the Amount of a Sinking Fund Payment by Table

In a sinking fund, the future value is known; therefore, we use the future value of an annuity table (Table 12-1) to calculate the amount of the payment.

STEPS FOR CALCULATING THE AMOUNT OF A SINKING FUND PAYMENT:

Step 1. Using the appropriate rate per period and number of periods of the sinking fund, find the future value table factor from Table 12-1.

Step 2. Calculate the amount of the sinking fund payment by

$$\text{Sinking fund payment} = \frac{\text{Future value of the sinking fund}}{\text{Future value table factor}}$$

EXAMPLE

What sinking fund payment is required at the end of each 6-month period, at 6% interest compounded semiannually, to amount to $12,000 in 4 years?

SOLUTION STRATEGY

Step 1. This sinking fund is for eight periods (4 years $\times$ 2 periods per year) at 3% per period (6% $\div$ 2 periods per year). From Table 12-1, eight periods, 3% per period gives a future value table factor of 8.89234.

Step 2. $$\text{Sinking fund payment} = \frac{\text{Future value of the sinking fund}}{\text{Future value table factor}}$$

$$\text{Sinking fund payment} = \frac{12{,}000}{8.89234} = \underline{\underline{\$1{,}349.48}}$$

Sinking funds enable businesses to plan for future purchases of expensive equipment.

TRY-IT | EXERCISE

7. Mollie Schlue wants to accumulate $8,000 in 5 years for a trip to Europe. If her bank is paying 12% interest compounded quarterly, how much must Mollie deposit at the end of each 3-month period to reach her desired goal?

Check your answer with the solution on page 437.

12-8 Calculating the Amount of an Amortization Payment by Table

Amortization is the process of paying off a financial obligation in a series of equal regular payments over a period of time. With amortization, the original amount of the loan or obligation is known (present value); therefore, we use the present value table (Table 12-2) to calculate the amount of the payment.

STEPS FOR CALCULATING THE AMOUNT OF AN AMORTIZATION PAYMENT:

Step 1. Using the appropriate rate per period and number of periods of the amortization, find the present value table factor from Table 12-2.

Step 2. Calculate the amount of the amortization payment by the formula

$$\text{Amortization payment} = \frac{\text{Original amount of obligation}}{\text{Present value table factor}}$$

EXAMPLE

What amortization payments are required each month, at 12% interest, to pay off a $10,000 loan in 2 years?

SOLUTION STRATEGY

Step 1. This amortization is for 24 periods (2 years × 12 periods per year) at 1% per period (12% ÷ 12 periods per year). From Table 12-2, 24 periods, 1% per period gives a present value table factor of 21.24339.

Step 2. $$\text{Amortization payment} = \frac{\text{Original amount of obligation}}{\text{Present value table}}$$

$$\text{Amortization payment} = \frac{10{,}000}{21.24339} = \underline{\underline{\$470.73}}$$

TRY-IT | EXERCISE

8. Captain Doug Black purchased a new fishing boat for $130,000. He made a $20,000 down payment and financed the balance at his bank for 7 years. What amortization payments are required every 3 months, at 16% interest, to pay off the boat loan?

Check your answer with the solution on page 437.

12-9 (Optional) Calculating Sinking Fund Payments by Formula

In addition to using Table 12-1, sinking fund payments are calculated by using the formula

$$\textbf{Sinking fund payment} = FV \times \frac{i}{(1+i)^n - 1}$$

where

FV = **amount needed in the future**

i = **interest rate per period (nominal rate ÷ periods per year)**

n = **number of periods (years × periods per year)**

Calculator Sequence:

1 [+] i [=] [y^x] n [−] 1 [=] [M+] i [÷] [MR] [×] FV [=] Sinking fund payment

EXAMPLE

Consolidated Widget Corporation needs $100,000 in 5 years to pay off a bond issue. What sinking fund payment is required at the end of each month, at 12% interest compounded monthly, to meet this financial obligation?

SOLUTION STRATEGY

To solve this sinking fund problem, we use 1% interest rate per period (12% ÷ 12) and 60 periods (5 years × 12 periods per year).

$$\text{Sinking fund payment} = \text{Future value} \times \frac{i}{(1+i)^n - 1}$$

$$\text{Sinking fund payment} = 100{,}000 \times \frac{.01}{(1+.01)^{60} - 1}$$

$$\text{Sinking fund payment} = 100{,}000 \times \frac{.01}{.8166967}$$

$$\text{Sinking fund payment} = 100{,}000 \times .0122444 = \underline{\underline{\$1{,}224.44}}$$

Calculator Sequence:

1 [+] .01 [=] [y^x] 60 [−] 1 [=] [M+] .01 [÷] [MR] [×] 100,000 [=] $1,224.44

TRY-IT | EXERCISE

9. What sinking fund payment is required at the end of each month, at 18% interest compounded monthly, to amount to $40,000 in 6 years?

Check your answer with the solution on page 437.

12-10 (Optional) Calculating Amortization Payments by Formula

Amortization payments are calculated by using the formula

$$\text{Amortization payment} = PV \times \frac{i}{1-(1+i)^{-n}}$$

where

PV = **amount of the loan or obligation**

i = **interest rate per period (nominal rate ÷ periods per year)**

n = **number of periods (years × periods per year)**

Calculator Sequence:

1 [+] i [=] [y^x] n [+/−] [=] [M+] 1 [−] [MR] [=] [M+] i [÷] [MR] [×] PV [=] Amortization payment

EXAMPLE

What amortization payment is required each month, at 18% interest, to pay off $5,000 in 3 years?

SOLUTION STRATEGY

To solve this amortization problem, we use 1.5% interest rate per period (18% ÷ 12) and 36 periods (3 years × 12 periods per year).

$$\text{Amortization payment} = \text{Present value} \times \frac{i}{1-(1+i)^{-n}}$$

$$\text{Amortization payment} = 5{,}000 \times \frac{.015}{1-(1+.015)^{-36}}$$

$$\text{Amortization payment} = 5{,}000 \times \frac{.015}{.4149103}$$

$$\text{Amortization payment} = 5{,}000 \times .0361524 = \$180.76$$

Calculator Sequence:

1 [+] .015 [=] [y^x] 36 [+/−] [=] [M+] 1 [−] [MR] [=] [M+] .015 [÷] [MR] [×] 5,000 [=] $180.76

TRY-IT EXERCISE

10. Mountainview Manufacturing recently purchased a new computer system for $150,000. What amortization payment is required each month, at 12% interest, to pay off this obligation in 8 years?

Check your answer with the solution on page 437.

REVIEW EXERCISES | CHAPTER 12—SECTION III

For the following sinking funds, use Table 12-1 to calculate the amount of the periodic payments needed to amount to the financial objective (future value of the annuity):

	Sinking Fund Payment	Payment Frequency	Time Period (years)	Nominal Rate (%)	Interest Compounded	Future Value (Objective)
1.	________	every 6 months	8	10	semiannually	$50,000
2.	________	every year	14	9	annually	$250,000
3.	________	every 3 months	5	12	quarterly	$1,500
4.	________	every month	$1\frac{1}{2}$	12	monthly	$4,000
5.	________	every 3 months	4	16	quarterly	$18,750

You have just been hired as a loan officer at the Eagle National Bank. Your first assignment is to calculate the amount of the periodic payment required to amortize (pay off) the following loans being considered by the bank (use Table 12-2):

	Loan Payment	Payment Period	Term of Loan (years)	Nominal Rate (%)	Present Value (Amount of Loan)
6.	________	every year	12	9	$30,000
7.	________	every 3 months	5	8	$5,500
8.	________	every month	$1\frac{3}{4}$	18	$10,000
9.	________	every 6 months	8	6	$13,660
10.	________	every month	1.5	12	$850

11. John Rose is planning a safari vacation in Africa in 4 years and will need $7,500 for the trip. He decides to set up a sinking fund savings account for the vacation. He intends to make regular payments at the end of each 3-month period into the account that pays 6% interest compounded quarterly. What periodic sinking fund payment will allow John to achieve his vacation goal?

12. Elizabeth Robinson bought a new Nissan Altima for $15,500. She made a $2,500 down payment and is financing the balance at the Mid-South Bank over a 3-year period at 12% interest. As her banker, calculate what equal monthly payments will be required by Elizabeth to amortize the car loan.

13. Green Thumb Landscaping buys new lawn equipment every 3 years. It is estimated that $25,000 will be needed for the next purchase. The company sets up a sinking fund to save for this obligation.

a. What equal payments must be deposited every 6 months if interest is 8% compounded semiannually?

b. What is the total amount of interest earned by the sinking fund?

14. Karen Moore is ready to retire and has saved up $200,000 for that purpose. She wants to amortize (liquidate) that amount in a retirement fund so that she will receive equal annual payments over the next 25 years. At the end of the 25 years, there will be no funds left in the account. If the fund earns 12% interest, how much will Karen receive each year?

15. West Coast Industries established a sinking fund to pay off a $10,000,000 bond issue that comes due in 8 years.

a. What equal payments must be deposited into the fund every 3 months at 6% interest compounded quarterly for West Coast to meet this financial obligation?

b. What is the total amount of interest earned in this sinking fund account?

(Optional) Solve the following exercises by using the sinking fund or amortization formulas:

16. Howard Lockwood purchased a new home for $225,000 with a 20% down payment and the remainder amortized over a 15-year period at 9% interest.

a. What is the amount of the house that was financed?

b. What equal monthly payments are required to amortize this loan over 15 years?

c. What equal monthly payments are required if Howard decides to take a 20-year loan rather than a 15?

17. The Beach Club Hotel has a financial obligation of $1,000,000 due in 5 years. A sinking fund is established to meet this obligation at 12% interest compounded monthly.

a. What equal monthly sinking fund payments are required to accumulate the needed amount?

b. What is the total amount of interest earned in the account?

BUSINESS DECISION

Don't Forget Inflation!

E3

18. You are the vice president of finance for Casablanca Enterprises, Inc., a manufacturer of office furniture. The company is planning a major plant expansion in 5 years. You have decided to start a sinking fund to accumulate the funds necessary for the project. Current bank rates are 8% compounded quarterly. It is estimated that $2,000,000 in today's dollars will be required; however, the inflation rate on construction costs and plant equipment is expected to average 5% per year for the next 5 years.

a. Use the compound interest concept from Chapter 11 to determine how much will be required for the project, taking inflation into account.

b. What sinking fund payments will be required at the end of every 3-month period to accumulate the necessary funds?

Everybody's Business

Real-World Connection

This Business Decision, "Don't Forget Inflation," is a good illustration of how inflation can affect long-range financial planning in business. Notice how much more the project will cost in 5 years because of rising prices.

CHAPTER FORMULAS

Future value (ordinary annuity) = Ordinary annuity table factor × Annuity payment

$$FV\text{ (ordinary annuity)} = \text{Payment} \times \frac{(1+i)^n - 1}{i}$$

Future value (annuity due) = Annuity due table factor × Annuity payment

$$FV\text{ (annuity due)} = \text{Payment} \times \frac{(1+i)^n - 1}{i} \times (1+i)$$

Present value (ordinary annuity) = Ordinary annuity table factor × Annuity payment

$$PV\text{ (ordinary annuity)} = \text{Payment} \times \frac{1-(1+i)^{-n}}{i}$$

Present value (annuity due) = Annuity due table factor × Annuity payment

$$PV\text{ (annuity due)} = \text{Payment} \times \frac{1-(1+i)^{-n}}{i} \times (1+i)$$

$$\text{Sinking fund payment} = \frac{\text{Future value of the sinking fund}}{\text{Future value table factor}}$$

$$\text{Sinking fund payment} = \text{Future value} \times \frac{i}{(1+i)^n - 1}$$

$$\text{Amortization payment} = \frac{\text{Original amount of obligation}}{\text{Present value table factor}}$$

$$\text{Amortization payment} = \text{Present value} \times \frac{i}{1-(1+i)^{-n}}$$

✦ SUMMARY CHART ✦

SECTION I: Future Value of an Annuity

Topic	P/O, Page	Important Concepts	Illustrative Examples
Calculating the Future Value of an Ordinary Annuity by Using Tables	12-1 410	An annuity is the payment or receipt of *equal* cash amounts per period for a specified amount of time.	Calculate the future value of an ordinary annuity of $500 every 6 months for 5 years at 12% interest compounded semiannually.

SECTION I: (continued)

Topic	P/O, Page	Important Concepts	Illustrative Examples
		1. Calculate the interest rate per period for the annuity (nominal rate ÷ periods per year). 2. Determine the number of periods of the annuity (years × periods per year). 3. From Table 12-1, locate the ordinary annuity table factor at the intersection of the rate column and the periods row. 4. Calculate the future value of an ordinary annuity by **Future value (ordinary annuity) = Table factor × Annuity payment**	Rate per period = 6% (12% ÷ 2 periods per year) Periods = 10 (5 years × 2 periods per year) Table factor 6%, 10 periods = 13.18079 Future value = 13.18079 × 500 Future value = $6,590.40
Calculating the Future Value of an Annuity Due by Using Tables	12-2 414	1. Calculate the number of periods of the annuity (years × periods per year), and add one period to the total. 2. Calculate the interest rate per period (nominal rate ÷ periods per year). 3. Locate the table factor at the intersection of the rate column and the periods row. 4. Subtract 1 from the ordinary annuity table factor to get the annuity due table factor. 5. Calculate the future value of an annuity due by **Future value (annuity due) = Table factor × Annuity payment**	Calculate the future value of an annuity due to $100 per month, for 2 years, at 12% interest compounded monthly. Periods = 24 (2 × 12) + 1 for a total of 25 Rate per period = 1% (12% ÷ 12) Table factor 1%, 25 periods = 28.24320 28.24320 − 1 = 27.24320 Future value = 27.24320 × 100 Future value = $2,724.32
(Optional) Calculating the Future Value of an Ordinary Annuity and an Annuity Due by Formula	12-3 415	***Future Value: Ordinary Annuity*** $FV = Pmt \times \frac{(1+i)^n - 1}{i}$ ***Future Value: Annuity Due*** $FV = Pmt \times \frac{(1+i)^n - 1}{i} \times (1+i)$ **where** FV **= future value** Pmt **= annuity payment** i **= interest rate per period (nominal rate ÷ periods per year)** n **= number of periods (years × periods per year)**	a. What is the future value of an *ordinary annuity* of $200 per month for 4 years at 12% interest compounded monthly? $FV = 200 \times \frac{(1+.01)^{48} - 1}{.01}$ $FV = 200 \times 61.222608$ $FV = \$12{,}244.52$ b. What is the future value of this investment if it was an *annuity due?* $FV = 12{,}244.52 \times (1 + .01)$ $FV = 12{,}244.52 \times 1.01$ $FV = \$12{,}366.97$

SECTION II: Present Value of an Annuity

<table>
<tr><th>Topic</th><th>P/O, Page</th><th>Important Concepts</th><th>Illustrative Examples</th></tr>
<tr><td>Calculating the Present Value of an Ordinary Annuity by Using Tables</td><td>12-4
419</td><td>1. Calculate the interest rate per period for the annuity (nominal rate ÷ periods per year).
2. Determine the number of periods of the annuity (years × periods per year).
3. From Table 12-2, locate the present value table factor at the intersection of the rate column and the periods row.
4. Calculate the present value of an ordinary annuity by
Present value (ordinary annuity) = Table factor × Annuity payment</td><td>How much must be deposited now, at 5% compounded annually, to yield an annuity payment of $1,000 at the end of each year, for 11 years?
Rate per period = 5%
(5% ÷ 1 period per year)
Number of periods = 11
(11 years × 1 period per year)
Table factor 5%, 11 periods is 8.30641
Present value = 8.30641 × 1,000
Present value = $8,306.41</td></tr>
<tr><td>Calculating the Present Value of an Annuity Due by Using Tables</td><td>12-5
421</td><td>1. Calculate the number of periods (years × periods per year), and subtract 1 from the total.
2. Calculate rate per period (nominal rate ÷ periods per year).
3. Locate the table factor at the intersection of the rate column and the periods row.
4. Add 1 to the ordinary annuity table factor to get the annuity due table factor.
5. Calculate the present value of an annuity due by
Present value (annuity due) = Table factor × Annuity payment</td><td>How much must be deposited now, at 8% compounded semiannually, to yield an annuity payment of $1,000 at the beginning of each 6-month period, for 5 years?
Number of periods = 10 (5 × 2) less 1 period = 9
Rate per period = 4% (8% ÷ 2)
Table factor 4%, 9 periods = 7.43533
7.43533 + 1 = 8.43533
Present value = 8.43533 × 1,000
Present value = $8,435.33</td></tr>
<tr><td>(Optional) Calculating the Present Value of an Ordinary Annuity and an Annuity Due by Formula</td><td>12-6
422</td><td>Present Value: Ordinary Annuity
$PV = Pmt \times \frac{1-(1+i)^{-n}}{i}$
Present Value: Annuity Due
$PV = Pmt \times \frac{1-(1+i)^{-n}}{i} \times (1+i)$
where
PV = present value
Pmt = annuity payment
i = interest rate per period (nominal rate ÷ periods per year)
n = number of periods (years × periods per year)</td><td>a. What is the present value of an ordinary annuity of $100 per month for 5 years at 12% interest compounded monthly?
$PV = 100 \times \frac{1-(1+.01)^{-60}}{.01}$
$PV = 100 \times 44.955039$
$PV = \$4,495.50$
b. What is the present value of this investment if it was an annuity due?
$PV_{\text{annuity due}} =$
$PV_{\text{ordiary annuity}} \times (1+i)$
$PV = 4,495.50 \times (1+.01)$
$PV = 4,495.50 \times 1.01$
$PV = \$4,540.46$</td></tr>
</table>

SECTION III: Sinking Funds and Amortization

Topic	P/O, Page	Important Concepts	Illustrative Examples
Calculating the Amount of a Sinking Fund Payment by Table	12-7 426	Sinking funds are accounts used to set aside equal amounts of money at the end of each period, at compound interest, for the purpose of saving for a known future financial obligation. 1. Using the appropriate rate per period and number of periods, find the future value table factor from Table 12-1. 2. Calculate the amount of the sinking fund payment by $\text{Sinking fund payment} = \dfrac{\text{Future value of sinking fund}}{\text{Future value table factor}}$	What sinking fund payment is required at the end of each 6-month period, at 10% interest compounded semiannually, to amount to $10,000 in 7 years? Number of periods = 14 (7 years × 2 periods per year) Rate per period = 5% (10% ÷ 2 periods per year) Table factor 14 periods, 5% = 19.59863 $\text{Payment} = \dfrac{10{,}000}{19.59863}$ Payment = $510.24
Calculating the Amount of an Amortization Payment by Table	12-8 427	Amortization is a financial arrangement whereby a lump-sum obligation is incurred now (present value) and is paid off or liquidated by a series of equal periodic payments for a specified amount of time. 1. Using the appropriate rate per period and number of periods of the amortization, find the present value table factor from Table 12-2. 2. Calculate the amount of the amortization payment by $\text{Amortization payment} = \dfrac{\text{Original amount obligation}}{\text{Present value table factor}}$	What amortization payments are required at the end of each month, at 18% interest, to pay off a $15,000 loan in 3 years? Number of periods = 36 (3 years × 12 periods per year) Rate per period = 1.5% (18% ÷ 12 periods per year) Table factor 36 periods, 1.5% = 27.66068 $\text{Amort. payment} = \dfrac{15{,}000}{27.66068}$ Amortization payment = $542.29
(Optional) Calculating Sinking Fund Payments by Formula	12-9 428	Sinking fund payments can be calculated by using the following formula $Pmt = FV \times \dfrac{i}{(1+i)^n - 1}$ where Pmt = sinking fund payment FV = future value, amount needed in the future i = interest rate per period (nominal rate ÷ periods per year) n = number of periods (years × periods per year)	What sinking fund payment is required at the end of each month, at 12% interest compounded monthly, to amount to $10,000 in 4 years? Rate per period = 1% (12% ÷ 12) Periods = 48 (4 × 12) $Pmt = 10{,}000 \times \dfrac{.01}{(1+.01)^{48} - 1}$ $Pmt = 10{,}000 \times \dfrac{.01}{.6122261}$ $Pmt = 10{,}000 \times .0163338$ Sinking fund payment = $163.34

SECTION III: (continued)

Topic	P/O, Page	Important Concepts	Illustrative Examples
(Optional) Calculating Amortization Payments by Formula	12-10 429	Amortization payments are calculated by using the following formula: $Pmt = PV \times \frac{i}{1-(1+i)^{-n}}$ **where** **Pmt = amortization payment** **PV = present value, amount of the loan or obligation** **i = interest rate per period (nominal rate ÷ periods per year)** **n = number of periods (years × periods per year)**	What amortization payment is required each month, at 18% interest, to pay off $3,000 in 2 years? Rate = 1.5% (18% ÷ 12) Periods = 24 (2 × 12) $Pmt = 3{,}000 \times \frac{.015}{1-(1+.015)^{-24}}$ $Pmt = 3{,}000 \times \frac{.015}{.3004561}$ $Pmt = 3{,}000 \times .0499241$ Amortization payment = $149.77

TRY-IT EXERCISE | SOLUTIONS

1. 2%, 24 periods
Future value = Table factor × Annuity payment
Future value = 30.42186 × 1,000 = $30,421.86

2. Periods = 20 (5 × 4) + 1 = 21

$$\text{Rate} = \frac{6\%}{4} = 1\frac{1}{2}\%$$

Table factor = 24.47052
− 1.00000
23.47052

Future value = Table factor × Annuity payment
Future value = 23.47052 × 1,000 = $23,470.52

3. a. 2%, 20 periods

$$FV = Pmt \times \frac{(1+i)^n - 1}{i}$$

$$FV = 250 \times \frac{(1+.02)^{20}-1}{.02} = 250 \times \frac{(1.02)^{20}-1}{.02}$$

$FV = 250 \times 24.297369 =$ $6,074.34

b. $FV_{\text{annuity due}} = (1+i) \times FV_{\text{ordinary annuity}}$
$FV_{\text{annuity due}} = (1+.02)6{,}074.34 =$ $6,195.83

4. 4%, 12 periods
Present value = Table factor × Annuity payment
Present value = 9.38507 × 20,000 = $187,701.40

5. Periods = 12 (3 × 4) − 1 = 11

$$\text{Rate} = \frac{6\%}{4} = 1\frac{1}{2}\%$$

Table factor = 10.07112
+ 1.00000
11.07112

Present value = Table factor × Annuity payment
Present value = 11.07112 × 10,000 = $110,711.20

6. a. 2%, 24 periods

$$PV = Pmt \times \frac{1-(1+i)^{-n}}{i}$$

$$PV = 500 \times \frac{1-(1+.02)^{-24}}{.02} = 500 \times \frac{1-.6217215}{.02}$$

$PV = 500 \times 18.913925 =$ $9,456.96

b. $PV_{\text{annuity due}} = (1+i) \times PV_{\text{ordinary annuity}}$
$PV_{\text{annuity due}} = (1+.02) \times 9{,}456.96 =$ $9,646.10

7. 3%, 20 periods

$$\text{Sinking fund payment} = \frac{\text{Future value of sinking fund}}{\text{Future value table factor}}$$

$$\text{Sinking fund payment} = \frac{8{,}000}{26.87037} = \$297.73$$

8. 4%, 28 periods

$$\text{Amortization payment} = \frac{\text{Original amount of obligation}}{\text{Present value table factor}}$$

$$\text{Amortization payment} = \frac{110{,}000}{16.66306} = \$6{,}601.43$$

9. $1\frac{1}{2}\%$, 72 periods

$$\text{Sinking fund payment} = FV \times \frac{i}{(1+i)^n - 1}$$

$$\text{Sinking fund payment} = 40{,}000 \times \frac{.015}{(1+.015)^{72}-1}$$

Sinking fund payment = 40,000 × .0078078 = $312.31

10. 1%, 96 periods

$$\text{Amortization payment} = PV \times \frac{i}{1-(1+i)^{-n}}$$

$$\text{Amortization payment} = 150{,}000 \times \frac{.01}{1-(1+.01)^{-96}}$$

Amortization payment = 150,000 × .0162528 = $2,437.93

Name ____________________

Class ____________________

Answers

1. ____________________
2. ____________________
3. ____________________
4. ____________________
5. ____________________
6. ____________________
7. ____________________
8. ____________________
9. ____________________
10. ____________________
11. ____________________
12. ____________________
13. ____________________

CHAPTER 12 | ASSESSMENT TEST

Use Table 12-1 to calculate the future value of the following ordinary annuities:

	Annuity Payment	Payment Frequency	Time Period (years)	Nominal Rate (%)	Interest Compounded	Future Value of the Annuity
1.	$4,000	every 3 months	6	8	quarterly	________
2.	$10,000	every year	20	5	annually	________

Use Table 12-1 to calculate the future value of the following annuities due:

	Annuity Payment	Payment Frequency	Time Period (years)	Nominal Rate (%)	Interest Compounded	Future Value of the Annuity
3.	$1,850	every 6 months	12	10	semiannually	________
4.	$200	every month	$1\frac{3}{4}$	12	monthly	________

Use Table 12-2 to calculate the present value of the following ordinary annuities:

	Annuity Payment	Payment Frequency	Time Period (years)	Nominal Rate (%)	Interest Compounded	Present Value of the Annuity
5.	$6,000	every year	9	5	annually	________
6.	$125,000	every 3 months	3	6	quarterly	________

Use Table 12-2 to calculate the present value of the following annuities due:

	Annuity Payment	Payment Frequency	Time Period (years)	Nominal Rate (%)	Interest Compounded	Present Value of the Annuity
7.	$700	every month	$1\frac{1}{2}$	12	monthly	________
8.	$2,000	every 6 months	6	4	semiannually	________

Use Table 12-1 to calculate the amount of the periodic payments needed to amount to the financial objective (future value of the annuity) for the following sinking funds:

	Sinking Fund Payment	Payment Frequency	Time Period (years)	Nominal Rate (%)	Interest Compounded	Future Value (Objective)
9.	________	every year	13	7	annually	$20,000
10.	________	every month	$2\frac{1}{4}$	12	monthly	$7,000

Use Table 12-2 to calculate the amount of the periodic payment required to amortize (pay off) the following loans:

	Loan Payment	Payment Period	Term of Loan (years)	Nominal Rate (%)	Interest Compounded	Present Value (Amount of Loan)
11.	________	every 3 months	8	8	quarterly	$6,000
12.	________	every month	$2\frac{1}{2}$	18	monthly	$20,000

13. How much will $800 deposited at the *end* of each month into a savings account be worth after 2 years at 6% interest compounded monthly?

Name ______________________

Class ______________________

Answers

14. ______________________

15. ______________________

16. ______________________

17. a. ______________________

b. ______________________

18. a. ______________________

b. ______________________

14. How much will \$3,500 deposited at the *beginning* of each 3-month period be worth after 7 years at 12% interest compounded quarterly?

15. What amount must be deposited now to withdraw \$200 at the *beginning* of each month for 3 years if interest is 12% compounded monthly?

16. How much must be deposited now to withdraw \$4,000 at the *end* of each year for 20 years if interest is 7% compounded annually?

17. A sinking fund is established by Infinity, Inc., at 8% interest compounded semiannually to meet a financial obligation of \$1,800,000 in 4 years.

a. What periodic sinking fund payment is required every 6 months to reach the company's goal?

b. How much greater would the payment be if the interest rate was 6% compounded semiannually rather than 8%?

18. The Carvers buy a home for \$120,500. After a 15% down payment, the balance is financed at 8% interest for 9 years.

a. What equal quarterly payments will be required to amortize this mortgage loan?

b. What is the total amount of interest the Carvers will pay on the loan?

Name ______________________

Class ______________________

Answers

19. a. ______________________

b. ______________________

20. a. ______________________

b. ______________________

(Optional) Use formulas and a financial calculator to solve the following:

19. The Presidio Bank is paying 9% interest compounded monthly.

a. If you deposit $100 at the beginning of each month into a savings plan, how much will it be worth in 10 years?

b. How much would the account be worth if the payments were made at the end of each month rather than at the beginning?

20. The town of Bay Harbor is planning to buy five new police cars in 4 years. The cars are expected to cost $18,500 each.

a. What equal monthly payments must the city deposit into a sinking fund at 6% interest compounded monthly to achieve its goal?

b. What is the total amount of interest earned in the account?

21. Santa Fe Savings & Loan is offering mortgages at 9% interest. What monthly payments would be required to amortize a loan of $200,000 for 25 years?

Name ______________

Class ______________

Answers

21. ______________

22. a. ______________

b. ______________

c. ______________

d. ______________

BUSINESS DECISION

Time Is Money!

22. You are one of the retirement counselors at Sun Trust Bank. You have been asked to give a presentation to a class of high school seniors about the importance of saving for retirement. Your boss, the vice president of the trust division, has designed an example for you to use in your presentation. The students are shown 5 retirement scenarios, and are asked to guess which yields the most money. *Note:* All annuities are *ordinary*. Although some stop investing, the money remains in the account at 10% interest compounded annually.

   a. Look over each scenario and make an educated guess as to which investor will have the largest accumulation of money invested at 10%, over the next 40 years. Then, for your presentation, calculate the final value for each scenario.

   - Melissa invests $1,200 per year and stops after 15 years.
   - Charles waits for 15 years, then invests $1,200 per year for 15 years, then stops.
   - Brian waits for 15 years, then invests $1,200 per year for 25 years.
   - Anita waits for 10 years, then invests $1,500 per year for 15 years, then stops.
   - Todd waits for 10 years, then invests $1,500 per year for 30 years.

   b. Based on the results, what message will this presentation convey to the students?

   c. Recalculate each scenario as an annuity due.

   d. How can the results be used in your presentation?

All the Math That's Fit to Learn

The Business Math Times

Volume XII | **Annuities** | One Dollar

Saving for College

If parents save and invest $10 per work day at 12% interest from the birth of their child, when their child is 18 and ready for college, they would have $150,000 accumulated through the power of compounding.

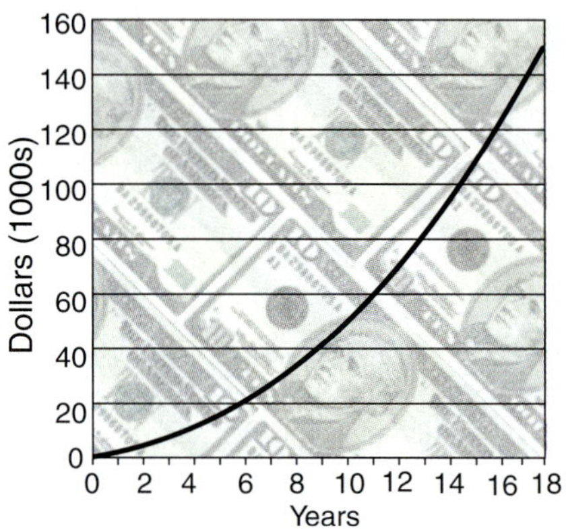

The Long View!

WHAT A DIFFERENCE 10 YEARS MAKES

Albert Einstein called compound interest the greatest invention of mankind. And the younger you start investing, the better.

If you start saving $4,000 annually at age 30, you will have $1.19 million by age 65, assuming a 10% average annual return. But waiting five years to begin saving shrinks your ending balance to $723,774. Similarly, waiting until age 40 reduces that nest egg by $759,780 to $432,727.

Hold the Anchovies!

According to financial planner Allyson Lewis, the author of *The Million Dollar Car and $250,000 Pizza*, if $20 spent on pizza were invested weekly in a mutual fund with a 9% annual return, it would be worth a quarter of a million dollars in 30 years.

The following table demonstrates what some small expenses would be worth after 20 years in a 401(k) earning 9%.

Item	Cost per week	Cost per year	20 years in 401(k)
ATM Fees	$2.50	$130	$7,280
Soda, Snacks	$3.75	$195	$10,192
Lottery Tickets	$5	$260	$13,302
Frozen Yogurt	$6	$312	$15,962
Mocha Latte	$15	$780	$43,682
Movie Tickets	$20	$1,040	$53,207
Dining Out	$100	$5,200	$291,214

"Quote . . . Unquote"

Plans are nothing; planning is everything.
—*Dwight D. Eisenhower*

Do you know the only thing that gives me pleasure? It's to see my dividends coming in.
—*John D. Rockefeller*

Retirement Annuity

The following chart shows the number of years a $1 million portfolio with an annual return of 8.7% can last based on percentage of assets withdrawn each year. Initial withdrawal is increased 3% each year for inflation.

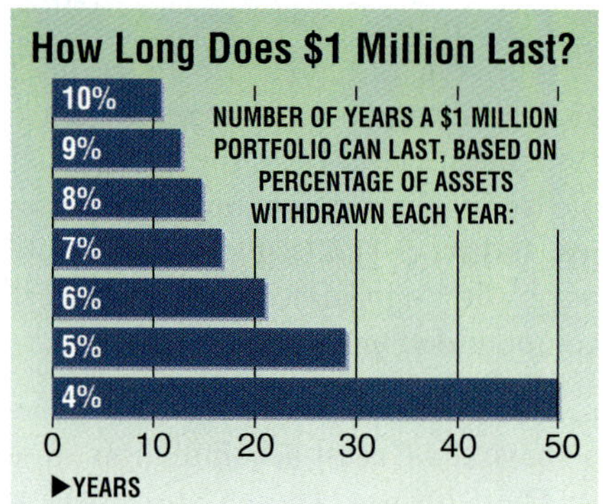

NEW YORK, NEW YORK—SOLUTION

(Please refer to p. 408.)

A. At 6%, the $24 would be worth more than $83 billion.

$$\$24(1 + .06)^{377} = \$83{,}276{,}500{,}000$$

B. At 8%, the $24 would be worth over $95 trillion.

$$\$24(1 + .08)^{377} = \$95{,}712{,}150{,}000{,}000$$

This is a dramatic example of how interest rates affect the time value of money.

Brainteaser

UP, UP, AND AWAY!

If a stack of 1,000 thousand-dollar bills ($1 million) is 4 inches thick, how high would the stack be if it was equal to $5.7 trillion, the national debt as of January 2002.

ANSWER TO LAST ISSUE'S BRAINTEASER

The room will be darkest at 1:11 and brightest at 10:08.

CHAPTER

13

Consumer and Business Credit

PERFORMANCE OBJECTIVES

Section I Open-End Credit—Charge Accounts, Credit Cards, and Lines of Credit

13-1 Calculating finance charge and new balance by the unpaid or previous month's balance method. (p. 447)

13-2 Calculating finance charge and new balance by using the average daily balance method. (p. 448)

13-3 Calculating the finance charge and new balance of business and personal lines of credit. (p. 450)

Section II Closed-End Credit—Installment Loans

13-4 Calculating the total deferred payment price and the amount of the finance charge of an installment loan. (p. 457)

13-5 Calculating the amount of the regular monthly payments of an installment loan by the add-on interest method. (p. 459)

13-6 Calculating the annual percentage rate of an installment loan by APR tables and by formula. (p. 460)

13-7 Calculating the finance charge and monthly payment of an installment loan by using the APR tables. (p. 465)

13-8 Calculating the finance charge rebate and the amount of the payoff when a loan is paid off early by using the sum-of-the-digits method. (p. 466)

SECTION I

OPEN-END CREDIT—CHARGE ACCOUNTS, CREDIT CARDS, AND LINES OF CREDIT

open-end credit
Loan arrangement in which there is no set number of payments. As the balance of the loan is reduced, the borrower can renew the amount of the loan up to a preapproved credit limit. A form of revolving credit.

finance charge
Dollar amount that is paid for credit. Total of installment payments for an item less the cost price of that item.

annual percentage rate (APR)
Effective or true annual interest rate being charged for credit. Must be revealed to borrowers under the Truth in Lending Act.

"Buy now, pay later" is a concept that has become an everyday part of the way individuals and businesses purchase goods and services. Merchants in all categories, and lending institutions alike, encourage us to just say "charge it!" Consumers are offered a wide variety of charge accounts with many extra services and incentives attached. Many businesses have charge accounts in the company name. These accounts may be used to facilitate employee travel and entertainment expenses or just to fill up the company delivery truck with gasoline, without having to deal with cash. Exhibit 13-1 shows a sample credit card and its parts.

Lending and borrowing money comprise a huge portion of the U.S. economic system. Over the years, as the practice became more and more prevalent, the federal government enacted various legislation to protect the consumer from being misled about credit and finance charges. One of the most important and comprehensive pieces of legislation, known as Regulation Z, covers both installment and **open-end credit.**

Regulation Z of the Consumer Credit Protection Act, 1969, also known as the Truth in Lending Act, requires that the lender fully disclose to the customer, in writing, the cost of the credit, particularly the finance charge and the annual percentage rate. The **finance charge** is the dollar amount that is paid for the credit. The **annual percentage rate,** also known as the **APR,** is the effective or true annual interest rate being charged.

The granting of credit involves a trust relationship between the borrower and the lender. The borrower promises to repay the loan, with interest, in one of many predetermined payment arrangements. Trust on the part of the lender is based on past lending experience with the borrower, the information provided on the credit application, and independent credit reports from credit bureaus. The degree and depth of lender investigation

EXHIBIT 13-1
Parts of a Credit Card

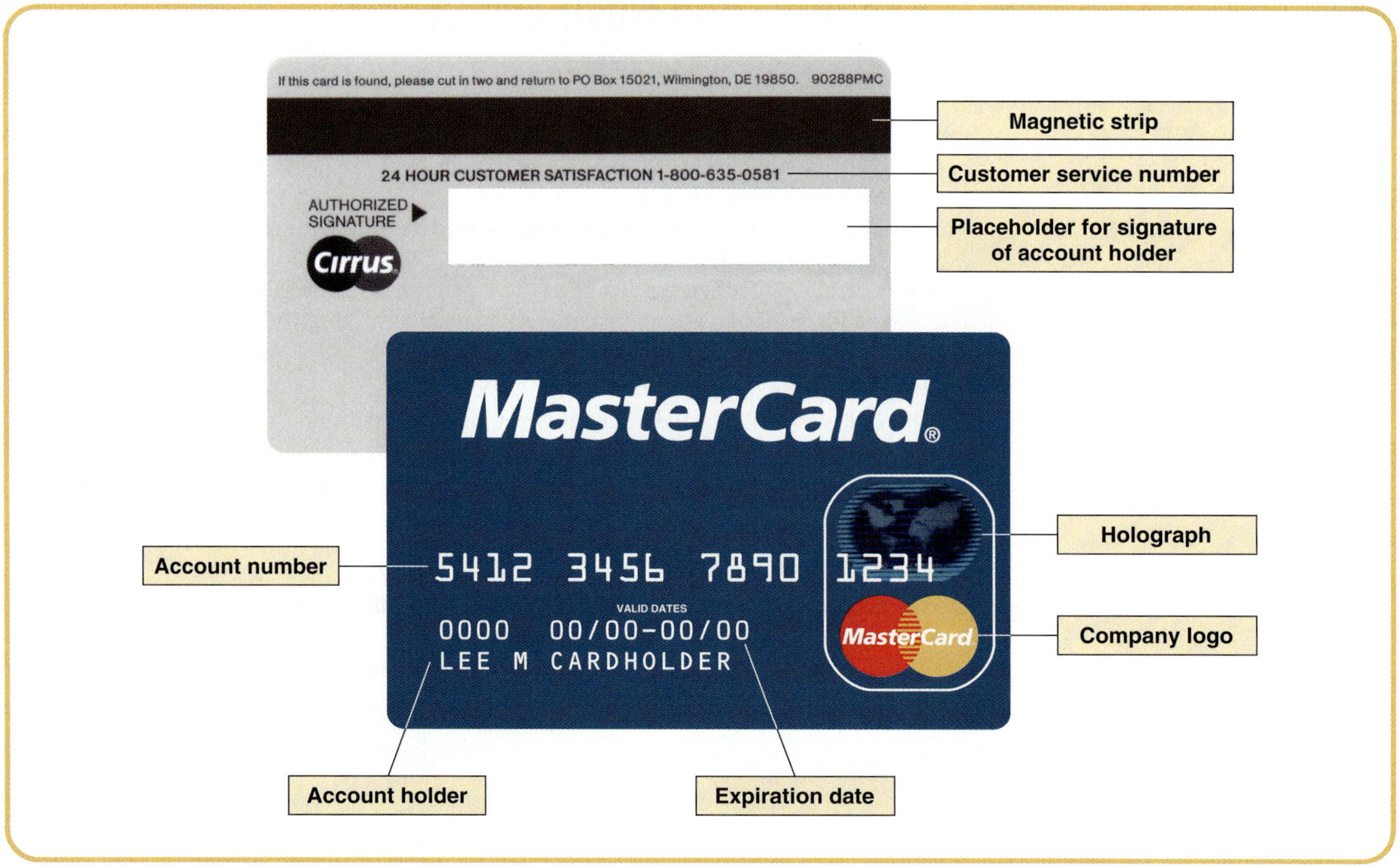

EXHIBIT 13-2
Typical Credit Application

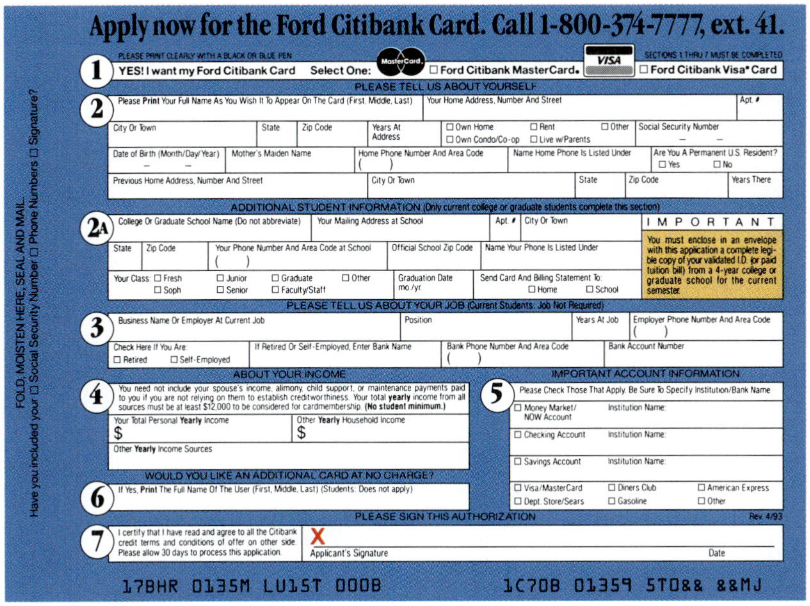

Apply now for the Ford Citibank Card. Call 1-800-374-7777, ext. 41.

PLEASE PRINT CLEARLY WITH A BLACK OR BLUE PEN — SECTIONS 1 THRU 7 MUST BE COMPLETED

1 YES! I want my Ford Citibank Card Select One: ☐ Ford Citibank MasterCard. ☐ Ford Citibank Visa® Card

PLEASE TELL US ABOUT YOURSELF

2 Please **Print** Your Full Name As You Wish It To Appear On The Card (First, Middle, Last) | Your Home Address, Number And Street | Apt. #
City Or Town | State | Zip Code | Years At Address | ☐ Own Home ☐ Rent ☐ Other ☐ Own Condo/Co-op ☐ Live w/Parents | Social Security Number
Date of Birth (Month/Day/Year) | Mother's Maiden Name | Home Phone Number And Area Code ( ) | Name Home Phone Is Listed Under | Are You A Permanent U.S. Resident? ☐ Yes ☐ No
Previous Home Address, Number And Street | City Or Town | State | Zip Code | Years There

ADDITIONAL STUDENT INFORMATION (Only current college or graduate students complete this section)

2A College Or Graduate School Name (Do not abbreviate) | Your Mailing Address at School | Apt. # | City Or Town
State | Zip Code | Your Phone Number And Area Code at School ( ) | Official School Zip Code | Name Your Phone Is Listed Under
Your Class: ☐ Fresh ☐ Soph ☐ Junior ☐ Senior ☐ Graduate ☐ Faculty/Staff ☐ Other | Graduation Date mo./yr. | Send Card And Billing Statement To: ☐ Home ☐ School

IMPORTANT
You must enclose in an envelope with this application a complete legible copy of your validated I.D. (or paid tuition bill) from a 4-year college or graduate school for the current semester.

PLEASE TELL US ABOUT YOUR JOB (Current Students: Job Not Required)

3 Business Name Or Employer At Current Job | Position | Years At Job | Employer Phone Number And Area Code ( )
Check Here If You Are: ☐ Retired ☐ Self-Employed | If Retired Or Self-Employed, Enter Bank Name | Bank Phone Number And Area Code ( ) | Bank Account Number

ABOUT YOUR INCOME

4 You need not include your spouse's income, alimony, child support, or maintenance payments paid to you if you are not relying on them to establish creditworthiness. Your total **yearly** income from all sources must be at least $12,000 to be considered for cardmembership. **(No student minimum.)**
Your Total Personal **Yearly** Income $ | Other **Yearly** Household Income $
Other **Yearly** Income Sources

IMPORTANT ACCOUNT INFORMATION

5 Please Check Those That Apply. Be Sure To Specify Institution/Bank Name
☐ Money Market/NOW Account Institution Name:
☐ Checking Account Institution Name:
☐ Savings Account Institution Name:
☐ Visa/MasterCard ☐ Diners Club ☐ American Express ☐ Dept. Store/Sears ☐ Gasoline ☐ Other

WOULD YOU LIKE AN ADDITIONAL CARD AT NO CHARGE?

6 If Yes, **Print** The Full Name Of The User (First, Middle, Last) (Students: Does not apply)

PLEASE SIGN THIS AUTHORIZATION — Rev. 4/93

7 I certify that I have read and agree to all the Citibank credit terms and conditions of offer on other side. Please allow 30 days to process this application. | X Applicant's Signature | Date

FOLD, MOISTEN HERE, SEAL AND MAIL.
Have you included your ☐ Social Security Number ☐ Phone Numbers ☐ Signature?

17BHR 0135M LU15T 000B 1C70B 01359 5T0&& &&MJ

is directly proportional to the amount of money being borrowed. Exhibit 13-2 is an example of a typical credit application used to secure consumer credit.

For many consumers and almost all businesses, credit is an important element of the financial plan. It allows borrowers the advantage of having an asset, and its use, before it is paid for. Credit should not be taken lightly nor used irresponsibly. Well-established credit and a good banking relationship should be long-term goals of businesses that plan to grow and prosper.

When loans are backed by a simple promise to repay, they are known as **unsecured loans.** Most open-end credit accounts are unsecured. Loans that are backed by tangible assets, such as car and boat loans and home mortgage loans, are known as **secured loans.** These loans are backed or secured by an asset that can be repossessed and sold by the lender if the borrower fails to comply with the rules of the loan. Secured loans are covered in Section II of this chapter and in Chapter 14.

Revolving credit is the most popular type of open-end credit. Under this agreement, the consumer has a prearranged credit limit and two payment options. The first option is to use the account as a regular charge account, whereby the balance is paid off at the end of the month with no finance charge. The second option is to make a minimum payment or portion of the payment but less than the full balance. This option leaves a carryover balance, which accrues finance charges by using the simple interest formula

$$\text{Interest} = \text{Principal} \times \text{Rate} \times \text{Time}$$

The name *revolving credit* comes from the fact that there is no set number of payments as with installment credit. The account revolves month-to-month, year-to-year—technically never being paid off as long as minimum monthly payments are made. Exhibit 13-3 illustrates a typical revolving credit monthly statement.

unsecured loan
Loan that is backed simply by the borrower's "promise" to repay, without any tangible asset pledged as collateral. These loans carry more risk for the lender and therefore have higher interest rates than secured loans.

secured loan
Loan that is backed by a tangible asset, such as a car, boat, or home, which can be repossessed and sold if the borrower fails to pay back the loan. These loans carry less risk for the lender and therefore have lower interest rates than unsecured loans.

revolving credit
Loans made on a continuous basis and billed periodically. Borrower makes minimum monthly payments or more and pays interest on the outstanding balance. A form of open-end credit extended by many retail stores and credit card companies.

Statement of Account

Bank of America

Payable upon Receipt in U.S. Dollars with a check drawn on a bank located in the U.S. or a money order.
Please enter Corporate Account Number on all checks and correspondence.

☐ Check here if address or telephone number has changed. Please note changes on reverse side.

ACCOUNT NUMBER	STATEMENT CLOSING DATE	TOTAL AMOUNT DUE
0000-657421-91226	**04-02-03**	**$166.61**

TRACY MORSE
301 COMMERCE ST.
FT WORTH TX 76102

MAIL PAYMENT TO:

BANK OF AMERICA
P.O. BOX 631
DALLAS TX 73563-0001

Detach here and return upper portion with check or money order. Do not staple or fold.

Summary of Account

Bank of America

Retain this portion for your files.

NEW BALANCE	PAYMENT DUE DATE	STATEMENT CLOSING DATE	CARDMEMBER NAME
$166.61	**04-22-03**	**04-02-03**	**TRACY MORSE**
TOTAL CREDIT LINE	TOTAL AVAILABLE CREDIT	CASH ACCESS LINE	ACCOUNT NUMBER
$3,100	**$2933.39**	**$2,600**	**0000-657421-91226**

Here is your Account Summary:

	PURCHASES	CASH	TOTAL
Previous Balance	$174.84	$0.00	$174.84
(–) Payments, Credits	174.84	0.00	174.84
(+) Purchases, Cash, Debits	166.61	0.00	166.61
(+) FINANCE CHARGES	0.00	0.00	0.00
(=) New Balance	166.61	0.00	166.61
Minimum Payment Due	$10.00	$0.00	$10.00

NEED TO KNOW YOUR CURRENT BALANCE OR AVAILABLE CREDIT? FOR INQUIRIES ABOUT YOUR ACCOUNT CALL TOLL FREE 1-800-635-0581.

Your charges and credits at a glance:

TRAN. DATE	POST DATE	REF. NO.	DESCRIPTION OF TRANSACTIONS			CREDITS	CHARGES
03/19	03/19	835078	Payment - Thank You			$174.84	
03/29	03/30	501065	McDonald's	Food/Beverage	Ft. Worth TX		3.97
03/03	03/04	501081	Wal-Mart	Apparel/Housewares/ACC	Ft. Worth TX		56.94
03/21	03/22	501069	American Artist	Publications	Marion OH		26.95
02/18	02/20	501065	Exxon Company USA	Fuel/Misc	Red Oak TX		13.30
03/29	03/30	501071	Amazon.com	Books	Dallas TX		16.00
03/29	03/30	501079	Sports Authority	Soccer ball	Dallas TX		18.00
03/29	03/30	501089	Texaco	Isle Sale	Dallas TX		15.25
03/29	03/30	501092	IMAX Theaters	Tickets	Arlington TX		16.20
					TOTAL CREDITS AND CHARGES	$174.84	
					BALANCE DUE		$166.61

Here's how we determined your Finance Charge*:

	PURCHASES	CASH
Monthly Periodic Rate	V 1.387%	V 1.629%
(–) Average Daily Balance	$0.00	$0.00
(+) Periodic FINANCE CHARGE	$0.00	$0.00
(=) Total FINANCE CHARGE	$0.00	$0.00

Nominal ANNUAL PERCENTAGE RATE (For Balances)	19.80%
ANNUAL PERCENTAGE RATE (For this billing period-adjusted to include any additional Finance Charges)	19.80%

*Please see reverse side for balance computation method and other important information.
Payments or credits received after closing date above will appear on next month's statement.

EXHIBIT 13-3

Typical Monthly Statement

13-1 Calculating Finance Charge and New Balance by the Unpaid or Previous Month's Balance Method

Open-end credit transactions are divided into time periods known as **billing cycles.** These cycles are commonly between 28 and 31 days. At the end of a billing cycle, a statement is sent to the account holder much like the one in Exhibit 13-3.

billing cycle
Time period, usually 28 to 31 days, used in billing revolving credit accounts. Account statements are sent to the borrower after each billing cycle.

STEPS TO CALCULATE THE FINANCE CHARGE AND NEW BALANCE BY USING THE UNPAID BALANCE METHOD:

Step 1. Divide the annual percentage rate by 12 to find the monthly or periodic interest rate. (Round to the nearest hundredth percent when necessary.)

$$\text{Periodic rate} = \frac{\text{Annual percentage rate}}{12}$$

Step 2. Calculate the finance charge by multiplying the previous month's balance by the periodic interest rate from Step 1.

$$\text{Finance charge} = \text{Previous month's balance} \times \text{Periodic rate}$$

Step 3. Total all the purchases and cash advances for the month.

Step 4. Total all the payments and credits for the month.

Step 5. Use the following formula to determine the new balance:

$$\text{New balance} = \text{Previous balance} + \text{Finance charge} + \text{Purchases and cash advances} - \text{Payments and credits}$$

EXAMPLE

Jack Calhoun has a revolving department store credit account, with an annual percentage rate of 18%. His previous balance from last month is $322.40. During the month, he purchased shirts for $65.60 and a baseball bat for $43.25. He returned a tie for a credit of $22.95 and made a $50 payment. If the department store uses the unpaid balance method, what is the amount of the finance charge on the account and what is Jack's new balance?

SOLUTION STRATEGY

Step 1.

$$\text{Periodic rate} = \frac{\text{Annual percentage rate}}{12}$$

$$\text{Periodic rate} = \frac{18\%}{12} = 1.5\%$$

Step 2.

$$\text{Finance charge} = \text{Previous month's balance} \times \text{Periodic rate}$$

$$\text{Finance charge} = 322.40 \times .015$$

$$\text{Finance charge} = 4.836 = \underline{\underline{\$4.84}}$$

Step 3. Total the purchases for the month:

$$\$65.60 + 43.25 = \$108.85$$

Step 4. Total the payments and credits for the month:

$$\$50.00 + \$22.95 = \$72.95$$

Step 5. Find the new balance for Jack's account by using the formula

$$\text{New balance} = \text{Previous balance} + \text{Finance charge} + \text{Purchases and cash advances} - \text{Payments and credits}$$

$$\text{New balance} = \$322.40 + \$4.84 + \$108.85 - \$72.95$$

$$\text{New balance} = \underline{\underline{\$363.14}}$$

TRY-IT | EXERCISE

1. **Heather Hogan has a Bank of America account with an annual percentage rate of 15%. Her previous month's balance is $214.90. During the month of July, Heather's account showed the following activity:**

Statement of Account — Bank of America

NAME	ACCOUNT NUMBER	BILLING CYCLE
HEATHER HOGAN	097440	JULY 1–31

DATE	DESCRIPTION OF TRANSACTIONS	CHARGES
07/06	Royal Cleaners	$35.50
07/09	Payment	40.00
07/15	Steve Madden Shoes	133.25
07/16	Andre's Restaurant	41.10
07/21	Walgreens	29.00
07/27	Walgreens (credit)	9.12

How much is the finance charge for July, and what is Heather's new balance?

Check your answers with the solutions on page 479.

13-2 Calculating Finance Charge and New Balance by Using the Average Daily Balance Method

average daily balance
In open-end credit, the most commonly used method for determining the account balance for a billing cycle. It is the total of the daily balances divided by the number of days in the cycle.

In business today, the method most widely used to calculate finance charge on a revolving credit account is known as the **average daily balance.** This method precisely tracks the activity in an account on a daily basis. Each day's balance of a billing cycle is totaled and then divided by the number of days in that cycle. This gives an average of all the daily balances.

For accounts in which many charges are made each month, the average daily balance method results in much higher interest than the unpaid balance method, because interest starts accruing on the day purchases are made or cash advances are taken.

STEPS TO CALCULATE THE FINANCE CHARGE AND NEW BALANCE BY USING THE AVERAGE DAILY BALANCE:

Step 1. Starting with the previous month's balance as the first unpaid balance, multiply each by the number of days that balance existed, until the next account transaction.

Step 2. At the end of the billing cycle, find the sum of all the daily balance figures.

Step 3. Find the average daily balance using the formula

$$\text{Average daily balance} = \frac{\text{Sum of daily balances}}{\text{Days in billing cycle}}$$

Step 4. Calculate the finance charge by

$$\text{Finance charge} = \text{Average daily balance} \times \text{Periodic rate}$$

Step 5. Compute the new balance as before, using

$$\text{New balance} = \text{Previous balance} + \text{Finance charge} + \text{Purchases and cash advances} - \text{Payments and credits}$$

EXAMPLE

John Hope has a Bank of America revolving credit account with a 15% annual percentage rate. The finance charge is calculated by using the average daily balance method. The billing date is the first day of each month, and the billing cycle is the number of days in that month. During the month of March, John's account showed the following activity:

Statement of Account

Bank of America

NAME
JOHN HOPE

ACCOUNT NUMBER
1229-3390-0038

BILLING CYCLE
MARCH 1–31

DATE	DESCRIPTION OF TRANSACTIONS	CHARGES
03/01	Previous month's balance	$215.60
03/07	Sports Authority	125.11
03/10	Exxon	23.25
03/12	Payment	75.00
03/17	Macy's (credit)	54.10
03/23	H.L. Mager, DDS	79.00
03/23	Exxon	19.43
03/24	Blockbuster Music	94.19

How much is the finance charge for March, and what is John's new balance?

SOLUTION STRATEGY

Steps 1 and 2. To calculate the daily balances and their sum, set up a chart such as the one below that lists the activity in the account by dates and number of days.

Dates	Number of Days	Activity/Amount	Unpaid Balance	Daily Balances (unpaid bal. × days)
March 1–6	6	Previous balance	$215.60	$1,293.60
March 7–9	3	Charge +$125.11	340.71	1,022.13
March 10–11	2	Charge +23.25	363.96	727.92
March 12–16	5	Payment −75.00	288.96	1,444.80
March 17–22	6	Credit −54.10	234.86	1,409.16
March 23	1	Charges +79.00		
		+19.43	333.29	333.29
March 24–31	8	Charge +94.19	427.48	3,419.84
	31 days in cycle			Total $9,650.74

Step 3. $$\text{Average daily balance} = \frac{\text{Sum of daily balances}}{\text{Days in billing cycle}} = \frac{\$9{,}650.74}{31} = \$311.31$$

Step 4. The periodic rate is 1.25% (15% ÷ 12).

$$\text{Finance charge} = \text{Periodic rate} \times \text{Average daily balance}$$

$$\text{Finance charge} = .0125 \times 311.31 = \underline{\underline{\$3.89}}$$

Step 5. $$\text{New balance} = \text{Previous balance} + \text{Finance charge} + \text{Purchases and cash advances} - \text{Payments and credits}$$

$$\text{New balance} = \$215.60 + \$3.89 + \$340.98 - \$129.10$$

$$\text{New balance} = \underline{\underline{\$431.37}}$$

Everybody's Business

Shortcut

"New Balance" can be calculated by adding the finance charge to the last "Unpaid Balance" of the month.

$427.28 + $3.89 = $431.37

TRY-IT | EXERCISE

2. Julie Conover has a Bank of America revolving credit account with an 18% annual percentage rate. The finance charge is calculated by using the average daily balance method. The billing date is the first day of each month, and the billing cycle is the number of days in that month. During the month of August, Julie's account showed the following activity:

Statement of Account — Bank of America

NAME: JULIE CONOVER
ACCOUNT NUMBER: 2967-39460-0098
BILLING CYCLE: AUGUST 1–31

DATE	DESCRIPTION OF TRANSACTIONS	CHARGES
08/01	Previous month's balance	$158.69
08/05	Nathan's Beauty Salon	55.00
08/11	Payment	100.00
08/15	Wal-Mart	43.22
08/17	Sunshine Auto Repair	54.10
08/20	Circuit City	224.50
08/26	Cash Advance	75.00

How much is the finance charge for August, and what is Julie's new balance?

Check your answers with the solutions on pages 479–480.

13-3 Calculating the Finance Charge and New Balance of Business and Personal Lines of Credit

line of credit
Pre-approved amount of open-end credit, based on borrower's ability to pay.

One of the most useful types of open-end credit is the business or personal **line of credit.** In this section, we investigate the unsecured credit line, which is based on your own merit. In Chapter 14, we discuss the home equity line of credit, which is secured by a home or other piece of real estate property.

A line of credit is an important tool for on-going businesses and responsible individuals. For those who qualify, unsecured lines of credit generally range from $2,500 to $250,000. The amount is based on your ability to pay as well as your financial and credit history. This pre-approved borrowing power essentially gives you the ability to become your own private banker. Once the line has been established, you can borrow money by simply writing a check. Lines of credit usually have an annual usage fee of between $50 and $100, and most lenders also require that you update your financial information each year.

prime rate
Lending rate at which the largest and most creditworthy corporations borrow money from banks. The interest rate of most lines of credit is tied to the movement of the prime rate.

With credit lines, you only pay interest on the outstanding average daily balance of your loan. For most lines and some credit cards, the interest rate is variable and is based on, or indexed to, the prime rate. The **prime rate** is the lending rate at which the largest and most creditworthy corporations in the country borrow money from banks. The current prime rate is published daily in *The Wall Street Journal* in a chart entitled "Money Rates." Exhibit 13-4 shows an example of this chart.

A typical line of credit quotes interest as the prime rate plus a fixed percent, such as "prime + 3%" or "prime + 6.8%." Some lenders have a minimum rate regardless of the prime rate, such as "prime + 3%, minimum 10%." In this case, when the prime is greater than 7%, the rate varies up and down. When the prime falls to less than 7%, the minimum 10% rate applies. This guarantees the lender at least a 10% return on funds loaned. Exhibit 13-5 is an example of a credit card rate disclosure indexed to the prime rate.

EXHIBIT 13-4

Money Rates Chart

MONEY RATES

Friday, January 18, 2002

The key U. S. and foreign annual interest rates below are a guide to general levels but don't always represent actual transactions.

PRIME RATE: 4.75% (effective 12/12/01). The base rate on corporate loans posted by at least 75% of the nation's 30 largest banks.

DISCOUNT RATE: 1.25% (effective 12/11/01). The charge on loans to depository institutions by the Federal Reserve Banks.

FEDERAL FUNDS: 8 % high, 1 9/16 % low, 7 % near closing bid, 10 % offered. Reserves traded among commercial banks for overnight use in amounts of $1 million or more. Source: Prebon Yamane(U.S.A) Inc. FOMC fed funds target rate 1.75% effective 12/11/01.

CALL MONEY: 3.50% (effective 12/12/01). The charge on loans to brokers on stock exchange collateral. Source: Reuters.

COMMERCIAL PAPER: Placed directly by General Electric Capital Corp.: 1.64% 30 to 63 days; 1.55% 64 to 87 days; 1.63% 88 to 119 days; 1.66% 120 to 179 days; 1.72% 180 to 209 days; 1.78% 210 to 239 days; 1.87% 240 to 270 days.

EURO COMMERCIAL PAPER: Placed directly by General Electric Capital Corp.: 3.32% 30 days; 3.31% two months; 3.31% three months; 3.31% four months; 3.31% five months; 3.31% six months.

DEALER COMMERCIAL PAPER: High-grade unsecured notes sold through dealers by major corporations: 1.62% 30 days; 1.63% 60 days; 1.64% 90 days.

CERTIFICATES OF DEPOSIT: Typical rates in the secondary market. 1.69% one month; 1.68% three months; 1.77% six months.

LONDON INTERBANK OFFERED RATES (LIBOR): 1.7500% one month; 1.7700% three months; 1.88125% six months; 2.2875% one year. British Banker's Association average of interbank offered rates for dollar deposits in the London market based on quotations at 16 major banks. Effective rate for contracts entered into two days from date appearing at top of this column.

EURO LIBOR: 3.34675% one month; 3.34375% three months; 3.34763% six months; 3.47500% one year. British Banker's Association average of interbank offered rates for euro deposits in the London market based on quotations at 16 major banks. Effective rate for contracts entered into two days from date appearing at top of this column.

EURO INTERBANK OFFERED RATES (EURIBOR): 3.349% one month; 3.345% three months; 3.351% six months; 3.475% one year. European Banking Federation-sponsored rate among 57 Euro zone banks.

FOREIGN PRIME RATES: Canada 3.75%; Germany 3.25%; Japan 1.375%; Switzerland 3.50%; Britain 4.00%. These rate indications aren't directly comparable; lending practices vary widely by location.

TREASURY BILLS: Results of the Monday, January 14, 2002, auction of short-term U.S. government bills, sold at a discount from face value in units of $1,000 to $1 million: 1.530% 13 weeks; 1.580% 26 weeks. Tuesday, January 15, 2002 auction: 1.605% 4 weeks.

OVERNIGHT REPURCHASE RATE: 1.67%. Dealer financing rate for overnight sale and repurchase of Treasury securities. Source: Reuters.

FREDDIE MAC: Posted yields on 30-year mortgage commitments. Delivery within 30 days 6.66%, 60 days 6.75%, standard conventional fixed-rate mortgages: 3.375%,2% rate capped one-year adjustable rate mortgages. Source: Reuters.

FANNIE MAE: Posted yields on 30 year mortgage commit-

EXHIBIT 13-5

American Express Credit Card Rate Disclosure Indexed to Prime Rate

DISCLOSURE

Annual Percentage Rate for purchases	Variable Rate Information	Grace Period for repayment of the balance for purchases	Method of computing the balance for purchases	Annual Fee	Minimum Finance Charge
• 3.9% Introductory APR for 6 months; thereafter, Prime + 9.99% (18.49% as of 4/30/01). Fixed rate of 23.99% for defaulted accounts.*	• Your Annual Percentage Rate (APR) may vary. The APR for purchases is determined by adding 9.99% to the Prime Rate.*	• 20 days for purchases if full balance is paid by due date.	• Average daily balance (including new purchases).	• $85; $30 if you are a qualified American Express® Consumer Charge Cardmember.†	• $0.50

Over-limit and late-payment fees: $0 to $29 as determined by applicable law. Fee for Cash Advances through Express Cash: 3% of each withdrawal with $3.00 minimum and no maximum. Withdrawal limit of $2,500 every 7 days per account, combining Basic and Additional Cardmember activity. Withdrawals are subject to network ATM restrictions and your Cardmember payment history. The minimum yearly income required to qualify for the Gold Delta SkyMiles® Credit Card is $20,000. The lines of credit offered with the Gold Delta SkyMiles Credit Card are from $2,000 to $100,000.

*The APR for Cash Advances is 21.49% as of 4/30/01. The APRs may vary and are determined monthly by adding 9.99% and 12.99% to the Prime Rate (PR) for purchases and Cash Advances, respectively. The APR is a fixed rate of 23.99% for defaulted accounts. The PR for billing periods ending in any month is the PR listed in the *Wall Street Journal* on the 15th day (or preceding business day) of the prior month. Your account is reviewed monthly and will be considered in default if minimum payments are not timely paid, your account is overlimit, any account terms are breached, or the account is otherwise in default as defined in the Cardmember Agreement, in each case during any portion of the 12-month period prior to the billing period ("review period"). Defaulted accounts will forfeit the introductory and any promotional rates. If a promotional rate is in effect, that rate will apply and expire according to the promotional terms disclosed to you when you were offered the account or promotional opportunity. Iowa and Puerto Rico are not currently within American Express Centurion Bank's Credit Card service area, therefore Cards cannot be issued to residents of these locations.

†The $85 fee for the Gold Delta SkyMiles Credit Card will be $30 annually, provided you maintain a qualified American Express Consumer Charge Card account in your name for which you are charged an annual fee. Qualified accounts include but are not limited to the Personal Card, the Gold Card, and the Platinum Card® First-year-free offer is valid for first-time Cardmembers and cannot be used in conjunction with any other offer. Offer expires in 90 days.

[1]Double Miles offer applies at qualifying stand-alone supermarkets, drugstores, gas stations, home improvement stores, and the U.S. Postal Service. Offer applies for wireless phone bill payments only. American Express® Cards are not currently accepted for bulk mail. [2]In each year of Cardmembership, your mileage earnings are limited to $100,000 of eligible spending, not including bonuses. However, only 1 SkyMile for each U.S. dollar of eligible spending on Delta charges will be awarded above the limit. Bonus miles will be posted to your Delta Skymiles account 6 to 12 weeks after the end of

A personal or business line of credit allows easy access to large amounts of money.

Just as with calculating finance charges and new balances on credit cards (see the steps on page 448), the finance charge on a line of credit is based on average daily balance and is calculated by

Finance charge = Average daily balance × Periodic rate

This means that interest begins as soon as you write a check for a loan. Typically, the loan is paid back on a flexible schedule. In most cases, balances of $100 or less must be paid in full. Larger balances require minimum monthly payments of $100 or 2% of the outstanding balance, whichever is greater. As you repay, the line of credit renews itself. The new balance of the line of credit is calculated by

New balance = Previous balance + Finance charge + Loans − Payments

EXAMPLE

Shari's Gift Shop has a $20,000 line of credit with The Executive National Bank. The annual percentage rate charged on the account is the current prime rate plus 4%. There is a minimum APR on the account of 10%. The starting balance on April 1 was $2,350. On April 9, Shari borrowed $1,500 to pay for a shipment of assorted gift items. On April 20, she made a $3,000 payment on the account. On April 26, another $2,500 was borrowed to pay for air conditioning repairs. The billing cycle for April has 30 days. If the current prime rate is 8%, what is the finance charge on the account, and what is Shari's new balance?

SOLUTION STRATEGY

To solve this problem, we must find the annual percentage rate, the periodic rate, the average daily balance, the finance charge, and finally the new balance.

Annual percentage rate: The annual percentage rate is prime plus 4%, with a minimum of 10%. Because the current prime is 8%, the APR on this line of credit is 12% (8% + 4%).

Periodic rate:

$$\text{Periodic rate} = \frac{\text{Annual percentage rate}}{12 \text{ months}} = \frac{12\%}{12} = 1\%$$

Average daily balance: From the information given, we construct the following chart showing the account activity.

Dates	Number of Days	Activity/Amount	Unpaid Balance	Daily Balances (unpaid balance × days)
April 1–8	8	Previous balance	$2,350.00	$18,800.00
April 9–19	11	Borrowed–$1,500	3,850.00	42,350.00
April 20–25	6	Payment–$3,000	850.00	5,100.00
April 26–30	5	Borrowed–$2,500	3,350.00	16,750.00
	30 days in cycle			Total $83,000.00

$$\text{Average daily balance} = \frac{\text{Sum of daily balances}}{\text{Days in billing cycle}} = \frac{83{,}000}{30} = \$2{,}766.67$$

Finance charge:

Finance charge = Periodic rate × Average daily balance

Finance charge = .01 × 2,766.67 = $27.67

New balance:

$$\text{New balance} = \frac{\text{Previous}}{\text{balance}} + \frac{\text{Finance}}{\text{charge}} + \frac{\text{Loan}}{\text{amounts}} - \text{Payments}$$

$$\text{New balance} = \$2{,}350.00 + \$27.67 + \$4{,}000.00 - \$3{,}000.00$$

$$\text{New balance} = \underline{\underline{\$3{,}377.67}}$$

TRY-IT EXERCISE

3. V.I.P. Industries has a $75,000 line of credit with Citicorp Bank. The annual percentage rate is the current prime rate plus 4.5%. The balance on November 1 was $12,300. On November 7, V.I.P. borrowed $16,700 to pay for a shipment of merchandise, and on November 21 it borrowed another $8,800. On November 26, a $20,000 payment was made on the account. The billing cycle for November has 30 days. If the current prime rate is $8\frac{1}{2}$%, what is the finance charge on the account, and what is V.I.P.'s new balance?

Check your answers with the solutions on page 480.

REVIEW EXERCISES | CHAPTER 13—SECTION I

Calculate the missing information on the following revolving charge accounts. Interest is calculated on the unpaid or previous month's balance:

	Previous Balance	Annual Percentage Rate (APR)	Monthly Periodic Rate	Finance Charge	Purchases and Cash Advances	Payments and Credits	New Balance
1.	$167.88	18%	______	______	$215.50	$50.00	______
2.	$35.00	12%	______	______	$186.40	$75.00	______
3.	$455.12	______	1.75%	______	$206.24	$125.00	______
4.	$2,390.00	______	$1\frac{1}{4}$%	______	$1,233.38	$300.00	______

5. Karl Hellman has a Bank of America account with an annual percentage rate of 12% calculated on the previous month's balance. Answer the questions that follow using the Visa monthly statement below:

Statement of Account — Bank of America

NAME: KARL HELLMAN

ACCOUNT NUMBER: 2290-0090-4959

BILLING CYCLE: SEPTEMBER 1–30

DATE	DESCRIPTION OF TRANSACTIONS	CHARGES
09/01	Previous month's balance	$120.00
09/08	Radio Shack	65.52
09/11	Payment	70.00
09/14	Texaco Oil	23.25
09/22	Cash Advance	60.00
09/26	Kroger Supermarket	59.16

a. What is the amount of the finance charge?

b. What is Karl's new balance?

Linda Blundell has a revolving charge account. The finance charge is calculated on the previous month's balance, and the annual percentage rate is 21%. Complete the following 5-month account activity table for Linda:

	Month	Previous Month's Balance	Finance Charge	Purchases and Cash Advances	Payments and Credits	New Balance End of Month
6.	March	$560.00	______	$121.37	$55.00	______
7.	April	______	______	$46.45	$65.00	______
8.	May	______	______	$282.33	$105.00	______
9.	June	______	______	$253.38	$400.00	______
10.	July	______	______	$70.59	$100.00	______

11. Calculate the average daily balance for the month of October of an account with a previous month's balance of $140.00 and the following activity:

Date	Activity	Amount
October 3	Cash advance	$50.00
October 7	Payment	$75.00
October 10	Purchase	$26.69
October 16	Credit	$40.00
October 25	Purchase	$122.70

12. Calculate the average daily balance for the month of February of an account with a previous month's balance of $69.50 and the following activity:

Date	Activity	Amount
February 6	Payment	$58.00
February 9	Purchase	$95.88
February 15	Purchase	$129.60
February 24	Credit	$21.15
February 27	Cash advance	$100.00

13. Carolyn Salkind has a Bank of America revolving credit account with a 15% annual percentage rate. The finance charge is calculated by using the average daily balance method. The billing date is the first day of each month, and the billing cycle is the number of days in that month. During the month of March, Carolyn's account showed the following activity:

Statement of Account Bank of America

NAME
CAROLYN SALKIND

ACCOUNT NUMBER
2967-39460

BILLING CYCLE
MARCH 1–31

DATE	DESCRIPTION OF TRANSACTIONS	CHARGES
03/01	Previous month's balance	$324.45
03/05	A Nose for Clothes	156.79
03/11	Payment	150.00
03/15	Office Depot	45.60
03/17	Delta Airlines	344.50

a. How much is the finance charge for March?

b. What is Carolyn's new balance?

14. The First National Bank of Commerce offers a business line of credit that has an annual percentage rate of prime rate plus 5.4%, with a minimum of 11%. What is the APR if the prime rate is

a. 7% **b.** 10.1% **c.** 9.25% **d.** $5\frac{3}{4}$%

15. The Rocky Mountain Corporation has a $30,000 line of credit with NationsBank. The annual percentage rate is the current prime rate plus 4.7%. The balance on March 1 was $8,400. On March 6, Rocky Mountain borrowed $6,900 to pay for a shipment of supplies, and on March 17 it borrowed another $4,500 for equipment repairs. On March 24, a $10,000 payment was made on the account. The billing cycle for March has 31 days. The current prime rate is 9%.

a. What is the finance charge on the account?

b. What is Rocky Mountain's new balance?

c. On April 1, how much credit does Rocky Mountain have left on the account?

BUSINESS DECISION

Pick the Right Plastic

16. On October 22, you plan to purchase a $3,000 computer by using one of your two credit cards. The Silver Card charges 18% interest and calculates interest on the previous month's balance. The Gold Card charges 18% interest and calculates interest based on the average daily balance. Both cards have a $0 balance as of October 1.

 Your plan is to make a $1,000 payment in November, a $1,000 payment in December, and pay off the remaining balance in January. All your payments will be received and posted on the 10th of each month. No other charges will be made on the account.

 a. Based on this information, calculate the interest charged by each card for this purchase.

 b. Which card is the better deal and by how much?

SECTION II

CLOSED-END CREDIT—INSTALLMENT LOANS

installment loan
Loan made for a specified number of equal monthly payments. A form of closed-end credit used for purchasing durable goods such as cars, boats, and furniture or services such as vacations or home improvements.

mortgage
Installment loans made for homes and other real estate property.

down payment
Percentage of the purchase price that the buyer must pay in a lump sum at the time of purchase.

Closed-end credit, in the form of installment loans, is used extensively today for the purchase of durable goods such as cars, boats, electronic equipment, furniture, and appliances, as well as services such as vacations and home improvements. **Installment loans** are lump-sum loans whereby the borrower repays the principal plus interest in a specified number of equal monthly payments. These loans generally range in time from 6 months to 10 years, depending on what is being financed.

When homes and other real estate property are financed, the installment loans are known as **mortgages.** Mortgages may be for as long as 30 years on homes and even longer on commercial property such as office buildings or factories. These loans, along with home equity loans, are discussed in Chapter 14.

Many installment loans are secured by the asset for which the loan was made. For example, when a bank makes a car loan for 3 years, the consumer gets the car to use and monthly payments to make, but the lender still owns the car. Only after the final payment is made on the loan does the lender turn over the title, or proof of ownership, to the borrower. An additional form of security for the lending institution is that borrowers are often asked to make a down payment as part of the loan agreement.

A **down payment** is a percentage of the purchase price that the buyer must pay in a lump sum at the time of purchase. Down payments on installment loans vary by category of merchandise and generally range from between 0% to 30% of the price of the item. Sometimes, the amount of the down payment is based on the credit rating of the borrower. Usually, the better the credit, the less the down payment.

As with open-end credit, installment loan consumers are protected by Regulation Z of the Truth in Lending Act. Not only must lenders make full disclosure of the terms in the loan agreement, but advertisers of installment loans, such as car dealers and furniture stores, must by law disclose in the ad the following information:

1. Amount or percentage of the down payment
2. Terms of the repayment of the loan

Until the loan on this car is repaid, the lending institution is technically the owner.

3. Annual percentage rate
4. Total payback over the life of the loan

13-4 Calculating the Total Deferred Payment Price and the Amount of the Finance Charge of an Installment Loan

Let's take a look at some of the terminology of installment loans. When a consumer buys goods or services without any financing, the price paid is known as the **cash price** or **purchase price.** When financing is involved, the **amount financed** is found by subtracting the down payment from the cash or purchase price. Sometimes, the down payment will be listed as a dollar amount, and other times it will be expressed as a percent of the purchase price.

$$\text{Amount financed} = \text{Purchase price} - \text{Down payment}$$

When the down payment is listed as a percent of the purchase price, it can be found by using

$$\text{Down payment} = \text{Purchase price} \times \text{Down payment percent}$$

A finance charge, including simple interest and any loan origination fees, is then added to the amount financed to give the total amount of installment payments.

$$\text{Total amount of installment payments} = \text{Amount financed} + \text{Finance charge}$$

The finance charge can be found by subtracting the amount financed from the total amount of installment payments.

$$\text{Finance charge} = \text{Total amount of installment payments} - \text{Amount financed}$$

When the amount of the monthly payments is known, the total amount of installment payments can be found by multiplying the monthly payment amount by the number of payments.

$$\text{Total amount of installment payments} = \text{Monthly payment amount} \times \text{Number of monthly payments}$$

The total deferred payment price is the sum of the total amount of installment payments plus the down payment. This represents the total out-of-pocket expenses incurred by the buyer for an installment purchase.

$$\text{Total deferred payment price} = \text{Total of installment payments} + \text{Down payment}$$

Everybody's Business
Real-World Connection

Secret No More!
After years of secrecy, "FICO" scores are finally available to consumers nationwide. This all-important credit scoring system, developed by Fair Isaac and Co., provides credit scores and other information to lending institutions everywhere. Most lenders rely heavily on these scores when making credit decisions, especially mortgages.

With proper "financial identification" and $12.50, you can get your FICO score and other personal credit information at

www.myfico.com

For $8 you can request a credit report from one of the three major credit bureaus listed below. If you have been denied credit, the report is free. These can be ordered online or by phone at

www.icreditreport.com

- Equifax—800-685-1111
- Experian—800-682-7654
- TransUnion—800-888-4213

cash or purchase price
Price paid for goods and services without the use of financing.

amount financed
After the down payment, the amount of money that is borrowed to complete a sale.

EXAMPLE

Peggy Estes is interested in buying a computer. At Computers USA, she picks out a computer and a printer for a total cash price of \$2,550.00. The salesperson informs her that if she qualifies for an installment loan she may pay 20% now, as a down payment, and finance the balance with payments of \$110.00 per month for 24 months.

a. What is the amount of the finance charge on this loan?
b. What is the total deferred payment price of Peggy's computer?

SOLUTION STRATEGY

a. Finance charge:

To calculate the finance charge on this loan, we must first find the amount of the down payment, the amount financed, and the total amount of the installment payments.

$$\text{Down payment} = \text{Purchase price} \times \text{Down payment percent}$$

$$\text{Down payment} = \$2{,}550.00 \times 20\% = 2{,}550.00 \times .2 = \underline{\$510.00}$$

$$\text{Amount financed} = \text{Purchase price} - \text{Down payment}$$

$$\text{Amount financed} = \$2{,}550.00 - \$510.00 = \underline{\$2{,}040.00}$$

$$\begin{matrix}\text{Total amount of} \\ \text{installment payments}\end{matrix} = \begin{matrix}\text{Monthly payment} \\ \text{amount}\end{matrix} \times \begin{matrix}\text{Number of} \\ \text{monthly payments}\end{matrix}$$

$$\text{Total amount of installment payments} = 110.00 \times 24 = \underline{\$2{,}640.00}$$

$$\text{Finance charge} = \text{Total amount of installment payments} - \text{Amount financed}$$

$$\text{Finance charge} = 2{,}640.00 - 2{,}040.00$$

$$\text{Finance charge} = \underline{\underline{\$600.00}}$$

b. Total deferred payment price:

$$\text{Total deferred payment price} = \text{Total of installment payments} + \text{Down payment}$$

$$\text{Total deferred payment price} = \$2{,}640.00 + \$510.00$$

$$\text{Total deferred payment price} = \underline{\underline{\$3{,}150.00}}$$

TRY-IT | EXERCISE

4. Steve Schoen found a car he wanted to buy at Friendly Motors. He had the option of paying \$12,500 in cash or financing the car with a 4-year installment loan. The loan required a 15% down payment and equal monthly payments of \$309.90 for 48 months.

a. What is the finance charge on the loan?

b. What is the total deferred payment price of Steve's car?

Check your answers with the solutions on page 480.

13-5 Calculating the Amount of the Regular Monthly Payments of an Installment Loan by the Add-On Interest Method

One of the most common methods of calculating the finance charge on an installment loan is known as **add-on interest.** Add-on interest is essentially the simple interest that we studied in Chapter 10. The term gets its name from the fact that the simple interest is computed and then added on to the amount financed to get the total of installment payments. The interest or finance charge is computed by using the simple interest formula

add-on interest
Popular method of calculating the interest on an installment loan. Found by adding the simple interest ($I = PRT$) to the amount financed.

$$\underset{(\textit{finance charge})}{\text{Interest}} = \underset{(\textit{amount financed})}{\text{Principal}} \times \text{Rate} \times \text{Time}$$

Everybody's Business
Real-World Connection
As with open-end credit, installment loan consumers are protected by Regulation Z of the Truth in Lending Act.

Advertisers of installment loans, such as car dealers and furniture stores, must disclose in the ad and the loan agreement the following information:

- down payment
- terms and payments
- annual percentage rate
- total payback

STEPS TO CALCULATE THE MONTHLY PAYMENT USING ADD-ON INTEREST:

Step 1. Calculate the amount to be financed by subtracting the down payment from the purchase price. *Note:* When the down payment is expressed as a percent, the amount financed can be found by the complement method, because the percent financed is 100% minus the down payment percent:

$$\text{Amount financed} = \text{Purchase price } (100\% - \text{Down payment percent})$$

Step 2. Compute the add-on interest finance charge by using $I = PRT$.

Step 3. Find the total of installment payments by adding the finance charge to the amount financed.

$$\text{Total of installment payments} = \text{Amount financed} + \text{Finance charge}$$

Step 4. Find the regular monthly payments by dividing the total of installment payments by the number of months of the loan.

$$\text{Regular monthly payments} = \frac{\text{Total of installment payments}}{\text{Number of months of the loan}}$$

EXAMPLE

Nick Speckman bought a new boat with a 7% add-on interest installment loan from his credit union. The purchase price of the boat was $19,500.00. The credit union required a 20% down payment and equal monthly payments for 5 years (60 months). How much are Nick's monthly payments?

SOLUTION STRATEGY

Step 1. Amount financed = Purchase price (100% − Down payment percent)

Amount financed = $19,500.00 (100% − 20%) = 19,500.00 × .8

Amount financed = $\underline{\$15,600.00}$

Step 2.

$$\underset{(\textit{finance charge})}{\text{Interest}} = \underset{(\textit{amount financed})}{\text{Principal}} \times \text{Rate} \times \text{Time}$$

Finance charge = 15,600.00 × .07 × 5

Finance charge = $\underline{\$5,460.00}$

Step 3. Total of installment payments = Amount financed + Finance charge

Total of installment payments = 15,600.00 + 5,460.00

Total of installment payments = $\underline{\$21,060.00}$

Step 4.

$$\text{Regular monthly payments} = \frac{\text{Total of installment payments}}{\text{Number of months of the loan}}$$

$$\text{Regular monthly payments} = \frac{\$21{,}060.00}{60}$$

$$\text{Regular monthly payments} = \underline{\underline{\$351.00}}$$

TRY-IT | EXERCISE

5. Noemi Medina bought a bedroom set from City Furniture with a 6% add-on interest installment loan from her bank. The purchase price of the furniture was $1,500.00. The bank required a 10% down payment and equal monthly payments for 2 years. How much are Noemi's monthly payments?

Check your answer with the solution on page 480.

13-6 Calculating the Annual Percentage Rate of an Installment Loan by APR Tables and by Formula

As mentioned before, the add-on interest calculated for an installment loan is the same as on the simple interest promissory note we studied in Chapter 10. Although the interest is calculated the same way, the manner in which the loans are repaid is different. With promissory notes, the principal plus interest is repaid at the end of the loan period. The borrower has the use of the principal for the full time period of the loan. With an installment loan, the principal plus interest is repaid in equal regular payments. Each month in which a payment is made, the borrower has less and less use of the principal.

For this reason, the effective or true interest rate on an installment loan is considerably higher than the simple add-on rate. As we learned in Section I of this chapter, the effective or true annual interest rate being charged on open- and closed-end credit is known as the APR.

The Federal Reserve Board has published APR tables that can be used to find the APR of an installment loan. APR tables, such as Table 13-1, have values representing the finance charge per $100 of the amount financed. To look up the APR of a loan, we must first calculate the finance charge per $100.

STEPS TO FIND THE ANNUAL PERCENTAGE RATE OF AN INSTALLMENT LOAN BY USING APR TABLES:

Step 1. Calculate the finance charge per $100 by

$$\textbf{Finance charge per \$100} = \frac{\textbf{Finance charge} \times \textbf{100}}{\textbf{Amount financed}}$$

Step 2. From Table 13-1, scan down the Number of Payments column to the number of payments for the loan in question.

Step 3. Scan to the right in that Number of Payments row to the table factor that most closely corresponds to the finance charge per $100 calculated in Step 1.

Step 4. Look to the top of the column containing the finance charge per $100 to find the APR of the loan.

ANNUAL PERCENTAGE RATE TABLE FOR MONTHLY PAYMENT PLANS
SEE INSTRUCTIONS FOR USE OF TABLES FRB-103-M

NUMBER OF PAYMENTS	10.00%	10.25%	10.50%	10.75%	11.00%	11.25%	11.50%	11.75%	12.00%	12.25%	12.50%	12.75%	13.00%	13.25%	13.50%	13.75%
	(FINANCE CHARGE PER $100 OF AMOUNT FINANCED)															
1	0.83	0.85	0.87	0.90	0.92	0.94	0.96	0.98	1.00	1.02	1.04	1.06	1.08	1.10	1.12	1.15
2	1.25	1.28	1.31	1.35	1.38	1.41	1.44	1.47	1.50	1.53	1.57	1.60	1.63	1.66	1.69	1.72
3	1.67	1.71	1.76	1.80	1.84	1.88	1.92	1.96	2.01	2.05	2.09	2.13	2.17	2.22	2.26	2.30
4	2.09	2.14	2.20	2.25	2.30	2.35	2.41	2.46	2.51	2.57	2.62	2.67	2.72	2.78	2.83	2.88
5	2.51	2.58	2.64	2.70	2.77	2.83	2.89	2.96	3.02	3.08	3.15	3.21	3.27	3.34	3.40	3.46
6	2.94	3.01	3.08	3.16	3.23	3.31	3.38	3.45	3.53	3.60	3.68	3.75	3.83	3.90	3.97	4.05
7	3.36	3.45	3.53	3.62	3.70	3.78	3.87	3.95	4.04	4.12	4.21	4.29	4.38	4.47	4.55	4.64
8	3.79	3.88	3.98	4.07	4.17	4.26	4.36	4.46	4.55	4.65	4.74	4.84	4.94	5.03	5.13	5.22
9	4.21	4.32	4.43	4.53	4.64	4.75	4.85	4.96	5.07	5.17	5.28	5.39	5.49	5.60	5.71	5.82
10	4.64	4.76	4.88	4.99	5.11	5.23	5.35	5.46	5.58	5.70	5.82	5.94	6.05	6.17	6.29	6.41
11	5.07	5.20	5.33	5.45	5.58	5.71	5.84	5.97	6.10	6.23	6.36	6.49	6.62	6.75	6.88	7.01
12	5.50	5.64	5.78	5.92	6.06	6.20	6.34	6.48	6.62	6.76	6.90	7.04	7.18	7.32	7.46	7.60
13	5.93	6.08	6.23	6.38	6.53	6.68	6.84	6.99	7.14	7.29	7.44	7.59	7.75	7.90	8.05	8.20
14	6.36	6.52	6.69	6.85	7.01	7.17	7.34	7.50	7.66	7.82	7.99	8.15	8.31	8.48	8.64	8.81
15	6.80	6.97	7.14	7.32	7.49	7.66	7.84	8.01	8.19	8.36	8.53	8.71	8.88	9.06	9.23	9.41
16	7.23	7.41	7.60	7.78	7.97	8.15	8.34	8.53	8.71	8.90	9.08	9.27	9.46	9.64	9.83	10.02
17	7.67	7.86	8.06	8.25	8.45	8.65	8.84	9.04	9.24	9.44	9.63	9.83	10.03	10.23	10.43	10.63
18	8.10	8.31	8.52	8.73	8.93	9.14	9.35	9.56	9.77	9.98	10.19	10.40	10.61	10.82	11.03	11.24
19	8.54	8.76	8.98	9.20	9.42	9.64	9.86	10.08	10.30	10.52	10.74	10.96	11.18	11.41	11.63	11.85
20	8.98	9.21	9.44	9.67	9.90	10.13	10.37	10.60	10.83	11.06	11.30	11.53	11.76	12.00	12.23	12.46
21	9.42	9.66	9.90	10.15	10.39	10.63	10.88	11.12	11.36	11.61	11.85	12.10	12.34	12.59	12.84	13.08
22	9.86	10.12	10.37	10.62	10.88	11.13	11.39	11.64	11.90	12.16	12.41	12.67	12.93	13.19	13.44	13.70
23	10.30	10.57	10.84	11.10	11.37	11.63	11.90	12.17	12.44	12.71	12.97	13.24	13.51	13.78	14.05	14.32
24	10.75	11.02	11.30	11.58	11.86	12.14	12.42	12.70	12.98	13.26	13.54	13.82	14.10	14.38	14.66	14.95
25	11.19	11.48	11.77	12.06	12.35	12.64	12.93	13.22	13.52	13.81	14.10	14.40	14.69	14.98	15.28	15.57
26	11.64	11.94	12.24	12.54	12.85	13.15	13.45	13.75	14.06	14.36	14.67	14.97	15.28	15.59	15.89	16.20
27	12.09	12.40	12.71	13.03	13.34	13.66	13.97	14.29	14.60	14.92	15.24	15.56	15.87	16.19	16.51	16.83
28	12.53	12.86	13.18	13.51	13.84	14.16	14.49	14.82	15.15	15.48	15.81	16.14	16.47	16.80	17.13	17.46
29	12.98	13.32	13.66	14.00	14.33	14.67	15.01	15.35	15.70	16.04	16.38	16.72	17.07	17.41	17.75	18.10
30	13.43	13.78	14.13	14.48	14.83	15.19	15.54	15.89	16.24	16.60	16.95	17.31	17.66	18.02	18.38	18.74
31	13.89	14.25	14.61	14.97	15.33	15.70	16.06	16.43	16.79	17.16	17.53	17.90	18.27	18.63	19.00	19.38
32	14.34	14.71	15.09	15.46	15.84	16.21	16.59	16.97	17.35	17.73	18.11	18.49	18.87	19.25	19.63	20.02
33	14.79	15.18	15.57	15.95	16.34	16.73	17.12	17.51	17.90	18.29	18.69	19.08	19.47	19.87	20.26	20.66
34	15.25	15.65	16.05	16.44	16.85	17.25	17.65	18.05	18.46	18.86	19.27	19.67	20.08	20.49	20.90	21.31
35	15.70	16.11	16.53	16.94	17.35	17.77	18.18	18.60	19.01	19.43	19.85	20.27	20.69	21.11	21.53	21.95
36	16.16	16.58	17.01	17.43	17.86	18.29	18.71	19.14	19.57	20.00	20.43	20.87	21.30	21.73	22.17	22.60
37	16.62	17.06	17.49	17.93	18.37	18.81	19.25	19.69	20.13	20.58	21.02	21.46	21.91	22.36	22.81	23.25
38	17.08	17.53	17.98	18.43	18.88	19.33	19.78	20.24	20.69	21.15	21.61	22.07	22.52	22.99	23.45	23.91
39	17.54	18.00	18.46	18.93	19.39	19.86	20.32	20.79	21.26	21.73	22.20	22.67	23.14	23.61	24.09	24.56
40	18.00	18.48	18.95	19.43	19.90	20.38	20.86	21.34	21.82	22.30	22.79	23.27	23.76	24.25	24.73	25.22
41	18.47	18.95	19.44	19.93	20.42	20.91	21.40	21.89	22.39	22.88	23.38	23.88	24.38	24.88	25.38	25.88
42	18.93	19.43	19.93	20.43	20.93	21.44	21.94	22.45	22.96	23.47	23.98	24.49	25.00	25.51	26.03	26.55
43	19.40	19.91	20.42	20.94	21.45	21.97	22.49	23.01	23.53	24.05	24.57	25.10	25.62	26.15	26.68	27.21
44	19.86	20.39	20.91	21.44	21.97	22.50	23.03	23.57	24.10	24.64	25.17	25.71	26.25	26.79	27.33	27.88
45	20.33	20.87	21.41	21.95	22.49	23.03	23.58	24.12	24.67	25.22	25.77	26.32	26.88	27.43	27.99	28.55
46	20.80	21.35	21.90	22.46	23.01	23.57	24.13	24.69	25.25	25.81	26.37	26.94	27.51	28.08	28.65	29.22
47	21.27	21.83	22.40	22.97	23.53	24.10	24.68	25.25	25.82	26.40	26.98	27.56	28.14	28.72	29.31	29.89
48	21.74	22.32	22.90	23.48	24.06	24.64	25.23	25.81	26.40	26.99	27.58	28.18	28.77	29.37	29.97	30.57
49	22.21	22.80	23.39	23.99	24.58	25.18	25.78	26.38	26.98	27.59	28.19	28.80	29.41	30.02	30.63	31.24
50	22.69	23.29	23.89	24.50	25.11	25.72	26.33	26.95	27.56	28.18	28.80	29.42	30.04	30.67	31.29	31.92
51	23.16	23.78	24.40	25.02	25.64	26.26	26.89	27.52	28.15	28.78	29.41	30.05	30.68	31.32	31.96	32.60
52	23.64	24.27	24.90	25.53	26.17	26.81	27.45	28.09	28.73	29.38	30.02	30.67	31.32	31.98	32.63	33.29
53	24.11	24.76	25.40	26.05	26.70	27.35	28.00	28.66	29.32	29.98	30.64	31.30	31.97	32.63	33.30	33.97
54	24.59	25.25	25.91	26.57	27.23	27.90	28.56	29.23	29.91	30.58	31.25	31.93	32.61	33.29	33.98	34.66
55	25.07	25.74	26.41	27.09	27.77	28.44	29.13	29.81	30.50	31.18	31.87	32.56	33.26	33.95	34.65	35.35
56	25.55	26.23	26.92	27.61	28.30	28.99	29.69	30.39	31.09	31.79	32.49	33.20	33.91	34.62	35.33	36.04
57	26.03	26.73	27.43	28.13	28.84	29.54	30.25	30.97	31.68	32.39	33.11	33.83	34.56	35.28	36.01	36.74
58	26.51	27.23	27.94	28.66	29.37	30.10	30.82	31.55	32.27	33.00	33.74	34.47	35.21	35.95	36.69	37.43
59	27.00	27.72	28.45	29.18	29.91	30.65	31.39	32.13	32.87	33.61	34.36	35.11	35.86	36.62	37.37	38.13
60	27.48	28.22	28.96	29.71	30.45	31.20	31.96	32.71	33.47	34.23	34.99	35.75	36.52	37.29	38.06	38.83

continued

✦ **TABLE 13-1** ✦

Annual Percentage Rate (APR) Finance Charge Per $100

ANNUAL PERCENTAGE RATE TABLE FOR MONTHLY PAYMENT PLANS
SEE INSTRUCTIONS FOR USE OF TABLES

FRB-104-M

NUMBER OF PAYMENTS	ANNUAL PERCENTAGE RATE															
	14.00%	14.25%	14.50%	14.75%	15.00%	15.25%	15.50%	15.75%	16.00%	16.25%	16.50%	16.75%	17.00%	17.25%	17.50%	17.75%
	(FINANCE CHARGE PER $100 OF AMOUNT FINANCED)															
1	1.17	1.19	1.21	1.23	1.25	1.27	1.29	1.31	1.33	1.35	1.37	1.40	1.42	1.44	1.46	1.48
2	1.75	1.78	1.82	1.85	1.88	1.91	1.94	1.97	2.00	2.04	2.07	2.10	2.13	2.16	2.19	2.22
3	2.34	2.38	2.43	2.47	2.51	2.55	2.59	2.64	2.68	2.72	2.76	2.80	2.85	2.89	2.93	2.97
4	2.93	2.99	3.04	3.09	3.14	3.20	3.25	3.30	3.36	3.41	3.46	3.51	3.57	3.62	3.67	3.73
5	3.53	3.59	3.65	3.72	3.78	3.84	3.91	3.97	4.04	4.10	4.16	4.23	4.29	4.35	4.42	4.48
6	4.12	4.20	4.27	4.35	4.42	4.49	4.57	4.64	4.72	4.79	4.87	4.94	5.02	5.09	5.17	5.24
7	4.72	4.81	4.89	4.98	5.06	5.15	5.23	5.32	5.40	5.49	5.58	5.66	5.75	5.83	5.92	6.00
8	5.32	5.42	5.51	5.61	5.71	5.80	5.90	6.00	6.09	6.19	6.29	6.38	6.48	6.58	6.67	6.77
9	5.92	6.03	6.14	6.25	6.35	6.46	6.57	6.68	6.78	6.89	7.00	7.11	7.22	7.32	7.43	7.54
10	6.53	6.65	6.77	6.88	7.00	7.12	7.24	7.36	7.48	7.60	7.72	7.84	7.96	8.08	8.19	8.31
11	7.14	7.27	7.40	7.53	7.66	7.79	7.92	8.05	8.18	8.31	8.44	8.57	8.70	8.83	8.96	9.09
12	7.74	7.89	8.03	8.17	8.31	8.45	8.59	8.74	8.88	9.02	9.16	9.30	9.45	9.59	9.73	9.87
13	8.36	8.51	8.66	8.81	8.97	9.12	9.27	9.43	9.58	9.73	9.89	10.04	10.20	10.35	10.50	10.66
14	8.97	9.13	9.30	9.46	9.63	9.79	9.96	10.12	10.29	10.45	10.62	10.78	10.95	11.11	11.28	11.45
15	9.59	9.76	9.94	10.11	10.29	10.47	10.64	10.82	11.00	11.17	11.35	11.53	11.71	11.88	12.06	12.24
16	10.20	10.39	10.58	10.77	10.95	11.14	11.33	11.52	11.71	11.90	12.09	12.28	12.46	12.65	12.84	13.03
17	10.82	11.02	11.22	11.42	11.62	11.82	12.02	12.22	12.42	12.62	12.83	13.03	13.23	13.43	13.63	13.83
18	11.45	11.66	11.87	12.08	12.29	12.50	12.72	12.93	13.14	13.35	13.57	13.78	13.99	14.21	14.42	14.64
19	12.07	12.30	12.52	12.74	12.97	13.19	13.41	13.64	13.86	14.09	14.31	14.54	14.76	14.99	15.22	15.44
20	12.70	12.93	13.17	13.41	13.64	13.88	14.11	14.35	14.59	14.82	15.06	15.30	15.54	15.77	16.01	16.25
21	13.33	13.58	13.82	14.07	14.32	14.57	14.82	15.06	15.31	15.56	15.81	16.06	16.31	16.56	16.81	17.07
22	13.96	14.22	14.48	14.74	15.00	15.26	15.52	15.78	16.04	16.30	16.57	16.83	17.09	17.36	17.62	17.88
23	14.59	14.87	15.14	15.41	15.68	15.96	16.23	16.50	16.78	17.05	17.32	17.60	17.88	18.15	18.43	18.70
24	15.23	15.51	15.80	16.08	16.37	16.65	16.94	17.22	17.51	17.80	18.09	18.37	18.66	18.95	19.24	19.53
25	15.87	16.17	16.46	16.76	17.06	17.35	17.65	17.95	18.25	18.55	18.85	19.15	19.45	19.75	20.05	20.36
26	16.51	16.82	17.13	17.44	17.75	18.06	18.37	18.68	18.99	19.30	19.62	19.93	20.24	20.56	20.87	21.19
27	17.15	17.47	17.80	18.12	18.44	18.76	19.09	19.41	19.74	20.06	20.39	20.71	21.04	21.37	21.69	22.02
28	17.80	18.13	18.47	18.80	19.14	19.47	19.81	20.15	20.48	20.82	21.16	21.50	21.84	22.18	22.52	22.86
29	18.45	18.79	19.14	19.49	19.83	20.18	20.53	20.88	21.23	21.58	21.94	22.29	22.64	22.99	23.35	23.70
30	19.10	19.45	19.81	20.17	20.54	20.90	21.26	21.62	21.99	22.35	22.72	23.08	23.45	23.81	24.18	24.55
31	19.75	20.12	20.49	20.87	21.24	21.61	21.99	22.37	22.74	23.12	23.50	23.88	24.26	24.64	25.02	25.40
32	20.40	20.79	21.17	21.56	21.95	22.33	22.72	23.11	23.50	23.89	24.28	24.68	25.07	25.46	25.86	26.25
33	21.06	21.46	21.85	22.25	22.65	23.06	23.46	23.86	24.26	24.67	25.07	25.48	25.88	26.29	26.70	27.11
34	21.72	22.13	22.54	22.95	23.37	23.78	24.19	24.61	25.03	25.44	25.86	26.28	26.70	27.12	27.54	27.97
35	22.38	22.80	23.23	23.65	24.08	24.51	24.94	25.36	25.79	26.23	26.66	27.09	27.52	27.96	28.39	28.83
36	23.04	23.48	23.92	24.35	24.80	25.24	25.68	26.12	26.57	27.01	27.46	27.90	28.35	28.80	29.25	29.70
37	23.70	24.16	24.61	25.06	25.51	25.97	26.42	26.88	27.34	27.80	28.26	28.72	29.18	29.64	30.10	30.57
38	24.37	24.84	25.30	25.77	26.24	26.70	27.17	27.64	28.11	28.59	29.06	29.53	30.01	30.49	30.96	31.44
39	25.04	25.52	26.00	26.48	26.96	27.44	27.92	28.41	28.89	29.38	29.87	30.36	30.85	31.34	31.83	32.32
40	25.71	26.20	26.70	27.19	27.69	28.18	28.68	29.18	29.68	30.18	30.68	31.18	31.68	32.19	32.69	33.20
41	26.39	26.89	27.40	27.91	28.41	28.92	29.44	29.95	30.46	30.97	31.49	32.01	32.52	33.04	33.56	34.08
42	27.06	27.58	28.10	28.62	29.15	29.67	30.19	30.72	31.25	31.78	32.31	32.84	33.37	33.90	34.44	34.97
43	27.74	28.27	28.81	29.34	29.88	30.42	30.96	31.50	32.04	32.58	33.13	33.67	34.22	34.76	35.31	35.86
44	28.42	28.97	29.52	30.07	30.62	31.17	31.72	32.28	32.83	33.39	33.95	34.51	35.07	35.63	36.19	36.76
45	29.11	29.67	30.23	30.79	31.36	31.92	32.49	33.06	33.63	34.20	34.77	35.35	35.92	36.50	37.08	37.66
46	29.79	30.36	30.94	31.52	32.10	32.68	33.26	33.84	34.43	35.01	35.60	36.19	36.78	37.37	37.96	38.56
47	30.48	31.07	31.66	32.25	32.84	33.44	34.03	34.63	35.23	35.83	36.43	37.04	37.64	38.25	38.86	39.46
48	31.17	31.77	32.37	32.98	33.59	34.20	34.81	35.42	36.03	36.65	37.27	37.88	38.50	39.13	39.75	40.37
49	31.86	32.48	33.09	33.71	34.34	34.96	35.59	36.21	36.84	37.47	38.10	38.74	39.37	40.01	40.65	41.29
50	32.55	33.18	33.82	34.45	35.09	35.73	36.37	37.01	37.65	38.30	38.94	39.59	40.24	40.89	41.55	42.20
51	33.25	33.89	34.54	35.19	35.84	36.49	37.15	37.81	38.46	39.12	39.79	40.45	41.11	41.78	42.45	43.12
52	33.95	34.61	35.27	35.93	36.60	37.27	37.94	38.61	39.28	39.96	40.63	41.31	41.99	42.67	43.36	44.04
53	34.65	35.32	36.00	36.68	37.36	38.04	38.72	39.41	40.10	40.79	41.48	42.17	42.87	43.57	44.27	44.97
54	35.35	36.04	36.73	37.42	38.12	38.82	39.52	40.22	40.92	41.63	42.33	43.04	43.75	44.47	45.18	45.90
55	36.05	36.76	37.46	38.17	38.88	39.60	40.31	41.03	41.74	42.47	43.19	43.91	44.64	45.37	46.10	46.83
56	36.76	37.48	38.20	38.92	39.65	40.38	41.11	41.84	42.57	43.31	44.05	44.79	45.53	46.27	47.02	47.77
57	37.47	38.20	38.94	39.68	40.42	41.16	41.91	42.65	43.40	44.15	44.91	45.66	46.42	47.18	47.94	48.71
58	38.18	38.93	39.68	40.43	41.19	41.95	42.71	43.47	44.23	45.00	45.77	46.54	47.32	48.09	48.87	49.65
59	38.89	39.66	40.42	41.19	41.96	42.74	43.51	44.29	45.07	45.85	46.64	47.42	48.21	49.01	49.80	50.60
60	39.61	40.39	41.17	41.95	42.74	43.53	44.32	45.11	45.91	46.71	47.51	48.31	49.12	49.92	50.73	51.55

continued

✦ TABLE 13-1 (continued)✦

Annual Percentage Rate (APR) Finance Charge Per $100

ANNUAL PERCENTAGE RATE TABLE FOR MONTHLY PAYMENT PLANS
SEE INSTRUCTIONS FOR USE OF TABLES FRB-105-M

NUMBER OF PAYMENTS	ANNUAL PERCENTAGE RATE															
	18.00%	18.25%	18.50%	18.75%	19.00%	19.25%	19.50%	19.75%	20.00%	20.25%	20.50%	20.75%	21.00%	21.25%	21.50%	21.75%
	(FINANCE CHARGE PER $100 OF AMOUNT FINANCED)															
1	1.50	1.52	1.54	1.56	1.58	1.60	1.62	1.65	1.67	1.69	1.71	1.73	1.75	1.77	1.79	1.81
2	2.26	2.29	2.32	2.35	2.38	2.41	2.44	2.48	2.51	2.54	2.57	2.60	2.63	2.66	2.70	2.73
3	3.01	3.06	3.10	3.14	3.18	3.23	3.27	3.31	3.35	3.39	3.44	3.48	3.52	3.56	3.60	3.65
4	3.78	3.83	3.88	3.94	3.99	4.04	4.10	4.15	4.20	4.25	4.31	4.36	4.41	4.47	4.52	4.57
5	4.54	4.61	4.67	4.74	4.80	4.86	4.93	4.99	5.06	5.12	5.18	5.25	5.31	5.37	5.44	5.50
6	5.32	5.39	5.46	5.54	5.61	5.69	5.76	5.84	5.91	5.99	6.06	6.14	6.21	6.29	6.36	6.44
7	6.09	6.18	6.26	6.35	6.43	6.52	6.60	6.69	6.78	6.86	6.95	7.04	7.12	7.21	7.29	7.38
8	6.87	6.96	7.06	7.16	7.26	7.35	7.45	7.55	7.64	7.74	7.84	7.94	8.03	8.13	8.23	8.33
9	7.65	7.76	7.87	7.97	8.08	8.19	8.30	8.41	8.52	8.63	8.73	8.84	8.95	9.06	9.17	9.28
10	8.43	8.55	8.67	8.79	8.91	9.03	9.15	9.27	9.39	9.51	9.63	9.75	9.88	10.00	10.12	10.24
11	9.22	9.35	9.49	9.62	9.75	9.88	10.01	10.14	10.28	10.41	10.54	10.67	10.80	10.94	11.07	11.20
12	10.02	10.16	10.30	10.44	10.59	10.73	10.87	11.02	11.16	11.31	11.45	11.59	11.74	11.88	12.02	12.17
13	10.81	10.97	11.12	11.28	11.43	11.59	11.74	11.90	12.05	12.21	12.36	12.52	12.67	12.83	12.99	13.14
14	11.61	11.78	11.95	12.11	12.28	12.45	12.61	12.78	12.95	13.11	13.28	13.45	13.62	13.79	13.95	14.12
15	12.42	12.59	12.77	12.95	13.13	13.31	13.49	13.67	13.85	14.03	14.21	14.39	14.57	14.75	14.93	15.11
16	13.22	13.41	13.60	13.80	13.99	14.18	14.37	14.56	14.75	14.94	15.13	15.33	15.52	15.71	15.90	16.10
17	14.04	14.24	14.44	14.64	14.85	15.05	15.25	15.46	15.66	15.86	16.07	16.27	16.48	16.68	16.89	17.09
18	14.85	15.07	15.28	15.49	15.71	15.93	16.14	16.36	16.57	16.79	17.01	17.22	17.44	17.66	17.88	18.09
19	15.67	15.90	16.12	16.35	16.58	16.81	17.03	17.26	17.49	17.72	17.95	18.18	18.41	18.64	18.87	19.10
20	16.49	16.73	16.97	17.21	17.45	17.69	17.93	18.17	18.41	18.66	18.90	19.14	19.38	19.63	19.87	20.11
21	17.32	17.57	17.82	18.07	18.33	18.58	18.83	19.09	19.34	19.60	19.85	20.11	20.36	20.62	20.87	21.13
22	18.15	18.41	18.68	18.94	19.21	19.47	19.74	20.01	20.27	20.54	20.81	21.08	21.34	21.61	21.88	22.15
23	18.98	19.26	19.54	19.81	20.09	20.37	20.65	20.93	21.21	21.49	21.77	22.05	22.33	22.61	22.90	23.18
24	19.82	20.11	20.40	20.69	20.98	21.27	21.56	21.86	22.15	22.44	22.74	23.03	23.33	23.62	23.92	24.21
25	20.66	20.96	21.27	21.57	21.87	22.18	22.48	22.79	23.10	23.40	23.71	24.02	24.32	24.63	24.94	25.25
26	21.50	21.82	22.14	22.45	22.77	23.09	23.41	23.73	24.04	24.36	24.68	25.01	25.33	25.65	25.97	26.29
27	22.35	22.68	23.01	23.34	23.67	24.00	24.33	24.67	25.00	25.33	25.67	26.00	26.34	26.67	27.01	27.34
28	23.20	23.55	23.89	24.23	24.58	24.92	25.27	25.61	25.96	26.30	26.65	27.00	27.35	27.70	28.05	28.40
29	24.06	24.41	24.77	25.13	25.49	25.84	26.20	26.56	26.92	27.28	27.64	28.00	28.37	28.73	29.09	29.46
30	24.92	25.29	25.66	26.03	26.40	26.77	27.14	27.52	27.89	28.26	28.64	29.01	29.39	29.77	30.14	30.52
31	25.78	26.16	26.55	26.93	27.32	27.70	28.09	28.47	28.86	29.25	29.64	30.03	30.42	30.81	31.20	31.59
32	26.65	27.04	27.44	27.84	28.24	28.64	29.04	29.44	29.84	30.24	30.64	31.05	31.45	31.85	32.26	32.67
33	27.52	27.93	28.34	28.75	29.16	29.57	29.99	30.40	30.82	31.23	31.65	32.07	32.49	32.91	33.33	33.75
34	28.39	28.81	29.24	29.66	30.09	30.52	30.95	31.37	31.80	32.23	32.67	33.10	33.53	33.96	34.40	34.83
35	29.27	29.71	30.14	30.58	31.02	31.47	31.91	32.35	32.79	33.24	33.68	34.13	34.58	35.03	35.47	35.92
36	30.15	30.60	31.05	31.51	31.96	32.42	32.87	33.33	33.79	34.25	34.71	35.17	35.63	36.09	36.56	37.02
37	31.03	31.50	31.97	32.43	32.90	33.37	33.84	34.32	34.79	35.26	35.74	36.21	36.69	37.16	37.64	38.12
38	31.92	32.40	32.88	33.37	33.85	34.33	34.82	35.30	35.79	36.28	36.77	37.26	37.75	38.24	38.73	39.23
39	32.81	33.31	33.80	34.30	34.80	35.30	35.80	36.30	36.80	37.30	37.81	38.31	38.82	39.32	39.83	40.34
40	33.71	34.22	34.73	35.24	35.75	36.26	36.78	37.29	37.81	38.33	38.85	39.37	39.89	40.41	40.93	41.46
41	34.61	35.13	35.66	36.18	36.71	37.24	37.77	38.30	38.83	39.36	39.89	40.43	40.96	41.50	42.04	42.58
42	35.51	36.05	36.59	37.13	37.67	38.21	38.76	39.30	39.85	40.40	40.95	41.50	42.05	42.60	43.15	43.71
43	36.42	36.97	37.52	38.08	38.63	39.19	39.75	40.31	40.87	41.44	42.00	42.57	43.13	43.70	44.27	44.84
44	37.33	37.89	38.46	39.03	39.60	40.18	40.75	41.33	41.90	42.48	43.06	43.64	44.22	44.81	45.39	45.98
45	38.24	38.82	39.41	39.99	40.58	41.17	41.75	42.35	42.94	43.53	44.13	44.72	45.32	45.92	46.52	47.12
46	39.16	39.75	40.35	40.95	41.55	42.16	42.76	43.37	43.98	44.58	45.20	45.81	46.42	47.03	47.65	48.27
47	40.08	40.69	41.30	41.92	42.54	43.15	43.77	44.40	45.02	45.64	46.27	46.90	47.53	48.16	48.79	49.42
48	41.00	41.63	42.26	42.89	43.52	44.15	44.79	45.43	46.07	46.71	47.35	47.99	48.64	49.28	49.93	50.58
49	41.93	42.57	43.22	43.86	44.51	45.16	45.81	46.46	47.12	47.77	48.43	49.09	49.75	50.41	51.08	51.74
50	42.86	43.52	44.18	44.84	45.50	46.17	46.83	47.50	48.17	48.84	49.52	50.19	50.87	51.55	52.23	52.91
51	43.79	44.47	45.14	45.82	46.50	47.18	47.86	48.55	49.23	49.92	50.61	51.30	51.99	52.69	53.38	54.08
52	44.73	45.42	46.11	46.80	47.50	48.20	48.89	49.59	50.30	51.00	51.71	52.41	53.12	53.83	54.55	55.26
53	45.67	46.38	47.08	47.79	48.50	49.22	49.93	50.65	51.37	52.09	52.81	53.53	54.26	54.98	55.71	56.44
54	46.62	47.34	48.06	48.79	49.51	50.24	50.97	51.70	52.44	53.17	53.91	54.65	55.39	56.14	56.88	57.63
55	47.57	48.30	49.04	49.78	50.52	51.27	52.02	52.76	53.52	54.27	55.02	55.78	56.54	57.30	58.06	58.82
56	48.52	49.27	50.03	50.78	51.54	52.30	53.06	53.83	54.60	55.37	56.14	56.91	57.68	58.46	59.24	60.02
57	49.47	50.24	51.01	51.79	52.56	53.34	54.12	54.90	55.68	56.47	57.25	58.04	58.84	59.63	60.43	61.22
58	50.43	51.22	52.00	52.79	53.58	54.38	55.17	55.97	56.77	57.57	58.38	59.18	59.99	60.80	61.62	62.43
59	51.39	52.20	53.00	53.80	54.61	55.42	56.23	57.05	57.87	58.68	59.51	60.33	61.15	61.98	62.81	63.64
60	52.36	53.18	54.00	54.82	55.64	56.47	57.30	58.13	58.96	59.80	60.64	61.48	62.32	63.17	64.01	64.86

TABLE 13-1 (continued)
Annual Percentage Rate (APR) Finance Charge Per $100

EXAMPLE

Mike Jordan purchased a used car for $7,000. He made a down payment of $1,000 and financed the remaining $6,000 for 36 months. With monthly payments of $200 each, the total finance charge on the loan was $1,200 ($200 × 36 = $7,200 − $6,000 = $1,200). Use Table 13-1 to find what annual percentage rate was charged on Mike's automobile loan.

SOLUTION STRATEGY

Step 1.

$$\text{Finance charge per \$100} = \frac{\text{Finance charge} \times 100}{\text{Amount financed}}$$

$$\text{Finance charge per \$100} = \frac{1{,}200 \times 100}{6{,}000} = \frac{120{,}000}{6{,}000}$$

$$\text{Finance charge per \$100} = \underline{\underline{\$20}}$$

Step 2. Using Table 13-1, scan down the number of payments column to 36 payments.

Step 3. Scan to the right in that number of payments row until we find $20, the finance charge per $100.

Step 4. Looking to the top of the column containing the $20, we find the annual percentage rate for the loan to be 12.25%.

TRY-IT | EXERCISE

6. Pamela Fuller purchased a living room set for $4,500 from Classic Furniture. She made a $500 down payment and financed the balance with an installment loan for 24 months. If her payments are $190 per month, what APR is she paying on the loan?

Check your answer with the solution on page 480–481.

Calculating APR by Formula

When APR tables are not available, the annual percentage rate can be closely approximated by the formula

$$\text{APR} = \frac{72I}{3P(n+1) + I(n-1)}$$

where

I = finance charge on the loan

P = principal, or amount financed

n = number of months of the loan

EXAMPLE

Refer to the previous example, Mike Jordan's car purchase. This time use the APR formula to find the annual percentage rate. How does it compare with the APR from the table?

SOLUTION STRATEGY

$$\text{APR} = \frac{72I}{3P(n+1) + I(n-1)}$$

$$\text{APR} = \frac{72(1{,}200)}{3(6{,}000)(36+1) + 1{,}200(36-1)} = \frac{86{,}400}{666{,}000 + 42{,}000} = \frac{86{,}400}{708{,}000}$$

$$\text{APR} = .1220338 = \underline{\underline{12.20\%}}$$

In comparing the two answers, we can see that using the formula gives a close approximation of the Federal Reserve Board's APR table value of 12.25%.

TRY-IT | EXERCISE

7. Kristin Carter repaid a $2,200 installment loan with 18 monthly payments of $140.00 each. Use the APR formula to determine the annual percentage rate of Kristin's loan.

Check your answer with the solution on page 481.

13-7 Calculating the Finance Charge and Monthly Payment of an Installment Loan by Using the APR Tables

When the annual percentage rate and number of months of an installment loan are known, the APR tables can be used in reverse to find the amount of the finance charge. Once the finance charge is known, the monthly payment required to amortize the loan can be calculated as before.

STEPS TO FIND THE FINANCE CHARGE AND THE MONTHLY PAYMENT OF AN INSTALLMENT LOAN BY USING THE APR TABLES:

Step 1. Using the APR and the number of payments of the loan, locate the table factor at the intersection of the APR column and the number of payments row. This factor represents the finance charge per $100 financed.

Step 2. The total finance charge of the loan can be found by

$$\text{Finance charge} = \frac{\text{Amount financed} \times \text{Table factor}}{100}$$

Step 3. The monthly payment can now be found by

$$\text{Monthly payment} = \frac{\text{Amount financed} + \text{Finance charge}}{\text{Number of months of the loan}}$$

EXAMPLE

Southwest Motors uses Fleet Bank to finance automobile and truck sales. This month Fleet is offering up to 48-month installment loans with an APR of 15.5%. For qualified buyers, no down payment is required. If Bob Woods wants to finance a new truck for $17,500, what are the finance charge and the amount of the monthly payment on Bob's loan?

SOLUTION STRATEGY

Step 1. The table factor at the intersection of the 15.5% APR column and the 48 payments row is $34.81.

Step 2.

$$\text{Finance charge} = \frac{\text{Amount financed} \times \text{Table factor}}{100}$$

$$\text{Finance charge} = \frac{17{,}500 \times 34.81}{100} = \frac{609{,}175}{100}$$

$$\text{Finance charge} = \underline{\underline{\$6{,}091.75}}$$

Step 3.

$$\text{Monthly payment} = \frac{\text{Amount financed} + \text{Finance charge}}{\text{Number of months of the loan}}$$

$$\text{Monthly payment} = \frac{17{,}500 + 6{,}091.75}{48} = \frac{23{,}591.75}{48}$$

$$\text{Monthly payment} = \underline{\underline{\$491.49}}$$

TRY-IT | EXERCISE

8. Computer Warehouse uses a finance company that is offering up to 24-month installment loans with an APR of 13.25%. For qualified buyers, no down payment is required. If Sandra Miller wants to finance a computer and printer for $3,550, what are the finance charge and the amount of the monthly payment on Sandra's loan?

Check your answers with the solutions on page 481.

13-8 Calculating the Finance Charge Rebate and the Amount of the Payoff when a Loan Is Paid Off Early by Using the Sum-of-the-Digits Method

finance charge rebate
Unearned portion of the finance charge that the lender returns to the borrower when an installment loan is paid off early.

Rule of 78, or sum-of-the-digits method
Widely accepted method for calculating the finance charge rebate. Based on the assumption that more interest is paid in the early months of a loan, when a greater portion of the principal is available to the borrower.

Frequently, borrowers choose to repay installment loans before the full time period of the loan has elapsed. When loans are paid off early, the borrower is entitled to a **finance charge rebate,** because the principal was not kept for the full amount of time on which the finance charge was calculated. At payoff, the lender must return or rebate any unearned portion of the finance charge to the borrower.

A widely accepted method for calculating the finance charge rebate is known as the **sum-of-the-digits method.** This method is based on the assumption that the lender earns more interest in the early months of a loan, when the borrower has the use of much of the principal, than in the later months, when most of the principal has already been paid back.

When using this method, the finance charge is assumed to be divided in parts equal to the sum of the digits of the months of the loan. Because the sum of the digits of a 12-month loan is 78, the technique has become known as the **Rule of 78.**

$$\text{Sum of the digits of } 12 = 1 + 2 + 3 + 4 + 5 + 6 + 7 + 8 + 9 + 10 + 11 + 12 = 78$$

The amount of finance charge in any given month is represented by a fraction whose numerator is the number of payments remaining, and the denominator is the sum of the digits of the number of months in the loan.

For a 12-month loan, for example, the fraction of the finance charge in the first month would be $\frac{12}{78}$. The numerator is 12, because in the first month no payments have been made; therefore, 12 payments remain. The denominator is 78 because the sum of the digits of 12 is 78. In the second month, the lender earns $\frac{11}{78}$; in the third month, $\frac{10}{78}$. This decline continues until the last month when only $\frac{1}{78}$ remains. Exhibit 13-6 illustrates the distribution of a $1,000 finance charge by using the sum-of-the-digits method.

With the sum-of-the-digits method, a **rebate fraction** is established based on when a loan is paid off. The numerator of the rebate fraction is the sum-of-the-digits of the number of remaining payments and the denominator is the sum of the digits of the total number of payments.

$$\text{Rebate fraction} = \frac{\text{Sum of the digits of the number of remaining payments}}{\text{Sum of the digits of the total number of payments}}$$

Although the sum of the digits is easily calculated by addition, it can become tedious for loans of 24, 36, or 48 months. For this reason, we shall use the sum-of-the-digits formula to find the numerator and denominator of the rebate fraction. In the formula, n represents the number of months.

$$\text{Sum of the digits} = \frac{n(n+1)}{2}$$

Installment financing is frequently used when consumers purchase big-ticket items such as appliances and electronic equipment.

rebate fraction
Fraction used to calculate the finance charge rebate. The numerator is the sum of the digits of the number of payments remaining when the loan is paid off; the denominator is the sum of the digits of the total number of payments of the loan.

STEPS TO CALCULATE THE FINANCE CHARGE REBATE AND LOAN PAYOFF:

Step 1. Calculate the rebate fraction by using the sum-of-the-digits formula for the numerator (number of remaining payments) and the denominator (total number of payments).

Step 2. Determine the finance charge rebate by

$$\text{Finance charge rebate} = \text{Rebate fraction} \times \text{Total finance charge}$$

Step 3. Find the loan payoff by

$$\text{Loan payoff} = \left(\text{Payments remaining} \times \text{Payment amount}\right) - \text{Finance charge rebate}$$

✦ **EXHIBIT 13-6** ✦
Distribution of a $1,000 Finance Charge over 12 Months

Month Number	Finance Charge Fraction	x	$1,000	Finance Charge
1	$\frac{12}{78}$	x	$1,000	$153.85
2	$\frac{11}{78}$	x	$1,000	$141.03
3	$\frac{10}{78}$	x	$1,000	$128.21
4	$\frac{9}{78}$	x	$1,000	$115.38
5	$\frac{8}{78}$	x	$1,000	$102.56
6	$\frac{7}{78}$	x	$1,000	$89.74
7	$\frac{6}{78}$	x	$1,000	$76.92
8	$\frac{5}{78}$	x	$1,000	$64.10
9	$\frac{4}{78}$	x	$1,000	$51.28
10	$\frac{3}{78}$	x	$1,000	$38.46
11	$\frac{2}{78}$	x	$1,000	$25.64
12	$\frac{1}{78}$	x	$1,000	$12.82

Everybody's Business
Real-World Connection
This table clearly illustrates that the majority of the finance charge on an installment loan is incurred in the first half of the loan.

EXAMPLE

Santiago Alan financed a $1,500 set of golf clubs with an installment loan for 12 months. The payments were $145 per month, and the total finance charge was $240. After 8 months, he decided to pay off the loan. How much is the finance charge rebate, and what is his loan payoff?

SOLUTION STRATEGY

Step 1. Rebate fraction:

Set up the rebate fraction by using the sum-of-the-digits formula. Because Santiago has already made eight payments, he has four payments remaining (12 − 8 = 4).

The *numerator* will be the sum of the digits of the number of remaining payments, 4.

$$\text{Sum of the digits of 4} = \frac{n(n+1)}{2} = \frac{4(4+1)}{2} = \frac{4(5)}{2} = \frac{20}{2} = \underline{10}$$

The *denominator* will be the sum of the digits of the total number of payments, 12.

$$\text{Sum of the digits of 12} = \frac{n(n+1)}{2} = \frac{12(12+1)}{2} = \frac{12(13)}{2} = \frac{156}{2} = \underline{78}$$

The rebate fraction is therefore $\frac{10}{78}$.

Step 2. Finance charge rebate:

$$\text{Finance charge rebate} = \text{Rebate fraction} \times \text{Total finance charge}$$

$$\text{Finance charge rebate} = \frac{10}{78} \times 240$$

$$\text{Finance charge rebate} = 30.7692 = \underline{\underline{\$30.77}}$$

Step 3. Loan payoff:

$$\text{Loan payoff} = (\text{Payments remaining} \times \text{Payment amount}) - \text{Finance charge rebate}$$

$$\text{Loan payoff} = (4 \times 145) - 30.77$$

$$\text{Loan payoff} = 580.00 - 30.77$$

$$\text{Loan payoff} = \underline{\underline{\$549.23}}$$

TRY-IT | EXERCISE

9. Adrienne Krysiuk financed a $4,000 piano with an installment loan for 36 months. The payments were $141 per month, and the total finance charge was $1,076. After 20 months Adrienne decided to pay off the loan. How much is the finance charge rebate, and how much is Adrienne's loan payoff?

Check your answers with the solutions on page 481.

REVIEW EXERCISES | CHAPTER 13—SECTION II

Calculate the amount financed, the finance charge, and the total deferred payment price for the following installment loans:

	Purchase (Cash) Price	Down Payment	Amount Financed	Monthly Payments	Number of Payments	Finance Charge	Total Deferred Payment Price
1.	$1,400	$350	______	$68.00	24	______	______
2.	$3,500	20%	______	$257.00	12	______	______
3.	$12,000	10%	______	$375.00	36	______	______
4.	$2,900	0	______	$187.69	18	______	______
5.	$8,750	15%	______	$198.33	48	______	______

Calculate the amount financed, the finance charge, and the amount of the monthly payments for the following add-on interest loans:

	Purchase (Cash) Price	Down Payment	Amount Financed	Add-On Interest	Number of Payments	Finance Charge	Monthly Payment
6.	$788	10%	______	8%	12	______	______
7.	$1,600	$250	______	10%	24	______	______
8.	$4,000	15%	______	$11\frac{1}{2}$%	30	______	______
9.	$17,450	$2,000	______	14%	48	______	______
10.	$50,300	25%	______	12.4%	60	______	______

Calculate the finance charge, finance charge per $100, and the annual percentage rate for the following installment loans by using the APR table, Table 13-1:

	Amount Financed	Number of Payments	Monthly Payment	Finance Charge	Finance Charge per $100	APR
11.	$2,300	24	$109.25	______	______	______
12.	$14,000	36	$495.00	______	______	______
13.	$1,860	18	$115.75	______	______	______
14.	$35,000	60	$875.00	______	______	______

Calculate the finance charge and the annual percentage rate for the following installment loans by using the APR formula:

	Amount Financed	Number of Payments	Monthly Payment	Finance Charge	APR
15.	$500	12	$44.25	______	______
16.	$2,450	36	$90.52	______	______
17.	$13,000	48	$373.75	______	______
18.	$100,000	72	$2,055.50	______	______

Calculate the finance charge and the monthly payment for the following loans by using the APR table, Table 13-1:

	Amount Financed	Number of Payments	APR	Table Factor	Finance Charge	Monthly Payment
19.	$5,000	48	13.5%			
20.	$7,500	36	12%			
21.	$1,800	12	11.25%			
22.	$900	18	14%			

Calculate the missing information for the following installment loans that are being paid off early:

	Number of Payments	Payments Made	Payments Remaining	Sum of Digits Payments Remaining	Sum of Digits Number of Payments	Rebate Fraction
23.	12	4				
24.	36	22				
25.	24	9				
26.	60	40				

You are the loan department supervisor for the Pacific National Bank. The following installment loans are being paid off early, and it is your task to calculate the rebate fraction, the finance charge rebate, and the payoff for each loan:

	Amount Financed	Number of Payments	Monthly Payment	Payments Made	Rebate Fraction	Finance Charge Rebate	Loan Payoff
27.	$3,000	24	$162.50	9			
28.	$1,600	18	$104.88	11			
29.	$9,500	48	$267.00	36			
30.	$4,800	36	$169.33	27			

31. Ana Luisa Bridges is interested in buying a dining room set for her home. At Styline Furniture, she picks out a seven-piece set for a total cash price of $1,899.00. The salesperson informs her that if she qualifies for an installment loan, she may pay 10% now, as a down payment, and finance the balance with payments of $88.35 per month for 24 months.

a. What is the amount of the finance charge on this loan?

b. What is the total deferred payment price of the dining room set?

32. Randy Iverson found a time-share condominium he wanted to buy in Orlando, Florida. He had the option of paying $7,600 in cash or financing the condo with a 2-year installment loan. The loan required a 20% down payment and equal monthly payments of $283.73.

a. What is the finance charge on Randy's loan?

b. What is the total deferred payment price of the condo?

33. Dan Neely bought fishing equipment with a 9% add-on interest installment loan from his credit union. The purchase price of the equipment was $1,450.00. The credit union required a 15% down payment and equal monthly payments for 48 months. How much are Dan's monthly payments?

34. Kelley Tyner financed a trip to Europe with a 5% add-on interest installment loan from her bank. The total price of the trip was $1,500.00. The bank required equal monthly payments for 2 years. How much are Kelley's monthly payments?

35. Fritz Schanz purchased a jet ski for $8,350. He made a down payment of $1,400 and financed the balance with monthly payments of $239.38 for 36 months.

a. What is the amount of the finance charge on the loan?

b. Use Table 13-1 to find what annual percentage rate was charged on Fritz's loan.

36. Van Mua purchased an artist's studio desk for $2,400. He made a $700 down payment and financed the balance with an installment loan for 48 months. If Van's payments are $42.50 per month, use the APR formula to calculate what annual percentage rate he is paying on the loan.

37. The Electronic Showcase uses the First American Bank to finance customer purchases. This month, the bank is offering 24-month installment loans with an APR of 15.25%. For qualified buyers, no down payment is required. If Alton Amidon wants to finance a complete stereo system for $1,300, use the APR tables to calculate the finance charge and the amount of the monthly payment on his loan.

38. At a recent boat show, MegaBank was offering boat loans for up to 5 years, with APRs of 13.5%. On new boats, a 20% down payment was required. Alan Hensley wanted to finance a $55,000 boat for 5 years.

a. What would be the finance charge on the loan?

b. What would be the amount of the monthly payment?

39. Find the sum of the digits of

a. 24 **b.** 30

40. a. What is the rebate fraction of a 36-month loan paid off after the 14th payment?

b. What is the rebate fraction of a 42-month loan paid off after the 19th payment?

41. Bob Googins financed a $3,500 Hobie-Cat sailboat with an 8% add-on interest installment loan for 24 months. The loan required a 10% down payment.

a. What is the amount of the finance charge on the loan?

b. How much are Bob's monthly payments?

c. What annual percentage rate is being charged on the loan?

d. If Bob decides to pay off the loan after 16 months, what is his loan payoff?

BUSINESS DECISION

Reading the Fine Print

The advertisement for Digital Warehouse shown here appeared in your local newspaper this morning. Answer the questions that follow based on the information in the ad:

42. a. If you purchased the TV on January 24th of this year and the billing date of the installment loan is the 15th of each month, when would your first payment be due?

b. What is the required amount of that payment?

c. If that payment is late or less than required, what happens and how much does that amount to?

d. If that payment is more than 30 days late, what happens and how much does that amount to?

e. Explain the advantages and disadvantages of this offer.

CHAPTER FORMULAS

$$\text{Periodic rate} = \frac{\text{Annual percentage rate}}{12}$$

Finance charge = Previous month's balance × Periodic rate

$$\text{Average daily balance} = \frac{\text{Sum of daily balances}}{\text{Days in billing cycle}}$$

Finance charge = Average daily balance × Periodic rate

$$\text{New balance} = \text{Previous balance} + \text{Finance charge} + \text{Purchases and cash advances} - \text{Payments and credits}$$

Amount financed = Purchase price − Down payment

Down payment = Purchase price × Down payment percent

Amount financed = Purchase price (100% − Down payment percent)

Total amount of installment payments = Amount financed + Finance charge

Finance charge = Total amount of installment payments − Amount financed

Total amount of installment payments = Monthly payment amount × Number of monthly payments

Total deferred payment price = Total of installment payments + Down payment

Interest (*finance charge*) = Principal (*amount financed*) × Rate × Time

$$\text{Regular monthly payments} = \frac{\text{Total of installment payments}}{\text{Number of months of loan}}$$

$$\text{APR} = \frac{72I}{3P(n + 1) + I(n - 1)}$$

$$\text{Finance charge} = \frac{\text{Amount financed} \times \text{APR table factor}}{100}$$

(continued)

$$\text{Sum of digits} = \frac{n(n+1)}{2}$$

$$\text{Rebate fraction} = \frac{\text{Sum of digits of remaining payments}}{\text{Sum of digits of total payment}}$$

$$\text{Finance charge rebate} = \text{Rebate fraction} \times \text{Total finance charge}$$

$$\text{Loan payoff} = (\text{Payments remaining} \times \text{Payment amount}) - \text{Finance charge rebate}$$

✦ SUMMARY CHART ✦

SECTION I: Open-End Credit—Charge Accounts, Credit Cards, and Lines of Credit

Topic	P/O, Page	Important Concepts	Illustrative Examples
Calculating Finance Charge and New Balance by Using Previous Month's Balance Method	13-1 447	1. Divide the annual percentage rate by 12 to find the monthly or periodic interest rate. 2. Calculate the finance charge by multiplying the previous month's balance by the periodic interest rate from Step 1. 3. Total all the purchases and cash advances for the month. 4. Total all the payments and credits for the month. 5. Use the following formula to determine the new balance: $\text{New bal} = \text{Prev bal} + \text{Fin chg} + \text{Purch \& csh} - \text{Pmts \& crd}$	Calculate the finance charge and the new balance of an account with an annual percentage rate of 15%. Previous month's bal = \$186.11 Purchases = \$365.77 Payments = \$200.00 Periodic rate $= \frac{15}{12} = 1.25\%$ Finance charge = 186.11 × .0125 = \$2.33 New balance = 186.11 + 2.33 + 365.77 − 200.00 = \$354.21
Calculating Finance Charge and New Balance by Using the Average Daily Balance Method	13-2 448	1. Starting with the previous month's balance, multiply each by the number of days that balance existed until the next account transaction. 2. At the end of the billing cycle, add all the daily balances × days figures. 3. $\text{Average daily balance} = \frac{\text{Sum of daily balances}}{\text{Number of days of billing cycle}}$ 4. $\text{Finance charge} = \text{Periodic rate} \times \text{Average daily balance}$ 5. $\text{New bal} = \text{Prev bal} + \text{Fin chg} + \text{Purch \& csh} - \text{Pmts \& crd}$	Calculate the finance charge and the new balance of an account with a periodic rate of 1%, a previous balance of \$132.26, and the following activity: May 5 Purchase \$45.60 May 9 Cash advance 100.00 May 15 Credit 65.70 May 23 Purchase 75.62 May 26 Payment 175.00 \$132.26 × 4 days = \$529.04 177.86 × 4 days = 711.44 277.86 × 6 days = 1,667.16 212.16 × 8 days = 1,697.28 287.78 × 3 days = 863.34 112.78 × 6 days = 676.68 31 days \$6,144.94 Average daily balance $= \frac{6{,}144.94}{31}$ = \$198.22 Finance charge = 1% × 198.22 = \$1.98 New balance = 132.26 + 1.98 + 221.22 − 240.70 = \$114.76

SECTION I: (continued)

Topic	P/O, Page	Important Concepts	Illustrative Examples
Calculating the Finance Charge and New Balance of Business and Personal Lines of Credit	13-3 450	With business and personal lines of credit, the annual percentage rate is quoted as the current prime rate plus a fixed percent. Once the APR rate is determined, the finance charge and new balance are calculated as before, using the average daily balance method. $\text{New bal} = \text{Previous balance} + \text{Finance charge} + \text{Loans} - \text{Payments}$	What are the finance charge and new balance of a line of credit with an APR of the current prime rate plus 4.6%? Previous balance = \$2,000 Average daily balance = \$3,200 Payments = \$1,500 Loans = \$3,600 Current prime rate = 7% APR = 7% + 4.6% = 11.6% Periodic rate = $\frac{11.6}{12}$ = .97% Finance charge = 3,200 × .0097 = \$31.04 New balance = 2,000 + 31.04 + 3,600 − 1,500 = \$4,131.04

SECTION II: Closed-End Credit—Installment Loans

Topic	P/O, Page	Important Concepts	Illustrative Examples
Calculating the Total Deferred Payment Price and the Amount of the Finance Charge of an Installment Loan	13-4 457	$\text{Finance charge} = \text{Total amount of installment pmts} - \text{Amount financed}$ $\text{Total deferred payment price} = \text{Total of installment payments} + \text{Down payment}$	Waterbed City sold a \$1,900 bedroom set to Tom Ash. Tom put down \$400 and financed the balance with an installation loan of 24 monthly payments of \$68.75 each. What are the finance charge and total deferred payment price of the bedroom set? Total amount of payments = \$68.75 × 24 = \$1,650 Finance charge = 1,650 − 1,500 = \$150 Total deferred payment price = 1,650 + 400 = \$2,050
Calculating the Regular Monthly Payment of a Loan by the Add-On Interest Method	13-5 459	1. Calculate the amount financed by subtracting the down payment from the purchase price. 2. Compute the add-on interest finance charge by using $I = PRT$. 3. Find the total of the installment payments by adding the interest to the amount financed. 4. Calculate the monthly payment by dividing the total of the installment payments by the number of months of the loan.	Cindy Young financed a new car with an 8% add-on interest loan. The purchase price of the car was \$13,540. The bank required a \$1,500 down payment and equal monthly payments for 48 months. How much are Cindy's monthly payments? Amount financed = 13,540 − 1,500 = \$12,040 Interest = 12,040 × .08 × 4 = \$3,852.80 Total of installment payments = 12,040 + 3,852.80 = \$15,892.80 Monthly payment = $\frac{15,892.80}{48}$ = \$331.10

SECTION II: (continued)

Topic	P/O, Page	Important Concepts	Illustrative Examples
Calculating the Annual Percentage Rate (APR) by Using APR Tables	13-6 460	1. Calculate the finance charge per $100 by $\frac{\textbf{Finance charge} \times 100}{\textbf{Amount financed}}$ 2. From Table 13-1, scan down the payments column to the number of payments of the loan. 3. Scan to the right in that row to the table factor that most closely corresponds to the finance charge per $100. 4. Look to the top of the column containing the finance charge per $100 to find the APR of the loan.	John Anderson purchased a snowmobile for $8,000. He made a $1,500 down payment and financed the remaining $6,500 for 30 months. If John's total finance charge is $1,858, what APR is he paying on the loan? Finance charge per $100 = $\frac{1{,}858 \times 100}{6{,}500} = \$28.58$ From Table 13-1, scan down the payments column to 30. Then scan right to the table factor closest to 28.58, which is 28.64. The top of that column shows the APR to be 20.5%.
Calculating the Annual Percentage Rate (APR) by Using the APR Formula	13-6 464	When APR tables are not available, the annual percentage rate can be approximated by the formula $\textbf{APR} = \frac{72I}{3P(n+1) + I(n-1)}$ **where** I **= finance charge on the loan** P **= principal; amount financed** n **= number of months of the loan**	Using the APR formula, verify the 20.5% found by the table in the previous example. $\text{APR} = \frac{72(1{,}858)}{3(6{,}500)(30+1) + 1{,}858(30-1)}$ $= \frac{133{,}776}{658{,}382} = .2031 = 20.3\%$
Calculating the Finance Charge and Monthly Payment of a Loan by Using APR Tables	13-7 465	1. From Table 13-1, locate the table factor at the intersection of the APR and number of payments of the loan. This table factor is the finance charge per $100. 2. **Total finance charge =** $\frac{\textbf{Amount financed} \times \textbf{Table factor}}{\textbf{100}}$ 3. $\textbf{Monthly payment} = \frac{\textbf{Amt. financed + Finance chg}}{\textbf{Number of months of the loan}}$	Contemporary Electronics uses the MegaBank to finance customer purchases. This month MegaBank is offering loans up to 36 months with an APR of 13.25%. For qualified buyers, no down payment is required. If Jacquelyn Carrillo wants to purchase a $2,350 large-screen TV on a 36-month loan, what are the finance charge and monthly payment of the loan? From Table 13-1, the table factor for 36 payments, 13.25% = 21.73 Total finance charge = $\frac{2{,}350 \times 21.73}{100} = \$510.66$ Monthly payment = $\frac{2{,}350 + 510.66}{36} = \$79.46$

SECTION II: (continued)

Topic	P/O, Page	Important Concepts	Illustrative Examples
Calculating the Finance Charge Rebate and Payoff for Loans Paid Off Early by Using the Sum-of-the-Digits, or Rule of 78, Method	13-8 466	1. Calculate the rebate fraction by using the sum-of-the-digits formula for the numerator (number of payments remaining) and the denominator (total number of payments). **Sum of digits** $= \dfrac{n(n+1)}{2}$ 2. Calculate the finance charge rebate by multiplying the rebate fraction by the total finance charge. 3. The payoff of the loan is found by multiplying the remaining number of payments by the payment amount, then subtracting the finance charge rebate.	Scott Stewart financed a $2,000 motorcycle with an installment loan for 24 months. The payments are $98.00 per month, and the total finance charge is $352.00. After 18 months, Scott decides to pay off the loan. How much is the finance charge rebate, and what is the amount of the loan payoff? Rebate fraction $= \dfrac{\text{Sum of digits of 6}}{\text{Sum of digits of 24}}$ Sum digits 6 $= \dfrac{6(7)}{2} = 21$ Sum digits 24 $= \dfrac{24(25)}{2} = 300$ Rebate fraction $= \dfrac{21}{300}$ Finance charge rebate $= \dfrac{21}{300} \times 352 = \underline{\underline{\$24.64}}$ Loan payoff $= (6 \times 98) - 24.64$ $= 588.00 - 24.64$ $= \underline{\underline{\$563.36}}$

TRY-IT EXERCISE | SOLUTIONS

1. Periodic rate $= \dfrac{\text{APR}}{12} = \dfrac{15\%}{12} = 1.25\%$

Finance charge = Previous balance × Periodic rate
Finance charge = 214.90 × .0125 = $\underline{\underline{\$2.69}}$

New balance = Previous balance + Finance charge + Purchases & cash advance − Payment & credits
New balance = 214.90 + 2.69 + 238.85 − 49.12 = $\underline{\underline{\$407.32}}$

2. Periodic rate $= \dfrac{\text{APR}}{12} = \dfrac{18\%}{12} = 1.5\%$

Dates	Days	Activity/Amount		Unpaid Balance	Daily Balances
Aug. 1–4	4	Previous balance	158.69	158.69	634.76
Aug. 5–10	6	Charge	55.00	213.69	1,282.14
Aug. 11–14	4	Payment	−100.00	113.69	454.76
Aug. 15–16	2	Charge	43.22	156.91	313.82
Aug. 17–19	3	Charge	54.10	211.01	633.03
Aug. 20–25	6	Charge	224.50	435.51	2,613.06
Aug. 26–31	6	Cash advance	75.00	510.51	3,063.06
	31				8,994.63

$$\text{Average daily balance} = \frac{\text{Daily balances}}{\text{Days}} = \frac{8{,}994.63}{31} = \$290.15$$

Finance charge = Average daily balance × Periodic rate
Finance charge = $290.15 × .015 = $4.35

New balance = Previous balance + Finance charge + Purchases & cash advance − Payments & credits
New balance = 158.69 + 4.35 + 451.82 − 100.00 = $514.86

3. APR = Prime rate + 4.5%
APR = 8.5 + 4.5 = 13%

$$\text{Periodic rate} = \frac{13\%}{12} = 1.08\%$$

Dates	Days	Activity/Amount		Unpaid Balance	Daily Balances
Nov. 1–6	6	Previous balance	12,300	12,300	73,800
Nov. 7–20	14	Loan	16,700	29,000	406,000
Nov. 21–25	5	Loan	8,800	37,800	189,000
Nov. 26–30	5	Payment	−20,000	17,800	89,000
	30				757,800

$$\text{Average daily balance} = \frac{757{,}800}{30} = \$25{,}260$$

Finance charge = 25,260 × .0108 = $272.81

New balance = Previous balance + Finance charge + Loan amounts − Payments
New balance = 12,300 + 272.81 + 25,500 − 20,000 = $18,072.81

4. a. Down payment = Purchase price × Down payment percent
Down payment = 12,500 × .15 = $1,875.00

Amount financed = Purchase price − Down payment
Amount financed = 12,500 − 1,875 = $10,625.00

Total amount of installment payments = Monthly payment × Number of payments
Total amount of installment payments = 309.90 × 48 = $14,875.20

Finance charge = Total amount of installment payments − Amount financed
Finance charge = 14,875.20 − 10,625.00 = $4,250.20

b. Total deferred payment price = Total amount of installment payments + Down payment
Total deferred payment price = 14,875.20 + 1,875.00 = $16,750.20

5. Amount financed = Purchase price (100% − Down payment %)
Amount financed = 1,500 × .9 = $1,350.00

Finance charge = Amount financed × Rate × Time
Finance charge = 1,350 × .06 × 2 = $162.00

Total of installment payments = Amount financed + Finance charge
Total of installment payments = 1,350.00 + 162.00 = $1,512.00

$$\text{Monthly payments} = \frac{\text{Total of installment payments}}{\text{Number of months of loan}}$$

$$\text{Monthly payments} = \frac{1{,}512}{24} = \$63.00$$

6. Amount financed = 4,500 − 500 = $4,000
Total payments = 190 × 24 = 4,560
Finance charge = 4,560 − 4,000 = $560.00

$$\text{Finance charge}/100 = \frac{\text{Finance charge} \times 100}{\text{Amount financed}} = \frac{560 \times 100}{4{,}000} = \$14.00$$

From Table 13-1 APR for \$14.00 = 13%

7. Total payments = 140 × 18 = 2,520

Finance charge = 2,520 − 2,200 = \$320.00

$$\text{APR} = \frac{72I}{3P(n+1) + I(n-1)}$$

$$\text{APR} = \frac{72(320)}{3(2{,}200)(18+1) + 320(18-1)} = \frac{23{,}040}{125{,}400 + 5{,}440}$$

$$\text{APR} = \frac{23{,}040}{130{,}840} = .17609 = 17.6\%$$

8. 13.25%, 24-month table factor = \$14.38

$$\text{Finance charge} = \frac{\text{Amount financed} \times \text{Table factor}}{100}$$

$$\text{Finance charge} = \frac{3{,}550.00 \times 14.38}{100} = \frac{51{,}049}{100} = \$510.49$$

$$\text{Monthly payment} = \frac{\text{Amount financed} + \text{Finance charge}}{\text{Number of months of loan}}$$

$$\text{Monthly payment} = \frac{3{,}550.00 + 510.49}{24} = \frac{4{,}060.49}{24}$$

Monthly payment = \$169.19

9. 16 months remaining; total of 36 months.

$$\text{Sum of digits 16} = \frac{n(n+1)}{2} = \frac{16(16+1)}{2} = \frac{272}{2} = 136$$

$$\text{Sum of digits 36} = \frac{n(n+1)}{2} = \frac{36(36+1)}{2} = \frac{1{,}332}{2} = 666$$

$$\text{Rebate fraction} = \frac{136}{666}$$

Finance charge rebate = Rebate fraction × Total finance charge = × 1,076

Finance charge rebate = \$219.72

Loan payoff = (Payments remaining × Payment amount) − Finance charge rebate

Loan payoff = (16 × 141.00) − 219.72 = 2,256.00 − 219.72

Loan payoff = \$2,036.28

Name ______________

Class ______________

Answers

1. a. ______________

b. ______________

c. ______________

2. a. ______________

b. ______________

CHAPTER 13 | ASSESSMENT TEST

1. Valerie Mebust's revolving charge account has an annual percentage rate of 16%. The previous month's balance was $345.40. During the current month, Valerie's purchases and cash advances amounted to $215.39, and her payments and credits totaled $125.00.

   a. What is the monthly periodic rate of the account?

   b. What is the amount of the finance charge?

   c. What is Valerie's new balance?

2. Tom Hall has a Bank of America account with an annual percentage rate of 12% calculated on the previous month's balance. In April, the account had the following activity.

Statement of Account — Bank of America

NAME
TOM HALL

ACCOUNT NUMBER
9595-55-607

BILLING CYCLE
APRIL 1–30

DATE	DESCRIPTION OF TRANSACTIONS	CHARGES
04/01	Previous month's balance	$301.98
04/08	Atlas Gym & Health Club	250.00
04/09	Payment	75.00
04/15	Lucky's Auto Repair	124.80
04/25	Cash Advance	100.00
04/28	Brandon's Western Wear	178.90

   a. What is the amount of the finance charge?

   b. What is Tom's new balance?

3. Annette Fear has a revolving charge account at Macy's. The finance charge is calculated on the previous month's balance, and the annual percentage rate is 20%. Complete the following 3-month account activity table for Annette:

Month	Previous Month's Balance	Finance Charge	Purchases and Cash Advances	Payments and Credits	New Balance End of Month
a. December	$267.00	______	$547.66	$95.00	______
b. January	______	______	$213.43	$110.00	______
c. February	______	______	$89.95	$84.00	______

4. Calculate the average daily balance for the month of January of a charge account with a previous month's balance of $480.94 and the following activity:

Date	Activity	Amount
January 7	Cash advance	$80.00
January 12	Payment	$125.00
January 18	Purchase	$97.64
January 24	Credit	$72.00
January 29	Purchase	$109.70
January 30	Purchase	$55.78

5. Mike Roche has a Bank of America account with a 13% annual percentage rate calculated on the average daily balance. The billing date is the first day of each month, and the billing cycle is the number of days in that month.

Statement of Account — Bank of America

NAME: MIKE ROCHE

ACCOUNT NUMBER: 4495-5607

BILLING CYCLE: SEPTEMBER 1–30

DATE	DESCRIPTION OF TRANSACTIONS	CHARGES
09/01	Previous month's balance	$686.97
09/04	Lord & Taylor's	223.49
09/08	Payment	350.00
09/12	Office Depot	85.66
09/21	United Airlines (credit)	200.00
09/24	Miller Paint and Body Shop	347.12
09/28	Ticketmasters	64.00

a. What is the average daily balance for September?

b. How much is the finance charge for September?

c. What is Mike's new balance?

Name ______________________

Class ______________________

Answers

3. a. ______________________

____

b. ______________________

____

____

c. ______________________

____

____

4. ______________________

5. a. ______________________

b. ______________________

c. ______________________

Name ______________________

Class ______________________

Answers

6. a. ______________________

b. ______________________

7. a. ______________________

b. ______________________

8. a. ______________________

b. ______________________

6. Precision Builders, Inc., has a $100,000 line of credit with the California National Bank. The annual percentage rate is the current prime rate plus $3\frac{1}{4}$%. The balance on June 1 was $52,900. On June 8, Precision borrowed $30,600 to pay for a shipment of lumber and roofing materials and on June 18 borrowed another $12,300 for equipment repairs. On June 28, a $35,000 payment was made on the account. The billing cycle for June has 30 days. The current prime rate is $7\frac{3}{4}$%.

   a. What is the finance charge on the account?

   b. What is Precision's new balance?

7. Stuart McPherson bought a motor home for a cash price of $29,200.00. He made a 15% down payment and financed the balance with payments of $579.00 per month for 60 months.

   a. What is the amount of the finance charge on this loan?

   b. What is the total deferred payment price of the motor home?

8. Lamar Hester bought a home exercise gym with a 9.3% add-on interest installment loan from the San Antonio bank. The purchase price of the gym was $1,290.00. The bank required a 15% down payment and equal monthly payments for 24 months.

   a. What is the total deferred payment price of the gym?

   b. How much are Lamar's monthly payments?

Name ____________

Class ____________

Answers

9. a. ____________
   b. ____________

10. a. ____________
    b. ____________

11. a. ____________
    b. ____________

9. Music City Recording Studio purchased a new digital recording console for $28,600. A down payment of $5,000 was made and the balance financed with monthly payments of $708.00 for 48 months.

a. What is the amount of the finance charge on the loan?

b. Use Table 13-1 to find what annual percentage rate was charged on the equipment loan.

10. A Pizza Palace franchise purchased a $7,590 pizza oven with a 36-month installment loan. The monthly payments are $261.44 per month.

a. Use the APR formula to calculate the annual percentage rate of the loan.

b. Use the APR tables to verify your answer from part a.

11. SkyHigh Aircraft Sales uses the Millennium Bank to finance customer aircraft purchases. This month, Millennium is offering 60-month installment loans with an APR of 11.25%. A 15% down payment is required. The KARVA Corporation president wants to finance the purchase of a company airplane for $250,000.

a. Use the APR tables to calculate the amount of the finance charge.

b. How much are the monthly payments on KARVA's aircraft loan?

Name ______________________

Class ______________________

Answers

12. a. ______________________

b. ______________________

13. a. ______________________

b. ______________________

c. ______________________

d. ______________________

12. After making 11 payments on a 36-month loan, you pay it off.

a. What is your rebate fraction?

b. If the finance charge was $1,300, what is the amount of your finance charge rebate?

13. Internet Solutions financed a $68,000 fiber-optic switcher with a $6\frac{1}{2}\%$ add-on interest installment loan for 48 months. The loan required a 20% down payment.

a. What is the amount of the finance charge on the loan?

b. How much are the monthly payments?

c. What annual percentage rate is being charged on the loan?

d. If the company decides to pay off the loan after 22 months, what is the amount of the loan payoff?

Name ____________________

Class ____________________

Answers

14. a. ____________________

b. ____________________

c. ____________________

15. a. ____________________

b. ____________________

c. ____________________

d. ____________________

e. ____________________

14. You are a salesperson for Grove Key Marina—Boat Sales. A customer is interested in purchasing the 23-foot Sea Ray shown in the accompanying ad and has asked you the following questions:

a. What is the APR of the loan? Use the formula to find the APR of the loan.

b. What is the total deferred payment price of the boat?

c. If the loan is paid off after 7 years, what would be the payoff?

15. Brian Joyner found the accompanying ad for a Honda S 2000 in his local newspaper. If the sales tax in his state is 7% and the tag and title fees are $62.50, calculate the following information for Brian:

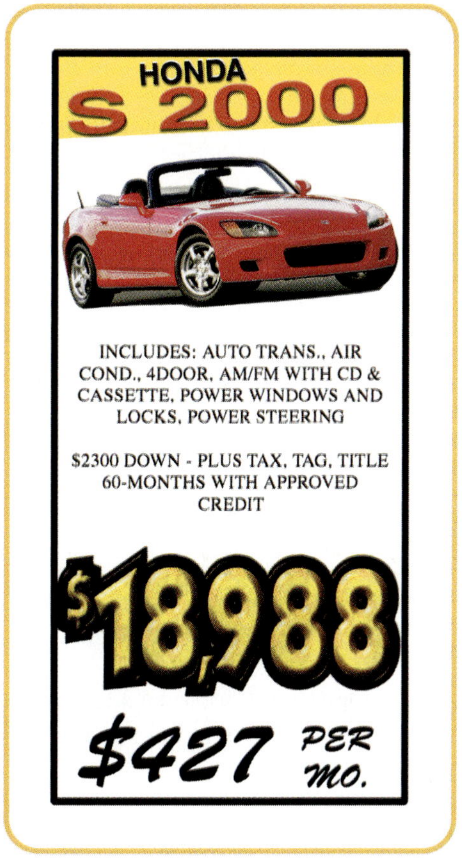

a. The total cost of the car including tax, tag, and title.

b. The amount financed.

c. The amount of the finance charge.

d. The total deferred price of the car.

e. The annual percentage rate of the loan.

Name ____________________

Class ____________________

Answers

16. a. ____________________

b. ____________________

c. ____________________

d. ____________________

e. ____________________

BUSINESS DECISION

Purchase vs. Lease

16. You are interested in getting a new car. You have decided to look into leasing, to see how it compares with buying. In recent years, you have noticed that advertised lease payments are considerably lower than those advertised for financing a purchase. It always seemed as if you would be getting "more car for the money!"

In your research, you have found that a closed-end vehicle lease is an agreement in which you make equal monthly payments based on your estimated usage for a set period of time. Then you turn the vehicle back in to the leasing dealer. No equity, no ownership, no asset at the end! You also have the option of purchasing the vehicle at an agreed-on price.

Leasing terminology is different from purchasing, but they are related. The *capitalized cost* is the purchase price; the *capitalized cost reduction* is the down payment; the *money factor* is the interest rate; the *residual value* is the expected market price of the vehicle at the end of the lease.

Use the advertisement and the purchase vs. lease worksheet that follow to compare the total cost of each option. The residual value of the car is estimated to be $13,650.00. The lease has no termination fees or charges. If you decide to purchase, your bank requires a down payment of $3,800 and will finance the balance with a 10.25% APR loan for 36 months. The sales tax in your state is 6.5%, and the tag and title charges are $75.00. The *opportunity cost* is the interest your down payment could have earned if you didn't purchase the new car. Currently, your money earns 4.5% in a savings account.

a. What is the total purchase price of the car, including tax, tag, and title?

b. How much are the monthly payments on the loan?

c. What is the total cost of purchasing?

d. What is the total cost of leasing?

e. In your own words, explain which of these financing choices is a better deal, and why.

f. (Optional) Choose an ad from your local newspaper for a lease offer on a vehicle you would like to have. Gather the necessary information needed to complete a purchase vs. lease worksheet. Use local dealers and banks to find the information you need, or do some research on the Internet. Report your findings and conclusions to the class.

Purchase vs. Lease Worksheet

Cost of Purchasing

1. Total purchase price, including tax, tag, and title _____
2. Down payment _____
3. Total of loan payments (monthly payment _____ × _____ months) _____
4. Opportunity cost on down payment (_____ % × _____ years × line 2) _____
5. Less: Expected market value of vehicle at the end of the loan _____
6. **Total cost of purchasing (lines 2 + 3 + 4 − 5)** _____

Cost of Leasing

1. Capitalized cost, including tax, tag, and title. _____
2. Down payment (capitalized cost reduction _____ + security deposit _____) _____
3. Total of lease payments (monthly payments _____ × _____ months) _____
4. Opportunity cost on down payment (_____ % × _____ years × line 2) _____
5. End-of-lease termination fees and charges (excess mileage or damage) _____
6. Less: Refund of security deposit _____
7. **Total cost of leasing (lines 2 + 3 + 4 + 5 − 6)** _____

All the Math That's Fit to Learn

The Business Math Times

Volume XIII | Consumer and Business Credit | One Dollar

"Quote . . . Unquote"

Education is when you read the fine print.
Experience is what you get if you don't.
—*Pete Seeger*

Debt is saving in reverse.
—*Peter Lynch*

1,562 Hippos!

A billion credit cards combined would weigh the same as 1,562 hippopotamuses. A billion cards laid end-to-end would reach around the earth 2.2 times. Stacked up, they would be taller than 2,667 Eiffel Towers!

In 2001, Visa reached the 1 billion card mark, with its cardholders purchasing more than \$1.6 trillion in products and services. Amazing growth, considering that in 1970 Visa had only 30 million credit card customers.

Then, it took more than 5 minutes to get a transaction authorized; now on average it takes less than 5 seconds—anywhere in the world. Visa's Payments Processing System handles more than 3,700 transactions every second during peak seasons, and can operate in 160 different currencies.

MasterCard is not far behind. Together with Visa and American Express, the three companies represent most of the world's market for "plastic" banking services. Today, credit cards are accepted at more than 23 million locations in more than 300 countries.

Pepper . . . and Salt

THE WALL STREET JOURNAL

"Well, here's your problem right here, Mr. Abbott. You didn't read the *finest* print."

Electronic Wallets

Soon, many credit cards will be "smart" cards, or cards embedded with an integrated circuit chip. These computer chips give the card the power to perform a number of different functions. Smart cards can contain multiple accounts and provide numerous services such as ID verification, merchant loyalty program tracking, and personal data storage.

Smart cards have been described as a PC in your wallet. They have the capability to store up to 80 times more information than magnetic stripe cards. The cards have processing capabilities that allow them to take a variety of factors into consideration and actually make a decision, such as authorizing a purchase or the amount of a promotional discount.

With a smart card, you can carry multiple currencies when traveling, make secure purchases over the Internet, pay for public transportation and public phone calls, and make traditional credit and debit purchases. Other uses include secure identification, driver's licenses, and carrying personal information such as health care or credit records.

Europeans use them everywhere. In various countries, you can stick them into parking meters, pay for a Big Mac, or use them to make pay phone calls.

In Germany, most citizens have a health insurance smart card the holds an insurance ID number and other basic data. Physicians insert the cards into readers to call up the information. This really reduces the amount of red tape that patients must deal with before getting to see the physician.

Student Debt on the Rise

In a recent survey by Nellie Mae, the national leader in student loans and services, the average credit card debt among students rose from \$1,879 to \$2,748 between 1998 and 2000. The study showed that nearly 25% of the students with credit card debt owe more than \$3,000 and that nearly 10% of students owe more than \$7,000.

More than 78% of today's college students use credit cards—95% for graduate students. The average number of credit cards per student is three. Thirty-two percent have four or more cards.

Brainteaser

WHICH SWITCH IS WHICH?

In the basement there are three light switches in the "off" position. Each switch controls one of three light bulbs on the floor above. You may turn any of the switches on or off, but you may only go upstairs one time. How can you determine which switch controls each light bulb?

ANSWER TO LAST ISSUE'S BRAINTEASER

The stack would be 359.84 miles high.
If 4 inches equals \$1 million, then a foot equals \$3 million and a mile equals \$15.84 billion.

$$\$1 \text{ trillion} = \frac{1{,}000}{15.84} = 63.13 \text{ miles}$$

$$5.7 \times 63.13 = 359.84 \text{ miles}$$

CHAPTER 14

Mortgages

PERFORMANCE OBJECTIVES

Section I Mortgages—Fixed-Rate and Adjustable-Rate

14-1 Calculating the monthly payment and total interest paid on a fixed-rate mortgage. (p. 493)
14-2 Preparing a partial amortization schedule of a mortgage. (p. 495)
14-3 Calculating the monthly PITI of a mortgage loan. (p. 497)
14-4 Understanding closing costs and calculating the amount due at closing. (p. 498)
14-5 Calculating the interest rate of an adjustable-rate mortgage (ARM). (p. 500)

Section II Second Mortgages—Home Equity Loans and Lines of Credit

14-6 Calculating the potential amount of credit available to a borrower. (p. 506)
14-7 Calculating the housing expense ratio and the total obligations ratio of a borrower. (p. 508)

SECTION I

MORTGAGES—FIXED-RATE AND ADJUSTABLE-RATE

real estate
Land, including any permanent improvements such as homes, apartment buildings, factories, hotels, shopping centers, or any other "real" structures.

mortgage
A loan in which real property is used as security for a debt.

Federal Housing Administration (FHA)
A government agency within the U.S. Department of Housing and Urban Development (HUD) that sets construction standards and insures residential mortgage loans made by approved lenders.

VA mortgage, or GI Loan
Long-term, low-down-payment home loans made by private lenders to eligible veterans, the payment of which is guaranteed by the Veterans Administration in the event of a default.

conventional loans
Real estate loans made by private lenders that are not FHA-insured or VA-guaranteed.

private mortgage insurance (PMI)
A special form of insurance primarily on mortgages for single-family homes, allowing the buyer to borrow more, by putting down a smaller down payment.

adjustable-rate mortgage (ARM)
A mortgage loan in which the interest rate changes periodically, usually in relation to a predetermined economic index.

Real estate is defined as land, including the air above and the earth below, plus any permanent improvements to the land, such as homes, apartment buildings, factories, hotels, shopping centers, or any other "real" property. Whether for commercial or residential property, practically all real estate transactions today involve some type of financing. The mortgage loan is the most popular method of financing real estate purchases.

A **mortgage** is any loan in which real property is used as security for a debt. During the term of the loan, the property becomes security or collateral for the lender, sufficient to ensure recovery of the amount loaned.

Mortgages today fall into one of three categories: FHA-insured, VA-guaranteed, and conventional. The National Housing Act of 1934 created the **Federal Housing Administration (FHA)** to encourage reluctant lenders to invest their money in the mortgage market, thereby stimulating the depressed construction industry. Today, the FHA is a government agency within the Department of Housing and Urban Development (HUD). The FHA insures private mortgage loans made by approved lenders.

In 1944, the Servicemen's Readjustment Act (GI Bill of Rights) was passed to help returning World War II veterans purchase homes. Special mortgages were established known as **Veterans Affairs (VA) mortgages** or **GI Loans.** Under this and subsequent legislation, the government guarantees payment of a mortgage loan made by a private lender to a veteran/buyer should the veteran default on the loan.

VA loans may be used by eligible veterans, surviving spouses, and active service members to buy, construct, or refinance homes, farm residences, or condominiums. Down payments by veterans are not required but are left to the discretion of lenders, whereas FHA and conventional loans require a down payment from all buyers.

Conventional loans are made by private lenders and generally have a higher interest rate than either FHA or VA loans. Most conventional lenders are restricted to loaning 80% of the appraised value of a property, thus requiring a 20% down payment. If the borrower agrees to pay the premium for **private mortgage insurance (PMI),** the conventional lender can lend up to 95% of the appraised value of the property.

Historically, high interest rates in the early 1980s caused mortgage payments to skyrocket beyond the financial reach of the average home buyer. To revitalize the slumping mortgage industry, the **adjustable-rate mortgage (ARM)** was created. These are mortgage loans under which the interest rate is periodically adjusted to more closely coincide with changing economic conditions. ARMs are very attractive, particularly to first-time buyers, because a low teaser rate may be offered for the first few years and

Mortgage loans are the most common form of loan made for real property purchases such as office buildings.

then adjusted upward to a higher rate later in the loan. Today, the adjustable-rate mortgage has become the most widely accepted option to the traditional 15- and 30-year fixed-rate mortgages.

Extra charges known as **mortgage discount points** are frequently added to the cost of a loan as a rate adjustment factor. This allows lenders to increase their yield without showing an increase in the mortgage interest rate. Each discount point is equal to 1% of the amount of the loan.

mortgage discount points
Extra charge frequently added to the cost of a mortgage, allowing lenders to increase their yield without showing an increase in the mortgage interest rate.

By their nature, mortgage loans involve large amounts of money, and long periods of time. Consequently, the monthly payments and the amount of interest paid over the years can be considerable. Exhibit 14-1 illustrates the 30-year mortgage rates in the United States from 1971 to 2001, and the monthly payment on a $100,000 mortgage, at various interest rate levels.

In reality, the higher interest mortgages would have been refinanced as rates declined, but consider the "housing affordability" factor. In 1982, payments on a $100,000 mortgage were $1,548 per month, compared with $600 in 2001!

In this section, you learn to calculate the monthly payments of a mortgage and prepare a partial amortization schedule of that loan. You also calculate the amount of property tax and insurance required as part of each monthly payment. In addition, you learn about the **closing,** the all-important final step in a real estate transaction, and the calculation of the closing costs. Finally, you learn about the important components of an adjustable-rate mortgage: the index, the lender's margin, the interest rate, and the cost caps.

closing
A meeting at which the buyer and seller of real estate conclude all matters pertaining to the transaction. At the closing, the funds are transferred to the seller, and the ownership or title is transferred to the buyer.

14-1 Calculating the Monthly Payment and Total Interest Paid on a Fixed-Rate Mortgage

In Chapter 12, we learned that amortization is the process of paying off a financial obligation in a series of equal regular payments over a period of time. We calculated the amount of an amortization payment by using the present value of an annuity table or the optional amortization formula.

Because mortgages run for relatively long periods of time, we can also use a special present-value table in which the periods are listed in years. The table factors represent the monthly payment required per $1,000 of debt to amortize a mortgage. The monthly payment includes mortgage interest and an amount to reduce the principal. See Table 14-1.

Everybody's Business
Real-World Connection

As a result of declining mortgage rates in recent years, a record 68% of families own their own homes today. That amounts to nearly 72 million households.

Purchasing and financing a home is one of the most important financial decisions a person will ever make. Substantial research should be done and much care taken in choosing the correct time to buy, the right property to buy, and the best financial offer to accept. (See Exhibit 14-2, "Mortgage Shopping Worksheet," pages 500–501.)

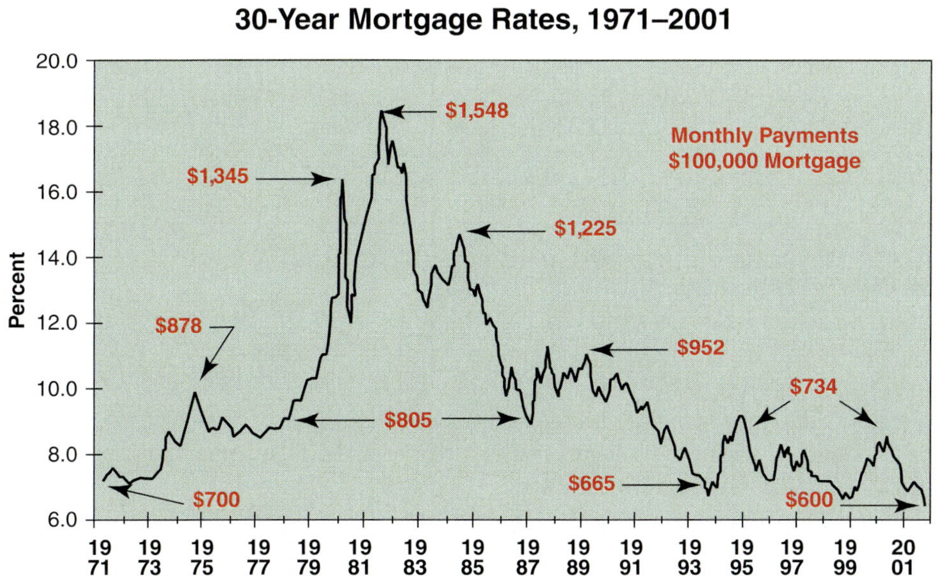

EXHIBIT 14-1
Historical Mortgage Rates and Monthly Payments

✦ TABLE 14-1 ✦

Monthly Payments to Amortize Principal and Interest per $1000 Financed

Everybody's Business

Learning Tip

Remember that the table values represent monthly payment "per $1,000" financed. When calculating the amount of the monthly payment, you must first determine the number of $1,000s being financed, then multiply that figure by the table factor.

Monthly Payments
(Necessary to amortize a loan of $1,000)

Interest Rate	5 Years	10 Years	15 Years	20 Years	25 Years	30 Years	35 Years	40 Years
5 %	18.88	10.61	7.91	6.60	5.85	5.37	5.05	4.83
5¼	18.99	10.73	8.04	6.74	6.00	5.53	5.21	4.99
5½	19.11	10.86	8.18	6.88	6.15	5.68	5.38	5.16
5¾	19.22	10.98	8.31	7.03	6.30	5.84	5.54	5.33
6	19.34	11.11	8.44	7.17	6.45	6.00	5.71	5.51
6¼	19.45	11.23	8.58	7.31	6.60	6.16	5.88	5.68
6½	19.57	11.36	8.72	7.46	6.76	6.33	6.05	5.86
6¾	19.69	11.49	8.85	7.61	6.91	6.49	6.22	6.04
7	19.81	11.62	8.99	7.76	7.07	6.66	6.39	6.22
7¼	19.92	11.75	9.13	7.91	7.23	6.83	6.57	6.40
7½	20.04	11.88	9.28	8.06	7.39	7.00	6.75	6.59
7¾	20.16	12.01	9.42	8.21	7.56	7.17	6.93	6.77
8	20.28	12.14	9.56	8.37	7.72	7.34	7.11	6.96
8¼	20.40	12.27	9.71	8.53	7.89	7.52	7.29	7.15
8½	20.52	12.40	9.85	8.68	8.06	7.69	7.47	7.34
8¾	20.64	12.54	10.00	8.84	8.23	7.87	7.66	7.53
9	20.76	12.67	10.15	9.00	8.40	8.05	7.84	7.72
9¼	20.88	12.81	10.30	9.16	8.57	8.23	8.03	7.91
9½	21.01	12.94	10.45	9.33	8.74	8.41	8.22	8.11
9¾	21.13	13.08	10.60	9.49	8.92	8.60	8.41	8.30
10	21.25	13.22	10.75	9.66	9.09	8.78	8.60	8.50
10¼	21.38	13.36	10.90	9.82	9.27	8.97	8.79	8.69
10½	21.50	13.50	11.06	9.99	9.45	9.15	8.99	8.89
10¾	21.62	13.64	11.21	10.16	9.63	9.34	9.18	9.09
11	21.75	13.78	11.37	10.33	9.81	9.53	9.37	9.29
11¼	21.87	13.92	11.53	10.50	9.99	9.72	9.57	9.49
11½	22.00	14.06	11.69	10.67	10.17	9.91	9.77	9.69
11¾	22.12	14.21	11.85	10.84	10.35	10.10	9.96	9.89
12	22.25	14.35	12.01	11.02	10.54	10.29	10.16	10.09
12¼	22.38	14.50	12.17	11.19	10.72	10.48	10.36	10.29
12½	22.50	14.64	12.33	11.37	10.91	10.68	10.56	10.49
12¾	22.63	14.79	12.49	11.54	11.10	10.87	10.76	10.70
13	22.76	14.94	12.66	11.72	11.28	11.07	10.96	10.90
13¼	22.89	15.08	12.82	11.90	11.47	11.26	11.16	11.10
13½	23.01	15.23	12.99	12.08	11.66	11.46	11.36	11.31
13¾	23.14	15.38	13.15	12.26	11.85	11.66	11.56	11.51
14	23.27	15.53	13.32	12.44	12.04	11.85	11.76	11.72

STEPS TO FIND THE MONTHLY MORTGAGE PAYMENT BY USING AN AMORTIZATION TABLE, AND TOTAL INTEREST:

Step 1. Find the number of $1,000s financed by

$$\text{Number of \$1,000s financed} = \frac{\text{Amount financed}}{1{,}000}$$

Step 2. Using Table 14-1, locate the table factor, monthly payment per $1,000 financed, at the intersection of the number of years column and the interest rate row.

Step 3. Calculate the monthly payment by

Monthly payment = Number of $1,000s financed × Table factor

Step 4. Find the total interest of the loan by

Total interest = (Monthly payment × Number of payments) − Amount financed

EXAMPLE

What is the monthly payment and total interest on a $50,000 mortgage at 8% for 30 years?

SOLUTION STRATEGY

Step 1. $\text{Number of \$1,000s financed} = \dfrac{\text{Amount financed}}{1{,}000} = \dfrac{50{,}000}{1{,}000} = 50$

Step 2. Table factor for 8%, 30 years is 7.34.

Step 3. Monthly payment = Number of $1,000s financed × Table factor

Monthly payment = 50 × 7.34

Monthly payment = $367.00

Step 4. Total interest = (Monthly payment × Number of payments) − Amount financed

Total interest = (367 × 360) − 50,000

Total interest = 132,120 − 50,000

Total interest = $82,120

TRY-IT | EXERCISE

1. What is the monthly payment and total interest on an $85,500 mortgage at 7% for 25 years?

Check your answers with the solutions on page 514.

14-2 Preparing a Partial Amortization Schedule of a Mortgage

Mortgages used to purchase residential property generally require regular, equal payments. A portion of the payment is used to pay interest on the loan; the balance of the payment is used to reduce the principal. This type of mortgage is called a **level-payment plan** because the amount of the payment remains the same for the duration of the loan. The amount of the payment that is interest gradually decreases while the amount that reduces the debt gradually increases.

level-payment plan
Mortgages with regular, equal payments over a specified period of time.

An **amortization schedule** is a chart that shows the status of the mortgage loan after each payment. The schedule illustrates month by month how much of the mortgage payment is interest and how much is left to reduce to principal. The schedule also shows the outstanding balance of the loan after each payment.

amortization schedule
A chart that shows the month-by-month breakdown of each mortgage payment into interest and principal, and the outstanding balance of the loan.

In reality, amortization schedules are long, because they show the loan status for each month. A 30-year mortgage, for example, would require a schedule with 360 lines (12 months × 30 years = 360 payments).

STEPS TO CREATE AN AMORTIZATION SCHEDULE FOR A LOAN:

Step 1. Use Table 14-1 to calculate the amount of the monthly payment.

Step 2. Calculate the amount of interest for the current month using $I = PRT$, where P is the current outstanding balance of the loan, R is the annual interest rate, and T is $\frac{1}{12}$.

continued

Everybody's Business

Real-World Connection

In most cases, mortgage interest expense is tax deductible. To increase your deductions for the current year, make your January mortgage payment by December 20. This will allow time for the payment to be credited to your account in December, giving you an extra month of interest deduction this year.

continued

Step 3. Find the portion of the payment used to reduce principal by

Portion of payment reducing principal = Monthly payment − Interest

Step 4. Calculate the outstanding balance of the mortgage loan by

Outstanding balance = Previous balance − Portion of pmt. reducing principal

Step 5. Repeat Steps 2, 3, and 4 for each succeeding month and enter the values on a schedule labeled as follows:

Payment Number	Monthly Payment	Monthly Interest	Portion Used to Reduce Principal	Loan Balance

EXAMPLE

Prepare an amortization schedule for the first 3 months of the $50,000 mortgage at 8% for 30 years from the previous example. Remember, you have already calculated the monthly payment to be $367.00.

SOLUTION STRATEGY

Step 1. $367.00 (from previous example, page 495)

Step 2. **Month 1:**

Interest = Principal × Rate × Time

Interest = $50,000 \times .08 \times \frac{1}{12}$

Interest = $333.33

Step 3. Portion of payment reducing principal = Monthly payment − Interest

Portion of payment reducing principal = $367.00 − $333.33

Portion of payment reducing principal = $33.67

Step 4. Outstanding balance = Previous balance − Portion of payment reducing principal

Outstanding balance = 50,000 − 33.67

Outstanding balance after one payment = $49,966.33

Step 5. Repeat Steps 2, 3, and 4, for two more payments and enter the values on the schedule.

Month 2:

Interest = $49{,}966.33 \times .08 \times \frac{1}{12}$ = $333.11

(*Note:* Although very slightly, interest decreased.)

Portion reducing principal = 367.00 − 333.11 = $33.89

Outstanding balance after 2 payments = 49,966.33 − 33.89 = $49,932.44

Month 3:

Interest = $49{,}932.44 \times .08 \times \frac{1}{12}$ = $332.88

Portion reducing principal = 367.00 − 332.88 = $34.12

Outstanding balance after three payments = 49,932.44 − 34.12 = $49,898.32

Amortization Schedule
$50,000 Loan, 8%, 30 years

Payment Number	Monthly Payment	Monthly Interest	Portion Used to Reduce Principal	Loan Balance
0				$50,000.00
1	$367.00	$333.33	$33.67	$49,966.33
2	$367.00	$333.11	$33.89	$49,932.44
3	$367.00	$332.88	$34.12	$49,898.32

TRY-IT | EXERCISE

2. Prepare an amortization schedule of the first four payments of a $75,000 mortgage at 9% for 15 years. Use Table 14-1 to calculate the amount of the monthly payment.

Check your answers with the solutions on pages 514–515.

14-3 Calculating the Monthly PITI of a Mortgage Loan

In reality, mortgage payments include four elements: principal, interest, taxes, and insurance—thus the abbreviation **PITI.** VA, FHA, and most conventional loans require borrowers to pay $\frac{1}{12}$ of the estimated annual property taxes and hazard insurance with each month's mortgage payment. Each month, the taxes and insurance portions of the payment are placed in a type of savings account for safekeeping known as an **escrow account.** Each year when the property taxes and hazard insurance premiums are due, the lender disburses those payments from the borrower's escrow account. During the next 12 months, the account again builds up to pay for the next year's taxes and insurance.

PITI
An abbreviation for the total amount of a mortgage payment; includes principal, interest, property taxes, and hazard insurance.

escrow account
Bank account used by mortgage lenders for the safekeeping of the funds accumulating to pay next year's property taxes and hazard insurance.

STEPS TO CALCULATE THE PITI OF A MORTGAGE:

Step 1. Calculate the principal and interest portion, PI, of the payment as before using the amortization table, Table 14-1.

Step 2. Calculate the monthly tax and insurance portion, TI:

$$\text{Monthly TI} = \frac{\text{Estimated property tax} + \text{Hazard insurance}}{12}$$

Step 3. Calculate the total monthly PITI:

$$\text{Monthly PITI} = \text{Monthly PI} + \text{Monthly TI}$$

Everybody's Business
Real-World Connection
Typically, over the years of a mortgage, property taxes and insurance premiums rise. When this happens, the lender must increase the portion set aside in the escrow account by increasing the taxes and insurance parts of the monthly payment.

EXAMPLE

Martha Cavalaris purchased a home with a mortgage of $87,500 at $7\frac{1}{2}$% for 30 years. The property taxes are $2,350.00 per year, and the hazard insurance premium is $567.48. What is the monthly PITI payment of Martha's loan?

SOLUTION STRATEGY

Step 1. From the amortization table, Table 14-1, the factor for $7\frac{1}{2}$%, 30 years is 7.00. When we divide the amount of Martha's loan by 1,000 we get 87.5 as the number of 1,000s financed. The principal and interest portion, PI, is therefore $87.5 \times 7.00 = \underline{\underline{\$612.50}}$.

Step 2. $$\text{Monthly TI} = \frac{\text{Estimated property tax} + \text{Hazard Insurance}}{12}$$

$$\text{Monthly TI} = \frac{2{,}350.00 + 567.48}{12} = \frac{2{,}917.48}{12} = \underline{\underline{\$243.12}}$$

Step 3. Monthly PITI = PI + TI

Monthly PITI = 612.50 + 243.12

Monthly PITI = $\underline{\underline{\$855.62}}$

TRY-IT | EXERCISE

3. Bryan Ellison purchased a home with a mortgage of \$125,600 at $9\frac{1}{4}$% for 20 years. The property taxes are \$3,250.00 per year, and the hazard insurance premium is \$765.00. What is the monthly PITI payment of Bryan's loan?

Check your answer with the solution on page 515.

14-4 Understanding Closing Costs and Calculating the Amount Due at Closing

The term closing, or settlement, is used to describe the final step in a real estate transaction. This is a meeting at which time documents are signed, the buyer pays the agreed purchase price, and the seller delivers the **title,** or right of ownership, to the buyer. The official document conveying ownership is known as the **deed.**

title, or deed
The official document representing the right of ownership of real property.

closing costs
Expenses incurred in conjunction with the sale of real estate, including loan origination fees, credit reports, appraisal fees, title search, title insurance, inspections, attorney's fees, recording fees, and broker's commission.

settlement or closing statement
A document that provides a detailed accounting of payments, credits, and closing costs of a real estate transaction.

Closing costs are the expenses incurred in conjunction with the sale of real estate. In the typical real estate transaction, both the buyer and the seller are responsible for a number of costs that are paid for at the time of closing. The party obligated for paying a particular closing cost is often determined by local custom or by negotiation. Some closing costs are expressed as dollar amounts, whereas others are a percent of the amount financed or the amount of the purchase price.

At closing, the buyer is responsible for the purchase price (mortgage + down payment) plus closing costs. The amount received by the seller, after all expenses have been paid, is known as the proceeds. The **settlement statement** or **closing statement** is a document, usually prepared by an attorney, that provides a detailed breakdown of the real estate transaction. This document itemizes closing costs and indicates how they are allocated between the buyer and the seller.

Exhibit 14-2, "Mortgage Shopping Worksheet," can be used to compare mortgage offers from various lenders. It provides a comprehensive checklist of important loan information, typical fees, closing and settlement costs, and other questions and considerations people should be aware of when shopping for a mortgage loan.

EXAMPLE

Rich and Linda Arrandt are purchasing a \$180,000 home. The down payment is 25%, and the balance will be financed with a 25-year fixed-rate mortgage at 10% and 2 discount points (each point is 1% of the amount financed). When Rich and Linda signed the sales contract, they put down a deposit of \$15,000, which will be credited to their down payment at the time of the closing. In addition, they must pay the following expenses: credit report, \$80; appraisal fee, \$150; title insurance premium, $\frac{1}{2}$% of amount financed; title search, \$200; and attorney's fees, \$450.

a. Calculate the amount due from Rich and Linda at the closing.

b. If the sellers are responsible for the broker's commission, which is 6% of the purchase price, \$900 in other closing costs, and the existing mortgage, with a balance of \$50,000, what proceeds will they receive on the sale of the property?

SOLUTION STRATEGY

a. Down payment = 180,000 × 25% = $45,000
Amount financed = 180,000 − 45,000 = $135,000

Closing Costs, Buyer	
Discount points (135,000 × 2%)	$2,700
Down payment (45,000 − 15,000 deposit)	$30,000
Credit report	$80
Appraisal fee	$150
Title insurance ($135{,}000 \times \frac{1}{2}\%$)	$675
Title search	$200
Attorney's fees	$450
Due at closing	$34,255

b.

Proceeds, Seller		
Sale price		$180,000
Less: Broker's commission:		
180,000 × 6%	$10,800	
Closing costs	$900	
Mortgage payoff	$50,000	
		− $61,700
Proceeds to seller:		$118,300

TRY-IT | EXERCISE

4. Kathi Albrecht is purchasing a townhouse for $120,000. The down payment is 20%, and the balance will be financed with a 15-year fixed-rate mortgage at 9% and 3 discount points (each point is 1% of the amount financed). When Kathi signed the sales contract, she put down a deposit of $10,000, which will be credited to her down payment at the time of the closing. In addition, she must pay the following expenses: loan application fee, $100; condominium transfer fee, $190; title insurance premium, $\frac{3}{4}$% of amount financed; hazard insurance premium, $420; prepaid taxes, $310; and attorney's fees, $500.

a. Calculate the amount due from Kathi at the closing.

b. If the seller is responsible for the broker's commission, which is $5\frac{1}{2}$% of the purchase price, $670 in other closing costs, and the existing mortgage balance of $65,000, what proceeds will he receive on the sale of the property?

Check your answers with the solutions on page 515.

✦ **EXHIBIT 14-2** ✦
Mortgage Shopping Worksheet

Mortgage Shopping Worksheet

	Lender 1		Lender 2	
Name of Lender:				
Name of Contact:				
Date of Contact:				
Mortgage Amount:				
	mortgage 1	mortgage 2	mortgage 1	mortgage 2
Basic Information on the Loans				
Type of Mortgage: fixed rate, adjustable rate, conventional, FHA, other? If adjustable, see below				
Minimum down payment required				
Loan term (length of loan)				
Contract interest rate				
Annual percentage rate (APR)				
Points (may be called loan discount points)				
Monthly Private Mortgage Insurance (PMI) premiums				
How long must you keep PMI?				
Estimated monthly **escrow** for taxes and hazard insurance				
Estimated monthly payment (Principal, Interest, Taxes, Insurance, PMI)				
Fees Different institutions may have different names for some fees and may charge different fees. We have listed some typical fees you may see on loan documents.				
Application fee or Loan processing fee				
Origination fee or Underwriting fee				
Lender fee or Funding fee				
Appraisal fee				
Attorney fees				
Document preparation and recording fees				
Broker fees (may be quoted as points, origination fees, or interest rate add-on)				
Credit report fee				
Other fees				
Other Costs at Closing/Settlement				
Title search/Title insurance For lender				
For you				
Estimated prepaid amounts for interest, taxes, hazard insurance, payments to escrow				
State and local taxes, stamp taxes, transfer taxes				
Flood determination				
Prepaid Private Mortgage Insurance (PMI)				
Surveys and home inspections				
Total Fees and Other Closing/Settlement Cost Estimates				

14-5 Calculating the Interest Rate of an Adjustable-Rate Mortgage

With a fixed-rate mortgage, the interest rate stays the same during the life of the loan. With an adjustable-rate mortgage (ARM), the interest rate changes periodically, usually in relation to an index, and payments may go up or down accordingly. In recent years, the ARM has become the most widely accepted alternative to the traditional 30-year fixed-rate mortgage.

✦ **EXHIBIT 14-2** ✦
(continued)

Mortgage Shopping Worksheet—continued

	Lender 1		Lender 2	
Name of Lender:				
	mortgage 1	mortgage 2	mortgage 1	mortgage 2
Other Questions and Considerations about the Loan				
Are any of the fees or costs waivable?				
Prepayment penalties				
Is there a prepayment penalty?				
If so, how much is it?				
How long does the penalty period last? (for example, 3 years? 5 years?)				
Are extra principal payments allowed?				
Lock-ins				
Is the lock-in agreement in writing?				
Is there a fee to lock-in?				
When does the lock-in occur—at application, approval, or another time?				
How long will the lock-in last?				
If the rate drops before closing, can you lock-in at a lower rate?				
If the loan is an adjustable rate mortgage:				
What is the initial rate?				
What is the maximum the rate could be next year?				
What are the rate and payment caps each year and over the life of the loan?				
What is the frequency of rate change and of any changes to the monthly payment?				
What is the index that the lender will use?				
What margin will the lender add to the index?				
Credit life insurance				
Does the monthly amount quoted to you include a charge for credit life insurance?				
If so, does the lender require credit life insurance as a condition of the loan?				
How much does the credit life insurance cost?				
How much lower would your monthly payment be without the credit life insurance?				
If the lender does not require credit life insurance, and you still want to buy it, what rates can you get from other insurance providers?				

The primary components of an ARM are the index, lender's margin, calculated interest rate, initial interest rate, and cost caps. With most ARMs, the interest rate and monthly payment change either every year, every 3 years, or every 5 years. The period between one rate change and the next is known as the **adjustment period.** A loan with an adjustment period of 1 year, for example, is called a 1-year ARM.

adjustment period
The amount of time between one rate change and the next on an adjustable-rate mortgage; generally 1, 2, or 3 years.

Most lenders tie ARM interest rate changes to changes in an **index rate.** These indexes usually go up and down with the general movement of interest rates in the nation's economy. When the index goes up, so does the mortgage rate, resulting in higher monthly payments. When the index goes down, the mortgage rate may or may not go down.

index rate
The economic index to which the interest rate on an adjustable-rate mortgage is tied.

margin, or spread
The percentage points added to an index rate to get the interest rate of an adjustable-rate mortgage.

To calculate the interest rate on an ARM, lenders add a few points called the **margin** or **spread** to the index rate. The amount of the margin can differ among lenders and can make a significant difference in the amount of interest paid over the life of a loan.

Calculated interest rate = Index rate + Lender's margin

calculated or initial interest rate
The interest rate of an adjustable-rate mortgage to which all future adjustments and caps apply.

teaser rate
A discounted interest rate for the first adjustment period of an adjustable-rate mortgage that is below the current market rate of interest.

interest-rate cap
Limit on the amount the interest rate can increase on an ARM.

periodic cap
Limit on the amount the interest rate of an ARM can increase per adjustment period.

overall cap
Limit on the amount the interest rate of an ARM can increase over the life of the loan.

The **calculated** or **initial interest rate** is usually the rate to which all future adjustments and caps apply, although this rate may be discounted by the lender during the first payment period to attract and qualify more potential borrowers. This low initial interest rate, sometimes known as a **teaser rate,** is one of the main appeals of the ARM; however, without some protection from rapidly rising interest rates, borrowers might be put in a position of not being able to afford the rising mortgage payments. To prevent this situation, standards have been established requiring limits or caps on increases.

Interest-rate caps place a limit on the amount the interest rate can increase. These may come in the form of **periodic caps,** which limit the increase from one adjustment period to the next, and **overall caps,** which limit the increase over the life of the mortgage. The following formulas can be used to find the maximum interest rates of an ARM:

Maximum rate per adjustment period = Previous rate + Periodic cap

Maximum overall rate of ARM = Initial rate + Overall cap

EXAMPLE

Gisela Halpern bought a home with an adjustable-rate mortgage. The margin on the loan is 2.5%, and the rate cap is 6% over the life of the loan.

a. If the current index rate is 4.9%, what is the calculated interest rate of the ARM?

b. What is the maximum overall rate of the loan?

SOLUTION STRATEGY

a. Because the loan interest rate is tied to an index, we use the formula

Calculated ARM interest rate = Index rate + Margin

Calculated ARM interest rate = 4.9% + 2.5%

Calculated ARM interest rate = 7.4%

b.

Maximum overall rate = Calculated rate + Overall cap

Maximum overall rate = 7.4% + 6%

Maximum overall rate = 13.4%

TRY-IT | EXERCISE

5. Sara Burstell bought a home with an adjustable-rate mortgage. The margin on the loan is 3.4%, and the rate cap is 7% over the life of the loan. The current index rate is 3.2%.

a. What is the initial interest rate of the ARM?

b. What is the maximum overall rate of the loan?

Check your answers with the solutions on page 515.

REVIEW EXERCISES | CHAPTER 14—SECTION I

Using Table 14-1 as needed, calculate the required information for the following mortgages:

	Amount Financed	Interest Rate (%)	Term of Loan (years)	Number of $1,000s Financed	Table Factor	Monthly Payment	Total Interest
1.	$80,000	9	20	______	______	______	______
2.	$72,500	10	30	______	______	______	______
3.	$130,900	$8\frac{1}{2}$	25	______	______	______	______
4.	$154,300	$9\frac{1}{4}$	15	______	______	______	______
5.	$96,800	$7\frac{3}{4}$	30	______	______	______	______

6. Mark Batchelor purchased a home with a $78,500 mortgage at 9% for 15 years. Calculate the monthly payment and prepare an amortization schedule for the first 4 months of Mark's loan.

Payment Number	Monthly Payment	Monthly Interest	Portion Used to Reduce Principal	Loan Balance
0				$78,500
1	______	______	______	______
2	______	______	______	______
3	______	______	______	______
4	______	______	______	______

Calculate the monthly principal and interest, PI, using Table 14-1, and the monthly PITI for the following mortgages:

	Amount Financed	Interest Rate (%)	Term of Loan (years)	Monthly PI	Annual Property Tax	Annual Insurance	Monthly PITI
7.	$76,400	8	20	______	$1,317	$866	______
8.	$128,800	10	15	______	$2,440	$1,215	______
9.	$174,200	$7\frac{1}{4}$	30	______	$3,505	$1,432	______
10.	$250,000	$9\frac{1}{2}$	25	______	$6,553	$2,196	______

11. Pam Jeffries bought a home with an adjustable-rate mortgage. The margin on the loan is 3.5%, and the rate cap is 8% over the life of the loan.

a. If the current index rate is 3.75%, what is the calculated interest rate of the ARM?

b. What is the maximum overall rate of Pam's loan?

12. Christine Balmori purchased a condominium for $88,000. She made a 20% down payment and financed the balance with a 30-year, 9% fixed-rate mortgage.

a. What is the amount of the monthly principal and interest portion, PI, of Christine's loan?

b. Construct an amortization schedule for the first 4 months of Christine's mortgage:

Payment Number	Monthly Payment	Monthly Interest	Portion Used to Reduce Principal	Loan Balance
0				______
1	______	______	______	______
2	______	______	______	______
3	______	______	______	______
4	______	______	______	______

c. If the annual property taxes are $1,650 and the hazard insurance premium is $780 per year, what is the total monthly PITI of Christine's loan?

13. Tom Glover is shopping for a 15-year mortgage for $150,000. Currently, the Fortune Bank is offering an $8\frac{1}{2}$% mortgage with 3 discount points; the Northern Trust Bank is offering a $8\frac{3}{4}$% mortgage with no points. Tom is unsure which mortgage is a better deal and has asked you to help him decide. (Remember, each discount point is equal to 1% of the amount financed.)

a. What is the total interest paid on each loan?

b. Taking into account the closing points, which bank is offering a better deal and by how much?

14. Eduardo Padron is interested in a fixed-rate mortgage for $100,000. He is undecided whether to choose a 15- or 30-year mortgage. The current mortgage rate is 10% for the 15-year mortgage and 11% for the 30-year mortgage.

a. What are the monthly principal and interest payments for each loan?

b. What is the total amount of interest paid on each loan?

c. Overall, how much more interest is paid by choosing the 30-year mortgage?

BUSINESS DECISION

The Closing

15. You are a real estate broker for Renaissance Realty. One of your clients, Paula Stephenson, has agreed to purchase one of the homes your office has listed for sale for a negotiated price of $235,000. The down payment is 20%, and the balance will be financed with a 15-year fixed-rate mortgage at $8\frac{3}{4}$% and $3\frac{1}{2}$ discount points. The annual property tax is $5,475, and the hazard insurance premium is $2,110. When Paula signed the original contract, she put down a deposit of $5,000, which will be credited to her down payment. In addition, at the time of closing Paula must pay the following expenses:

Appraisal fee	$215.00
Credit report	$65.00
Roof inspection	$50.00
Mortgage insurance premium	$\frac{1}{2}$% of amount financed
Title search	$125.00
Attorney's fees	$680.00
Escrow fee	$210.00
Prepaid interest	$630.00

As Paula's real estate broker, she has asked you the following:

a. What is the total monthly PITI of the mortgage loan?

b. What is the total amount of interest that will be paid on the loan?

c. How much is due from Paula at the time of the closing?

d. If your real estate office is entitled to a commission of $6\frac{1}{2}\%$ of the price of the home from the seller, how much commission is made on the sale?

SECTION II

SECOND MORTGAGES—HOME EQUITY LOANS AND LINES OF CREDIT

Home equity loans and home equity lines of credit are becoming more popular each year. By using the equity in a home, a borrower may qualify for a sizable amount of credit at an interest rate that is relatively low. In addition, under the tax law, the interest may be a tax deduction because the debt is secured by your home.

home equity loan
A lump-sum second mortgage loan made on the available equity in a home.

home equity line
A revolving credit second mortgage loan made on the available equity in a home.

credit limit
A pre-approved limit on the amount of a home equity line of credit.

A **home equity loan** is a lump-sum second mortgage loan made on the available equity in your home. A **home equity line** is a form of revolving credit, also based on the available equity. Because the home is likely to be a consumer's largest asset, many homeowners use these loans and credit lines only for major expenditures such as debt consolidation, education, home improvements, business expansion, medical bills, or vacations.

With home equity lines of credit, the borrower will be approved for a specific amount of credit known as the **credit limit.** This is the maximum amount that can be borrowed at any one time on that line of credit.

Exhibit 14-3 illustrates some typical bank literature used to promote home equity loans. Note that with the tax deductibility advantage of these loans, a considerable amount of money can be saved on interest over installment loans or credit cards.

14-6 Calculating the Potential Amount of Credit Available to a Borrower

Most lenders set the credit limit on a home equity loan or line by taking a percentage of the appraised value of the house and subtracting the balance owed on the existing mortgage. In determining your actual credit limit, the lender also will consider your ability to repay by looking at your income, debts, and other financial obligations, as well as your credit history.

STEPS TO CALCULATE THE POTENTIAL AMOUNT OF CREDIT AVAILABLE TO A BORROWER:

Step 1. Calculate the percentage of appraised value by

Percentage of appraised value = Appraised value × Lender's percentage

Step 2. Find the potential amount of credit available by

Potential credit = Percentage of appraised value − First mortgage balance

✦ **EXHIBIT 14-3** ✦

Bank Loan Promotional Literature

Does It Make Sense To Consolidate My Debt With A Home Equity Loan?

Product	Current Monthly Debts					Home Equity Loan To Refinance All Current Debt	
	Installment Loan	Credit Card #1	Credit Card #2	=	Total Of Current Debts	Home Equity Loan	Interest & Tax Savings
Remaining Amount Owed	$8,000	$3,000	$5,000	=	$16,000	$16,000	
Annual Percentage Rate	12.00%	18.00%	16.00%			10.50%	
Monthly Payment	$178	$76	$122	=	$376	$344	
Total Interest To Pay Off	$2,677	$1,571	$2,295	=	$6,544	$4,634	$1,920
Deductible Interest*	$0	$0	$0	=	$0	$4,634	
Total Tax Savings Over Term Of Loan	$0	$0	$0	=	$0	$1,298	$1,298
						Total Savings By Consolidating Debt	$3,218

For demonstration purposes only. Individual circumstances may vary. Tax savings based on 28% tax bracket.

Can A Home Equity Loan Save Me Money When I Buy A New Car?

Product	New Car Loan (5-year term)	VS.	Home Equity To Purchase A Car (5-year term)
Amount Borrowed	$12,000		$12,000
Annual Percentage Rate	11.37%		10.50%
Monthly Payment	$263		$258
Total Interest Paid	$3,788		$3,476
Deductible Interest*	$0		$3,476
Total Tax Savings Over Term Of Loan	$0		$973
Interest Savings Over Term Of Loan			$312
Total Savings			$1,285

For demonstration purposes only. Individual circumstances may vary. Tax savings based on 28% tax bracket.

How Much Can I Save With A Home Equity Loan To Pay Off My Credit Cards?

Product	Credit Card Loan (5-year term)	VS.	Home Equity Loan To Pay Off Debt (5-year term)
Amount Borrowed	$5,000		$5,000
Annual Percentage Rate	18.50%		10.50%
Monthly Payment	$127		$107
Total Interest Paid	$2,618		$1,448
Deductible Interest*	$0		$1,448
Total Tax Savings Over Term Of Loan	$0		$405
Interest Savings Over Term Of Loan			$1,170
Total Savings			$1,575

For demonstration purposes only. Individual circumstances may vary. Tax savings based on 28% tax bracket.

Everybody's Business

Real-World Connection

This exhibit illustrates how banks promote home equity loans to consolidate debts, buy cars, and pay off credit cards.

Note how banks first entice people to use credit cards and then advertise home equity loans to pay them off when people "overcharge."

Keep in mind the responsibility involved with using credit. It should be used wisely! As with all financial transactions, be aware with whom you are dealing. Remember that bad credit stays on your record for 7 years.

EXAMPLE

Pat Kelley owns a house that was recently appraised for $115,700. The balance on her existing mortgage is $67,875. If her bank is willing to loan up to 75% of the appraised value, what is the potential amount of credit available to Pat on a home equity loan?

SOLUTION STRATEGY

Step 1. Percentage of appraised value = Appraised value × Lender's percentage

Percentage of appraised value = 115,700 × .75

Percentage of appraised value = $86,775

Step 2. Potential credit = Percentage of appraised value − First mortgage balance

Potential credit = 86,775 − 67,875

Potential credit = $\underline{\underline{\$18,900}}$

TRY-IT | EXERCISE

6. Craig Johnson owns a home that was recently appraised for $92,900. The balance on his existing first mortgage is $32,440. If his credit union is willing to loan up to 80% of the appraised value, what is the potential amount of credit available to Craig on a home equity line of credit?

Check your answer with the solution on page 515.

14-7 Calculating the Housing Expense Ratio and the Total Obligations Ratio of a Borrower

qualifying ratios
Ratios used by lenders to determine whether borrowers have the economic ability to repay loans.

housing expense ratio
The ratio of a borrower's monthly housing expense (PITI) to monthly gross income.

total obligations ratio
The ratio of a borrower's total monthly financial obligations to monthly gross income.

Mortgage lenders use ratios to determine whether borrowers have the economic ability to repay the loan. FHA, VA, and conventional lenders all use monthly gross income as the base for calculating these **qualifying ratios.** Two important ratios used for this purpose are the **housing expense ratio** and the **total obligations ratio.** These ratios are expressed as percents and are calculated by using the following formulas:

$$\text{Housing expense ratio} = \frac{\text{Monthly housing expense (PITI)}}{\text{Monthly gross income}}$$

$$\text{Total obligations ratio} = \frac{\text{Total monthly financial obligations}}{\text{Monthly gross income}}$$

The mortgage business uses widely accepted guidelines for these ratios that should not be exceeded. The ratio guidelines are as follows:

LENDING RATIO GUIDELINES

Mortgage Type	Housing Expense Ratio	Total Obligations Ratio
FHA	29%	41%
Conventional	28%	36%

Note that the ratio formulas are an application of the percentage formula; the ratio is the rate, the PITI or total obligations are the portion, and the monthly gross income is the base. With this in mind, we are able to solve for any of the variables.

EXAMPLE

Jennifer Bernhard earns a gross income of $2,490.00 per month. She has made application for a mortgage with a monthly PITI of $556.00. Jennifer has other financial obligations totaling $387.50 per month.

a. What is Jennifer's housing expense ratio?

b. What is Jennifer's total obligations ratio?

c. According to the lending ratio guidelines above, what type of mortgage would she qualify for, if any?

SOLUTION STRATEGY

a. $$\text{Housing expense ratio} = \frac{\text{Monthly housing expense (PITI)}}{\text{Monthly gross income}}$$

$$\text{Housing expense ratio} = \frac{556}{2{,}490}$$

$$\text{Housing expense ratio} = .2232 = \underline{\underline{22.3\%}}$$

b. $$\text{Total obligations ratio} = \frac{\text{Total monthly financial obligations}}{\text{Monthly gross income}}$$

$$\text{Total obligations ratio} = \frac{556 + 387.50}{2{,}490} = \frac{943.50}{2{,}490}$$

$$\text{Total obligations ratio} = .3789 = \underline{\underline{37.9\%}}$$

c. According to the lending ratio guidelines, Jennifer would qualify for an FHA mortgage but not a conventional mortgage; her total obligations ratio is 37.9%, which is above the limit for conventional mortgages.

TRY-IT | EXERCISE

7. Bob Lynch earns a gross income of $3,100.00 per month. He has made application for a mortgage with a monthly PITI of $669.00. Bob has other financial obligations totaling $375.00 per month.

a. What is Bob's housing expense ratio?

b. What is Bob's total obligations ratio?

c. According to the ratio guidelines, what type of mortgage would he qualify for, if any?

Check your answers with the solutions on page 516.

REVIEW EXERCISES | CHAPTER 14—SECTION II

For the following second mortgage applications, calculate the percentage of appraised value and the potential credit:

	Appraised Value	Lender's Percentage	Percentage of Appraised Value	Balance of First Mortgage	Potential Credit
1.	$118,700	75%	________	$67,900	________
2.	$89,400	65%	________	$37,800	________
3.	$141,200	80%	________	$99,100	________
4.	$324,600	75%	________	$197,500	________
5.	$98,000	65%	________	$66,000	________

For the following mortgage applications, calculate the housing expense ratio and the total obligations ratio:

	Applicant	Monthly Gross Income	Monthly (PITI) Expense	Other Monthly Financial Obligations	Housing Expense Ratio (%)	Total Obligations Ratio (%)
6.	Johnson	$2,000	$455	$380	______	______
7.	Wilson	$3,700	$530	$360	______	______
8.	Turnberry	$3,100	$705	$720	______	______
9.	Gomez	$4,800	$1,250	$430	______	______
10.	Black	$2,900	$644	$290	______	______

11. From the lending ratio guidelines on page 508,

a. Which of the applicants in Questions 6–10 would *not* qualify for a conventional mortgage?

b. Which of the applicants in Questions 6–10 would *not* qualify for any mortgage?

12. The Hamptons own a home that was recently appraised for $219,000. The balance on their existing first mortgage is $143,250. If their bank is willing to loan up to 65% of the appraised value, what is the potential amount of credit available to the Hamptons on a home equity loan?

1

13. Roxanne Pierce is thinking about building an addition on her home. The house was recently appraised at $154,000, and the balance on her existing first mortgage is $88,600. If Roxanne's bank is willing to loan 70% of the appraised value, does she have enough equity in the house to finance a $25,000 addition?

BUSINESS DECISION

Qualifying the Borrower

3

14. You are a mortgage loan officer at The Gold Mine Bank. One of your customers, Butch Porter, has submitted an application for a mortgage with a monthly PITI of $1,259.00. His other financial obligations total $654.50 per month. Butch earns a gross income of $4,890.00 per month.

a. What is his housing expense ratio?

b. What is his total obligations ratio?

c. According to the lending ratio guidelines on page 508, for what type of mortgage would Butch qualify, if any?

d. If Butch decided to get a part time job so that he could qualify for a conventional mortgage, how much additional monthly income would he need?

CHAPTER FORMULAS

Monthly payment = Number of \$1,000s financed × Table 14-1 factor

Total interest = (Monthly payment × Number of payments) − Amount financed

$$\text{Monthly taxes and insurance (TI)} = \frac{\text{Estimated property tax} + \text{Hazard insurance}}{12}$$

Monthly PITI = Monthly PI + Monthly TI

ARM-Calculated interest rate = Index rate + Lender's margin

ARM-Maximum rate per adjustment period = Previous rate + Periodic cap

ARM-Maximum overall rate = Initial rate + Overall cap

Percentage of appraised value = Appraised value × Lender's percentage

Second mortgage potential credit = Percentage of appraised value − First mtg. balance

$$\text{Housing expense ratio} = \frac{\text{Monthly housing expense (PITI)}}{\text{Monthly gross income}}$$

$$\text{Total obligations ratio} = \frac{\text{Total monthly financial obligations}}{\text{Monthly gross income}}$$

✦ SUMMARY CHART ✦

SECTION I: Mortgages—Fixed-Rate and Adjustable-Rate

Topic	P/O, Page	Important Concepts	Illustrative Examples
Calculating the Monthly Payment and Total Interest Paid on a Fixed-Rate Mortgage	14-1 493	1. Find the number of \$1,000s financed by $\text{Number of \$1,000s} = \frac{\text{Amount financed}}{1,000}$ 2. From Table 14-1, locate the table factor, monthly payment per \$1,000 financed, at the intersection of the number of years column and the interest rate row. 3. Calculate the monthly payment by **Monthly payment = Number of 1,000s financed × Table factor** 4. Find the total interest of the loan by $\text{Total interest} = \left(\text{Monthly payments} \times \text{Number of payments}\right) - \text{Amount financed}$	What is the monthly payment and total interest on a \$100,000 mortgage at $9\frac{1}{2}\%$ for 30 years? $\text{Number of 1,000s} = \frac{100,000}{1,000} = 100$ Table factor: $9\frac{1}{2}\%$, 30 years = 8.41 Monthly payment = 100 × 8.41 = <u>\$841.00</u> Total interest of the loan = (841 × 360) − 100,000 = 302,760 − 100,000 = <u>\$202,760</u>

SECTION I: (continued)

<table>
<tr><th>Topic</th><th>P/O, Page</th><th>Important Concepts</th><th>Illustrative Examples</th></tr>
<tr><td>Preparing a Partial Amortization Schedule of a Mortgage</td><td>14-2
495</td><td>1. Calculate the monthly payment of the loan as before.
2. Calculate the amount of interest for the current month using $I = PRT$, where P is the current outstanding balance of the loan, R is the annual interest rate, and T is $\frac{1}{12}$.
3. Find the portion of the payment used to reduce principal by
$\text{Portion of payment reducing principal} = \text{Monthly payment} - \text{Interest}$
4. Calculate outstanding balance of the loan by
$\text{Outstanding balance} = \text{Previous balance} - \text{Portion of payment reducing principal}$
5. Repeat Steps 2, 3, and 4 for each succeeding month and enter the values on a schedule labeled appropriately.</td><td>Prepare an amortization schedule for the first month of a $70,000 mortgage at 9% for 20 years.
Using Table 14-1, we find the monthly payment of the mortgage to be <u>$630</u>.
Month 1:
Interest = Principal × Rate × Time
Interest = $70{,}000 \times .09 \times \frac{1}{12}$
Interest = <u>$525.00</u>
Portion of payment reducing principal 630.00 − 525.00 = <u>$105.00</u>
Outstanding balance after one payment = 70,000.00 − 105.00 = <u>$69,895.00</u>
An amortization schedule can now be prepared from these data.</td></tr>
<tr><td>Calculating the Monthly PITI of a Mortgage</td><td>14-3
497</td><td>In reality, mortgage payments include four elements: principal, interest, taxes, and insurance, thus the abbreviation PITI.
Monthly PITI of a mortgage:
1. Calculate the principal and interest portion (PI) of the payment as before, using Table 14-1.
2. Calculate the monthly tax and insurance portion (TI) by
$\text{Monthly TI} = \frac{\text{Estimated property tax} + \text{Hazard Insurance}}{12}$
3. Calculate the total monthly PITI by
$\text{Monthly PITI} = \text{Monthly PI} + \text{Monthly TI}$</td><td>Bridget Burghy purchased a home for $97,500 with a mortgage at $8\frac{1}{2}\%$ for 15 years. The property taxes are $1,950 per year, and the hazard insurance premium is $466. What is the monthly PITI payment of Bridget's loan?
Using a table factor of 9.85 from Table 14-1, we find the monthly PI for this $8\frac{1}{2}\%$, 15-year mortgage to be $960.38.
$\text{Monthly TI} = \frac{1{,}950 + 466}{12} = \frac{2{,}416}{12} = \$201.33$
Monthly PITI = PI + TI = 960.38 + 201.33 = <u>$1,161.71</u></td></tr>
</table>

SECTION I: (continued)

Topic	P/O, Page	Important Concepts	Illustrative Examples
Calculating the Amount Due at Closing	14-4 498	Closing costs are the expenses incurred in conjunction with the sale of real estate. Both buyer and seller are responsible for certain of these costs. The party responsible for paying a particular closing cost is often determined by local custom or by negotiation. Some closing costs are expressed as dollar amounts, whereas others are a percent of the amount financed or the amount of the purchase price. At closing, the buyer is responsible for the purchase price (mortgage + down payment) plus closing costs. The amount received by the seller after all expenses have been paid is known as the proceeds.	*Typical Closing Costs* *Buyer:* Attorney's fee, inspections, credit report, appraisal fee, hazard insurance premium, title exam and insurance premium, escrow fee, prepaid taxes and interest. *Seller:* Attorney's fee, broker's commission, survey expense, inspections, abstract of title, certificate of title, escrow fee, prepayment penalty–existing loan, documentary stamps.
Calculating the Interest Rate of an Adjustable-Rate Mortgage (ARM)	14-5 500	Use the following formulas to find the various components of an ARM: **Calculated interest rate = Index rate + Lender's margin** **Max rate per period = Previous rate + Periodic cap** **Maximum overall rate of ARM = Initial rate + Overall cap**	Wendy DiLeonardo bought a home with an adjustable-rate mortgage. The margin on the loan is 3.5%, and the rate cap is 8% over the life of the loan. If the current index rate is 3.6%, what is the calculated interest rate and the maximum overall rate of the loan? Calculated interest rate = 3.6% + 3.5% = <u>7.1%</u> Maximum overall rate = 7.1% + 8% = <u>15.1%</u>

SECTION II: Second Mortgages—Home Equity Loans and Lines of Credit

Topic	P/O, Page	Important Concepts	Illustrative Examples
Calculating the Potential Amount of Credit Available to a Borrower	14-6 506	Most lenders set the credit limit on a home equity loan or line by taking a percentage of the appraised value of the home and subtracting the balance owed on the existing first mortgage. In determining your actual credit limit, the lender also will consider your ability to repay by looking at your income, debts, and other financial obligations, as well as your credit history. *Potential amount of credit available to borrower:* 1. Calculate the percentage of appraised value by **Percentage of appraised value = Appraised value × Lender's percentage** 2. Find the potential amount of credit available by **Potential credit = Percentage of appraised value − First mortgage debt**	The Jacksons own a home that was recently appraised for $134,800. The balance on their existing first mortgage is $76,550. If their bank is willing to loan up to 70% of the appraised value, what is the potential amount of credit available to the Jacksons on a home equity loan? Percentage of appraised value = 134,800 × .70 = $94,360 Potential credit = 94,360 − 76,550 = <u>$17,810</u>

SECTION II: (continued)

Topic	P/O, Page	Important Concepts	Illustrative Examples
Calculating the Housing Expense Ratio and the Total Obligations Ratio of a Borrower	14-7 508	Mortgage lenders use ratios to determine if borrowers have the economic ability to repay the loan. Two important ratios used for this purpose are the housing expense ratio and the total obligations ratio. These ratios are expressed as percents and are calculated by using the following formulas: $\text{Housing expense ratio} = \dfrac{\text{Monthly housing expense (PITI)}}{\text{Monthly gross income}}$ $\text{Total obligations ratio} = \dfrac{\text{Total monthly financial obligations}}{\text{Monthly gross income}}$	Renee McKim earns a gross income of \$3,750.00 per month. She has made application for a mortgage with a monthly PITI of \$956.00. Renee has other financial obligations totaling \$447.00 per month. a. What is her housing expense ratio? b. What is her total obligations ratio? c. According to the ratio guidelines on page 508, for what type of mortgage would Renee qualify, if any? Housing exp. ratio = $\dfrac{956}{3,750} = \underline{\underline{25.5\%}}$ Tot. oblig. ratio = $\dfrac{1,403}{3,750} = \underline{\underline{37.4\%}}$ According to the ratio guidelines, Renee would qualify for an FHA mortgage but not a conventional mortgage; her total obligations ratio is 37.4%, which is above the limit for conventional mortgages.

TRY-IT EXERCISE | SOLUTIONS

1. $\text{Number of 1,000s financed} = \dfrac{\text{Amount financed}}{1,000}$

$\text{Number of 1,000s financed} = \dfrac{85,500}{1,000} = 85.5$

Table factor 7%, 25 years = 7.07

Monthly payment = Number of 1,000s financed × Table factor
Monthly payment = 85.5 × 7.07 = $\underline{\$604.49}$

Total interest = (Monthly payment × Number of payments) − Amount financed
Total interest = (604.49 × 300) − 85,500
Total interest = 181,347 − 85,500 = $\underline{\underline{\$95,847}}$

2. $\text{Number of 1,000s financed} = \dfrac{75,000}{1,000} = 75$

Table factor 9%, 15 years = 10.15
Monthly payment = 75 × 10.15 = 761.25

Month 1

$I = PRT = 75,000 \times .09 \times \dfrac{1}{12} = \$562.50$

Portion of payment reducing principal = 761.25 − 562.50 = \$198.75
Outstanding balance = 75,000 − 198.75 = \$74,801.25

Month 2

$I = PRT = 74{,}801.25 \times .09 \times \frac{1}{12} = \$561.01$

Portion of payment reducing principal = 761.25 − 561.01 = $200.24
Outstanding balance = 74,801.25 − 200.24 = $74,601.01

Month 3

$I = PRT = 74{,}601.01 \times .09 \times \frac{1}{12} = \$559.51$

Portion of payment reducing principal = 761.25 − 559.51 = $201.74
Outstanding balance = 74,601.01 − 201.74 = $74,399.27

Month 4

$I = PRT = 74{,}399.27 \times .09 \times \frac{1}{12} = \$557.99$

Portion of payment reducing principal = 761.25 − 557.99 = $203.26
Outstanding balance = 74,399.27 − 203.26 = $74,196.01

Armortization Schedule
$75,000, 9%, 15 years

Payment Number	Monthly Payment	Monthly Interest	Portion Used to Reduce Principal	Loan Balance
0				$75,000.00
1	$761.25	$562.50	$198.75	$74,801.25
2	$761.25	$561.01	$200.24	$74,601.01
3	$761.25	$559.51	$201.74	$74,399.27
4	$761.25	$557.99	$203.26	$74,196.01

3. Number of 1,000s $= \frac{125{,}600}{1{,}000} = 125.6$

Table factor $9\frac{1}{4}\%$, 20 years = 9.16

Monthly payment (PI) = 125.6 × 9.16 = $1,150.50

Monthly TI $= \frac{\text{Property Tax} + \text{Hazard insurance}}{12}$

Monthly TI $= \frac{3{,}250 + 765}{12} = \frac{4{,}015}{12} = \$334.58$

Monthly PITI = PI + TI = 1,150.50 + 334.58 = $1,485.08

4. a. Down payment = 120,000 × 20% = $24,000
Amount financed = 120,000 − 24,000 = $96,000

Closing Costs, Buyer:

Discount points (96,000 × 3%)	$2,880.00
Down payment (24,000 − 10,000)	$14,000.00
Application fee	$100.00
Condominium transfer fee	$190.00
Title insurance (96,000 × 3/4%)	$720.00
Hazard insurance	$420.00
Prepaid taxes	$310.00
Attorney's fees	$500.00
Due at closing:	$19,120.00

b. *Proceeds, Seller:*

Purchase price		$120,000.00
Less: Broker's commission		
$120{,}000 \times 5\frac{1}{2}\%$	$6,600.00	
Closing costs	$670.00	
Mortgage payoff	$65,000.00	
		− $72,270.00
Proceeds to seller:		$47,730.00

5. a. Calculated ARM rate = Index rate + Margin
Calculated ARM rate = 3.2 + 3.4 = 6.6%

b. Maximum overall rate = Calculated rate + Overall cap
Maximum overall rate = 6.6 + 7.0 = 13.6%

6. Percentage of appraised value = Appraised value × Lender's percentage
Percentage of appraised value = 92,900 × 80% = $74,320
Potential credit = Percentage of appraised value − First mtg. balance
Potential credit = 74,320 − 32,440 = $41,880.00

7. a. $$\text{Housing expense ratio} = \frac{\text{Monthly housing expense (PITI)}}{\text{Monthly gross income}}$$

$$\text{Housing expense ratio} = \frac{669}{3{,}100} = \underline{\underline{21.6\%}}$$

b. $$\text{Total obligations ratio} = \frac{\text{Total monthly financial obligations}}{\text{Monthly gross income}}$$

$$\text{Total obligations ratio} = \frac{669 + 375}{3{,}100} = \frac{1{,}044}{3{,}100} = \underline{\underline{33.7\%}}$$

c. According to guidelines, Bob would qualify for both <u>FHA and conventional mortgages.</u>

CHAPTER 14 | ASSESSMENT TEST

Name ____________________

Class ____________________

You are one of the branch managers of the Fuji Bank. Today, two loan applications were submitted to your office. Calculate the requested information for each loan:

	Amount Financed	Interest Rate (%)	Term of Loan	Number of $1,000s Financed	Table Factor	Monthly Payment	Total Interest
1.	$134,900	$7\frac{3}{4}$	25 years	______	______	______	______
2.	$79,500	$8\frac{1}{4}$	20 years	______	______	______	______

3. Jennifer Majors purchased a home with a $146,100 mortgage at $11\frac{1}{2}$% for 30 years. Calculate the monthly payment and prepare an amortization schedule for the first 3 months of Jennifer's loan.

Payment Number	Monthly Payment	Monthly Interest	Portion Used to Reduce Principal	Loan Balance
0				$146,100.00
1	______	______	______	______
2	______	______	______	______
3	______	______	______	______

Calculate the monthly principal and interest by using Table 14-1 and the monthly PITI for the following mortgages:

	Amount Financed	Interest Rate (%)	Term of Loan	Monthly PI	Annual Property Tax	Annual Insurance	Monthly PITI
4.	$54,200	9	25 years	______	$719	$459	______
5.	$132,100	$8\frac{3}{4}$	15 years	______	$2,275	$1,033	______

For the following second mortgage applications, calculate the percentage of appraised value and the potential credit:

	Appraised Value	Lender's Percentage	Percentage of Appraised Value	Amount of First Mortgage	Potential Credit
6.	$114,500	65	______	$77,900	______
7.	$51,500	80	______	$27,400	______
8.	$81,200	70	______	$36,000	______

For the following mortgage applications, calculate the housing expense ratio and the total expense ratio:

	Applicant	Monthly Gross Income	Monthly (PITI) Expense	Other Monthly Financial Obligations	Housing Expense Ratio (%)	Total Obligations Ratio (%)
9.	Morgan	$5,300	$1,288	$840	______	______
10.	Willow	$3,750	$952	$329	______	______

11. As a loan officer using the lending ratio guidelines on page 508, what type of mortgage can you offer Morgan and Willow, from Exercises 9 and 10?

Answers

1. ____________________

2. ____________________

3. ____________________

4. ____________________

5. ____________________

6. ____________________

7. ____________________

8. ____________________

9. ____________________

10. ____________________

11. ____________________

Name ____________________

Class ____________________

Answers

12. a. ____________________

b. ____________________

13. a. ____________________

b. ____________________

c. ____________________

d. ____________________

14. ____________________

12. Andrew Zorich bought a home with an adjustable-rate mortgage. The margin on the loan is 3.9%, and the rate cap is 6% over the life of the loan.

a. If the current index rate is 4.45%, what is the calculated interest rate of the ARM?

b. What is the maximum overall rate of Andrew's loan?

13. Royal Properties purchased a 24-unit apartment building for $650,000. After a 20% down payment, the balance was financed with a 20-year, $10\frac{1}{2}$% fixed-rate mortgage.

a. What is the amount of the monthly principal and interest portion of the loan?

b. Construct an amortization schedule for the first 2 months of Royal's mortgage:

Payment Number	Monthly Payment	Monthly Interest	Portion Used to Reduce Principal	Loan Balance
0				________
1	________	________	________	________
2	________	________	________	________

c. If the annual property taxes are $9,177 and the hazard insurance premium is $2,253 per year, what is the total monthly PITI of the loan?

d. If each apartment rents for $425 per month, how much income will Royal make per month after the PITI is paid on the building?

14. John Paulson purchased a ski lodge in Mountain Peak for $74,900. His bank is willing to finance 70% of the purchase price. As part of the mortgage closing costs, John had to pay $4\frac{1}{4}$ discount points. How much did this amount to?

15. A Burger King franchisee is looking for a 20-year mortgage, with 90% financing, to purchase a new location costing \$775,000. The Red River Bank is offering a $10\frac{1}{4}$% mortgage with $1\frac{1}{2}$ discount points; Sterling Savings and Loan is offering a 10% mortgage with 4 closing points. The franchisee is unsure which mortgage is a better deal and has asked for your help.

a. What is the total interest paid on each loan?

b. Taking into account the discount points, which lender is offering a better deal and by how much?

16. How much more total interest will be paid on a 30-year fixed-rate mortgage for \$100,000 at 11% compared with a 15-year mortgage at $9\frac{1}{2}$%?

17. The Waltons own a home that recently appraised for \$161,400. The balance on their existing first mortgage is \$115,200. If their bank is willing to loan up to 70% of the appraised value, what is the potential amount of credit available to the Waltons on a home equity line of credit?

Name ______________________

Class ______________________

Answers

15. a. ______________________

____

b. ______________________

16. ______________________

17. ______________________

Name ____________

Class ____________

Answers

18. a. ____________

b. ____________

c. ____________

d. ____________

19. a. ____________

18. Cheryl Kabb is purchasing a $134,000 home. The down payment is 20%, and the balance will be financed with a 20-year fixed-rate mortgage at $8\frac{3}{4}\%$ and 3 discount points. The annual property tax is $1,940, and the hazard insurance premium is $1,460. When Cheryl signed the original sales contract, she put down a deposit of $10,000, which will be credited to her down payment. In addition, at the time of closing she must pay the following expenses:

Appraisal fee	$165.00
Credit report	$75.00
Attorney's fees	$490.00
Roof inspection	$50.00
Mortgage insurance premium	1.2% of amount financed
Termite inspection	$88.00
Title search	$119.00
Documentary stamps	$\frac{1}{4}\%$ of amount financed

As Cheryl's real estate agent, she has asked you the following:

a. What is the total monthly PITI of the mortgage loan?

b. What is the total amount of interest that will be paid on the loan?

c. How much is due at the time of the closing?

d. If the sellers are responsible for the 6% broker's commission, $900 in closing costs, and the existing first mortgage with a balance of $45,000, what proceeds will be received on the sale of the property?

19. Chuck Wells earns a gross income of $5,355.00 per month. He has submitted an application for a fixed-rate mortgage with a monthly PITI of $1,492.00. Chuck has other financial obligations totaling $625.00 per month.

a. What is his housing expense ratio?

b. What is his total obligations ratio?

Name ____________

Class ____________

c. According to the lending ratio guidelines on page 508, for what type of mortgage would Chuck qualify, if any?

Answers

19. b. ____________

c. ____________

20. a. ____________

b. ____________

c. ____________

BUSINESS DECISION

What Size Mortgage Can You Qualify For?

20. You are applying for a conventional mortgage from the First National Bank. Your monthly gross income is $3,500, and the bank uses the 28% housing expense ratio guideline.

a. What is the highest PITI you can qualify for? *Hint:* Solve the housing expense ratio formula for PITI. (Remember, this is an application of the percentage formula, Portion = Rate × Base, where PITI is the portion, the expense ratio is the rate, and your monthly gross income is the base.)

b. Based on your answer from part **a,** if you are applying for a 30-year, 9% mortgage, and the taxes and insurance portion of PITI is $175 per month, use Table 14-1 to calculate what size mortgage you qualify for. *Hint:* Subtract TI from PITI. Divide the PI by the appropriate table factor to determine how many $1,000s you qualify to borrow.

c. Based on your answer from part **b,** if you are planning on a 20% down payment, what is the most expensive house you can afford? *Hint:* Use the percentage formula again. The purchase price of the house is the base, the amount financed is the portion, and the percent financed is the rate.

All the Math That's Fit to Learn

The Business Math Times

Volume XIV | Mortgages | One Dollar

Mortgage Shopping

COMPARE, NEGOTIATE

Home loans are available from several types of lenders, including savings and loan institutions, commercial banks, mortgage companies, and credit unions. You can also get a mortgage through a mortgage broker.

Mortgage brokers find a lender for you. A broker's access to several lenders can mean a wider selection of loan products and terms from which to choose. Brokers are usually paid a fee for their services that may be separate from and in addition to the lender's origination or other fees.

Whether it's a home purchase, a refinancing, or a home equity loan, mortgages are products, just as cars are, so the price and terms may be negotiable. You should compare all the costs involved in obtaining a mortgage. Shopping, comparing, and negotiating may save you thousands of dollars.

A LITTLE EXTRA SAVES A LOT!

The amount of interest paid and the length of the mortgage can be dramatically reduced by paying a "little extra" with each monthly payment.

The chart above and table below provide the dramatic evidence of the "time value of money" concept. They illustrate how much would be saved in time and money on a 30-year, 8% mortgage by paying an extra $100 or $200 per month.

30-Year, 8%, $100,000 Mortgage

Extra Payment	Interest Savings	Time Savings
$100	$62,456	9.8 years
$200	$88,259	14.25 years

"We don't need to ask questions; everything we need to know is on the computer."

"Quote . . . Unquote"

You are the C.E.O. of your life.
—*unknown*

Nowadays, people can be divided into three classes, the Haves, the Have-Nots, and the Have-Not-Paid-for-What-They-Haves.
—*Earl Wilson*

Extra Payment Scenarios: $100,000, 30-Year, 8% Mortgage

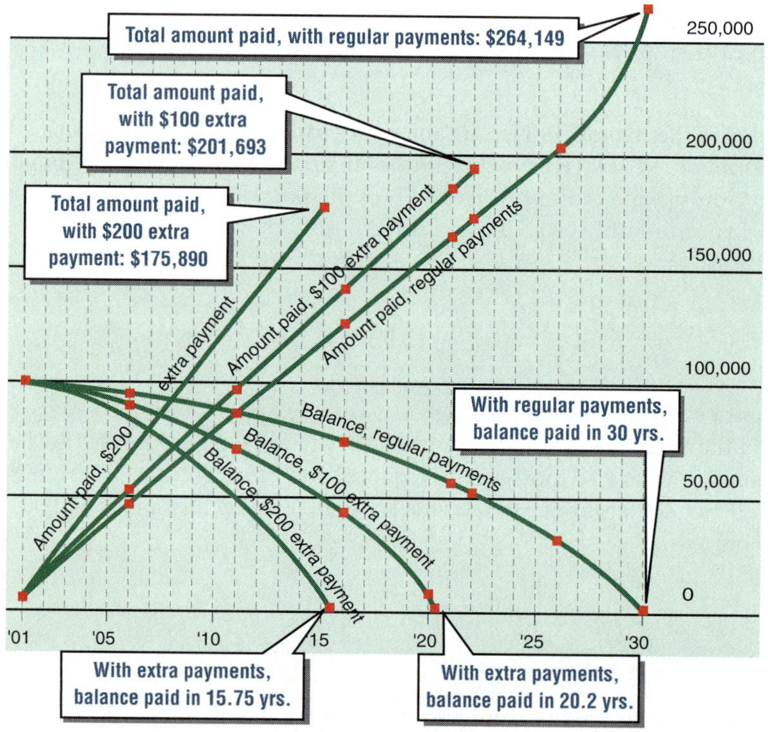

Brainteaser

BUY THE NUMBERS

You recently purchased a 100-unit apartment building. As part of a "fix-up" project you have decided to install new numbers on each front door.

If the apartments are numbered consecutively from 1 to 100, how many nines will you need to buy?

ANSWER TO LAST ISSUE'S BRAINTEASER

Turn any one switch to the on position for 5 minutes, then turn that switch off. Quickly turn any other switch to the on position and run up stairs.

Feel the two lights that are off. One of them will be hot because it was on for 5 minutes. Obviously, the "hot" bulb is controlled by the first switch you turned on. The light that is currently on is controlled by the switch you last turned on. The "cold" bulb that is off is controlled by the only switch left.

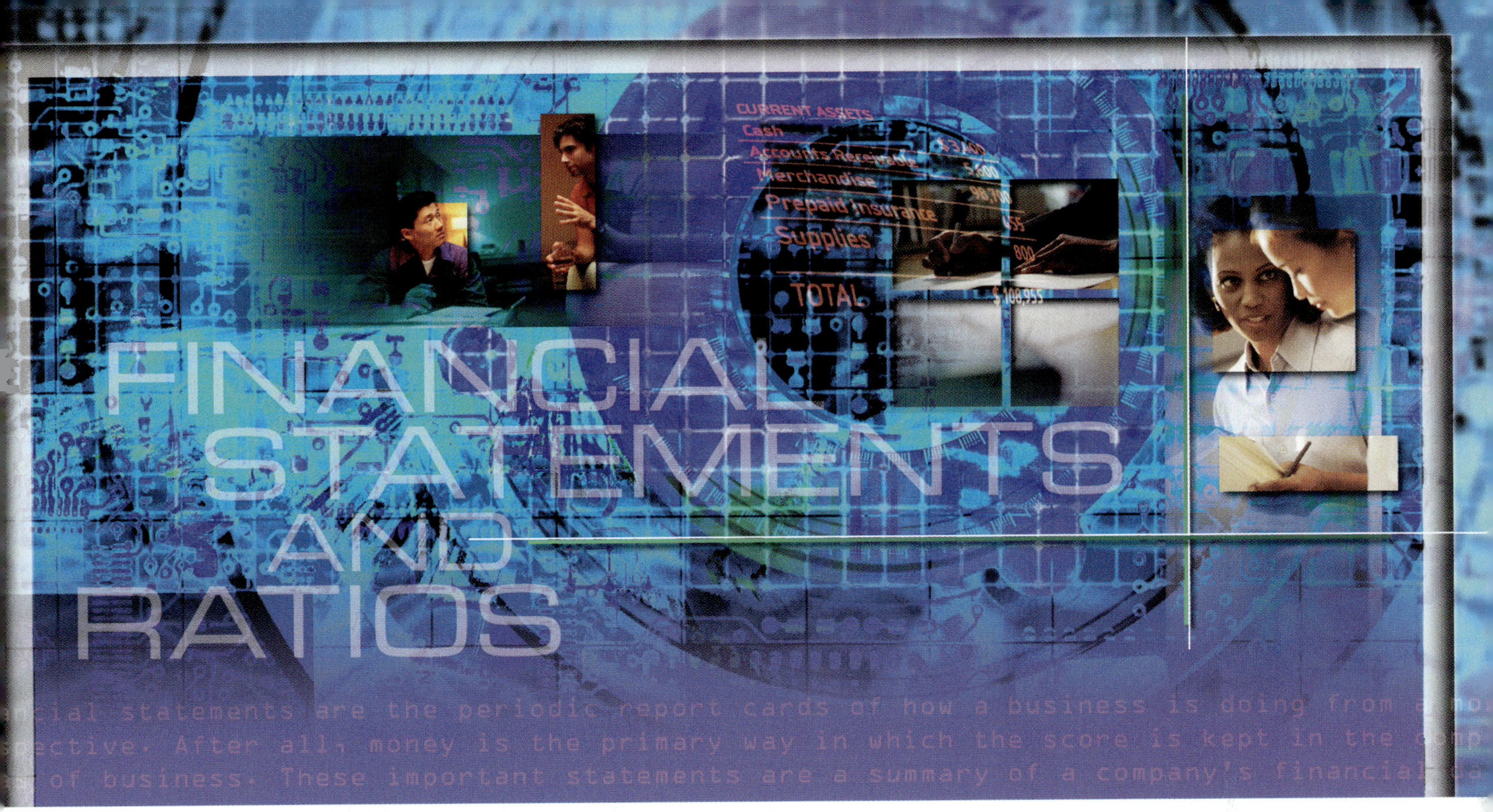

CHAPTER

15

Financial Statements and Ratios

PERFORMANCE OBJECTIVES

Section I The Balance Sheet

15-1 Preparing a balance sheet. (p. 525)
15-2 Preparing a vertical analysis of a balance sheet. (p. 529)
15-3 Preparing a horizontal analysis of a balance sheet. (p. 531)

Section II The Income Statement

15-4 Preparing an income statement. (p. 537)
15-5 Preparing a vertical analysis of an income statement. (p. 541)
15-6 Preparing a horizontal analysis of an income statement. (p. 542)

Section III Financial Ratios and Trend Analysis

15-7 Calculating financial ratios. (p. 547)
15-8 Preparing a trend analysis chart and graph of financial data. (p. 552)

financial statements
A series of accounting reports summarizing a company's financial data compiled from business activity over a period of time. The four most common are the balance sheet, the income statement, the owner's equity statement, and the cash flow statement.

Financial statements are the periodic report cards of how a business is doing from a monetary perspective. After all, money is the primary way in which the score is kept in the competitive arena of business. These important statements are a summary of a company's financial data compiled from business activity over a period of time.

The four major financial statements used in business today are the balance sheet, the income statement, the owner's equity statement, and the cash flow statement. Together, they tell a story about how a company has performed in the past and is likely to perform in the near future. In this chapter, we focus our attention on the preparation and analysis of the balance sheet and the income statement. The Business Decisions at the ends of the review exercises and the Assessment Test feature actual financial statements from recent annual reports of well-known companies representing various industries. They provide an opportunity to examine real-world statements and apply your own analytical skills.

Typically, a company's accounting department prepares financial statements quarterly for the purpose of management review and government reporting of income tax information. At the end of each year, the accounting department prepares annual financial statements to present the company's yearly financial position and performance. Public corporations, those whose stock can be bought and sold by the general investing public, are required by law to make their statements available to the stockholders and the financial community in the form of quarterly and annual reports. Because it is public information, condensed versions of these reports often appear in financial publications such as *The Wall Street Journal, Business Week, Forbes,* and *Fortune.*

financial analysis
The assessment of a company's past, present, and anticipated future financial condition based on the information found on the financial statements.

balance sheet
A financial statement illustrating the financial position of a company in terms of assets, liabilities, and owner's equity as of a certain date.

Financial analysis is the assessment of a company's past, present, and anticipated future financial condition based on the information found on the financial statements. Financial ratios are the primary tool of this analysis. These ratios are a way of standardizing financial data so that they may be compared with ratios from previous operating periods of the same firm or from other similar-size firms in the same industry.

Internally, owners and managers rely on this analysis to evaluate a company's financial strengths and weaknesses and to help make sound business decisions. From outside the firm, creditors and investors use financial statements and ratios to determine a company's creditworthiness or investment potential.

SECTION I

THE BALANCE SHEET

financial position
The economic resources owned by a company and the claims against those resources at a specific point in time.

creditor
One to whom money is owed.

liabilities
Debts or obligations of a business resulting from past transactions that require the company to pay money, provide goods, or perform services in the future.

owner's equity
The resources claimed by the owner against the assets of a business: Owner's equity = Assets − Liabilities. Also called proprietorship, capital, or net worth.

assets
Economic resources, such as cash, inventories, and land, buildings, and equipment owned by a business.

The **balance sheet** is the financial statement that lists a company's financial position on a certain date, usually at the end of a month, a quarter, or a year. To fully understand the balance sheet, we must first examine some basic accounting theory.

Financial position refers to the economic resources owned by a company and the claims against those resources at a specific point in time. *Equities* is another term for claims. Keep in mind that a firm's economic resources must always be equal to its equities. A business enterprise can therefore be pictured as an equation:

Economic resources = Equities

There are two types of equities: the rights of the **creditors** (those who are owed money by the business) and the rights of the owners. The rights of the creditors are known as **liabilities** and represent debts of the business. The rights of the owners are known as **owner's equity.** Owner's equity represents the resources invested in the business by the owners. Theoretically, owner's equity is what would be left over after all the liabilities were paid to the creditors. We can now enhance our equation:

Economic resources = Liabilities + Owner's equity

In accounting terminology, the economic resources owned by a business are known as the **assets.** Our equation now becomes

Assets = Liabilities + Owner's Equity

This all-important equation is known as the **accounting equation.** The balance sheet is a visual presentation of this equation at a point in time. Some balance sheets display the assets on the left and the liabilities and owner's equity on the right. Another popular format lists the assets on the top and the liabilities and owner's equity below. Remember, on a balance sheet the assets must always be equal to the liabilities plus owner's equity.

accounting equation
Algebraic expression of a company's financial position:
Assets = Liabilities + Owner's equity.

15-1 Preparing a Balance Sheet

Let's begin by looking at an example of a typical balance sheet and then examining each section and its components more closely. A balance sheet for a corporation, Hypothetical Enterprises, Inc., follows. Carefully look over the statement. Next, read the descriptions of the Balance Sheet Components, pages 526–527, and the Steps to Prepare a Balance Sheet, page 527. Then follow the Example and attempt the Try-It Exercise.

Hypothetical Enterprises, Inc.
Balance Sheet
December 31, 200X

Assets		
Current Assets		
Cash	$ 13,000	
Accounts Receivable	32,500	
Merchandise Inventory	50,600	
Prepaid Expenses	1,200	
Supplies	4,000	
Total Current Assets		$101,300
Property, Plant, and Equipment		
Land	40,000	
Buildings	125,000	
Machinery and Equipment	60,000	
Total Property, Plant, and Equipment		225,000
Investments and Other Assets		
Investments	10,000	
Intangible Assets	5,000	
Total Investments and Other Assets		15,000
Total Assets		$341,300
Liabilities and Owner's Equity		
Current Liabilities		
Accounts Payable	$ 17,500	
Salaries Payable	5,400	
Taxes Payable	6,500	
Total Current Liabilities		$29,400
Long-Term Liabilities		
Mortgage Payable	115,000	
Debenture Bond	20,000	
Total Long-Term Liabilities		135,000
Total Liabilities		164,400
Stockholder's Equity		
Capital Stock	126,900	
Retained Earnings	50,000	
Total Stockholder's Equity		176,900
Total Liabilities and Stockholder's Equity		$341,300

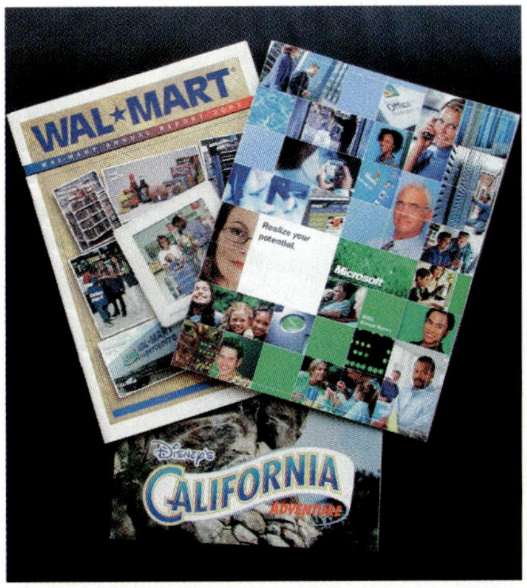

A company's annual report is like a report card of how the company is doing financially.

> **Everybody's Business**
> **Learning Tip**
> Don't be overwhelmed by the amount of new terminology associated with financial statements. Start by understanding the function and basic structure of each statement.
> Next, learn the purpose of each major category. This should help you determine in which category of the statement each component is listed.

Balance Sheet Components

Assets. The asset section of a balance sheet is divided into three components: Current Assets; Property, Plant, and Equipment; and Investments and Other Assets.

Current Assets Assets that are cash or will be sold, used, or converted to cash within 1 year. The following are typical examples of current assets:

- Cash—Cash on hand in the form of bills, coins, checking accounts, and savings accounts.
- Marketable securities—Investments in short-term securities that can be quickly converted to cash, such as stocks and bonds.
- Accounts receivable—Money owed by customers to the firm for goods and services sold on credit.
- Notes receivable—Money owed to the business involving promissory notes.
- Merchandise inventory—The cost of goods a business has on hand for resale to its customers.
- Prepaid expenses—Money paid in advance by the firm for benefits and services not yet received, such as prepaid insurance premiums or prepaid rent.
- Supplies—Cost of assets used in the day-to-day operation of the business. These might include office supplies such as paper, pencils, pens, and computer diskettes or maintenance supplies such as paper towels, soap, lubricants, light bulbs, and batteries.

Property, Plant, and Equipment Also known as fixed or long-term assets. These assets will be used by the firm in the operation of the business for a period of time longer than 1 year. Some examples follow:

- Land—The original purchase price of land owned by the company. Land is an asset that does not depreciate or lose its value over a period of time.
- Buildings—The cost of the buildings owned by the firm less the accumulated depreciation, or total loss in value, on those buildings since they were new. This is known as the book value of the buildings.
- Machinery and equipment—The book value or original cost less accumulated depreciation of all machinery, fixtures, vehicles, and equipment used in the operation of a business.

Investments and Other Assets This category lists the firm's investments and all other assets.

- Investments—These are investments made by the firm and held for periods longer than 1 year.
- Other assets—This catch-all category is for any assets not previously listed.
- Intangibles—Long-term assets that have no physical substance but have a value based on rights and privileges claimed by the owner. Some examples are copyrights, patents, royalties, and goodwill.

Liabilities. The liabilities section of the balance sheet lists the current and long-term liabilities incurred by the company.

Current Liabilities Debts and financial obligations of the company that are due to be paid within 1 year. Some examples follow:

- Accounts payable—Debts owed by the firm to creditors for goods and services purchased with less than 1 year credit. These might include 30-, 60-, or 90-day terms of sale extended by suppliers and vendors.

- Notes payable—Debts owed by the firm involving promissory notes. An example would be a short-term loan from a bank.
- Salaries payable—Compensation to employees that has been earned but not yet paid.
- Taxes payable—Taxes owed by the firm but not yet paid by the date of the statement.

Long-Term Liabilities Debts and financial obligations of the company that are due to be paid in 1 year or more or are to be paid out of noncurrent assets. Some examples follow:

- Mortgage payable—The total obligation a firm owes for the long-term financing of land and buildings.
- Debenture bonds—The total amount a firm owes on bonds at maturity to bondholders for money borrowed on the general credit of the company.

Equity. That portion of a balance sheet representing an owner's *net worth* or claim against the assets of the business. From the accounting equation, it is the difference between the total assets and the total liabilities.

Owner's Equity When a business is organized as a sole proprietorship or partnership, the equity section of the balance sheet is known as owner's equity. The ownership is labeled with the name of the owners or business and the word *capital.* Some examples follow:

- John Smith, capital
- Handy Hardware Store, capital.

Stockholder's Equity When the business is a corporation, the equity section of the balance sheet is known as stockholder's equity. The ownership is represented in two categories, capital stock and retained earnings.

- Capital stock—This represents money acquired by selling stock to investors who become stockholders. Capital stock is divided into preferred stock, which has preference over common stock regarding dividends, and common stock, representing the most basic rights to ownership of a corporation.
- Retained earnings—Profits from the operation of the business that have not been distributed to the stockholders in the form of dividends.

Pepper . . . and Salt

THE WALL STREET JOURNAL

"Feelings of self-worth are important, but never confuse them with *net* worth."

STEPS TO PREPARE A BALANCE SHEET:

Step 1. Centered at the top of the page, write the company name, type of statement, and date.

Step 2. In a section labeled ASSETS, list and total all the Current Assets; Property, Plant, and Equipment; and Investments and Other Assets.

Step 3. Add the three components of the Assets section to get Total Assets.

Step 4. Double underline Total Assets.

Step 5. In a section labeled LIABILITIES AND OWNER'S EQUITY, list and total all Current Liabilities and Long-Term Liabilities.

Step 6. Add the two components of the Liabilities section to get Total Liabilities.

Step 7. List and total the Owner's or Stockholder's Equity.

Step 8. Add the Total Liabilities and Owner's Equity.

Step 9. Double underline Total Liabilities and Owner's Equity.

Note: In accordance with the accounting equation, check to be sure that

Assets = Liabilities + Owner's Equity

EXAMPLE

Use the following financial information to prepare a balance sheet for Delta Plumbing Supply, Inc., as of June 30, 2002: cash, $3,400; accounts receivable, $5,600; merchandise inventory, $98,700; prepaid insurance, $455; supplies, $800; land and building, $147,000; fixtures, $8,600; delivery vehicles, $27,000; forklift, $7,000; goodwill, $10,000; accounts payable, $16,500; notes payable, $10,000; mortgage payable, $67,000; common stock, $185,055; and retained earnings, $30,000.

SOLUTION STRATEGY

The balance sheet for Delta Plumbing Supply, Inc., follows. Note that the assets are equal to the liabilities plus stockholder's equity.

Delta Plumbing Supply, Inc.
Balance Sheet
June 30, 2002

Assets		
Current Assets		
Cash	$ 3,400	
Accounts and Notes Receivable	5,600	
Merchandise Inventory	98,700	
Prepaid Insurance	455	
Supplies	800	
Total Current Assets		$108,955
Property, Plant, and Equipment		
Land and Building	$147,000	
Fixtures	8,600	
Delivery Vehicles	27,000	
Forklift	7,000	
Total Property, Plant, and Equipment		189,600
Investments and Other Assets		
Goodwill	10,000	
Total Investments and Other Assets		10,000
Total Assets		$308,555
Liabilities and Owner's Equity		
Current Liabilities		
Accounts Payable	$ 16,500	
Notes Payable	10,000	
Total Current Liabilities		$ 26,500
Long-Term Liabilities		
Mortgage Payable	67,000	
Total Long-Term Liabilities		67,000
Total Liabilities		93,500
Stockholder's Equity		
Common Stock	185,055	
Retained Earnings	30,000	
Total Stockholder's Equity		215,055
Total Liabilities and Stockholder's Equity		$308,555

Everybody's Business
Real-World Connection
The owners of a corporation are the stockholders; therefore, the *owner's equity* on the balance sheet of a corporation is called *stockholder's equity.*

TRY-IT | EXERCISE

1. Use the following financial information to prepare a balance sheet as of December 31, 2002, for Lee's Auto Repair, a sole proprietorship, owned by Lee Parker: cash, \$5,200; accounts receivable, \$2,800; merchandise inventory, \$2,700; prepaid salary, \$235; supplies, \$3,900; land, \$35,000; building, \$74,000; fixtures, \$1,200; tow truck, \$33,600; tools and equipment, \$45,000; accounts payable, \$6,800; notes payable, \$17,600; taxes payable, \$3,540; mortgage payable, \$51,000; Lee Parker, capital, \$124,695.

Check your balance sheet with the solution on page 564.

15-2 Preparing a Vertical Analysis of a Balance Sheet

Once the balance sheet has been prepared, a number of analytical procedures can be applied to the data to further evaluate a company's financial condition. One common method of analysis of a single financial statement is known as **vertical analysis.** In vertical analysis, each item on the balance sheet is expressed as a percent of total assets (total assets = 100%).

Once the vertical analysis has been completed, the figures show the relationship of each item on the balance sheet to total assets. For analysis purposes, these percents can then be compared with previous statements of the same company, with competitor's figures, or with published industry averages for similar-size companies.

A special form of balance sheet known as a common-size balance sheet is frequently used in financial analysis. **Common-size balance sheets** list only the vertical analysis percentages, not the dollar figures.

vertical analysis
A percentage method of analyzing financial statements whereby each item on the statement is expressed as a percent of a base amount. On balance sheet analysis, the base is total assets; on income statement analysis, the base is net sales.

common-size balance sheet
A special form of balance sheet that lists only the vertical analysis percentages, not the dollar figures. All items are expressed as a percent of total assets.

STEPS TO PREPARE A VERTICAL ANALYSIS OF A BALANCE SHEET:

Step 1. Use the percentage formula, Rate = Portion ÷ Base, to find the percentage of each item on the balance sheet. Use each individual item as the portion and total assets as the base.

Step 2. Round each answer to the nearest tenth percent. *Note:* A 0.1% differential may sometimes occur due to rounding.

Step 3. List the percent of each balance sheet item in a column to the right of the monetary amount.

EXAMPLE

Prepare a vertical analysis balance sheet for Hypothetical Enterprises, Inc., using the balance sheet found on page 525.

SOLUTION STRATEGY

Using the steps for vertical analysis, perform the following calculation for each balance sheet item and enter the results on the statement:

Everybody's Business
Learning Tip
In vertical analysis, remember that each individual item on the balance sheet is the *portion,* and Total Assets is the *base.*

Because of rounding, the percents may not always add up to exactly 100%. There may be a .1% differential.

$$\frac{\text{Cash}}{\text{Total assets}} = \frac{13{,}000}{341{,}300} = .038 = \underline{\underline{3.8\%}}$$

Hypothetical Enterprises, Inc.
Balance Sheet
December 31, 200X

Assets		
Current Assets		
Cash	$ 13,000	3.8
Accounts Receivable	32,500	9.5
Merchandise Inventory	50,600	14.8
Prepaid Expenses	1,200	0.4
Supplies	4,000	1.2
Total Current Assets	101,300	29.7
Property, Plant, and Equipment		
Land	40,000	11.7
Buildings	125,000	36.6
Machinery and Equipment	60,000	17.6
Total Property, Plant, and Equipment	225,000	65.9
Investments and Other Assets		
Investments	10,000	2.9
Intangible Assets	5,000	1.5
Total Investments and Other Assets	15,000	4.4
Total Assets	$341,300	100.0%

Liabilities and Owner's Equity		
Current Liabilities		
Accounts Payable	$ 17,500	5.1
Salaries Payable	5,400	1.6
Taxes Payable	6,500	1.9
Total Current Liabilities	29,400	8.6
Long-Term Liabilities		
Mortgage Payable	115,000	33.7
Debenture Bond	20,000	5.9
Total Long-Term Liabilities	135,000	39.6
Total Liabilities	164,400	48.2
Stockholder's Equity		
Capital Stock	126,900	37.2
Retained Earnings	50,000	14.6
Total Stockholder's Equity	176,900	51.8
Total Liabilities and Stockholder's Equity	$341,300	100.0%

TRY-IT | EXERCISE

2. Prepare a vertical analysis of the balance sheet for Delta Plumbing Supply, Inc., on page 528.

Check your statement with the solution on page 565.

15-3 Preparing a Horizontal Analysis of a Balance Sheet

Frequently, balance sheets are prepared with the data from the current year or operating period side-by-side with the figures from one or more previous periods. This type of presentation is known as a **comparative balance sheet** because the data from different periods can be readily compared. This information provides managers, creditors, and investors with important data concerning the progress of the company over a period of time, financial trends that may be developing, and the likelihood of future success.

Comparative balance sheets use horizontal analysis to measure the increases and decreases that have taken place in the financial data between two operating periods. In **horizontal analysis,** each item of the current period is compared in dollars and percent with the corresponding item from a previous period.

comparative balance sheet
Balance sheet prepared with the data from the current year or operating period side-by-side with the figures from one or more previous periods.

horizontal analysis
Method of analyzing financial statements whereby each item of the current period is compared in dollars and percent with the corresponding item from a previous period.

STEPS TO PREPARE A HORIZONTAL ANALYSIS OF A BALANCE SHEET:

Step 1. Set up a comparative balance sheet format with the current period listed first and the previous period listed next.

Step 2. Label the next two columns:

Increase/Decrease	
Amount	Percent

Step 3. For each item on the balance sheet, calculate the dollar difference between the current and previous period and enter this figure in the Amount column. Enter all decreases in parentheses.

Step 4. Calculate the percent change (increase or decrease) using the percentage formula:

$$\text{Percent change (rate)} = \frac{\text{Amount of change, Step 3 (portion)}}{\text{Previous period amount (base)}}$$

Step 5. Enter the percent change, rounded to the nearest tenth percent, in the Percent column. Once again, enter all decreases in parentheses.

EXAMPLE

Using the comparative balance sheet for the Albrecht Construction Company, as of December 31, 2002 and 2003, prepare a horizontal analysis of this balance sheet for Mr. Albrecht.

Albrecht Construction Company
Comparative Balance Sheet
December 31, 2002 and 2003

Assets	**2003**	**2002**
Current Assets		
Cash	$ 3,500	$ 2,900
Accounts Receivable	12,450	7,680
Supplies	2,140	3,200
Total Current Assets	$ 18,090	$ 13,780
Property, Plant, and Equipment		
Land	$ 15,000	$ 15,000
Buildings	54,000	61,000
Machinery and Equipment	134,200	123,400
Total Property, Plant, and Equipment	$203,200	$199,400
Total Assets	$221,290	$213,180

Liabilities and Owner's Equity	2003	2002
Current Liabilities		
Accounts Payable	$ 5,300	$ 4,100
Notes Payable	8,500	9,400
Total Current Liabilities	$ 13,800	$ 13,500
Long-Term Liabilities		
Mortgage Payable	$ 26,330	$ 28,500
Note Payable on Equipment (5-year)	10,250	11,430
Total Long-Term Liabilities	$ 36,580	$ 39,930
Total Liabilities	$ 50,380	$ 53,430
Owner's Equity		
Bob Albrecht, Capital	$170,910	$159,750
Total Liabilities and Owner's Equity	$221,290	$213,180

SOLUTION STRATEGY

Using the steps for horizontal analysis, perform the following operation on all balance sheet items and then enter the results on the statement.

Cash

$$2003 \text{ amount} - 2002 \text{ amount} = 3{,}500 - 2{,}900 = \$600 \text{ increase}$$

$$\text{Percent change} = \frac{\text{Amount of change}}{\text{Previous period amount}} = \frac{600}{2{,}900} = .20689 = 20.7\%$$

Albrecht Construction Company
Comparative Balance Sheet
December 31, 2002 and 2003

Assets	2003	2002	Increase/Decrease Amount	Increase/Decrease Percent
Current Assets				
Cash	$ 3,500	$ 2,900	$ 600	20.7
Accounts Receivable	12,450	7,680	4,770	62.1
Supplies	2,140	3,200	(1,060)	(33.1)
Total Current Assets	$ 18,090	$ 13,780	4,310	31.3
Property, Plant, and Equipment				
Land	$ 15,000	$ 15,000	0	0
Buildings	54,000	61,000	(7,000)	(11.5)
Machinery and Equipment	134,200	123,400	10,800	8.8
Total Property, Plant, and Equipment	$203,200	$199,400	3,800	1.9
Total Assets	$221,290	$213,180	$8,110	3.8
Liabilities and Owner's Equity				
Current Liabilities				
Accounts Payable	$ 5,300	$ 4,100	$ 1,200	29.3
Notes Payable	8,500	9,400	(900)	(9.6)
Total Current Liabilities	$ 13,800	$ 13,500	300	2.2
Long-Term Liabilities				
Mortgage Payable	$ 26,330	$ 28,500	(2,170)	(7.6)
Note Payable on Equipment (5-year)	10,250	11,430	(1,180)	(10.3)
Total Long-Term Liabilities	$ 36,580	$ 39,930	(3,350)	(8.4)
Total Liabilities	$ 50,380	$ 53,430	(3,050)	(5.7)
Owner's Equity				
Bob Albrecht, Capital	$170,910	$159,750	11,160	7.0
Total Liabilities and Owner's Equity	$221,290	$213,180	$8,110	3.8

TRY-IT | EXERCISE

3. Complete the following comparative balance sheet with horizontal analysis for Figueroa Industries, Inc.

Figueroa Industries, Inc.
Comparative Balance Sheet
December 31, 2002 and 2003

			Increase/Decrease	
Assets	**2003**	**2002**	**Amount**	**Percent**
Current Assets				
Cash	$ 8,700	$ 5,430		
Accounts Receivable	23,110	18,450		
Notes Receivable	2,900	3,400		
Supplies	4,540	3,980		
Total Current Assets				
Property, Plant, and Equipment				
Land	$34,000	$34,000		
Buildings	76,300	79,800		
Machinery and Equipment	54,700	48,900		
Total Property, Plant, and Equipment				
Investments and Other Assets	54,230	49,810		
Total Assets				
Liabilities and Owner's Equity				
Current Liabilities				
Accounts Payable	$15,330	$19,650		
Salaries Payable	7,680	7,190		
Total Current Liabilities				
Long-Term Liabilities				
Mortgage Payable	$53,010	$54,200		
Note Payable (3-year)	32,400	33,560		
Total Long-Term Liabilities				
Total Liabilities				
Stockholder's Equity				
Figueroa Industries, Common Stock				
Total Liabilities and Stockholder's Equity				

Check your statement with the solution on page 565–566.

REVIEW EXERCISES | CHAPTER 15—SECTION I

Calculate the following values according to the accounting equation:

	Assets	Liabilities	Owner's Equity
1.	$283,000	$121,400	
2.		$335,900	$213,000
3.	$45,300		$16,300

For the following balance sheet items, check the appropriate category:

	Current Asset	Fixed Asset	Current Liability	Long-Term Liability	Owner's Equity
4. Land	_____	_____	_____	_____	_____
5. Supplies	_____	_____	_____	_____	_____
6. Marketable securities	_____	_____	_____	_____	_____
7. Retained earnings	_____	_____	_____	_____	_____
8. Buildings	_____	_____	_____	_____	_____
9. Mortgage payable	_____	_____	_____	_____	_____
10. Cash	_____	_____	_____	_____	_____
11. Notes payable	_____	_____	_____	_____	_____
12. Equipment	_____	_____	_____	_____	_____
13. Note receivable (3-month)	_____	_____	_____	_____	_____
14. Prepaid expenses	_____	_____	_____	_____	_____
15. Merchandise inventory	_____	_____	_____	_____	_____
16. Common stock	_____	_____	_____	_____	_____
17. Trucks	_____	_____	_____	_____	_____
18. Debenture bonds	_____	_____	_____	_____	_____
19. Accounts receivable	_____	_____	_____	_____	_____
20. Salaries payable	_____	_____	_____	_____	_____
21. R. Smith, capital	_____	_____	_____	_____	_____
22. Savings account	_____	_____	_____	_____	_____
23. Preferred stock	_____	_____	_____	_____	_____
24. Note payable (2-year)	_____	_____	_____	_____	_____
25. Taxes payable	_____	_____	_____	_____	_____

Prepare the following statements on separate sheets of paper.

26. a. Use the following financial information to calculate the owner's equity and prepare a balance sheet with vertical analysis as of December 31, 2002, for Gary's Gifts, a sole proprietorship owned by Gary Robbins: current assets, $157,600; property, plant, and equipment, $42,000; investments and other assets, $35,700; current liabilities, $21,200; long-term liabilities, $53,400.

Gary's Gifts
Balance Sheet
December 31, 2002

b. The following financial information is for Gary's Gifts as of December 31, 2003: current assets, $175,300; property, plant, and equipment, $43,600; investments and other assets, $39,200; current liabilities, $27,700; long-term liabilities, $51,000.

Calculate the owner's equity for 2003 and prepare a comparative balance sheet with horizontal analysis for 2002 and 2003.

Gary's Gifts
Comparative Balance Sheet
December 31, 2002 and 2003

27. a. Use the following financial information to prepare a balance sheet with vertical analysis as of June 30, 2002, for Northern Industries, Inc.: cash, $44,300; accounts receivable, $127,600; merchandise inventory, $88,100; prepaid maintenance, $4,100; office supplies, $4,000; land, $154,000; building, $237,000; fixtures, $21,400; vehicles, $64,000; computers, $13,000; goodwill, $20,000; investments, $32,000; accounts payable, $55,700; salaries payable, $23,200; notes payable (6-month), $38,000; mortgage payable, $91,300; debenture bonds, $165,000; common stock, $350,000; and retained earnings, $86,300.

Northern Industries, Inc.
Balance Sheet
June 30, 2002

b. The following financial information is for Northern Industries as of June 30, 2003: cash, $40,200; accounts receivable, $131,400; merchandise inventory, $92,200; prepaid maintenance, $3,700; office supplies, $6,200; land, $154,000; building, $231,700; fixtures, $23,900; vehicles, $55,100; computers, $16,800; goodwill, $22,000; investments, $36,400; accounts payable, $51,800; salaries payable, $25,100; notes payable (6-month), $19,000; mortgage payable, $88,900; debenture bonds, $165,000; common stock, $350,000; and retained earnings, $113,800.

Prepare a comparative balance sheet with horizontal analysis for 2002 and 2003.

Northern Industries, Inc.
Comparative Balance Sheet
June 30, 2002 and 2003

BUSINESS DECISION

The Balance Sheet

28. From the consolidated balance sheets for Wal-Mart on page 536.

a. Prepare a horizontal analysis of the Current Assets section comparing 2000 and 2001.

b. Prepare a vertical analysis of the Current Liabilities section for 2001.

WAL★MART
Annual Report 2001

Consolidated Balance Sheets

(Amounts in millions) January 31,	2001	2000
Assets		
Current Assets:		
Cash and cash equivalents	$ 2,054	$ 1,856
Receivables	1,768	1,341
Inventories		
At replacement cost	21,644	20,171
Less LIFO reserve	202	378
Inventories at LIFO cost	21,442	19,793
Prepaid expenses and other	1,291	1,366
Total Current Assets	26,555	24,356
Property, Plant, and Equipment, at Cost:		
Land	9,433	8,785
Building and improvements	24,537	21,169
Fixtures and equipment	12,964	10,362
Transportation equipment	879	747
	47,813	41,063
Less accumulated depreciation	10,196	8,224
Net property, plant, and equipment	37,617	32,839
Property Under Capital Lease:		
Property under capital lease	4,620	4,285
Less accumulated amortization	1,303	1,155
Net property under capital leases	3,317	3,130
Other Assets and Deferred Charges:		
Net goodwill and other acquired intangible assets	9,059	9,392
Other assets and deferred charges	1,582	632
Total Assets	$ 78,130	$ 70,349
Liabilities and Shareholders' Equity		
Current Liabilities:		
Commercial paper	$ 2,286	$ 3,323
Accounts payable	15,092	13,105
Accrued liabilities	6,355	6,161
Accrued income taxes	841	1,129
Long-term debt due within one year	4,234	1,964
Obligations under capital leases due within one year	141	121
Total Current Liabilities	28,949	25,803
Long-Term Debt	12,501	13,672
Long-Term Obligations Under Capital Leases	3,154	3,002
Deferred Income Taxes and Other	1,043	759
Minority Interest	1,140	1,279
Shareholders' Equity:		
Preferred stock ($0.10 par value; 100 shares authorized, none issued)		
Common stock ($0.10 par value; 11,000 shares authorized, 4,470 and 4,457 issued and outstanding in 2001 and 2000, respectively)	447	446
Capital in excess of par value	1,411	714
Retained earnings	30,169	25,129
Other accumulated comprehensive income	(684)	(455)
Total Shareholders' Equity	31,343	25,834
Total Liabilities and Shareholders' Equity	$ 78,130	$ 70,349

SECTION II

THE INCOME STATEMENT

The Bottom Line

When it is all said and done, the question is "how well did the business do?" The real score is found on the income statement. An **income statement** is a summary of the operations of a business over a period of time—usually a month, a quarter, or a year. For any business to exist, it must have earnings and also expenses, either in the form of cash or credit. The income statement shows the **revenue** or earnings of the business from the sale of goods and services; the **expenses,** the costs incurred to generate that revenue; and the bottom line **profit** or **loss,** the difference between revenue and expenses.

For any operating period, when a company earns more than the expenses incurred there is a profit; when it incurs more expenses than it earns there is a loss. As with the balance sheet, a simple equation can be used to illustrate the structure of the statement.

income, operating, or profit and loss statement
Financial statement summarizing the operations of a business over a period of time. Illustrates the amount of revenue earned, expenses incurred, and the resulting profit or loss:
Revenue − Expenses = Profit (or loss).

$$\text{Profit (or Loss)} = \text{Revenue} - \text{Total Expenses}$$

where:

Revenue = Earnings (either cash or credit) from sales during the period
Total expenses = Cost of goods sold + Operating expenses + Taxes

revenue
The primary source of money, both cash and credit, flowing into the business from its customers for goods sold or services rendered over a period of time.

expenses
Costs incurred by a business in the process of earning revenue.

profit or loss
The difference between revenue earned and expenses incurred during an operating period. Profit when revenue is greater than expenses; loss when expenses are greater than revenue. Profit is also known as earnings or income.

15-4 Preparing an Income Statement

Once again, let's begin by looking at a typical income statement. As before, we shall use Hypothetical Enterprises, Inc., to illustrate. Carefully look over the following income statement and then read the descriptions of each section and its components.

As with the balance sheet, do not try to memorize the parts of the statement. Your understanding will increase very quickly with some practice. After you have reviewed the Steps for Preparing an Income Statement, carefully follow the Example and Solution Strategy, then work the Try-It Exercise.

Hypothetical Enterprises, Inc.
Income Statement
For the year ended December 31, 200X

Revenue		
Gross sales	$923,444	
Less: Sales Returns and Allowances	22,875	
Sales Discounts	3,625	
Net Sales		$896,944
Cost of Goods Sold		
Merchandise Inventory, Jan. 1	220,350	
Net Purchases	337,400	
Freight In	12,350	
Goods Available for Sale	570,100	
Less: Merchandise Inventory, Dec. 31	88,560	
Cost of Goods Sold		481,540
Gross Margin		415,404
Operating Expenses		
Salaries and Benefits	152,600	
Rent and Utilities	35,778	
Advertising and Promotion	32,871	
Insurance	8,258	
General and Administrative Expenses	41,340	
Depreciation	19,890	
Miscellaneous Expenses	14,790	
Total Operating Expenses		305,527
Income before Taxes		109,877
Income Tax		18,609
Net Income		$ 91,268

Everybody's Business
Learning Tip
Keep in mind that an income statement covers a "period" of time, whereas a balance sheet covers a "moment" in time.

Income Statement Components

Revenue. The revenue section of the income statement represents the primary source of money, both cash and credit, flowing into the business from its customers for goods sold or services rendered.

Gross sales
− Sales returns and allowances
− Sales discounts
Net sales

- Gross sales—Total sales of goods and services achieved by the company during the operating period.
- Sales returns and allowances—Amount of merchandise returned for cash or credit by customers for various reasons.
- Sales discounts—Cash discounts given to customers by the business as an incentive for early payment of an invoice. For example, 3/15, n/45, where there is a 3% extra discount if the invoice is paid within 15 days, rather than the net date, 45 days.
- Net sales—Amount received after taking into consideration returned goods, allowances, and sales discounts.

Cost of Goods Sold. The cost of goods sold section represents the cost to the business of the merchandise that was sold during the operating period.

Merchandise inventory (beginning)
+ Net purchases
+ Freight in
Goods available for sale
− Merchandise inventory (ending)
Cost of goods sold

- Merchandise inventory (beginning of operating period)—Total value of the goods in inventory at the beginning of the operating period. This *beginning inventory* is last period's ending inventory.
- Net purchases—Amount, at cost, of merchandise purchased during the period for resale to customers after deducting purchase returns and allowances and purchase discounts earned.
- Freight in—Total amount of the freight or transportation charges incurred for the net purchases.
- Goods available for sale—The total amount of the goods available to be sold during the operating period. It is the sum of beginning inventory, net purchases, and freight in.
- Merchandise inventory (end of operating period)—Total value of the goods remaining in inventory at the end of the operating period. This *ending inventory* is next period's beginning inventory.
- Cost of goods sold—Total value of the goods that were sold during the period. It is the difference between goods available for sale and the ending merchandise inventory.

Gross Margin. Gross margin, also known as gross profit, represents the difference between net sales and cost of goods sold.

Net sales
− Cost of goods sold
Gross margin

Total Operating Expenses. The sum of all the expenses incurred by the business during the operating period, except the cost of goods sold and taxes. Operating expenses differ from company to company. Some typical examples are salaries and benefits, sales commissions, rent and utilities, advertising and promotion, insurance, general and administrative expenses, depreciation, and miscellaneous expenses.

Everybody's Business

Real-World Connection

The phrase "all to the good" is derived from an old accounting term. The word *good* was used in the nineteenth century to mean *profit*. Thus, after expenses and so forth were taken out, the rest "went to the good!"

Income before Taxes. This figure represents the money a company made before paying income tax. It is the difference between gross margin and total operating expenses.

Gross margin
− Total operating expenses
Income before taxes

Income Tax. This expense figure is the amount of income tax, both state and federal, that is paid by the business during the operating period.

Net Income, Net Profit (or Net Loss). Literally the bottom line of the income statement. It is the difference between income before taxes and the income tax paid.

Income before taxes
− Income tax
Net income (loss)

STEPS TO PREPARE AN INCOME STATEMENT:

Step 1. Centered at the top of the page, write the company name, type of statement, and period of time covered by the statement (example "Year ended Dec. 31, 2002" or "April 2002").

Step 2. In a two-column format, as illustrated on page 541, calculate:

A. *Net Sales*, using

Gross sales
− Sales returns and allowances
− Sales discounts
Net sales

B. *Cost of Goods Sold,* using

Merchandise inventory (beginning)
+ Net purchases
+ Freight in
Goods available for sale
− Merchandise inventory (ending)
Cost of goods sold

C. *Gross Margin,* using

Net sales
− Cost of goods sold
Gross margin

D. *Total Operating Expenses*—Sum of all operating expenses

E. *Income before Taxes,* using

Gross margin
− Total operating expenses
Income before taxes

F. *Net Income,* using

Income before taxes
− Income tax
Net income (loss)

Everybody's Business

Real-World Connection

The popular business term *bottom line* literally comes from the structure of an income statement:

Total revenue
− Total expenses
Income (loss) ⟵ Bottom line

EXAMPLE

Use the following financial information to prepare an income statement for Delta Plumbing Supply, Inc., for the year ended December 31, 2002: gross sales, $458,400; sales returns and allowances, $13,200; sales discounts, $1,244; merchandise inventory, Jan. 1, 2002, $198,700; merchandise inventory, Dec. 31, 2002, $76,400; net purchases, $86,760; freight in, $875; salaries, $124,200; rent, $21,000; utilities, $1,780; advertising, $5,400; insurance, $2,340; administrative expenses, $14,500; miscellaneous expenses, $6,000; and income tax, $17,335.

SOLUTION STRATEGY

The income statement for Delta Plumbing Supply, Inc., follows.

Delta Plumbing Supply, Inc.
Income Statement
For the year ended December 31, 2002

Revenue		
Gross Sales	$458,400	
Less: Sales Returns and Allowances	13,200	
Sales Discounts	1,244	
Net Sales		$443,956
Cost of Goods Sold		
Merchandise Inventory, Jan. 1	198,700	
Net Purchases	86,760	
Freight In	875	
Goods Available for Sale	286,335	
Less: Merchandise Inventory, Dec. 31	76,400	
Cost of Goods Sold		209,935
Gross Margin		234,021
Operating Expenses		
Salaries	124,200	
Rent	21,000	
Utilities	1,780	
Advertising	5,400	
Insurance	2,340	
Administrative Expenses	14,500	
Miscellaneous Expenses	6,000	
Total Operating Expenses		175,220
Income before Taxes		58,801
Income Tax		17,335
Net Income		$ 41,466

TRY-IT | EXERCISE

4. Use the following financial information to prepare an income statement for Westminster Manufacturing, Inc., for the year ended December 31, 2003: gross sales, $1,356,000; sales returns and allowances, $93,100; sales discounts, $4,268; merchandise inventory, Jan. 1, 2003, $324,800; merchandise inventory, Dec. 31, 2003, $179,100; net purchases, $255,320; freight in, $3,911; salaries, $375,900; rent, $166,000; utilities, $7,730; advertising, $73,300; insurance, $22,940; administrative expenses, $84,500; miscellaneous expenses, $24,900; and income tax, $34,760.

Check your income statement with the solution on page 566.

15-5 Preparing a Vertical Analysis of an Income Statement

Vertical analysis can be applied to the income statement just as it was to the balance sheet. Each figure on the income statement is expressed as a percent of net sales (net sales = 100%). The resulting figures describe how net sales were distributed among the expenses and what percent was left as net profit. For analysis purposes, this information can then be compared with the figures from previous operating periods for the company, with competitor's figures, or with published industry averages for similar-size companies.

As with balance sheets, income statements with vertical analysis can be displayed in the format known as **common-size,** in which all figures on the statement appear as percentages.

common-size income statement
A special form of income statement that lists only the vertical analysis percentages, not the dollar figures. All items are expressed as a percent of net sales.

STEPS TO PREPARE A VERTICAL ANALYSIS OF AN INCOME STATEMENT:

Step 1. Use the percentage formula, Rate = Portion ÷ Base, to find the rate of each item on the income statement. Use each individual item as the portion and net sales as the base.

Step 2. Round each answer to the nearest tenth percent. *Note:* A 0.1% differential may sometimes occur due to rounding.

Step 3. List the percentage of each statement item in a column to the right of the monetary amount.

EXAMPLE

Prepare a vertical analysis income statement for Hypothetical Enterprises, Inc., on page 537.

SOLUTION STRATEGY

Using the steps for vertical analysis, perform the following calculation for each income statement item and enter the results on the income statement as follows.

$$\frac{\text{Gross sales}}{\text{Net sales}} = \frac{923{,}444}{896{,}944} = 1.0295 = \underline{\underline{103.0\%}}$$

Hypothetical Enterprises, Inc.
Income Statement
For the year ended December 31, 200X

Revenue		
Gross Sales	$923,444	103.0
Less: Sales Returns and Allowances	22,875	2.6
Sales Discounts	3,625	.4
Net Sales	896,944	100.0%
Cost of Goods Sold		
Merchandise Inventory, Jan. 1	220,350	24.6
Net Purchases	337,400	37.6
Freight In	12,350	1.4
Goods Available for Sale	570,100	63.6
Less: Merchandise Inventory, Dec. 31	88,560	9.9
Cost of Goods Sold	481,540	53.7
Gross Margin	415,404	46.3
Operating Expenses		
Salaries and Benefits	152,600	17.0
Rent and Utilities	35,778	4.0
Advertising and Promotion	32,871	3.7
Insurance	8,258	.9
General and Administrative Expenses	41,340	4.6
Depreciation	19,890	2.2
Miscellaneous Expenses	14,790	1.6
Total Operating Expenses	305,527	34.1
Income before Taxes	109,877	12.3
Income Tax	18,609	2.1
Net Income	$ 91,268	10.2%

TRY-IT | EXERCISE

5. Prepare a vertical analysis of the income statement for Delta Plumbing Supply, Inc., on page 540.

Check your statement with the solution on page 566.

15-6 Preparing a Horizontal Analysis of an Income Statement

As with the balance sheet, the income statement can be prepared in a format that compares the financial data of the business from one operating period to another. This horizontal analysis provides percent increase or decrease information for each item on the income statement. Information such as this provides a very useful progress report of the company. As before, the previous or original period figure is the base.

STEPS TO PREPARE A HORIZONTAL ANALYSIS OF AN INCOME STATEMENT:

Step 1. Set up a comparative income statement format with the current period listed first and the previous period listed next.

Step 2. Label the next two columns: **Increase/Decrease** — **Amount** | **Percent**

Step 3. For each item on the income statement, calculate the dollar difference between the current and previous period and enter this figure in the Amount column. Enter all decreases in parentheses.

Step 4. Calculate the percent change (increase or decrease) by the percentage formula:

$$\text{Percent change (rate)} = \frac{\text{Amount of change, Step 3 (portion)}}{\text{Previous period amount (base)}}$$

Step 5. Enter the percent change, rounded to the nearest tenth percent, in the Percent column. Once again, enter all decreases in parentheses.

EXAMPLE

A comparative income statement for Fisher Island Electronics, Inc., for the years 2001 and 2002, follows. Prepare a horizontal analysis of the statement for the company.

Fisher Island Electronics, Inc.
Comparative Income Statement
For the years ended December 31, 2001 and 2002

	2002	2001
Revenue		
Gross Sales	$623,247	$599,650
Less: Sales Returns and Allowances	8,550	9,470
Sales Discounts	3,400	1,233
Net Sales	611,297	588,947
Cost of Goods Sold		
Merchandise Inventory, Jan. 1	158,540	134,270
Purchases	117,290	111,208
Freight In	2,460	1,980
Goods Available for Sale	278,290	247,458
Less: Merchandise Inventory, Dec. 31	149,900	158,540
Cost of Goods Sold	128,390	88,918
Gross Margin	482,907	500,029

Operating Expenses		
Salaries and Benefits	165,300	161,200
Rent and Utilities	77,550	76,850
Depreciation	74,350	75,040
Insurance	4,560	3,900
Office Expenses	34,000	41,200
Warehouse Expenses	41,370	67,400
Total Operating Expenses	397,130	425,590
Income before Taxes	85,777	74,439
Income Tax	27,400	19,700
Net Income	$ 58,377	$ 54,739

SOLUTION STRATEGY

Using the steps for horizontal analysis, perform the following operation on all income statement items and then enter the results on the statement.

Gross Sales

2002 amount − 2001 amount = Amount of change

623,247 − 599,650 = $23,597 increase

$$\text{Percent change} = \frac{\text{Amount of change}}{\text{Previous period amount}} = \frac{23{,}597}{599{,}650} = 3.9\%$$

Fisher Island Electronics, Inc.
Comparative Income Statement
For the years ended December 31, 2001 and 2002

			Increase/Decrease	
	2002	**2001**	**Amount**	**Percent**
Revenue				
Gross Sales	$623,247	$599,650	23,597	3.9
Less: Sales Returns and Allowances	8,550	9,470	(920)	(9.7)
Sales Discounts	3,400	1,233	2,167	175.8
Net Sales	611,297	588,947	22,350	3.8
Cost of Goods Sold				
Merchandise Inventory, Jan. 1	158,540	134,270	24,270	18.1
Purchases	117,290	111,208	6,082	5.5
Freight In	2,460	1,980	480	24.2
Goods Available for Sale	278,290	247,458	30,832	12.5
Less: Merchandise Inventory, Dec. 31	149,900	158,540	(8,640)	(5.4)
Cost of Goods Sold	128,390	88,918	39,472	44.4
Gross Margin	482,907	500,029	(17,122)	(3.4)
Operating Expenses				
Salaries and Benefits	165,300	161,200	4,100	2.5
Rent and Utilities	77,550	76,850	700	.9
Depreciation	74,350	75,040	(690)	(.9)
Insurance	4,560	3,900	660	16.9
Office Expenses	34,000	41,200	(7,200)	(17.5)
Warehouse Expenses	41,370	67,400	(26,030)	(38.6)
Total Operating Expenses	397,130	425,590	(28,460)	(6.7)
Income before Taxes	85,777	74,439	11,338	15.2
Income Tax	27,400	19,700	7,700	39.1
Net Income	$ 58,377	$ 54,739	$ 3,638	6.6

TRY-IT | EXERCISE

6. Complete the following comparative income statement with horizontal analysis for Winkler's Grocery Store, Inc.

Winkler's Grocery Store, Inc.
Comparative Income Statement
For the years ended December 31, 2001 and 2002

			Increase/Decrease	
	2002	**2001**	**Amount**	**Percent**
Revenue				
Gross Sales	$1,223,000	$996,500	______	______
Less: Sales Returns and Allowances	121,340	99,600	______	______
Sales Discounts	63,120	51,237	______	______
Net Sales	______	______	______	______
Cost of Goods Sold				
Merchandise Inventory, Jan. 1	311,200	331,000	______	______
Purchases	603,290	271,128	______	______
Freight In	18,640	13,400	______	______
Goods Available for Sale	______	______	______	______
Less: Merchandise Inventory, Dec. 31	585,400	311,200	______	______
Cost of Goods Sold	______	______	______	______
Gross Margin	______	______	______	______
Operating Expenses				
Salaries and Benefits	215,200	121,800	______	______
Rent and Utilities	124,650	124,650	______	______
Depreciation	43,500	41,230	______	______
Insurance	24,970	23,800	______	______
Administrative Store Expenses	58,200	33,900	______	______
Warehouse Expenses	42,380	45,450	______	______
Total Operating Expenses	______	______	______	______
Income before Taxes	______	______	______	______
Income Tax	66,280	41,670	______	______
Net Income	______	______	______	______

Check your statement with the solution on page 567.

REVIEW EXERCISES | CHAPTER 15—SECTION II

Calculate the missing information based on the format of the income statement:

3

	Net Sales	Cost of Goods Sold	Gross Margin	Operating Expenses	Net Profit
1.	$334,500	$132,300	______	$108,000	______
2.	$1,640,000	______	$760,000	$354,780	______
3.	______	$257,000	$418,530	______	$84,370

4. For the third quarter of 2002, Carpet Boutique had gross sales of $315,450; sales returns and allowances of $23,100; and sales discounts of $18,700. What were the net sales?

5. For the month of August, Far East Imports, Inc., had the following financial information: merchandise inventory, August 1, $244,500; merchandise inventory, August 31, $193,440; gross purchases, $79,350; purchase returns and allowances, $8,700; and freight in, $970.

   a. What is the amount of the goods available for sale?

   b. What is the cost of goods sold for August?

   c. If net sales were $335,000, what was the gross margin for August?

   d. If total operating expenses were $167,200, what was the net profit?

Prepare the following statements on separate sheets of paper.

6. **a.** As the assistant accounting manager for Kwik-Mix Concrete, Inc., construct an income statement with vertical analysis for the first quarter of 2002 from the following information: gross sales, $240,000; sales discounts, $43,500; beginning inventory, Jan. 1, $86,400; ending inventory, March 31, $103,200; net purchases, $76,900; total operating expenses, $108,000; income tax, $14,550.

   Kwik-Mix Concrete, Inc.
   Income Statement
   January 1 to March 31, 2002

   b. You have just received a report with the second quarter figures. Prepare a comparative income statement with horizontal analysis for the first and second quarter of 2002: gross sales, $297,000; sales discounts, $41,300; beginning inventory, April 1, $103,200; ending inventory, June 30, $96,580; net purchases, $84,320; total operating expenses, $126,700; income tax, $16,400.

   Kwik-Mix Concrete, Inc.
   Comparative Income Statement
   First and Second Quarter, 2002

7. a. Use the following financial information to construct a 2002 income statement with vertical analysis for the Tasty Treats Food Wholesalers, Inc.: gross sales, $2,249,000; sales returns and allowances, $143,500; sales discounts, $54,290; merchandise inventory, Jan. 1, 2002, $875,330; merchandise inventory, Dec. 31, 2002, $716,090; net purchases, $546,920; freight in, $11,320; salaries, $319,800; rent, $213,100; depreciation, $51,200; utilities, $35,660; advertising, $249,600; insurance, $39,410; administrative expenses, $91,700; miscellaneous expenses, $107,500; and income tax, $38,450.

Tasty Treats Food Wholesalers, Inc.
Income Statement
2002

b. The following data represents Tasty Treats' operating results for 2003. Prepare a comparative income statement with horizontal analysis for 2002 and 2003: gross sales, $2,125,000; sales returns and allowances, $126,400; sales discounts, $73,380; merchandise inventory, Jan. 1, 2003, $716,090; merchandise inventory, Dec. 31, 2003, $584,550; net purchases, $482,620; freight in, $9,220; salaries, $340,900; rent, $215,000; depreciation, $56,300; utilities, $29,690; advertising, $217,300; insurance, $39,410; administrative expenses, $95,850; miscellaneous expenses, $102,500; and income tax, $44,530.

Tasty Treats Food Wholesalers, Inc.
Comparative Income Statement
2002 and 2003

BUSINESS DECISION

The Income Statement

8. From the following income statements for Microsoft Corporation,

a. Prepare a horizontal analysis of the operating income section comparing 2000 and 2001.

b. Prepare a vertical analysis of the operating expenses section for 2000.

Microsoft—2001 Annual Report

Income Statements

In Millions, Except Earnings per Share/Year Ended June 30	1999	2000	2001
Revenue	$19,747	$22,956	$25,296
Operating Expenses:			
Cost of Revenue	2,814	3,002	3,455
Research and Development	2,970	3,772	4,379
Sales and Marketing	3,238	4,126	4,885
General and Administrative	715	1,050	857
Total Operating Expenses	9,737	11,950	13,576
Operating Income	10,010	11,006	11,720
Losses on Equity Investees and Other	(70)	(57)	(159)
Investment Income/(loss)	1,951	3,326	(36)
Income before Income Taxes	11,891	14,275	11,525
Provision for Income Taxes	4,106	4,854	3,804
Income before Accounting Change	7,785	9,421	7,721
Cumulative Effect of Accounting Change (net of income taxes of $185)	—	—	(375)
Net Income	$ 7,785	$ 9,421	$ 7,346

SECTION III

FINANCIAL RATIOS AND TREND ANALYSIS

In addition to vertical and horizontal analysis of financial statements, managers, creditors, and investors also study comparisons among various components on the statements. These comparisons are expressed as ratios and are known as **financial ratios.**

financial ratios
A series of comparisons of financial statement components in ratio form used by analysts to evaluate the operating performance of a company.

Basically, financial ratios represent an effort by analysts to standardize financial information, which in turn makes comparisons more meaningful. The fundamental purpose of ratio analysis is to indicate areas requiring further investigation. Think of them as signals indicating areas of potential strength or weakness of the firm. Frequently, financial ratios have to be examined more closely to discover their true meaning. A high ratio, for example, might indicate that the numerator figure is too high or the denominator figure is too low.

Financial ratios fall into four major categories:

Liquidity ratios tell how well a company can pay off its short-term debts and meet unexpected needs for cash.

Efficiency ratios indicate how effectively a company uses its resources to generate sales.

Leverage ratios show how and to what degree a company has financed its assets.

Profitability ratios tell how much of each dollar of sales, assets, and stockholder's investment resulted in bottom-line net profit.

Everybody's Business
Real-World Connection
To be most meaningful, financial ratios should be compared with ratios from previous operating periods of the company and with industry statistics for similar-sized companies.

This information can be found in an annual publication called *Industry Norms and Ratios,* produced by Dun and Bradstreet, or *The Survey of Current Business,* published by the U. S. Department of Commerce.

15-7 Calculating Financial Ratios

As we learned in Chapter 5, a **ratio** is a comparison of one amount to another. A financial ratio is simply a ratio whose numerator and denominator are financial information taken from the balance sheet, income statement, or other important business data.

ratio
A comparison of one amount to another.

Ratios may be stated in a number of ways. For example, a ratio of credit sales, $40,000, to total sales, $100,000, in a retail store may be stated as

a. Credit sales ratio is $\frac{40,000}{100,000}$, or 4 to 10, or 2 to 5 (written 2:5).

b. Credit sales are $\frac{4}{10}$, or 40% of total sales.

c. For every $1.00 of sales, $.40 is on credit.

Managers analyze financial statement data to determine a business's strengths and weaknesses.

Conversely, the ratio of total sales, $100,000, to credit sales, $40,000, may be stated as

a. Total sales ratio is $\frac{100{,}000}{40{,}000}$, or 10 to 4, or 2.5 to 1 (written 2.5:1).

b. Total sales are $\frac{10}{4}$, or 250% of credit sales.

c. For every $2.50 of sales, $1.00 is on credit.

To illustrate how ratios are used in financial analysis, let's apply this analysis to Hypothetical Enterprises, Inc., a company introduced in Sections I and II of this chapter.

EXAMPLE

Calculate the financial ratios for Hypothetical Enterprises, Inc., using the data from the financial statements presented on pages 525 and 537.

SOLUTION STRATEGY

Liquidity Ratios

liquidity ratios Financial ratios that tell how well a company can pay off its short-term debts and meet unexpected needs for cash.

working capital The difference between current assets and current liabilities at a point in time. Theoretically, the amount of money left over if all the current liabilities were paid off by current assets.

current ratio, or working capital ratio The comparison of a firm's current assets to current liabilities.

Businesses must have enough cash on hand to pay their bills as they come due. The **liquidity ratios** examine the relationship between a firm's current assets and its maturing obligations. The amount of a firm's working capital and these ratios are good indicators of a firm's ability to pay its bills over the next few months. Short-term creditors pay particular attention to these figures.

The term **working capital** refers to the difference between current assets and current liabilities at a point in time. Theoretically, it is the amount of money that would be left over if all the current liabilities were paid off by current assets.

$$\text{Working capital} = \text{Current assets} - \text{Current liabilities}$$

Current ratio or working capital ratio is the comparison of a firm's current assets to current liabilities. This ratio indicates the amount of current assets available to pay off $1 of current debt. A current ratio of 2:1 or greater is considered by banks and other lending institutions to be an acceptable ratio.

$$\text{Current ratio} = \frac{\text{Current assets}}{\text{Current liabilities}}$$

Hypothetical Enterprises, Inc.:

$$\text{Working capital} = 101{,}300 - 29{,}400 = \underline{\underline{\$71{,}900}}$$

$$\text{Current ratio} = \frac{101{,}300}{29{,}400} = 3.45 = \underline{\underline{3.45:1}}$$

Analysis: This ratio shows that Hypothetical has $3.45 in current assets for each $1.00 it owes in current liabilities. A current ratio of 3.45:1 indicates that the company has more than sufficient means of covering short-term debt and is therefore in a strong liquidity position.

acid test, or quick ratio A ratio that indicates a firm's ability to quickly liquidate assets to pay off current debt.

Acid test or quick ratio indicates a firm's ability to quickly liquidate assets to pay off current debt. This ratio recognizes that a firm's inventories are one of the least liquid current assets. Merchandise inventories and prepaid expenses are not part of quick assets because they are not readily convertible to cash. An acid test ratio of 1:1 or greater is considered to be acceptable.

$$\text{Quick assets} = \text{Cash} + \text{Marketable securities} + \text{Receivables}$$

$$\text{Acid test ratio} = \frac{\text{Quick Assets}}{\text{Current liabilities}}$$

Hypothetical Enterprises, Inc. (*Note:* Hypothetical has no marketable securities):

$$\text{Quick assets} = 13{,}000 + 32{,}500 = \underline{\$45{,}500}$$

$$\text{Acid test ratio} = \frac{45{,}500}{29{,}400} = 1.55 = \underline{\underline{1.55{:}1}}$$

Analysis: An acid test ratio of 1.55:1 also indicates a strong liquidity position. It means that Hypothetical has the ability to meet all short-term debt obligations immediately if necessary.

Efficiency Ratios

Efficiency ratios provide the basis for determining how effectively the firm is using its resources to generate sales. A firm with $500,000 in assets producing $1,000,000 in sales is using its resources more efficiently than a firm producing the same sales with $2,000,000 invested in assets.

efficiency ratios
Financial ratios that indicate how effectively a company uses its resources to generate sales.

Average collection period indicates how quickly a firm's credit accounts are being collected and is a good measure of how efficiently a firm is managing its accounts receivable. *Note:* When credit sales figures are not available, net sales may be used instead.

average collection period
Indicator of how quickly a firm's credit accounts are being collected. Expressed in days.

$$\textbf{Average collection period} = \frac{\textbf{Accounts receivable} \times \textbf{365}}{\textbf{Credit sales}}$$

Hypothetical Enterprises, Inc.:

$$\text{Average collection period} = \frac{32{,}500 \times 365}{896{,}944} = \frac{1{,}186{,}250}{896{,}944} = 13.23 = \underline{\underline{13\text{ days}}}$$

Analysis: This ratio tells us that, on the average, Hypothetical's credit customers take 13 days to pay their bills. Because most industries average between 30 and 60 days, the firm's 13-day collection period is favorable and shows considerable efficiency in handling credit accounts.

Inventory turnover is the number of times during an operating period that the average inventory was sold.

inventory turnover
The number of times during an operating period that the average inventory was sold.

$$\textbf{Average inventory} = \frac{\textbf{Beginning inventory} + \textbf{Ending inventory}}{\textbf{2}}$$

$$\textbf{Inventory turnover} = \frac{\textbf{Cost of goods sold}}{\textbf{Average inventory}}$$

Hypothetical Enterprises, Inc.:

$$\text{Average inventory} = \frac{220{,}350 + 88{,}560}{2} = \underline{\$154{,}455}$$

$$\text{Inventory turnover} = \frac{481{,}540}{154{,}455} = 3.12 = \underline{\underline{3.1\text{ times}}}$$

Analysis: Inventory turnover is one ratio that should be compared with the data from previous operating periods and with published industry averages for similar-sized firms in the same industry to draw any meaningful conclusions. When inventory turnover is below average, it may be a signal that the company is carrying too much inventory. Carrying excess inventory can lead to extra expenses such as warehouse costs and insurance. It also ties up money that could be used more efficiently elsewhere.

asset turnover ratio
Ratio that tells the number of dollars in sales a firm generates from each dollar it has invested in assets.

Asset turnover ratio tells the number of dollars in sales the firm generates from each dollar it has invested in assets. This ratio is an important measure of a company's efficiency in managing its assets.

$$\textbf{Asset turnover ratio} = \frac{\textbf{Net sales}}{\textbf{Total assets}}$$

Hypothetical Enterprises, Inc.:

$$\text{Asset turnover ratio} = \frac{896{,}944}{341{,}300} = 2.63 = \underline{\underline{2.63:1}}$$

Analysis: Asset turnover is another ratio best compared with those of previous operating periods and industry averages to reach any meaningful conclusions. Hypothetical's 2.63:1 ratio means that the company is generating $2.63 in sales for every $1.00 in assets.

Leverage Ratios

leverage ratios
Financial ratios that show how and to what degree a company has financed its assets.

debt-to-assets ratio
Ratio that measures to what degree the assets of the firm have been financed with borrowed funds, or leveraged.

When firms borrow money to finance assets, they are using financial leverage. Investors and creditors alike are particularly interested in the **leverage ratios** because the greater the leverage a firm has used, the greater the risk of default on interest and principal payments. Such situations could lead the firm into eventual bankruptcy.

Debt-to-assets ratio measures to what degree the assets of the firm have been financed with borrowed funds, or leveraged. This ratio identifies the claim on assets by the creditors. It is commonly expressed as a percent.

$$\textbf{Debt-to-assets ratio} = \frac{\textbf{Total liabilities}}{\textbf{Total assets}}$$

Hypothetical Enterprises, Inc.:

$$\text{Debt-to-assets ratio} = \frac{164{,}400}{341{,}300} = .4817 = \underline{\underline{48.2\%}}$$

Analysis: This ratio indicates that Hypothetical's creditors have claim to 48.2% of the company, assets, or for each $1.00 of assets, the company owes $.48 to its creditors.

debt-to-equity ratio
A ratio that compares the total debt of a firm to the owner's equity.

Debt-to-equity ratio is used as a safety-factor measure for potential creditors. The ratio compares the total debt of the firm with the owner's equity. It tells the amount of debt incurred by the company for each $1.00 of equity. It is commonly expressed as a percent.

$$\textbf{Debt-to-equity ratio} = \frac{\textbf{Total liabilities}}{\textbf{Owner's equity}}$$

Hypothetical Enterprises, Inc.:

$$\text{Debt-to-equity ratio} = \frac{164{,}400}{176{,}900} = .929 = \underline{\underline{.93:1 \text{ or } 92.9\%}}$$

Analysis: This ratio indicates that for each $1.00 of owner's equity, Hypothetical has financed $.93 in assets. As the debt-to-equity ratio increases, so does the risk factor to potential creditors and investors. This ratio should be compared with previous periods and industry norms.

Profitability Ratios

The **profitability ratios** are important to anyone whose economic interests are tied to the long-range success of the firm. Investors expect a return on their investment in the form of dividends and stock price appreciation. Without adequate profits, firms quickly fall out of favor with current and future investors.

profitability ratios
Financial ratios that tell how much of each dollar of sales, assets, and owner's investment resulted in net profit.

Gross profit margin is an assessment of how well the cost of goods sold category of expenses was controlled. This measure particularly spotlights a firm's management of its purchasing and pricing functions. Gross profit margin is expressed as a percent of net sales.

gross profit margin
An assessment of how well the cost of goods sold category of expenses was controlled. Expressed as a percent of net sales.

$$\text{Gross profit margin} = \frac{\text{Gross profit}}{\text{Net sales}}$$

Hypothetical Enterprises, Inc.:

$$\text{Gross profit margin} = \frac{415{,}404}{896{,}944} = .463 = 46.3\%$$

Analysis: Hypothetical's gross profit constitutes 46.3% of the company's sales, which means that for each $1.00 of sales, $.46 remains as gross margin. For a meaningful analysis, this ratio should be compared with previous operating periods and industry averages.

Net profit margin is an assessment of management's overall ability to control the cost of goods sold and the operating expenses of the firm. This ratio is the bottom-line score of a firm's profitability and is one of the most important and most frequently used. Net profit margin can be calculated either before or after income tax. As with gross profit margin, it is expressed as a percent.

net profit margin
An assessment of management's overall ability to control the cost of goods sold and the operating expenses of a firm. Expressed as a percent of net sales.

$$\text{Net profit margin} = \frac{\text{Net income}}{\text{Net sales}}$$

Hypothetical Enterprises, Inc.:

$$\text{Net profit margin} = \frac{91{,}268}{896{,}944} = .1018 = 10.2\%$$

Analysis: This means that for each $1.00 of net sales, Hypothetical was able to generate $.10 in net profit. Most firms today have net profit margins between 1% and 8%, depending on the industry. Regardless of industry, Hypothetical's 10.2% net profit margin would be considered very profitable.

Return on investment is the amount of profit generated by the firm in relation to the amount invested by the owners. Abbreviated ROI, this ratio is commonly expressed as a percent.

return on investment
The amount of profit generated by a firm in relation to the amount invested by the owners. Expressed as a percent of owner's equity.

$$\text{Return on investment} = \frac{\text{Net income}}{\text{Owner's equity}}$$

Hypothetical Enterprises, Inc.:

$$\text{Return on investment} = \frac{91{,}268}{176{,}900} = .5159 = 51.6\%$$

Analysis: This ratio indicates that Hypothetical generated $.52 in net profit for each $1.00 invested by the owners. Most investors would consider 51.6% an excellent return on their money.

TRY-IT | EXERCISE

7. Use the balance sheet and income statement on pages 528 and 540 to calculate the financial ratios for Delta Plumbing Supply, Inc.

Check your answers with the solutions on pages 567–568.

15-8 Preparing a Trend Analysis Chart and Graph of Financial Data

In Sections I and II of this chapter, we used horizontal analysis to calculate and report the *amount* and *percent* change in various balance sheet and income statement items from one operating period to another. When these percentage changes are tracked for a number of successive periods, it is known as **trend analysis.** Trend analysis introduces the element of time into financial analysis. Whereas data from one statement gives a firm's financial position at a given point in time, trend analysis provides a dynamic picture of the firm by showing its financial direction over a period of time.

trend analysis
The use of index numbers to calculate percentage changes of a company's financial data for several successive operating periods.

index numbers
Numbers used in trend analysis indicating changes in magnitude of financial data over a period of time. Calculated by setting a base period equal to 100% and calculating other periods in relation to the base period.

Index numbers are used in trend analysis to show the percentage change in various financial statement items. With index numbers, a base year is chosen and is equal to 100%. All other years' figures are measured as a percentage of the base year. Once again, we encounter the now familiar percentage formula, Rate = Portion ÷ Base. The index number should be expressed as a percent, rounded to the nearest tenth.

$$\text{Index number (rate)} = \frac{\text{Yearly amount (portion)}}{\text{Base year amount (base)}}$$

For example, if a company had sales of \$50,000 in the base year and \$60,000 in the index year, the index number would be 1.2 or 120% (60,000 ÷ 50,000). The index number means the sales for the index year were 1.2 times or 120% of the base year.

STEPS FOR PREPARING A TREND ANALYSIS:

Step 1. Choose a base year and let it equal 100%.

Step 2. Calculate the index number for each succeeding year by using

$$\text{Index number} = \frac{\text{Yearly amount}}{\text{Base year amount}}$$

Step 3. Round each index number to the nearest tenth percent.

EXAMPLE

From the following data, prepare a 5-year trend analysis of net sales, net income, and total assets for Hypothetical Enterprises, Inc.

Hypothetical Enterprises, Inc.
5-Year Selected Financial Data

	2002	2001	2000	1999	1998
Net Sales	896,944	881,325	790,430	855,690	825,100
Net Income	91,268	95,550	56,400	75,350	70,100
Total Assets	341,300	320,100	315,600	314,200	303,550

SOLUTION STRATEGY

To prepare the trend analysis, we shall calculate the index number for each year by using the percentage formula and then enter the figures in a trend analysis table. The earliest year, 1998, will be the base year (100%). The first calculation, 1999 net sales index, is as follows:

$$1999 \text{ net sales index number} = \frac{855{,}690}{825{,}100} = 1.037 = \underline{\underline{103.7\%}}$$

Trend Analysis (in percentages)

	2002	2001	2000	1999	1998
Net Sales	108.7	106.8	95.8	103.7	100.0
Net Income	130.2	136.3	80.5	107.5	100.0
Total Assets	112.4	105.5	104.0	103.5	100.0

In addition to the table form of presentation, trend analysis frequently uses charts to visually present the financial data. Multiple-line charts are a particularly good way of presenting comparative data. For even more meaningful analysis, company data can be graphed on the same coordinates as industry averages.

The chart below illustrates Hypothetical's trend analysis figures in a multiple-line-chart format.

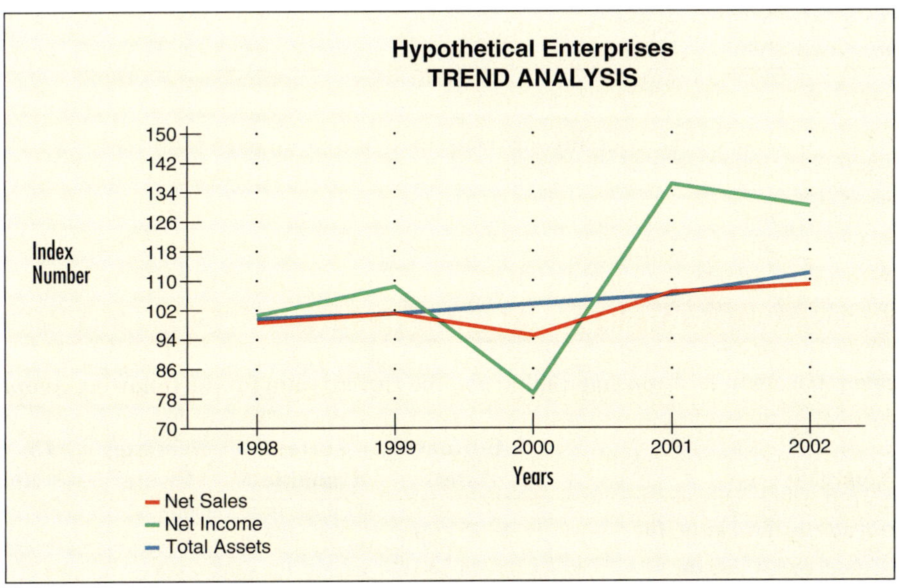

Everybody's Business

Real-World Connection

Tables illustrate specific data better than charts; however, charts are able to show "relationships" among data more clearly and visually.

Frequently in business presentations they are used together, with the chart used to clarify or reinforce facts presented in a table.

TRY-IT | EXERCISE

8. Prepare a trend analysis chart from the following financial data for the Scarborough Corporation and prepare a multiple-line graph of the net sales, total assets, and stockholder's equity.

Scarborough Corporation
5-Year Selected Financial Data

	2003	2002	2001	2000	1999
Net Sales	245,760	265,850	239,953	211,231	215,000
Total Assets	444,300	489,320	440,230	425,820	419,418
Stockholder's Equity	276,440	287,500	256,239	223,245	247,680

Scarborough Corporation
Trend Analysis Chart

	2003	2002	2001	2000	1999
Net Sales	_______	_______	_______	_______	_______
Total Assets	_______	_______	_______	_______	_______
Stockholder's Equity	_______	_______	_______	_______	_______

Check your answers with the solutions on page 568.

REVIEW EXERCISES | CHAPTER 15—SECTION III

Calculate the amount of working capital and the current ratio for the following companies:

	Company	Current Assets	Current Liabilities	Working Capital	Current Ratio
2	**1.** Roadway Trucking, Inc.	$125,490	$74,330	_______	_______
	2. Camera Corner, Inc.	14,540	19,700	_______	_______
	3. Royal Dry Cleaners	3,600	1,250	_______	_______
	4. Computer Warehouse, Inc.	1,224,500	845,430	_______	_______

Use the additional financial information below to calculate the quick assets and acid test ratio for the companies in Questions 1–4.

	Company	Cash	Marketable Securities	Accounts Receivable	Quick Assets	Acid Test Ratio
3	**5.** Roadway Trucking, Inc.	$12,320	$30,000	$53,600	_______	_______
	6. Camera Corner, Inc.	2,690	0	4,330	_______	_______
	7. Royal Dry Cleaners	1,180	0	985	_______	_______
	8. Computer Warehouse, Inc.	24,400	140,000	750,300	_______	_______

9. Calculate the average collection period for Roadway Trucking, Inc., from Exercise 5 if the credit sales for the year amounted to $445,000.

10. a. Calculate the average collection period for Computer Warehouse, Inc., from Exercise 8 if the credit sales for the year amounted to $8,550,000.

b. If the industry average for similar firms is 48 days, evaluate the company's ratio.

Calculate the average inventory and inventory turnover ratio for the following companies:

Company	Beginning Inventory	Ending Inventory	Average Inventory	Cost of Goods Sold	Inventory Turnover
11. The Bookworm	$121,400	$89,900		$659,000	
12. Eastern Wholesalers	856,430	944,380		3,437,500	
13. Alliance Corporation	90,125	58,770		487,640	
14. Walgreens Pharmacy	313,240	300,050		4,356,470	

15. Lakewood Enterprises had net sales of $1,354,600 last year. If the total assets of the company are $2,329,500, what is the asset turnover ratio?

Calculate the amount of owner's equity and the two leverage ratios for the following companies:

Company	Total Assets	Total Liabilities	Owner's Equity	Debt-to-Assets Ratio	Debt-to-Equity Ratio
16. Big Ben Clock Company	$232,430	$115,320			
17. Far East Furniture	512,900	357,510			
18. Magnum Industries	2,875,000	2,189,100			

Calculate the gross and net profits and the two profit margins for the following companies:

Company	Net Sales	Cost of Goods Sold	Gross Profit	Operating Expenses	Net Profit	Gross Profit Margin (%)	Net Profit Margin (%)
19. Ace Manufacturing	$743,500	$489,560		$175,410			
20. Europa Cafe	324,100	174,690		99,200			
21. Pet Supermarket	316,735	203,655		85,921			

Using the owner's equity information below, calculate the return on investment for the companies in Exercises 19–21:

	Owner's Equity	Return on Investment (%)
22. Ace Manufacturing	$434,210	______
23. Europa Cafe	615,400	______
24. Pet Supermarket	397,000	______

25. Prepare a trend analysis chart from the following financial data for the King Tire Company.

King Tire Company
5-year Selected Financial Data

	2002	2001	2000	1999	1998
Net Sales	$238,339	$282,283	$239,448	$215,430	$221,800
Net Income	68,770	71,125	55,010	57,680	55,343
Total Assets	513,220	502,126	491,100	457,050	467,720
Stockholder's Equity	254,769	289,560	256,070	227,390	240,600

King Tire Company
Trend Analysis Chart

	2002	2001	2000	1999	1998
Net Sales	______	______	______	______	______
Net Income	______	______	______	______	______
Total Assets	______	______	______	______	______
Stockholder's Equity	______	______	______	______	______

BUSINESS DECISION

Financial Ratios

26. Use the financial information for Dell on page 557 to answer **a** through **e**.

a. Calculate the asset turnover ratio for 2000 and 2001.

b. Calculate the net profit margin for 1999, 2000, and 2001.

Dell—Selected Financial Data

	Fiscal Year Ended				
	February 2, 2001 (a)	January 28, 2000 (b)	January 29, 1999	February 1, 1998	February 2, 1997
	(in millions, except per share data)				
Results of Operations Data:					
Net Revenue	$31,888	$25,265	$18,243	$12,327	$7,759
Gross Margin	6,443	5,218	4,106	2,722	1,666
Operating Income	2,663	2,263	2,046	1,316	714
Income before Extraordinary Loss	2,236	1,666	1,460	944	531
Income before Cumulative Effect of Change in Accounting Principle (c)	2,236	1,666	1,460	944	518
Net Income	$ 2,177	$ 1,666	$ 1,460	$ 944	$ 518
Earnings per Common Share (d):					
Before Cumulative Effect of Change in Accounting Principle					
Basic	$ 0.87	$ 0.66	$ 0.58	$ 0.36	$ 0.19
Diluted	$ 0.81	$ 0.61	$ 0.53	$ 0.32	$ 0.17
After Cumulative Effect of Change in Accounting Principle					
Basic	$ 0.84	$ 0.66	$ 0.58	$ 0.36	$ 0.19
Diluted	$ 0.79	$ 0.61	$ 0.53	$ 0.32	$ 0.17
Number of Weighted Average Shares Outstanding:					
Basic	2,582	2,536	2,531	2,631	2,838
Diluted	2,746	2,728	2,772	2,952	3,126
Balance Sheet Data:					
Working Capital	$ 2,948	$ 2,489	$ 2,112	$ 758	$ 891
Total Assets	13,435	11,471	6,877	4,268	2,993
Long-Term Debt	509	508	512	17	18
Total Stockholders' Equity	$ 5,622	$ 5,308	$ 2,321	$ 1,293	$ 806

c. Calculate the return on investment for 1999, 2000, and 2001.

d. Prepare a trend analysis chart of net sales and total assets for 1997 through 2001.

e. Extra credit: Prepare a trend analysis graph for the information in part d.

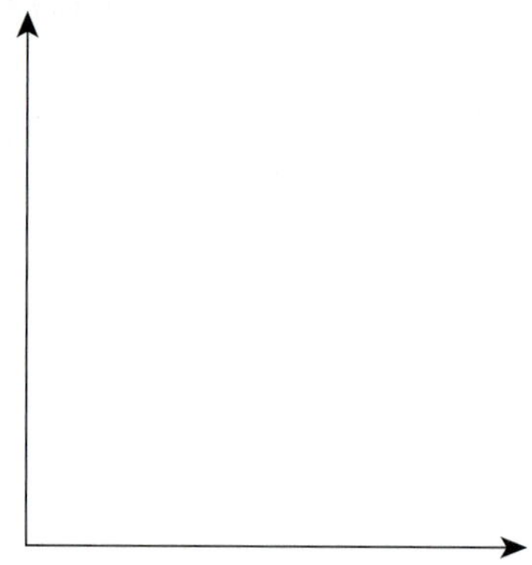

CHAPTER FORMULAS

Liquidity Ratios

$$\text{Working capital} = \text{Current assets} - \text{Current liabilities}$$

$$\text{Current ratio} = \frac{\text{Current assets}}{\text{Current liabilities}}$$

$$\text{Quick assets} = \text{Cash} + \text{Marketable securities} + \text{Receivables}$$

$$\text{Acid test ratio} = \frac{\text{Quick assets}}{\text{Current liabilities}}$$

Efficiency Ratios

$$\text{Average collection period} = \frac{\text{Accounts receivable} \times 365}{\text{Credit sales}}$$

$$\text{Average inventory} = \frac{\text{Beginning inventory} + \text{Ending inventory}}{2}$$

$$\text{Inventory turnover} = \frac{\text{Cost of goods sold}}{\text{Average inventory}}$$

$$\text{Asset turnover ratio} = \frac{\text{Net sales}}{\text{Total assets}}$$

Leverage Ratios

$$\text{Debt-to-assets ratio} = \frac{\text{Total liabilities}}{\text{Total assets}}$$

$$\text{Debt-to-equity ratio} = \frac{\text{Total liabilities}}{\text{Owner's equity}}$$

Profitability Ratios

$$\text{Gross profit margin} = \frac{\text{Gross profit}}{\text{Net sales}}$$

$$\text{Net profit margin} = \frac{\text{Net income}}{\text{Net sales}}$$

$$\text{Return on investment} = \frac{\text{Net income}}{\text{Owner's equity}}$$

✦ SUMMARY CHART ✦
SECTION I: The Balance Sheet

Topic	P/O, Page	Important Concepts	Illustrative Examples
Preparing a Balance Sheet	15-1 525	The balance sheet is a financial statement that shows a company's financial position on a certain date. It is based on the fundamental accounting equation: Assets = Liabilities + Owner's equity *Balance sheet preparation:* 1. *List and total:* Current assets + Property, plant, and equipment + Investments and other assets Total assets 2. *List and total:* Current liabilities + Long-term liabilities Total liabilities 3. *List and total:* Owner's equity 4. Add the Total liabilities and the Owner's equity. This total should equal the Total assets.	*Land'n'Sea Exporters* Balance Sheet December 31, 2002 Assets Cash $ 24,000 Receivables 92,000 Inventory 68,500 Supplies 12,100 Total current assets $196,600 Land and building $546,700 Fixtures & equip. 88,400 Vehicles 124,200 Total prop. & equip. $759,300 Total assets $955,900 Liabilities & Owner's Equity Accounts payable $ 82,400 Note payable (3-month) 31,300 Total current liab. $113,700 Mortgage payable $213,400 Note payable (2-year) 65,800 Total long-term liab. $279,200 Total liabilities $392,900 Owner's equity 563,000 Total liabilities & owner's equity $955,900
Preparing a Vertical Analysis of a Balance Sheet	15-2 529	In vertical analysis, each item on the balance sheet is expressed as a percent of total assets. *Vertical analysis preparation:* 1. Use the percentage formula, **Rate = Portion ÷ Base** Use each balance sheet item as the portion and total assets as the base. 2. Round each answer to the nearest tenth percent. *Note:* A 0.1% differential may occur due to rounding.	*Land'n'Sea Exporters* Balance Sheet—Asset Section Cash $ 24,000 2.5 Receivables 92,000 9.6 Inventory 68,500 7.2 Supplies 12,100 1.3 Current assets $196,600 20.6 Land & building $546,700 57.2 Fixtures & equip. 88,400 9.2 Vehicles 124,200 13.0 Prop. & equip. $759,300 79.4 Total assets $955,900 100.0

SECTION I: (continued)

Topic	P/O, Page	Important Concepts	Illustrative Examples
Preparing a Horizontal Analysis of a Comparative Balance Sheet	15-3 531	Comparative balance sheets display data from the current period side-by-side with the figures from one or more previous periods. In horizontal analysis, each item of the current period is compared in dollars and percent with the corresponding item from the previous period. *Horizontal analysis preparation:* 1. Set up a comparative balance sheet format with the current period listed first. 2. Label the next two columns: **Increase/Decrease** **Amount Percent** 3. For each item, calculate the dollar difference between the current and previous period and enter this figure in the amount column. Enter all decreases in parentheses. 4. Calculate the percent change using: $\text{Percent change (rate)} = \dfrac{\text{Amount of change (portion)}}{\text{Previous period amount (base)}}$ 5. Enter the percent change in the Percent column. Round to the nearest tenth percent. Enter all decreases in parentheses.	If the 2001 cash figure for Land'n'Sea Exporters was \$21,300, the comparative balance sheet horizontal analysis would be listed as follows: Cash Increase/Decrease 2002 | 2001 | Amount | Percent 24,000 | 21,300 | 2,700 | 12.7 $\dfrac{2,700}{21,300} = 12.7\%$ For a comprehensive example of a comparative balance sheet with horizontal analysis, see pages 531 and 532, Albrecht Construction Company.

SECTION II: The Income Statement

Topic	P/O, Page	Important Concepts	Illustrative Examples
Preparing an Income Statement	15-4 537	An income statement is a summary of the operations of a business over a period of time. It is based on the equation **Profit = Revenue − Total expenses** *Income Statement preparation:* 1. Label the top of the statement with the company name and period of time covered. 2. In a two-column format, calculate a. *Net Sales,* using **Gross sales** **− Sales returns & allow.** **− Sales discounts** **Net sales** b. *Cost of goods sold,* using **Beginning inventory** **+ Net purchases** **+ Freight in** **Goods available for sale** **− Ending inventory** **Cost of goods sold** c. *Gross margin,* using **Net sales** **− Cost of goods sold** **Gross margin**	*Land'n'Sea Exporters* Income Statement Year Ended December 31, 2002 (000) Gross sales \$435.3 Sales returns 11.1 Sales discounts 8.0 Net sales \$416.2 Inventory, Jan. 1 124.2 Net purchases 165.8 Freight in 2.7 Goods available 292.7 Inventory, Dec. 31. 118.1 Cost of goods sold 174.6 Gross margin 241.6

SECTION II: (continued)

Topic	P/O, Page	Important Concepts	Illustrative Examples
		d. *Net income,* using **Gross margin** **− Total operating expenses** **Net income**	Salaries 87.6 Rent & utilities 22.5 Other expenses 101.7 Total op. expenses 211.8 Net income $ 29.8
Preparing a Vertical Analysis of an Income Statement	15-5 541	In vertical analysis of an income statement, each figure is expressed as a percent of net sales. *Vertical analysis preparation:* 1. Use the percentage formula, **Rate = Portion ÷ Base** Use each income statement item as the portion and net sales as the base. 2. Round each answer to the nearest tenth percent. *Note:* A 0.1% differential may occur due to rounding.	*Land'n'Sea Exporters* Income Statement—2002 (000) Gross sales $435.3 104.6 Sales returns 11.1 2.7 Sales discounts 8.0 1.9 Net sales 416.2 100.0 Inventory, Jan. 1. 124.2 29.8 Net purchases 165.8 39.8 Freight in 2.7 .6 Goods available for sale 292.7 70.3 Inventory, Dec. 31. 118.1 28.4 Cost of goods sold 174.6 42.0 Gross margin 241.6 58.0 Salaries 87.6 21.0 Rent & utilities 22.5 5.4 Other expenses 101.7 24.4 Total op. expenses 211.8 50.9 Net income $ 29.8 7.2
Preparing a Horizontal Analysis of a Comparative Income Statement	15-6 542	In horizontal analysis of a comparative income statement, each item of the current period is compared in dollars and percent with the corresponding item from the previous period. *Horizontal analysis preparation:* 1. Set up a comparative income statement format with the current period listed first. 2. Label the next two columns: **Increase/Decrease** **Amount Percent** 3. For each item, calculate the dollar difference between the current and previous period and enter this figure in the amount column. Enter all decreases in parentheses. 4. Calculate the percent change by using $\text{Percent change (rate)} = \frac{\text{Amount of change (portion)}}{\text{Previous period amount (base)}}$ 5. Enter the percent change in the Percent column. Round to the nearest tenth percent. Enter all decreases in parentheses.	If the 2001 net income figure for Land'n'Sea Exporters was $23,100, the comparative income statement horizontal analysis would be listed as follows: Net Income **Increase/Decrease** **2002** **2001** **Amount** **Percent** 28,800 23,100 5,700 24.7 $\frac{5{,}700}{23{,}100} = 24.7\%$ For a comprehensive example of \a comparative income statement with horizontal analysis, see pages 542–543, Fisher Island Electronics, Inc.

SECTION III: Financial Ratios and Trend Analysis

Topic	P/O, Page	Important Concepts	Illustrative Examples
Calculating Financial Ratios	15-7 547	Financial ratios are standardized comparisons of various items from the balance sheet and the income statement. When compared with ratios of previous operating periods and industry averages, they can be used as signals to analysts of potential strengths or weaknesses of the firm.	A company had net sales of \$100,000 and net income of \$10,000. Express these data as a ratio. $\frac{100{,}000}{10{,}000} = 10$ 1. The ratio of sales to income is 10 to 1, written 10:1. 2. Net income is $\frac{1}{10}$ or 10% of net sales. 3. For every \$1.00 of net sales, the company generates \$.10 in net income.
Liquidity Ratios	15-7 548	Liquidity ratios examine the relationship between a firm's current assets and its maturing obligation. They are a good indicator of a firm's ability to pay its bills over the next few months. $\text{Current ratio} = \frac{\text{Current assets}}{\text{Current liabilities}}$ $\text{Acid test ratio} = \frac{\text{Cash} + \text{Marketable securities} + \text{Accounts receivable}}{\text{Current liabilities}}$	Land'n'Sea Exporters Financial Ratios 2002 Current ratio = $\frac{196{,}600}{113{,}700} = 1.73 = \underline{\underline{1.73:1}}$ Acid test ratio = $\frac{24{,}000 + 92{,}000}{113{,}700} = 1.02 = \underline{\underline{1.02:1}}$
Efficiency Ratios	15-7 549	Efficiency ratios provide the basis for determining how effectively a firm uses its resources to generate sales. $\text{Average collection period} = \frac{\text{Accounts receivable} \times 365}{\text{Credit sales}}$ $\text{Inventory turnover} = \frac{\text{Cost of goods sold}}{\frac{\text{Beg inventory} + \text{End inventory}}{2}}$ $\text{Asset turnover ratio} = \frac{\text{Net sales}}{\text{Total assets}}$	Credit sales for Land'n'Sea are 50% of net sales. Average collection period = $\frac{92{,}000 \times 365}{208{,}100} = \underline{\underline{161 \text{ days}}}$ Inventory turnover = $\frac{174{,}600}{\frac{124{,}200 + 118.1}{2}} = \underline{\underline{1.44 \text{ times}}}$ Asset turnover ratio = $\frac{416{,}200}{955{,}900} = .44 = \underline{\underline{.44:1}}$
Leverage Ratios	15-7 550	Leverage ratios provide information about the amount of money a company has borrowed to finance its assets. $\text{Debt-to-assets ratio} = \frac{\text{Total liabilities}}{\text{Total assets}}$ $\text{Debt-to-equity ratio} = \frac{\text{Total liabilities}}{\text{Owner's equity}}$	Debt-to-assets ratio = $\frac{392{,}900}{955{,}900} = .411 = \underline{\underline{41.1\%}}$ Debt-to-equity ratio = $\frac{392{,}900}{563{,}000} = .698 = \underline{\underline{69.8\%}}$

SECTION III: (continued)

Topic	P/O, Page	Important Concepts	Illustrative Examples
Profitability Ratios	15-7 551	Profitability ratios show a firm's ability to generate profits and provide its investors with a return on their investment. $\text{Gross profit margin} = \frac{\text{Gross profit}}{\text{Net sales}}$ $\text{Net profit margin} = \frac{\text{Net income}}{\text{Net sales}}$ $\text{Return on investment} = \frac{\text{Net income}}{\text{Owner's equity}}$	Gross profit margins = $\frac{241{,}600}{416{,}200} = .580 = \underline{\underline{58.0\%}}$ Net profit margin = $\frac{29{,}800}{416{,}200} = .072 = \underline{\underline{7.2\%}}$ Return on investment = $\frac{29{,}800}{563{,}000} = .053 = \underline{\underline{5.3\%}}$
Preparing Trend Analysis Charts and Graphs	15-8 552	Trend analysis is the process of tracking changes in financial statement items for three or more operating periods. Trend analysis figures can be displayed on a chart using index numbers or more visually as a line graph or bar chart. *Trend analysis chart preparation:* 1. Choose a base year (usually the earliest year) and let it equal 100%. 2. Calculate the index number for each succeeding year by using $\text{Index number (rate)} = \frac{\text{Yearly amount (portion)}}{\text{Base year amount (base)}}$ 3. Round each index number to the nearest tenth percent. 4. *Optional:* Graph the index numbers or the raw data on a line graph.	Prepare a trend analysis chart for Land'n'Sea Exporters' net sales data. Land'n'Sea Exporters Net Sales (000) **2002 2001 2000 1999 1998** 416.2 401.6 365.4 388.3 375.1 For this trend analysis, we shall use 1998 as the base year, 100%. Each succeeding year's index number is calculated by using the yearly amount as the portion and the 1998 amount as the base. For example, 1999 index number = $\frac{388.3}{375.1} = 103.5$ **2002 2001 2000 1999 1998** 111.0 107.1 97.4 103.5 100.0 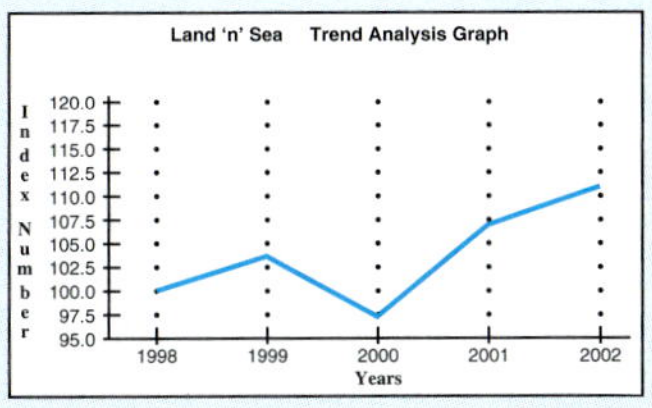

TRY-IT EXERCISE | SOLUTIONS

1.

Lee's Auto Repair
Balance Sheet
December 31, 2002

Assets		
Current Assets		
Cash	$ 5,200	
Accounts Receivable	2,800	
Merchandise Inventory	2,700	
Prepaid Salary	235	
Supplies	3,900	
Total Current Assets		$ 14,835
Property, Plant, and Equipment		
Land	35,000	
Building	74,000	
Fixtures	1,200	
Tow Truck	33,600	
Tools and Equipment	45,000	
Total Property, Plant, and Equipment		188,800
Total Assets		$203,635

Liabilities and Owner's Equity		
Current Liabilities		
Accounts Payable	$ 6,800	
Notes Payable	17,600	
Taxes Payable	3,540	
Total Current Liabilities		$ 27,940
Long-Term Liabilities		
Mortgage Payable	51,000	
Total Long-Term Liabilities		51,000
Owner's Equity		
Lee Parker, Capital	124,695	
Total Owner's Equity		124,695
Total Liabilities and Owner's Equity		$203,635

2.

Delta Plumbing Supply, Inc.
Balance Sheet
June 30, 2002

Assets		
Current Assets		
Cash	$ 3,400	1.1
Accounts and Notes Receivable	5,600	1.8
Merchandise Inventory	98,700	32.0
Prepaid Insurance	455	.1
Supplies	800	.3
Total Current Assets	108,955	35.3
Property, Plant, and Equipment		
Land and Building	147,000	47.6
Fixtures	8,600	2.8
Delivery Vehicles	27,000	8.8
Forklift	7,000	2.3
Total Property, Plant, and Equipment	189,600	61.4
Investments and Other Assets		
Goodwill	10,000	3.2
Total Investments and Other Assets	10,000	3.2
Total Assets	$308,555	100%
Liabilities and Owner's Equity		
Current Liabilities		
Accounts Payable	$ 16,500	5.3
Notes Payable	10,000	3.2
Total Current Liabilities	26,500	8.6
Long-Term Liabilities		
Mortgage Payable	67,000	21.7
Total Long-Term Liabilities	67,000	21.7
Total Liabilities	93,500	30.3
Stockholder's Equity		
Common Stock	185,055	60.0
Retained Earnings	30,000	9.7
Total Stockholder's Equity	215,055	69.7
Total Liabilities and Stockholder's Equity	$308,555	100%

3.

Figueroa Industries, Inc.
Comparative Balance Sheet
December 31, 2002 and 2003

			Increase/Decrease	
Assets	**2003**	**2002**	**Amount**	**Percent**
Current Assets				
Cash	$ 8,700	$ 5,430	$3,270	60.2
Accounts Receivable	23,110	18,450	4,660	25.3
Notes Receivable	2,900	3,400	(500)	(14.7)
Supplies	4,540	3,980	560	14.1
Total Current Assets	39,250	31,260	7,990	25.6
Property, Plant, and Equipment				
Land	$ 34,000	$ 34,000	0	0
Buildings	76,300	79,800	(3,500)	(4.4)
Machinery and Equipment	54,700	48,900	5,800	11.9
Total Prop., Plant, and Equip.	165,000	162,700	2,300	1.4
Investments and Other Assets	54,230	49,810	4,420	8.9
Total Assets	258,480	243,770	14,710	6.0

Liabilities and Owner's Equity	2003	2002	Increase/Decrease Amount	Percent
Current Liabilities				
Accounts Payable	$ 15,330	$ 19,650	(4,320)	(22.0)
Salaries Payable	7,680	7,190	490	6.8
Total Current Liabilities	23,010	26,840	(3,830)	(14.3)
Long-Term Liabilities				
Mortgage Payable	$ 53,010	$ 54,200	(1,190)	(2.2)
Note Payable (3-year)	32,400	33,560	(1,160)	(3.5)
Total Long-Term Liabilities	85,410	87,760	(2,350)	(2.7)
Total Liabilities	108,420	114,600	(6,180)	(5.4)
Stockholder's Equity				
Figueroa Industries, Common Stock	150,060	129,170	20,890	16.2
Total Liabilities and Stockholder's Equity	258,480	243,770	14,710	6.0

4.

Westminster Manufacturing, Inc.
Income Statement
For the year ended December 31, 2003

Revenue		
Gross Sales	$1,356,000	
Less: Sales Returns and Allowances	93,100	
Sales Discounts	4,268	
Net Sales		1,258,632
Cost of Goods Sold		
Merchandise Inv., Jan. 1	324,800	
Net Purchases	255,320	
Freight In	3,911	
Goods Available for Sale	584,031	
Less: Merchandise Inv., Dec. 31	179,100	
Cost of Goods Sold		404,931
Gross Margin		853,701
Operating Expenses		
Salaries	375,900	
Rent	166,000	
Utilities	7,730	
Advertising	73,300	
Insurance	22,940	
Administrative Expenses	84,500	
Miscellaneous Expenses	24,900	
Total Operating Expenses		755,270
Income before Taxes		98,431
Income Tax		34,760
Net Income		$ 63,671

5.

Delta Plumbing Supply, Inc.
Income Statement
For the year ended December 31, 2002

Revenue		
Gross Sales	$458,400	103.3
Less: Sales Returns and Allowances	13,200	3.0
Sales Discounts	1,244	.3
Net Sales	$443,956	100.0%
Cost of Goods Sold		
Merchandise Inventory, Jan. 1	198,700	44.8
Net Purchases	86,760	19.5
Freight In	875	.2
Goods Available for Sale	286,335	64.5
Less: Merchandise Inventory, Dec. 31	76,400	17.2
Cost of Goods Sold	209,935	47.3
Gross Margin	234,021	52.7
Operating Expenses		
Salaries	124,200	28.0
Rent	21,000	4.7
Utilities	1,780	.4
Advertising	5,400	1.2
Insurance	2,340	.5
Administrative Expenses	14,500	3.3
Miscellaneous Expenses	6,000	1.4
Total Operating Expenses	175,220	39.5
Income before Taxes	58,801	13.2
Income Tax	17,335	3.9
Net Income	$41,466	9.3

6.

Winkler's Grocery Store, Inc.
Comparative Income Statement
For the years ended December 31, 2001 and 2002

	2002	2001	Increase/Decrease Amount	Increase/Decrease Percent
Revenue				
Gross Sales	$1,223,000	$996,500	$226,500	22.7%
Less: Sales Returns and Allowances	121,340	99,600	21,740	21.8
Sales Discounts	63,120	51,237	11,883	23.2
Net Sales	1,038,540	845,663	192,877	22.8
Cost of Goods Sold				
Merchandise Inventory, Jan. 1	311,200	331,000	(19,800)	(6.0)
Purchases	603,290	271,128	332,162	122.5
Freight In	18,640	13,400	5,240	39.1
Goods Available for Sale	933,130	615,528	317,602	51.6
Less: Merchandise Inventory, Dec. 31	585,400	311,200	274,200	88.1
Cost of Goods Sold	347,730	304,328	43,402	14.3
Gross Margin	690,810	541,335	149,475	27.6
Operating Expenses				
Salaries and Benefits	215,200	121,800	93,400	76.7
Rent and Utilities	124,650	124,650	0	0
Depreciation	43,500	41,230	2,270	5.5
Insurance	24,970	23,800	1,170	4.9
Administrative Store Expenses	58,200	33,900	24,300	71.7
Warehouse Expenses	42,380	45,450	(3,070)	(6.8)
Total Operating Expenses	508,900	390,830	118,070	30.2
Income before Taxes	181,910	150,505	31,405	20.9
Income Tax	66,280	41,670	24,610	59.1
Net Income	$115,630	$108,835	$ 6,795	6.2

7. *Delta Plumbing Supply—Financial Ratios 2002*

$$\text{Current ratio} = \frac{\text{Current assets}}{\text{Current liabilities}} = \frac{108{,}955}{26{,}500} = \underline{\underline{4.11:1}}$$

$$\text{Acid test ratio} = \frac{\text{Cash} + \text{Marketable securities} + \text{Receivables}}{\text{Current liabilities}} = \frac{3{,}400 + 5{,}600}{26{,}500} = \underline{\underline{.34:1}}$$

$$\text{Average collection period} = \frac{\text{Accounts receivable} \times 365}{\text{Net sales}} = \frac{5{,}600 \times 365}{443{,}956} = \underline{\underline{4.6 \text{ days}}}$$

$$\text{Average inventory} = \frac{\text{Beginning inventory} + \text{Ending inventory}}{2} = \frac{198{,}700 + 76{,}400}{2} = \underline{\underline{\$137{,}550}}$$

$$\text{Inventory turnover} = \frac{\text{Cost of goods sold}}{\text{Average inventory}} = \frac{209{,}935}{137{,}550} = \underline{\underline{1.5 \text{ times}}}$$

$$\text{Asset turnover ratio} = \frac{\text{Net sales}}{\text{Total assets}} = \frac{443{,}956}{308{,}555} = \underline{\underline{1.44:1}}$$

$$\text{Debt-to-assets ratio} = \frac{\text{Total liabilities}}{\text{Total assets}} = \frac{93{,}500}{308{,}555} = .303 = \underline{\underline{30.3\%}}$$

$$\text{Debt-to-equity ratio} = \frac{\text{Total liabilities}}{\text{Owner's equity}} = \frac{93{,}500}{215{,}055} = .435 = \underline{\underline{43.5\%}}$$

$$\text{Gross profit margin} = \frac{\text{Gross profit}}{\text{Net sales}} = \frac{234{,}021}{443{,}956} = .527 = \underline{\underline{52.7\%}}$$

$$\text{Net profit margin} = \frac{\text{Net income}}{\text{Net sales}} = \frac{41{,}466}{443{,}956} = .093 = \underline{\underline{9.3\%}}$$

$$\text{Return on investment} = \frac{\text{Net income}}{\text{Owner's equity}} = \frac{41{,}466}{215{,}055} = .193 = \underline{\underline{19.3\%}}$$

8.

Scarborough Corporation
Trend Analysis Chart

	2003	2002	2001	2000	1999
Net Sales	114.3	123.7	111.6	98.2	100.0
Total Assets	105.9	116.7	105.0	101.5	100.0
Stockholder's Equity	111.6	116.1	103.5	90.1	100.0

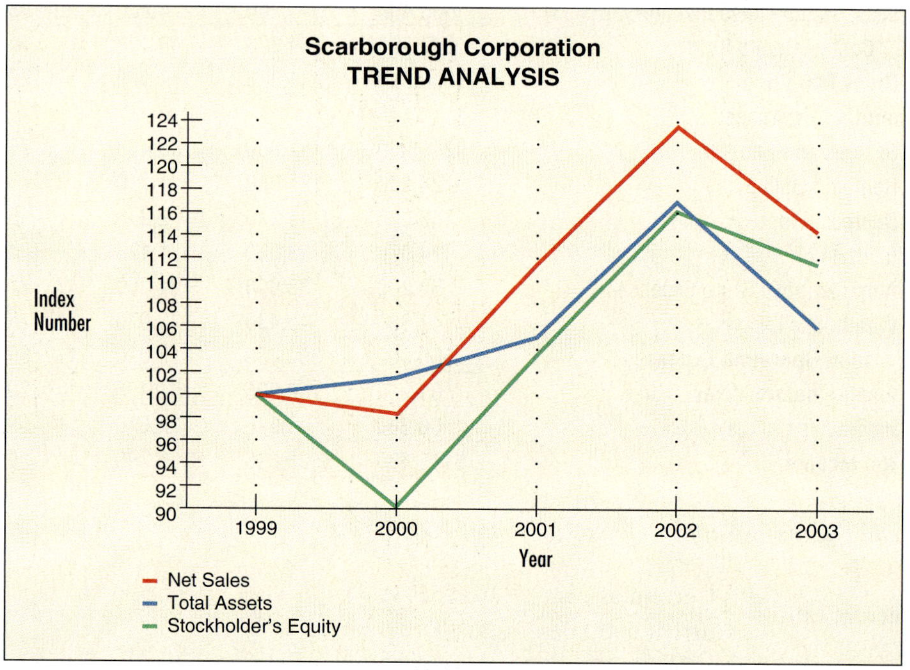

CHAPTER 15 | ASSESSMENT TEST

Name ______________________

Class ______________________

Answers

3. ______________________

Prepare the following statements on separate sheets of paper.

1. a. Use the following financial information to calculate the owner's equity and prepare a balance sheet with vertical analysis as of December 31, 2002, for Service Master Carpet Cleaning, a sole proprietorship owned by Al Mosley: current assets, $132,500; property, plant, and equipment, $88,760; investments and other assets, $32,400; current liabilities, $51,150; long-term liabilities, $87,490.

Service Master Carpet Cleaning
Balance Sheet
As of December 31, 2002

b. The following financial information is for Service Master as of December 31, 2003. Calculate the owner's equity for 2003, and prepare a comparative balance sheet with horizontal analysis for 2002 and 2003: current assets, $154,300; property, plant, and equipment, $124,650; investments and other assets, $20,000; current liabilities, $65,210; long-term liabilities, $83,800.

Service Master Carpet Cleaning
Comparative Balance Sheet
As of December 31, 2002 and 2003

2. a. Use the following financial information to prepare a balance sheet with vertical analysis as of October 31, 2002, for General Industries, Inc.: cash, $45,260; accounts receivable, $267,580; merchandise inventory, $213,200; prepaid expenses, $13,400; supplies, $5,300; land, $87,600; building, $237,200; equipment, $85,630; vehicles, $54,700; computers, $31,100; investments, $53,100; accounts payable, $43,200; salaries payable, $16,500; notes payable (6-month), $102,400; mortgage payable, $124,300; notes payable (3-year), $200,000; common stock, $422,000; and retained earnings, $185,670.

General Industries, Inc.
Balance Sheet
As of October 31, 2002

b. The following financial information is for General Industries as of October 31, 2003. Prepare a comparative balance sheet with horizontal analysis for 2002 and 2003: cash, $47,870; accounts receivable, $251,400; merchandise inventory, $223,290; prepaid expenses, $8,500; supplies, $6,430; land, $87,600; building, $234,500; equipment, $88,960; vehicles, $68,800; computers, $33,270; investments, $55,640; accounts payable, $48,700; salaries payable, $9,780; notes payable (6-month), $96,700; mortgage payable, $121,540; notes payable (3-year), $190,000; common stock, $450,000; and retained earnings, $189,540.

General Industries, Inc.
Consolidated Balance Sheet
As of October 31, 2002 and 2003

3. For the second quarter of 2003, the Quality Picture Frame Company had gross sales of $214,300, sales returns and allowances of $26,540, and sales discounts of $1,988. What were Quality's net sales?

Name ______________________

Class ______________________

Answers

4. a. ______________________

b. ______________________

c. ______________________

d. ______________________

4. For the month of January, Premier Manufacturing, Inc., had the following financial information: merchandise inventory, January 1, $322,000; merchandise inventory, January 31, $316,400; gross purchases, $243,460; purchase returns and allowances, $26,880; and freight in, $3,430.

   a. What are Premier's goods available for sale?

   b. What is the cost of goods sold for January?

   c. If net sales were $389,450 what was the gross margin for January?

   d. If total operating expenses were $179,800, what was the net profit?

Prepare the following statements on separate sheets of paper.

5. a. From the following third quarter 2003 information for Abbey Road Restaurant Supply, construct an income statement with vertical analysis: gross sales, $224,400; sales returns and allowances, $14,300; beginning inventory, July 1, $165,000; ending inventory, September 30, $143,320; net purchases, $76,500; total operating expenses, $68,600; income tax, $8,790.

Abbey Road Restaurant Supply
Income Statement
Third Quarter, 2003

   b. The following financial information is for the fourth quarter of 2003 for Abbey Road Restaurant Supply. Prepare a comparative income statement with horizontal analysis for the third and fourth quarters: gross sales, $218,200; sales returns and allowances, $9,500; beginning inventory, October 1, $143,320; ending inventory, December 31, $125,300; net purchases, $81,200; total operating expenses, $77,300; income tax, $11,340.

Abbey Road Restaurant Supply
Comparative Income Statement
Third and Fourth Quarters, 2003

6. a. Use the following financial information to construct a 2002 income statement with vertical analysis for Omega Optical, Inc.: gross sales, $1,243,000; sales returns and allowances, $76,540; sales discounts, $21,300; merchandise inventory, Jan. 1, 2002, $654,410; merchandise inventory, Dec. 31, 2002, $413,200; net purchases, $318,000; freight in, $3,450; salaries, $92,350; rent, $83,100; depreciation, $87,700; utilities, $21,350; advertising, $130,440; insurance, $7,920; miscellaneous expenses, $105,900; and income tax, $18,580.

Omega Optical, Inc.
Income Statement
For the year ended December 31, 2002

Name ______________________

Class ______________________

b. The following data represent Omega's operating results for 2003. Prepare a comparative income statement with horizontal analysis for 2002 and 2003: gross sales, $1,286,500; sales returns and allowances, $78,950; sales discounts, $18,700; merchandise inventory, Jan. 1, 2003, $687,300; merchandise inventory, Dec. 31, 2003, $401,210; net purchases, $325,400; freight in, $3,980; salaries, $99,340; rent, $85,600; depreciation, $81,200; utilities, $21,340; advertising, $124,390; insurance, $8,700; miscellaneous expenses, $101,230; and income tax, $12,650.

Omega Optical, Inc.
Comparative Income Statement
For the years ended December 31, 2002 and 2003

As the accounting manager of Niagara Industries, Inc., you have been asked to calculate the following financial ratios for the company's 2002 annual report. Use the balance sheet and income statement for Niagara, on page 572:

7. Working capital:

8. Current ratio:

9. Acid test ratio:

10. Average collection period (credit sales are 60% of net sales):

11. Inventory turnover:

12. Asset turnover ratio:

13. Debt-to-assets ratio:

14. Debt-to-equity ratio:

15. Gross profit margin:

16. Net profit margin:

17. Return on investment:

Answers

7. ______________________

8. ______________________

9. ______________________

10. ______________________

11. ______________________

12. ______________________

13. ______________________

14. ______________________

15. ______________________

16. ______________________

17. ______________________

Niagara Industries, Inc.
Balance Sheet
As of December 31, 2002

Assets		
Cash	$ 250,000	
Accounts Receivable	325,400	
Merchandise Inventory	416,800	
Marketable Securities	88,700	
Supplies	12,100	
Total Current Assets		$1,093,000
Land and Building	1,147,000	
Fixtures and Equipment	868,200	
Total Property, Plant, and Equipment		2,015,200
Total Assets		$3,108,200
Liabilities and Owner's Equity		
Accounts Payable	$286,500	
Notes Payable (6-month)	153,200	
Total Current Liabilities		$ 439,700
Mortgage Payable	325,700	
Notes Payable (4-year)	413,100	
Total Long-Term Liabilities		738,800
Total Liabilities		1,178,500
Owner's Equity		1,929,700
Total Liabilities and Owner's Equity		$3,108,200

Niagara Industries, Inc.
Income Statement, 2002

Net Sales		$1,695,900
Merchandise Inventory, Jan. 1	$ 767,800	
Net Purchases	314,900	
Freight In	33,100	
Goods Available for Sale	1,115,800	
Merchandise Inventory, Dec. 31	239,300	
Cost of Goods Sold		876,500
Gross Margin		819,400
Total Operating Expenses		702,300
Income before Taxes		117,100
Taxes		35,200
Net Income		$ 81,900

18. Prepare a trend analysis chart from the financial data listed below for ATM Systems, Inc.

ATM Systems, Inc.
4-year Selected Financial Data

	2002	2001	2000	1999
Net Sales	$898,700	$829,100	$836,200	$801,600
Net Income	96,300	92,100	94,400	89,700
Total Assets	2,334,000	2,311,000	2,148,700	1,998,900
Stockholder's Equity	615,000	586,000	597,200	550,400

ATM Systems, Inc.
Trend Analysis Chart

	2002	2001	2000	1999
Net Sales	______	______	______	______
Net Income	______	______	______	______
Total Assets	______	______	______	______
Stockholder's Equity	______	______	______	______

19. As part of the trend analysis for ATM Systems, Inc., prepare a multiple-line chart for the annual report comparing net sales and net income for the years 1999 through 2002.

20. From the following consolidated statements of earnings for Office Depot, prepare a vertical analysis in the form of a common-size income statement (percentages only) for 2000.

Consolidated Statements of Earnings
Office Depot

(in thousands, except per share amounts)	2000	1999	1998
Sales	$11,569,696	$10,272,060	$9,007,051
Cost of Goods Sold and Occupancy costs	8,479,698	7,450,310	6,484,464
Gross Profits	3,089,998	2,821,750	2,522,587
Store and Warehouse Operating and Selling Expenses	2,361,301	1,969,817	1,651,355
Pre-Opening Expenses	13,465	23,628	17,150
General and Administrative Expenses	501,700	381,611	330,194
Merger and Restructuring Costs	(6,732)	(7,104)	119,129
Facility Closure Costs	110,038	40,425	
Operating Profit	110,226	413,373	404,759
Other Income (expenses):			
Interest Income	11,502	30,176	25,309
Interest Expense	(33,901)	(26,148)	(22,356)
Miscellaneous Income (expense), Net	4,632	(3,514)	(18,985)
Earnings before Income Taxes	92,459	413,887	388,727
Income Taxes	43,127	156,249	155,531
Net Earnings	$ 49,332	$ 257,638	$ 233,196
Earnings per Share:			
Basic	$.16	$.71	$.64
Diluted	.16	.69	.61

Name ______________________

Class ______________________

Answers

21. a. ______________________

____

b. ______________________

____

c. ______________________

____

d. ______________________

____

e. ______________________

____

f. ______________________

____

g. ______________________

____

h. ______________________

____

____

____

____

____

____

i. ______________________

BUSINESS DECISION

Evaluating Financial Performance

21. From the consolidated statements of earnings and balance sheets of Winn-Dixie Stores on page 575, prepare the following financial ratios for 2000 and 2001.

a. Current ratio

b. Acid test ratio (*Note:* Winn-Dixie has no marketable securities.)

c. Asset turnover ratio

d. Debt-to-assets ratio

e. Debt-to-equity ratio

f. Net profit margin

g. Return on investment

h. Based on your calculations of the financial ratios for Winn-Dixie in the annual report in Question 21 above, determine for each ratio whether the 2001 figure was better or worse than the 2000 figure.

i. How would you rate Winn-Dixie's financial performance from 2000 to 2001?

Consolidated Statements of Earnings
Winn-Dixie Stores

Years ended June 27, 2001 and June 28, 2000	2001	2000
	Amounts in thousands except per share data	
Net Sales	**$12,903,373**	13,697,547
Cost of Sales, Including Warehousing and Delivery Expense	**9,449,346**	9,970,497
Gross Profit on Sales	**3,454,027**	3,727,050
Operating and Administrative Expenses	**3,180,297**	3,586,351
Restructuring and Other Nonrecurring Charges	**147,245**	396,029
Operating Income (loss)	**126,485**	(255,330)
Interest Expense	**52,843**	47,081
Earnings (loss) before Income Taxes	**73,642**	(302,411)
Income Taxes	**28,331**	(73,516)
Net Earnings (loss)	**$ 45,311**	(228,895)
Basic Earnings (loss) per Share	**$ .32**	(1.57)
Diluted Earnings (loss) per Share	**$ .32**	(1.57)

Consolidated Balance Sheets

Years ended June 27, 2001 and June 28, 2000

Assets	2001	2000
	Amounts in thousands	
Current Assets:		
Cash and Cash Equivalents	**$ 121,061**	29,576
Trade and Other Receivables, Net	**109,159**	107,425
Merchandise Inventories, less LIFO Reserve	**1,198,602**	1,141,405
Prepaid Expenses	**34,643**	58,739
Deferred Income Taxes	**135,736**	134,777
Total Current Assets	**1,599,201**	1,471,922
Cash Surrender Value of Life Insurance, Net	**16,876**	14,035
Property, Plant, and Equipment, Net	**1,146,654**	1,016,292
Intangible Assets, Net	**92,875**	18,606
Noncurrent Deferred Income Taxes	**106,145**	166,449
Other Assets, Net	**79,919**	59,789
Total Assets	**$3,041,670**	2,747,093
Liabilities and Shareholders' Equity		
Current Liabilities	**1,149,907**	1,421,553
Obligations under Capital Leases	**28,953**	32,239
Long-Term Debt	**697,414**	—
Long-Term Restructuring Expenses	**118,745**	143,188
Defined Benefit Plan	**49,027**	45,241
Reserve for Insurance Claims and Self-Insurance	**147,964**	141,251
Other Liabilities	**78,006**	95,786
Shareholders' Equity	**771,654**	867,835
Total Liabilities and Shareholders' Equity	**$3,041,670**	2,747,093

All the Math That's Fit to Learn

The Business Math Times

Volume XV | **Financial Statements and Ratios** | One Dollar

The Accountant

Managers require up-to-date financial information to make important business decisions. Accountants prepare, analyze, and verify financial reports and taxes, and monitor information systems that furnish this information to managers in all business, industrial, and government organizations.

Accounting is the process used by organizations to "track" their income and assets over periods of time. Because accountants spend a lot of time looking under the hoods of businesses, they develop a keen understanding of how business works. It is no surprise that many successful people in business began their careers as accountants.

The premier achievement in public accounting is becoming a Certified Public Accountant (CPA). The CPA must fulfill certain state education and experience requirements, and pass a rigorous examination.

You are most likely to start your career at a public accounting firm. After a few years of that excellent training and experience, many accountants move on to their own practices or other accounting-related business or government careers.

For more information about accounting careers, visit: www.contemporarymath.com

Pepper . . . and Salt

THE WALL STREET JOURNAL

"Great annual report. Scratch and sniff and it smells like money!"

"Quote . . . Unquote"

The engine which drives enterprises is not thrift, but profit.
—John Maynard Keynes

Profit is like breathing,
if you can't do that, you can forget about doing anything else.
—Robert Mercer

The "Big Five" Accounting Firms

Company	Revenue (in millions)	Offices	Total Employees	Major Clients
PricewaterhouseCoopers	$8,878	186	45,767	Kodak, Ford, Nike, Disney, AT&T, IBM
Deloitte & Touche	$5,838	103	26,667	Microsoft, Boeing, Sears, GM
KPMG	$5,400	145	27,500	PepsiCo, Xerox, JC Penney, BMW
Ernst & Young	$4,270	82	22,637	Apple, McDonald's, Wal-Mart, Coke
Anderson	$3,600	80	25,860	American Express, Chemical Bank

Accounting Salaries

The median entry-level salary in public accounting is more than $30,000. After four years, you can expect to make between $40,000 and $55,000. Salaries are usually similar in the private sector and slightly lower in government. They tend to be higher in major cities.

On an overall basis, median incomes are highest for accounting managers in the fields of taxation, audit, financial analysis/planning, and cost accounting; lowest in general accounting and payroll.

Accounting/Financial Field Salary Survey—2001

Accounting Position	Median Income	Years Experience
Entry Level	$ 23,900	first year
Junior Staff	29,500	1–2
Senior Staff	42,300	3–5
Manager	55,700	5–7
Senior Mgr.	81,300	7+
Partner	250,000	10+

The Future is Bright

According to the Bureau of Labor Statistics, the accounting profession is expanding at a rapid pace. They project a 34% increase in job openings in accounting by 2005.

Supervising accountants are paid best in taxation, auditing, cost accounting, and general accounting functions; least in the accounts payable and accounts receivable functions.

Brainteaser

LEAP FROG

A frog is standing 20 feet away from a wall. If each time it jumps it covers exactly half the distance left to the wall, how many jumps will it take the frog to reach the wall?

ANSWER TO LAST ISSUE'S BRAINTEASER

20
Don't forget 90, 91, 92, 93, . . . 99!

CHAPTER 16

Inventory

PERFORMANCE OBJECTIVES

Section I Inventory Valuation

16-1 Pricing inventory by using the first-in, first-out (FIFO) method. (p. 579)
16-2 Pricing inventory by using the last-in, first-out (LIFO) method. (p. 582)
16-3 Pricing inventory by using the average cost method. (p. 583)
16-4 Pricing inventory by using the lower-of-cost-or-market (LCM) rule. (p. 584)

Section II Inventory Estimation

16-5 Estimating the value of ending inventory by using the retail method. (p. 588)
16-6 Estimating the value of ending inventory by using the gross profit method. (p. 590)

Section III Inventory Turnover and Targets

16-7 Calculating inventory turnover rate at retail. (p. 594)
16-8 Calculating inventory turnover rate at cost. (p. 595)
16-9 Calculating target inventories based on industry standards. (p. 596)

inventory
Goods that a company has in its possession at any given time. May be in the form of raw materials, partially finished goods, or goods available for sale.

merchandise inventory
Goods purchased by wholesalers and retailers for resale.

In business, the term **inventory** is used to describe the goods that a company has in its possession at any given time. For companies engaged in manufacturing activities, inventories are divided into raw materials (used to make other products), partially completed products (work in process), and finished goods (ready for sale to the trade).

Manufacturers sell their finished goods to wholesalers and retailers. These goods, purchased and held expressly for resale, are commonly known as **merchandise inventory.** For wholesalers and retailers, the primary source of revenue is from the sale of this merchandise. In terms of dollars, merchandise inventory is one of the largest and most important assets of a merchandising company. As an expense, the cost of goods sold is the largest deduction from sales in the determination of a company's profit, often larger than the total of operating or overhead expenses.

Interestingly, the merchandise inventory is the only account that is found on both the balance sheet and the income statement. The method used to determine the value of this inventory has a significant impact on a company's bottom-line results. In addition to appearing on the financial statements, the value of the merchandise inventory must also be determined for income tax purposes, insurance, and as a business indicator to management.

SECTION I

INVENTORY VALUATION

periodic inventory system
Inventory system in which merchandise is physically counted at least once a year to determine the value of the goods available for sale.

perpetual inventory system
Inventory system in which goods available for sale are updated on a continuous basis by computer. Purchases by the company are added to inventory, whereas sales to customers are subtracted from inventory.

book inventory
The balance of a perpetual inventory system at any given time. Must be confirmed with an actual physical count at least once a year.

To place a value on a merchandise inventory, we must first know the quantity and the cost of the goods remaining at the end of an operating period. Merchandise held for sale must be physically counted at least once a year. Many businesses take inventory on a quarterly or even monthly basis. This is known as a **periodic inventory system,** because the physical inventory is counted periodically.

Today, more and more companies use computers to keep track of merchandise inventory on a continuous or perpetual basis. This is known as a **perpetual inventory system.** For each merchandise category, the purchases made by the company are added to inventory, whereas the sales to customers are subtracted. These balances are known as **book inventories** of the items held for sale. As accurate as the perpetual system may be, it must be confirmed with an actual physical count at least once a year.

Taking inventory consists of physically counting, weighing, or measuring the items on hand; placing a price on each item; and multiplying the number of items by the price to

When a cashier scans a product being purchased, a low-power laser reads the universal product code (UPC), a 12-digit bar code on each product's package or label. The digits identify the manufacturer, the product, the size, and product attributes, such as flavor or color. The tracking information is used for maintaining perpetual inventory systems. See *The Business Math Times*, page 610.

determine the total cost. The counting part of taking inventory, although tedious, is not difficult. The pricing part, however, is an important and often controversial business decision. To this day, accountants have varying opinions on the subject of inventory valuation techniques.

In most industries, the prices paid by businesses for goods frequently change. A hardware store, for example, may buy a dozen light bulbs for $10.00 one month and $12.50 the next. A gasoline station may pay $.75 per gallon on Tuesday and $.69 on Thursday. When taking inventory, it is virtually impossible to determine what price items are left. This means that the *flow of goods* in and out of a business does not always match the *flow of costs* in and out of the business.

The one method of pricing inventory that actually matches the flow of costs to the flow of goods is known as the **specific identification method.** This method is feasible only when the variety of merchandise carried in stock and the volume of sales are relatively low, such as with automobiles or other expensive items. Each car, for example, has a specific vehicle identification number or serial number that makes inventory valuation accurate. A list of the actual vehicles in stock at any given time, and their corresponding costs, can easily be totaled to arrive at an inventory figure.

specific identification method
Inventory valuation method in which each item in inventory is matched or coded with its actual cost. Feasible only for low-volume merchandise flow such as automobiles, boats, or other expensive items.

In reality, most businesses have a wide variety of merchandise and find this method too expensive, because implementation would require sophisticated computer bar-coding systems. For this reason, it is customary to use an assumption as to the flow of costs of merchandise in and out of the business. The three most common cost flow assumptions or inventory pricing methods are as follows:

1. **First in, first-out (FIFO):** Cost flow is in the order in which the costs were incurred.
2. **Last-in, first-out (LIFO):** Cost flow is in the reverse order in which the costs were incurred.
3. **Average cost:** Cost flow is an average of the costs incurred.

Everybody's Business
Real-World Connection
The value placed on inventory can have a significant effect on the *net income* of a company. Because net income is the basis of calculating federal income tax, accountants frequently must decide whether to value inventory to reflect higher net profit to entice investors or lower net profit to minimize income taxes.

Although cost is the primary basis for the valuation of inventory, when market prices or current replacement costs fall below the actual cost of those in inventory, the company has incurred a loss. For example, let's say a computer retailer purchases a large quantity of DVD drives at a cost of $200 each. A few months later, due to advances in technology, a faster model is introduced costing only $175 each. Under these market conditions, companies are permitted to choose a method for pricing inventory known as the lower-of-cost-or-market (LCM) rule.

All the inventory valuation methods listed above are acceptable for both income tax reporting and a company's financial statements. As we see in this section, each of these methods has advantages and disadvantages. Economic conditions, such as whether merchandise prices are rising (inflation) or falling (deflation), play an important role in the decision of which method to adopt.

For income tax reporting, once a method has been chosen, the Internal Revenue Service (IRS) requires that it be used consistently from one year to the next. Any changes in the method used for inventory valuation must be for a good reason and must be approved by the IRS.

16-1 Pricing Inventory by Using the First-In, First-Out (FIFO) Method

The **first-in, first-out (FIFO) method** assumes that the items purchased *first* are the *first* items sold. The items in inventory at the end of the year are matched with the costs of items of the same type that were most recently purchased. This method closely approximates the manner in which most businesses reduce their inventory, especially when the merchandise is perishable or subject to frequent style or model changes.

first-in, first-out (FIFO) method
Inventory valuation method that assumes the items purchased by the company *first* are the *first* items to be sold. Items remaining in ending inventory at the end of an accounting period are therefore the most recently purchased.

Essentially, this method involves taking physical inventory at the end of the year or accounting period and assigning cost in reverse order in which the purchases were received.

FIFO

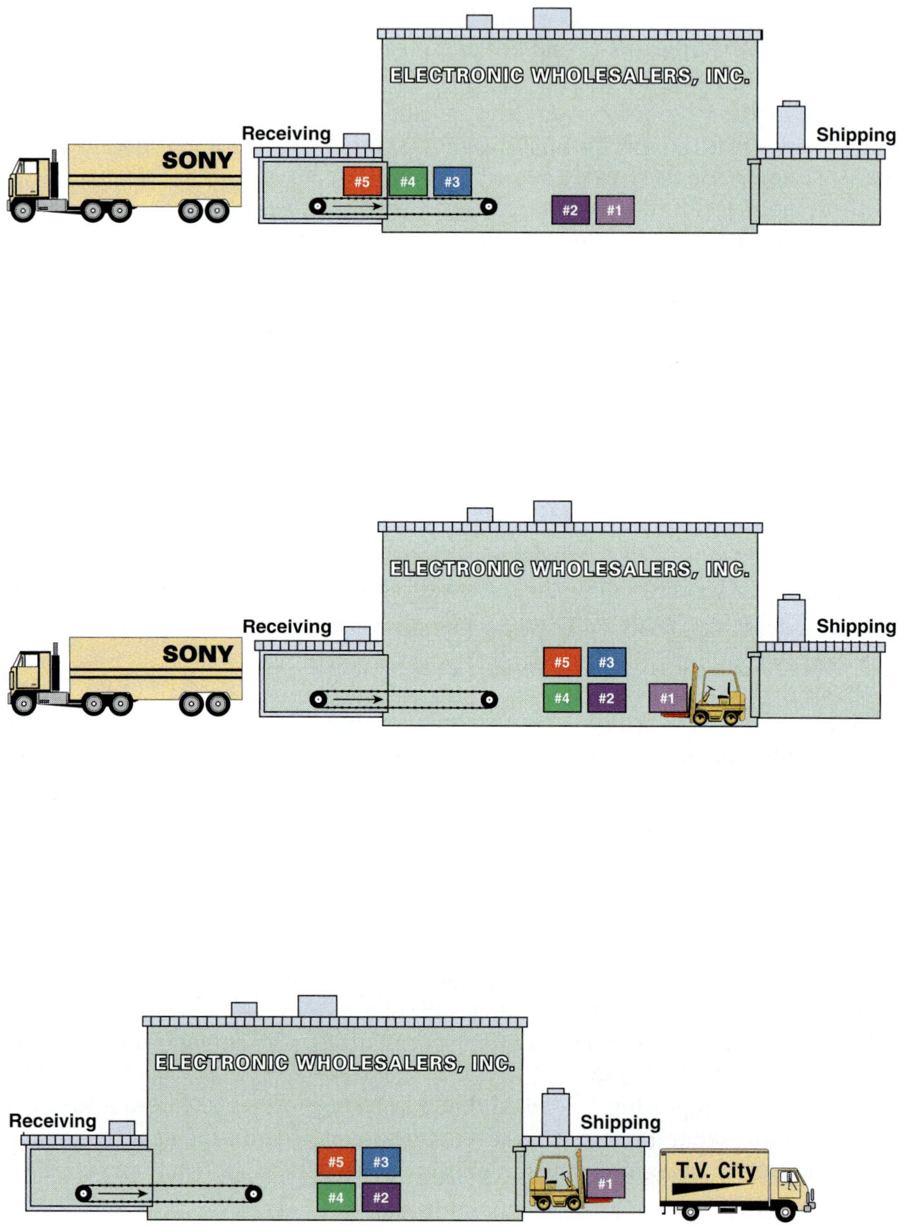

✦ **EXHIBIT 16-1** ✦
FIFO

STEPS TO CALCULATE THE VALUE OF ENDING INVENTORY BY USING FIFO:

Step 1. List the number of units on hand at the end of the year and their corresponding costs, starting with the ending balance and working *backward* through the incoming shipments.

Step 2. Multiply the number of units by the corresponding cost per unit for each purchase.

Step 3. Calculate the value of ending inventory by totaling the extensions from Step 2.

To illustrate the application of the FIFO method of inventory pricing, as well as the other methods in this section, we shall use the following annual inventory data for 12-inch clay pots at a Kmart Garden Center.

Kmart Garden Center

January 1	Beginning Inventory	400 units @ $5.00	$2,000
April 9	Purchase	200 units @ $6.00	1,200
July 19	Purchase	500 units @ $7.00	3,500
October 15	Purchase	300 units @ $8.00	2,400
December 8	Purchase	200 units @ $9.00	1,800
12-inch clay pots available for sale during the year		1,600	$10,900

Everybody's Business

Real-World Connection

Although the material in this chapter essentially deals with accounting, anyone who plans to own or manage a business involving merchandise should have a conceptual understanding of inventory valuation methods.

EXAMPLE

When physical inventory of the 12-inch clay pots was taken at Kmart on December 31, it was found that 700 remained in inventory. Using the FIFO method of inventory pricing, what is the dollar value of this ending inventory?

SOLUTION STRATEGY

With the assumption under FIFO that the inventory cost flow is made up of the *most recent* costs, the 700 clay pots in ending inventory would be valued as follows:

Step 1. Set up a table listing the 700 pots with costs in reverse order of acquisition.

200 units @ $9.00 from the December 8 purchase
300 units @ $8.00 from the October 15 purchase
200 units @ $7.00 from the July 19 purchase
700 Inventory, December 31

Steps 2 & 3. Next we extend each purchase, multiplying the number of units by the cost per unit, and find the total of the extensions.

Units	Cost/Unit	Total	
200	$9.00	$1,800	
300	8.00	2,400	
200	7.00	1,400	
700		$5,600	Ending inventory using FIFO

TRY-IT | EXERCISE

1. You are the merchandise manager of Circuit City. The following data represent your records of the annual inventory figures for DVD players.

Circuit City

January 1	Beginning Inventory	200 units @ $8.00	$1,600
May 14	Purchase	100 units @ $8.50	850
August 27	Purchase	250 units @ $9.00	2,250
November 18	Purchase	300 units @ $8.75	2,625
DVD players available for sale		850	$7,325

Using the FIFO method of inventory pricing, what is the dollar value of ending inventory if there were 380 DVD players on hand on December 31?

Check your answer with the solution on page 604.

16-2 Pricing Inventory by Using the Last-In, First-Out (LIFO) Method

last-in, first-out (LIFO) method Inventory valuation method that assumes the items purchased by the company *last* are the *first* items to be sold. Items remaining in ending inventory at the end of an accounting period are therefore the oldest goods.

The **last-in, first-out (LIFO) method** assumes that the items purchased *last* are sold or removed from inventory *first.* The items in inventory at the end of the year are matched with the cost of items of the same type that were purchased earliest. Therefore, items included in your ending inventory are considered to be those from the beginning inventory plus those acquired first from purchases.

This method involves taking physical inventory at the end of the year or accounting period and assigning cost in the same order in which the purchases were received.

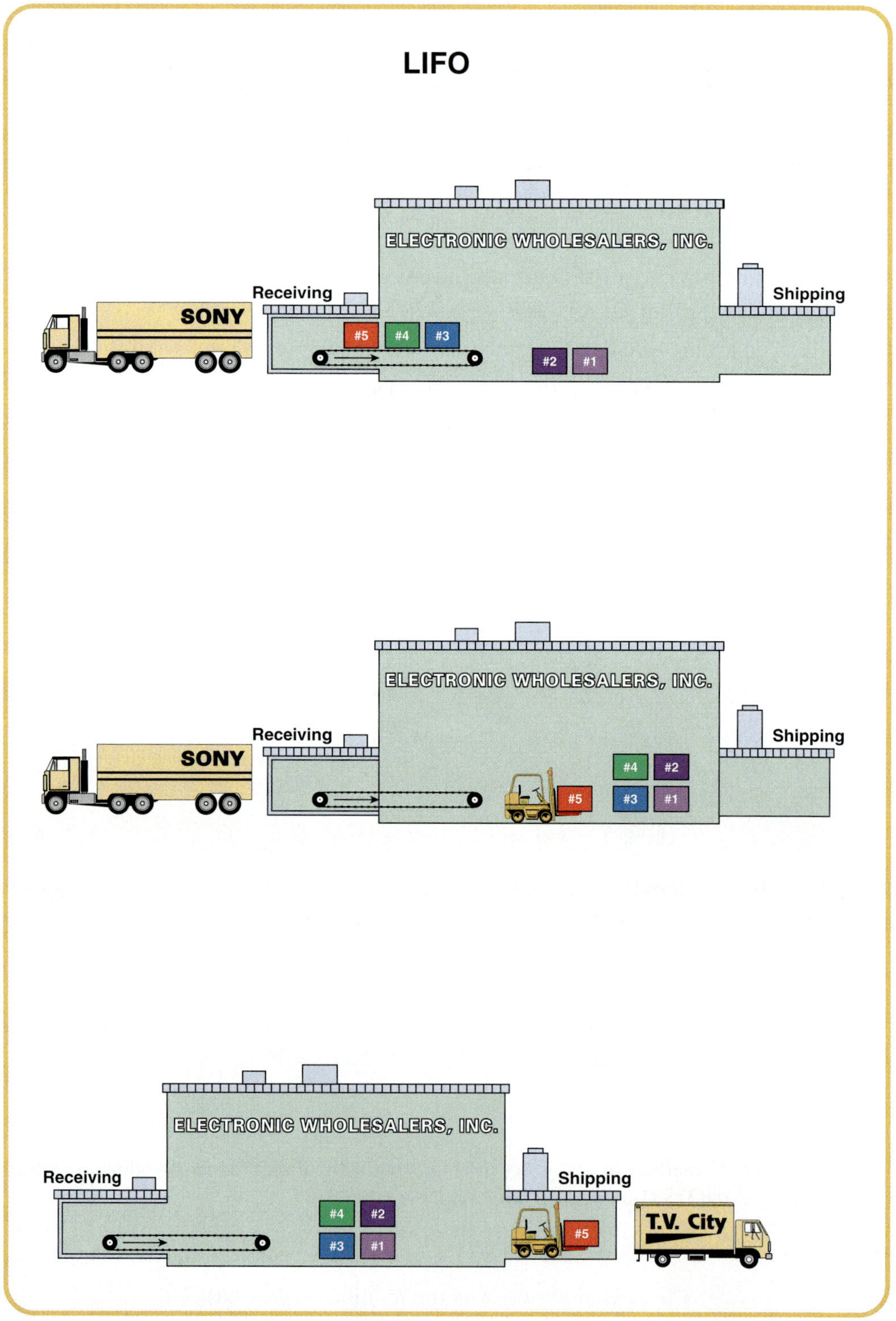

✦ **EXHIBIT 16-2** ✦
LIFO

STEPS TO CALCULATE THE VALUE OF ENDING INVENTORY BY USING LIFO:

Step 1. List the number of units on hand at the end of the year and their corresponding costs starting with the beginning inventory and working *forward* through the incoming shipments.

Step 2. Multiply the number of units by the corresponding cost per unit for each purchase.

Step 3. Calculate the value of ending inventory by totaling the extensions from Step 2.

Everybody's Business

Real-World Connection

One of the main reasons for choosing a particular inventory valuation method is for the calculation of *income* for tax purposes.

- When costs are rising:
  - FIFO → Higher gross profit
  - LIFO → Lower gross profit
- When costs are decreasing:
  - FIFO → Lower gross profit
  - LIFO → Higher gross profit

EXAMPLE

Let's return to the previous example about the 12-inch clay pots from Kmart, page 581. Once again, when physical inventory was taken on December 31, it was found that 700 remained in inventory. Using the LIFO method of inventory pricing, what is the dollar value of this ending inventory?

SOLUTION STRATEGY

With the assumption under LIFO that the inventory cost flow is made up of the *earliest* costs, the 700 clay pots in ending inventory would be valued as follows:

Step 1. Set up a table listing the 700 pots with costs in the order in which they were acquired.

400 units @ $5.00 from the January 1 beginning inventory
200 units @ $6.00 from the April 9 purchase
100 units @ $7.00 from the July 19 purchase
700 Inventory, December 31

Steps 2 & 3. Next, we extend each purchase, multiplying the number of units by the cost per unit, and find the total of the extensions.

Units	Cost/Unit	Total	
400	$5.00	$2,000	
200	6.00	1,200	
100	7.00	700	
700		$3,900	Ending inventory using LIFO

TRY-IT EXERCISE

2. Let's return to Try-It Exercise 1, Circuit City. Use the data from page 581 to calculate the dollar value of the 380 DVD players in ending inventory by using the LIFO method.

Check your answer with the solution on page 604.

16-3 Pricing Inventory by Using the Average Cost Method

The **average cost method,** also known as the **weighted average method,** assumes that the cost of each unit of inventory is the *average* cost of all goods available for sale during that accounting period. It is a weighted average because it takes into consideration not only the cost per unit in each purchase but also the number of units purchased at each cost.

average cost, or weighted average, method
Inventory valuation method that assumes the cost of each unit of inventory is the *average* cost of all goods available for sale during that accounting period.

STEPS TO CALCULATE THE VALUE OF ENDING INVENTORY BY USING AVERAGE COST:

Step 1. Calculate the average cost per unit by using the following formula:

$$\text{Average cost per unit} = \frac{\text{Cost of goods available for sale}}{\text{Total units available for sale}}$$

Step 2. Calculate the value of ending inventory by multiplying the number of units in ending inventory by the average cost per unit.

$$\text{Ending inventory} = \text{Units in ending inventory} \times \text{Average cost per unit}$$

EXAMPLE

Let's return once again to the example of the 12-inch clay pots from Kmart, page 581. Using the average cost method of inventory pricing, what is the dollar value of the 700 units on hand in ending inventory?

SOLUTION STRATEGY

Under the weighted average cost method, the 700 clay pots in ending inventory would be valued as follows:

Step 1. Calculate the average cost per unit:

$$\text{Average cost per unit} = \frac{\text{Cost of goods available for sale}}{\text{Total units available for sale}}$$

$$\text{Average cost per unit} = \frac{10{,}900}{1{,}600} = \$6.81$$

Step 2. Ending inventory = Units in ending inventory × Average cost per unit

Ending inventory = 700 × 6.81 = $4,767.00

TRY-IT | EXERCISE

3. **Once again, let's use the Circuit City example. This time use the data from page 581 to calculate the value of the 380 DVD players in ending inventory by using the average cost method.**

Check your answer with the solution on page 604.

16-4 Pricing Inventory by Using the Lower-of-Cost-or-Market (LCM) Rule

The three methods of pricing inventory discussed to this point—FIFO, LIFO, and weighted average—have been based on the cost of the merchandise. When the market price or current replacement price of an inventory item declines below the actual price paid for that item, companies are permitted to use a method known as the **lower-of-cost-or-market (LCM) rule.** This method takes into account such market conditions as severely falling prices, changing fashions or styles, or obsolescence of inventory items. The use of the LCM rule assumes that decreases in replacement costs will be accompanied by proportionate decreases in selling prices.

lower-of-cost-or-market (LCM) rule Inventory valuation method whereby items in inventory are valued either at their actual cost or current replacement value, whichever is lower. This method is permitted under conditions of falling prices or merchandise obsolescence.

The lower-of-cost-or-market means comparing the market value (current replacement cost) of each item on hand with its cost, using the lower amount as its inventory value. Under ordinary circumstances, market value means the usual price paid, based on the volume of merchandise normally ordered by the firm.

STEPS TO CALCULATE THE VALUE OF ENDING INVENTORY BY USING THE LOWER-OF-COST-OR-MARKET RULE:

Step 1. Calculate the cost for each item in the inventory by using one of the acceptable methods: FIFO, LIFO, or weighted average.

Step 2. Determine the market price or current replacement cost for each item.

Step 3. For each item, select the basis for valuation, cost or market, by choosing the lower figure.

Step 4. Calculate the total amount for each inventory item by multiplying the number of items by the valuation price chosen in Step 3.

Step 5. Calculate the total value of the inventory by adding all the figures in the Amount column.

EXAMPLE

The following data represent the inventory figures of the Exotica Boutique. Use the lower-of-cost-or-market rule to calculate (a) the extended amount for each item and (b) the total value of the inventory.

Item	Description	Quantity	Unit Price Cost	Unit Price Market	Valuation Basis	Amount
Blouses	Style #44	40	$27.50	$31.25	______	______
	Style #54	54	36.40	33.20	______	______
Slacks	Style #20	68	42.10	39.80	______	______
	Style #30	50	57.65	59.18	______	______
Jackets	Suede	30	141.50	130.05	______	______
	Wool	35	88.15	85.45	______	______
					Total Value of Inventory:	______

SOLUTION STRATEGY

In this example, the cost and market price are given. We begin by choosing the lower of cost or market and then extending each item to the Amount column. For example, the Style #44 blouse will be valued at the cost, $27.50, because it is less than the market price, $31.25. The extension would be 40 × $27.50 = $1,100.00.

Item	Description	Quantity	Unit Price Cost	Unit Price Market	Valuation Basis	Amount
Blouses	Style #44	40	$27.50	$31.25	Cost	$1,100.00
	Style #54	54	36.40	33.20	Market	1,792.80
Slacks	Style #20	68	42.10	39.80	Market	2,706.40
	Style #30	50	57.65	59.18	Cost	2,882.50
Jackets	Suede	30	141.50	130.05	Market	3,901.50
	Wool	35	88.15	85.45	Market	2,990.75
					Total Value of Inventory:	$15,373.95

TRY-IT | EXERCISE

4. Determine the value of the following inventory for the Galleria Gift Shop by using the lower-of-cost-or-market rule.

Description	Quantity	Unit Price Cost	Unit Price Market	Valuation Basis	Amount
Picture Frames	75	$ 9.50	$ 9.20	______	______
Ash Trays	120	26.30	27.15	______	______
16" Vases	88	42.40	39.70	______	______
12" Vases	64	23.65	21.40	______	______
Fruit Bowls	42	36.90	42.00	______	______
				Total Value of Inventory:	______

Check your answers with the solutions on page 604.

REVIEW EXERCISES | CHAPTER 16—SECTION I

1. Calculate the total number of units available for sale and the cost of goods available for sale from the following inventory of oil filters for Action Auto Parts:

Action Auto Parts
Oil Filter Inventory

Date	Units Purchased	Cost per Unit	Total Cost
Beginning Inventory, Jan. 1	160	$1.45	______
Purchase, March 14	210	1.65	______
Purchase, May 25	190	1.52	______
Purchase, August 19	300	1.77	______
Purchase, October 24	250	1.60	______
Total units available:	______	Cost of goods available for sale:	______

2. When the merchandise manager of Action Auto Parts took physical inventory of the oil filters on December 31, it was found that 550 remained in inventory.

a. What is the dollar value of the oil filter inventory by using FIFO?

b. What is the dollar value of the oil filter inventory by using LIFO?

c. What is the dollar value of the filters by using the average cost method?

3. The following data represent the inventory figures for 55-gallon fish tanks at Something's Fishy:

Something's Fishy
55-Gallon Fish Tanks Inventory

			Amount
January 1	Beginning Inventory	42 units @ $38.00	________
March 12	Purchase	80 units @ $36.50	________
July 19	Purchase	125 units @ $39.70	________
September 2	Purchase	75 units @ $41.75	________
	Fish tanks available for sale: ____	Cost of tanks available for sale:	________

a. How many fish tanks did Something's Fishy have available for sale?

b. What is the total cost of the tanks available for sale?

c. If physical inventory on December 31 was 88 tanks on hand, what is the value of those tanks by using FIFO?

d. What is the value of the 88 tanks by using LIFO?

e. What is the value of the 88 tanks by using the average cost method?

4. Determine the amount of the following inventory for True Value Hardware by using the lower-of-cost-or-market rule:

True Value Hardware
Power Tool Inventory

		Unit Price		Valuation	
Description	**Quantity**	**Cost**	**Market**	**Basis**	**Amount**
$\frac{3}{8}$" Drill	15	$25.60	$22.40	________	________
$\frac{1}{2}$" Drill	19	42.33	39.17	________	________
7" Circle Saw	12	32.29	34.50	________	________
$\frac{3}{8}$" Router	8	55.30	54.22	________	________
5" Rotary Sander	15	27.60	27.10	________	________
9" Belt Sander	9	33.59	34.51	________	________
				Total value of inventory:	________

BUSINESS DECISION

In or Out?

5. You are the accounting manager for Marcel Industries. One of your junior accountants is working on the December 31, 2002, year-end inventory figures, and has asked for help in determining which units represent actual inventory. From the following inventory scenarios, choose which *should* be included in the year-end inventory and which *should not*. *Hint:* Refer to Exhibit 7-3, Freight Terminology, page 212.

   a. Marcel shipped 4,650 units FOB shipping point on December 31, 2002. They were picked up by the freight company at 11:30 p.m.

   b. On December 27, Franklin Supply Company returned 1,200 units to Marcel that were the wrong merchandise. The replacement order is scheduled to be shipped on January 6, 2003.

   c. Marcel has moved 4,500 units from the warehouse to the packing department for shipment on January 3, 2003, to Castlewood, Inc.

   d. Merchandise that Marcel shipped to Brantley Distributors FOB shipping point was picked up by the freight company on December 26, 2002, but was not delivered at its destination until January 5, 2003.

   e. On December 19, 2002, Marcel received 25 units from Dorsey Discount for warranty repair. These are scheduled to be returned to Dorsey on January 15, 2003.

   f. Marcel shipped 3,400 units FOB destination on December 29, 2002, which arrived on January 3, 2003.

SECTION II

INVENTORY ESTIMATION

Everybody's Business

Real-World Connection

In business today, it is common practice for retail stores to use the retail method of inventory valuation, whereas manufacturers and wholesalers use the gross profit method.

In Section I of this chapter, we learned to calculate the value of ending inventory by several methods using a physical count at the end of the accounting year. Most companies, however, require inventory figures more frequently than the once-a-year physical inventory. Monthly and quarterly financial statements, for example, may be prepared with inventory estimates, rather than expensive physical counts or perpetual inventory systems. In addition, when physical inventories are destroyed by fire or other disasters, estimates must be made for insurance claims purposes.

The two generally accepted methods for *estimating* the value of an inventory are the retail method and the gross profit method. For these methods to closely approximate the actual value of inventory, the markup rate for all items bought and sold by the company must be consistent. If they are not, the estimates should be calculated separately for each product category. For example, if a toy store gets a 30% markup on tricycles and 50% on bicycles, these categories should be calculated separately.

16-5 Estimating the Value of Ending Inventory by Using the Retail Method

retail method
Method of inventory estimation used by most retailers based on a comparison of goods available for sale at cost and at retail.

The **retail method** of inventory estimation is used by retail businesses of all types and sizes, from Wal-Mart and Sears to the corner grocery store. To use this method, the company must have certain figures in its accounting records, including the following:

a. *Beginning inventory* at cost price and at retail (selling price).

b. *Purchases* during the period at cost price and at retail.

c. *Net sales* for the period.

From these figures, the goods available for sale are determined at both cost and retail. We then calculate a ratio known as the **cost to retail price ratio,** or simply **cost ratio,** by the formula:

cost to retail price ratio, or cost ratio Ratio of goods available for sale at cost to the goods available for sale at retail. Used in the retail method of inventory estimation to represent the *cost* of each dollar of retail sales.

$$\text{Cost ratio} = \frac{\text{Goods available for sale at cost}}{\text{Goods available for sale at retail}}$$

This ratio represents the cost of each dollar of retail sales. For example, if the cost ratio for a company is .6 or 60%, this means that $.60 is the cost of each $1.00 of retail sales.

STEPS TO ESTIMATE THE VALUE OF ENDING INVENTORY BY USING THE RETAIL METHOD:

Step 1. List beginning inventory and purchases at both cost and retail.

Step 2. Add purchases to beginning inventory to determine goods available for sale at both cost and retail.

Beginning inventory
\+ Purchases
Goods available for sale

Step 3. Calculate the cost ratio:

$$\text{Cost ratio} = \frac{\text{Goods available for sale at cost}}{\text{Goods available for sale at retail}}$$

Step 4. Subtract net sales from goods available for sale at retail to get ending inventory at retail:

Goods available for sale at retail
− Net sales
Ending inventory at retail

Step 5. Convert ending inventory at retail to ending inventory at cost by multiplying the ending inventory at retail by the cost ratio.

$$\text{Ending inventory at cost} = \text{Ending inventory at retail} \times \text{Cost ratio}$$

EXAMPLE

Using the retail method, estimate the value of the ending inventory at cost on June 30, from the following information for Western Distributors, Inc.

Western Distributors, Inc.
Financial Highlights
June 1–June 30

	Cost	Retail
Beginning Inventory	$200,000	$400,000
Net Purchases (June)	150,000	300,000
Net Sales (June) $500,000		

SOLUTION STRATEGY

Steps 1 & 2. List the beginning inventory and purchases and calculate the goods available for sale.

	Cost	Retail
Beginning Inventory	$200,000	$400,000
+ Net Purchases (June)	+ 150,000	+ 300,000
Goods Available for Sale	$350,000	$700,000

Step 3. $\text{Cost ratio} = \dfrac{\text{Goods available for sale at cost}}{\text{Goods available for sale at retail}}$

$$\text{Cost ratio} = \frac{350{,}000}{700{,}000} = .5 = 50\%$$

Remember, this 50% figure means that \$.50 was the cost of each \$1.00 of retail sales.

Step 4. Next, find ending inventory at retail:

Goods available for sale at retail		\$700,000
− Net sales		− 500,000
Ending inventory at retail	=	\$200,000

Step 5. Now, convert the inventory at retail to inventory at cost by using the cost ratio:

$$\text{Ending inventory at cost} = \text{Ending inventory at retail} \times \text{Cost ratio}$$

$$\text{Ending inventory at cost} = 200{,}000 \times .5 = \underline{\underline{\$100{,}000}}$$

TRY-IT | EXERCISE

5. Using the retail method, estimate the value of the ending inventory at cost on August 31, from the following information for Fancy Fruit Wholesalers, Inc.:

Fancy Fruit Wholesalers, Inc.
Financial Highlights
August 1–August 31

	Cost	Retail
Beginning Inventory	\$600,000	\$800,000
Net Purchases (August)	285,000	380,000
Net Sales (August) \$744,000		

Check your answer with the solution on page 605.

16-6 Estimating the Value of Ending Inventory by Using the Gross Profit Method

gross profit or gross margin method Method of inventory estimation using a company's gross margin percent to estimate the ending inventory. This method assumes that a company maintains approximately the same gross margin from year to year.

The **gross profit** or **gross margin method** uses a company's gross margin percent to estimate the ending inventory. This method assumes that a company maintains approximately the same gross margin from year to year. Inventories estimated in this manner are frequently used for interim reports and insurance claims; however, this method is not acceptable for inventory valuation on a company's annual financial statements.

From Chapter 15, remember that net sales is comprised of the cost of goods sold and gross margin.

Net sales (100%) = Cost of goods sold (%) + Gross margin (%)

From this equation, we see that when the gross margin percent is known, the cost of goods sold percent would be its complement, because together they equal net sales, which is 100%.

Cost of goods sold percent = 100% − Gross margin percent

Knowing the cost of goods sold percent is the key to this calculation. We use this percent to find the cost of goods sold, which, when subtracted from goods available for sale, gives us the estimated ending inventory.

STEPS TO ESTIMATE THE VALUE OF ENDING INVENTORY BY USING THE GROSS PROFIT METHOD:

Step 1. Calculate the goods available for sale:

Beginning inventory
+ Net purchases
Goods available for sale

Step 2. Find the estimated cost of goods sold by multiplying net sales by the cost of goods sold percent (complement of gross margin percent).

Estimated cost of goods sold = Net sales (100% − Gross margin %)

Step 3. Calculate the estimate of ending inventory by subtracting the estimated cost of goods sold from the goods available for sale.

Goods available for sale
− Estimated cost of goods sold
Estimated ending inventory

EXAMPLE

Wilbur Fishing Supply, Inc., maintains a gross margin of 45% on all its wholesale supplies. In April, Wilbur had a beginning inventory of $80,000, net purchases of $320,000, and net sales of $500,000. Use the gross profit method to estimate Wilbur's cost of ending inventory.

SOLUTION STRATEGY

Step 1.

Beginning inventory (April 1)	$ 80,000
+ Net purchases	320,000
Goods available for sale	$400,000

Step 2. Estimated cost of goods sold = Net sales (100% − Gross margin %)

Estimated cost of goods sold = $500,000 (100% − 45%) = $275,000

Step 3.

Goods available for sale	$400,000
− Estimated cost of goods sold	275,000
Estimated ending inventory (April 30)	$125,000

TRY-IT | EXERCISE

6. European Beauty Supply, Inc., maintains a gross margin of 39% on all its wholesale beauty supplies. In November, the company had a beginning inventory of $137,000, net purchases of $220,000, and net sales of $410,000. Use the gross profit method to estimate the cost of ending inventory for November.

Check your answer with the solution on page 605.

REVIEW EXERCISES | CHAPTER 16—SECTION II

2 **1.** Using the retail method, estimate the value of the ending inventory at cost on September 30 from the following information for Contemporary Furniture Designs, Inc. Round the cost ratio to the nearest tenth percent.

Contemporary Furniture Designs, Inc.
September 1–September 30

	Cost	Retail
Beginning Inventory, Sept. 1	$150,000	$450,000
Purchases (September)	90,000	270,000
Net Sales (September) $395,000		

1 **2.** Precision Fitness Equipment, Inc., maintains a gross margin of 55% on all its weight training products. In April, Precision had a beginning inventory of $146,000, net purchases of $208,000, and net sales of $437,000. Use the gross profit method to estimate the cost of ending inventory.

3. The following data represent the inventory figures for Marathon Welding Supply, Inc. Using the retail method, estimate the value of the ending inventory at cost on January 31. Round the cost ratio to the nearest tenth percent.

Marathon Welding Supply, Inc.
January 1–January 31

	Cost	Retail
Beginning Inventory, Jan. 1	$50,000	$120,000
Purchases (January)	90,000	216,000
Net Sales (January) $188,000		

4. You are the warehouse manager for the Carpet Boutique, Inc. On a Sunday in May, you receive a phone call from the owner. He states that the entire building and contents were destroyed by fire. For the police report and the insurance claim, the owner has asked you to estimate the value of the lost inventory. Your records, which luckily were backed up on the hard drive of your home computer, indicate that at the time of the fire the net sales to date were $615,400 and the purchases were $232,600. The beginning inventory, on January 1, was $312,000. For the past 3 years, the company has operated at a gross margin of 60%. Use the gross profit method to calculate your answer.

BUSINESS DECISION

Over or Under?

5. You own Anchor Marine, a retailer of boats, motors, and marine accessories. The store manager has just informed you that the amount of the physical inventory was incorrectly reported as $540,000 instead of the correct amount of $450,000. Unfortunately, yesterday you sent the quarterly financial statements to the stockholders. Now you must send revised statements and a letter of explanation.

   a. What effect did the error have on the items of the balance sheet for Anchor Marine? Express your answer as *overstated* or *understated* for the items affected by the error.

   b. What effect will the error have on the items of the income statement for Anchor Marine?

   c. Did this error make the Anchor Marine quarterly results look better or worse than they actually are?

SECTION III

INVENTORY TURNOVER AND TARGETS

In Chapter 15, we learned to use inventory turnover as one of the financial statement efficiency ratios. To review, **inventory turnover** or **stock turnover** is the number of times during an operating period that the average dollar invested in merchandise inventory was theoretically sold out or turned over.

inventory or stock turnover
The number of times during an operating period that the average dollar invested in merchandise inventory was theoretically sold out or turned over. May be calculated in retail dollars or in cost dollars.

Generally, the more expensive the item, the lower the turnover rate. For example, furniture and fine jewelry items might have a turnover rate of three or four times per year, whereas a grocery store might have a turnover of 15 or 20 times per year, or more. In this section, we revisit the concept of inventory turnover and learn to calculate it at retail and at cost.

Although a company must maintain inventory quantities large enough to meet the day-to-day demands of its operations, it is important to keep the amount invested in inventory to a minimum. In this section, we also learn to calculate target inventories for companies based on published industry standards.

Regardless of the method used to determine inventory turnover, the procedure always involves dividing some measure of sales volume by a measure of the typical or average inventory. This **average inventory** is commonly found by adding the beginning and ending inventories of the operating period, and dividing by 2.

average inventory
An estimate of a company's typical inventory at any given time, calculated by dividing the total of all inventories taken during an operating period by the number of times inventory was taken.

$$\text{Average inventory} = \frac{\text{Beginning inventory} + \text{Ending inventory}}{2}$$

Whenever possible, additional interim inventories should be used to increase the accuracy of the average inventory figure. For example, if a mid-year inventory was taken, this figure would be added to the beginning and ending inventories and the total divided by 3. If monthly inventories were available, they would be added and the total divided by 12.

16-7 Calculating Inventory Turnover Rate at Retail

When inventory turnover rate is calculated at retail, the measure of sales volume used is net sales. The average inventory is expressed in retail sales dollars by using the beginning and ending inventories at retail. The inventory turnover rate is expressed in number of *times* the inventory was sold out during the period.

STEPS TO CALCULATE INVENTORY TURNOVER RATE AT RETAIL:

Step 1. Calculate average inventory at retail:

$$\text{Average inventory}_{\text{at retail}} = \frac{\text{Beginning inventory at retail} + \text{Ending inventory at retail}}{2}$$

Step 2. Calculate the inventory turnover at retail:

$$\text{Inventory turnover}_{\text{at retail}} = \frac{\text{Net sales}}{\text{Average inventory at retail}}$$

Inventory turnover rates are important business indicators.

Everybody's Business

Real-World Connection

Inventory turnover is an important business indicator, particularly when compared with turnover rates from previous operating periods and with published industry statistics for similar-sized companies.

EXAMPLE

Hobby Town had net sales of $650,900 for the year. If the beginning inventory at retail was $143,000 and the ending inventory at retail was $232,100, what are the average inventory at retail and the inventory turnover at retail, rounded to the nearest tenth?

SOLUTION STRATEGY

Step 1. $\text{Average inventory}_{\text{at retail}} = \dfrac{\text{Beginning inventory at retail} + \text{Ending inventory at retail}}{2}$

$\text{Average inventory}_{\text{at retail}} = \dfrac{143{,}000 + 232{,}100}{2} = \dfrac{375{,}100}{2} = \underline{\underline{\$187{,}550}}$

Step 2. $\text{Inventory turnover}_{\text{at retail}} = \dfrac{\text{Net sales}}{\text{Average inventory at retail}}$

$\text{Inventory turnover}_{\text{at retail}} = \dfrac{650{,}900}{187{,}550} = 3.47 = \underline{\underline{3.5\text{ times}}}$

TRY-IT EXERCISE

7. Security Aluminum Windows, Inc., had net sales of $260,700 for the year. If the beginning inventory at retail was $65,100 and the ending inventory at retail was $52,800, what are (a) the average inventory and (b) the inventory turnover rounded to the nearest tenth?

Check your answers with the solutions on page 605.

16-8 Calculating Inventory Turnover Rate at Cost

Frequently, the inventory turnover rate of a company is expressed in terms of cost dollars rather than selling price or retail dollars. When this is the case, the cost of goods sold is used as the measure of sales volume and becomes the numerator in the formula. The denominator, average inventory, is calculated at cost.

STEPS TO CALCULATE INVENTORY TURNOVER RATE AT COST:

Step 1. Calculate the average inventory at cost:

$$\text{Average inventory}_{\text{at cost}} = \frac{\text{Beginning inventory at cost} + \text{Ending inventory at cost}}{2}$$

Step 2. Calculate the inventory turnover at cost:

$$\text{Inventory turnover}_{\text{at cost}} = \frac{\text{Cost of goods sold}}{\text{Average inventory at cost}}$$

EXAMPLE

Metro Hydraulics, Inc., had cost of goods sold of $416,200 for the year. If the beginning inventory at cost was $95,790 and the ending inventory at cost was $197,100, what are the average inventory at cost and the inventory turnover at cost, rounded to the nearest tenth?

SOLUTION STRATEGY

Step 1. $$\text{Average inventory}_{\text{at cost}} = \frac{\text{Beginning inventory at cost} + \text{Ending inventory at cost}}{2}$$

$$\text{Average inventory}_{\text{at cost}} = \frac{95{,}790 + 197{,}100}{2} = \frac{292{,}890}{2} = \underline{\underline{\$146{,}445}}$$

Step 2. $$\text{Inventory turnover}_{\text{at cost}} = \frac{\text{Cost of good sold}}{\text{Average inventory at cost}}$$

$$\text{Inventory turnover}_{\text{at cost}} = \frac{416{,}200}{146{,}445} = 2.84 = \underline{\underline{2.8 \text{ times}}}$$

TRY-IT | EXERCISE

8. E-Z Kwik Grocery Store had cost of goods sold of \$756,400 for the year. If the beginning inventory at cost was \$43,500 and the ending inventory at cost was \$59,300, what are (a) the average inventory at cost and (b) the inventory turnover rounded to the nearest tenth?

Check your answers with the solutions on page 605.

16-9 Calculating Target Inventories Based on Industry Standards

When inventory turnover is below average for a firm its size, it may be a signal that the company is carrying too much inventory. Carrying extra inventory can lead to extra expenses, such as warehousing costs and insurance. It also ties up money the company could use more efficiently elsewhere. In certain industries, some additional risks of large inventories would be losses due to price declines, obsolescence, or deterioration of the goods.

Trade associations and the federal government publish a wide variety of important industry statistics, ratios, and standards for every size company. When such inventory turnover figures are available, merchandise managers can use the following formulas to calculate the **target average inventory** required by their firm to achieve the published industry standards for a company with similar sales volume.

target average inventory
Inventory standards published by trade associations and the federal government for companies of all sizes and in all industries. Used by managers as *targets* for the ideal amount of inventory to carry for maximum efficiency.

$$\textbf{Target average inventory}_{\text{at cost}} = \frac{\textbf{Cost of goods sold}}{\textbf{Published inventory turnover at cost}}$$

$$\textbf{Target average inventory}_{\text{at retail}} = \frac{\textbf{Net sales}}{\textbf{Published inventory turnover at retail}}$$

Everybody's Business
Real-World Connection

✦ If industry figures are published at "cost," target inventory is calculated by using *cost of goods sold.*

✦ If industry figures are published at "retail," target inventory is calculated by using *net sales.*

EXAMPLE

WorldWide Photo, Inc., a wholesale photo supply business, had cost of goods sold of \$950,000 for the year. The beginning inventory at cost was \$245,000 and the ending inventory at cost amounted to \$285,000. According to the noted business research firm Dun & Bradstreet, the inventory turnover rate at cost for a photo business of this size is five times. (a) Calculate the average inventory and actual inventory turnover for WorldWide. (b) If the turnover is less than five times, calculate the target average inventory needed by WorldWide to theoretically come up to industry standards.

SOLUTION STRATEGY

(a)

Step 1. $$\text{Average inventory}_{\text{at cost}} = \frac{\text{Beginning inventory at cost} + \text{Ending inventory at cost}}{2}$$

$$\text{Average inventory}_{\text{at cost}} = \frac{245{,}000 + 285{,}000}{2} = \frac{530{,}000}{2} = \underline{\underline{\$265{,}000}}$$

Step 2. $$\text{Inventory turnover}_{\text{at cost}} = \frac{\text{Cost of goods sold}}{\text{Average inventory at cost}}$$

$$\text{Inventory turnover}_{\text{at cost}} = \frac{950{,}000}{265{,}000} = 3.58 = \underline{\underline{3.6 \text{ times}}}$$

(b)

Step 3. The actual inventory turnover for WorldWide is *3.6 times* per year compared with the industry standard of five times. This indicates that the company is carrying too much inventory. Let's calculate the target average inventory WorldWide should carry to meet industry standards.

$$\text{Target average inventory}_{\text{at cost}} = \frac{\text{Cost of goods sold}}{\text{Published inventory turnover at cost}}$$

$$\text{Target average inventory}_{\text{at cost}} = \frac{950{,}000}{5} = \underline{\underline{\$190{,}000}}$$

The actual average inventory carried by WorldWide for the year was $265,000 compared with the target inventory of $190,000. This indicates that, at any given time, the inventory for WorldWide averaged about $75,000 higher than that of its competition.

TRY-IT | EXERCISE

9. Mobile Communications, Inc., had net sales of $2,650,000 for the year. The beginning inventory at retail was $495,000, and the ending inventory at retail amounted to $380,000. The inventory turnover at retail published as the standard for a business of this size is seven times. (a) Calculate the average inventory and actual inventory turnover for the company. (b) If the turnover is less than seven times, calculate the target average inventory needed to theoretically come up to industry standards.

Check your answers with the solutions on page 605.

REVIEW EXERCISES | CHAPTER 16—SECTION III

Assuming that all net sales figures are at *retail* and all cost of goods sold figures are at *cost*, calculate the average inventory and inventory turnover for the following. If the actual turnover is less than the published rate, calculate the target average inventory necessary to come up to industry standards:

	Net Sales	Cost of Goods Sold	Beginning Inventory	Ending Inventory	Average Inventory	Inventory Turnover	Published Rate	Target Average Inventory
1.	$ 500,000		$ 50,000	$ 70,000	______	______	10.0	______
2.		$335,000	48,000	56,000	______	______	6.0	______
3.		1,200,000	443,000	530,000	______	______	3.5	______
4.	4,570,000		854,000	650,300	______	______	8.2	______

5. Quality Brakes and Parts, Inc., had net sales of $145,900 for the year. The beginning inventory at retail was $24,000, and the ending inventory at retail was $32,900.

a. What is the average inventory at retail?

b. What is the inventory turnover, rounded to the nearest tenth?

6. The Gourmet's Delight, a cooking equipment wholesaler, had cost of goods sold of $458,900 for the year. The beginning inventory at cost was $83,600, and the ending inventory at cost was $71,700.

a. What is the average inventory at cost?

b. What is the inventory turnover, rounded to the nearest tenth?

3 **7.** Modern Molding Corporation had cost of goods sold for the year of $1,250,000. The beginning inventory at cost was $135,000, and the ending inventory at cost amounted to $190,900. The inventory turnover rate published as the industry standard for a business of this size is 9.5 times.

a. Calculate the average inventory and actual inventory turnover rate for the company.

b. If the turnover rate is less than 9.5 times, calculate the target average inventory needed to theoretically come up to industry standards.

8. Trophy Masters had net sales for the year of $145,000. The beginning inventory at retail was $36,000, and the ending inventory at retail amounted to $40,300. The inventory turnover rate published as the industry standard for a business of this size is 4.9 times.

a. Calculate the average inventory and actual inventory turnover rate for the company.

b. If the turnover rate is less than 4.9 times, calculate the target average inventory needed to theoretically come up to industry standards.

BUSINESS DECISION

Keep Your Eye on the Feet

9. Another way to look at the concept of inventory turnover is by measuring sales per square foot. Taking the average inventory at retail and dividing it by the number of square feet devoted to a particular product will give you *average sales per square foot*. When you multiply this figure by the inventory turnover rate you get the *annual sales per square foot*.

It is important to know the amount of sales per square foot your merchandise is producing, both on the average and annually. These figures should be tracked monthly, and compared with industry standards for businesses of similar size and type.

You own Mega Music, a large multiproduct music store in a regional mall. Mega has 10,000 square feet of selling space divided into five departments.

a. From the table below, calculate the average and annual sales per square foot. Then, calculate the annual sales for each department and the total sales for the whole store.

b. If industry standards for this size store and type of merchandise is $200 per square foot in annual sales, which departments are below standards? What can be done to improve the situation?

c. (Optional) Use the Internet to research and share with the class the current "industry standard" sales per square foot and inventory turnover rates for the merchandise categories of your store.

Department	Square Feet	Average Inventory at Retail	Average Sales per Sq. Foot	Inventory Turnover	Annual Sales per Sq. Foot	Departmental Annual Sales
CDs	3,500	$153,000	________	5.2	________	________
DVDs	2,800	$141,000	________	4.6	________	________
Video Tapes	2,100	$38,500	________	4.1	________	________
Audio Tapes	500	$12,700	________	2.3	________	________
Accessories	1,100	$45,000	________	4.7	________	________
					Total Sales:	

Everybody's Business
Real-World Connection

DVD PLAYER SALES SET TO OUTPACE VCRS

VCRs are expected to outpace DVD players until 2004 when experts say the trend will reverse.

Sales of DVD players and VCRs
IN MILLIONS OF UNITS SHIPPED

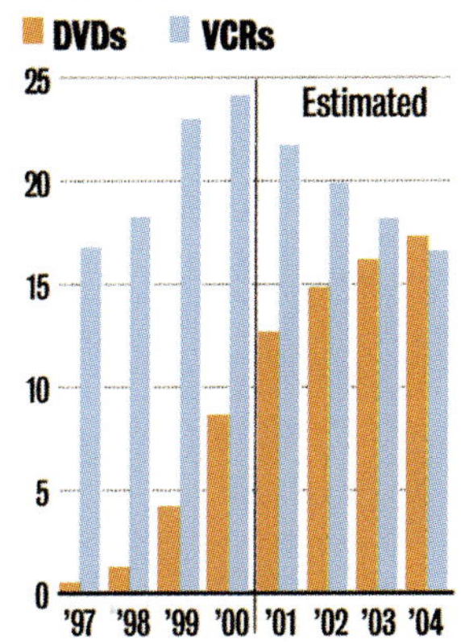

SOURCE: Consumer Electronics Association Market Research

CHAPTER FORMULAS

Inventory Valuation—Average Cost Method

$$\text{Average cost per unit} = \frac{\text{Cost of goods available for sale}}{\text{Total units available for sale}}$$

$$\text{Ending inventory} = \text{Units in ending inventory} \times \text{Average cost per unit}$$

Inventory Estimation—Retail Method

$$\text{Cost ratio} = \frac{\text{Goods available for sale at cost}}{\text{Goods available for sale at retail}}$$

$$\text{Estimated ending inventory at cost} = \text{Ending inventory at retail} \times \text{Cost ratio}$$

Inventory Estimation—Gross Profit Method

$$\text{Estimated cost of goods sold} = \text{Net sales } (100\% - \text{Gross margin } \%)$$

Inventory Turnover—Retail

$$\text{Average inventory}_{retail} = \frac{\text{Beginning inventory}_{retail} + \text{Ending inventory}_{retail}}{2}$$

$$\text{Inventory turnover}_{retail} = \frac{\text{Net sales}}{\text{Average inventory}_{retail}}$$

Inventory Turnover—Cost

$$\text{Average inventory}_{cost} = \frac{\text{Beginning inventory}_{cost} + \text{Ending inventory}_{cost}}{2}$$

$$\text{Inventory turnover}_{cost} = \frac{\text{Cost of goods sold}}{\text{Average inventory}_{cost}}$$

Target Inventory

$$\text{Target average inventory}_{cost} = \frac{\text{Cost of goods sold}}{\text{Published inventory turnover}_{cost}}$$

$$\text{Target average inventory}_{retail} = \frac{\text{Net sales}}{\text{Published inventory turnover}_{retail}}$$

✦ SUMMARY CHART ✦

SECTION I: Inventory Valuation

Topic	P/O, Page	Important Concepts	Illustrative Examples
Pricing Inventory by Using the First-In, First-Out (FIFO) Method	16-1 579	FIFO assumes that the items purchased first are the first items sold. The items in inventory at the end of the year are matched with the cost of items of the same type that were purchased most recently. *Inventory Pricing—FIFO* 1. List the number of units on hand at the end of the year and their corresponding costs, starting with the ending balance and working *backward* through the incoming shipments. 2. Multiply the number of units by the corresponding cost per unit for each purchase. 3. Calculate the value of ending inventory by totaling all the extensions from Step 2.	The following data represent the inventory figures for imported ceramic bowls at The Gift Express: **Date** / / **Units** / **Cost per Unit** Jan. 1 Beg. Inv. 55 $12.30 Mar. 9 Purch. 60 13.50 Aug. 12 Purch. 45 13.90 Nov. 27 Purch. 75 14.25

SECTION I: (continued)

Topic	P/O, Page	Important Concepts	Illustrative Examples
			On December 31, physical inventory revealed 130 bowls in stock. Calculate the value of the ending inventory by using FIFO. With the assumption under FIFO that the inventory cost flow is made up of the most recent costs, the 130 bowls would be valued as follows: **Date / Units / Cost / Total** Nov. 27 / 75 / @ 14.25 / 1,068.75 Aug. 12 / 45 / @ 13.90 / 625.50 Mar. 9 / 10 / @ 13.50 / 135.00 130 / $1,829.25
Pricing Inventory by Using the Last-In, First-Out (LIFO) Method	16-2 582	LIFO assumes that the items purchased last are sold or removed from inventory first. The items in inventory at the end of the year are matched with the cost of the same type items purchased earliest. *Inventory Pricing—LIFO:* 1. List the number of units on hand at the end of the year and their corresponding costs, starting with the beginning inventory and working *forward* through the incoming shipments. 2. Multiply the number of units by the corresponding cost per unit for each purchase. 3. Calculate the value of ending inventory by totaling all the extensions from Step 2.	Using the data above for The Gift Express, calculate the value of the 130 bowls in ending inventory by using LIFO. With the assumption under LIFO that the inventory cost flow is made up of the earliest costs, the 130 bowls would be valued as follows: **Date / Units / Cost / Total** Jan. 1 / 55 / @ 12.30 / 676.50 Mar. 9 / 60 / @ 13.50 / 810.00 Aug. 12 / 15 / @ 13.90 / 208.50 130 / $1,695.00
Pricing Inventory by Using the Average Cost Method	16-3 583	The average cost method, also known as the weighted average method, assumes that the cost of each unit of inventory is the average cost of all goods available for sale during that accounting period. 1. Calculate the average cost per unit by $\text{Average cost} = \frac{\text{Cost of goods available for sale}}{\text{Total units available for sale}}$ 2. Calculate the value of ending inventory by multiplying the number of units in ending inventory by the average cost per unit.	Using the average cost method of inventory pricing, what is the dollar value of the 130 bowls in ending inventory for The Gift Express? First, we shall extend and sum each purchase to find the total units available and the total cost of those units available for sale. **Date / Units / Cost per Unit / Total** Jan. 1 / 55 / $12.30 / $676.50 Mar. 9 / 60 / 13.50 / 810.00 Aug. 12 / 45 / 13.90 / 625.50 Nov. 27 / 75 / 14.25 / 1,068.75 235 / $3,180.75 $\text{Av. cost} = \frac{3{,}180.75}{235} = \$13.54$ End. inv. = 130 × 13.54 = $1,760.20

SECTION I: (continued)

<table>
<tr><th>Topic</th><th>P/O, Page</th><th>Important Concepts</th><th>Illustrative Examples</th></tr>
<tr><td>Pricing Inventory by Using the Lower-of-Cost-or-Market (LCM) Rule</td><td>16-4
584</td><td>When the market price or current replacement price of an inventory item declines below the actual price paid for that item, a company is permitted to use the lower-of-cost-or-market rule.
1. Choose lower of cost or market as valuation basis.
2. Multiply the number of units by the valuation basis price.
3. Add the extended totals in the Amount column to get the value of ending inventory.</td><td>From the following inventory data for small, medium, and large lamps at The Gift Express, calculate the value of the ending inventory by using the LCM rule.

Units | Unit Price: Cost | Unit Price: Market | Valuation Basis | Amount
small
34 | $40 | $43 | Cost | 1,360
medium
55 | 70 | 65 | Market | 3,575
large
47 | 99 | 103 | Cost | 4,653
Ending Inventory = $9,588</td></tr>
</table>

SECTION II: Inventory Estimation

<table>
<tr><td>Estimating the Value of Ending Inventory by Using the Retail Method</td><td>16-5
588</td><td>When it is too costly or not feasible to take a physical inventory count, inventory can be estimated. The retail method, as the name implies, is used by retail operations of all sizes.
1. List beginning inventory and purchases at both cost and retail.
2. Add purchases to beginning inventory to determine goods available for sale.
3. Calculate the cost ratio by
$$\text{Cost ratio} = \frac{\text{Goods available for sale at cost}}{\text{Goods available for sale at retail}}$$
4. Calculate ending inventory at retail by subtracting net sales from goods available for sale at retail.
5. Convert ending inventory at retail to ending inventory at cost by multiplying the ending inventory at retail by the cost ratio.</td><td>Estimate the value of the ending inventory at cost on July 31 from the following information for Allstate Distributors, Inc.

| Cost | Retail
Beg. Inv. | $300,000 | $450,000
Net Purch. | 100,000 | 150,000
Net Sales $366,000

| Cost | Retail
Beg. Inv. | $300,000 | $450,000
Net Purch. | +100,000 | +150,000
Goods Avail. | $400,000 | $600,000

$$\text{Cost ratio} = \frac{400{,}000}{600{,}000} = .67$$
Goods avail. at retail $600,000
−Net sales −366,000
Ending inv. at retail = $234,000

Ending inventory at cost =
234,000 × .67 = $156,780</td></tr>
<tr><td>Estimating the Value of Ending Inventory by Using the Gross Profit Method</td><td>16-6
590</td><td>The gross profit or gross margin method uses a company's gross margin percent to estimate the ending inventory. This method assumes that a company maintains approximately the same gross margin from year to year.
1. Calculate the goods available for sale.

Beginning inventory
+ Net purchases
Goods available for sale</td><td>The Stereo Connection maintains a gross margin of 60% on all speakers. In June, the beginning inventory was $95,000, net purchases were $350,600, and net sales were $615,000. What is the estimated cost of ending inventory, using the gross profit method?

Beginning inv. $95,000
+ Net purchases + 350,600
Goods available = $445,600</td></tr>
</table>

SECTION II: (continued)

Topic	P/O, Page	Important Concepts	Illustrative Examples
		2. Find the estimated cost of goods sold by multiplying net sales by the cost of goods sold percent (complement of gross margin percent). 3. Calculate the estimate of ending inventory by Goods available for sale − Estimated cost of goods sold Estimated ending inventory	Estimated cost of goods sold = Net sales (100% − Gr. margin %) = 615,000 (100% − 60%) = $246,000 Goods available $445,600 − Estimated CGS − 246,000 Est. ending inv. = $199,600

SECTION III: Inventory Turnover and Targets

Topic	P/O, Page	Important Concepts	Illustrative Examples
Calculating Inventory Turnover Rate at Retail	16-7 594	Inventory or stock turnover rate is the number of times during an operating period that the average inventory is sold out or turned over. Average inventory may be expressed either at retail or at cost. 1. Calculate the average inventory at retail by $\text{Average inventory}_{\text{at retail}} = \dfrac{\text{Beginning inventory at retail} + \text{Ending inventory at retail}}{2}$ 2. Calculate the inventory turnover at retail by $\text{Inventory turnover}_{\text{at retail}} = \dfrac{\text{Net sales}}{\text{Average inventory at retail}}$	Royal Rugs had net sales of $66,000 for the year. If the beginning inventory at retail was $24,400 and the ending inventory at retail was $19,600, what are the average inventory and the inventory turnover rate? Average inventory at retail = $\dfrac{24{,}400 + 19{,}600}{2} = \underline{\underline{\$22{,}000}}$ Inventory turnover at retail = $\dfrac{66{,}000}{22{,}000} = \underline{\underline{3 \text{ times}}}$
Calculating Inventory Turnover Rate at Cost	16-8 595	Inventory turnover may also be calculated at cost by using cost of goods sold and the average inventory at cost. 1. Calculate average inventory at cost by $\text{Average inventory}_{\text{at cost}} = \dfrac{\text{Beginning inventory at cost} + \text{Ending inventory at cost}}{2}$ 2. Calculate the inventory turnover at cost by $\text{Inventory turnover}_{\text{at cost}} = \dfrac{\text{Cost of goods sold}}{\text{Average inventory at cost}}$	Astro Enterprises had $426,000 in cost of goods sold. The beginning inventory at cost was $75,000, and the ending inventory at cost was $95,400. What are Astro's average inventory at cost and inventory turnover rate? Average inventory at cost = $\dfrac{75{,}000 + 95{,}400}{2} = \underline{\underline{85{,}200}}$ Inventory turnover at cost = $\dfrac{426{,}000}{85{,}200} = \underline{\underline{5 \text{ times}}}$

SECTION III: (continued)

Topic	P/O, Page	Important Concepts	Illustrative Examples
Calculating Target Average Inventories Based on Industry Standards	16-9 596	When inventory turnover is below average, based on published industry standards, it may be a signal that a company is carrying too much inventory. This can lead to extra expenses such as warehousing and insurance. The following formulas can be used to calculate target average inventories at cost or retail to theoretically achieve the published turnover rate. $\text{Target inventory at cost} = \frac{\text{Cost of goods sold}}{\text{Published rate at cost}}$ $\text{Target inventory at retail} = \frac{\text{Net sales}}{\text{Published rate at retail}}$	Eveready Distributing had cost of goods sold of $560,000 for the year. The beginning inventory at cost was $140,000, and the ending inventory was $180,000. The published rate for a firm this size is four times. Calculate the average inventory and turnover rate for Eveready. If the rate is less than four times, calculate the target average inventory. Average inventory at cost = $\frac{140{,}000 + 180{,}000}{2} = \underline{\underline{\$160{,}000}}$ Inventory turnover at cost= $\frac{560{,}000}{160{,}000} = \underline{\underline{3.5 \text{ times}}}$ Target average inventory = $\frac{560{,}000}{4} = \underline{\underline{\$140{,}000}}$

TRY-IT EXERCISE | SOLUTIONS

1. FIFO Inventory Valuation

Units	Cost/Unit	Total
300	$8.75	$2,625
80	9.00	720
380		$3,345

2. LIFO Inventory Valuation

Units	Cost/Unit	Total
200	$8.00	$1,600
100	8.50	850
80	9.00	720
380		$3,170

3. Average Cost Method

$$\text{Average cost/unit} = \frac{\text{Cost of goods available}}{\text{Total units available}} = \frac{7{,}325}{850} = \$8.62$$

Ending inventory = Units in inv. × Av. cost/unit

Ending inventory = 380 × 8.62 = $3,275.60

4. LCM Rule

The Galleria Gift Shop

Item	Quantity	Valuation/Basis	Price	Amount
Frames	75	Market	$ 9.20	$ 690.00
Ash trays	120	Cost	26.30	3,156.00
16" Vases	88	Market	39.70	3,493.60
12" Vases	64	Market	21.40	1,369.60
Bowls	42	Cost	36.90	1,549.80
				$10,259.00

5.

	Cost	Retail
Beginning Inventory	\$600,000	\$800,000
+ Net Purchases	+ 285,000	+ 380,000
Goods Available for Sale	\$885,000	\$1,180,000

$$\text{Cost ratio} = \frac{\text{Goods available}_{\text{cost}}}{\text{Goods available}_{\text{retail}}} = \frac{885{,}000}{1{,}180{,}000} = .75 = 75\%$$

Goods available$_{\text{retail}}$	1,180,000
− Net sales	− 744,000
Ending inventory$_{\text{retail}}$	\$436,000

$$\text{Ending inventory}_{\text{cost}} = \text{Ending inventory}_{\text{retail}} \times \text{Cost ratio}$$
$$\text{Ending inventory}_{\text{cost}} = 436{,}000 \times .75 = \underline{\underline{\$327{,}000}}$$

6.

Beginning inventory	\$137,000
+ Net purchases	+ 220,000
Goods available for sale	\$357,000

Estimated cost of goods sold = Net sales (100% − Gross margin %)
Estimated cost of goods sold = 410,000 (100% − 39%)
Estimated cost of goods sold = 410,000 (.61) = \$250,100

Goods available for sale	\$357,000
− Estimated cost of goods sold	− 250,100
Estimated ending inventory	\$106,900

7. a. $$\text{Average inventory}_{\text{retail}} = \frac{\text{Beginning inventory}_{\text{retail}} + \text{Ending inventory}_{\text{retail}}}{2}$$

$$\text{Average inventory}_{\text{retail}} = \frac{65{,}100 + 52{,}800}{2} = \underline{\underline{\$58{,}950}}$$

b. $$\text{Inventory turnover}_{\text{retail}} = \frac{\text{Net sales}}{\text{Average inventory}_{\text{retail}}}$$

$$\text{Inventory turnover}_{\text{retail}} = \frac{260{,}700}{58{,}950} = \underline{\underline{4.4}}$$

8. a. $$\text{Average inventory}_{\text{cost}} = \frac{\text{Beginning inventory}_{\text{cost}} + \text{Ending inventory}_{\text{cost}}}{2}$$

$$\text{Average inventory}_{\text{cost}} = \frac{43{,}500 + 59{,}300}{2} = \underline{\underline{\$51{,}400}}$$

b. $$\text{Inventory turnover}_{\text{cost}} = \frac{\text{Cost of goods sold}}{\text{Average inventory}_{\text{cost}}}$$

$$\text{Inventory turnover}_{\text{cost}} = \frac{756{,}400}{51{,}400} = \underline{\underline{14.7}}$$

9. a. $$\text{Average inventory} = \frac{\text{Beginning inventory} + \text{Ending inventory}}{2}$$

$$\text{Average inventory} = \frac{495{,}000 + 380{,}000}{2} = \underline{\underline{\$437{,}500}}$$

$$\text{Inventory turnover} = \frac{\text{Net sales}}{\text{Average inventory}_{\text{retail}}} = \frac{2{,}650{,}000}{437{,}500} = \underline{\underline{6.1}}$$

b. $$\text{Target average inventory} = \frac{\text{Net sales}}{\text{Published turnover}}$$

$$\text{Target average inventory} = \frac{2{,}650{,}000}{7} = \underline{\underline{\$378{,}571.43}}$$

Name ____________________

Class ____________________

Answers

1. ____________________

____

2. a. ____________________

b. ____________________

c. ____________________

3. ____________________

CHAPTER 16 | ASSESSMENT TEST

1. Calculate the total number of units available for sale and the cost of goods available for sale from the following inventory of imported silk ties for Downtown Fashions, Inc.:

Date	Units Purchased	Cost per Unit	Total Cost
Beginning Inventory, January 1	59	$46.10	______
Purchase, March 29	75	43.50	______
Purchase, July 14	120	47.75	______
Purchase, October 12	95	50.00	______
Purchase, December 8	105	53.25	______
Total units available:	____	Cost of goods available for sale:	______

2. As the manager of Downtown Fashions (Exercise 1), you took physical inventory of the ties on December 31 and found that 128 were still in stock.

a. What is the dollar value of the ending inventory by using FIFO?

b. What is the dollar value of the ending inventory by using LIFO?

c. What is the dollar value of the ending inventory by using the average cost method?

2

3. Determine the value of the following inventory for The Rainbow Tile Company by using the lower-of-cost-or-market rule.

Description	Quantity in Square Feet	Unit Price Cost	Unit Price Market	Valuation Basis	Amount
Terracotta 12"	8,400	$4.55	$5.10	______	______
Super Saltillo 16"	7,300	8.75	8.08	______	______
Monocottura 10"	4,500	3.11	2.90	______	______
Glazed Ceramic	6,200	4.50	5.25	______	______
Brick Pavers	12,700	3.25	3.15	______	______
				Total value of inventory:	______

4. Using the retail method, estimate the value of the ending inventory at cost on May 31 from the following information for Quality Shutters, Inc. Round the cost ratio to the nearest tenth percent.

Quality Shutters, Inc.
May 1–May 31

	Cost	Retail
Beginning Inventory, May 1	$145,600	$196,560
Purchases	79,000	106,650
Net Sales $210,800		

5. On July 24, a tornado destroyed Midwest Wholesalers' main warehouse and all its contents. Company records indicate that at the time of the tornado the net sales to date were $535,100 and the purchases were $422,900. The beginning inventory, on January 1, was $319,800. For the past 3 years, the company has maintained a gross margin of 35%. Use the gross profit method to estimate the inventory loss for the insurance claim.

Assuming that all net sales figures are at *retail* and all cost of goods sold figures are at *cost*, calculate the average inventory and inventory turnover for Exercises 6–7. If the actual turnover is below the published rate, calculate the target average inventory necessary to come up to industry standards:

	Net Sales	Cost of Goods Sold	Beginning Inventory	Ending Inventory	Average Inventory	Inventory Turnover	Published Rate	Target Average Inventory
6.	$290,000		$88,000	$94,000	______	______	4.4	______
7.		$760,000	184,000	123,000	______	______	6.8	______

8. Midway Electronics had net sales of $435,900 for the year. The beginning inventory at retail was $187,600, and the ending inventory at retail was $158,800.

a. What is the average inventory at retail?

b. What is the inventory turnover rounded to the nearest tenth?

c. If the turnover rate for similar-sized competitors is 3.8 times, calculate the target average inventory needed to theoretically come up to industry standards.

Name ______________________

Class ______________________

Answers

4. ______________________

5. ______________________

6. ______________________

____

____

7. ______________________

____

____

8. a. ______________________

b. ______________________

c. ______________________

Name ______________________

Class ______________________

Answers

9. a. ______________________

b. ______________________

c. ______________________

10. a. FIFO: ______________________

LIFO: ______________________

Average cost: ______________________

9. The Fabric Warehouse had cost of goods sold for the year of $884,000. The beginning inventory at cost was $305,500, and the ending inventory at cost amounted to $414,200. The inventory turnover rate published as the industry standard for a business of this size is five times.

a. What is the average inventory at cost?

b. What is the inventory turnover rounded to the nearest tenth?

c. What is the target average inventory needed to theoretically come up to the industry standard?

Everybody's Business

Real-World Connection

This Business Decision, "Inventory Valuation and the Bottom Line," clearly illustrates how the various inventory methods can affect a company's profit picture. Note the significant variation in net income among the three methods.

BUSINESS DECISION

Inventory Valuation and the Bottom Line

10. You are the chief accountant of Dollar Time Industries, Inc. In anticipation of the upcoming annual stockholders meeting, the president of the company asked you to determine the effect of the FIFO, LIFO, and average inventory valuation methods on the company's income statement.

Beginning inventory, January 1, was 10,000 units at $5.00 each. Purchases during the year consisted of 15,000 units at $6.00 on April 15, 20,000 units at $7.00 on July 19, and 25,000 units at $8.00 on November 2.

a. If ending inventory on December 31 was 40,000 units, calculate the value of this inventory by using the three valuation methods:

FIFO: ________ LIFO ________ Average Cost: ________

Name ______________________

Class ______________________

b. Complete the comparative income statement for the year by using the following information and the format below:

Net sales	30,000 units at $12 each
Operating expenses	$100,000
Income tax rate	30%

Dollar Time Industries, Inc.
Comparative Income Statement

	FIFO	LIFO	Average Cost
Net sales			
Beginning inventory			
Purchases			
Cost of goods available for sale			
Ending inventory			
Cost of goods sold			
Gross profit			
Operating expenses			
Income before taxes			
Income tax			
Net income			

c. Which inventory method should be used if the objective is to pay the least amount of taxes?

d. Which method should be used if the objective is to show the greatest amount of profit to the shareholders in the annual report?

Answers

9. b. ______________________

c. ______________________

d. ______________________

All the Math That's Fit to Learn

The Business Math Times

Volume XVI | Inventory | One Dollar

The ABCs of UPCs

If you look in your pantry or refrigerator right now, you will find that just about every package you see has a UPC bar code printed on it. In fact, nearly every item that you purchase from a grocery store, department store, or mass merchandiser has a UPC bar code on it somewhere.

17 OZ NATURE VALLEY FRUIT GRANOLA UPC #

0 16000 65110 4

"UPC" stands for Universal Product Code. UPC bar codes were originally created in the early 1970s to help grocery stores speed up the check-out process and keep better track of inventory. The new system quickly spread to all other retail products because it was so successful.

The bar code is a 12-digit number that identifies the manufacturer and the product. In general, every item the manufacturer sells, as well as every size and type of package gets its own code.

"Well, when can I buy your 'always in stock' products?"

"Quote . . . Unquote"

It's easy to change cash into inventory . . .
the challenge is to turn inventory back into cash!
—*Effective Inventory Management, Inc.*

Nothing is particularly hard if you divide it into small jobs.
—*Henry Ford*

Much Smarter Labels!

Long checkout lines at the grocery store are one of the biggest complaints about the shopping experience. According to writer Kevin Bonsor, by 2005, these lines could disappear when the ubiquitous UPC bar code is replaced by smart labels, also called radio frequency identification (RFID) tags.

RFID tags are intelligent bar codes that can talk to a networked system to track every product that you put in your shopping cart. Imagine going to the grocery store, filling up your cart, and walking right out the door. No longer will you have to wait as someone rings up each item in your cart.

Instead, these RFID tags will communicate with an electronic reader that will detect every item in the cart and ring each up almost instantly. The reader will be connected to a large network that will send information on your products to the retailer and product manufacturers. Your bank will then be notified and the amount of the bill will be deducted from your account. No lines, no waiting.

This technology, once limited to tracking cattle, railroad cars, airline baggage, and highway tolls, will soon be tracking trillions of consumer products worldwide.

The First Swipe

At 8:01 a.m. on June 26, 1974, a customer at Marsh's supermarket in Troy, Ohio, made the first purchase of a product with a bar code, a 10-pack of Wrigley's Juicy Fruit Gum. That pack of gum took its place in American history, and is now on display at the Smithsonian Institute's National Museum of American History in Washington, D.C.

Inventory Pie

According to an Accounting Trends and Techniques survey by the American Institute of Certified Public Accountants (AICPA), the following is the breakdown of inventory valuation methods used by the 600 largest U.S. companies.

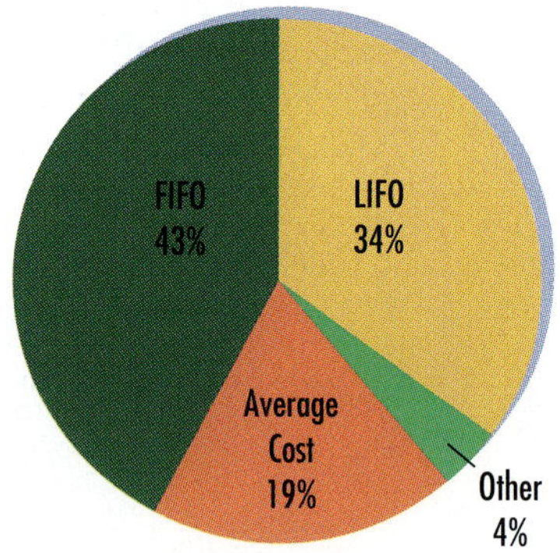

Brainteaser

TAKE INVENTORY!

How much dirt is in a hole 15 feet long by 10 feet wide by 5 feet deep?

ANSWER TO LAST ISSUE'S BRAINTEASER

The frog will *never* reach the wall.

CHAPTER 17

Depreciation

PERFORMANCE OBJECTIVES

Section I Traditional Depreciation—Methods Used for Financial Statement Reporting

17-1 Calculating depreciation by the straight-line method. (p. 613)
17-2 Calculating depreciation by the sum-of-the-years' digits method. (p. 614)
17-3 Calculating depreciation by the declining-balance method. (p. 616)
17-4 Calculating depreciation by the units-of-production method. (p. 618)

Section II Asset Cost Recovery Systems—IRS Prescribed Methods for Income Tax Reporting

17-5 Calculating depreciation by using the Modified Accelerated Cost Recovery System (MACRS). (p. 623)
17-6 Calculating the periodic depletion cost of natural resources. (p. 625)

long-term or long-lived assets
Relatively fixed or permanent assets such as land, buildings, tools, equipment, and vehicles that companies acquire in the course of operating a business.

depreciation, or depreciation expense
The decrease in value from the original cost of a long-term asset over its useful life.

book value
The value of an asset at any given time. It is the original cost less the accumulated depreciation to that point.

total cost, or original basis
The total amount a company pays for an asset, including freight, handling, and setup charges.

residual, scrap, salvage, or trade-in value
The value of an asset at the time it is taken out of service.

useful life
The length of time an asset is expected to generate revenue.

In Chapter 15, we learned a firm's assets are divided into three categories: current assets; property, plant, and equipment; and investments and other assets. This chapter deals with the valuation of the **long-term** or **long-lived assets** of the firm: the property, plant, and equipment. Companies acquire these relatively fixed or permanent assets in the course of building and operating a business. Some examples of these assets would be land, buildings, equipment, machinery, vehicles, furniture, fixtures, and tools.

As time goes by, the usefulness or productivity of these assets, except land, decreases. Think of this decrease as a loss of revenue earning power. Accordingly, the cost of these assets is distributed over their useful life to coincide with the revenue earned. This cost write-off is known as **depreciation.** On the income statement, depreciation is listed under operating expenses as **depreciation expense.** On the balance sheet, it is used to determine the current **book value** of an asset, whereby

Book value = Original cost − Accumulated depreciation

Assets depreciate for a number of reasons. They may physically wear out from use and deterioration or they may depreciate because they have become inadequate and obsolete. Four important factors must be taken into account to determine the amount of depreciation expense of an asset.

1. The **total cost,** or **original basis** of the asset. This amount includes such items as freight, handling, and set-up charges.
2. The asset's estimated **residual value** at the time that it is taken out of service. This is also known as **scrap value, salvage value,** or **trade-in value.**
3. An estimate of the **useful life** of the asset or the length of time it is expected to generate revenue. To be depreciated, an asset must have a life greater than 1 year.
4. The method of calculating depreciation must match the way in which the asset will depreciate. Some assets depreciate evenly over the years (straight-line depreciation), whereas others depreciate more quickly at first and then slow down in the later years (accelerated depreciation). Regardless of which method a company chooses, at the end of the useful life of an asset, the total amount of depreciation expense write-off will be the same.

This chapter examines the various methods used to depreciate assets. In Section I, we learn to calculate depreciation by the four traditional methods: straight-line; sum-of-the-years' digits; declining-balance; and units-of-production. Any of these methods may be used for financial statement reporting. However, once a method has been implemented, it cannot be changed.

Frequently, the amount of depreciation reported by a company on its financial statements will differ from the amount reported to the IRS for income tax purposes, because the IRS allows additional options for calculating depreciation expense. Today, the most widely used method for tax purposes is known as the modified accelerated cost recovery system (MACRS). This method is covered in Section II.

SECTION I

TRADITIONAL DEPRECIATION—METHODS USED FOR FINANCIAL STATEMENT REPORTING

Depreciation is most frequently based on time, how many years an asset is expected to last. Certain assets, however, are depreciated more accurately on the basis of some productivity measure such as units of output for production machinery, or mileage for vehicles, regardless of time. This section deals with both time- and productivity-based depreciation methods.

17-1 Calculating Depreciation by the Straight-Line Method

The **straight-line depreciation** method is by far the most widely used in business today. It provides for equal periodic charges to be written off over the estimated useful life of the asset.

Once the annual depreciation has been determined, we can set up a **depreciation schedule.** The depreciation schedule is a chart illustrating the depreciation activity of the asset for each year of its useful life. The chart shows the amount of depreciation each year, the accumulated depreciation to date, and the book value of the asset.

straight-line depreciation
A method of depreciation that provides for equal periodic charges to be written off over the estimated useful life of an asset.

depreciation schedule
Chart showing the depreciation activity (depreciation, accumulated depreciation, and book value) of an asset for each year of its useful life.

STEPS TO PREPARE A DEPRECIATION SCHEDULE BY THE STRAIGHT-LINE METHOD:

Step 1. Determine the total cost and salvage value of the asset.

Step 2. Subtract salvage value from total cost to find the total amount of depreciation.

$$\text{Total depreciation} = \text{Total cost} - \text{Salvage value}$$

Step 3. Calculate the annual amount of depreciation by dividing the total depreciation by the useful life of the asset.

$$\text{Annual depreciation} = \frac{\text{Total depreciation}}{\text{Estimated useful life (years)}}$$

Step 4. Set up the depreciation schedule in the form of a chart with the following headings:

End of Year	Annual Depreciation	Accumulated Depreciation	Book Value

Everybody's Business
Learning Tip
On a depreciation schedule, the starting book value is the *original cost* of the asset, and the last book value is the *salvage value* of the asset.

EXAMPLE

Barton Enterprises purchased a computer system for $9,000. Shipping charges were $125, and setup and programming amounted to $375. The system is expected to last 4 years and has a residual value of $1,500. If Barton elects to use the straight-line method of depreciation for the computer, calculate the total cost, total depreciation, and annual depreciation. Prepare a depreciation schedule for its useful life.

SOLUTION STRATEGY

Step 1.

$$\text{Total cost} = \text{Cost} + \text{Freight} + \text{Setup expenses}$$

$$\text{Total cost} = 9{,}000 + 125 + 375 = \underline{\underline{\$9{,}500}}$$

Step 2.

$$\text{Total depreciation} = \text{Total cost} - \text{Salvage value}$$

$$\text{Total depreciation} = 9{,}500 - 1{,}500 = \underline{\underline{\$8{,}000}}$$

Step 3.

$$\text{Annual depreciation} = \frac{\text{Total depreciation}}{\text{Estimated useful life (years)}}$$

$$\text{Annual depreciation} = \frac{8{,}000}{4} = \underline{\underline{\$2{,}000}}$$

Step 4.

Depreciation Schedule
Barton Enterprises, Computer System

End of Year	Annual Depreciation	Accumulated Depreciation	Book Value
			$9,500 (original cost)
1	$2,000	$2,000	7,500
2	2,000	4,000	5,500
3	2,000	6,000	3,500
4	2,000	8,000	1,500 (salvage value)

Expensive assets such as this semi-truck are considered long-lived assets, the value of which depreciates over time.

TRY-IT | EXERCISE

1. Holsum Bakery purchased a new bread oven for $125,000. Shipping charges were $1,150.00, and installation amounted to $750.00. The oven is expected to last 5 years and has a trade-in value of $5,000. If Holsum elects to use the straight-line method, calculate the total cost, total depreciation, and annual depreciation of the oven. Prepare a depreciation schedule for its useful life.

Check your answers with the solutions on pages 631–632.

17-2 Calculating Depreciation by the Sum-of-the-Years' Digits Method

accelerated depreciation
Depreciation methods that assume an asset depreciates more in the early years of its useful life than in the later years.

sum-of-the-years' digits
A method of accelerated depreciation that allows an asset to depreciate the most during the first year, with decreasing amounts each year thereafter. Total depreciation is based on the total cost of an asset less its salvage value.

The sum-of-the-years' digits and the declining-balance methods of calculating depreciation are the two **accelerated depreciation** methods. These methods assume that an asset depreciates more in the early years of its useful life than in the later years. Under the sum-of-the-years' digits method, the yearly charge for depreciation declines steadily over the estimated useful life of the asset because a successively smaller fraction is applied each year to the total depreciation (total cost − salvage value).

This fraction is known as the **sum-of-the-years' digits** fraction. The denominator of the fraction is the sum of the digits of the estimated life of the asset. This number does not change. The numerator of the fraction is the number of years of useful life remaining. This number changes every year as the asset gets older and older. This sum-of-the-years' digits depreciation rate fraction can be expressed as

$$\text{SYD depreciation rate fraction} = \frac{\text{Years of useful life remaining}}{\text{Sum-of-the-digits of the useful life}}$$

The denominator (the sum of the years' digits) can be calculated by adding all the digits of the years, or by the following formula:

$$\text{SYD} = \frac{n(n+1)}{2}$$

where

$$n = \text{the number of years of useful life of the asset}$$

For example, let's compute the depreciation rate fractions for an asset that has a useful life of 4 years. The denominator, the sum of the digits of 4, is 10. This is calculated by 4 + 3 + 2 + 1 = 10 or by the SYD formula, 4(4 + 1) ÷ 2 = 10. Remember, the denominator does not change. The numerator of the fractions will be 4, 3, 2, and 1 for each succeeding year.

Year	Depreciation Rate Fraction	Depreciation Rate	
		Decimal	Percent
1	4/10	.40	40%
2	3/10	.30	30%
3	2/10	.20	20%
4	1/10	.10	10%

From this chart, we can see that an asset with 4 years of useful life will depreciate $\frac{4}{10}$ or 40% in the first year, $\frac{3}{10}$ or 30% in the second year, and so on. The accelerated rate of 40% depreciation write-off in the first year gives the business a reduced tax advantage and therefore an incentive to invest in new equipment.

STEPS TO PREPARE A DEPRECIATION SCHEDULE BY USING THE SUM-OF-THE-YEARS' DIGITS METHOD:

Step 1. Find the total depreciation of the asset by

$$\text{Total depreciation} = \text{Total cost} - \text{Salvage value}$$

Step 2. Calculate the SYD depreciation rate fraction for each year by

$$\text{SYD depreciation rate fraction} = \frac{\text{Years of useful life remaining}}{\frac{n(n+1)}{2}}$$

Step 3. Calculate the depreciation for each year by multiplying the total depreciation by that year's depreciation rate fraction.

$$\text{Annual depreciation} = \text{Total depreciation} \times \text{Depreciation rate fraction}$$

Step 4. Set up a depreciation schedule in the form of a chart with the following headings:

End of Year	Total Depreciation	×	Depreciation Rate Fraction	=	Annual Depreciation	Accumulated Depreciation	Book Value

EXAMPLE

All City Wholesalers purchased a delivery truck for $35,000. The truck is expected to have a useful life of 5 years and a trade-in value of $5,000. Using the sum-of-the-years' digits method, prepare a depreciation schedule for All City.

SOLUTION STRATEGY

Following the steps for preparing a depreciation schedule by using sum-of-the-years' digits:

Step 1. Total depreciation = Total cost − Salvage value

Total depreciation = 35,000 − 5,000 = $30,000

Step 2. Year 1: SYD depreciation rate fraction $= \dfrac{\text{Years of useful life remaining}}{\frac{n(n+1)}{2}}$

$$\text{SYD depreciation rate fraction} = \frac{5}{\frac{5(5+1)}{2}} = \frac{5}{15}$$

The depreciation rate fraction for year 1 is $\frac{5}{15}$. The depreciation fractions for the remaining years will have the same denominator, 15 (the sum of the digits of 5). Only the numerators will change, in descending order. The depreciation fractions for the remaining years are $\frac{4}{15}$, $\frac{3}{15}$, $\frac{2}{15}$, and $\frac{1}{15}$.

Note how accelerated this SYD method is: $\frac{5}{15}$, or $\frac{1}{3}$ of the asset (33.3%), is allowed to be written off in the first year. This is compared with only $\frac{1}{5}$ (20%) per year by using the straight-line method.

Step 3. Annual depreciation = Total depreciation × Depreciation rate fraction

$$\text{Annual depreciation (year 1)} = 30{,}000 \times \frac{5}{15} = \$10{,}000$$

$$\text{Annual depreciation (year 2)} = 30{,}000 \times \frac{4}{15} = \$8{,}000$$

Continue this calculation for each of the remaining 3 years. Then prepare the schedule.

Step 4.

All City Wholesalers
SYD Depreciation Schedule
Delivery Truck

End of Year	Total Depreciation	×	Depreciation Rate Fraction	=	Annual Depreciation	Accumulated Depreciation	Book Value
							(new) $35,000
1	30,000	×	$\frac{5}{15}$	=	10,000	10,000	25,000
2	30,000	×	$\frac{4}{15}$	=	8,000	18,000	17,000
3	30,000	×	$\frac{3}{15}$	=	6,000	24,000	11,000
4	30,000	×	$\frac{2}{15}$	=	4,000	28,000	7,000
5	30,000	×	$\frac{1}{15}$	=	2,000	30,000	5,000

TRY-IT | EXERCISE

2. StyleCraft Furniture Manufacturers purchased new production-line machinery for a total of $44,500. The company expects this machinery to last 6 years and have a residual value of $2,500. Using the sum-of-the-years' digits method, prepare a depreciation schedule for StyleCraft.

Check your answers with the solutions on page 632.

17-3 Calculating Depreciation by the Declining-Balance Method

declining-balance
A method of accelerated depreciation that uses a multiple (125%, 150%, or 200%) of the straight-line rate to calculate depreciation. Further accelerated because depreciation is based on the original cost of the asset, with salvage value only being considered in the last year.

double-declining balance
Name given to the declining-balance method of depreciation when the straight-line multiple is 200%.

The second widely accepted method of accelerated depreciation in business is known as the **declining-balance** method. This method uses a *multiple* of the straight-line rate to calculate depreciation. The most frequently used multiples are 1.25, 1.5, and 2. When 1.25 is used, it is known as the 125% declining balance, when 1.5 is used it is known as the 150% declining balance. When 2 is the multiple, the method is known as the **double-declining balance.**

To calculate the declining-balance rate, we first determine the straight-line rate by dividing 1 by the number of years of useful life, then multiplying by the appropriate declining-balance multiple. For example, when using the double-declining balance, an asset with a useful life of 4 years would have a straight-line rate of 25% per year ($1 \div 4 = \frac{1}{4} =$ 25%). This rate is then multiplied by the declining-balance multiple, 2, to get 50%, the double-declining rate. The following formula should be used for this calculation:

$$\textbf{Declining-balance rate} = \frac{1}{\textbf{Useful life}} \times \textbf{Multiple}$$

To further accelerate the depreciation, this declining-balance rate is applied to the original total cost of the asset. Salvage value is not considered until the last year of depreciation. When preparing a depreciation schedule by using the declining-balance method, the depreciation stops when the book value of the asset reaches the salvage value. By IRS regulations, the asset cannot be depreciated below the salvage value.

STEPS TO PREPARE A DEPRECIATION SCHEDULE BY USING THE DECLINING-BALANCE METHOD:

Step 1. Calculate the declining-balance rate by the formula

$$\text{Declining-balance rate} = \frac{1}{\text{Useful life}} \times \text{Multiple}$$

Step 2. Calculate the depreciation for each year by applying the rate to each year's beginning book value, which is the ending book value of the previous year.

Depreciation for the year = Beginning book value × Declining-balance rate

Step 3. Calculate the ending book value for each year by subtracting the depreciation for the year from the beginning book value:

Ending book value = Beginning book value − Depreciation for the year

Step 4. When the ending book value equals the salvage value, the depreciation is complete.

Step 5. Set up a depreciation schedule in the form of a chart with the following headings:

End of Year	Beginning Book Value	Depreciation Rate	Depreciation for the Year	Accumulated Depreciation	Ending Book Value

Everybody's Business

Real-World Connection

From Chapter 15, Financial Statements, remember that depreciation appears on both the balance sheet and the income statement.

- *Balance sheet*—Used to determine book value of an asset.
- *Income statement*—Listed as an operating expense.

EXAMPLE

Continental Shipping bought a forklift for $20,000. It is expected to have a 5-year useful life and a trade-in value of $2,000. Prepare a depreciation schedule for this asset by using the double-declining balance method.

SOLUTION STRATEGY

Step 1. $\text{Declining-balance rate} = \frac{1}{\text{Useful life}} \times \text{Multiple}$

$\text{Declining-balance rate} = \frac{1}{5} \times 2 = .20 \times 2 = .40 = \underline{\underline{40\%}}$

Step 2. Depreciation for the year = Beginning book value × Declining-balance rate

Depreciation: Year 1 = 20,000 × .40 = $\underline{\underline{\$8,000}}$

Step 3. Ending book value = Beginning book value − Depreciation for the year

Ending book value: Year 1 = 20,000 − 8,000 = $\underline{\underline{\$12,000}}$

Repeat Steps 2 and 3 for years 2, 3, 4, and 5.

Step 4. In year 5, although the calculated depreciation is $1,036.80 (2,592 × .4), the allowable depreciation is limited to $592 (2,592 − 2,000), because the book value has reached the $2,000 salvage value. At this point, the depreciation is complete.

Step 5.

Continental Shipping, Inc.
Depreciation Schedule
5-year, double-declining balance

End of Year	Beginning Book Value	Depreciation Rate	Depreciation for the Year	Accumulated Depreciation	Ending Book Value
					(new) $20,000
1	20,000	40%	8,000	8,000	12,000
2	12,000	40%	4,800	12,800	7,200
3	7,200	40%	2,880	15,680	4,320
4	4,320	40%	1,728	17,408	2,592
5	2,592	40%	592*	18,000	2,000

*Maximum allowable to reach salvage value.

TRY-IT | EXERCISE

3. Southwest Air Service bought a small commuter airplane for \$386,000. It is expected to have a useful life of 4 years and a trade-in value of \$70,000. Prepare a depreciation schedule for the airplane by using the 150% declining-balance method.

Check your answers with the solutions on page 632.

17-4 Calculating Depreciation by the Units-of-Production Method

units-of-production
Depreciation method based on how much an asset is used, such as miles, hours, or units produced, rather than the passage of time.

When the useful life of an asset is more accurately defined in terms of how much it is used rather than the passage of time, we may use the **units-of-production** method to calculate depreciation. To apply this method, the life of the asset is expressed in productive capacity, such as miles driven, units produced, or hours used. Some examples of assets typically depreciated by using this method would be cars, trucks, airplanes, production-line machinery, engines, pumps, and electronic equipment.

To calculate depreciation by using this method, we begin by determining the depreciation per unit. This number is found by dividing the amount to be depreciated (cost − salvage value) by the estimated units of useful life:

$$\textbf{Depreciation per unit} = \frac{\textbf{Cost} - \textbf{Salvage value}}{\textbf{Units of useful life}}$$

For example, let's say that a hole-punching machine on a production line had a cost of \$35,000 and a salvage value of \$5,000. If we estimate that the machine had a useful life of 150,000 units of production, the depreciation per unit would be calculated as follows:

$$\text{Depreciation per unit} = \frac{\text{Cost} - \text{Salvage value}}{\text{Units of useful life}} = \frac{35{,}000 - 5{,}000}{150{,}000} = \frac{30{,}000}{150{,}000} = \underline{\underline{\$.20 \text{ per unit}}}$$

Once we have determined the depreciation per unit, we can find the annual depreciation by multiplying the depreciation per unit by the number of units produced each year.

$$\textbf{Annual depreciation} = \textbf{Depreciation per unit} \times \textbf{Units produced}$$

In the previous example, if the hole-punching machine produced 30,000 in a year, the annual depreciation for that year would be as follows:

$$\text{Annual depreciation} = \text{Depreciation per unit} \times \text{Units produced} = .20 \times 30{,}000 = \underline{\underline{\$6{,}000}}$$

STEPS TO CALCULATE DEPRECIATION BY USING THE UNITS-OF-PRODUCTION METHOD:

Step 1. Determine the depreciation per unit by using

$$\textbf{Depreciation per unit} = \frac{\textbf{Cost} - \textbf{Salvage value}}{\textbf{Units of useful life}}$$

(Round to the nearest tenth of a cent when necessary.)

Step 2. Calculate the annual depreciation by using

$$\textbf{Annual depreciation} = \textbf{Depreciation per unit} \times \textbf{Units produced}$$

Step 3. Set up the depreciation schedule in the form of a chart with the following headings:

End of Year	Depreciation per Unit	Units Produced	Annual Depreciation	Accumulated Depreciation	Book Value

EXAMPLE

Precision Printing purchased a new printing press for $8,500 with a salvage value of $500. For depreciation purposes, the press is expected to have a useful life of 5,000 hours. From the following estimate of hours of use, prepare a depreciation schedule for the printing press by using the units-of-production method.

Year	Hours of Use
1	1,500
2	1,200
3	2,000
4	500

SOLUTION STRATEGY

Step 1. $$\text{Depreciation per unit (hours)} = \frac{\text{Cost} - \text{Salvage value}}{\text{Hours of useful life}}$$

$$\text{Depreciation per unit} = \frac{8{,}500 - 500}{5{,}000} = \frac{8{,}000}{5{,}000} = \underline{\underline{\$1.60 \text{ per hour}}}$$

Step 2. $$\text{Annual depreciation} = \text{Depreciation per unit} \times \text{Units produced}$$

$$\text{Annual depreciation (year 1)} = 1.60 \times 1{,}500 = \underline{\underline{\$2{,}400}}$$

$$\text{Annual depreciation (year 2)} = 1.60 \times 1{,}200 = \underline{\underline{\$1{,}920}}$$

Continue this procedure for the remaining years.

Step 3.

Precision Printing, Inc.
Depreciation Schedule, Printing Press
Units-of-Production Method (5,000 hours)

End of Year	Depreciation per Hour	Hours Used	Annual Depreciation	Accumulated Depreciation	Book Value
					(new) $8,500
1	$1.60	1,500	$2,400	$2,400	6,100
2	1.60	1,200	1,920	4,320	4,180
3	1.60	2,000	3,200	7,520	980
4	1.60	500	480*	8,000	500

*Maximum allowable to reach salvage value.

TRY-IT | EXERCISE

4. Hyde Park Industries purchased a delivery truck with an expected useful life of 75,000 miles. The cost of the truck was $54,500, and the residual value was $7,500. If the truck was driven the following amounts of miles per year, prepare a depreciation schedule by using the units-of-production method.

Year	Miles Driven
1	12,500
2	18,300
3	15,900
4	19,100
5	12,400

Check your answers with the solutions on pages 632–633.

REVIEW EXERCISES | CHAPTER 17—SECTION I

Calculate the total cost, total depreciation, and annual depreciation for the following assets by using the straight-line method:

	Cost	Freight Charges	Setup Charges	Total Cost	Salvage Value	Estimated Useful Life (years)	Total Depreciation	Annual Depreciation
1.	$45,000	$150	$500	________	$3,500	10	________	________
2.	$88,600	$625	$2,500	________	$9,000	7	________	________
3.	$158,200	$0	$1,800	________	$20,000	5	________	________
4.	$750,000	$0	$10,300	________	$70,000	15	________	________

5. The Fluffy Laundry purchased new washing machines and dryers for $57,000. Freight charges were $470, and installation amounted to $500. The machines are expected to last 5 years and have a residual value of $2,000. If Fluffy elects to use the straight-line method of depreciation, prepare a depreciation schedule for these machines.

Fluffy Laundry
Depreciation Schedule
Straight-line Method

End of Year	Annual Depreciation	Accumulated Depreciation	Book Value
		(new)	________
1	________	________	________
2	________	________	________
3	________	________	________
4	________	________	________
5	________	________	________

6. Carson Supply Company purchases warehouse shelving for $18,600. Freight charges were $370, and assembly and setup amounted to $575. The shelves are expected to last for 7 years and have a scrap value of $900. Using the straight-line method of depreciation,

a. What is the annual depreciation expense of the shelving?

b. What is the accumulated depreciation after the third year?

c. What is the book value of the shelving after the fifth year?

Complete Exercises 7–9 as they relate to the sum-of-the-years' digits method of depreciation:

	Useful Life (years)	Sum-of-the-Years' Digits	Depreciation Rate Fraction Year 1	Year 3	Year 5
7.	5	________	________	________	________
8.	7	________	________	________	________
9.	10	________	________	________	________

10. New Age Manufacturing, Inc., purchased production-line machinery for $445,000. It is expected to last for 6 years and have a trade-in value of $25,000. Using the sum-of-the-years' digits method, prepare a depreciation schedule for New Age.

New Age Manufacturing, Inc.
Machinery—SYD Depreciation Schedule

End of Year	Total Depreciation	Depreciation Rate Fraction	Annual Depreciation	Accumulated Depreciation	Book Value
				(new)	______
1	______	______	______	______	______
2	______	______	______	______	______
3	______	______	______	______	______
4	______	______	______	______	______
5	______	______	______	______	______
6	______	______	______	______	______

Complete Exercises 11–13 as they relate to the declining-balance method of depreciation:

	Years	Straight-Line Rate (%)	Multiple (%)	Declining-Balance Rate (%)
11.	4	______	125	______
12.	6	______	200	______
13.	10	______	150	______

14. Service America, Inc., bought a fleet of new cars for $180,000. The fleet is expected to have an 8-year useful life and a trade-in value of $35,000. Prepare a depreciation schedule by using the 150% declining-balance method for the cars.

Service America, Inc.
Depreciation Schedule—Service Fleet
8-year, 150% declining-balance

End of Year	Beginning Book Value	Depreciation Rate	Depreciation for the Year	Accumulated Depreciation	Ending Book Value
				(new)	______
1	______	______	______	______	______
2	______	______	______	______	______
3	______	______	______	______	______
4	______	______	______	______	______
5	______	______	______	______	______
6	______	______	______	______	______
7	______	______	______	______	______
8	______	______	______	______	______

Complete the following as they relate to the units-of-production method of depreciation (round to the nearest tenth of a cent when necessary):

	Asset	Cost	Salvage Value	Units of Useful Life	Depreciation per Unit
15.	Pump	$15,000	$2,800	100,000 hours	______
16.	Automobile	$27,400	$3,400	60,000 miles	______
17.	Assembly robot	$775,000	$25,000	3,000,000 units	______

18. Millennium Manufacturing purchased a new stamping machine for $45,000 with a salvage value of $5,000. For depreciation purposes, the machine is expected to have a useful life of 250,000 units of production. Complete the following depreciation schedule by using the units-of-production method:

Millennium Manufacturing, Inc.
Depreciation Schedule, Units-of-Production
Stamping Machine—250,000 Units

End of Year	Depreciation per Unit	Units Produced	Annual Depreciation	Accumulated Depreciation	Book Value
				(new)	________
1	________	50,000	________	________	________
2	________	70,000	________	________	________
3	________	45,000	________	________	________
4	________	66,000	________	________	________
5	________	30,000	________	________	________

BUSINESS DECISION

The Revised Estimate

19. You are the accountant for Simplex Industries, a manufacturer of plastic gears for electric motors. The company's production facility in Pittsburgh has a cost of $3,800,000, an estimated residual value of $400,000, and an estimated useful life of 40 years. You are using the straight-line method of depreciation for this asset.

a. What is the amount of the annual depreciation?

b. What is the book value of the property at the end of the twentieth year of use?

c. If at the start of the twenty-first year you revise your estimate so that the remaining useful life is 15 years and the residual value is $120,000, what should be the depreciation expense for each of the remaining 15 years?

SECTION II

ASSET COST RECOVERY SYSTEMS—IRS PRESCRIBED METHODS FOR INCOME TAX REPORTING

Section I of this chapter described the depreciation methods used by businesses for the preparation of financial statements. For income tax purposes, the Internal Revenue Service (IRS), through federal tax laws, prescribes how depreciation must be taken.

As part of the Economic Recovery Act of 1981, the IRS introduced a depreciation method known as the accelerated cost recovery system (ACRS), which allowed businesses to depreciate assets more quickly than they could with traditional methods. Faster write-offs encouraged businesses to invest in new equipment and other capital assets more frequently, thereby sparking needed economic growth. Essentially, ACRS discarded the concepts of estimated useful life and residual value. In their place, it required that business compute a **cost recovery allowance.**

cost recovery allowance
Term used under MACRS meaning the amount of depreciation of an asset that may be written off for tax purposes in a given year.

After the ACRS was modified by the Tax Equity and Fiscal Responsibility Act of 1982 and the Tax Reform Act of 1984, it was significantly overhauled by the Tax Reform Act of

3-Year Property	5-Year Property	7-Year Property
Over-the-road tractors Some horses and hogs Special handling devices for the manufacture of food and beverages Specialty tools used in the manufacture of motor vehicles Specialty tools used in the manufacture of finished products made of plastic, rubber, glass, and metal	Automobiles and taxis Buses and trucks Computers and peripherals Office machinery Research and experimental equipment Breeding or dairy cattle Sheep and goats Airplanes (except those in commercial use) Drilling and timber-cutting equipment Construction equipment	Office furniture and fixtures Railroad cars and engines Commercial airplanes Equipment used in mining, petroleum drilling, and natural gas exploration Equipment used in the manufacture of wood, pulp, and paper products Equipment used to manufacture aerospace products
10-Year Property	**15-Year Property**	**20-Year Property**
Vessels, barges, and tugs Single-purpose agricultural structures Trees and vines bearing fruits or nuts Equipment for grain, sugar, and vegetable oil products	Depreciable improvements made to land such as shrubbery, fences, roads, and bridges Equipment used to manufacture cement Gas utility pipelines	Farm buildings Railroad structures and improvements Communication cable and long-line systems Water utility plants and equipment
	31.5-Year Property	**39-Year Property**
	Placed into service before May 13, 1993: Nonresidential real estate Office in the home	*Placed into service after May 12, 1993:* Nonresidential real estate Office in the home

TABLE 17-1
MACRS Property Classes General Depreciation System

1986. The resulting method was known as the **modified accelerated cost recovery system (MACRS).** This is the system we shall use to calculate depreciation for federal income tax purposes.

modified accelerated cost recovery system (MACRS)
A 1986 modification of the property classes and the depreciation rates of the accelerated depreciation method; used for assets put into service after 1986.

17-5 Calculating Depreciation by Using the Modified Accelerated Cost Recovery System (MACRS)

According to the IRS, the modified accelerated cost recovery system (MACRS) is the name given to tax rules for getting back or recovering through depreciation deductions the cost of property used in a trade or business, or to produce income. These rules generally apply to tangible property placed in service *after 1986.* MACRS consists of two systems that determine how property is to be depreciated. The primary system is known as the **general depreciation system (GDS),** while the secondary system is called the **alternative depreciation system (ADS).**

Unless the ADS is specifically required by law, such as with tangible property used predominantly *outside* the United States during the year, the GDS should be used to calculate the depreciation deduction. The main difference between the two systems is that the GDS allows shorter recovery periods for each property class, and therefore greater write-offs each year.

Table 17-1 exhibits the eight main property classes, with some examples of assets included in each class under the GDS.

Once the **property class** for the asset has been identified, the amount of depreciation each year can be manually calculated or found by using percentage tables. As a general rule, the 3-, 5-, 7-, and 10-year property class assets are depreciated by using the 200% declining-balance method; the 15- and 20-year classes use the 150% declining-balance method; and the 31.5- and 39-year classes use straight-line depreciation.

general depreciation system (GDS)
One of two MACRS depreciation systems. Most tangible depreciable property falls within the rules of the GDS, which permits the use of declining-balance depreciation and shorter recovery periods than the alternative depreciation system.

alternative depreciation system (ADS)
One of two MACRS depreciation systems. Primarily for property used *outside* the United States during the year or for tax-exempt property. Uses straight-line depreciation and generally longer recovery periods than the GDS.

property class
One of several time categories to which property is assigned under MACRS showing how many years are allowed for cost recovery.

TABLE 17-2

Cost Recovery Percentage Table MACRS

Recovery Year	Depreciation Rate for Property Class					
	3-year	5-year	7-year	10-year	15-year	20-year
1	33.33%	20.00%	14.29%	10.00%	5.00%	3.750%
2	44.45	32.00	24.49	18.00	9.50	7.219
3	14.81	19.20	17.49	14.40	8.55	6.677
4	7.41	11.52	12.49	11.52	7.70	6.177
5		11.52	8.93	9.22	6.93	5.713
6		5.76	8.92	7.37	6.23	5.285
7			8.93	6.55	5.90	4.888
8			4.46	6.55	5.90	4.522
9				6.56	5.91	4.462
10				6.55	5.90	4.461
11				3.28	5.91	4.462
12					5.90	4.461
13					5.91	4.462
14					5.90	4.461
15					5.91	4.462
16					2.95	4.461
17						4.462
18						4.461
19						4.462
20						4.461
21						2.231

Everybody's Business

Learning Tip

In MACRS, the entire asset is depreciated. There is no salvage value.

Note that the percents for any given property class in the Cost Recovery Percentage Table add up to 100%.

cost recovery percentage
An IRS-prescribed percentage that is multiplied by the original basis of an asset to determine the depreciation deduction for a given year. Based on property class and year of asset life.

half-year convention
IRS rule under MACRS that assumes all property is placed in service or taken out of service at the midpoint of the year, regardless of the actual time.

Because these calculations were already covered in Section I of this chapter, we shall focus on using one of the **cost recovery percentage** tables provided by the IRS. Table 17-2 is such a table.

Note that the number of recovery years is one greater than the property class. This is due to a rule known as the **half-year convention,** which assumes that the asset was placed in service in the middle of the first year and therefore begins depreciating at that point. Quarterly tables are listed in IRS Publication 534 for assets placed in service at other times of the year.

STEPS TO PREPARE A DEPRECIATION SCHEDULE BY USING MACRS:

Step 1. Use Table 17-1 to determine the property class for the asset in question.

Step 2. Multiply the cost recovery percentages for each year, from Table 17-2, by the original basis of the asset.

Depreciation deduction = Original basis (cost) × Cost recovery percentage

Step 3. Set up the depreciation schedule in the form of a chart with the following headings:

End of Year	Original Basis (cost)	Cost Recovery Percentage	Cost Recovery (depreciation)	Accumulated Depreciation	Book Value

EXAMPLE

Fantasy Tours purchased a new sightseeing bus for $185,000. Prepare a depreciation schedule for this new asset by using MACRS.

SOLUTION STRATEGY

From Table 17-1, we find that buses are listed in the 5-year property class. Table 17-2 provides the percentages for each recovery year. Note once again, the extra year is to allow for the assumption that the asset was placed in service at mid-year.

Fantasy Tours, Inc.
MACRS Depreciation Schedule
Sightseeing Bus

End of Year	Original Basis (cost)	Cost Recovery Percentage	Cost Recovery (depreciation)	Accumulated Depreciation	Book Value
					(new) $185,000
1	$185,000	20.00%	$37,000	$37,000	148,000
2	185,000	32.00	59,200	96,200	88,800
3	185,000	19.20	35,520	131,720	53,280
4	185,000	11.52	21,312	153,032	31,968
5	185,000	11.52	21,312	174,344	10,656
6	185,000	5.76	10,656	185,000	0

TRY-IT | EXERCISE

5. Allied Van Lines purchased an over-the-road tractor for $88,400. As the accountant for the company, you are asked to prepare a depreciation schedule for this new asset by using MACRS.

Check your answers with the solutions on page 633.

17-6 Calculating the Periodic Depletion Cost of Natural Resources

Just as depreciation is used to write off the useful life of plant assets such as trucks, equipment, and buildings, depletion is used to account for the consumption of natural resources such as coal, petroleum, timber, natural gas, and minerals. **Depletion** is the proportional allocation of the cost of natural resources to the units used up or depleted per accounting period. In accounting, natural resources are also known as **wasting assets,** because they are considered to be exhausted or to be used up as they are converted into inventory by mining, pumping, or cutting.

Depletion of natural resources is calculated in the same way as the units-of-production method of depreciation for plant assets. To calculate the depletion allocation, we must determine the following:

a. *Total cost of the natural resource package,* including the original purchase price, exploration expenses, and extraction or cutting expenses.

b. *Residual or salvage value* of the property after resources have been exhausted.

c. *Estimated total number of units* (tons, barrels, board feet) of resource available.

depletion
The proportional allocation or write-off of the cost of natural resources to the units used up or depleted per accounting period. Calculated in the same way as units-of-production depreciation.

wasting assets
An accounting term used to describe natural resources that are exhausted or used up as they are converted into inventory by mining, pumping, or cutting.

STEPS TO CALCULATE THE PERIODIC DEPLETION COST OF NATURAL RESOURCES:

Step 1. Compute the average depletion cost per unit by

$$\text{Average depletion cost per unit} = \frac{\text{Total cost of resource} - \text{Residual value}}{\text{Estimated total units available}}$$

(Round to the nearest tenth of a cent when necessary.)

Step 2. Calculate the periodic depletion cost by

$$\text{Periodic depletion cost} = \text{Units produced in current period} \times \text{Average depletion cost per unit}$$

Natural resources are also known as wasting assets, because they are considered to be used up when converted into inventory.

EXAMPLE

Sunday Oil, Inc., purchased a parcel of land containing an estimated 2 million barrels of crude oil for $850,000. Two oil wells were drilled at a cost of $340,000. The residual value of the property and equipment is $50,000. Calculate the periodic depletion cost for the first year of operation if 325,000 barrels were extracted.

SOLUTION STRATEGY

Step 1. $\text{Average depletion cost per unit} = \dfrac{\text{Total cost of resource} - \text{Residual value}}{\text{Estimated total units available}}$

$$\text{Average depletion cost per barrel} = \frac{(850{,}000 + 340{,}000) - 50{,}000}{2{,}000{,}000} = \$.57 \text{ per barrel}$$

Step 2. Periodic depletion cost = Units produced in current period × Average depl. cost per unit

$$\text{Periodic depletion cost} = 325{,}000 \times .57 = \underline{\underline{\$185{,}250}}$$

TRY-IT | EXERCISE

6. Northwest Mining Company paid $5,330,000 for a parcel of land, including the mining rights. In addition, the company spent $900,000 on labor and equipment to prepare the site for mining operations. After mining is completed, it is estimated that the land and equipment would have a residual value of $400,000. Geologists estimated that the mine contains 7,000,000 tons of coal. If Northwest mined 1,500,000 tons of coal in the first year, what is the amount of the depletion cost?

Check your answer with the solution on page 633.

REVIEW EXERCISES | CHAPTER 17—SECTION II

1. Nationwide Nursing Services purchased a computer system for $24,300. What is the amount of the first year's depreciation by using the modified accelerated cost recovery system?

2. Atlantis Fantasy Company constructed roads and a bridge at AtlantisWorld in Orlando, Florida, at a cost of $15,000,000. Atlantis uses MACRS for tax purposes.

a. What is the second year's depreciation expense?

b. What is the ninth year's depreciation expense?

3. Minute Maid Orange Groves planted fruit trees valued at $250,000.

a. What is the property class for this asset under MACRS?

b. What is the percentage for the sixth year of depreciation for this property?

c. What is the amount of the depreciation expense in the final year of write-off?

4. Island Hoppers Airways of Hawaii purchased a new commercial airplane for $2,400,000. As the accountant for the company, prepare a depreciation schedule for the asset by using MACRS.

5. Lake Tahoe Timber Company purchased land containing an estimated 6,500,000 board feet of lumber for $3,700,000. The company invested another $300,000 to construct access roads and a company depot. The residual value of the property and equipment is estimated to be $880,000.

a. What is the average depletion cost per board foot of lumber?

b. If 782,000 board feet were cut in the second year of operation, what is the amount of the depletion cost for that year?

BUSINESS DECISION

Intangible Write-offs

6. As you have seen in this chapter, companies depreciate or write off the expense of *tangible assets*, such as trucks and equipment, over a period of their useful lives. Many companies also have *intangible assets* that must be accounted for as an expense over a period of time.

Intangible assets are resources that benefit the company, but do not have any physical substance. Some examples are copyrights, franchises, patents, trademarks, and leases. In accounting, intangible assets are written off in a procedure known as asset amortization. This is much like straight-line depreciation, but there is no salvage value.

You are the accountant for Bayview Pharmaceuticals, Inc. In January 1996, the company purchased the patent rights for a new medication from Novae, Inc., for $9,000,000. The patent had 15 years remaining as its useful life. In January 2001, Bayview Pharmaceuticals successfully defended its right to the patent in a lawsuit at a cost of $550,000 in legal fees.

a. Using the straight-line method, calculate the patent's annual amortization expense for the years before the lawsuit.

b. Calculate the amortization expense per year for the remaining years after the lawsuit.

CHAPTER FORMULAS

Straight-Line Method

$$\text{Total cost} = \text{Cost} + \text{Freight} + \text{Setup expenses}$$

$$\text{Total depreciation} = \text{Total cost} - \text{Salvage value}$$

$$\text{Annual depreciation} = \frac{\text{Total depreciation}}{\text{Estimated useful life (years)}}$$

Sum-of-the-Years' Digits Method

$$\text{SYD depreciation rate fraction} = \frac{\text{Years of useful life remaining}}{\frac{n(n+1)}{2}}$$

$$\text{Annual depreciation} = \text{Total depreciation} \times \text{Depreciation rate fraction}$$

Declining-Balance Method

$$\text{Declining-balance rate} = \frac{1}{\text{Useful life}} \times \text{Multiple}$$

$$\text{Beginning book value} = \text{Ending book value of the previous year}$$

$$\text{Ending book value} = \text{Beginning book value} - \text{Depreciation for the year}$$

Units-of-Production Method

$$\text{Depreciation per unit} = \frac{\text{Cost} - \text{Salvage value}}{\text{Units of useful life}}$$

$$\text{Annual depreciation} = \text{Depreciation per unit} \times \text{Units produced}$$

MACRS Depreciation

$$\text{Depreciation deduction} = \text{Original basis} \times \text{Cost recovery percentage}$$

Natural Resource Depletion

$$\text{Average depletion cost per unit} = \frac{\text{Total cost of resource} - \text{Residual value}}{\text{Estimated total units available}}$$

$$\text{Periodic depletion cost} = \text{Units produced in current period} \times \text{Average depletion cost per unit}$$

✦ SUMMARY CHART ✦

SECTION I: Traditional Depreciation—Methods Used for Financial Statement Reporting

Topic	P/O, Page	Important Concepts	Illustrative Examples
Calculating Depreciation by the Straight-Line Method	17-1 613	Straight-line depreciation provides for equal periodic charges to be written off over the estimated useful life of the asset. 1. Determine the total cost and residual value of the asset. 2. Subtract residual value from total cost to find the total amount of depreciation. **Total depreciation = Total cost − Residual value** 3. Calculate the annual depreciation by dividing the total depreciation by the useful life of the asset. $\textbf{Annual depreciation} = \dfrac{\textbf{Total depreciation}}{\textbf{Useful life of asset}}$ 4. Set up a depreciation schedule in the form of a chart. End of Year / Annual Depreciation / Accumulated Depreciation / Book Value	The Diamond Bank purchased a closed-circuit television system for \$45,000. Shipping charges were \$325, and installation expenses amounted to \$2,540. The system is expected to last 5 years and has a residual value of \$3,500. Prepare a depreciation schedule for the system. Total cost = 45,000 + 325 + 2,540 = \$47,865 Total depr. = 47,865 − 3,500 = \$44,365 $\text{Annual depr.} = \dfrac{44{,}365}{5} = \$8{,}873$ End of Year / Annual Depr / Accum Depr / Book Value: — / — / (new) / 47,865 1 / 8,873 / 8,873 / 38,992 2 / 8,873 / 17,746 / 30,119 3 / 8,873 / 26,619 / 21,246 4 / 8,873 / 35,492 / 12,373 5 / 8,873 / 44,365 / 3,500
Calculating Depreciation by the Sum-of-the-Years' Digits Method	17-2 614	The sum-of-the-years' digits method is one of the accelerated methods of calculating depreciation. 1. Find the total depreciation of the asset: **Total depreciation = Total cost − Residual value** 2. Calculate the SYD depreciation rate fraction for each year: $\textbf{Rate fraction} = \dfrac{\textbf{Years of life remaining}}{\frac{n(n+1)}{2}}$ 3. Calculate the depreciation for each year: **Annual depreciation = Total depreciation × Depreciation rate fraction**	Il Piccolo Cafe purchased new equipment for \$45,000 with a 4-year useful life and salvage value of \$3,000. Using the sum-of-the-years' digits method, calculate the depreciation expense for year 1 and year 3. Total depr. = 45,000 − 3,000 = 42,000 $\text{Rate fract. yr 1} = \dfrac{4}{\frac{4(4+1)}{2}} = \dfrac{4}{10}$ $\text{Depr. year 1} = 42{,}000 \times \dfrac{4}{10}$ = \$16,800 $\text{Rate fract. year 3} = \dfrac{2}{\frac{4(4+1)}{2}} = \dfrac{2}{10}$ $\text{Depr. year 3} = 42{,}000 \times \dfrac{2}{10}$ = \$8,400

SECTION I: (continued)

<table>
<tr><th>Topic</th><th>P/O, Page</th><th>Important Concepts</th><th>Illustrative Examples</th></tr>
<tr><td>Calculating Depreciation by the Declining-Balance Method</td><td>17-3
616</td><td>Declining-balance depreciation, the second accelerated method, uses a multiple of the straight-line rate, such as 125%, 150%, and 200%. Salvage value is not considered until the last year.
1. Calculate the declining-balance rate:
Declining-balance rate = $\frac{1}{\text{Useful life}}$ × Multiple
2. Calculate the depreciation for each year by applying the rate to each year's beginning book value.
Depreciation for year = Beginning book value × Declining balance rate
3. Calculate the ending book value for each year by subtracting the depreciation for the year from the beginning book value.
Ending book value = Beginning book value − Depreciation for year
4. The depreciation is complete when the ending book value equals the salvage value.</td><td>The Fitness Factory purchased a treadmill for $5,000. It is expected to last 4 years and have a salvage value of $1,000. Use 150% declining-balance depreciation to calculate the book value after each year.
Decl. bal. rate = $\frac{1}{4} \times 1.5 = .375$
Year 1:
Depr. = 5,000 × .375 = 1,875
Book value = 5,000 − 1,875 = $3,125
Year 2:
Depr. = 3,125 × .375 = 1,172
Book value = 3,125 − 1,172 = $1,953
Year 3:
Depr. = 1,953 × .375 = 732
Book value = 1,953 − 732 = $1,221
Year 4:
Depr. = 1,221 × .375 = 458
Book value = 1,221 − 221 = $1,000*
*Note: In year 4, the calculated depreciation is $458. Because the book value of an asset cannot fall below the salvage value, the allowable depreciation is limited to $221 (1,221 − 1,000 = 221).</td></tr>
<tr><td>Calculating Depreciation by the Units-of-Production Method</td><td>17-4
618</td><td>When the useful life of an asset is more accurately defined in terms of how much it is used, such as miles driven or units produced, we may apply the units-of-production method.
1. Determine the depreciation cost per unit by using
Depreciation per unit = $\frac{\text{Cost} - \text{Salvage value}}{\text{Units of useful life}}$
2. Calculate the depreciation for each year by using
Annual depreciation = Depreciation per unit × Units produced</td><td>Campbell purchased a new canning machine for one of its chicken soup production lines at a cost of $455,000. The machine has an expected useful life of 1,000,000 cans and a residual value of $25,000. In the first year, the machine produced 120,000 cans. Calculate the depreciation on the machine for year 1.
Depreciation per unit = $\frac{455{,}000 - 25{,}000}{1{,}000{,}000} = \$.43$
Depreciation year 1 = 120,000 × .43 = $51,600</td></tr>
</table>

SECTION II: Asset Cost Recovery Systems—IRS Prescribed Methods for Income Tax Reporting

Topic	P/O, Page	Important Concepts	Illustrative Examples
Calculating Depreciation by Using the Modified Accelerated Cost Recovery System (MACRS)	17-5 623	MACRS is used for assets placed in service after 1986. This system uses property classes, Table 17-1, and recovery percentages, Table 17-2. 1. Use Table 17-1 to determine the property class for the asset in question. 2. Multiply the cost recovery percentages for each year, Table 17-2, by the original cost of the asset. **Depreciation deduction = Original cost × Recovery percentage**	Captain Morgan purchased a tug boat for \$650,000. As his accountant, use MACRS to calculate the depreciation expense for the second and fifth year. Using Table 17-1, we find that tug boats are considered 10-year property. *MACRS Depreciation Expense:* *Year 2* 650,000 × .18 = \$117,000 *Year 5* 650,000 × .0922 = \$59,930
Calculating the Periodic Depletion Cost of Natural Resources	17-6 625	Depletion is the proportional allocation of natural resources to the units used up or depleted, per accounting period. Depletion is calculated in the same way as the units-of-production method of depreciation. 1. Compute the average depletion cost per unit: $\textbf{Average depletion/unit} = \dfrac{\textbf{Total cost} - \textbf{Salvage}}{\textbf{Total units available}}$ 2. Calculate the periodic depletion cost: **Periodic depletion cost = Current units × Average depletion per unit**	The Continental Mining Company purchased a parcel of land containing an estimated 800,000 tons of iron ore. The cost of the asset was \$2,000,000. An additional \$350,000 was spent to prepare the property for mining. The estimated residual value of the asset is \$500,000. If the first year's output was 200,000 tons, what is the amount of the depletion allowance? Av. depl. per unit = $\dfrac{2{,}350{,}000 - 500{,}000}{800{,}000}$ = \$2.31 per ton Depletion cost: Year 1 = 200,000 × 2.31 = \$462,000

TRY-IT EXERCISE | SOLUTIONS

1.

$$\text{Total cost} = \text{Cost} + \text{Freight} + \text{Setup}$$
$$\text{Total cost} = 125{,}000 + 1{,}150 + 750 = \underline{\underline{\$126{,}900}}$$

$$\text{Total depreciation} = \text{Total cost} - \text{Salvage value}$$
$$\text{Total depreciation} = 126{,}900 - 5{,}000 = \underline{\underline{\$121{,}900}}$$

$$\text{Annual depreciation} = \frac{\text{Total depreciation}}{\text{Estimated useful life}}$$

$$\text{Annual depreciation} = \frac{121{,}900}{5} = \underline{\underline{\$24{,}380}}$$

Holsum Bakery—Bread Oven

End of Year	Annual Depreciation	Accumulated Depreciation	Book Value
			$126,900 (cost)
1	$24,380	$24,380	102,520
2	24,380	48,760	78,140
3	24,380	73,140	53,760
4	24,380	97,520	29,380
5	24,380	121,900	5,000 (salvage value)

2. Total depreciation = Total cost − Salvage value

Total depreciation = 44,500 − 2,500 = $42,000

$$\text{SYD depreciation rate fraction} = \frac{\text{Years of useful life remaining}}{\frac{n(n+1)}{2}}$$

$$\text{Rate fraction year 1} = \frac{6}{\frac{6(6+1)}{2}} = \frac{6}{\frac{42}{2}} = \frac{6}{21}$$

StyleCraft Furniture

End of Year	Total Depreciation	Rate Fraction	Annual Depreciation	Accumulated Depreciation	Book Value
					$44,500 (cost)
1	$42,000	$\frac{6}{21}$	$12,000	$12,000	32,500
2	42,000	$\frac{5}{21}$	10,000	22,000	22,500
3	42,000	$\frac{4}{21}$	8,000	30,000	14,500
4	42,000	$\frac{3}{21}$	6,000	36,000	8,500
5	42,000	$\frac{2}{21}$	4,000	40,000	4,500
6	42,000	$\frac{1}{21}$	2,000	42,000	2,500 (salvage value)

3. $$\text{Declining-balance rate} = \frac{1}{\text{Useful life}} \times \text{Multiple}$$

$$\text{Declining-balance rate} = \frac{1}{4} \times 1.5 = .375$$

Southwest Air Service

End of Year	Regular Book Value	Depreciation Rate	Depreciation for Year	Accumulated Depreciation	Ending Book Value
					$386,000 (new)
1	$386,000.00	.375	$144,750.00	$144,750.00	241,250.00
2	241,250.00	.375	90,468.75	235,218.75	150,781.25
3	150,781.25	.375	56,542.97	291,761.72	94,238.28
4	94,238.28	.375	24,238.28*	316,000.00	70,000.00 (salvage value)

*Maximum allowable to reach salvage value

4. $$\text{Depreciation per unit} = \frac{\text{Cost} - \text{Salvage value}}{\text{Units of useful life}}$$

$$\text{Depreciation per unit} = \frac{54{,}500 - 7{,}500}{75{,}000} = \$.627/\text{mile}$$

Hyde Park Industries

End of Year	Depreciation per Mile	Miles Used	Annual Depreciation	Accumulated Depreciation	Book Value
					$54,500 (new)
1	$.627	12,500	$7,837.50	$7,837.50	46,662.50
2	.627	18,300	11,474.10	19,311.60	35,188.40
3	.627	15,900	9,969.30	29,280.90	25,219.10
4	.627	19,100	11,975.70	41,256.60	13,243.40
5	.627	12,400	5,743.40*	47,000.00	7,500.00 (salvage value)

*Maximum allowable to reach salvage value

5. MACRS 3-Year Property

Allied Van Lines
Over-the-Road Tractor

End of Year	Original Basis	Cost Recovery Percentage	Cost Recovery	Accumulated Depreciation	Book Value
					(new) $88,400.00
1	$88,400.00	33.33	$29,463.72	$29,463.72	58,936.28
2	88,400.00	44.45	39,293.80	68,757.52	19,642.48
3	88,400.00	14.81	13,092.04	81,849.56	6,550.44
4	88,400.00	7.41	6,550.44	88,400.00	0

6. $$\text{Average depletion cost/unit} = \frac{\text{Total cost} - \text{Residual value}}{\text{Estimated total units available}}$$

$$\text{Average depletion cost/unit} = \frac{(5{,}330{,}000 + 900{,}000) - 400{,}000}{7{,}000{,}000} = \frac{5{,}830{,}000}{7{,}000{,}000} = \$.833$$

$$\text{Periodic depletion cost} = \text{Units produced} \times \text{Average depletion cost/unit}$$

$$\text{Periodic depletion cost (1st year)} = 1{,}500{,}000 \times .833 = \underline{\underline{\$1{,}249{,}500}}$$

Name ____________________

Class ____________________

Answers

1. ____________________
____
____

2. ____________________
____
____

3. ____________________

4. ____________________
____
____
____

5. ____________________
____
____
____

6. ____________________

CHAPTER 17 | ASSESSMENT TEST

Calculate the total cost, total depreciation, and annual depreciation for the following assets by using the straight-line method:

	Cost	Freight Charges	Setup Charges	Total Cost	Salvage Value	Estimated Useful Life (years)	Total Depreciation	Annual Depreciation
1.	$5,600	$210	$54	______	$600	6	______	______
2.	$16,900	$310	0	______	$1,900	4	______	______

3. Modern Manufacturing, Inc., purchased new equipment totaling $648,000. Freight charges were $2,200, and installation amounted to $1,800. The equipment is expected to last 4 years and have a residual value of $33,000. If the company elects to use the straight-line method of depreciation, prepare a depreciation schedule for these assets.

Modern Manufacturing, Inc.
Depreciation Schedule
Straight-line Method

End of Year	Annual Depreciation	Accumulated Depreciation	Book Value
		(new)	______
1	______	______	______
2	______	______	______
3	______	______	______
4	______	______	______

Complete the following as they relate to the sum-of-the-years' digits method of depreciation:

	Useful life (years)	Sum-of-the-Years' Digits	Depreciation Rate Fraction Year 2	Year 4	Year 6
4.	7	______	______	______	______
5.	9	______	______	______	______

6. Appliance Masters purchased a service truck for $32,400. It has an estimated useful life of 3 years and a trade-in value of $3,100. Using the sum-of-the-years' digits method, prepare a depreciation schedule for the truck.

Appliance Masters
Service Truck, SYD—Depreciation Schedule

End of Year	Total Depreciation	Depreciation Rate Fraction	Annual Depreciation	Accumulated Depreciation	Book Value
				(new)	______
1	______	______	______	______	______
2	______	______	______	______	______
3	______	______	______	______	______

Name ______________________

Class ______________________

Complete the following as they relate to the declining-balance method of depreciation (round answers to thousandths where applicable):

	Years	Straight-Line Rate (%)	Multiple (%)	Declining-Balance Rate (%)
7.	9	________	125	________
8.	6	________	200	________

9. Academy Trophy bought a computerized engraving machine for $33,800. It is expected to have a 6-year useful life and a trade-in value of $2,700. Prepare a depreciation schedule for the *first 3 years* by using the 125% declining-balance method for the machine.

Academy Trophy
Depreciation Schedule
6-year, 125% declining-balance

End of Year	Beginning Book Value	Depreciation Rate	Depreciation for the Year	Accumulated Depreciation	Ending Book Value
				(new)	________
1	________	________	________	________	________
2	________	________	________	________	________
3	________	________	________	________	________

Complete the following as they relate to the units-of-production method of depreciation (round answers to the nearest tenth of a cent):

	Asset	Cost	Salvage Value	Units of Useful Life	Depreciation per Unit
10.	Pump	$8,900	$250	500,000 gallons	________
11.	Copier	3,900	0	160,000 copies	________

12. The Main Street Movie Theater purchased a new projector for $155,000 with a salvage value of $2,000. Delivery and installation amounted to $580. The projector is expected to have a useful life of 15,000 hours. Complete the following depreciation schedule for the *first 4 years* of operation by using the units-of-production method:

Main Street Movie Theater
Depreciation Schedule, Units-of-Production
Projector—15,000 Hours

End of Year	Depreciation per Hour	Hours	Annual Depreciation	Accumulated Depreciation	Book Value
				(new)	________
1	________	2,300	________	________	________
2	________	1,890	________	________	________
3	________	2,160	________	________	________
4	________	2,530	________	________	________

Answers

7. ______________________

____

8. ______________________

____

9. ______________________

10. ______________________

11. ______________________

12. ______________________

Name ____________________

Class ____________________

Answers

13. ____________________

14. a. ____________________

b. ____________________

15. a. ____________________

13. Custom Concrete Corporation purchased cement manufacturing equipment valued at $320,000. As the accountant for the company, prepare a depreciation schedule for the *first 5 years* of operation of this equipment by using MACRS.

Custom Concrete, Inc.
Depreciation Schedule, MACRS
Cement Manufacturing Equipment

End of Year	Original Basis (cost)	Cost Recovery Percentage	Cost Recovery (depreciation)	Accumulated Depreciation	Book Value
				(new)	______
1	______	______	______	______	______
2	______	______	______	______	______
3	______	______	______	______	______
4	______	______	______	______	______
5	______	______	______	______	______

14. The Platinum Touch Mining Company paid $4,000,000 for a parcel of land, including the mining rights. In addition, the company spent $564,700 to prepare the site for mining operations. When mining is completed, it is estimated that the residual value of the asset will be $800,000. Scientists estimate that the site contains 150,000 ounces of platinum.

a. What is the average depletion cost per ounce?

b. If 12,200 ounces were mined in the first year of operation, what is the amount of the depletion cost?

BUSINESS DECISION

A Dispute with the IRS

15. You are the accountant for the Carnival Corporation. Last year, the company purchased a $2,500,000 corporate jet to be used for executive travel. To help offset the cost of the airplane, your company occasionally rents the jet to the executives of two other corporations when it is not in use by Carnival.

When the corporate tax return was filed this year, you began depreciating the jet by using the MACRS. Today, you received a letter from the IRS informing you that because your company occasionally rents the airplane to others, it is considered a commercial aircraft and must be depreciated as such. The corporate lawyers are considering disputing this IRS ruling and have asked you the following:

a. How much depreciation did you claim this year?

Everybody's Business
Real-World Connection
This Business Decision, "A Dispute with the IRS," clearly illustrates how an IRS- prescribed change in property class under MACRS can affect the bottom line of a company's income statement.

b. Under the new category, how much depreciation would be claimed?

c. If the company pays 30% income tax, what effect will this change have on the amount of tax owed, assuming the company made a net profit this year?

Name ____________________

Class ____________________

Answers

15. b. ____________________

c. ____________________

All the Math That's Fit to Learn

The Business Math Times

Volume XVII | **Depreciation** | One Dollar

Upside Down!

If you are not careful, you can be "upside-down" in a loan. This means that the asset you financed, such as a car or a boat, is depreciating or losing market value faster than the loan is being paid off. With new car purchases, for example, as soon as you drive away from the dealership, you have lost about 10% of the new car's value to depreciation.

Being upside-down means that your loan balance is greater than the current market value of the asset you have financed. Amazingly, at that point you would have to pay money to dispose of it!

To avoid this situation, you could purchase brands that hold their value better, make a larger down payment, or finance the asset for a shorter period of time.

The Bottom Line

If you were able to depreciate your automobile, would you have more cash? No!

Similarly, when businesses depreciate assets each period for accounting purposes, there is no cash outlay. For that reason, depreciation does not influence cash flow. Depreciation is an expense, however, and therefore does affect a company's bottom line, net income!

A Taxing Matter

If you have property that was purchased either to use in your trade or business or to produce income, and this property has a useful life substantially beyond the tax year, you can depreciate it.

"All in favor of taking action, please submit a report."

"Quote . . . Unquote"

Life is a work of art, designed by the one who lives it.
—*Dove Chocolate*

I have no use for bodyguards, but I have a very special use for two highly trained certified public accountants.
—*Elvis Presley*

The kinds of property you can depreciate include machinery, equipment, buildings, vehicles, and furniture. You cannot claim depreciation on property held for personal purposes. If you use property, such as a car, for both business and personal purposes, only the business use portion may be depreciated.

According to the IRS, you may depreciate property if it meets all three of the following criteria:

- It must be used in business or other income-producing activity.
- It must be something that wears out, decays, gets used up, becomes obsolete, or loses value from natural causes.
- It must have a determinable useful life substantially beyond the tax year.

Group Rates

When accountants determine that the useful life of a delivery truck for example is five years, that means the *average* of that type truck is expected to last five years. In reality, some may last only two or three years, and others may last six or seven years, or even longer. For that reason, in accounting, similar assets are grouped together when calculating depreciation. This is called *group depreciation*. Most companies today use this method for all or part of their plant assets.

Depreciation Pie

According to an Accounting Trends and Techniques survey conducted by the American Institute of Certified Public Accountants (AICPA), here is the breakdown of depreciation methods used by the 600 largest U.S. companies.

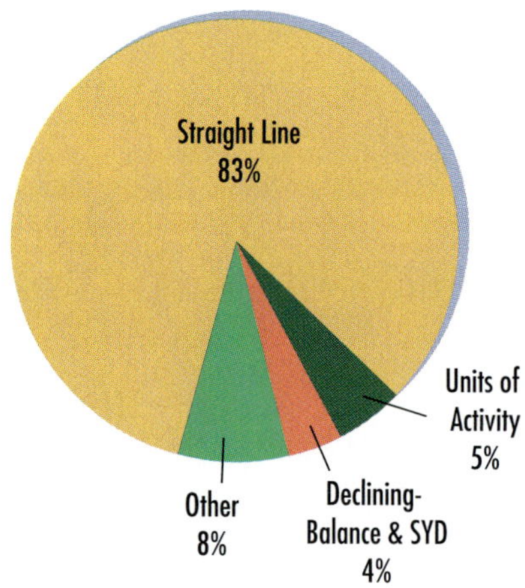

For additional information or examples, visit our web site at:
www.contemporarymath.com

Brainteaser

CYBER CHARGE

Sandra pays an online service provider a fixed monthly fee plus an hourly charge for connect time. Her December bill was $24.96. Her January bill, for which she used twice as much connect time as in December, was $31.08. What is the fixed monthly fee?

ANSWER TO LAST ISSUE'S BRAINTEASER

None

There is no dirt in a hole.

CHAPTER

18

Taxes

PERFORMANCE OBJECTIVES

Section I Sales and Excise Taxes

18-1 Determining sales tax by using sales tax tables. (p. 641)
18-2 Calculating sales tax by using the percent method. (p. 642)
18-3 Calculating selling price and amount of sales tax when total purchase price is known. (p. 643)
18-4 Calculating excise tax. (p. 643)

Section II Property Tax

18-5 Calculating the amount of property tax. (p. 647)
18-6 Calculating tax rate necessary in a community to meet budgetary demands. (p. 649)

Section III Income Tax

18-7 Calculating taxable income for individuals. (p. 653)
18-8 Using the Tax Table to determine tax liability. (p. 656)
18-9 Using the Tax Rate Schedule to determine tax liability. (p. 662)
18-10 Calculating an individual's tax refund or amount of tax owed. (p. 663)
18-11 Calculating corporate income tax and net income after taxes. (p. 666)

taxation
The imposition of a mandatory levy or charge by a government unit to provide financing for public services.

Benjamin Franklin wrote that "nothing can be said to be certain except death and taxes." **Taxation** is the imposition of a mandatory levy on the citizens of a country by their government. In 1904, Supreme Court Justice Oliver Wendell Holmes, Jr. defined taxes as "the price we pay for living in a civilized society." In almost all countries, tax revenue is the major source of financing for publicly provided services. In a democracy, a majority of citizens or their representatives vote to impose taxes on themselves in order to finance, through the public sector, services on which they place value but that they believe cannot be adequately provided by market processes.

In addition to generating revenue to finance public services, taxation can be used for other objectives, such as income redistribution, economic stabilization, and the regulating of consumption of certain commodities or services. In this chapter we shall focus our attention on the three major categories of taxation: sales and excise tax, property tax, and individual and corporate income tax.

SECTION I

SALES AND EXCISE TAXES

sales tax
A tax based on the retail selling or rental price of tangible personal property, collected by the retailer at the time of purchase, and paid to the state or local government.

sales tax rate
Sales tax expressed in its most common form, as a percent of the retail price of an item.

excise tax
A tax levied by federal, state, and local governments on certain luxury or nonessential products and services such as alcoholic beverages, furs, tobacco products, telephone service, and airline and cruise ship tickets.

A tax based on the retail selling or rental price of tangible personal property is called a **sales tax.** This tax may also be imposed on admission charges to places of amusement, sport, and recreation, as well as on certain services. Most states, and many other taxing units such as cities, counties, and municipalities, levy or charge a tax on sales. Businesses that purchase merchandise for resale to others are normally exempt from this tax. Only final buyers pay sales tax. Many states allow a sales tax exemption for food, prescription drugs, household medicines, and other selected items.

The liability for the sales tax is incurred at the time the sale is made. Retail merchants act as agents, collecting sales taxes and periodically remitting them to the proper tax agency. The **sales tax rate** is expressed as a percent and varies from state to state.

Another type of tax levied by federal, state, and local governments on certain products and services is known as an **excise tax.** This tax, which is paid in addition to the sales tax, is imposed on so-called luxury or nonessential items. Some typical examples would be tires, alcoholic beverages, jewelry (except watches), gasoline, furs, firearms, certain recreational equipment and sporting goods, tobacco products, telecommunications services, airline and cruise ship transportation, and telephone service.

Everybody's Business
Real-World Connection
The cost of a civilized society: In 2001, federal, state, and local governments in the United States collected $11,116 in tax revenue for every man, woman, and child in the country!

That amounts to 39% of the income of a median two-income family. A one-income family paid 37.6%.

Revenue from taxes helps pay for many public services, such as the maintenance of highways and roads.

18-1 Determining Sales Tax by Using Sales Tax Tables

Many state and local governments provide retailers with sales tax tables such as those in Exhibit 18-1. These tables are used by employees of businesses that do not have computer cash register systems that automatically compute the proper amount of sales tax.

STEPS TO DETERMINE SALES TAX DUE ON AN ITEM BY USING SALES TAX TABLES:

Step 1. Locate the taxable retail price in the Amount of Sale column.

Step 2. Scan to the right to locate the amount of tax due in the Tax column.

Note: Exhibit 18-1 is only a partial listing. Complete sales tax tables are available in most states from the Department of Revenue.

Everybody's Business

Real-World Connection

Currently, 45 states have a sales tax, with rates that range from 3% to 8%. In many areas, city and county rates add an additional .5% to 6%.

States with the highest sales tax rates are Tennessee, Alabama, Mississippi, and Missouri. Among the lowest are Vermont, Massachusetts, Maryland, Indiana, and Iowa.

Alaska, Delaware, Montana, New Hampshire, and Oregon have no sales tax.

EXAMPLE

Elizabeth Robinson purchased a can of hair spray at Walgreens for $3.29. Use Exhibit 18-1 to determine the amount of sales tax on this item.

SOLUTION STRATEGY

Step 1. From Exhibit 18-1 we find that the retail price of the hair spray, $3.29, falls in the range of $3.24 to $3.38.

Step 2. Scanning to the right, we find the tax due on this item is $.22.

SALES TAX BRACKETS
ON ALL 6 1/2% TAXABLE TRANSACTIONS
(FLORIDA DEPT. OF REVENUE)

Amount of Sale	Tax	Amount of Sale	Tax
.10- .15	.01	5.08- 5.23	.34
.16- .30	.02	5.24- 5.38	.35
.31- .46	.03	5.39- 5.53	.36
.47- .61	.04	5.54- 5.69	.37
.62- .76	.05	5.70- 5.84	.38
.77- .92	.06	5.85- 6 09	.39
.93- 1.07	.07	6.10- 6.15	.40
1.08- 1.23	.08	6.16- 6.30	.41
1.24- 1.38	.09	6.31- 6.46	.42
1.39- 1.53	.10	6.47- 6.61	.43
1.54- 1.69	.11	6.62- 6.76	.44
1.70- 1.84	.12	6.77- 6.92	.45
1.85- 2.09	.13	6.93- 7.07	.46
2.10- 2.15	.14	7.08- 7.23	.47
2.16- 2.30	.15	7.24- 7.38	.48
2.31- 2.46	.16	7.39- 7.53	.49
2.47- 2.61	.17	7.54- 7.69	.50
2.62- 2.76	.18	7.70- 7.84	.51
2.77- 2.92	.19	7.85- 8.09	.52
2.93- 3.07	.20	8.10- 8.15	.53
3.08- 3.23	.21	8.16- 8.30	.54
3.24- 3.38	.22	8.31- 8.46	.55
3.39- 3.53	.23	8.47- 8.61	.56
3.54- 3.69	.24	8.62- 8.76	.57
3.70- 3.84	.25	8.77- 8.92	.58
3.85- 4.09	.26	8.93- 9.07	.59
4.10- 4.15	.27	9.08- 9.23	.60
4.16- 4.30	.28	9.24- 9.38	.61
4.31- 4.46	.29	9.39- 9.53	.62
4.47- 4.61	.30	9.54- 9.69	.63
4.62- 4.76	.31	9.70- 9.84	.64
4.77- 4.92	.32	9.85- 10.09	.65
4.93- 5.07	.33		

SALES TAX BRACKETS
ON ALL 6 1/2% TAXABLE TRANSACTIONS
(FLORIDA DEPT. OF REVENUE)

Amount of Sale	Tax	Amount of Sale	Tax
10.10- 10.15	.66	15.08- 15.23	.99
10.16- 10.30	.67	15.24- 15.38	1.00
10.31- 10.46	.68	15.39- 15.53	1.01
10.47- 10.61	.69	15.54- 15.69	1.02
10.62- 10.76	.70	15.70- 15.84	1.03
10.77- 10.92	.71	15.85- 16.09	1.04
10.93- 11.07	.72	16.10- 16.15	1.05
11.08- 11.23	.73	16.16- 16.30	1.06
11.24- 11.38	.74	16.31- 16.46	1.07
11.39- 11.53	.75	16.47- 16.61	1.08
11.54- 11.69	.76	16.62- 16.76	1.09
11.70- 11.84	.77	16.77- 16.92	1.10
11.85- 12.09	.78	16.93- 17.07	1.11
12.10- 12.15	.79	17.08- 17.23	1.12
12.16- 12.30	.80	17.24- 17.38	1.13
12.31- 12.46	.81	17.39- 17.53	1.14
12.47- 12.61	.82	17.54- 17.69	1.15
12.62- 12.76	.83	17.70- 17.84	1.16
12.77- 12.92	.84	17.85- 18.09	1.17
12.93 13.07	.85	18.10- 18.15	1.18
13.08- 13.23	.86	18.16- 18.30	1.19
13.24- 13.38	.87	18.31- 18.46	1.20
13.39- 13.53	.88	18.47- 18.61	1.21
13.54- 13.69	.89	18.62- 18.76	1.22
13.70- 13.84	.90	18.77- 18.92	1.23
13.85- 14.09	.91	18.93- 19.07	1.24
14.10- 14.15	.92	19.08- 19.23	1.25
14.16- 14.30	.93	19.24- 19.38	1.26
14.31- 14.46	.94	19.39- 19.53	1.27
14.47- 14.61	.95	19.54- 19.69	1.28
14.62- 14.76	.96	19.70- 19.84	1.29
14.77- 14.92	.97	19.85- 20.09	1.30
14.93- 15.07	.98		

EXHIBIT 18-1
Sales Tax Brackets

TRY-IT | EXERCISE

1. Use Exhibit 18-1 to determine the amount of sales tax on a calculator with a retail price of $12.49.

Check your answer with the solution on page 676.

18-2 Calculating Sales Tax by Using the Percent Method

When sales tax tables are not available, the percent method may be used to calculate the sales tax on an item or service. Other nontaxable charges, such as packing, delivery, handling, or setup, are added after the sales tax has been computed.

Everybody's Business

Learning Tip

Remember, there is no sales tax on packing, shipping, handling, or setup charges for merchandise purchased. These charges should be added *after* the sales tax has been computed.

STEPS TO CALCULATE SALES TAX AND TOTAL PURCHASE PRICE BY USING THE PERCENT METHOD:

Step 1. Calculate the sales tax by multiplying the selling price of the good or service by the sales tax rate:

Sales tax = Selling price × Sales tax rate

Step 2. Compute the total purchase price by adding the selling price, the sales tax, and any other additional charges.

Total purchase price = Selling price + Sales tax + Other charges

EXAMPLE

Donald Waller purchased a riding lawnmower for $488.95 at a Wal-Mart store in Atlanta, Georgia. The store charges $25.00 for delivery and $15.00 for assembly. If the state sales tax in Georgia is 5%, and Atlanta has a 1.5% city tax, what is the amount of sales tax on the lawnmower and what is the total purchase price?

SOLUTION STRATEGY

In this example, the sales tax rate will be the total of the state and city taxes,

Sales tax rate = 5% + 1.5% = 6.5%

Step 1. Sales tax = Selling price × Sales tax rate

Sales tax = 488.95 × .065 = $31.78

Step 2. Total purchase price = Selling price + Sales tax + Other charges

Total purchase price = 488.95 + 31.78 + (25.00 + 15.00)

Total purchase price = $560.73

TRY-IT | EXERCISE

2. Chris Mengel purchased a car for $18,600 at Auto City in Boulder, Colorado. If the dealer preparation charges are $240 and the sales tax rate in Colorado is 8%, what is the amount of sales tax on the car and what is the total purchase price?

Check your answers with the solutions on page 676.

18-3 Calculating Selling Price and Amount of Sales Tax When Total Purchase Price Is Known

From time to time, merchants and customers may want to know the actual selling price of an item when the total purchase price, including sales tax, is known.

STEPS TO CALCULATE SELLING PRICE AND AMOUNT OF SALES TAX:

Step 1. Calculate the selling price of an item by dividing the total purchase price by 100% plus the sales tax rate:

$$\textbf{Selling price} = \frac{\textbf{Total purchase price}}{\textbf{100\% + Sales tax rate}}$$

Step 2. Determine the amount of sales tax by subtracting the selling price from the total purchase price:

$$\textbf{Sales tax = Total purchase price − Selling price}$$

EXAMPLE

Eric Sandburg bought a television set for a total purchase price of $477. If his state has a 6% sales tax, what were the actual selling price of the TV and the amount of sales tax?

SOLUTION STRATEGY

Step 1.

$$\text{Selling price} = \frac{\text{Total purchase price}}{100\% + \text{Sales tax rate}}$$

$$\text{Selling price} = \frac{477}{100\% + 6\%} = \frac{477}{1.06} = \underline{\underline{\$450}}$$

Step 2.

$$\text{Sales tax} = \text{Total purchase price} - \text{Selling price}$$

$$\text{Sales tax} = 477 - 450 = \underline{\underline{\$27.00}}$$

TRY-IT EXERCISE

3. At the end of a business day, the cash register at Gary's Gift Shop showed total sales, including sales tax, of $3,520.00. If the state and local sales taxes amounted to $8\frac{1}{2}$%, what is the amount of Gary's actual sales? How much sales tax did he collect that day?

Check your answers with the solutions on page 676.

18-4 Calculating Excise Tax

As with the sales tax, an excise tax is usually expressed as a percentage of the purchase price. In certain cases, however, the excise tax may be expressed as a fixed amount per unit purchased, such as $5 per passenger on a cruise ship, or $.15 per gallon of gasoline.

When both sales tax and excise tax are imposed on merchandise at the retail level, the excise taxes are *not included* in the selling price when computing the sales tax. Each tax should be calculated independently on the actual selling price.

Everybody's Business

Real-World Connection

The government "takes its cut" is a good description of the **excise** or **tax** charged on various goods considered luxury items.

The word *excise* is from *excidere,* Latin for "to cut out." In essence, the government cuts out its share!

In 2000, the federal government collected $54.8 billion in excise tax.

Everybody's Business

Learning Tip

Don't tax the tax! The excise tax is *not included* in the selling price when computing the sales tax. Each tax should be calculated *separately* on the actual selling price.

STEPS TO CALCULATE THE AMOUNT OF EXCISE TAX:

Step 1. *When expressed as a percent:* Multiply the selling price of the item by the excise tax rate:

Excise tax = Selling price × Excise tax rate

When expressed as a fixed amount per unit: Multiply the number of units by the excise tax per unit.

Excise tax = Number of units × Excise tax per unit

Step 2. Calculate total purchase price by adding the selling price plus sales tax plus excise tax:

Total purchase price = Selling price + Sales tax + Excise tax

EXAMPLE

The round-trip airfare from Miami to New York is $379.00. If the federal excise tax on airline travel is 10% and the Florida state sales tax is 6%, what are the amounts of each tax and the total purchase price of the ticket?

SOLUTION STRATEGY

Step 1. Sales tax = Selling price × Sales tax rate

Sales tax = 379 × .06 = $22.74

Excise tax = Selling price × Excise tax rate

Excise tax = 379 × .10 = $37.90

Step 2. Total purchase price = Selling price + Sales tax + Excise tax

Total purchase price = 379.00 + 22.74 + 37.90 = $439.64

TRY-IT | EXERCISE

4. A bow and arrow set at The Sports Authority in Cincinnati, Ohio, has a retail price of $129.95. The sales tax in Ohio is 5% and the federal excise tax on this type of sporting goods is 11%. What is the amount of each tax, and what is the total purchase price of the bow and arrow set?

Check your answers with the solutions on page 676.

REVIEW EXERCISES | CHAPTER 18—SECTION I

Use Exhibit 18-1 to determine the sales tax and calculate the total purchase price for the following items:

	Item	Selling Price	Sales Tax	Total Purchase Price
1.	flashlight	$8.95	______	______
2.	candy	.79	______	______
3.	notebook	4.88	______	______
4.	calculator	18.25	______	______

Calculate the missing information for the following purchases:

	Item	Selling Price	Sales Tax Rate	Sales Tax	Excise Tax Rate	Excise Tax	Total Purchase Price	
5.	computer	$1,440.00	7%	________	1.1%	________	________	2
6.	sofa	$750.00	5	________	0	0	________	
7.	fishing rod	$219.95	$4\frac{1}{2}$	________	10	________	________	
8.	tire	$109.99	6	________	5	________	________	3
9.	automobile	________	$5\frac{1}{4}$	________	0	0	$18,785.00	
10.	book	________	8	________	0	0	$15.12	

11. Kate Purnell purchased a refrigerator at Sears for $899.90. The delivery charge was $20 and the ice maker hookup amounted to $55.00. The state sales tax is $6\frac{1}{2}$% and the city tax is 1.3%.

a. What is the total amount of sales tax on the refrigerator?

b. What is the total purchase price?

12. Tod Switzer purchased supplies at Office Depot for a total purchase price of $46.71. The state has a 4% sales tax.

a. What was the selling price of the supplies?

b. What was the amount of sales tax?

13. Last month, The Sweet Tooth Candy Shops had total sales, including sales tax, of $57,889.00. The stores are located in a state that has a sales tax of $5\frac{1}{2}$%. As the accountant for The Sweet Tooth, calculate: 2

a. The amount of sales revenue for the shops last month.

b. The amount of sales taxes that must be sent to the state Department of Revenue.

14. Penny Lane purchased a diamond necklace for $17,400 at Abby Road Jewelers. The state sales tax is 8% and the federal excise tax on this type of jewelry is 10% on amounts over $10,000. 3

a. What is the amount of the sales tax?

b. What is the amount of the federal excise tax?

c. What is the total purchase price of the necklace?

15. The federal excise tax on commercial aviation fuel is 14.1 cents per gallon. If Universal Airlines used a total of 6,540,000 gallons of fuel last month, how much excise tax was paid?

BUSINESS DECISION

Splitting the Tax

16. You are the owner of Fast Forward, a chain of women's clothing boutiques. Your state has a sales tax of 6% and your city has an additional sales tax of 1.5%. Each quarter you are responsible for making these tax deposits to the city and state. Last quarter your stores had total revenue, including sales tax, of $376,250.

a. How much of this revenue was sales and how much was sales tax?

b. How much tax should be sent to the city?

c. How much tax should be sent to the state?

SECTION II

PROPERTY TAX

ad valorem or property tax
A tax based on the assessed value of property, generally collected at the city or county level as the primary source of revenue for counties, municipalities, school districts, and special taxing districts.

real estate, or real property
Land, buildings, and all other permanent improvements situated thereon.

Most states have laws that provide for the annual assessment and collection of ad valorem taxes on real and personal property. **Ad valorem tax** means a tax based upon the assessed value of property. The term **property tax** is used interchangeably with the term ad valorem tax. Property taxes are assessed and collected at the county level as the primary source of revenue for counties, municipalities, school districts, and special taxing districts.

Real estate, or **real property** is defined as land, buildings, and all other permanent improvements situated thereon. Real estate is broadly classified based on land use and includes the following:

- Single-family and multifamily residential, condominiums, townhouses, and mobile homes
- Vacant residential and unimproved acreage
- Commercial and industrial land and improvements
- Agriculture

personal property
For ad valorem tax purposes, divided into tangible personal property such as business equipment, fixtures, and supplies and household goods such as clothing, furniture, and appliances.

Personal property is divided into two categories for ad valorem tax purposes:

- Tangible personal property—such as business fixtures, supplies, and equipment and machinery for shop, plant, and farm.
- Household goods (exempt from property tax in most states)—apparel, furniture, appliances, and other items usually found in the home.

assessed value
The value of property for tax purposes, generally a percentage of the fair market value.

fair market value
A value placed on property based on location, size, cost, replacement value, condition, and income derived from its use.

tax assessor, or property appraiser
The city or county official designated to determine assessed values of property.

The value of property for tax purposes is known as the **assessed value.** In some states assessed value of the property is a specified percentage of the **fair market value,** while in other states it is fixed by law at 100%. Typical factors considered in determining the fair market value of a piece of property are location, size, cost, replacement value, condition, and income derived from its use.

The assessed value is determined each year by the **tax assessor** or **property appraiser.** Most states allow specific discounts for early payment of the tax and have serious penalties for delinquency. The Department of Revenue in each state has the responsibility of insuring that all property is assessed and taxes are collected in accordance with the law.

18-5 Calculating the Amount of Property Tax

On the basis of the fair market value, less all applicable exemptions, the property tax due is computed by applying the tax rates established by the taxing authorities within that area to the assessed value of the property.

Property tax = Assessed value of property × Tax rate

Property tax rates may be expressed in the following ways:

a. Decimal or percent of assessed value—for example, .035 or 3.5%

b. Per \$100 of assessed value—for example, \$3.50 per \$100

c. Per \$1,000 of assessed value—for example, \$35.00 per \$1,000

d. Mills (one one-thousandth of a dollar)—for example, 35 mills

Let's look at the steps to calculate the property tax due when the same tax is expressed in each of the four different ways on a house with an assessed value of \$250,000.

Everybody's Business

Real-World Connection

Property taxes vary greatly from area to area. Among the highest are Lansing, Michigan; Buffalo, New York; Jersey City, New Jersey; Providence, Rhode Island; and Milwaukee, Wisconsin.

Among the lowest are Honolulu and Hilo, Hawaii; Mobile, Alabama; Baton Rouge, Louisiana; and Colorado Springs, Colorado.

A. STEPS TO CALCULATE PROPERTY TAX WHEN THE TAX IS EXPRESSED AS A PERCENT:

Step 1. Convert the tax rate percent to a decimal by moving the decimal point 2 places to the left.

Step 2. Multiply the assessed value by the tax rate as a decimal.

Property tax = Assessed value × Tax rate

Property taxes are the primary source of income for most school districts.

EXAMPLE A

Calculate the tax due on a house with an assessed value of \$250,000. The tax rate is 7.88% of the assessed value.

SOLUTION STRATEGY

Step 1. Convert tax percent to decimal form: 7.88% = .0788.

Step 2. Property tax = Assessed value × Tax rate

Property tax = 250,000 × .0788 = \$19,700

TRY-IT EXERCISE

5a. Calculate the tax due on a condominium with an assessed value of \$160,000. The property tax rate is 6.3%.

Check your answer with the solution on page 677.

B. STEPS TO CALCULATE PROPERTY TAX WHEN THE TAX IS EXPRESSED PER $100 OF ASSESSED VALUE:

Step 1. Divide the assessed value by $100 to determine the number of $100 the assessed value contains.

$$\text{Number of \$100} = \frac{\text{Assessed value}}{100}$$

Step 2. Calculate the property tax by multiplying the number of $100 times the tax per $100.

$$\text{Property tax} = \text{Number of \$100} \times \text{Tax per \$100}$$

EXAMPLE B

Calculate the tax due on a house with an assessed value of $250,000. The tax rate is $7.88 per $100 of assessed value.

SOLUTION STRATEGY

Step 1. $$\text{Number of \$100} = \frac{\text{Assessed value}}{100} = \frac{250{,}000}{100} = 2{,}500$$

Step 2. $$\text{Property tax} = \text{Number of \$100} \times \text{Tax per \$100}$$

$$\text{Property tax} = 2{,}500 \times 7.88 = \underline{\underline{\$19{,}700}}$$

TRY-IT | EXERCISE

5b. Calculate the tax due on a three-acre parcel of land with an assessed value of $50,800. The property tax rate is $3.60 per $100 of assessed value.

Check your answer with the solution on page 677.

C. STEPS TO CALCULATE PROPERTY TAX WHEN THE TAX IS EXPRESSED PER $1,000 OF ASSESSED VALUE:

Step 1. Divide the assessed value by $1,000 to determine the number of $1,000 the assessed value contains.

$$\text{Number of \$1,000} = \frac{\text{Assessed value}}{1{,}000}$$

Step 2. Calculate the tax due by multiplying the number of $1,000 times the tax per $1,000.

$$\text{Property tax} = \text{Number of \$1,000} \times \text{Tax per \$1,000}$$

EXAMPLE C

Calculate the tax due on a house with an assessed value of $250,000. The tax rate is $78.80 per $1,000 of assessed value.

SOLUTION STRATEGY

Step 1. $$\text{Number of \$1,000} = \frac{\text{Assessed value}}{1{,}000} = \frac{250{,}000}{1{,}000} = 250$$

Step 2. $$\text{Property tax} = \text{Number of \$1,000} \times \text{Tax per \$1,000}$$

$$\text{Property tax} = 250 \times 78.80 = \underline{\underline{\$19{,}700}}$$

TRY-IT | EXERCISE

5c. Calculate the tax due on a warehouse with an assessed value of $325,400. The property tax rate is $88.16 per $1,000 of assessed value.

Check your answer with the solution on page 677.

D. STEPS TO CALCULATE PROPERTY TAX WHEN THE TAX IS EXPRESSED IN MILLS:

Step 1. Since mills means $\frac{1}{1000}$ (.001) of a dollar, convert tax rate in mills to tax rate in decimal form by multiplying mills times .001.

Tax rate in decimal form = Tax rate in mills × .001

Step 2. Calculate the tax due by multiplying the assessed value times the tax rate in decimal form:

Property tax = Assessed value × Tax rate in decimal form

EXAMPLE D

Calculate the tax due on a house with an assessed value of $250,000. The tax rate is 78.8 mills.

SOLUTION STRATEGY

Step 1. Tax rate in decimal form = Tax rate in mills × .001

Tax rate in decimal form = 78.8 × .001 = .0788

Step 2. Property tax = Assessed value × Tax rate in decimal form

Property tax = 250,000 × .0788 = $19,700

TRY-IT | EXERCISE

5d. Calculate the tax due on a farm with an assessed value of $85,300. The property tax rate is 54.1 mills.

Check your answer with the solution on page 677.

18-6 Calculating Tax Rate Necessary in a Community to Meet Budgetary Demands

Each year local taxing units such as counties and cities must estimate the amount of tax dollars required to pay for all governmental services provided. Typical examples include public schools, law enforcement, fire protection, hospitals, public parks and recreation, roads and highways, sanitation services, and many others. The tax rate necessary to meet these budgetary demands is determined by two factors: (1) the total taxes required, and (2) the total assessed value of the property in the taxing unit. The tax rate is computed by the following formula:

$$\text{Tax rate per dollar (decimal form)} = \frac{\text{Total taxes required}}{\text{Total assessed property value}}$$

As before, the tax rate may be expressed as a percent, per \$100 of assessed value, per \$1,000 of assessed value, or in mills.

Everybody's Business

Learning Tip

When calculating tax rate per dollar, remember to round your answer to ten-thousandths (4 decimal places) and always round up, even if the next digit is less than 5.

STEPS TO COMPUTE TAX RATE:

Step 1. Calculate tax rate per dollar of assessed property value by dividing the total taxes required by the total assessed property value:

$$\text{Tax rate per dollar (decimal form)} = \frac{\text{Total taxes required}}{\text{Total assessed property value}}$$

Round your answer to ten-thousandths (4 decimal places). In most states, the rounding is always up, even if the next digit is less than 5.

Step 2. *To convert tax rate per dollar to:*

a. percent, move the decimal point 2 places to the right and add a percent sign;
b. tax rate per \$100, multiply by 100;
c. tax rate per \$1,000, multiply by 1,000;
d. mills, divide by .001.

EXAMPLE

The budget planners for Mountainview have determined that \$5,700,000 will be needed to provide all government services for next year. If the total assessed property value in Mountainview is \$68,000,000, what tax rate is required to meet the budgetary demands? Express your answer in each of the four ways.

SOLUTION STRATEGY

Step 1.

$$\text{Tax rate per dollar} = \frac{\text{Total tax required}}{\text{Total assessed property value}}$$

$$= \frac{5{,}700{,}000}{68{,}000{,}000} = .0838235 = \underline{\underline{\$.0839}}$$

Step 2. a. To express tax rate as a percent, move the decimal point 2 places to the right, and add a percent sign. Tax rate $= \underline{\underline{8.39\%}}$.

b. Tax rate expressed per \$100 = .0839 × 100 = $\underline{\underline{\$8.39}}$.

c. Tax rate expressed per \$1,000 = .0839 × 1,000 = $\underline{\underline{\$83.90}}$.

d. Tax rate expressed in mills $= \frac{.0839}{.001} = \underline{\underline{83.9 \text{ mills.}}}$

TRY-IT | EXERCISE

6. The budget planners for Century City have determined that \$3,435,000 will be needed to provide governmental services for next year. The total assessed property value in Century City is \$71,800,000. As the tax assessor, you have been asked by the city council to determine what tax rate will need to be imposed to meet these budgetary demands. Express your answer in each of the four ways.

Check your answers with the solutions on page 677.

REVIEW EXERCISES | CHAPTER 18—SECTION II

Calculate the assessed value and the property tax due on the following properties:

	Fair Market Value	Assessment Rate	Assessed Value	Property Tax Rate	Property Tax Due	
1.	$76,000	100%		3.44%		
2.	125,000	100		$1.30 per $100		1
3.	248,000	80		$25.90 per $1,000		
4.	54,600	30		45.5 mills		
5.	177,400	60		$2.13 per $100		
6.	2,330,000	100		13.22 mills		2
7.	342,900	77		5.3%		
8.	90,230	90		$12.50 per $1,000		

Calculate the property tax rate required to meet the budgetary demands of the following communities:

		Community	Total Assessed Property Valuation	Total Taxes Required	Property Tax Rate			
					Percent	Per $100	Per $1,000	Mills
2	**9.**	Glendale	$657,000,000	$32,300,000				
	10.	Paxton	338,000,000	19,900,000				
3	**11.**	Golden Isles	57,000,000	2,100,000				
	12.	Bayside	880,000,000	13,600,000				

13. Shelley Krane purchased a home with a market value of $125,000 in Cherokee Valley. The assessment rate in that county is 70% and the tax rate is 19.44 mills.

a. What is the assessed value of the home?

b. What is the amount of property tax?

14. As the tax assessor for San Fernando County you have been informed that due to budgetary demands a tax increase will be necessary next year. The total market value of the property in the county is $600,000,000. Currently the assessment rate is 45% and the tax rate is 30 mills. The county commission increases the assessment rate to 55% and the tax rate to 35 mills.

a. How much property tax was collected under the old rates?

b. How much more tax revenue will be collected under the new rates?

BUSINESS DECISION

Early Payment, Late Payment

15. You own a house with an assessed value of \$185,400. The tax rate is \$2.20 per \$100 of assessed value.

a. What is the amount of property tax?

b. If the state offers a 4% discount for early payment, how much would the tax bill amount to if you paid early?

c. If the state charges a mandatory $3\frac{1}{2}\%$ penalty for late payments, how much would the tax bill amount to if you paid late?

SECTION III

INCOME TAX

"The Congress shall have power to lay and collect taxes on incomes, from whatever source derived. . . ." These are the words of the Sixteenth Amendment to the Constitution of the United States. Passed by Congress in 1909 and ratified in 1913, this amendment paved the way for the evolution of the federal income tax system as we know it today. Income taxes, both personal and corporate, compose the largest source of receipts for our federal government. In 2000, individuals paid more than \$1 trillion in federal income taxes and corporations paid more than \$202 billion. In addition to the federal income tax, many state governments have also imposed income taxes on their citizens to finance government activities.

income tax
A pay-as-you-go tax based on the amount of income of an individual or corporation.

tax return
The official Internal Revenue Service forms used to report and pay income tax for income earned during the previous calendar year.

Income tax is a pay-as-you-go tax. The tax is paid as you earn or receive income throughout the year. As we learned in Chapter 9, payment is accomplished through income tax withholdings made by employers on wages and salaries paid to employees, and quarterly estimated tax payments made by people earning substantial income other than wages and salaries, such as interest income and business profits.

For those individuals subject to personal income tax, a **tax return** must be filed on the appropriate IRS form before midnight on April 15th. The tax return pertains to income earned during the previous calendar year. As the income tax filing deadline approaches, taxpayers must begin the preparation of their tax returns. Although tax preparation services are available to help with this annual task, you still have to keep and organize the records necessary for the return. Keep in mind, even if someone else prepares your return, you are ultimately responsible for its accuracy!

Exhibit 18-5, Form 1040, U. S. Individual Income Tax Return, is the most widely used form for individuals filing tax returns. It is known as the "long form." Based on tax filing options, individuals may qualify to use one of the "short forms," 1040A or 1040EZ. Although the tax rules and forms change almost every year, the method for calculating the amount of income tax due remains generally the same. For the purpose of this chapter, we shall divide the task into two components: (a) calculating the taxable income; and (b) determining the amount of income tax due. The figures and tables used in this section reflect IRS requirements for tax year 2001. For the most recent tax information and tables, consult the instruction booklet that accompanies this year's income tax forms.

18-7 Calculating Taxable Income for Individuals

Taxable income is the amount of income that tax rates are applied to in order to calculate the amount of tax owed for the year. Exhibit 18-2 is a schematic diagram of the procedure used to calculate taxable income. Look it over carefully, and then use the following steps to calculate taxable income.

taxable income
The amount of income that tax rates are applied to in order to calculate the amount of tax owed for the year.

STEPS TO CALCULATE TAXABLE INCOME FOR INDIVIDUALS:

Step 1. Determine **total income** by adding all sources of taxable income.

Step 2. Calculate **adjusted gross income** by subtracting the sum of all adjustments to income from total income.

Step 3. Subtract the sum of the **itemized deductions** or the **standard deduction** (whichever is larger) from the adjusted gross income.

2001 Standard Deductions:

Single	$4,550
Married, filing jointly or Qualifying widow(er)	7,600
Married, filing separately	3,800
Head of household	6,650
65 or older, and/or blind	See IRS instructions to find standard deduction

Step 4. *If adjusted gross income is $99,725 or less:*

Multiply $2,900 by the total number of exemptions claimed and subtract from the amount in Step 3. The result is **taxable income.**

If adjusted gross income is over $99,725:
See IRS instructions to find exemption amounts.

Everybody's Business
Real-World Connection

The current standard deductions, tax tables and forms can be found in the IRS publication: *1040 Forms and Instructions.*

This and other tax forms and publications can be obtained by calling the IRS at 1-800-TAX FORM, or from their Web site, www.irs.gov.

For help with doing your taxes, the taxpayer help lines, 1-800-829-1040, are open 24 hours a day, 7 days a week. For recorded tax information and to check on a tax refund, call TeleTax at 1-800-829-4477.

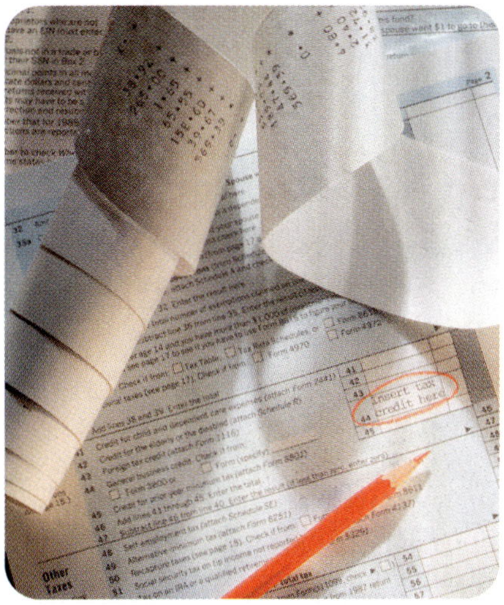

Federal income tax forms must be filed before midnight on April 15th.

Everybody's Business
Real-World Connection

There are three basic rules to follow when doing your taxes to avoid arousing IRS suspicion.

1. *Don't Be Greedy*—The IRS uses 35% of your income as the point at which they would like to "take a look" at what you have deducted. Be sure you always **document** your write-offs as fully as possible.
2. *Don't Be Sloppy*—Tax returns that are **incomplete** or have a number of **math errors** will "raise some questions."
3. *Don't "Forget" Income*—The IRS receives **income information** from **all** employers, as well as **all** banks, brokerage houses and other financial institutions that pay interest, dividends or distribute profits of any kind.

According to Kiplinger's *Personal Finance* magazine and *CCH Standard Federal Tax Reporter*, these are your audit odds:

All individuals
1 in 200
High income ($100,000-plus)
1 in 100
Chance of owing more after an audit
8 in 10
Chance of getting a refund after an audit
1 in 27

EXAMPLE

John and Sally Worthington are married and file a joint tax return. John is a manager and earned $43,500 last year. Sally worked as a secretary and earned $24,660. In addition, they earned $540 interest on their savings account. They each contributed $2,500 to a retirement account, and John paid alimony of $4,700 to his first wife. Itemized deductions amounted to $2,340 in real estate taxes, $4,590 in mortgage interest, $325 in charitable contributions, and $120 in unreimbursed employee expenses (above 2% of adjusted gross income). The Worthingtons claim three exemptions: one each for themselves and one for their dependent son Billy. From this information, calculate the Worthingtons' taxable income.

Income	Wages, salaries, bonuses, commissions, tips, gratuities Interest and dividend income Rents, royalties, partnerships, S corporations, trusts Pensions and annuities Business income (or loss) Capital gain (or loss) from the sale or exchange of property Farm income Unemployment compensation, social security benefits Contest prizes, gambling winnings
Less	
Adjustments to Income	Alimony payments Retirement fund payments—IRA, Keogh, 401K One-half of self-employment tax Self-employment health insurance Penalty on early withdrawal of savings
Equals	
Adjusted Gross Income	Used in determining limits on certain itemized deductions, such as medical, dental, and employee expenses
Less	
Deductions: Standard or Itemized	Medical and dental expenses (above 7.5% of adjusted gross income) Taxes paid: state and local income taxes; real estate taxes Home mortgage interest and points Charitable contributions Casualty and theft losses Moving expenses Unreimbursed employee expenses—union dues, job travel, education (above 2.0% of adjusted gross income)
and	
Exemptions	Personal exemptions Dependents' exemptions
Equals	
Taxable Income	Income on which the amount of income tax due is based. Used for Tax Table look-up or Tax Rate Schedule computation

EXHIBIT 18-2
Procedure to Calculate Taxable Income

SOLUTION STRATEGY

Step 1. Total Income:

\$43,500	John's income
+ 24,660	Sally's income
+ 540	Interest from savings account
\$68,700	Total income

Step 2. Adjusted Gross Income:

\$68,700	Total income
− 9,700	Deductions from total income
\$59,000	Adjusted gross income

\$2,500	John's retirement payments
+ 2,500	Sally's retirement payments
+ 4,700	Alimony payments
\$9,700	Deductions from total income

Step 3. Deductions:

\$2,340	Real estate taxes
+ 4,590	Mortgage interest
+ 325	Charitable contributions
+ 120	Unreimbursed employee expenses (above 2% of adjusted gross income)
\$7,375	Total itemized deductions

Since the total itemized deductions, \$7,375, is less than the standard deduction for married filing jointly (\$7,600) we shall use the standard deduction amount for John and Sally's tax return.

Step 4. Exemptions:
Since the Worthingtons' adjusted gross income is less than \$99,725, multiply \$2,900 by the number of exemptions, three:

\$59,000	Adjusted gross income
− 7,600	Total itemized deductions
− 8,700	\$2,900 × 3 exemptions
\$42,700	Taxable income

TRY-IT EXERCISE

7. Nick Bontempo is single, claiming two exemptions. He is a welder, earning \$35,000 in wages per year. Last year, he also earned \$1,200 in cash dividends from his investments portfolio. Nick contributed \$1,500 to his individual retirement account and gained \$5,000 from the sale of 100 shares of Consolidated Widget stock. His itemized deductions amounted to medical expenses of \$1,000 in excess of IRS exclusions; \$1,945 in real estate taxes; \$2,500 in mortgage interest; and \$300 in charitable contributions. From this information, calculate Nick's taxable income.

Check your answer with the solution on page 677.

18-8 Using the Tax Table to Determine Tax Liability

Tax Table
The IRS chart used to find the amount of income tax due for individuals with taxable income of under $100,000.

Tax Rate Schedules
The IRS chart used to calculate the amount of income tax due for individuals with taxable income of $100,000 or more.

If taxable income is less than $100,000, the Tax Table must be used to figure the tax liability. When the taxable income is $100,000 or more, the Tax Rate Schedule for the appropriate filing status must be used. Exhibit 18-3 illustrates a portion of the 2001 **Tax Table** and Exhibit 18-4 shows the 2001 **Tax Rate Schedules.** The most current version of these may be found in *Instructions for Form 1040,* published by the IRS.

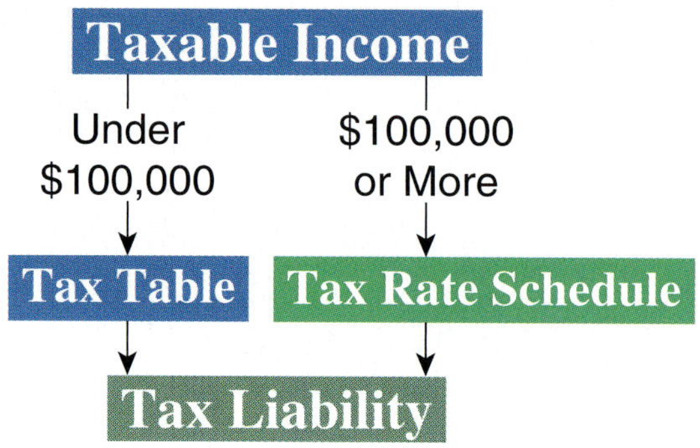

STEPS TO CALCULATE TAX LIABILITY USING THE TAX TABLE, TAXABLE INCOME UNDER $100,000:

Step 1. Read down the "If line 39 (taxable income) is—" columns and find the line that includes the amount of taxable income. *Note:* Line 39 refers to the line on the 1040 tax form where taxable income is listed.

Step 2. Find the tax liability by scanning across to the "And you are—" column containing the appropriate filing status.

EXAMPLE

Troy Reeves is single with taxable income of $37,440. Use the Tax Table, Exhibit 18-3, to calculate his tax liability.

SOLUTION STRATEGY

Step 1. From the Tax Table, Exhibit 18-3, we read down the "If line 39 (taxable income) is—" column to find Troy's taxable income, $37,440, listed between 37,400 and 37,450.

Step 2. Scan across the "And you are—Single" column to locate Troy's tax liability, $6,911.

2001 Tax Table **Caution.** Dependents, see the worksheet on page 33.

If line 39 (taxable income) is— At least	But less than	And you are— Single	Married filing jointly *	Married filing separately	Head of a household
		Your tax is—			
23,000					
23,000	**23,050**	3,454	3,454	3,507	3,454
23,050	**23,100**	3,461	3,461	3,521	3,461
23,100	**23,150**	3,469	3,469	3,534	3,469
23,150	**23,200**	3,476	3,476	3,548	3,476
23,200	**23,250**	3,484	3,484	3,562	3,484
23,250	**23,300**	3,491	3,491	3,576	3,491
23,300	**23,350**	3,499	3,499	3,589	3,499
23,350	**23,400**	3,506	3,506	3,603	3,506
23,400	**23,450**	3,514	3,514	3,617	3,514
23,450	**23,500**	3,521	3,521	3,631	3,521
23,500	**23,550**	3,529	3,529	3,644	3,529
23,550	**23,600**	3,536	3,536	3,658	3,536
23,600	**23,650**	3,544	3,544	3,672	3,544
23,650	**23,700**	3,551	3,551	3,686	3,551
23,700	**23,750**	3,559	3,559	3,699	3,559
23,750	**23,800**	3,566	3,566	3,713	3,566
23,800	**23,850**	3,574	3,574	3,727	3,574
23,850	**23,900**	3,581	3,581	3,741	3,581
23,900	**23,950**	3,589	3,589	3,754	3,589
23,950	**24,000**	3,596	3,596	3,768	3,596
24,000					
24,000	**24,050**	3,604	3,604	3,782	3,604
24,050	**24,100**	3,611	3,611	3,796	3,611
24,100	**24,150**	3,619	3,619	3,809	3,619
24,150	**24,200**	3,626	3,626	3,823	3,626
24,200	**24,250**	3,634	3,634	3,837	3,634
24,250	**24,300**	3,641	3,641	3,851	3,641
24,300	**24,350**	3,649	3,649	3,864	3,649
24,350	**24,400**	3,656	3,656	3,878	3,656
24,400	**24,450**	3,664	3,664	3,892	3,664
24,450	**24,500**	3,671	3,671	3,906	3,671
24,500	**24,550**	3,679	3,679	3,919	3,679
24,550	**24,600**	3,686	3,686	3,933	3,686
24,600	**24,650**	3,694	3,694	3,947	3,694
24,650	**24,700**	3,701	3,701	3,961	3,701
24,700	**24,750**	3,709	3,709	3,974	3,709
24,750	**24,800**	3,716	3,716	3,988	3,716
24,800	**24,850**	3,724	3,724	4,002	3,724
24,850	**24,900**	3,731	3,731	4,016	3,731
24,900	**24,950**	3,739	3,739	4,029	3,739
24,950	**25,000**	3,746	3,746	4,043	3,746
25,000					
25,000	**25,050**	3,754	3,754	4,057	3,754
25,050	**25,100**	3,761	3,761	4,071	3,761
25,100	**25,150**	3,769	3,769	4,084	3,769
25,150	**25,200**	3,776	3,776	4,098	3,776
25,200	**25,250**	3,784	3,784	4,112	3,784
25,250	**25,300**	3,791	3,791	4,126	3,791
25,300	**25,350**	3,799	3,799	4,139	3,799
25,350	**25,400**	3,806	3,806	4,153	3,806
25,400	**25,450**	3,814	3,814	4,167	3,814
25,450	**25,500**	3,821	3,821	4,181	3,821
25,500	**25,550**	3,829	3,829	4,194	3,829
25,550	**25,600**	3,836	3,836	4,208	3,836
25,600	**25,650**	3,844	3,844	4,222	3,844
25,650	**25,700**	3,851	3,851	4,236	3,851
25,700	**25,750**	3,859	3,859	4,249	3,859
25,750	**25,800**	3,866	3,866	4,263	3,866
25,800	**25,850**	3,874	3,874	4,277	3,874
25,850	**25,900**	3,881	3,881	4,291	3,881
25,900	**25,950**	3,889	3,889	4,304	3,889
25,950	**26,000**	3,896	3,896	4,318	3,896
26,000					
26,000	**26,050**	3,904	3,904	4,332	3,904
26,050	**26,100**	3,911	3,911	4,346	3,911
26,100	**26,150**	3,919	3,919	4,359	3,919
26,150	**26,200**	3,926	3,926	4,373	3,926
26,200	**26,250**	3,934	3,934	4,387	3,934
26,250	**26,300**	3,941	3,941	4,401	3,941
26,300	**26,350**	3,949	3,949	4,414	3,949
26,350	**26,400**	3,956	3,956	4,428	3,956
26,400	**26,450**	3,964	3,964	4,442	3,964
26,450	**26,500**	3,971	3,971	4,456	3,971
26,500	**26,550**	3,979	3,979	4,469	3,979
26,550	**26,600**	3,986	3,986	4,483	3,986
26,600	**26,650**	3,994	3,994	4,497	3,994
26,650	**26,700**	4,001	4,001	4,511	4,001
26,700	**26,750**	4,009	4,009	4,524	4,009
26,750	**26,800**	4,016	4,016	4,538	4,016
26,800	**26,850**	4,024	4,024	4,552	4,024
26,850	**26,900**	4,031	4,031	4,566	4,031
26,900	**26,950**	4,039	4,039	4,579	4,039
26,950	**27,000**	4,046	4,046	4,593	4,046
27,000					
27,000	**27,050**	4,054	4,054	4,607	4,054
27,050	**27,100**	4,064	4,061	4,621	4,061
27,100	**27,150**	4,078	4,069	4,634	4,069
27,150	**27,200**	4,092	4,076	4,648	4,076
27,200	**27,250**	4,106	4,084	4,662	4,084
27,250	**27,300**	4,119	4,091	4,676	4,091
27,300	**27,350**	4,133	4,099	4,689	4,099
27,350	**27,400**	4,147	4,106	4,703	4,106
27,400	**27,450**	4,161	4,114	4,717	4,114
27,450	**27,500**	4,174	4,121	4,731	4,121
27,500	**27,550**	4,188	4,129	4,744	4,129
27,550	**27,600**	4,202	4,136	4,758	4,136
27,600	**27,650**	4,216	4,144	4,772	4,144
27,650	**27,700**	4,229	4,151	4,786	4,151
27,700	**27,750**	4,243	4,159	4,799	4,159
27,750	**27,800**	4,257	4,166	4,813	4,166
27,800	**27,850**	4,271	4,174	4,827	4,174
27,850	**27,900**	4,284	4,181	4,841	4,181
27,900	**27,950**	4,298	4,189	4,854	4,189
27,950	**28,000**	4,312	4,196	4,868	4,196
28,000					
28,000	**28,050**	4,326	4,204	4,882	4,204
28,050	**28,100**	4,339	4,211	4,896	4,211
28,100	**28,150**	4,353	4,219	4,909	4,219
28,150	**28,200**	4,367	4,226	4,923	4,226
28,200	**28,250**	4,381	4,234	4,937	4,234
28,250	**28,300**	4,394	4,241	4,951	4,241
28,300	**28,350**	4,408	4,249	4,964	4,249
28,350	**28,400**	4,422	4,256	4,978	4,256
28,400	**28,450**	4,436	4,264	4,992	4,264
28,450	**28,500**	4,449	4,271	5,006	4,271
28,500	**28,550**	4,463	4,279	5,019	4,279
28,550	**28,600**	4,477	4,286	5,033	4,286
28,600	**28,650**	4,491	4,294	5,047	4,294
28,650	**28,700**	4,504	4,301	5,061	4,301
28,700	**28,750**	4,518	4,309	5,074	4,309
28,750	**28,800**	4,532	4,316	5,088	4,316
28,800	**28,850**	4,546	4,324	5,102	4,324
28,850	**28,900**	4,559	4,331	5,116	4,331
28,900	**28,950**	4,573	4,339	5,129	4,339
28,950	**29,000**	4,587	4,346	5,143	4,346
29,000					
29,000	**29,050**	4,601	4,354	5,157	4,354
29,050	**29,100**	4,614	4,361	5,171	4,361
29,100	**29,150**	4,628	4,369	5,184	4,369
29,150	**29,200**	4,642	4,376	5,198	4,376
29,200	**29,250**	4,656	4,384	5,212	4,384
29,250	**29,300**	4,669	4,391	5,226	4,391
29,300	**29,350**	4,683	4,399	5,239	4,399
29,350	**29,400**	4,697	4,406	5,253	4,406
29,400	**29,450**	4,711	4,414	5,267	4,414
29,450	**29,500**	4,724	4,421	5,281	4,421
29,500	**29,550**	4,738	4,429	5,294	4,429
29,550	**29,600**	4,752	4,436	5,308	4,436
29,600	**29,650**	4,766	4,444	5,322	4,444
29,650	**29,700**	4,779	4,451	5,336	4,451
29,700	**29,750**	4,793	4,459	5,349	4,459
29,750	**29,800**	4,807	4,466	5,363	4,466
29,800	**29,850**	4,821	4,474	5,377	4,474
29,850	**29,900**	4,834	4,481	5,391	4,481
29,900	**29,950**	4,848	4,489	5,404	4,489
29,950	**30,000**	4,862	4,496	5,418	4,496
30,000					
30,000	**30,050**	4,876	4,504	5,432	4,504
30,050	**30,100**	4,889	4,511	5,446	4,511
30,100	**30,150**	4,903	4,519	5,459	4,519
30,150	**30,200**	4,917	4,526	5,473	4,526
30,200	**30,250**	4,931	4,534	5,487	4,534
30,250	**30,300**	4,944	4,541	5,501	4,541
30,300	**30,350**	4,958	4,549	5,514	4,549
30,350	**30,400**	4,972	4,556	5,528	4,556
30,400	**30,450**	4,986	4,564	5,542	4,564
30,450	**30,500**	4,999	4,571	5,556	4,571
30,500	**30,550**	5,013	4,579	5,569	4,579
30,550	**30,600**	5,027	4,586	5,583	4,586
30,600	**30,650**	5,041	4,594	5,597	4,594
30,650	**30,700**	5,054	4,601	5,611	4,601
30,700	**30,750**	5,068	4,609	5,624	4,609
30,750	**30,800**	5,082	4,616	5,638	4,616
30,800	**30,850**	5,096	4,624	5,652	4,624
30,850	**30,900**	5,109	4,631	5,666	4,631
30,900	**30,950**	5,123	4,639	5,679	4,639
30,950	**31,000**	5,137	4,646	5,693	4,646
31,000					
31,000	**31,050**	5,151	4,654	5,707	4,654
31,050	**31,100**	5,164	4,661	5,721	4,661
31,100	**31,150**	5,178	4,669	5,734	4,669
31,150	**31,200**	5,192	4,676	5,748	4,676
31,200	**31,250**	5,206	4,684	5,762	4,684
31,250	**31,300**	5,219	4,691	5,776	4,691
31,300	**31,350**	5,233	4,699	5,789	4,699
31,350	**31,400**	5,247	4,706	5,803	4,706
31,400	**31,450**	5,261	4,714	5,817	4,714
31,450	**31,500**	5,274	4,721	5,831	4,721
31,500	**31,550**	5,288	4,729	5,844	4,729
31,550	**31,600**	5,302	4,736	5,858	4,736
31,600	**31,650**	5,316	4,744	5,872	4,744
31,650	**31,700**	5,329	4,751	5,886	4,751
31,700	**31,750**	5,343	4,759	5,899	4,759
31,750	**31,800**	5,357	4,766	5,913	4,766
31,800	**31,850**	5,371	4,774	5,927	4,774
31,850	**31,900**	5,384	4,781	5,941	4,781
31,900	**31,950**	5,398	4,789	5,954	4,789
31,950	**32,000**	5,412	4,796	5,968	4,796

* This column must also be used by a qualifying widow(er).

(Continued on page 63)

EXHIBIT 18-3

Tax Table

Caution. Dependents, see the worksheet on page 33. **2001 Tax Table—*Continued***

If line 39 (taxable income) is— At least	But less than	And you are— Single	Married filing jointly *	Married filing sepa-rately	Head of a house-hold
		Your tax is—			
32,000					
32,000	**32,050**	5,426	4,804	5,982	4,804
32,050	**32,100**	5,439	4,811	5,996	4,811
32,100	**32,150**	5,453	4,819	6,009	4,819
32,150	**32,200**	5,467	4,826	6,023	4,826
32,200	**32,250**	5,481	4,834	6,037	4,834
32,250	**32,300**	5,494	4,841	6,051	4,841
32,300	**32,350**	5,508	4,849	6,064	4,849
32,350	**32,400**	5,522	4,856	6,078	4,856
32,400	**32,450**	5,536	4,864	6,092	4,864
32,450	**32,500**	5,549	4,871	6,106	4,871
32,500	**32,550**	5,563	4,879	6,119	4,879
32,550	**32,600**	5,577	4,886	6,133	4,886
32,600	**32,650**	5,591	4,894	6,147	4,894
32,650	**32,700**	5,604	4,901	6,161	4,901
32,700	**32,750**	5,618	4,909	6,174	4,909
32,750	**32,800**	5,632	4,916	6,188	4,916
32,800	**32,850**	5,646	4,924	6,202	4,924
32,850	**32,900**	5,659	4,931	6,216	4,931
32,900	**32,950**	5,673	4,939	6,229	4,939
32,950	**33,000**	5,687	4,946	6,243	4,946
33,000					
33,000	**33,050**	5,701	4,954	6,257	4,954
33,050	**33,100**	5,714	4,961	6,271	4,961
33,100	**33,150**	5,728	4,969	6,284	4,969
33,150	**33,200**	5,742	4,976	6,298	4,976
33,200	**33,250**	5,756	4,984	6,312	4,984
33,250	**33,300**	5,769	4,991	6,326	4,991
33,300	**33,350**	5,783	4,999	6,339	4,999
33,350	**33,400**	5,797	5,006	6,353	5,006
33,400	**33,450**	5,811	5,014	6,367	5,014
33,450	**33,500**	5,824	5,021	6,381	5,021
33,500	**33,550**	5,838	5,029	6,394	5,029
33,550	**33,600**	5,852	5,036	6,408	5,036
33,600	**33,650**	5,866	5,044	6,422	5,044
33,650	**33,700**	5,879	5,051	6,436	5,051
33,700	**33,750**	5,893	5,059	6,449	5,059
33,750	**33,800**	5,907	5,066	6,463	5,066
33,800	**33,850**	5,921	5,074	6,477	5,074
33,850	**33,900**	5,934	5,081	6,491	5,081
33,900	**33,950**	5,948	5,089	6,504	5,089
33,950	**34,000**	5,962	5,096	6,518	5,096
34,000					
34,000	**34,050**	5,976	5,104	6,532	5,104
34,050	**34,100**	5,989	5,111	6,546	5,111
34,100	**34,150**	6,003	5,119	6,559	5,119
34,150	**34,200**	6,017	5,126	6,573	5,126
34,200	**34,250**	6,031	5,134	6,587	5,134
34,250	**34,300**	6,044	5,141	6,601	5,141
34,300	**34,350**	6,058	5,149	6,614	5,149
34,350	**34,400**	6,072	5,156	6,628	5,156
34,400	**34,450**	6,086	5,164	6,642	5,164
34,450	**34,500**	6,099	5,171	6,656	5,171
34,500	**34,550**	6,113	5,179	6,669	5,179
34,550	**34,600**	6,127	5,186	6,683	5,186
34,600	**34,650**	6,141	5,194	6,697	5,194
34,650	**34,700**	6,154	5,201	6,711	5,201
34,700	**34,750**	6,168	5,209	6,724	5,209
34,750	**34,800**	6,182	5,216	6,738	5,216
34,800	**34,850**	6,196	5,224	6,752	5,224
34,850	**34,900**	6,209	5,231	6,766	5,231
34,900	**34,950**	6,223	5,239	6,779	5,239
34,950	**35,000**	6,237	5,246	6,793	5,246

If line 39 (taxable income) is— At least	But less than	And you are— Single	Married filing jointly *	Married filing sepa-rately	Head of a house-hold
		Your tax is—			
35,000					
35,000	**35,050**	6,251	5,254	6,807	5,254
35,050	**35,100**	6,264	5,261	6,821	5,261
35,100	**35,150**	6,278	5,269	6,834	5,269
35,150	**35,200**	6,292	5,276	6,848	5,276
35,200	**35,250**	6,306	5,284	6,862	5,284
35,250	**35,300**	6,319	5,291	6,876	5,291
35,300	**35,350**	6,333	5,299	6,889	5,299
35,350	**35,400**	6,347	5,306	6,903	5,306
35,400	**35,450**	6,361	5,314	6,917	5,314
35,450	**35,500**	6,374	5,321	6,931	5,321
35,500	**35,550**	6,388	5,329	6,944	5,329
35,550	**35,600**	6,402	5,336	6,958	5,336
35,600	**35,650**	6,416	5,344	6,972	5,344
35,650	**35,700**	6,429	5,351	6,986	5,351
35,700	**35,750**	6,443	5,359	6,999	5,359
35,750	**35,800**	6,457	5,366	7,013	5,366
35,800	**35,850**	6,471	5,374	7,027	5,374
35,850	**35,900**	6,484	5,381	7,041	5,381
35,900	**35,950**	6,498	5,389	7,054	5,389
35,950	**36,000**	6,512	5,396	7,068	5,396
36,000					
36,000	**36,050**	6,526	5,404	7,082	5,404
36,050	**36,100**	6,539	5,411	7,096	5,411
36,100	**36,150**	6,553	5,419	7,109	5,419
36,150	**36,200**	6,567	5,426	7,123	5,426
36,200	**36,250**	6,581	5,434	7,137	5,434
36,250	**36,300**	6,594	5,441	7,151	5,444
36,300	**36,350**	6,608	5,449	7,164	5,458
36,350	**36,400**	6,622	5,456	7,178	5,472
36,400	**36,450**	6,636	5,464	7,192	5,486
36,450	**36,500**	6,649	5,471	7,206	5,499
36,500	**36,550**	6,663	5,479	7,219	5,513
36,550	**36,600**	6,677	5,486	7,233	5,527
36,600	**36,650**	6,691	5,494	7,247	5,541
36,650	**36,700**	6,704	5,501	7,261	5,554
36,700	**36,750**	6,718	5,509	7,274	5,568
36,750	**36,800**	6,732	5,516	7,288	5,582
36,800	**36,850**	6,746	5,524	7,302	5,596
36,850	**36,900**	6,759	5,531	7,316	5,609
36,900	**36,950**	6,773	5,539	7,329	5,623
36,950	**37,000**	6,787	5,546	7,343	5,637
37,000					
37,000	**37,050**	6,801	5,554	7,357	5,651
37,050	**37,100**	6,814	5,561	7,371	5,664
37,100	**37,150**	6,828	5,569	7,384	5,678
37,150	**37,200**	6,842	5,576	7,398	5,692
37,200	**37,250**	6,856	5,584	7,412	5,706
37,250	**37,300**	6,869	5,591	7,426	5,719
37,300	**37,350**	6,883	5,599	7,439	5,733
37,350	**37,400**	6,897	5,606	7,453	5,747
37,400	**37,450**	6,911	5,614	7,467	5,761
37,450	**37,500**	6,924	5,621	7,481	5,774
37,500	**37,550**	6,938	5,629	7,494	5,788
37,550	**37,600**	6,952	5,636	7,508	5,802
37,600	**37,650**	6,966	5,644	7,522	5,816
37,650	**37,700**	6,979	5,651	7,536	5,829
37,700	**37,750**	6,993	5,659	7,549	5,843
37,750	**37,800**	7,007	5,666	7,563	5,857
37,800	**37,850**	7,021	5,674	7,577	5,871
37,850	**37,900**	7,034	5,681	7,591	5,884
37,900	**37,950**	7,048	5,689	7,604	5,898
37,950	**38,000**	7,062	5,696	7,618	5,912

If line 39 (taxable income) is— At least	But less than	And you are— Single	Married filing jointly *	Married filing sepa-rately	Head of a house-hold
		Your tax is—			
38,000					
38,000	**38,050**	7,076	5,704	7,632	5,926
38,050	**38,100**	7,089	5,711	7,646	5,939
38,100	**38,150**	7,103	5,719	7,659	5,953
38,150	**38,200**	7,117	5,726	7,673	5,967
38,200	**38,250**	7,131	5,734	7,687	5,981
38,250	**38,300**	7,144	5,741	7,701	5,994
38,300	**38,350**	7,158	5,749	7,714	6,008
38,350	**38,400**	7,172	5,756	7,728	6,022
38,400	**38,450**	7,186	5,764	7,742	6,036
38,450	**38,500**	7,199	5,771	7,756	6,049
38,500	**38,550**	7,213	5,779	7,769	6,063
38,550	**38,600**	7,227	5,786	7,783	6,077
38,600	**38,650**	7,241	5,794	7,797	6,091
38,650	**38,700**	7,254	5,801	7,811	6,104
38,700	**38,750**	7,268	5,809	7,824	6,118
38,750	**38,800**	7,282	5,816	7,838	6,132
38,800	**38,850**	7,296	5,824	7,852	6,146
38,850	**38,900**	7,309	5,831	7,866	6,159
38,900	**38,950**	7,323	5,839	7,879	6,173
38,950	**39,000**	7,337	5,846	7,893	6,187
39,000					
39,000	**39,050**	7,351	5,854	7,907	6,201
39,050	**39,100**	7,364	5,861	7,921	6,214
39,100	**39,150**	7,378	5,869	7,934	6,228
39,150	**39,200**	7,392	5,876	7,948	6,242
39,200	**39,250**	7,406	5,884	7,962	6,256
39,250	**39,300**	7,419	5,891	7,976	6,269
39,300	**39,350**	7,433	5,899	7,989	6,283
39,350	**39,400**	7,447	5,906	8,003	6,297
39,400	**39,450**	7,461	5,914	8,017	6,311
39,450	**39,500**	7,474	5,921	8,031	6,324
39,500	**39,550**	7,488	5,929	8,044	6,338
39,550	**39,600**	7,502	5,936	8,058	6,352
39,600	**39,650**	7,516	5,944	8,072	6,366
39,650	**39,700**	7,529	5,951	8,086	6,379
39,700	**39,750**	7,543	5,959	8,099	6,393
39,750	**39,800**	7,557	5,966	8,113	6,407
39,800	**39,850**	7,571	5,974	8,127	6,421
39,850	**39,900**	7,584	5,981	8,141	6,434
39,900	**39,950**	7,598	5,989	8,154	6,448
39,950	**40,000**	7,612	5,996	8,168	6,462
40,000					
40,000	**40,050**	7,626	6,004	8,182	6,476
40,050	**40,100**	7,639	6,011	8,196	6,489
40,100	**40,150**	7,653	6,019	8,209	6,503
40,150	**40,200**	7,667	6,026	8,223	6,517
40,200	**40,250**	7,681	6,034	8,237	6,531
40,250	**40,300**	7,694	6,041	8,251	6,544
40,300	**40,350**	7,708	6,049	8,264	6,558
40,350	**40,400**	7,722	6,056	8,278	6,572
40,400	**40,450**	7,736	6,064	8,292	6,586
40,450	**40,500**	7,749	6,071	8,306	6,599
40,500	**40,550**	7,763	6,079	8,319	6,613
40,550	**40,600**	7,777	6,086	8,333	6,627
40,600	**40,650**	7,791	6,094	8,347	6,641
40,650	**40,700**	7,804	6,101	8,361	6,654
40,700	**40,750**	7,818	6,109	8,374	6,668
40,750	**40,800**	7,832	6,116	8,388	6,682
40,800	**40,850**	7,846	6,124	8,402	6,696
40,850	**40,900**	7,859	6,131	8,416	6,709
40,900	**40,950**	7,873	6,139	8,429	6,723
40,950	**41,000**	7,887	6,146	8,443	6,737

* This column must also be used by a qualifying widow(er).

-63-

EXHIBIT 18-3

Tax Table (continued)

2001 Tax Table— **Caution.** Dependents, see the worksheet on page 33.

If line 39 (taxable income) is— At least	But less than	And you are— Single	Married filing jointly *	Married filing separately	Head of a household
		Your tax is—			
59,000					
59,000	59,050	12,851	10,582	13,539	11,701
59,050	59,100	12,864	10,596	13,554	11,714
59,100	59,150	12,878	10,609	13,569	11,728
59,150	59,200	12,892	10,623	13,585	11,742
59,200	59,250	12,906	10,637	13,600	11,756
59,250	59,300	12,919	10,651	13,615	11,769
59,300	59,350	12,933	10,664	13,630	11,783
59,350	59,400	12,947	10,678	13,646	11,797
59,400	59,450	12,961	10,692	13,661	11,811
59,450	59,500	12,974	10,706	13,676	11,824
59,500	59,550	12,988	10,719	13,691	11,838
59,550	59,600	13,002	10,733	13,707	11,852
59,600	59,650	13,016	10,747	13,722	11,866
59,650	59,700	13,029	10,761	13,737	11,879
59,700	59,750	13,043	10,774	13,752	11,893
59,750	59,800	13,057	10,788	13,768	11,907
59,800	59,850	13,071	10,802	13,783	11,921
59,850	59,900	13,084	10,816	13,798	11,934
59,900	59,950	13,098	10,829	13,813	11,948
59,950	60,000	13,112	10,843	13,829	11,962
60,000					
60,000	60,050	13,126	10,857	13,844	11,976
60,050	60,100	13,139	10,871	13,859	11,989
60,100	60,150	13,153	10,884	13,874	12,003
60,150	60,200	13,167	10,898	13,890	12,017
60,200	60,250	13,181	10,912	13,905	12,031
60,250	60,300	13,194	10,926	13,920	12,044
60,300	60,350	13,208	10,939	13,935	12,058
60,350	60,400	13,222	10,953	13,951	12,072
60,400	60,450	13,236	10,967	13,966	12,086
60,450	60,500	13,249	10,981	13,981	12,099
60,500	60,550	13,263	10,994	13,996	12,113
60,550	60,600	13,277	11,008	14,012	12,127
60,600	60,650	13,291	11,022	14,027	12,141
60,650	60,700	13,304	11,036	14,042	12,154
60,700	60,750	13,318	11,049	14,057	12,168
60,750	60,800	13,332	11,063	14,073	12,182
60,800	60,850	13,346	11,077	14,088	12,196
60,850	60,900	13,359	11,091	14,103	12,209
60,900	60,950	13,373	11,104	14,118	12,223
60,950	61,000	13,387	11,118	14,134	12,237
61,000					
61,000	61,050	13,401	11,132	14,149	12,251
61,050	61,100	13,414	11,146	14,164	12,264
61,100	61,150	13,428	11,159	14,179	12,278
61,150	61,200	13,442	11,173	14,195	12,292
61,200	61,250	13,456	11,187	14,210	12,306
61,250	61,300	13,469	11,201	14,225	12,319
61,300	61,350	13,483	11,214	14,240	12,333
61,350	61,400	13,497	11,228	14,256	12,347
61,400	61,450	13,511	11,242	14,271	12,361
61,450	61,500	13,524	11,256	14,286	12,374
61,500	61,550	13,538	11,269	14,301	12,388
61,550	61,600	13,552	11,283	14,317	12,402
61,600	61,650	13,566	11,297	14,332	12,416
61,650	61,700	13,579	11,311	14,347	12,429
61,700	61,750	13,593	11,324	14,362	12,443
61,750	61,800	13,607	11,338	14,378	12,457
61,800	61,850	13,621	11,352	14,393	12,471
61,850	61,900	13,634	11,366	14,408	12,484
61,900	61,950	13,648	11,379	14,423	12,498
61,950	62,000	13,662	11,393	14,439	12,512

If line 39 (taxable income) is— At least	But less than	And you are— Single	Married filing jointly *	Married filing separately	Head of a household
		Your tax is—			
62,000					
62,000	62,050	13,676	11,407	14,454	12,526
62,050	62,100	13,689	11,421	14,469	12,539
62,100	62,150	13,703	11,434	14,484	12,553
62,150	62,200	13,717	11,448	14,500	12,567
62,200	62,250	13,731	11,462	14,515	12,581
62,250	62,300	13,744	11,476	14,530	12,594
62,300	62,350	13,758	11,489	14,545	12,608
62,350	62,400	13,772	11,503	14,561	12,622
62,400	62,450	13,786	11,517	14,576	12,636
62,450	62,500	13,799	11,531	14,591	12,649
62,500	62,550	13,813	11,544	14,606	12,663
62,550	62,600	13,827	11,558	14,622	12,677
62,600	62,650	13,841	11,572	14,637	12,691
62,650	62,700	13,854	11,586	14,652	12,704
62,700	62,750	13,868	11,599	14,667	12,718
62,750	62,800	13,882	11,613	14,683	12,732
62,800	62,850	13,896	11,627	14,698	12,746
62,850	62,900	13,909	11,641	14,713	12,759
62,900	62,950	13,923	11,654	14,728	12,773
62,950	63,000	13,937	11,668	14,744	12,787
63,000					
63,000	63,050	13,951	11,682	14,759	12,801
63,050	63,100	13,964	11,696	14,774	12,814
63,100	63,150	13,978	11,709	14,789	12,828
63,150	63,200	13,992	11,723	14,805	12,842
63,200	63,250	14,006	11,737	14,820	12,856
63,250	63,300	14,019	11,751	14,835	12,869
63,300	63,350	14,033	11,764	14,850	12,883
63,350	63,400	14,047	11,778	14,866	12,897
63,400	63,450	14,061	11,792	14,881	12,911
63,450	63,500	14,074	11,806	14,896	12,924
63,500	63,550	14,088	11,819	14,911	12,938
63,550	63,600	14,102	11,833	14,927	12,952
63,600	63,650	14,116	11,847	14,942	12,966
63,650	63,700	14,129	11,861	14,957	12,979
63,700	63,750	14,143	11,874	14,972	12,993
63,750	63,800	14,157	11,888	14,988	13,007
63,800	63,850	14,171	11,902	15,003	13,021
63,850	63,900	14,184	11,916	15,018	13,034
63,900	63,950	14,198	11,929	15,033	13,048
63,950	64,000	14,212	11,943	15,049	13,062
64,000					
64,000	64,050	14,226	11,957	15,064	13,076
64,050	64,100	14,239	11,971	15,079	13,089
64,100	64,150	14,253	11,984	15,094	13,103
64,150	64,200	14,267	11,998	15,110	13,117
64,200	64,250	14,281	12,012	15,125	13,131
64,250	64,300	14,294	12,026	15,140	13,144
64,300	64,350	14,308	12,039	15,155	13,158
64,350	64,400	14,322	12,053	15,171	13,172
64,400	64,450	14,336	12,067	15,186	13,186
64,450	64,500	14,349	12,081	15,201	13,199
64,500	64,550	14,363	12,094	15,216	13,213
64,550	64,600	14,377	12,108	15,232	13,227
64,600	64,650	14,391	12,122	15,247	13,241
64,650	64,700	14,404	12,136	15,262	13,254
64,700	64,750	14,418	12,149	15,277	13,268
64,750	64,800	14,432	12,163	15,293	13,282
64,800	64,850	14,446	12,177	15,308	13,296
64,850	64,900	14,459	12,191	15,323	13,309
64,900	64,950	14,473	12,204	15,338	13,323
64,950	65,000	14,487	12,218	15,354	13,337

If line 39 (taxable income) is— At least	But less than	And you are— Single	Married filing jointly *	Married filing separately	Head of a household
		Your tax is—			
65,000					
65,000	65,050	14,501	12,232	15,369	13,351
65,050	65,100	14,514	12,246	15,384	13,364
65,100	65,150	14,528	12,259	15,399	13,378
65,150	65,200	14,542	12,273	15,415	13,392
65,200	65,250	14,556	12,287	15,430	13,406
65,250	65,300	14,569	12,301	15,445	13,419
65,300	65,350	14,583	12,314	15,460	13,433
65,350	65,400	14,597	12,328	15,476	13,447
65,400	65,450	14,611	12,342	15,491	13,461
65,450	65,500	14,624	12,356	15,506	13,474
65,500	65,550	14,638	12,369	15,521	13,488
65,550	65,600	14,653	12,383	15,537	13,502
65,600	65,650	14,668	12,397	15,552	13,516
65,650	65,700	14,683	12,411	15,567	13,529
65,700	65,750	14,698	12,424	15,582	13,543
65,750	65,800	14,714	12,438	15,598	13,557
65,800	65,850	14,729	12,452	15,613	13,571
65,850	65,900	14,744	12,466	15,628	13,584
65,900	65,950	14,759	12,479	15,643	13,598
65,950	66,000	14,775	12,493	15,659	13,612
66,000					
66,000	66,050	14,790	12,507	15,674	13,626
66,050	66,100	14,805	12,521	15,689	13,639
66,100	66,150	14,820	12,534	15,704	13,653
66,150	66,200	14,836	12,548	15,720	13,667
66,200	66,250	14,851	12,562	15,735	13,681
66,250	66,300	14,866	12,576	15,750	13,694
66,300	66,350	14,881	12,589	15,765	13,708
66,350	66,400	14,897	12,603	15,781	13,722
66,400	66,450	14,912	12,617	15,796	13,736
66,450	66,500	14,927	12,631	15,811	13,749
66,500	66,550	14,942	12,644	15,826	13,763
66,550	66,600	14,958	12,658	15,842	13,777
66,600	66,650	14,973	12,672	15,857	13,791
66,650	66,700	14,988	12,686	15,872	13,804
66,700	66,750	15,003	12,699	15,887	13,818
66,750	66,800	15,019	12,713	15,903	13,832
66,800	66,850	15,034	12,727	15,918	13,846
66,850	66,900	15,049	12,741	15,933	13,859
66,900	66,950	15,064	12,754	15,948	13,873
66,950	67,000	15,080	12,768	15,964	13,887
67,000					
67,000	67,050	15,095	12,782	15,979	13,901
67,050	67,100	15,110	12,796	15,994	13,914
67,100	67,150	15,125	12,809	16,009	13,928
67,150	67,200	15,141	12,823	16,025	13,942
67,200	67,250	15,156	12,837	16,040	13,956
67,250	67,300	15,171	12,851	16,055	13,969
67,300	67,350	15,186	12,864	16,070	13,983
67,350	67,400	15,202	12,878	16,086	13,997
67,400	67,450	15,217	12,892	16,101	14,011
67,450	67,500	15,232	12,906	16,116	14,024
67,500	67,550	15,247	12,919	16,131	14,038
67,550	67,600	15,263	12,933	16,147	14,052
67,600	67,650	15,278	12,947	16,162	14,066
67,650	67,700	15,293	12,961	16,177	14,079
67,700	67,750	15,308	12,974	16,192	14,093
67,750	67,800	15,324	12,988	16,208	14,107
67,800	67,850	15,339	13,002	16,223	14,121
67,850	67,900	15,354	13,016	16,238	14,134
67,900	67,950	15,369	13,029	16,253	14,148
67,950	68,000	15,385	13,043	16,269	14,162

* This column must also be used by a qualifying widow(er).

-66-

EXHIBIT 18-3

Tax Table (continued)

Caution. Dependents, see the worksheet on page 33. **2001 Tax Table**

If line 39 (taxable income) is— At least	But less than	Single	Married filing jointly *	Married filing sepa-rately	Head of a house-hold
		Your tax is—			
68,000					
68,000	**68,050**	15,400	13,057	16,284	14,176
68,050	**68,100**	15,415	13,071	16,299	14,189
68,100	**68,150**	15,430	13,084	16,314	14,203
68,150	**68,200**	15,446	13,098	16,330	14,217
68,200	**68,250**	15,461	13,112	16,345	14,231
68,250	**68,300**	15,476	13,126	16,360	14,244
68,300	**68,350**	15,491	13,139	16,375	14,258
68,350	**68,400**	15,507	13,153	16,391	14,272
68,400	**68,450**	15,522	13,167	16,406	14,286
68,450	**68,500**	15,537	13,181	16,421	14,299
68,500	**68,550**	15,552	13,194	16,436	14,313
68,550	**68,600**	15,568	13,208	16,452	14,327
68,600	**68,650**	15,583	13,222	16,467	14,341
68,650	**68,700**	15,598	13,236	16,482	14,354
68,700	**68,750**	15,613	13,249	16,497	14,368
68,750	**68,800**	15,629	13,263	16,513	14,382
68,800	**68,850**	15,644	13,277	16,528	14,396
68,850	**68,900**	15,659	13,291	16,543	14,409
68,900	**68,950**	15,674	13,304	16,558	14,423
68,950	**69,000**	15,690	13,318	16,574	14,437
69,000					
69,000	**69,050**	15,705	13,332	16,589	14,451
69,050	**69,100**	15,720	13,346	16,604	14,464
69,100	**69,150**	15,735	13,359	16,619	14,478
69,150	**69,200**	15,751	13,373	16,635	14,492
69,200	**69,250**	15,766	13,387	16,650	14,506
69,250	**69,300**	15,781	13,401	16,665	14,519
69,300	**69,350**	15,796	13,414	16,680	14,533
69,350	**69,400**	15,812	13,428	16,696	14,547
69,400	**69,450**	15,827	13,442	16,711	14,561
69,450	**69,500**	15,842	13,456	16,726	14,574
69,500	**69,550**	15,857	13,469	16,741	14,588
69,550	**69,600**	15,873	13,483	16,757	14,602
69,600	**69,650**	15,888	13,497	16,772	14,616
69,650	**69,700**	15,903	13,511	16,787	14,629
69,700	**69,750**	15,918	13,524	16,802	14,643
69,750	**69,800**	15,934	13,538	16,818	14,657
69,800	**69,850**	15,949	13,552	16,833	14,671
69,850	**69,900**	15,964	13,566	16,848	14,684
69,900	**69,950**	15,979	13,579	16,863	14,698
69,950	**70,000**	15,995	13,593	16,879	14,712
70,000					
70,000	**70,050**	16,010	13,607	16,894	14,726
70,050	**70,100**	16,025	13,621	16,909	14,739
70,100	**70,150**	16,040	13,634	16,924	14,753
70,150	**70,200**	16,056	13,648	16,940	14,767
70,200	**70,250**	16,071	13,662	16,955	14,781
70,250	**70,300**	16,086	13,676	16,970	14,794
70,300	**70,350**	16,101	13,689	16,985	14,808
70,350	**70,400**	16,117	13,703	17,001	14,822
70,400	**70,450**	16,132	13,717	17,016	14,836
70,450	**70,500**	16,147	13,731	17,031	14,849
70,500	**70,550**	16,162	13,744	17,046	14,863
70,550	**70,600**	16,178	13,758	17,062	14,877
70,600	**70,650**	16,193	13,772	17,077	14,891
70,650	**70,700**	16,208	13,786	17,092	14,904
70,700	**70,750**	16,223	13,799	17,107	14,918
70,750	**70,800**	16,239	13,813	17,123	14,932
70,800	**70,850**	16,254	13,827	17,138	14,946
70,850	**70,900**	16,269	13,841	17,153	14,959
70,900	**70,950**	16,284	13,854	17,168	14,973
70,950	**71,000**	16,300	13,868	17,184	14,987

If line 39 (taxable income) is— At least	But less than	Single	Married filing jointly *	Married filing sepa-rately	Head of a house-hold
		Your tax is—			
71,000					
71,000	**71,050**	16,315	13,882	17,199	15,001
71,050	**71,100**	16,330	13,896	17,214	15,014
71,100	**71,150**	16,345	13,909	17,229	15,028
71,150	**71,200**	16,361	13,923	17,245	15,042
71,200	**71,250**	16,376	13,937	17,260	15,056
71,250	**71,300**	16,391	13,951	17,275	15,069
71,300	**71,350**	16,406	13,964	17,290	15,083
71,350	**71,400**	16,422	13,978	17,306	15,097
71,400	**71,450**	16,437	13,992	17,321	15,111
71,450	**71,500**	16,452	14,006	17,336	15,124
71,500	**71,550**	16,467	14,019	17,351	15,138
71,550	**71,600**	16,483	14,033	17,367	15,152
71,600	**71,650**	16,498	14,047	17,382	15,166
71,650	**71,700**	16,513	14,061	17,397	15,179
71,700	**71,750**	16,528	14,074	17,412	15,193
71,750	**71,800**	16,544	14,088	17,428	15,207
71,800	**71,850**	16,559	14,102	17,443	15,221
71,850	**71,900**	16,574	14,116	17,458	15,234
71,900	**71,950**	16,589	14,129	17,473	15,248
71,950	**72,000**	16,605	14,143	17,489	15,262
72,000					
72,000	**72,050**	16,620	14,157	17,504	15,276
72,050	**72,100**	16,635	14,171	17,519	15,289
72,100	**72,150**	16,650	14,184	17,534	15,303
72,150	**72,200**	16,666	14,198	17,550	15,317
72,200	**72,250**	16,681	14,212	17,565	15,331
72,250	**72,300**	16,696	14,226	17,580	15,344
72,300	**72,350**	16,711	14,239	17,595	15,358
72,350	**72,400**	16,727	14,253	17,611	15,372
72,400	**72,450**	16,742	14,267	17,626	15,386
72,450	**72,500**	16,757	14,281	17,641	15,399
72,500	**72,550**	16,772	14,294	17,656	15,413
72,550	**72,600**	16,788	14,308	17,672	15,427
72,600	**72,650**	16,803	14,322	17,687	15,441
72,650	**72,700**	16,818	14,336	17,702	15,454
72,700	**72,750**	16,833	14,349	17,717	15,468
72,750	**72,800**	16,849	14,363	17,733	15,482
72,800	**72,850**	16,864	14,377	17,748	15,496
72,850	**72,900**	16,879	14,391	17,763	15,509
72,900	**72,950**	16,894	14,404	17,778	15,523
72,950	**73,000**	16,910	14,418	17,794	15,537
73,000					
73,000	**73,050**	16,925	14,432	17,809	15,551
73,050	**73,100**	16,940	14,446	17,824	15,564
73,100	**73,150**	16,955	14,459	17,839	15,578
73,150	**73,200**	16,971	14,473	17,855	15,592
73,200	**73,250**	16,986	14,487	17,870	15,606
73,250	**73,300**	17,001	14,501	17,885	15,619
73,300	**73,350**	17,016	14,514	17,900	15,633
73,350	**73,400**	17,032	14,528	17,916	15,647
73,400	**73,450**	17,047	14,542	17,931	15,661
73,450	**73,500**	17,062	14,556	17,946	15,674
73,500	**73,550**	17,077	14,569	17,961	15,688
73,550	**73,600**	17,093	14,583	17,977	15,702
73,600	**73,650**	17,108	14,597	17,992	15,716
73,650	**73,700**	17,123	14,611	18,007	15,729
73,700	**73,750**	17,138	14,624	18,022	15,743
73,750	**73,800**	17,154	14,638	18,038	15,757
73,800	**73,850**	17,169	14,652	18,053	15,771
73,850	**73,900**	17,184	14,666	18,068	15,784
73,900	**73,950**	17,199	14,679	18,083	15,798
73,950	**74,000**	17,215	14,693	18,099	15,812

If line 39 (taxable income) is— At least	But less than	Single	Married filing jointly *	Married filing sepa-rately	Head of a house-hold
		Your tax is—			
74,000					
74,000	**74,050**	17,230	14,707	18,114	15,826
74,050	**74,100**	17,245	14,721	18,129	15,839
74,100	**74,150**	17,260	14,734	18,144	15,853
74,150	**74,200**	17,276	14,748	18,160	15,867
74,200	**74,250**	17,291	14,762	18,175	15,881
74,250	**74,300**	17,306	14,776	18,190	15,894
74,300	**74,350**	17,321	14,789	18,205	15,908
74,350	**74,400**	17,337	14,803	18,221	15,922
74,400	**74,450**	17,352	14,817	18,236	15,936
74,450	**74,500**	17,367	14,831	18,251	15,949
74,500	**74,550**	17,382	14,844	18,266	15,963
74,550	**74,600**	17,398	14,858	18,282	15,977
74,600	**74,650**	17,413	14,872	18,297	15,991
74,650	**74,700**	17,428	14,886	18,312	16,004
74,700	**74,750**	17,443	14,899	18,327	16,018
74,750	**74,800**	17,459	14,913	18,343	16,032
74,800	**74,850**	17,474	14,927	18,358	16,046
74,850	**74,900**	17,489	14,941	18,373	16,059
74,900	**74,950**	17,504	14,954	18,388	16,073
74,950	**75,000**	17,520	14,968	18,404	16,087
75,000					
75,000	**75,050**	17,535	14,982	18,419	16,101
75,050	**75,100**	17,550	14,996	18,434	16,114
75,100	**75,150**	17,565	15,009	18,449	16,128
75,150	**75,200**	17,581	15,023	18,465	16,142
75,200	**75,250**	17,596	15,037	18,480	16,156
75,250	**75,300**	17,611	15,051	18,495	16,169
75,300	**75,350**	17,626	15,064	18,510	16,183
75,350	**75,400**	17,642	15,078	18,526	16,197
75,400	**75,450**	17,657	15,092	18,541	16,211
75,450	**75,500**	17,672	15,106	18,556	16,224
75,500	**75,550**	17,687	15,119	18,571	16,238
75,550	**75,600**	17,703	15,133	18,587	16,252
75,600	**75,650**	17,718	15,147	18,602	16,266
75,650	**75,700**	17,733	15,161	18,617	16,279
75,700	**75,750**	17,748	15,174	18,632	16,293
75,750	**75,800**	17,764	15,188	18,648	16,307
75,800	**75,850**	17,779	15,202	18,663	16,321
75,850	**75,900**	17,794	15,216	18,678	16,334
75,900	**75,950**	17,809	15,229	18,693	16,348
75,950	**76,000**	17,825	15,243	18,709	16,362
76,000					
76,000	**76,050**	17,840	15,257	18,724	16,376
76,050	**76,100**	17,855	15,271	18,739	16,389
76,100	**76,150**	17,870	15,284	18,754	16,403
76,150	**76,200**	17,886	15,298	18,770	16,417
76,200	**76,250**	17,901	15,312	18,785	16,431
76,250	**76,300**	17,916	15,326	18,800	16,444
76,300	**76,350**	17,931	15,339	18,815	16,458
76,350	**76,400**	17,947	15,353	18,831	16,472
76,400	**76,450**	17,962	15,367	18,846	16,486
76,450	**76,500**	17,977	15,381	18,861	16,499
76,500	**76,550**	17,992	15,394	18,876	16,513
76,550	**76,600**	18,008	15,408	18,892	16,527
76,600	**76,650**	18,023	15,422	18,907	16,541
76,650	**76,700**	18,038	15,436	18,922	16,554
76,700	**76,750**	18,053	15,449	18,937	16,568
76,750	**76,800**	18,069	15,463	18,953	16,582
76,800	**76,850**	18,084	15,477	18,968	16,596
76,850	**76,900**	18,099	15,491	18,983	16,609
76,900	**76,950**	18,114	15,504	18,998	16,623
76,950	**77,000**	18,130	15,518	19,014	16,637

* This column must also be used by a qualifying widow(er).

EXHIBIT 18-3

Tax Table (continued)

2001 Tax Rate Schedules

CAUTION Use **only** if your taxable income (Form 1040, line 39) is $100,000 or more. If less, use the **Tax Table.** Even though you cannot use the Tax Rate Schedules below if your taxable income is less than $100,000, all levels of taxable income are shown so taxpayers can see the tax rate that applies to each level.

Schedule X—Use if your filing status is **Single**

If the amount on Form 1040, line 39, is: *Over—*	*But not over—*	Enter on Form 1040, line 40	*of the amount over—*
$0	$27,050	--------- 15%	$0
27,050	65,550	$4,057.50 + 27.5%	27,050
65,550	136,750	14,645.00 + 30.5%	65,550
136,750	297,350	36,361.00 + 35.5%	136,750
297,350	---------	93,374.00 + 39.1%	297,350

Schedule Y-1—Use if your filing status is **Married filing jointly** or **Qualifying widow(er)**

If the amount on Form 1040, line 39, is: *Over—*	*But not over—*	Enter on Form 1040, line 40	*of the amount over—*
$0	$45,200	--------- 15%	$0
45,200	109,250	$6,780.00 + 27.5%	45,200
109,250	166,500	24,393.75 + 30.5%	109,250
166,500	297,350	41,855.00 + 35.5%	166,500
297,350	---------	88,306.75 + 39.1%	297,350

CAUTION

Dependents, see the worksheet on page 33.

Schedule Y-2—Use if your filing status is **Married filing separately**

If the amount on Form 1040, line 39, is: *Over—*	*But not over—*	Enter on Form 1040, line 40	*of the amount over—*
$0	$22,600	--------- 15%	$0
22,600	54,625	$3,390.00 + 27.5%	22,600
54,625	83,250	12,196.88 + 30.5%	54,625
83,250	148,675	20,927.50 + 35.5%	83,250
148,675	---------	44,153.38 + 39.1%	148,675

Schedule Z—Use if your filing status is **Head of household**

If the amount on Form 1040, line 39, is: *Over—*	*But not over—*	Enter on Form 1040, line 40	*of the amount over—*
$0	$36,250	--------- 15%	$0
36,250	93,650	$5,437.50 + 27.5%	36,250
93,650	151,650	21,222.50 + 30.5%	93,650
151,650	297,350	38,912.50 + 35.5%	151,650
297,350	---------	90,636.00 + 39.1%	297,350

-71-

EXHIBIT 18-4
Tax Rate Schedules

TRY-IT | EXERCISE

8. John Coleman and his wife, Louise, had taxable income last year amounting to $64,425. The Colemans' filing status is married, filing jointly. Using the Tax Table, determine their tax liability.

Check your answer with the solution on page 677.

Everybody's Business

Real-World Connection

The federal individual income tax began relatively modestly in 1913 with 400 pages of rules and a basic rate of 1 percent. From the beginning, CCH Inc. has published an annual collection of federal tax rules containing the tax code, tax regulations, and summaries of federal tax pronouncements. The number of pages in this publication has grown from 400 in 1913 to 45,662 in 2001, representing an annual average growth rate of 5.5 percent. According to CCH, with another 88 years of growth at this rate, a set of federal tax rules will cover 5 million pages!

18-9 Using the Tax Rate Schedule to Determine Tax Liability

If taxable income is $100,000 or more, the appropriate Tax Rate Schedule must be used to calculate the tax liability. Exhibit 18-4 contains the 2001 Tax Rate Schedules.

STEPS TO CALCULATE TAX LIABILITY USING THE TAX RATE SCHEDULE, TAXABLE INCOME $100,000 OR ABOVE:

Step 1. Locate the tax rate schedule corresponding to the appropriate filing status:

Schedule X	Single
Schedule Y-1	Married filing jointly or qualifying widow(er)
Schedule Y-2	Married filing separately
Schedule Z	Head of household

Step 2. Read down the "If the amount on Form 1040, line 39, is—" column to find the range containing the taxable income.

Step 3. Subtract the lower number of the range from the taxable income.

Step 4. Multiply the result from Step 3 by the tax rate listed for that range.

Step 5. Calculate the tax liability by adding the result from Step 4 to the dollar amount of tax indicated for that range.

EXAMPLE

Maybelline Williams had taxable income last year of $121,334. For income tax purposes she files as married, filing separately. Use the appropriate Tax Rate Schedule to calculate her tax liability.

SOLUTION STRATEGY

Step 1. Since Maybelline files as married, filing separately, we shall use Tax Rate Schedule Y-2.

Step 2. Reading down the "If the amount on Form 1040, line 39, is—" column, we find Maybelline's taxable income in the range "Over $83,250, but not over $148,675."

Step 3.

121,334.00	Taxable income
− 83,250.00	Lower number of the range
38,084.00	

Step 4.

38,084.00	Result from Step 3
× .355	Tax rate for that range
$13,519.82	

Step 5.

13,519.82	Result from Step 4
+ 20,927.50	Dollar amount of tax indicated for that range
$34,447.32	Tax liability

TRY-IT EXERCISE

9. Abdul Hamza had taxable income of $123,545 last year. If he files as head of household, what is his tax liability?

Check your answer with the solution on page 677.

18-10 Calculating an Individual's Tax Refund or Amount of Tax Owed

Once the tax liability has been determined, we must consider the final three items in income tax preparation: tax credits, other taxes, and payments. The following formula is used to complete the tax preparation process. *Note:* When the result is a positive number, it is the amount of tax owed. When the result is a negative number, it indicates a tax overpayment by that amount. When an overpayment occurs, the taxpayer has the option of receiving a refund or applying the amount of the overpayment to next year's estimated tax.

Refund (−) or amount owed (+) = Tax liability − Credits + Other taxes − Payments

Tax Credits. Tax credits are a dollar-for-dollar subtraction from the tax liability. A **tax credit** of one dollar saves a full dollar in taxes, whereas a tax deduction of one dollar results in less than a dollar in tax savings (the amount depends on the tax rate). Some examples are credit for child and dependent care expenses, credit for the elderly or disabled, and the foreign tax credit.

tax credit
Dollar-for-dollar subtractions from an individual's or corporation's tax liability. Some examples for individuals would be the credit for child and dependent care expenses, the credit for the elderly or disabled, and the foreign tax credit.

Other Taxes. In addition to the tax liability from the Tax Table or Tax Rate Schedules, other taxes may also be due. These taxes are added to the tax liability. Some examples would be self-employment taxes and Social Security and Medicare taxes on tip income.

Payments. This calculation involves subtracting payments such as employees' federal income tax withheld by employers, estimated tax payments made quarterly, excess Social Security and Medicare paid, and the Earned Income Credit (considered a payment). The Earned Income Credit is available to those taxpayers with a child and adjusted gross income of less than $26,473.

Form **1040** Department of the Treasury—Internal Revenue Service
U.S. Individual Income Tax Return **2001** (L)
IRS Use Only—Do not write or staple in this space.

Label (See instructions on page 19.)
Use the IRS label. Otherwise, please print or type.
LABEL HERE

For the year Jan. 1–Dec. 31, 2001, or other tax year beginning , 20 | OMB No. 1545-0074

Your first name and initial	Last name	**Your social security number**
If a joint return, spouse's first name and initial	Last name	**Spouse's social security number**
Home address (number and street). If you have a P.O. box, see page 19.	Apt. no.	▲ **Important!** ▲ You **must** enter your SSN(s) above.
City, town or post office, state, and ZIP code. If you have a foreign address, see page 19.		

Presidential Election Campaign (See page 19.)
Note. Checking "Yes" will not change your tax or reduce your refund.
Do you, or your spouse if filing a joint return, want $3 to go to this fund? ▶ You ☐ Yes ☐ No Spouse ☐ Yes ☐ No

Filing Status

Check only one box.

1 ☐ Single
2 ☐ Married filing joint return (even if only one had income)
3 ☐ Married filing separate return. Enter spouse's social security no. above and full name here. ▶
4 ☐ Head of household (with qualifying person). (See page 19.) If the qualifying person is a child but not your dependent, enter this child's name here. ▶
5 ☐ Qualifying widow(er) with dependent child (year spouse died ▶). (See page 19.)

Exemptions

6a ☐ **Yourself.** If your parent (or someone else) can claim you as a dependent on his or her tax return, **do not** check box 6a
b ☐ **Spouse**
c **Dependents:**

If more than six dependents, see page 20.

(1) First name Last name	(2) Dependent's social security number	(3) Dependent's relationship to you	(4) ✓ if qualifying child for child tax credit (see page 20)
			☐
			☐
			☐
			☐
			☐
			☐

d Total number of exemptions claimed

No. of boxes checked on 6a and 6b
No. of your children on 6c who:
• lived with you
• did not live with you due to divorce or separation (see page 20)
Dependents on 6c not entered above
Add numbers entered on lines above ▶

Income

Attach Forms W-2 and W-2G here. Also attach Form(s) 1099-R if tax was withheld.

If you did not get a W-2, see page 21.

Enclose, but do not attach, any payment. Also, please use Form 1040-V.

Line	Description		Line
7	Wages, salaries, tips, etc. Attach Form(s) W-2		7
8a	**Taxable** interest. Attach Schedule B if required		8a
b	**Tax-exempt** interest. **Do not** include on line 8a	8b	
9	Ordinary dividends. Attach Schedule B if required		9
10	Taxable refunds, credits, or offsets of state and local income taxes (see page 22)		10
11	Alimony received		11
12	Business income or (loss). Attach Schedule C or C-EZ		12
13	Capital gain or (loss). Attach Schedule D if required. If not required, check here ▶ ☐		13
14	Other gains or (losses). Attach Form 4797		14
15a	Total IRA distributions 15a	b Taxable amount (see page 23)	15b
16a	Total pensions and annuities 16a	b Taxable amount (see page 23)	16b
17	Rental real estate, royalties, partnerships, S corporations, trusts, etc. Attach Schedule E		17
18	Farm income or (loss). Attach Schedule F		18
19	Unemployment compensation		19
20a	Social security benefits 20a	b Taxable amount (see page 25)	20b
21	Other income. List type and amount (see page 27)		21
22	Add the amounts in the far right column for lines 7 through 21. This is your **total income** ▶		22

Adjusted Gross Income

Line	Description		Line
23	IRA deduction (see page 27)	23	
24	Student loan interest deduction (see page 28)	24	
25	Archer MSA deduction. Attach Form 8853	25	
26	Moving expenses. Attach Form 3903	26	
27	One-half of self-employment tax. Attach Schedule SE	27	
28	Self-employed health insurance deduction (see page 30)	28	
29	Self-employed SEP, SIMPLE, and qualified plans	29	
30	Penalty on early withdrawal of savings	30	
31a	Alimony paid b Recipient's SSN ▶	31a	
32	Add lines 23 through 31a		32
33	Subtract line 32 from line 22. This is your **adjusted gross income** ▶		33

For Disclosure, Privacy Act, and Paperwork Reduction Act Notice, see page 72. Cat. No. 12600W Form **1040** (2001)

✦ **EXHIBIT 18-5** ✦

Form 1040

Form 1040 (2001) Page 2

Tax and Credits

Standard Deduction for—

- People who checked any box on line 35a or 35b **or** who can be claimed as a dependent, see page 31.
- All others:

Single, $4,550

Head of household, $6,650

Married filing jointly or Qualifying widow(er), $7,600

Married filing separately, $3,800

34 Amount from line 33 (adjusted gross income) 34

35a Check if: ☐ **You** were 65 or older, ☐ Blind; ☐ **Spouse** was 65 or older, ☐ Blind.
Add the number of boxes checked above and enter the total here . . . . ▶ 35a

b If you are married filing separately and your spouse itemizes deductions, or you were a dual-status alien, see page 31 and check here . . . . ▶ 35b ☐

36 **Itemized deductions** (from Schedule A) **or** your **standard deduction** (see left margin) . . 36

37 Subtract line 36 from line 34 37

38 If line 34 is $99,725 or less, multiply $2,900 by the total number of exemptions claimed on line 6d. If line 34 is over $99,725, see the worksheet on page 32 38

39 **Taxable income.** Subtract line 38 from line 37. If line 38 is more than line 37, enter -0- . 39

40 **Tax** (see page 33). Check if any tax is from a ☐ Form(s) 8814 b ☐ Form 4972 . . . 40

41 **Alternative minimum tax** (see page 34). Attach Form 6251 41

42 Add lines 40 and 41 . . . . ▶ 42

43 Foreign tax credit. Attach Form 1116 if required 43

44 Credit for child and dependent care expenses. Attach Form 2441 44

45 Credit for the elderly or the disabled. Attach Schedule R . . 45

46 Education credits. Attach Form 8863 46

47 Rate reduction credit. See the worksheet on page 36 47

48 Child tax credit (see page 37) 48

49 Adoption credit. Attach Form 8839 49

50 Other credits from: a ☐ Form 3800 b ☐ Form 8396
c ☐ Form 8801 d ☐ Form (specify) ________ 50

51 Add lines 43 through 50. These are your **total credits** 51

52 Subtract line 51 from line 42. If line 51 is more than line 42, enter -0- . . . . . . ▶ 52

Other Taxes

53 Self-employment tax. Attach Schedule SE 53

54 Social security and Medicare tax on tip income not reported to employer. Attach Form 4137 . . 54

55 Tax on qualified plans, including IRAs, and other tax-favored accounts. Attach Form 5329 if required . 55

56 Advance earned income credit payments from Form(s) W-2 56

57 Household employment taxes. Attach Schedule H 57

58 Add lines 52 through 57. This is your **total tax** . . . . ▶ 58

Payments

If you have a qualifying child, attach Schedule EIC.

59 Federal income tax withheld from Forms W-2 and 1099 . . 59

60 2001 estimated tax payments and amount applied from 2000 return . 60

61a **Earned income credit (EIC)** 61a

b Nontaxable earned income . . | 61b |

62 Excess social security and RRTA tax withheld (see page 51) 62

63 Additional child tax credit. Attach Form 8812 63

64 Amount paid with request for extension to file (see page 51) 64

65 Other payments. Check if from a ☐ Form 2439 b ☐ Form 4136 65

66 Add lines 59, 60, 61a, and 62 through 65. These are your **total payments** . . . . ▶ 66

Refund

Direct deposit? See page 51 and fill in 68b, 68c, and 68d.

67 If line 66 is more than line 58, subtract line 58 from line 66. This is the amount you **overpaid** 67

68a Amount of line 67 you want **refunded to you** . . . . ▶ 68a

▶ b Routing number ☐☐☐☐☐☐☐☐☐ ▶ c Type: ☐ Checking ☐ Savings

▶ d Account number ☐☐☐☐☐☐☐☐☐☐☐☐☐☐☐☐☐

69 Amount of line 67 you want **applied to your 2002 estimated tax** ▶ 69

Amount You Owe

70 **Amount you owe.** Subtract line 66 from line 58. For details on how to pay, see page 52 ▶ 70

71 Estimated tax penalty. Also include on line 70 71

Third Party Designee

Do you want to allow another person to discuss this return with the IRS (see page 53)? ☐ **Yes.** Complete the following. ☐ **No**

Designee's name ▶ Phone no. ▶ ( ) Personal identification number (PIN) ▶

Sign Here

Joint return? See page 19.

Keep a copy for your records.

Under penalties of perjury, I declare that I have examined this return and accompanying schedules and statements, and to the best of my knowledge and belief, they are true, correct, and complete. Declaration of preparer (other than taxpayer) is based on all information of which preparer has any knowledge.

Your signature	Date	Your occupation	Daytime phone number ( )
Spouse's signature. If a joint return, **both** must sign.	Date	Spouse's occupation	

Paid Preparer's Use Only

Preparer's signature	Date	Check if self-employed ☐	Preparer's SSN or PTIN
Firm's name (or yours if self-employed), address, and ZIP code		EIN	
		Phone no. ( )	

*U.S. Government Printing Office: 2001 — 474-058

Form **1040** (2001)

EXHIBIT 18-5

Form 1040 (continued)

Everybody's Business

Real-World Connection

When it comes to income tax, there is a move toward paperless filing and plastic payments. The IRS has the goal of receiving 80% of all tax returns **electronically** within 10 years.

Among today's most popular tax-preparation software programs are Kiplinger's TaxCut, and Quicken's TurboTax and MacinTax.

The IRS will electronically—with your permission—debit your checking account for your income tax payment on April 15th or credit your account with your refund.

You may also use your American Express Card, Discover Card, or MasterCard to make tax payments. Call toll free or access by Internet one of the service providers listed below and follow the instructions of the provider. Each provider will charge a convenience fee based on the amount you are paying.

- Official Payments Corporation 1-800-2PAY-TAX (1-800-272-9829) www.officialpayments.com
- PhoneCharge, Inc. 1-888-ALLTAXX (1-888-255-8229) www.About1888ALLTAXX.com

STEPS TO CALCULATE AN INDIVIDUAL'S TAX REFUND OR AMOUNT OF TAX OWED:

Step 1. Subtract total credits from the tax liability.

Step 2. Add total of other taxes to the tax liability to get total tax.

Step 3. If total payments are greater than total tax, a refund of the difference is due. If total payments are less than total tax, the difference is the tax owed.

EXAMPLE

After preparing her taxes for last year, Pat Reese determined that she had a tax liability of $5,326. In addition, she owed other taxes of $575. Because of her mother, Pat was entitled to a credit for the elderly of $1,412. If her employer withheld $510 from her paycheck each month, is Pat entitled to a refund or does she owe additional taxes? How much?

SOLUTION STRATEGY

Steps 1 & 2.

$5,326	Tax liability
− 1,412	Tax credits
+ 575	Other taxes
$4,489	Total tax owed

Step 3. Payments: Federal income tax withheld was $510 × 12 months = $6,120.

$6,120	Payments
− 4,489	Total tax
$1,631	Overpayment

Since Pat's payments are greater than her total tax owed, she has made an overpayment by the amount of the difference, and is therefore entitled to a tax refund of $1,631.

TRY-IT | EXERCISE

10. Lisa Goodrich had a tax liability of $14,600 last year. In addition, she owed other taxes of $2,336. She was entitled to a credit for child care of $668 and a foreign tax credit of $1,719. If her employer withheld $270 per week for 52 weeks, does Lisa qualify for a refund or owe more taxes? How much?

Check your answers with the solutions on page 677.

18-11 Calculating Corporate Income Tax and Net Income after Taxes

Corporate Tax Rate Schedule The IRS chart used to calculate the amount of income tax due from corporations.

Just as with individuals, corporations are also taxable entities that must file tax returns and are taxed directly on their earnings. In Chapter 15, we learned to prepare a balance sheet and an income statement based on the operating figures of a company over a period of time. At the bottom of the income statement the net income before taxes was determined. Now let's use the 2001 **Corporate Tax Rate Schedule,** Exhibit 18-6 on page 667, to figure the amount of corporate income tax due.

EXHIBIT 18-6
Corporate Tax Rate Schedule

Corporate Tax Rate Schedule

If taxable income (line 30, Form 1120, or line 26, Form 1120-A) on page 1 is:

Over—	*But not over—*	*Tax is:*	*Of the amount over—*
$0	$50,000	**15%**	$0
50,000	75,000	**$7,500 + 25%**	50,000
75,000	100,000	**13,750 + 34%**	75,000
100,000	335,000	**22,250 + 39%**	100,000
335,000	10,000,000	**113,900 + 34%**	335,000
10,000,000	15,000,000	**3,400,000 + 35%**	10,000,000
15,000,000	18,333,333	**5,150,000 + 38%**	15,000,000
18,333,333	- - - - -	**35%**	0

STEPS TO CALCULATE CORPORATE INCOME TAX AND NET INCOME AFTER TAXES:

Step 1. Using the Corporate Tax Rate Schedule, read down the "Over—" and "But not over—" columns to find the range containing the taxable income of the corporation.

Step 2. Subtract the lower number of the range from the taxable income.

Step 3. Multiply the result from Step 2 by the tax rate listed for that range.

Step 4. Calculate the tax liability by adding the result from Step 3 to the dollar amount of tax indicated for that range.

Step 5. Calculate income after taxes by subtracting the tax liability from the net income before taxes.

Everybody's Business

Real-World Connection

A qualifying domestic corporation with 35 or fewer shareholders may elect to be treated as an **S-corporation,** thus eliminating all corporate liability for federal income taxes.

Instead, any taxable income or loss will be allocated proportionately among the shareholders, who will be responsible for reporting the amounts on their personal income tax returns.

EXAMPLE

The Strand Corporation had net income before taxes of $7,550,000. Use the Corporate Tax Rate Schedule to calculate the amount of income tax due. Also calculate the company's net income after taxes.

SOLUTION STRATEGY

Step 1. Strand's net income falls in the range 335,000 to 10,000,000.

Step 2.

7,550,000	Income before taxes
− 335,000	Lower number of the range
7,215,000	

Step 3.

7,215,000	Step 2 result
× .34	Tax rate for that range
2,453,100	

Step 4.

2,453,100	Result from Step 3
+ 113,900	Dollar amount of tax indicated for that range
$2,567,000	Tax liability

Step 5.

7,550,000	Income before taxes
− 2,567,000	Tax liability
$4,983,000	Net income after taxes

TRY-IT | EXERCISE

11. The Bar BQ Barn had taxable income of $311,200 last year. Use the Corporate Tax Rate Schedule to calculate the amount of income tax due. Also, calculate the company's net income after taxes.

Check your answers with the solutions on page 677.

REVIEW EXERCISES | CHAPTER 18—SECTION III

As a tax return preparer for The Walzer Tax & Accounting Service, you have been asked to calculate the missing information for eight of the firm's tax clients:

	Name	Filing Status (exemptions)	Income	Adjustments to Income	Adjusted Gross Income	Standard Deduction (circle your choice)	Itemized Deductions (circle your choice)	Exemption Allowances	Taxable Income
1.	Roman	Single (1)	$34,300	$2,120	______	______	$4,870	______	______
2.	Wilson	Married filing jointly (3)	______	1,244	47,228	______	5,329	______	______
3.	Kirk	Qualifying widow (2)	45,670	1,760	______	______	3,870	______	______
4.	Bright	Single (2)	______	3,410	51,290	______	6,860	______	______
5.	Garcia	Married filing separately (1)	66,210	______	59,430	______	2,245	______	______
6.	Haines	Married filing jointly (5)	52,130	1,450	______	______	5,610	______	______
7.	Lee	Head of household (3)	88,600	______	84,520	______	21,230	______	______
8.	Montero	Married filing jointly (4)	______	696	37,550	______	8,400	______	______

9. Maria Barrios sells wholesale school supplies for Crayola Corporation. She is single, claiming three exemptions. For income tax purposes, she qualifies as a head of household. Last year she earned a total of $54,300 in salary and commission. She contributed $2,500 to her retirement plan and had the following itemized deductions: $1,231 in real estate taxes, $3,450 in mortgage interest, $2,000 in mortgage loan closing points, $420 in charitable contributions, and $3,392 in unreimbursed job expenses above the 2% adjusted gross income exclusion. From this information, calculate Maria's taxable income.

Use the Tax Table, Exhibit 18-3, to calculate the tax liability for the following taxpayers earning under $100,000:

	Name	Filing Status	Taxable Income	Tax Liability
10.	Randall	Married, Separately	$27,665	________
11.	Denner	Head of household	74,804	________
12.	Butler	Single	38,150	________
13.	Mesa	Married, Jointly	69,915	________

Use the Tax Rate Schedules, Exhibit 18-4, to calculate the tax liability for the following taxpayers earning $100,000 or above:

	Name	Filing Status	Taxable Income	Tax Liability
14.	Crenshaw	Married, Jointly	$121,430	________
15.	Brandon	Single	247,619	________
16.	Lowell	Head of household	185,188	________
17.	Perez	Married, Separately	334,515	________

As a newly hired IRS trainee, you have been asked to calculate the amount of tax refund or tax owed for the following taxpayers:

	Name	Tax Liability	Tax Credits	Other Taxes	Payments	Refund/Owe (circle one)	Amount	
18.	Grant	$5,320	$2,110	$325	$4,650	Refund/Owe	________	2
19.	Stonewall	3,229	750	0	3,130	Refund/Owe	________	
20.	Gonzalez	12,280	2,453	1,232	9,540	Refund/Owe	________	3
21.	Youmans	6,498	1,221	885	7,600	Refund/Owe	________	

22. Peter and Christina Anderson had combined income of $97,320 last year. For tax purposes the Andersons claim four exemptions and their filing status is married, filing jointly. They contributed $5,000 to their retirement plan and had total itemized deductions of $17,200. In addition, the Andersons had a tax credit for the disabled of $3,430. If their combined income tax withheld last year amounted to $10,887, calculate:

a. Adjusted gross income.

b. Taxable income.

c. Tax liability.

d. Are the Andersons entitled to a refund or do they owe additional taxes? How much?

Calculate the amount of corporate income tax due and the net income after taxes for the following corporations:

	Name	Taxable Income	Tax Liability	Net Income after Taxes
23.	Northwest Supply, Inc.	$ 88,955	______	______
24.	Grambling Corp.	14,550,000	______	______
25.	Kroger, Inc.	955,000,000	______	______

BUSINESS DECISION

Investing Your Tax Savings

26. You are a merchandise manager for a chain of department stores. You earn $50,000 per year, and are in the 28% federal income tax bracket. Each year you contribute $2,500 tax free to your individual retirement account, IRA. The account earns 8% annual interest. In addition, the amount of tax that you save each year by making these "pre-tax" contributions is invested in a taxable aggressive growth mutual fund averaging 15%.

a. How much tax do you save each year by making the retirement fund contributions?

b. How much will the retirement fund be worth in 30 years?

c. Although the income from this investment is taxable each year, how much will the "tax savings" fund be worth in 30 years?

CHAPTER FORMULAS

Sales and Excise Taxes

Sales tax = Selling price × Sales tax rate

Total purchase price = Selling price + Sales tax + Other charges

$$\text{Selling price} = \frac{\text{Total purchase price}}{100\% + \text{Sales tax rate}}$$

Sales tax = Total purchase price − Selling price

Excise tax = Selling price × Excise tax rate

Excise tax = Number of units × Excise tax per unit

Total purchase price = Selling price + Sales tax + Excise tax

Property Tax

a. Expressed as a Percent

Property tax = Assessed value of property × Tax rate

b. Expressed per $100 of Assessed Value

Property tax = Number of $100 of assessed value × Tax per $100

c. Expressed per $1,000 of Assessed Value

Property tax = Number of $1,000 of assessed value × Tax per $1,000

d. Expressed in Mills

Tax rate in decimal form = Tax rate in mills × .001

Property tax = Assessed value × Tax rate in decimal form

Community Tax Rate

$$\text{Tax rate per dollar (decimal form)} = \frac{\text{Total taxes required}}{\text{Total assessed property value}}$$

Income Tax

Refund (−) or amount owed (+) = Tax liability − Credits + Other taxes − Payments

✦ SUMMARY CHART ✦
SECTION I: Sales and Excise Taxes

Topic	P/O, Page	Important Concepts	Illustrative Examples
Determining Sales Tax by Using Sales Tax Tables	18-1 641	Sales tax is a tax based on the total retail price of tangible personal property and certain services and admissions. Exhibit 18-1 is an example of a $6\frac{1}{2}$% sales tax table. *Sales tax tables* 1. Locate the taxable retail price in the Amount of Sale column. 2. Scan to the right to locate the amount of tax due in the Tax column.	Bill Gates purchased 3 rolls of film at The Shutterbug for a total of $16.23. The sales tax in that state is $6\frac{1}{2}$%. Use Exhibit 18-1 to determine the amount of sales tax due on this sale. From Exhibit 18-1 we find that the retail price of the film, $16.23, falls in the range of $16.16 to $16.30. Scanning to the right, we find the tax due on this sale is $1.06.

SECTION I: (continued)

Topic	P/O, Page	Important Concepts	Illustrative Examples
Calculating Sales Tax by Using the Percent Method	18-2 642	Sales tax is expressed as a percentage of the retail selling price. *Percent Method* 1. Calculate the sales tax by multiplying the retail selling price by the sales tax rate: **Sales tax = Selling price × Sales tax rate** 2. Compute total purchase price by adding the selling price, the sales tax, and any other additional charges: **Total purchase price = Selling price + Sales tax + Other charges**	Bob Rich purchased a barbecue grill for \$179.95 at JCPenney. The store charged \$12.00 for assembly. If the state sales tax is 4% and the city adds an additional $3\frac{1}{2}$%, what is the amount of sales tax on the grill and what is Bob's total purchase price? Sales tax rate $= 4 + 3\frac{1}{2} = 7\frac{1}{2}\%$ Sales tax = 179.95 × .075 = \$13.50 Total purchase price = 179.95 + 13.50 + 12.00 = \$205.45
Calculating Selling Price and Amount of Sales Tax When Total Purchase Price Is Known	18-3 643	When the total purchase price of an item or items, including sales tax, is known, actual selling price and amount of sales tax is calculated by: 1. Calculate the selling price of an item by dividing the total purchase price by 100% plus the sales tax rate: **Selling price = $\frac{\text{Total purchase price}}{100\% + \text{Sales tax rate}}$** 2. Determine the amount of sales tax by subtracting the selling price from the total purchase price: **Sales tax = Total purchase price − Selling price**	At the end of the day, the cash register at Winkler's Knitting Salon showed total purchases, including sales tax, of \$2,251.83. If the sales tax rate in that state is 5%, calculate Winkler's actual sales revenue and sales tax collected. Sales revenue = $\frac{2{,}251.83}{1.05}$ = \$2,144.60 Sales tax = 2,251.83 − 2,144.60 = \$107.23
Calculating Excise Tax	18-4 643	An excise tax is a tax levied by federal, state, and local governments on certain products and services deemed to be luxury or nonessential items. Excise tax is paid in addition to sales tax and is expressed as a percentage of the purchase price or as a fixed amount per unit purchased. *Percentage:* **Excise tax = Selling price × Excise tax rate** *Per Unit:* **Excise tax = Units × Excise tax per unit**	Larry Limbaugh purchased fishing equipment for \$244.00. The sales tax in his state is 4% and the federal excise tax on fishing equipment is 11%. What is the amount of each tax and the total purchase price of the equipment? Sales tax = 244.00 × .04 = \$9.76 Excise tax = 244.00 × .11 = \$26.84 Total purchase price = 244.00 + 9.76 + 26.84 = \$280.60

SECTION II: Property Tax

Topic	P/O, Page	Important Concepts	Illustrative Examples
Calculating Property Tax Due with Tax Rate Expressed **a. As a Percent**	18-5a 647	A tax levied on the assessed value of real and certain personal property is known as property tax. *Expressed as a percent* 1. Convert the tax rate to a decimal. 2. Calculate property tax: **Property tax = Assessed value × Tax rate**	A house with an assessed value of \$120,000 is subject to a property tax of 2.31%. What is the amount of property tax due? Property tax = 120,000 × .0231 = \$2,772
b. Per \$100 of Assessed Value	18-5b 648	*Per \$100 of assessed value* 1. Calculate number of \$100: $\text{Number of \$100} = \frac{\text{Assessed value}}{100}$ 2. Calculate property tax: **Property tax = Number of \$100 × Tax per \$100**	A house with an assessed value of \$120,000 is subject to a property tax of \$2.31 per \$100 of assessed value. What is the amount of property tax due? Number of \$100 = $\frac{120{,}000}{100} = 1{,}200$ Property tax = 1,200 × 2.31 = \$2,772
c. Per \$1,000 of Assessed Value	18-5c 648	*Per \$1,000 of assessed value* 1. Calculate number of \$1,000: $\text{Number of \$1,000} = \frac{\text{Assessed Value}}{1{,}000}$ 2. Calculate property tax: **Property tax = Number of \$1,000 × Tax per \$1,000**	A house with an assessed value of \$120,000 is subject to a property tax of \$23.10 per \$1,000 of assessed value. What is the amount of property tax due? Number of \$1,000 = $\frac{120{,}000}{1{,}000} = 120$ Property tax = 120 × 23.10 = \$2,772
d. In Mills	18-5d 649	*Expressed in mills* 1. Multiply tax rate in mills by .001 to get tax rate as a decimal: **Tax rate (decimal) = Tax rate in mills × .001** 2. Calculate property tax: **Property tax = Assessed value × Tax rate**	A house with an assessed value of \$120,000 is subject to a property tax of 23.1 mills. What is the amount of property tax due? Tax rate (decimal) = 23.1 × .001 = .0231 Property tax = 120,000 × .0231 = \$2,772
Calculating Tax Rate Necessary in a Community to Meet Budgetary Demands	18-6 649	1. $\text{Tax rate per dollar of assessed value} = \frac{\text{Total taxes required}}{\text{Total assessed property value}}$	A town requires \$5,000,000 for its annual budget. If the total assessed property value of the town is \$80,000,000, what property tax rate is needed to meet those demands? Express your answer in each of the four ways.

SECTION II: (continued)

Topic	P/O, Page	Important Concepts	Illustrative Examples
		2. To convert tax rate per dollar to: a. *Percent*—move the decimal point 2 places to the right and add a percent sign. b. *Tax rate per $100*—multiply by 100. c. *Tax rate per $1,000*—multiply by 1,000. d. *Mills*—divide by .001.	Tax rate $= \frac{5{,}000{,}000}{80{,}000{,}000} = .0625$ Percent = 6.25% Per $100 = .0625 × 100 = $6.25 per $100 Per $1,000 = .0625 × 1,000 = $62.50 per $1,000 Mills $= \frac{.0625}{.001} =$ 62.5 mills

SECTION III: Income Tax

Topic	P/O, Page	Important Concepts	Illustrative Examples
Computing Taxable Income for Individuals	18-7 653	Taxable income is the amount of income that tax rates are applied to in order to calculate the amount of tax owed for the year. Use Exhibit 18-2 and the following steps to compute taxable income. 1. Determine *gross income* by adding all sources of taxable income. 2. Calculate *adjusted gross income* by subtracting the sum of all adjustments to income from the gross income. 3. Subtract the sum of the *itemized deductions* or the *standard deduction* (whichever is larger) from the adjusted gross income. See Step 3, page 653, for standard deduction amounts. 4. If adjusted gross income is $99,725 or less, multiply $2,900 by the number of exemptions claimed and subtract from the amount in Step 3. The result is *taxable income.* For adjusted gross incomes over $99,725 see IRS instructions to find exemption amounts.	Richard and Cindy Greer are married. For income tax purposes they file jointly and claim four exemptions. Last year they earned a total of $45,460. They had adjustments to income of $3,241, and itemized deductions of $8,776. What is the amount of their taxable income? $45,460 Total income − 3,241 Adjustments to income $42,219 Adjusted gross income Since the itemized deductions are greater than the $7,600 allowed as the standard deduction for married, filing jointly, we shall use the itemized figure. The exemption allowance is 2,900 × 4 = $11,600. $42,219 Adjusted gross income − 8,776 Itemized deductions − 11,600 Exemption allowance $21,843 Taxable income
Using the Tax Table to Determine Personal Income Tax Liability	18-8 656	If taxable income is under $100,000, the Tax Table must be used to figure the tax liability. Exhibit 18-3 illustrates a portion of the 2001 Tax Table. 1. Read down the "If line 39 (taxable income) is—" columns and find the line that includes the amount of taxable income. 2. Find the tax liability by scanning across to the "And you are—" column containing the appropriate filing status.	Laurenzo Picata files his taxes as a head of household. If his taxable income last year was $35,552, what was his tax liability? From Exhibit 18-3, we find Laurenzo's taxable income in the range 35,550 to 35,600. Scanning across to the Head of Household column, we find that Laurenzo's tax liability is $5,336.

SECTION III: (continued)

Topic	P/O, Page	Important Concepts	Illustrative Examples
Using the Tax Rate Schedule to Calculate Personal Income Tax Liability	18-9 662	When taxable income is $100,000 or more, the appropriate Tax Rate Schedule must be used to calculate the tax liability. Exhibit 18-4 contains the 2001 Tax Rate Schedules. 1. Locate the tax rate schedule corresponding to the appropriate filing status. 2. Read down the first column to find the range containing the taxable income. 3. Subtract the lower number of the range from the taxable income. 4. Multiply the result from Step 3 by the tax rate listed for that range. 5. Calculate tax liability by adding the result from Step 4 to the dollar amount of tax indicated for that range.	Albert Hall had taxable income last year of $145,000. For income tax purposes he files as married, filing separately. Use the appropriate Tax Rate Schedule to calculate his tax liability. *Step 1.* For Albert's filing status, we shall use Schedule Y-2. *Step 2.* His taxable income is in the range, "83,250 to 148,675" *Step 3.* $145,000 Taxable income − 83,250 Lower number of range 61,750 *Step 4.* $61,750 Result from Step 3 × .355 Tax rate for that range $21,921.25 *Step 5.* $21,921.25 Result from Step 4 + 20,927.50 Dollar amount $42,848.75 Tax liability
Calculating Tax Refund or Income Tax Owed	18-10 663	To calculate the refund or tax owed, we must finally consider tax credits, other taxes, and payments. 1. Subtract total credits from the tax liability. 2. Add total of other taxes to the tax liability to get total tax. 3. If total payments are greater than total tax, a refund of the difference is due. If total payments are less than total tax, the difference is the tax owed.	After preparing his taxes, Gene Hamilton determined that he had a tax liability of $7,370. In addition, he owed other taxes of $1,225 and was entitled to a tax credit of $3,420. If Gene's employer withheld $445 each month for income tax, is Gene entitled to a refund or does he owe additional taxes? How much? $7,370 Tax liability − 3,420 Tax credits + 1,225 Other taxes $5,175 Total tax Payments = 445 × 12 = $5,340 $5,340 Payments − 5,175 Total tax $165 Tax refund due (may be applied to next year's taxes)

SECTION III: (continued)

Topic	P/O, Page	Important Concepts	Illustrative Examples
Calculating Corporate Income Tax and Net Income after Taxes	18-11 666	Corporate income tax is calculated using the Corporate Tax Rate Schedule, Exhibit 18-6. 1. Read down the "Over—" and "But not over—" columns to find the range containing the taxable income. 2. Subtract the lower number of the range from the taxable income. 3. Multiply the result from Step 2 by the tax rate listed for that range. 4. Calculate the tax liability by adding the result from Step 3 to the dollar amount of tax indicated for that range. 5. Calculate the net income after taxes by subtracting the tax liability from the taxable income. **Net income after taxes = Income before tax − Tax liability**	The Card Shop, Inc., had net income before taxes of $62,000. What is the amount of income tax due and the net income after taxes? *Step 1.* The taxable income falls in the range 50,000 to 75,000. *Step 2.* $62,000 Taxable income − 50,000 Lower number of range 12,000 *Step 3.* $12,000 Result from Step 2 × .25 Tax rate for that range $3,000 *Step 4.* $3,000 Result from Step 3 + 7,500 Dollar amount $10,500 Tax liability *Step 5.* $62,000 Income before taxes − 10,500 Tax liability $51,500 Net income after taxes

TRY-IT EXERCISE | SOLUTIONS

1. From Exhibit 18-1, sales tax on $12.49 = $.82

2. Sales tax = Selling price × Sales tax rate
Sales tax = 18,600 × .08 = $1,488.00

Total purchase price = Selling price + Sales tax + Other charges
Total purchase price = 18,600 + 1,488 + 240 = $20,328.00

3. $\text{Selling price} = \dfrac{\text{Total purchase price}}{100\% + \text{Sales tax rate}}$

$\text{Selling price} = \dfrac{3{,}520.00}{100\% + 8\frac{1}{2}\%} = \dfrac{3{,}520.00}{1.085} = \$3{,}244.24$

Sales tax = Total purchase price − Selling price
Sales tax = 3,520.00 − 3,244.24 = $275.76

4. Sales tax = Selling price × Sales tax rate
Sales tax = 129.95 × .05 = $6.50

Excise tax = Selling price × Excise tax rate
Excise tax = 129.95 × .11 = $14.29

Total purchase price = Selling price + Sales tax + Excise tax
Total purchase price = 129.95 + 6.50 + 14.29 = $150.74

5. a. Tax rate = 6.3% = .063

Property tax = Assessed value × Tax rate

Property tax = 160,000 × .063 = $10,080.00

b. $\text{Number of \$100} = \frac{\text{Assessed value}}{100} = \frac{50,800}{100} = 508$

Property tax = Number of $100 × Tax per $100

Property tax = 508 × 3.60 = $1,828.80

c. $\text{Number of \$1,000} = \frac{\text{Assessed value}}{1,000} = \frac{325,400}{1,000} = 325.4$

Property tax = Number of $1,000 × Tax per $1,000

Property tax = 325.4 × 88.16 = $28,687.26

d. Tax rate in decimal form = Tax rate in mills × .001
Tax rate in decimal form = 54.1 × .001 = .0541
Property tax = Assessed value × Tax rate in decimal form
Property tax = 85,300 × .0541 = $4,614.73

6. $\text{Tax rate per dollar} = \frac{\text{Total tax required}}{\text{Total assessed property value}}$

$\text{Tax rate per dollar} = \frac{3,435,000}{71,800,000} = .0478412 = \$.0479$

a. *Percent* .0479 = 4.79%

b. *Per $100* .0479 × 100 = $4.79

c. *Per $1000* .0479 × 1000 = $47.90

d. *Mills* $\frac{.0479}{.001} = 47.9 \text{ mills}$

7.

$35,000	Wages
+ 1,200	Cash dividends
+ 5,000	Sale of stock (gain)
$41,200	Total income

$41,200	Total income
− 1,500	Retirement contributions
$39,700	Adjusted gross income

$1,000	Medical expenses
1,945	Real estate taxes
2,500	Mortgage interest
+ 300	Charitable contributions
5,745	Itemized deductions

$39,700	Adjusted gross income
− 5,745	Itemized deductions
− 5,800	($2,900 × 2) exemptions
$28,155	Taxable income

8. Using Exhibit 18-3, Tax liability,
John and Louise Coleman = $12,067

9. Using Tax Rate Schedule Z, Exhibit 18-4

123,545	Taxable Income
−93,650	Lower number of range
$29,895	

29,895	
× .305	Tax rate for that range
9,117.98	Computed tax
+ 21,222.50	Dollar amount for that range
$30,340.48	Tax liability

10.

$14,600	Tax liability
+ 2,336	Other taxes
− 668	Child care credit
− 1,719	Foreign tax credit
$14,549	Total tax

Employer withheld 270 × 52 = $14,040
Tax owed = Total tax − Payments
Tax owed = 14,549 − 14,040 = $509

11. Using Corporate Tax Rate Schedule, Exhibit 18-6:

$311,200	Income before taxes
−100,000	Lower number of range
$211,200	
× .39	Tax rate
82,368	Computed tax
+ 22,250	Dollar amount for that range
$104,618	Tax liability

$311,200	Income before taxes
−104,618	Tax liability
$206,582	Net income after tax

Name ______________________

Class ______________________

Answers

1. ______________________

____

2. ______________________

____

3. ______________________

____

4. ______________________

____

____

5. ______________________

____

____

6. ______________________

____

7. a. ______________________

b. ______________________

8. a. ______________________

b. ______________________

9. a. ______________________

____

b. ______________________

____

c. ______________________

CHAPTER 18 | ASSESSMENT TEST

Use Exhibit 18-1 to determine the sales tax and calculate the total purchase price for the following items:

Item	Selling Price	Sales Tax	Total Purchase Price
1. alarm clock	$17.88	________	________
2. magazine	2.90	________	________

Calculate the missing information for the following purchases:

Item	Selling Price	Sales Tax Rate	Sales Tax	Excise Tax Rate	Excise Tax	Total Purchase Price
3. ceiling fan	$135.00	4.9%	________	0	0	________
4. cable TV bill	24.40	5	________	4.2	________	________
5. fur coat	17,550	$6\frac{3}{4}$	________	10% (over $10,000)	________	________
6. scanner	________	$7\frac{1}{2}$	________	0	0	$1,277.10

7. Travis Wagner purchased a dishwasher at Sears for $345.88. The delivery charge was $25.00 and the installation amounted to $75.00. The state sales tax is $6\frac{1}{4}$% and the county tax is 1.1%.

a. What is the total amount of sales tax on the dishwasher?

b. What is the total purchase price?

8. Last week Porch & Patio Furniture had total sales, including sales tax, of $16,502.50. The store is located in a state that has a sales tax of $6\frac{3}{4}$%. As the accountant for the store, calculate:

a. The amount of sales revenue.

b. The amount of sales taxes that must be sent to the state Department of Revenue.

9. Transport Services, Inc., purchased 580 tires rated at 50 pounds each for its fleet of trucks. The tires had a retail price of $85.00 each. The sales tax is 4.5% and the federal excise tax is $.15 per pound.

a. What are the amount of sales tax per tire and the total sales tax?

b. What are the amount of federal excise tax per tire and the total excise tax?

c. What is the total purchase price of the tires?

Name ____________

Class ____________

Calculate the assessed value and the property tax due on the following properties:

	Fair Market Value	Assessment Rate	Assessed Value	Property Tax Rate	Property Tax Due
10.	$92,200	80%	________	2.33%	________
11.	74,430	70	________	$12.72 per $1,000	________
12.	2,450,900	100	________	$2.16 per $100	________
13.	165,230	50	________	28.98 mills	________

Calculate the property tax rate required to meet the budgetary demands of the following communities:

	Community	Total Assessed Property Valuation	Total Taxes Required	Property Tax Rate			
				Percent	Per $100	Per $1,000	Mills
14.	Cherry Hill	$860,000,000	$32,400,000	_____	_____	_____	_____
15.	Mill Valley	438,000,000	7,200,000	_____	_____	_____	_____

16. The Valdes family is considering the purchase of a home. They have narrowed the choice down to a $162,000 home in Palm Springs and a $151,200 home in Weston. With regard to property taxes, Palm Springs has an assessment rate of 90% and a tax rate of 22.45 mills, while Weston has a 100% assessment rate and a tax rate of $2.60 per $100 of assessed value. Which house has the higher property tax, and by how much?

17. As the tax assessor for Golden County you have been informed that an additional $4,500,000 in taxes will be required next year for new street lighting and bridge repairs. If the total assessed value of the property in Golden County is $6,500,000,000, how much will this add to property taxes?

a. As a percent

b. Per $100 of assessed value

c. Per $1,000 of assessed value

d. In mills

Answers

10. ____________

____

11. ____________

____

12. ____________

____

13. ____________

____

14. ____________

____

____

____

15. ____________

____

____

____

16. ____________

17. a. ____________

b. ____________

c. ____________

d. ____________

Calculate the missing information for the following taxpayers:

	Name	Filing Status (exemptions)	Income	Adjustments to Income	Adjusted Gross Income	Standard Deduction (circle your choice)	Itemized Deductions (circle your choice)	Exemption Allowance	Taxable Income
18.	Albert	Single (1)	$34,900	$660	______	______	$5,480	______	______
19.	Stiber	Married filing jointly (3)	______	2,180	63,823	______	6,850	______	______
20.	Chong	Head of household (4)	38,100	______	35,650	______	5,930	______	______

Name ______________________

Class ______________________

Answers

18. ______________________

19. ______________________

20. ______________________

21. ______________________

22. ______________________

23. ______________________

24. ______________________

25. ______________________

26. ______________________

27. ______________________

28. ______________________

29. a. ______________________

b. ______________________

c. ______________________

d. ______________________

Use the Tax Table, Exhibit 18-3, or the Tax Rate Schedule, Exhibit 18-4, whichever is appropriate, to calculate the tax liability for the following taxpayers:

	Name	Filing Status	Taxable Income	Tax Liability
21.	Siemans	Head of household	$184,112	______
22.	Jones	Single	70,890	______
23.	Gomez	Married, Jointly	24,938	______
24.	Williams	Head of household	125,202	______
25.	Herbert	Married, Separately	213,280	______
26.	Cuesta	Single	38,216	______

Calculate the amount of tax refund or tax owed for the following taxpayers:

	Name	Tax Liability	Tax Credits	Other Taxes	Payments	Refund/Owe (circle one)	Amount
27.	Brown	$6,540	$1,219	0	$5,093	Refund/Owe	______
28.	Mager	25,112	7,650	2,211	21,200	Refund/Owe	______

29. Neil Rogers is the promotions director for Power 96, a local radio station. He is single and claims two exemptions. Last year Neil earned a salary of $2,450 per month from the station and received a $1,000 Christmas bonus. In addition, he earned royalties of $3,250 from a song he wrote, which was recorded and made popular by a famous musical group. Neil's itemized deductions amounted to $1,850 and he is entitled to a tax credit of $1,765. If the radio station withheld $325 per month for income tax, what is Neil's:

a. Adjusted gross income?

b. Taxable income?

c. Tax liability?

d. Is Neil entitled to a refund or does he owe additional taxes? How much?

Name ______________

Class ______________

30. You are the tax consultant for Macintosh Associates, Inc. If the company had taxable income of $875,500 last year, calculate:

a. Corporate tax liability.

b. Net income after taxes.

BUSINESS DECISION

The 90% Rule, Happy New Year!

31. Scott Stewart, a successful sales manager for a large company, earns a gross income of $6,000 per month. Scott is single, claims one exemption, and uses the standard deduction. Throughout last year, his company withheld $1,000 each month from his paycheck for federal income tax.

Today is January 4th. As Scott's accountant, you just informed him that although his tax return is due at the IRS by April 15, 90% of the income tax due for last year must be paid by January 15, or a penalty would be imposed.

a. Calculate the amount of tax Scott owes for the year.

b. Did his company withhold enough from each paycheck to cover the 90% requirement?

c. How much should Scott send the IRS by January 15 so he will not be penalized?

d. If Scott waits until April 15 to send the balance of his taxes to the IRS, how much will he be penalized, if the penalty is 18% per year, or 1.5% per month on the shortfall up to 90%? (*Hint:* Use the simple formula, $I = PRT$, with exact interest.)

e. If Scott gets a 10% raise, all other factors being the same, how much should he tell his payroll department to withhold from each month's paycheck so that 90% of the tax due will have been taken out?

Answers

30. a. ______________

b. ______________

31. a. ______________

b. ______________

c. ______________

d. ______________

e. ______________

Everybody's Business

Real-World Connection

Every year the Internal Revenue Service publicizes a taxpayer's right to apply for a four-month extension past April 15, a request rarely denied. In 2000, more than 7 million tax payers took advantage of this provision by filing an IRS Form 4868.

Not as well known is that these late filers can also get an additional two months extension, until October 15, by filing a Form 2688 or writing a letter of explanation to the IRS.

For many of the late filers, the extension amounts to a free loan from Uncle Sam, as long as they have paid at least 90 percent of their taxes in withholding or installments.

All the Math That's Fit to Learn

The Business Math Times

Volume XVIII | **Taxes** | One Dollar

Tax Freedom Day

In 2001, Tax Freedom Day arrived on the 123rd day, May 3. This is the longest Americans had to work to pay their taxes.

Tax Freedom Day is the day each year when Americans have finally earned enough money to pay off their tax bills for the year. All taxes at all levels of government are included: federal, state, and local.

The following chart uses the number of days worked as a yardstick to measure the price of government against the price of other important categories of consumer spending. Note that Americans have to work longer to afford federal taxes (86 days) than on any of the other major budget items.

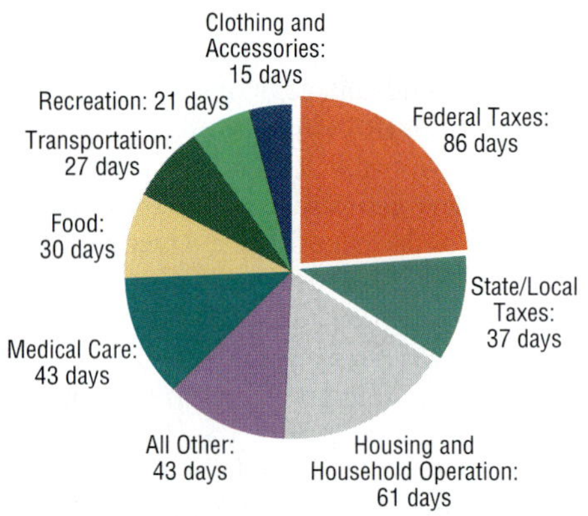

"Quote . . . Unquote"

If you are truly serious about preparing your child for the future, don't teach him to subtract—teach him to deduct.
—*Fran Lebowitz*

Income tax returns are the most imaginative fiction being written today.
—*Herman Wouk*

How Tax Rates Will Decline in Coming Years

	28% rate reduced to:	31% rate reduced to:	36% rate reduced to:	39.6% rate reduced to:
2001	27.5%	30.5%	35.5%	39.1%
2002–2003	27.0%	30.0%	35.0%	38.6%
2004–2005	26.0%	29.0%	34.0%	37.6%
2006 and later	25.0%	28.0%	33.0%	35.0%

Easy Come, Easy Go!

In fiscal year 2000, the Internal Revenue Service reported that federal income was $2,025 billion and outlays were $1,789 billion, leaving a surplus of $239 billion.

The following charts show the relative sizes of the major categories of federal income and outlays for fiscal year 2000.

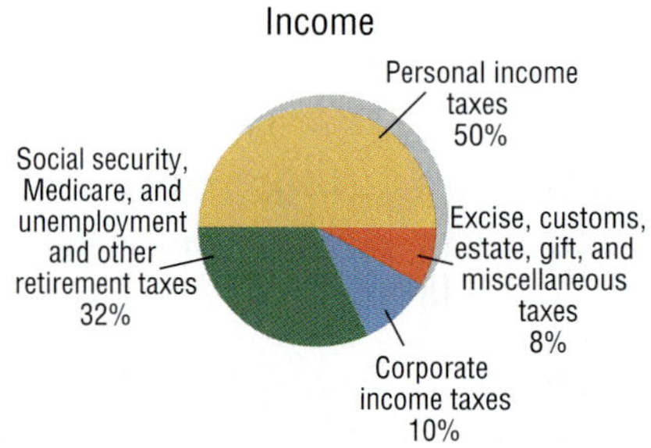

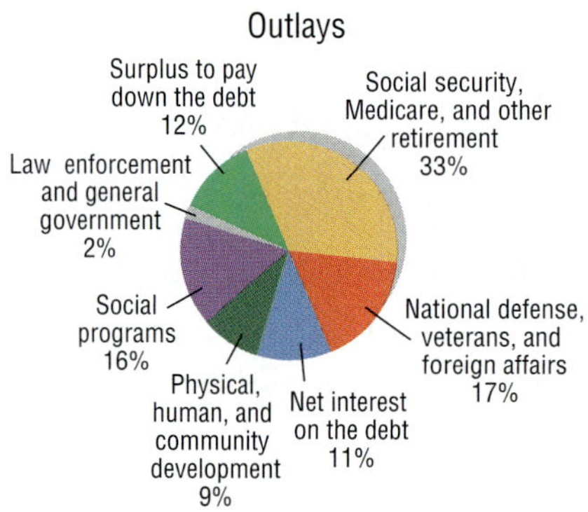

Filing Tips

- Check your math
- Write legibly
- Copy your withholding accurately from your W-2 forms.
- Get the exemptions right
- Be sure that you use the correct column in the tax rate tables
- Photocopy your return (IRS copies cost $23)
- Sign and date your return. Spouse also must sign if filing jointly.

Brainteaser

THE RECESSION

During a particularly slow business period, the sales tax collected by a state fell by 20% in April. If collections fell an additional 25% in May, what was the percent decrease in the entire two-month period?

ANSWER TO LAST ISSUE'S BRAINTEASER

$18.84

The difference between the January and December bills is $6.12 (31.08 − 24.96). This equals the hourly charge in December. Therefore, the fixed monthly fee is:

$24.96 − $6.12 = $18.84.

CHAPTER 19

Insurance

PERFORMANCE OBJECTIVES

Section I Life Insurance

19-1 Understanding life insurance and calculating typical premiums for various types of policies. (p. 685)
19-2 Calculating the value of various nonforfeiture options. (p. 689)
19-3 Calculating the amount of life insurance needed to cover dependents' income shortfall. (p. 691)

Section II Property Insurance

19-4 Understanding property insurance and calculating typical fire insurance premiums. (p. 694)
19-5 Calculating premiums for short-term policies and the refunds due on canceled policies. (p. 696)
19-6 Understanding coinsurance and computing compensation due in the event of a loss. (p. 698)
19-7 Determining each company's share of a loss when liability is divided among multiple carriers. (p. 699)

Section III Motor Vehicle Insurance

19-8 Understanding motor vehicle insurance and calculating typical premiums. (p. 703)
19-9 Computing the compensation due following an accident. (p. 706)

Insurance is the promise to substitute future economic certainty for uncertainty and to replace the unknown with a sense of security. It is a mechanism for reducing financial risk and spreading financial loss due to unexpected events such as the death or disability of an individual, a home or business fire, a flood, an earthquake, an automobile accident, a negligence lawsuit, or an illness. These are only a few of the uncertainties that businesses and individuals can protect against by purchasing insurance. Companies may even purchase business interruption insurance, which covers the loss of income that may occur as a result of a multitude of perils.

insurance
A mechanism for reducing financial risk and spreading financial loss due to unexpected events.

Insurance is a very large and important segment of the U.S. economic system. Today, there are more than 6,000 insurance companies, employing more than 2 million persons and collecting close to $225 billion in annual premiums. The insurance industry is second only to commercial banking as a source of investment funds, because insurance companies invest the billions of premium dollars they receive each year in a wide range of investments.

Insurance is based on the theory of **shared risk,** which means that insurance protection is purchased by many whose total payments are pooled together to pay off those few who actually incur a particular loss. Insurance companies use statisticians known as **actuaries** to calculate the **probability** or chance of a certain insurable event occurring. Based on a series of complicated calculations, insurance rates are then set. The rates are high enough to cover the cost of expected loss payments in the future and to provide a profit for the insurance company.

shared risk
The theory on which insurance is based; protection is purchased by many whose total payments are pooled together to pay off those few who actually incur a particular loss.

actuaries
Statisticians employed by insurance companies who calculate the probability or chance of a certain insurable event occurring.

probability
A number expressing the likelihood or chance that a certain event will occur.

This chapter covers three major categories of insurance: life insurance, property insurance, and motor vehicle insurance. Within these three categories are several hundred different products or lines. Each year, companies market new insurance products to meet the needs of a changing society. Recently, for example, insurance was made available to cover the loss of communication satellites during launch, space travel, and reentry.

Let's start with some basic terminology of the insurance industry. The company offering the insurance protection and assuring payment in the event of a loss is known as the **insurer, carrier,** or **underwriter.** The individual or business purchasing the protection is the **insured** or **policyholder.** The document stipulating the terms of the contract between the insurer and the insured is the **policy.** The amount of protection provided by the policy is the **face value,** and the amount paid at regular intervals to purchase this protection is known as the **premium.** The **beneficiary** is the person or institution to whom the proceeds of the policy are paid in the event that a loss occurs.

insurer, carrier, or underwriter
The company offering the insurance protection and assuring payment in the event of a loss.

insured, or policyholder
The individual or business purchasing the insurance protection.

policy
The document stipulating the terms of the contract between the insurer and the insured.

face value
The amount of protection provided by the policy.

premium
The amount paid at regular intervals to purchase insurance protection.

beneficiary
The person or institution to whom the proceeds of the policy are paid in the event that a loss occurs.

The insurance industry is regulated by a number of authorities, including federal, state, and some inside the industry itself. This regulation is designed to promote the public

The average household is covered by $189,800 in life insurance.

welfare by maintaining the solvency of insurance companies, providing consumer protection, and ensuring fair trade practices as well as fair contracts at fair prices.

Insurance regulations, procedures, and laws vary widely from state to state. Most states have insurance commissions, departments, divisions, or boards that regulate all aspects of the insurance industry. Some of their responsibilities include premium structure and computation, insurance requirements, and salesperson education and licensing. This chapter focuses on calculating the premiums and the payouts of typical life, property, and motor vehicle insurance policies.

SECTION I

LIFE INSURANCE

19-1 Understanding Life Insurance and Calculating Typical Premiums for Various Types of Policies

Most individuals enjoy feeling that they are in control of their financial destiny. Few products are more important to that sense of security than life insurance. **Life insurance** guarantees a specified sum of money to the surviving beneficiaries on the death of the person who is insured. Over the years, the average amount of life insurance per insured household has been steadily increasing. In 1960, for example, each insured household had an average of $13,000 in life insurance. By 1970, the average had doubled to about $26,000. By 1980, it doubled again, to more than $50,000. Today, the average insured household has more than $189,800 in life insurance coverage.

There are two basic types of policies: those that pay only if the policyholder dies **(term insurance)** and those that pay whether the policyholder lives or dies **(permanent insurance).** Today, many insurance policies combine an investment component with risk protection to provide the policyholder with both a death benefit if he or she dies and attractive investment returns if he or she lives. In this section, we examine five popular types of life insurance policies: term, whole life, limited payment life, endowment, and nontraditional.

life insurance
A type of insurance that guarantees a specified sum of money to the surviving beneficiaries upon the death of the person who is insured.

term insurance
A type of life insurance that offers pure insurance protection, paying the face value of the policy to the beneficiaries upon the death of the insured.

permanent insurance
A type of insurance that combines an investment component with risk protection in order to provide the policyholder with both a death benefit and attractive investment returns.

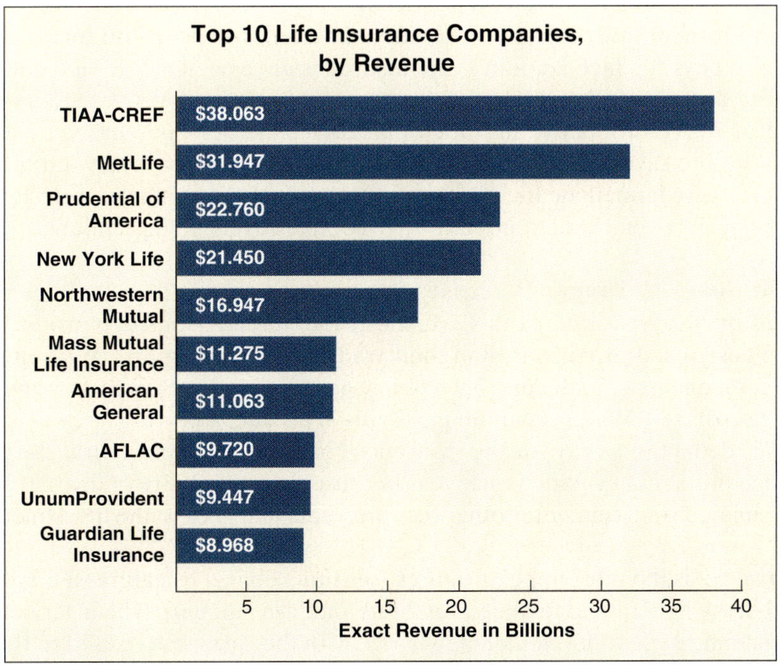

EXHIBIT 19-1
Top 10 Life Insurance Companies, by Revenue

Types of Life Insurance

Term Insurance. This type of life insurance offers pure insurance protection, paying the face value of the policy to the beneficiaries on the death of the insured. With term insurance, there is no investment component. All the premium goes toward purchasing the risk coverage. With most term policies, the premium increases periodically, because the risk of death of the insured increases with age. Term policies may be purchased with premiums increasing every year, every 5 years, every 10 years, and so on.

Renewable term insurance allows the policyholder the option of renewing the policy for another 5- or 10-year period, regardless of his or her health. The premiums on these policies are higher than nonrenewable term insurance. Because it is impossible to predict one's future health, many persons opt for the renewable policy. Another common type of insurance, known as convertible term, allows the policyholder to trade in or convert the term policy for permanent insurance with an investment element and cash value, without having to prove one's health status.

Everybody's Business
Real-World Connection

Here are some rules to remember when buying life insurance:

- Evaluate and understand your needs.
- Buy from a company licensed in your state.
- Select an agent who is competent and trustworthy.
- Shop around to compare costs and benefits.
- Buy only the amount you need and can afford.
- Ask about lower premiums for nonsmokers.
- Read and understand your policy.
- Inform your beneficiaries about the insurance you own.
- Keep your policy in a safe place at home and keep the company's name and policy number in a safe deposit box.

For additional information and assistance, contact

- National Insurance Consumer Helpline, 1-800-942-4242
- Insurance Information Institute, 1-800-331-9146

For Internet links to Web sites that offer comparison rate quotes from many companies, visit TOPICS on our Web site at www.contemporarymath.com.

Whole Life Insurance. Whole life, also known as ordinary life and straight life, is the most common type of permanent insurance. With whole life insurance, policyholders agree to pay premiums for their entire lives. Whole life insurance offers a guaranteed premium and death benefit as well as a guaranteed minimum cash value, which can be borrowed against if necessary. When the insured dies, the beneficiaries receive the face value of the policy. Having cash value is like having a savings account within the policy that grows each year. If the policyholder lives long enough, the cash value can be received as an annuity to supplement retirement income in later years.

Limited Payment Life Insurance. Limited payment life policies have level premiums that are limited to a certain period of time. After this period, usually 10, 20, or 30 years, the policy is paid up, and the insured is covered for the rest of his or her life. The premiums charged for limited payment policies are higher than premiums for whole life policies because they are paid for a shorter period of time. A variation of the limited payment policy is the life paid-up at 65 policy. This type is one in which the premiums are payable until the insured reaches age 65, after which no more premiums are owed.

Endowment Insurance. Endowment insurance is a combination of life insurance and an accelerated savings plan. The emphasis of the endowment policy is the accumulation of money. Endowment insurance pays the face amount of the policy on the death of the insured. It also pays the face amount if the insured is alive as of a specified date, known as the maturity date. Typical endowment periods are 10, 15, or 20 years or to a specified age such as 65 or 70. Traditionally, this type of insurance has been purchased by families with young children to save money for college education or by those who want to set up a retirement fund with immediate life insurance protection. Because they are designed to build cash values quickly, endowment policies have comparatively high premiums.

Nontraditional Insurance. In recent years, certain nontraditional policies have been introduced by insurance companies. Most of these interest-sensitive products are more flexible in design and provisions than their traditional counterparts. With these policies, the basic components of a life insurance policy, insurance (protection) and savings (investment), are separated. When premium payments are made, a portion known as the *mortality charge* is deducted to pay for the insurance coverage. This mortality charge increases with the age of the policyholder each year because the probability of death increases with age. The remaining amount, after other fees are deducted, goes to the investment *side fund.*

- *Universal life* is the most popular interest-sensitive policy. It features a minimum guaranteed death benefit and flexible premiums and face amounts. The insurance company decides on the type of investments to make, with the earnings credited to the side fund.
- *Variable life* is a higher-risk interest-sensitive policy that allows the policyholder to choose how the side fund will be invested. Typical choices include stocks, bonds,

✦ **TABLE 19-1** ✦
Annual Life Insurance Premiums (Per $1,000 of Face Value)

	Term Insurance				Permanent Insurance					
	5-Year Term		10-Year Term		Whole Life		20-Payment Life		20-Year Endowment	
Age	Male	Female	Male	Female	Male	Female	Male	Female	Male	Female
18	$ 2.32	$ 1.90	$ 4.33	$ 4.01	$13.22	$11.17	$23.14	$19.21	$33.22	$29.12
19	2.38	1.96	4.42	4.12	13.60	11.68	24.42	20.92	33.68	30.04
20	2.43	2.07	4.49	4.20	14.12	12.09	25.10	21.50	34.42	31.28
21	2.49	2.15	4.57	4.29	14.53	12.53	25.83	22.11	34.90	31.79
22	2.55	2.22	4.64	4.36	14.97	12.96	26.42	22.89	35.27	32.40
23	2.62	2.30	4.70	4.42	15.39	13.41	27.01	23.47	35.70	32.93
24	2.69	2.37	4.79	4.47	15.90	13.92	27.74	24.26	36.49	33.61
25	2.77	2.45	4.85	4.51	16.38	14.38	28.40	25.04	37.02	34.87
26	2.84	2.51	4.92	4.60	16.91	14.77	29.11	25.96	37.67	35.30
27	2.90	2.58	5.11	4.69	17.27	15.23	29.97	26.83	38.23	35.96
28	2.98	2.64	5.18	4.77	17.76	15.66	30.68	27.54	38.96	36.44
29	3.07	2.70	5.23	4.84	18.12	16.18	31.52	28.09	39.42	37.21
30	3.14	2.78	5.30	4.93	18.54	16.71	32.15	28.73	40.19	37.80
35	3.43	2.92	6.42	5.35	24.19	22.52	37.10	33.12	43.67	39.19
40	4.23	3.90	7.14	6.24	27.21	25.40	42.27	36.29	48.20	42.25
45	6.12	5.18	8.81	7.40	33.02	29.16	48.73	39.08	51.11	46.04
50	9.72	8.73	14.19	9.11	37.94	33.57	56.31	44.16	58.49	49.20
55	16.25	12.82	22.03	13.17	45.83	37.02	61.09	49.40	71.28	53.16
60	24.10	19.43	37.70	24.82	53.98	42.24	70.43	52.55	79.15	58.08

money market accounts, and real estate funds. Although this policy has a guaranteed death benefit, it does not have a guaranteed cash value like universal life.

✦ *Variable/universal life* is a recently introduced policy that combines features of both variable life and universal life. These policies offer flexible premiums and guaranteed death benefits, both of which can be adjusted by the policyholder. The cash value is not guaranteed and depends on the investment performance of the funds selected by the policyholder.

✦ **TABLE 19-2** ✦
Life Insurance—Premium Factors

Premium Paid	Percent of Annual Premium
Semiannually	52%
Quarterly	26%
Monthly	9%

Calculating Premiums

Insurance premiums are based on the age and sex of the insured as well as the type of policy being purchased. Premiums are less expensive for younger people because their probability of dying is lower than for older people. Females pay lower rates than males of the same age because they have a longer life expectancy than males.

Life insurance is purchased in increments of $1,000 of face value. The actuaries at insurance companies generate comprehensive rate tables, listing the premiums per $1,000 of insurance for males and females of all ages. Table 19-1 is a typical example of such a table.

Annual life insurance premiums are calculated by first determining the number of $1,000 of insurance desired and then multiplying the number of $1,000 by the rate per $1,000 found in Table 19-1. When the insured desires to pay the premiums more frequently than annually, such as semiannually, quarterly, or monthly, a small surcharge is added to account for the increased cost of billing, handling, and bookkeeping. Table 19-2 illustrates typical **premium factors** used by insurance companies for this purpose.

premium factor
A small surcharge added to the cost of insurance policies when the insured chooses to pay the premiums more frequently than annually; takes into account the increased cost of billing, handling, and bookkeeping.

STEPS TO CALCULATE LIFE INSURANCE PREMIUMS:

Step 1. Calculate the number of $1,000 of insurance desired by dividing the face value of the policy by $1,000.

$$\text{Number of \$1,000} = \frac{\text{Face value of policy}}{\$1,000}$$

Step 2. Locate the appropriate premium rate per $1,000 from Table 19-1. Choose the rate based on the type of policy desired and the age and sex of the applicant.

Step 3. Calculate annual premium by multiplying the number of $1,000 of insurance desired by the Table 19-1 rate.

$$\text{Annual premium} = \text{Number of \$1,000} \times \text{Rate per \$1,000}$$

Step 4. For premiums other than annual, multiply the appropriate Table 19-2 premium factor by the annual premium.

$$\text{Premium other than annual} = \text{Annual premium} \times \text{Premium factor}$$

EXAMPLE

Madalenna Bridges is 24 years old. She is interested in purchasing a whole life insurance policy with a face value of $50,000. As her insurance agent, calculate the annual and monthly insurance premiums for this policy.

SOLUTION STRATEGY

Step 1. $\text{Number of \$1,000} = \frac{\text{Face value of policy}}{\$1,000} = \frac{50,000}{1,000} = 50$

Step 2. From Table 19-1, we find the premium per $1,000 for whole life insurance for a 24-year-old woman to be $13.92.

Step 3. Annual premium = Number of $1,000 × Rate per $1,000 = 50 × 13.92 = $\underline{\underline{\$696.00}}$

Step 4. Monthly premium = Annual premium × Monthly premium factor

Monthly premium = 696 × .09 = $\underline{\underline{\$62.64}}$

TRY-IT | EXERCISE

1. Michael O'Brian, age 26, wants to purchase a 10-year term insurance policy with a face value of $75,000. Calculate his annual and quarterly premiums. How much more will Michael pay per year if he chooses quarterly payments?

Check your answers with the solutions on page 714.

19-2 Calculating the Value of Various Nonforfeiture Options

Because all life insurance policies (except term) build up a **cash value** after the first 2 or 3 years, they should be viewed as being property with a value. Policyholders in effect own these properties and therefore have certain **ownership rights.** For example, policyholders, or policyowners, have the right to change beneficiaries, designate how the death benefits will be paid, borrow money against the policy, assign ownership to someone else, or cancel the policy.

Let's take a closer look at what happens when a policyowner decides to cancel a policy or allows it to terminate or **lapse** by failing to make the required premium payments within 31 days of the due date. The amount of cash value that has accumulated to that point is based on the size of the policy and the amount of time it has been in force. Most policies give the policyowner three choices, known as **nonforfeiture options.**

cash value
The amount of money that begins to build up in a permanent life insurance policy after the first 2 or 3 years.

ownership rights
The rights of life insurance policyholders, including the right to change beneficiaries, designate how the death benefits will be paid, borrow money against the policy, assign ownership to someone else, or cancel the policy.

lapse
Allowing an insurance policy to terminate by failing to make the required premium payments within 31 days of the due date.

nonforfeiture options
The options available to the policyholder on termination of a permanent life insurance policy with accumulated cash value; these include receiving the cash value, using the cash value to purchase a reduced paid-up insurance policy of the same type, or purchasing term insurance with the same face value as the original policy, for as long a time period as the cash value will purchase.

Option 1—Cash Value or Cash Surrender Option. Once a policy has accumulated cash value, the policyowner may choose to surrender (give up) the policy to the company and receive its cash value. At this point, the policy is terminated. If the insured wants to maintain the insurance coverage, the amount of the cash value may be borrowed and later repaid with interest.

Option 2—Reduced Paid-Up Insurance. The second option is that the available cash value is used to purchase a reduced level of paid-up insurance. This policy is of the same type as the original and continues for the life of the policyowner, with no further premiums due.

Option 3—Extended Term Insurance. With this option, the policyholder elects to use the cash value to purchase a term policy with the same face value as the original policy. The new policy will last for as long a time period as the cash value will purchase. When a policyowner simply stops paying on a policy and does not choose a nonforfeiture option, the insurance company automatically implements this extended term option.

Table 19-3 illustrates typical nonforfeiture options per $1,000 of face value, for a policy issued to a woman at age 20.

TABLE 19-3
Nonforfeiture Options (Per $1,000 of Face Value Issued to a Woman at Age 20)

	Whole Life Options				20-Payment Life Options				20-Year Endowment Options			
	1	2	3		1	2	3		1	2	3	
			Extended Term				Extended Term				Extended Term	
End of Year	Cash Value	Reduced Paid-up Insurance	Years	Days	Cash Value	Reduced Paid-up Insurance	Years	Days	Cash Value	Reduced Paid-up Insurance	Years	Days
3	$ 11	$ 25	2	17	$ 29	$ 90	4	217	$ 39	$ 97	7	132
5	32	64	9	23	73	212	14	86	91	233	19	204
7	54	99	13	142	101	367	23	152	186	381	26	310
10	98	186	17	54	191	496	30	206	324	512	32	117
15	157	314	21	218	322	789	34	142	647	794	37	350
20	262	491	25	77	505	1,000	-Life-		1,000	1,000	-Life-	

Everybody's Business

Real-World Connection

It is important to check your insurance coverage periodically or whenever your situation changes to be sure it meets your current needs.

Some changes that require insurance review might include increased income, getting married, or having a change in family size.

Many insurable things are tied to inflation and therefore require periodic increases.

- *Life insurance*—Cost of living increases such as food, clothing, and transportation.
- *Property insurance*—Rising real estate values and cost of replacement materials.
- *Health care insurance*—Cost increases in physician, hospital, and other medical-related items.

STEPS TO CALCULATE THE VALUE OF VARIOUS NONFORFEITURE OPTIONS:

Step 1. Calculate the number of \$1,000 of insurance by dividing the face value of the policy by \$1,000.

Step 2. *Option 1—Cash Value.* Locate the appropriate dollars per \$1,000 in the *cash value* column of Table 19-3, and multiply this figure by the number of \$1,000 of insurance.

Option 2—Reduced Paid-Up Insurance. Locate the appropriate dollars per \$1,000 in the *reduced paid-up insurance* column of Table 19-3, and multiply this figure by the number of \$1,000 of insurance.

Option 3—Extended Term. Locate the length of time of the new extended term policy in the *years* and *days* columns of Table 19-3.

EXAMPLE

Kimberly Kilmer purchased a \$30,000 whole life insurance policy when she was 20 years old. She is now 35 years old and wants to investigate her nonforfeiture options. As her insurance agent, use Table 19-3 to calculate the value of Kimberly's three options.

SOLUTION STRATEGY

Step 1. $\text{Number of \$1,000} = \dfrac{\text{Face value of policy}}{\$1,000} = \dfrac{30,000}{1,000} = 30$

Step 2. *Option 1—Cash Value.* From Table 19-3, we find that after being in force for 15 years, a whole life policy issued to a woman at age 20 has a cash value of \$157 per \$1,000 of insurance.

$$\text{Number of \$1,000} \times \text{Table value} = 30 \times \$157 = \underline{\underline{\$4,710.00}}$$

Kimberly's cash value option is to receive \$4,710.00 in cash from the company and have no further insurance coverage.

Option 2—Reduced Paid-Up Insurance. From Table 19-3, we find that after being in force for 15 years, a whole life policy issued to a woman at age 20 will have enough cash value to buy \$314 in paid-up whole life insurance per \$1,000 of face value.

$$\text{Number of \$1,000} \times \text{Table value} = 30 \times 314 = \underline{\underline{\$9,420.00}}$$

Kimberly's reduced paid-up insurance option is to receive a \$9,420 whole life policy, effective for her entire life, with no further payments.

Option 3—Extended Term Insurance. From Table 19-3, we find that after being in force for 15 years, a whole life policy issued to a woman at age 20 will have enough cash value to buy \$30,000 of term insurance for a period of 21 years and 218 days.

TRY-IT | EXERCISE

2. Gigi LeBlanc purchased a \$100,000 20-payment life insurance policy when she was 20 years old. She is now 30 years old and wants to investigate her nonforfeiture options. As her insurance agent, use Table 19-3 to determine the value of Gigi's three options.

Check your answers with the solutions on page 714.

19-3 Calculating the Amount of Life Insurance Needed to Cover Dependents' Income Shortfall

Evaluating your life insurance needs is a fundamental part of sound financial planning. The amount of insurance and type of policy you should purchase are much less obvious. Life insurance is needed if you keep a household running, support a family, have a mortgage or other major debts, or expect the kids to go to college. Insurance should be used to fill the financial gap a family may incur by the death or disability of the insured.

One so-called rule of thumb is that you carry between seven and ten times your annual income, depending on your lifestyle, number of dependents, and other sources of income. Another estimator of the amount of insurance to purchase is based on a family's additional income requirements needed in the event of the death of the insured. These additional requirements are known as the **income shortfall.**

income shortfall
The difference between the total living expenses and the total income of a family after the death of the insured; used as an indicator of how much life insurance to purchase.

Let's say, for example, that a family has \$30,000 in living expenses per year. If the family's total income, after the death of the insured, decreases to only \$20,000, the income shortfall would be \$10,000 (\$30,000 − \$20,000). The theory is to purchase enough life insurance so that the face value of the policy, collected by the family on the death of the insured, can be invested at the prevailing interest rate to generate the additional income needed to overcome the \$10,000 shortfall. When prevailing interest rates are low, large amounts of insurance are needed to cover the shortfall. As interest rates rise, less insurance will be needed.

STEPS TO CALCULATE INSURANCE NEEDED TO COVER DEPENDENTS' INCOME SHORTFALL:

Step 1. Determine the dependents' total annual living expenses, including mortgages.

Step 2. Determine the dependents' total annual sources of income, including salaries, investments, and social security.

Step 3. Subtract the income from the living expenses to find the income shortfall.

$$\text{Income shortfall} = \text{Total living expenses} - \text{Total income}$$

Step 4. Calculate the insurance needed to cover the shortfall by dividing the shortfall by the prevailing interest rate (round to the nearest \$1,000).

$$\text{Insurance needed} = \frac{\text{Income shortfall}}{\text{Prevailing interest rate}}$$

EXAMPLE

With a prevailing interest rate of 6%, how much life insurance is required to cover dependents' income shortfall if their living expenses amount to \$48,000 per year and their total income sources amount to \$33,000 per year?

SOLUTION STRATEGY

Step 1. Living expenses per year are \$48,000 (given).

Step 2. Dependents' total income is \$33,000 (given).

Step 3. Income shortfall = Total expenses − Total income = \$48,000 − \$33,000 = \$15,000

Step 4. $\text{Insurance needed} = \dfrac{\text{Shortfall}}{\text{Prevailing rate}} = \dfrac{\$15{,}000}{.06} = \underline{\underline{\$250{,}000}}$

TRY-IT | EXERCISE

3. Robert Kelly is evaluating his life insurance needs. His family's total living expenses are $54,000 per year. Mary, his wife, earns $38,000 per year in salary and receives another $5,000 per year from an endowment fund. If the prevailing interest rate is currently 5%, how much life insurance should Robert purchase to cover his dependents' income shortfall?

Check your answer with the solution on page 714.

REVIEW EXERCISES | CHAPTER 19—SECTION I

Calculate the annual, semiannual, quarterly, and monthly premiums for the following life insurance policies:

	Face Value of Policy	Sex and Age of Insured	Type of Policy	Annual Premium	Semiannual Premium	Quarterly Premium	Monthly Premium
1.	$ 5,000	Male—24	Whole Life	_____	_____	_____	_____
2.	10,000	Female—35	10-Year Term	_____	_____	_____	_____
3.	25,000	Male—19	20-Year Endowment	_____	_____	_____	_____
4.	75,000	Male—50	20-Payment Life	_____	_____	_____	_____
5.	100,000	Female—29	5-Year Term	_____	_____	_____	_____
6.	40,000	Male—35	Whole Life	_____	_____	_____	_____
7.	35,000	Male—30	20-Payment Life	_____	_____	_____	_____
8.	250,000	Female—45	20-Year Endowment	_____	_____	_____	_____

Calculate the value of the nonforfeiture options for the following life insurance policies:

	Face Value of Policy	Years in Force	Type of Policy	Cash Value	Reduced Paid-Up Insurance	Extended Term Years	Extended Term Days
9.	$ 50,000	10	Whole Life	_____	_____	_____	_____
10.	250,000	7	20-Year Endowment	_____	_____	_____	_____
11.	35,000	15	Whole Life	_____	_____	_____	_____
12.	100,000	3	20-Payment Life	_____	_____	_____	_____

13. Herbert Love is 35 years old and is interested in purchasing a 20-year endowment insurance policy with a face value of $120,000.

a. Calculate the annual premium for this policy.

b. Calculate the semiannual premium.

14. Tina Gildewell, age 27, wants to purchase a 5-year term insurance policy with a face value of $25,000. As her insurance agent, answer the following:

a. What is the annual premium for this policy?

b. What is the monthly premium?

c. How much more will Tina pay per year if she chooses monthly payments?

15. Libby Bailey purchased a $75,000, 20-payment life insurance policy when she was 20 years old. She is now 30 years old and wants to investigate her nonforfeiture options. As her insurance agent, calculate the value of Libby's three options.

16. Michael McDonald is evaluating his life insurance needs. His family's total living expenses are $37,500 per year. Vickie, his wife, earns $14,900 per year in salary and receives another $3,500 annually in disability benefits from an insurance settlement for an accident. If the prevailing interest rate is $7\frac{1}{2}\%$, how much life insurance should Michael purchase to cover his dependents' income shortfall? Round to nearest $1,000.

BUSINESS DECISION

The Consultation

17. Stacy Spencer, a single mother, is 20 years old. She has called on you for an insurance consultation. Her objective is to purchase life insurance protection for the next 10 years while her children are growing up. Stacy tells you that she can afford about $250 per year for insurance premiums. You have suggested either a 10-year term policy or a whole life policy.

a. Rounded to the nearest thousand, how much insurance coverage can Stacy purchase under each policy? *Hint:* Divide her annual premium allowance by the rate per $1,000 for each policy.

b. If she should die in the next 10 years, how much more will her children receive under the term insurance?

c. If she should live beyond the 10th year, what are her nonforfeiture options with the whole life policy?

SECTION II

PROPERTY INSURANCE

19-4 Understanding Property Insurance and Calculating Typical Fire Insurance Premiums

Businesses and homeowners alike need insurance protection for the financial losses that may occur to their property from such perils as fire, lightning, wind, water, negligence, burglary, and vandalism. Although the probability that a particular peril will occur is small, no homeowner or business can afford the risk of not having **property insurance.** Most mortgage lenders, in fact, require that sufficient property insurance is purchased by the borrower as a condition for obtaining a mortgage.

property insurance
Insurance protection for the financial losses that may occur to business and homeowner's property from such perils as fire, lightning, wind, water, negligence, burglary, and vandalism.

In addition to the items listed above, most property insurance policies today have provisions for liability coverage, medical expenses, and additional expenses that may be incurred while the damaged property is being repaired. For example, a business may have to move to a temporary location during reconstruction, or a family may have to stay in an apartment or motel while their house is being repaired. Insurance companies offer similar policies to meet the needs of apartment and home renters, as well as condominium owners.

In this section, we focus our attention on fire insurance and how these premiums are determined. Fire insurance rates are quoted as an amount per $100 of insurance coverage purchased. Rates are separated into two categories: (a) the structure or building itself and (b) the contents within the building.

A *building's* fire insurance rates are determined by a number of important factors:

1. The *dollar amount* of insurance purchased on the property.
2. The *location of the property*—city, suburbs, and rural areas.
3. The *proximity* and *quality* of fire protection available.
4. The *type of construction* materials used—masonry (brick) or wood (frame).

The *contents* portion of the fire insurance rate is based on

1. The *dollar amount* or value of the contents.
2. The *flammability* of the contents.

From this rate structure, we can see that a building made of concrete, bricks, and steel, located 2 or 3 miles from a fire station, would have a considerably lower rate than a building of the same value, with wood frame construction, located in a rural area, 12 miles from the nearest fire-fighting equipment. Or for that matter, a warehouse filled with explosive chemicals would cost more to insure than the same warehouse filled with Coca-Cola.

Table 19-4 illustrates typical annual fire insurance premiums. Note that the rates are per $100 of insurance coverage. The building and contents are listed separately and divided by the structural class of the building and the location (area rating).

Most businesses and homeowners carry special insurance policies to protect against loss due to fire.

STEPS TO CALCULATE TYPICAL FIRE INSURANCE PREMIUMS:

Step 1. From Table 19-4, locate the appropriate rate, based on *structural class* and *area rating,* for both the building and the contents.

Step 2. Calculate the number of $100 of insurance coverage desired for both the building and the contents by dividing the amount of coverage for each by $100.

Step 3. Multiply the number of $100 for both the building and contents by the rates from Step 1 to find the annual premium for each.

Step 4. Add the annual premiums for the building and the contents to find the total annual premium.

Total annual fire premium = Building premium + Contents premium

EXAMPLE

What is the total annual fire insurance premium on a building valued at $200,000 with structural classification B and area rating 4 and contents valued at $40,000?

SOLUTION STRATEGY

Step 1. From Table 19-4, we find the following rates for structural class B and area rating 4:

Building— $.76 per $100 of coverage

Contents—$.83 per $100 of coverage

Step 2. Number of $100 of coverage:

$$\text{Building} = \frac{\text{Amount of coverage}}{\$100} = \frac{200{,}000}{100} = 2{,}000$$

$$\text{Contents} = \frac{\text{Amount of coverage}}{\$100} = \frac{40{,}000}{100} = 400$$

Step 3. Annual fire insurance premiums:

Building = Number of $100 × Table rate = 2,000 × .76 = $1,520.00

Contents = Number of $100 × Table rate = 400 × .83 = $332.00

Step 4. Total annual fire premium = Building premium + Contents premium

Total annual fire premium = 1,520.00 + 332.00 = $1,852.00

Everybody's Business

Real-World Connection

Before the concept of insurance was invented, people were helped by their neighbors and friends when fire or other peril caused damage to their property.

There was an unwritten code that when someone incurred a loss, such as a house or barn burning down, the people of the town would volunteer labor time and donate materials to help rebuild the property and defray the cost.

This concept is similar to insurance as we know it today; the *many,* each helping a little, to aid the *few* who need it.

TABLE 19-4

Annual Fire Insurance Premiums (Per $100 of Face Value)

	Structural Classification							
	A		B		C		D	
Area Rating	Building	Contents	Building	Contents	Building	Contents	Building	Contents
1	$.21	$.24	$.32	$ .37	$ .38	$ .42	$ .44	$ .48
2	.38	.42	.39	.48	.43	.51	.57	.69
3	.44	.51	.55	.66	.69	.77	.76	.85
4	.59	.68	.76	.83	.87	1.04	.98	1.27
5	.64	.73	.92	1.09	1.08	1.13	1.39	1.43

TRY-IT | EXERCISE

4. You are the insurance agent for McCready Enterprises, Inc. The owner, Fred McCready, would like you to give him a quote on the total annual premium for a property insurance policy on a new warehouse in the amount of $420,000 and contents valued at $685,000. The warehouse is structural classification A and area rating 2.

Check your answer with the solution on page 714.

19-5 Calculating Premiums for Short-Term Policies and the Refunds Due on Canceled Policies

short-term policy
An insurance policy for less than 1 year.

short-rate
The premium charged when a policy is canceled by the insured or is written for less than 1 year.

From time to time, businesses and individuals cancel insurance policies or require **short-term policies** of less than 1 year. For example, a family might sell their home 2 months after paying the annual premium, or a business may require coverage for a shipment of merchandise that will be sold within a few months. When a policy is canceled by the insured or is written for less than 1 year, the premium charged is known as the **short-rate.**

Short-Rate Refund

Table 19-5 illustrates typical short-term policy rate factors. These rate factors should be used to calculate the premiums and refunds for short-term policies canceled by the insured. Note that these rate factors are a percentage of the annual premium.

STEPS TO CALCULATE SHORT-RATE REFUNDS—POLICIES CANCELED BY INSURED:

Step 1. Calculate the short-term premium using the short-rate from Table 19-5:

$$\text{Short-rate premium} = \text{Annual premium} \times \text{Short-rate}$$

Step 2. Calculate the short-rate refund by subtracting the short-rate premium from the annual premium:

$$\text{Short-rate refund} = \text{Annual premium} - \text{Short-rate premium}$$

✦ TABLE 19-5 ✦
Property Insurance Short-Rate Schedule

Time Policy Is in Force	Percent of Annual Premium	Time Policy Is in Force (months)	Percent of Annual Premium
5 days	8	4	50
10 days	10	5	60
15 days	14	6	70
20 days	16	7	75
25 days	18	8	80
		9	85
1 month	20	10	90
2 months	30	11	95
3 months	40	12	100

EXAMPLE

A property insurance policy has an annual premium of \$500. What is the short-rate refund if the policy is canceled by the insured after 3 months?

SOLUTION STRATEGY

Step 1. Short-rate premium = Annual premium $\times$ Short-rate

Short-rate premium = $500 \times 40\% = \underline{\$200}$

Step 2. Short-rate refund = Annual premium − Short-rate premium

Short-rate refund = $500 - 200 = \underline{\underline{\$300}}$

TRY-IT | EXERCISE

5. A property insurance policy has an annual premium of \$850. What is the short-rate refund if the policy is canceled by the insured after 8 months?

Check your answer with the solution on page 714.

Regular Refund

When a policy is canceled by the insurance company, rather than the insured, the company must refund the entire unused portion of the premium. This short-term refund calculation is based on the fraction of a year that the policy was in force and is known as a regular refund.

STEPS TO CALCULATE REGULAR REFUNDS—POLICIES CANCELED BY COMPANY:

Step 1. Calculate the premium for the period of time the policy was in force, by using either

$$\textbf{Exact time: Annual premium} \times \frac{\textbf{Days policy in force}}{\textbf{365}}$$

or

$$\textbf{Approximate time: Annual premium} \times \frac{\textbf{Months policy in force}}{\textbf{12}}$$

Step 2. Calculate refund by subtracting premium for period in force from the annual premium:

Regular refund = Annual premium − Premium for period

Everybody's Business

Real-World Connection

In addition to homeowners, insurance companies offer similar policies to meet the needs of apartment and home renters, as well as condominium owners.

- *Renter's insurance*—Insurance that covers the renter's personal property and liability. The property owner pays the insurance for the building.
- *Condominium insurance*—Insurance that covers the interior walls, wiring, and contents of the condominium. The exterior walls and roof are covered under a separate policy purchased by the condominium association and paid for from the monthly condominium maintenance fees.

EXAMPLE

A property insurance policy has an annual premium of \$500. What is the regular refund if the policy is canceled by the insurance company after 3 months?

SOLUTION STRATEGY

Step 1. Premium for period = Annual premium $\times \dfrac{\text{Months policy in force}}{12}$

Premium for period = $500 \times \dfrac{3}{12} = \underline{\$125}$

Step 2. Regular refund = Annual premium − Premium for period

Regular refund = $500 - 125 = \underline{\underline{\$375}}$

TRY-IT | EXERCISE

6. A property insurance policy has an annual premium of \$850. What is the regular refund if the policy is canceled by the insurance company after 8 months?

Check your answer with the solution on page 714.

19-6 Understanding Coinsurance and Computing Compensation Due in the Event of a Loss

Knowing that most fires do not totally destroy the insured property, many businesses, as a cost-saving measure, insure their buildings and contents for less than the full value. Insurance companies, to protect themselves from having more claims than premiums collected, write a **coinsurance clause** into most business policies. This clause stipulates a minimum amount of coverage required for a claim to be paid in full. The coinsurance minimum is stated as a percent of the replacement value of the property and is usually between 70% and 90%.

coinsurance clause
A clause in a property insurance policy stipulating a minimum amount of coverage required for a claim to be paid in full. This requirement is stated as a percent of the replacement value of the property.

Here is an example of how coinsurance works. Let's say that a building has a replacement value of \$100,000. If the insurance policy has an 80% coinsurance clause, the building must be insured for \$80,000 (80% of the \$100,000) to be fully covered for any claim, up to the face value of the policy. Any coverage less than the required 80% would be paid out in proportion to the coverage ratio. The **coverage ratio** is a ratio of the amount of insurance carried by the insured to the amount of insurance required by the insurance company.

coverage ratio
A ratio of the amount of insurance carried by the insured to the amount of insurance required according to the coinsurance clause of the insurance policy.

$$\text{Coverage ratio} = \frac{\text{Insurance carried}}{\text{Insurance required}}$$

If, for example, the owner had purchased only \$40,000, rather than the required \$80,000, the insurance company would only be obligated to pay half, or 50%, of any claim. This is because the ratio of insurance carried to insurance required was 50%.

$$\text{Coverage ratio} = \frac{\$40{,}000}{\$80{,}000} = \frac{1}{2} = 50\%$$

STEPS TO CALCULATE AMOUNT OF LOSS TO BE PAID WITH A COINSURANCE CLAUSE:

Step 1. Determine the amount of insurance required by the coinsurance clause:

$$\text{Insurance required} = \text{Replacement value of property} \times \text{Coinsurance percent}$$

Step 2. Calculate the amount of the loss to be paid by the insurance company by multiplying the coverage ratio times the amount of the loss:

$$\text{Amount of loss paid by insurance} = \frac{\text{Insurance carried}}{\text{Insurance required}} \times \text{Amount of the loss}$$

EXAMPLE

The Castlerock Corporation had property valued at \$500,000 and insured for \$300,000. If the fire insurance policy contained an 80% coinsurance clause, how much would be paid by the insurance company in the event of a \$100,000 fire?

SOLUTION STRATEGY

Step 1. Insurance required = Value of the property × Coinsurance percent

Insurance required = 500,000 × .80 = \$400,000

Step 2. $$\text{Amount of loss paid by insurance} = \frac{\text{Insurance carried}}{\text{Insurance required}} \times \text{Amount of loss}$$

$$\text{Amount of loss paid by insurance} = \frac{300{,}000}{400{,}000} \times 100{,}000 = \underline{\underline{\$75{,}000}}$$

TRY-IT | EXERCISE

7. Consolidated Materials Corporation had property valued at \$850,000 and insured for \$400,000. If the fire insurance policy contained a 70% coinsurance clause, how much would be paid by the insurance company in the event of a \$325,000 fire?

Check your answer with the solution on page 714.

19-7 Determining Each Company's Share of a Loss when Liability Is Divided among Multiple Carriers

Sometimes businesses are covered by fire insurance policies from more than one company at the same time, which is known as having **multiple carriers.** This situation occurs when one insurance company is unwilling or unable to carry the entire liability of a particular property or because additional coverage was purchased from different insurance companies over a period of time as the business expanded and became more valuable.

multiple carriers
A situation in which a business is covered by fire insurance policies from more than one company at the same time.

Assuming that all coinsurance clause requirements have been met, when a claim is made against multiple carriers, each carrier is responsible for its portion of the total coverage carried. To calculate that portion, we divide the amount of each company's policy by the total insurance carried. This portion is expressed as a percent of the total coverage.

For example, if an insurance company was one of multiple carriers and had a \$30,000 fire policy written on a business that had a total of \$200,000 in coverage, that insurance company would be responsible for $\frac{30{,}000}{200{,}000}$, or 15%, of any loss.

STEPS TO DETERMINE EACH COMPANY'S SHARE OF A LOSS WHEN LIABILITY IS SHARED AMONG MULTIPLE CARRIERS:

Step 1. Calculate each carrier's portion by dividing the amount of each policy by the total insurance carried:

$$\textbf{Carrier's percent of total coverage} = \frac{\textbf{Amount of carrier's policy}}{\textbf{Total amount of insurance}}$$

Step 2. Determine each carrier's share of a loss by multiplying the amount of the loss by each carrier's percent of the total coverage:

Carrier's share of loss = Amount of loss × Carrier's percent of total coverage

EXAMPLE

Omega International had multiple carrier fire insurance coverage in the amount of $400,000, as follows:

Travelers—$ 80,000	policy
State Farm—$120,000	policy
Allstate—$200,000	policy
$400,000	total coverage

Assuming that all coinsurance clause stipulations have been met, how much would each carrier be responsible for in the event of a $50,000 fire?

SOLUTION STRATEGY

Step 1. $$\text{Carrier's percent of total coverage} = \frac{\text{Amount of carrier's policy}}{\text{Total amount of insurance}}$$

$$\text{Travelers} = \frac{80{,}000}{400{,}000} = \underline{20\%}$$

$$\text{State Farm} = \frac{120{,}000}{400{,}000} = \underline{30\%}$$

$$\text{Allstate} = \frac{200{,}000}{400{,}000} = \underline{50\%}$$

Step 2. Carrier's share of loss = Amount of loss × Carrier's percent of total coverage

$$\text{Travelers Share} = 50{,}000 \times .20 = \underline{\underline{\$10{,}000}}$$

$$\text{State Farm Share} = 50{,}000 \times .30 = \underline{\underline{\$15{,}000}}$$

$$\text{Allstate Share} = 50{,}000 \times .50 = \underline{\underline{\$25{,}000}}$$

TRY-IT | EXERCISE

8. Elite Industries, Inc., had multiple carrier fire insurance coverage in the amount of $125,000, as follows:

Aetna — $ 20,000	policy
USF&G — $ 45,000	policy
John Hancock — $ 60,000	policy
$125,000	total coverage

Assuming that all coinsurance clause stipulations have been met, how much would each carrier be responsible for in the event of a $16,800 fire?

Check your answers with the solutions on page 714.

REVIEW EXERCISES | CHAPTER 19—SECTION II

Calculate the building, contents, and total property insurance premiums for the following policies:

	Area Rating	Structural Class	Building Value	Building Premium	Contents Value	Contents Premium	Total Premium
1.	4	B	$ 88,000	_______	$21,000	_______	_______
2.	2	C	124,000	_______	35,000	_______	_______
3.	1	A	215,000	_______	29,000	_______	_______
4.	5	D	518,000	_______	90,000	_______	_______
5.	3	C	309,000	_______	57,000	_______	_______

Calculate the short-term premium and refund for each of the following policies:

	Annual Premium	Canceled After	Canceled By	Short-Term Premium	Short-Term Refund
6.	$ 450	3 months	insurance company	_______	_______
7.	560	20 days	insured	_______	_______
8.	1,280	9 months	insured	_______	_______
9.	322	5 months	insurance company	_______	_______
10.	630	5 days	insured	_______	_______

Calculate the amount to be paid by the insurance company for each of the following claims:

	Replacement Value of Building	Face Value of Policy	Coinsurance Clause (%)	Amount of Loss	Amount of Loss Insurance Company Will Pay
11.	$200,000	$160,000	80	$ 75,000	_______
12.	350,000	300,000	90	125,000	_______
13.	70,000	50,000	70	37,000	_______
14.	125,000	75,000	80	50,000	_______
15.	500,000	300,000	80	200,000	_______

16. You are the insurance agent for Southeast Furniture Manufacturing, Inc. The owner, Michael Chang, would like you to give him a quote on the total annual premium for property insurance on a new production facility in the amount of $1,640,000 and equipment and contents valued at $955,000. The building is structural classification B and area rating 4.

17. A property insurance policy has an annual premium of $1,350. What is the short-rate refund if the policy is canceled by the insured after 9 months?

18. Drake Enterprises has a property insurance policy with an annual premium of $1,320. In recent months, Drake has filed four different claims against the policy: a fire, two burglaries, and a vandalism incident. The insurance company has elected to cancel the policy, which has been in effect for 310 days. What is the regular refund due to Drake?

2 19. Midway Electronics had multiple carrier fire insurance coverage in the amount of $500,000, as follows:

Aetna—	$300,000 policy
State Farm—	$125,000 policy
Liberty Mutual—	$ 75,000 policy
	$500,000 total coverage

Assuming that all coinsurance clause stipulations have been met, how much would each carrier be responsible for in the event of a $95,000 fire?

BUSINESS DECISION

Business Interruption Insurance

20. As the owner of a successful business, you have just purchased an additional type of property insurance coverage known as *business interruption insurance*. This insurance protects the profits that a company would have earned had there been no problem. Business interruption insurance covers damages caused by all types of perils such as fires, tornadoes, hurricanes, lightning, or any other disaster except floods and earthquakes.

    This insurance pays for "economic" losses incurred when business operations suddenly cease. These include loss of income due to the interruption and additional expenses incurred such as leases; relocation to temporary facilities; overtime to keep up with production demands; recompiling of business, financial and legal records; and even the salaries of key employees.

Your coverage provides insurance reimbursement for 80% of any losses. Your company pays the other 20%. The annual premium is 2% of the income and extra expenses that you insure.

a. If you have purchased coverage amounting to $20,000 per month, what is the amount of your annual premium?

b. If a tornado put your company out of business for $5\frac{1}{2}$ months, what would be the amount of the insurance reimbursement for your economic loss?

SECTION III

MOTOR VEHICLE INSURANCE

19-8 Understanding Motor Vehicle Insurance and Calculating Typical Premiums

With the steadily increasing costs of automobile and truck repairs and replacement, as well as all forms of medical services, **motor vehicle insurance** today is an absolute necessity! In fact, most states require a certain minimum amount of insurance before a vehicle may even be registered.

Motor vehicle insurance rates, regulations, and requirements vary widely from state to state, but the basic structure is the same. Vehicle insurance is divided into three main categories: **liability, collision,** and **comprehensive.**

motor vehicle insurance
Insurance protection for the financial losses that may be incurred due to a motor vehicle accident or damage caused by fire, vandalism, or other perils.

liability
A portion of motor vehicle insurance that includes payment for bodily injury to other persons and damages to the property of others resulting from the insured's negligence.

collision
A portion of motor vehicle insurance that covers damage sustained by the insured's vehicle in an accident.

comprehensive
Insurance coverage that protects the insured's vehicle for damage caused by fire, wind, water, theft, vandalism, and other perils not caused by accident.

Liability. This category includes (a) payment for bodily injury to other persons resulting from the insured's negligence and (b) damages to the property of others resulting from the insured's negligence. This property may be other vehicles damaged in the accident or other objects such as fences, landscaping, or buildings.

Most states require motor vehicle insurance.

deductible
A premium reduction measure in collision insurance whereby the insured pays a stipulated amount of the damage first, the *deductible,* and the insurance company pays any amount over that; common deductibles are $100, $250, $500, and $1,000.

Collision. This category covers damage sustained by the insured's vehicle in an accident. As a premium reduction measure, collision coverage is often sold with a **deductible** amount, for example, $250 deductible. This means that the insured pays the first $250 in damages for each occurrence, and the insurance company pays the amount over $250. As the deductible amount increases, the premium for the insurance decreases.

Comprehensive. This insurance coverage protects the insured's vehicle for damage caused by fire, wind, water, theft, vandalism, and other perils not caused by an accident.

Most insurance companies also offer policyholders the option of purchasing policy extras such as uninsured motorist's protection and coverage while driving a rented or borrowed car. Some policies even offer to pay towing expenses in the event of a breakdown or cover the cost for a rental car while the insured's vehicle is being repaired after an accident.

Liability rates are based on three primary factors: *who* is driving the vehicle, *where* the vehicle is being driven, and the *amount* of insurance coverage desired. Table 19-6 illustrates typical annual liability premiums for bodily injury and property damage. Note that the rates are listed by driver classification (age, sex, and marital status of the driver), territory (metropolitan area, suburbs, small town, rural or farm area), and amount (in thousands of dollars).

Motor vehicle liability premiums are typically stated in a three-number format, such as 50/100/50, with the numbers given in thousands of dollars. The first two numbers, 50/100, refer to the bodily injury portion and means the policy will pay up to $50,000 for bodily injury caused by the insured's vehicle to any one person, with $100,000 maximum per accident, regardless of the number of persons injured. The third number, 50 ($50,000), represents the maximum property damage benefits to be paid per single accident.

rating factors
Multiples of the base rates for motor vehicles; used by insurance companies to adjust premiums upward (factors greater than 1) or downward (factors less than 1), depending on the amount of risk involved in the coverage.

Table 19-7 illustrates typical collision and comprehensive premiums. Note that these rates are listed according to model class (type of vehicle—compact, luxury, truck, or van), vehicle age, territory (where driven), and the amount of the deductible.

Insurance companies often adjust premiums upward or downward by the use of **rating factors,** which are multiples of the base rates found in the tables. For example, if a vehicle is used for business purposes, the risk of an accident is increased and therefore a rating factor of, say, 1.5 might be applied to the base rate to adjust for this risk. A $200 base-rate premium would increase to $300, $200 times the rating factor of 1.5. However, a vehicle driven less than 3 miles to work each way would have less chance of having an accident and might have a rating factor of .9 to lower the rate.

TABLE 19-6
Motor Vehicle Liability Insurance Premiums
Annual—Bodily Injury and Property Damage Rates

		Bodily Injury (000)					Property Damage (000)				
Territory	Driver Class	10/20	15/30	25/50	50/100	100/300	5	10	25	50	100
1	1	$61	$73	$ 88	$ 92	$113	$46	$49	$53	$58	$ 64
	2	63	75	81	94	116	48	51	55	61	66
	3	65	78	84	98	118	52	54	58	63	69
	4	69	81	86	101	121	54	56	60	65	71
2	1	66	75	83	93	114	56	63	68	73	77
	2	69	77	88	98	117	58	64	70	75	79
	3	75	82	92	104	119	59	66	71	76	82
	4	78	86	95	109	122	62	67	73	78	84
3	1	73	77	84	95	116	64	65	72	76	81
	2	78	83	86	99	119	66	69	74	80	83
	3	84	88	92	103	124	70	73	77	82	85
	4	87	93	95	106	128	72	78	81	85	89
4	1	77	81	86	99	118	76	78	83	88	92
	2	81	86	93	103	121	79	83	87	91	95
	3	87	92	100	106	126	80	84	88	93	97
	4	90	94	103	111	132	84	86	91	94	100

STEPS TO CALCULATE TYPICAL MOTOR VEHICLE INSURANCE PREMIUMS:

Step 1. Use Table 19-6 to find the appropriate base premiums for bodily injury and property damage.

Step 2. Use Table 19-7 to find the appropriate base premiums for collision and comprehensive.

Step 3. Add all the individual premiums to find the total base premium.

Step 4. Multiply the total base premium by the rating factor, if any.

Total annual premium = Total base premium × Rating factor

Everybody's Business

Real-World Connection

Many insurance companies give money-saving *rating factor* discounts to students who have good grade point averages, usually over 3.0 out of 4.0, or safe-driving records—without tickets or accidents.

EXAMPLE

Evie Irvin wants to purchase a motor vehicle insurance policy with bodily injury and property damage coverage in the amounts of 25/50/25. In addition, she wants collision coverage with $500 deductible and comprehensive with no deductible. Evie is in driver classification 3 and lives in territory 1. Her vehicle, a Ford Mustang, is in model class P and is 3 years old. Because she has taken driver training classes, Evie qualifies for a .95 rating factor. As Evie's insurance agent, calculate her total annual premium.

SOLUTION STRATEGY

Step 1. From Table 19-6, we find the bodily injury premium to be $84 and the property damage premium to be $58.

Step 2. From Table 19-7, we find collision to be $101 and comprehensive to be $83.

Step 3. Total base premium = Bodily injury + Property damage + Collision + Comprehensive

Total base premium = 84 + 58 + 101 + 83 = $326

Step 3. Total annual premium = Total base premium × Rating factor

Total annual premium = 326 × .95 = $309.70

TABLE 19-7

Motor Vehicle Insurance Premiums Annual—Collision and Comprehensive Rates

		Territory 1 & 2				Territory 3 & 4			
		Collision		Comprehensive		Collision		Comprehensive	
Model Class	Vehicle Age	$250 Deductible	$500 Deductible	Full Coverage	$100 Deductible	$250 Deductible	$500 Deductible	Full Coverage	$100 Deductible
A–G	0–1	$ 89	$ 81	$ 63	$ 59	$ 95	$ 88	$ 67	$ 61
	2–3	87	79	60	57	93	84	63	58
	4–5	86	77	58	54	89	81	60	57
	6+	84	76	55	50	86	78	57	52
H–L	0–1	96	92	78	71	104	95	83	75
	2–3	93	89	76	68	101	90	80	72
	4–5	89	85	74	66	96	87	78	68
	6+	86	81	70	64	92	84	74	66
M–R	0–1	108	104	86	83	112	106	91	88
	2–3	104	101	83	79	109	104	88	82
	4–5	100	98	79	75	104	101	84	77
	6+	94	90	75	71	100	96	80	74
S–Z	0–1	120	115	111	108	124	116	119	113
	2–3	116	112	106	104	121	114	115	109
	4–5	111	107	101	99	116	110	111	106
	6+	108	103	98	96	111	107	108	101

TRY-IT | EXERCISE

9. Don Robinson, owner of High Performance Marine, wants to purchase truck insurance with bodily injury and property damage coverage in the amounts of 100/300/100. Don also wants $250 deductible collision and $100 deductible comprehensive. He is in driver classification 4 and lives in territory 3. His vehicle, a Chevy Blazer, is in model class F and is 4 years old. Because Don uses his truck to make dockside calls and haul boats to his shop, the insurance company has assigned a 2.3 rating factor to his policy. What is Don's total annual premium?

Check your answer with the solution on page 715.

19-9 Computing the Compensation Due Following an Accident

When the insured is involved in a motor vehicle accident in which he or she is at fault, his or her insurance company must pay out the claims resulting from that accident. Any amounts of bodily injury or property damage that exceed the limits of the policy coverage are the responsibility of the insured.

THE LOCKHORNS

"They shouldn't call it a drive-in window if they don't mean it."

EXAMPLE

Bill Bradley has motor vehicle insurance in the following amounts: liability, 15/30/5; $500 deductible collision; and $100 deductible comprehensive. Recently, Bill was at fault in an accident in which his van hit a car stopped at a traffic light. Two individuals in the other vehicle, Angel and Martha Cordero, were injured. Angel's bodily injuries amounted to $6,300, whereas Martha's more serious injuries totaled $18,400. In addition, their car sustained $6,250 in damages. Although he was not physically injured, the damage to Bill's van amounted to $4,788.

a. How much will the insurance company have to pay and to whom?

b. What part of the settlement will be Bill's responsibility?

SOLUTION STRATEGY

Liability Portion:

Bill's liability coverage is limited to $15,000 per person. The insurance company will pay the $6,300 for Angel's injuries; however, Bill is responsible for Martha's expenses above the limit.

$18,400	Martha's medical expenses
− $15,000	Insurance limit—bodily injury
$3,400	Bill's responsibility

Property Damage Portion:
The property damage limit of $5,000 is not sufficient to cover the damage to Angel's car. Bill will have to pay the portion above the limit.

$6,250	Angel's car repairs
−$5,000	Insurance limit—property damage
$1,250	Bill's responsibility

The damage to Bill's van will be paid by the insurance company, except for the $500 deductible.

$4,788	Van repairs
−$500	Deductible
$4,288	Insurance company responsibility

TRY-IT | EXERCISE

10. Joy Miller has automobile liability insurance in the amount of 25/50/10 and also carries $250 deductible collision and full-coverage comprehensive. Recently, Joy was at fault in an accident in which her Oldsmobile went out of control on a rainy day and hit two cars, a fence, and the side of a house. The first car, a Lexus, had $8,240 in damages. The second car, a Ford Taurus, sustained damages of $2,540. The repairs to Joy's car amounted to $3,542. In addition, the fence repairs came to $880, and the house damages were estimated at $5,320.

a. How much will the insurance company have to pay and to whom?

b. What part of the settlement will be Joy's responsibility?

Check your answers with the solutions on page 715.

REVIEW EXERCISES | CHAPTER 19—SECTION III

As an insurance agent, calculate the annual premium for the following clients:

Name	Territory	Driver Class	Bodily Injury	Property Damage	Model Class	Vehicle Age	Comprehensive Deductible	Collision Deductible	Rating Factor	Annual Premium
1. Rosen	2	4	50/100	25	J	3	$100	$250	None	______
2. Maples	1	2	10/20	10	R	1	Full Coverage	500	1.5	______
3. Lopez	3	1	25/50	5	U	5	Full Coverage	250	3.0	______
4. Zahn	2	3	100/300	25	C	4	$100	250	None	______
5. Nadler	4	2	50/100	100	H	2	Full Coverage	500	1.7	______
6. Maui	1	4	15/30	50	M	3	$100	250	2.5	______
7. Hale	2	1	10/20	10	Q	6	$100	250	3.9	______
8. Coll	3	3	100/300	100	Z	1	Full Coverage	500	None	______

9. Shaun Taylor wants to purchase an automobile insurance policy with bodily injury and property damage coverage in the amounts of 50/100/50. In addition, he wants collision coverage with $250 deductible and comprehensive with no deductible. Shaun is in driver classification 4 and lives in territory 3. His vehicle, a Mercedes 190S, is in model class B and is 1 year old. Shaun has had two accidents and one ticket in the past 12 months and is therefore considered to be a high risk. Consequently, the insurance company has assigned a rating factor of 4.0 to his policy. As his automobile insurance agent, calculate the total annual premium for Shaun's policy.

10. Howard Marshall's Corvette was hit by a palm tree during a hurricane. The damage was estimated at $1,544. If Howard carried $250 deductible collision and $100 deductible comprehensive, how much of the damages does the insurance company have to pay?

11. Len Hawkins has motor vehicle liability insurance in the amount of 50/100/50 and also carries $250 deductible collision coverage and full-coverage comprehensive. Recently, he was at fault in an accident in which his camper hit a bus. Five individuals were injured on the bus and were awarded the following settlements by the courts: Hart, $13,500; Black, $11,700; Garner, $4,140; Williams, $57,800; and Morgan, $3,590. The damage to the bus was $12,230, and Len's camper sustained $3,780 in damages.

    a. How much will the insurance company have to pay and to whom?

    b. What part of the settlement will be Len's responsibility?

BUSINESS DECISION

Insuring the Fleet

12. The Yellow Cab Company of Statesville is interested in purchasing $250 deductible collision insurance and full-coverage comprehensive insurance to cover its fleet of 10 taxi cabs. As a requirement for the job, all drivers already carry their own liability coverage in the amount of 100/300/100. Statesville is rated as territory 2. Five of the cabs are 4-year-old Checker Towncars, model class Y. Three of them are 2-year-old Chrysler station wagons, model class R. The remaining two are new Buick sedans, in model class C. Because the vehicles are on the road almost 24 hours a day, they are considered to be very high risk and carry a rating factor of 5.2. They are, however, subject to an 18% multivehicle fleet discount.

a. As the insurance agent for Yellow Cab, calculate the total annual premium for the fleet.

b. When the owner saw your rate quote, he exclaimed, "Too expensive! How can I save some money on this insurance?" At that point, you suggested changing the coverage to $500 deductible collision and $100 deductible comprehensive. How much can you save Yellow Cab by using the new coverage?

CHAPTER FORMULAS

Life Insurance

$$\text{Number of \$1,000} = \frac{\text{Face value of policy}}{1{,}000}$$

Annual premium = Number of $1,000 × Rate per $1,000

Premium other than annual = Annual premium × Premium factor

Income shortfall = Total living expenses − Total income

$$\text{Insurance needed} = \frac{\text{Income shortfall}}{\text{Prevailing interest rate}}$$

Property Insurance

Total annual fire premium = Building premium + Contents premium

Short-rate premium = Annual premium × Short-rate

Short-rate refund = Annual premium − Short-rate premium

Regular refund = Annual premium − Premium for period in force

$$\text{Coinsurance coverage ratio} = \frac{\text{Insurance carried}}{\text{Insurance required}}$$

$$\text{Amount of loss paid by insurance} = \frac{\text{Insurance carried}}{\text{Insurance required}} \times \text{Amount of loss}$$

$$\text{Carrier's percent of total coverage} = \frac{\text{Amount of carrier's policy}}{\text{Total amount of insurance}}$$

Carrier's share of loss = Amount of loss × Carrier's percent of total coverage

✦ SUMMARY CHART ✦

Section I: Life Insurance

Topic	P/O, Page	Important Concepts	Illustrative Examples
Calculating Various Types of Life Insurance Premiums	19-1 685	Life insurance guarantees a specified sum of money to the surviving beneficiaries, on the death of the insured. It is purchased in increments of $1,000. Calculating premiums: 1. Calculate the number of $1,000 of insurance desired by dividing the face value of the policy by $1,000. 2. Locate the appropriate premium rate per $1,000 in Table 19-1. 3. Calculate the total annual premium by multiplying the number of $1,000 by the Table 19-1 rate. 4. For premiums other than annual, multiply the annual premium by the appropriate Table 19-2 premium factor.	Pamela Boyd is 20 years old. She is interested in purchasing a 20-payment life insurance policy with a face value of $25,000. Calculate her annual and monthly premium. Number of \$1,000 = $\frac{25{,}000}{1{,}000}$ = 25 Table 20-1 rate = $21.50. Annual premium = 25 × 21.50 = $537.50 Monthly premium = 537.50 × 9% = $48.38

SECTION I: (continued)

Topic	P/O, Page	Important Concepts	Illustrative Examples
Calculating Life Insurance Nonforfeiture Options	19-2 689	Life insurance policies with accumulated cash value may be converted to one of three nonforfeiture options. Use Table 19-3 and the number of $1,000 of insurance to determine the value of each option. Option 1—Take the cash value of the policy, and cancel the insurance coverage. Option 2—Reduced, paid-up amount of the same insurance. Option 3—Term policy for a certain number of years and days, with the same face value as the original policy.	Barbara Seinfeld, 30 years old, purchased a $50,000 whole life insurance policy at age 20. What is the value of her nonforfeiture options? Number of \$1,000 $= \frac{50{,}000}{1{,}000} = 50$ Option 1: 50 × \$98 = <u>\$4,900 Cash</u> Option 2: 50 × \$186 = <u>\$9,300 Reduced Paid-up Insurance</u> Option 3: <u>17 years, 54 days Term Policy</u>
Determining the Amount of Life Insurance Needed to Cover Dependents' Income Shortfall	19-3 691	When one of the wage-earners in a household dies, the annual living expenses of the dependents may exceed the annual income. This difference is known as the income shortfall. To calculate the amount of insurance needed to cover the shortfall, use **Insurance needed = $\frac{\text{Income shortfall}}{\text{Prevailing interest rate}}$**	With a prevailing interest rate of 5%, how much life insurance will be needed to cover dependents' income shortfall if the annual living expenses amount to \$37,600 and the total income is \$21,200? Income shortfall = 37,600 − 21,200 = <u>\$16,400</u> Insurance needed at 5% = $\frac{16{,}400}{.05}$ = <u>\$328,000</u>

SECTION II: Property Insurance

Topic	P/O, Page	Important Concepts	Illustrative Examples
Calculating Typical Fire Insurance Premiums	19-4 694	Fire insurance premiums are based on type of construction, location of the property, and availability of fire protection. Fire insurance premiums are quoted per \$100 of coverage, with buildings and contents listed separately. Use Table 19-4 to calculate fire insurance premiums: **Premium = Number of \$100 × Table rate**	What is the total annual fire insurance premium on a building valued at \$120,000, with structural class C and area rating 3, and contents valued at \$400,000? Building: 120 × .69 = <u>\$82.80</u> Contents: 400 × .77 = <u>\$308.00</u> Total annual fire premium = 82.80 + 308.00 = <u>\$390.80</u>

SECTION II: (continued)

Topic	P/O, Page	Important Concepts	Illustrative Examples
Computing Short-Rate Premiums and Canceled Policy Refunds	19-5 696	Fire policies for less than 1 year are known as short-rate. Use Table 19-5 for these policies. a. Short-rate refund (Policy canceled by insured): **Short-rate premium = Annual premium × Table factor** **Short-rate refund = Annual premium − Short-rate premium** b. Regular refund (Policy canceled by insurance company): **Premium for time in force =** $\textbf{Annual premium} \times \dfrac{\textbf{Months in force}}{\textbf{12}}$ **Regular refund = Annual premium − Premium for time in force**	The Atlas Company has property insurance with State Farm. The annual premium is \$3,000. a. If Atlas cancels the policy after 2 months, what is the short-rate refund? b. If State Farm cancels the policy after 2 months, what is the regular refund? a. Short-rate refund Short-rate premium = 3,000 × 30% = \$900 Short-rate refund = 3,000 − 900 = \$2,100 b. Regular refund Time in force premium = $3{,}000 \times \dfrac{2}{12} = \$500$ Regular refund = 3,000 − 500 = \$2,500
Calculating Compensation Due by Using Coinsurance Clause	19-6 698	A coinsurance clause stipulates the minimum amount of coverage required for a claim to be paid in full. If less than the coinsurance requirement is carried, the payout is proportionately less. **Amount of insurance required = Replacement value × Coinsurance %** **Amount of loss paid =** $\dfrac{\textbf{Insurance carried}}{\textbf{Insurance required}} \times \textbf{Amount of loss}$	The Novell Corporation has a \$150,000 fire insurance policy on a property valued at \$250,000. If the policy has an 80% coinsurance clause, how much would be paid in the event of a \$50,000 fire? Insurance required = 250,000 × .8 = \$200,000 Amount of loss paid = $\dfrac{150{,}000}{200{,}000} \times 50{,}000 = \$37{,}500$
Determining a Company's Share of a Loss When Multiple Carriers Are Used	19-7 699	When more than one insurance company covers a piece of property, the property has multiple carriers. In the event of a claim, each company is responsible for its portion of the total insurance carried. **Carrier's % of total =** $\dfrac{\textbf{Amount of carrier's policy}}{\textbf{Total insurance}}$ **Carrier's share = Amount of loss × Carrier's %**	West Industries had multiple carrier fire insurance on its property as follows: Southwest Mutual . . . . . . \$300,000 Travelers . . . . \$100,000 Total . . . . . \$400,000 Assuming that all coinsurance requirements have been met, how much will each carrier be responsible for in a \$20,000 fire? Southwest Mutual: $\dfrac{300{,}000}{400{,}000} \times 20{,}000 = \$15{,}000$ Travelers: $\dfrac{100{,}000}{400{,}000} \times 20{,}000 = \$5{,}000$

Section III: Motor Vehicle Insurance

Topic	P/O, Page	Important Concepts	Illustrative Examples
Computing Typical Motor Vehicle Insurance Premiums	19-8 703	Motor vehicle insurance is divided into three main categories: Liability—Covers bodily injury and property damage to others. Use Table 19-6 for these rates. Collision—Covers damage to the insured's vehicle from an auto accident. Use Table 19-7. Comprehensive—Covers damage to the insured's vehicle from fire, wind, water, vandalism, theft, and so on. Use Table 19-7. Rates may be adjusted up or down by multiplying the total table rate by a rating factor.	Roni Salkind wants auto liability coverage of 25/50/25, $250 deductible collision, and $100 deductible comprehensive. She is in driver class 2 and lives in territory 3. Her vehicle, a new SL 500, is in model class L and has a sports car rating factor of 1.7. What is Roni's total auto premium? $86 Bodily injury Table 19-6 $74 Property damage Table 19-6 $104 Collision Table 19-7 + $75 Comprehensive Table 19-7 $339 Total base × 1.7 Rating factor $576.30 Total premium
Computing the Compensation Due Following an Accident	19-9 706	When the policyholder is at fault in an accident, his or her insurance company is responsible for all settlements, up to the limits and deductibles of the policy. Any settlement amounts greater than the policy coverage are the responsibility of the insured.	Warner Johnson has auto liability coverage of 50/100/50, no deductible comprehensive, and $250 deductible collision. Recently, Warner ran a red light and broadsided Sylvia Norton's car. In the court settlement, Sylvia was awarded $75,000 for bodily injury and $14,500 in property damages. Warner's car sustained $7,500 in damages. How much will the insurance company be responsible to pay? How much of the settlement is Warner's responsibility? Liability: Warner's policy limit for bodily injury liability is $50,000. $75,000 Court settlement −$50,000 Paid by insurance $25,000 Paid by Warner The policy limit for property damage is $50,000, therefore the insurance company will pay the full $14,500. Collision: $7,500 Collision damage −250 Deductible $7,250 Paid by insurance

TRY-IT EXERCISE | SOLUTIONS

1. $\text{Number of \$1,000} = \dfrac{\text{Face value of policy}}{1{,}000}$

$\text{Number of \$1,000} = \dfrac{75{,}000}{1{,}000} = 75$

Table 19-1 rate = $4.92 per $1,000
Annual premium = Number of 1,000 × Rate per $1,000
Annual premium = 75 × 4.92 = $369.00

Quarterly premium = Annual premium × Quarterly factor
Quarterly premium = 369 × .26 = $95.94

Total payment = Quarterly payment × 4 payments
Total payment = $95.94 × 4 = $383.76
Michael will pay $14.76 ($383.76 − $369.00) more if paid quarterly.

2. $\text{Number of \$1,000} = \dfrac{\text{Face value of policy}}{1{,}000} = \dfrac{100{,}000}{1{,}000} = 100$

Option 1
Cash value = 100 × 191 = $19,100

Option 2
Reduced paid-up insurance = 100 × 496 = $49,600

Option 3
Extended term = 30 years, 206 days

3. Total income = 38,000 + 5,000 = 43,000
Income shortfall = Total expenses − Total income
Income shortfall = 54,000 − 43,000 = $11,000

$\text{Insurance needed} = \dfrac{\text{Shortfall}}{\text{Prevailing rate}}$

$\text{Insurance needed} = \dfrac{11{,}000}{.05} = \$220{,}000$

4. From Table 19-4
Building: .38
Contents: .42

$\text{Building} = \dfrac{\text{Amount of coverage}}{100} = \dfrac{420{,}000}{100} = 4{,}200$

$\text{Contents} = \dfrac{\text{Amount of coverage}}{100} = \dfrac{685{,}000}{100} = 6{,}850$

Building = Number of $100 × Rate = 4,200 × .38 = $1,596
Contents = Number of $100 × Rate = 6,850 × .42 = $2,877

Total premium = Building + Contents
Total premium = 1,596 + 2,877 = $4,473

5. From Table 19-5, 8 months = 80%
Short-rate premium = Annual premium × Short-rate
Short-rate premium = 850 × .8 = $680
Short-rate refund = Annual premium − Short-rate premium
Short-rate refund = 850 − 680 = $170

6. $\text{Premium for period} = \text{Annual premium} \times \dfrac{\text{Months in force}}{12}$

$\text{Premium for period} = 850 \times \dfrac{8}{12} = \$566.67$

Regular refund = Annual premium − Premium for period
Regular refund = 850.00 − 566.67 = $283.33

7. Insurance required = Value of property × Coinsurance percent
Insurance required = 850,000 × .7 = $595,000

$\text{Amount of loss paid} = \dfrac{\text{Insurance carried}}{\text{Insurance required}} \times \text{Loss}$

$\text{Amount of loss paid} = \dfrac{400{,}000}{595{,}000} \times 325{,}000 = \$218{,}487.39$

8. $\text{Carrier's percent of total} = \dfrac{\text{Amount of carrier's policy}}{\text{Total amount of insurance}}$

$\text{Aetna} = \dfrac{20{,}000}{125{,}000} = 16\%$

$\text{USF\&G} = \dfrac{45{,}000}{125{,}000} = 36\%$

$\text{Hancock} = \dfrac{60{,}000}{125{,}000} = 48\%$

Carrier's share of loss = Amount of loss × Carrier's percent
Aetna = 16,800 × .16 = $2,688
USF&G = 16,800 × .36 = $6,048
Hancock = 16,800 × .48 = $8,064

9. Base premium = Bodily injury + Property damage + Collision + Comprehensive

Base premium = 128 + 89 + 89 + 57 = $363

Total annual premium = Base premium × Rating factor

Total annual premium = 363 × 2.3 = $834.90

10.

a. Insurance Pays

$10,000	Property damage
+3,292	Joy's car *less* deductible
$13,292	Total insurance responsibility

b. Joy Pays

$8,240	Lexus
2,540	Taurus
880	Fence
+ 5,320	House
16,980	Total property damage
−10,000	Insurance
$6,980	Joy's portion
+ 250	Collision deductible
$7,230	Joy's responsibility

Name ______________________

Class ______________________

Answers

1. ______________________

2. ______________________

3. ______________________

4. ______________________

5. ______________________

6. ______________________

7. a. ______________________

b. ______________________

c. ______________________

8. a. ______________________

b. ______________________

CHAPTER 19 | ASSESSMENT TEST

Calculate the annual, semiannual, quarterly, and monthly premiums for the following life insurance policies:

	Face Value of Policy	Sex and Age of Insured	Type of Policy	Annual Premium	Semiannual Premium	Quarterly Premium	Monthly Premium
1.	$80,000	Male, 29	20-Payment Life				
2.	55,000	Female, 21	20-Year Endowment				
3.	38,000	Female, 40	5-Year Term				
4.	175,000	Male, 30	Whole Life				

Calculate the value of the nonforfeiture options for the following life insurance policies:

	Face Value of Policy	Years in Force	Type of Policy	Cash Value	Reduced Paid-up Insurance	Extended Term	
						Years	Days
5.	$130,000	15	Whole Life				
6.	60,000	5	20-Payment Life				

7. Tom Finlay is 19 years old and is interested in purchasing a whole life insurance policy with a face value of $80,000.

a. Calculate the annual insurance premium for this policy.

b. Calculate the monthly insurance premiums.

c. How much more will Tom pay per year if he chooses monthly payments?

8. Gail Lobanoff purchased a $45,000 20-year endowment life insurance policy when she was 20 years old. She is now 35 years old and wants to look into her nonforfeiture options. As her insurance agent, calculate the value of Gail's three options.

a. Option 1

b. Option 2

c. Option 3

9. Carl McAdams is evaluating his life insurance needs. His family's total annual living expenses are $54,500. Darlene, his wife, earns $28,900 per year in salary. If the prevailing interest rate is 5%, how much life insurance should Carl purchase to cover his dependents' income shortfall in the event of his death?

Calculate the building, contents, and total property insurance premiums for the following property insurance policies:

	Area Rating	Structural Class	Building Value	Building Premium	Contents Value	Contents Premium	Total Premium
10.	4	B	$ 47,000	______	$ 93,000	______	______
11.	2	A	125,000	______	160,000	______	______
12	3	C	980,000	______	1,500,000	______	______

Calculate the short-term premium and refund for the following policies:

	Annual Premium	Canceled After	Canceled By	Short-Term Premium	Short-Term Refund
13.	$260	8 months	insurance company	______	______
14.	720	15 days	insured	______	______

Calculate the amount to be paid by the insurance company for each of the following claims:

	Replacement Value of Building	Face Value of Policy	Coinsurance Clause (%)	Amount of Loss	Amount of Loss Insurance Company Will Pay
15.	$260,000	$105,000	80	$12,000	______
16.	490,000	450,000	90	80,000	______

17. You are the insurance agent for Seacoast International, a company that imports men's and women's clothing from Europe and the Far East. The owner, Bill Benzinger, wants you to give him a quote on the total annual premium for property insurance on a new warehouse and showroom facility in the amount of $320,000. The building is structural classification B and area rating 4. In addition, Bill will require contents insurance in the amount of $1,200,000.

18. "Movers of the Stars" has been contracted by Premier Events, Inc., to transport the stage and sound equipment for a 4-month rock-and-roll tour by the Rolling Stones. The moving company purchased property insurance to cover this valuable equipment for an annual premium of $12,500. What is the short-rate premium due for this coverage?

Name ______________________

Class ______________________

Answers

8. c. ______________________
9. ______________________
10. ______________________
11. ______________________
12. ______________________
13. ______________________
14. ______________________
15. ______________________
16. ______________________
17. ______________________
18. ______________________

Name ____________

Class ____________

19. The Professional Medical Center had property valued at $750,000 and insured for $600,000. The fire insurance policy contained an 80% coinsurance clause. One evening, an electrical short circuit caused a $153,000 fire. How much of the damages will be paid by the insurance company?

Answers

19. ____________

20. Bubbly Cola Bottling Company had multiple carrier fire insurance coverage on its plant and equipment in the amount of $2,960,000, as follows:

Kemper	$1,350,000 policy
Metropolitan	921,000 policy
The Hartford	689,000 policy
	$2,960,000 total coverage

Assuming that all coinsurance clause stipulations have been met, how much would each carrier be responsible for in the event of a $430,000 fire? (Round to the nearest whole percent.)

a. Kemper

b. Metropolitan

c. The Hartford

20. a. ____________

b. ____________

c. ____________

21. ____________

22. ____________

23. ____________

24. ____________

As an insurance agent, calculate the annual premium for the following clients:

	Name	Territory	Driver Class	Bodily Injury	Property Damage	Model Class	Vehicle Age	Comprehensive Deductible	Collision Deductible	Rating Factor	Annual Premium
21.	Wills	3	2	50/100	25	X	1	$100	$500	0.9	______
22.	Benson	1	1	10/20	5	Q	4	Full Cov.	250	2.2	______
23.	Mays	2	4	100/300	100	F	7	$100	500	1.7	______

24. Kathleen Sharp wants to purchase an automobile insurance policy with bodily injury and property damage coverage in the amounts of 25/50/25. In addition, she wants collision coverage with $250 deductible and comprehensive with $100 deductible. Kathleen is in driver classification 2 and lives in territory 3. Her vehicle, a new Toyota Camry, is in model class B. Because the car has an airbag, an alarm, and antilock brakes, the insurance company has assigned a rating factor of .95 to the policy. As her auto insurance agent, calculate Kathleen's total annual premium.

25. Winston Hill has automobile liability insurance in the amount of 50/100/50. He also carries $250 deductible collision and full comprehensive coverage. Recently, he was at fault in an accident in which his car went out of control in the rain and struck four pedestrians. In an out-of-court settlement, they were awarded the following: Goya, $45,000; Truman, $68,000; Copeland, $16,000; and Kelly, $11,000. Damages to Winston's car amounted to $3,900.

a. How much will the insurance company pay and to whom?

b. What part of the settlement will be Winston's responsibility?

Name ______________

Class ______________

Answers

25. a. ______________

b. ______________

26. a. ______________

b. ______________

c. ______________

BUSINESS DECISION

Group Insurance

26. Many employers purchase group insurance on behalf of their employees. Under a group insurance plan, a master contract issued to the company provides either life insurance, health insurance, or both for the employees who choose to participate. Most plans also provide coverage for dependents of employees. The two major benefits of group plans are lower premiums than individual insurance of the same coverage and no medical exams.

You are the owner of Superior Industries, Inc., a small manufacturing company with 250 employees. The company has just instituted a group health insurance plan for employees. Under the plan, the employees pay 30% of the premium and the company pays 70%. The insurance company reimburses 80% of all medical expenses over the deductible. The annual rates and deductibles from the insurance company are as follows:

	Annual Premium	Deductible
Employee with no dependents	$1,200	$300
Employee with one dependent	$1,400	$500
Employee with multiple dependents	$1,800	$800

a. If all 250 employees opt for the group health plan, what is the annual cost to the company assuming: 100 employees have no dependents, 80 employees have one dependent, and 70 have multiple dependents?

b. If your employees are paid biweekly, how much should be deducted from each paycheck for each of the three categories?

c. If Maggie Diaz chooses the multiple dependent option, and has a total of $3,400 in medical bills for the year, how much will be reimbursed by the insurance company?

All the Math That's Fit to Learn

The Business Math Times

Volume XIX | Insurance | One Dollar

Career Track: Insurance Agent

Insurance agents and brokers are professionals who sell individuals and businesses insurance policies that provide protection against loss. They help individuals, families, and businesses select the policies that best provide insurance protection for their lives and health, as well as for their automobiles, personal valuables, household items, businesses, and other properties.

Agents and brokers prepare reports, maintain records, and help policyholders settle insurance claims. An increasing number of insurance agents offer comprehensive financial planning services to their clients, such as retirement planning and counseling. As a result, many also are licensed to sell mutual funds, annuities, and other securities.

For jobs selling insurance, companies prefer college graduates, particularly those who have majored in business or economics. Courses in finance, mathematics, accounting, business law, and government enable insurance agents to understand changes in tax laws and government regulations that can affect the insurance needs of clients. In addition, courses in psychology, sociology, and public speaking are useful in improving sales techniques.

All insurance agents and brokers must obtain a license in the states where they plan to sell insurance. In most states, licenses are issued only to applicants who have completed specified courses and passed written examinations covering insurance fundamentals and state insurance laws.

Pepper . . . and Salt

THE WALL STREET JOURNAL

"It's nothing personal, sir—we're just going through our files and cancelling every other policy."

"Quote . . . Unquote"

Here's why insurance companies are mostly indestructible:
The cost of damages most times is less than the deductible.
—*G. Sterling Lieby*

Life lived for tomorrow will always be just a day away from being realized.
—*Leo Buscaglia*

September 11, 2001
Insurance Industry Loss Estimates* ($ billions)

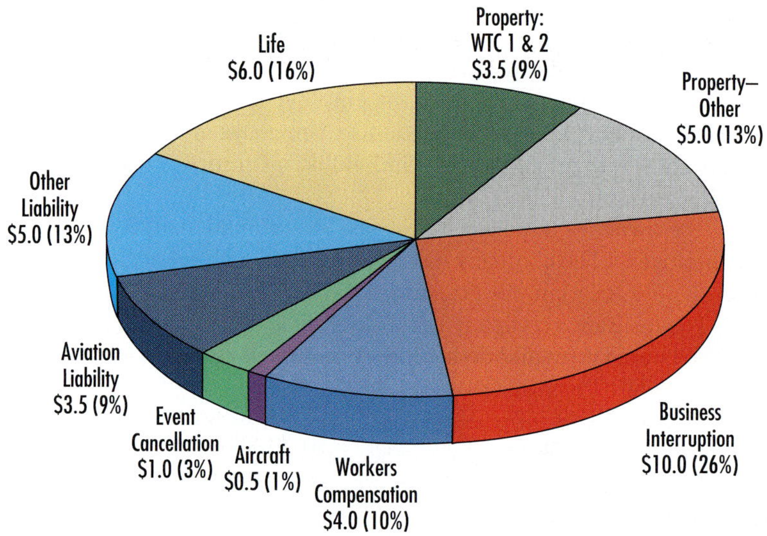

*As of January, 2002

For additional information, visit our web site at: www.contemporarymath.com

http://www

Did You Know?

The word policy comes from the Greek word "polyptychon" meaning "a piece of writing with many folds."

Braineteaser

LIGHT AT THE END

How long will it take a train 1 mile long to get through a tunnel 1 mile long if the train is traveling at 15 miles per hour?

ANSWER TO LAST ISSUE'S BRAINTEASER

40%

100 − 20% = 80
80 − 25% = 60
100 − 60 = 40%

CHAPTER 20

Investments

PERFORMANCE OBJECTIVES

Section I Stocks

20-1 Understanding stocks and distributing dividends on preferred and common stock. (p. 722)
20-2 Reading stock quotations. (p. 726)
20-3 Calculating current yield for a stock. (p. 728)
20-4 Determining the price-earnings ratio of a stock. (p. 729)
20-5 Computing the cost, proceeds, and gain (or loss) on a stock transaction. (p. 729)

Section II Bonds

20-6 Understanding bonds and reading bond quotations. (p. 734)
20-7 Computing the cost of purchasing bonds and the proceeds from the sale of bonds. (p. 737)
20-8 Calculating the current yield for a bond. (p. 739)

Section III Mutual Funds

20-9 Understanding mutual funds and reading mutual fund quotations. (p. 742)
20-10 Calculating the sales charge and sales charge percent of a mutual fund. (p. 744)
20-11 Calculating the net asset value of a mutual fund. (p. 745)
20-12 Calculating the number of shares purchased of a mutual fund. (p. 746)
20-13 Calculating return on investment. (p. 747)

financial risk
The chance you take of either making or losing money on an investment.

conservative investments
Low-risk investments, such as government bonds or certificates of deposit.

speculative investments
High-risk investments, such as stocks in new companies, junk bonds, or options and futures.

diversified portfolio
An investment strategy that is a mixture of stocks, bonds, cash equivalents, and other types of investments.

stocks, or equities
An investment that is an ownership share of a corporation.

Financial risk is the chance you take of either making or losing money on an investment. In most cases, the greater the risk, the more money you stand to gain or lose. Investment opportunities range from low-risk **conservative investments,** such as government bonds or certificates of deposit, to high-risk **speculative investments,** such as stocks in new companies, junk bonds, or options and futures. Selecting the right investment depends on personal circumstances as well as general market conditions. See Exhibit 20-1.

Investments are based on *liquidity,* which indicates how easy it is to get your money out; *safety,* how much risk is involved; and *return,* how much you can expect to earn. Investment advice is available from stockbrokers, financial planners, and many other sources. It is generally agreed that over the long run, a **diversified portfolio,** with a mixture of stocks, bonds, cash equivalents, and sometimes other types of investments, is a sensible choice. Determining the correct portfolio mix is a decision that should be based on the amount of assets available, the age of the investor, and the amount of risk desired.

In this chapter, we investigate three major categories of investments: **stocks,** also known as **equities,** which represent an *ownership share* of a corporation; bonds, or debt, which represent IOUs for money borrowed from the investor; and mutual funds, which are investment *pools* of money with a wide variety of investment goals.

SECTION I

STOCKS

20-1 Understanding Stocks and Distributing Dividends on Preferred and Common Stock

share
One unit of stock or ownership in a corporation.

stock certificate
The official document that represents an ownership share in a corporation.

Corporations are built and expanded with money known as capital, which is raised by issuing and selling **shares** of stock. Investors' ownership in a company is measured by the number of shares they own. Each ownership portion, or share, is represented by a **stock certificate.** In the past, these certificates were sent to the investor, confirming the stock purchase transaction. Today, however, this confirmation comes in the form of a computerized book entry on

Everybody's Business
Real-World Connection
History has demonstrated repeatedly that a well-diversified portfolio of investments based on careful planning and a focused strategy reduces risk and provides an opportunity for solid returns.

Changing investments too frequently—overreacting to daily economic data or the latest Wall Street fads—can distract investors from reaching their specific goals.

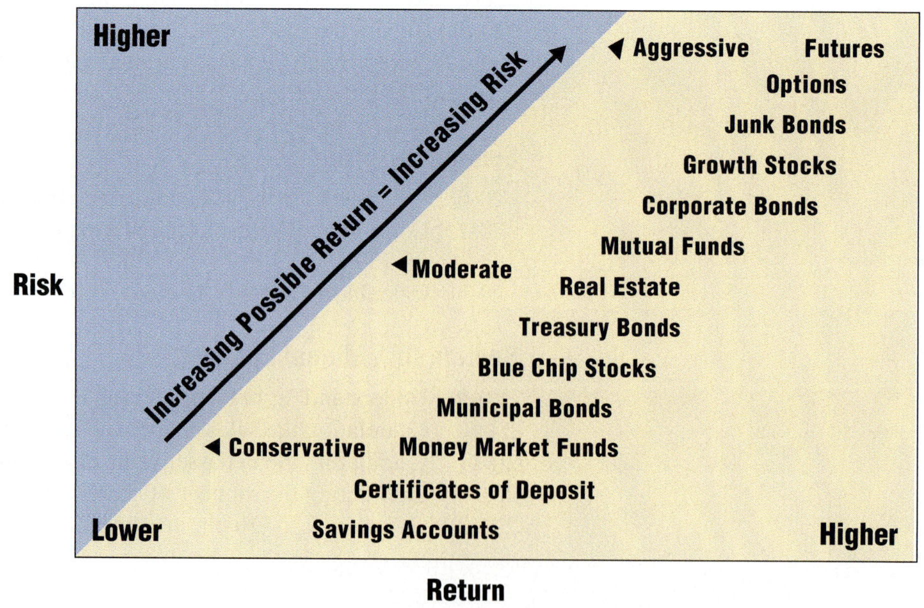

EXHIBIT 20-1
Risk and Return

an account statement. Investors who actually want to hold their certificates are charged extra service fees. Exhibit 20-2 is an example of a stock certificate.

Generally, if the company does well, the investor or **shareholder** will receive **dividends,** which are a distribution of the company's profits. If the share price goes up, the stockholder can sell the stock at a profit. Today, more than 50 million persons in the United States own stock in thousands of **publicly held corporations.**

Many companies offer two classes of stock to appeal to different types of investors. These classes are known as common and preferred. With **common stock,** an investor shares directly in the success or failure of the business. When the company does well, the dividends and price of the stock may rise, and the investors make money. When the company does poorly, it does not pay dividends and the price of the stock may fall.

With **preferred stock,** the dividends are fixed, regardless of how the company is doing. When the board of directors of a company declare a dividend, the preferred stockholders are paid before the common. If the company goes out of business, the preferred stockholders have priority over the common as far as possibly getting back some of their investment.

Preferred stock is issued either with or without a **par value.** When the stock has a par value, the dividend is specified as a percent of par. For example, each share of 8%, $100 par value preferred stock pays a dividend of $8.00 per share (100 × .08) per year. The dividend is usually paid on a quarterly basis, in this case, $2.00 each quarter. When preferred stock is **no-par value,** the dividend is stated as a dollar amount.

Cumulative preferred stock receives a dividend each year. When no dividends are paid one year, the amount owed, known as **dividends in arrears,** accumulates. Common stockholders cannot receive any dividends until all the dividends in arrears have been paid to cumulative preferred stockholders.

Preferred stock is further divided into categories known as nonparticipating, which means the stockholders receive only the fixed dividend and no more; and participating, which means the stockholders may receive additional dividends if the company does well. Convertible preferred means the stock may be exchanged for a specified number of common shares in the future.

shareholder
The person who owns shares of stock in a corporation.

dividends
A distribution of a company's profits to its shareholders.

publicly held corporation
A corporation whose stock is available to be bought and sold by the general investing public. The opposite of a privately held corporation.

common stock
A class of corporate stock in which the investor has voting rights and shares directly in the success or failure of the business.

preferred stock
A class of corporate stock in which the investor has preferential rights over the common shareholders to dividends and a company's assets.

par value
An arbitrary monetary figure specified in the corporate charter for each share of stock and printed on each stock certificate. The dividend for par value preferred stock is quoted as a percent of the par value.

no-par value stock
Stock that does not have a par value. The dividend for no-par value preferred stock is quoted as a dollar amount per share.

cumulative preferred stock
A type of preferred stock that receives a dividend each year. When no dividends are paid one year, the amount owed accumulates and must be paid to cumulative preferred shareholders before any dividends can be paid to common shareholders.

dividends in arrears
The amount of dividends that accumulate and are owed to cumulative preferred shareholders for past years in which no dividends were paid.

STEPS TO DISTRIBUTE DIVIDENDS ON PREFERRED AND COMMON STOCK:

Step 1. If the preferred stock is *cumulative,* any dividends that are in arrears are paid first; then the preferred dividend is paid for the current period. When the dividend per share is stated in dollars (no-par stock), go to Step 2. When the dividend per share is stated as a percent (par stock), multiply the par value by the dividend rate.

$$\text{Dividend per share (preferred)} = \text{Par value} \times \text{Dividend rate}$$

Step 2. Calculate the total amount of the preferred stock dividend by multiplying the number of preferred shares by the dividend per share.

$$\text{Total preferred dividend} = \text{Number of shares} \times \text{Dividend per share}$$

Step 3. Calculate the total common stock dividend by subtracting the total preferred stock dividend from the total dividend declared.

$$\text{Total common dividend} = \text{Total dividend} - \text{Total preferred dividend}$$

Step 4. Calculate the dividends per share for common stock by dividing the total common stock dividend by the number of shares of common stock.

$$\text{Dividend per share (common)} = \frac{\text{Total common dividend}}{\text{Number of shares (common)}}$$

EXHIBIT 20-2
Stock Certificate

EXAMPLE

The Eastman Corporation has 2,500,000 shares of common stock outstanding. If a dividend of $4,000,000 was declared by the company directors last year, what are the dividends per share of common stock?

SOLUTION STRATEGY

Because Eastman has no preferred stock, the common shareholders will receive the entire dividend. We go directly to Step 4.

$$\text{Dividend per share (common)} = \frac{\text{Total common dividend}}{\text{Number of shares (common)}} = \frac{4{,}000{,}000}{2{,}500{,}000} = \underline{\underline{\$1.60 \text{ per share}}}$$

TRY-IT | EXERCISE

1. **Forsythe Computer, Inc., has 1,400,000 shares of common stock outstanding. If a dividend of $910,000 was declared by the company directors last year, what is the dividend per share of common stock?**

Check your answer with the solution on page 755.

EXAMPLE

The board of directors of Waterways Developers, Inc., have declared a dividend of $300,000. The company has 60,000 shares of preferred stock that pay $.50 per share and 100,000 shares of common stock. Calculate the amount of dividends due the preferred shareholders and the dividend per share of common stock.

SOLUTION STRATEGY

Step 1. Because the preferred dividend is stated in dollars ($.50 per share), we skip to Step 2.

Step 2.

$$\text{Total preferred dividend} = \text{Number of shares} \times \text{Dividend per share}$$

$$\text{Total preferred dividend} = 60{,}000 \times .50 = \underline{\underline{\$30{,}000}}$$

Step 3.

$$\text{Total common dividend} = \text{Total dividend} - \text{Total preferred dividend}$$

$$\text{Total common dividend} = 300{,}000 - 30{,}000 = \underline{\underline{\$270{,}000}}$$

Step 4.

$$\text{Dividend per share (common)} = \frac{\text{Total common dividend}}{\text{Number of shares (common)}} = \frac{270{,}000}{100{,}000} = \underline{\underline{\$2.70 \text{ per share}}}$$

TRY-IT | EXERCISE

2. The board of directors of Analog Technology, Inc., has declared a dividend of $2,800,000. The company has 600,000 shares of preferred stock that pay $1.40 per share and 1,000,000 shares of common stock. Calculate the amount of dividends due the preferred shareholders and the dividend per share of common stock.

Check your answer with the solution on page 755.

EXAMPLE

Galaxy Enterprises has 100,000 shares of $100 par value, 6%, cumulative preferred stock and 2,500,000 shares of common stock. Although no dividend was declared last year, a $5,000,000 dividend has been declared this year. Calculate the amount of dividends due the preferred shareholders and the dividend per share of common stock.

SOLUTION STRATEGY

Step 1. Because the preferred stock is cumulative and the company did not pay a dividend last year, the preferred shareholders are entitled to the dividends in *arrears* and the dividends for the *current period.*

$$\text{Dividend per share (preferred)} = \text{Par value} \times \text{Dividend rate}$$

$$\text{Dividend per share (preferred)} = 100 \times .06 = \underline{\underline{\$6.00 \text{ per share}}}$$

Step 2.

$$\text{Total preferred dividend (per year)} = \text{Number of shares} \times \text{Dividend per share}$$

$$\text{Total preferred dividend (per year)} = 100{,}000 \times 6.00 = \underline{\underline{\$600{,}000}}$$

$$\text{Total preferred dividend} = 600{,}000 \text{ (arrears)} + 600{,}000 \text{ (current year)} = \underline{\underline{\$1{,}200{,}000}}$$

Step 3.

$$\text{Total common dividend} = \text{Total dividend} - \text{Total preferred dividend}$$

$$\text{Total common dividend} = 5{,}000{,}000 - 1{,}200{,}000 = \underline{\underline{\$3{,}800{,}000}}$$

Step 4.

$$\text{Dividend per share (common)} = \frac{\text{Total common dividend}}{\text{Number of shares (common)}} = \frac{3{,}800{,}000}{2{,}500{,}000} = \underline{\underline{\$1.52}}$$

TRY-IT EXERCISE

3. Fuller Laboratories has 300,000 shares of $100 par value, 7.5%, cumulative preferred stock and 5,200,000 shares of common stock. Although no dividend was declared for last year, a $7,000,000 dividend has been declared for this year. Calculate the amount of dividends due the preferred shareholders and the dividend per share of common stock.

Check your answers with the solutions on page 755.

Everybody's Business

Real-World Connection

The New York Stock Exchange began trading stocks in dollars and cents rather than fractions in 2000. For investors, the move to decimals meant that the spreads—the difference between the price of a stock and what a broker will charge investors to buy it—were narrowed.

The minimum spread using fractions was one-eighth, or 12.5 cents. With decimal pricing, the spread could be as little as a penny.

20-2 Reading Stock Quotations

Stock quotation tables found in the business section of most newspapers provide investors with a daily summary of what happened in the stock market on the previous trading day. Let's take a column-by-column look at a typical day's listing for Wal-Mart. Exhibit 20-3 is a portion of such a table, reprinted from *The Wall Street Journal.*

Stock prices on these tables are listed in dollars and cents. The first step in reading the stock quotation table is to locate the alphabetical listing of the company whose stock you want to look up, in this case, Wal-Mart. Each line is divided into 11 columns as follows:

Column 1 (YTD % Chg +3.4) Indicates the Year-to-date percentage change. In this case the value of the stock has risen 3.4% for the year.

Column 2 (Hi—58.75) Highest price of the stock during the preceding 52-week period.

Column 3 (Lo—41.50) Lowest price of the stock during the preceding 52-week period.

Column 4 (Stock—Wal-Mart) Company name and type of stock. If no symbol appears after a name, it is common stock. A "pf" after the name indicates it is preferred stock.

Column 5 (Sym—WMT) Symbol used to identify a particular stock on the stock exchange's ticker and on other references such as information systems and computer databases.

Column 6 (Div—.28) The amount of dividend paid out on the stocks last year. When there were no dividends, the column is blank.

Column 7 (Yld %—.5) Yield percent. Last year's dividend as a percent of the current prices of the stock. Found by dividing last year's dividend by the current price of the stock. When there were no dividends, the column shows " . . . "

Column 8 (PE—38) Price-earnings ratio, which indicates investor confidence in a stock. It is the ratio of the current price of the stock to the earnings per share of the company for the past four quarters. When a company has no earnings, the column shows " . . . "; "dd" indicates a loss.

Column 9 (Vol 100s—87671) Indicates the volume or number of shares, in hundreds, traded for the day. For example, 87671 would mean 8,767,100 shares (87671 × 100). Listings that are *underlined* indicate unusually large trading activity or volume.

Column 10 (Last—54.94) The last price of the trading day.

Column 11 (Net Chg +1.04) Indicates the difference, or net change, between the last price and the previous day's last price.

◆ EXHIBIT 20-3 ◆

***The Wall Street Journal* New York Stock Exchange Composite Transactions**

1 2 3 4 5 6 7 8 9 10 11

YTD % CHG	52 WEEKS HI	52 WEEKS LO	STOCK (SYM)	DIV	YLD %	PE	VOL 100S	LAST	NET CHG
▲+ 2.0	15.10	15	Viasys wi n		...	...	76	15.30	+ 0.30
− 86.0	17.63	0.35	ViaSystems **VG**		...	dd	1477	1.16	− 0.04
− 16.5	17.88	6.80	VdshSnchr ADS **VSL** s	2.13e	20.4	...	97	10.44	...
▲+ 38.6	20.50	12.06	Vimpel ADR **VIP**		...	dd	1071	20.62	+ 0.51
...	48.10	36.31	VinaConc ADR **VCO**	.60e	1.5	...	26	39.01	+ 0.27
− 22.1	23.50	14.75	VintagePete **VPI**	.14	.8	4	1815	16.75	+ 0.29
+ 24.4	31.50	13.75♣	Vishay **VSH**		...	13	17488	18.81	− 0.17
+ 6.8	21.72	9.75	Visteon	.24	2.0	dd	6627	12.28	+ 0.22
+ 14.4	25.70	8.75	Visx **EYE**		...	cc	958	11.94	+ 0.46
− 8.1	3.62	1.81	Vitro ADR **VTO**	.16e	7.1	...	15	2.24	− 0.01
− 1.4	39.50	37	VvndiEnvrADS **VE** n		...	...	114	38.50	+ 0.70
− 25.0	76	37.30	VivndUnvsl ADS **V** s	.90p	...	...	2354	48.98	+ 0.67
− 29.0	**42.63**	**17.97**	**Vodafon ADR VOD**	**.21e**	**.8**	**...**	**59288**	**25.41**	**+ 1.29**
− 45.5	28.10	10.50♣	VoltInfoSci **VOL**		...	19	222	11.30	− 0.40
+ 4.9	41.60	34.38	Vornado **VNO**	2.64f	6.6	17	2387	40.20	+ 0.82
+ 11.7	17.25	11.25	VotorCel ADS	.73p	...	...	140	15.57	+ 0.05
− 9.1	55.30	37.50♣	VulcanMat **VMC**	.90	2.1	20	1915	43.53	+ 0.23
			-W-W-W-						
+ 5.7	15.24	8.81	WABTEC **WAB**	.04	.3	19	313	12.42	+ 0.11
− 9.3	31.50	25.25♣	WGL Hldgs **WGL**	1.26	4.6	15	769	27.62	+ 0.16
+ 94.7	2.25	0.69	WHX Cp **WHX**		...	dd	69	1.46	− 0.03
+ 17.0	20.70	13.50	WMC ADR **WMC**	76e	3.8	...	81	19.75	+ 0.25
− 5.6	32.64	13.44	WMS Ind **WMS**		...	19	1626	19	+ 0.78
+ 20.4	22.50	16.25♣	WP Carey A **WPC**	1.70f	7.8	21	125	21.80	− 0.08
− 5.2	39	30.06	WPS Res **WPS**	2.10	6.0	14	610	34.89	+ 0.09
− 9.5	29.63	18.01	WP Stewart **WPL** n	1.20	5.1	12	395	23.52	+ 0.32
− 13.0	13.33	6.32	WabashNtl **WNC**	.04m	.5	dd	397	7.50	− 0.14
+ 9.3	36.60	23.50	Wachovia **WB**	.96	3.2	19	20843	30.40	+ 0.96
+ 98.4	27.40	11.44♣	Wacknhut **WAK**	j	...	69	238	26.79	− 0.04
+ 134.2	20.75	6.81♣	Wacknhut B **WAKB**	j	...	34	349	20.20	− 0.11
+ 103.3	16.60	5.88♣	WacknhutCorr **WHC**		...	17	287	14.99	− 0.05
− 29.1	38.88	23	WaddlReed A **WDR**	.35	1.3	17	1211	26.68	+ 0.07
− 24.2	45.75	28.70	Walgreen **WAG**	.14f	.4	37	32600	31.68	+ 0.20
− 2.1	20	13.69	WallaceCS **WCS**	.66	4.0	13	741	16.64	+ 0.29
+ 3.4	58.75	41.50	WalMart **WMT**	.28	.5	38	87671	54.94	+ 1.04
+ 52.7	**14.65**	**5.81**	**Walterind WLT**	**.12**	**1.0**	**dd**	**539**	**11.45**	**+ 0.82**
− 13.8	42.99	26.52	WashMut **WM** s	.96f	3.1	10	66305	30.50	− 0.23
− 11.6	94.67	62.80	WashMut PIES n	4.00	5.8	...	54	69.50	+ 0.04
− 14.5	651.50	470	WashPost B **WPO**	5.60	1.1	20	45	527.45	+ 8.53
+ 1.3	25.52	19.75♣	WashREIT **WRE**	1.33	5.6	18	758	23.94	− 0.11
− 8.6	31.85	19.25	WasteMgt **WMI**	.01	...	cc	26856	25.35	+ 0.46
+ 16.3	9.75	5.75	WtrPikTch **PIK**		...	9	156	8.14	+ 0.09
− 55.4	85.38	22.33♣	WatersCp **WAT**		...	31	6816	37.25	+ 1.09
+ 10.2	14.50	9	Watsco **WSO**	.10	.8	23	453	12.70	+ 0.25
− 6.1	66.39	42.25	WatsnPharm **WPI**		...	78	11049	48.08	− 0.42
− 16.0	28.20	14.30	WatsonWyatt A **WW**		...	14	288	19.75	+ 0.50
− 2.0	18.19	10.06	WattsInd A **WTS**	.24	1.8	16	39	13.60	− 0.29
+ 4.2	14	7.85	WausaMosin **WMO**	.34	3.2	88	644	10.55	+ 0.10
− 30.8	60.35	22.71♣	Weatherford **WFT**		...	64	16511	32.70	− 0.05
− 29.4	3.38	1.35	WeiderNutrtn A **WNI**	.15	10.0	dd	12	1.50	− 0.05
+ 13.1	50.65	38.78♣	WeingtnRlty **WRI**	3.16	6.4	19	1797	49.50	+ 0.71
+ 22.0	23.90	12.88	Westcorp **WES**	.44	2.4	10	87	18.30	+ 0.81
+ 64.1	6.25	1.95	WstnDgtl **WDC**		...	dd	8983	4	+ 0.17
− 6.0	43.50	21.63♣	WestGasRes **WGR**	.20	.6	12	838	31.65	...
− 32.5	25.88	15.62♣	WstnRes **WR**	1.20	7.2	dd	2505	16.74	...
▲+ 7.2	39.10	29.36	WestpacBk **WBK**	2.31e	5.9	...	73	39.47	+ 0.47
− 67.3	10.15	0.96	WstptStvn **WXS**	j	...	dd	1118	2.45	− 0.04
− 21.6	32.09	12.60	WestportRes **WRC**		...	8	491	17.19	+ 0.15
− 12.1	32.10	22.68	Westvaco **W**	.88	3.4	16	1772	25.65	+ 0.09
+ 39.1	**37.30**	**15.38**	**WestwdOne WON**		**...**	**67**	**2185**	**26.87**	**+ 1.37**
+ 2.3	63.50	40.50	Weyerhsr **WY**	1.60	3.1	20	3905	51.90	+ 0.45
+ 33.2	71.93	37.38	Whirlpool **WHR**	1.36	2.1	73	6440	63.51	+ 1.99
+ 15.4	392	243.88	WhiteMtnIns **WTM**	1.00m	.3	7	107	368	+ 4.00
+ 15.7	12.13	6	WhthlJwlr **JWL**		...	20	144	8.17	− 0.12
− 5.8	23.89	17.90	WileyJn A **JWA**	.18	.9	21	516	20.25	− 0.35
− 3.1	23.75	18.05	WileyJn B **JWB**	.18	.9	...	28	20.35	− 0.30
+ 0.7	50.65	34	Willamet **WLL**	.92	1.9	18	5464	47.25	− 0.01
+ 136.9	17	4.38	WillbrosGp **WG**		...	cc	377	15.10	+ 0.52
+ 46.1	15	6.63	WilLyonHms **WLS**		...	4	163	13.70	+ 0.10
+ 80.0	21.99	7.50	WillmCoal un	2.51e	17.3	6	682	14.51	− 0.19
− 87.3	20.63	1.11	WillmsComm **WCG**		...	dd	22208	1.49	...
− 20.9	43.71	24.74	WillmsCos **WMB**	.72f	2.5	11	14667	29.01	...
+ 68.8	42.49	23	WilliamsEngy **WEG** n	2.31f	5.7	...	139	40.50	+ 0.50
+ 49.7	39.70	16	WillmSnoma **WSM**		...	35	4396	29.93	+ 0.03
+ 49.9	26.29	15.50	WillisGrp **WSH** n		...	...	1329	24.89	+ 0.39
− 5.1	67	49.88	WilmTr **WL**	1.92	3.3	16	689	58.90	+ 0.67
+ 9.1	33.38	17.26	WilsGrtbtchTch **GB**		...	52	781	30.83	− 0.47
− 42.7	33.12	10.22	WinnDixie **WIN**	1.02	9.2	26	2974	11.11	− 0.01
+ 47.8	30.75	10.75♣	Winnebago **WGO**	.20	.8	12	399	25.95	+ 0.24
+ 14.8	10.77	6.76	WinstonHtl **WXH**	1.12	13.7	15	469	8.18	+ 0.08
− 53.8	68.44	16.99	Wipro ADS **WIT**	.01e	...	...	333	23.15	+ 0.95
+ 1.4	24.62	18.44	WI Engy **WEC**	.80	3.5	13	1187	22.88	+ 0.18
+ 4.6	10.10	3.94	WiserOil **WZR**		...	3	367	5.49	− 0.21
− 8.4	38	26	Wolseley ADS **WOS** n	1.36e	4.2	...	5	32.75	+ 0.75
+ 5.9	17.65	9.84	WolvTube **WLV**		...	12	386	12.70	− 0.40
− 2.3	19.56	10.25	WlvrinWrld **WWW**	.16	1.1	15	917	14.90	...
+ 96.3	15.38	6	WldFuelSvc **INT**	.30a	2.2	9	378	13.74	− 0.54
− 26.6	22	10.31	WWF Ent **WWF**		...	69	590	11.74	+ 0.15
+ 0.8	25.14	23.20	Worldcom CorTS n	.62p	...	...	10	24.50	− 0.10
− 26.7	2.13	0.87	WldwdRest **SZ**		...	22	346	1.10	− 0.01
+ 61.2	14.88	6.38	WorthgtnInd **WOR**	.64	4.9	30	2338	13	+ 0.05
▲+ 10.4	52.68	38.84	Wrigley **WWY** s	.76	1.4	34	3057	52.90	+ 0.62
− 66.3	3	0.50	Wyndhm A **WYN**		...	dd	5927	0.59	+ 0.02
			-X-Y-Z-						
▲+ 10.0	95	61.50♣	XL Cap A **XL**	1.84	1.9	dd	22414	96.12	+ 1.74
− 8.5	3.15	1.66	Xanser **XNR** s		...	4	244	2.06	+ 0.06
+ 1.5	31.85	24.19♣	XcelEngy **XEL**	1.50a	5.1	13	7608	29.50	+ 0.13
+ 55.9	11.35	3.75	Xerox **XRX**		...	dd	17425	7.21	+ 0.10
+ 105.9	22.30	6.38	Xerox CorTS **KTX**	2.00e	11.4	...	15	17.50	...
− 7.8	21.73	11.58♣	XTO Engy **XTO** s	.04	.2	7	3700	17.05	+ 0.07
− 43.2	35	16.05	YPF Soc ADR **YPF**	2.00f	11.8	...	20	17	...

EXAMPLE

From the following stock quotation table, explain the information listed for RadioShack.

+ 55.7	13.53	7.91	RPM **RPM**	.50	3.8	19	2561	13.33	+ 0.10
− 36.8	17.75	5.60	RTI IntMtls **RTI**		...	27	570	9.05	+ 0.05
− 4.5	43.87	26.91	RadianGrp **RDN** s	.08	.2	10	3411	35.86	− 0.13
− 31.2	58.94	20.10	RadioShack **RSH**	.22	.7	21	13801	29.47	+ 0.77
+ 19.4	20.85	13.81	RalcpHldg **RAH**		...	15	411	19.55	+ 0.05
+ 24.2	33	23.13	RalstonPur **RAL**	.28	.9	32	21987	32.45	− 0.12
+ 27.4	18.50	12.81	RmcoGrshn **RPT**	1.68	10.2	12	85	16.48	+ 0.13
− 41.2	**7.13**	**3.96♣**	**RangeRes RRC**	**j**	**...**	**4**	**3409**	**4.04**	**− 0.28**
− 7.8	41.35	23.36	RayJamFnl **RJF**	.36	1.1	16	1370	32.16	− 0.14
+ 14.9	47.70	34	Rayonier **RYN**	1.44	3.1	20	558	45.76	+ 0.28
+ 12.1	25.25	11.69	Rayovac **ROV**		...	28	2308	15.90	+ 0.72

SOLUTION STRATEGY

According to the listing, the year-to-date percentage change is −31.2. The 52-week high for RadioShack was $58.94 and the low was $20.10. The ticker symbol is RSH. The dividend last year was $.22 per share, the yield is .7%, and the PE ratio is 21. The volume for the day was 1,380,100 shares; and the last price was $29.47, up $.77 from the previous day.

TRY-IT | EXERCISE

4. From the following stock quotation table, explain the information listed for the common stock of Harley Davidson.

−44.8	**46.06**	**19**	**HanovrCmprsr**	**HC**		**...**	**...**	**15492**	**24.59**	**−3.41**
−0.1	40	24	♣Hanson	**HAN**	1.10e	3.2	...	78	34.23	+0.54
+45.8	24.90	12.25	Harland	**JH** x	.30	1.5	23	589	20.60	+0.35
+21.7	54.35	32	HarleyDav	**HDI**	.12	.2	36	17968	48.36	+1.08
+11.2	46.12	23.28	HarmanInt	**HAR**	.10	.2	46	1099	40.60	−0.32
+29.9	38.29	22	HarrahEntn	**HET**		...	dd	8375	34.25	...
+4.4	37	20.80	Harris	**HRS** x	.20	.6	29	2984	31.98	+0.02

Check your answers with the solutions on page 755.

20-3 Calculating Current Yield for a Stock

current yield
A percentage measure of how much an investor is earning on a stock compared with other investments. It is calculated by dividing the annual dividend per share by the current price of the stock.

One way to measure how much you are earning on a stock compared with other investments is by calculating the **current yield.** In the stock quotations, this is listed in the yield % column. The current yield is a way of evaluating the current value of a stock. It tells you how much dividend you get as a percentage of the current price of the stock. When a stock pays no dividend, there is no current yield.

STEPS TO DETERMINE THE CURRENT YIELD OF A STOCK:

Step 1. Divide the annual dividend per share by the current price of the stock:

$$\text{Current yield} = \frac{\text{Annual dividend per share}}{\text{Current price of the stock}}$$

Step 2. Convert the answer to a percent, rounded to the nearest tenth.

Everybody's Business
Real-World Connection
Investors are using their computers to trade stocks in record numbers. In 2001, roughly one in five stock trades originated from orders that were placed online. There were more than 20 million online brokerage accounts, up from just 1.5 million in 1996, according to Gomez Advisors, an Internet consulting firm in Lincoln, Massachusetts. The number of accounts is expected to top 50 million in 2004, estimates Forrester Research, of Cambridge, Massachusetts.

EXAMPLE

Calculate the current yield for Apex Corporation stock, which pays a dividend of $1.60 per year and is currently selling at $34.06 per share.

SOLUTION STRATEGY

$$\text{Current yield} = \frac{\text{Annual dividend per share}}{\text{Current price of the stock}}$$

$$\text{Current yield} = \frac{1.60}{34.06} = .0469759 = \underline{\underline{4.7\%}}$$

TRY-IT | EXERCISE

5. The Wellington Corporation paid a dividend of $.68 per share last year. If yesterday's last price was $12.84, what is the current yield on the stock?

Check your answer with the solution on page 755.

20-4 Determining the Price-Earnings Ratio of a Stock

One of the most widely used tools for analyzing a stock is the price-to-earnings ratio, commonly called the **price-earnings ratio** or **PE ratio.** This number shows the relationship between the price of a stock and the company's earnings for the past 12 months. The price-earnings ratio is an important indicator because it reflects buyer confidence in a particular stock compared with the stock market as a whole. For example, a PE ratio of 20, or 20:1, means that buyers are willing to pay 20 times the current earnings for a share of stock.

The price-earnings ratio of a stock is most useful when compared with the PE ratios of the company in previous years and with the ratios of other companies in the same industry.

price-earnings ratio, or PE ratio A ratio that shows the relationship between the price of a stock and a company's earnings for the past 12 months; one of the most widely used tools for analyzing stock.

STEPS TO DETERMINE THE PRICE-EARNINGS RATIO OF A STOCK:

Step 1. Divide the current price of the stock by the earnings per share for the past 12 months:

$$\text{Price-earnings ratio} = \frac{\text{Current price per share}}{\text{Earnings per share}}$$

Step 2. Round answer to the nearest whole number (may be written as a ratio, *X*:1).

Everybody's Business

Real-World Connection

A **bull market** is when investors *buy* in anticipation that stock prices will go up. A **bear market** is when investors *sell* in anticipation that stock prices will go down.

Many factors go into the performance of stocks. Profits and expectations of success are one area; another is the overall economic climate.

Investors are generally positive, or **bullish,** during periods of abundant money, low interest rates, tax cuts, political stability, and high employment.

Investors are generally negative, or **bearish,** during periods of tight money, high interest rates, increasing taxes, political unrest, and high unemployment.

EXAMPLE

Monarch stock is currently selling at $104.75. If the company had earnings per share of $3.60 last year, calculate the price-earnings ratio of the stock.

SOLUTION STRATEGY

$$\text{Price-earnings ratio} = \frac{\text{Current price per share}}{\text{Earnings per share}}$$

$$\text{Price-earnings ratio} = \frac{104.75}{3.60} = 29.09722 = \underline{\underline{29}} \text{ or } \underline{\underline{29:1}}$$

This means investors are currently willing to pay 29 times the earnings for one share of Monarch stock.

TRY-IT | EXERCISE

6. Sterling Industries is currently selling for $37.19 per share. If the company had earnings per share of $6.70 in the past 12 months, what is the price-earnings ratio for Sterling?

Check your answer with the solution on page 755.

20-5 Computing the Cost, Proceeds, and Gain (or Loss) on a Stock Transaction

Investors take on the risks of purchasing stocks in the hope of making money. Although they are more risky than many other types of investment, over the years stocks have shown they are capable of generating spectacular returns in some periods and steady returns in the long run. One investment strategy is to buy stocks and keep them for the dividends paid by the company each quarter. Another strategy is to make money from the profit (or

Stock exchanges are where brokers execute investors' requests to buy and sell shares of stock.

loss) of buying and selling the stock. Simply put, investors generally want to buy low and sell high! The gain or loss is the difference between the cost of purchasing the stock and the **proceeds** received when selling the stock.

Gain (or loss) on stock = Proceeds − Total cost

Stocks are generally purchased and sold through a **stockbroker.** Brokers have representatives at various **stock exchanges,** which are like a marketplace where stocks are bought and sold in the form of an auction. When you ask your broker to buy or sell a stock, the order is transmitted to the representative on the floor of the exchange. It is there that your request is *executed* or transacted.

The charge for this service is a **commission,** which is a percent of the cost of the transaction. Commission rates are competitive and vary from broker to broker. **Full-service brokers,** who provide additional services such as research data and investment advice, charge higher commissions than **discount brokers,** who simply execute the transactions.

proceeds
The amount of money that an investor receives after selling a stock. It is calculated as the value of the shares less the broker's commission.

stockbroker
A professional in stock market trading and investments who acts as an agent in the buying and selling of stocks or other securities.

stock exchanges
Marketplaces where stocks, bonds, and mutual funds are bought and sold in the form of an auction.

stockbroker's commission
The fee a stockbroker charges for assisting in the purchase or sale of shares of stock; a percent of the cost of the stock transaction.

full-service broker
Stockbrokers who provide services such as research and investment advice in addition to assisting in the purchase or sale of stock. Commissions generally range from 3% to 5% of the cost of the transaction.

discount broker
Minimum service stockbrokers who simply execute stock purchase and sale transactions. Commissions generally range from 1% to 2% of the cost of the transaction.

STEPS TO COMPUTE THE COST, PROCEEDS, AND GAIN (OR LOSS) ON A STOCK TRANSACTION:

Cost of purchasing stock

Step 1. Calculate the cost of the shares:

Cost of shares = Price per share × Number of shares

Step 2. Compute the amount of the broker's commission:

Broker's commission = Cost of shares × Commission rate

Step 3. Determine the total cost of the stock purchase:

Total cost = Cost of shares + Broker's commission

Proceeds from selling stock

Step 1. Calculate the value of shares on sale:

Value of shares = Price per share × Number of shares

Step 2. Compute the amount of the broker's commission.

Step 3. Determine the proceeds by subtracting the commission from the value of the shares:

Proceeds = Value of shares − Broker's commission

Gain (or loss) on the transaction

Gain (or loss) on transaction = Proceeds − Total cost

Another factor affecting the commission is whether the amount of shares purchased is a **round lot,** a multiple of 100, or an **odd lot,** less than 100. The commission rate on an odd lot is usually a bit higher than on a round lot. For example, the commission on a 400-share transaction might be 3%, while the commission on a 40-share transaction might be 4%.

round lot
Shares of stock purchased in multiples of 100.

odd lot
The purchase of less than 100 shares of stock.

EXAMPLE

You purchase 350 shares of General Dynamo common stock at $46.50 per share. A few months later, you sell the shares at $54.31. Your stockbroker charges 3% commission on round lots and 4% on odd lots. Calculate (a) the total cost, (b) the proceeds, and (c) the gain or loss on the transaction.

SOLUTION STRATEGY

a. *Cost of purchasing stock*

Step 1.

$$\text{Cost of shares} = \text{Price per share} \times \text{Number of shares}$$

$$\text{Cost of shares} = 46.50 \times 350 = \underline{\$16{,}275.00}$$

Step 2.

$$\text{Broker's commission} = \text{Cost of shares} \times \text{Commission rate}$$

$$\text{Round lot commission} = 300 \text{ shares} \times 46.50 \times .03 = \$418.50$$

$$\text{Odd lot commission} = 50 \text{ shares} \times 46.50 \times .04 = \$93.00$$

$$\text{Broker's commission} = 418.50 + 93.00 = \underline{\$511.50}$$

Step 3.

$$\text{Total cost} = \text{Cost of shares} + \text{Broker's commission}$$

$$\text{Total cost} = 16{,}275 + 511.50 = \underline{\underline{\$16{,}786.50}}$$

b. *Proceeds from selling stock*

Step 1.

$$\text{Value of shares} = 54.31 \times 350 = \underline{\$19{,}008.50}$$

Step 2.

$$\text{Broker's commission} = \text{Cost of shares} \times \text{Commission rate}$$

$$\text{Round lot commission} = 300 \text{ shares} \times 54.31 \times .03 = \$488.79$$

$$\text{Odd lot commission} = 50 \text{ shares} \times 54.31 \times .04 = \$108.62$$

$$\text{Broker's commission} = 488.79 + 108.62 = \underline{\$597.41}$$

Step 3.

$$\text{Proceeds} = \text{Value of shares} - \text{Broker's commission}$$

$$\text{Proceeds} = 19{,}008.50 - 597.41 = \underline{\underline{\$18{,}411.09}}$$

c. *Gain (or loss) on the transaction*

$$\text{Gain (or loss) on transaction} = \text{Proceeds} - \text{Total cost}$$

$$\text{Gain (or loss) on transaction} = 18{,}411.09 - 16{,}786.50 = \underline{\underline{\$1{,}624.59}}$$

Everybody's Business
Learning Tip
Remember, when purchasing stock, commissions are *added* to the cost of the stock to get total cost; when selling, the commissions are *deducted* by the brokerage firm from the sale price to get the proceeds of the sale.

TRY-IT | EXERCISE

7. You purchase 225 shares of Anchor Corporation common stock at $44.80 per share. A few months later, you sell the shares at $53.20. Your stockbroker charges 2% commission on round lots and 3% on odd lots. Calculate (a) the total cost, (b) the proceeds, and (c) the gain or loss on the transaction.

Check your answers with the solutions on page 756.

REVIEW EXERCISES | CHAPTER 20—SECTION I

Calculate the preferred and common dividend per share for the following companies:

	Company	Common Stock Shares	Preferred Stock Shares	Preferred Stock Div. or Par	Preferred Stock Cum.	Dividend Declared	Arrears	Preferred Div./Share	Common Div./Share
1.	Intel	5,000,000		none		$ 3,000,000	none	______	______
2.	Alcoa	10,000,000	3,000,000	$5.50	no	25,000,000	none	______	______
3.	Pepsi	8,000,000	2,000,000	$100 6%	no	10,000,000	none	______	______
4.	Wrigley	4,000,000	1,000,000	$100 4%	yes	14,000,000	1 year	______	______
5.	IBM	20,000,000	4,000,000	$6.25	yes	none	1 year	______	______

− 5.8	77.84	58.10	TotalFinaElf	**TOT**	1.46e	2.1	...	4612	68.48	− 1.12
− 29.3	**15.48**	**5.87**	**TowerAuto**	**TWR**		...	**dd**	**2063**	**6.36**	**− 0.49**
+ 9.5	22.40	16.94	TownCntry	**TCT**	1.72	8.1	24	224	21.15	+ 0.15
− 19.9	83.40	46.60	ToyotaMtr ADS	**TM**	.38e	.8	...	347	50.45	− 1.45
+ 26.1	31	14.50	ToysRUs	**TOY**		...	31	6487	21.05	+ 0.05
− 21.0	26.56	16.25	TPG ADS	**TP**	.33e	1.7	...	146	19.41	− 0.84
− 29.1	14	8.60	TramelCrow	**TCC**		...	24	255	9.57	+ 0.04
− 11.0	16.61	12.98	Transalta	**TAC** n		...	...	55	14.30	+ 0.18
+ 23.8	90.05	61	TransatlHldg	**TRH** s	.38	.4	72	125	87.35	+ 0.30
+ 9.5	13.41	9.31♣	TransCan g	**TRP**	.90g	...	...	564	12.59	− 0.01
+ 85.0	16.85	8.19	TrancntlRlty	**TCI**	j	...	4	37	16.42	+ 0.02
− 32.4	57.69	23.05♣	Transocean	**RIG**	.12	.4	49	29773	31.10	+ 0.20
− 26.8	13.95	4.61	TrMMex ADR	**TMM**	j	...	...	225	8.05	− 0.17
− 16.0	13.60	4	TMMexA ADR	**TMMA**	j	...	...	188	7.98	− 0.02
− 29.8	8.15	4.45	TrGasSur ADR	**TGS**	.59e	12.1	...	48	4.87	+ 0.05
+ 15.1	**3.80**	**1.85**	**TransPro**	**TPR**		...	**dd**	**21**	**2.95**	**+ 0.25**
+ 245.1	14.80	2.63	TransTch	**TT**	j	...	...	38	11	+ 0.08
− 3.4	21.96	14.69♣	TredegrCp	**TG**	.16	.9	19	192	16.85	− 0.05
− 11.8	40.60	27.25	Tremont	**TRE**	.28	1.0	7	10	28.18	+ 0.02
− 63.9	27.13	5.50	TrenwickGp	**TWK**	.16	1.8	dd	3158	8.96	− 0.17
− 40.5	31.20	12.29	TrexCo	**TWP**		...	17	363	14.98	− 0.04
− 18.6	37.50	23.60	TriadHosp	**TRI**		...	dd	3611	26.50	...
− 4.5	26.62	21.80	Triarc A	**TRY**		...	dd	212	23.15	− 0.05
− 16.6	45.90	29.71	Tribune	**TRB**	.44	1.2	cc	8509	35.25	+ 0.05
− 35.9	16.50	4.80	Tricom ADS	**TDR**		...	dd	87	5.15	...
+ 54.0	52.40	29.38	Tricon	**YUM**		...	17	4024	50.82	− 0.09
− 20.4	81.50	46.90♣	TrigonHlthcr A	**TGH**		...	25	2959	61.96	+ 0.33
+ 2.5	27.98	17.35	TrinityInd	**TRN**	.72	2.8	dd	517	25.63	− 0.38
− 6.5	51.91	26.56	Triton A	**TPC**		...	dd	1125	31.72	+ 0.02
− 34.2	50	21.60	TriumphGp	**TGI**		...	9	528	26.98	− 0.24
− 1.5	19.30	13.25	TrizecHahn	**TZH**	.35g	2.3	cc	2080	14.90	+ 0.20
− 45.1	3.13	0.83	TrumpHtls	**DJT**		...	dd	695	1.03	− 0.09
+ 1.9	26	16.94	Tupperware	**TUP**	.88	4.2	22	968	20.83	+ 0.08
− 76.9	**104.07**	**5.90**	**Turkcell ADS**	**TKC** s	**.65e**	**4.4**	...	**694**	**14.70**	**+ 1.07**
+ 15.1	19.57	13.13	21CentIns	**TW**	.32	2.0	91	276	16.40	+ 0.05

Answer Exercises 6–10 based on the stock quotation table to the left:

6. Tupperware—High and low for the past 52 weeks: ________________

7. Town & Country—Ticker symbol, PE ratio, and last price: ________________

8. Transocean—Dividend, volume, net change: ________________

9. Tribune—Percent yield, volume, last price: ________________

10. Toyota Motors—Dividend, percent yield, 52-week low: ________________

Calculate the missing information for the following stocks:

	Company	Earnings per Share	Annual Dividend	Current Price per Share	Current Yield	Price-Earnings Ratio
11.	Sears	$6.59	$1.60	$46.13	_____	_____
12.	Wendy's	.77	.24	17.63	_____	_____
13.	Rubbermaid	_____	.45	27.50	_____	21
14.	Ford	4.92	1.60	_____	2.5%	_____
15.	Disney	_____	_____	42.38	.7%	30

Calculate the total cost, proceeds, and gain (or loss) for the following stock market transactions:

	Company	Number of Shares	Purchase Price	Selling Price	Commissions Buy	Commissions Sell	Commissions Odd Lot	Total Cost	Proceeds	Gain (or Loss)
16.	DuPont	100	$47.20	$56.06	3%	3%		______	______	______
17.	Wal-Mart	350	18.42	29.19	2	2	add 1%	______	______	______
18.	Heinz	900	28.37	36.25	3	3		______	______	______
19.	Goodyear	775	37.75	34.50	1.5	1.5	add 1%	______	______	______
20.	AmExpress	500	25.11	28.86	3	3		______	______	______

21. The Maxtor Corporation has 500,000 shares of common stock outstanding. If a dividend of $425,000 was declared by the company directors last year, what is the dividend per share of common stock?

22. The board of directors of Saratoga, Inc., has declared a dividend of \$3,000,000. The company has 700,000 shares of preferred stock that pay \$.90 per share and 1,600,000 shares of common stock.

 a. What are the dividends due the preferred shareholders?

 b. What is the dividend per share of common stock?

23. Keller Corporation has 1,800,000 shares of \$100 par value, 5%, cumulative preferred stock and 9,750,000 shares of common stock. Although no dividend was declared for the past 2 years, a \$44,000,000 dividend has been declared for this year.

 a. How much is due the preferred shareholders?

 b. What is the dividend per share of common stock?

24. Alpha Airlines is currently selling at \$47.35. The earnings per share is \$3.14, and the dividend is \$1.70.

 a. What is the current yield of the stock?

 b. What is the price-earnings ratio?

25. You purchase 650 shares of Prism Corporation common stock at \$44.25 per share. A few months later, you sell the shares at \$57.29. Your stockbroker charges 3% commission on round lots and an extra $1\frac{1}{2}$% on odd lots.

 a. What is the total cost of the purchase?

 b. What are the proceeds on the sale?

 c. What is the gain or loss on the transaction?

BUSINESS DECISION

Dollar-Cost Averaging

26. Though investing all at once works best when stock prices are rising, *dollar-cost averaging* can be a good way to take advantage of a fluctuating market. Dollar-cost averaging is an investment strategy designed to reduce volatility in which securities are purchased in *fixed dollar amounts at regular intervals*, regardless of what direction the market is moving. This strategy is also called *the constant dollar plan.*

You are considering a hypothetical $1,200 investment in Polynomial Corporation stock. Your choice is to invest the money all at once or dollar-cost average at the rate of $100 per month for one year.

a. If you invested all of the money in January, and bought the shares for $10.00 each, how many shares could you buy?

b. From the following chart of share prices, calculate the number of shares that would be purchased each month using dollar-cost averaging and the total shares for the year.

Month	Amount Invested	Cost per Share	Shares Purchased	Month	Amount Invested	Cost per Share	Shares Purchased
January	$100	$10.00	______	July	$100	$11.50	______
February	100	9.55	______	August	100	10.70	______
March	100	8.80	______	September	100	9.80	______
April	100	7.75	______	October	100	10.60	______
May	100	9.15	______	November	100	9.45	______
June	100	10.25	______	December	100	10.15	______

c. What is the average price you pay per share if you purchase them all in January?

d. What is the average price you pay per share if you purchase them using dollar-cost averaging?

SECTION II

BONDS

20-6 Understanding Bonds and Reading Bond Quotations

bond
A loan or an IOU in the form of an interest-bearing note, in which the bond buyer lends money to the bond issuer. Used by corporations and governments to borrow money on a long-term basis.

secured bonds
Bonds that are backed by a lien on specific collateral such as a plant, equipment, or other corporate asset.

A **bond** is a loan, or an IOU, where the bond buyer lends money to the bond issuer. With stock, the investor becomes a part-owner of the corporation; with bonds, the investor becomes a creditor. Bonds are known as fixed-income securities because the issuer promises to pay a specified amount of interest on a regular basis, usually semiannually. Although stock is issued only by corporations, bonds are issued by corporations and governments. The federal government, as well as states and local municipalities, issues bonds. The funds raised are used to finance general operations and specific projects such as schools, highways, bridges, and airports. An example of a bond certificate is shown in Exhibit 20-4.

Corporate bonds represent the number one source of corporate borrowing for both large and small companies. Corporations use the money raised from bonds to finance modernization and expansion programs. **Secured bonds** are backed by a lien on a plant,

Bonds were issued to pay part of the construction costs of the Golden Gate Bridge.

equipment, or other corporate asset. **Unsecured bonds,** also known as **debentures,** are backed only by the general credit of the issuing corporation. Some bonds are **convertible,** which means they can be converted into, or exchanged for, a specified number of shares of common stock. **Callable** bonds give the issuer the right to call or redeem the bonds before the maturity date. Calling bonds might occur when interest rates are falling and the company can issue new bonds at a lower rate.

When bonds are issued by a corporation, they may be purchased by investors at par value, usually $1,000, and held until the maturity date; or they may be bought and sold through a broker on the secondary or resale market. Bonds pay a fixed interest rate, also known as the **coupon rate.** This rate is a fixed percentage of the par value that will be paid to the bondholder on a regular basis.

unsecured bonds, or debentures
Bonds that are backed only by the general credit of the issuing corporation, not on specific collateral pledged as security.

convertible bonds
Bonds that can be converted or exchanged at the owner's option for a certain number of shares of common stock.

callable bonds
Bonds that the issuer has the right to call or repurchase before the maturity date. Bonds are called when interest rates are falling and the company can issue new bonds at a lower rate.

coupon rate
A fixed percentage of the par value of a bond that is paid to the bondholder on a regular basis.

EXHIBIT 20-4
Bond Certificate

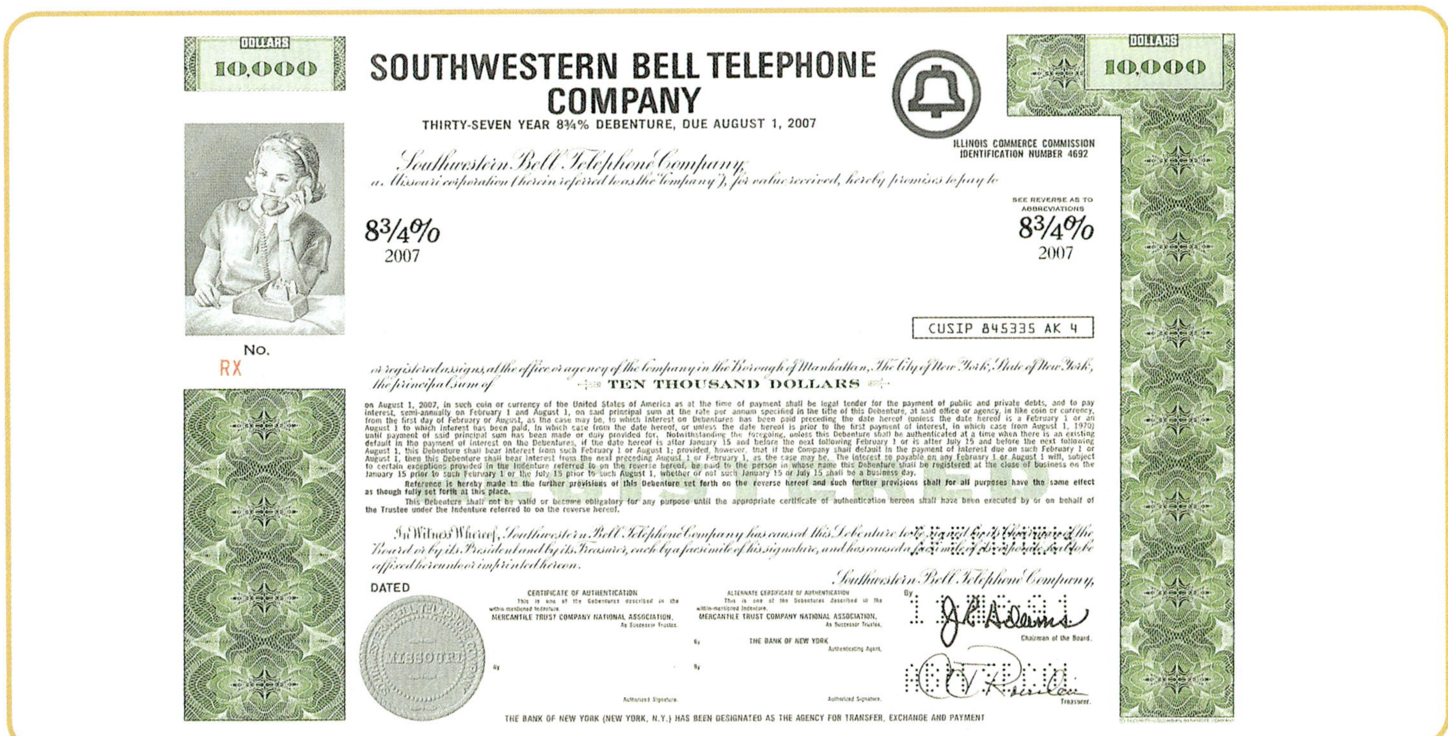

For example, a company might issue a $1,000 par value, 7% bond, maturing in the year 2025. The bondholder in this case would receive a fixed interest payment of $70 per year (1,000 × .07), or $35 semiannually, until the bond matures. At maturity, the company repays the loan by paying the bondholder the par value of the bond.

During the period between the issue date and the maturity date, bond prices fluctuate in the opposite direction of prevailing interest rates. Let's say you buy a bond with a coupon rate of 8%. If interest rates in the marketplace fall to 7%, newly issued bonds will have a rate lower than yours, thus making yours more attractive and driving the price above the par value. When this occurs, the bonds are said to be selling at a **premium.** However, if interest rates rise to 9%, new bonds would have a higher rate than yours, thus making yours less attractive and pushing the price down, below par. If bonds sell below par, it is known as selling at a **discount.** Remember, at maturity the bond returns to its par value.

premium
When a bond is selling for more than its par value, it is said to be selling at a premium. This occurs during periods when prevailing interest rates are declining.

discount
When a bond is selling for less than its par value, it is said to be selling at a discount. This occurs during periods when prevailing interest rates are rising.

Just as with stocks, bond prices are listed in the financial section of most newspapers. Bonds are identified alphabetically by the abbreviated name of the issuer. Let's take a column-by-column look at a typical day's listing for Ryder $9\frac{7}{8}$17. Exhibit 20-5 is a portion of such a table, reprinted from *The Wall Street Journal.*

Column 1 (Bonds—Ryder $9\frac{7}{8}$17) Specifically identifies the issuing company, the coupon rate, and the last two numbers of the maturity date of the bond. For example, Ryder $9\frac{7}{8}$17 means Ryder bond, with a coupon rate of $9\frac{7}{8}$%, maturing in the year 2017.

Column 2 (Cur Yld—8.1) The current percent yield of the bond. The yield for the Ryder bond is 8.1%. As with stocks, the yield fluctuates with the current price of the bond. A "cv" in this column indicates the bond is convertible.

Column 3 (Vol—10) Indicates the volume or number of bonds sold. Ten Ryder bonds were sold.

Column 4 (Close—108) The closing or last price of the trading day. Bond prices are listed as a percent of the par value of $1,000. For example, the Ryder bond, listed at 108, is selling for $1,080.00 (1,000 × 1.08). A bond selling for 126 would be $1,260 (1,000 × 1.26).

Column 5 (Net Chg.—2) Indicates the difference in price from the previous close. As with closing prices, the net change is listed as a percent of the par value. The Ryder bond closed down 2, or $20 (1,000 × .02).

◆ EXHIBIT 20-5 ◆
The Wall Street Journal
New York Exchange Bonds

1	2	3	4	5
BONDS	CUR YLD.	VOL.	CLOSE	NET CHG.
Consec 8⅛03	9.9	81	82	+ ⅜
Conseco 10½04	12.5	40	84	− 1
Conseco 10¼02	11.0	106	93 15/32	+ 15/32
CnNG 6⅝08	6.7	4	99½	+ 1½
ConPort 11s06	13.6	3	81	+ 1
CoxCm 3s30	cv	2	46	− 2
CrownC 7⅛02	11.3	228	63	− 1
CrwnCk 7⅜26	16.8	50	44	...
CypSemi 4s05	cv	6	91	+ 1⅜
DVI 9⅞04	10.0	135	98½	...
DelcoR 8⅝07	8.7	15	99	− 1
DevonE 4.9s08	cv	11	101⅜	+ ⅛
DevonE 4.95s08	cv	55	102½	+ 2¼
Dole 7s03	6.9	20	101	...
Dole 7⅞13	7.9	45	99¼	− ½
DukeEn 6¾25	6.7	25	100⅜	...
DukeEn 7½25	7.1	7	105⅝	+ 1⅞
DukeEn 7s33	7.0	2	100½	− 1⅝
FedDS 8½03	8.0	50	106⅛	− ⅛
FordCr 6⅜08	6.4	10	100	+ ½
GBCB 8⅜07	8.8	10	95¾	...
GMA 6⅜01	6.4	5	100	+ 5/32
GMA 5½01	5.5	8	99 15/16	...
GMA 7s02	6.9	10	101 5/16	...
GMA 6⅛08	6.2	5	99	− 1⅜
GMA dc6s11	6.4	20	93⅞	− ¾
NYTel 7s33	6.9	18	101¾	− ⅛
OreStl 11s03	11.5	209	96	+ 4
ParkerD 5½04	cv	1	88⅛	+ ½
PhilPt 7.92s23	7.6	13	104	...
PrmHsp 9¼06	9.1	20	101¾	− ¼
PSEG 6½04	6.2	70	104⅝	+ ⅞
PSvEG 7s24	7.0	15	100¼	+ ⅛
Quanx 6.88s07	cv	157	100⅞	+ ¾
RalsP 8⅝22	7.3	10	118¼	− 1⅞
ReynTob 8⅝02	7.7	6	103⅜	+ ⅜
ReynTob 7⅝03	7.4	10	102½	− ¼
ReynTob 8¾04	8.4	155	103¾	− 1
ReynTob 8¾05	8.3	5	106	...
ReynTob 8¾07	8.3	10	105¼	− ⅛
ReynTob 9¼13	8.5	3	109	+ 1
Ryder 9⅞17	8.1	10	108	− 2
Safwy 10s01	10.0	5	100	...
Safwy 9.65s04	8.8	5	109⅝	− ⅛
Safwy 9.3s07	8.0	5	115⅝	− 2⅜
SalSB 03t	...	10	99⅛	+ ⅛
SilicnGr 5¼04	cv	95	49½	− ¼
Sizeler 8s03	cv	70	98	+ ¾
Solectrn zrM20	...	10	52	− 1
StdCmcl 07	cv	57	91	+ ½
StdPac 8½07	8.7	283	97¼	+ ¾
TVA 8¼42	6.9	3	120	+ 3¼
Tenet 6s05	cv	15	100	+ ¼

Everybody's Business
Real-World Connection

Treasury bonds are fully guaranteed by the U.S. government and therefore have lower interest rates than those of other issuers such as corporations and municipalities.

Because corporate and municipal bonds carry a "risk factor," prospective purchasers can use **bond ratings** to evaluate how safe one bond is compared with another.

Bonds with lower ratings carry a higher risk and therefore must offer higher interest rates to attract investors. Bonds with low ratings are often referred to as **junk bonds.**

EXAMPLE

From the following bond quotation table, explain the information listed for Dole:

Dole 7⅞13	8.1	95	97¾	+	2¼	PSEG 6⅞03	6.7	100	103	+	¾
DukeEn 6¾25	6.8	12	99½	−	½	PSvEG 7s24	6.9	10	101⅞	+	1⅜
FedDS 8⅛02	7.8	10	103¾		...	Quanx 6.88s07	cv	60	101	+	½
FnclFed 4½05	cv	42	98		...	RalsP 7⅞25	7.0	15	112	+	3⅝
FordCr 6⅜08	6.4	25	99½		...	ReynTob 8⅝02	7.8	75	102⅜	−	⅝
Fortune 8½03	8.1	70	105	−	½	ReynTob 7⅝03	7.4	5	103⅜	+	⅞
FourSeas zr29	...	8	24⅜	+	⅜	ReynTob 8¾05	8.3	5	104⅞	+	⅛
GBCB 8⅜07	8.8	26	95¾	+	2	ReynTob 9¼13	8.6	10	107⅞	+	1
GMA 5½01	5.5	5	99 15/16		...	Safwy 10s01	10.0	5	100 5/32	+	1/16

SOLUTION STRATEGY

According to the listing, the Dole bond has a coupon rate of $7\frac{7}{8}\%$ and will mature in the year 2013. The current yield is 8.1%, and the volume for the day was 95 bonds traded. The bond is selling for \$977.50 (1,000 × .9775). The net change in price from the previous trading day is up $2\frac{1}{4}$ or \$22.50 (1,000 × .0225).

TRY-IT EXERCISE

8. From the bond quotation table above, explain the information listed for Fortune:

Check your answers with the solutions on page 756.

20-7 Computing the Cost of Purchasing Bonds and the Proceeds from the Sale of Bonds

Similar to stocks, when bonds are bought and sold a brokerage charge is commonly added to the price of each bond. Although there is no standard commission, the charge is generally between \$5 and \$10 per bond. As noted earlier, bonds pay interest semiannually, such as on January 1 and July 1. When bonds are traded between the stated interest payment dates, the interest accumulated from the last payment date must be paid to the seller by the buyer. This interest due to the seller is known as the **accrued interest.**

Accrued interest of a bond is calculated by using the simple interest formula, $I = PRT$, where P is the face value of the bond, R is the coupon rate, and T is the number of days since the last payment date divided by 360. When time is stated in months, divide by 12.

accrued interest When bonds are traded between the stated interest payment dates, the interest accumulated from the last payment date that must be paid to the seller by the buyer.

STEPS TO CALCULATE THE COST OF PURCHASING A BOND:

Step 1. Calculate the accrued interest on the bond since the last payment date using $I = PRT$.

Step 2. Calculate the price to purchase the bond:

Price per bond = Current market price + Accrued interest + Commission

Step 3. Calculate total purchase price:

Total purchase price = Price per bond × Number of bonds purchased

EXAMPLE

What is the purchase price of 10 Crystal Corporation bonds with a coupon rate of $9\frac{1}{2}$ and a current market price of 107? The commission charge is \$5.00 per bond. The date of the transaction is April 1, and the bond pays interest on January 1 and July 1.

SOLUTION STRATEGY

Step 1. Because the time since the last payment is 3 months, we shall use $T = \frac{3}{12}$.

$$\text{Accrued interest} = 1{,}000 \times .095 \times \frac{3}{12} = \underline{\$23.75}$$

Step 2. Price per bond = Current market price + Accrued interest + Commission

Price per bond = 1,070.00 + 23.75 + 5.00 = $\underline{\$1{,}098.75 \text{ per bond}}$

Step 3. Total purchase price = Price per bond × Number of bonds

Total purchase price = 1,098.75 × 10 = $\underline{\underline{\$10{,}987.50}}$

TRY-IT | EXERCISE

9. What is the purchase price of 20 SilverLake Corporation bonds with a coupon rate of $6\frac{1}{4}$ and a current market price of $91\frac{3}{8}$? The commission charge is $10.00 per bond. The date of the transaction is October 1, and the bond pays interest on February 1 and August 1.

Check your answer with the solution on page 756.

STEPS TO CALCULATE THE PROCEEDS FROM THE SALE OF A BOND:

Step 1. Calculate the accrued interest on the bond since the last payment date by using $I = PRT$.

Step 2. Calculate the proceeds per bond by

Proceeds = Current market price + Accrued interest − Commission

Step 3. Calculate the total proceeds from the sale by

Total proceeds = Proceeds per bond × Number of bonds sold

EXAMPLE

What are the proceeds of the sale of 15 Tornado Corporation bonds with a coupon rate of $7\frac{1}{8}$ and a current market price of 111? The commission charge is $7.50 per bond. The date of the transaction is 71 days since the last interest payment.

SOLUTION STRATEGY

Step 1.

$$\text{Accrued interest} = 1{,}000 \times .07125 \times \frac{71}{360} = \underline{\$14.05}$$

Step 2. Proceeds per bond = Current market price + Accrued interest − Commission

Proceeds per bond = 1,110.00 + 14.05 − 7.50 = $\underline{\$1{,}116.55}$

Step 3. Total proceeds = Proceeds per bond × Number of bonds sold

Total proceeds = 1,116.55 × 15 = $\underline{\underline{\$16{,}748.25}}$

TRY-IT | EXERCISE

10. What are the proceeds of the sale of five Mercantile Corporation bonds with a coupon rate of $8\frac{7}{8}$ and a current market price of 99? The commission charge is \$10.00 per bond. The date of the transaction is 122 days since the last interest payment.

Check your answer with the solution on page 756.

20-8 Calculating the Current Yield for a Bond

Just as with stocks, the current yield of a bond is a simple measure of the return on investment based on the current market price. When bonds are purchased at par, the current yield is equal to the coupon rate. For example, a bond purchased at par for \$1,000, with a coupon rate of 7%, pays interest of \$70 per year (1,000 × .07), and has a yield of 7% ($\frac{70}{1,000} = .07$). If the bond is purchased at a discount, say, \$875, it still pays \$70; however, the yield is 8% ($\frac{70}{875} = .08$). If the bond is purchased at a premium, say, \$1,165, it still pays \$70; however, now the yield is only 6% ($\frac{70}{1,165} = .06$).

STEPS TO CALCULATE CURRENT YIELD FOR A BOND:

Step 1. Calculate the annual interest and current price of the bond.

Step 2. Divide the annual interest of the bond by the current market price:

$$\text{Current yield} = \frac{\text{Annual interest}}{\text{Current market price}}$$

Step 3. Convert the answer to a percent, rounded to the nearest tenth.

Everybody's Business

Learning Tip

Remember, bond interest is always constant, regardless of what you paid for the bond; the yield is what varies, depending on the current price of the bond.

EXAMPLE

Calculate the current yield for a Revco Electronics bond with a coupon rate of $13\frac{1}{2}\%$ and currently selling at a premium of $107\frac{1}{4}$.

SOLUTION STRATEGY

Annual interest = Par value × Coupon rate = 1,000 × .135 = $\underline{\$135}$

Current price = Par value × Price percent = 1,000 × 1.0725 = $\underline{\$1,072.50}$

$$\text{Current yield} = \frac{\text{Annual interest}}{\text{Current market price}} = \frac{135}{1,072.50} = .12587 = \underline{\underline{12.6\%}}$$

TRY-IT | EXERCISE

11. Calculate the current yield for a Wakefield Industries bond with a coupon rate of $9\frac{3}{8}\%$ and currently selling at a discount of $84\frac{3}{4}$.

Check your answer with the solution on page 756.

REVIEW EXERCISES | CHAPTER 20—SECTION II

Answer Exercises 1–10 based on the following bond quotation table:

CORPORATION BONDS

Bonds	Cur Yld.	Vol.	Close	Net Chg.
AES05	...	13	93⅛	− 2⅞
AMR 9s16	7.6	32	118	+ ½
ATT 6¾04	6.4	35	105⅝	− ⅛
ATT 7s05	6.6	1	106⅝	− 1⅛
ATT 7½06	6.7	65	111¼	− ⅜
ATT 8⅛22	7.6	24	107⅝	...
ATT 8⅛24	7.5	20	107¾	...
ATT 8⅝31	7.7	10	112⅝	− 1⅜
Aames 10½02	11.6	23	90⅝	− ⅜
Aetna 6⅜03	6.4	60	100	+ ⅝
Alza 5s06	cv	3	143⅛	− ¾
Amresco 8¾05	8.8	50	99¼	+ 23/32
Amresco 10s03	12.1	5	82½	− ¾
Amresco 10s04	12.5	158	80¼	+ ¼
AnnTaylr 8¾04	8.6	115	101¼	− ⅛
Apache 9¼02	8.4	10	110	+ 3½
Argosy 12s01	cv	50	103	− 1
Argosy 13¼04	11.8	100	112¾	...
HlthcrR 6.55s02	cv	35	90½	...
Hlthso 9½06	9.3	15	102½	− 1
HewlPkd zr17	...	15	56½	+ ¼
Hexcel 7s03	cv	80	90	− 2
Hills 12½03f	...	10	95½	− 1
Hilton 5s06	cv	115	96⅝	...
HomeDpt 3¼09	cv	5	236	− 1
IRT Pr 7.3s03	cv	15	98	− 1¾
InldStl 7.9s07	8.0	10	98⅝	− ¾
IntgHlth 5¾06	cv	373	75½	− 6½
IBM 6⅜10	6.3	5	101½	...
IBM 7¼11	6.9	10	105	− ¼
IBM 7s25	6.5	5	107¼	+ ⅛
IBM 6½28	6.1	15	106	+ 3
JCPL 7½23	7.2	10	104½	+ ½
KCS En 8⅞08	20.9	366	42½	− ½
KaufB 9⅜03	9.2	10	102¼	...
KaufB 7¾04	7.8	92	100	− ⅜
KaufB 9⅝06	9.0	45	106⅞	− ⅜
KentE 4½04	cv	145	77½	-- ⅛

1. Aetna—Coupon rate and current yield: ______________________

2. IBM $6\frac{1}{2}28$—Closing price and net change: ______________________

3. AnnTaylr—Maturity year and volume: ______________________

4. Apache—Volume and closing price: ______________________

5. AMR—Coupon rate, maturity year, and net change: ______________________

6. Aames—Current yield and closing price: ______________________

7. Which bonds are selling for exactly par value? ______________________

8. Which bond has the highest current yield? ______________________

9. Which bond had the greatest net change? How much? ______________________

10. Which bond had the highest price? How much? ______________________

Calculate the accrued interest and the total purchase price of the following bond purchases:

	Company	Coupon Rate	Market Price	Time Since Last Interest	Accrued Interest	Commission per Bond	Bonds Purchased	Total Price
11.	Xerox	$5\frac{1}{2}$	$86\frac{1}{4}$	2 months	________	$5.00	1	________
12.	U.S. West	$7\frac{1}{4}$	$102\frac{1}{2}$	78 days	________	4.50	5	________
13.	AT&T	$8\frac{3}{8}$	95	5 months	________	10.00	8	________
14.	Hilton	$9\frac{1}{2}$	$79\frac{3}{4}$	23 days	________	9.75	15	________
15.	Ford	$6\frac{5}{8}$	$111\frac{7}{8}$	3 months	________	8.00	10	________

Calculate the accrued interest and the total proceeds of the following bond sales:

	Company	Coupon Rate	Market Price	Time Since Last Interest	Accrued Interest	Commission per Bond	Bonds Solds	Total Proceeds
16.	Textron	$6\frac{1}{4}$	$91\frac{1}{2}$	21 days	______	$6.00	10	______
17.	Apple	$8\frac{1}{2}$	$108\frac{3}{4}$	4 months	______	8.50	4	______
18.	USX	$10\frac{5}{8}$	77	85 days	______	12.00	15	______
19.	Mobil	$9\frac{3}{4}$	$89\frac{3}{8}$	1 month	______	7.25	7	______
20.	Nabisco	$6\frac{5}{8}$	$104\frac{1}{8}$	39 days	______	9.00	20	______

Calculate the annual interest and current yield for the following bonds:

	Company	Coupon Rate	Annual Interest	Market Price	Current Yield	
21.	Kroger	$6\frac{5}{8}$	______	$91\frac{1}{8}$	______	1
22.	Bordens	$9\frac{1}{4}$	______	108	______	
23.	Blockbuster	$7\frac{1}{2}$	______	$125\frac{1}{4}$	______	2
24.	McDonald's	$11\frac{7}{8}$	______	$73\frac{1}{2}$	______	
25.	Pacific Telesis	$5\frac{3}{8}$	______	$84\frac{3}{8}$	______	

26. On March 1, Kimberly Lipscomb bought 10 Slick Oil Company bonds with a coupon rate of $9\frac{1}{8}$. The purchase price was $88\frac{7}{8}$, and the commission was $6.00 per bond. Slick Oil bonds pay interest on February 1 and August 1.

a. What is the current yield of the bond?

b. What is the total purchase price of the bonds?

c. If Kimberly sold the bonds on November 1 for $93\frac{7}{8}$, what are the proceeds from the sale?

BUSINESS DECISION

Taxable or Tax-free Bonds

27. More than 50,000 state and local governments and their agencies borrow money by issuing **municipal bonds** to build, repair, or improve schools, streets, highways, hospitals, sewer systems, and so on. When the federal income tax law was adopted in 1913, interest on municipal bonds was excluded from federal taxation. As a result, municipal bond investors are willing to accept lower yields than those they can obtain from taxable bonds.

As part of your portfolio, you are considering investing $50,000 in bonds. You have the choice of investing in tax-exempt municipal bonds yielding 5.5% or corporate bonds yielding 7.5% in taxable interest income.

a. What is the annual interest income and tax status of the municipal bond investment?

b. What is the annual interest income and tax status of the corporate bond investment?

c. If you are in the 30% marginal tax bracket for federal income taxes and your state and local taxes on that income amount to an additional 6%, what is the after-tax income on the corporate bonds?

d. What is the actual percent yield realized on the corporate bonds after taxes?

SECTION III

MUTUAL FUNDS

20-9 Understanding Mutual Funds and Reading Mutual Fund Quotations

mutual funds, or investment trusts Corporations that are investment pools of money with a wide variety of investment goals.

Mutual funds are a very popular way of investing. Essentially, mutual funds are professionally managed investment companies that pool the money from many individuals and invest it in stocks, bonds, and other securities. Most individual investors do not have the time or the ability to research the literally thousands of investment possibilities. By pooling the financial resources of thousands of shareholders, mutual funds can use the expertise of the country's top professional money managers.

Mutual funds are corporations known as **investment trusts.** Their assets are stocks and bonds purchased with the hope that the value of the securities will increase. Investors purchase shares of stock of the fund. If the fund is successful in its investments, it pays dividends and capital gains to its shareholders.

With mutual funds, instead of choosing individual stocks and bonds, investors pick a fund with financial goals similar to their own. These range from high-risk aggressive growth goals, such as investing in new and unproven companies and industries, to more moderate-risk goals, such as steady income and balanced growth and income, which is achieved by investing in large and established companies. Most mutual fund companies offer several different funds known as a *family.* Investors are free to move their money back and forth among them as their investment goals or market conditions change.

Just as with the stock prices of other corporations, mutual fund stock prices fluctuate up and down on a daily basis and can be tracked in the financial section of most newspapers. Let's take a column-by-column look at a typical day's listing for a mutual fund in the GT Global family, known as Amer p. Exhibit 20-6 is a portion of such a table, as listed in *The Wall Street Journal.*

Everybody's Business

Real-World Connection

In 1998, a milestone was reached: Mutual fund assets crossed $5 trillion for the first time, according to the Investment Company Institute, the fund industry's main trade group.

That sum, which rivals the deposits Americans have in banks, was up from $4.5 trillion at the end of 1997, $1.1 trillion at the end of 1990, and less than $300 billion in 1982.

	Inv. Obj.	NAV	Offer Price	NAV Chg.	Total Return YTD	Total Return 39 wks	Total Return 5 yrs	R
LtdGv	BST	9.70	NL	+0.04	−1.4	0.0	+7.9	C
LTG	BND	10.83	NL	+0.14	−10.3	−7.3	NS	..
MD Mu	SSM	9.62	NL	+0.07	−5.9	NA	NS	..
MunIn r	GLM	10.08	NL	+0.07	−6.1	−1.4	NS	..
NJHY r	MNJ	10.94	NL	+0.07	−5.9	−1.9	+8.3	C
NYHY r	DNY	10.29	NL	+0.09	−6.1	−2.4	NS	..
PAHY r	MPA	10.29	NL	+0.07	−4.9	−0.4	+8.6	B
ShtInc	BST	9.36	NL	−0.02	−4.3	−1.2	NS	..
SIntGv	BST	9.53	NL	+0.04	−2.0	−0.4	NS	..
ShtMu	STM	9.80	NL	+0.03	−1.7	+1.0	+6.5	B
FiduCap	GRO	18.46	NL	+0.13	−6.0	+2.0	+10.3	C
59 Wall St:								
EuroEq	ITL	30.02	30.02	+0.01	−5.2	+17.1	NS	..
PacBsn	ITL	39.06	39.06	−0.64	−15.3	+26.9	NS	..
Sm Co	SML	11.61	11.61	+0.20	−7.1	−0.1	NS	..
TxFSI	STM	10.14	10.14	+0.02	−1.0	+1.0	NS	..
FinHorGv t	BND	10.53	10.53	+0.09	−3.5	−2.3	+10.1	A
FinHorMu	GLM	10.34	10.34	+0.13	−8.8	NA	+7.1	E
First American Cl A:								
AstAll p	S&B	10.21	10.69	+0.13	−3.2	+1.1	NS	..
Balanced p	S&B	10.46	10.95	+0.12	−1.8	+2.4	NS	..
EqIdxA p	G&I	10.34	10.83	+0.15	−3.3	+1.5	NS	..
FxdInc p	BND	10.70	11.12	+0.05	−2.5	−0.3	+9.2	C
GovBd p	BIN	9.16	9.44	+0.04	−1.9	−0.2	+7.2	E
IntInc p	BIN	9.73	10.11	+0.03	−1.7	−0.3	NS	..
LtdInc	BST	9.92	10.12	−0.01	−0.1	+1.6	NS	..
MtgSec p	BND	9.96	10.35	+0.02	−2.0	+0.5	NS	..
MunBd p	IDM	10.43	10.75	+0.06	−3.0	+0.1	+6.4	E
RegEq p	SML	11.83	12.39	+0.08	−3.1	+6.0	NS	..
SpecEq p	CAP	15.51	16.24	+0.07	−0.8	+6.9	+11.1	C
Stock p	G&I	15.97	16.72	+0.24	−0.4	+5.8	+11.2	B
First American Cl C:								
AstAllI	S&B	10.20	NL	+0.12	NS	NS	NS	..
BalanceI	S&B	10.46	NL	+0.12	NS	NS	NS	..
EqIdxI	G&I	10.34	NL	+0.15	NS	NS	NS	..
FxdIncI	BND	10.70	NL	+0.05	NS	NS	NS	..
GovBdI	BIN	9.16	NL	+0.04	NS	NS	NS	..
IntIncI	BIN	9.73	NL	+0.03	NS	NS	NS	..
LtdIncI	BST	9.92	NL	−0.01	NS	NS	NS	..
MunBd	IDM	10.43	NL	+0.06	NS	NS	NS	..
MtgSecI	BND	9.96	NL	+0.02	NS	NS	NS	..
ReqEq	SML	11.83	NL	+0.08	NS	NS	NS	..
SpecEqI	CAP	15.50	NL	+0.06	NS	NS	NS	..
StockI	G&I	15.97	NL	+0.25	NS	NS	NS	..
FtBosIG	BND	9.32	9.56	+0.06	−3.1	−1.7	NS	..

1	2	3	4	5	6	7	8	9
	Inv. Obj.	NAV	Offer Price	NAV Chg.	Total Return YTD	Total Return 39 wks	Total Return 5 yrs	R
S&S PM	G&I	35.45	NL	+0.48	−4.2	+0.8	+11.1	B
GE Funds:								
IncomeA	BIN	11.57	12.08	+0.07	−2.8	NS	NS	..
Global C	WOR	18.35	NL	+0.10	−2.2	+15.7	NS	..
IntlEqD	...	14.47	NL	+0.03	NA	NA	NA	..
Strag C	S&B	15.31	NL	+0.13	−4.0	+0.6	NS	..
US Eq A	G&I	15.55	16.33	+0.21	−4.4	NS	NS	..
US Eq C	G&I	15.57	NL	+0.21	−4.2	+0.8	NS	..
US Eq D	G&I	15.58	NL	+0.21	−4.2	NS	NS	..
GIT Invst:								
EqSpc	SML	19.26	NL	+0.05	−2.5	+8.6	+7.5	E
TFNatl	HYM	10.02	NL	+0.06	−7.2	−3.5	+6.5	E
TFVA	SSM	10.86	NL	+0.08	−6.7	−2.9	+6.8	E
GT Global:								
Amer p	GRO	17.98	18.88	+0.09	+4.7	+23.2	+16.0	A
EmMktA	ITL	14.95	15.70	−0.02	−14.1	+24.7	NS	..
EmMktB	ITL	14.90	14.90	−0.02	−14.3	+24.2	NS	..
EuroA p	ITL	10.56	11.09	+0.02	−2.6	+12.5	+4.2	D
EuroB	ITL	10.49	10.49	+0.02	−2.8	+11.9	NS	..
GvIncA p	WBD	9.04	9.49	+0.03	−10.8	−1.6	+9.5	B
GovIncB	WBD	9.04	9.04	+0.03	−11.0	−2.1	NS	..
GrIncA p	WOR	6.04	6.34	...	−5.0	+7.8	NS	..
GrIncB	WOR	6.04	6.04	...	−5.3	+7.0	NS	..
HltCr p	SEC	17.51	18.38	+0.25	−7.7	+4.0	NS	..
HltCrB	SEC	17.42	17.42	+0.24	−7.9	+3.5	NS	..
HiIncA	WBD	11.32	11.88	−0.19	−24.8	−9.0	NS	..
HiIncB	WBD	11.31	11.31	−0.19	−24.9	−9.4	NS	..
IntlA p	ITL	10.33	10.85	−0.01	−6.3	+12.2	+7.3	C
IntlB	ITL	10.27	10.27	−0.01	−6.5	+11.5	NS	..
Japan p	ITL	12.92	13.56	−0.14	+11.3	+16.3	+2.1	E
LatAmG	ITL	19.23	20.19	+0.16	−16.9	+16.6	NS	..
LatAmGB	ITL	19.17	19.17	+0.16	−17.0	+16.2	NS	..
PacifA p	ITL	13.04	13.69	−0.12	−17.8	+10.8	+9.3	B
PacifB	ITL	12.96	12.96	−0.12	−17.9	+10.2	NS	..
StratA p	WBD	10.51	11.03	−0.08	−21.2	−7.2	+9.8	B
StratB	WBD	10.52	10.52	−0.07	−21.3	−7.6	NS	..
Telecom	WOR	16.04	16.84	+0.15	−6.6	+14.2	NS	..
TeleB	WOR	15.95	15.95	+0.14	−6.7	+13.6	NS	..
Wldw p	WOR	16.51	17.33	+0.02	−5.5	+7.2	+9.8	B
WldwB	WOR	16.40	16.40	+0.02	−5.7	+6.6	NS	..
Gabelli Funds:								
ABC p	GRO	10.08	10.29	+0.01	+0.5	+7.6	NS	..
Asset p	GRO	22.31	NL	+0.15	−4.2	+3.8	+10.5	C
CnvSc	S&B	11.39	NL	+0.02	−1.1	+2.6	NS	..
EqInc p	EQI	11.33	11.86	+0.07	−1.6	+4.1	NS	..

EXHIBIT 20-6

***The Wall Street Journal* Mutual Fund Quotations**

Column 1 Mutual fund companies are listed alphabetically by the fund's family name (GT Global) and in subcategories by the various funds available within that family (Amer p).

Column 2 (Inv. Obj.—GRO) Investment objective is the stated goal of the fund. *The Wall Street Journal* lists 27 abbreviated objectives. The most common objectives follow:

CAP—Capital Appreciation	EQI—Equity Income
G&I—Growth and Income	S&B—Stocks and Bonds
GRO—Growth	BND—General U.S. Taxable Bonds
SML—Small Company Growth	GLM—General Municipal Bonds

Column 3 (NAV—17.98) **Net asset value** is the dollar value of one share of the fund's stock. This is the price you receive when you sell your shares of the fund.

net asset value (NAV)
The dollar value of one share of a mutual fund's stock. It is the price investors receive when they sell their shares of the fund.

Column 4 (Offer Price—18.88) **Offer price** is the price per share investors pay when purchasing the fund. The offer price includes the net asset value plus a broker's commission charge known as a load. NL in the offer price column means no load, or no commission, when purchasing the fund. There may, however, be a sales charge when selling the shares.

offer price
The price per share investors pay when purchasing a mutual fund. Offer price includes the net asset value plus the broker's commission.

Column 5 (NAV Chg.—+0.09) This is the dollar change in the net asset value of the fund since the previous quotation.

Total Return These columns indicate the performance and ranking of the fund.

> **Everybody's Business**
> **Real-World Connection**
> Today, there are more than 8,000 mutual funds being offered to the investing public.
>
> To bolster your knowledge and improve your odds of investing success, call the Securities and Exchange Commission's (SEC) Office of Investor Education and Assistance at 800-SEC-0330 to get its free brochure called *Invest Wisely: An Introduction to Mutual Funds.*
>
> Among other things, the booklet explains the fees that funds charge and gives tips on comparing fund performance. Cyberinvestors can download the brochure from the SEC's home page at www.sec.gov.

Column 6 (YTD—+4.7) This is the year-to-date percent return on investment of the fund.

Columns 7 & 8 Each day *The Wall Street Journal* lists different past performance data in these columns. Exhibit 20-6, a Friday, lists the 39-week (+23.2) and annualized 5-year return (+16.0) of the fund. On Tuesdays, for example, these columns list the 4-week and 1-year percent returns of the fund.

Column 9 (R—A) This column lists the fund's ranking compared with other funds with the same investment objectives: A = top 20%; B = next 20%; C = middle 20%, D = next 20%; E = bottom 20%.

EXAMPLE

From the following mutual fund quotation table, explain the information listed for the Robertson Stephens—Em Gr fund.

	Inv. Obj.	NAV	Offer Price	NAV Chg.	– Total Return – YTD	26 wks	4 yrs	R
TNMuOb	SSM	9.92	10.23	...	−4.3	NA	NS	..
Robertson Stephens:								
Contra	GRO	12.27	12.27	+0.06	+7.5	+22.5	NS	..
Em Gr p	SML	18.53	NL	−0.23	+3.1	+12.4	+15.6	B
Val Pl	SML	13.55	NL	−0.13	+3.8	+8.2	NS	..

SOLUTION STRATEGY

According to the listing, the investment objective of this fund is investing in small growth companies. The net asset value is $18.53, and the offer price is the same as the NAV because this is a no-load fund. The change in net asset value from the previous trading session is down $.23. Regarding return on investment, this fund is up 3.1% for the year-to-date; up 12.4% for the past 26 weeks; and up 15.6% on an annualized basis for the past 4 years. The fund has a ranking of B compared with similar funds.

TRY-IT | EXERCISE

12. **From the following mutual fund quotation table, explain the information listed for the Oppenheimer Fd: EqIncA fund.**

	Inv. Obj.	NAV	Offer Price	NAV Chg.	– Total Return – YTD	26 wks	4 yrs	R
SmCoGr	SML	16.56	NL	−0.14	−3.7	−2.4	+14.5	C
TFBdA	GLM	9.71	NL	...	−2.2	−2.1	NS	..
Oppenheimer Fd:								
AsetA p	S&B	12.55	13.32	−0.07	−3.2	−0.1	+9.3	D
CA TE A p	MCA	10.10	10.60	...	−6.4	−5.4	+7.8	D
ChHY p	BHI	12.64	13.27	−0.03	−1.2	+3.7	+16.4	B
Disc p	SML	35.69	37.87	−0.60	−9.6	−9.3	+18.2	B
EqIncA p	EQI	9.61	10.20	−0.05	−2.9	−2.7	+8.4	D
EqIncB t	...	9.58	9.58	−0.05	NA	NA	NA	..

Check your answers with the solutions on page 756.

20-10 Calculating the Sales Charge and Sales Charge Percent of a Mutual Fund

load
The sales charge or broker's commission on a mutual fund.

front-end load
The sales charge or commission on a mutual fund when it is paid at the time of purchase.

back-end load
The sales charge or commission on a mutual fund when it is paid at the time of sale.

With mutual funds, the sales charge or broker's commission is known as the **load.** These charges vary from 1% to more than 8% of the amount invested. The load is paid either when purchasing the stock, in a **front-end load,** or when selling the stock, in a **back-end load.** Some mutual funds do not charge a commission and are known as no-load funds. For load funds, the difference between the offer price and the net asset value is the sales charge.

STEPS TO CALCULATE MUTUAL FUND SALES CHARGE AND SALES CHARGE PERCENT:

Step 1. Calculate mutual fund sales charge by subtracting the net asset value from the offer price:

$$\textbf{Mutual fund sales charge} = \textbf{Offer price} - \textbf{Net asset value}$$

Step 2. Calculate sales charge percent by dividing the sales charge by the net asset value:

$$\textbf{Sales charge percent} = \frac{\textbf{Sales charge}}{\textbf{Net asset value}}$$

EXAMPLE

A mutual fund has an offer price of $6.75 per share and a net asset value of $6.44. What are the sales charge and the sales charge percent?

SOLUTION STRATEGY

Step 1. Mutual fund sales charge = Offer price − Net asset value

Mutual fund sales charge = 6.75 − 6.44 = $.31 per share

Step 2.

$$\text{Sales charge percent} = \frac{\text{Sales charge}}{\text{Net asset value}}$$

$$\text{Sales charge percent} = \frac{.31}{6.44} = .0481 = 4.8\%$$

TRY-IT EXERCISE

13. What are the sales charge and the sales charge percent for a mutual fund with an offer price of $9.85 per share and net asset value of $9.21?

Check your answers with the solutions on page 756.

20-11 Calculating the Net Asset Value of a Mutual Fund

The assets of a mutual fund consist of the total current value of the stocks or bonds that the fund owns. As stated earlier, a mutual fund's net asset value is the per share price of the fund's stock.

STEPS TO CALCULATE NET ASSET VALUE OF A MUTUAL FUND:

Step 1. Calculate net asset value by subtracting the total liabilities from the total assets of the fund and dividing by the number of shares outstanding.

$$\textbf{Net asset value (NAV)} = \frac{\textbf{Total assets} - \textbf{Total liabilities}}{\textbf{Number of shares outstanding}}$$

Step 2. Round the answer to dollars and cents.

EXAMPLE

A mutual fund has total assets of $40,000,000 and liabilities of $6,000,000. If there are 12,000,000 shares outstanding, what is the net asset value of the fund?

SOLUTION STRATEGY

$$\text{Net asset value} = \frac{\text{Total assets} - \text{Total liabilities}}{\text{Number of shares outstanding}}$$

$$\text{Net asset value} = \frac{40{,}000{,}000 - 6{,}000{,}000}{12{,}000{,}000} = \underline{\underline{\$2.83 \text{ per share}}}$$

TRY-IT | EXERCISE

14. A mutual fund has total assets of $80,000,000 and liabilities of $5,000,000. If there are 17,000,000 shares outstanding, what is the net asset value of the fund?

Check your answer with the solution on page 756.

20-12 Calculating the Number of Shares Purchased of a Mutual Fund

Investors frequently purchase shares of mutual funds by using lump-sum amounts of money. To accommodate this practice, most funds sell fractional shares of their stock.

STEPS TO CALCULATE NUMBER OF SHARES PURCHASED OF A MUTUAL FUND:

Step 1. Calculate number of shares by dividing the amount of the investment by the offer price of the fund. For no-load funds, use the net asset value as the denominator.

$$\textbf{Number of shares purchased} = \frac{\textbf{Total investment}}{\textbf{Offer price}}$$

Step 2. Round the answer to thousandths (three decimal places).

EXAMPLE

Chris Kentner invested a lump sum of $5,000 in a mutual fund with an offer price of $6.55. How many shares did Chris purchase?

SOLUTION STRATEGY

$$\text{Number of shares purchased} = \frac{\text{Total investment}}{\text{Offer price}}$$

$$\text{Number of shares purchased} = \frac{5{,}000}{6.55} = \underline{\underline{763.359 \text{ shares}}}$$

TRY-IT | EXERCISE

15. Melanie Foye invested $10,000 in a no-load mutual fund with a net asset value of $12.25. How many shares did she purchase?

Check your answer with the solution on page 756.

20-13 Calculating Return on Investment

Regardless of whether you are investing in stocks, bonds, or mutual funds, the basic measure of how well your investments are doing is known as the **return on investment (ROI).** This performance yardstick allows investors to compare various investments on an equal basis. Return on investment takes into account all transaction charges, such as broker's commissions and fees, as well as income received, such as dividends and interest payments. ROI is expressed as a percent, rounded to the nearest tenth.

return on investment (ROI)
The basic measure of how well an investment is doing. Used to compare various investments on an equal basis. Calculated as a percent, by dividing the total gain on the investment by the total purchase price.

STEPS TO CALCULATE RETURN ON INVESTMENT:

Step 1. Calculate the dollar gain (or loss) on the sale of the investment by subtracting the total cost from the proceeds of the sale.

Gain (or loss) on investment = Proceeds − Total cost

Step 2. Compute total gain by adding any dividends received on stocks, or interest received on bonds, to the gain or loss on sale.

Total gain (or loss) = Gain (or loss) + Dividends or interest

Step 3. Calculate return on investment by dividing the total gain by the total cost of purchase. Round your answer to the nearest tenth percent.

$$\text{Return on investment (ROI)} = \frac{\text{Total gain}}{\text{Total cost of purchase}}$$

Everybody's Business

Real-World Connection

The nineties were one of the best decades of the century for return on investment on stocks; according to *Kiplinger's Personal Finance Magazine*, nobody did better than Dell Computer's stockholders.

If you purchased Dell shares in 1990, and held onto them through 1999, you would have reaped an annualized return of 107%—doubling your investment and then some every year. Over the decade this amounts to an astounding total return of 57,282%!

EXAMPLE

Ben Bean purchased 1,000 shares of Utah Valley Mutual Fund for an offer price of $5.30 per share. He later sold the shares at a net asset value of $5.88 per share. During the time Ben owned the shares, Utah Valley paid a dividend of $.38 per share. What is Ben's return on investment?

SOLUTION STRATEGY

Step 1.

Total cost of purchase = 1,000 shares × 5.30 = $5,300
Proceeds from sale = 1,000 shares × 5.88 = $5,880
Gain on sale = Proceeds − Total cost
Gain on sale = 5,880 − 5,300 = $580

Step 2. In addition to the gain on sale, Ben also made $380 (1,000 × .38) in dividends.

Total gain = Gain on sale + Dividends
Total gain = 580 + 380 = $960

Step 3. $\text{Return on investment} = \frac{\text{Total gain}}{\text{Total cost of purchase}} = \frac{960}{5{,}300} = .18113 = 18.1\%$

TRY-IT EXERCISE

16. Bob Leshin purchased 2,000 shares of Homestead National Mutual Fund for an offer price of $8.60 per share. He later sold the shares at a net asset value of $9.18 per share. During the time Bob owned the shares, Homestead National paid dividends of $.27 and $.42 per share. What is Bob's return on investment?

Check your answer with the solution on page 756.

REVIEW EXERCISES | CHAPTER 20—SECTION III

Answer Exercises 1–12 based on the following mutual fund quotation table:

	Inv. Obj.	NAV	Offer Price	NAV Chg.	Total Return YTD	Total Return 39 wks	Total Return 5 yrs	R
Rembrandt Funds:								
AsiaTI	...	9.26	NL	−0.14	NA	NA	NA	..
Bal Tr	S&B	9.65	NL	+0.08	−3.3	+0.4	NS	..
GIFxInTr	WBD	10.10	NL	+0.01	−3.2	+3.2	NS	..
Gwth Tr	GRO	10.05	NL	+0.12	−1.2	+0.8	NS	..
IntlEqTr	ITL	12.61	NL	−0.08	+0.2	+15.4	NS	..
SIGvFITr	BST	9.67	NL	+0.03	−3.0	−1.6	NS	..
SmCapTr	SML	9.84	NL	+0.06	−3.8	+5.4	NS	..
TE FITr	GLM	9.63	9.63	+0.06	−4.8	−1.8	NS	..
Tax FI Tr	BIN	9.76	9.76	+0.05	−3.4	−1.0	NS	..
ValueTr	GRO	9.95	NL	+0.05	−2.6	−0.9	NS	..
Retire Invst Trust:								
Balanced	S&B	16.76	16.76	+0.21	−4.6	−2.1	+8.0	E
EqGro	GRO	17.70	17.70	+0.30	−4.9	−1.4	+8.3	D
EqIncom	EQI	17.77	17.77	+0.24	−4.0	−0.6	+8.2	D
Income	BND	15.44	15.44	+0.10	−4.2	−2.5	+7.8	E
Rey BC	G&I	13.88	NL	+0.39	−6.3	−2.2	+7.0	E
Rightime Group:								
BlueC p	G&I	32.72	34.35	−0.03	+0.2	+4.2	+10.2	C
RT fp	G&I	35.27	NL	−0.10	−0.1	+4.9	+9.6	D
GvSc p	BND	13.33	13.99	+0.16	−0.8	−0.7	+5.9	E
Grth p	GRO	25.69	26.97	+0.16	−0.4	−0.2	+4.8	E
SpEquitII	SML	10.37	10.37	+0.12	−3.9	+4.4	NS	..
Smith Barney A:								
CapApA	CAP	13.53	14.17	+0.40	−6.7	−2.0	NS	..
GIGvtA	WBD	12.16	12.67	+0.02	−3.9	+2.8	NS	..
IncGrA p	G&I	12.63	13.23	+0.12	−4.4	+0.9	+9.5	D
IncRetA	BST	9.49	9.63	...	+0.3	+1.5	+7.7	C
IntlA	ITL	17.34	18.16	−0.04	−7.3	+25.1	+16.1	A
MoGvtA	BND	12.29	12.80	+0.08	−2.2	−1.6	+9.9	B
MuCalA	MCA	12.23	12.74	+0.06	−4.7	−1.2	+8.5	A
MuFl A	MFL	12.82	13.35	+0.10	−4.5	−0.5	NS	..
MuLtd A	IDM	6.53	6.66	+0.02	−2.7	+0.7	+7.6	B
MunNtA	GLM	13.30	13.85	+0.08	−4.8	−0.8	+9.1	A
MuNJ A	MNJ	13.20	13.75	+0.07	−5.6	−1.8	NS	..
MuNY A	DNY	12.80	13.33	+0.08	−4.9	−1.1	+8.8	A
SHTSY	BST	4.04	4.04	+0.01	−1.6	−0.1	NS	..
USGvtA	BND	13.09	13.64	+0.09	−2.3	−1.6	+9.9	B
UtltyA p	SEC	12.53	13.12	+0.13	−3.7	−4.4	NS	..
Smith Barney B & C:								
CapApB	CAP	13.39	13.39	+0.40	−6.9	−2.6	NS	..
IntlB	ITL	17.18	17.18	−0.05	−7.5	+24.6	NS	..
MuLtd B	IDM	6.53	6.53	+0.03	−2.9	NA	NS	..
IntlC	ITL	17.33	17.33	−0.04	−7.4	+25.1	NS	..

1. Smith Barney A: MuCalA—Offer price and 39-week return: ____________

2. Retirement Investment Trust: Balanced—Objective and net asset value: ____________

3. Rightime Group: BlueC—NAV change and 5-year return: ____________

4. Which Rembrandt fund has the only positive return in the year-to-date? ____________

5. Which Rightime Group fund is a bond fund? What is its ranking? ____________

6. Which Smith Barney A funds have the best and worst 39-week returns? ____________

7. What does NL mean in the offer price of some funds? ____________

8. Which Rembrandt fund has the best 39-week return? ____________

Fund	Offer Price	Net Asset Value	Sales Charge	Sales Charge %
9. Smith Barney A: MuFl A	______	______	______	______
10. Retire Invst Trust: Income	______	______	______	______
11. Rightime Group: Grth	______	______	______	______
12. Smith Barney A: USGvtA	______	______	______	______

Calculate the net asset value and number of shares purchased for the following funds (round shares to thousandths, three decimal places):

	Total Assets	Total Liabilities	Shares Outstanding	Net Asset Value	Offer Price	Total Investment	Shares Purchased
13.	$80,000,000	$2,300,000	5,000,000	________	$16.10	$10,000	________
14.	52,000,000	1,800,000	6,100,000	________	9.50	5,000	________
15.	95,400,000	4,650,000	8,500,000	________	11.15	50,000	________
16.	15,000,000	750,000	1,300,000	________	NL	25,000	________

Calculate the total cost, proceeds, total gain or loss, and return on investment for the following mutual fund investments. The offer price is the purchase price of the shares, and the net asset value is the price at which the shares were later sold:

	Shares	Offer Price	Total Cost	Net Asset Value	Proceeds	Per Share Dividends	Total Gain (or Loss)	Return on Investment (%)
17.	100	$15.30	________	$18.80	________	$.45	________	________
18.	500	10.40	________	12.90	________	.68	________	________
19.	1,000	4.85	________	6.12	________	1.25	________	________
20.	700	7.30	________	5.10	________	0	________	________

21. A mutual fund has an offer price of $13.10 and a net asset value of $12.35.

a. What is the sales charge?

b. What is the sales charge percent?

22. A mutual fund has total assets of $25,000,000 and liabilities of $3,500,000. If there are 8,600,000 shares outstanding, what is the net asset value of the fund?

23. William Stokes invested a lump sum of $10,000 in a mutual fund with an offer price of $14.50. How many shares did he purchase?

24. Charlie Beavin purchased 500 shares of Advantage Resource Fund for an offer price of $8.90 per share. He later sold the shares at a net asset value of $10.50 per share. During the time that he owned the shares the fund paid a dividend of $.75 per share three times. What is Charlie's return on investment?

BUSINESS DECISION

Capital Gains

25. There are many tax rules and regulations that you should be aware of when investing; whether it be in stocks, bonds, or mutual funds. **Capital gains** are proceeds derived from your investments. Unless they are specified as being tax-free, such as municipal bonds, you must pay capital gains taxes on these funds.

Capital gains are taxed in one of two ways. If the investment was held for one year or less, this is considered **short-term** and is taxed as ordinary income at your regular income tax rate. If the investment was held for more than one year, it is considered **long-term**, and qualifies for various tax discounts, as follows:

Capital Gains Rates

Stocks Held	15% tax bracket	Over 15% bracket
1 year or less	15%	27%–38.6%
Over 1 year, less than 5	10%	20%
5 years or more	8%	18%*

*If purchased after January 1, 2001

a. If you are in the 15% tax bracket, how much tax would be saved by waiting for an investment to become long-term before selling, if your taxable profit from this investment was $25,000?

b. How much would you save if you were in the 37.6% tax bracket?

c. How much additional tax savings would you get if you kept the investment for more than 5 years?

CHAPTER FORMULAS

Stocks

$$\text{Dividend per share (preferred)} = \text{Par value} \times \text{Dividend rate}$$

$$\text{Dividend per share (common)} = \frac{\text{Total common dividend}}{\text{Number of shares (common)}}$$

$$\text{Current yield} = \frac{\text{Annual dividend per share}}{\text{Current price of the stock}}$$

$$\text{Price-earnings ratio} = \frac{\text{Current price per share}}{\text{Earnings per share}}$$

$$\text{Gain (or loss) on stock} = \text{Proceeds} - \text{Total cost}$$

Bonds

$$\text{Price per bond} = \text{Current market price} + \text{Accrued interest} + \text{Commission}$$

$$\text{Proceeds} = \text{Current market price} + \text{Accrued interest} - \text{Commission}$$

$$\text{Current yield} = \frac{\text{Annual interest}}{\text{Current market price}}$$

Mutual funds

$$\text{Mutual fund sales charge} = \text{Offer price} - \text{Net asset value}$$

$$\text{Sales charge percent} = \frac{\text{Sales charge}}{\text{Net asset value}}$$

$$\text{Net asset value (NAV)} = \frac{\text{Total assets} - \text{Total liabilities}}{\text{Number of shares outstanding}}$$

$$\text{Number of shares purchased} = \frac{\text{Total investment}}{\text{Offer price}}$$

$$\text{Return on investment (ROI)} = \frac{\text{Total gain}}{\text{Total cost of purchase}}$$

✦ SUMMARY CHART ✦

SECTION I: Stocks

Topic	P/O, Page	Important Concepts	Illustrative Examples
Distributing Dividends on Preferred and Common Stock	20-1 722	Companies raise capital by selling stock. Common stock shares in the success or failure of the business. Preferred stock receives a fixed dividend and is paid before common. Cumulative preferred receives dividends in arrears, those not paid in past years. Preferred dividends are stated as a percent of par value or as a dollar amount for no-par preferred. Dividends are distributed as follows: 1. Preferred—Arrears 2. Preferred—Current period 3. Common—Current period	Kensington Corp. has 100,000 shares of \$100 par, 7%, cumulative preferred and 300,000 shares of common stock. No dividend was declared last year. This year, a \$2,000,000 dividend was declared. Distribute the dividends among the two classes of stock. Preferred stockholders receive 100 × .07 = \$7.00 per share. Preferred—Arrears: 100,000 shares × 7 = \$700,000

SECTION I: (continued)

Topic	P/O, Page	Important Concepts	Illustrative Examples
			Preferred—Current: 100,000 shares × 7 = $700,000 Total due preferred = $1,400,000 Common: $2,000,000 Total dividend − 1,400,000 Preferred dividend $600,000 Common dividend $\text{Div. per share} = \frac{600{,}000}{300{,}000} = \$2.00$
Calculating Current Yield for a Stock	20-3 728	Current yield is a measure of how much you are earning on a stock compared with other investments. $\text{Current Yield} = \frac{\text{Annual dividend}}{\text{Current price}}$	What is the current yield for Calder Corporation stock, which pays a dividend of $2.35 per share and is currently selling for $57.25? $\text{Current Yield} = \frac{2.35}{57.25} = 4.1\%$
Determining the Price-Earnings Ratio of a Stock	20-4 729	The price-earnings ratio of a stock shows the relationship between the price of a stock and the company's earnings for the past 12 months. $\text{PE ratio} = \frac{\text{Current price per share}}{\text{Earnings per share}}$	Trendy Toy stock is selling at $34.35. If the company had earnings per share of $4.27, calculate the price-earnings ratio. $\text{PE ratio} = \frac{34.35}{4.27} = 8.04 = 8$
Computing the Cost, Proceeds, and Gain (or Loss) on a Stock Transaction	20-5 729	Stocks are purchased and sold through stockbrokers, who charge a commission for these services. Round lots are purchases in multiples of 100 shares. Odd lots are purchases of less than 100 shares. Extra commission is usually charged for odd lots. **Total cost of purchase = Cost of shares + Broker's comm.** **Proceeds = Value of shares − Broker's comm.** **Gain (or loss) = Proceeds − Total cost**	You purchase 450 shares of G-Tech common stock at $19.75 per share. A few months later, you sell the shares at $27.50. Your stockbroker charges 3% on round lots and 4% on odd lots. What are the total cost, the proceeds, and the gain or loss on your investment? *Purchase* Cost of shares = 450 × 19.75 = $8,887.50 Commission = 400 × 19.75 × .03 = $237.00 50 × 19.75 × .04 = 39.50 Total Comm = $276.50 Total cost of purchase = 8,887.50 + 276.50 = $9,164.00 *Sale* Value of shares = 450 × 27.50 = $12,375.00

SECTION I: (continued)

Topic	P/O, Page	Important Concepts	Illustrative Examples
			Commission = $400 \times 27.50 \times .03 = \$330.00$ $50 \times 27.50 \times .04 = 55.00$ Total commission = $385.00 Proceeds = $12{,}375 - 385.00 = \$11{,}990.00$ *Gain* $11{,}990.00 - 9{,}164.00 = \$2{,}826.00$

SECTION II: Bonds

Topic	P/O, Page	Important Concepts	Illustrative Examples
Computing the Cost of Purchasing Bonds	20-7 737	Bonds are loans to companies or governments that pay fixed interest semiannually. *Buying Bonds:* 1. Calculate accrued interest since last payment by $I = PRT$. 2. Calculate the price to the bond: **Puchase price per bond = Current price + Accrued interest + Commission** 3. Calculate total purchase price: **Total purchase price = Price per bond × Number of bonds**	What is the purchase price of 10 Tiffany bonds with a coupon rate of $5\frac{1}{2}$ and a current market price of $96\frac{1}{4}$? The commission charge is $6.00 per bond. The date of the purchase is November 1; the bond pays interest on Jan. 1 and July 1. Accrued interest = $1{,}000 \times .055 \times \frac{4}{12} = \$18.33$ Price per bond = $962.50 + 18.33 + 6.00 = \$986.83$ Total purchase price = $986.83 \times 10 = \$9{,}868.30$
Computing Proceeds from the Sale of Bonds	20-7 738	*Selling Bonds:* 1. Calculate accrued interest since last payment by $I = PRT$. 2. Calculate the proceeds per bond by adding the accrued interest to the current market price and subtracting the broker's commission. 3. **Total proceeds = Proceeds per bond × Number of bonds**	Marvin Mai sold 5 Procter & Gamble bonds with a coupon rate of $6\frac{3}{8}$ and a current market price of $107\frac{3}{4}$. The commission charge is $8 per bond. The date of sale is 100 days since the last interest payment. What are Marvin's proceeds? Accrued interest = $1{,}000 \times .06375 \times \frac{100}{360} = \$17.71$ Proceeds per bond = $1{,}077.50 + 17.71 - 8.00 = \$1{,}087.21$ Total proceeds = $1{,}087.21 \times 5 = \$5{,}436.05$

SECTION II: (continued)

Topic	P/O, Page	Important Concepts	Illustrative Examples
Calculating the Current Yield for a Bond	20-8 739	Current yield is a simple measure of the return on investment based on the current market price of the bond. **Annual interest = Par value × Coupon rate** $\text{Current yield} = \frac{\text{Annual interest}}{\text{Market price}}$	Calculate the current yield for a Universal Foods bond with a coupon rate of $9\frac{1}{4}\%$ and currently selling at a premium of $112\frac{1}{2}$. Annual interest = $1{,}000 \times .0925 = \underline{\$92.50}$ $\text{Current yield} = \frac{92.50}{1{,}125} = \underline{\underline{8.2\%}}$

SECTION III: Mutual Funds

Topic	P/O, Page	Important Concepts	Illustrative Examples
Calculating the Sales Charge and the Sales Charge Percent of a Mutual Fund	20-10 744	Mutual fund sales charge or load may vary from 1% to 8% of the amount invested. When it is paid at the time of purchase, it is known as a front-end load. It is the difference between the offer price and the net asset value of the fund. **Sales charge = Offer price − NAV** $\text{Sales charge\%} = \frac{\text{Sales charge}}{\text{Net asset value}}$	What are the sales charge and the sales charge percent for a mutual fund with an offer price of \$12.35 per share and a net asset value of \$11.60? Sales charge = $12.35 - 11.60 = \underline{\$.75 \text{ per share}}$ $\text{Sales charge \%} = \frac{.75}{11.60} = \underline{\underline{6.5\%}}$
Calculating Net Asset Value of a Mutual Fund	20-11 745	The assets of a mutual fund are the total current value of its investments. The net asset value is the per share figure. $\text{Net asset value (NAV)} = \frac{\text{Total assets} - \text{Total liabilities}}{\text{Number of shares outstanding}}$	A mutual fund has total assets of \$20,000,000 and liabilities of \$5,000,000. If there are 4,000,000 shares outstanding, what is the net asset value of the fund? Net asset value = $\frac{20{,}000{,}000 - 5{,}000{,}000}{4{,}000{,}000} = \underline{\underline{\$3.75}}$
Computing Number of Shares Purchased of a Mutual Fund	20-12 746	Mutual fund stock is sold in fractional shares to accommodate those investing lump sums of money. Shares are rounded to thousandths (three decimal places). $\text{Number of shares} = \frac{\text{Total investment}}{\text{Offer price}}$ *Note:* For no-load funds, use net asset value as the denominator.	Mike Matthews invested a lump sum of \$10,000 in a mutual fund with an offer price of \$8.75. How many shares did he purchase? Number of shares = $\frac{10{,}000}{8.75} = \underline{\underline{1{,}142.857}}$

SECTION III: (continued)

Topic	P/O, Page	Important Concepts	Illustrative Examples
Calculating Return on Investment	20-13 747	Return on investment is the basic measure of how your stocks, bonds, or mutual fund investments are doing. 1. Calculate the gain (or loss) on the investment: **Gain (or loss) = Proceeds − Total cost** 2. Compute total gain (or loss) by adding any dividends received on stocks or interest received on bonds. **Total gain = Gain + Dividends or interest** 3. $\textbf{Return on investment} = \dfrac{\textbf{Total gain}}{\textbf{Total cost of purchase}}$	Gene Gomberg purchased 1,000 shares of Continental Group mutual fund for an offer price of \$7.50 per share. He later sold the shares at a net asset value of \$8.75. During the time he owned the shares, Continental paid a dividend of \$.85 per share. What is Gene's return on investment? Total cost = 1,000 × 7.50 = $\underline{\$7{,}500}$ Proceeds = 1,000 × 8.75 = $\underline{\$8{,}750}$ Gain = 8,750 − 7,500 = $\underline{\$1{,}250}$ Dividends = 1,000 × .85 = $\underline{\$850}$ Total gain = 1,250 + 850 = $\underline{\$2{,}100}$ $\text{ROI} = \dfrac{2{,}100}{7{,}500} = .28 = \underline{\underline{28\%}}$

TRY-IT EXERCISE | SOLUTIONS

1. $\text{Dividend per share} = \dfrac{\text{Total dividend}}{\text{Number of shares}}$

$\text{Dividend per share} = \dfrac{910{,}000}{1{,}400{,}000} = \underline{\underline{\$.65}}$

2. Total preferred dividend = Number of shares × Dividend per share

Total preferred dividend = 600,000 × 1.40 = $\underline{\underline{\$840{,}000}}$

Total common dividend = Total dividend − Total preferred dividend

Total common dividend = 2,800,000 − 840,000 = \$1,960,000

$\text{Dividend per share} = \dfrac{\text{Total common dividend}}{\text{Number of shares}}$

$\text{Dividend per share} = \dfrac{1{,}960{,}000}{1{,}000{,}000} = \underline{\underline{\$1.96}}$

3. Dividend per share = Par value × Dividend rate

Dividend per share = 100 × 7.5% = \$7.50

Total preferred div. (per year) = Number of shares × Div. per share

Total preferred div. (per year) = 300,000 × 7.50 = \$2,250,000

Total preferred div. = 2,250,000 (arrears) + 2,250,000 (this year) = $\underline{\underline{\$4{,}500{,}000}}$

Total common div. = Total div. − Preferred div.

Total common div. = 7,000,000 − 4,500,000 = \$2,500,000

$\text{Dividend per share} = \dfrac{2{,}500{,}000}{5{,}200{,}000} = \underline{\underline{\$.48}}$

4. *Harley Davidson: Stock*

YTD % Chg	+21.7
52-week high	\$54.35
52-week low	\$32.00
Ticker symbol	HDI
Dividend	\$.12 per share
Yield	.2%
PE ratio	36
Volume	1,796,800 shares traded
Last for day	\$48.36
Change	up 1.08 points

5. $\text{Current yield} = \dfrac{\text{Annual dividend per share}}{\text{Current price of stock}}$

$\text{Current yield} = \dfrac{.68}{12.84} = \underline{\underline{5.3\%}}$

6. $\text{Price-earnings ratio} = \dfrac{\text{Current price per share}}{\text{Earnings per share}}$

$\text{Price-earnings ratio} = \dfrac{37.19}{6.70} = 5.55 = \underline{\underline{6}}$

7. a. *Cost of stock:*

Cost of shares = Price per share × Number of shares
Cost of shares = 44.80 × 225 = $10,080.00

Broker's commission = Cost of shares × Comm. Rate
Round lot = 200 × 44.80 × .02 = $179.20
Odd lot = 25 × 44.80 × .03 = $33.60
Total commission = 179.20 + 33.60 = $212.80

Total cost = Cost of shares + Commission
Total cost = 10,080.00 + 212.80 = $10,292.80

b. *Proceeds from sale:*

Value of shares = Price per share × Number of shares
Value of shares = 53.20 × 225 = $11,970.00

Commission:
Round lot = 200 × 53.20 × .02 = $212.80
Odd lot = 25 × 53.20 × .03 = $39.90
Total commission = 212.80 + 39.90 = $252.70

Proceeds = Value of shares − Broker's commission
Proceeds = 11,970.00 − 252.70 = $11,717.30

c. *Gain on transaction:*

Gain = Proceeds − Total cost
Gain = 11,717.30 − 10,292.80 = $1,424.50

8. *Fortune: Bond*

Coupon rate	8.5%
Maturing in	2003
Current yield	8.1%
Volume	70 Bonds
Closing price	105, $1,050 (1,000 × 1.05)
Net change	down $\frac{1}{2}$, $5 (1,000 × .005)

9. Accrued interest = $1{,}000 \times .0625 \times \frac{2}{12} = \$10.42$

Price per bond = Market price + Accrued int + Comm.
Price per bond = 913.75 + 10.42 + 10.00 = $934.17

Total purchase price = Price per bond × Number of bonds
Total purchase price = 934.17 × 20 = $18,683.40

10. Accrued interest = $1{,}000 \times .08875 \times \frac{122}{360} = \$30.08$

Proceeds per bond =
Market price + Accrued interest − Comm.
Proceeds per bond = 990 + 30.08 − 10.00 = $1,010.08

Total proceeds = Proceeds per bond × Number of bonds
Total proceeds = 1,010.08 × 5 = $5,050.40

11. Annual interest = Par value × Coupon rate
Annual interest = 1,000 × .09375 = $93.75

Current price = Par value × Price percent
Current price = 1,000 × .8475 = $847.50

$$\text{Current yield} = \frac{\text{Annual interest}}{\text{Market price}}$$

$$\text{Current yield} = \frac{93.75}{847.50} = .1106 = 11.1\%$$

12. *Oppenheimer Fund: EqInc A: Mutual Fund*

Investment objective	Equity income
Net asset value	$9.61
Offer price	$10.20
NAV change	down $.05
Year-to-date return	−2.9%
26-week return	−2.7%
4-year return	+8.4%
Rating	D

13. Mutual fund sales charge = Offer price − Net asset value
Mutual fund sales charge = 9.85 − 9.21 = $.64

$$\text{Sales charge percent} = \frac{\text{Sales charge}}{\text{NAV}} = \frac{.64}{9.21} = 6.9\%$$

14. $$\text{Net asset value} = \frac{\text{Total assets} - \text{Total liabilities}}{\text{Number of shares}}$$

$$\text{Net asset value} = \frac{80{,}000{,}000 - 5{,}000{,}000}{17{,}000{,}000} = \$4.41$$

15. $$\text{Number of shares purchased} = \frac{\text{Total investment}}{\text{Offer price}}$$

$$\text{Number of shares purchased} = \frac{10{,}000}{12.25} = 816.327 \text{ shares}$$

16. Total cost of purchase = 2,000 × 8.60 = $17,200
Proceeds from sale = 2,000 × 9.18 = $18,360

Gain on sale = Proceeds − Total cost
Gain on sale = 18,360 − 17,200 = $1,160

Dividends: 2,000 × .27 = $540
2,000 × .42 = $840
Total dividends = 540 + 840 = $1,380

Total gain = Gain on sale + Dividends
Total gain = 1,160 + 1,380 = $2,540

$$\text{Return on investment} = \frac{\text{Total gain}}{\text{Total cost of purchase}}$$

$$\text{ROI} = \frac{2{,}540}{17{,}200} = .1476 = 14.8\%$$

Name ______________

Class ______________

CHAPTER 20 | ASSESSMENT TEST

Calculate the preferred and common stock dividend per share for the following companies:

Company	Common Stock Shares	Preferred Stock: Shares	Preferred Stock: Div. or Par.	Preferred Stock: Cum.	Dividend Declared	Arrears	Preferred Div./Share	Common Div./Share
1. Goodyear	22,000,000		none		$ 7,900,000	none	______	______
2. Hasbro	5,000,000	1,000,000	$3.20	yes	8,500,000	1 year	______	______
3. Chrysler	80,000,000	3,400,000	$100, 5%	yes	58,000,000	2 years	______	______

Answer Questions 4–7 based on the following stock quotation table:

−50.2	37.90	13.55	GlblPwrEquip **GEG** n	...	...		310	15.65	+0.17
+22.6	**6.35**	**3.25**	**GlblTch GAI**	**e**	**...**	**19**	**68**	**4.75**	**−0.25**
+85.1	12.65	5.25♣	Goldcp g **GG**	.20eg	...	...	1981	11.22	+0.01
−20.1	35.43	23.50	GldnState **GSB**	.40	1.6	9	4799	25.12	−0.03
−28.0	70.90	45.02	GldnWstFnl **GDW**	.29f	.6	11	8124	48.60	−0.15
−17.6	120	63.27	GoldmanSachs **GS**	.48	.5	20	22153	88.10	+1.24
−37.2	44.50	15.91	Goodrich **GR**	1.10	4.8	6	7590	22.86	−0.20
− 6.1	6.75	4.50	GoodrichPet **GDP**		...	22	71	4.81	+0.05
−16.8	32.10	16.70	Goodyear **GT**	48m	2.5	dd	4016	19.13	−0.09
−40.8	6.20	2.25♣	Gottschks **GOT**		...	61	34	2.44	...
−47.3	4.63	1.25	GraceWR **GRA**		...	dd	786	1,68	+0.05
+13.8	36.15	22.33♣	Graco **GGG** s	.40	1.3	15	532	31.40	−0.60
+22.0	48	29.51	Grainger **GWW**	.70	1.6	26	3544	44.53	−0.46
+33.5	31.10	17.04	GranitCnstr **GVA** s	.32	1.2	20	577	25.75	+0.09
−57.7	24.20	5.25♣	GrantPrid **GRP**		...	dd	4165	9.29	−0.03
+294.7	7.20	1.06	GrphPclnt A **GPK**		...	...	54	4.44	+0.09
−20.8	19.05	12.35	GrayComm **GCS**	.08	.6	dd	36	12.52	+0.01
− 9.5	19.63	16.59	GreatAmFnl **GFR**	.10	.6	...	30	17.30	...
+167.4	20.36	6	GtAtlPac **GAP**	j	...	dd	691	18.72	+0.30
−40.4	39.19	20	GtLakesChm **GLK**	.32	1.4	dd	1182	22.16	−0.30
−11.1	18.58	14.89♣	GtLksREIT **GL**	1.60	10.4	9	348	15.44	+0.20
+28.3	77	52	GtNorlron **GNI**	8.60e	12.5	11	12	68.80	+0.50
− 9.1	28.19	23.19	GrtPlnsEngy **GXP**	1.66	6.7	20	1235	24.95	−0.38
+ 8.8	25.70	21.19	GrtWstLf **GWL**	1.81	7.2	...	16	25.15	−0.05

+ 8.3	16.24	12.20	JonsLngLaSal **JLL**		...	dd	390	15.03	+0.23
+10.5	18.50	14.98	JrnlRgstr **JRC**		...	7	770	17.75	−0.15
+ 1.1	25.75	24.40	LehCBTCS 2001-15 n	.38p	...	...	38	25.32	...
			-K-K-K-						
− 3.2	38.31	24.67	KB Home **KBH**	.30	.9	6	6856	32.62	+1.50
−12.1	10.50	1.88	KCS Engy **KCS**	j	...	1	671	3.57	−0.16
−59.7	**27**	**6.95**	**KLM KLM**	**.52e**	**5.7**	**...**	**867**	**9.07**	**−0.59**
− 3.5	77.90	52.31	KN Engy PEPS un	3.55f	5.5	...	100	64.65	−0.18
−60.0	19.31	1.85	KPN **KPN**	e	...	...	601	4.45	+0.07
− 1.7	39.94	16	KV Pharm A **KVA**		...	30	121	24.58	−0.01
+13.8	39.81	16	KV Pharm B **KVB**		...	54	79	27.60	+0.25
−25.4	12	5.06	K2 **KTO**		...	dd	30	5.97	+0.07
−48.7	5.06	1.56	KaiserAlum **KLU**		...	1	287	1.89	+0.32
+36.8	44.12	26	KanPipLP **KPP**	3.00f	7.1	...	136	42.14	+0.14
+24.5	19.10	13.87	KanebServs **KSL** n	.36e	1.9	...	166	18.67	−0.17
+18.5	16.75	7.38	KanCtySo **KSU**		...	36	1346	12	−0.44
−48.3	10	2.95	Katylnd **KT**	j	...	dd	175	3.10	−0.10
−22.0	28.25	17.80	Kaydon **KDN**	.48	2.5	92	189	19.40	+0.10
−59.3	69.60	11.95	Keithlylnstr **KEI**	.15	.9	17	1374	17.52	−0.04
+15.9	34	23.19	Kellogg **K**	1.01	3.3	27	8185	30.42	−0.09
+ 2.5	25.50	17.30	Kellwood **KWD**	.64	3.0	10	1117	21.65	+0.70
+13.7	27.63	13.75	KemetCp **KEM**		...	8	6078	17.20	−0.18
+27.9	39.79	25.30♣	Kennmetl **KMT**	.68	1.8	20	1355	37.24	−0.46

4. Goodrich—Dividend, volume, net change: ______________________

5. Kellogg—Dividend, percent yield, 52-week low: ______________________

6. Grainger—Ticker symbol, PE ratio, and 52-week high: ______________________

7. Kaydon—YTD %Chg, volume, last price: ______________________

Calculate the missing information for the following stocks:

Company	Earnings per Share	Annual Dividend	Current Price per Share	Current Yield (%)	Price-Earnings Ratio
8. Federal Express	$3.20	$1.50	$69.25	______	______
9. Merck	______	$1.12	$33.50	______	16
10. Office Depot	$2.10	$.48	______	1.2	______
11. Loews Corp.	______	______	$89.75	1.9	10

Calculate the total cost, proceeds, and gain (or loss) for the following stock market transactions:

Company	Number of Shares	Purchase Price	Selling Price	Commissions: Buy	Commissions: Sell	Commissions: Odd Lot	Total Cost	Proceeds	Gain (or Loss)
12. Olin	400	$39.25	$44.75	2%	2%	—	______	______	______
13. Limited	630	24.13	19.88	3	3	add 1%	______	______	______
14. Exxon	200	61.50	71.25	2	2	—	______	______	______
15. IBM	850	45.50	53.75	$1\frac{1}{2}$	$1\frac{1}{2}$	add 1%	______	______	______

16. The board of directors of Contempo Furniture has declared a dividend of $16,000,000. The company has 800,000 shares of preferred stock that pay $4.90 per share and 8,200,000 shares of common stock.

a. What are the dividends due the preferred shareholders?

Answers

1. ______________

2. ______________

3. ______________

4. ______________

5. ______________

6. ______________

7. ______________

8. ______________

9. ______________

10. ______________

11. ______________

12. ______________

13. ______________

14. ______________

15. ______________

16. a. ______________

Name ______________

Class ______________

Answers

16. b. ______________

17. a. ______________

b. ______________

18. a. ______________

b. ______________

19. a. ______________

b. ______________

c. ______________

b. What is the dividend per share of common stock?

17. Great Eastern Financial has 500,000 shares of $100 par value, $6\frac{1}{2}\%$, cumulative preferred stock and 8,400,000 shares of common stock. Although no dividend was declared for the past 3 years, a $19,000,000 dividend has been declared for this year.

a. How much is due the preferred shareholders?

b. What is the dividend per share of common stock?

18. Webster Electronics is currently selling at $27.48. The earnings per share are $2.69, and the dividend is $.70.

a. What is the current yield of the stock?

b. What is the price-earnings ratio?

19. You purchase 350 shares of General Merchandise common stock at $12.38 per share. A few months later, you sell the shares at $9.88. Your stockbroker charges 3% commission on round lots and an extra $1\frac{1}{2}\%$ on odd lots.

a. What is the total cost of the purchase?

b. What are the proceeds on the sale?

c. What is the gain or loss on the transaction?

Name ______________________

Class ______________________

Answer Questions 20–25 based on the bond quotation table below:

CORPORATION BONDS

Bonds	Cur Yld.	Vol.	Close	Net Chg.
AES05	...	13	96¼	+ 1¼
AMR 9s16	7.7	27	117	...
ATT 5⅛02	5.1	60	99⅞	− ⅛
ATT 7⅛03	6.8	99	104⅛	...
ATT 6¾04	6.4	112	105⅛	...
ATT 7s05	6.6	20	106⅜	− ¼
ATT 8.2s05	7.9	97	104⅜	+ ½
ATT 7½06	6.7	39	111⅛	+ ⅞
ATT 8⅛22	7.6	55	107⅜	+ ¼
ATT 8⅛24	7.5	27	107¾	...
ATT 8⅝31	7.7	70	111⅞	− 1¼
Aames 10½02	11.4	115	92½	+ ½
Aetna 6⅜03	6.3	38	101⅞	+ 1⅞
AlldC zr2003	...	12	91⅜	− ⅛
AlldC zr04	...	5	85¾	− ¼
AlldC zr05	...	35	67	+ ¾
GMA zr12	...	26	398⅝	− 1¾
GMA zr15	...	23	325⅝	− 2¾
GaPw 6⅛07	6.1	20	100	...
GrnTrFrr 10¼02	9.6	20	106¼	+ ⅞
Hallwd 7s05	7.3	10	95½	...
HlthcrR 6.55s02	cv	12	90½	+ ½
HewlPkd zr17	...	5	56⅛	− ⅛
Hexcel 7s03	cv	75	89	...
Hills 12½03f	...	34	96⅜	+ ⅞
Hilton 5s06	cv	26	96½	+ ⅞
Hollngr 9¼06	9.1	14	102⅛	− 1¾
HuntPly 11¾04	11.0	2	107	+ 1
IBM 6⅜08	6.3	80	101⅝	+ ½
IBM 7½13	6.5	5	115½	...
IBM 7s25	6.5	23	106⅞	− ⅜
IBM 6½28	6.3	41	103⅜	+ 3¼
KCS En 8⅞08	23.8	70	37¼	− 2¾
KaufB 9⅜03	9.2	33	102¼	...
KaufB 7¾04	7.7	177	100¼	− ¼

20. AMR—Maturity year and volume: ______________________

21. Hilton—Closing price and net change: ______________________

22. Aetna—Coupon rate, maturity year, and net change: ______________________

23. IBM $6\frac{1}{2}$ 28—Volume and closing price: ______________________

24. GaPw—Coupon rate and current yield: ______________________

25. Which ATT bond is selling at the greatest discount? ______________________

Calculate the accrued interest and the total purchase price of the following bond purchases:

	Company	Coupon Rate	Market Price	Time Since Last Interest	Accrued Interest	Commission per Bond	Bonds Purchased	Total Price
26.	Conagra	$8\frac{1}{4}$	$95\frac{3}{8}$	65 days	________	$5.00	10	________
27.	Dell	$7\frac{3}{8}$	$78\frac{1}{2}$	100 days	________	9.50	5	________
28.	Chevron	$5\frac{5}{8}$	$105\frac{3}{4}$	3 months	________	7.00	15	________

Calculate the accrued interest and the total proceeds of the following bond sales:

	Company	Coupon Rate	Market Price	Time Since Last Interest	Accrued Interest	Commission per Bond	Bonds Sold	Total Proceeds
29.	Upjohn	$7\frac{3}{8}$	$94\frac{1}{2}$	10 days	________	$6.00	10	________
30.	Brunswick	$8\frac{7}{8}$	$109\frac{1}{4}$	4 months	________	5.00	20	________
31.	Pet	$9\frac{1}{4}$	98	85 days	________	8.00	5	________

Calculate the annual interest and current yield for the following bonds:

	Company	Coupon Rate	Annual Interest	Market Price	Current Yield
32.	Duracell	$5\frac{3}{8}$	________	$94\frac{1}{8}$	________
33.	Seaboard	$9\frac{1}{2}$	________	$105\frac{3}{4}$	________

Answers

20. ______________________

21. ______________________

22. ______________________

23. ______________________

24. ______________________

25. ______________________

26. ______________________

27. ______________________

28. ______________________

29. ______________________

30. ______________________

31. ______________________

32. ______________________

33. ______________________

Name ____________________

Class ____________________

Answers

34. a. ____________________

b. ____________________

c. ____________________

35. ____________________

36. ____________________

37. ____________________

38. ____________________

34. On May 1, Perry Herbert bought 10 Satellite bonds with a coupon rate of $7\frac{7}{8}$. The purchase price was $101\frac{3}{8}$, and the commission was $8.00 per bond. Satellite bonds pay interest on April 1 and October 1.

a. What is the current yield of the bond?

b. What is the total purchase price of the bonds?

c. If Perry sold the bonds on August 1 for $109\frac{1}{2}$, what are the proceeds from the sale?

Answer Questions 35–40 by using the following mutual fund quotation table:

	Inv. Obj.	NAV	Offer Price	NAV Chg.	Total Return YTD	Total Return 13 wks	Total Return 3 yrs	R
GlGrB t	WOR	9.22	9.22	−0.07	−2.9	−3.2	NS	..
GrInB t	G&I	12.95	12.95	+0.01	−3.6	−5.0	NS	..
HlthB t	SEC	24.56	24.56	−0.12	−7.1	−9.3	NS	..
HiYldB t	BHI	12.47	12.47	−0.01	−3.2	−4.4	NS	..
IncmB t	BND	6.74	6.74	...	−4.3	−4.9	NS	..
InvB t	GRO	7.59	7.59	−0.08	−6.6	−8.8	NS	..
MATXB t	DMA	8.99	8.99	−0.01	−5.7	−5.8	NS	..
MuniB t	GLM	8.67	8.67	−0.02	−6.0	−6.0	NS	..
NJTxB t	MNJ	8.74	8.74	−0.02	−6.0	−6.1	NS	..
NwOpB t	GRO	22.44	22.44	−0.36	−8.5	−10.0	NS	..
NYTxB t	DNY	8.63	8.63	−0.01	−7.2	−7.0	NS	..
OTC B t	SML	10.19	10.19	−0.21	−10.5	−10.5	NS	..
TxExB t	GLM	8.65	8.65	−0.02	−7.4	−7.3	NS	..
TFHYB t	HYM	14.13	14.13	−0.02	−5.3	−5.4	+8.6	B
TFInB t	ISM	14.50	14.50	−0.03	−6.3	−6.3	+6.5	E
USGvB t	BND	12.59	12.59	+0.01	−4.1	−4.4	NS	..
UtilB t	SEC	9.09	9.09	+0.04	−6.9	−5.9	NS	..
VstaB t	SML	7.02	7.02	−0.11	−6.3	−7.6	NS	..
VoyB t	CAP	10.70	10.70	−0.10	−9.4	−10.0	NS	..
Quantitative Group:								
BostFor	ITL	10.42	10.42	−0.03	+9.8	+8.0	+7.3	D
BostGrInc	G&I	13.66	13.66	−0.02	−5.6	−6.4	+6.6	D
BostNumA	SML	15.04	15.04	−0.27	−2.3	−4.6	NS	..
BostNumO	SML	14.91	14.91	−0.26	−2.5	−4.7	NS	..
Quest For Value:								
CA TE	MCA	10.36	10.88	−0.01	−6.6	−6.9	+7.3	C
PATxA p	MPA	7.60	7.98	−0.01	−7.2	−7.5	+7.2	D
SCTxA	SSM	7.68	8.06	−0.02	−7.0	−7.1	+6.6	E
US Gvt A p	BND	6.84	7.18	...	−3.0	−3.5	+7.0	D
H Yd B A p	BHI	6.60	6.93	−0.04	−2.4	−3.5	+16.2	C
Sentinel Group:								
Balan p	S&B	14.44	15.20	...	−4.2	−4.9	+7.7	D
Bond p	BND	6.13	6.45	+0.01	−5.2	−5.9	+9.2	B
Com S p	G&I	28.34	29.83	+0.03	−4.0	−5.3	+7.4	D
EmGr p	SML	5.31	5.59	−0.03	−7.2	−6.7	NS	..
GvSecs p	BND	9.71	10.22	+0.01	−4.8	−5.3	+7.7	C
Grwth p	GRO	16.17	17.02	−0.09	−9.0	−8.9	+2.7	E
PA TF p	MPA	12.87	13.55	−0.01	−5.0	−5.0	+7.0	E
TF Inc p	GLM	12.93	13.61	−0.01	−5.9	−6.1	+7.9	B
World p	ITL	12.67	13.34	−0.05	+0.3	−0.5	NS	..
Sentry	GRO	14.67	NL	+0.04	−1.2	−1.4	+7.0	C
Sequoia	GRO	54.82	NL	+0.24	+0.3	−0.5	+12.9	A
Seven Seas Series:								
MatrixEq	GRO	11.32	NL	...	−4.7	−5.8	NS	..
SP500	G&I	10.10	NL	...	−4.4	−6.2	NS	..
S&P Mid	SML	11.18	NL	−0.14	−5.9	−6.4	NS	..
ST Gvt	BST	9.68	NL	...	−0.9	−1.2	NS	..
Yldpl	BST	9.99	NL	...	+0.9	+0.8	NS	..
1784 Funds:								
Gov Med	BIN	9.43	NL	+0.01	−4.1	−4.5	NS	..
Gr In	G&I	10.17	NL	−0.12	−4.5	−5.6	NS	..
MATEIn	DMA	9.66	NL	−0.03	−5.7	−5.7	NS	..

35. Sentinel Group: Balan—Objective, net asset value, and ranking: ____________________

36. Quantitative Group: BostGrinc—Offer price and 13-week return: ____________________

37. Quest for Value: CA TE—NAV, NAV change, and 3-year return: ____________________

38. Which Seven Seas Series funds have the best and worst YTD returns? ____________________

Name ____________

Class ____________

Fund	Offer Price	Net Asset Value (NAV)	Sales Charge	Sales Charge %
39. Quest for Value: CA TE	______	______	______	______
40. Sentinel Group: EmGr	______	______	______	______

Calculate the net asset value and number of shares purchased for the following funds (round shares to thousandths, three decimal places):

	Total Assets	Total Liabilities	Shares Outstanding	Net Asset Value (NAV)	Offer Price	Total Investment	Shares Purchased
41.	$30,000,000	$1,800,000	4,000,000	______	$7.80	$50,000	______
42.	58,000,000	3,700,000	7,100,000	______	NL	25,000	______

Calculate the total cost, proceeds, total gain or loss, and return on investment for the following mutual fund investments. The offer price is the purchase price of the shares and the net asset value is the price at which the shares were later sold.

	Shares	Offer Price	Total Cost	Net Asset Value (NAV)	Proceeds	Per Share Dividends	Total Gain (or Loss)	Return on Investment (%)
43.	100	$13.40	______	$11.80	______	$.75	______	______
44.	500	12.65	______	15.30	______	.63	______	______
45.	1,000	9.40	______	12.82	______	.96	______	______

46. A mutual fund has an offer price of $8.90 and a net asset value of $8.35.

a. What is the sales charge?

b. What is the sales charge percent?

Answers

39. ____________

40. ____________

41. ____________

42. ____________

43. ____________

44. ____________

45. ____________

46. a. ____________

b. ____________

Name ______________________

Class ______________________

Answers

47. ______________________

48. ______________________

49. ______________________

50. a. ______________________

47. A mutual fund has total assets of $25,000,000 and liabilities of $1,500,000. If there are 2,600,000 shares outstanding, what is the net asset value of the fund?

48. Melinda Gross invested a lump sum of $20,000 in a mutual fund with an offer price of $11.80. How many shares did she purchase?

3

49. Rick Ungerman purchased 800 shares of Premium Value Fund for an offer price of $6.90 per share. He later sold the shares at a net asset value of $8.60 per share. During the time he owned the shares, the fund paid dividends of $.24 and $.38 per share. What is Rick's return on investment?

BUSINESS DECISION

Paper Profit

50. You have received your investment portfolio year-end statement from your broker, Rich Waldman. All investments were purchased at the January prices and held the entire year.

Portfolio Year-End Statement

Investment	Number	Dividend	Price—Jan. 1	Price—Dec. 31
Disney	400 shares	$.30	38.38	45.75
Federal Express	500 shares	0	74.50	70.13
McDonald's	200 shares	.24	27.88	29.25
Exxon	300 shares	3.00	68.75	64.63
AT&T $7\frac{1}{8}$ 02	20 bonds		98.50	101.38
Ryder $9\frac{7}{8}$ 17	10 bonds		103.88	100.75

a. Calculate how much profit or loss you made for the year, including stock dividends and bond interest.

b. What was the total return on investment for your portfolio?

Name ______________________

Class ______________________

Answers

50. b. ______________________

c. ______________________

d. ______________________

c. Using a broker's commission of 3% buying and 3% selling on the stocks, and $5.00 buying and $5.00 selling per bond, how much profit or loss would you make if you liquidated your entire portfolio at the December 31 prices?

d. What would be the return on investment?

All the Math That's Fit to Learn

The Business Math Times

Volume XX | **Investments** | One Dollar

"Quote . . . Unquote"

It is not the return on my investment that I am concerned about;
it is the return of my investment.
—*Will Rogers*

October. This is one of the peculiarly dangerous months to speculate in stocks. The others are July, January, September, April, November, May, March, June, December, August and February.
—*Mark Twain*

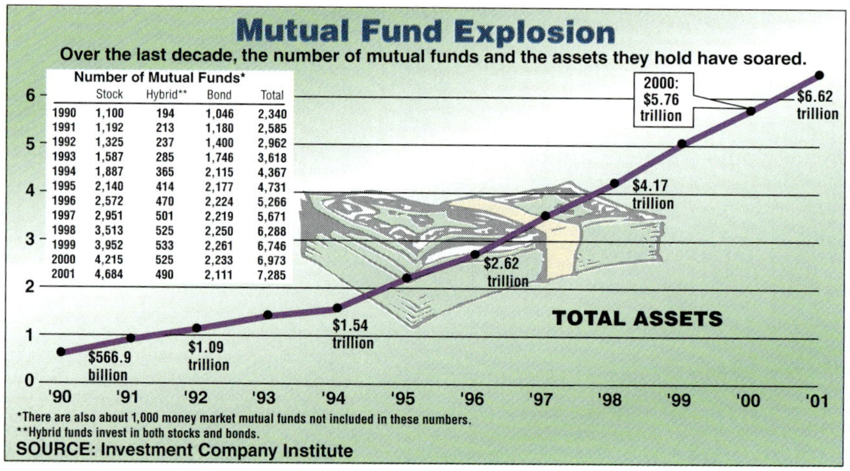

Number of Mutual Funds*

	Stock	Hybrid**	Bond	Total
1990	1,100	194	1,046	2,340
1991	1,192	213	1,180	2,585
1992	1,325	237	1,400	2,962
1993	1,587	285	1,746	3,618
1994	1,887	365	2,115	4,367
1995	2,140	414	2,177	4,731
1996	2,572	470	2,224	5,266
1997	2,951	501	2,219	5,671
1998	3,513	525	2,250	6,288
1999	3,952	533	2,261	6,746
2000	4,215	525	2,233	6,973
2001	4,684	490	2,111	7,285

*There are also about 1,000 money market mutual funds not included in these numbers.
**Hybrid funds invest in both stocks and bonds.
SOURCE: Investment Company Institute

Stockbroker

CAREER TRACK

Most investors, whether they are individuals with a few hundred dollars to invest or larger institutions with millions, use stockbrokers to handle the transactions when buying or selling stocks, bonds, mutual funds, or other financial products. In most cases, the brokers relay the buy or sell order through their firms' offices to the floor of a securities exchange, such as the New York Stock Exchange.

Stockbrokers also provide many related services for their customers, such as financial counseling, portfolio management, and supplying information about various securities their clients are interested in, as well as giving current price quotations.

Because stockbrokers must be well informed about economic conditions and trends, a college education, with emphasis in business administration, economics, and finance is increasingly important.

Stockbrokers must meet state licensing requirements, which generally include passing examinations and, in some cases, furnishing a personal bond. In addition, they must serve a four-month apprenticeship and pass an exam administered by the National Association of Securities Dealers, Inc., before they are officially registered as representatives of their brokerage firms.

Median annual earnings of securities, commodities, and financial services sales representatives are about $50,000. The middle half earned between $31,400 and $103,040. The lowest 10% earned less than $22,600; the top 10%, more than $124,800.

Brokers who work for discount brokerage firms that promote the use of telephone and online trading services are usually paid a salary. Sometimes the salary is boosted by bonuses that reflect the profitability of the office.

For further information
visit "Business Careers" at:
www.contemporarymath.com

THE WALL STREET JOURNAL

"Stock prices fell sharply today on the fear that stock prices would fall sharply."

Wall Street

The street in New York City where the New York Stock Exchange (NYSE), American Stock Exchange (AMEX), the National Association of Securities Dealers Automated Quotations (NASDAQ), and many brokerage firms are located is Wall Street.

The term is often used to describe the stock market itself. "How did Wall Street do today?"

Brainteaser

PEPPERONI & CHEESE—PLEASE!

Two hungry friends were at a Pizza King. If they wanted the most pizza for their money, and the prices were the same, should they order a 10-inch round pizza or a 9-inch square pizza?

ANSWER TO LAST ISSUE'S BRAINTEASER

8 Minutes

At 15 mph, the train is traveling at 1 mile every 4 minutes. To get through a 1-mile-long tunnel, the train must travel a total of 2 miles: 1 mile in, and 1 mile out. The total travel time, therefore, is $4 \times 2 = 8$ minutes.

CHAPTER

21

Business Statistics and Data Presentation

PERFORMANCE OBJECTIVES

Section I Data Interpretation and Presentation

Section II Measures of Central Tendency and Dispersion—Ungrouped Data

Section III Frequency Distributions—Grouped Data

Information, the Name of the Game!

Statistical ideas and methods are used in almost every aspect of human activity, from the natural sciences to the social sciences. Statistics has special applications in such areas as medicine, psychology, education, engineering, and agriculture. In business, statistical methods are applied extensively in production, marketing, finance, and accounting.

business statistics
The systematic process of collecting, interpreting, and presenting numerical data about business situations.

descriptive statistics
Statistical procedures that deal with the collection, classification, summarization, and the tabular or graphical presentation of data.

statistical inference
The process of arriving at conclusions, predictions, forecasts, or estimates based on the data under study.

Business statistics is the systematic process of collecting, interpreting, and presenting numerical data about business situations. In business, statistics is organized into two categories, descriptive statistics and statistical inference. **Descriptive statistics** deals with the tabular or graphical presentation of data, whereas **statistical inference** is the process of arriving at conclusions, predictions, forecasts, or estimates based on that data. To make sound managerial decisions, today's managers must understand the meaning and implications of vast amounts of numerical data generated by their companies.

Business statistics starts with the collection of raw data concerning a particular business situation or question. For example, if management wants the next annual report to present a comparison chart of company sales and profit figures with current industry trends, two types of information would be required. First are the company records of sales and profits. These data would be readily available from *internal* company sources. Most large corporations today use a vast array of computer systems to collect and store incredible amounts of information relating to all aspects of business activity. Management information systems are then used to deliver these data, on request, in an electronic instant.

Information gathered from sources outside the firm, such as current industry statistics, are known as *external* data and are readily available from a variety of private and government publications. The federal government is by far the largest researcher and publisher of business data. The Departments of Commerce and Labor periodically publish information relating to all aspects of the economy and the country. Some of these publications are the *Statistical Abstract of the United States, Survey of Current Business, Monthly Labor Review, Federal Reserve Bulletin, Census of the United States,* and the *Census of Business.*

Private statistical services such as Moody's Investors Service and Standard and Poor's offer a wealth of information for business decision making. Other private sources are periodicals such as *The Wall Street Journal, Fortune, Business Week, Forbes,* and *Money,* as well as hundreds of industry and trade publications, and Web sites.

Everybody's Business
Real-World Connection

The material in this chapter presents concepts and procedures that will help you understand and evaluate statistical information that you encounter as both a consumer and businessperson.

Statistical information may be in the form of daily media, such as radio and television reports or newspaper and magazine articles, or they may be business-related statistics such as company reports, presentations, budgets, and schedules.

Government publications, financial journals, and news sources are excellent resources for business and financial data.

SECTION I

DATA INTERPRETATION AND PRESENTATION

Numerical data form the raw material on which analyses, forecasts, and managerial plans are based. In business, tables and charts are used extensively to summarize and display data in a clear and concise manner. In this section, you learn to read, interpret, and construct information from tables and charts.

21-1 Reading and Interpreting Information from Tables

Tables are a collection of related data arranged for ease of reference or comparison, usually in parallel columns with meaningful titles. They are a very useful tool in summarizing statistical data and are found everywhere in business. Once the data have been obtained from the table, they can be compared with other data by arithmetic or percentage analysis.

tables
A collection of related data arranged for ease of reference or comparison, usually in parallel columns with meaningful titles.

STEPS TO READING TABLES:

Step 1. Scan the titles above the columns for the category of information being sought.

Step 2. Look down the column for the specific fact required.

Table 21-1 shows the sales figures in dollars for Magnum Enterprises over a 6-month period. Magnum manufactures and sells standard and deluxe computer components. Note that the table is divided into columns representing sales per month of each product type by territory.

	January		February		March		April		May		June	
	Standard	Deluxe	Standard	Deluxe	Standard	Deluxe	Standard	Deluxe	Standard	Deluxe	Standard	Deluxe
Northwest	$123,200	$ 86,400	$115,800	$ 73,700	$133,400	$ 91,100	$136,700	$ 92,600	$112,900	$ 65,300	$135,000	$ 78,400
Northeast	214,700	121,300	228,400	133,100	246,600	164,800	239,000	153,200	266,100	185,000	279,300	190,100
Southwest	88,300	51,000	72,100	45,700	97,700	58,300	104,000	67,800	125,000	78,300	130,400	74,500
Southeast	143,200	88,700	149,900	91,300	158,400	94,500	127,700	70,300	145,700	79,400	162,000	88,600

TABLE 21-1
Magnum Enterprises 6-Month Sales Report

EXAMPLE

Answer the following questions about Magnum Enterprises from Table 21-1:

1. What were the sales of deluxe units in April in the Northeast?
2. What were the sales of standard units in May in the Southwest?
3. What were the total sales for February and March in the Southeast?
4. What months showed a decrease in sales of deluxe units in the Northwest?
5. How many more standard units were sold companywide in June than in January?
6. What percent of the total units sold in March were deluxe?

SOLUTION STRATEGY

Questions 1, 2, and 4 can be answered by inspection. Questions 3, 5, and 6 require numerical or percentage calculations.

1. Deluxe unit sales in April in the Northeast = $153,200
2. Standard unit sales in May in the Southwest = $125,000
3. Total sales in February and March in the Southeast:

$$149{,}900 + 91{,}300 + 158{,}400 + 94{,}500 = \$494{,}100$$

4. Decrease in sales of deluxe units in the Northwest occurred in February and May.
5. Standard unit sales in January = \$569,400
   Standard unit sales in June = \$706,700

$$706{,}700 - 569{,}400 = \underline{\underline{\$137{,}300}} \text{ more in June}$$

6. To solve this problem, we use the percentage formula Rate = Portion ÷ Base. In this case, the rate is the unknown, the total sales in March is the base, and the deluxe sales in March is the portion.

$$\text{Rate} = \frac{408{,}700}{1{,}044{,}800} = .3911 = \underline{\underline{39.1\%}}$$

TRY-IT | EXERCISES

Answer the following questions about Magnum Enterprises from Table 21-1:

1. What were the sales of standard units in February in the Northeast?
2. What were the sales of deluxe units in April in the Southeast?
3. What were the total sales for May and June in the Northwest?
4. What months showed an increase in sales of standard units in the Southwest?
5. How many more deluxe units were sold companywide in May than in April?
6. What percent of the total units sold in the Northwest were standard?

Check your answers with the solutions on page 805.

21-2 Reading and Constructing Line Charts

line chart
A series of data points on a grid, continuously connected by straight lines, that display a picture of selected data changing over a period of time.

***x*-axis**
The horizontal axis of a chart, usually used to measure units of time such as days, weeks, months, or years.

***y*-axis**
The vertical axis of a chart, usually used to measure the quantity or magnitude of something, such as sales dollars or production units. The *y*-axis is frequently used to measure the percentage of something.

Charts are used to display a picture of the relationships among selected data. **Line charts** show data changing over a period of time. A single glance at a line chart gives the viewer a general idea of the direction or trend of the data: up, down, or up and down.

The horizontal or ***x*-axis** is used to measure units of time, such as days, weeks, months, or years, whereas the vertical or ***y*-axis** depicts magnitude, such as sales dollars or production units. Frequently, the *y*-axis is used to measure the percentage of something.

Line charts are actually a series of data points on a grid, continuously connected by straight lines. They may contain a single line, representing the change of one variable such as interest rates; or they may contain multiple lines, representing the change of interrelated variables such as interest rates and stock prices or sales and profits.

STEPS FOR READING LINE CHARTS:

Step 1. Scan either the *x*- or *y*-axis for the known variable: *x* for time, *y* for amount.

Step 2. Draw a perpendicular line from that axis to the point where it intersects the chart.

Step 3. Draw a line from that point perpendicular to the opposite axis.

Step 4. The answer is read where that line intersects the opposite axis.

Exhibit 21-1 and Exhibit 21-2 are examples of single- and multiple-line charts.

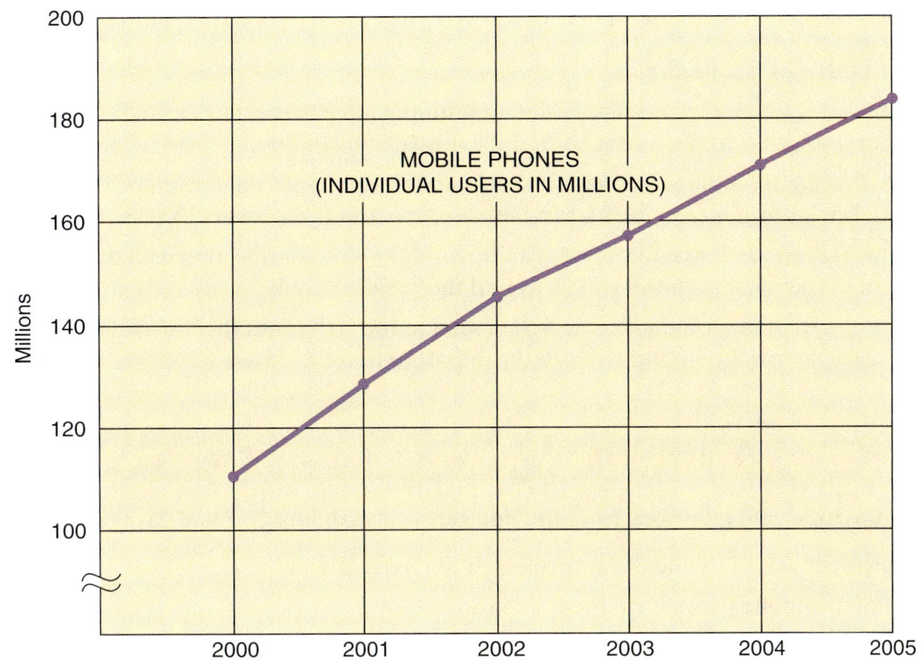

EXHIBIT 21-1
Single-Line Chart

> **Everybody's Business**
> **Learning Tip**
> Sometimes the x- or y-axis of a chart is "shortened" to better display the required scale. A pair of wavy lines (≈) intersecting the axis are used to indicate when this occurs. See Exhibit 21-1.

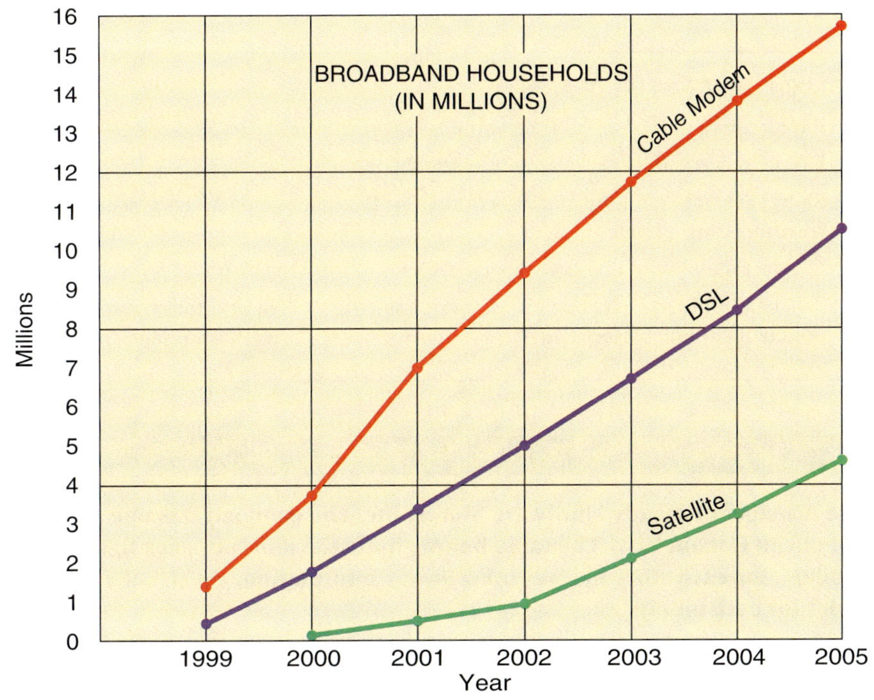

EXHIBIT 21-2
Multiple-Line Chart

> **Everybody's Business**
> **Real-World Connection**
> Tables illustrate specific data better than line charts; however, line charts are able to show relationships among data more clearly.
> Frequently, in business presentations they are used together, with the chart used to clarify or reinforce facts presented in a table.

EXAMPLES

Answer the following questions from the charts in Exhibits 21-1 and 21-2:

1. How many mobile phones were projected for 2002?

2. In what year were DSL households projected to reach 5 million?

3. How many cable modem households were there in 2001?
4. In what year was the number of mobile phones projected to reach 172 million?

SOLUTION STRATEGY

1. Locate 2002 on the *x*-axis and the scan up until the line chart is intersected. Look to the left, perpendicular to the *y*-axis, to find the answer, 145 million.
2. Locate 5 million on the *y*-axis and then scan to the right until the line chart is intersected. Look down, perpendicular to the *x*-axis, to find the answer, 2002.
3. Locate 2001 on the *x*-axis and then scan up until the line chart is intersected. Look to the left, perpendicular to the *y*-axis, to find the answer, 7 million.
4. Locate 172 million on the *y*-axis and then scan to the right until the line chart is intersected. Look down, perpendicular to the *x*-axis, to find the answer, 2004.

TRY-IT | EXERCISES

Answer the following questions from the line charts in Exhibits 21-1 and 21-2:

7. In what year were satellite dishes projected to pass 3 million?
8. How many mobile phones are projected for 2005?
9. In 2005, how many *more* cable modems than DSL connections will there be?

Check your answers with the solutions on page 805.

STEPS TO CONSTRUCT A LINE CHART:

Step 1. Evenly space and label the time variable on the *x*-axis.

Step 2. Evenly space and label the amount variable on the *y*-axis.

Step 3. Show each data point by placing a dot above the time period and across from the corresponding amount.

Step 4. Connect the plotted points with straight lines to form the chart.

Step 5. When multiple lines are displayed, they should be labeled or differentiated by various colors or line patterns.

EXAMPLE

You are the manager of Handy Hardware Stores, Inc. The company has one store in Centerville and one in Carson City. The table below shows the monthly sales figures, in thousands of dollars, for each store last year. From this information, construct a line chart of the total sales for each month.

Handy Hardware: Monthly Sales Report (000)

	Jan.	Feb.	Mar.	Apr.	May	June	July	Aug.	Sept.	Oct.	Nov.	Dec.
Centerville	16	18	24	21	15	14	17	18	16	23	24	20
Carson City	8	11	14	12	10	15	13	13	9	13	14	17
Total	24	29	38	33	25	29	30	31	25	36	38	37

SOLUTION STRATEGY

For this chart, show the months on the *x*-axis and the sales on the *y*-axis. Use a range of 0 to 40 on the *y*-axis. Plot each month with a dot and connect all the dots with straight lines.

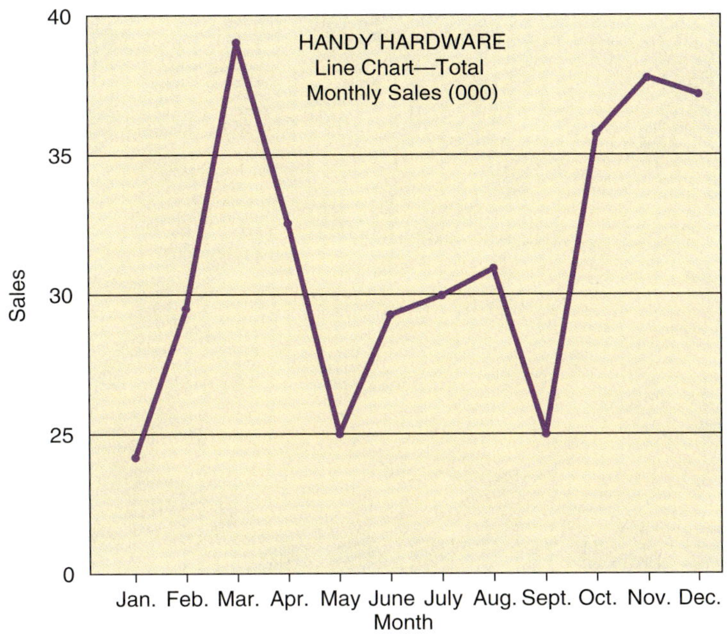

TRY-IT | EXERCISE

10. The following data represent the audience statistics for a circus that performed in your town last week. Use the grid below to draw a line chart of the total attendance for each day.

Circus Attendance

	Monday	Tuesday	Wednesday	Thursday	Friday	Saturday	Sunday
Adults	2,300	2,100	1,900	2,200	2,400	2,700	2,600
Children	3,300	2,600	2,400	1,900	2,700	3,100	3,600
Total	5,600	4,700	4,300	4,100	5,100	5,800	6,200

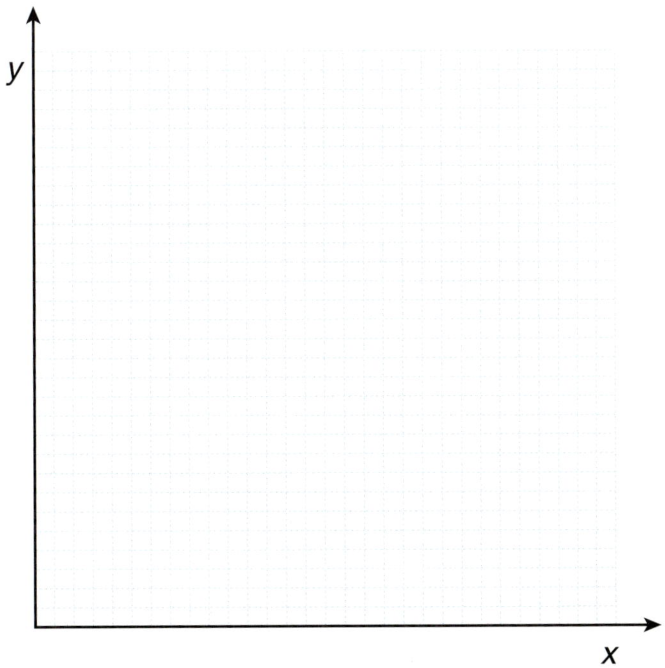

Check your chart with the solution on page 805.

Statistical information is recorded and used in many different ways at sporting events, including measuring attendance and athlete performance.

EXAMPLE

From the Handy Hardware table on page 770 construct a multiple-line chart of the monthly sales for each of the stores. Show the Centerville store with a solid line and the Carson City store with a dashed line.

SOLUTION STRATEGY

As in the last example, the x-axis, time, will be months. The y-axis should range from 0 to 25 to include all the data.

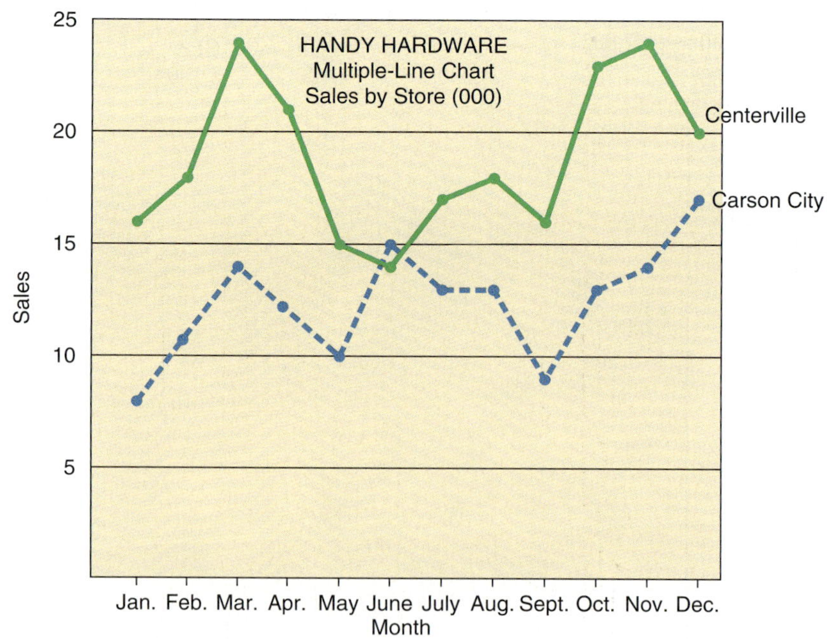

TRY-IT | EXERCISE

11. From the Circus Attendance table on page 771 draw a multiple-line chart showing the number of adults and children attending the circus last week. Use a solid line for the adults and a dashed line for the children.

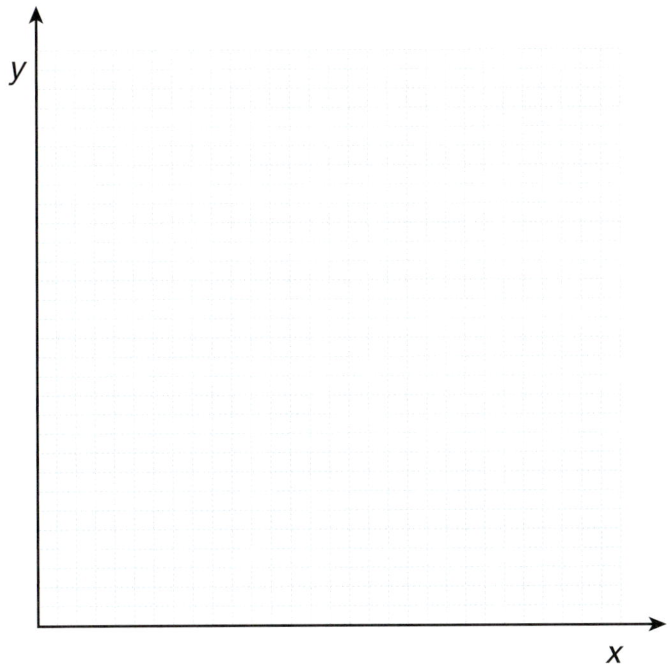

Check your chart with the solution on page 805.

21-3 Reading and Constructing Bar Charts

Bar charts represent quantities or percentages by the length of horizontal or vertical bars. As with line charts, bar charts often illustrate increases or decreases in magnitude of a certain variable or the relationship between similar variables. Bar charts may or may not be based on the movement of time.

Bar charts are divided into three categories: standard, comparative, and component. **Standard bar charts** are used to illustrate the change in magnitude of one variable. See Exhibit 21-3.

Comparative bar charts are used to illustrate two or more related variables. The bars representing each variable should be shaded or colored differently to make the chart easy to read and interpret. See Exhibit 21-4.

bar chart
Graphical presentations that represent quantities or percentages by the length of horizontal or vertical bars. These charts may or may not be based on the movement of time.

standard bar chart
A bar chart that illustrates increases or decreases in magnitude of one variable.

comparative bar chart
A bar chart used to illustrate the relationship between two or more similar variables.

One of the most common uses of statistical information and data interpretation is for business presentations.

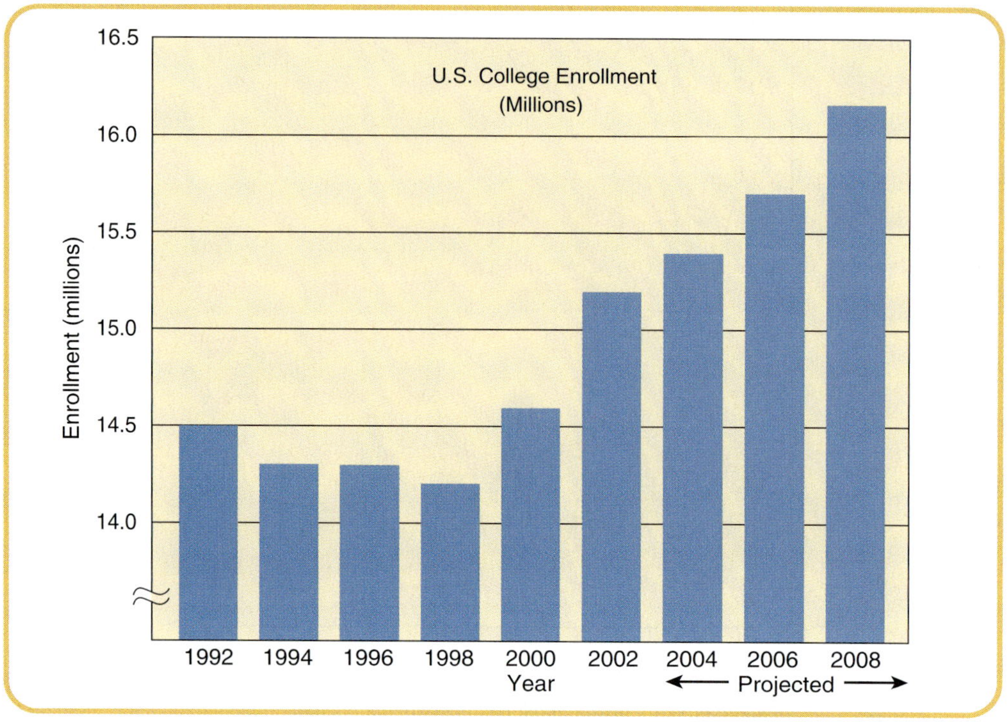

EXHIBIT 21-3
Standard Bar Chart

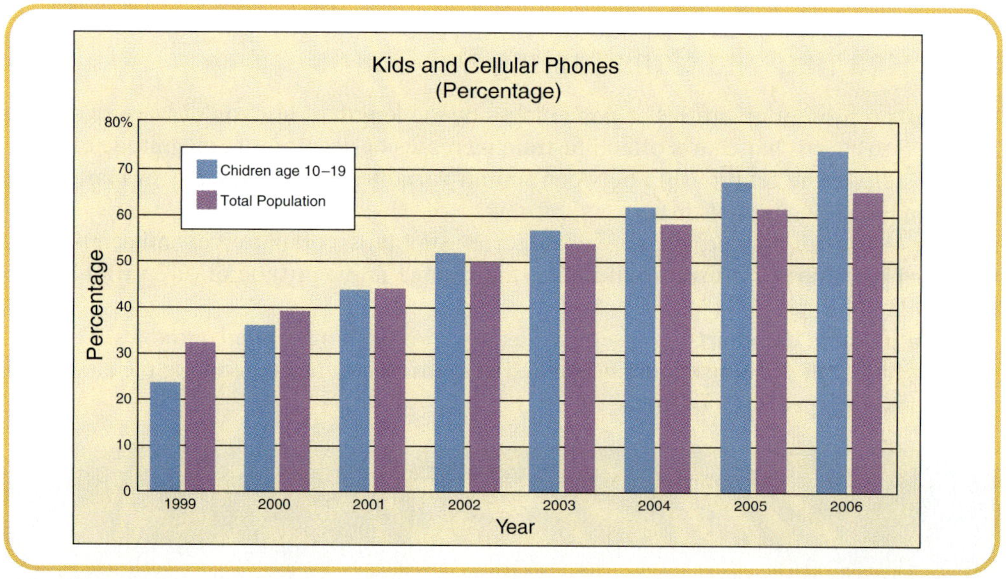

EXHIBIT 21-4
Comparative Bar Chart

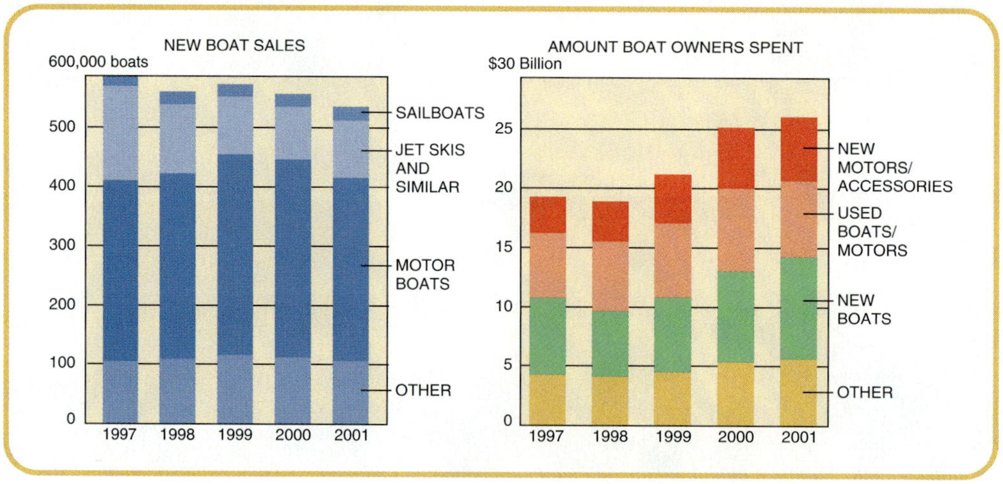

EXHIBIT 21-5
Component Bar Charts

Component bar charts are used to illustrate parts of something that add to a total. Each bar is divided into the components, stacked on top of each other and shaded or colored differently. See Exhibit 21-5.

component bar chart
A bar chart used to illustrate the parts of something that add to a total; each bar is divided into the components stacked on top of each other and shaded or colored differently.

STEPS FOR READING BAR CHARTS:

Step 1. Scan the x- or y-axis for a known variable.

Step 2. Read the answer on the opposite axis directly across from the top of the appropriate bar.

EXAMPLES

From the bar charts in Exhibits 21-3, 21-4, and 21-5, answer the following questions:

1. What was the college enrollment in 2002?

2. In what year is the college enrollment projected to surpass 15.5 million?

3. In 2000, what percent of children age 10 to 19 had cellular phones?

4. What is the first year it is projected that more than 50% of the total population will have cell phones?

5. In what year did the total number of new recreational boats exceed 600,000?

6. How much did boat owners spend in 2000 on boats and motors?

SOLUTION STRATEGY

1. Locate 2002 on the x-axis and scan up to the top of the bar; then scan left to the y-axis for the answer, 15.2 million.

2. Locate 15.5 million on the y-axis and scan right until a bar is intersected; now look down to the x-axis for the answer, 2006.

3. Locate the bar representing children age 10 to 19 in 2000 on the x-axis and scan up to the top of the bar; then scan left to the y-axis for the answer, 35%.

4. Locate 50% on the y-axis and scan right until a bar is intersected; now look down to the x-axis for the answer, 2003.

5. Locate 600,000 on the y-axis and scan right until a bar is intersected; now look down to the x-axis for the answer, 1997.

6. Locate 2000 on the x-axis and scan up to the top of the bar; then scan left to the y-axis for the answer, \$25 billion.

TRY-IT | EXERCISES

From the bar charts in Exhibits 21-3, 21-4, and 21-5, answer the following questions:

12. What was the college enrollment in 1992?

13. In what year did children age 10 to 19 surpass the total population in cell phones?

14. How many new recreational boats were sold in 2001?

15. In what year did spending on new boats and motors decrease from the previous year?

Check your answers with the solutions on page 806.

Everybody's Business

Learning Tip

The steps shown here are used to construct charts with *vertical* bars. For charts with *horizontal* bars, lay out the bars on the *y*-axis and the magnitude variable on the *x*-axis.

STEPS TO CONSTRUCT A BAR CHART:

Step 1. Evenly space and label the *x*-axis. The space between bars should be one-half the width of the bars.

Step 2. Evenly space and label the *y*-axis. Be sure to include the full range of values needed to represent the variable. The lowest values should start at the bottom of the *y*-axis and increase upward.

Step 3. Draw each bar up from the *x*-axis to the point opposite the *y*-axis that corresponds to its value.

Step 4. For comparative and component bar charts, differentiate the bars by color or shading pattern. For complex presentations, provide a key or legend that shows which pattern or color represents each variable. This will help the reader to interpret the chart.

EXAMPLE

From the Handy Hardware sales report table on page 770, construct a standard bar chart of total sales for January through June.

SOLUTION STRATEGY

For this chart, the time variable, January through June, is shown on the *x*-axis. A range of 0 to 40 is used on the *y*-axis.

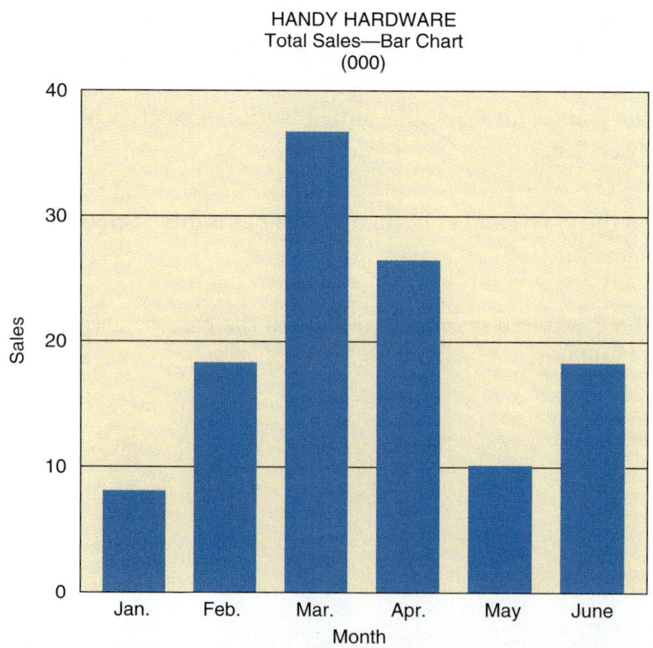

TRY-IT EXERCISE

16. From the table for Circus Attendance on page 771 use the following grid to construct a standard bar chart of the total attendance for each day.

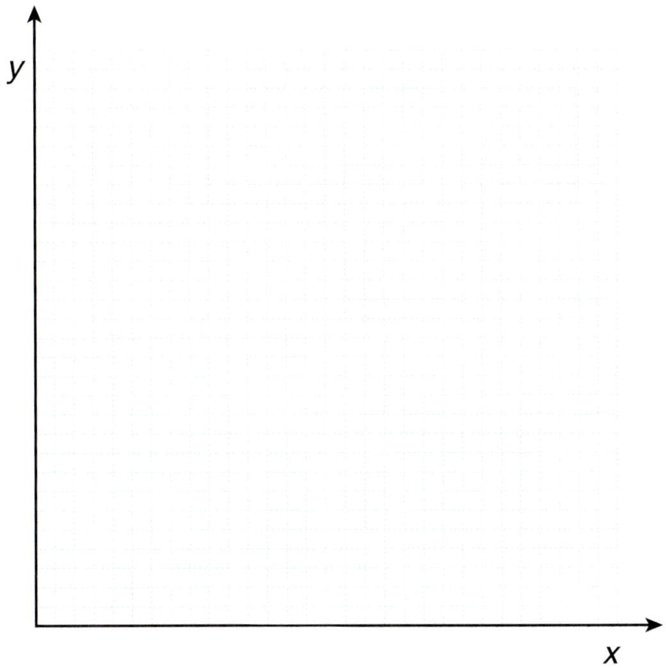

Check your chart with the solution on page 806.

EXAMPLE

From the table for Circus Attendance on page 771 construct a component bar chart that displays the adults and the children as components of each day's total audience. Plot the adults at the bottom of the bars in dark shading, and the children stacked above the adults in light shading.

SOLUTION STRATEGY

For this chart, the time variable, Monday through Sunday, is shown on the x-axis. A range of 0 to 7,000 is used on the y-axis.

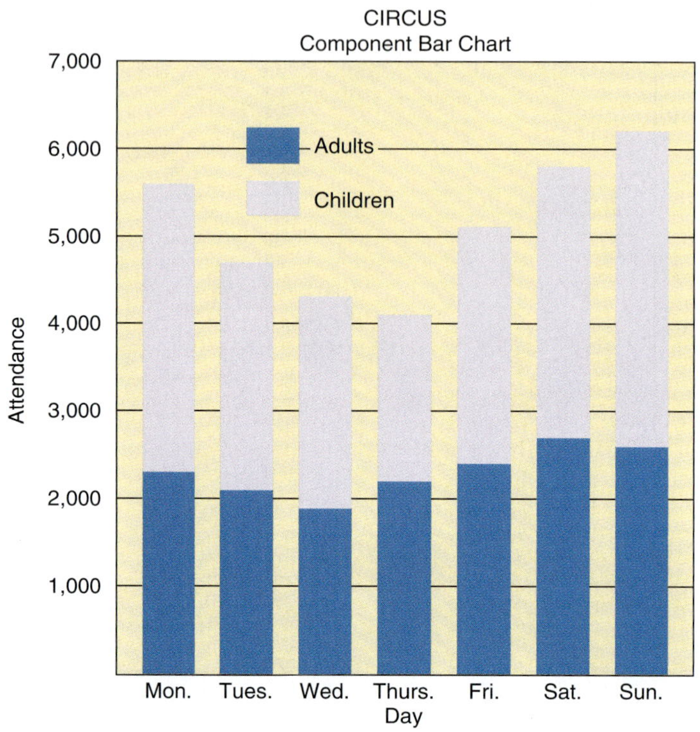

TRY-IT | EXERCISE

17. From the Handy Hardware sales report table on page 770 construct a component bar chart that displays the Centerville and the Carson City stores as components of the total monthly sales for July through December.

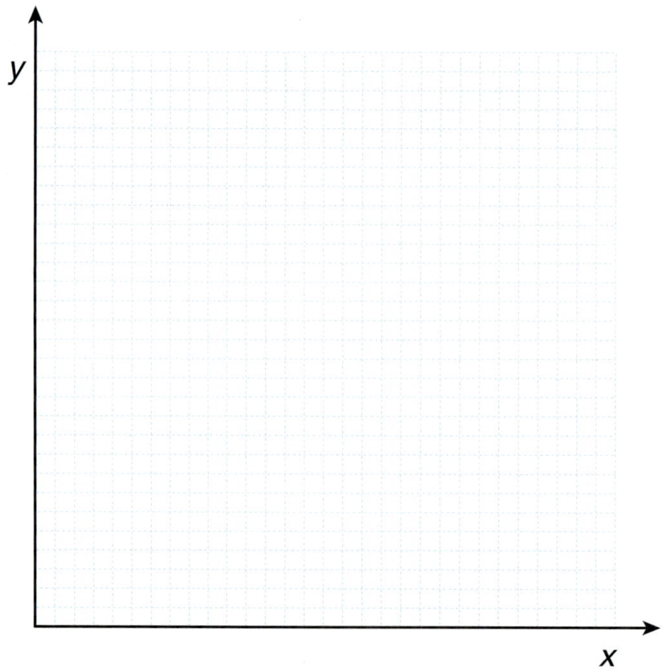

Check your chart with the solution on page 806.

EXAMPLE

From the table below, construct a comparative bar chart of the freshmen and sophomore enrollment. Let the x-axis represent the time variable. For each term, group the bars together and differentiate them by shading.

Interstate Business College: Annual Enrollment

	Fall	Winter	Spring	Summer
Freshmen	1,800	1,400	1,350	850
Sophomores	1,200	1,200	1,150	700
Juniors	1,200	1,100	750	650
Seniors	850	700	500	400

SOLUTION STRATEGY

This chart is constructed in the same way as the standard bar chart except that the variables being compared are drawn side by side. The space between the bars is one-half the width of each bar. The y-axis ranges from 0 to 2,000 students. Note that the bars are shaded to differentiate the variables and that an explanation key is provided.

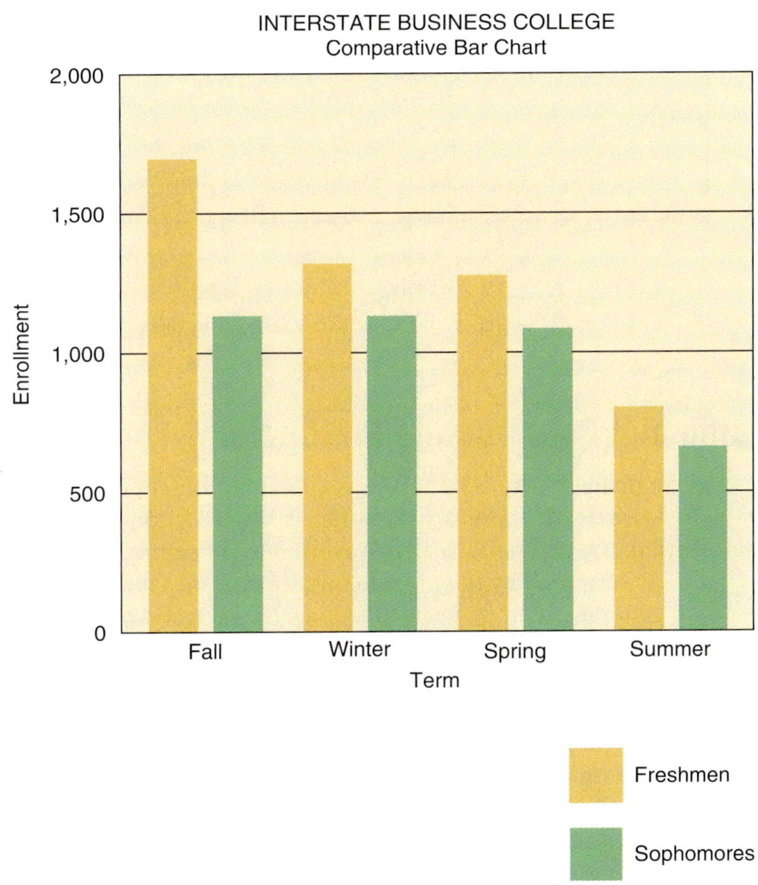

Everybody's Business

Real-World Connection

Many popular software programs, such as Microsoft's Excel and PowerPoint, Lotus 123, and Harvard Graphics, are designed to generate data in visually appealing chart form. These can be used to enhance your homework assignments at school or business presentations at work.

TRY-IT | EXERCISE

18. From the Interstate Business College enrollment figures in the table on page 779, construct a comparative bar chart of the junior and senior enrollment. Let the *x*-axis represent the time variable. For each term, group the bars together and differentiate them by shading.

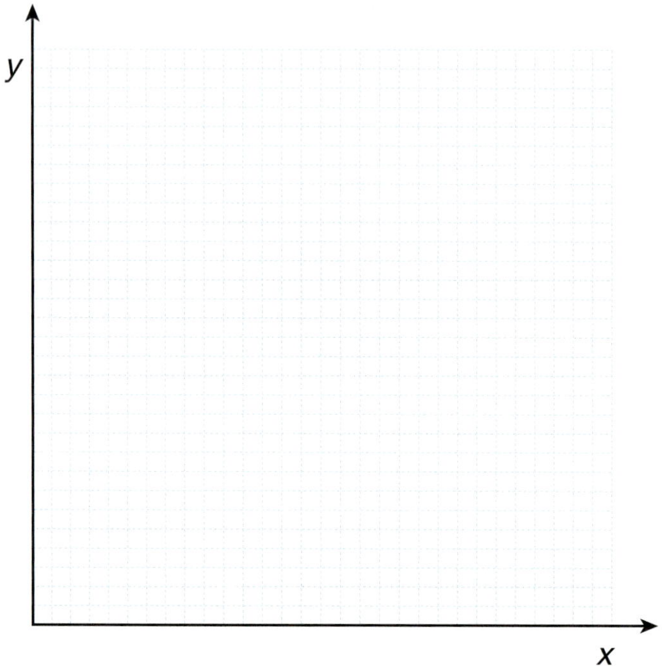

Check your chart with the solution on page 806.

21-4 Reading and Constructing Pie Charts

pie chart
A circle divided into sections, usually expressed in percentage form, representing the component parts of a whole.

The **pie chart** is a circle divided into sections representing the component parts of a whole. The whole, 100%, is the circle; the parts are the wedge-shaped sections of the circle. When this type of chart is used, the data are usually converted to percentages. The size of each section of the circle is determined by the portion or percentage each component is of the whole. Pie charts are generally read by inspection because each component of the data is clearly labeled by category and percent. Exhibit 21-6 illustrates examples of pie charts.

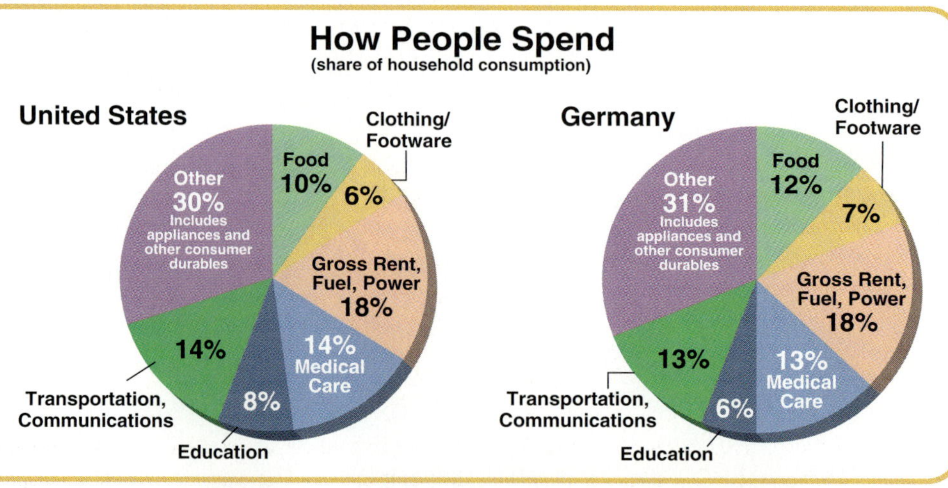

EXHIBIT 21-6
Pie Charts

EXAMPLES

From the pie charts in Exhibit 21-6, answer the following:

1. In the United States, what percent of household consumption is spent on education?

2. What category of household consumption is the same in the United States and Germany?

SOLUTION STRATEGY

By inspection,

1. 8% of U.S. household consumption is spent on education.

2. Gross rent, fuel, and power (18%) is the same in the United States and Germany.

TRY-IT EXERCISE

19. From the pie charts in Exhibit 21-6, answer the following:

a. What is the combined percent of Germany's household consumption of food and clothing?

b. How much more, in percent, does a U. S. household spend on transportation and communications than a German household?

Check your answers with the solutions on page 806.

STEPS TO CONSTRUCT A PIE CHART:

Step 1. Convert the amount of each component to a percent by using the percentage formula Rate = Portion ÷ Base. Let the portion be the amount of each component and the base the total amount. Round each percent to hundredths.

Step 2. Because a full circle is made up of 360° representing 100%, multiply each component's percent (decimal form) by 360° to determine how many degrees each component's slice will be. Round to the nearest whole degree.

Step 3. Draw a circle with a compass and mark the center.

Step 4. Using a protractor, mark off the number of degrees on the circle that represents each component.

Step 5. Connect each point on the circle with the center by a straight line to form a segment or slice for each component.

Step 6. Label the segments clearly by name, color, or shading.

Pepper . . . and Salt

THE WALL STREET JOURNAL

"The secret to a crowd-pleasing pie chart is the crust."

EXAMPLE

Cycle World sold 80 bicycles last week: 30 racing bikes, 20 off-road bikes, 15 standard bikes, and 15 tricycles. Construct a pie chart showing the sales breakdown for the shop.

SOLUTION STRATEGY

For this chart, we must first convert the component amounts to percents and then multiply the decimal form of the percents by 360° as follows:

$$\textit{Racing bikes:}\quad \frac{30}{80} = .375 = 37.5\% \qquad .375 \times 360^\circ = 135^\circ$$

$$\textit{Off-road bikes:}\quad \frac{20}{80} = .25 = 25\% \qquad .25 \times 360^\circ = 90^\circ$$

$$\textit{Standard bikes:}\quad \frac{15}{80} = .1875 = 18.75\% \qquad .1875 \times 360^\circ = 67.5^\circ$$

$$\textit{Tricycles:}\quad \frac{15}{80} = .1875 = 18.75\% \qquad .1875 \times 360^\circ = 67.5^\circ$$

Next, draw a circle and use a protractor to mark the degree points of each component. Connect the points with the center of the circle to form the segments, and label each appropriately. The completed chart follows.

> **Everybody's Business**
> **Learning Tip**
> Although a full circle has exactly 360°, sometimes, as in this example, the total may be slightly higher or lower than 360° because of rounding.

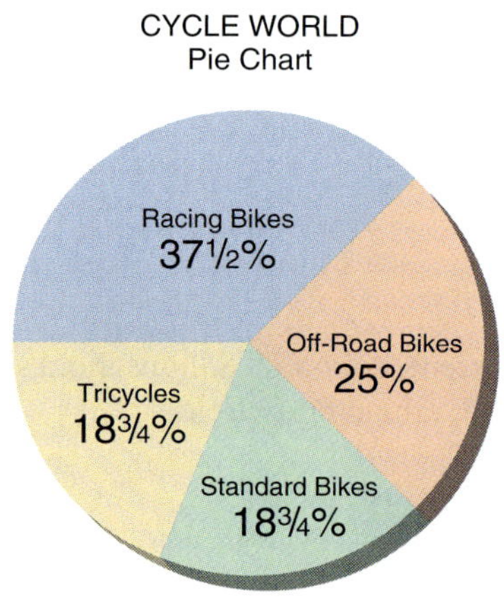

TRY-IT | EXERCISE

20. From the Interstate Business College enrollment figures in the table on page 779, construct a pie chart illustrating the winter term enrollment.

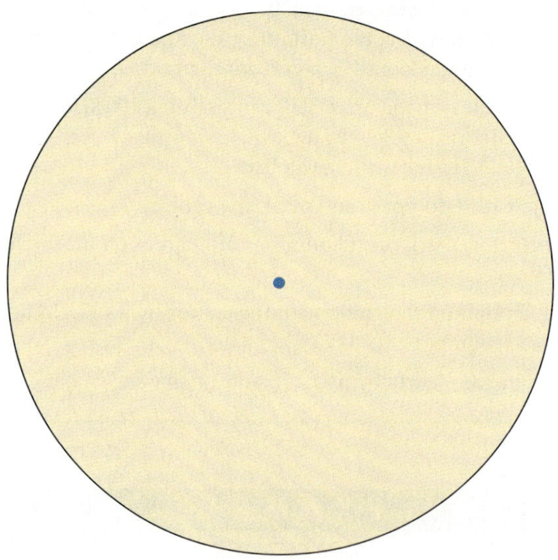

Check your chart with the solution on page 806.

REVIEW EXERCISES | CHAPTER 21—SECTION I

As the sales manager for Magnum Enterprises, you have been asked by the president to prepare the following charts for the shareholders' meeting next week. Use the 6-month sales report, Table 21-1, as the database for these charts. Calculate totals as required:

1. Single-line chart of the total company sales per month.

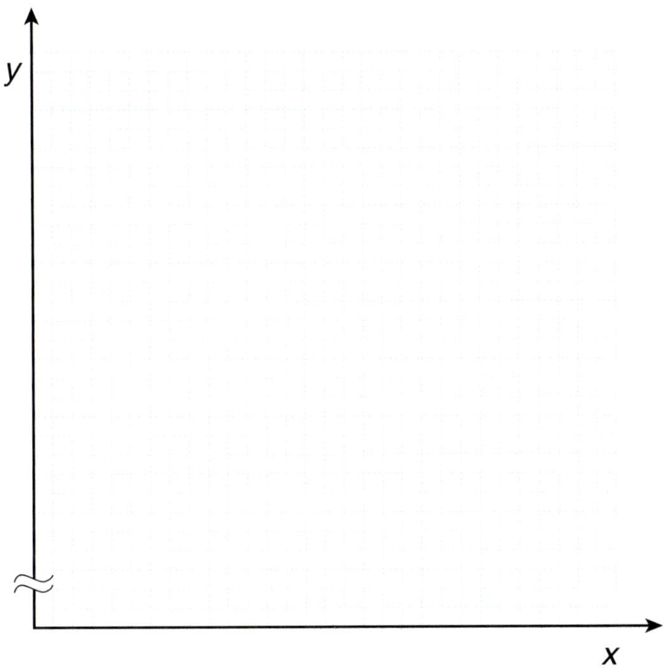

2. Multiple-line chart of the total sales per month of each model, standard and deluxe.

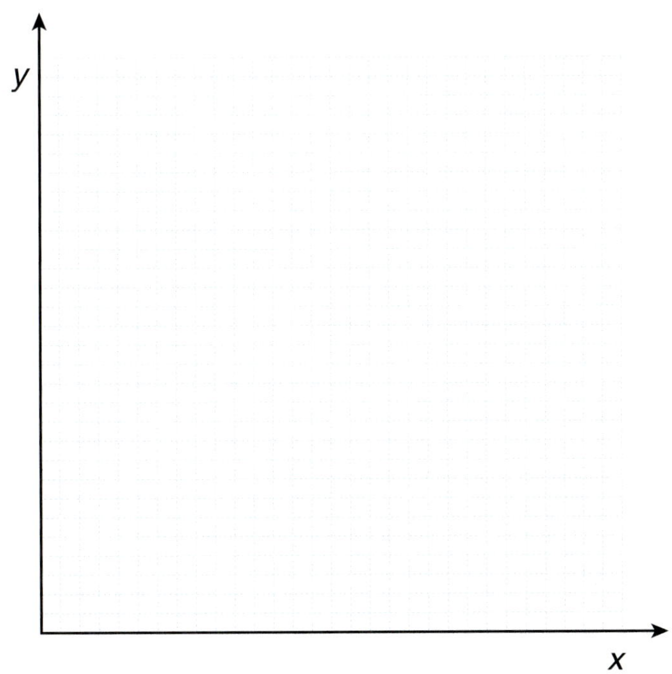

3. Standard bar chart of the deluxe sales per month in the Southeast territory.

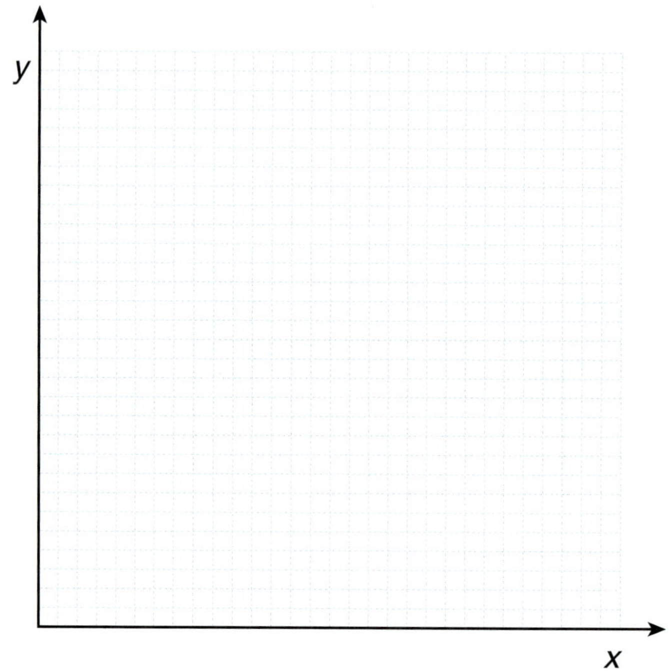

4. Component bar chart of the standard and deluxe model sales as components of total monthly sales in the Northeast territory.

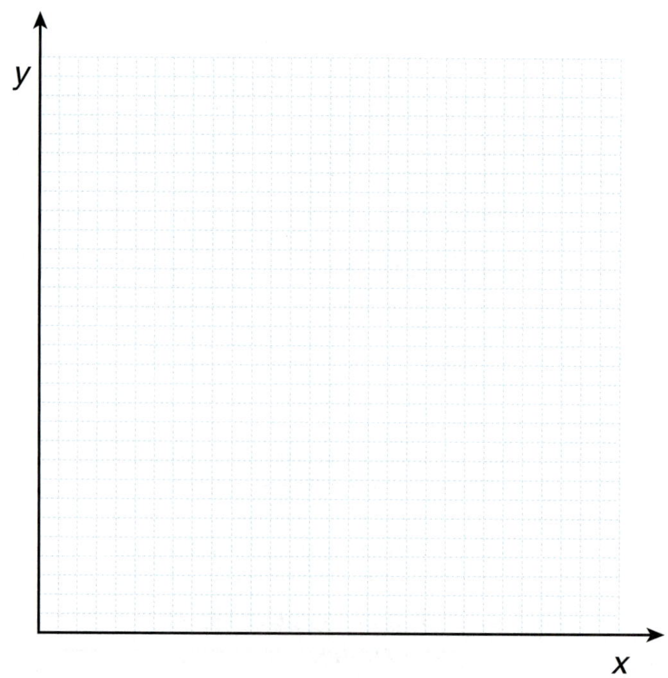

5. Comparative bar chart of the standard and deluxe model sales per month in the Northwest territory.

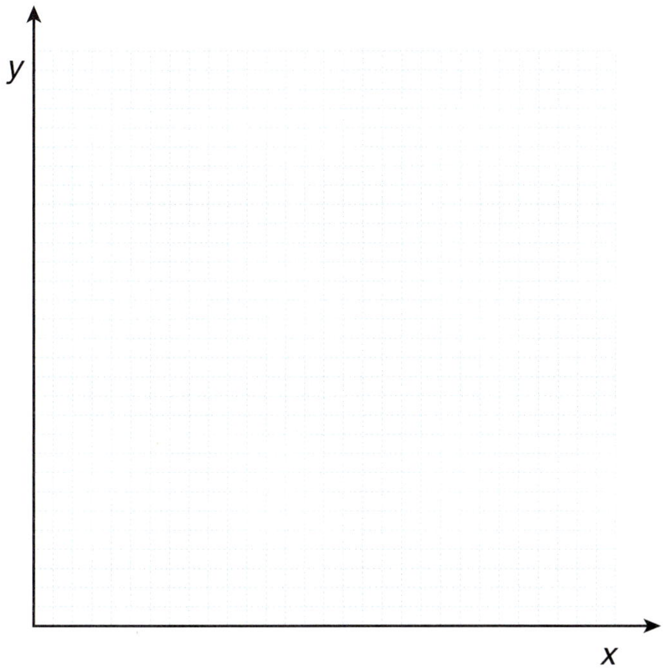

6. Pie chart of the total 6-month sales of the four territories.

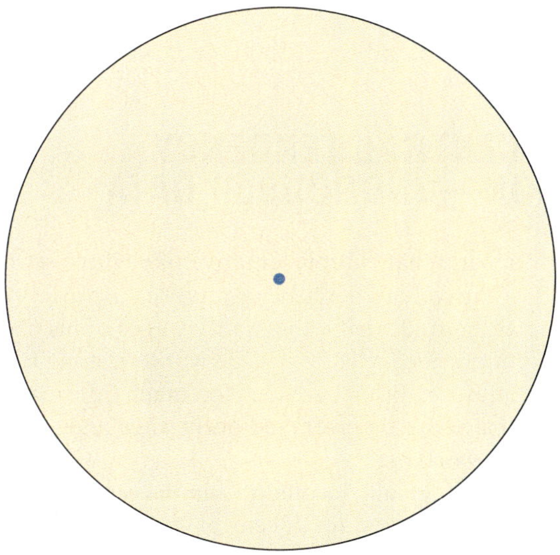

BUSINESS DECISION

Choosing a Chart

7. You have been asked to prepare a chart of stock prices for the upcoming semiannual stockholders' meeting for Magnum Enterprises. The following table shows Magnum's stock prices on the first day of each month. Choose and prepare a chart that best illustrates this information.

Month	Stock Price
January	35.50
February	32.75
March	37.25
April	38.50
May	40.25
June	39.75

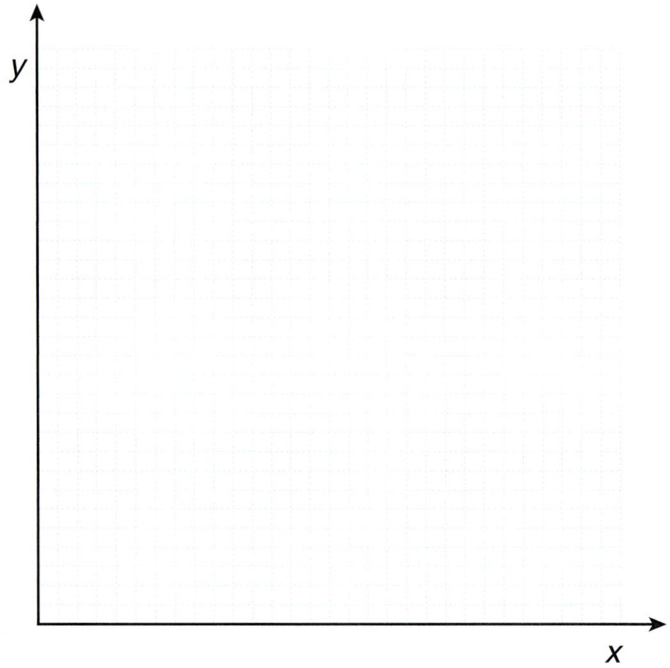

SECTION II

MEASURES OF CENTRAL TENDENCY AND DISPERSION—UNGROUPED DATA

average
A numerical value that is representative of a whole set of values.

A numerical **average** is a value that is representative of a whole set of values. In business, managers use averages extensively to describe or represent a variety of situations. Imagine a payroll director being asked to describe the hourly wages of his 650 factory workers. On the one extreme, he might produce a list of his 650 workers along with their hourly wages. This action answers the question, but it provides too much information. A more appropriate response might be to calculate the average hourly wage and report that "$9.75 was the average hourly wage of the workers."

Because an average is numerically located within the range of values that it represents, averages are often referred to as measures of central tendency. In this section, we study the three most commonly used averages in business statistics: the arithmetic mean, the median, and the mode. We also study a measure of dispersion known as the range.

21-5 Calculating the Arithmetic Mean of Ungrouped Data

mean, or arithmetic mean
The sum of the values of a set of data divided by the number of values in that set.

The **arithmetic mean** corresponds to the generally accepted meaning of the word *average.* It is customary to abbreviate the term *arithmetic mean* and refer to this average simply as the **mean.**

STEPS TO CALCULATE THE ARITHMETIC MEAN OF UNGROUPED DATA:

Step 1. Find the sum of all the values in the data set.

Step 2. Divide the sum in Step 1 by the number of values in the set.

$$\text{Mean} = \frac{\text{Sum of values}}{\text{Number of values}}$$

Everybody's Business

Real-World Connection

Your grade point average (GPA) is actually the *mean* of your grades. It is calculated by assigning a "value" to each grade, such as A=4, B=3, C=2, and multiplying those values by the number of credits earned for each.

The sum of those values divided by the number of credits earned is your GPA.

EXAMPLE

A travel agency had daily sales of $4,635 on Monday, $3,655 on Tuesday, $3,506 on Wednesday, $2,870 on Thursday, $4,309 on Friday, and $5,475 on Saturday. What is the mean sales per day?

SOLUTION STRATEGY

To calculate the mean (average sales per day), we find the sum of the values (sales per day) and divide this sum by the number of values (6 days).

$$\text{Mean} = \frac{\text{Sum of values}}{\text{Number of values}}$$

$$\text{Mean} = \frac{4{,}635 + 3{,}655 + 3{,}506 + 2{,}870 + 4{,}309 + 5{,}475}{6} = \frac{24{,}450}{6} = \underline{\underline{\$4{,}075}}$$

TRY-IT | EXERCISE

21. The attendance figures for a series of management seminars are as follows: 432, 247, 661, 418, and 512. What was the average number of individuals attending per seminar?

Check your answer with the solution on page 807.

21-6 Calculating the Median

Another measure of central tendency, and a very useful way of describing a large quantity of data, is the median. The **median** of a set of numbers is the *midpoint* value when the numbers are ranked in ascending or descending order. The median is a more useful measure of central tendency than the mean when one or more of the values of the set is significantly higher or lower than the rest of the set. For example, if the ages of five individuals in a group are 22, 26, 27, 31, and 69, the mean of this set is 35. However, the median is 27, a value that better describes the set.

median
The *midpoint* value of a set of data when the numbers are ranked in ascending or descending order.

When there is an odd number of values in the set, the middle value is the median. For example, in a set of seven ranked values, the fourth value is the midpoint. There are three values greater than and three values less than the median.

When there is an even number of values in the set, the median is the midpoint or average between the two middle values. For example, in a set with 10 values, the median is the midpoint between the fifth and the sixth value.

STEPS TO DETERMINE THE MEDIAN:

Step 1. Rank the numbers in ascending or descending order.

Step 2a. For an *odd number of values*—The median is the middle value.

Step 2b. For an *even number of values*—The median is the average or midpoint of the two middle values.

$$\textbf{Median} = \frac{\textbf{Middle value} + \textbf{Middle value}}{\textbf{2}}$$

EXAMPLE

Find the median for the following set of values:

2 8 5 13 11 6 9 15 4

SOLUTION STRATEGY

Step 1. Rank the data in ascending order as follows:

2 4 5 6 8 9 11 13 15

Step 2. Because the number of values in this set is *odd* (nine), there are four values below and four values above the median. Therefore, the median is the fifth value, $\underline{\underline{8}}$.

TRY-IT | EXERCISE

22. Determine the median for the following set of values:

4,589 6,558 4,237 2,430 3,619 5,840 1,220

Check your answer with the solution on page 807.

EXAMPLE

Find the median for the following set of values:

56 34 87 12 45 49

SOLUTION STRATEGY

Step 1. Rank the data in ascending order:

12 34 45 49 56 87

Step 2. Because the number of values in this set is *even* (six), the median is the midpoint between the third and the fourth values, 45 and 49.

$$\text{Median} = \frac{\text{Middle value} + \text{Middle value}}{2} = \frac{45 + 49}{2} = \frac{94}{2} = \underline{\underline{47}}$$

TRY-IT | EXERCISE

23. Determine the median for the following set of values:

12 33 42 13 79 29 101 54 76 81

Check your answer with the solution on page 807.

21-7 Determining the Mode

The **mode** is the third measure of central tendency that we consider. It is the value or values in a set that occur *most often*. It is possible for a set of data to have more than one mode or no mode at all.

mode
The value or values in a set of data that occur *most often*.

STEPS TO DETERMINE THE MODE:

Step 1. Count the number of times each value in a set occurs.

Step 2a. If one value occurs more times than any other, it is the mode.

Step 2b. If two or more values occur more times than any other, they are all modes of the set.

Step 2c. If all values occur the same number of times, there is no mode.

One common business application of the mode is in merchandising, in which it is used to keep track of the most frequently purchased goods, as in the following example. Note that the mean and median of this set of data would provide little useful information regarding sales.

Everybody's Business
Real-World Connection
The *mode* is used extensively in marketing research to measure the most frequent responses on survey questions. In advertising, the mode translates into persuasive headlines, "4 Out of 5 Doctors Recommend . . . . "

It is interesting to note that the mean and median do not necessarily occur within a set of numbers; but the mode, if there is one, does.

EXAMPLE

Find the mode of the following set of values representing the wattage of light bulbs sold in a hardware store:

25 25 60 60 60 75 75 75 75 100 100 150

SOLUTION STRATEGY

From these data, we see that the mode is 75 watts, because the value 75 occurs most often. This would indicate to the retailer that 75-watt bulbs were the most frequently purchased.

TRY-IT | EXERCISE

24. Calculate the mode of the following set of values representing the size, in gallons, of fish tanks sold in a pet shop:

10 10 20 10 55 20 10 65 85 20 10 20 55 10 125 55 10 20

Check your answer with the solution on page 807.

21-8 Determining the Range

range
The difference between the lowest and the highest values in a data set; used as a measure of *dispersion*.

Although it does not measure central tendency like the mean, median, and mode, the range is another useful measure in statistics. The **range** is a measure of *dispersion;* it is the difference between the lowest and the highest values in a data set. It is used to measure the scope or broadness of a set of data. A small range indicates that the data in a set are narrow in scope; the values are close to each other. A large range indicates that the data in a set are wide in scope; the values are spread far apart.

STEPS TO CALCULATE THE RANGE:

Step 1. Locate the highest and lowest values in a set of numbers.

Step 2. Subtract the lowest from the highest to get the range.

Range = Highest value − Lowest value

EXAMPLE

Find the range of the following shirt prices in a department store:

\$37.95 \$15.75 \$24.75 \$18.50 \$33.75 \$42.50 \$14.95 \$27.95 \$19.95

SOLUTION STRATEGY

To find the range of shirt prices, subtract the lowest price from the highest price:

Range = Highest value − Lowest value = 42.50 − 14.95 = \$27.55

Note that the range for shirts, \$27.55, is relatively large. It might be said that customers shopping in this shirt department have a wide range of prices to choose from.

TRY-IT | EXERCISE

25. Find the range of the following temperature readings from the oven of a bakery:

367° 351° 349° 362° 366° 358° 369° 355° 354°

Check your answer with the solution on page 807.

REVIEW EXERCISES | CHAPTER 21—SECTION II

Calculate the mean of the following sets of values (round to the nearest tenth when applicable):

1. 4 6 1 8 9 2 3 5 5 6 8 9 10

2. 324 553 179 213 423 336 190 440 382 111 329 111 397

3. .87 .32 1.43 2.3 5.4 3.25 .5

Determine the median of the following sets of values (round to the nearest tenth when applicable):

4. 57 38 29 82 71 90 11 94 26 18 18

5. $2.50 $3.25 $4.35 $1.22 $1.67 $4.59

6. 35% 51% 50% 23% 18% 67% 44% 52%

Find the mode of the following sets of values:

7. 21 57 46 21 34 76 43 68 21 76 18 12

8. $1,200 $7,300 $4,500 $3,450 $1,675

9. 4 9 3 5 4 7 1 9 9 4 7 1 8 1 4 6 7 4 6 9 9 2

Find the range of the following sets of values:

10. 12 42 54 28 112 76 95 27 36 11 96 109 210

11. $2.35 $4.16 $3.42 $1.29 $.89 $4.55

12. 1,099 887 1,659 1,217 2,969 790

13. The following numbers represent the gallons of chocolate syrup used per month by a Haagen-Däzs Ice Cream Shop to make milk shakes and hot fudge sundaes:

Jan.—225	Feb.—254	March—327	April—370	May—425	June—435
July—446	Aug.—425	Sept.—359	Oct.—302	Nov.—270	Dec.—241

a. What is the mean of this set of data?

b. What is the median of this set of data?

c. What is the mode of this set of data?

d. What is the range of this set of data?

14. You are the owner of The Dependable Delivery Service. Your company has four vehicles: a large and a small van and a large and a small truck. The following set of data represents the number of packages delivered last week:

	Monday	Tuesday	Wednesday	Thursday	Friday
Small Van	67	86	94	101	86
Large Van	142	137	153	165	106
Small Truck	225	202	288	311	290
Large Truck	322	290	360	348	339

a. What is the mean number of packages delivered for each van?

b. What is the median number of packages delivered for each truck?

c. What is the mean number of packages delivered on Monday?

d. What is the median number of packages delivered on Thursday?

e. What is the mode of all the packages delivered during the week?

f. What is the range of all the packages delivered during the week?

BUSINESS DECISION

Interpreting the Numbers

15. You are the manager of a production plant that makes computer hard drives for Maxtor Corporation. Last week your plant had the following production numbers during a 6-day production run:

2,300 2,430 2,018 2,540 2,675 4,800

a. What is the mean, median, mode, and range of this set of production data?

b. Which average best describes the production at your plant? Why?

SECTION III

FREQUENCY DISTRIBUTIONS—GROUPED DATA

In the previous section, the values in the sets are listed individually and are known as **ungrouped data.** Frequently, business statistics deals with hundreds or even thousands of values in a set. In dealing with such a large amount of values, it is often easier to represent the data by dividing the values into equal-size groups known as classes, creating **grouped data.**

The number of values in each class is called the **frequency,** with the resulting chart called a **frequency distribution** or **frequency table.** The purpose of a frequency distribution is to organize large amounts of data into a more compact form without changing the essential information contained in those values.

ungrouped data
Data that have not been grouped into a distribution-type format.

grouped data
Data that have been divided into equal-size groups known as classes. Frequently used to represent data when dealing with large amounts of values in a set.

frequency
The number of values in each class of a frequency distribution.

frequency distribution, or frequency table
The chart obtained by dividing data into equal-size classes; used to organize large amounts of data into a more compact form without changing the essential information contained in those values.

21-9 Constructing a Frequency Distribution

STEPS TO CONSTRUCT A FREQUENCY DISTRIBUTION:

Step 1. Divide the data into equal-size classes. Be sure to use a range that includes all values in the set.

Step 2. Use tally marks to record the frequency of values within each class.

Step 3. Rewrite the tally marks for each class numerically in a column labeled "frequency (*f*)." The data are now grouped.

EXAMPLE

From the following ungrouped data representing the weight of packages shipped by Monarch Manufacturing this month, construct a frequency distribution by using classes with an interval of 10 pounds each.

13	16	65	45	44	35	22	46	36	49	56	26
68	27	35	15	43	62	32	57	48	23	43	44

SOLUTION STRATEGY

First, we find the range of the data by subtracting the lowest value, 13, from the highest value, 68. This gives a range of 55 pounds. Second, by using 60 pounds as the range for the classes of our frequency distribution we are sure to include all values in the set. Class intervals of 10 pounds each allow for six equal classes:

Frequency Distribution for Monarch Manufacturing

Class (lb)	Tally	Frequency *(f)*
10 to 19	III	3
20 to 29	IIII	4
30 to 39	IIII	4
40 to 49	~~IIII~~ III	8
50 to 59	II	2
60 to 69	III	3

TRY-IT | EXERCISE

26. You are the manager of The Dress Code Boutique. From the following ungrouped data representing the dollar sales of each transaction at the store today, construct a frequency distribution using classes with an interval of \$10 each.

14	19	55	47	44	39	22	71	35	49	64	22	88	78	16
88	37	29	71	74	62	54	59	18	93	49	74	26	66	75

Check your answer with the solution on page 807.

21-10 Computing the Mean of Grouped Data

Just as with ungrouped data, we can calculate the arithmetic mean of grouped data in a frequency distribution. Keep in mind, however, that the means for grouped data are calculated by using the midpoints of each class rather than the actual values of the data and are therefore only approximations. Because the actual values of the data in each class of the distribution are lost, we must make the assumption that the midpoints of each class closely approximate the values in that class. In most cases, this is true because some class values fall below the midpoint and some above, thereby canceling the inaccuracy.

STEPS TO CALCULATE THE MEAN OF A FREQUENCY DISTRIBUTION:

Step 1. Add a column to the frequency distribution listing the midpoints of each class. Label it "midpoints" (m).

Step 2. In a column labeled $(f \times m)$, multiply the frequency for each class by the midpoint of that class.

Step 3. Find the sum of the frequency column.

Step 4. Find the sum of the $(f \times m)$ column.

Step 5. Find the mean by dividing the sum of the $(f \times m)$ column by the sum of the frequency column.

$$\textbf{Mean of grouped data} = \frac{\textbf{Sum of (frequency} \times \textbf{midpoint)}}{\textbf{Sum of frequency}}$$

EXAMPLE

Calculate the mean of the grouped data from the frequency distribution for Monarch Manufacturing in the previous example.

SOLUTION STRATEGY

Begin by attaching the midpoint (m) and frequency $\times$ midpoint $(f \times m)$ columns to the frequency distribution as follows:

Frequency Distribution for Monarch Manufacturing

Class (lb)	Tally	Frequency (f)	Midpoint (m)	$f \times m$
10 to 19	III	3	14.5	43.5
20 to 29	IIII	4	24.5	98.0
30 to 39	IIII	4	34.5	138.0
40 to 49	~~IIII~~ III	8	44.5	356.0
50 to 59	II	2	54.5	109.0
60 to 69	III	3	64.5	193.5
		24		938.0

After finding the sum of the frequency and $f \times m$ columns, use these sums to calculate the mean of the grouped data:

$$\text{Mean of grouped data} = \frac{\text{Sum of (frequency} \times \text{midpoint)}}{\text{Sum of frequency}} = \frac{938}{24} = \underline{\underline{39.1 \text{ lb}}}$$

TRY-IT EXERCISE

27. From the frequency distribution previously prepared in Try-It Exercise 26 for The Dress Code Boutique, calculate the mean of the grouped data.

Check your answer with the solution on page 807.

21-11 Preparing a Histogram of a Frequency Distribution

histogram
A special type of bar chart, without space between the bars, that is used to display the data from a frequency distribution.

A **histogram** is a special type of bar chart that is used in business to display the data from a frequency distribution. A histogram is drawn in the same way as a standard bar chart but without space between the bars.

Everybody's Business
Learning Tip
Because a frequency distribution has classes whose numbers are continuous, the histogram bars depicting that distribution are made to look continuous by drawing them adjacent to each other—no space between them.

STEPS TO PREPARE A HISTOGRAM OF A FREQUENCY DISTRIBUTION:

Step 1. Locate the classes of the frequency distribution adjacent to each other along the x-axis, increasing from left to right.

Step 2. Evenly space the frequencies on the y-axis, increasing from bottom to top.

Step 3. Plot the frequency for each class in the form of a rectangular bar whose top edge is opposite the frequency of that class on the y-axis.

EXAMPLE

Prepare a histogram from the Monarch Manufacturing frequency distribution on page 794.

SOLUTION STRATEGY

Below is the histogram prepared from the data in the Monarch Manufacturing frequency distribution. Note that the x-axis displays the adjacent classes and the y-axis displays their frequencies.

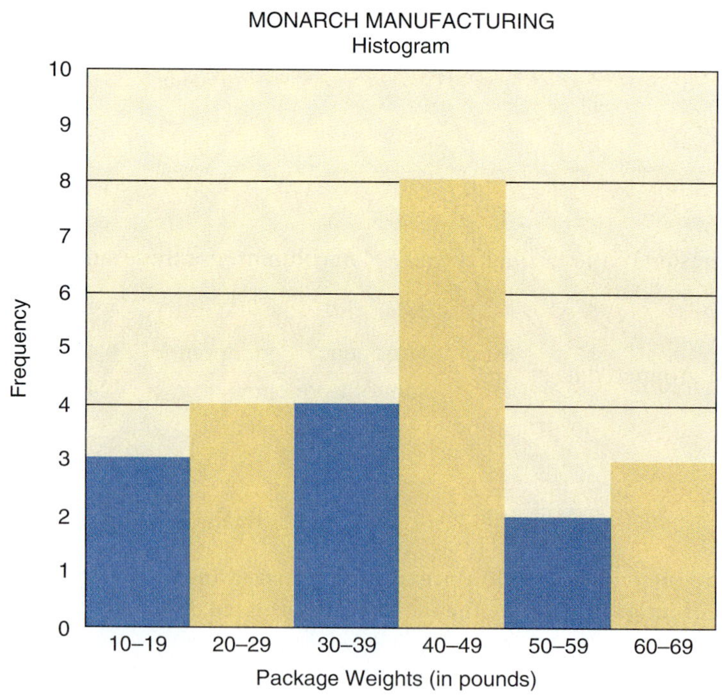

TRY-IT EXERCISE

28. Using the graph provided below, construct a histogram from the data in The Dress Code Boutique frequency distribution you prepared in Try-It Exercise 26.

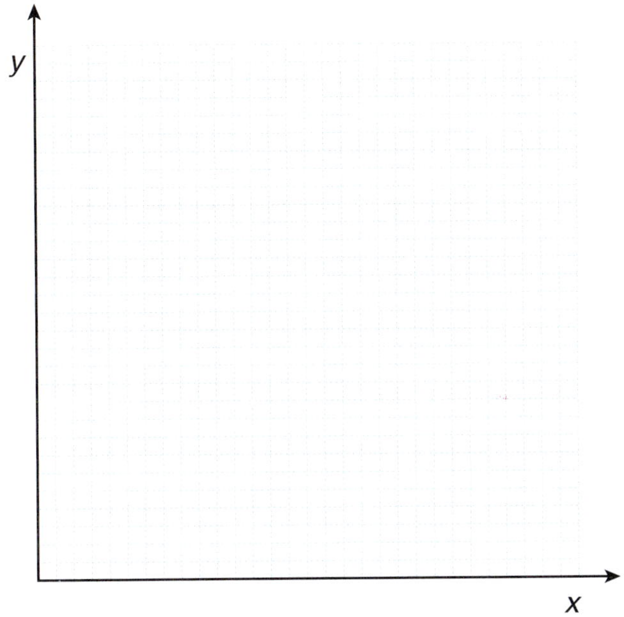

Check your answer with the solution on page 807.

REVIEW EXERCISES | CHAPTER 21—SECTION III

1. You are the sales manager of the Esquire Sportswear Company. Last week, your 30 salespeople reported the following automobile mileage while making sales calls to retail stores around the state:

385	231	328	154	283	86	415	389	575	117	75	173	247	316	357
211	432	271	93	515	376	328	183	359	136	88	438	282	375	637

a. Group the data into seven classes of equal size (0–99, 100–199, 200–299, 300–399, etc.) and construct a frequency distribution of the mileage.

b. Calculate the mean of the grouped data by using 49.5, 149.5, 249.5, etc., as the midpoints.

c. Using the grid provided below, prepare a histogram of these data to graphically illustrate your salespeoples' mileage.

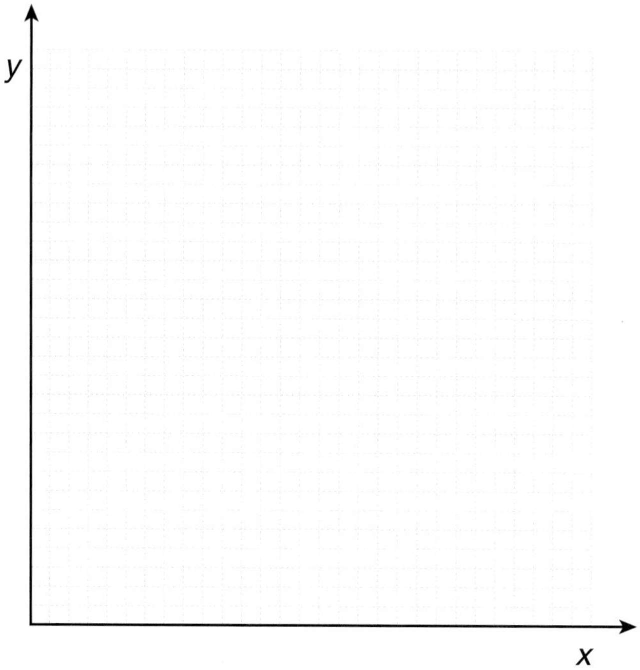

2. You are the payroll manager for the Bilt-Rite Construction Company. Your boss has asked that you review the hourly wages of your workers and give him a report to be presented at this afternoon's board meeting. The following are the hourly wages of your construction crew:

\$4.15	\$5.60	\$4.95	\$6.70	\$5.40	\$7.15	\$6.45	\$8.25	\$7.60	\$6.25
\$5.50	\$4.90	\$7.60	\$6.40	\$7.75	\$5.25	\$6.70	\$8.45	\$7.10	\$8.80
\$9.65	\$8.40	\$6.50	\$5.25	\$6.75	\$8.50	\$5.35	\$6.80	\$4.25	\$9.95

a. Group the wages into six classes of equal size (\$4.00–\$4.99, \$5.00–\$5.99, etc.) and construct a frequency distribution.

b. Calculate the mean of the grouped data.

c. Using the grid provided below, prepare a histogram of the hourly wages for your boss to present at his meeting.

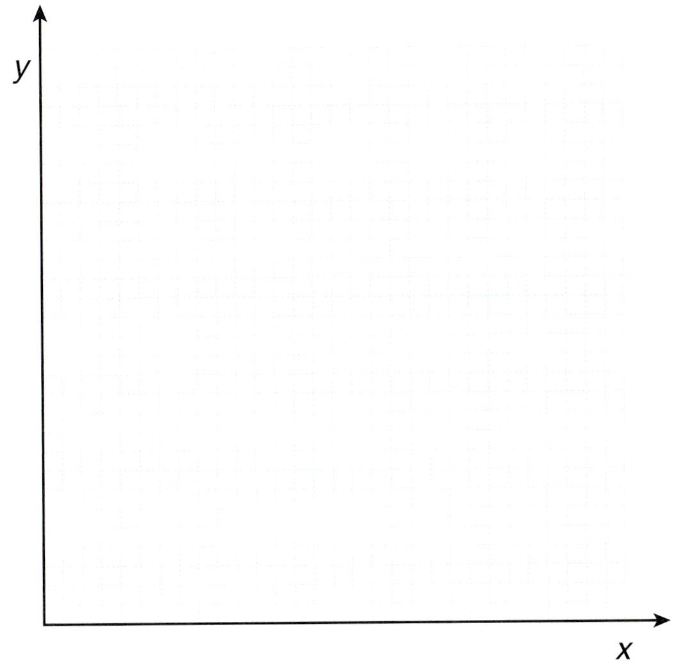

BUSINESS DECISION

Relative Frequency Distribution

3. In business, percents are frequently used to express the number of observations in a frequency distribution of business data. A **relative frequency distribution** expresses the distribution as percents. To convert a frequency distribution to a relative frequency distribution, each of the class frequencies (portion) is divided by the total number of observations (base). Remember, rate = portion ÷ base.

a. From the frequency distribution you constructed in Exercise 2a, convert each class frequency to a relative class frequency; percents. Round your answers to tenths.

b. What percent of the workers were paid between $5.00 and $5.99?

c. What percent were paid $7.00 or more?

d. What percent was paid less than $8.00?

CHAPTER FORMULAS

Ungrouped Data

$$\text{Mean} = \frac{\text{Sum of values}}{\text{Number of values}}$$

$$\text{Median (odd number of values)} = \text{Middle value}$$

$$\text{Median (even number of values)} = \frac{\text{Middle value} + \text{Middle value}}{2}$$

$$\text{Mode} = \text{Value or values that occur most frequently}$$

$$\text{Range} = \text{Highest value} - \text{Lowest value}$$

Grouped Data

$$\text{Mean} = \frac{\text{Sum of (frequency} \times \text{midpoint)}}{\text{Sum of frequency}}$$

✦ SUMMARY CHART ✦

SECTION I: Data Interpretation and Presentation

<table>
<tr><th>Topic</th><th>P/O, Page</th><th>Important Concepts</th><th>Illustrative Examples</th></tr>
<tr>
<td>Reading and Interpreting Information from Tables</td>
<td>21-1
767</td>
<td>Tables are a collection of related data arranged for ease of reference or comparison, usually in parallel columns with meaningful titles. They are a very useful tool in summarizing statistical data and are found everywhere in business.
Reading tables:
1. Scan the titles above the columns for the category of information being sought.
2. Look down the column for the specific fact required.</td>
<td>FRIENDLY AUTO SALES
90-Day Sales Report
(Thousands of Dollars)
<table>
<tr><th></th><th>April</th><th>May</th><th>June</th></tr>
<tr><td>Autos</td><td>56</td><td>61</td><td>64</td></tr>
<tr><td>Trucks</td><td>68</td><td>58</td><td>66</td></tr>
<tr><td>Parts</td><td>32</td><td>41</td><td>37</td></tr>
<tr><td>Total</td><td>156</td><td>160</td><td>167</td></tr>
</table>
</td>
</tr>
<tr>
<td>Reading and Constructing Line Charts</td>
<td>21-2
768</td>
<td>Charts are used to display a picture of the relationships among selected data. Line charts show data changing over a period of time. They are a graph of series of data points on a grid, continuously connected by straight lines.
Reading line charts:
1. Scan either the x- or y-axis for the known variable; x for time or y for amount.
2. Draw a perpendicular line from that axis to the point where it intersects the chart.
3. Draw a line from that point perpendicular to the opposite axis.
4. The answer is read where that line intersects the opposite axis.
Constructing line charts:
1. Evenly space and label the time variable on the x-axis.
2. Evenly space and label the amount variable on the y-axis.
3. Show each data point by placing a dot above the time period and across from the corresponding amount.
4. Connect the plotted points with straight lines to form the chart.
5. Lines should be differentiated by various line patterns or colors.</td>
<td>Single-Line Chart
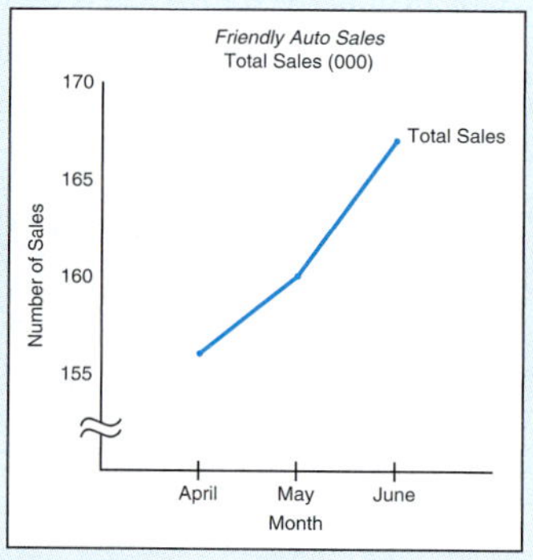

Multiple-Line Chart
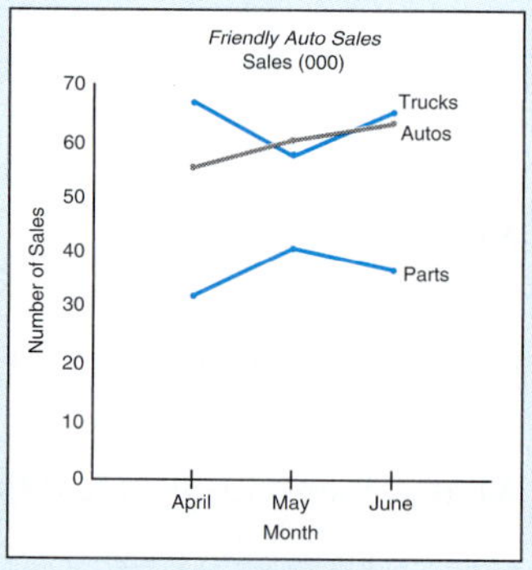

</td>
</tr>
</table>

SECTION I: (continued)

<table>
<tr><th>Topic</th><th>P/O, Page</th><th>Important Concepts</th><th>Illustrative Examples</th></tr>
<tr>
<td>Reading and Constructing Bar Charts</td>
<td>21-3
773</td>
<td>
Bar charts represent data by the length of horizontal bars or vertical columns. As with line charts, bar charts often illustrate increases or decreases in magnitude of a certain variable, or the relationship between similar variables.

Comparative bar charts illustrate two or more related variables. In this chart, the bars of the related variables are drawn next to each other but do not touch.

Component bar charts illustrate parts of something that add to a total. Each bar is divided into components stacked on top of each other and shaded or colored differently.

Reading bar charts:

1. Scan the x- or y-axis for a known variable.
2. Read the answer on the opposite axis directly across from the top of the appropriate bar.

Constructing bar charts:

1. Evenly space and label the x-axis. The space between bars should be one-half the width of the bars.
2. Evenly space and label the y-axis.
3. Draw each bar up from the x-axis to the point opposite the y-axis that corresponds to its value.
4. For comparative and component bar charts, differentiate the bars by color or shading pattern.
</td>
<td>
Standard Bar Chart

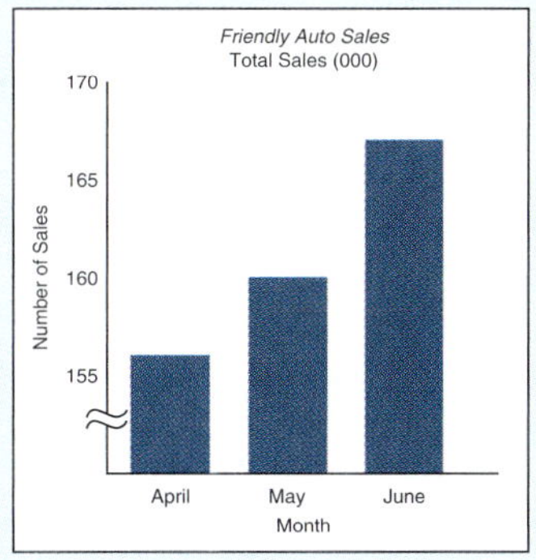

Comparative Bar Chart

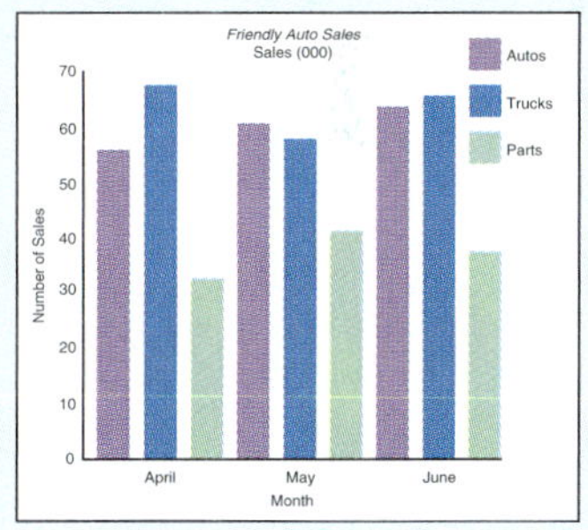

Component Bar Chart

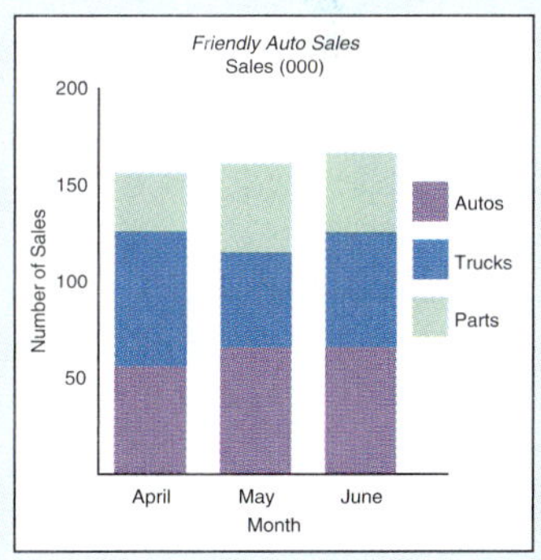

</td>
</tr>
</table>

SECTION I: (continued)

Topic	P/O, Page	Important Concepts	Illustrative Examples
Reading and Constructing Pie Charts	21-4 780	The pie chart is a circle divided into sections representing the component parts of a whole, usually in percentage terms. Constructing pie charts: 1. Convert the amount of each component to a percent using the formula Rate = Portion ÷ Base. Let the percentage be the amount of each component, and the base the total amount. Round each percent to hundredths. 2. Because a full circle is made up of 360° representing 100%, multiply each component's percent (decimal form) by 360° to determine how many degrees each component's slice will be. Round to the nearest whole degree. 3. Draw a circle with a compass and mark the center. 4. Using a protractor, mark off the number of degrees on the circle that represents each component. 5. Connect each point on the circle with the center by a straight line to form a segment or slice for each component. 6. Label the segments clearly by name, color, or shading.	April $= \frac{156}{483} = .323 = 32.3\%$ April $= .323 \times 360° = 116°$ May $= \frac{160}{483} = .331 = 33.1\%$ May $= .331 \times 360° = 119°$ June $= \frac{167}{483} = .346 = 34.6\%$ June $= .346 \times 360° = 125°$ *Pie Chart* 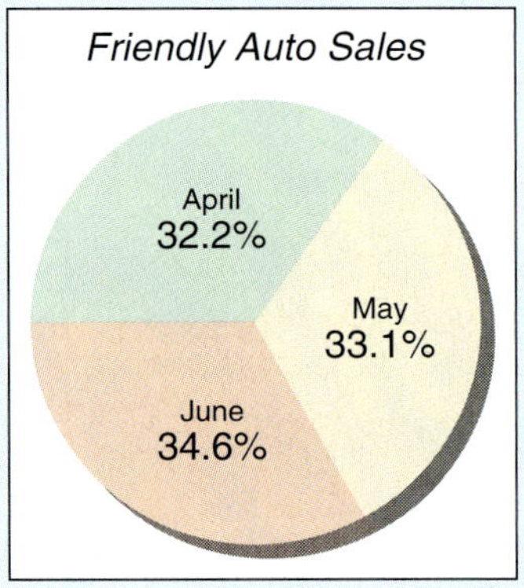

SECTION II: Measures of Central Tendency and Dispersion—Ungrouped Data

Calculating the Arithmetic Mean	21-5 786	A numerical average is a value that is representative of a whole set of values. The arithmetic mean corresponds to the generally accepted meaning of the word *average.* Computing the mean: 1. Find the sum of all the values in the set. 2. Divide by the number of values in the set. **Mean = $\frac{\text{Sum of values}}{\text{Number of values}}$**	If a grocery store had sales of \$4,600 on Monday, \$3,650 on Tuesday, and \$3,500 on Wednesday, what is the mean sales for the 3 days? Mean $= \frac{4,600 + 3,650 + 3,500}{3}$ $= \frac{11,750}{3} = \$3,916.67$

SECTION II: (continued)

Topic	P/O, Page	Important Concepts	Illustrative Examples
Calculating the Median	21-6 787	Another measure of central tendency, and a very useful way of describing a large quantity of data, is the median. The median of a set of numbers is the *midpoint* value when the numbers are ranked in increasing or decreasing order. Determining the median: 1. Rank the numbers in increasing or decreasing order. 2a. For an *odd number* of values in the set, the median is the middle value. 2b. For an *even number* of values in the set, the median is the average or midpoint of the two middle values. $\text{Median} = \frac{\text{Middle value} + \text{Middle value}}{2}$	Example 1: Find the median for the following set of values: 2 8 5 13 11 6 9 15 4 Rank the data as follows: 2 4 5 6 8 9 11 13 15 Because the number of values in the set is odd (nine), the median is the middle value, 8. Example 2: Find the median for the following set of values: 56 34 87 12 45 49 Rank the data as follows: 12 34 45 49 56 87 Because the number of values in this set is even (six), the median is the midpoint between the third and the fourth values, 45 and 49. $\text{Median} = \frac{45 + 49}{2} = \frac{94}{2} = \underline{\underline{47}}$
Determining the Mode	21-7 789	The mode is the third measure of central tendency. It is the value or values in a set that occur most often. It is possible for a set of data to have more than one mode or no mode at all. Determining the mode: 1. Count the number of times each value in a set occurs. 2a. If one value occurs most often, it is the mode. 2b. If more than one value occur the same number of times, they are all modes of the set. 2c. If all values occur only once, there is no mode.	Find the mode of the following set representing television screen sizes sold in a Circuit City store yesterday: 25 25 27 25 17 19 12 12 17 25 17 5 25 From these data, we see that the mode is 25 inches, because the value 25 occurs most often.
Determining the Range	21-8 790	The range is a measure of dispersion, equal to the difference between the lowest and the highest values in a set. It is used to measure the scope or broadness of a set of data. Determining the range: 1. Locate the highest and lowest values in a set of numbers. 2. Subtract these values to determine the range. **Range = Highest value − Lowest value**	Find the range of the following modem prices at Computers USA: 237 215 124 185 375 145 199 Highest = \$375 Lowest = \$124 Range = 375 − 124 = \$251

SECTION III: Frequency Distributions—Grouped Data

Topic	P/O, Page	Important Concepts	Illustrative Examples

Topic: **Constructing a Frequency Distribution**

P/O, Page: 21-9, 793

Important Concepts:

Business statistics frequently deals with hundreds or even thousands of values in a set. In dealing with large amounts of values, it is often easier to represent the data by dividing the values into equal-size groups known as classes, forming grouped data. The number of values in each class is called the frequency, with the resulting chart called a frequency distribution.

Constructing a frequency distribution:

1. Divide the data into equal-size classes. Be sure to use a range that includes all values in the set.
2. Use tally marks to record the frequency of values within each class.
3. Rewrite the tally marks for each class numerically in a column labeled "frequency." The data are now grouped.

Illustrative Examples:

The following ungrouped data represent the number of sales calls made by the sales force of Northwest Supply Company last month. Construct a frequency distribution of these data by using six equal classes with an interval of ten.

13	26	65	45	44	35	46
36	49	56	16	68	27	35
43	62	32	57	23	43	44

Class	Tally	Freq *(f)*
10 to 19	II	2
20 to 29	III	3
30 to 39	IIII	4
40 to 49	~~IIII~~ II	7
50 to 59	II	2
60 to 69	III	3

Topic: **Computing the Mean of Grouped Data**

P/O, Page: 21-10, 794

Important Concepts:

Calculating the mean of a frequency distribution:

1. Add a column to the frequency distribution listing the midpoints of each class.
2. In a column labeled $(f \times m)$, multiply the frequency for each class by the midpoint of that class.
3. Find the sum of the frequency column.
4. Find the sum of the $(f \times m)$ column.
5. Find the mean by dividing the sum of the $(f \times m)$ column by the sum of the frequency column.

$$\text{Mean} = \frac{\text{Sum of } (f \times m)}{\text{Sum of frequencies}}$$

Illustrative Examples:

Calculate the mean number of sales calls for Northwest Supply. The mean of the grouped data is computed by first attaching the midpoint *(m)* and frequency × midpoint $(f \times m)$ columns to the frequency distribution as follows:

Class	Freq *(f)*	Midpt *(m)*	$f \times m$
10–19	2	14.5	29.0
20–29	3	24.5	73.5
30–39	4	34.5	138.0
40–49	7	44.5	311.5
50–59	2	54.5	109.0
60–69	3	64.5	193.5
	21		854.5

$$\text{Mean} = \frac{854.5}{21} = \underline{\underline{40.7 \text{ calls}}}$$

Topic: **Preparing a Histogram of a Frequency Distribution**

P/O, Page: 21-11, 796

Important Concepts:

A histogram is a special type of bar chart that is used in business to display the data from a frequency distribution. A histogram is drawn in the same way as a standard bar chart except there are no spaces between the bars.

Constructing a histogram:

1. Locate the classes of the frequency distribution adjacent to each other along the *x*-axis, increasing from left to right.
2. Evenly space the frequencies on the *y*-axis, increasing from bottom to top.
3. Plot each class's frequency in the form of a rectangular bar whose top edge is opposite the frequency of that class.

Illustrative Examples:

Histogram

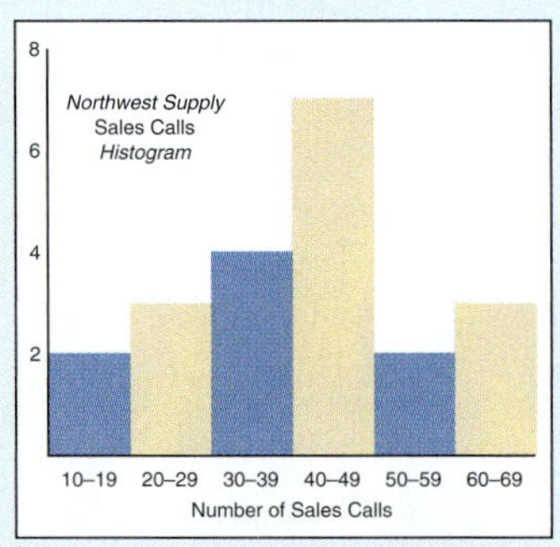

TRY-IT EXERCISE | SOLUTIONS

1. Standard units—February—Northeast = 228,400

2. Deluxe units—April—Southeast = 70,300

3. Total sales—May and June—Northwest

May = 112,900 + 65,300 = 178,200
June = 135,000 + 78,400 = 213,400
Total = 391,600

4. Months with increase in standard unit sales—Southwest

March, April, May, June

5. April—Deluxe = 92,600 + 153,200 + 67,800 + 70,300 = 383,900

May—Deluxe = 65,300 + 185,000 + 78,300 + 79,400 = 408,000

408,000 − 383,900 = 24,100

6. Northwest—Percent standard units = $\frac{\text{Standard units}}{\text{Total units}}$

Northwest—Percent standard units = $\frac{757{,}000}{1{,}244{,}500}$ = .6082 = 60.8%

7. 2004

8. 185 million

9. Approximately 5 million more cable modems

10.

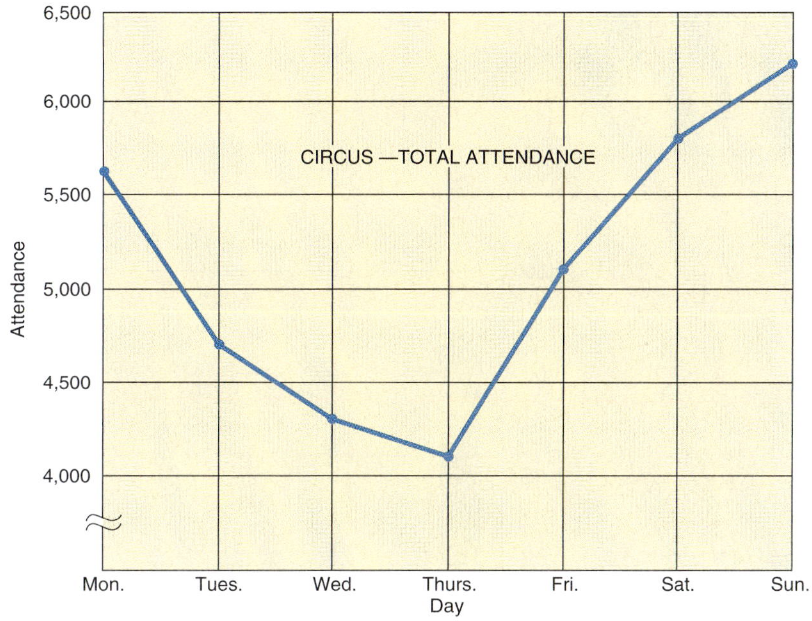

11.

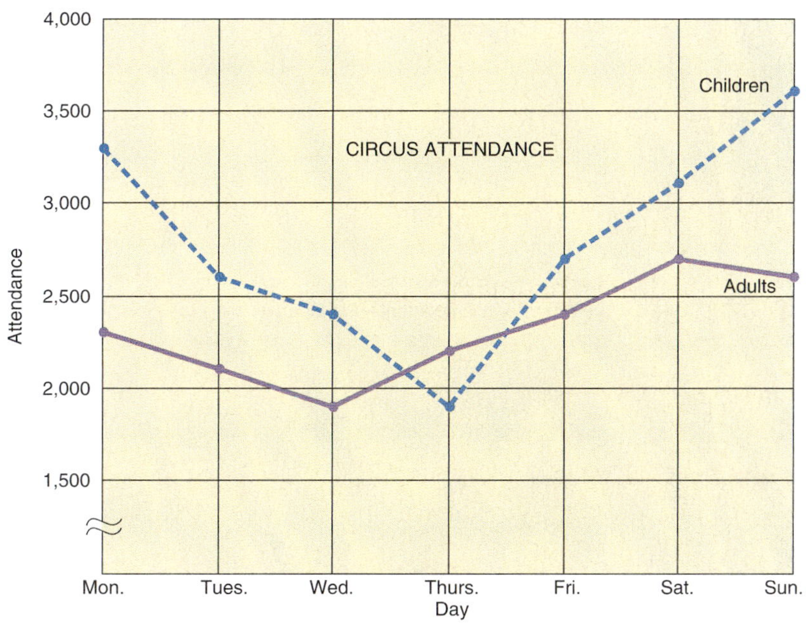

12. 14.5 million **13.** 2002 **14.** 540,000 **15.** 1998

16.

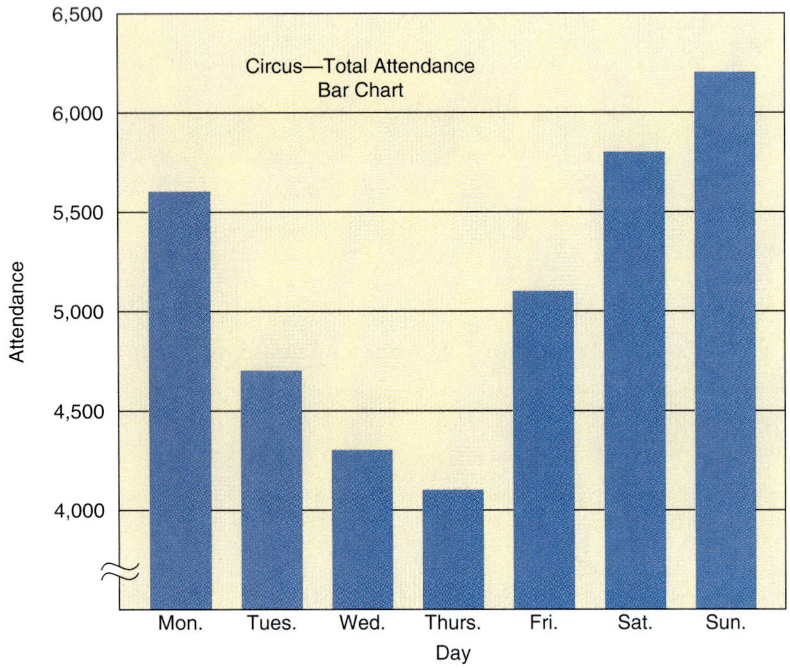

17.

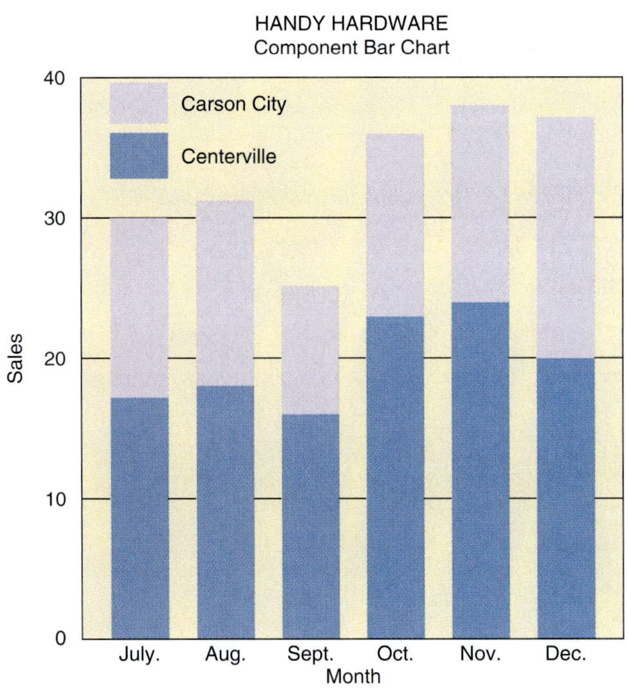

18.

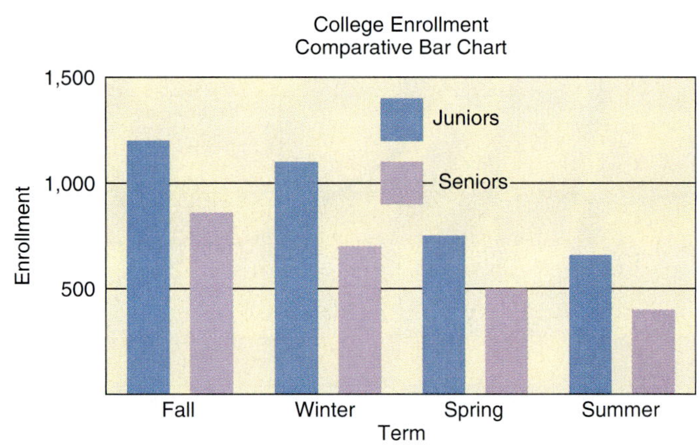

19. a. Food 12% + Clothing 7% = 19%

b. U. S. 14% − Germany 13% = 1%

20. Freshmen $= \frac{1,400}{4,400} = .318 = 31.8\%$ $.318 \times 360° = 114°$

Sophomores $= \frac{1,200}{4,400} = .273 = 27.3\%$ $.273 \times 360° = 98°$

Juniors $= \frac{1,100}{4,400} = .25 = 25\%$ $.25 \times 360° = 90°$

Seniors $= \frac{700}{4,400} = .159 = 15.9\%$ $.159 \times 360° = 57°$

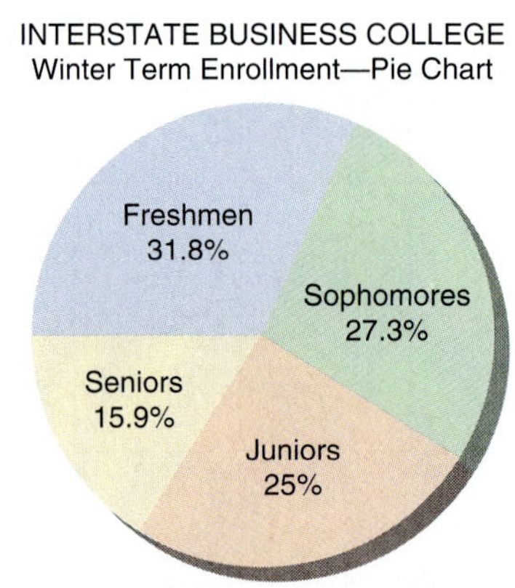

21. $\text{Mean} = \dfrac{\text{Sum of values}}{\text{Number of values}}$

$\text{Mean} = \dfrac{432 + 247 + 661 + 418 + 512}{5} = \dfrac{2{,}270}{5} = \underline{\underline{454}}$

22. Ranked in increasing order:

1,220 2,430 3,619 4,237 4,589 5,840 6,558

Median is midpoint of odd number of values = 4,237

23. Ranked in increasing order:

12 13 29 33 42 54 76 79 81 101

For even number of values, median is midpoint of the two middle values.

$\text{Midpoint} = \dfrac{42 + 54}{2} = \dfrac{96}{2} = \underline{\underline{48}}$

24. 10 = 7 20 = 5 55 = 3 65 = 1 85 = 1 125 = 1

The mode of these values is 10 because it occurred the most number of times, seven.

25. Range = Highest value − Lowest value

Range = 369° − 349° = 20°

26. *The Dress Code*

Frequency Distribution

$ Sales per transaction

Class ($)	Tally	Frequency
10–19	IIII	4
20–29	IIII	4
30–39	III	3
40–49	IIII	4
50–59	III	3
60–69	III	3
70–79	~~IIII~~ I	6
80–89	II	2
90–99	I	1

27. *The Dress Code* *$ Sales per transaction*

Class ($)	Tally	Freq *(f)*	Midpoint *(m)*	*(f* x *m)*
10–19	IIII	4	14.5	58.0
20–29	IIII	4	24.5	98.0
30–39	III	3	34.5	103.5
40–49	IIII	4	44.5	178.0
50–59	III	3	54.5	163.5
60–69	III	3	64.5	193.5
70–79	~~IIII~~ I	6	74.5	447.0
80–89	II	2	84.5	169.0
90–99	I	1	94.5	94.5
		30		1,505.0

$\text{Mean} = \dfrac{\text{Sum of } (f \times m)}{\text{Sum of frequency}}$

$\text{Mean} = \dfrac{1{,}505}{30} = 50.166 = \underline{\underline{\$50.17}}$

28.

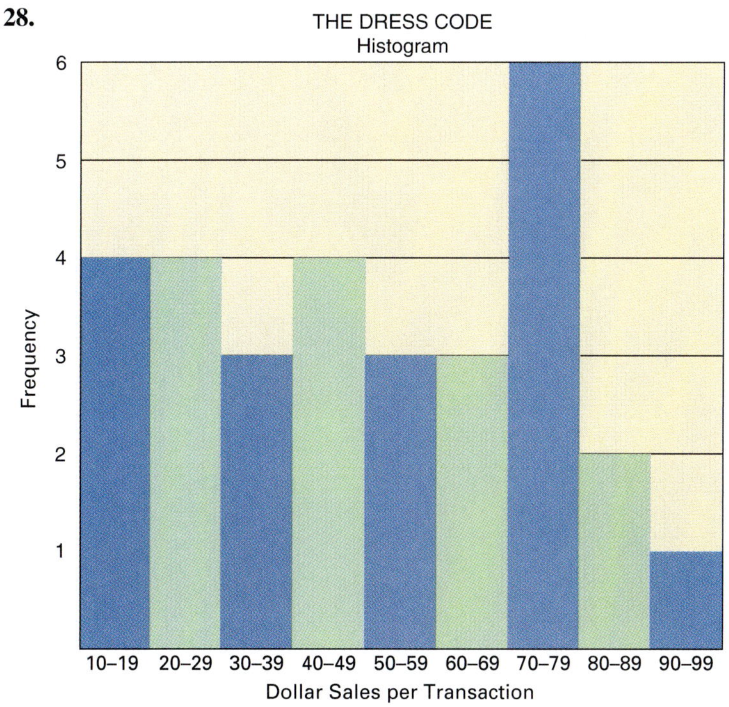

Name ______________________

Class ______________________

Answers

1. a. and b.

Please use the grid below the problem to provide your answers.

CHAPTER 21 | ASSESSMENT TEST

1. The following data represent the monthly sales figures, in thousands, for the New York and California branches of the Discovery Corporation:

	April	May	June	July	August	September
New York	121	254	218	156	255	215
California	88	122	211	225	248	260

a. Construct a multiple-line chart depicting the monthly sales for the two branches. Show the New York branch as a solid line and the California branch as a dashed line.

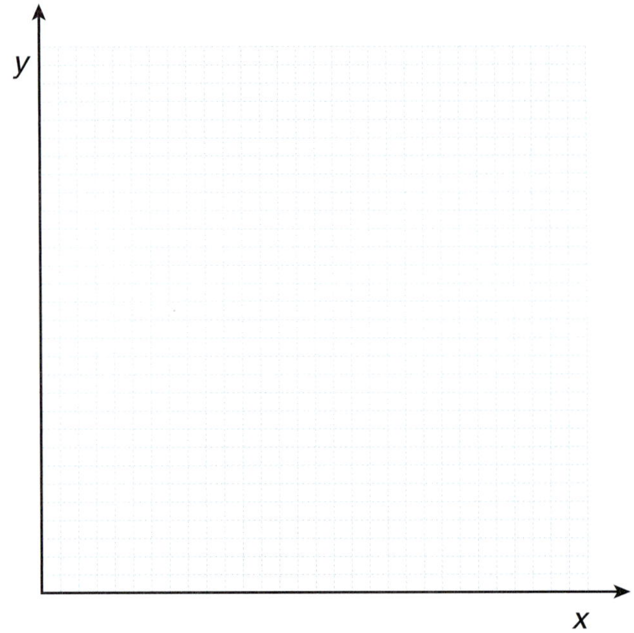

b. Construct a comparative bar chart for the same data. Highlight the bars for each branch differently.

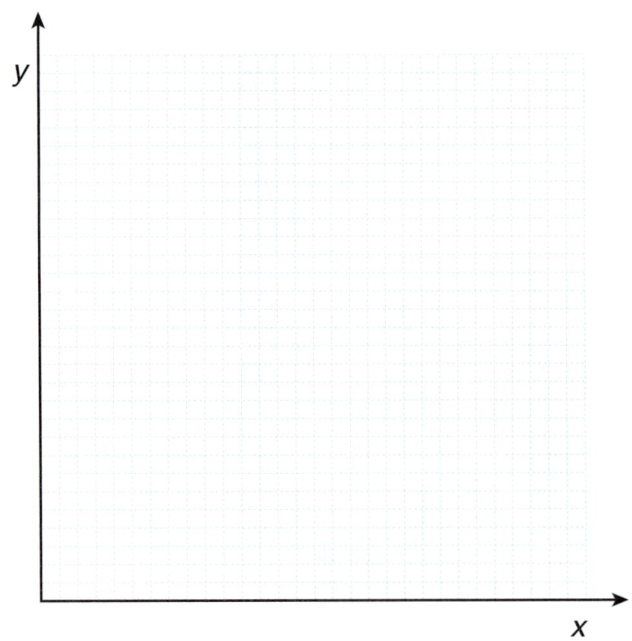

2. Construct a pie chart from the following information compiled in a recent survey of the buying habits of children aged 8 to 17.

Category	Percentage
Clothing	35%
Fast food, snacks, candy	20%
Electronics products	15%
Entertainment	10%
School supplies	10%
Personal care	7%
Other	3%

3. Last month, Computer Village sold $150,000 in standard computers, $75,000 in portable computers, $30,000 in software, $37,500 in printers, and $7,500 in accessories.

a. What percent of the total sales does each category of merchandise represent?

b. Construct a pie chart showing the percentage breakdown of sales by merchandise category.

4. You have just been hired as the quality control manager by Blue Diamond Manufacturing, a company producing fuel injection systems for General Motors, Ford, and Chrysler. Top management has requested a status report on the number of defective units produced each day. You decide to keep track of the number of defects each day for 30 days. The following are the results of your survey:

Blue Diamond Manufacturing—Defects per day—Survey 1

11	13	17	13	15	9	14	11	13	15	11	10	14	12	15
19	15	13	17	9	20	13	14	18	16	15	14	17	18	13

Name ________________

Class ________________

Answers

2. Please use the grid below the problem to provide your answers.

3. a. ________________

b. ________________

Name ______________

Class ______________

Answers

4. a. ______________

____

____

____

b. ______________

____

____

____

c. ______________

____

d. ______________

e. ______________

5. a. ______________

____

a. Find the mean, median, mode, and range of these data for your report to top management.

After implementing your suggestions for improved quality on the production line, you decide to survey the defects for another 30 days with the following results:

Blue Diamond Manufacturing—Defects per day—Survey 2

11	9	12	7	8	10	12	8	9	10	9	7	11	12	8
7	9	11	8	6	12	10	8	8	7	9	6	10	9	11

b. Find the mean, median, mode, and range of the new data.

c. If defective units cost the company $75.00 each to fix, use the *means* of each survey to calculate the average cost per day for defects, before and after your improvements.

d. Theoretically, how much will your improvements save the company in a 300-day production year?

e. Congratulations! The company has awarded you a bonus amounting to 15% of the first year's savings. How much is your bonus check?

5. You are the personnel director for Supreme Industries. Forty applicants for employment were given an assessment test in math and English with the following results:

87	67	81	83	94	72	84	68	33	56
91	79	88	95	84	75	46	27	69	97
69	57	66	81	87	19	76	54	78	91
78	72	75	89	74	92	45	59	85	72

a. What are the range and mode of these scores?

b. Group the data into nine classes of equal size (11–20, 21–30, etc.) and construct a frequency distribution.

Name ______________________

Class ______________________

Answers

5. c. ______________________

d. ______________________

c. Calculate the mean of the grouped data by using 15.5, 25.5, etc., as the midpoints.

d. If company policy is to consider only those who score *10 points higher* than the mean of the data or better, how many from this group are still being considered for the job?

e. Construct a histogram of the assessment test scores frequency distribution.

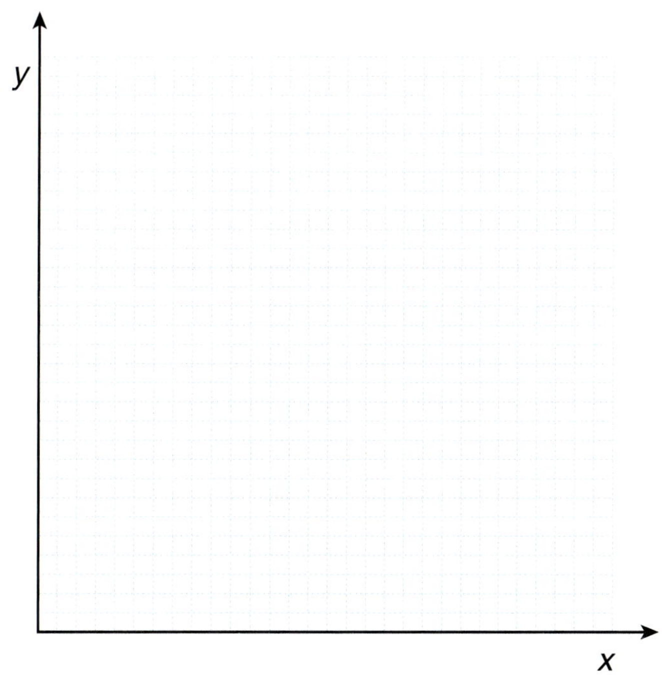

Name ______________

Class ______________

Answers

6. ______________

____

____

____

____

BUSINESS DECISION

Beat the Mean Bonus!

6. You are the owner of Supreme Imports, Inc., a car dealership specializing in expensive pre-owned automobiles, such as Mercedes Benz, BMW, and Lexus. You have a unique and quite motivating bonus plan that has worked well over the years.

   Each quarter, the mean number of cars sold is calculated. The first time a salesperson sells more cars than the mean, he or she earns a \$100 bonus for each car *over the mean* in that quarter. If a salesperson beats the mean a second time in a year, the bonus increases to \$150 per car for that quarter. Three times over the mean in 1 year and the bonus is \$200 per car for that quarter. If anyone beats the mean all four quarters, the fourth quarter bonus is \$300 per car. Remember, the bonus is paid only for the number of cars over the mean.

   Each year, the program starts all over again. All bonuses are paid once per year, in January, for the previous year. The following table represents the number of cars sold by your five salespeople for each quarter last year. Calculate the bonus each person should receive for last year.

	First Quarter	Second Quarter	Third Quarter	Fourth Quarter
Evans	16	23	14	23
Chen	12	20	16	25
Walker	15	13	26	19
Black	22	20	27	19
Sanchez	25	19	32	24

All the Math That's Fit to Learn

The Business Math Times

Volume XXI | **Business Statistics and Data Presentation** | One Dollar

The Ultimate Survey

Fact-finding is one of America's oldest activities. In the early 1600s, a census was taken in Virginia, and people were counted in nearly all of the British colonies that became the United States. Following independence, there was an almost immediate need for a census of the entire nation. The first census was taken in 1790. The census counted 3.9 million inhabitants.

The U.S. Constitution (Article 1, Sec. 2) requires a census every 10 years to apportion seats in the House of Representatives. Census numbers also are used to distribute more than $200 billion in federal and state money.

The 1990 census cost $2.6 billion. The 2000 census cost more than $6 billion. The single largest expense is paying enumerators to follow up with nonresponding households.

The decennial census is the largest peacetime mobilization of American resources and personnel. In 1990, about 500,000 temporary and 6,800 permanent Census Bureau employees took part in conducting the census. For the 2000 census, the bureau used 6,000 permanent employees and hired more than 850,000 temporary workers.

The national 67% final response rate for Census 2000 exceeds the 65% response rate from the 1990 census; it far exceeds the expected 61% response rate.

"Quote . . . Unquote"

I have not failed. I've just found 10,000 ways that won't work.
—*Thomas Alva Edison*

Get your facts straight first. Then you can distort them as much as you like.
—*Mark Twain*

Census 2000—Facts & Figures

- ✦ Population, 2000. 281,421,906
- ✦ Percent change from 1990. . . . +13.1%
- ✦ Males 49.1% . . . . Females 50.9%
- ✦ Median age. 35.3
- ✦ Households 105,480,101
- ✦ Persons per household 2.59
- ✦ Average family size. 3.14
- ✦ Homeownership rate 66.2%
- ✦ Land area (sq. miles) 3,537,411
- ✦ Persons per sq. mile 79.6
- ✦ Nonfarm businesses 7,008,444
- ✦ Retail sales ($1,000) . . . $2,460,886,012

The National Data Book

The Statistical Abstract of the United States is our national data book. Published annually since 1878, it is the standard summary of statistics on the social, political, and economic organization of the United States.

It is designed to serve as a convenient volume for statistical reference and as a guide to other statistical publications and sources. Available in all libraries and most bookstores, it's even available on CD-ROM and on the Internet at www.census.gov.

"I figured out how we can double our quarterly sales. From now on, each quarter will last six months."

Ancient Origins

GRAPH

Frequently, the word *graph* is used instead of chart. Graph is short for graphic formula. That is, a means of providing information graphically rather than in words. Graph is from the Greek, *graphein*, to draw!

AVERAGE

The word *average* is derived from maritime laws dating back to the 16th century. When a cargo vessel was in danger of sinking during a storm at sea, the heavy cargo was usually thrown overboard to save the ship.

By law, the cost of the lost or damaged goods was equally divided among all the concerned parties. In French, this practice was known as *avarié*, which later became the English word *average*.

Brainteaser*

THE MISSING GRADE

An absent-minded professor misplaced the business math test scores of his five students. However, he did remember that the mode was 90, the median was 85, and the mean was 83. If the grades ranged from 0 to 100, what is the lowest possible grade from the missing set of scores?

*Solution to this brainteaser is at the end of Appendix A, Collaborative Learning Activities, which follows Chapter 21.

ANSWER TO LAST ISSUE'S BRAINTEASER

9-Inch square

Area of a square = side^2
Area = 9 × 9 = 81 sq. in.

Area of a circle = πr^2
Area = 3.14 × 5 × 5 = 78.5 sq. in.

Collaborative Learning Activities

APPENDIX

A

The following collaborative learning activities are designed to supplement and enhance your business math learning experience. They will introduce you to real-world business applications of the material presented in each chapter as well as professionals who use these applications each day in their work.

Although the activities can be done on an individual basis, it is recommended that students break into teams of two, three, or four, and work together to accomplish each task.

For maximum effectiveness, each team's findings should be shared with the rest of the class.

COLLABORATIVE LEARNING ACTIVITY | CHAPTER 1

USING MATH IN BUSINESS

As a team, discuss and list the ways that math is used in the following businesses. Report your findings to the class.

a. Supermarket

b. Car dealership

c. Beauty Salon

d. Restaurant

e. Additional choice: ______________________

COLLABORATIVE LEARNING ACTIVITY | CHAPTER 2

KNOWING FRACTIONS IS HALF THE BATTLE

As a team, investigate and share with the class how fractions are used in the following:

a. Stock market

b. Manufacturing

c. Cooking

d. Medicine or pharmacy

e. Architecture and building construction

f. Additional choice: ______________________

COLLABORATIVE LEARNING ACTIVITY | CHAPTER 3

SPORTS MATH

As a team, choose two sports.

a. Investigate how fractions and decimals are used in their record keeping and statistics.

b. Prepare a visual presentation to share with the class.

COLLABORATIVE LEARNING ACTIVITY | CHAPTER 4

CHOOSING A CHECKING ACCOUNT

Have each team member call a local bank, credit union, or other financial institution offering checking accounts and ask for a brochure describing the types of checking accounts they have and other banking services they offer. As a team, look over the material, and answer the following:

a. How do they compare regarding monthly service charges, interest paid, account minimums, ATM charges, and other rules and regulations?

b. Do they offer any incentives, such as a no-fee Visa or MasterCard, bounce-proof checking, or a line of credit?

c. Based on your team's research, which one seems like the best deal for a
   - College student? Why?
   - Small business? Why?
   - Large corporation? Why?

COLLABORATIVE LEARNING ACTIVITY | CHAPTER 5

USING FORMULAS IN BUSINESS

Have each member of the team speak with someone in one of the following professions to determine how he or she uses equations and formulas in the business:

a. Store owner or manager

b. Real estate or insurance salesperson

c. Advertising or marketing manager

d Production manager

e. Accountant

f. Banker

g. Additional choice: ______________________

COLLABORATIVE LEARNING ACTIVITY | CHAPTER 6

PERCENTS—THE LANGUAGE OF BUSINESS!

As we learned in Chapter 6, percents are one of the most common and useful business math tools. As a team, find ten examples of their application in business from each of the following sources:

a. Business sections of your local newpaper

b. Business newspapers, such as *The Wall Street Journal* or *Barrons*

c. Business magazines, such as *Fortune* or *Business Week*

d. Company annual reports

COLLABORATIVE LEARNING ACTIVITY | CHAPTER 7

COMPARING INVOICES AND DISCOUNTS

1. As a team, collect invoices from a number of businesses in different industries in your area.
   a. How are they similar?
   b. How are they different?

2. Have each member of the team speak with a wholesaler or a retailer in your area.
   a. What are the typical trade discounts in that industry?
   b. What are the typical cash discounts in that industry?

COLLABORATIVE LEARNING ACTIVITY | CHAPTER 8

THE "SHOPPING" TRIP

1. As a team, collect newspaper advertisements for merchandise that is "on sale" at the following types of retail stores in your area. Calculate the amount of the markdown, the markdown percent, or the original price—whichever is *not* given in the ad. How do the figures compare among the categories?
   a. Supermarket
   b. Drugstore
   c. Department store
   d. Specialty shop
   e. Additional choice: ______________________
2. Have each member of the team visit one of the stores advertising "sale" merchandise in Question 1, and answer the following:
   a. Were the items marked correctly with the advertised sale price?
   b. Did the stores make any attempt to feature the sale merchandise using in-store displays, such as signs or other eye-catching devices?
   c. Were the employees aware of the sale?
   d. Would you say the stores did a good job of coordinating their newspaper advertising with their "in-store" efforts?
   e. Overall, what can you and your team conclude about markdowns and "sales" from this "shopping" trip?

COLLABORATIVE LEARNING ACTIVITY | CHAPTER 9

THE JOB HUNT

1. As a team, collect help wanted ads from the classifed section of your local newpaper. (*Note:* Sunday editions are usually best.) Find examples of various jobs paid by salary, hourly rate, piece rate, and commission, and answer the following:
   a. How much do they pay?
   b. What pay periods are used?
   c. What fringe benefits do they offer?
   d. Did you notice any trends among similar jobs?
2. As a team, go to the library or to the Internet to research the following:
   a. Personal income of employees in various industries and in government occupations.
   b. Personal and household income by area of the country. How does your area compare?
   c. Starting salaries by amount of education, in various fields of study.
   d. Where did your team find this information?

For additional information, visit our Web site at: www.contemporarymath.com

COLLABORATIVE LEARNING ACTIVITY | CHAPTER 10

THE CAR LOAN

As a team, choose a particular type of vehicle category that you want to research (such as sport utility vehicle, sports car, or luxury sedan). Then have each member of the team choose a different manufacturer's competitive model within that category.

For example, if the team picked sport utility vehicles, then individual choices might be Nissan Pathfinder, Toyota 4Runner, Ford Explorer, and Chevy Blazer.

a. From your local newspaper, collect advertisements for the purchase of the model you picked.

b. Visit an automobile dealership for the vehicle you picked. Speak with a salesperson about the types of deals currently being offered on that model.
   - What loan rates and terms are available through the dealer?
   - Who is the actual lender?
   - How much does the dealer make on the financing?

c. Contact various lending institutions (banks, finance companies, credit unions) and inquire about automobile loans.
   - What rates and terms are being offered?
   - Which one is offering the best deal?
   - How do these compare with those from the dealership?

COLLABORATIVE LEARNING ACTIVITY | CHAPTER 11

PUTTING YOUR MONEY TO WORK!

As a team, research the financial institutions and brokerage houses in your area to determine the various deals being offered on certificates of deposit. Assume that you want to invest $10,000, for up to 24 months.

a. What interest rates do these CDs pay? How often is interest compounded?
b. What is the early withdrawal penalty?
c. Which offers a better deal: bank CDs or brokerage house CDs?
d. Are these CDs insured? By whom? For how much?
e. Overall, which CD would be worth the most money after 24 months?

COLLABORATIVE LEARNING ACTIVITY | CHAPTER 12

THE "PERSONAL" SINKING FUND

1. As a team, design a "personal" sinking fund for something you want to save for in the future.
   a. What is the amount and the purpose of the fund?
   b. What interest rate is currently available in savings accounts? (Check with local lending institutions.)
   c. At that rate, calculate what monthly payment would be required to accumulate the desired amount in 1 year, 2 years, 5 years?

2. As a team, research the annual reports or speak with accountants of corporations that are using sinking funds to accumulate money for a future obligation. Answer the following questions about those funds:
   a. What is the name of the corporation?
   b. What is the purpose and the amount of the sinking fund?
   c. For how many years is the fund?
   d. How much are the periodic payments?
   e. At what interest rate are these funds growing?

COLLABORATIVE LEARNING ACTIVITY | CHAPTER 13

PLASTIC CHOICES

1. Have each member of the team contact a local bank, credit union, or retail store in your area that offers a credit card. Get a brochure and/or a copy of the credit agreement.
   a. For each card, determine the following information:

- Annual interest rate
- Method used for computing interest
- Credit limit
- Annual fee
- "Fine-print" features

b. Based on your research, which cards are the best and worst deals?

2. Contact CardTrack (www.cardtrack.com); (1-800-344-7714), a company that publishes a monthly consumer newsletter that lists the banks currently offering the best credit card rates and features in the country.
   a. Order a copy of CardTrack ($5.00)
   b. Compare your local banks' offers to those in the newsletter.

3. As a team, go to the library or to the Internet to research the rules, regulations, and recent changes in the following:
   a. The Fair Credit Reporting Act, a federal law that spells out the rules that govern credit-card issuers.
   b. Laws in your state relating to credit cards.

COLLABORATIVE LEARNING ACTIVITY I CHAPTER 14

THE "HYPOTHETICAL" MORTGAGE

As a team, contact several lending institutions in your area that offer mortgage loans. Speak with loan officers, and ask for their help with a class project in business math.

Your assignment is to research the various types of financing deals currently being offered for a hypothetical home you plan to buy. The following assumptions apply to this project:

- The purchase price of the house you plan to buy is $100,000.
- The house was recently appraised for $105,000.
- You plan to make a 25% down payment ($25,000) and are seeking a $75,000 mortgage.
- You have a job that qualifies you for that size mortgage.

Your assignment, as a team, is to compare the current interest rates, costs, and features associated with a 15-year fixed-rate mortgage, a 30-year fixed-rate mortgage, and an adjustable-rate mortgage.

a. What are the current interest rates and discount points of the 15- and 30-year fixed-rate mortgages?
b. What are the monthly payments of the fixed-rate mortgages?
c. What is the teaser rate, discount points, adjustment period, rate caps, margin, and index for the adjustable-rate mortgage?
d. What are the fees or charges for the loan application, property appraisal, survey, credit report, inspections, title search, title insurance, and document preparation?
e. What other charges or fees can be expected at closing?
f. As a team, decide which type of mortgage is the best deal at this time? Why?
g. Which bank would you and your team choose for the mortgage? Why?

For additional information, visit our Web site at: www.contemporarymath.com

COLLABORATIVE LEARNING ACTIVITY | CHAPTER 15

ANALYZING A COMPANY

As a team, choose an industry you want to research, such as airline, beverage, computer, entertainment, food, motor vehicle, retail, or wholesale. Next, choose three public companies that directly compete in that industry.

Using the reference section of your library or the Internet, research key business ratios and other available information about that industry. This may be found in the government's publication, *The Survey of Current Business,* or from private sources, such as *Moody's Index, Dun & Bradstreet,* or *Standard & Poors.*

Next, obtain the most recent financial statements for each company. These may be found in the sources mentioned above, or, if possible, contact a stockbroker or the company directly, and obtain a copy of the most recent annual report and quarterly reports. Based on the information your team has accumulated:

a. Calculate the current and previous years' financial ratios for each company.

b. Compare each company's ratios to the industry averages.

c. Evaluate each company's financial condition regarding liquidity, efficiency, leverage, and profitability.

d. If you and your team were going to invest in only one of these companies, which would you choose? Why?

COLLABORATIVE LEARNING ACTIVITY | CHAPTER 16

THE COUNTING GAME!

As a team, choose two or three competitive retail stores in your area, such as supermarkets, drug stores, general merchandisers, or hardware stores. Speak with an accounting and/or merchandise manager for each, and determine the following:

a. How many different items are carried in inventory?

b. What is their average inventory?

c. How often is a physical inventory count taken? Who does it?

d. Does the company have a computerized perpetual inventory system? How does it work?

e. What is the inventory turnover ratio? How does this compare with the published industry figures for a company that size? (Where did you find the published figures?)

f. What method of inventory valuation is being used? Why?

g. Which of the companies your team researched has the most efficient inventory system? Why?

COLLABORATIVE LEARNING ACTIVITY | CHAPTER 17

GOING, GOING, GONE!

1. Have each member of your team choose his or her favorite automobile and determine the price of a new one from a dealership. Then check the classified ads of your local newspaper or a publication of used car prices. Determine the price of the same car model at one, two, three, four, and five years old.
    a. Prepare a depreciation schedule based on the information found.
    b. Calculate what percent of its original value was lost in each year.
    c. Construct a line graph of the five years of depreciation of the car.
    d. Does it seem to be straight-line or accelerated?
    e. Compare the depreciation for each team member's car. Which models depreciated the fastest? The slowest?
    f. Can any conclusions be drawn from this research?

2. Choose a local industry, and have each member of the team pick a different company within that industry and speak with an accountant who works there. Identify three major assets that are being depreciated, such as a truck, production-line equipment, a computer, office furniture and fixtures, etc. For each asset, determine the following:
   a. Original purchase price
   b. Useful life
   c. Salvage value
   d. Depreciation method used for financial statement reporting
   e. Depreciation method used for income tax purposes
   f. Can any conclusions be drawn from this research?

COLLABORATIVE LEARNING ACTIVITY I CHAPTER 18

"YOUR TAX DOLLARS AT WORK"

In Chapter 18, Taxes, the primary focus has been on calculating the amount of taxes that are due. Now, as a team, do some research into how your tax dollars are being spent, both at the local and state level.

1. *Local level.* As we have learned, local tax dollars are generally raised from property and local sales taxes. Is this true in your area? Contact your local tax assessors office and determine the following:
   a. What are the local taxing units? City, county, municipality, district, province, parish, other?
   b. How are local taxes derived for each unit?
   c. What are the tax rates for each unit?
   d. How have the rates changed over the past five years?
   e. What is the latest tax budget for each unit and how is the money being spent?
   f. List five major projects in your area that are currently, recently, or soon-to-be funded by your tax dollars.
   g. As a team, what is your overall opinion of "your local tax dollars at work"?
2. *State level.* Tax revenue in most states is derived either from sales tax, state income tax, or a combination of both. Is this true in your state? As a team, contact your state taxing authority and determine the following:
   a. How are state taxes derived?
   b. What are the tax rates?
   c. How have the rates changed over the past five years?
   d. What is the latest tax budget and how is the money being spent?
   e. List five or more major projects in your state that are currently, recently, or soon-to-be funded by tax dollars.
   f. As a team, what is your overall opinion of "your state tax dollars at work"?

COLLABORATIVE LEARNING ACTIVITY I CHAPTER 19

INSURANCE FOR SWEETIE PIE

As a team, you and your partners hypothetically are going to start a company called The Sweetie Pie Corporation, a bakery that makes and distributes pies, cakes, cookies, and donuts to restaurants and food stores in your area.

The company will have property and a building valued at $200,000, baking and production-line equipment valued at $400,000, office equipment and fixtures worth $100,000, and four delivery trucks valued at $25,000 each. There will be 10 employees and 4 partners, including yourself.

Each team member is to consult with a different insurance agent to put together a "package" of business insurance for Sweetie Pie Corporation, including property insurance, liability insurance, and business interruption insurance.

In addition, look into a health insurance program for the partners and the employees, as well as $100,000 "key man" insurance for each partner. What other types of coverage does the agent recommend?

It is only fair that you tell the agents this is a project for your business math class and that you are seeking their help on this hypothetical company. After each team member has done his or her research, collaborate on which insurance agent offered the best package and rates, and why. Share your findings with the class.

COLLABORATIVE LEARNING ACTIVITY | CHAPTER 20

YESTERDAY, TODAY, AND TOMORROW!

In this activity, you and your team will research the meaning and direction of some of the more important investment and money indicators in our economy. Your best sources of information for this project will be the library, stockbrokers, and financial newspapers such as *The Wall Street Journal*, *Barron's,* or *The New York Times.* Divide the indicators among the team members and do the following:

a. Research and explain what the indicators mean, and how they are derived.

b. Look up the current figure for each indicator.

c. Look up historical figures (every 3 or 6 months) and prepare a visual presentation (line chart or bar chart) of each indicator's performance trend since January 2002.

d. As a team, discuss and report what each trend indicates.

Economic Indicator	January, 2002
Dow Jones Industrial Average	9,771.85
Standard & Poor's 500	1,127.58
Nasdaq Composite Average	1,939.49
30-year U.S. Treasury Bond*	5.38%
10-year U.S. Treasury Note	4.95%
Japanese yen (per U.S. dollar)	132.61
Euro (in U.S. dollars)	$.8844
Canadian dollar (in U.S. dollars)	$.6195
Gold (troy oz.)	$283.10
Oil, W. Texas (per barrel)	$18.36
Prime rate	4.75%
Certificates of deposit (6-month)	1.77%
30-year mortgage	6.44%
Consumer price index (C.P.I.)	176.7

*None issued since 2001

COLLABORATIVE LEARNING ACTIVITY | CHAPTER 21

CONDUCTING A MARKETING RESEARCH SURVEY

You and your team have been hired to conduct a marketing research survey by a company that is interested in advertising its products to college students in your area. They want to know the media preferences of the students at your school, and specifically would like answers to the following questions:

- What radio station, if any, do you listen to in the morning?
- What television local news program, if any, do you watch in the evening?
- What newspaper, if any, do you read each day?

a. As a team, design a questionnaire for this research survey. For each question, list all of the local media choices, with a place for easy check-off response. Be sure to include "no preference" and "none of the above" as choices. In addition to the survey questions, design some easy check-off demographic information questions, such as male/female, age group, ethnic group, income range, and marital status.
b. Individually, have each member of the research team personally interview about 25 or 30 students. (Questionnaires can be handed out, and then collected.)
c. As a team, tabulate the results of each survey and demographic question.
d. Calculate the mean, median, and mode for each of the demographic questions.
e. Prepare a visual presentation for the class of the results of the survey questions.
f. As a team, do you think the results of your survey are valid? Why? Why not?

Answer to the Brainteaser for Chapter 21

Answer 66

The most common score (mode) was 90, so at least two scores were 90s. The middle score (median) was 85, so at least one score was 85 and the remaining two must be less than 85. The mean was 83, so the sum of all five test scores was 5×83, or 415.

$415 - 2(90) - 85 = 150$. If one score was 84, the other would be 66.

Answers to Odd-Numbered Exercises

(Except Business Decisions)

APPENDIX

B

CHAPTER 1 WHOLE NUMBERS

REVIEW EXERCISES | CHAPTER 1—SECTION I

1. 22,938—twenty-two thousand, nine hundred thirty-eight **3.** 184—one hundred eighty-four **5.** 2,433,590—two million, four hundred thirty-three thousand, five hundred ninety **7.** 183,622 **9.** 1,936 **11.** d **13.** a **15.** 1,760 **17.** 235,400 **19.** 8,000,000 **21.** 1,300,000,000 **23.** 19,000,000,000

REVIEW EXERCISES | CHAPTER 1—SECTION II

1. 91 **3.** 19,943 **5.** 37,648 **7.** 70,928 **9.** 43,100 estimate—41,844 exact **11a.** 7,000 **11b.** 6,935 **13.** 3,236 grand total **15.** \$1,627 **17.** 4,629 **19.** 278,091 **21.** \$138 **23.** \$139 **25.** 3,490,700 **27.** \$20,220 **29.** 378

REVIEW EXERCISES | CHAPTER 1—SECTION III

1. 11,191 **3.** 294,300 **5.** 56,969,000 **7.** 13,110 **9.** 100,000 estimate—98,980 exact **11.** 200 estimate—187 exact **13.** 399 **15.** 70,350 **17.** 13 R67 **19.** 55 **21.** 2 R300 estimate—2 R339 exact **23.** 6 **25.** \$924

CHAPTER 1 | ASSESSMENT TEST

1. 200,049—two hundred thousand, forty-nine **3.** 316,229 **5.** 18,300 **7.** 260,000 **9.** 99 **11.** 44 R28 **13.** 22,258 **15.** 714 **17.** \$14,524 **19a.** 19 **19b.** 25 **21a.** \$11,340 **21b.** \$36 **23.** \$1,003 **25.** \$49,260 **27.** 5,040 **29.** 15

CHAPTER 2 FRACTIONS

REVIEW EXERCISES | CHAPTER 2—SECTION I

1. mixed fraction, twenty-three and four-fifths **3.** improper fraction, fifteen-ninths **5.** mixed fraction, two and one-eighth **7.** $3\frac{1}{3}$ **9.** $4\frac{4}{15}$ **11.** $1\frac{2}{31}$ **13.** $\frac{59}{5}$ **15.** $\frac{149}{8}$ **17.** $\frac{1{,}001}{4}$ **19.** $\frac{3}{4}$ **21.** $\frac{27}{115}$ **23.** $\frac{1}{8}$ **25.** $\frac{19}{65}$ **27.** $\frac{13}{16}$ **29.** $\frac{5}{18}$ **31.** $\frac{36}{48}$ **33.** $\frac{44}{64}$ **35.** $\frac{42}{98}$ **37.** $\frac{40}{64}$ **39.** $\frac{126}{182}$ **41.** $\frac{16}{72}$ **43.** $\frac{3}{5}$

REVIEW EXERCISES | CHAPTER 2—SECTION II

1. 15 **3.** 12 **5.** 300 **7.** $1\frac{1}{3}$ **9.** $1\frac{7}{16}$ **11.** $1\frac{13}{20}$ **13.** $2\frac{3}{20}$ **15.** $11\frac{13}{24}$ **17.** $10\frac{17}{40}$ **19.** $10\frac{19}{30}$ **21.** $\frac{2}{3}$ **23.** $\frac{11}{18}$ **25.** $8\frac{4}{15}$ **27.** $26\frac{29}{45}$ **29.** $35\frac{13}{15}$ **31a.** $45\frac{11}{30}$ **31b.** $90\frac{19}{30}$ **33.** $\frac{5}{16}$

REVIEW EXERCISES | CHAPTER 2—SECTION III

1. $\frac{8}{15}$ **3.** $\frac{2}{9}$ **5.** $\frac{10}{19}$ **7.** $2\frac{2}{5}$ **9.** $21\frac{13}{15}$ **11.** $\frac{1}{125}$ **13a.** $\frac{5}{8}$ **13b.** 2,750 **15.** $43\frac{15}{16}$ **17.** $317\frac{9}{10}$ **19.** $2\frac{2}{9}$ **21.** $1\frac{1}{15}$ **23.** $\frac{2}{5}$ **25.** $5\frac{17}{35}$ **27.** 19 **29.** $\frac{5}{14}$ **31.** 46 **33a.** 240 **33b.** 90 **35.** 213 **37.** 55

CHAPTER 2 | ASSESSMENT TEST

1. improper fraction, eighteen elevenths **3.** proper fraction, thirteen sixteenths **5.** 25 **7.** $\frac{86}{9}$ **9.** $\frac{2}{5}$ **11.** $\frac{18}{78}$ **13.** $\frac{25}{36}$ **15.** $5\frac{1}{3}$ **17.** $4\frac{3}{10}$ **19.** $13\frac{1}{3}$ **21.** 69 **23.** $23\frac{5}{8}$ **25a.** $18\frac{3}{8}$ **25b.** $183,750.00 **27a.** $588,000 **27b.** $49,000 **29.** 15 ounces, pasta; 4 tablespoons, garlic; $3\frac{1}{8}$ cups, tomatoes; $6\frac{1}{4}$ tablespoons, cheese **31a.** $4\frac{15}{16}$ **31b.** $9\frac{5}{8}$

CHAPTER 3 DECIMALS

REVIEW EXERCISES | CHAPTER 3—SECTION I

1. twenty-one hundredths **3.** ninety-two thousandths **5.** ninety-eight thousand forty-five and forty-five thousandths **7.** nine hundred thirty-eight hundred-thousandths **9.** fifty-seven and one half hundred-thousandths **11.** .8 **13.** 67,309.04 **15.** 183,000.0183 **17.** 123.007 **19.** .01004 **21.** $14.60 **23.** 43.01 **25.** 46

REVIEW EXERCISES | CHAPTER 3—SECTION II

1. 58.033 **3.** $45.27 **5.** 152.784494 **7.** 16.349 **9.** $.87 **11.** 779.75 **13.** $138.37 **15.** 2.693 **17a.** 2.3091 **17b.** 1.6309 **19.** $1,636.24 **21.** 549.24 **23.** 7.3952 **25.** .04848 **27.** 45,007.9 **29.** 1.29 **31.** .02 **33.** 3.7 **35.** 1,555 **37.** $7,946.50 **39a.** $45.70 **39b.** $11.40 **41.** 316 **43a.** $45.72 **43b.** $10.06 **45a.** 15 **45b.** 27 **45c.** $39.96

REVIEW EXERCISES | CHAPTER 3—SECTION III

1. $\frac{1}{8}$ **3.** $\frac{1}{125}$ **5.** $14\frac{41}{50}$ **7.** 5.67 **9.** 1.22 **11.** 58.43 **13.** 5 **15a.** 16 **15b.** $190.24 **17a.** $278.66 **17b.** 25.7¢ **19.** $13.10

CHAPTER 3 | ASSESSMENT TEST

1. sixty-one hundredths **3.** one hundred nineteen dollars and eighty-five cents **5.** four hundred ninety-five ten-thousandths **7.** 5.014 **9.** $16.57 **11.** 995.070 **13.** 4.7 **15.** $37.19 **17.** 7.7056 **19.** .736 **21.** .000192 **23.** .4 **25.** $20.06 **27.** $\frac{441}{10{,}000}$ **29.** 3.11 **31.** $1,127.85 **33.** $1,500.36 **35a.** $1.11 **35b.** $1.86 **35c.** 5¢ **35d.** Sale price **37.** $21,773.77 **39a.** 23 **39b.** $41.17

CHAPTER 4 CHECKING ACCOUNTS

REVIEW EXERCISES | CHAPTER 4—SECTION I

1. $345.54 **3.** $644.30 **5.** Your Signature, 099-506-8 Blank Endorsement **7.** $9,998.67 net deposit **9.** #439—$90.68 Bal. Fwd, #440—$317.90 Bal. Fwd, #441—$864.50 Bal. Fwd.

REVIEW EXERCISES | CHAPTER 4—SECTION II

1. \$1,485.90 reconciled balance **3.** \$471.84 reconciled balance

CHAPTER 4 | ASSESSMENT TEST

1. \$24,556.00 **3.** \$935.79 net deposit **5.** \$324.57 reconciled balance

CHAPTER 5 USING EQUATIONS TO SOLVE BUSINESS PROBLEMS

REVIEW EXERCISES | CHAPTER 5—SECTION I

1. $B = 13$ **3.** $S = 90$ **5.** $K = 3$ **7.** $Y = 7\frac{1}{2}$ **9.** $G = 4$ **11.** $A = 3$ **13.** $X = 4$ **15.** $D = 5$ **17.** $Q = 1$ **19.** $5F + 33$ **21.** $HP + 550$ **23.** $8Y - 128$ **25.** $\frac{3}{4}B + 40$ **27.** $X = 5B + C$ **29.** $\$5.75R = \$28.75$ **31.** $5X + 4 + 2X = X + 40$

REVIEW EXERCISES | CHAPTER 5—SECTION II

1. 47 Karen, 39 Kathy **3.** 114 cartons **5.** 18 units **7.** \$22,400 Robbin, \$67,200 Bryant **9.** 288 total transactions **11.** 14 extended, 42 standard **13a.** 220 peanut butter, 310 oatmeal **13b.** \$352 peanut butter, \$403 oatmeal **15.** \$2.60 per piece **17.** \$777 **19.** \$114.10 **21.** 27 inches **23.** 18,850 **25a.** 256 **25b.** \$9.52

CHAPTER 5 | ASSESSMENT TEST

1. $T = 65$ **3.** $K = 15$ **5.** $X = 8$ **7.** $B = 8$ **9.** $X = 15$ **11.** $4R - 108$ **13.** $ZW + 24$ **15.** $X = 4C + L$ **17.** $3F - 14 = 38$ **19.** 14 Blue Water, 19 Atlas **21.** \$55 **23.** 95 watts **25.** \$1.15 **27a.** 200 banana splits, 800 sundaes **27b.** \$850 banana splits, \$2,880 sundaes **29.** \$104,000 **31.** \$1,365 **33.** 60 ft.

CHAPTER 6 PERCENTS AND THEIR APPLICATIONS IN BUSINESS

REVIEW EXERCISES | CHAPTER 6—SECTION I

1. .28 **3.** .134 **5.** .4268 **7.** .0002 **9.** 1.2517 **11.** 350% **13.** 4,600% **15.** .935% **17.** 16,400% **19.** 533% **21.** $\frac{1}{20}$ **23.** $\frac{89}{100}$ **25.** $\frac{19}{50}$ **27.** $\frac{5}{8}$ **29.** $1\frac{1}{4}$ **31.** 75% **33.** 240% **35.** 125% **37.** 18.75% **39.** 35%

REVIEW EXERCISES | CHAPTER 6—SECTION II

1. 57 **3.** 90 **5.** 85.5 **7.** 64.77 **9.** 56.88 **11.** 32% **13.** 250% **15.** 13.5% **17.** 29.9% **19.** 26.0% **21.** 460 **23.** 34.86 **25.** 363.64 **27.** 400 **29.** \$53.65 **31.** \$59,200 **33.** \$165,000 **35.** \$13,650 **37.** \$142.35 **39.** 10 **41.** 1,700 **43.** \$61,230.75 **45a.** 16,666,700 **45b.** 360 **45c.** Women 294,667 Men 216,000

REVIEW EXERCISES | CHAPTER 6—SECTION III

1. 37.5% **3.** 25.2% **5.** 60 **7.** 15 **9.** 10,000 **11.** 7% **13a.** 1,105 **13b.** 442 graphite, 663 wood **15.** 29.4% **17a.** $110,000 **17b.** $105,600 **19.** 22.7%

CHAPTER 6 | ASSESSMENT TEST

1. .88 **3.** .5968 **5.** .005625 **7.** 68.1% **9.** 2,480% **11.** $\frac{19}{100}$ **13.** $\frac{93}{1,250}$ **15.** $\frac{127}{500}$ **17.** 55.56% **19.** 5,630% **21.** 408 **23.** 103.41 **25.** 180% **27.** 69 **29.** 2,960 **31.** 1,492 **33.** $122.48 **35.** 50% **37.** 21.0% **39a.** 500 lbs **39b.** 72.2% **41.** 18.1% **43a.** 367,500 **43b.** 69.4% **45.** 40,583.33 **47a.** Land 7%; concrete and steel, 20.1%; plumbing and electrical, 28.5%; carpentry and roof, 24.6%; other, 19.9% **47b.** $318,292.50

CHAPTER 7 INVOICES, TRADE DISCOUNTS, AND CASH DISCOUNTS

REVIEW EXERCISES | CHAPTER 7—SECTION I

1. box **3.** drum **5.** gross **7.** thousand **9.** Frasier Mfg. **11.** June 16, 200x **13.** J. M. Hardware Supply **15.** 2051 W. Adams Blvd, Nashville, TN 96133 **17.** Gilbert Trucking **19.** $61.45 **21.** $4,415.12

REVIEW EXERCISES | CHAPTER 7—SECTION II

1. $258 **3.** $7.93 **5.** $44.13 **7.** $53.92 - $80.87 **9.** $527.45 - $431.55 **11.** 76%, $429.65 **13.** 87.25%, $4.01 **15.** $120.50, $34.9% **17.** $239.99 **19.** $1,950 **21a.** $494.80 **21b.** $192.97 **21c.** $301.83 **23.** $1,512 **25a.** Pro-Chef, $233.75 **25b.** $7,125.00.

REVIEW EXERCISES | CHAPTER 7—SECTION III

1. .792, $285.12 **3.** .648, $52.97 **5.** .57056, $4.14 **7.** .765, .235 **9.** .59288, .40712 **11.** .51106, .48894 **13.** .6324, .3676, $441.12, $758.88 **15.** .65666, .34334, $303.34, $580.16 **17.** .5292, .4708, $1,353.53, $1,521.42 **19.** .49725 **21a.** .6 **21b.** $54,300.00 **23a.** .57375 **23b.** .42625 **25a.** $324.19 **25b.** .53687 **27a.** $232.96 **27b.** $291.20 **29a.** $1,494.90 **29b.** $687.65 **29c.** $807.25

REVIEW EXERCISES | CHAPTER 7—SECTION IV

1. $474, $15,326 **3.** $96.84, $2,324.16 **5.** $319.25, $8,802.19 **7.** $474.23, $870.37 **9.** $5,759.16, $1,472.92 **11.** May 8, June 22 **13.** 2%, Feb 8, 1%, Feb 18, Mar 30 **15.** Jan 10, Jan 30 **17.** Oct 23, Nov 12 **19.** June 25, July 15 **21a.** April 27, May 27 **21b.** $21.24 **21c.** $1,148.76 **23a.** Mar 22 **23b.** Apr 11 **25a.** $23,095.36 **25b.** June 24 **25c.** $24,134.65

CHAPTER 7 | ASSESSMENT TEST

1. Sunshine Patio Furniture Manufacturers **3.** 4,387 **5.** $46.55 **7.** $2,558 **9.** $11,562.45 **11.** $1,485 **13.** 33.76% **15.** Ideal Shoes, $340.56, Fancy Footwear, $335.30 (lower net price) **17a.** .6052 **17b.** .3948 **19a.** April 24 **19b.** May 9 **19c.** May 15 **19d.** June 4

CHAPTER 8 MARKUP AND MARKDOWN

REVIEW EXERCISES | CHAPTER 8—SECTION I

1. $138.45, 85.7% **3.** $6,944.80, 77.8% **5.** $156.22, $93.73 **7.** $2,149, 159.2% **9.** $.75, $1.33 **11.** $85.90 **13.** $195 **15a.** $4.19 **15b.** 71.7% **17.** $21.88 **19.** $583.92 **21a.** $60.63 **21b.** 104.1% **23a.** $11.76 **23b.** $8.23

REVIEW EXERCISES | CHAPTER 8—SECTION II

1. $115, 43.5% **3.** $61.36, $136.36 **5.** 37.5% **7.** $94.74, 133%, 57.1% **9.** $9,468.74, $24,917.74, 61.3% **11.** 60% **13a.** $455.99 **13b.** 45.6% **15.** $366.12 **17a.** $2.87 **17b.** $1.12 **17c.** 39% **19.** 75.4% **21a.** $30.49 **21b.** 141.8% **21c.** 58.6%

REVIEW EXERCISES | CHAPTER 8—SECTION III

1. $161.45, 15% **3.** $1.68, 23.2% **5.** $41.10, $16.44 **7.** $80.27, 30.7% **9.** $559.96, $1,039.92 **11a.** $45.80 **11b.** 19.4% **13a.** $.70 **13b.** 41.4% **13c.** $1.39 **15.** $30.00 **17.** $115.00 **19.** $469.68 **21.** $233.99 **23a.** 20% **23b.** $159.99

CHAPTER 8 | ASSESSMENT TEST

1. $152.60 **3.** $18.58 **5a.** $81.50 **5b.** 71.6% **5c.** 41.7% **7.** $15.95 **9a.** 63% **9b.** $84.98 **11.** $216.06 **13a.** $56.25 **13b.** $64.68 **15a.** $2,499.99 **15b.** $1,000.00 **15c.** 60% **15d.** 36%

CHAPTER 9 PAYROLL

REVIEW EXERCISES | CHAPTER 9—SECTION I

1. $1,250, $625, $576.92, $288.46 **3.** $8,333.33, $4,166.67, $3,846.15, $1,923.08 **5.** $34,800, $2,900, $1,338.46, $669.23 **7.** $17,420, $1,451.67, $725.83, $670 **9.** $166,666.67 **11.** $491.55 **13.** 36, 0, $205.20, 0, $205.20 **15.** 48, 8, $290, $87.00, $377.00 **17.** $572 **19.** $433 **21.** $739.90 **23.** $3,664.50 **25.** $3,336 **27.** $629.97

REVIEW EXERCISES | CHAPTER 9—SECTION II

1. $51.15, social security; $11.96, Medicare **3a.** $545.60, social security; $127.60, Medicare **3b.** October **3c.** $353.40, social security; $127.60, Medicare **5.** $212.16, $49.62 **7.** $104.47, $68.15 **9.** $53.77 **11.** $735.06 **13.** $191.24 **15.** $2,133.51 **17.** $151.53 **19.** $702.21

REVIEW EXERCISES | CHAPTER 9—SECTION III

1a. $806, social security; $188.50, Medicare **1b.** $10,478, social security; $2,450.50, Medicare **3.** $347.20, social security; $81.20, Medicare **5a.** $378 **5b.** $56 **7a.** $950.13, SUTA; $140.76, FUTA **7b.** $183.87, SUTA; $27.24, FUTA **9a.** $34,725.00, 1st QTR; $26,652.60, 2nd QTR; $25,425.00 3rd & 4th QTR **9b.** 1040-ES

CHAPTER 9 | ASSESSMENT TEST

1a. $67,200 **1b.** $2,584.62 **3.** $491.70 **5a.** $305.40 **5b.** $209.30 **5c.** $602.40 **7.** $3,300.10 **9.** $2,284.10 **11.** $44.95, social security; $10.51, Medicare **13a.** $1,709.22 **13b.** $1,793.02 **13c.** $2,038.99 **15.** $1,225.19 **17a.** $1,693.03, social security; $395.95, Medicare **17b.** $44,018.78, social security; $10,294.70, Medicare **19a.** $378 **19b.** $56 **21a.** $58,589.20 **21b.** 20.8% **21c.** $3,046,638.40

CHAPTER 10 SIMPLE INTEREST AND PROMISSORY NOTES

REVIEW EXERCISES | CHAPTER 10—SECTION I

1. $800 **3.** $19,050 **5.** $206.62 **7.** $1,602.74, $1,625 **9.** $1,839.79, $1,865.34 **11.** $15.16, $15.38 **13.** $60.82, $61.67 **15.** $882.88, $895.15 **17.** $12,852, $66,852 **19.** $2,362.50, $36,112.50 **21.** $1,770 **23.** $1,330,000 **25.** 98 **27.** 289 **29.** Dec. 3 **31.** June 24 **33.** Feb. 23 **35.** $62,005.48 **37.** $403.89

REVIEW EXERCISES | CHAPTER 10—SECTION II

1. $1,250 **3.** $50,000 **5.** $12,000 **7.** 14% **9.** 12.8% **11.** 158 days **13.** 308 days **15.** 180 days **17.** $13,063.16, $13,403.16 **19.** $2,390.63, $27,890.63 **21a.** 166 days **21b.** Sept. 29 **23.** $10,000 **25.** 11.6% **27.** $6,147.56 **29a.** 12.5 years **29b.** 10 years

REVIEW EXERCISES | CHAPTER 10—SECTION III

1. $292.50, $4,207.50 **3.** $231.25, $1,618.75 **5.** $232.38, $7,567.62 **7.** 84 days, $171.50, $4,828.50 **9.** 100 days, $34.31, $1,265.69 **11.** $132.30, $2,567.70, 14.72% **13.** $214.28, $3,585.72, 15.37% **15.** $4,683.85, $52,816.15, 13.88% **17.** Jan. 31, $4,057.78, 12 days, $4,037.49 **19a.** $23,533.33 **19b.** April 10 **21a.** Dec. 16 **21b.** $41,266.67 **21c.** Nov. 21 **21d.** $40,836.81

CHAPTER 10 | ASSESSMENT TEST

1. $641.10 **3.** $672.93 **5.** $24,648 **7.** 107 **9.** Jan. 24 **11.** $11,666.67 **13.** 9.1% **15.** 72 days **17.** 190 days, $13,960 **19.** 15.2%, $2,795 **21.** Jan. 20, $20,088.54, $854,911.46 **23.** $10,544.72, $279,455.28, 12.35% **25.** Aug. 25, $5,642.31, 34 days, $5,569.30 **27.** $99.37 **29.** 15.3% **31.** $9,393.88 **33a.** $28,970.83 **33b.** Nov. 12 **33c.** 13.46%

CHAPTER 11 COMPOUND INTEREST AND PRESENT VALUE

REVIEW EXERCISES | CHAPTER 11—SECTION I

1. 3, 13% **3.** 24, 4% **5.** 16, 3.5% **7.** 3, 3% **9.** $11,255.09, $1,255.09 **11.** $11,413.29, $4,413.29 **13.** $6,721.67, $1,421.67 **15.** $119,614.75, $94,614.75 **17.** $29,799.88, $20,999.88 **19.** 12.17218, $231,271.42 **21.** 132.78160, $1,327,816 **23.** $512.50, 10.25% **25.** $4,565.88, 12.68% **27a.** 6.14% **27b.** $4,288.50 **29.** $673,925

REVIEW EXERCISES | CHAPTER 11—SECTION II

1. $4,633.08, $1,366.92 **3.** $437.43, $212.57 **5.** $3,680.50, $46,319.50 **7.** $6,107.07, $3,692.93 **9.** $209.10, $40.90 **11.** .20829, $2,499.48 **13.** .24200, $338.80 **15.** .26355, $28,990.50 **17a.** $2,549.58 **17b.** $950.42 **19a.** $10,927 **19b.** $14,073

CHAPTER 11 | ASSESSMENT TEST

1. $31,530.66, $17,530.66 **3.** $3,586.86, $586.86 **5.** 5.61652, $112,330.40 **7.** $1,078.06, 12.68% **9.** $6,930, $143,070 **11.** $658.35, 241.65 **13.** .62027, $806.35 **15.** $81,392.40, $45,392.40 **17.** $17,150.85, compound amount; $2,150.85, compound interest **19.** $32,342 **21a.** 12.55% **21b.** $17,888.55 **23.** $48,545.40 **25a.** $37,243.34 **25b.** $14,243.34

CHAPTER 12 ANNUITIES

REVIEW EXERCISES | CHAPTER 12—SECTION I

1. $18,639.29 **3.** $151,929.30 **5.** $74,951.37 **7.** $13,680.33 **9.** $100,226.90 **11.** $2,543.20 **13.** $15,934.37

REVIEW EXERCISES | CHAPTER 12—SECTION II

1. $2,969.59 **3.** $27,096.86 **5.** $79,773.10 **7.** $16,819.32 **9.** $110,997.88 **11.** $9,025.15 **13.** $380,773

REVIEW EXERCISES | CHAPTER 12—SECTION III

1. $2,113.50 **3.** $55.82 **5.** $859.13 **7.** $336.36 **9.** $1,087.48 **11.** $418.24 **13a.** $3,769.04 **13b.** $2,385.76

CHAPTER 12 | ASSESSMENT TEST

1. $121,687.44 **3.** $86,445.14 **5.** $42,646.92 **7.** $11,593.58 **9.** $993.02 **11.** $255.66 **13.** $20,345.57 **15.** $6,081.72 **17a.** $195,350.02 **17b.** $7,071.39 **19a.** $19,496.56 **19b.** $19,351.43 **21.** $1,678.39

CHAPTER 13 CONSUMER AND BUSINESS CREDIT

REVIEW EXERCISES | CHAPTER 13—SECTION I

1. 1.5%, $2.52, $335.90 **3.** 21%, $7.96, $544.32 **5a.** $1.20 **5b.** $259.13 **7.** $636.17, $11.13, $628.75 **9.** $817.08, $14.30, $684.76 **11.** $152.29 **13a.** $6.89 **13b.** $728.23 **15a.** $157.14 **15b.** $9,957.14 **15c.** $20,042.86

REVIEW EXERCISES | CHAPTER 13—SECTION II

1. \$1,050, \$582, \$1,982 **3.** \$10,800, \$2,700, \$14,700 **5.** \$7,437.50, \$2,082.34, \$10,832.34 **7.** \$1,350, \$270, \$67.50 **9.** \$15,450, \$8,652, \$502.13 **11.** \$322, \$14, 13% **13.** \$223.50, \$12.02, 14.75% **15.** \$31, 11.25% **17.** \$4,940, 16.6% **19.** 29.97, \$1,498.50, \$135.39 **21.** 6.20, \$111.60, \$159.30 **23.** 8, 36, 78, $\frac{36}{78}$ **25.** 15, 120, 300, $\frac{120}{300}$ **27.** $\frac{120}{300}$, \$360, \$2,077.50 **29.** $\frac{78}{1,176}$, \$219.94, \$2,984.06 **31a.** \$411.30 **31b.** \$2,310.30 **33.** \$34.92 **35a.** \$1,667.68 **35b.** 14.5% **37.** \$216.45, finance charge, \$63.19, monthly payment **39a.** 300 **39b.** 465 **41a.** \$504.00 **41b.** \$152.25 **41c.** 14.75%, table; 14.64%, formula **41d.** \$1,157.52

CHAPTER 13 | ASSESSMENT TEST

1a. 1.33% **1b.** \$4.59 **1c.** \$440.38 **3a.** \$4.46, \$724.12 **3b.** \$724.12, \$12.09, \$839.64 **3c.** \$839.64, \$14.02, \$859.61 **5a.** \$694.76 **5b.** \$7.50 **5c.** \$864.74 **7a.** \$9,920 **7b.** \$39,120 **9a.** \$10,384 **9b.** 19.25% **11a.** \$66,300 **11b.** \$4,646.67 **13a.** \$14,144 **13b.** \$1,428 **13c.** 11.75% **13d.** \$32,906.45 **15a.** \$20,379.66 **15b.** \$18,079.66 **15c.** \$7,540.34 **15d.** \$27,920.00 **15e.** 14.75%

CHAPTER 14 MORTGAGES

REVIEW EXERCISES | CHAPTER 14—SECTION I

1. 80, 9.00, \$720, \$92,800 **3.** 130.9, 8.06, \$1,055.05, \$185,615.00 **5.** 96.8, 7.17, \$694.06, \$153,061.60 **7.** \$639.47, \$821.39 **9.** \$1,189.79, \$1,601.21 **11a.** 7.25% **11b.** 15.25% **13a.** Fortune Bank, \$115,950; Northern Trust Bank, \$120,000 **13b.** Fortune Bank, \$120,450; Northern Trust Bank, \$120,000 (better deal by \$450.00)

REVIEW EXERCISES | CHAPTER 14—SECTION II

1. \$89,025, \$21,125 **3.** \$112,960, \$13,860.00 **5.** \$63,700, 0 **7.** 14.32%, 24.05% **9.** 26.04%, 35% **11a.** Johnson and Turnberry **11b.** Johnson and Turnberry **13.** no, potential credit only \$19,200

CHAPTER 14 | ASSESSMENT TEST

1. 134.9, 7.56, \$1,019.84, \$171,052 **3.** monthly payment, \$1,447.85; loan balance after 3 payments, \$145,955.46 **5.** \$1,321.00, \$1,596.67 **7.** \$41,200, \$13,800 **9.** 24.3%, 40.15% **11.** Morgan, FHA; Willow, FHA and conventional **13a.** \$5,194.80 **13b.** loan balance after 2 payments, \$518,704.76 **13c.** \$6,147.30 **13d.** \$4,052.70 **15a.** Red River Bank, \$946,368; Sterling Savings & Loan, \$919,584 **15b.** Sterling is a better deal by \$9,346.50 **17.** 0 **19a.** 27.86% **19b.** 39.53% **19c.** FHA

CHAPTER 15 FINANCIAL STATEMENTS AND RATIOS

REVIEW EXERCISES | CHAPTER 15—SECTION I

1. $161,600 **3.** $29,000 **5.** current asset **7.** owner's equity **9.** long-term liability **11.** current liability **13.** current asset **15.** current asset **17.** fixed asset **19.** current asset **21.** owner's equity **23.** owner's equity **25.** current liability

27a.

Northern Industries, Inc.
Balance Sheet
June 30, 2002

Assets		
Current Assets		**Percent***
Cash	$ 44,300	5.5
Accounts Receivable	127,600	15.8
Merchandise Inventory	88,100	10.9
Prepaid Maintenance	4,100	.5
Office Supplies	4,000	.5
Total Current Assets	268,100	33.2
Property, Plant and Equipment		
Land	154,000	19.0
Buildings	237,000	29.3
Fixtures	21,400	2.6
Vehicles	64,000	7.9
Computers	13,000	1.6
Total Property, Plant and Equipment	489,400	60.4
Investments and Other Assets		
Investments	32,000	4.0
Goodwill	20,000	2.5
Total Assets	$809,500	100%
Liabilities and Owner's Equity		
Current Liabilities		
Accounts Payable	55,700	6.9
Salaries Payable	23,200	2.9
Notes Payable	38,000	4.7
Total Current Liabilities	116,900	14.5
Long-Term Liabilities		
Mortgage Payable	91,300	11.3
Debenture Bonds	165,000	20.4
Total Long-Term Liabilities	256,300	31.7
Total Liabilities	373,200	46.2
Owner's Equity		
Common Stock	350,000	43.2
Retained Earnings	86,300	10.7
Total Owner's Equity	436,300	53.9
Total Liabilities and Owner's Equity	$809,500	100%

*Percents may vary by .1 due to rounding

27b.

Northern Industries, Inc.
Comparative Balance Sheet
June 30, 2002 and 2003

Assets	2003	2002	Increase/Decrease Amount	Increase/Decrease Percent
Current Assets				
Cash	$ 40,200	$ 44,300	($4,100)	(9.3)
Accounts Receivable	131,400	127,600	3,800	3.0
Merchandise Inventory	92,200	88,100	4,100	4.7
Prepaid Maintenance	3,700	4,100	(400)	(9.8)
Office Supplies	6,200	4,000	2,200	55.0
Total Current Assets	273,700	268,100	5,600	2.1
Property, Plant and Equipment				
Land	154,000	154,000	0	0
Buildings	231,700	237,000	(5,300)	(2.2)
Fixtures	23,900	21,400	2,500	11.7
Vehicles	55,100	64,000	(8,900)	(13.9)
Computers	16,800	13,000	3,800	29.2
Total Property, Plant and Equipment	481,500	489,400	7,900	1.6
Investments and Other Assets				
Investments	36,400	32,000	4,400	13.8
Goodwill	22,000	20,000	2,000	10.0
Total Assets	$813,600	$809,500	4,100	.5
Liabilities and Owner's Equity				
Current Liabilities				
Accounts Payable	51,800	55,700	(3,900)	(7.0)
Salaries Payable	25,100	23,200	1,900	8.2
Notes Payable	19,000	38,000	(19,000)	(50.0)
Total Current Liabilities	95,900	116,900	(21,000)	(18.0)
Long-Term Liabilities				
Mortgage Payable	88,900	91,300	(2,400)	(2.6)
Debenture Bonds	165,000	165,000	0	0
Total Long-Term Liabilities	253,900	256,300	(2,400)	(.9)
Total Liabilities				
Owner's Equity	349,800	373,200	(23,400)	(6.3)
Common Stock	350,000	350,000	0	0
Retained Earnings	113,800	86,300	27,500	31.9
Total Owner's Equity	463,800	436,300	27,500	6.3
Total Liabilities and Owner's Equity	$813,600	$809,500	4,100	.5

REVIEW EXERCISES | CHAPTER 15—SECTION II

1. $202,200, $94,200 **3.** $675,530, $334,160 **5a.** $316,120 **5b.** $122,680 **5c.** $212,320 **5d.** $45,120

7a.

Tasty Treats Food Wholesalers, Inc.
Income Statement
For the year ended December 31, 2002

Revenue		
Gross Sales	$2,249,000	109.6
Less: Sales Returns and Allowances	143,500	7.0
Sales Discounts	54,290	2.6
Net Sales	$2,051,210	100.0
Cost of Goods sold		
Merchandise Inventory, Jan.1	875,330	42.7
Net Purchases	546,920	26.7
Freight In	11,320	.6
Goods Available for Sale	1,433,570	69.9
Less: Merchandise Inventory, Dec. 31	716,090	34.9
Cost of Goods Sold	717,480	35.0
Gross Margin	1,333,730	65.0
Operating Expenses		
Salaries	319,800	15.6
Rent	213,100	10.4
Depreciation	51,200	2.5
Utilities	35,660	1.7
Advertising	249,600	12.2
Insurance	39,410	1.9
Administrative Expenses	91,700	4.5
Miscellaneous Expenses	107,500	5.2
Total Operating Expenses	1,107,970	54.0
Income before Taxes	225,760	11.0
Income Tax	38,450	1.9
Net Income	$ 187,310	9.1

7b.

Tasty Treats Food Wholesalers, Inc.
Comparative Income Statement
For the years ended December 31, 2002 and 2003

	2003	2002	Increase/Decrease Amount	Increase/Decrease Percent
Revenue				
Gross Sales	$2,125,000	$2,249,000	($124,000)	(5.5)
Less: Sales Returns and Allowances	126,400	143,500	(17,100)	(11.9)
Sales Discounts	73,380	54,290	19,090	35.2
Net Sales	1,925,220	2,051,210	(125,990)	(6.1)
Cost of Goods Sold				
Merchandise Inventory, Jan. 1	716,090	875,330	(159,240)	(18.2)
Net Purchases	482,620	546,920	(64,300)	(11.8)
Freight In	9,220	11,320	(2,100)	(18.6)
Goods Available for Sale	1,207,930	1,433,570	(225,640)	(15.7)
Less: Merchandise Inventory, Dec. 31	584,550	716,090	(131,540)	(18.4)
Cost of Goods Sold	623,380	717,480	(94,100)	(13.1)
Gross Margin	1,301,840	1,333,730	(31,890)	(2.4)
Operating Expenses				
Salaries	340,900	319,800	21,100	7.0
Rent	215,000	213,100	1,900	.9
Depreciation	56,300	51,200	5,100	10.0
Utilities	29,690	35,660	(5,970)	(16.7)
Advertising	217,300	249,600	(32,300)	(13.0)
Insurance	39,410	39,410	0	0
Administrative Expenses	95,850	91,700	4,150	4.5
Miscellaneous Expenses	102,500	107,500	(5,000)	(4.7)
Total Operating Expenses	1,096,950	1,107,970	(11,020)	(1.0)
Income before Income Tax	204,890	225,760	(20,870)	(9.2)
Income Tax	44,530	38,450	6,080	15.8
Net Income	$ 160,360	$ 187,310	(26,950)	(14.4)

REVIEW EXERCISES | CHAPTER 15—SECTION III

1. $51,160, 1.69:1 **3.** $2,350, 2.88:1 **5.** $95,920, 1.29:1 **7.** $2,165, 1.73:1 **9.** 44 days **11.** $105,650, 6.2 times **13.** $74,447.50, 6.6 times **15.** .58:1 **17.** $155,390, .7:1, 2.3:1 **19.** $253,940, $78,530, 34.2%, 10.6% **21.** $113,080, $27,159, 35.7%, 8.6% **23.** 8.2%

25.

King Tire Company
Trend Analysis Chart

	2002	2001	2000	1999	1998
Net Sales	107.5	127.3	108.0	97.1	100.0
Net Income	124.3	128.5	99.4	104.2	100.0
Total Assets	109.7	107.4	105.0	97.7	100.0
Stockholder's Equity	105.9	120.3	106.4	94.5	100.0

CHAPTER 15 | ASSESSMENT TEST

1a.

Service Master Carpet Cleaning
Balance Sheet
December 31, 2002

Assets		**Percent**
Current Assets	$132,500	52.2
Property, Plant and Equipment	88,760	35.0
Investments and Other Assets	32,400	12.8
Total Assets	$253,660	100%
Liabilities		
Current Liabilities	51,150	20.2
Long-Term Liabilities	87,490	34.5
Total Liabilities	138,640	54.7
Owner's Equity		
Al Mosley, Equity	115,020	45.3
Total Liabilities and Owner's Equity	$253,660	100%

1b.

Service Master Carpet Cleaning
Comparative Balance Sheet
December 31, 2002 and 2003

			Increase/Decrease	
	2003	**2002**	**Amount**	**Percent**
Assets				
Current Assets	$154,300	$132,500	$21,800	16.5
Property, Plant and Equipment	124,650	88,760	35,890	40.4
Investments and Other Assets	20,000	32,400	(12,400)	(38.3)
Total Assets	$298,950	$253,660	45,290	17.9
Liabilities				
Current Liabilities	65,210	51,150	14,060	27.5
Long-Term Liabilities	83,800	87,490	(3,690)	(4.2)
Total Liabilities	149,010	138,640	10,370	7.5
Owner's Equity				
Al Mosley Equity	149,940	115,020	34,920	30.4
Total Liabilities and Owner's Equity	$298,950	$253,660	45,290	17.9

3. $185,772

5a.

Abbey Road Restaurant Supply
Income Statement
Third Quarter, 2003

Revenue		
Gross Sales	$224,400	106.8
Less: Sales Returns and Allowances	14,300	6.8
Net Sales	210,100	100.0
Cost of Goods sold		
Merchandise Inventory, July 1	165,000	78.5
Net Purchases	76,500	36.4
Goods Available for Sale	241,500	114.9
Less: Merchandise Inventory, Sept. 30	143,320	68.2
Cost of Goods Sold	98,180	46.7
Gross Margin	111,920	53.3
Operating Expenses	68,600	32.7
Income before Taxes	43,320	20.6
Income Tax	8,790	4.2
Net Income	$ 34,530	16.4

5b.

Abbey Road Restaurant Supply
Comparative Income Statement
Third and Fourth Quarter – 2003

			Increase/Decrease	
	4th Qtr.	**3rd Qtr.**	**Amount**	**Percent**
Revenue				
Gross Sales	$218,200	$224,400	($6,200)	(2.8)
Less: Sales Returns and Allowances	9,500	14,300	(4,800)	(33.6)
Net Sales	208,700	210,100	1,400	.7
Cost of Goods Sold				
Merchandise Inventory, Beginning	143,320	165,000	(21,680)	(13.1)
Net Purchases	81,200	76,500	4,700	6.1
Goods Available for Sale	224,520	241,500	(16,980)	(7.0)
Less: Merchandise Inventory, Ending	125,300	143,320	(18,020)	(12.6)
Cost of Goods Sold	99,220	98,180	1,040	1.0
Gross Margin	109,480	111,920	(2,440)	(2.2)
Operating Expenses	77,300	68,600	8,700	12.7
Income before Income Tax	32,180	43,320	(11,140)	(25.7)
Income Tax	11,340	8,790	2,550	29.0
Net Income	$ 20,840	$ 34,530	(13,690)	(39.6)

7. $653,300 **9.** 1.02:1 **11.** 1.74 times **13.** 37.9% **15.** 48.3% **17.** 4.2%

19.

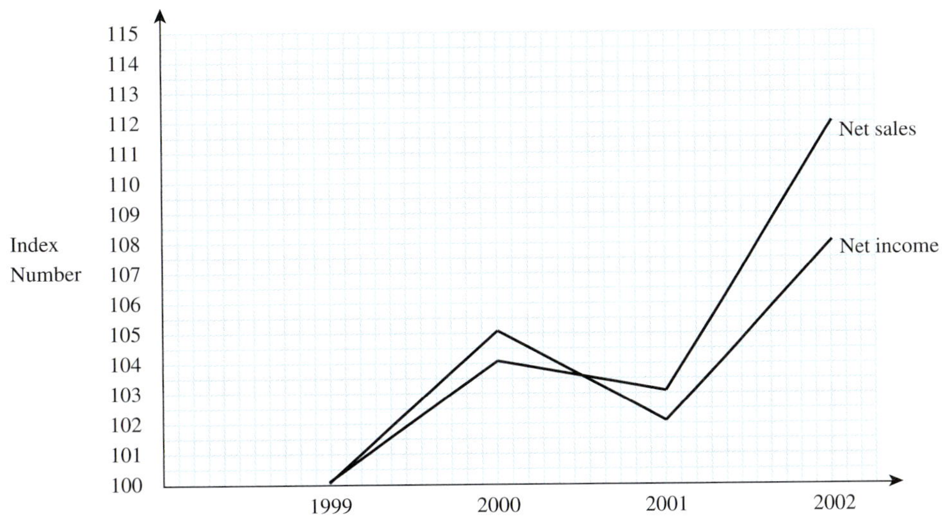

CHAPTER 16 INVENTORY

REVIEW EXERCISES | CHAPTER 16—SECTION I

1. 1,110 units available, $1,798.30, cost of goods **3a.** 322 **3b.** $12,609.75 **3c.** $3,647.35 **3d.** $3,275.00 **3e.** $3,446.08

REVIEW EXERCISES | CHAPTER 16—SECTION II

1. $108,225 **3.** $61,716

REVIEW EXERCISES | CHAPTER 16—SECTION III

1. $60,000, 8.3 times, $50,000 **3.** $486,500, 2.5 times, $342,857.14 **5a.** $28,450 **5b.** 5.1 times **7a.** $162,950, 7.7 times **7b.** $131,578.95

CHAPTER 16 | ASSESSMENT TEST

1. 454 units, $22,053.65 cost of goods **3.** $178,159 **5.** $394,885 **7.** $153,500, 5 times, $111,764.71 **9a.** $359,850 **9b.** 2.5 times **9c.** $176,800

CHAPTER 17 DEPRECIATION

REVIEW EXERCISES | CHAPTER 17—SECTION I

1. $45,650, $42,150, $4,215 **3.** $160,000, $140,000, $28,000

5.

Fluffy Laundry
Depreciation Schedule
Straight-line Method

End of Year	Annual Depreciation	Accumulated Depreciation	Book Value
			(new) $57,970.00
1	$11,194.00	$11,194.00	46,776.00
2	11,194.00	22,388.00	35,582.00
3	11,194.00	33,582.00	24,388.00
4	11,194.00	44,776.00	13,194.00
5	11,194.00	55,970.00	2,000.00

7. 15, $\frac{5}{15}$, $\frac{3}{15}$, $\frac{1}{15}$ **9.** 55, $\frac{10}{55}$, $\frac{8}{55}$, $\frac{6}{55}$ **11.** 25%, 31.25% **13.** 10%, 15% **15.** $.122 **17.** $.25

REVIEW EXERCISES | CHAPTER 17—SECTION II

1. $4,860 **3a.** 10-year property **3b.** 7.37% **3c.** $8,200 **5a.** $.48 **5b.** $375,360

CHAPTER 17 | ASSESSMENT TEST

1. $5,864, $5,264, $877.33

3.

Modern Manufacturing, Inc.
Depreciation Schedule
Straight-line Method

End of Year	Annual Depreciation	Accumulated Depreciation	Book Value
			(new) $652,000
1	$154,750	$154,750	497,250
2	154,750	309,500	342,500
3	154,750	464,250	187,750
4	154,750	619,000	33,000

5. 45, $\frac{8}{45}$, $\frac{6}{45}$, $\frac{4}{45}$ **7.** 11.111%, 13.889%

9.

Academy Trophy
Depreciation Schedule
6-year, 125% declining-balance

End of Year	Beginning Book Value	Depreciation Rate	Depreciation for the Year	Accumulated Depreciation	Ending Book Value
					(new) $33,800.00
1	$33,800.00	20.833	$7,041.55	$7,041.55	26,758.45
2	26,758.45	20.833	5,574.59	12,616.14	21,183.86
3	21,183.86	20.833	4,413.23	17,029.37	16,770.63

11. $.024

13.

Custom Concrete, Inc.
Depreciation Schedule, MACRS
Cement Manufacturing Equipment

End of Year	Original Basis (cost)	Cost Recovery Percentage	Cost Recovery (depreciation)	Accumulated Depreciation	Book Value
					(new) $320,000
1	$320,000	5	$16,000	$16,000	304,000
2	320,000	9.5	30,400	46,400	273,600
3	320,000	8.55	27,360	73,760	246,240
4	320,000	7.70	24,640	98,400	221,600
5	320,000	6.93	22,176	120,576	199,424

CHAPTER 18 TAXES

REVIEW EXERCISES | CHAPTER 18—SECTION I

1. $.59, $9.54 **3.** $.32, $5.20 **5.** $100.80, $15.84, $1,556.64 **7.** $9.90, $22, $251.85 **9.** $17,847.98, $937.02 **11a.** $70.19 **11b.** $1,045.09 **13a.** $54,871.09 **13b.** $3,017.91 **15.** $922,140

REVIEW EXERCISES | CHAPTER 18—SECTION II

1. $76,000, $2,614.40 **3.** $198,400, $5,138.56 **5.** $106,440, $2,267.17 **7.** $264,033, $13,993.75 **9.** 4.92%, $4.92, $49.20, 49.2 **11.** 3.68%, $3.68, $36.80, 36.8 **13a.** $87,500 **13b.** $1,701

REVIEW EXERCISES | CHAPTER 18—SECTION III

1. $32,180, $4,550, ($4,870), $2,900, $24,410 **3.** $43,910, ($7,600), $5,800, $30,510 **5.** $6,780, ($3,800), $2,900, $52,730 **7.** $4,080, $6,650, ($21,230), $8,700, $54,590 **9.** $32,607 **11.** $16,046 **13.** $13,579 **15.** $75,719.50 **17.** $116,816.82 **19.** refund, $651.00 **21.** refund, $1,438.00 **23.** $18,494.70, $70,460.30 **25.** $334,250,000, $620,750,000

CHAPTER 18 | ASSESSMENT TEST

1. $1.17, $19.05 **3.** $6.62, $141.62 **5.** $1,184.63, $755, $19,489.63 **7a.** $25.42 **7b.** $471.30 **9a.** $3.83, $2,221.40 **9b.** $7.50, $4,350 **9c.** $55,871.40 **11.** $52,101, $662.72 **13.** $82,615, $2,394.18 **15.** 1.64%, $1.64, $16.40, 16.4 **17a.** .07% **17b.** $.07 **17c.** $.70 **17d.** .7 **19.** $66,003, $7,600, $8,700, $47,523 **21.** $50,436.51 **23.** $3,739.00 **25.** $69,413.94 **27.** owe, $228.00 **29a.** $33,650 **29b.** $23,300 **29c.** $1,734 **29d.** refund, $2,166

CHAPTER 19 INSURANCE

REVIEW EXERCISES | CHAPTER 19—SECTION I

1. $79.50, $41.34, $20.67, $7.16 **3.** $842, $437.84, $218.92, $75.78 **5.** $270, $140.40, $70.20, $24.30 **7.** $1,125.25, $585.13, $292.57, $101.27 **9.** $4,900, $9,300, 17 years, 54 days **11.** $5,495.00, $10,990, 21 years, 218 days **13a.** $5,240.40 **13b.** $2,725.01 **15.** $14,325.00 cash value; $37,200 reduced paid-up ins.; 30 years, 206 days extended term

REVIEW EXERCISES | CHAPTER 19—SECTION II

1. \$668.80, \$174.30, \$843.10 **3.** \$451.50, \$69.60, \$521.10 **5.** \$2,132.10, \$438.90, \$2,571 **7.** \$89.60, \$470.40 **9.** \$134.17, \$187.83 **11.** \$75,000 **13.** \$37,000 **15.** \$150,000 **17.** \$202.50 **19.** Aetna: \$57,000, State Farm: \$23,750, Liberty Mutual: \$14,250

REVIEW EXERCISES | CHAPTER 19—SECTION III

1. \$343 **3.** \$1,125 **5.** \$625.60 **7.** \$1,146.60 **9.** \$1,412 **11a.** Hart: \$13,500, Black: \$11,700, Garner: \$4,140, Williams: \$50,000, Morgan: \$3,590, bus: \$12,230, camper: \$3,530 **11b.** Williams: \$7,800, deductible: \$250

CHAPTER 19 | ASSESSMENT TEST

1. \$2,521.60, \$1,311.23, \$655.62, \$226.94 **3.** \$148.20, \$77.06, \$38.53, \$13.34 **5.** \$20,410 cash value, \$40,820 reduced paid-up ins.; 21 years, 218 days extended term **7a.** \$1,088.00 **7b.** \$97.92 **7c.** \$87.04 **9.** \$512.000 **11.** \$475, \$672, \$1,147 **13.** \$173.33, \$86.67 **15.** \$6,057.69 **17.** \$12,392 **19.** \$153,000 **21.** \$361.80 **23.** \$564.40 **25a.** Goya: \$45,000, Truman: \$50,000, Copeland: \$5,000, Kelly: 0, Winston's car: \$3,650 **25b.** Truman: \$18,000, Copeland: \$11,000, Kelly: \$11,000, deductible: \$250

CHAPTER 20 INVESTMENTS

REVIEW EXERCISES | CHAPTER 20—SECTION I

1. none, \$.60 **3.** \$5.00, 0 **5.** 0, 0 **7.** TCT, 24, \$21.15 **9.** 1.2%, 850,900 shares, \$35.25 **11.** 3.5%, 7 **13.** \$1.31, 1.6% **15.** \$1.41, \$.30 **17.** \$6,585.15, \$9,997.57, \$3,412.42 **19.** \$29,723.41, \$26,310.56, (\$3,412.85) **21.** \$.85 **23a.** \$27,000,000 **23b.** \$1.74 **25a.** \$29,658.56 **25b.** \$36,078.38 **25c.** \$6,419.82

REVIEW EXERCISES | CHAPTER 20—SECTION II

1. $6\frac{3}{8}$%%, 6.4% **3.** 2004, 115 **5.** 9%, 2016, up $\frac{1}{2}$ **7.** Aetna, KaufB $7\frac{3}{4}$04 **9.** IntgHlth, down $6\frac{1}{2}$ **11.** \$9.17, \$876.67 **13.** \$34.90, \$7,959.20 **15.** \$16.56, \$11,433.10 **17.** \$28.33, \$4,429.32 **19.** \$8.13, \$6,262.41 **21.** \$66.25, 7.3% **23.** \$75, 6% **25.** \$53.75, 6.4%

REVIEW EXERCISES | CHAPTER 20—SECTION III

1. \$12.74, 1.2% **3.** −0.03, +10.2% **5.** GVScp, E **7.** no load **9.** \$13.35, \$12.82, \$.53, 4.1% **11.** \$26.97, \$25.69, \$1.28, 5% **13.** \$15.54, 621.118 **15.** \$10.68, 4,484.305 **17.** \$1,530, \$1,880, \$395, 25.8% **19.** \$4,850, \$6,120, \$2,520, 52% **21a.** \$.75 **21b.** 6.1% **23.** 689.655

CHAPTER 20 | ASSESSMENT TEST

1. none, \$.36 **3.** \$15, \$.09 **5.** \$1.01, 3.3%, \$23.19 **7.** −22.0%, 18,900, \$19.40 **9.** \$2.09, 3.3% **11.** \$8.98, \$1.71 **13.** \$15,665.20, \$12,142.70, (\$3,522.50) **15.** \$39,277.88, \$44,975.31, \$5,697.43 **17a.** \$13,000,000 **17b.** \$.71 **19a.** \$4,472.28 **19b.** \$3,346.85 **19c.** \$1,125.43 **21.** $96\frac{1}{2}$, up $\frac{7}{8}$ **23.** 41, $103\frac{3}{8}$ **25.** ATT $5\frac{1}{8}$02 Price $99\frac{7}{8}$ **27.** \$20.49,

$4,074.95 **29.** $2.05, $9,410.50 **31.** $21.84, $4,969.20 **33.** $95, 9% **35.** stocks & bonds, $14.44, D **37.** $10.36, −0.01, 7.3% **39.** $10.88, $10.36, $.52, 5% **41.** $7.05, 6,410.256 **43.** $1,340, $1,180, ($85), −6.3% **45.** $9,400, $12,820, $4,380, 46.6% **47.** $9.04 **49.** 33.6%

CHAPTER 21 BUSINESS STATISTICS AND DATA PRESENTATION

REVIEW EXERCISES I CHAPTER 21—SECTION I

1.

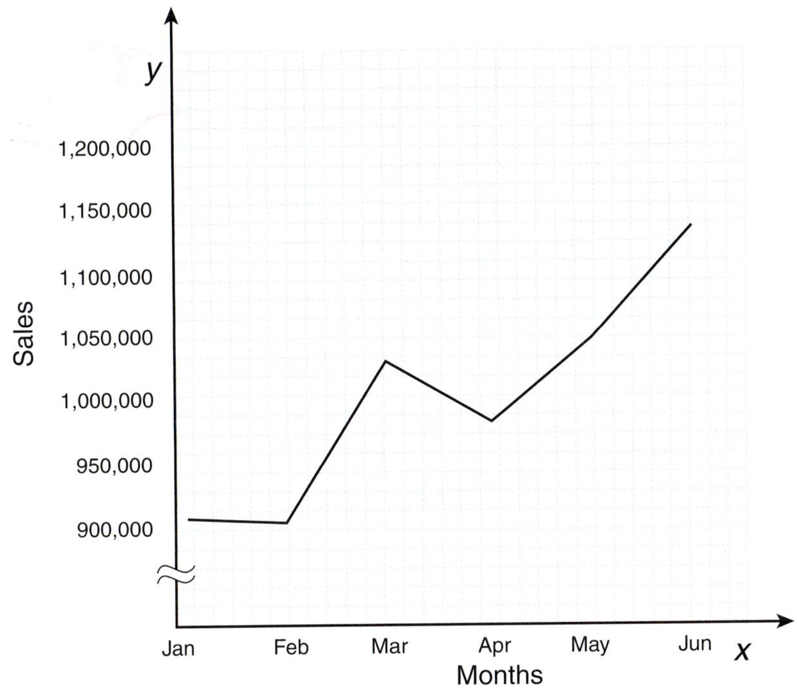

3.

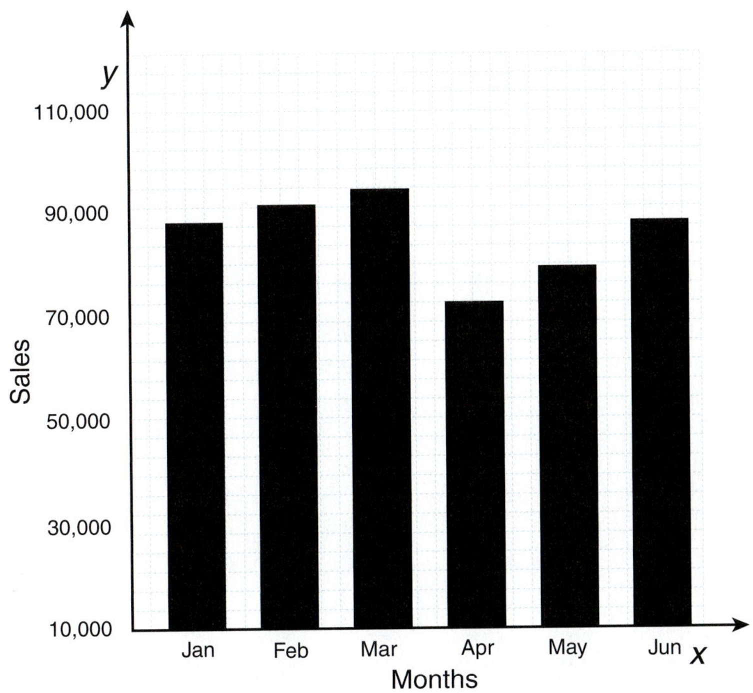

5.

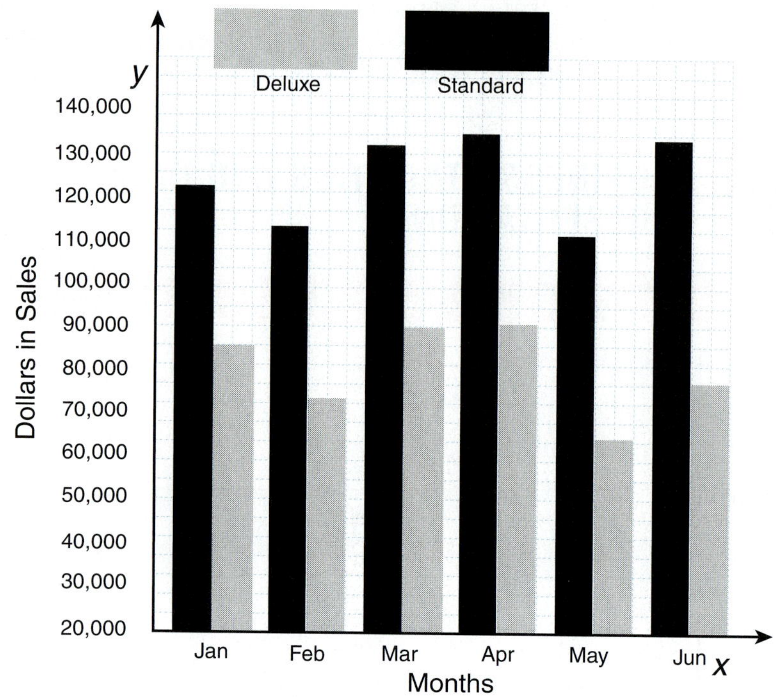

REVIEW EXERCISES | CHAPTER 21—SECTION II

1. 5.8 **3.** 2 **5.** \$2.88 **7.** 21 **9.** 4 and 9 **11.** \$3.66 **13a.** 339.9 **13b.** 343 **13c.** 425 **13d.** 221

REVIEW EXERCISES | CHAPTER 21—SECTION III

1a.

Class	Tally	Frequency
0–99	IIII	4
100–199	~~IIII~~	5
200–299	~~IIII~~ I	6
300–399	~~IIII~~ IIII	9
400–499	III	3
500–599	II	2
600–699	I	1

1b.

Class	Tally	Frequency (f)	Midpoint (m)	f × m
0–99	IIII	4	49.5	198
100–199	~~IIII~~	5	149.5	747.5
200–299	~~IIII~~ I	6	249.5	1,497
300–399	~~IIII~~ IIII	9	349.5	3,145.5
400–499	III	3	449.5	1,348.5
500–599	II	2	549.5	1,099
600–699	I	1	649.5	649.5
		30		8,685.0

$$\text{Mean} = \frac{8,685}{30} = 289.5$$

1c.

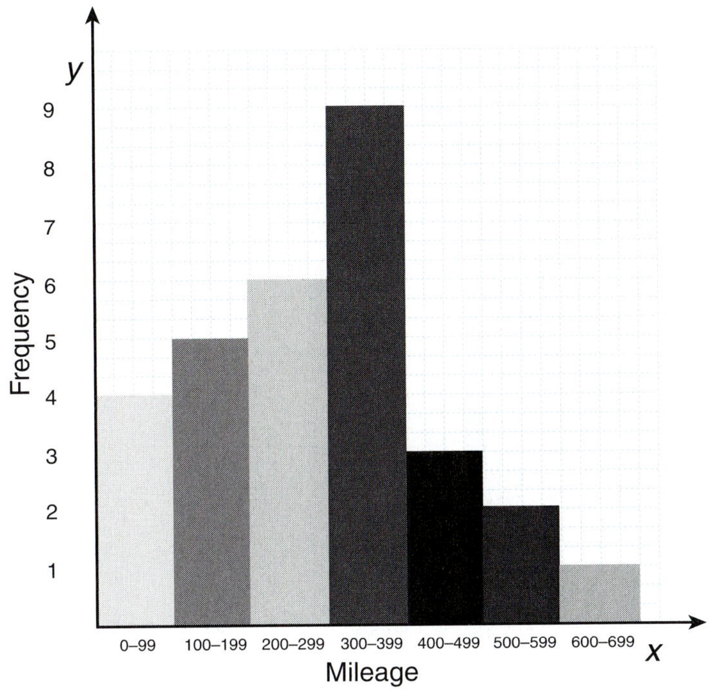

CHAPTER 21 | ASSESSMENT TEST

1a.

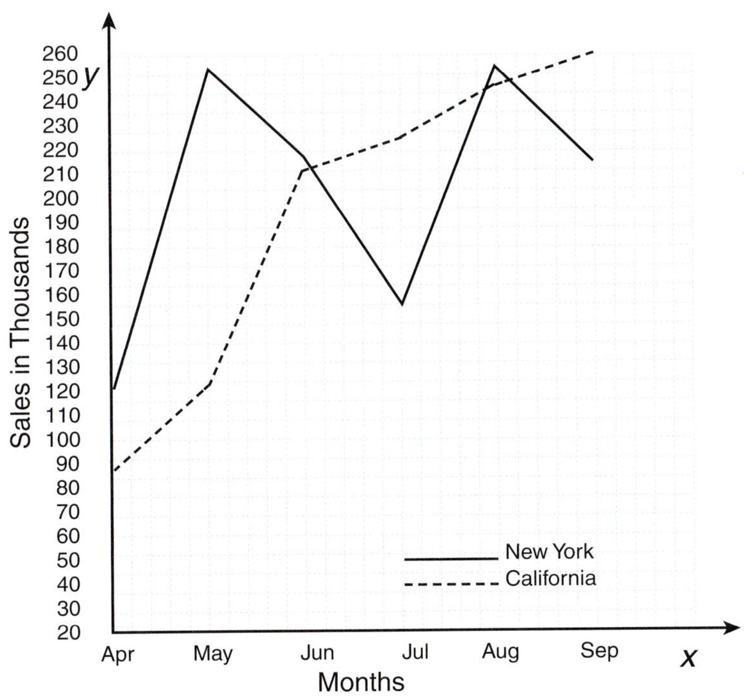

1b.

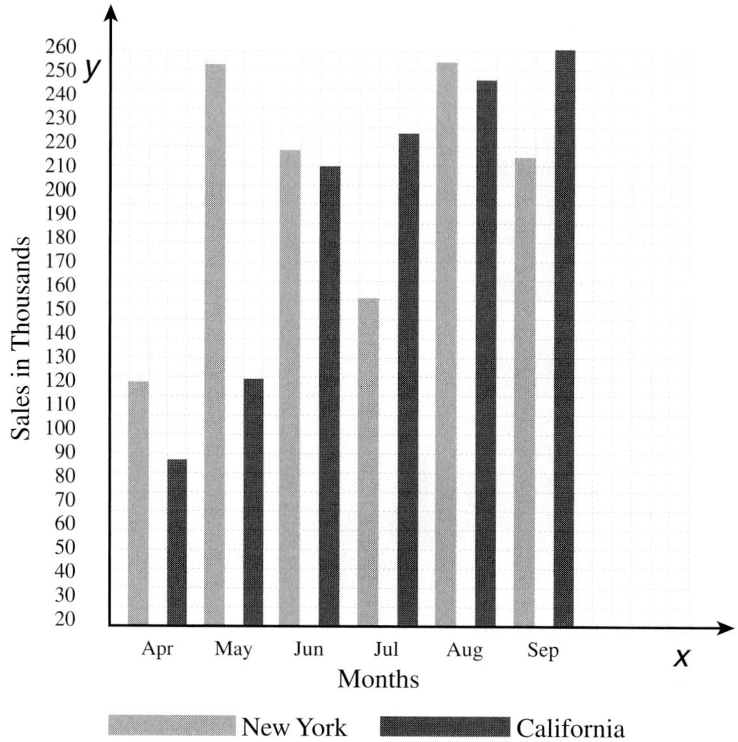

3a. standard: 50%, portable: 25%, software: 10%, printers: 12.5%, accessories: 2.5%

3b.

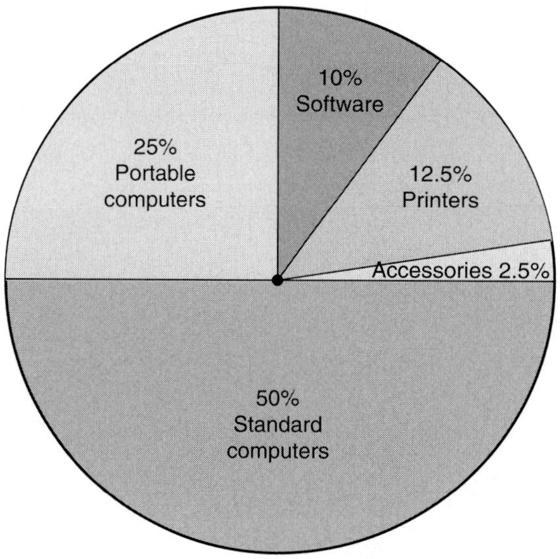

5a. range: 78, mode: 72

5b.

Class	Tally	Frequency
11–20	I	1
21–30	I	1
31–40	I	1
41–50	II	2
51–60	IIII	4
61–70	卌	5
71–80	卌 卌	10
81–90	卌 卌	10
91–100	卌 I	6

5c. mean = 72.5

Class	Tally	Frequency (f)	Midpoint (m)	$f \times m$
11–20	I	1	15.5	15.5
21–30	I	1	25.5	25.5
31–40	I	1	35.5	35.5
41–50	II	2	45.5	91.0
51–60	IIII	4	55.5	222.0
61–70	卌	5	65.5	327.5
71–80	卌 卌	10	75.5	755.0
81–90	卌 卌	10	85.5	855.0
91–100	卌	6	95.5	573.0
		40		2,900.0

$$\text{Mean} = \frac{2{,}900}{40} = \underline{\underline{72.5}}$$

5d. 14

5e.

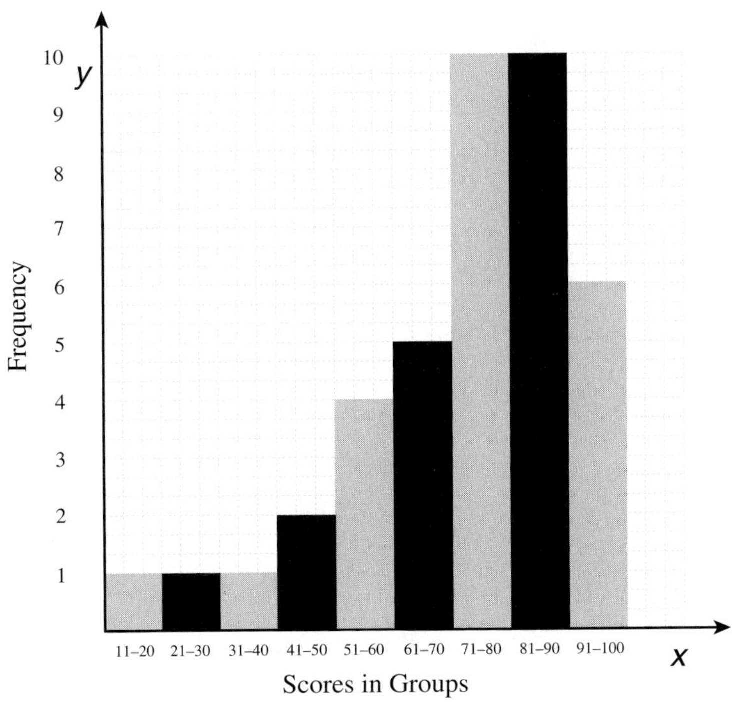

CREDITS

Photos

P. 2 © Jean Louis Batt/FPG/Getty Images; P. 5 www.irs.gov/forms_pubs/index.html; PP. 31, 72, 261, 262, 268, 269, 270, 276, 278, 279, 285, 286, 287, 288, 451, 456, 457, 474, 547, 613, 684: PhotoDisc; P. 36 © John Boykin/Index Stock Photography/PictureQuest; P. 38 © AP Wide World Photos/Bob Child; P. 75 © M. David Leeds/AllSport; P. 100 © Michael Newman/PhotoEdit; P. 103 © Eric Kamp/Index Stock Photography; P. 137 © Fabricius & Taylor/Photo Network/PictureQuest;PP. 174, 256: © Bonnie Kamin/PhotoEdit; P. 190 © David Young-Wolff/PhotoEdit; P. 211 © Zephyr Pictures/Index Stock Photography; P. 271 © George Bergeman; P. 292 Photo courtesy of Lathem Time. To learn about Lathem products, visit www.lathem.com; PP. 303, 316, 487, 492, 525, 735: © Bob Brechner; P. 340 © AP Wide World Photos/Martin Ruetschi; P. 426 © AP Wide World Photos/Jonny Mattsson; P.467 © Don Couch Photography; P. 487 Photo courtesy of American Honda Motor Corporation; P. 489 Photo courtesy of Volkswagen of America; P. 490 Hippopotamus © Ronn Maratea/International Stock; P. 501 © Wallace Garrison/Index Stock Photography; P . 578 © Michael Newman/PhotoEdit; P. 585 *Fortune Magazine*; P. 594 © Laima Druskis/Stock, Boston/PictureQuest; P. 599 Miami Herald by Consumer Electronics Association. © 2001 by Miami Herald. Reproduced with permission of Miami Herald in the format Textbook via Copyright Clearance Center; P. 626 © Jan Stromme/PhotoEdit; P. 640 © Edward Slater/Index Stock Photography; P. 647 © David Young-Wolff/PhotoEdit; P. 656 © Peter Gregoire/Index Stock Photography; P. 695 © AP Wide World Photos/Independent Record; P. 703 © Comstock Images; P. 724 Courtesy Home Depot, Inc.; P. 730 © Spencer Platt/Newsmakers; PP. 727, 728, 732, 736, 737, 740, 743, 744, 748, 757, 759, 760: *Wall Street Journal*. Eastern Edition (Staff produced copy only) by *Wall Street Journal*. © 2001 by Dow Jones & Co Inc. in the format Textbook via Copyright Clearance Center. P. 735 Courtesy Southwestern Bell; P. 766 © Tomas del Amo/Index Stock Photography; P. 772 © AP Wide World Photos/Bill Kostroun; P. 773 © Jon Feingersh/Corbis Stock Market

Cartoons

PP. 6, 46: © Cabisco Mathematics/Carolina Biological Supply Company, Burlington, North Carolina;PP. 32, 98, 134 338, 706: © 2001 William Hoest Enterprises, courtesy of Bunny Hoest; P. 70 ® used by permission of Hank Ketcham Enterprises and © by North America Syndicate; P. 148 © Tribune Media Services; P. 172 © R.F. May;PP. 208, 254, 274, 610, 638: © 2001 Ted Goff, www.tedgoff.com; P. 290 From *The Wall Street Journal*, January 5, 1999, page A23. Reprinted by permission of Cartoon Features Syndicate;PP. 313, 442, 813: © Randy Glasbergen, www.glasbergen.com; P. 378 From *The Wall Street Journal*, January 8, 2001, page A33. Reprinted by permission of Cartoon Features Syndicate; P. 382 Wit of the World reprinted by permission of Arnould and Cartoonist and Writers Syndicate. © 1992 Arnould.; P. 408 From *The Wall Street Journal*, August 3, 2000, page A15. Reprinted by permission of Cartoon Features Syndicate; P. 445 © Mark Litzler; P. 490 From *The Wall Street Journal*, January 1, 2001, page A23. Reprinted by permission of Cartoon Features Syndicate; P. 522 From *The Wall Street Journal*, August 5, 1997, page A19. Reprinted by permission of Cartoon Features Syndicate; PP. 527, 646: Harley Schwadron; P. 576 From *The Wall Street Journal*, July 31, 2000, page A23. Reprinted by permission of Cartoon Features Syndicate; P. 662 Jeff MacNelly; P. 720 Peter Hesse; P. 760 Mark Litzler; P. 764 Sidney Harris

The Business Math Times

Chapter 3: Moore's Law chart courtesy of Intel Corporation, P. 98. **Chapter 9:** Tax Facts, SOURCE: *Wall Street Journal*. Eastern Edition (Staff produced copy only) by *Wall Street Journal*. © 2000 by Dow Jones & Co Inc. Reproduced with permission of Dow Jones & Co Inc. in the format Textbook via Copyright Copy Center, P. 338 **Chapter 12:** Saving for College, SOURCE: http://library.thinkquest.org.; The Long View!, SOURCE: Reprinted with permission. © 2002 Investor's Business Daily, Inc. Content is not to be redistributed, downloaded, sold or used in any print media or on any other site without prior express written permission of Investor's Business Daily, Inc. Rights to content are not transferable. 401K Chart, SOURCE: *Modern Maturity*, July–August 2000. How Long Does $1Million Last?, , SOURCE: *Business Week*. Money rates chart, SOURCE: *Wall Street Journal*. Eastern Edition (Staff produced copy only) by *Wall Street Journal*, P. 442 **Chapter 14:** 30-Year Mortgage Rates, SOURCE: www.economagic.com, P. 522. **Chapter 17:** Depreciation Pie, SOURCE: American Institute of Certified Public Accountants, P. 638 **Chapter 18:** Tax Freedom Day, SOURCE: www.taxfoundation.org, P. 662 **Chapter 19:** Insurance Loss Chart, SOURCE: Morgan Stanley: Insurance Information Institute, P. 720

INDEX